THE LAW OF SET-OFF

THE LAW OF SET-OFF

Third Edition

RORY DERHAM

OXFORD

UNIVERSITY PRESS

OXFORD
UNIVERSITY PRESS

Great Clarendon Street, Oxford OX2 6DP

Oxford University Press is a department of the University of Oxford.
It furthers the University's objective of excellence in research, scholarship,
and education by publishing worldwide in

Oxford New York

Auckland Bangkok Buenos Aires Cape Town Chennai
Dar es Salaam Delhi Hong Kong Istanbul Karachi Kolkata
Kuala Lumpur Madrid Melbourne Mexico City Mumbai Nairobi
São Paulo Shanghai Taipei Tokyo Toronto

Oxford is a registered trade mark of Oxford University Press
in the UK and in certain other countries

Published in the United States
by Oxford University Press Inc., New York

British Library Cataloguing in Publication Data

Data available

Library of Congress Cataloging in Publication Data
Derham, S. R.
Set-off/Rory Derham.—3rd ed.
p. cm.
Includes bibliographical references and index.
1. Set-off and counterclaim—Great Britain. 2. Debtor and creditor—Great Britain.
3. Bankruptcy—Great Britain. I. Title.
KD7458 .D47 2002   346.4107'7—dc21   2002038164
ISBN 0–19–829800–5

3 5 7 9 10 8 6 4 2

Typeset by Hope Services (Abingdon) Ltd
Printed in Great Britain
on acid-free paper by
Biddles Ltd, Guildford and King's Lynn

To Heather, Ryan, Kate and Stephen

CONTENTS—SUMMARY

CONTENTS

PREFACE

Six years have elapsed since the second edition of this book. In that period a considerable number of cases concerning set-off have come before the courts, particularly in the context of equitable set-off. Probably the most significant of the recent cases however is *Re Bank of Credit and Commerce International SA (No 8)* [1998] AC 214, in which the House of Lords rejected the view previously accepted by Millett J (as he then was) in *Re Charge Card Services Ltd* [1987] 1 Ch 150, and by the Court of Appeal in *BCCI (No 8)* [1996] Ch 245, that it is conceptually impossible for a debtor (typically a bank) to take a charge over its own debt. As a consequence of the rejection of the conceptual impossibility argument, there is now no difficulty in a bank taking as security for a facility a charge over a deposit made with the bank. It is not necessary for the bank to rely instead on set-off rights. Initially the House of Lords' view met with opposition in Australia (see *Wily v Rothschild Australia Ltd* (1999) 47 NSWLR 555), but Spigelman CJ later adopted it in the New South Wales Court of Appeal in *Cinema Plus Ltd v Australia and New Zealand Banking Group Ltd* (2000) 49 NSWLR 513, 517–21, and it should now also represent the law in that country.

The third edition generally follows the same format as the second. However the first chapter of the second edition, which dealt with set-off before insolvency, has been divided into four. This has allowed greater discussion of some issues of practical importance, for example the circumstances in which the parties to a transaction will be taken to have agreed to exclude defences of set-off. The question whether or not set-off has been excluded in a particular case could have a significant effect on cash flow.

New Civil Procedure Rules have now come into force. It is suggested in the principal commentary on the rules (*Civil Procedure* (Autumn 2001) vol 1, para 16.6.1) that the courts may take the opportunity afforded by the new rules to define set-off differently in the future. The new rules should not affect the position, however. The Civil Procedure Act 1997, s 1(1) only permitted the making of rules governing the practice and procedure of the courts. Set-off, particularly under the Statutes of Set-off, has procedural aspects to it, and indeed the statutory defence is commonly referred to as a procedural defence. Set-off nevertheless is a defence, and because it is a defence it is not wholly a matter of procedure. The availability of a defence can have a substantive effect on the rights of third parties, such as assignees of debts, who take subject to equities, which include defences. Because set-off has substantive as well as procedural aspects, the circumstances in which the defence is available should not be affected by the new rules, which relate only to matters of practice and procedure. This point is made, with references to the issues raised, in the first chapter.

Under the Civil Procedure Rules, a person who commences an action is called a "claimant" rather than a "plaintiff". The new terminology is used when discussing cases decided under the new rules, and also in general discussion of the principles of set-off under English law. The term "plaintiff" is retained however when the discussion relates to cases decided under former rules of court, or to the position in England before the new rules, or when it concerns other jurisdictions.

The scope of set-off before insolvency has been criticized. Set-off is permitted under the Statutes of Set-off when both demands are liquidated, even if they are unconnected, and a set-off may occur in equity if one or both of the demands is unliquidated and they are sufficiently connected to give rise to an equitable set-off, but there may not be a set-off if one of the claims is unliquidated and the claims are not connected. This has been described as unsatisfactory and lacking logic and sense. See *Axel Johnson Petroleum AB v MG Mineral Group AG* [1992] 1 WLR 270, 274, *per* Leggatt LJ, 275–276, *per* Staughton LJ. But in considering that criticism it should be appreciated that an extension in the scope of the defence of set-off to unconnected damages claims could have important consequences. It would affect third parties, such as assignees of debts, who take subject to defences. An expansion in the scope of the defence would increase the range of cross-claims to which assignees and other such persons take subject, and would diminish their rights accordingly. Moreover, an expansion in the scope of the defence could affect cash flow, which in some industries such as building and construction is vital. The criticism of the state of the defence of set-off before insolvency is addressed at the conclusion of chapter 5.

As in the case of the first two editions, I have tried to write this book from both an English and an Australian perspective. As a consequence I have cited a large number of Australian cases, more than one usually finds in an English text. The principles generally are the same in both countries. Where they differ, or where discussion of a point is relevant only to Australia, I have tried to make it clear in section headings or in the text.

I have attempted to state the law on the basis of the reported law available to me on 1 September 2002.

RORY DERHAM

PREFACE TO THE FIRST EDITION

Set-off is an area of the law that, for some unknown reason, has not proved attractive for academic writers. In the early part of the nineteenth century Babington and Montagu each published monographs on the subject, but since then it has received remarkably little attention. This is surprising given the importance that the business community does attach to the right to set cross-demands against each other, particularly in the event of an insolvency. The avowed aim of this book is to provide an exposition of some of the more important principles of the law of set-off. It had its genesis in a thesis for which the author was awarded the degree of Doctor of Philosophy, and subsequently also a Yorke Prize, at the University of Cambridge. The thesis was entitled 'The Law of Set-off in Bankruptcy and Company Liquidation', and more and less constitutes the material set out in Chapters 2 to 12 of the present book. The first chapter, dealing with equitable set-off and the final chapter, on a surety's right of set-off, have been added in order to expand the scope of the work for the purpose of publication.

The emphasis throughout is on the question of when a right of set-off is available. Questions of pleading and procedure are not dealt with. For these, the appropriate rules of court, and commentaries thereon, should be consulted. Moreover the book is concerned with the *principles* of set-off. It does not purport to provide an exhaustive list of the myriad situations in which the courts in the past have allowed a right of set-off. Rather the aim is to indicate the principles upon which the decided case law is based.

During my period of research at Cambridge I was fortunate to have as my supervisors Professor Gareth Jones, of Trinity College, and Michael Prichard, of Gonville and Caius College. I am grateful to these gentlemen for their advice and assistance. The thesis was examined by Dr Len Sealy, of Gonville and Gaius College, and Professor Roy Goode, of Queen Mary College in London. Their comments and criticisms, and the encouragement they gave me to publish this book, are greatly appreciated. Of course none of these people is in any way responsible for any errors of omission or commission that may be contained in the ensuing pages.

The discussion of the various principles of set-off is based primarily upon English case and statute law, though reference is also made to suitable authorities from Australia and New Zealand. There are also extensive cross-references to the relevant Australian statutory provisions. The law is stated on the basis of the available reported law as at 31 December 1986. However for the second impression of the book cases reported after that date and before 30 September 1988 have been included, but by way of brief reference only in the footnotes. Unfortunately it has not been possible to discuss these cases in any great depth.

R. D.

TABLE OF CASES

TABLES OF LEGISLATION, TREATIES AND CONVENTIONS

AUSTRALIA

Commonwealth

1

INTRODUCTION

A. The Meaning of Set-off

It is difficult to give a comprehensive definition of set-off without reference to the **1.01** various forms that it can take, but on a general level it can be defined as the setting of money cross-claims[1] against each other to produce a balance. It provides a defence to an action, although, depending on the form of set-off, the issue need not arise in that context. The essence of set-off, in this sense of the word, is the existence of cross-demands.[2] The term 'set-off' is also commonly used in a different sense, to describe a situation in which the damages payable by a defendant to a claimant may be reduced because of a benefit incidentally accruing to the claimant as a result of the defendant's breach.[3] This is not a case of cross-demands, but rather of calculating the true measure of damages. It is not therefore a set-off,

---

[1] Set-off is concerned with money claims. See *Tony Lee Motors Ltd v M S McDonald & Son (1974) Ltd* [1981] 2 NZLR 281, 288; *Hamilton Ice Arena Ltd v Perry Developments Ltd* [2002] 1 NZLR 309, 311. See also CPR 16.6, and para 3.02 below.

[2] *Re Dalco, ex p Dalco and Deputy Commissioner of Taxation (NSW)* (1986) 17 ATR 906, 913; *Buttrose v Versi* (NSW SC, Young J, 14 May 1992). Compare *Bedford Steamship Co Ltd v Navico AG (The Ionian Skipper)* [1977] 2 Lloyd's Rep 273, 279.

[3] See eg *Nadreph Ltd v Willmett & Co* [1978] 1 WLR 1537; *Ocean Glory Compania Naviera SA v A/S PV Christensen (The Ioanna)* [1985] 2 Lloyd's Rep 164; *Christianos v Westpac Banking Corp* (1991) 5 WAR 336; *Brown v KMR Services Ltd* [1995] 2 Lloyd's Rep 513, 555; *Longden v British Coal Corp* [1998] AC 653. When a defendant who has not been guilty of fraud or negligence has incurred expenses in good faith with respect to goods the subject of an action for detention, and the goods have been delivered up to the plaintiff, who consequently has the benefit of the expenses, the defendant is entitled to have the expenses taken into account in any assessment of damages for detention. See *Peruvian Guano Co Ltd v Dreyfus Brothers & Co* [1892] AC 166; *Hill v Ziymack* (1908) 7 CLR 352; *Halsbury's Laws of England* (4th edn, 1999) vol 45, 398 para 625. In *Re Baldwin (A Bankrupt), and Tasman Fruit-Packers Ltd, ex p Official Assignee* [1940] NZLR 848, it was held that the value of the interest of a member of a society registered under the Industrial and Provident Societies Act 1908 (NZ) could only be ascertained by deducting the amount of the member's indebtedness to the society. This was independent of any principle of set-off.

in the sense in which that term is used in this book. A similar comment may be made in relation to the action for money had and received. The action is based on the principle of unjust enrichment, and it cannot be asserted without the claimant at the same time giving credit for any payments that he received from the defendant.[4] The net sum represents the amount of the enrichment, as opposed to the product of bringing together cross-claims. A running account should also be distinguished. A true running account is not within the ambit of the law of set-off[5] because there are not independent cross-demands between the parties requiring to be set off. Rather, there is only one cause of action for the balance.[6]

B. The Importance of Set-off

Insolvency

1.02 A right of set-off may be crucial in the event of an insolvency. If there are cross-demands between a creditor and a debtor who has become insolvent, the creditor, in the absence of a set-off, may be obliged to pay the full amount of his own indebtedness, and yet be confined to receiving a dividend along with the other creditors for the amount for which the insolvent debtor is indebted to him. If a set-off is available, however, only the balance remaining after deducting one claim from the other would be payable. Therefore, if the debtor's claim against the creditor exceeds in value the creditor's claim against the debtor, the creditor in effect would obtain payment in full for his claim in the form of a deduction from his liability, and would only be obliged to pay the balance. Alternatively the creditor's claim may be the greater, in which case the creditor would receive payment in full to the extent of his liability to the debtor and he would only be confined to a dividend in respect of the balance.

Counterclaim

1.03 A set-off also may have advantages in the absence of insolvency. In that context, it is often important to distinguish between set-off and counterclaim.

1.04 A defendant's right to counterclaim against the claimant in the claimant's action originated in the Supreme Court of Judicature Act 1873, section 24(3).[7] It differs

---

[4] *Westdeutsche Landesbank v Islington BC* [1994] 4 All ER 890, 940–941 (Hobhouse J).

[5] Compare *Rolls Razor Ltd v Cox* [1967] 1 QB 552, 575; *Opal Maritime Agencies Pty Ltd v Baltic Shipping Co* (1998) 158 ALR 416, 421 (contrast *Opal Maritime Agencies Pty Ltd v 'Skulptor Konenkov'* (2000) 98 FCR 519, 567–568).

[6] *Cottam v Partridge* (1842) 4 Man & G 271, 293–294, 134 ER 111, 120; *Re Armour, ex p Official Receiver v Commonwealth Trading Bank of Australia* (1956) 18 ABC 69, 75; *Re Convere Pty Ltd* [1976] VR 345, 349; *Re Charge Card Services Ltd* [1987] 1 Ch 150, 174.

[7] See now the Supreme Court Act 1981, s 49, and CPR r 20.4. The Judicature Acts in introducing a right of counterclaim did not confer any new right of set-off. See *Hanak v Green* [1958] 2 QB 9, 22.

from set-off in that it does not give rise to a defence, but rather it constitutes a procedural device by which the court may consider independent cross-actions in the same proceedings. The cross-actions are treated as independent actions for all purposes except execution.[8] Since a set-off gives rise to a defence to the claimant's claim, there is only one judgment for the balance.[9] In the case of a counterclaim, the courts, particularly in the early years after the Judicature Acts, would sometimes enter only a single judgment for the balance,[10] although the usual practice is to enter separate judgments on both the claim and the counterclaim,[11] but with execution issuing only for the balance.[12]

In an application by a claimant for summary judgment against the defendant,[13] **1.05** the existence of a cross-claim not amounting to a set-off ordinarily is not sufficient to prevent judgment being entered, although the court in its discretion can stay enforcement on the judgment until the defendant's cross-action has been tried. Under former rules of court, the question whether the court should exercise its discretion to grant a stay depended on a number of factors, such as the degree of connection between the claim and the cross-claim, the strength of the cross-claim, and the ability of the claimant to satisfy any judgment on the cross-claim.[14] It has been suggested that, under the new Civil Procedure Rules 1998, the courts may be prepared to grant summary judgment and a delay on enforcement more

---

[8] *Stumore v Campbell & Co* [1892] 1 QB 314, 317, *per* Lord Esher MR. See also *Beddall v Maitland* (1881) 17 Ch D 174.

[9] If the cross-demand of a defendant asserting a set-off is greater in value than the claimant's claim against the defendant, the defendant may employ the cross-demand in a set-off to the extent of, and in order to defeat, the claimant's claim, and counterclaim for the balance.

[10] See eg *Stooke v Taylor* (1880) 5 QBD 569, 581; *Provincial Bill Posting Co v Low Moor Iron Co* [1909] 2 KB 344, 351; *Chell Engineering Ltd v Unit Tool and Engineering Co Ltd* [1950] 1 All ER 378, 380 (referring to the *Annual Practice* (1948), 410).

[11] *Sharpe v Haggith* (1912) 106 LT 13; *Stumore v Campbell & Co* [1892] 1 QB 314, 317; *McDonnell & East Ltd v McGregor* (1936) 56 CLR 50, 62; *Chell Engineering Ltd v Unit Tool and Engineering Co Ltd* [1950] 1 All ER 378; *Hanak v Green* [1958] 2 QB 9.

[12] *Stumore v Campbell & Co* [1892] 1 QB 314, 317. This practice should not apply when the beneficial ownership of the cross-claims is in different hands in consequence of an assignment of one of them. See *John Dee Group Ltd v WMH (21) Ltd* [1998] BCC 972, 976, CA.

[13] See CPR Part 24.

[14] *The Supreme Court Practice* (1999) 178–9 para 14/4/14, referring to *A B Contractors Ltd v Flaherty Brothers Ltd* (1978) 16 BLR 8, CA and *Drake and Fletcher Ltd v Batchelor* (1986) 83 LS Gaz 1232, *per* Sir Neil Lawson. See also *State Bank of Victoria v Parry* [1989] WAR 240, 246; *Exmar BV v National Iranian Tanker Co (The Trade Fortitude)* [1992] 1 Lloyd's Rep 169, 177; *Aectra Refining and Manufacturing Inc v Exmar NV* [1994] 1 WLR 1634, 1652. For instances in which a stay was refused, see eg *Anglian Building Products Ltd v W & C French (Construction) Ltd* (1972) 16 BLR 1 and *Century Textiles and Industry Ltd v Tomoe Shipping (Singapore) Pte Ltd (The Aditya Vaibhav)* [1991] 1 Lloyd's Rep 573. Compare Dillon LJ in *Schofield v Church Army* [1986] 1 WLR 1328, 1334–1335, who said that a summary judgment 'ought to be stayed' until after the trial of a counterclaim if the counterclaim is not frivolous, and see also Croom Johnson LJ at 1337. Compare also *L U Simon Builders Pty Ltd v H D Fowles* [1992] 2 VR 189, 196, though that was in the context of a cross-claim that was closely connected with the plaintiff's claim.

frequently than hitherto,[15] but those factors should still be relevant in determining whether to grant a stay. On the other hand, a defendant whom the court considers has a real prospect of establishing a set-off overtopping the claimant's claim ordinarily could expect to be granted leave to defend,[16] either unconditionally or subject to conditions,[17] so that the defendant would not be the subject of an adverse judgment.

Costs

1.06 The distinction between set-off and counterclaim is relevant to the question of costs. Costs are within the discretion of the court, but the general rule is that the unsuccessful party pays the costs of the successful party.[18] Since a set-off gives rise to a defence, it follows that, if the defendant's cross-claim the subject of the set-off exceeded the claimant's claim, the defendant will have succeeded in defending the action, and accordingly the defendant, rather than the claimant, ordinarily would be entitled to an order for costs.[19] A counterclaim on the other hand ordinarily results in two judgments. The approach of the courts usually has been that the claimant is entitled to the costs of his claim, if successful, and the defendant is awarded the costs of a successful counterclaim.[20] The circumstances of a particular case may warrant different orders,[21] but these are the prima facie positions.

---

[15] *Civil Procedure* (Autumn 2001) vol 1, para 24.2.6.

[16] CPR r 24.2. See eg *Morgan & Son Ltd v S Martin Johnson & Co Ltd* [1949] 1 KB 107; *James Lamont & Co Ltd v Hyland Ltd* [1950] 1 KB 585; *Re K L Tractors Ltd* [1954] VLR 505, 509; *Edward Ward & Co v McDougall* [1972] VR 433; *Mottram Consultants Ltd v Bernard Sunley & Sons Ltd* [1975] 2 Lloyd's Rep 197, 212, 214; *Petersville Ltd v Rosgrae Distributors Pty Ltd* (1975) 11 SASR 433; *General Credits (Finance) Pty Ltd v Stoyakovich* [1975] Qd R 352; *United Dominions Corp Ltd v Jaybe Homes Pty Ltd* [1978] Qd R 111; *Paynter Ltd v Ben Candy Investments Ltd* [1987] 1 NZLR 257. Compare the proposed order in *Standard Chartered Bank v Pakistan National Shipping Corp* [1995] 2 Lloyd's Rep 365, 375 (judgment on the plaintiff's claim, with damages to be assessed, with the defendant left to advance its cross-claim and, if appropriate, to set it off before a money judgment was entered in favour of the plaintiff). Ordinarily the defendant should quantify the value of his set-off to justify leave to defend. Compare *Asco Developments Ltd v Gordon* (1978) 248 EG 683.

[17] As in *General Credits (Finance) Pty Ltd v Stoyakovich* [1975] Qd R 352.

[18] See CPR r 44.3, and the Supreme Court Act 1981, s 51.

[19] *Baines v Bromley* (1881) 6 QBD 691, 694, *per* Brett LJ; *Baylis Baxter Ltd v Sabath* [1958] 1 WLR 529, 538, *per* Parker LJ; *Hanak v Green* [1958] 2 QB 9.

[20] *Stooke v Taylor* (1880) 5 QBD 569 (overruling *Staples v Young* (1877) 2 Ex D 324); *Shrapnel v Laing* (1888) 20 QBD 334; *Sharpe v Haggith* (1912) 106 LT 13; *McDonnell & East Ltd v McGregor* (1936) 56 CLR 50, 62; *Chell Engineering Ltd v Unit Tool and Engineering Co Ltd* [1950] 1 All ER 378; *E Reynolds & Sons (Chingford) Ltd v Hendry Brothers (London) Ltd* [1955] 1 Lloyd's Rep 258. Compare para 5.152 below.

[21] See the matters referred to in CPR 44.3. In relation to set-off, see also *Box v Midland Bank Ltd* [1981] 1 Lloyd's Rep 434 and *Hanak v Green* [1958] 2 QB 9, 27. In the case of a counterclaim not amounting to a set-off, where the plaintiff's claim was admitted and the only point that was litigated was the counterclaim, see *Childs v Gibson* [1954] 1 WLR 809, 812–813. Compare *Nicholson v Little* [1956] 1 WLR 829. There may be a special order as to costs in the case of a counterclaim where the issues on the claim and the counterclaim are interlocked. See *Chell Engineering Ltd v Unit Tool and Engineering Co Ltd* [1950] 1 All ER 378, 383 (Denning LJ); *Childs v Gibson* at 815.

Assignments

An assignee of a debt takes subject to defences available to the debtor against the assignor before the debtor received notice of the assignment. These defences include the defence of set-off.[22] An assignee does not take subject to a debtor's cross-claim against the assignor if the cross-claim could not have been raised as a set-off in an action by the assignor, although a contrary view has been expressed in Australia.[23]

1.07

Arbitration

The importance of set-off has come into prominence in the context of commercial arbitrations. Arbitration as a means of settling disputes is generally considered to be quicker and less expensive than proceeding through the courts, and it is common for commercial contracts to stipulate that any 'dispute' arising under the contract should be referred to arbitration. It may be that a person being sued for the price of services performed or of goods delivered pursuant to a contract containing an arbitration clause has a cross-claim against the claimant for damages for breach of contract. If the cross-claim could be marshalled as an equitable set-off the defendant would have a substantive defence[24] to the claimant's claim, so that the sum claimed by the claimant would be in dispute. The defendant in such a case could apply for a stay of the action,[25] and have both the claim and the cross-claim referred to arbitration. If on the other hand the cross-claim for damages could not be employed in a set-off, the defendant would not be entitled to a stay of the claimant's action, so that only the cross-claim would be referred to arbitration.[26]

1.08

---

[22] See ch 17 below.
[23] See paras 17.05–17.08 below.
[24] See paras 4.29–4.43 below.
[25] See the Arbitration Act 1996, s 9.
[26] See generally *Compania Sud Americana de Vapores v Shipmair BV (The Teno)* [1977] 2 Lloyd's Rep 289; *A/S Gunnstein & Co K/S v Jensen, Krebs and Nielsen (The Alfa Nord)* [1977] 2 Lloyd's Rep 434; *Nova (Jersey) Knit Ltd v Kammgarn Spinnerei GmbH* [1977] 1 WLR 713; *Federal Commerce & Navigation Co Ltd v Molena Alpha Inc* [1978] 1 QB 927, 974; *SL Sethia Liners Ltd v Naviagro Maritime Corp (The Kostas Melas)* [1981] 1 Lloyd's Rep 18, 27; *Cleobulos Shipping Co Ltd v Intertanker Ltd (The Cleon)* [1983] 1 Lloyd's Rep 586. See also *Ellis Mechanical Services Ltd v Wates Construction Ltd* [1978] 1 Lloyd's Rep 33; *R M Douglas Construction Ltd v Bass Leisure Ltd* (1990) 53 BLR 119; *Hermcrest plc v G Percy Trentham Ltd* (1991) 53 BLR 104. Compare *Russell v Pellegrini* (1856) 6 El & Bl 1020, 119 ER 1144 (which was followed in *Seligmann v Le Boutillier* (1866) LR 1 CP 681), although Lord Wilberforce in the *Nova Knit* case (and see also *The Alfa Nord*) thought that *Russell v Pellegrini* should only be regarded as correct, if at all, on the basis of the particularly wide arbitration clause there in issue. On other occasions it has been said that *Russell v Pellegrini* should not be followed. See Bramwell B in *Daunt v Lazard* (1858) LJ 27 Ex 399, 400 and Lord Russell of Killowen in *Nova Knit* at 733. *Quaere* whether there was a 'dispute' in *Graham v Seagoe* [1964] 2 Lloyd's Rep 564, in view of the general principle that an equitable set-off is not available against a claim on a negotiable instrument. See paras 5.25–5.32 below.

1.09   In order to preserve cash flow, arbitrators may be called upon to make a prompt interim award and to decide that a minimum sum at least is payable by one party to the other. In doing so the arbitrators may decide to award only such sum as proves not be in dispute after taking into account the extent of a claim for an equitable set-off.[27] Alternatively, it is open to arbitrators, when awarding a minimum sum as due and payable, to reject a claim for an equitable set-off if the party advancing the claim cannot satisfy them that he is seeking to exercise the right in good faith and on reasonable grounds. If the arbitrators reject the claim for a set-off on that ground, the cross-claim nevertheless may be made out later on fuller evidence when the arbitrators proceed to a final award in the case. The fact that arbitrators have rejected a claim for a set-off in an interim award is not inconsistent with a finding that the cross-claim is valid when they have the full evidence before them at a later date.[28]

C. The Forms of Set-off

1.10   There are various forms of set-off.

1.11   In the case of parties, neither of whom is bankrupt or is a company in liquidation, a set-off may proceed under the right of set-off derived from the Statutes of Set-off enacted in 1729[29] and 1735[30] if the case is one of mutual debts. Alternatively, a set-off may be available in accordance with the principles developed independently by courts of equity. Set-off in equity is both broader and narrower than set-off under the Statutes. It is broader in that it extends to claims for damages, while it is narrower in that generally it is necessary to show a sufficient connection between the cross-demands. Set-off under the Statutes, on the other hand, does not require any connection between the debts.[31] Further, in the particular case of contracts for the sale of goods with a warranty or for the performance of work pursuant to a contract, a common law principle, known as abatement, may apply, so as to reduce the price payable in the event that there has been a breach of warranty in relation to the goods or a breach of the contract for the performance of the work.[32] These forms of set-off, including the common law principle of abatement, are the subject of discussion in chapters 2, 3 and 4. If one of the parties to

---

[27] See eg *Exmar BV v National Iranian Tanker Co (The Trade Fortitude)* [1992] 1 Lloyd's Rep 169, and the cases referred to in the judgment.

[28] *SL Sethia Liners Ltd v Naviagro Maritime Corporation (The Kostas Melas)* [1981] 1 Lloyd's Rep 18; *Industriebeteiligungs & Handelsgesellschaft v Malaysian International Shipping Corporation Berhad (The Bunga Melawis)* [1991] 2 Lloyd's Rep 271.

[29] (1729) 2 Geo II, c 22, s 13.

[30] (1735) 8 Geo II, c 24, s 5.

[31] *Axel Johnson Petroleum AB v MG Mineral Group AG* [1992] 1 WLR 270, 272; *Fuller v Happy Shopper Markets Ltd* [2001] 1 WLR 1681, 1690 para 21.

[32] See paras 2.87–2.97 below.

the cross-demands is a person who is bankrupt or is a company in liquidation, the right of set-off is governed by the set-off section (or, as it is sometimes called, the mutual credit provision) in the insolvency legislation.[33] Insolvency set-off is discussed in the fifth and succeeding chapters.

In addition to those forms of set-off, there are certain rights which are distinct **1.12** from set-off but which have an analogous effect. Two such rights, combination of bank accounts[34] and the rule in *Cherry v Boultbee*,[35] receive detailed consideration. Combination of bank accounts, as the name suggests, relates to bank accounts, and refers to a bank's right[36] to look upon various accounts held by a customer as combined to produce a single debt. The rule in *Cherry v Boultbee* applies in the situation in which a person who is entitled to receive a distribution from a fund is also obliged to contribute to the fund. It entitles the administrator of the fund to direct the person to satisfy his entitlement to a distribution from a particular asset of the fund, in the form of his own obligation to contribute.

D. Civil Procedure Rules

Set-off is dealt with in r 16.6 of the new Civil Procedure Rules 1998 made pur- **1.13** suant to the Civil Procedure Act 1997. While there are some differences in the drafting, the substance of the rule is the same as the former RSC O 18 r 17. In relation to the former rule and its predecessors, the courts emphasized that the rule itself did not determine the availability of a set-off,[37] but merely laid down a procedure for claiming the defence outside bankruptcy and company liquidation. In other words, the circumstances in which a set-off was available depended upon the interpretation of the Statutes of Set-off and the set-off section in the insolvency legislation, and, in other cases, upon an examination of the substantive principles developed by the courts independently of the rules.

It has been suggested that the courts may take the opportunity afforded by the **1.14** new rule to define set-off differently in the future.[38] There is no reason why this

---

[33] Currently the Insolvency Act 1986, s 323 in the case of bankruptcy, and for company liquidation the Insolvency Rules 1986, r 4.90.

[34] See ch 15 below.

[35] (1839) 4 My & Cr 442, 41 ER 171. See ch 14 below.

[36] And also the customer. See para 15.31 below.

[37] *In re Milan Tramways Co, ex p Theys* (1882) 22 Ch D 122, 126; *Pellas v Neptune Marine Insurance Co* (1879) 5 CPD 34, 40; *Stumore v Campbell & Co* [1892] 1 QB 314, 316–317; *Smail v Zimmerman* [1907] VLR 702; *Hanak v Green* [1958] 2 QB 9, 22; *Bank of Boston Connecticut v European Grain and Shipping Ltd* [1989] 1 AC 1056, 1109; *Griffiths v Commonwealth Bank of Australia* (1994) 123 ALR 111, 124. See also *Westwind Air Charter Pty Ltd v Hawker de Havilland Ltd* (1990) 3 WAR 71, 84; *Hazcor Pty Ltd v Kirwanon Pty Ltd* (1995) 12 WAR 62. Compare the position in Victoria. See paras 2.64–2.66 below.

[38] *Civil Procedure* (Autumn 2001) vol 1, para 16.6.1.

should be the case, however. Like their predecessors, the Civil Procedure Rules relate only to matters of practice and procedure.[39] While the right of set-off, particularly pursuant to the Statutes of Set-off, has procedural aspects to it, it is nevertheless a defence, and because it is a defence it is not a matter of pure procedure.[40] Thus, the scope of the defence can have a substantive effect on the rights of third parties, such as assignees, who take subject to defences available to the debtor against the assignor.[41] Since set-off is not simply a question of practice and procedure, rules of court which are confined to matters of practice and procedure on their own cannot enlarge the defence. Indeed, it is questioned later whether the defence should be expanded.[42]

E. Applicable Law for Determining the Existence of a Cross-Claim

1.15   The question whether there is a defence to a claim governed by English law is also to be determined by English law. English law in this context includes the rules of private international law, and any foreign law which English law would regard as applicable pursuant to those rules. Therefore, where a defendant asserts a cross-claim against the claimant arising out of a contract which is governed by a foreign law, the question whether there is a cross-claim must be determined by reference to the foreign law.[43]

---

[39]   The Civil Procedure Act 1997, s 1(1), pursuant to which the new Civil Procedure Rules were made, provided that: 'There are to be rules of court . . . governing the practice and procedure . . .', and CPR r 1.1(1) states that 'These Rules are a new procedural code . . .'.

[40]   See paras 2.35–2.38 below.

[41]   See ch 17 below.

[42]   See paras 5.139–5.153 below.

[43]   *ISS Machinery Services Ltd v Aeolian Shipping SA (The Aeolian)* [2001] 2 Lloyd's Rep 641, esp at 644, *per* Potter LJ, referring to *Meridien BIAO Bank GmbH v Bank of New York* [1997] 1 Lloyd's Rep 437, 446, *per* Millett LJ.

2

SET-OFF BETWEEN SOLVENT PARTIES: COMMON LAW

A. Early Development

Prior to the enactment of the first Statute of Set-off in 1729[1] there was no general **2.01** right of set-off available to a defendant in a common law action when he was being sued by a solvent plaintiff, as opposed to the assignees of a bankrupt.[2] This denial of a set-off was consistent with the adoption of strict rules of pleading and of forms of action, which were designed to reduce the question to be decided by the court as far as possible to a single, well-defined issue.[3] There are instances in the late seventeenth and early eighteenth centuries in which equity enforced set-offs of unconnected debts by means of an injunction to restrain the plaintiff in an action

---

[1] (1729) 2 Geo II, c 22, s 13.

[2] For a discussion of the early development of set-off in English and Roman Law, see Loyd, 'The Development of Set-off' (1916) 64 University of Pennsylvania Law Review 541 and Tigar, 'Automatic Extinction of Cross-Demands: *Compensatio* From Rome to California' (1965) 53 California Law Review 224.

[3] See Loyd, 'The Development of Set-off' (1916) 64 University of Pennsylvania Law Review 541, 544, and also Lord Mansfield in *Green v Farmer* (1768) 4 Burr 2214, 2220, 98 ER 154, 157.

at law from proceeding with his claim against the defendant until he had given credit for his own indebtedness to the defendant. Those cases however should not be taken as evidence of a general equitable jurisdiction to set off cross-debts. Equitable relief usually was founded upon a custom that the accounts should be balanced,[4] or alternatively an implied agreement to that effect.[5] There is an early decision that seems to indicate a general equitable jurisdiction. In 1699, Sir John Trevor MR in *Arnold v Richardson*[6] ordered that a plaintiff in an action at law for payment of a debt on a bond should bring into account his own indebtedness to the defendant for food and lodging, even though 'there was no Agreement for that Purpose'. The reporter has attributed to the Master of the Rolls a remark that 'a Discount was natural Justice in all cases'. However, the judgment of Sir Joseph Jekyll MR some twenty-three years later in *Jeffs v Wood*[7] suggests that, in the absence of an insolvency, equity at that time ordinarily would look for evidence, however slight, of an agreement for a set-off.

2.02   There were also certain discrete situations in which rights akin to set-offs were recognized by the common law courts.[8] By this it is meant that the common law would allow the defendant in an action to plead the existence of certain facts as a means of reducing the amount which otherwise would be awarded to the plaintiff, when those facts could have formed the basis of a separate action by the defendant against the plaintiff. For example, a bailiff who was entitled to receive rent from the manor could obtain payment by recoupment from his obligation to account to his master.[9] Further, if a landlord disseised his tenant and the tenant then brought a writ of assise against the landlord, the landlord was entitled to deduct from the damages payable any rent which the tenant was required to pay for the period of the disseisin.[10] Similarly, if the holder of a rent-charge disseised the owner of the land, the former's right to receive payment under the charge for the period of the disseisin could be recouped from his obligation to pay damages to the landlord.[11] The holder of the rent-charge was given this right in order to

---

[4]   See *Curson v African Co* (1682) 1 Vern 121, 23 ER 358.

[5]   *Downam v Matthews* (1721) Prec Ch 580, 24 ER 260; *Hawkins v Freeman* 2 Eq Ca Abr 10, 22 ER 8. See also *Sir William Darcy's Case* (1677) 2 Freeman 28, 22 ER 1037; *Jeffs v Wood* (1723) 2 P Wms 128, 24 ER 668.

[6]   (1699) 1 Eq Ca Abr 8, 21 ER 833.

[7]   (1723) 2 P Wms 128, 24 ER 668.

[8]   A number of cases are collected in *Viner's Abridgment* (2nd edn, 1741) vol 8, 556–7. See also the discussion in Loyd, 'The Development of Set-off' (1916) 64 University of Pennsylvania Law Review 541, 544–6.

[9]   See *Viner's Abridgment* (2nd edn, 1741) vol 8, 557, and also the note to *Gybson v Searls* (1607) Cro Jac 176, 178, 79 ER 154, 155, citing 20 Hen 7, pl 5.

[10]   *Coulter's Case* 5 Co Rep 30a, 30b, 77 ER 98 (discussed in Loyd, 'The Development of Set-off' (1916) 64 University of Pennsylvania Law Review 541, 545). Only rent owing for the period of the disseisin could be deducted. Arrears of rent owing from before then could not be recouped in this manner. See *Viner's Abridgment* (2nd edn, 1741) vol 8, 556, citing 9 E 3.8.

[11]   See *Viner's Abridgment* (2nd edn, 1741) vol 8, 556, and *Coulter's Case* 5 Co Rep 30a, 31a, 77 ER 98, 100.

avoid circuity of action.[12] It should be compared to the right recognized by Gawdy J in 1591 in *Taylor v Beal*[13] in the situation in which a landlord under an obligation to repair premises failed to do so. In that circumstance, it was said that the tenant himself could undertake the repairs and deduct the expenses from his rent.[14] The tenant's right in this situation was not based upon a desire to avoid circuity of action, but rather Gawdy J said that 'the law giveth this liberty to the lessee to expend the rent in reparations, for he shall be otherwise at great mischief, for the house may fall upon his head before it be repaired; and therefore the law alloweth him to repair it, and recoupe the rent'.

Customary law provides another instance. According to the custom of foreign attachment, if a plaint was entered in the court of the mayor or the sheriff of the City of London against a defendant, and the process was returned *nihil*, and thereupon the plaintiff suggested that another person within London was indebted to the defendant, the debtor was warned, and if he did not deny that he was so indebted the debt was attached in his hands as payment to the plaintiff.[15] The custom apparently contemplated the attachment of a debt owing by the plaintiff himself to the defendant,[16] which in effect would have operated as a set-off of the plaintiff's debt against that of the defendant. It appears however that this custom has fallen into disuse.[17] **2.03**

B. Statutes of Set-off

(1) Introduction

The Statutes of Set-off were enacted in 1729 and 1735. The title of the first **2.04**
Statute, 'An Act for the Relief of Debtors with respect to the Imprisonment of their Persons',[18] suggests that their purpose was to assist debtors who were liable to be sent to debtors' prison for non-payment of debts, although Willes CJ not long after their enactment considered that they were designed to avoid circuity of

---

[12] See *Viner's Abridgment* (2nd edn, 1741) vol 8, 556, and *Coulter's Case* 5 Co Rep 30a, 31a, 77 ER 98, 100.

[13] (1591) Cro Eliz 222, 78 ER 478.

[14] The report suggests that Clench J agreed with this view, though he held against the tenant on a question of pleading. Fenner J on the other hand said that the tenant had to bring a separate action.

[15] See *Comyns' Digest* (5th edn, 1822) vol 1, 713–14.

[16] See Brandon, *The Customary Law of Foreign Attachment* (1861) 60–1, 143 n s, and *Comyns' Digest* (5th edn, 1822) vol 1, 716, although compare Bayley J in *Nonell v Hullett and Widder* (1821) 4 B & Ald 646, 106 ER 1073.

[17] See *Halsbury's Laws of England* (4th edn, 1998) vol 12(1), 180 para 628 n 13.

[18] (1729) 2 Geo II, c 22, s 13.

action and multiplicity of suits.[19] The first Statute was a temporary provision intended to last for a period of five years. It provided that:

> [W]here there are mutual Debts between the Plaintiff and Defendant, or if either Party sue or be sued as Executor or Administrator, where there are mutual Debts between the Testator or Intestate and either Party, one Debt may be set against the other, and such Matter may be given in Evidence upon the General Issue, or pleaded in Bar, as the Nature of the Case shall require, so as at the Time of his pleading the General Issue, where any such Debt of the Plaintiff, his Testator or Intestate, is intended to be insisted on in Evidence, Notice shall be given of the particular Sum or Debt so intended to be insisted on, and upon what Account if became due, or otherwise such Matter shall not be allowed in Evidence upon such General Issue.

2.05 Several questions arose upon the construction of this provision, for example, whether debts of a different nature (ie simple and specialty debts) could be set off against each other, and whether in the case of a bond the penalty was to be considered as the debt.[20] Therefore, when the right of set-off conferred by the first Statute of Set-off was made permanent in 1735 by the second Statute (8 Geo II, c 24, s 4), the Act went on to provide, in section 5, that mutual debts could be set off notwithstanding that in law they were deemed to be of a different nature, and further that, if either of the debts accrued by reason of a penalty in a bond, the amount to be included in the set-off was the amount 'truly and justly due'.[20a]

2.06 The Statutes were repealed in England in 1879 by section 2 of the Civil Procedure Acts Repeal Act in so far as they applied to the newly founded Supreme Court of Judicature, though it was expressly provided that the repeal was not to affect any 'jurisdiction or principle or rule of law or equity established or confirmed, or right or privilege acquired'.[21] This has been interpreted as preserving the right of set-off originally conferred by the Statutes.[22] Recently in the Court of Appeal Clarke LJ (with whose judgment Otton and Kennedy LJJ agreed) suggested that the Statutes of Set-off were replaced by the rules of court.[23] A more accurate statement

---

[19] *Hutchinson v Sturges* (1741) Willes 261, 262, 125 ER 1163; *Pilgrim v Kinder* (1744) 7 Mod 463, 467, 87 ER 1357, 1360. See also *Forster v Wilson* (1843) 12 M & W 191, 203, 152 ER 1165, 1171; *Ex parte Cleland, re Davies* (1867) LR 2 Ch App 808, 812–813; *Re Unit 2 Windows Ltd* [1985] 1 WLR 1383, 1387; *Fuller v Happy Shopper Markets Ltd* [2001] 1 WLR 1681, 1690 para 21.

[20] See the discussion in *Hutchinson v Sturges* (1741) Willes 261, 125 ER 1163.

[20a] See para 2.34 below.

[21] Civil Procedure Acts Repeal Act 1879, s 4(1)(b).

[22] *Re Daintrey* [1900] 1 QB 546, 548; *Hanak v Green* [1958] 2 QB 9, 22; *Southern Textile Converters Pty Ltd v Stehar Knitting Mills Pty Ltd* [1979] 1 NSWLR 692, 697–698; *Walker v Department of Social Security* (1995) 56 FCR 354, 374. See also, eg, *Henriksens Rederi A/S v THZ Rolimpex (The Brede)* [1974] 1 QB 233, 246, 252. There was a similar repeal and saving of the right of set-off in relation to courts other than the Supreme Court of Judicature, in the Statute Law Revision and Civil Procedure Act 1883 (which in turn was repealed by the Supreme Court of Judicature (Consolidation) Act 1925). See now the Courts and Legal Services Act 1990, s 3 (which was substituted for the County Courts Act 1984, s 38).

[23] *Glencore Grain Ltd v Agros Trading Co* [1999] 2 Lloyd's Rep 410, 417.

would be that the right of set-off conferred by the Statutes has been preserved, though the procedure for giving effect to it is now set out in the rules.[24]

Australia

In Australia, the operation of the Statutes of Set-off varies between the states. The **2.07** application of the Statutes in Australia is considered later.[25]

(2) When Must the Set-off be Available?

Prior to the Judicature Acts the courts applied the principle that a set-off under the **2.08** Statutes could only be pleaded in bar to the plaintiff's action if the set-off was available at the commencement of the action, as opposed to when the defence was delivered. In other words, at the date of the commencement of the action there had to be a presently existing and payable debt owing by the plaintiff to the defendant.[26] The principle was confirmed in *Richards v James*.[27] The plaintiff in that case became indebted to the defendant after the plaintiff had commenced proceedings against the defendant for payment of a debt. The defendant pleaded that, because of the cross-debt, the plaintiff ought not further to maintain his action. Pollock CB said that: 'The novelty of the plea is supported by no precedent, and there is nothing to warrant us in so construing the statute, so as to enable a defendant to set off a debt which has arisen since the commencement of the action.'[28] Subsequently, Farwell LJ in *Bennett v White*[29] referred to the form of plea for the right of set-off given in the third edition of Bullen and Leake in 1868, in terms that 'the plaintiff, *at the commencement of this suit*, was and still is indebted to the defendant'.[30] He said that it 'was at that time and always has been the proper form'.

Richards v James should no longer apply. After the Judicature Acts the Supreme **2.09** Court Rules[31] permitted a defendant to rely on a ground of defence which arose after the action was commenced, and in *Wood v Goodwin*[32] Mathew J applied that principle in relation to a defence of set-off. The Rules of the Supreme Court 1965

---

[24] See para 1.13 above.

[25] See paras 2.55–2.67 below.

[26] *Pilgrim v Kinder* (1744) 7 Mod 463, 87 ER 1357 (plaintiff's debt existing but not payable until after action commenced); *Evans v Prosser* (1789) 3 TR 186, 100 ER 524; *Richards v James* (1848) 2 Ex 471, 154 ER 577. See also *Rogerson v Ladbroke* (1822) 1 Bing 93, 130 ER 39; *Leman v Gordon* (1838) 8 Car & P 392, 173 ER 546; *Dendy v Powell* (1838) 3 M & W 442, 444, 150 ER 1218, 1219; *Lee v Lester* (1849) 7 CB 1008, 1017, 137 ER 399, 403; *Maw v Ulyatt* (1861) 31 LJ Ch 33.

[27] (1848) 2 Ex 471, 154 ER 577.

[28] (1848) 2 Ex 471, 473, 154 ER 577, 578.

[29] [1910] 2 KB 643, 648.

[30] Bullen and Leake, *Precedents of Pleadings* (3rd edn, 1868) 682 (emphasis added by Farwell LJ).

[31] The first such rule was the Rules of Court O 21 r 1 set out in the Supreme Court of Judicature Act 1875, First Schedule.

[32] [1884] WN 17. See also *Toke v Andrews* (1882) 8 QBD 428, 431.

similarly contained a provision to that effect, in O 18 r 9. While it has not been re-produced in the new Civil Procedure Rules 1998, there is nothing to suggest that the principle itself will not be continued. On the other hand, if a defendant wishes to amend his defence after it has been served, the Civil Procedure Rules now require the defendant to obtain either the written consent of all the other parties or the permission of the court.[33]

2.10 Farwell LJ's comment in *Bennett v White* (above) was made in a different context. The defendant in an action for payment of a debt sought to set off a debt originally due from the plaintiff to a third party, who had assigned it to the defendant. The plaintiff argued that the plea of set-off was bad, since set-off under the Statutes required that the debts originally should have existed between the plaintiff and the defendant. Farwell LJ did not refer to the pleading in Bullen and Leake in order to draw a distinction between debts arising before and after the commencement of the suit, but rather to show that it was not necessary that the plaintiff's debt should have been owing from its inception to the defendant. Of greater concern is *Edmunds v Lloyds Italico SpA*,[34] in which Sir John Donaldson MR referred to *Richards v James* in terms suggesting that it was regarded as still representing the law. The effect of the Supreme Court Rules after the Judicature Acts was not considered, however, and as a matter of policy it is difficult to see why a right of set-off arising after the commencement of the claimant's action should not be able to be relied on as a defence. There is support for that view in Australia,[35] and moreover Lord Hoffmann commented in passing in *Stein v Blake*[36] that set-off under the Statutes is confined to debts which are liquidated and due and payable 'at the time when the defence of set-off is filed'.[37]

2.11 The view that *Richards v James* no longer represents the law means that a cross-debt which arises after the commencement of the claimant's action may be pleaded as a set-off. This is not inconsistent with the principle discussed later, that a cross-debt owing by a claimant to the defendant must be enforceable at the commencement of the claimant's action in order to be available as a set-off.[38] The issue

---

[33] CPR Part 17.

[34] [1986] 1 WLR 492.

[35] Angas Parsons J in *Rex v Ray ex p Chapman* [1936] SASR 241, 247 noted without adverse comment the views of Farwell LJ in *Bennett v White*, which suggests that the principle in *Richards v James* was thought to be still applicable. In *Ingleton v Coates* (1896) 2 ALR 154, on the other hand, Madden CJ in the Victorian Supreme Court held that the Supreme Court Rules permitted the defendant to plead a set-off in respect of an indebtedness of the plaintiff assigned to him after commencement of the plaintiff's action. Powell J in *McColl's Wholesale Pty Ltd v State Bank of NSW* [1984] 3 NSWLR 365, 381 expressed a similar view in relation to the procedure in force at that time in New South Wales.

[36] [1996] AC 243, 251.

[37] In *Hoverd Industries Ltd v Supercool Refrigeration and Air Conditioning (1991) Ltd* [1995] 3 NZLR 577, 587 the New Zealand Court of Appeal referred to debts 'which can be ascertained with certainty at the time of pleading'.

[38] See paras 2.49–2.51 below.

of enforceability may arise, for example, in relation to a debt which is unenforceable because of the expiration of a time bar. The notion that unenforceability is determined as at the date of the claimant's action has the opposite effect to that which would follow from *Richards v James*. *Richards v James* unduly restricts the availability of the defence. On the other hand, the determination of the enforceability of a pre-existing cross-debt under a statute of limitation as at the commencement of the claimant's action, rather than the later date when the set-off is pleaded, expands the class of claims which can be set off under the Statutes.

2.12 The above discussion relates to a debt of the claimant that arises or becomes due and payable after commencement of the action and before judgment. If the debt arises after judgment, it generally does not provide a ground for restraining the claimant from enforcing the judgment.[39]

(3) Mutuality

2.13 For the Statutes of Set-off to apply there must be mutuality. Mutuality is considered later.[40]

(4) The Requirement of Debts

2.14 The Statutes only apply when there is a debt on each side of the account. The debts, and the transactions giving rise to them, need not be connected in any way.[41] But because of the requirement of 'debts', a claim for the return of goods,[42] or an entitlement to a statutory benefit which does not create a debt enforceable by action,[43] is not susceptible to a defence of set-off under the Statutes.

What is a 'debt'?

2.15 The word 'debt' is not used in the strict sense of a claim which could have been the subject of the old action of debt.[44] Rather, Cockburn CJ in *Stooke v Taylor*[45] said that the plea of set-off under the Statutes 'is available only where the claims on both sides are in respect of liquidated debts, or money demands which can be readily and without difficulty ascertained'.[46] Each of the demands accordingly

---

[39] *Maw v Ulyatt* (1861) 31 LJ Ch 33. See para 2.77 below.
[40] See ch 11 below.
[41] *Axel Johnson Petroleum AB v M G Mineral Group AG* [1992] 1 WLR 270, 272; *Courage Ltd v Crehan* [1999] 2 EGLR 145, 155; *Fuller v Happy Shopper Markets Ltd* [2001] 1 WLR 1681, 1690 para 21.
[42] *Green v Farmer* (1768) 4 Burr 2214, 98 ER 154.
[43] *Walker v Department of Social Security* (1995) 56 FCR 354.
[44] *Morley v Inglis* (1837) 4 Bing (NC) 58, 71, 132 ER 711, 716; *Victorian WorkCover Authority v Esso Australia Ltd* (2001) 182 ALR 321, 330 [30], HCA.
[45] (1880) 5 QBD 569, 575.
[46] Formerly it was said that a test for considering whether a plea of set-off was admissible in an action on an agreement was whether the agreement was such that *indebitatus assumpsit* would lie upon it. See Hill J in *Crampton v Walker* (1860) 3 El & El 321, 330–331, 121 ER 463, 466, referring to Tindal CJ in *Morley v Inglis* (1837) 4 Bing (NC) 58, 72, 132 ER 711, 716.

must be capable of being liquidated or ascertained with precision at the time of pleading,[47] or, as Lord Hoffmann expressed it in delivering the judgment of the House of Lords in *Stein v Blake*,[48] they must be 'either liquidated or in sums capable of ascertainment without valuation or estimation'. A recent illustration is *Axel Johnson Petroleum AB v MG Mineral Group AG*.[49] The defendant in an action for payment of a sum certain asserted that the plaintiff had agreed to buy all such oil as the defendant itself bought from a third party, the contract price being the same as the price paid by the defendant to the third party together with a sum of US$1.00 per tonne to cover 'local expenses'. The Court of Appeal held that the price payable by the plaintiff under the arrangement was liquidated, and accordingly could give rise to a defence under the Statutes so as to entitle the defendant to leave to defend. It was not necessary that the price should be capable of being computed by reference to the contract without investigation.

2.16   If the quantum of the claim sought to be set off by the defendant can only be ascertained by litigation or arbitration it generally will be unliquidated, and it makes no difference that an estimate has been made by an expert.[50] On the other hand, a cross-demand may still be regarded as liquidated notwithstanding that the defendant is unable to state at the present time what the precise value of the demand is. It would suffice that, when full particulars are known, the matter simply would be one of addition and subtraction. In a case in Victoria,[51] the defendant in an action on a cheque pleaded that the plaintiffs had been his agents for the sale of tallow, and in breach of their duty as agents they purchased the defendant's tallow themselves and sold it on their own account at enhanced prices without accounting for the difference in price. The defendant alleged that the difference in price amounted to more than the value of the cheque sued upon, though he said that he was not at present able to give further particulars. Although the amount was still uncertain, it was held that the demand nevertheless was pleadable as a set-off, because by its nature it was a liquidated demand.

2.17   If the defendant's cross-claim in its nature is liquidated, a set-off will not be denied simply because the cross-claim is disputed by the claimant as to all or part on grounds that require determination by litigation or arbitration. The defendant in such a case may plead the cross-claim as a defence to an action brought against

---

[47]   *Morley v Inglis* (1837) 4 Bing (NC) 58, 71, 132 ER 711, 716; *Henriksens Rederi A/S v THZ Rolimpex (The Brede)* [1974] 1 QB 233, 246; *Axel Johnson Petroleum AB v MG Mineral Group AG* [1992] 1 WLR 270, 272; *Courage Ltd v Crehan* [1999] 2 EGLR 145, 155.

[48]   [1996] AC 243, 251. See also Hoffmann LJ's earlier comment in *Aectra Refining and Manufacturing Inc v Exmar NV* [1994] 1 WLR 1634, 1649 ('either liquidated or capable of being quantified by reference to ascertainable facts which do not in their nature require estimation or valuation'), and *Fuller v Happy Shopper Markets Ltd* [2001] 1 WLR 1681, 1690 para 21.

[49]   [1992] 1 WLR 270.

[50]   *B Hargreaves Ltd v Action 2000 Ltd* [1993] BCLC 1111 (estimate by a surveyor of the amount claimed in respect of faulty workmanship).

[51]   *Woodroffe & Co v J W Moss* [1915] VLR 237.

him for payment of a debt, and in an application by the claimant for summary judgment the defendant may be granted leave to defend.[52] As Hirst LJ remarked in *Aectra Refining and Manufactuiring Inc v Exmar BV*,[53] when Cockburn CJ in *Stooke v Taylor* spoke of 'money demands which can be readily and without difficulty ascertained', he was referring to ascertainment of the quantum of the demand, and not to the amount which might ultimately be held recoverable after all the defences put forward have been considered.

Alternative causes of action

If the claim of one of the parties has both a liquidated and an unliquidated component, a set-off may proceed against the liquidated part.[54] Further, if the claimant's claim in truth is for a liquidated sum, so that prior to the Judicature Acts he could have maintained an action in *indebitatus assumpsit*, he should not be able to deprive the defendant of a right of set-off by framing his claim instead as an action for damages,[55] although there is authority to the contrary.[56] *Hutchinson v Reid*[57] is not inconsistent with that view. The plaintiff in that case sold goods to the defendant in consideration of the defendant's agreeing to accept a bill of exchange for the price, the bill to be payable in two months. The defendant refused to accept the bill whereupon the plaintiff, within the two-month period, commenced an action. As a defence the defendant pleaded a set-off in respect of a debt owing by the plaintiff. The defence failed, because the plaintiff was not suing for the price but rather for damages for failure to accept the bill. However, Lord Ellenborough emphasized in his judgment that the action had been brought within the two-month period. If the plaintiff had sued after the time of payment, the claim in effect would have been for the price, in which case his Lordship indicated that a set-off would have been available.

2.18

Demands closely analogous to debts

The test formulated by Cockburn CJ in *Stooke v Taylor*[58] has two aspects. It encompasses not only liquidated debts but also money demands which can be

2.19

---

[52] *Aectra Refining and Marketing Inc v Exmar NV* [1994] 1 WLR 1634, CA, leave to appeal refused [1995] 1 WLR 526.
[53] [1994] 1 WLR 1634, 1647.
[54] *Crampton v Walker* (1860) 3 El & El 321, 121 ER 463.
[55] *Birch v Depeyester* (1816) 4 Camp 385, 171 ER 122; *Crampton v Walker* (1860) 3 El & El 321, 331–332, 121 ER 463, 466–467. This is also consistent with the approach adopted by the Court of Appeal in a different context in *G L Baker Ltd v Barclays Bank Ltd* [1956] 1 WLR 1409.
[56] See eg *Colson v Welsh* (1795) 1 Esp 378, 170 ER 391; *Cooper v Robinson* (1818) 2 Chit 161; *Thorpe v Thorpe* (1832) 3 B & Ad 580, 584, 585, 110 ER 211, 212–213; *Hill v Smith* (1844) 12 M & W 618, 631, 152 ER 1346, 1351; *Halsbury's Laws of England* (4th edn, 1999) vol 42, 250 para 421.
[57] (1813) 3 Camp 329, 170 ER 1400.
[58] (1880) 5 QBD 569, 575.

readily and without difficulty ascertained. The better view, which was favoured by Hirst LJ in *Aectra Refining and Marketing Inc v Exmar NV*,[59] is that this second aspect refers to demands that are closely analogous to debts and which can be readily ascertained. It encompasses the old *indebitatus* counts,[60] including claims in *quantum meruit* and *quantum valebat* where work had been performed or goods sold without a price having been agreed.[61] In an appropriate case it may also include a demand that strictly sounds in damages, if indeed it is ascertainable with precision.[62] The classic example is a liquidated damages clause. It was settled in the eighteenth century that the obligation pursuant to a clause in a contract for the payment of liquidated damages in the event of a breach gives rise to a debt for the purpose of the Statutes.[63] Thus, a sum specified in a shipping contract as being payable by way of demurrage constitutes liquidated damages,[64] and the Court of Appeal in *Axel Johnson* recognized that it could be the subject of a set-off. That view should be compared to *Seeger v Duthie*,[65] in which a claim arising out of a delay in loading a ship was held not to come within the terms of the demurrage clause. Accordingly, it was a claim for unliquidated damages which could not be set off under the Statutes.

2.20   It is not intended to go through the catalogue of cases which illustrate whether various classes of claims are regarded as liquidated for the purpose of the Statutes. However a question of particular interest to the commercial community is whether a claim on a guarantee or an indemnity may be set off under the Statutes.

Claims on guarantees

2.21   Traditionally it has been thought that a claim on a guarantee is not susceptible to a set-off.

2.22   The difficulty with a set-off lies in the nature of a guarantor's liability. In *Moschi v Lep Air Services Ltd*[66] Lord Diplock explained that, by the beginning of the nineteenth century, it had come to be accepted in English law that the obligation assumed by a guarantor under the contract of guarantee is to see to it that the debtor

---

[59] [1994] 1 WLR 1634, 1647, approving of the explanation of counsel (at 1645).

[60] See *Howlet v Strickland* (1774) 1 Cowp 56, 57, 98 ER 965; *Victorian WorkCover Authority v Esso Australia Ltd* (2001) 182 ALR 321, 330 [30], HCA.

[61] See the discussion by Farwell LJ in *Lagos v Grunwaldt* [1910] 1 KB 41, 48 in relation to the meaning of the expression 'debt or liquidated demand', referred to in *Aectra Refining and Marketing Inc v Exmar NV* [1994] 1 WLR 1634, 1647.

[62] In *Axel Johnson Petroleum AB v MG Mineral Group AG* [1992] 1 WLR 270, 272 Leggatt LJ said that: 'For set-off to be available at law the claim and cross-claim must be mutual, but they need not be connected. They need not be debts strictly so called, but may sound in damages.' See also *B Hargreaves Ltd v Action 2000 Ltd* [1993] BCLC 1111, 1113.

[63] *Fletcher v Dyche* (1787) 2 TR 32, 100 ER 18. This assumes that the clause is not a penalty.

[64] *President of India v Lips Maritime Corporation* [1988] 1 AC 395.

[65] (1860) 8 CB(NS) 45, 141 ER 1081.

[66] [1973] AC 331, 348–349.

performs his obligation to the creditor. Accordingly, even if the subject of the guarantee is the payment of a debt, the creditor's remedy against the guarantor lies in damages for breach of contract. Thus, before the Judicature Acts, the creditor's action against the guarantor was in special *assumpsit*, rather than *indebitatus assumpsit*. Consistent with that view, in *Morley v Inglis*[67] the Common Pleas held that a claim on a guarantee could not be employed by the defendant in a set-off under the Statutes of Set-off, even though the obligation the subject of the guarantee itself was a debt. In particular, Tindal CJ said that the liability was not ascertained because the guarantor's liability for interest and expenses had not been ascertained by a jury.[68] Nevertheless, given the broad meaning that has now been ascribed to the word 'debts' in the Statutes,[69] *Morley v Inglis* is likely to be reconsidered. In that regard, Leggatt LJ in *Axel Johnson*[70] framed the principle in terms suggesting that a liability on a guarantee could be set off under the Statutes if the amount of the liability in respect of which the guarantee was given has been 'established'. But whatever the position in England, *Morley v Inglis* would not represent the law in Australia in light of comments by Mason CJ in the High Court in *Sunbird Plaza Pty Ltd v Maloney*.[71] The Chief Justice said of Lord Diplock's analysis that, while it may be correct as a matter of history, it does not accord with the modern view, that the guarantor of a debt may be sued for the money sum which the debtor has failed to pay. This should have as a consequence that a set-off should be available in Australia against a guarantor's liability when the subject of the liability is a debt.

There are indeed two cases which support a right of set-off in this situation, **2.23** though neither provides strong authority. In *National Bank of Australasia v Swan*,[72] Stawell CJ in the Victorian Supreme Court held that a set-off could occur against a guarantor's liability in respect of a debt. However, his Honour based his conclusion on the earlier decision in *Brown v Tibbitts*,[73] which in truth was concerned with an indemnity rather than a guarantee. Moreover, the case may be explained on the basis of the language of the guarantee in issue, by which the defendant promised to pay all advances which were made by the plaintiff to a third party in case of default. This seems to have been a conditional agreement to pay,

---

[67] (1837) 4 Bing (NC) 58, 132 ER 711. See also *Crawford v Stirling* (1802) 4 Esp 207, 170 ER 693; *Williams v Flight* (1842) 2 Dowl NS 11, 16–17. Compare *Bank of Ireland v Martin* [1937] IR 189, 191, *per* Meredith J, 205, *per* Fitzgibbon J, on appeal.

[68] (1837) 4 Bing (NC) 58, 72, 132 ER 711, 716.

[69] See para 2.15 above.

[70] [1992] 1 WLR 270, 272, referring to *Morley v Inglis*.

[71] (1988) 166 CLR 245, 255–256. Deane, Dawson and Toohey JJ agreed with Mason CJ's judgment. See also *Hawkins v Bank of China* (1992) 26 NSWLR 562; *Sandtara Pty Ltd v Abigroup Ltd* (1996) 42 NSWLR 491, 498.

[72] (1872) 3 VR (L) 168.

[73] (1862) 11 CB (NS) 855, 142 ER 1031.

in the sense discussed by Lord Reid in *Moschi*[74] and by Mason CJ in *Sunbird Plaza v Maloney*,[75] so that, when the condition occurred (ie default), the 'guarantor' himself became liable to pay the advances, as opposed to the usual promise of a guarantor to see to it that the principal debtor performs his payment obligation. The second case is *The Raven*,[76] in which Parker J seemed to accept that there could be a set-off against a claim under a guarantee.[77] *Morley v Inglis* was not discussed however, and moreover it is not clear from the judgment whether Parker J had in mind set-off under the Statutes or equitable set-off.

2.24   The above discussion relates to a guarantee of a debt. If the guarantee is in respect of another obligation, breach of which would give rise to a liability in damages, the claim of the person holding the guarantee against the guarantor similarly would be in damages,[78] and accordingly it could not be set off under the Statutes.

Indemnities

2.25   Indemnities similarly are not free from difficulty.

2.26   A promise of indemnity is regarded as a promise to hold the indemnified person harmless against a specified loss or expense. Consistent with that view, an action on a contract of indemnity is characterized at common law as an action for unliquidated damages, arising from the failure of the indemnifier to prevent the indemnified person from suffering damage.[79] A classic illustration is a policy of indemnity insurance. Save in the case of a valued policy where there has been a total loss,[80] a claim on the policy for a long time has been regarded as being for unliquidated damages.[81] That remains so even after the loss has been adjusted,

---

[74] [1973] AC 331, 344–345.

[75] (1988) 166 CLR 245, 256–257.

[76] *Banco Central SA v Lingoss & Falce Ltd (The Raven)* [1980] 2 Lloyd's Rep 266.

[77] See the discussion at [1980] 2 Lloyd's Rep 266, 271–272.

[78] *Sunbird Plaza Pty Ltd v Maloney* (1988) 166 CLR 245, 255.

[79] *Firma C-Trade SA v Newcastle Protection and Indemnity Association* [1991] 2 AC 1, 35–36, *per* Lord Goff of Chieveley. See also *Ventouris v Mountain (The Italia Express (No 2))* [1992] 2 Lloyd's Rep 281, 291–292 (in which Hirst J accepted that Lord Goff's statement of the law in *Firma C-Trade* was of general application); *Re Dixon* [1994] 1 Qd R 7, 18.

[80] *Irving v Manning* (1848) 6 CB 391, 422, 136 ER 1302, 1314 ('liquidated damages'); *Alexander v Ajax Insurance Co Ltd* [1956] VLR 436, 445–446; *Odyssey Re (Bermuda) v Reinsurance Australia* (2001) 19 ACLC 987, 992 para 16.

[81] *Luckie v Bushby* (1853) 13 CB 864, 138 ER 1443; *Pellas v Neptune Marine Insurance Co* (1879) 5 CPD 34; *William Pickersgill & Sons Ltd v London and Provincial Marine and General Insurance Co Ltd* [1912] 3 KB 614, 622; *Jabbour v Custodian of Israeli Absentee Property* [1954] 1 WLR 139, 145; *Chandris v Argo Insurance Co Ltd* [1963] 2 Lloyd's Rep 65, 73–74; *Edmunds v Lloyds Italico* [1986] 1 WLR 492, 493; *Accident Compensation Commission v C E Heath Underwriting & Insurance (Aust) Pty Ltd* [1990] VR 224, 231; *Penrith City Council v Government Insurance Office* (1991) 24 NSWLR 564, 568; *I M Properties plc v Cape & Dalgleish* [1999] QB 297, 304; *Odyssey Re (Bermuda) v Reinsurance Australia* (2001) 19 ACLC 987.

because the adjustment is said to be merely evidence of the amount due.[82] Given the nature of a claim on an indemnity, the courts have said that the claim may not be the subject of a set-off under the Statutes.[83] Nevertheless, as Pearson J once remarked,[84] the word 'damages' is used in a somewhat unusual sense in this context, and, at least if the loss has been adjusted, it is difficult as a matter of substance to see why a set-off should be denied. The argument that an adjustment is merely evidence of the amount of the loss, so that it may be rebutted, eg by proof of a mistake,[85] is not a convincing reason for disallowing a set-off if the adjustment is accepted by both parties. Further, it has been suggested in Victoria that a claim under a policy of liability insurance in relation to an ascertained liability might not attract the same constraint in relation to set-off.[86]

In any event, there is no such difficulty when non-indemnity insurance is in issue. **2.27** The action in this instance is brought to recover a liquidated sum due under the contract, in which case there is no reason for denying a right of set-off under the Statutes against the claim.[87]

A less restrictive approach has also been adopted in relation to an indemnity given **2.28** for costs and expenses incurred.[88] If costs and expenses coming within the indemnity have been both incurred and paid, the courts have accepted that the resulting claim on the indemnity for reimbursement may be the subject of a set-off.[89] Similarly it has been said that there may be a set-off in the situation in which an indemnity is given to an accommodation acceptor of a bill of exchange, and the acceptor makes a claim on the indemnity for the amount that he has had to pay on the bill.[90] If on the other hand the sums in question have not been paid, a claim for payment pursuant to the indemnity has been said to be unliquidated so that it

---

[82] *Luckie v Bushby* (1853) 13 CB 864, 138 ER 1443; *Jabbour v Custodian of Israeli Absentee Property* [1954] 1 WLR 139, 143. Compare *Alexander v Ajax Insurance Co Ltd* [1956] VLR 436, 446.

[83] *Grant v Royal Exchange Assurance Co* (1815) 5 M & S 439, 105 ER 1111; *Castelli v Boddington* (1852) 1 El & Bl 66, 118 ER 361 (affirmed (1853) 1 El & Bl 879, 118 ER 665); *Luckie v Bushby* (1853) 13 CB 864, 138 ER 1443; *Pellas & Co v Neptune Marine Insurance Co* (1879) 5 CPD 34.

[84] *Jabbour v Custodian of Israeli Absentee Property* [1954] 1 WLR 139, 144.

[85] See *Jabbour v Custodian of Israeli Absentee Property* [1954] 1 WLR 139, 145.

[86] *Accident Compensation Commission v C E Heath Underwriting & Insurance (Aust) Pty Ltd* [1990] VR 224, 231. Tadgell J suggested that this especially may be the case in Victoria in view of the Supreme Court Rules, r 13.14. See paras 2.64–2.66 below.

[87] *Blackley v National Mutual Life Association (No 2)* [1973] 1 NZLR 668, 672.

[88] Compare *Cooper v Robinson* (1818) 2 Chit 161.

[89] *Hutchinson v Sydney* (1854) 10 Ex 438, 156 ER 508; *Brown v Tibbitts* (1862) 11 CB(NS) 855, 142 ER 1031. Compare *Attwooll v Attwooll* (1853) 2 El & Bl 23, 118 ER 677, though that case should be understood as turning on a peculiarity of a claim on a penal bond. See Leggatt LJ in *Axel Johnson* [1992] 1 WLR 270, 273–274.

[90] A suggestion to that effect in *Hardcastle v Netherwood* (1821) 5 B & Ald 93, 106 ER 1027 was adopted in later cases. See *Brown v Tibbitts* (1862) 11 CB(NS) 855, 867, 142 ER 1031, 1036; *Crampton v Walker* (1860) 3 El & El 321, 121 ER 463.

cannot be the subject of a set-off,[91] although there is authority in Australia which suggests a more liberal view.[92] If the claim on the indemnity has both a liquidated and an unliquidated component, a set-off under the Statutes may proceed against the liquidated component.[93]

(5) Due and Payable

2.29   A set-off under the Statutes is only available in respect of cross-debts that are due and payable.[94] A debt which is payable *in futuro*,[95] or which is merely contingent,[96] cannot be employed in a set-off.

2.30   When a debt is payable on demand, the requirement of a demand is not regarded as creating a contingency if the liability in question is primary rather than secondary,[97] unless, it would seem, if the effect of the demand is to change the nature of the liability.[98] This may arise, for example, when a notice turns a liability to pay by instalments into a liability to pay the whole at once.[99] A classic example of a secondary liability is a liability under a guarantee. In that case, the requirement of a demand renders the liability contingent upon the making of a demand. But if the guarantee stipulates that the guarantor is to be liable as a principal debtor, the liability is primary, and the debt is not then contingent upon a demand.[100]

2.31   The question of when the debt must be due and payable was considered earlier.[101] Prior to the Judicature Acts, the courts applied the principle that a set-off could only be pleaded in bar to the plaintiff's action if the set-off was available at the

---

[91]   *Crampton v Walker* (1860) 3 El & El 321, 121 ER 463 (esp at 329–330, 466 referring to *Hardcastle v Netherwood* (1821) 5 B & Ald 93, 106 ER 1027).

[92]   *Kostka v Addison* [1986] 1 Qd R 416 (on the assumption that the clause conferred a true indemnity).

[93]   *Crampton v Walker* (1860) 3 El & El 321, 121 ER 463, and see also *Brown v Tibbitts* (1862) 11 CB(NS) 855, 867, 142 ER 1031, 1036. Compare *Cooper v Robinson* (1818) 2 Chit 161.

[94]   *Stein v Blake* [1996] 1 AC 243, 251; *Hoverd Industries Ltd v Supercool Refrigeration and Air Conditioning (1991) Ltd* [1995] 3 NZLR 577, 587 ('presently due'); *Fuller v Happy Shopper Markets Ltd* [2001] 1 WLR 1681, 1690 para 21. Compare *NZ Factors Ltd v Farmers Trading Co Ltd* [1992] 3 NZLR 703, 710.

[95]   *Pilgrim v Kinder* (1744) 7 Mod 463, 87 ER 1357; *Smith, Fleming & Co's Case* (1866) LR 1 Ch App 538 (which was decided before the bankruptcy set-off section was imported into the law of company liquidation); *Rex v Ray ex p Chapman* [1936] SASR 241, 247; *Hoverd Industries Ltd v Supercool Refrigeration and Air Conditioning (1991) Ltd* [1995] 3 NZLR 577, 587.

[96]   *Fromont v Coupland* (1824) 2 Bing 170, 130 ER 271; *Leman v Gordon* (1838) 8 Car & P 392, 173 ER 546. Compare *Agra & Masterman's Bank v Hoffman* (1864) 34 LJ Ch 285, although the injunction to restrain the action at law in that case was granted on the basis of an equitable set-off, as opposed to a set-off under the Statutes.

[97]   See Hoffmann LJ, and Dillon LJ in the Court of Appeal, in *M S Fashions Ltd v Bank of Credit and Commerce International SA* [1993] Ch 425, 436, 447–448, and the cases there referred to.

[98]   *Esso Petroleum Co Ltd v Alstonbridge Properties Ltd* [1975] 1 WLR 1474, 1483.

[99]   *Esso Petroleum Co Ltd v Alstonbridge Properties Ltd* [1975] 1 WLR 1474, 1483.

[100]   *M S Fashions Ltd v Bank of Credit and Commerce International SA* [1993] Ch 425, 436, 447–448.

[101]   See paras 2.08–2.12 above.

commencement of the action.[102] That should no longer be the case, however. A defendant should be able to plead a set-off in respect of matters arising subsequent to the action,[103] so that it should suffice if the plaintiff's cross-debt is due and payable when the defence of set-off is filed.

(6) Freight and Negotiable Instruments

It has been suggested that a defence of set-off under the Statutes of Set-off is not **2.32** available in an action against the issuer of a negotiable instrument, or against a claim for the payment of freight under a voyage charterparty or a bill of lading. The better view is that there are no such restrictions.[104]

(7) Procedural Defence

While the right of set-off derived from the Statutes of Set-off operates as a defence **2.33** to an action at law for payment of a debt, it is commonly described as a procedural defence.[105] By this it is meant that separate and distinct debts remain in existence until there is judgment for a set-off[106] and, moreover, unlike the substantive defence of equitable set-off,[107] prior to judgment the rights consequent upon being a creditor still attach, as do the obligations and liabilities consequent upon being a debtor. For example, the statute (1605) 3 Jac 1, c 15 provided that, if a debtor living within the city of London owed a debt of 40s or less (other than certain specified debts), it had to be sued for in the court of requests, failing which the plaintiff was not entitled to costs of the action. The courts held that the amount owing had to be measured irrespective of any right of set-off available to the defendant under the Statutes,[108] the reason being that the mutual debts were still subsisting at the commencement of the action.[109]

---

[102] *Richards v James* (1848) 2 Ex 471, 154 ER 577.

[103] See *Wood v Goodwin* [1884] WN 17.

[104] See paras 5.17–5.22 (freight), and paras 5.35–5.40 (negotiable instruments) below.

[105] In addition to the cases referred to below, see *Fuller v Happy Shopper Markets Ltd* [2001] 1 WLR 1681, 1690 para 21 ('procedural device'). Compare McCracken, *The Banker's Remedy of Set-off* (2nd edn, 1998) 133–5. *Smit Tek International v Selco Salvage Ltd* [1988] 2 Lloyd's Rep 398, 404–405 is difficult to follow in this regard.

[106] *Briscoe v Hill* (1842) 10 M & W 735, 738, 152 ER 668, 670, *per* Parke B, *arguendo* ('The meaning of a plea of set-off is, that the plaintiff was and still is indebted to the defendant in a larger amount than his demand against the defendant, and in order to make that defence available, it should be equally true at the time of the trial as at the time of pleading.'); *Lee v Lester* (1849) 7 CB 1008, 1015, 137 ER 399, 402 (Maule J, *arguendo*); *Stooke v Taylor* (1880) 5 QBD 569, 575; *Re Hiram Maxim Lamp Company* [1903] 1 Ch 70, 74; *Re K L Tractors Ltd* [1954] VLR 505, 507; *Stehar Knitting Mills Pty Ltd v Southern Textile Converters Pty Ltd* [1980] 2 NSWLR 514, 518; *Covino v Bandag Manufacturing Pty Ltd* [1983] 1 NSWLR 237, 238; *Glencore Grain Ltd v Agros Trading Co* [1999] 2 Lloyd's Rep 410. See also *Stein v Blake* [1996] 1 AC 243, 251; *Ciavarella v Balmer* [1983] 2 NSWLR 439, 442. For other authorities in support of this proposition, see Wood, *English and International Set-off* (1989) 43–4.

[107] See paras 4.29–4.43 below.

[108] *Pitts v Carpenter* (1743) 1 Wils KB 19, 95 ER 469; *Gross v Fisher* (1770) 3 Wils KB 48, 95 ER 926.

[109] *Gross v Fisher* (1770) 3 Wils KB 48, 49, 95 ER 926.

2.34 In considering this point two lines of authority should be distinguished. In the first place, in some early cases in which the question of arrest for non-payment of a debt was in issue, it was accepted that the balance only after setting off any mutual debt owing by the creditor to the debtor was the amount for which the creditor could procure the debtor's arrest.[110] The fact that this was so before judgment for a set-off is indicative of a substantive defence. The cases, however, involved the special question of a person's liberty, and on that basis they should be regarded as exceptions to the general principle that set-off under the Statutes is a procedural defence. It is also necessary to explain another line of cases concerning claims on penal bonds. If a bond provided for payment of a penalty in the event of default in the payment of a sum of money, and the defendant, having defaulted in payment to the plaintiff, nevertheless was a creditor of the plaintiff for a greater amount, the plaintiff could not obtain judgment for the penalty.[111] This may suggest that a set-off was thought to have already occurred against the required payment, so that there was no default and therefore no justification for suing for the penalty, which in turn would suggest that the set-off was thought to operate substantively. The cases however turned upon a special provision in the second Statute of Set-off[112] that, if one of the debts in a set-off accrued by reason of a penalty contained in a bond or specialty, judgment could be entered 'for no more than shall appear to be truly and justly due to the plaintiff, after one debt being set against the other'. If the plaintiff himself was indebted to the defendant for an amount which exceeded the amount in respect of which the defendant had defaulted, there was nothing 'truly and justly due to the plaintiff', so that the plaintiff was not entitled to judgment for the amount of the penalty.

The substantive aspects of the defence

2.35 While set-off under the Statutes is described as a procedural defence, it should be appreciated nevertheless that it is not wholly a matter of procedure.[113]

2.36 The fundamental point is that the right of set-off derived from the Statutes is a defence. In that sense it differs from counterclaim, which merely provides a mechanism by which separate actions may be tried in the same proceedings. Counterclaim is not a defence, and is properly described as being wholly procedural. But because the Statutes provided a defence, the right in question is not wholly a matter of procedure. It can have a substantive effect upon the rights and interests of third parties. For example, an assignee of a debt takes subject to

---

[110] *Dronefield v Archer* (1822) 5 B & Ald 513, 106 ER 1278; *Austin v Debnam* (1824) 3 B & C 139, 107 ER 686. Compare the earlier decision in *Brown v Pigeon* (1811) 2 Camp 594, 170 ER 1263.

[111] *Collins v Collins* (1755) 2 Burr 820, 97 ER 579; *Lee v Lester* (1849) 7 CB 1008, 137 ER 399. See also *Rodgers v Maw* (1846) 15 M & W 444, 153 ER 924.

[112] (1735) 8 Geo II, c 24, s 5.

[113] See also McCracken, *The Banker's Remedy of Set-off* (2nd edn, 1998) 111 *et seq.*

defences, including rights of set-off, [114] which were available to the debtor against the assignor before the debtor received notice of the assignment.[115] This includes the case of a secured creditor pursuant to a crystallized floating charge, because the creditor is regarded as an equitable assignee of any debt owing to the company which comes within the ambit of the charge.[116] Similarly, when an undisclosed principal sues on a contract entered into by his agent, the principal may be met by any right of set-off under the Statutes, or any other defence, that would have been available to the defendant against the agent before the defendant had notice of the agency.[117] A similar situation may arise in relation to an action by a party with sub-rogation rights, for example a subrogated insurer,[118] or where a judgment creditor is seeking to attach a debt owing by a third party to the judgment debtor by way of a garnishee order, in circumstances where the third party would have had a defence of set-off available in an action brought against him by the judgment debtor for payment of the debt.[119]

If the availability of a defence of set-off can affect the interests of third parties in this manner, the right could hardly be described as wholly procedural.[120] Admittedly, for the purpose of private international law set-off has been said to be a matter of procedure, with the result that it is governed by the *lex fori*.[121] However **2.37**

---

[114] See, for example, *Roxburghe v Cox* (1881) 17 Ch D 520, 526, *per* James LJ (an assignee 'takes subject to all rights of set-off and other defences which were available against the assignor'); *White & Tudor's Leading Cases in Equity* (9th edn, 1928) vol 1, 136; *Edward Nelson & Co Ltd v Faber & Co* [1903] 2 KB. 367, 375 *per* Joyce J ('It is a general rule with respect to a chose in action that an assignee takes it subject to all equities—in other words, whatever defence by way of set-off or otherwise the debtor would be entitled to set up against the assignor's claim up to the time of his receiving notice of the assignment . . .').

[115] See ch 17 below. There are some nineteenth century cases that have been interpreted in Australia as supporting a proposition that an assignee of a debt may take subject to an unliquidated cross-demand available to the debtor against the assignor, notwithstanding that it would not have given rise to a defence as between those parties, if it arose out of the same contract or transaction as the assigned debt. The point in relation to that interpretation is that it is not generally regarded as sufficient to give rise to an equitable set-off that the cross-demands arose out of the same contract or transaction. The impeachment test for equitable set-off, which still generally applies in Australia (see paras 4.21–4.28 below), requires something more than that. See para 4.16 below. The proposition inherent in that interpretation, that a cross-demand that is not available as a set-off against an assignor can bind the assignee, was rejected by the House of Lords in *Bank of Boston Connecticut v European Grain and Shipping Ltd* [1989] 1 AC 1056, 1105–1106, 1109–1111, and it seems incorrect, both historically and as a matter or principle. See paras 17.05–17.09 below.

[116] *N W Robbie & Co Ltd v Witney Warehouse Co Ltd* [1963] 1 WLR 1324. See para 17.74 below.

[117] See paras 13.71–13.91 below.

[118] See *Sydney Turf Club v Crowley* [1971] 1 NSWLR 724, 734, *per* Mason JA. ('When an insurer is subrogated to the rights of the insured against a third party . . . [the action] is brought in the name of the insured and it is subject to all the defences which would be available if the action had been brought by the insured for his own benefit'), and also Derham, *Subrogation in Insurance Law* (1985), 122–3.

[119] See paras 17.104–17.112 below.

[120] See Derham, 'Set-off in Victoria' (1999) 73 Australian Law Journal 754, 760–4.

[121] *Meyer v Dresser* (1864) 16 CB(NS) 646, 665, 666, 143 ER 1280, 1287–1288; *Maspons y Hermano v Mildred Goyeneche & Co* (1882) 9 QBD 530.

this principle should be approached with caution in other contexts, because English private international lawyers in the past have tended to give a wide meaning to the term 'procedure' in order to evade unsatisfactory choice of law rules.[122] Merely because something is regarded as a matter of procedure for the purpose of private international law does not mean that it is matter of procedure for all other purposes. In Victoria, for example, *William Cook Pty Ltd v Read*[123] concerned the question whether the power conferred on the Governor in Council by s 5 of the Justices Act 1958 (Vic) to make rules as to practice and procedure included a power to make rules as to evidence. O'Bryan J in the Victorian Supreme Court held that it did not, even though in private international law the rules of evidence are regarded as a matter of procedure.[124]

2.38 In Australia, Meagher, Gummow and Lehane expressed the view that, while rights of set-off are procedural in so far as they depend on entry of judgment for their effect, in so far as they operate as 'pleas in bar, they seem to be substantive rights'.[125] Hoffmann LJ made a similar point in *Aectra Refining and Manufacturing Inc v Exmar NV*.[126] In drawing a distinction between the substantive defence of equitable (or, as it is sometimes called, transaction) set-off,[127] and set-off under the Statutes of Set-off (which he termed independent set-off, and which he referred to generally as having a procedural basis[128]), he said that: 'It would not be entirely true to say that transaction set-off was substantive while independent set-off was procedural, because independent set-off does operate as a substantive reduction or extinction of the debt owed to the plaintiff. But it arrives at this result by procedural means.' This thesis is also reflected in Lord Hoffmann's later comment in the House of Lords in *Stein v Blake*,[129] that 'Legal set-off does not affect the substantive rights of the parties against each other, at any rate until both causes of action have been merged in a judgment of the court.' Thus, the result is substantive, but the means of achieving it are procedural.

Concepts inherent in describing the defence as procedural

2.39 There are two concepts inherent in the notion that set-off under the Statutes is a procedural defence. The first is that legal proceedings are required in order to

---

[122] Dicey and Morris, *The Conflict of Laws* (13th edn, 2000) vol 1, 157, and see also McCracken, *The Banker's Remedy of Set-off* (2nd edn, 1998) 113 where this point is made in relation to set-off.

[123] [1940] VLR 214.

[124] [1940] VLR 214, 218–219.

[125] Meagher, Gummow and Lehane, *Equity Doctrines and Remedies* (3rd edn, 1992) 825 para 3714.

[126] [1994] 1 WLR 1634, 1650.

[127] See ch 4 below.

[128] Hoffmann LJ said (at [1994] 1 WLR 1634, 1650) that: 'The procedural basis of independent set-off is reflected in the rule that the mere existence of liquidated cross-claims does not automatically extinguish the smaller debt.'

[129] [1996] 1 AC 243, 251.

bring about a set-off, so that one of the parties to mutual debts cannot act unilaterally to achieve that result.[130] As Brett LJ once remarked,[131] 'the right of set-off only arises where there is an action between parties. It is a statutable remedy which only is given in the case of an action'. The fact that the debts are not set off until judgment is evident from the old form of pleading for set-off under the Statutes, that 'the plaintiff, before and at the time of the commencement of his suit was and from thence hitherto hath been *and still is* indebted to the defendant'.[132] The plea was bad if it was not stated that the plaintiff 'still is' indebted.[133] It should be compared to a defence that the plaintiff and the defendant had agreed prior to the action that the two debts should be set off. In that circumstance, the defendant would plead accord and satisfaction rather than set-off.[134]

The second concept is that the Statutes only authorized a set-off in legal proceed-   **2.40**
ings where the set-off was being pleaded in those proceedings as a *defence*.[135] The second Statute[135a] provided that 'mutual debts may be set against each other, either by being pleaded in bar, or given in evidence on the general issue . . .'. Both the general issue and a special plea in bar were pleas which denied a cause of complaint.[136] The general issue was a plea which imported an absolute and general denial of what was alleged in the plaintiff's declaration, without offering any special matter whereby it was evaded. A special plea in bar, on the other hand, set forth the particular facts which comprised the defence. Rules made in Hilary Term, 4 Will 4, had the effect that henceforth set-off had to be specially pleaded, and it could not be given in evidence under the general issue.[137] The point remains, however, that those pleas were the only means contemplated in the second Statute for bringing about a set-off. While the pleas themselves are now obsolete, it is clear that the Statutes only applied where a set-off was pleaded as a defence.

---

[130]   *Aectra Refining and Marketing Inc v Exmar NV* [1994] 1 WLR 1634, 1650; *Glencore Grain Ltd v Agros Trading Co* [1999] 2 Lloyd's Rep 410. Similarly, in the case of an assignment of a debt, notice of the assignment to the debtor does not effect a set-off of the debts. See *Glencore v Agros* at 417–419. It is difficult to follow Kerr LJ's suggestion in *BICC plc v Burndy Corporation* [1985] 1 Ch 232, 254–255 that Burndy could have acted unilaterally to bring about a set-off so as to extinguish BICC's claim (the case concerned legal set-off under the Statutes (see *per* Dillon LJ at 247 and *per* Kerr LJ at 256 and 259) and so presumably the comment was intended to apply in that context).

[131]   *Re Anglo-French Co-operative Society, ex p Pelly* (1882) 21 Ch D 492, 507. While the *Pelly* case concerned a company in liquidation, Brett LJ's reference later in that paragragh to the 'statute of set-off' suggests that he had in mind the Statutes rather than the insolvency set-off section.

[132]   See Chitty's *Precedents in Pleadings* (2nd edn, 1847) 390.

[133]   *Dendy v Powell* (1838) 3 M & W 442, 150 ER 1218.

[134]   Chitty's *Precedents in Pleadings* (2nd edn, 1847) 237–8.

[135]   See eg Parke B in *Graham v Partridge* (1836) 1 M & W 395, 401, 150 ER 488, 490 ('The legislature constituted it a defence . . .'). In *Stein v Blake* [1996] 1 AC 243, 253 Lord Hoffmann said that set-off under the Statutes 'can be invoked only by the filing of a defence in an action'.

[135a]   (1735) 8 Geo II, c 24, s5.

[136]   See generally *Blackstone's Commentaries* (1768) vol 3, 305–306.

[137]   *Fidgett v Penny* (1834) 1 C M & R 108, 149 ER 1014; *Graham v Partridge* (1836) 1 M & W 395, 150 ER 488.

2.41   These concepts nevertheless have not always been applied. Two cases are of particular interest in this regard.[138] The first is *Shipton v Casson*,[139] the relevant facts of which may be summarized as follows. The plaintiffs and the defendant had agreed that a debt should be payable by instalments, but that, in the event of default in the payment of any one instalment, the plaintiffs could accelerate the debt so that the full amount was payable. The plaintiffs alleged that the first instalment had not been paid in full, and accordingly they sued for the full debt. The defendant pleaded that he had sold some goods to the plaintiffs, and that the plaintiffs' indebtedness for the price could be set off against the unpaid part of the instalment. On that basis, it was said that the instalment should be regarded as having been paid in full, and that the plaintiffs therefore were not entitled to accelerate the debt. The defendant's plea was successful, but the decision is difficult to explain. The defendant's right of set-off only entitled him to a defence to an action at law. But this should not have helped the defendant, because the point remained that he had not paid the first instalment on time. Payment of the instalment by way of a set-off would not have occurred until there was judgment for a set-off. On that basis there had been a default, and therefore the plaintiffs prima facie should have been entitled to accelerate. One can appreciate the justice of the result, but the difficulty is in explaining it.[140] In some cases it may be possible to interpret the contract as not permitting acceleration unless the creditor could have obtained judgment for payment of the outstanding instalment. This approach was adopted in a case in Victoria.[141] In issue in that case was a contract which entitled one party to terminate it if the other failed to pay any sum payable to the first party. Byrne J in the Victorian Supreme Court interpreted this as referring to a non-payment of a sum in respect of which the first party could have obtained judgment, so that non-payment in circumstances where the second party had a defence of set-off to an action for payment did not justify termination.

2.42   The second case is *Parker v Jackson*.[142] The plaintiffs were the trustees of the will of John Parker. Prior to his death Parker had mortgaged a property to secure a debt of £700 to Mrs Williams. After Parker's death, his solicitor took a transfer of the mortgage. In addition the solicitor, once again after the death, received a sum of £2,000 constituting the proceeds of an investment made on behalf of the estate. This sum was payable to the plaintiffs as trustees of the estate. The position

---

[138] Other cases referred to in Wood, *English and International Set-off* (1989) 44–50 may be explained on other grounds. The cases referred to in Wood, *op cit* 50–1 should be considered in the context of combination of bank accounts rather than the Statutes of Set-off. See ch 15 below.

[139] (1826) 5 B & C 378, 108 ER 141.

[140] There would be no such difficulty however in the case of a substantive defence of equitable set-off. See para 4.36 below.

[141] *Auspac Trade International Pty Ltd v Victorian Dairy Industry Authority* (Vic SC, 30 June 1993, at pp 69–71), *per* Byrne J. His Honour's comments on set-off were affirmed on appeal (22 February 1994 at p 39).

[142] [1936] 2 All ER 281.

accordingly was that the solicitor was a creditor of the estate to the extent of £700 on the mortgage, but at the same time was liable to hand over £2,000. Subsequently, the solicitor transferred the mortgage to a client. The client as transferee gave notice of the transfer to the plaintiffs, requesting that all interest henceforth should be paid to her. The plaintiffs then brought this action seeking a declaration that the mortgage debt had been discharged, and an order for the de-livery up of the mortgage deed and the documents of title. The impetus for this was that the solicitor was insolvent, so that a claim by the trustees for payment of the £2,000 would not have been satisfied. Equally, if the plaintiffs succeeded in the action so that the mortgage was discharged, the transferee would have lost the mortgage and would have been left with a worthless claim against the solicitor. As Farwell J remarked, this was a case in which one of two innocent parties had to suffer. His Lordship held in favour of the plaintiffs. He said that, before the solic-itor transferred the mortgage, the plaintiffs as trustees of the estate were entitled to direct the solicitor to apply part of the £2,000 in discharge of the mortgage. This was regarded as a right of set-off.[143] While the plaintiffs in fact did not give a direction to that effect, the transferee nevertheless took subject to the right to do so on the basis of the principle that an assignee takes subject to equities.

It is difficult to support Farwell J's view, that the trustees of the estate had a right **2.43** of set-off which entitled them to direct the solicitor to satisfy the mortgage debt out of the money owing to the estate. His Lordship would appear to have had in mind a set-off under the Statutes, though the Statutes only provide a procedural defence. They do not entitle one party to mutual debts to act unilaterally to bring about a set-off by notice to the other party. The set-off requires a judgment. Indeed, the view expressed by Farwell J sits uneasily with the principle that inter-est on a mortgage debt continues to accrue even though there may be a debt for a greater amount owing by the mortgagee to the mortgagor on another account. The mortgagor cannot avoid that result simply by requesting the mortgagee to apply the cross-debt in discharge of the mortgage debt.[144] It is also inconsistent with a dictum of Megarry J in *Samuel Keller (Holdings) Ltd v Martins Bank Ltd.*[145] In the *Samuel Keller* case, mortgaged premises had been sold, and debts owing to first and second mortgagees had been satisfied from the proceeds. The third mort-gagee said that the remaining proceeds should be paid to it, while the mortgagor argued that the proceeds should be paid into court pending the determination of a damages action which the mortgagor had commenced against the third

---

[143] See the judgment at [1936] 2 All ER 281, 289, 291 ('as in this case the mortgagors had an un-doubted right of set-off against the assignor . . .').

[144] *Garforth v Bradley* (1755) 2 Ves Sen 675, 678, 28 ER 430, 432; *Fisher and Lightwood's Law of Mortgage* (11th edn, 2002) 791 para 28.37. See also *Pettat v Ellis* (1804) 9 Ves Jun 563, 32 ER 721, although in any event a set-off under the Statutes was not available in that case.

[145] [1971] 1 WLR 43, 48. Russell LJ on appeal in the Court of Appeal (at 51) quoted this passage with approval.

mortgagee, on the basis that the mortgage debt had been satisfied by the mortgagor's unilateral appropriation to it of the damages cross-claim. In holding in favour of the mortgagee Megarry J said:

> Unless and until the mortgage in this case is discharged in the appropriate way on actual payment and acceptance of the sum due, I think that the mortgage remains a mortgage . . . .[146]

and:

> Even where there is a claim which is both liquidated and admitted, and it exceeds the mortgage debt in amount, it may be to the interest of one party or the other, or both, that the mortgage and the mortgage debt should continue in existence. The rate of interest may be attractively high or seductively low; there may be fiscal advantages in keeping the mortgage alive; there may be new projects to be financed which make liquid cash preferable to the satisfaction of mortgage debts; and so on. Nor have I heard any reason why it should be the mortgagor who is to have a unilateral power to discharge the mortgage debt by appropriation without payment.[147]

2.44 While the trustees in *Parker v Jackson* in truth would not have been entitled to act unilaterally to bring about a set-off, it has been suggested that the case was still correctly decided, on the ground that they had a *right* of set-off against the solicitor, and the court therefore could give a judgment for a set-off which was binding on the transferees in accordance with the usual principles governing set-off against assignees.[148] There are two difficulties with that view, however.[149]

2.45 The first is that the plaintiffs were seeking a declaration that the mortgage had been discharged and an order for redemption. The Statutes of Set-off, on the other hand, only authorized a set-off in legal proceedings where the set-off was pleaded as a defence. Since a set-off was not being raised as a defence in *Parker v Jackson*, the case would not appear to have been within the ambit of the Statutes.[150] If a mortgagee sues for the mortgage debt, he may be met by a set-off. But consistent with the view of Megarry J in the *Samuel Keller* case, if the mortgagee does not sue for payment, and instead relies on the security as a lever in order to obtain a perceived commercial advantage from requiring payment of the mortgage debt and interest in accordance with the contract, he should be permitted to do so.

2.46 *Unity Joint Stock Mutual Banking Association v King*[151] does not support the contrary view. Sir John Romilly suggested in that case that, where two sons were

---

[146] [1971] 1 WLR 43, 48–49.

[147] [1971] 1 WLR 43, 49.

[148] Wood, *English and International Set-off* (1989) 45. See ch 17 below in relation to assignments.

[149] This is in addition to any difficulty that would have arisen if the solicitor had held the proceeds of the investment on trust. See ch 10 below.

[150] In *P Rowe Graphics Pty Ltd v Scanagraphix Pty Ltd* (NSW Supreme Court, 6 September 1988), Young J doubted that a declaration is available in the case of a procedural defence, such as that provided by the Statutes of Set-off.

[151] (1858) 25 Beav 72, 53 ER 563.

indebted to their father, and at the same time the sons were entitled to an equitable charge or lien on the father's land on the basis of an equitable proprietary estoppel arising from the expenditure of money on improvements, 'the father would be entitled to set off any sum [owing to him by the sons] against any sum due to them upon the security of this land, and that this Court would enforce such right, and cause them to deliver up the land free from any charge upon it'.[152] Those remarks however should be understood in the context of the set-off in issue, which was an equitable set-off permitted in circumstances where the father himself was not indebted to the sons for the expenditure.[153] Since the equitable charge was not security for a debt as such, but rather it was an interest in the land which the court considered that it was appropriate that the sons should have in order to satisfy the equity which arose in their favour as a result of the expenditure of money on improvements, the reasons adduced by Megarry J in the *Samuel Keller* case for not allowing a mortgagor to appropriate a cross-debt in extinction of the mortgage debt were not applicable.

The second objection to the view that the court in *Parker v Jackson* could have **2.47** given a judgment for a set-off in the action before it is that, in the particular circumstances of the case, it is difficult to see how the Statutes of Set-off could have applied in any event. The solicitor's liability to the estate arose after the death when the proceeds of sale were received, and equally the solicitor obtained a claim after the death when the mortgage was transferred to him. A set-off would not have been available under the Statutes as between the deceased and the solicitor, because the Statutes required that the debts should originally have existed between two living persons.[154] Nor was there a set-off available as between the solicitor and the plaintiffs in their capacity as executors because, while the receipt of the proceeds of sale by the solicitor could be regarded as a debt owing to the plaintiffs in that capacity,[155] the plaintiffs themselves were not liable for payment of the mortgage debt. There was not therefore mutuality.[156] If indeed a set-off had been available to the plaintiffs under the Statutes as against the solicitor, they could have waited until the transferee sued for payment, and then defended that action on the ground that the transferee took subject to the right of set-off.[157] That would have provided adequate protection to the plaintiffs. In the circumstances however that course of action would not appear to have been open in *Parker v Jackson*.

---

[152] (1858) 25 Beav 72, 79–80, 53 ER 563, 566.

[153] See Sir John Romilly's judgment at (1858) 25 Beav 72, 78, 53 ER 563, 565, and also Lord Denning's discussion of the case in *Hussey v Palmer* [1972] 1 WLR 1286, 1290.

[154] See para 13.122 below.

[155] See *Rees v Watts* (1855) 11 Ex 410, 415, 156 ER 891, 893 in relation to the plaintiff administrator's claim for money had and received by the defendant for the use of the plaintiff as administrator.

[156] The demands would not have been sufficiently closely connected to give rise to an equitable set-off, for which mutuality is not a strict requirement. See paras 4.48–4.54 below.

[157] See ch 17 below.

Equitable remedies

2.48 While the Statutes only provided a procedural defence to an action, so that separate and distinct debts remain in existence until there is judgment for a set-off, a court of equity may take into account the availability of a right of set-off when considering whether to grant an equitable remedy consequent upon the existence of a debt. Prior to judgment for a set-off, when the debts retain their separate identities, the availability of a right pursuant to the Statutes may constitute a ground for refusing the equitable relief sought.[158] An illustration is *BICC plc v Burndy Corp*.[159] The plaintiff and the defendant were the joint owners of various patents and other rights. The plaintiff was primarily responsible for paying the costs and fees in relation to the rights, subject to a right of reimbursement of one-half by the defendant. If the defendant failed to reimburse, the plaintiff could require the defendant to transfer to it all its interest in the joint rights. The defendant failed to pay an invoice forwarded to it for its share of the costs, but asserted that it was entitled to do so because the plaintiff was also indebted to it, and therefore it had a set-off under the Statutes for an amount which exceeded its own liability. The plaintiff then brought this action seeking specific performance of the assignment. The Court of Appeal held that a right of set-off under the Statutes constituted a defence to an application for specific performance,[160] and that, in any event, the set-off provided grounds for relief against forfeiture of the rights. This should not be taken as authority for the proposition that, because of the availability of the set-off, there had not been default.[161] Rather, given that a claim by the plaintiff for payment would have failed because of the defence of the set-off, it was considered inappropriate that a claim for equitable relief which depended upon non-payment instead should be available.[162] Equally, the fact that there was a defence to a claim for payment constituted grounds for equitable intervention in the form of relief against forfeiture.[163]

---

[158] In addition to *BICC v Burndy Corporation* (below), see *Dodd v Lydall* (1842) 1 Hare 331, 66 ER 1060 (decree of foreclosure), in which the set-off in issue appears to have been an equitable set-off arising by analogy with the Statutes of Set-off. See para 3.06 below.

[159] [1985] 1 Ch 232.

[160] *Quaere* whether this is strictly correct, or whether the availability of a set-off under the Statutes instead constitutes a factor relevant to the exercise of the court's discretion in determining whether to grant the equitable relief sought. See the discussion of *BICC v Burndy* in paras 5.68–5.70 below.

[161] Compare McCracken, *The Banker's Remedy of Set-off* (2nd edn, 1998) 135.

[162] See the 'crucial question' framed by Dillon LJ at [1985] 1 Ch 232, 248, and also *Glencore Grain Ltd v Agros Trading Co* [1999] 2 Lloyd's Rep 410, 419.

[163] *Quaere* whether relief against forfeiture indeed was appropriate in this instance. See Note (1985) 101 LQR 145, 146.

(8) Cross-Debt Must be Enforceable

Because the defence of set-off under the Statutes is merely procedural, the **2.49**
cross-debt sought to be set off must be enforceable by action.[164] It should be distinguished in that regard from a substantive defence of equitable set-off.[165] The
point was made earlier in relation to the statutory defence that it should not be
necessary that the cross-debt be in existence at the date of the commencement of
the claimant's action. It should suffice if the defence is available when the defence
of set-off is filed.[166] A corollary of that view is that the cross-debt should be
enforceable at that time.[167]

Limitation Act

A different principle applies in some circumstances under section 35 of the **2.50**
Limitation Act 1980 in the context of limitation periods. The basic principle is set
out in section 35(1). Essentially, it provides that a 'new claim', in the form of a set-off or a counterclaim,[168] is deemed to be a separate action and to have been commenced on the same date as the original action. Prima facie, then, any question as
to the expiration of a limitation period for the cross-debt the subject of a proposed
set-off should be determined by reference to that date.[169] A similar principle is
adopted in the legislation of other jurisdictions.[170] However section 35(3) goes on
to provide for a different approach if the set-off is not an 'original set-off', in other
words if the person asserting the set-off has previously made a claim in the action,
in the sense that he has previously made a claim for some form of relief.[171] Section

---

[164] *Owens v Denton* (1835) 1 C M & R 711, 149 ER 1266; *Walker v Clements* (1850) 15 QB
1046, 117 ER 755; *McDonnell & East Ltd v McGregor* (1936) 56 CLR 50, 57; *Re Elgar Heights Pty
Ltd* [1985] VR 657, 665; *Aectra Refining and Marketing Inc v Exmar NV* [1994] 1 WLR 1634,
1650–1651; *Glencore Grain Ltd v Agros Trading Co* [1999] 2 Lloyd's Rep 410, 417, 420.

[165] See para 4.39 below.

[166] *Stein v Blake* [1996] AC 243, 251. See paras 2.08–2.11 above.

[167] Compare *Glencore Grain Ltd v Agros Trading Co* [1999] 2 Lloyd's Rep 410, 417, where the
Court of Appeal referred to the commencement of the plaintiff's action.

[168] See s 35(2).

[169] The word 'set-off' in s 35 encompasses a set-off under the Statutes of Set-off, but it does not
include a substantive defence of equitable set-off. See *Westdeutsche Landesbank v Islington BC*
[1994] 4 All ER 890, 943–946, *per* Hobhouse J, and para 4.39 below.

[170] See, eg, the Limitation of Actions Act 1958 (Vic), s 30 and the Limitation Act 1969 (NSW),
s 74, and *McDonnell & East Ltd v McGregor* (1936) 56 CLR 50, 57. Those provisions apply in the
case of a cross-claim pleaded as a set-off in the original defence. If it is sought to amend a defence to
include a set-off, the operation of the relevant rules of court in relation to amendment of pleadings
would also require consideration. See *JFS (UK) Ltd v DWR Cymru Cyf* [1999] 1 WLR 231,
235–236 in relation to the position formerly applying in England. In the *JFS (UK) Ltd* case, the
Court of Appeal held that the Limitation Act 1980, s 35(3) (see below) has widened the court's jurisdiction so that, in an application under the rules to amend a defence, the court in its discretion
may allow a new claim which is an original set-off or counterclaim to be made, even though it is
founded on a cause of action which is statute-barred.

[171] Compare *JFS (UK) Ltd v Dwr Cymru Cyf* [1999] 1 WLR 231.

35(3) stipulates that, save as provided by section 33 (which deals with actions in respect of personal injuries or death) or by rules of court,[172] the court shall not allow a claim by way of set-off that is not an original set-off to be made in the course of an action after the expiration of the time limit under the Act which would affect a new action to enforce that claim. Therefore, in the case of a set-off which is not an original set-off, the limitation period is determined by reference to the date that the set-off is included in the defence.

Unenforceable on other grounds

2.51 The courts have held that a set-off under the Statutes may not be based upon a debt which is unenforceable, not only because of the expiration of a limitation period,[173] but also because of the operation of moratorium legislation,[174] or because the plaintiff contracted the debt during his infancy,[175] or because of the Statute of Frauds,[176] or because the plaintiff had obtained a discharge under insolvent debtors' legislation.[177] There are two exceptions to the principle, however. The first arises in relation to the statutory provision that a solicitor must deliver a bill of costs in the proper form before he can bring an action to recover the costs.[178] A solicitor may employ the debt for costs in a set-off even though he has not complied with the requirement.[179] In *Rawley v Rawley*[180] Mellish LJ sought to explain this result on the ground that the statute in question merely postponed the remedy of bringing action until a bill of costs was delivered, and left other remedies untouched,[181] although in Australia and Canada it has been held in other contexts that the principle that the debt sought to be set off must be enforceable by action also applies during any period when the remedy of bringing an action is suspended.[182] The second exception arises in relation to an alien enemy. As a matter of public policy an alien enemy cannot sue as claimant in English courts while the

---

[172] The rules of court must comply with certain conditions. See s 35(4).

[173] *Remington v Stevens* (1748) 2 Str 1271, 93 ER 1175; *Walker v Clements* (1850) 15 QB 1046, 117 ER 755. See also *Smith v Betty* [1903] 2 KB 317; *Re Morris, Deceased, Coneys v Morris* [1922] 1 IR 136. The comments in *Strachan v Marriott* [1995] 3 NZLR 272, 291–292 in relation to a statute-bar should be considered as having had in contemplation equitable set-off.

[174] *Rex v Ray ex p Chapman* [1936] SASR 241.

[175] *Rex v Ray ex p Chapman* [1936] SASR 241; *Rawley v Rawley* (1876) 1 QBD 460.

[176] *Salisbury Jones v Southwood and Co* (KB, Goddard LJ, 9 December 1941), unreported but noted at 193 LT 48.

[177] *Francis v Dodsworth* (1847) 4 CB 202, 136 ER 482.

[178] Solicitors Act 1974, s 69.

[179] *Brown v Tibbitts* (1862) 11 CB(NS) 855, 142 ER 1031; *Robinson v Vale* [1905] VLR 405; *Currie v The Law Society* [1977] 1 QB 990, 995. See also *Ex parte Cooper* (1854) 14 CB 663, 139 ER 273.

[180] (1876) 1 QBD 460.

[181] (1876) 1 QBD 460, 468.

[182] *Rex v Ray ex p Chapman* [1936] SASR 241; *Atlantic Acceptance Corporation Ltd v Burns & Dutton Construction (1962) Ltd* (1970) 14 DLR (3d) 175 (though note the criticism of that case in Palmer, *The Law of Set-off in Canada* (1993) 29–30).

state of hostilities subsists.[183] On the other hand, when he is being sued as a defendant, he is entitled to appear and be heard in his defence.[184] This includes defending an action by way of set-off.[185] Pleading a cross-demand as a set-off is permitted, because it cannot result in an order for payment to the alien enemy.[186] It should be distinguished from counterclaim. An alien enemy is not permitted to counterclaim because it may result in a larger sum being payable to the alien enemy than would be payable by him to the claimant.[187] One writer has suggested that the right of an alien enemy to plead a set-off should be confined to the substantive form of equitable set-off considered in chapter 4.[188] But if the justification for allowing a set-off is that it cannot result in an order for payment to the enemy alien, there is no reason for restricting the availability of the defence to equitable set-off.

(9) Cross-Debt Must be Able to be Determined in the Plaintiff's Action

Consistent with the notion that set-off under the Statutes of Set-off is a procedural **2.52** defence, a dispute on the cross-debt sought to be set off must be able to be determined by the court in the claimant's action. Therefore, in an application by a claimant for summary judgment, leave to defend will not be granted on the basis of a set-off under the Statutes if the court in the claimant's action would refuse to try the merits of the case on the cross-debt, for example because the cross-debt is the subject of an arbitration clause or a foreign jurisdiction clause to which the court would give effect.[189] On the other hand, the court has a discretion in such a case to stay execution on a judgment given in favour of the claimant until the cross-debt is determined by the appropriate tribunal.[190]

Unlike set-off under the Statutes, equitable set-off (and, in England, common law **2.53** abatement[191]) is regarded as a substantive defence.[192] Because it is not procedural, in the sense in which that expression is used in relation to the Statutes,[193] there is

---

[183] *Robinson & Co v Continental Insurance Co of Mannheim* [1915] 1 KB 155, 159.

[184] *Porter v Freudenberg* [1915] 1 KB 857, 883.

[185] *Re Stahlwerk Becker Aktiengesellschaft's Patent* [1917] 2 Ch 272, 273, 275–276.

[186] *Re Stahlwerk Becker Aktiengesellschaft's Patent* [1917] 2 Ch 272, 276.

[187] *Re Stahlwerk Becker Aktiengesellschaft's Patent* [1917] 2 Ch 272, 276.

[188] See Wood, *English and International Set-off* (1989) 755, who describes this form of set-off as a transaction set-off.

[189] *Aectra Refining and Marketing Inc v Exmar NV* [1994] 1 WLR 1634; *Glencore Grain Ltd v Agros Trading Co* [1999] 2 Lloyd's Rep 410 (esp at 417). See also Berg, 'Arbitration: Legal Set-off and Enforcing Admitted Claims' [2000] LMCLQ 153.

[190] *Aectra Refining and Marketing Inc v Exmar NV* [1994] 1 WLR 1634, 1652.

[191] See paras 2.87–2.97 below. There is authority in Australia which suggests that abatement is a procedural defence, although the prevailing view in England is that it is substantive. See para 2.93 below.

[192] See paras 4.29–4.43 below.

[193] See paras 2.33–2.48 above.

no such objection to the court giving effect to the defence in the face of an arbitration clause or a foreign jurisdiction clause applicable to the cross-claim.[194]

(10) Trustees

2.54 A trustee may hold a debt as trust property, and also may have incurred a debt to the debtor in his capacity as trustee. The question whether these debts can be set off under the Statutes of Set-off is considered later.[195]

C. The Statutes of Set-off in Australia

2.55 The Statutes of Set-off were originally incorporated into the laws of the various Australian jurisdictions[196] and of New Zealand[197] and, with the exception of New South Wales and Queensland, they are still part of the laws of those jurisdictions.[198]

(1) New South Wales and Queensland

2.56 In New South Wales the Statutes were repealed by the Imperial Acts Application Act 1969 (NSW). The Statutes have also been repealed in England, by the Civil Procedure Acts Repeal Act 1879, though the English legislation contained a provision which has been interpreted as preserving the right of set-off originally conferred by the Statutes.[199] The New South Wales Act on the other hand did not have a similar saving provision, so that the operation of the Statutes of Set-off has not

---

[194] *Aectra Refining and Marketing Inc v Exmar NV* [1994] 1 WLR 1634, 1649–1650 (referring to *Gilbert-Ash (Northern) Ltd v Modern Engineering (Bristol) Ltd* [1974] AC 689 (esp at 720, 726)); *Bim Kemi AB v Blackburn Chemicals Ltd* [2001] 2 Lloyd's Rep 93, 96 para 9. See also *Glencore Grain Ltd v Agros Trading Co* [1999] 2 Lloyd's Rep 410, 416–417.

[195] See paras 17.92–17.95 below.

[196] See, for example, *Day & Dent Constructions Pty Ltd v North Australian Properties Pty Ltd* (1981) 34 ALR 595, 599, 600 (Northern Territory). For New South Wales and Queensland see, respectively, *Stehar Knitting Mills Pty Ltd v Southern Textile Converters Pty Ltd* [1980] 2 NSWLR 514, 522, and *Phillips v Mineral Resources Developments Pty Ltd* [1983] 2 Qd R 138, though note the discussion below of the present position in those states. In the case of South Australia and Western Australia, the incorporation would have resulted from their being 'settled colonies'. For other jurisdictions, see the Australian Courts Act 1828 (9 Geo. 4, c 83), s 24. See generally Castles, 'The Reception and Status of English Law in Australia' (1963) 2 Adelaide Law Review 1. In the Australian Capital Territory, the operation of the Statutes has been expressly preserved, by the Imperial Acts Application Ordinance 1986, s 5 (together with Sch 3 Pts 15 and 16).

[197] *Grant v NZMC Ltd* [1989] 1 NZLR 8, 11, and see the Imperial Laws Application Act 1988 (NZ), s 3.

[198] In Victoria the Statutes were repealed by the Imperial Acts Application Act 1922, s 7 (and see also the Imperial Acts Application Act 1980), though the legislation had a saving provision similar to that in the English legislation (the Civil Procedure Acts Repeal Act 1879, s 2) which repealed the Statutes in England. See para 2.06 above. The current position in Victoria in relation to set-off is considered below.

[199] *Hanak v Green* [1958] 2 QB 9, 22. See para 2.06 above.

been preserved in New South Wales. On the other hand, the former Pt 15 r 25 of the Supreme Court Rules (NSW) contemplated that a monetary cross-demand possessed by the defendant against the plaintiff, whether for an ascertained sum or not, could be included in the defence and set off against the plaintiff's claim. In *Stehar Knitting Mills Pty Ltd v Southern Textile Converters Pty Ltd*[200] Hutley and Glass JJA[201] said that Pt 15 r 25 should take effect according to its literal terms. As a result, it appeared that in New South Wales *any* monetary cross-demand which was due and payable, whether it was liquidated or unliquidated and whether or not it was connected with the plaintiff's claim, could be the subject of a set-off in an action at law.[202] It was not necessary to show mutual debts or, if one of the demands was unliquidated, that the cross-demands were sufficiently closely connected so as to give rise to an equitable set-off. In 1984, however, Pt 15 r 25 was omitted from the Supreme Court Rules.[203] Accordingly, the position outlined in the *Stehar Knitting Mills* case would no longer apply. Since the Statutes of Set-off are no longer in force in New South Wales, the current position[204] would appear to be that the only right of set-off available in that state prior to bankruptcy or liquidation is the form of equitable set-off in which there is a sufficiently close connection between the demands.[205]

Notwithstanding that the *Stehar Knitting Mills* case no longer sets out the position **2.57** in New South Wales, the view that the Supreme Court Rules themselves could determine when a cross-demand may be set up as a defence is of general interest, particularly in Queensland where the Statutes of Set-off similarly no longer apply,[206] and in Victoria where it has been suggested that the distinction between set-off and counterclaim has been abolished in the ordinary case.[207] The analysis adopted in the *Stehar Knitting Mills* case therefore justifies further examination.

---

[200] [1980] 2 NSWLR 514.

[201] Mahoney JA not considering the issue.

[202] See Hutley JA at [1980] 2 NSWLR 514, 523.

[203] Supreme Court Rules (Amendment No 154) 1984.

[204] The New South Wales Law Reform Commission has recommended that a plain English restatement of the Statutes of Set-off be enacted in New South Wales. See the New South Wales Law Reform Commission Report No 94, 'Set-off', February 2000.

[205] *McIntyre v Perkes* (1990) 22 FCR 260, 272; *Sydmar Pty Ltd v Statewise Developments Pty Ltd* (1987) 73 ALR 289, 292; *Roadshow Entertainment Pty Ltd v (ACN 053 006 269) Pty Ltd* (1997) 42 NSWLR 462, 481–482. See also *APM Wood Products Pty Ltd v Kimberley Homes Pty Ltd* NSW Supreme Court, Cole J, 17 February 1989; *Buttrose v Versi* NSW Supreme Court, Young J, 14 May 1992; *Abignano v Wenkart* (1998) 9 BPR 16,765, 16,772. Compare Burton, 'Negotiability: Set-offs and Counterclaims,' *Directions in Finance Law* (1990) 70, and also *Akki Pty Ltd v Martin Hall Pty Ltd* (1994) 35 NSWLR 470, 479 in which Windeyer J assumed that a right of set-off existed in the case of mutual debts.

[206] See para 2.63 below.

[207] See para 2.64 below.

Criticism of the *Stehar Knitting Mills* case

2.58   The essence of the approach in the *Stehar Knitting Mills* case was that the Statutes were wholly procedural in their operation,[208] in which case it was said that there was no reason why Supreme Court Rules made pursuant to legislation which contained a rule-making power with respect to matters of practice and procedure could not be the source of a similar right. This reasoning is beset with difficulty. In the first place, there is ample authority in England for the proposition that the Judicature Acts, and the Rules of the Supreme Court made pursuant to those Acts and their successors, themselves did not alter the rights of the parties and, in particular, did not confer any new rights of set-off.[209] In the *Stehar Knitting Mills* case Hutley JA sought to distinguish the position in New South Wales from that in England on the ground that, in contrast to New South Wales, the repealing legislation in England preserved the right itself. It is difficult to follow this. If the question was whether the right of set-off in the case of mutual debts survived in New South Wales notwithstanding the repeal of the Statutes, the English position would have been distinguishable. But that was not the question. Hutley and Glass JJA said that the Supreme Court Rules under consideration allowed a cross-demand to be employed in a set-off in circumstances that were considerably broader than the right allowed by the Statutes. It is not clear why the question whether the rules should be interpreted literally so as to allow a right of set-off in those enlarged circumstances should depend upon the survival or otherwise of the right of set-off originally conferred by the Statutes in the limited case of mutual debts.

The defence is not wholly procedural

2.59   Of greater concern is the conclusion that the right of set-off conferred by the Statutes in the case of mutual debts is wholly procedural in its operation. [210] Set-off under the Statutes admittedly is described as a procedural defence.[211] By this it is meant that separate and distinct debts remain in existence until judgment for a set-off and, moreover, as between the parties to the cross-demands, the defence

---

[208]   See also *Kennedy v General Credits Ltd* (1982) 2 BPR 9456, 9464, *per* Hope JA, with whose judgment Mahoney JA agreed.

[209]   *Halsbury's Laws of England* (4th edn, 1999) vol 42, 243 para 404; *Re Milan Tramways Co, ex p Theys* (1882) 22 Ch D 122, 126; *Stumore v Campbell & Co* [1892] 1 QB 314, 316–317; *Hanak v Green* [1958] 2 QB 9, 22, *per* Morris LJ ('the Judicature Acts conferred no new rights of set-off'); *Bank of Boston Connecticut v European Grain and Shipping Ltd* [1989] 1 AC 1056, 1109. See also in Western Australia *Westwind Air Charter Pty Ltd v Hawker De Havilland Ltd* (1990) 3 WAR 71, 84, *per* Murray J ('reference to the rules does not aid one to understand a full statement of the law' of set-off). In New South Wales see *West Street Properties Pty Ltd v Jamison* [1974] 2 NSWLR 435, 438, and in relation to the Federal Court Rules see *Griffiths v Commonwealth Bank of Australia* (1994) 123 ALR 111, 124. Compare *Edward Ward & Co v McDougall* [1972] VR 433, 436.

[210]   See generally Derham, 'Set-off in Victoria' (1999) 73 Australian Law Journal 753.

[211]   See paras 2.33–2.48 above.

has no effect until judgment. Prior to judgment the rights consequent upon being a creditor still attach, as do the obligations and liabilities consequent upon being a debtor. It should be distinguished from the form of equitable set-off in which there is a sufficiently close connection between the demands.[212] This is properly described as a substantive defence, in the sense that prior to judgment it is unconscionable for the creditor to regard the debtor as being indebted while circumstances continue to exist which support an equitable set-off.[213] But, notwithstanding that distinction, the right of set-off derived from the Statutes is still a defence, and for that reason the point was made earlier that it is not wholly procedural.[214] In particular, it can have a substantive effect on the rights of third parties.[215]

Thus Meagher, Gummow and Lehane, in expressing reservation about the **2.60** reasoning in the *Stehar Knitting Mills* case, commented that, in so far as rights of set-off operate as 'pleas in bar, they seem to be substantive rights'.[216] Similarly in *Aectra Refining and Manufacturing Inc v Exmar NV*[217] Hoffmann LJ said that set-off under the Statutes of Set-off (which he termed independent set-off[218]) 'does operate as a substantive reduction or extinction of the debt owed to the plaintiff. But it arrives at this result by procedural means'.

The result is substantive, though the means of achieving it are procedural. But if **2.61** the result is a matter of substance, so should be the question of the circumstances in which that result is able to be brought about. Thus, it can be said on the basis of that distinction that a rule-making power limited to matters of practice and procedure would allow the making of rules as to the *means* of achieving a set-off, because that is a question of procedure. On the other hand, the power should not enable the making of rules as to the circumstances in which an extinction of cross-demands by way of set-off can be brought about, because that relates to a matter of substance.[219] This should be so notwithstanding the views expressed in the *Stehar Knitting Mills* case.

---

[212] See ch 4 below.

[213] See paras 4.29–4.43 below.

[214] See paras 2.35–2.38 above.

[215] See ch 17 below.

[216] Meagher, Gummow and Lehane, *Equity Doctrines and Remedies* (3rd edn, 1992) 825 para 3714.

[217] [1994] 1 WLR 1634, 1650.

[218] Hoffmann LJ (at [1994] 1 WLR 1634, 1650) said that the procedural basis of set-off under the Statutes is reflected in the rule that the mere existence of liquidated cross-claims does not automatically extinguish the smaller debt. Hutley JA relied on a similar argument in *Stehar Knitting Mills* [1980] 2 NSWLR 514, 518. See para 2.62 below.

[219] Earlier in his judgment in *Aectra Refining* (at [1994] 1 WLR 1634, 1649), Hoffmann LJ referred to the Statutes of Set-off, 'whose effect is now to be found in RSC Ord 18, r 17'. It is unlikely however that Hoffmann LJ had in mind that the rule itself was the source of the right of set-off. O 18 r 17 on its face extended to an unrelated damages cross-claim, but Hoffmann LJ did not suggest that the rule applied in that manner. Indeed, in 1879 Bramwell LJ rejected an argument to that effect in

2.62 Hutley JA in the *Stehar Knitting Mills* case said that it is only if the rules governing set-off work an automatic discharge that they cease to be procedural.[220] With respect, it is not clear why that should be necessary, if the substantive quality of the defence is evident from other factors. Thus, equitable set-off, which is regarded as a substantive defence, does not operate as an automatic extinction of cross-demands.[221]

2.63 The right of set-off derived from the Statutes of Set-off is not purely procedural, and on that basis it is difficult to support the reasoning in the *Stehar Knitting Mills* case. The ascertainment of the ambit of the right of set-off ordinarily is not a matter solely of interpreting the rules of court, and it should not make any difference whether in a particular jurisdiction the operation of the Statutes has or has not been preserved. This is relevant to the position in Queensland. Rule 173(1) of the Uniform Civil Procedure Rules provides that: 'A defendant may rely on set-off (whether or not of an ascertained amount) as a defence to all or part of a claim made by the plaintiff whether or not it is also included as a counterclaim.' In a number of cases concerned with the rule in force in Queensland before the current rule,[222] it was assumed that the principle accepted in England also applied in Queensland, so that the rule itself did not determine when there could be a set-off, and that regard had to be had instead to the established principles of set-off.[223] In 1984 however the Statutes of Set-off were repealed in Queensland, by the Imperial Acts Application Act 1984. This legislation was similar to the corresponding repealing Act in New South Wales (the Imperial Acts Application Act 1969), in that it did not expressly preserve the principle of set-off originally conferred by the Statutes. As a result, it would appear that in Queensland there is no longer a right of set-off in the case of mutual debts.[224] Nor, for the reasons given above, should the repeal without an express preservation of the right mean that the rules of court instead can provide a source of rights of set-off,[225] notwithstanding the decision in the *Stehar Knitting Mills* case. But even apart from the criticism of that case, rule 173(1) in its terms does not purport to expand the scope

---

relation to the rule in the 1875 Judicature Act, in *Pellas v Neptune Marine Insurance Co* (1879) 5 CPD 34, 40–41. Similar comments may be made in relation to the current CPR r 16.6.

[220] [1980] 2 NSWLR 514, 518. Hoffmann LJ expressed a similar view in *Aectra Refining and Manufacturing Inc v Exmar NV* [1994] 1 WLR 1634, 1650.

[221] See para 4.30 below.

[222] O 22 r 3 SCR (Qld).

[223] *Knockholt Pty Ltd v Graff* [1975] Qd R 88 (esp at 90); *General Credits (Finance) Pty Ltd v Stoyakovich* [1975] Qd R 352; *Eversure Textiles Co Ltd v Webb* [1978] Qd R 347 (esp at 348). See also *Phillips v Mineral Resources Developments Pty Ltd* [1983] 2 Qd R 138.

[224] In *Walker v Department of Social Security* (1995) 56 FCR 354, 374 (and see also *Cockerill v Westpac Banking Corp* (Federal Court of Australia, 20 December 1996, at p 93) Cooper J said that there is 'a serious question' whether the 1984 legislation brought about this result.

[225] The principal rule-making power in Queensland relates to 'the practices and procedures' of the court. See the Supreme Court of Queensland Act 1991, s 118(1)(a).

of the defence. It does not provide a description of the circumstances in which a set-off is available, but rather it assumes the existence of the right. It simply provides that set-off can be relied on as a defence. The procedure recognized by the rule is important for equitable set-off, which before the Judicature Acts was given effect by way of an injunction to restrain proceedings at law,[226] but which now can be pleaded directly as a defence in the plaintiff's action.

(2) Victoria

The view that the Supreme Court Rules do not alter substantive rights is subject **2.64** to legislation which provides to the contrary. Consider in that regard the position in Victoria.[227] In 1986 the judges of the Victorian Supreme Court made new Supreme Court Rules. Set-off was dealt with in r 13.14, which allowed a defendant to include in the defence and set off against the plaintiff's claim any claim that the defendant in turn had against the plaintiff for the recovery of a debt or damages. Tadgell J in the Victorian Supreme Court expressed the view that r 13.14 allowed a cross-claim that would not have given rise to a set-off according to traditional principles to be included in the defence. [228] In particular, he said that the 1986 rule made 'great inroads' upon the principle that an unliquidated pecuniary claim could not be set off by way of defence unless the defendant's claim impeached the plaintiff's legal demand or equity was on some other basis disposed to intervene.[229] This view is also accepted in the principal commentary on the Victorian Supreme Court rules.[230] and in a number of cases it has been assumed, although without discussion, that r 13.14 itself confers the defence.[231] The basis of the argument is that the 1986 rules were 'ratified, validated and approved' by section 41(1) of the Supreme Court (Rules of Procedure) Act 1986. When the Bill for the Act was introduced into Parliament, the Minister in the second reading

---

[226] See para 3.01 below.

[227] See Derham, 'Set-off in Victoria' (1999) 73 Australian Law Journal 754.

[228] *Moffat v Pinewood Resources Ltd* (Vic SC, 7 April 1989); *MEK Nominees Pty Ltd v Billboard Entertainments Pty Ltd* (1993) V Conv R 54–468 at p 65,465. See also *Accident Compensation Commission v C E Heath Underwriting & Insurance (Aust) Pty Ltd* [1990] VR 224, 231.

[229] *Moffat v Pinewood Resources Ltd* (Vic SC, 7 April 1989, at p 5a). See ch 4 below in relation to equitable set-off.

[230] Williams, *Civil Procedure Victoria* (looseleaf) vol 1, para 13.14.25 ('The rule abolishes the distinction between set-off and counterclaim in the ordinary case'). Compare *L U Simon Builders Pty Ltd v H D Fowles* [1992] 2 VR 189, 195, in which Smith J left aside the issue of the extent to which r 13.14 may change the substantive law.

[231] *John Holland Construction and Engineering Pty Ltd v Majorca Projects Pty Ltd* (Vic SC, 27 July 1995, at p 12) *per* Hansen J; *Westpac Banking Corp v Market Services International Pty Ltd* (Vic SC, Batt J 1 October 1996) at p 60; *Novawest Contracting Pty Ltd v Taras Nominees Pty Ltd* [1998] VSC 205 at [22] and [23]. In each of these cases however the circumstances in any event would appear to have been such as to give rise to a set-off under established principles (in the case of *John Holland* and *Novawest*, if set-off otherwise had not been excluded by the contract).

speech[232] noted that some of the rules arguably changed the substantive law, and he said that: 'It is of particular importance to remove any doubt that this . . . category of rule is within the rule-making power of the judges.' Regard may be had to a second reading speech in interpreting an Act of Parliament,[233] and the question therefore is whether r 13.14 was one of the rules that was intended to change the substantive law.

2.65 The notion that r 13.14 was intended to have that effect gives rise to a complication. According to Tadgell J,[234] r 13.14 was not intended to be taken wholly literally. For example, he said that the rule should not be interpreted as overturning the principles that a claim for unliquidated damages cannot be pleaded as a defence to a claim upon a bill of exchange[235] or a claim for freight.[236] But that proposition would be far from clear if one were to accept the view that the rule has expanded the scope of the defence. In considering the scope of r 13.14, the relevant question should be whether it was one of the new rules which, according to the second reading speech for the Supreme Court (Rules of Procedure) Act 1986, was intended to change the substantive law. If it was not, it could hardly be correct to say that the rule has had the effect suggested, because set-off in truth is not a matter of pure procedure. If on the other hand r 13.14 was intended to alter substantive law, it is not easy from a plain reading of the rule to justify an interpretation that the principles by which an unliquidated cross-demand cannot be pleaded as a set-off against a claim on a bill of exchange or a claim for freight have remained untouched.[237] On the assumption that the rule was intended to operate substantively, there is nothing in its language to suggest that those principles still apply.[238] This suggests that r 13.14 was not intended to change substantive law. Indeed, Tadgell J also commented that: 'rule 13.14 is after all a rule of procedure, and it would not ordinarily be construed in a way that would abrogate or interfere with

---

[232] The speech was delivered by Mr Mathews, the Minister for the Arts, in the Victorian Legislative Assembly on 7 May 1986.

[233] Interpretation of Legislation Act 1984 (Vic), s 35(b).

[234] *Moffat v Pinewood Resources Ltd* (Vic SC, 7 April 1989, pp 6–8).

[235] See paras 5.25–5.31 below.

[236] See paras 5.02–5.16 below.

[237] In *L U Simon Builders Pty Ltd v H D Fowles* [1992] 2 VR 189, 195 Smith J noted the qualifications discussed by Tadgell J, though he declined to express a view on the subject.

[238] Tadgell J's view in relation to bills of exchange and freight should be contrasted with the approach of the courts in New South Wales in interpreting the Common Law Procedure Act 1899, s 79, which provided that matters which were the subject of a cross-action between the parties could by leave of a judge be pleaded by way of set-off. Section 79 was repealed in 1970 by the Supreme Court Act, but before the repeal the courts accepted that it permitted a damages claim to be pleaded by way of set-off against a claim on a promissory note if the demands arose out of the same transaction. See *Karbowsky v Redaelli* (1914) 31 WN (NSW) 80; *Richardson v Hill* (1922) 22 SR (NSW) 326. The requirement that the demands should have originated in the same transaction followed from a requirement that the courts held was inherent in s 79 and applied generally. See *Assets & General Finance Co v Crick* (1911) 28 WN (NSW) 91; *Austral Bronze Co Ltd v Sleigh* (1916) 34 WN (NSW) 143.

substantive rights'.[239] That comment serves to emphasize the point under discussion. The question of the availability of a set-off is not wholly a matter of procedure. It is a defence which operates as a substantive reduction or extinction of the plaintiff's claim.[239a] Therefore a rule which purported to expand the scope of the defence would constitute an interference with substantive rights in the same way that a rule which purported to change the principles with respect to bills of exchange and freight would interfere with substantive rights.

The judgement therefore proceeded on a false assumption, that set-off is simply a **2.66** rule of procedure. If it is followed, however, it raises the question of the effect that it may have on third party rights.[240] It would be of little assistance to say that the rule ordinarily should not be construed in a way that would abrogate or interfere with the substantive rights of third parties if the characterization of a cross-claim as giving rise to a defence would have that consequence. This issue is considered later in the context of assignments of debts.[241]

Furthermore, for reasons set out later,[242] it is suggested that it is undesirable to **2.67** expand the defence of set-off to include *any* monetary cross-demand, whether liquidated or unliquidated and whether or not it is connected with the plaintiff's claim.

D. Connected Cross-Demands at Common Law

In *Green v Farmer*[243] Lord Mansfield commented: 'Where the nature of the em- **2.68** ployment, transaction, or dealings, necessarily constitutes an account consisting of receipts and payments, debts and credits; it is certain that only the balance can be the debt; and by the proper forms of proceeding in Courts of Law or Equity, the balance only can be recovered.' *Green v Farmer* subsequently was cited in the third edition of *Halsbury's Laws of England*[244] as authority for the following proposition: 'Where opposing demands are connected by originating in the same transaction the balance has always been regarded by the common law as the debt so that no question of set-off arises . . . .'

---

[239] *Moffat v Pinewood Resources Ltd* (Vic SC, 7 April 1989) at p 6a.
[239a] *Aectra Refining and Manufacturing Inc v Exmar NV* [1994] 1 WLR 1634, 1650, and see para 2.38 above.
[240] See para 2.36 above.
[241] See paras 17.14 & 17.15 below.
[242] See paras 5.139–5.153 below. This was also the view of the New South Wales Law Reform Commission in its report on 'Set-off', No 94, February 2000, paras 4.10–4.13, 5.10–5.12.
[243] (1768) 4 Burr 2214, 2221.
[244] *Halsbury's Laws of England* (3rd edn, 1960) vol 34, 396 para 673 n *(l)*.

2.69   Lord Denning referred to that passage in *Halsbury's Laws* with evident approval in *Henriksens Rederi A/S v THZ Rolimpex (The Brede)*.[245] Indeed, its substance has a long history which can be traced back to similar statements in early books on set-off, by Babington in 1827[246] and Montague in 1828.[247] On the other hand, the proposition for which *Green v Farmer* was cited in the third edition of *Halsbury's Laws* is questioned in the fourth edition.[248] In truth, it is difficult to find evidence which supports a general common law principle that a balance may be struck, without recourse to the principles of set-off, in a case in which there are opposing demands which originated in the same transaction. With the exception of *Dale v Sollett*[249] (see below), the cases to which Babington and Montague referred were instances in which there was an agreement between the parties for payment of a liability,[250] or alternatively there was a custom by which payment could be effected by way of a deduction.[251] What Lord Mansfield may have had in mind in *Green v Farmer* is the action for money had and received,[252] as exemplified by *Dale v Sollett*. Alternatively, he may have contemplated a running account. However a running account is not a case of opposing demands. Rather, it involves a series of debits and credits which gives rise to a single debt for the balance.[253]

2.70   There are, nevertheless, certain specific instances in which the common law has recognized that connected cross-demands may produce a balance outside the ambit of the established principles of set-off, though these constitute exceptions rather than the rule. One such case is common law abatement, which may arise in an action for the agreed price of goods sold with a warranty, or of work to be performed pursuant to a contract, in circumstances where the defendant asserts that the goods by reason of non-compliance with the warranty, or the work as a result of failure to perform in accordance with the contract, is diminished in value or is of no value. This defence of abatement is discussed below.[254] Another instance is to be found in a judgment of Lord Mansfield which was handed down the year

---

[245] [1974] 1 QB 233, 246.
[246] Babington, *The Law of Set-off and Mutual Credit* (1827) 4.
[247] Montague, *Summary of the Law of Set-off* (2nd edn, 1828) 1.
[248] *Halsbury's Laws of England* (4th edn, 1999) vol 42, 250 para 421 n 3. See also, in New South Wales, *P Rowe Graphics Pty Ltd v Scanagraphix Pty Ltd* (NSW SC, 6 Sept 1988), *per* Young J.
[249] (1767) 4 Burr 2133, 98 ER 154.
[250] See *Dobson v Lockhart* (1793) 5 TR 133, 101 ER 77; *James v Kynnier* (1799) 5 Ves Jun 108, 31 ER 496; *Sturdy v Arnaud* (1790) 3 TR 599, 100 ER 754; *Roper v Bumford* (1810) 3 Taunt 76, 128 ER 31. See also *Le Loir v Bristow* (1815) 4 Camp 134, 171 ER 43.
[251] *Bamford v Harris* (1816) 1 Stark 343, 171 ER 492.
[252] This seems to have been the view of Young J in the New South Wales Supreme Court in *McCosker v Lovett* (1995) 12 BCL 146, 149, 7 BPR 14,507, 14,510.
[253] See para 1.01 above.
[254] See paras 2.87–2.97 below.

before his judgment in *Green v Farmer*. In *Dale v Sollett*[255] the King's Bench held that an agent who recovered money on behalf of his principal could deduct from the proceeds an amount sufficient to recompense him for his labour and service in relation to the recovery. This was not by way of a set-off as such, but rather it was characterized as a common law right of deduction.[256] Lord Mansfield explained the result on the ground that:[257]

> This is an action for money had and received to the plaintiff's use. The plaintiff can recover no more than he is in conscience and equity entitled to: which can be no more than what remains after deducting all just allowances which the defendant has a right to retain out of the very sum demanded. This is not in the nature of a cross-demand or mutual debt: it is a charge, which makes the sum of money received for the plaintiff's use so much less.

The action was for money had and received,[258] which is based on the principle of unjust enrichment. It cannot be asserted without the claimant at the same time giving credit for any payments received from the defendant.[259]

E. Judgments

Questions of set-off typically arise in the situation in which there are two unlitigated cross-claims. It may be the case however that one or both of the claims has proceeded to judgment, and the judgment creditor is seeking to rely on the judgment debt as a defence to an action by the judgment debtor to enforce another debt. Alternatively, enforcement of a judgment properly obtained at law may be sought to be stayed on the basis of an unlitigated cross-claim. A third possibility is that a judgment debtor may seek to set off the judgment against a judgment that he has obtained in separate proceedings against the judgment creditor. Each of these situations is considered in turn.   **2.71**

(1) Pleading a Judgment Debt as a Defence Under the Statutes

A judgment for payment of a sum of money gives rise to a debt,[260] and accordingly it should be able to form the basis of a defence of set-off under the Statutes to an   **2.72**

---

[255] (1767) 4 Burr 2133, 98 ER 112.

[256] See the discussion in *Re Sutcliffe and Sons Ltd* [1933] 1 DLR 562, 566.

[257] (1767) 4 Burr 2133, 2134, 98 ER 112, 113.

[258] The action for money had and received, though of an equitable nature, is a common law action. See *Roxborough v Rothmans of Pall Mall Australia Ltd* (2001) 76 ALJR 203, 223 [96]-[99] *per* Gummow J, 244 [202]-[203], *per* Callinan J.

[259] *Westdeutsche Landesbank v Islington BC* [1994] 4 All ER 890, 940–941 (Hobhouse J). See also *Moses v Macferlan* (1760) 2 Burr 1005, 1010, 97 ER 676, 679. Similarly the claimant may be required to give credit for expenditure incurred by the defendant which benefited the claimant. See *Ex parte Elliott, Re Jermyn* (1838) 3 Deac 343, 345.

[260] *Hodsoll v Baxter* (1858) El Bl & El 884, 120 ER 739.

action by the judgment debtor for payment of a separate debt owing to him by the judgment creditor.[261] The case would be one of mutual debts for the purpose of the Statutes. Moreover, this should apply equally when the judgment arose out of an action for unliquidated damages. When judgment is given the unliquidated claim is replaced by a judgment debt,[262] which should be within the ambit of the Statutes. However in *Lawrence v Hayes*[263] Acton and Talbot JJ seem to have assumed that the judgment debt in that case could not have been employed in a set-off unless the damages claim in respect of which the judgment had been obtained gave rise to an equitable set-off.[263a]

(2) Stay on Enforcement of a Judgment on the Basis of an Unlitigated Cross-Claim

2.73 Subject to the discussion below of equitable set-off, a judgment debtor cannot extinguish or reduce the amount of the judgment by setting off an unlitigated simple contract debt owing to him by the judgment creditor.[264] However the question may arise whether an unlitigated cross-claim may provide a ground for staying enforcement of the judgment. In that regard, a distinction must be drawn between a judgment which has been obtained pursuant to the procedure for summary judgment, and a judgment which the claimant obtained after the case went to trial.

2.74 Summary judgment is available where it appears that the defendant has no real prospect of successfully defending the claim, and there is no other reason why the matter should not be disposed of at trial.[265] In such a case however the court in its discretion, and depending on such factors as the degree of connection between the claim and an alleged cross-claim and the ability of the claimant to satisfy any judgement on the cross-claim,[266] may order a stay on enforcement of the judgment.[267]

---

[261] *Watkins v Clark* (1862) 12 CB (NS) 277, 142 ER 1149. See also *Baskerville v Brown* (1761) 2 Burr 1229, 97 ER 804; *Russell v May* (1828) 7 LJOSKB 88; *Cochrane v Green* (1860) 9 CB(NS) 448, 142 ER 176; *Lawrence v Hayes* [1927] 2 KB 111. Formerly, if a judgment creditor had taken the body of the judgment debtor in execution pursuant to a writ of *capias ad satisfaciendum*, the judgment creditor could not set off the judgment as a defence to an action brought by the debtor on a cross-demand. See *Taylor v Waters* (1816) 5 M & S 103, 105 ER 989; *Tidd's Practice* (9th edn, 1828) vol 2, 1029. See also, and compare, *Thompson v Parish* (1859) 28 LJCP 153 (overruling *Peacock v Jeffrey* (1809) 1 Taunt 426, 127 ER 899). However, this principle turned upon a peculiarity of the writ, that the taking of a debtor's body in execution constituted a bar to any other remedy against the debtor during his life, which included employing the judgment debt in a set-off.

[262] Compare *Jones v Thompson* (1858) El Bl & El 63, 120 ER 430 and *R v Hopkins* [1896] 1 QB 652.

[263] [1927] 2 KB 111.

[263a] See ch4 below.

[264] *Philipson v Caldwell* (1815) 6 Taunt 176, 128 ER 1001; *Hawkins v Baynes and Ireland* (1823) 1 LJOSKB 167; *Chitty's Practice* (3rd edn, 1837) vol 1, 140. See also *Newton v Newton* (1832) 8 Bing 202, 203, 131 ER 378.

[265] CPR r 24.2.

[266] See para 1.05 above.

Subject to the various discretionary factors, the circumstances in which a stay would be ordered under former rules of court were expressed in various terms, such as that the cross-claim appeared to be so far plausible that it was not unreasonably possible for it to succeed, or that it was impossible to say that the cross-claim had no prospect of success, or that it was by no means frivolous.[268] These were not rigorous tests, and indeed it has been suggested that under the new Civil Procedure Rules the courts may grant summary judgment and a delay on enforcement more frequently than hitherto.[269] This approach to the question of a stay has been justified on the ground that a summary judgment is a judgment obtained at the very outset of proceedings before the defendant has had an opportunity to litigate his cross-claim.[270] The position is different if the action in respect of which judgment was given had proceeded to trial. In such a case, the defendant will not obtain a stay simply by showing that he has an arguable cross-claim.[271] Rather, he must show special circumstances which render it inexpedient to enforce the judgment.[272] The point is illustrated by *Schofield v Church Army*.[273] The appellant had dismissed the respondent from his employment for allegedly stealing money. An industrial tribunal found that the dismissal was unfair, and ordered the appellant to pay him compensation. The respondent obtained an ex parte order in the county court to enforce the tribunal's order, and also a garnishee order nisi attaching the appellant's bank account. The amount standing to the credit of the account was paid into court, and the respondent applied for an order that the money be paid to him. Meanwhile the appellant had commenced a civil action against the respondent alleging theft, and opposed the payment to the respondent. The Court of Appeal[274] considered that the question whether the money should be handed over should be determined by the same principles applicable to whether execution on a judgment by writ of *fieri facias* should be stayed under RSC O 47 r 1. The court may order a stay in that situation if the applicant can show special circumstances.[275] In the instant case, there were indeed special circumstances sufficient to support a stay. The

---

[267] *Civil Procedure* (Autumn 2001) vol 1, paras 24.2.6 and 24.6.3, and see CPR rr 3.1(3) and 24.6, and para 5.1 of the Practice Direction supplementing CPR Part 24.

[268] *Schofield v Church Army* [1986] 1 WLR 1328, 1334–1335, *per* Dillon LJ, referring to Lord Esher and Lindley LJ in *Sheppards and Co v Wilkinson and Jarvis* (1889) 6 TLR 13.

[269] *Civil Procedure* (Autumn 2001) vol 1, para 24.2.6.

[270] *Schofield v Church Army* [1986] 1 WLR 1328, 1335, *per* Dillon LJ.

[271] *Wagner v Laubscher Bros & Co* [1970] 2 QB 313, 317, *per* Lord Denning MR.

[272] *Schofield v Church Army* [1986] 1 WLR 1328, 1335; *State Bank of Victoria v Parry* [1989] WAR 240, 246. Compare *Akki Pty Ltd v Martin Hall Pty Ltd* (1994) 35 NSWLR 470, 479, in which Windeyer J considered that it was likely that a stay would be granted, although that was in the context of a case of mutual debts. Generally it would take less time for a defendant to establish, and obtain judgment for, a debt owing to him, as opposed to prosecuting a damages claim, and in that circumstance the courts may be more sympathetic to a stay.

[273] [1986] 1 WLR 1328.

[274] Dillon and Croom-Johnson LLJ.

[275] RSC O 47 r 1(a).

industrial tribunal had no jurisdiction to entertain the appellant's allegation of theft as a counterclaim to the respondent's claim for unfair dismissal. Nor was there any suggestion that the appellant had been dilatory in prosecuting its claim. Under the circumstances, it was considered to be inappropriate that the money be paid out before the civil action against the respondent came on for trial.

Equitable set-off

2.75   Consider that the cross-demands are such as to give rise to an equitable set-off,[276] either on the basis of equity acting by analogy with the legal right of set-off conferred by the Statutes of Set-off when the demands are mutual having regard to equitable rights,[277] or alternatively when there is a substantive defence of equitable set-off arising from a sufficiently close connection between the demands.[278] In *Jenner v Morris*,[279] a judgment had been obtained at common law but the assistance of a court of equity was required to enforce the judgment, and an equitable set-off was allowed to be raised in those proceedings. The plaintiff had recovered judgment against the defendant, and filed a bill in equity for the purpose of enforcing the judgment against a life interest of the defendant in some real estate. The defendant argued as a defence that he had made loans to the plaintiff's wife so that she could purchase necessaries, the wife having been deserted by the plaintiff. While a person who supplied necessaries to a deserted wife could sue the husband at common law, the common law did not recognize a similar right in a person who merely lent money to the wife for the purpose of acquiring necessaries. It was held in *Jenner v Morris* that the lender in that circumstance had a claim in equity against the husband, on the basis that the lender could stand in the shoes of the supplier in respect of the supplier's remedy against the husband and, further, that the defendant could set off against the judgment the plaintiff's liability to him in equity arising from the advances. In allowing a set-off equity acted by analogy with the legal right of set-off in the case of mutual debts, in that there was a debt due at common law from the defendant to the plaintiff in the form of the judgment, and a debt in equity owing by the plaintiff to the defendant.[280]

2.76   More generally, prior to the Judicature Acts equitable set-offs could be enforced by means of a common injunction restraining execution on a judgment obtained at

---

[276]   See also the common law case of *Alliance Bank of London and Liverpool v Holford* (1864) 16 CB(NS) 460, 143 ER 1207, in which the demands originated from the one transaction.

[277]   See para 3.06 below.

[278]   See ch 4 below.

[279]   (1860) 1 Dr & Sm 218, 62 ER 362, affirmed (1861) 3 De G F & J 45, 45 ER 795.

[280]   See the comments by Kindersley VC in other proceedings between the same parties (*Jenner v Morris* (1860) 1 Dr & Sm 334, 336, 62 ER 407, 408) in relation to his earlier decision in the instant case, which was the subject of the appeal to Lord Campbell and Turner LJ. Lord Campbell remarked in his judgment ((1861) 3 De G F & J 45, 53–54, 45 ER 795, 798) that the cross-demands were wholly unconnected, so that it is clear that a substantive defence of equitable set-off was not in issue.

common law.[281] Since the Judicature Acts a defendant in an action at law has been able to plead an equitable set-off as a defence in that action, and an equitable set-off after judgment would be given effect by way of a stay of execution. In Australia there is authority which suggests that a defendant who could have employed a cross-claim as a set-off in the plaintiff's action but failed to do so in some cases could be estopped from bringing a later action in respect of it.[282] But apart from the question of estoppel, if a defendant seeks to pursue an equitable set-off in re-spect of an unlitigated cross-claim after the plaintiff has obtained judgment, it may be necessary, in the post-Judicature Acts system where a cross-claim can be pleaded directly as a defence in the plaintiff's action, for the defendant to show special circumstances in order to obtain a stay of execution.[283] This may be diffi-cult to satisfy if the defendant has not diligently pursued his cross-claim.[284] Other circumstances may mitigate against a stay. In *Rawson v Samuel*[285] the applicants sought a common injunction to restrain execution on a judgment at law for dam-ages for breach of contract until an account could be taken of amounts due under the contract. Lord Cottenham pointed out that the account would be long and complicated,[286] and it could not be assumed that the balance would be in favour of the applicants. If the balance in fact should be found to be in favour of the plaintiff at law, he might not be adequately compensated for the delay in enforc-ing the judgment. Accordingly, the applicants did not have a sufficient equitable ground to support an injunction.

Cross-claim accruing after judgment

2.77 Enforcement of a judgment will not generally be stayed on the basis of a cross-claim that accrued after the judgment.[287] It is not considered reasonable that a sub-sequently acquired cross-demand should delay the plaintiff from the benefit of his judgment until the validity of the cross-demand can be tested.[288] However this

---

[281] See, eg, *Hamp v Jones* (1840) 9 LJ Ch 258; *Smith v Parkes* (1852) 16 Beav 115, 51 ER 720.

[282] See paras 5.133–5.136 below. This is not the prevailing view in England, however. See para 5.132 below.

[283] See para 2.74 above. Compare Meagher, Gummow and Lehane, *Equity Doctrines and Remedies* (3rd edn, 1992) 825 (referring to *Smith v Parkes* (1852) 16 Beav 115, 51 ER 720).

[284] *J C Scott Constructions v Mermaid Waters Tavern Pty Ltd* [1983] 2 Qd R 255, 259. Compare *Masterman v Malin* (1831) 7 Bing 435, 131 ER 168, in which the hearing of the cross-claim was ready to proceed, so that there would only have been a 'brief suspension' of the plaintiff's right to obtain the benefit of the judgment.

[285] (1841) Cr & Ph 161, 41 ER 451. See also *Preston v Strutton* (1792) 1 Anst 50, 145 ER 797; *Hill v Ziymak* (1908) 7 CLR 352.

[286] Compare *Clark v Cort* (1840) Cr & Ph 154, 41 ER 449, in which an account was also re-quired to be taken, though apparently it was less complicated than that in *Rawson v Samuel* because Lord Cottenham held that the claim could be the subject of a set-off.

[287] *Whyte v O'Brien* (1824) 1 Sim & St 551, 57 ER 218; *Maw v Ulyatt* (1861) 31 LJ Ch 33. Compare *Gale v Luttrell* (1826) 1 Y & J 180, 148 ER 636; *R (on the Application of Bateman) v Legal Services Commission* [2001] EWHC Admin 797; *Klein v Jeffcoat* [1996] EWCA Civ 686.

[288] See Sir John Leach in *Whyte v O'Brien* (1824) 1 Sim & St 551, 57 ER 218.

restriction may not apply if the demands are otherwise sufficiently closely connected to give rise to a substantive equitable set-off.[289]

(3) Setting Off Judgments and Orders[290]

2.78 It has been the practice of the common law courts since the eighteenth century to
allow one judgment or order for the payment of a sum of money to be set off
against another.[291] This practice extends to a judgment for damages,[292] as well as
to an order for the costs,[293] including costs in bankruptcy proceedings.[294]
Furthermore, it is not an objection that one of the judgments had existed at the
commencement of the other action, and might have been pleaded as a defence in
that action.[295] The set-off in these cases is not pursuant to the Statutes of Set-off,[296]
but rather it is allowed in the discretion of the court as part of its inherent jurisdiction.[297] It has been described as a form of 'equitable' jurisdiction possessed by
the common law courts for the purpose of preventing absurdity or injustice.[298] In

---

[289] See ch 4 below. Compare *Roadshow Entertaninment Pty Ltd v (ACN 053 006 269) Pty Ltd*
(1997) 42 NSWLR 462, 489. See on the other hand *Alliance Bank of London and Liverpool v Holford*
(1864) 16 CB(NS) 460, 143 ER 1207, which was decided at common law, although it is not clear
from the report when the cross-claims accrued.

[290] For set-off of judgments and orders in the county court, or a judgment or order in the county
court against a judgment or order in the High Court, see the County Courts Act 1984, s 72 and
CPR Sched 2, CCR O 22 r 11.

[291] See eg *Thrustout v Crafter* (1772) 2 Wm Bl 826, 96 ER 487. Montague, *Summary of the Law
of Set-off* (2nd edn, 1828) 4 note n, dates the practice from 23 Geo II (1750), while according to
Babington (*The Law of Set-off and Mutual Credit* (1827) 95–6), it became entrenched after 24 Geo
II. Prior to then, the courts had refused to allow judgments to be set off. See eg *Butler v Inneys* (1731)
2 Stra 891, 93 ER 921; *Tito v Duthie* (1744) 2 Stra 1203, 93 ER 1128. In an appropriate case an
order for costs may be on terms that payment is stayed pending the outcome of other proceedings
pending between the parties. See *R (on the Application of Bateman) v Legal Services Commission*
[2001] EWHC Admin 797, and *Klein v Jeffcoat* [1996] EWCA Civ 686.

[292] *Edwards v Hope* (1885) 14 QBD 922, 926.

[293] *Reid v Cupper* [1915] 2 KB 147; *R v Leeds County Court, ex p Morris* [1990] 1 QB 523; *Preston
v Nikolaides* (NSW Supreme Court, Young J, 25 July 1996). See now CPR r 44.3(9), and in
Queensland UCPR 734. Under CPR r 44.3(9), where a party entitled to costs is also liable to pay
costs, the court may assess the costs which he is liable to pay, and either set off the amount to which
he is entitled or delay the issue of a certificate for the costs to which he is entitled until he has paid
the amount for which he is liable.

[294] *Re A Debtor, No 21 of 1950 (No 2)* [1951] 1 Ch 612.

[295] *Barker v Braham* (1773) 2 Wm Bl 869, 96 ER 512.

[296] *Mitchell v Oldfield* (1791) 4 TR 123, 100 ER 929.

[297] *Re A Debtor, No 21 of 1950 (No 2)* [1951] 1 Ch 612, 617–618. As Lord Campbell CJ remarked in *Simpson v Lamb* (1857) 7 El & Bl 84, 89, 119 ER 1179, 1181, 'There is no strict right to
such a set-off . . .'. In New South Wales, see also *Wentworth v Wentworth* Young J, 12 December
1994, affirmed by the Court of Appeal, 21 February 1996.

[298] *Edwards v Hope* (1885) 14 QBD 922, 926; *Reid v Cupper* [1915] 2 KB 147, 149; *Kostka v
Addison* [1986] 1 Qd R 416, 420. See also *Simpson v Lamb* (1857) 7 El & Bl 84, 89, 90, 119 ER
1179, 1181. In *Barker v Braham* (1773) 2 Wm Bl 869, 872, 96 ER 512, 513 Blackstone J in the
Common Pleas described it as an 'equitable remedy', while Lord Kenyon in the King's Bench in
Mitchell v Oldfield (1791) 4 TR 123, 100 ER 929 referred to it as 'an equitable part of [the court's]
jurisdiction'.

allowing a set-off the court is at liberty to impose such terms as it considers reasonable and just.[299]

The nature of the set-off

In *Lockley v National Blood Transfusion Service*[300] the Court of Appeal character-ized the set-off in question as an equitable set-off arising from a close connection between the claims. In delivering the judgment of the Court,[301] Scott LJ said that the 'broad criterion' for determining the availability of the set-off is whether:[302] '[T]he plaintiff's claim and the defendant's claim are so closely connected that it would be inequitable to allow the plaintiff's claim without taking into account the defendant's claim. As it has sometimes been put, the defendant's claim must, in equity, impeach the plaintiff's claim.' This view has been accepted on other occa-sions.[303] Applying that principle, Scott LJ considered that interlocutory costs which a plaintiff is ordered to pay to the defendant in the progress of an action for trial in general would impeach in equity the right of the plaintiff to recover costs of the action which the defendant is ordered to pay to the plaintiff.[304] He said in relation to that proposition that:[305] 'A set-off of costs against costs, when all are incurred in the prosecution or defence of the same action, seems so natural and equitable as not to need any special justification. I would expect a party objecting to the set-off to give some special reason for that objection.' On the other hand, while Scott LJ commented that it is not wrong in principle to order that inter-locutory costs payable by a person should be set off against any damages to which the person is or may become in the future entitled, he nevertheless warned that it was 'less obvious that a set-off of costs against damages would always be justified'.[306] **2.79**

The difficulty with the *Lockley* case is the proposition that the set-off is an equitable set-off. In truth, it was applied by the common law courts long before the Judicature Acts.[307] It is true that the set-off has been described as an 'equitable' jurisdiction,[308] but that expression was used in the sense of justice and fairness, as **2.80**

---

[299] *Edwards v Hope* (1885) 14 QBD 922, 927.

[300] [1992] 1 WLR 492, 496–497.

[301] Farquharson and Scott LJJ and Sir John Megaw.

[302] [1992] 1 WLR 492, 496–497.

[303] *Klein v Jeffcoat* [1996] EWCA Civ 686; *Gorman v Carter* [1998] EWCA Civ 1038 (Mummery LJ and Sir John Knox).

[304] See also CPR r 44.3(9).

[305] [1992] 1 WLR 492, 497.

[306] [1992] 1 WLR 492, 497.

[307] See eg *Thrustout v Crafter* (1772) 2 Wm Bl 826, 96 ER 487, King's Bench; *Hall v Ody* (1799) 2 Bos & Pul 28, 126 ER 1136, Common Pleas; *Howell v Harding* (1807) 8 East 362, 103 ER 382, King's Bench; *Bridges v Smyth* (1831) 8 Bing 29, 131 ER 311, Common Pleas.

[308] See above.

opposed to a reference to the jurisdiction of the Court of Chancery.[309] The basis of the set-off is the general jurisdiction of the court over the suitors in it.[310] Indeed, it has long been accepted that the jurisdiction is not confined to judgments in the same action (or in the same court),[311] without any suggestion that the claims nevertheless should be closely connected. In so far as the Court of Appeal was reticent to accept that a set-off of costs against damages would always be justified, it is nevertheless the case that the courts in the past have been prepared to order a set-off of costs against a judgment for damages and costs, or of costs against a judgment for debt and costs,[312] or, more recently, of costs against any future sums which may be ordered to be paid on the taking of a partnership account between the parties.[313]

Mutuality

2.81 A set-off of judgments generally will not be permitted if the judgments, although between the same parties, nevertheless are in different rights, as where one of the parties is merely a trustee in relation to one judgment but in the other is interested in his own right.[314] Even before the Judicature Acts the common law courts would take notice of a trust and deny a set-off on this ground.[315] Conversely, the common law courts in the exercise of their 'equitable' jurisdiction would look

---

[309] In the same way, Lord Mansfield in *Moses v Macferlan* (1760) 2 Burr 1005, 1012, 97 ER 676, 680–681 referred to the common law action for money had and received as a 'kind of equitable action, to recover back money, which ought not in justice to be kept', and as being based upon 'ties of natural justice and equity'. However the action is a common law action. See *Roxborough v Rothmans of Pall Mall Australia Ltd* (2001) 76 ALJR 203, 223 [96]–[99], *per* Gummow J, 244 [202]–[203], *per* Callinan J.

[310] *Mitchell v Oldfield* (1791) 4 TR 123, 100 ER 929, *per* Lord Kenyon.

[311] *Edwards v Hope* (1885) 14 QBD 922, 927, *per* Bowen LJ. See, eg, *Mitchell v Oldfield* (1791) 4 TR 123, 100 ER 929 (to the extent that the set-off was not defeated by the solicitor's lien); *Glaister v Hewer* (1798) 8 TR 69, 101 ER 1271 (in which the actions appear to have been unrelated); *O'Connor v Murphy* (1791) 1 H Bl 657, 126 ER 375; *Bridges v Smyth* (1831) 8 Bing 29, 131 ER 311; *Bristowe v Needham* (1844) 7 Man & G 648, 649, 135 ER 261; *Edwards v Hope* (1885) 14 QBD 922, 926 ('distinct actions'); *Preston v Nikolaides* (NSW SC, Young J, 25 July 1996) ('The ordinary rule is that where there are costs owing and payable by two parties, even in different pieces of litigation, that there is a set-off, unless there are strong reasons to the contrary'); Babington, *The Law of Set-off and Mutual Credit* (1827) 95 ('To assist the parties in the recovery of costs, and do justice between them, they are allowed to deduct or set off the costs, or debt and costs in one action against those in another'). Compare *Throckmorton v Crowley* (1866) LR 3 Eq 196, 199 and *Collett v Preston* (1852) 15 Beav 458, 51 ER 615, which concerned the effect of a solicitor's lien, for which see below. Different considerations also applied when the debtor's body had been taken in execution. See *Taylor v Waters* (1816) 5 M & S 103, 105 ER 989 and *Thompson v Parish* (1859) 5 CB (NS) 685, 141 ER 276.

[312] See eg *Lang v Webber* (1815) 1 Price 375, 145 ER 1434 (costs against damages); *Thrustout v Crafter* (1772) 2 Wm Bl 826, 96 ER 487 (set-off against judgment for debt and costs); *Howell v Harding* (1807) 8 East 362, 103 ER 382 (interlocutory costs set off against a judgment for debt and costs). See also *Goldsborough Mort & Co Ltd v Quin* (1910) 10 CLR 674.

[313] *Klein v Jeffcoat* [1996] EWCA Civ 686. See also *R (on the Application of Bateman) v Legal Services Commission* [2001] EWHC Admin 797.

[314] *David v Rees* [1904] 2 KB 435, 443, 445–446; *Bristowe v Needham* (1844) 7 Man & G 648, 135 ER 261. See also *John Dee Group Ltd v WMH (21) Ltd* [1998] BCC 972, 976.

[315] *Bristowe v Needham* (1844) 7 Man & G 648, 135 ER 261.

behind the parties on the record and allow a set-off of judgments if, having regard to the parties truly interested in the judgments, it was considered just that a set-off should occur.[316] This applied, for example, where A was a judgment creditor of B on one claim, and A had agreed to indemnify C against a judgment obtained against him by B on another claim, so that A was the party who as a matter of substance had the burden of this second judgment.[317]

The principle that the cross-judgments should be held in the same right does not **2.82** preclude a set-off in the situation in which one of the parties died after obtaining judgment.[318] It does prevent a set-off, however, if one of the judgments was assigned to a third party, and notice of the assignment was given before the cross-judgment was obtained against the assignor.[319] It also applies if one of the parties is bankrupt, and the judgment was obtained in an action brought by the trustee in bankruptcy.[320] In such a case the cross-demands may be such that a set-off would be available in any event under the insolvency legislation. But if a bankruptcy has intervened, and for some reason the set-off section in the insolvency legislation is not applicable to the cross-actions in respect of which the judgments were obtained, Lord Ellenborough warned that the courts have a 'strong disinclination' to allow a set-off of the judgments pursuant to their equitable jurisdiction.[321] Indeed, it is unlikely that a set-off would ever be permitted in that circumstance today.

Where A has a judgment against B and C, and B has a separate judgment against **2.83** A, the courts have been prepared to set off the judgments.[322] In the cases where this occurred there was no question of a bankruptcy, and it was also emphasized that

---

[316] See eg *O'Connor v Murphy* (1791) 1 H Bl 657, 126 ER 375; *Standeven v Murgatroyd* (1858) 27 LJ Ex 425. See also, and compare, *Currie & Co v The Law Society* [1977] 1 QB 990 (assignment of judgment to the debtor on another judgment).

[317] *Schoole v Noble, Lett, and Byrne* (1788) 1 H Bl 23, 126 ER 15; *O'Connor v Murphy* (1791) 1 H Bl 657, 126 ER 375; *Bourne v Benett* (1827) 4 Bing 423, 130 ER 831; *Standeven v Murgatroyd* (1858) 27 LJ Ex 425.

[318] *Bridges v Smyth* (1831) 8 Bing 29, 131 ER 311.

[319] See, and compare, *Simpson v Lamb* (1857) 7 El & Bl 84, 119 ER 1179, where the assignment occurred between verdict and judgment, though it seems clear that the court would have reached the same conclusion on this point if the assignment had occurred after the judgment. Compare also *Bank of New South Wales v Preston* (1894) 20 VLR 1, in which the assignment occurred after the cross-judgment had been obtained, and the assignee was aware of all the circumstances. It was held that he took subject to a set-off.

[320] *Doe v Darnton* (1802) 3 East 149, 102 ER 554.

[321] *Doe v Darnton* (1802) 3 East 149, 150, 102 ER 554, although compare the special circumstances in *Alliance Bank of London & Liverpool Ltd v Holford* (1864) 16 CB(NS) 460, 143 ER 1207. Note that, when there have been orders in the same suit for payment of costs by each party to the other, the court subsequently may order that the costs be set off notwithstanding an intervening liquidation of one of the parties. See *J Earle Hermann Ltd v Municipality of North Sydney* (1914) 31 WN (NSW) 166.

[322] *Roberts v Biggs* (1754) Barnes 146, 94 ER 848; *Mitchell v Oldfield* (1791) 4 TR 123, 100 ER 929; *Dennie v Elliott* (1795) 2 H Bl 587, 126 ER 719. Compare *Bourne v Benett* (1827) 4 Bing 423, 130 ER 831, 1 Moo & P 141, in which there was the additional element that one of the defendants against whom judgment was given had agreed to indemnify the other defendants against the

the set-off did not depend upon the Statutes of Set-off but upon the court's 'equitable' jurisdiction.[323] If, however, B has become bankrupt, and the separate action against A was brought by his trustee in bankruptcy for the benefit of his general body of creditors, a set-off will not be permitted in respect of judgments upon the cross-actions in circumstances where a set-off is not available under the set-off section in the insolvency legislation.[324]

Solicitor's lien

2.84   A solicitor who conducts a case to trial has a charge (or lien) over the proceeds of a judgment obtained by his client for his costs in relation to the action.[325] If however the judgment were subject to a set-off, the fund available to satisfy the lien would be reduced to the extent of the set-off, to the evident detriment of the solicitor. At one time it seems that the various common law courts adopted different attitudes to the treatment of a solicitor's lien in an application to set off judgments.[326] Thus, the Court of King's Bench held that the set-off was subject to the lien, so that the lien had to be satisfied before the set-off could take effect,[327] except, it would seem, where the orders arose in the same suit.[328] The Court of

---

judgment, so that he was principally liable *inter se*. It was held that the judgment should be set off against a separate judgment obtained by that defendant against the plaintiff. In allowing the set-off Park J emphasized this additional element, although the earlier cases referred to above suggest that a set-off may have been available in any event.

[323]   *Mitchell v Oldfield* (1791) 4 TR 123, 124, 100 ER 929. Lord Kenyon therefore rejected an argument that, since one debt was due to the plaintiff alone whereas the other was the joint debt of the plaintiff and another to the defendant, the court should not interfere. Compare the discussion of mutuality in paras 12.02–12.07 below.

[324]   *Doe v Darnton* (1802) 3 East 149, 102 ER 554. See also *Loughnan v O'Sullivan* [1922] 1 IR 103 (affirmed [1922] 1 IR 160), in which A had become bankrupt.

[325]   It is commonly said that a solicitor's lien is simply a right in the solicitor to ask for the court's intervention for his protection when, having obtained judgment for the client, there is a probability that he will be deprived of his costs. See *Halvanon Insurance Co Ltd v Central Reinsurance Corp* [1988] 3 All ER 857, 862; *Fairfold Properties Ltd v Exmouth Docks Co Ltd* [1993] Ch 196, 200–201; *Halsbury's Laws of England* (4th edn (reissue) 1995) vol 44(1), 208 para 253. In Australia, it is regarded as more than a mere personal equity, and it is said that the assistance of the court is invoked not to create rights but to enforce them. See *Worrell v Power & Power* (1993) 46 FCR 214 (preference claim against solicitors who transferred the proceeds of a judgment from their trust account to their general account in satisfaction of the client's liability for costs); *Philippa Power & Associates v Primrose Couper Cronin Rudkin* [1997] 2 Qd R 266.

[326]   *Reid v Cupper* [1915] 2 KB 147, 155–156, *per* Pickford LJ.

[327]   *Mitchell v Oldfield* (1791) 4 TR 123, 100 ER 929; *Randle v Fuller* (1795) 6 TR 456, 101 ER 646; *Mercer v Graves* (1872) LR 7 QB 499, 503. In *Mercer v Graves* a set-off in fact was allowed, but that was because of a peculiar circumstance, that the plaintiff was required to bring an action in England in order to enforce the judgment that he had obtained in Ireland. The lien that the plaintiff's solicitor had over the judgment for his costs was not such as to give rise to a relationship of trustee and beneficiary as between the plaintiff and the solicitor, and therefore there was no equitable ground for disallowing the set-off that otherwise was available to the defendant under the Statutes of Set-off in the plaintiff's action.

[328]   *Howell v Harding* (1807) 8 East 362, 103 ER 382; *R v Burke* (1824) 7 LJOSKB 330. Compare *Aspinall v Stamp* (1824) 3 B & C 108, 107 ER 674. It appears that the Court of Chancery

Common Pleas said that the lien should be disregarded, on the basis that the solicitor should look in the first instance to the personal security of his client for payment.[329] In so far as the Court of Exchequer was concerned, it has been said that it would exercise its discretion according to the circumstances.[330] The modern view is that a set-off of judgments should not be refused on account of a solicitor's lien, if as between the parties themselves a set-off would be fair and just, and if no fraud or imposition has been practised upon the solicitor by collusion between the parties.[331]

Legal aid

When one party is legally aided, the Court of Appeal in *Lockley v National Blood Transfusion Service*[332] said that the question of set-off is no different from, and is no more extensive than, the availability of set-off to or against parties who are not legally aided.[333] The court therefore can order that interlocutory costs ordered in favour of one party who is not legally aided be set off against any costs to which the other party, who is legally aided, has become, or may in the future become, entitled in the action. **2.85**

Subsequently a set-off was denied in the context of legal aid in *Brookes v Harris*,[334] although the circumstances were exceptional. The plaintiff obtained judgment against the defendant for £130,000, and issued a writ of *fieri facias*. Pursuant to the writ the sheriff entered into possession of a collection of music records, tapes and compact discs belonging to the defendant. The defendant, who was legally aided, successfully argued that the collection constituted tools of his trade, as a presenter of music programmes, so that the execution was unlawful.[335] The plaintiff accordingly was ordered to pay his costs. The plaintiff then sought to have the costs set off against the unsatisfied judgment. Ferris J held that a set-off was **2.86**

---

exercised its discretion in the same way as the King's Bench. See *Reid v Cupper* [1915] 2 KB 147, 156 (Pickford LJ), and also *Throckmorton v Crowley* (1866) LR 3 Eq 196, 199, referring to *Collett v Preston* (1852) 15 Beav 458, 51 ER 615.

[329] *Hall v Ody* (1799) 2 Bos & Pul 28, 126 ER 1136; *Bridges v Smyth* (1831) 8 Bing 29, 131 ER 311; Babington, *The Law of Set-off and Mutual Credit* (1827) 111. Compare however *Thompson v Parish* (1859) 5 CB (NS) 685, 695–696.

[330] *Reid v Cupper* [1915] 2 KB 147, 156, *per* Pickford LJ.

[331] *Puddephatt v Leith (No 2)* [1916] 2 Ch 168; *Currie v The Law Society* [1977] 1 QB 990, 999. See also *Re A Debtor, No 21 of 1950 (No 2)* [1951] 1 Ch 612, and *Knight v Knight* [1925] 1 Ch 835. In Australia, see *Butcher v Colonial Wholesale Meat Co Ltd* (1920) 38 WN(NSW) 24; *Miller & Co Machinery Pty Ltd v Bear* [1934] VLR 85; *Akki Pty Ltd v Martin Hall Pty Ltd* (1994) 35 NSWLR 470. In Queensland, UCPR 734(2) provides that cross-costs may be set off, even though a solicitor for a party has a lien for his costs of the proceeding.

[332] [1992] 1 WLR 492. See also *Klein v Jeffcoat* [1996] EWCA Civ 686; *Gorman v Carter* [1998] EWCA Civ 1038.

[333] [1992] 1 WLR 492, 496.

[334] [1995] 1 WLR 918.

[335] See the Supreme Court Act 1981, s 138(3A).

inappropriate in the circumstances. The defendant had sought to preserve his property from an illegal execution, and for that he required legal aid. Pursuant to the Legal Aid Act 1988, section 16(6), however, the Legal Aid Board had a charge on the collection, as property preserved in the proceedings, as security for the payment of a contribution in respect of the cost of the legal aid. Therefore, unless the plaintiff paid the costs ordered against him, the Legal Aid Board would have had the right to enforce a charge over the very property which was saved from the illegal execution. In his Lordship's opinion, it would not have been a just result if, having been guilty of unjustified conduct which lead to the statutory charge being brought into existence, the plaintiff were to be allowed a set-off which would have prevented the amount secured by the charge being satisfied otherwise than by realization of the property in question.

F. Common Law Abatement

2.87 It used to be the practice of the common law courts in an action for the agreed price of goods sold with a warranty, or of work to be performed according to a contract, to allow the plaintiff to recover the stipulated sum while leaving the defendant to a cross-action for damages for any breach of warranty or contract by the plaintiff.[336] Compliance with the warranty, or proper performance of every portion of the work contracted for, was not regarded as a condition precedent to payment of the stipulated price.[337] However, in the latter part of the eighteenth century and the early part of the nineteenth century the courts began to develop a different practice, by which the defendant in these cases was permitted to show that the goods by reason of non-compliance with the warranty, or the work in consequence of the improper performance of the contract, was diminished in value or was of no value.[338] This was not in the nature of raising the cross-demand as a set-off,[339] because at common law the only right of set-off available

---

[336] See for example *Broom v Davis* (1794) 7 East 480n, 103 ER 186.

[337] The ensuing discussion concerns an action for an agreed price. If the claimant is suing for a quantum meruit rather than for a specific agreed sum, he must show what the work was worth, and it is open to the defendant in such a case to show that the work in fact was not worth as much as the claimant claims. See *Basten v Butter* (1806) 7 East 479, 103 ER 185; *Farnsworth v Garrard* (1807) 1 Camp 38, 170 ER 867; *Riverside Motors Pty Ltd v Abrahams* [1945] VLR 45.

[338] *King v Boston* (1789) 7 East 481n, 103 ER 186; *Germaine v Burton* (1821) 3 Stark 32, 171 ER 757 (sale by sample); *Poulton v Lattimore* (1829) 9 B & C 259, 109 ER 96; *Street v Blay* (1831) 2 B & Ad 456, 109 ER 1212; *Thornton v Place* (1832) 1 M & Rob 218, 174 ER 74 (plaintiff only entitled to the agreed price of work minus the sum necessary for the defendant to expend to complete the work according to the specifications); *Allen v Cameron* (1833) 1 C & M 832, 149 ER 635 (breach of obligation to tend trees the subject of a sale); *Cousins v Paddon* (1835) 2 C M & R 547, 150 ER 234; *Dicken v Neale* (1836) 1 M & W 556, 150 ER 556.

[339] *Bright v Rogers* [1917] 1 KB 917; *Hanak v Green* [1958] 2 QB 9, 17, 23; *Henriksens Rederi A/S v THZ Rolimpex (The Brede)* [1974] 1 QB 233, 252, 260; *United Dominions Corp Ltd v Jaybe Homes*

was under the Statutes of Set-off, and the Statutes required liquidated cross-demands in the form of mutual debts. Rather, the defendant was permitted to defend himself[340] by showing how much less the subject-matter of the contract was worth by reason of the breach, and to obtain an abatement of the price accordingly.[341] The revised practice received the imprimatur of the Court of Exchequer[342] in the leading case of *Mondel v Steel*,[343] and it is now firmly established.[344] Indeed, in the case of a sale of goods the right has been enshrined in the sale of goods legislation.[345] On the other hand it is tightly confined, being restricted to contracts for the sale of goods and for work and labour.[346] It is unlikely, for example, that it would be extended to a contract for the sale of shares with a warranty.[347]

The principle of abatement applies to building contracts,[348] including shipbuild- **2.88**
ing contracts.[349] At one time it was thought that the defence is not available in building cases in which the price is to be paid by instalment on certificate,[350] though that view is no longer current.[351] On the other hand, Parke B emphasized in *Mondel v Steel*[352] that the principle does not apply to all contracts for work and

---

Pty Ltd [1978] Qd R 111, 115–116; *R v McKay, ex p Cassaniti* [1993] 2 Qd R 95. See also *A Cameron Ltd v John Mowlem & Co plc* (1990) 52 BLR 24, 33. Compare *BICC plc v Burndy Corp* [1985] 1 Ch 232, 246. Abatement is independent of the doctrine of equitable set-off. See *Gilbert-Ash (Northern) Ltd v Modern Engineering (Bristol) Ltd* [1974] AC 689, 717.

[340] The order as to costs should follow accordingly. See for example *Lowe v Holme* (1883) 10 QBD 286, though compare *Chell Engineering Ltd v Unit Tool and Engineering Co Ltd* [1950] 1 All ER 378.

[341] *Mondel v Steel* (1841) 8 M & W 858, 870–872, 151 ER 1288, 1293–1294, *per* Parke B.

[342] Parke B, Alderson B, Gurney B and Rolfe B.

[343] (1841) 8 M & W 858, 151 ER 1288.

[344] In addition to the cases cited below, see *Parson v Sexton* (1847) 4 CB 899, 136 ER 763; *Dawson v Collis* (1851) 10 CB 523, 138 ER 208 and *Towerson v The Aspatria Agricultural Co-Operative Society Ltd* (1872) 27 LT 276 (sale by sample); *Webber v Aarons* [1972] 2 NSWLR 95. There cannot be both an award of damages for defective work and an abatement of the price, since it would result in payment twice over. See *Hutchinson v Harris* (1978) 10 BLR 19.

[345] Sale of Goods Act 1979, s 53(1)(a).

[346] *Gilbert-Ash (Northern) Ltd v Modern Engineering (Bristol) Ltd* [1974] AC 689, 717, *per* Lord Diplock; *Aries Tanker Corp v Total Transport Ltd* [1977] 1 WLR 185, 190; *Sim v Rotherham Metropolitan BC* [1987] 1 Ch 216, 258–259.

[347] The issue was referred to, but not decided, in *Intag Microelectronics Pty Ltd v AWA Ltd* (1995) 18 ACSR 284, 287.

[348] See eg *Gilbert-Ash (Northern) Ltd v Modern Engineering (Bristol) Ltd* [1974] AC 689; *Acsim (Southern) Ltd v Danish Contracting & Development Co Ltd* (1989) 47 BLR 55. An employer who has wrongfully repudiated a building contract is not precluded from relying on abatement for defective work. See *Slater v C A Duquemin Ltd* (1992) 29 Con LR 24.

[349] *Mondel v Steel* (1841) 8 M & W 858, 151 ER 1288.

[350] *Dawnays Ltd v F G Minter Ltd* [1971] 1 WLR 1205.

[351] *Gilbert-Ash (Northern) Ltd v Modern Engineering (Bristol) Ltd* [1974] AC 689. See para 5.49 below.

[352] (1841) 8 M & W 858, 871, 151 ER 1288, 1293.

labour.[353] It does not apply, for example, to a contract of carriage,[354] including carriage by sea.[355] Further, Parke B accepted that it did not extend to an attorney, unless no benefit whatever was derived from the work.[356] Consistent with that view, the Court of Appeal in *Hutchinson v Harris*[357] doubted whether abatement extends to fees for professional services,[358] in that case for an architect.[359] This view has also been expressed in relation to a consulting engineer.[360] On the other hand, a cross-claim for professional negligence and breach of duty in such a case may give rise to an equitable set-off.[361]

---

[353] *Quaere* whether the common law defence of abatement ever extended to a claim for wages under a contract of employment. In *Sagar v H Ridehalgh and Son Ltd* [1931] 1 Ch 310, 326 Lord Hanworth MR accepted that it does, although Scott J left the question open in *Sim v Rotherham Metropolitan BC* [1987] 1 Ch 216, 255–259, commenting (at 257) that Lord Hanworth's remarks were obiter and seemed inconsistent with the restrictive comments about the nature of the defence made by Lord Diplock in *Gilbert-Ash (Northern) Ltd v Modern Engineering (Bristol) Ltd* [1974] AC 689, 717. For set-off in relation to contracts of employment, see paras 5.53–5.55 below.

[354] *Aries Tanker Corp v Total Transport Ltd* [1977] 1 WLR 185, 190.

[355] *Mondel v Steel* (1841) 8 M & W 858, 871, 151 ER 1288, 1293 (freight); *Aries Tanker Corp v Total Transport Ltd* [1977] 1 WLR 185. Nor is the defence available to defeat a claim for hire under a time charter of a ship. See *Century Textiles and Industry Ltd v Tomoe Shipping Co (Singapore) Pte Ltd (The Aditya Vaibhav)* [1991] 1 Lloyd's Rep 573, 575.

[356] (1841) 8 M & W 858, 871, 151 ER 1288, 1293, referring to *Templer v M'Lachlan* (1806) 2 Bos & Pul (NR) 136, 127 ER 576.

[357] (1978) 10 BLR 19, 31–32, *per* Stephenson LJ, with whom Waller and Cumming-Bruce LJJ agreed.

[358] Compare *Foster Wheeler Group Engineering Ltd v Chevron UK Ltd* [1996] EWHC QB 381 at paras 296–324. The contract in that case was for a variety of services, mainly but not exclusively of an engineering nature. Judge Humphrey Lloyd QC held on the facts that the contract was for work and labour rather than for professional services, so that the defence of abatement applied. In *Hutchinson v Harris* (1978) 10 BLR 19, 31 Stephenson LJ noted the decision in *Hoenig v Isaacs* [1952] 2 All ER 176, in which the Court of Appeal allowed an abatement in relation to a contract with an interior decorator and designer of furniture. The complaint in that case however related to some articles of furniture which the designer supplied and which were said to be faulty and defective. In Victoria, the question whether abatement extends to fees for professional services was noted, but not decided, in *Hyder Consulting (Victoria) Pty Ltd v Transfield Pty Ltd* (2000) 17 BCL 129, 134. It has been suggested that abatement nevertheless may apply in this context as regards work not done. See *Keating on Building Contracts* (7th edn, 2001) 572.

[359] One of the complaints against the architect was that she had incorrectly certified work as having been completed by a builder, and the plaintiff therefore sought to abate the architect's fees to the extent of the cost to remedy the work. Stephenson LJ (at (1978) 10 BLR 19, 31–32) pointed out, however, that the subject-matter of the architect's contract was not the same as that of the builder. The fact that work that the architect certified had not been done by the builder did not necessarily mean that the architect had not done the equivalent amount of her own work.

[360] *Cathery v Lithodomos Ltd* (1987) 41 BLR 76, 82. In Victoria, the question of the application of the principle of abatement has been left open in the context of a design engineer (*Hyder Consulting (Victoria) Pty Ltd v Transfield Pty Ltd* (2000) 17 BCL 129, 134), and in relation to a contract for the provision of contract management consulting services. See *Leighton Contractors Pty Ltd v East Gippsland Catchment Management Authority* (2000) 17 BCL 35, 40–41[25]. On the other hand, in *Dames & Moore Pty Ltd v Jovista Pty Ltd* (1998) 14 BCL 421 Master Sanderson in the Western Australian Supreme Court accepted, in a summary judgment application, that abatement may apply to a contract to design the materials and equipment for a conveying and crushing system.

[361] *Cathery v Lithodomos Ltd* (1987) 41 BLR 76, 82. See also the *Cathery* case in relation to security for costs in such a case.

If a bill of exchange is given as payment for the purchase of goods or for the per- **2.89**
formance of work, the bill must be honoured irrespective of any breach of contract
by the vendor which amounts only to a partial failure of consideration.[362]
Similarly the defence does not apply where the price of goods was paid by means
of a loan from the vendor secured by a mortgage, so that the vendor's action is for
repayment of the loan rather than for payment of the price.[363]

It was held in *Mondel v Steel* that the defendant in an action for the agreed price of **2.90**
work and labour, and for goods sold and delivered, is only entitled to an abatement to the extent that, at the time of delivery, the value of the subject-matter of
the contract[364] has been reduced as a result of the breach of warranty or contract.[365]
All claims beyond that, for example on account of a subsequent necessity for more
extensive repairs,[366] or for damages for delay,[367] or for misrepresentation not
amounting to a breach of warranty,[368] will not result in an abatement under the
common law principle. Two points should be noted however in relation to this
limitation. The first is that, following the expansion in recent times of the defence
of equitable set-off,[369] a damages claim which could not form the subject of an
abatement in any event may well give rise now to a defence under the equitable
principle.[370] The second is that, in the case of a sale of goods, section 53(1)(a) of
the Sale of Goods Act 1979 may have taken the matter further than the common
law position. Section 53(1)(a) provides that a damages claim for breach of warranty by a seller may be set up in diminution or extinction of the price. One of the
warranties set out in the Act is that the buyer will enjoy quiet possession of the

---

[362] See paras 5.25–5.31 below.

[363] *Bow, McLachlan & Co Ltd v Ship 'Camosun'* [1909] AC 597, 610–613. See para 4.87 below.

[364] In the case of a sale of goods, the defence of abatement is only available when the claimant's
action is for the price of the same goods in which the defect occurred. See *W Pope & Co Pty Ltd v
Edward Souery & Co Pty Ltd* [1983] WAR 117 and *Bayview Quarries Pty Ltd v Castley Development
Pty Ltd* [1963] VR 445 in relation to equitable set-off.

[365] In addition to the cases cited below, see *Bow, McLachlan & Co Ltd v Ship 'Camosun'* [1909]
AC 597, 605; *Henriksens Rederi A/S v THZ Rolimpex (The Brede)* [1974] 1 QB 233, 248; *Hotel
Services Ltd v Hilton International Hotels (UK) Ltd* [2000] BLR 235, 239 (referring to *Mellowes
Archital Ltd v Bell Projects Ltd* (1997) 87 BLR 26).

[366] As in *Mondel v Steel* (1841) 8 M & W 858, 151 ER 1288. See also *Davis v Hedges* (1871) LR
6 QB 687, 691; *R v McKay ex p Cassaniti* [1993] 2 Qd R 95, 100.

[367] See *Oastler v Pound* (1863) 7 LT 852; *Henriksens Rederi A/S v THZ Rolimpex (The Brede)*
[1974] 1 QB 233, 248; *Mellowes Archital Ltd v Bell Projects Ltd* (1997) 87 BLR 26. This is also implicit in *Hermcrest plc v G Percy Trentham Ltd* (1991) 53 BLR 104 (esp at 112–113). Compare
Windeyer J in *Healing (Sales) Pty Ltd v Inglis Electrix Pty Ltd* (1968) 121 CLR 584, 618.

[368] *Intag Microelectronics Pty Ltd v AWA Ltd* (1995) 18 ACSR 284, 287, NSW SC, *per* Young J.
Similarly, a claim for damages for breach of the Trade Practices Act 1974 (Cth), not amounting to
a breach of contract, will not give rise to a defence of abatement. See *Intag v AWA* at 287.

[369] See ch 4 below.

[370] *R v McKay, ex p Cassaniti* [1993] 2 Qd R 95, 100; *Henriksens Rederi A/S v THZ Rolimpex (The
Brede)* [1974] 1 QB 233, 248. Thus, a cross-demand for damages for delay may be employed in a
set-off. See eg *Young v Kitchin* (1878) 3 Ex D 127; *Mitchell v Purnell Motors Pty Ltd* [1961] NSWR
165; *Galambos & Son Pty Ltd v McIntyre* (1974) 5 ACTR 10; *Henriksens Rederi v Rolimpex* at 248.

goods.[371] In Australia the High Court has held that this encompasses a subsequent interference with the goods by the seller and, further, that this breach could be set up in diminution of the price pursuant to the New South Wales equivalent of section 53(1)(a).[372] Yet, this could hardly be regarded as evidencing a reduction in the value of the goods as they were delivered. The notion that this breach of warranty comes within the ambit of section 53(1)(a) is difficult to reconcile with the view that section 53(1)(a) is merely a codification of the law laid down in *Mondel v Steel*.[373]

2.91 The measure of the abatement, in the case of a contract for the sale of goods, is prima facie the difference between the value of the goods at the time of delivery and the value they would have had if they had complied with the warranty.[374] In the case of a contract for work and labour, ordinarily it would be the cost of remedial work required to correct defects in the work.[375]

2.92 The defendant in an action for the agreed price of goods or of work and labour is not bound to set up the claim for breach of warranty or for failure to perform the work properly as a defence in that action. He may choose to pay the price and bring a separate action of his own for damages.[376] In the case of a contract for the sale of goods, this principle is reflected in section 53(1)(b) of the Sale of Goods Act 1979. Alternatively, the purchaser of the goods or services may sue for damages *before* paying the price. In such a case there is no principle of abatement to which the vendor may have recourse as a means of reducing the damages award. He is not entitled to an 'abatement' from his liability for damages to the extent of the unpaid price.[377]

Substantive or procedural?

2.93 A question in respect of which conflicting views have been expressed is whether common law abatement is a procedural or a substantive defence. Historically it

---

[371] Sale of Goods Act 1979, s 12(2).

[372] *Healing (Sales) Pty Ltd v Inglis Electrix Pty Ltd* (1968) 121 CLR 584. Indeed, Barwick CJ and Menzies J said in their joint judgment (at 595) that s 53(1)(a) allows a buyer to set up any breach of warranty against the price.

[373] See eg *Benjamin's Sale of Goods* (5th edn, 1997) 932 para 17-047, and also the minority view of Windeyer J in *Healing v Inglis* (1968) 121 CLR 584, 617–618.

[374] See the Sale of Goods Act 1979, s 53(3).

[375] *Thornton v Place* (1832) 1 M & Rob 218, 174 ER 74; *Hoenig v Isaacs* [1952] 2 All ER 176, 180, 181. See also *Argento v Cooba Developments Pty Ltd* (1987) 13 FCR 579, 584, 589; *Barnett v Peter Cox Group Ltd* (1995) 45 Con LR 131, and the commentary by the editors of the *Building Law Reports* on *C A Duquemin Ltd v Raymond Slater* (1993) 65 BLR 124, 126–127 (criticizing the judgment of Judge John Newey QC in that case).

[376] *Davis v Hedges* (1871) LR 6 QB 687 (disapproving of Lord Ellenborough in *Fisher v Samuda* (1808) 1 Camp 190, 191, 170 ER 925); *Healing (Sales) Pty Ltd v Inglis Electrix Pty Ltd* (1968) 121 CLR 584; *Henriksens Rederi A/S v THZ Rolimpex (The Brede)* [1974] 1 QB 233, 248; *Sidney Raper Pty Ltd v Commonwealth Trading Bank of Australia* [1975] 2 NSWLR 227, 238. See also *Rigge v Burbidge* (1846) 15 M & W 598, 153 ER 988.

[377] *Healing (Sales) Pty Ltd v Inglis Electrix Pty Ltd* (1968) 121 CLR 584.

seems that the justification for its introduction was to avoid circuity of action,[378] which is consistent with a procedural defence. This indeed would appear to be the prevailing view in Australia, where it has been referred to, in that country's highest court, as a 'procedural concession' which 'the law has come to concede for the sake of convenience'.[379] In England however the defence has been described as substantive.[380]

In *Aectra Refining and Marketing Inc v Exmar NV*[381] Hoffmann LJ (as he then was) equated abatement with the substantive defence of equitable set-off, and in contradistinction to the procedural defence provided by the Statutes of Set-off.[382] Equitable set-off is said to be a substantive defence because, unlike the Statutes, it does not require a judgment for a set-off in order to give effect to it. It may be set up by a debtor, not merely as a means of preventing a creditor from obtaining judgment, but as an immediate answer to liability. When circumstances exist which support an equitable set-off, it is unconscionable for a creditor to regard the debtor as being indebted to the extent of the debtor's cross-demand, and the creditor cannot take any action against the debtor which is predicated upon the debtor having failed to pay. A court of equity can protect the debtor's position by means of an injunction and a declaration.[383] It is not clear on the other hand how the substantive quality arises at common law in relation to the defence of abatement. The notion that abatement is substantive would not mean that a debt for the price does not arise to the extent of the reduction in value caused by the breach, as perhaps may be suggested by statements to the effect that abatement at common law reduces or diminishes or extinguishes the claim.[384] If that indeed were the case, it is difficult to see how separate claims could be regarded as subsisting at common law so as to entitle the purchaser to elect to pay the full price and to sue separately for the damages.[385] Nor does the purchaser himself, simply by electing to rely on the

2.94

---

[378] *Street v Blay* (1831) 2 B & Ad 456, 462–463, 109 ER 1212, 1214; *Allen v Cameron* (1833) 1 C & M 832, 840, 149 ER 635, 639; *Mondel v Steel* (1841) 8 M & W 858, 869–870, 151 ER 1288, 1293; *Davis v Hedges* (1871) LR 6 QB 687, 691; *Bow, McLachlan & Co Ltd v Ship 'Camosun'* [1909] AC 597, 611, 613; *Healing (Sales) Pty Ltd v Inglis Electrix Pty Ltd* (1968) 121 CLR 584, 614–615.

[379] See Kitto J in *Healing (Sales) Pty Ltd v Inglis Electrix Pty Ltd* (1968) 121 CLR 584, 601. The tenor of the judgment of Windeyer J suggests that he agreed with this view. See also *Cellulose Products Pty Ltd v Truda* (1970) 92 WN (NSW) 561, 570. Compare *Newman v Cook* [1963] VR 659.

[380] See eg *Gilbert-Ash (Northern) Ltd v Modern Engineering (Bristol) Ltd* [1974] AC 689, 717; *Aectra Refining and Marketing Inc v Exmar NV* [1994] 1 WLR 1634, 1650.

[381] [1994] 1 WLR 1634, 1649–1650.

[382] See paras 4.29–4.43 below in relation to equitable set-off, and paras 2.33–2.48 above in relation to the Statutes of Set-off.

[383] See para 4.30 below.

[384] See eg *Dole Dried Fruit and Nut Co v Trustin Kerwood Ltd* [1990] 2 Lloyd's Rep 309, 311, *per* Lloyd LJ; *Aectra Refining and Marketing Inc v Exmar NV* [1994] 1 WLR 1634, 1650, *per* Hoffmann LJ.

[385] See para 2.92 above, and *Healing (Sales) Pty Ltd v Inglis Electrix Pty Ltd* (1968) 121 CLR 584, 601.

defence, bring about an extinction or diminution in the debt.[386] The substantive view may be based on the notion that the availability of the defence is determined as at the date of delivery of the goods or completion of the work. In other words, the value of the goods delivered or of the work performed as at that date is reduced because of the breach of contract, and the nature of the defence is such that the purchaser, if he so chooses, can defend himself in a subsequent action for the price by showing the true value of what in fact was received as at that date. But if this were the justification for ascribing a substantive operation to the defence, one would have thought that it would continue to apply if the damages claim subsequently ceased to exist as a result of the expiration of a limitation period which has the effect of taking away, not only the remedy, but also the right itself. That eventuality would not affect the proposition that the value of the goods at the time of delivery or the value of the work that was actually performed was of diminished value. Yet, Lord Wilberforce in *Aries Tanker Corporation v Total Transport Ltd*[387] said that a claim which has ceased to exist cannot be introduced into legal proceedings as a defence, and his Lordship would seem to have had in mind common law abatement as well as equitable set-off. Certainly that was assumed by Mustill LJ in his discussion of the *Aries Tanker Corporation* case in the Court of Appeal in *Bank of Boston Connecticut v European Grain and Shipping Ltd*.[388]

2.95 Whatever the explanation of the substantive view, one situation in which the procedural and the substantive theories would produce different results is where the damages claim itself remains in existence although unenforceable, as, for example, where the expiration of a limitation period merely affects the remedy. If abatement were simply a procedural defence designed to avoid circuity of action, there would be no reason for allowing a defence in the situation where the claim for breach of warranty in any event could not be enforced.[389] This may be the position in Australia, where the defence has been described as a 'procedural concession'.[390] In England, however, both Lord Denning and Roskill LJ in *Henriksens Rederi A/S*

---

[386] *Healing (Sales) Pty Ltd v Inglis Electrix Pty Ltd* (1968) 121 CLR 584, 602–603. Compare Robert Goff J in *Impex Transport Aktieselskabet v AG Thames Holdings Ltd* [1981] 2 Lloyd's Rep 566, 570 ('plead by way of defence that the debt is extinguished, on the principle in *Mondel v Steel*').

[387] [1977] 1 WLR 185, 188.

[388] [1989] 1 AC 1056, 1071.

[389] See the discussion by Roskill LJ in *Henriksens Rederi A/S v THZ Rolimpex (The Brede)* [1974] 1 QB 233, 259, referring to Kitto J in *Healing (Sales) Pty Ltd v Inglis Electrix Pty Ltd* (1968) 121 CLR 584, 601.

[390] See para 2.93 above. In *Buttrose v Versi* (NSW SC, 14 May 1992), Young J, after noting that the defence was based upon circuity of action, said that if the defendants in that case could not sue for the damages they had suffered they could not abate the loss against the price, though that was in the context of a loss in respect of which there was no cause of action, as opposed to a right to sue which was unenforceable. Compare *Sidney Raper Pty Ltd v Commonwealth Trading Bank of Australia* [1975] 2 NSWLR 227, 238, in which Moffitt P said that a defence of abatement can be used outside a time limitation period.

v THZ Rolimpex (The Brede)[391] considered that the defence of abatement is not defeated by the expiration of a limitation period, a view which was shared by the Canadian Federal Court of Appeal in *The Didymi*.[392]

The question whether abatement is a procedural or a substantive defence in most **2.96** cases would be of little practical consequence. Following the expansion and development of equitable set-off,[393] the equitable defence to a considerable extent now overlaps the common law defence of abatement, and the tendency in recent cases in which the plaintiff was suing for the price of work done or of goods sold and delivered has been to consider both equitable set-off and common law abatement when the defendant sets up a defence that the plaintiff himself had breached the contract on which he sued.[394] Indeed, Lord Salmon remarked in *Aries Tanker Corporation v Total Transport Ltd*:[395] 'Whether [the defence] stems from the development of the common law in the last century or from equitable defences or equitable set-off, as it is sometimes called, or from both, seems to me to be only of academic interest since the passing of the Judicature Act 1873 made equitable defences available in common law courts.'[396] Consequently, if in a particular case the question arises whether the defence raised is procedural or substantive, the court may decide that it is substantive by reference to principles of equitable set-off without the need to have recourse to abatement.[397]

Abatement where there is no set-off

But while in the majority of cases Lord Salmon's comment no doubt would be cor- **2.97** rect, there may be circumstances in which abatement is available but not equitable set-off.[398] Thus, the contract between the parties may have excluded the right of the defendant to assert a set-off but not have affected the right to rely on the common law defence of abatement.[399] Further, abatement is a common law defence

---

[391] [1974] 1 QB 233, 248, 260.

[392] *Atlantic Lines & Navigation Co Inc v The Ship 'Didymi' (The Didymi)* [1988] 1 Lloyd's Rep 97, 102.

[393] See para 4.05 below.

[394] See eg *Gilbert-Ash (Northern) Ltd v Modern Engineering (Bristol) Ltd* [1974] AC 689. See also *Compania Sud Americana de Vapores v Shipmair BV (The Teno)* [1977] 2 Lloyd's Rep 289, 297, and the judgment of Hudson J in *Newman v Cook* [1963] VR 659.

[395] [1977] 1 WLR 185, 194.

[396] See also *Federal Commerce & Navigation Co Ltd v Molena Alpha Inc* [1978] 1 QB 927, 974; *Sim v Rotherham Metropolitan BC* [1987] 1 Ch 216, 257, 259.

[397] Compare *Newman v Cook* [1963] VR 659, in which Hudson J considered that equitable set-off but not common law abatement provided a substantive defence to which the purchaser could have recourse in order to defeat the claim to exercise a power of sale. Herring CJ and Dean J on the other hand decided the case by reference to the common law defence.

[398] Compare the view of Scott J in *Sim v Rotherham Metropolitan BC* [1987] 1 Ch 216, 259 that, if the circumstances of the case do not warrant equitable set-off, they would not establish an abatement.

[399] As in *Acsim (Southern) Ltd v Danish Contracting and Development Co Ltd* (1989) 47 BLR 59. See also *Mellowes Archital Ltd v Bell Projects Ltd* (1997) 87 BLR 26.

available as of right.[400] It is not subject to discretionary factors relevant to equitable set-off.[401] There may also be cases where the party being sued has not suffered a loss as a result of defective performance, for example where A entered into a contract for the renovation of premises which were not owned by him but by a family company, B Co, which bore the cost of remedial work. If A is sued for the price, he would not have suffered any loss so as to give rise to a cross-claim available by way of set-off. On the other hand, he should still be able to defend the action for payment on the ground that the work was of less value because of the defects.[402]

---

[400]   *Gilbert-Ash (Northern) Ltd v Modern Engineering (Bristol) Ltd* [1974] AC 689, 717.
[401]   See para 4.41 below.
[402]   As in *C A Duquemin Ltd v Raymond Slater* [1993] 65 BLR 124 (see esp at 130).

3

SET-OFF BETWEEN SOLVENT PARTIES: EQUITABLE SET-OFF

A. Introduction	3.01	B. The Forms of Equitable Set-off	3.03

A. Introduction

Prior to the Judicature Acts, equitable set-offs generally were enforced by means **3.01** of an injunction to restrain the plaintiff at law from either proceeding with an action or enforcing a judgment against the defendant until he had given credit to the defendant for the amount of a cross-demand.[1] This could also include an order for delivery up of documents.[2] Since the Judicature Acts the defendant has been permitted to plead the set-off directly as a defence in the claimant's action.[3]

Money demands

As in the case of other forms of set-off, equitable set-off is concerned with money **3.02** demands.[4] In *Smith v Bridgend County BC*[5] Lord Hoffmann said that a person could not retain an asset by way of equitable set-off against a money claim. If it were otherwise, he said that every creditor in effect would have a lien over any property of the debtor that was in his possession.

---

[1] Hobhouse LJ described the practice in *Schiffahrtsgesellschaft Detlev von Appen GmbH v Voest Alpine Intertrading GmbH* [1997] 2 Lloyd's Rep 279, 286.

[2] See eg *Ex parte Hanson* (1811) 18 Ves Jun 232, 34 ER 305.

[3] See now the Supreme Court Act 1981, s 49, and CPR r 16.6. The Supreme Court of Judicature Act 1873, s 24(5) abolished the common injunction as a means of restraining a cause or proceeding pending in the High Court or before the Court of Appeal. However an injunction may still be available if the action against the defendant is brought in another jurisdiction which does not recognize the defendant's equitable set-off. See *Schiffahrtsgesellschaft Detlev Von Appen GmbH v Voest Alpine Intertrading GmbH* [1997] 2 Lloyd's Rep 279, 286.

[4] *Tony Lee Motors Ltd v M S McDonald & Son (1974) Ltd* [1981] 2 NZLR 281, 288; *Hamilton Ice Arena Ltd v Perry Developments Ltd* [2002] 1 NZLR 309, 311. See ch 9 below.

[5] [2002] 1 AC 336, 351 para 36.

B. The Forms of Equitable Set-off

Implied agreement

3.03 An equitable set-off can take a number of forms. There are some early cases in which debts were set off in equity based upon an implied agreement that a set-off should occur,[6] and indeed Sir Joseph Jekyll once said that 'the least evidence of an agreement for a [set-off] will do', and that 'equity will take hold of a very slight thing to do both parties right'.[7] This principle was applied recently in New Zealand in relation to a cheque swapping arrangement between two parties for a monthly settlement of their mutual dealings. Pursuant to the arrangement, either party could refuse to provide a cheque in respect of its indebtedness if it was not at the same time provided with a cheque in respect of what it was owed. Hammond J commented that, even if this did not amount to a contract *strictu sensu*, it nevertheless was an arrangement that equity would recognize.[8]

Equitable proprietary estoppel

3.04 Another instance has arisen in the context of equitable proprietary estoppel. If A as a result of the expenditure of money in respect of B's land is entitled to an equitable charge or lien on the land, but A also happens to be personally indebted to B, B may set off the debt owing to him against the sum secured by the charge, so that the amount that must be paid by B in order to take the land free of the charge is the amount secured on the land less the debt.[9] The set-off does not apply however in the converse situation, in which B is suing for payment of the debt. In that circumstance, it has been said that A cannot set off the amount for which he has a charge on the land.[10]

3.05 In *Unity Joint Stock Mutual Banking Association v King*[11] A (in the example) had granted security over his interest in the land to a purchaser for value without notice before A became indebted to B, as a result of B having made a payment under a guarantee given in respect of A's liabilities. Lord Romilly held that the set-off did not arise until after the purchaser obtained its interest, and therefore the purchaser

---

[6] *Downam v Matthews* (1721) Prec Ch 580, 24 ER 260; *Hawkins v Freeman* 2 Eq Ca Abr 10, 22 ER 8; *Jeffs v Wood* (1723) 2 P Wms 128, 24 ER 668; *Wallis v Bastard* (1853) 4 De G M & G 251, 43 ER 503. See also *Whitaker v Rush* (1761) Amb 407, 408, 27 ER 272, 273.

[7] *Jeffs v Wood* (1723) 2 P Wms 128, 130, 24 ER 668, 669.

[8] *Commercial Factors Ltd v Maxwell Printing Ltd* [1994] 1 NZLR 724, 740.

[9] *Unity Joint Stock Mutual Banking Association v King* (1858) 25 Beav 72, 79–80, 53 ER 563, 566, and see also *Baillie v Edwards* (1848) 2 HLC 74, 9 ER 1020, in which it had been agreed that advances made on account of the estate would give rise to a right of repayment only from the estate itself. *Baillie v Edwards* is discussed in paras 4.54 & 6.19 below.

[10] Lord Lyndhurst expressed this view during argument in *Baillie v Edwards* (1848) 2 HLC 74, 81, 9 ER 1020, 1023.

[11] (1858) 25 Beav 72, 79–80, 53 ER 563, 566.

took free of the set-off, notwithstanding that A gave the guarantee to B before the grant of the security.

Acting by analogy with the Statutes

Equity may act by analogy with the legal right of set-off conferred by the Statutes **3.06** of Set-off when liquidated cross-demands are mutual having regard to equitable rights. This may arise because one of the debts itself is a matter of equitable juris-diction,[12] other than for payment of a trust fund, a claim for which generally cannot be met by a set-off under the Statutes.[13] Alternatively, it may arise because a common law debt is held on trust or has been the subject of an equitable assign-ment, so that the requirement of mutuality is satisfied only by reference to the equitable titles.[14] If special circumstances render it unjust that a set-off should occur, a court of equity in the exercise of its discretion nevertheless may refuse to allow a set-off by analogy with the Statutes.[15] On the other hand, when there are mutual liquidated cross-demands having regard to equitable rights, it is not necessary for the defendant to show some additional equity in order to give rise to a set-off. Suggestions to the contrary[16] are difficult to support.[17]

The right of set-off available pursuant to the Statutes is procedural in its opera- **3.07** tion.[18] It provides a defence to an action for payment, and the debts remain sepa-rate and distinct debts until there is judgment for a set-off. Further, as Lord Eldon once remarked, the construction of the Statutes is the same in equity as at law, un-less there is a natural equity going beyond the Statutes.[19] A natural equity would arise if the cross-demands are sufficiently closely connected to give rise to the sub-stantive form of equitable set-off discussed in the next chapter. Ordinarily, how-ever, the Statutes receive the same construction in equity. This proposition brings into question the decision of Street J in the New South Wales Supreme Court in *Stewart v Latec Investments Ltd*.[20] A company had executed a trust deed in order to

---

[12] *Kostka v Addison* [1986] 1 Qd R 416. Thus, the amount which a defaulting trustee is bound to pay to make good a breach of trust has been described as an equitable debt. See *Webb v Stenton* (1883) 11 QBD 518, 530; *Wickstead v Browne* (1992) 30 NSWLR 1, 14.

[13] See ch 10 below. On the other hand, when a person has a right to participate in a trust fund, and also has an obligation to contribute to it, the rule in *Cherry v Boultbee* (1839) 4 My & Cr 442, 41 ER 171 may apply. See ch 14 below.

[14] See eg *Clark v Cort* (1840) Cr & Ph 154, 41 ER 449; *Cochrane v Green* (1860) 9 CB(NS) 448, 142 ER 176; *Thornton v Maynard* (1875) LR 10 CP 695; *Manley & Sons Ltd v Berkett* [1912] 2 KB 329, 333; *High v Bengal Brass Co* (1921) 21 SR (NSW) 232, 238; *Tony Lee Motors Ltd v M S MacDonald & Son (1974) Ltd* [1981] 2 NZLR 281.

[15] See Spry, *Equitable Remedies* (6th edn, 2001) 175.

[16] *Middleton v Pollock, ex p Nugee* (1875) LR 20 Eq 29, 36–37, and see *Welton v Harnett* (1886) 7 NSWR 74.

[17] *Tony Lee Motors Ltd v M S MacDonald (1974) Ltd* [1981] 2 NZLR 281, 287–288.

[18] See paras 2.33–2.48 above.

[19] *Ex parte Stephens* (1805) 11 Ves Jun 24, 27, 32 ER 996, 997.

[20] [1968] 1 NSWR 432.

regulate the issue of debenture stock. The trust deed was in a common form, by which the trustee appointed under the deed was constituted the creditor of the company in respect of the issued stock, while each individual stockholder was the beneficial owner of his stock. In the event of a transfer of stock, the deed provided that, upon registration of the transfer, the transferee should be recognized as entitled to the stock free from any equity, set-off, or counterclaim possessed by the company against the transferor. The court was asked to determine a question of law, whether the company was bound to register a transferee as the owner of stock when the transferor was indebted to the company on an independent transaction. The perceived difficulty for the transferee was that the trust deed only stipulated that a transferee took free from equities after registration had been effected, and so it was held that the company could assert a set-off against the transferee before then in order to prevent registration.[21] When the company received the formal transfer, it credited the principal and interest payable in respect of the debenture stock against the transferor's indebtedness. Street J said that this book-keeping entry itself amounted to a valid redemption of the debenture.[22] Consistent with that view, *Stewart v Latec Investments* has been referred to as showing a species of equitable set-off having a substantive operation independently of any court order.[23]

3.08 The decision in *Stewart v Latec Investments* is difficult to justify. There was no question of the demands being sufficiently closely connected to give rise to a substantive equitable set-off of the kind considered in the next chapter.[24] Further, because of the interposition of the trustee, there was not mutuality at law as between the company and the transferor for the purpose of the Statutes of Set-off. There was on the other hand mutuality in equity, so that equity would have acted by analogy with the Statutes. But the Statutes should have received the same construction as at law, given that there does not appear to have been a natural equity taking the case beyond the Statutes. The right of set-off therefore should have been regarded as merely procedural, in the sense that it merely provided a defence to an action for payment, and it should not have permitted the company to bring about a set-off itself by making an entry to that effect in its books. Street J relied in his judgment on the earlier decision of Buckley J in *Re Palmer's Decoration & Furniture Co*,[25] which concerned a similar trust deed. The cases are distinguish-

---

[21] See eg *Re Richard Smith & Co Ltd* [1901] 1 IR 73.

[22] Street J commented (at [1968] 1 NSWR 432, 437) that 'when Latec Investments Ltd purported, on 13 July 1962, to credit the principal and interest payable in respect of the debenture stock against Mr Stewart's indebtedness to it this amounted to a valid redemption of the debenture'.

[23] See Gummow and von Doussa JJ in the Federal Court of Australia in *McIntyre v Perkes* (1990) 22 FCR 260, 270.

[24] See ch 4 below.

[25] [1904] 2 Ch 743.

able, however. In the *Palmer* case the transferor's title was defective,[26] in that he had obtained the debentures from the company by misrepresentation, and it was held that the transferee took subject to this defect in title. While the question in issue was whether the transferee was entitled to be paid, Buckley J also said that the defect of title would have provided a ground for the company to refuse to register the transfer. The nature of the equity in that case should be compared to the equity which arises under the Statutes of Set-off. This provides a procedural defence to an action but does not give rise to a defect in the title to the debt in question. The tenor of Buckley J's judgment admittedly suggests that the principle in that case was thought to apply to equities generally,[27] but the particular nature of the defence of set-off under the Statutes was not considered.[28]

Substantive equitable set-off

There is another form of equitable set-off which is both broader and narrower **3.09** than the Statutes of Set-off. It is broader in that it is not confined to the case of mutual debts, but can arise when one or both of the demands is for damages. On the other hand it is narrower, in that there must be some connection between the demands. The Statutes by contrast do not require any such connection. This form of equitable set-off has another characteristic which has come into prominence in recent years, and which distinguishes it from the Statutes, and that is that it operates substantively, as opposed to providing merely a procedural defence. The substantive equitable defence is dealt with separately in chapter 4 below.

---

[26] Buckley J expressed it ([1904] 2 Ch 743, 751) in terms that, 'by reason of the company's equity the title is not clear'.

[27] See also *Palmer's Company Precedents* (16th edn, 1952) Part 3 ('Debentures') 18, 235, 236.

[28] *Re Goy & Co Ltd* [1900] 2 Ch 149, which Buckley J discussed in his judgment in *Palmer's Decoration* [1904] 2 Ch 743, 749–751, was concerned with the rule in *Cherry v Boultbee* (1839) 4 My & Cr 442, 41 ER 171 (see para 14.65 below) rather than set-off under the Statutes.

4

SUBSTANTIVE EQUITABLE SET-OFF

There is a substantive[1] defence of equitable set-off which is not confined to **4.01** mutual debts,[2] and which has attracted considerable attention in recent years. It is the most elusive, but at the same time the most important, of the various forms of equitable set-off.

A. The Traditional Formulation

The seminal authority on this form of equitable set-off is Lord Cottenham's **4.02** judgment in *Rawson v Samuel*.[3] The Lord Chancellor said that the mere existence of cross-demands is not sufficient to give rise to a set-off. Rather, he said that the

---

[1] See paras 4.29–4.43 below.

[2] In a number of cases in Australia the view was put forward that an unliquidated demand may not be employed in a set-off. See eg *McDonnell & East Ltd v McGregor* (1936) 56 CLR 50, 62; *Classic Ceramic Importers Pty Ltd v Ceramica Antiga SA* (1994) 13 ACSR 263, 269. However, this is incorrect in so far as it relates to equitable set-off. See eg *Beasley v Darcy* (1800) 2 Sch & Lef 403n (in which the Lord Chancellor ordered that the defendant's cross-claim for damages be assessed by a jury); *Galambos & Son Pty Ltd v McIntyre* (1974) 5 ACTR 10 (in which the cases are discussed); *Knockholt Pty Ltd v Graff* [1975] Qd R 88; *United Dominions Corp Ltd v Jaybe Homes Pty Ltd* [1978] Qd R 111; *British Anzani (Felixstowe) Ltd v International Marine Management (UK) Ltd* [1980] 1 QB 137, 145–146.

[3] (1841) Cr & Ph 161, 41 ER 451.

applicant for relief must show some good equitable grounds for being protected against the plaintiff's demand, such that the plaintiff's title to his demand is impeached.[4] In *Rawson v Samuel*, the plaintiff at law was suing for damages for breach of contract.[5] The defendant at law (the plaintiff in equity) sought an account of transactions under the contract, and an injunction to restrain the plaintiff at law from executing any judgment obtained at law until he had given credit for any balance that may be found to be due to the defendant on the account. Lord Cottenham said that 'The object and subject matters are . . . totally distinct', and that 'the fact that the agreement was the origin of both does not form any bond of union for the purpose of supporting an injunction.'[6] The result was that the absence of a sufficient equity prevented a set-off despite the fact that both demands had their origin in the same contract.

4.03 The traditional basis of this form of equitable set-off is that the title of the plaintiff to his demand is impeached. The concept of impeachment has not been precisely defined. In general terms, what it requires, in the absence of some other equitable ground for being protected such as fraud,[7] is that there be a sufficiently close connection between the demands. In its traditional sense this was not simply a question whether the demands arose out of the same transaction,[8] although the principle has been expressed in those terms, including in the House of Lords.[9] It involves a consideration of the circumstances of the particular case, and indeed a close connection may not suffice to impeach the title if there are other discretionary factors which militate against equitable relief.[10] The closeness of the connection that courts of equity traditionally required has been expressed in various terms, for example that the cross-demand must go to the very root of the plaintiff's claim,[11] or that it must call in question, impugn, disparage or impede the title to the claim,[12] or that there must be some equitable ground for protection such as

---

[4] (1841) Cr & Ph 161, 178–180, 41 ER 451, 458–459. See also *Hanak v Green* [1958] 2 QB 9, 18–19. In *Ex parte Branwhite; re The West of England and South Wales District Bank* (1879) 40 LT 652, 654 Fry J commented that equitable set-off 'only arises when there are certain equitable circumstances which give a right to the person who sets them up against his antagonist'. In 1761, Sir Thomas Clarke MR said in *Whitaker v Rush* (1761) Amb 407, 408, 27 ER 272 that equity required that there should be a connection between the demands.

[5] An equitable set-off may be pleaded as a defence to an action for damages. See eg *Hanak v Green* [1958] 2 QB 9; *Filross Securities Ltd v Midgeley* [1998] 3 EGLR 43; *Bim Kemi AB v Blackburn Chemicals Ltd* [2001] 2 Lloyd's Rep 93, 98–99 paras 21–23.

[6] (1841) Cr & Ph 161, 178, 41 ER 451, 458.

[7] See *Ex parte Stephens* (1805) 11 Ves Jun 24, 32 ER 996; *Vuillamy v Noble* (1817) 3 Mer 593, 36 ER 228.

[8] See para 4.16 below.

[9] *Bank of Boston Connecticut v European Grain and Shipping Ltd* [1989] 1 AC 1056, 1102–1103, 1110–1111. See para 4.15 below.

[10] See paras 4.44–4.47 below.

[11] *British Anzani (Felixstowe) Ltd v International Marine Management (UK) Ltd* [1980] 1 QB 137, 145.

[12] *MEK Nominees Pty Ltd v Billboard Entertainments Pty Ltd* (1993) V Conv R 54–468 at p 65,466, Vic SC, *per* Tadgell J.

inseparability,[13] or, as the New Zealand Court of Appeal expressed it, that the link between the demands must be such that the two in effect are interdependent.[14] It is the nature of the cross-claim relative to the claim, rather than the amount of the damages recoverable or the severity of the breach, that matters.[15] The fact that the claimant is insolvent by itself does not give rise to an equity sufficient to support an equitable set-off.[16] Further, *Rawson v Samuel* illustrates that it is not sufficient that the demands arose out of the same contract.[17] Nor is the claimant's demand necessarily regarded as impeached because the cross-claim is in some way related to the transaction which gave rise to the claim,[18] or because the claim and the cross-claim turn on similar findings of fact.[19] If on the other hand cross-demands arise out of separate transactions, they usually would not be sufficiently closely connected so as to justify an equitable set-off.[20]

In *Rawson v Samuel* Lord Cottenham referred to a number of cases which illus-   **4.04** trate the impeachment principle. In *Beasley v Darcy*[21] a tenant was allowed to set off against his liability for rent a damages claim that he had against the landlord for damage suffered as a result of timber on the demised land being cut down and carried away. Lord Cottenham said that the equity against the landlord was that he should not recover possession of the farm for non-payment of rent when he owed to the tenant a sum for damage to that same farm, although on other occasions it has been suggested that the decision in the *Beasley* case may be justified on the ground that the produce of the farm may have been lessened as a result of the landlord's conduct, which in turn may have affected the tenant's ability to pay the rent.[22] In *Piggott v Williams*[23] a solicitor filed a bill for foreclosure of an estate pledged as security for costs. The relief sought by the solicitor was denied to him

---

[13]   *Tooth v Brisbane City Council* (1928) 41 CLR 212, 224, *per* Isaacs J.

[14]   *Grant v NZMC Ltd* [1989] 1 NZLR 8, 13. See also *Hoverd Industries Ltd v Supercool Refrigeration and Air Conditioning (1991) Ltd* [1995] 3 NZLR 577, 586; *Hamilton Ice Arena Ltd v Perry Developments Ltd* [2002] NZLR 309, 312.

[15]   *Sim v Rotherham Metropolitan BC* [1987] 1 Ch 216, 262.

[16]   *Rawson v Samuel* (1841) Cr & Ph 161, 175, 41 ER 451, 457. Compare *Clarkson v Smith and Goldberg* [1926] 1 DLR 509, 511.

[17]   See in particular (1841) Cr & Ph 161, 178, 41 ER 451, 458, *per* Lord Cottenham, and also *Best v Hill* (1872) LR 8 CP 10; *Re K L Tractors Ltd* [1954] VLR 505, 507–508; *The Raven* [1980] 2 Lloyd's Rep 266, 272; *Covino v Bandag Manufacturing Pty Ltd* [1983] 1 NSWLR 237, 238 (claim for the price of goods supplied and cross-claim for damages for breach of warranty as regards territorial monopoly not set off); *Westwind Air Charter Pty Ltd v Hawker De Havilland Ltd* (1990) 3 WAR 71.

[18]   *Hanak v Green* [1958] 2 QB 9, 23.

[19]   *Bim Kemi AB v Blackburn Chemicals Ltd* [2001] 2 Lloyd's Rep 93, 98 para 19.

[20]   *Re Convere Pty Ltd* [1976] VR 345, 349. See also *Abignano v Wenkart* (1998) 9 BPR 16,765, 16,773.

[21]   (1800) 2 Sch & Lef 403n. See the discussion of the case in *British Anzani (Felixstowe) Ltd v International Marine Management (UK) Ltd* [1980] 1 QB 137, 149–151.

[22]   *O'Mahony v Dickson* (1805) 2 Sch & Lef 400, 412, *per* Lord Redesdale; *Stimson v Hall* (1857) 1 H & N 831, 835–836, 156 ER 1436, *per* Bramwell B.

[23]   (1821) 6 Madd 95, 56 ER 1027.

because of a set-off held to be available to the client. The cross-claim was based upon an allegation of negligence, and it was argued that the costs claimed would not have been incurred were it not for the negligence. This was a case in which the plaintiff's own breach of duty brought about, or at least contributed to the existence of, the defendant's liability to him.[24] There was also *Lord Cawdor v Lewis*.[25] In that case a claim for compensation for improvements effected to another's land was set off against a cross-claim for mesne profits, in circumstances where the party claiming title to the land had stood by and watched the other spend money on the improvements without giving the other notice of his title. On the other hand, Lord Cottenham was critical of the decision in *Williams v Davies*.[26] The plaintiff had obtained judgment at law against the defendant upon some promissory notes, and the defendant had obtained judgment at law against the plaintiff for damages for wrongful distress. The plaintiff applied to the Court of King's Bench to set off the judgments pursuant to the court's inherent jurisdiction.[27] The application was refused, and so the plaintiff sought an injunction in equity. This succeeded before Sir Lancelot Shadwell, who said that it was right that the judgments should be set off. It is unclear, however, why equitable relief should have been available when a remedy had been refused at law, and Lord Cottenham doubted in *Rawson v Samuel* whether there was a sufficient equity to support an equitable set-off.[28]

4.05 The rigour with which the impeachment test originally was applied has weakened over time, so that in some more recent cases it is difficult to see what the basis for the set-off was apart from the fact that both demands arose out of the same contract or transaction. This would appear to be a consequence of the view that has been expressed,[29] that the courts should not be astute to restrict the right of set-off,

---

[24] See also *Popular Homes Ltd v Circuit Developments Ltd* [1979] 2 NZLR 642, 659–660; *Long Leys Co Pty Ltd v Silkdale Pty Ltd* (1991) 5 BPR 11,512, 11,519; *Ling v Commonwealth* (1996) 68 FCR 180, 191. Similarly, in an action by an employer under a building contract against the contractor arising out of a delay in completion, a cross-claim available to the contractor against the employer for hindering or preventing the contractor's performance may give rise to an equitable set-off. See *Hanak v Green* [1958] 2 QB 9; *Rosehaugh Stanhope (Broadgate Phase 6) plc v Redpath Dorman Long Ltd* (1990) 50 BLR 75; *Beaufort House Development Ltd v Zimmcor (International) Inc* (1990) 50 BLR 91. In some such cases a defence of circuity of action may be available. See eg *Post Office v Hampshire County Council* [1980] 1 QB 124. This defence is limited, however. It only applies in a situation in which, if the claimant recovered against the defendant, the defendant would recover exactly the same sum, or if damages exactly the same measure of damages, against the plaintiff. See *Aktieselskabet Ocean v B Harding and Sons Ltd* [1928] 2 KB 371, 385; *McCamley v Harris* (1998) NSW Conv R 55–827 at p 56,479.

[25] (1835) 1 Y & C Ex 427, 160 ER 174. Compare *Tai Te Whetu v Scandlyn* [1952] NZLR 30.

[26] (1829) 2 Sim 461, 57 ER 860.

[27] See paras 2.78–2.86 above.

[28] (1841) Cr & Ph 161, 178, 41 ER 451, 458. See also *Stimson v Hall* (1857) I H & N 831, 836, 156 ER 1436, 1438; *Aboussafy v Abacus Cities Ltd* (1981) 124 DLR 3d 150, 160; *J C Scott Constructions v Mermaid Waters Tavern Pty Ltd (No 1)* [1983] 2 Qd R 243.

[29] *Hanak v Green* [1958] 2 QB 9, 29, *per* Sellers LJ. Compare paras 5.139–5.153 below.

but rather should develop it as a discouragement to litigation. In particular, two Court of Appeal decisions have been referred to as illustrating a departure from the principle originally applied by Lord Cottenham.[30] The defendant in *Morgan & Son Ltd v S Martin Johnson & Co Ltd*[31] had delivered a number of vehicles to the plaintiff for the purpose of storage. The plaintiff subsequently claimed a sum for storage charges, and applied for summary judgment. The defendant resisted the application on the basis of an alleged damages claim for non-delivery of one of the vehicles. The Court of Appeal held that the facts set out in the defendant's affidavit supported a claim to an equitable set-off, and that accordingly the defendant should be granted unconditional leave to defend. That conclusion could hardly be questioned if the set-off had been confined to the charges for storing the particular vehicle which was the subject of the cross-action. The equity in favour of a set-off in such a case would be that the plaintiff should not be permitted to sue for the cost of storing a vehicle when the plaintiff failed to account for it.[32] In relation to the part of the storage charges which related to the other vehicles, however, it is not clear what the connection was other than that all the vehicles seem to have been stored under the one contract. The decision nevertheless has been referred to subsequently with evident approval,[33] and indeed there are other cases which support the availability of a set-off in analogous circumstances.[34] The second case, *Hanak v Green*,[35] concerned a building contract. The plaintiff sued the defendant builder for breach of contract for failing to complete or properly complete certain items of work. The defendant counterclaimed or claimed by way of set-off, (1) on a *quantum meruit* in respect of extra work done outside the contract, (2) on the ground that loss was caused by the plaintiff's refusal to admit the defendant's workmen, and (3) for trespass to the defendant's tools. It may be accepted that the second of these items exhibited a good equitable ground sufficient

---

[30] See Spry, 'Equitable Set-offs' (1969) 43 Australian Law Journal 265, 269–270; Meagher Gummow and Lehane, *Equity Doctrines and Remedies* (3rd edn, 1992) 822.

[31] [1949] 1 KB 107, *per* Tucker and Cohen LJJ.

[32] In this respect the case would have been analogous to *Beasley v Darcy* (1800) 2 Sch & Lef 403n, referred to above.

[33] See eg *Hale v Victoria Plumbing Co Ltd* [1966] 2 QB 746, 751, CA; *Federal Commerce & Navigation Co Ltd v Molena Alpha Inc* [1978] 1 QB 927, 975, *per* Lord Denning; *Newman v Cook* [1963] VR 659, 674.

[34] See *Parsons v Sovereign Bank of Canada* [1913] AC 160 (see para 4.63 below), *Kaps Transport Ltd v McGregor Telephone & Power Construction Co Ltd* (1970) 73 WWR 549 (in which the set-off claimed in respect of the damage to the appellant's equipment does not appear to have been confined to the claim for the price of the trucking services relating to the particular contract for the carriage of that equipment), and *John Dee Group Ltd v WMH (21) Ltd* [1997] BCC 518, 531 (referring to *Business Computers Ltd v Anglo-African Leasing Ltd* [1977] 1 WLR 578, 585). See also *Marubeni Corp v Sea Containers Ltd* (QBD, Waller J, 17 May 1995), in which it seems to have been accepted that a set-off would have been available against the claim for the price by reason of defects in other containers delivered under the same contract, were it not for the clause which was held to have excluded set-offs.

[35] [1958] 2 QB 9 (Hodson, Morris and Sellers LJJ).

to impeach the plaintiff's title to her demand if her refusal to admit the defendant's workmen was one of the reasons why the defendant had not completed the work. In that circumstance, the plaintiff's own conduct may have contributed to the existence of the defendant's liability to her.[36] A similar comment may be made in respect of the third item.[37] On the other hand, it is not clear what connection the first item had with the plaintiff's claim, in the sense considered by Lord Cottenham. The Court of Appeal however held that it could be set off. *Hanak v Green* has since become a leading case in the area, and Morris LJ's judgment in particular has been described as authoritative[38] and a masterly account of the subject.[39]

4.06   In the course of his judgment in *Rawson v Samuel* Lord Cottenham said that:[40]

> It was said that the subjects of the suit in this Court, and of the action at law, arise out of the same contract; but the one is for an account of transactions under the contract, and the other for damages for the breach of it. The object and subject-matters are, therefore, totally distinct; and the fact that the agreement was the origin of both does not form any bond of union for the purpose of supporting an injunction.

This should not be taken to mean that a claim for a sum of money payable under a contract cannot be met by a set-off in respect of a damages claim for breach of the contract.[41] Situations of that kind indeed are a prime source of equitable set-offs.[42] Lord Cottenham's statement should be understood in the context of the case before him. It concerned an agreement by which the defendant was to consign goods to some mercantile houses in which the plaintiffs had an interest for the purpose of sale. Part of the agreement was that, upon each shipment of goods, the defendant should be at liberty to draw bills of exchange upon the plaintiffs for

---

[36]   As in *Piggott v Williams* (1821) 6 Madd 95, 56 ER 1027.

[37]   The status of the third item was not considered by Hodson and Morris LJJ, the first and second items when added together being sufficient to overtop the plaintiff's claim. However Sellers LJ thought that it could be marshalled as a set-off.

[38]   *BICC plc v Burndy Corporation* [1985] 1 Ch 232, 247, *per* Dillon LJ.

[39]   Lord Diplock in *Gilbert-Ash (Northern) Ltd v Modern Engineering (Bristol) Ltd* [1974] AC 689, 717, and see also *Compania Sud Americana de Vapores v Shipmair BV (The Teno)* [1977] 2 Lloyd's Rep 289, 297; *British Anzani (Felixstowe) Ltd v International Marine Management (UK) Ltd* [1980] 1 QB 137, 144; *Dole Dried Fruit and Nut Co v Trustin Kerwood Ltd* [1990] 2 Lloyd's Rep 309, 310.

[40]   (1841) Cr & Ph 161, 178, 41 ER 451, 458.

[41]   *AWA Ltd v Exicom Australia Pty Ltd* (1990) 19 NSWLR 705, 713–714.

[42]   For example, in the case of at time charter of a ship there is ample authority for the proposition that a claim for hire may be met by a damages claim for breach of contract which deprives the charterer of the full use of the vessel. See *The Teno* (n 39 above) [1977] 2 Lloyd's Rep 289, 297; *Federal Commerce & Navigation Co Ltd v Molena Alpha Inc* [1978] 1 QB 927, 976. Similarly, a damages claim for breach of a building contract may be set off against a claim for moneys otherwise due under the contract. See eg *Young v Kitchin* (1878) 3 Ex D 127; *Government of Newfoundland v Newfoundland Railway Co* (1888) 13 App Cas 199. A claim for payment of fees charged for the performance of services may be impeached by a cross claim for negligence in the performance of the services. See *Re Kostezky* (1996) 67 FCR 101, 106.

the amount of his charges and disbursements in respect of the shipments. After the agreement had run for some time the plaintiffs refused to accept bills in accordance with the agreement, whereupon the defendant sued at common law for damages. The plaintiffs sought an injunction restraining execution on any judgment that may be obtained at law. Their bill sought an account of the dealings and transactions between the parties under the agreement, and an order setting off against their damages liability the amount which, upon taking the accounts, should be found due from the defendant to the plaintiffs. In this case the subject-matters of the claims were distinct, and Lord Cottenham was concerned to emphasize that the fact that they arose out of the same agreement was not sufficient to give rise to an equitable set-off.

This explanation of *Rawson v Samuel* appears not to have been appreciated in *Best* **4.07** *v Hill*.[43] The defendant had consigned goods to the plaintiffs for sale, the agreement between them being that the plaintiffs should make advances to the defendant against the goods, and that the plaintiffs should sell the goods and obtain payment from the proceeds for the advances and their expenses and commission. The plaintiffs sued for money lent and paid and commission in respect of the goods. The defendant pleaded as a defence on equitable grounds a cross-claim for damages for negligence in the care of part of the goods and for negligence in the management of the sale. The allegation was that the plaintiffs were guilty of such negligence and improper conduct in the care of the goods and the conduct of the sale that the goods fetched less than they ought to, such that the amount recovered was insufficient to satisfy the advances, expenses and commission. The Court of Common Pleas held that the plea was bad. One reason given was that the proceedings to ascertain the amount of damages would have involved considerable delay. But in addition Bovill CJ held, on the authority of *Rawson v Samuel*, that an equitable set-off was not available because, 'although these cross claims in one sense are connected . . . this does not appear to be sufficient, according to the doctrine of equity in relation to set-off; one claim arises out of the performance of the contract, the other out of its breach.'[44] As a general proposition for denying an equitable set-off, this is difficult to support. One would have thought that, apart from the discretionary consideration concerning delay in the assessment of the damages, the cross-claims were sufficiently connected to give rise to an equitable set-off. This would seem to have been the case notwithstanding that the Court of Exchequer in *Atterbury v Jarvie*[45] previously had denied a defence on equitable grounds in similar circumstances. The advances, commission and expenses the subject of the plaintiffs' claim in *Best v Hill* were intended to be satisfied out of the

---

[43] (1872) LR 8 CP 10.
[44] (1872) LR 8 CP 10, 15.
[45] (1857) 2 H & N 114, 157 ER 47.

proceeds of sale. The substance of the cross-claim against the plaintiffs was that, as a result of their own negligence and misconduct, the amount received from the sale was insufficient to satisfy the debts. This cross-claim would appear to have impeached the title of the plaintiffs to sue. As counsel unsuccessfully argued in *Best v Hill*, it was similar to *Beasley v Darcy*.[46] In that case the landlord's claim for rent was impeached by a cross-claim against him for damage done in cutting timber on the demised land, because this reduced the produce of the farm and therefore affected the tenant's ability to pay the rent.

Equitable set-off in relation to debts

4.08   Equitable set-offs commonly arise when there is a claim for a contract debt on one side of the account and on the other a claim for damages in either contract or tort which, in the traditional formulation, impeaches the title to the debt. Usually the damages claim is asserted as a defence to an action to enforce the debt, but the defence similarly may be available in the converse situation in which a debt is raised as a defence to an action for damages.[47] Furthermore, equitable set-off is not confined to cases involving a debt and a damages claim, but in an appropriate case may apply when both demands are liquidated.[48] The fact that there are mutual debts which would give rise to a procedural defence under the Statutes of Set-off[49] does not mean that a substantive defence of equitable set-off is not also available if the debts are sufficiently closely connected.[50] Thus, in an action involving a tenant who had failed to pay rent, Lightman J held that a cross-claim by the tenant for repayment of some earlier overpayments of rent gave rise to an equitable set-off, so as to deny the landlord the right to levy distress for unpaid rent.[51] Similarly it has been held that an overpayment of royalties may be the subject of an equitable set-off against future royalties.[52] An equitable set-off may also arise when the debt owing to a creditor is the source from which the creditor's own debt to the

---

[46]   (1800) 2 Sch & Lef 403n.

[47]   *Filross Securities Ltd v Midgeley* [1983] 3 EGLR 43. In *Cullinane v British 'Rema' Manufacturing Co Ltd* [1953] 2 All ER 1257, 1271 Sir Raymond Everted MR was prepared to assume (without deciding) that a set-off was available in this situation. See also *Hanak v Green* [1958] 2 QB 9 (cross-claim based on quantum meruit set off in an action for damages). Compare *McCreagh v Judd* [1923] WN 174, DC, and also *Rawson v Samuel* (1841) Cr & Ph 161, 41 ER 451 (in which the claims were insufficiently connected to give rise to an equitable set-off). Compare para 2.92 above in relation to the common law defence of abatement.

[48]   See eg *Coba Industries Ltd v Millie's Holdings (Canada) Ltd* [1985] 6 WWR 14; *Telford v Holt* (1987) 41 DLR (4th) 385; *Roadshow Entertainment Pty Ltd v (ACN 053 006 269) Pty Ltd* (1997) 42 NSWLR 462. The liquidated cross-demand need not be payable when the plaintiff commences proceedings. See *Roadshow Entertainment* at 489.

[49]   See paras 2.33–2.48 above.

[50]   *Fuller v Happy Shopper Markets Ltd* [2001] 1 WLR 1681, 1692 para 26.

[51]   *Fuller v Happy Shopper Markets Ltd* [2001] 1 WLR 1681.

[52]   *Philip Collins Ltd v Davis* [2000] 3 All ER 808 (esp at 830–832).

debtor is to be satisfied.[53] In *Ralston v South Greta Colliery Co*[54] A had leased a coal mine to B, the consideration for which included the payment of a royalty by B in respect of the coal won. In consideration of work and labour done by C, A agreed to pay C a part of the royalty that A received from time to time, and C then assigned this right to B. When A sued B for payment of the royalty, the New South Wales Supreme Court held that B had a set-off to the extent of the portion of the royalty that had been assigned back to him.[55] This was not a case of mutual debts under the Statutes of Set-off, because until A actually received payment there was no debt owing to B. The set-off was regarded instead as an equitable set-off. Sir William Cullen CJ said that there was 'a good equity in the defendant to restrain the prosecution of so much of the demand as the plaintiff has parted with and which has come back into the hands of the original debtor'.[56]

Contingent debts, and debts not yet payable

A set-off under the Statutes of Set-off is not available in respect of a debt that is not **4.09** yet payable,[57] and it has been suggested that set-off in equity is subject to a similar restriction.[58] This should be the case when equity acts by analogy with the Statutes of Set-off,[59] but it should not represent an inflexible principle when the peculiarly equitable form of set-off arising from an impeachment of title is in issue. Rather, the fact that the debt is not yet payable should constitute a factor to be taken into consideration in the exercise of the court's discretion.[60] In particular, equitable relief may not be available if the cross-demand is not payable for a long time, or terms may be imposed as a condition of relief.[61] It would be more difficult to

---

[53] See also the analogous circumstances in issue in *Safa Ltd v Banque du Caire* [2000] 2 Lloyd's Rep 600, 609, where the bank paying the beneficiary under the letter of credit would have been entitled to immediate reimbursement. *Quaere* whether this could also have been explained on the basis of circuity of action. See n 55 below.

[54] (1912) 13 SR (NSW) 6.

[55] The defence in *Ralston v South Greta Colliery Co* (n 54 above) was based upon set-off (see the discussion at (1912) 13 SR (NSW) 6, 15–16), as opposed to circuity of action. In the circumstances, a defence of circuity of action would appear not to have been available. In the first place, it is said that the defence only applies when the cross-claim arises *directly* between the parties to the proceeding in which it is used as a defence. See *Aktieselskabet Ocean v B Harding and Sons Ltd* [1928] 2 KB 371, 384–385, *per* Scrutton LJ and *Co-operative Retail Services Ltd v Taylor Young Partnership* [2000] BLR 461, 474–475, although compare *Schenker & Co (Aust) Pty Ltd v Maplas Equipment and Services Pty Ltd* [1990] VR 834, 849. In the *Ralston* case, on the other hand, there was an intervening assignment. Moreover, the defence only applies in circumstances where, if the claimant recovered against the defendant, the defendant could recover exactly the same sum from the claimant. See the *Aktieselskabet Ocean* case at 385; *McCamley v Harris* (1998) NSW Conv R 55–827 at p 56,479. However in the *Ralston* case only part of the amount payable by B to A was assigned.

[56] (1912) 13 SR (NSW) 6, 16.

[57] See para 2.29 above.

[58] *Manzanilla Ltd v Corton Property and Investments Ltd* [1996] EWCA Civ 942 at para 42.

[59] See paras 3.06–3.08 above.

[60] See *Roadshow Entertainment Pty Ltd v (ACN 053 006 269) Pty Ltd* (1997) 42 NSWLR 462, 489, and para 4.44 below in relation to discretion.

[61] *Roadshow Entertainment Pty Ltd v (ACN 053 006 269) Pty Ltd* (1997) 42 NSWLR 462, 489.

justify an equitable set-off in the case of a debt which is merely contingent,[62] because there is not in such a case an existing debt until the contingency occurs, although there may be cases when a set-off nevertheless would be appropriate. An example is *Ralston v South Greta Colliery Co*[63] (above), in which B's claim against A on the assigned debt was contingent upon B having first paid the royalty to A. An equitable set-off should not be available on the other hand when a debtor has merely a contingent right of reimbursement from the creditor, in circumstances where the right only arises upon payment by the debtor to a third party, and at the time when the question of set-off falls to be determined the debtor has not made the payment. Until such time as the debtor takes the step of paying the third party so as to crystallize his right of reimbursement from the creditor, the circumstances ordinarily would not be such as to render it unconscionable for the creditor to regard the debtor as being indebted to him. This situation arose in *Sloan Stanley Estate Trustees v Barribal.*[64] A tenant of a farm was liable under the Land Drainage Act 1976 to pay a drainage rate, although he was entitled to recover the amount paid from the landlord. The tenant argued that he was entitled to an equitable set-off against rent even before he had paid the rate, so that he could not be evicted for non-payment of rent.[65] The Court of Appeal held that a set-off was not available until the tenant himself had paid.

B. New Approaches

4.10 In recent years the courts have sought to redefine the basis upon which an equitable set-off may arise, the effect of which generally has been to expand the scope of the defence.

4.11 In *Henriksens Rederi A/S v THZ Rolimpex (The Brede)*[66] Lord Denning cited *Morgan v Johnson* and *Hanak v Green* as authorities for the proposition that equitable set-off 'is available whenever the cross-claim arises out of the same transaction as the claim; or out of a transaction that is closely related to the claim'.[67] There was no mention of an additional requirement of some equitable ground sufficient to impeach the plaintiff's title to his demand, and to this extent his statement of the law would appear to represent a broader basis for the defence than that originally contemplated by Lord Cottenham. Thus, Lord Denning accepted that 'with

---

[62] *Manzanilla Ltd v Corton Property and Investments Ltd* [1996] EWCA Civ 942 at para 42.

[63] (1912) 13 SR (NSW) 6. See also *Safa Ltd v Banque du Caire* [2000] 2 Lloyd's Rep 600, 609.

[64] [1994] 2 EGLR 8.

[65] This would have been a consequence of the substantive nature of equitable set-off. See paras 4.29–4.43 below.

[66] [1974] 1 QB 233.

[67] [1974] 1 QB 233, 248. See also *Box v Midland Bank Ltd* [1981] 1 Lloyd's Rep 434, 437, where Lord Denning allowed an equitable set-off on the basis that the 'claim and counterclaim arose out of a whole series of transactions in regard to the obtaining of the loan'.

any breach by the plaintiff of the self-same contract, the defendant can in equity set up his loss in diminution or extinction of the contract price',[68] whereas Lord Cottenham emphasized in *Rawson v Samuel*[69] that the fact that the one contract was the origin of both demands is not sufficient to found an equitable set-off.[70] However the traditional approach was reiterated in *Aries Tanker Corporation v Total Transport Ltd*.[71] The House of Lords in that case affirmed the principle that freight owing under a voyage charter must be paid without deduction.[72] Accordingly, the charterers could not deduct a sum for short delivery of cargo. But even apart from that principle, Lord Simon of Glaisdale said that an equitable set-off would not have been available on the facts. He said that, in order to succeed, the equity of the bill would have had to impeach the title to the legal demand, and the title to a claim for freight is not impeached by short delivery unless it amounts to a repudiation of the contract of carriage.[73] Similarly, Lord Wilberforce referred to *Rawson v Samuel* as setting out the relevant principle, and the courts on other occasions since then have adopted the impeachment test.[74]

After the *Aries Tanker* case there were some important observations on equitable **4.12** set-off in the Court of Appeal in *Federal Commerce & Navigation Co Ltd v Molena Alpha Inc*,[75] particularly by Lord Denning. In contrast with his earlier judgment in *Henriksens Rederi v Rolimpex*, Lord Denning acknowledged that there must be some equitable ground sufficient to impeach the plaintiff's demand.[76] In doing so however he rejected the notion that the categories of equitable grounds should be ascertained by examining the practice of the courts in matters of set-off prior to the Judicature Acts.[77] Instead he said that the relevant question is: 'what should we do now so as to ensure fair dealing between the parties?'[78] He then went on to explain the circumstances that would give rise to an equitable set-off today:

---

[68] [1974] 1 QB 233, 249.

[69] (1841) Cr & Ph 161, 175, 41 ER 451, 457.

[70] See para 4.55 below.

[71] [1977] 1 WLR 185.

[72] See paras 5.02–5.24 below.

[73] However the fact that the shipowner may have repudiated the charterparty does not preclude the operation of the principle that freight which has been earned must be paid without deduction. See *Bank of Boston Connecticut v European Grain and Shipping Ltd* [1989] 1 AC 1056, and para 5.04 below.

[74] See eg *British Anzani (Felixstowe) Ltd v International Marine Management (UK) Ltd* [1980] 1 QB 137, 145; *BICC plc v Burndy Corp* [1985] Ch 232, 258, 259; *Sim v Rotherham Council* [1987] 1 Ch 216, 261; *Atlantic Lines & Navigation Co Inc v The Ship 'Didymi' (The Didymi)* [1988] 1 Lloyd's Rep 97, Canadian Federal Court of Appeal; *Exmar BV v National Iranian Tanker Co (The Trade Fortitude)* [1992] 1 Lloyd's Rep 169, 172; *Aectra Refining and Marketing Inc v Exmar NV* [1994] 1 WLR 1634, 1649; *Courage Ltd v Crehan* [1999] 2 EGLR 145, 156.

[75] [1978] 1 QB 927.

[76] [1978] 1 QB 927, 974.

[77] See also *British Anzani (Felixstowe) Ltd v International Marine Management (UK) Ltd* [1980] 1 QB 137, 155.

[78] [1978] 1 QB 927, 974. In *A B Contractors Ltd v Flaherty Brothers Ltd* (1978) 16 BLR 8, 11, Cumming-Bruce LJ considered whether the dealings were so connected 'as to make it fair and sensible' that a set-off occur. See also *per* Stephenson LJ at 14.

> [I]t is not every cross-claim which can be deducted. It is only cross-claims that arise out of the same transaction or are closely connected with it. And it is only cross-claims which go directly to impeach the plaintiff's demands, that is, so closely connected with his demands that it would be manifestly unjust to allow him to enforce payment without taking into account the cross-claim.[79]

Parker J earlier had expressed the principle in similar terms in *The Teno* case,[80] and it has since been widely adopted.[81]

4.13 On Lord Denning's approach, two things must be established in order for equitable set-off to apply: first, the cross-claim must arise out of the same transaction as the claim or be closely connected with it; and, second, the relationship between the respective claims must be such that it would be manifestly unjust to allow one claim to be enforced without regard to the other.[82] In relation to the prevention of manifest injustice, or fairness, there is nothing new in that element. In truth, it has always been the concept underlying equitable set-off. The proper inquiry is, what are the circumstances in which equity regards it as unjust or unfair that one claim should be enforced without reference to another, and traditionally this has been expressed in terms that, in the absence of some other equitable ground for being protected,[83] the claims must be connected such that the title to sue is impeached. It is apparent from Lord Denning's reference to impeachment that his formulation was not intended to replace the impeachment test as such,[84] but rather to define it in terms which may be more familiar to the courts today. There is one situation in which he was careful not to extend the ambit of the defence. He said that, 'as at present advised', he would limit the right of a time charterer to make

---

[79] [1978] 1 QB 927, 974–975. Similarly, Goff LJ commented in *Federal Commerce* (n 75 above) at 981 that: 'The circumstances must be such as to make it unfair for the creditor to be paid his claim without allowing that of the debtor if and so far as well founded and thus to raise an equity against the creditor or, as it has been expressed, impeach his title to be paid.'

[80] *Compania Sud Americana de Vapores v Shipmair BV (The Teno)* [1977] 2 Lloyd's Rep 289, 297.

[81] See eg *British Anzani (Felixstowe) Ltd v International Marine Management (UK) Ltd* [1980] 1 QB 137, 145; *SL Sethia Liners Ltd v Naviagro Maritime Corp (The Kostas Melas)* [1981] 1 Lloyd's Rep 18, 25; *Dole Dried Fruit and Nut Co v Trustin Kerwood Ltd* [1990] 2 Lloyd's Rep 309, 311; *Esso Petroleum Co Ltd v Milton* [1997] 1 WLR 938, 950; *Peninsular and Oriental Steam Navigation Co v Youell* [1997] 2 Lloyd's Rep 136, 144; *Courage Ltd v Crehan* [1999] 2 EGLR 145, 155. In *National Westminster Bank plc v Skelton* [1993] 1 WLR 72, 76 Slade LJ said that, in deciding whether to allow a set-off, 'the court will be much influenced by what it regards as the essential requirements of justice'. In *Federal Commerce v Molena* [1978] 1 QB 927, 987 Goff LJ described Parker J's analysis in *The Teno* as 'impeccable'. See also *BICC plc v Burndy Corp* [1985] Ch 232, 250; *Sim v Rotherham Metropolitan BC* [1987] Ch 216, 261–262.

[82] *Esso Petroleum Co Ltd v Milton* [1997] 1 WLR 938, 950, *per* Simon Brown LJ; *Star Rider Ltd v Inntrepreneur Pub Co* [1998] 1 EGLR 53, 56.

[83] For example, fraud. See *Vuillamy v Noble* (1817) 3 Mer 593, 36 ER 228 and *Ex parte Stephens* (1805) 11 Ves Jun 24, 32 ER 996.

[84] Similarly Parker J in *Compania Sud Americana de Vapores v Shipmair BV (The Teno)* [1977] 2 Lloyd's Rep 289, 297 acknowledged that the cross-claim must be such as to impeach the plaintiff's title, but then went on to express the principle in terms whether it was manifestly unjust to allow the claimant to recover without taking into account the cross-claim.

deductions from hire to cases where the shipowner has wrongfully deprived the charterer of the use of the vessel or has prejudiced him in the use of it. He said that he would not extend it to other breaches or defaults of the shipowner, such as damage to cargo arising from the negligence of the crew.[85] This is consistent with the traditional approach, because depriving a charterer of the use of the ship or prejudicing the charterer's use is the very type of circumstance that would impeach a claim for hire.[86] It suggests a narrower view than that expressed in his earlier judgment in *Henriksens Rederi v Rolimpex*, that an equitable set-off is available whenever cross-claims arise out of the same transaction. But leaving that aside, the definition of impeachment in terms of a flexible concept such as fairness, or the prevention of manifest injustice, would tend to expand the scope of the defence, a proposition that may be illustrated by *Dole Dried Fruit and Nut Co v Trustin Kerwood Ltd*,[87] in which the Court of Appeal allowed an equitable set-off on the basis of Lord Denning's formulation in circumstances that would not appear to have satisfied the traditional test.[88]

A difficulty with a formulation based on 'justice' or 'fairness' is that it is conducive **4.14** to uncertainty, given that the determination of what is fair to a large extent is subjective, depending on from whose perspective the matter is looked at. As Professor Birks has observed, words such as 'fair' and 'just' and 'unconscionable' are so unspecific that they simply conceal a private and intuitive evaluation.[89] This element of subjectivity is reflected in Thorpe LJ's comment in *Esso Petroleum Co Ltd v Milton*[90] that: 'claims to equitable set-off ultimately depend upon the judge's assessment of the result that justice requires'. On the other hand, Hobhouse J in *The Leon* case[91] rejected the notion that the test is simply one of fairness. He said that, while

> equitable principles derive from a sense of what justice and fairness demand . . . this does not mean that equitable set-off has been reduced to an exercise of discretion. Since the merging of equity and law, equitable set-off gives rise to a legal defence. This defence does not vary according to the length of the Lord Chancellor's, or arbitrator's, foot. The defence has to be granted or refused by an application of legal principle.

---

[85] [1978] 1 QB 927, 976. Goff LJ (at 981) expressed a similar view. See also *Aliakmon Maritime Corporation v Trans Ocean Continental Shipping Ltd (The Aliakmon Progress)* [1978] 2 Lloyd's Rep 499, 501.

[86] See also *Leon Corporation v Atlantic Lines and Navigation Co Ltd (The Leon)* [1985] 2 Lloyd's Rep 470, 475; *Exmar BV v National Iranian Tanker Co (The Trade Fortitude)* [1992] 1 Lloyd's Rep 169, 172.

[87] [1990] 2 Lloyd's Rep 309.

[88] See paras 4.65 and 4.67 below.

[89] Birks, 'Equity in the Modern Law: An Exercise in Taxonomy' (1996) 26 University of Western Australia Law Review 1, 16–17.

[90] [1997] 1 WLR 938, 953.

[91] *Leon Corp v Atlantic Lines and Navigation Co Inc (The Leon)* [1985] 2 Lloyd's Rep 470, 474.

He went on to emphasize that the relevant principle is identified in Lord Cottenham's judgment in *Rawson v Samuel.*

4.15   After the *Federal Commerce* case, the House of Lords considered the question of equitable set-off in *Bank of Boston Connecticut v European Grain and Shipping Ltd.*[92] Lord Brandon of Oakbrook delivered the judgment of the Law Lords.[93] He said that the concept of impeachment is not a familiar one today. Instead, he approved a formulation that the Privy Council had expressed in *Government of Newfoundland v Newfoundland Railway Co,*[94] that an equitable set-off may occur if there is a cross-claim 'flowing out of and inseparably connected with the dealings and transactions which also give rise' to the claim.[95]

4.16   Lord Brandon did not regard that formulation as a departure from the impeachment test set out in *Rawson v Samuel.* Indeed, he affirmed that, in the determination today of whether a particular cross-claim can give rise to an equitable set-off, it is still necessary to see whether it is of such a character that it would have led a court of equity before the Judicature Acts to prohibit by injunction the enforcement of the plaintiff's claim.[96] This seems a rejection of the approach advocated by Lord Denning in the *Federal Commerce* case, that we should no longer ask ourselves what the courts of equity would have done before the Judicature Acts, but rather we should ask what should be done now so as to ensure fair dealing between the parties.[97] Nevertheless, it has been said in later cases that the authority of the *Federal Commerce* case has not been diminished by the *Bank of Boston* case,[98] and that the test enunciated by Lord Brandon was 'broadly similar' to and 'essentially the same as' that in *Federal Commerce v Molena.*[99] Lord Brandon went on to say that the test approved by the House of Lords was merely a 'different version' of the impeachment test,[100] while Lloyd LJ later characterized it as 'the same test in different language'.[101] This view is debatable, however. The notion that an equitable set-off may arise whenever the cross-claim is inseparably connected with the transaction founding the plaintiff's claim would not appear to reflect the the concept of impeachment as it was originally developed. Thus, it is difficult to see how

---

[92]   *Bank of Boston Connecticut v European Grain and Shipping Ltd* [1989] 1 AC 1056.
[93]   Lord Brandon, Lord Keith of Kinkel, Lord Oliver of Aylmerton, Lord Goff of Chieveley and Lord Jauncey of Tullichettle.
[94]   (1888) 13 App Cas 199.
[95]   See in particular the judgment at [1989] 1 AC 1056, 1102–1103, 1110–1111. See also *Kaps Transport Ltd v McGregor Telephone & Power Construction Co Ltd* (1970) 73 WWR 549.
[96]   [1989] 1 AC 1056, 1101.
[97]   [1978] 1 QB 927, 974.
[98]   *Dole Dried Fruit and Nut Co v Trustin Kerwood Ltd* [1990] 2 Lloyd's Rep 309, 311, *per* Lloyd LJ.
[99]   See Potter LJ in *Peninsular and Oriental Steam Navigation Co v Youell* [1997] 2 Lloyd's Rep 136, 144 and in *Bim Kemi AB v Blackburn Chemicals Ltd* [2001] 2 Lloyd's Rep 93, 100 para 27.
[100]   [1989] 1 AC 1056, 1102.
[101]   *Dole Dried Fruit and Nut Co v Trustin Kerwood Ltd* [1990] 2 Lloyd's Rep 309, 310.

the *Bank of Boston* approach would ever operate to deny an equitable set-off when the same transaction is the source of both demands,[102] yet it has been emphasized in the context of the impeachment test that it is not sufficient that the cross-demands arose out of the same transaction.[103] As Bramwell B once expressed the principle, 'where there is a transaction between two parties, and cross claims originate from it, a court of equity will *in some cases* interfere to prevent the one party from enforcing his claim without allowing the claim of the other'.[104]

Whatever the position in that regard, the Court of Appeal[105] reached the correct **4.17** decision in *Guinness plc v Saunders*.[106] The second defendant, through a company controlled by him, received payment from the plaintiff for services performed. The second defendant was also a director of the plaintiff, and it was held that the payment was received in breach of his fiduciary duty to the plaintiff and that he held it as constructive trustee. He said that he nevertheless had a valid defence based upon a cross-claim for quantum meruit in respect of the services. However the cross-demand did not impeach the trust, the plaintiff's claim being for the return of its money improperly received by the second defendant. An equitable set-off accordingly was not available.

Similarly, the Court of Appeal was correct in rejecting an argument for a set-off in **4.18** *Peninsular and Oriental Steam Navigation Co v Youell*.[107] Underwriters had paid P & O in respect of various claims made on a policy of liability insurance for the 1992/1993 year, but alleged that they had been induced to do so by fraud or

---

[102] In *A B Contractors Ltd v Flaherty Brothers Ltd* (1978) 16 BLR 8, 12 Cumming-Bruce LJ seemed to regard it as sufficient if 'the issue on a defence and counterclaim arises out of the same transaction, the same contract, as the issues on the claim'.

[103] *Leon Corp v Atlantic Lines and Navigation Co Inc (The Leon)* [1985] 2 Lloyd's Rep 470, 474; *Century Textiles and Industry Ltd v Tomoe Shipping Co (Singapore) Pte Ltd (The Aditya Vaibhav)* [1991] 1 Lloyd's Rep 573 (esp at 574); *Halsbury's Laws of England* (4th edn, 1999) vol 42, 254 para 430, *per* Sir Anthony Mason. In the Court of Appeal in *Bank of Boston* [1989] 1 AC 1056, 1075 (n 92 above) Mustill LJ said in relation to equitable set-off that 'the fact that the origin of the demands lay in the same transaction was plainly not enough'. In Australia, see *Re K L Tractors Ltd* [1954] VLR 505, 508; *Davkot Pty Ltd v Custom Credit Corp Ltd* (New South Wales Supreme Court, Wood J, 28th March 1991); *Griffiths v Commonwealth Bank of Australia* (1994) 123 ALR 111, 124 (in which Lee J held that a claim against a bank in tort for interference in the customer's contractual relations with a second bank was not impeached by the first bank's claim for repayment of a loan advanced to the customer, notwithstanding that Lee J agreed (at 124) that the bank's claim was part of the transaction which lead to its conduct the subject of the claim against it); *Walker v Department of Social Security* (1995) 56 FCR 354, 364 (referring to *James v Commonwealth Bank of Australia* (1992) 37 FCR 445). See also Spry, 'Equitable Set-offs' (1969) 43 Australian Law Journal 265, 268, referred to in *Popular Homes Ltd v Circuit Developments Ltd* [1979] 2 NZLR 642, 659 and *Parry v Grace* [1981] 2 NZLR 273, 276, 277.

[104] *Stimson v Hall* (1857) 1 H & N 831, 835, 156 ER 1436, 1438 (emphasis added).

[105] Fox and Glidewell LJJ, and Sir Frederick Lawton.

[106] [1988] 1 WLR 863, affirmed on different grounds, without reference to the set-off point, at [1990] 2 AC 663. See also *Zemco Ltd v Jerrom-Pugh* [1993] BCC 275, and *Neptune (Vehicle Washing Equipment) Ltd v Fitzgerald* [1996] Ch 274, 278.

[107] [1997] 2 Lloyd's Rep 136.

mistake. They sought to plead their claim for repayment as a defence to an action brought by P & O on a separate policy in respect of a similar claim for the years 1991/1992. But as Potter LJ in delivering the judgment of the Court[108] pointed out, different insurance contracts were in issue relating to different years. The fact that they may have been part of an overall insurance program was not a sufficient connection to support an equitable set-off.[109]

4.19   After the *Peninsular and Oriental* case, Potter LJ, once again delivering the judgment of the Court of Appeal, reviewed the authorities on equitable set-off in *Bim Kemi AB v Blackburn Chemicals Ltd.*[110] In the first place, he adopted the test approved by the House of Lords in the *Bank of Boston* case, in terms whether the cross-claim flows out of and is inseparably connected with the dealings and transactions which gave rise to the claim. He said that this emphasizes that the degree of closeness required for an equitable set-off is that of 'inseparable connection'.[111] But the availability of a set-off does not rest solely upon the determination of that issue. He said that in addition it is appropriate in every case to give separate consideration to the question of manifest injustice. He pointed out that, in *Federal Commerce v Molena*,[112] the question whether it would be manifestly unjust to allow a set-off was presented as the criterion by which to judge the closeness of the connection. The issue of closeness has since been determined by the House of Lords in the *Bank of Boston* case without reference to manifest injustice, although if the *Bank of Boston* test is satisfied Potter LJ said that it would be difficult to envisage in what circumstances it would be other than just to allow a set-off. Nevertheless he considered that it is still appropriate in every case to give separate consideration to the question.[113] This approach is likely to be adopted generally by English courts.[114]

4.20   The claimant in the *Bim Kemi* case was suing the defendant for damages for repudiation of an exclusive distribution agreement alleged to have been made in 1994, by which the claimant was to have the exclusive right to sell the defendant's product in Denmark, Norway and Finland for three years. By way of defence, the defendant asserted a set-off. It alleged that the claimant had breached a technology trademark and licensing agreement entered into in 1984, pursuant to which the

---

[108] Nourse, Potter and Mummery LJJ.

[109] A claim under a policy of indemnity insurance is a claim for unliquidated damages, and therefore a set-off would not have been available under the Statutes of Set-off. See para 2.26 above.

[110] [2001] 2 Lloyd's Rep 93, *per* Potter and Jonathan Parker LJJ, and Sedley J.

[111] [2001] 2 Lloyd's Rep 93, 100 para 29.

[112] *Sub nom The Nanfri.* See para 4.12 above.

[113] [2001] 2 Lloyd's Rep 93, 102 paras 38 and 39.

[114] Potter LJ referred to the *Bim Kemi* case in his later judgment in *ISS Machinery Services Ltd v Aeolian Shipping SA (The Aeolian)* [2001] 2 Lloyd's Rep 641, 646 para 20 (claim for the price of spare parts required to repair machinery and cross-claim for damages for breach of a term as to the quality of the machinery in the contract for the sale of the machinery, where the delivery of spare parts was only necessary because of the defect in the machinery).

defendant granted the claimant a licence to use the defendant's technology to process a chemical concentrate made by the defendant and to sell the product. The defence included an allegation that the claimant had promoted a competing product made by its subsidiary at the expense of the defendant's product. The claimant then applied to have the pleaded set-off struck out as not amounting to a defence and/or for summary judgment. The cross-claims concerned separate contracts made ten years apart, and the contracts related to different products, but the Court of Appeal considered that the claims were sufficiently connected to satisfy the *Bank of Boston* test. The parties in this case had a single trading relationship, and it has been said that a single relationship does not suffice to support an equitable set-off.[115] Potter LJ nevertheless considered that the principle stated in the *Bank of Boston* case is apt to cover a case where there are claims and cross-claims for damages in respect of different but closely connected contracts arising out of a longstanding trading relationship which is terminated. He went on to comment that this circumstance would not *per se* establish the requisite connection, but in an appropriate case it may well be manifestly unjust to allow one claim to be enforced without taking into account the other. In the present case, Potter LJ accepted that both agreements contemplated a continuing expansion and exploitation of the market for the defendant's products in Scandinavia, and the 1994 agreement supplemented rather than replaced the 1984 agreement. In those circumstances, the claimant's conduct in promoting its subsidiary's product at the expense of the defendant's product was considered to be in breach of obligations contained in both agreements, which he said gave rise to the 'close and inseparable connection' necessary for an equitable set-off.[116] Further, there were no competing factors which militated against the justice and fairness of recognizing a set-off.

C. Equitable Set-off in Australia

In Australia the courts[117] have been more prepared to emphasize impeachment of **4.21** title as the basis of equitable set-off,[118] and generally they have tended to be more

---

[115] *Esso Petroleum Co Ltd v Milton* [1997] 1 WLR 938, 951.

[116] [2001] 2 Lloyd's Rep 93, 102 para 37.

[117] The Federal Court of Australia is a court of equity (see the Federal Court of Australia Act 1976 (Cth), s 5(2), and *Scarel Pty Ltd v City Loan & Credit Corp Pty Ltd* (1988) 17 FCR 344, 349), and as such it should have jurisdiction in relation to equitable set-off in respect of matters that are otherwise within its jurisdiction. Compare *Intag Microelectronics Pty Ltd v AWA Ltd* (1995) 18 ACSR 284, 287. This has been assumed in a number of cases. See eg *Westpac Banking Corp v Eltran* (1987) 14 FCR 541; *Tomlinson v Cut Price Deli Pty Ltd* (1992) 38 FCR 490; *James v Commonwealth Bank of Australia* (1992) 37 FCR 445; *Griffiths v Commonwealth Bank* (1994) 123 ALR 111, 124; *Walker v Department of Social Security* (1995) 56 FCR 354, 368, 375.

[118] In addition to the cases referred to below, see *Stephenson Nominees Pty Ltd v Official Receiver* (1987) 16 FCR 536, 558 (claim by agent against the principal impeached by the agent's own

conservative on questions of equitable set-off than their English counterparts. In *Hill v Ziymack*[119] the plaintiff at law had obtained judgment for damages for conversion against the defendant, and the High Court held that the plaintiff's title to issue execution was not impeached by a cross-claim for an account between the parties of sums paid by the defendant on behalf of the plaintiff in satisfaction of a number of promissory notes given in payment for the property the subject of the conversion claim. A claim for a set-off also failed in *Bayview Quarries Pty Ltd v Castley Development Pty Ltd*.[120] The plaintiff was suing for the price of goods delivered to the defendant pursuant to an arrangement involving a running account between the parties. Sholl J held that a cross-claim for damages arising out of defects in other earlier deliveries did not constitute a sufficient reason in equity to protect the defendant from the plaintiff's demand, even though, because of payments made pursuant to the running account, the defendant had already paid for the defective goods.[121]

4.22 In a case such as *Bayview Quarries*, in which there are various contracts for the sale of goods, in principle the result should be the same when the contracts are subject to an overriding master agreement which governs their trading relationship, and which sets out the terms applicable to all the contracts. The contracts are still separate transactions. There is, however, authority in Victoria which suggests that damages payable for breach of one contract in that circumstance can be set off in equity against the price payable under another contract.[122]

4.23 The case law concerning equitable set-off was the subject of an extensive review by Woodward J in *Galambos & Son Pty Ltd v McIntyre*.[123] The case involved an action for payment of the balance due on a building contract. It was held that cross-

---

liability to account to the principal for misapplied funds); *Signature Resorts Pty Ltd v DHD Constructions Pty Ltd* (1995) 18 ACSR 627, 635 (claim for costs payable in a winding up not impeached by a cross-claim for damages for breach of contract); *Re Kostezky* (1996) 67 FCR 101, 106.

[119] (1908) 7 CLR 352.
[120] [1963] VR 445.
[121] See also *W Pope & Co Pty Ltd v Edward Souery & Co Pty Ltd* [1983] WAR 117. Compare *Edward Ward & Co v McDougall* [1972] VR 433, which involved a claim by share brokers for the balance due on moneys paid to the defendant's use as the purchase price of shares or as stamp duty, and for brokerage charged on work done in buying and selling shares, and a cross-claim for damages for negligence or breach of contract in respect of the purchase of some of the shares and the sale of others. Gowans J said that there was a real case in law to be investigated as to whether this gave rise to a defence.
[122] *Auspac Trade International Pty Ltd v Victorian Dairy Industry Authority* (Vic SC, Byrne J, 30 June 1993, at pp 67–70). On appeal, the Appeal Division of the Victorian Supreme Court (Southwell, Nathan and O'Bryan JJ) expressed approval of his Honour's observations on set-off. See *Auspac Trade International v Victorian Dairy Industry Authority* (22 December 1994, at p 39). Compare that view with *Century Textiles and Industry Ltd v Tomoe Shipping Co (Singapore) Pte Ltd (The Aditya Vaibhav)* [1991] 1 Lloyd's Rep 573, for which see para 4.80 below. Compare also paras 4.64–4.67 below in relation to the repudiation of an overriding agreement which governs the trading relationship between the parties to it.
[123] (1974) 5 ACTR 10.

claims possessed by the defendant against the plaintiff relating to non-performance of the contract or defective work, requiring remedial work or directly reducing the value of the work done, constituted matters of pure defence sufficient to defeat the plaintiff's claim. Further, his Honour said that a claim for damages for loss of enjoyment of the premises was so closely connected with the plaintiff's claim that it would have been appropriate, as a matter of equity, to set it off, had it been so pleaded and had it been necessary to do so.[124] Woodward J considered generally the situation in which there is a claim for money under a contract and a cross-claim for damages for breach of the same contract. These cross-claims may be set off *provided* that the equity of the case requires that this should be so. This was said to depend upon how closely the respective claims are related, particularly as to time and subject-matter, and also upon the general conduct of the respective parties.[125] But when cross-claims arise out of the same contract and are closely related to each other, he suggested that a set-off should normally be allowed.[126]

Since the *Galambos* case, a set-off has been denied in a case in which the plaintiff **4.24** was suing for money due under a mortgage of land given by the defendant to the plaintiff, and the defendant asserted a cross-claim against the plaintiff for breach of an alleged agreement by the plaintiff to lend other moneys to the defendant on the security of other lands purchased by the defendant from the plaintiff.[127] On another occasion it was held that a purchaser of land and dwelling-house could not set off against the price a damages claim that the purchaser had against the vendor for failure to assign a policy of insurance which indemnified the insured against loss of and damage to the dwelling and its contents.[128] Further, in a claim for the price of goods sold, a set-off was thought not to be available based upon a cross-claim arising out of a breach by the vendor of a promise under a franchise agreement to grant a territorial monopoly to the purchaser, notwithstanding that the claims had their respective origins in the same agreement.[129] In Western Australia, a vendor of land claimed possession of the land from the purchaser, as a result of the purchaser's failure to pay the purchase price on the settlement date. The purchaser asserted that the vendor held moneys on trust for it, and that it was entitled to complete the contract by tendering a reduced amount after setting off the amount of the trust moneys. However, Kennedy J (with whom Malcolm CJ and Murray J agreed) held that the tendering of the reduced amount could not be justified on the basis of an equitable set-off, since the moneys said to be held on

---

[124] In fact it was not necessary, because the defendant's cross-claims for non-performance of the contract and for defective work were sufficient to overtop the plaintiff's claim.

[125] (1974) 5 ACTR 10, 26.

[126] (1974) 5 ACTR 10, 22.

[127] *United Dominions Corporation Ltd v Jaybe Homes Pty Ltd* [1978] Qd R 111.

[128] *Eagle Star Nominees Ltd v Merril* [1982] VR 557.

[129] *Covino v Bandag Manufacturing Pty Ltd* [1983] 1 NSWLR 237 (see esp Hutley JA at 238).

trust were unconnected with the contract of sale out of which the vendor's claim arose.[130]

4.25 On the other hand, when a plaintiff applied for summary judgment on a claim for payment of his charges for the performance of earth-moving works, the Queensland Supreme Court said that there was at least an arguable case that an equitable set-off could arise in relation to a cross-claim for sums incurred by the defendant in repairing the plaintiff's machinery, so that the plaintiff could perform the work contracted for.[131] Moreover, Moffitt P in *Sidney Raper Pty Ltd v Commonwealth Trading Bank of Australia*,[132] as an alternative basis for his decision, held that a customer of a bank could not sue for the proceeds of a bank cheque issued to him by the bank without giving credit for a dishonoured cheque deposited by him with the bank, and which he had used in order to obtain the issue of the bank cheque.[133] Similarly, an impeachment of title would arise when a vendor of property is suing for the price, and the purchaser has a cross-claim for damages for breach of a warranty in the contract of sale which directly affects the value of the property sold.[134] In this situation, however, if the property in question consists of goods a common law defence of abatement in any event may be available.[135]

4.26 There have been instances in which Australian judges have adopted tests similar to Lord Denning's formulation in *Federal Commerce v Molena*.[136] In *Tooth & Co Ltd v Smith*[137] Clarke J said that: 'no general rule can be laid down except by stating that [an equitable] set-off will arise when there exist circumstances which make it unjust or inequitable that a plaintiff should be permitted to proceed with his claim'.[138] Wood J later remarked that, as presently advised, he could not see any fault with this.[139] Subsequently Giles J in *AWA Ltd v Exicom Australia Pty Ltd*,[140] after referring to these cases, said that the 'ultimate question' is whether it would

---

[130] *Hazcor Pty Ltd v Kirwanon Pty Ltd* (1995) 12 WAR 62. Indeed, it appears that the entitlement to some of the trust moneys was assigned to the purchaser by a third party a month after the settlement date.

[131] *Phillips v Mineral Resources Developments Pty Ltd* [1983] 2 Qd R 138.

[132] [1975] 2 NSWLR 227.

[133] In fact the customer had paid the bank cheque to a company, and the company was the party suing on the cheque. However, the company held the cheque as trustee for the customer, and so a set-off in equity was still available to the bank.

[134] *Altarama Ltd v Camp* (1980) 5 ACLR 513, 519–520. Compare the situation in which the purchaser's indebtedness for the price is satisfied by a loan from the vendor secured by a mortgage or other security, and the vendor is suing for repayment of the loan. See para 4.87 below.

[135] See paras 2.87–2.97 above.

[136] [1978] 1 QB 927, 975. See para 4.12 above.

[137] NSW SC, 5 September 1984.

[138] See also *Sydmar Pty Ltd v Statewise Developments Pty Ltd* (1987) 73 ALR 289, 295.

[139] *Tooth & Co Ltd v Rosier* (NSW SC, 7 June 1985). Wood J repeated this view in *Davkot v Custom Credit Corporation Ltd* (NSW SC, 28 March 1991). See also *Sydmar Pty Ltd v Statewise Developments Pty Ltd* (1987) 73 ALR 289, 295.

[140] (1990) 19 NSWLR 705, 712.

be 'unjust or inequitable' that the plaintiff should be permitted to proceed with his claim, an approach that has been referred to with approval in later cases.[141] More recently, however, the courts have tended to emphasize the traditional formulation.[142] In *MEK Nominees Pty Ltd v Billboard Entertainments Pty Ltd*[143] Tadgell J said that a dilution of the requirement of impeachment has not occurred in the Victorian Supreme Court, and this would also appear to be the case in Western Australia.[144] In particular, Kennedy J (with whose judgment Malcolm CJ and Murray J agreed) in *Hazcor Pty Ltd v Kirwanon Pty Ltd*[145] said that he was, 'quite unable to accept . . . that the test is no more than whether the set-off is reasonable in the interests of justice and fair dealing'. In the Federal Court,[146] the impeachment test was affirmed by Gummow J in *James v Commonwealth Bank of Australia*,[147] by Lee J in *Griffiths v Commonwealth Bank of Australia*,[148] and by Cooper J (with whom Spender J agreed) in *Walker v Department of Social Security*,[149] though Gummow J in the *James* case nevertheless emphasized that the requirement of impeachment has not been narrowly construed.[150] In the *James* case, a receiver claimed an indemnity from his appointing banks in respect of certain debts and liabilities that he had incurred. The banks in their cross-claim alleged that these debts and liabilities were the result of the personal neglect or default of the receiver, and that this gave rise to a cross-claim for damages which could be set off against their indemnity obligation. While for other reasons it was not necessary to decide the point, Gummow J nevertheless said that the cross-claim would have impeached the receiver's demand, since his demand owed its

---

[141] *Australian Mutual Provident Society v Specialist Funding Consultants Pty Ltd* (1991) 24 NSWLR 326, 328–329, *per* Rogers CJ; *Lambert Pty Ltd v Papadatos Pty Ltd* (1991) 5 ACSR 468, 470–471, *per* McLelland J; *Westmex Operations Pty Ltd (in liq) v Westmex Ltd (in liq)* (1992) 8 ACSR 146, 153, *per* McLelland J (affirmed (1993) 12 ACLC 106). See also *Signature Resorts Pty Ltd v DHD Constructions Pty Ltd* (1995) 18 ACSR 627, 634, *per* Bryson J, and *Opal Maritime Agencies Pty Ltd v Baltic Shipping Co* (1998) 158 ALR 416, 423, *per* Tamberlin J. In Victoria, see *Auspac Trade International Pty Ltd v Victorian Dairy Industry Authority* (Vic SC, Byrne J, 30 June 1993).

[142] In addition to the cases referred to below, see *General Credits (Finance) Pty Ltd v Stoyakovich* [1975] Qd R 352, 355 (Queensland); *W Pope & Co Pty Ltd v Edward Souery & Co Pty Ltd* [1983] WAR 117, 122.

[143] (1993) V Conv R 54–468 at p 65,466. See also *Eagle Star Nominees Ltd v Merril* [1982] VR 557, 561; *Indrisie v General Credits Ltd* [1985] VR 251, 254; *Doherty v Murphy* [1996] 2 VR 553, 565; *Mirvac Hotels Pty Ltd v 333 Collins Street Pty Ltd* (Vic SC, Byrne J, 20 December 1994, at p 12).

[144] *Westwind Air Charter Pty Ltd v Hawker De Havilland Ltd* (1990) 3 WAR 71; *Geraldton Building Co Pty Ltd v Christmas Island Resort Pty Ltd* (1992) 11 WAR 40. See also *Hazcor Ltd v Kirwanon Pty Ltd* (1995) 12 WAR 62, 67–68.

[145] (1995) 12 WAR 62, 68.

[146] In addition to the cases referred to below, see *Westpac Banking Corp v Eltran Pty Ltd* (1987) 14 FCR 541, 547–548; *Cunningham v National Australia Bank Ltd* (1987) 15 FCR 495.

[147] (1992) 37 FCR 445.

[148] (1994) 123 ALR 111, 124.

[149] (1995) 56 FCR 354, 375. Compare the discussion by Drummond J in his dissenting judgment at 363–370.

[150] (1992) 37 FCR 445, 458.

existence to, or at least it was contributed to by, his own breach of duty to the banks.

4.27   In a similar vein, the New South Wales Court of Appeal in *Lord v Direct Acceptance Corp Ltd*[151] accepted that it is still an indispensable requirement of equitable set-off in that state that the set-off 'impeach' the title of the plaintiff. Subsequently a differently constituted Court of Appeal in New South Wales considered equitable set-off in *Roadshow Entertainment Pty Ltd v (ACN 053 006 269) Pty Ltd*.[152] The *Roadshow Entertainment* case concerned a receivership, which is governed by the same principles which apply to an equitable assignment of a debt.[153] On the one hand, the Court of Appeal reiterated the impeachment principle for equitable set-off.[154] On the other, the Court also adopted the principle approved by the Privy Council in *Government of Newfoundland v Newfoundland Railway Company*,[155] and more recently by the House of Lords in the *Bank of Boston* case,[156] that an unliquidated cross-demand may be set off against an assignee if it flows out of and is inseparably connected with the dealings and transactions which also gave rise to the subject of the assignment.[157] In light of that formulation, the Court of Appeal in the *Roadshow Entertainment* case accepted that a cross-claim for unliquidated damages arising out of the contract which gave rise to the assigned debt could be the subject of a set-off,[158] even though it is generally said in the context of the traditional impeachment test that it is not sufficient for equitable set-off that the cross-claims arose out of the same contract.[159] However the Court of Appeal's acceptance of the *Government of Newfoundland* formulation appears not to have been on the basis that it set out the circumstances in which an equitable set-off is available as between a debtor and a creditor.[160] Rather, its acceptance seems to have been in the context of a view which has found favour in Australia, that an assignee cannot recover moneys owing under the contract without being met by a counterclaim for breach by the assignor of the same contract, whether or not the breach

---

[151]   (1993) 32 NSWLR 362, *per* Kirby P, Meagher and Sheller JJA. See also *Covino v Bandag Manufacturing Pty Ltd* [1983] 1 NSWLR 237, 238; *Signature Resorts Pty Ltd v DHD Constructions Pty Ltd* (1995) 18 ACSR 627, 635; *Horrobin v Australia and New Zealand Banking Group Ltd* (1996) 40 NSWLR 89, 100; *Perpetual Trustees (WA) Ltd v Equus Corp Pty Ltd* (NSW SC, Young J, 5 March 1998, at p 12); *Abignano v Wenkart* (1998) 9 BPR 16,765, 16,773 (different transactions); *Metal Manufacturers Ltd v Hall* (2002) 41 ACSR 446, 471.

[152]   (1997) 42 NSWLR 462.

[153]   (1997) 42 NSWLR 462, 483. See generally paras 17.73–17.87 below.

[154]   (1997) 42 NSWLR 462, 481.

[155]   (1888) 13 App Cas 199.

[156]   [1989] 1 AC 1056, 1102–1103, 1110.

[157]   See para 4.15 above.

[158]   (1997) 42 NSWLR 462, 482. See also *McDonnell & East Ltd v McGregor* (1936) 56 CLR 50, 60. That view nevertheless is curious, because the Privy Council in *Government of Newfoundland* (1888) 13 App Cas 199, 212 itself acknowledged that: 'There is no universal rule that claims arising out of the same contract may be set against each other in all circumstances.'

[159]   See para 4.55 below.

[160]   Compare *Lord v Direct Acceptance Corporation Ltd* (1993) 32 NSWLR 362, 367.

would have given rise to an equitable set-off as between the original parties.[161] The proposition inherent in that analysis, that an assignee may take subject to a counterclaim available to the debtor that would not have given rise to a defence of set-off as against the assignor, was rejected by the House of Lords in the *Bank of Boston* case,[162] and the view is expressed later that it is incorrect.[163]

Notwithstanding the breadth of the language used by Giles J in *AWA v Exicom*,[164] **4.28** the circumstances in issue in that case lent themselves to an equitable set-off on both the traditional and the more recent formulations. AWA had sold a business to the defendant, and was suing for moneys due under the contract by way of adjustments consequent upon the transfer of the business. The adjustments arose out of orders which had been accepted and contracts which had been undertaken prior to completion but which were incomplete as at the date of completion. The defendant claimed damages for breach of warranty which went to the value of the business. Giles J held that this gave rise to an equitable set-off, on the basis that it would have been unjust or inequitable to permit AWA to proceed with its claim. The same result would have been achieved applying the formulation approved by the House of Lords in the *Bank of Boston* case, because the cross-claim was inseparably connected with the transaction which gave rise to the claim.[165] Further, the impeachment test would appear to have been satisfied. If the claim had been for the price itself, the cross-claim certainly would have given rise to an equitable set-off under this formulation. Instead, the claim related to adjustments to take into account incomplete contracts. Nevertheless, as Giles J noted, it affected what the defendant as the purchaser had to pay, and in such a case it should not make any difference that the adjustments were treated separately in the contract rather than being built into the price.

D. The Substantive Nature of Equitable Set-off

The right of set-off derived from the Statutes of Set-off is commonly described as **4.29** a procedural defence.[166] By this it is meant that separate and distinct debts remain in existence until judgment for a set-off, and, moreover, the defence has no effect

---

[161] See Gummow J in *James v Commonwealth Bank of Australia* (1992) 37 FCR 445, 461–462, referring to Dixon J in *McDonnell & East Ltd v McGregor* (1936) 56 CLR 50, 59–60 and Spry, 'Equitable Set-offs' (1969) 43 Australian Law Journal 265, 268–70, and the *Roadshow Entertainment* case (1997) 42 NSWLR 462, 482.

[162] [1989] 1 AC 1056, 1105–1106, 1109–1111, approving of the analysis of Hobhouse J at first instance [1987] 1 Lloyd's Rep 239, 254–257.

[163] See paras 17.05–17.09 below, and also Derham, 'Recent Issues in Relation to Set-off' (1994) 68 Australian Law Journal 331, 334–7.

[164] (1990) 19 NSWLR 705.

[165] See Giles J at (1990) 19 NSWLR 705, 707.

[166] See paras 2.33–2.48 above.

until judgment. Prior to judgment the rights consequent upon being a creditor still attach, as do the obligations and liabilities consequent upon being a debtor. A similar analysis should apply when equity acts by analogy with the Statutes.[167] However, a characteristic of the form of equitable set-off under discussion which has emerged in recent years is that it operates as a true, or substantive, defence.[168] It may be invoked independently of any order of the court or of arbitrators.[169] It may be set up by a person indebted to another, not merely as a means of preventing that other person from obtaining judgment, but also as an immediate answer to his liability to pay the debt otherwise due.[170] While it is only recently that the substantive nature of this defence has come into prominence,[171] it is consistent with the tenor of Lord Cottenham's judgment in *Rawson v Samuel.*[172] The Lord Chancellor referred to earlier cases in which an equitable set-off had been allowed as cases in which 'the equity of the bill impeached the title to the legal demand'. It was not merely the right to obtain judgment on the demand that was impeached, but the title to the demand itself.

What is meant by 'substantive'?

4.30 Notwithstanding various judicial statements which may suggest the contrary,[173] the view that the defence is substantive does not mean that it operates as an auto-

---

[167] Compare *Stewart v Latec Investments Ltd* [1968] 1 NSWR 432. See para 3.07 above.

[168] In addition to the cases referred to below, see *Newman v Cook* [1963] VR 659, 674–675; *AWA Ltd v Exicom Australia Pty Ltd* (1990) 19 NSWLR 705, 711; *Long Leys Co Pty Ltd v Silkdale Pty Ltd* (1991) 5 BPR 11,512, 11,520 ('equitable set-off . . . operates to absolve the appellant in whole or in part from liability'); *Fuller v Happy Shopper Markets Ltd* [2001] 1 WLR 1681, 1690 para 22. Compare the judgments of Cairns and Roskill LJJ in *Henriksens Rederi A/S v THZ Rolimpex (The Brede)* [1974] 1 QB 233, and *Re K L Tractors Ltd* [1954] VLR 505, 507 (although O'Bryan J relied upon some observations by Byrne J in *Re Hiram Maxim Lamp Company* [1903] 1 Ch 70 which were concerned with the Statutes of Set-off). Since the prevailing view is that the defence is substantive, it has been suggested that it is better described as an equitable defence rather than a set-off. See *Henriksens Rederi v Rolimpex* at 248; *Sidney Raper Pty Ltd v Commonwealth Trading Bank of Australia* [1975] 2 NSWLR 227, 236, 238. See also *Altarama Ltd v Camp* (1980) 5 ACLR 513, 519.

[169] *SL Sethia Liners Ltd v Naviagro Maritime Corporation (The Kostas Melas)* [1981] 1 Lloyd's Rep 18, 26, *per* Robert Goff J.

[170] *Federal Commerce & Navigation Co Ltd v Molena Alpha Inc* [1978] 1 QB 927, 982, *per* Goff LJ.

[171] As Cumming-Bruce LJ remarked in *Federal Commerce v Molena* [1978] 1 QB 927, 997, 'it is probably true to say that it was only Morris LJ's judgment in *Hanak v Green* [1958] 2 QB 9 that brought clearly to the attention of the legal profession and the commercial world the possibilities of equitable set-off as a defence.'

[172] (1841) Cr & Ph 161, 179, 41 ER 451, 458.

[173] See eg *Covino v Bandag Manufacturing Pty Ltd* [1983] 1 NSWLR 237, 238; *AWA Ltd v Exicom Australia Pty Ltd* (1990) 19 NSWLR 705, 710–711. In *Hanak v Green* [1958] 2 QB 9, 29 Sellers LJ commented that: 'If there is a set-off at all each claim goes against the other and either extinguishes it or reduces it.' Similarly Scott LJ commented in the Court of Appeal in *Barclays Bank plc v Gruffydd* (30 October 1992) that: 'A set-off, whether legal or equitable, available to the principal debtor extinguishes, or reduces pro tanto, the amount of the creditor's claim.' See also *Lockley v National Blood Transfusion Service* [1992] 1 WLR 492, 495; *TSB Bank plc v Platts* [1998] 2 BCLC 1, 9.

matic extinction of cross-demands. Rather, the creditor's conscience is affected, so that the creditor is not permitted in equity to treat the debtor as being indebted to him to the extent of the debtor's cross-claim. At law the cross-demands remain in existence and retain their separate identities[174] until extinguished by judgment or agreement.[175] But as far as equity is concerned, it is unconscionable for the creditor even before judgment to regard the debtor as a debtor to the extent of debtor's cross-demand, or to treat the debtor as having defaulted in payment to that extent, if circumstances exist which support an equitable set-off.[176] In this sense, it operates in equity as a complete or a partial defeasance of the plaintiff's claim.[177] A court of equity can protect the debtor's position by means of an injunction, and the debtor's right may be the subject of a declaration.[178] This explains how equitable set-off can operate substantively without working an automatic discharge.[179]

The notion that the claimant's claim is not extinguished prior to judgment for a **4.31** set-off is reflected in one of the grounds for the decision of the House of Lords in *Aries Tanker Corporation v Total Transport Ltd.*[180] Charterers of a vessel were being sued for payment of freight, and argued as a defence that they had an equitable set-off arising from a damages claim that they had against the owners for short delivery. The defence failed, for two reasons. The first was on the basis of a long-standing principle, that a damages claim in respect of cargo cannot be asserted by way of deduction from freight.[181] But as an alternative ground, which the House of Lords in the *Bank of Boston* case later described as the primary ground

---

[174] In Australia, see *National Australia Bank Ltd v Market Holdings Pty Ltd* (2000) 35 ACSR 572, 577–578 [33].

[175] Before the Judicature Acts, the permanency of an equitable set-off was achieved by way of a perpetual injunction.

[176] This view has been accepted in Australia. See *Roadshow Entertainment Pty Ltd v (ACN 053 006 269) Pty Ltd* (1997) 42 NSWLR 462, 481 (Court of Appeal); *Re Kleiss, ex p Kleiss v Capt'n Snooze Pty Ltd* (1996) 61 FCR 436, 440. See also *Re Sgambellone, ex p Jaques* (1994) 53 FCR 275, 280.

[177] *Aectra Refining and Manufacturing Inc v Exmar NV* [1994] 1 WLR 1634, 1649; *Fuller v Happy Shopper Markets Ltd* [2001] 1 WLR 1681, 1690 para 22.

[178] See *Sim v Rotherham Metropolitan BC* [1987] 1 Ch 216 (discussed below at para 4.33) and, in New South Wales, *P Rowe Graphics Pty Ltd v Scanagraphix Pty Ltd* (NSW SC, Young J, 6 September 1988). In the case of a periodic payment obligation, the declaration may relate to future payments. See *Sim v Rotherham* (para 4.33 below), and see also *Philip Collins Ltd v Davis* [2000] 3 All ER 808 (esp at 830–832) (royalties).

[179] See in this regard the discussion of *Beasley v Darcy* (1800) 2 Sch & Lef 403n in *O'Mahoney v Dickson* (1805) 2 Sch & Lef 400, 408, 412, where it was acknowledged that the rent had been due in *Beasley*. In *Westpac Banking Corp v Eltran Pty Ltd* (1987) 14 FCR 541, 549 Fox and Burchett JJ in their joint judgment said that: 'Equity permits certain privileged cross-claims to put on the armour of a set-off, but they do not therefore lose the character of cross-claims. They operate to extinguish the debt, not by ceasing to be cross-claims, but by virtue of being cross-claims which possess additional features.' Compare however *Stehar Knitting Mills Pty Ltd v Southern Textile Converters Pty Ltd* [1980] 2 NSWLR 514, 518.

[180] [1977] 1 WLR 185.

[181] See paras 5.02–5.22 below.

for the decision,[182] the point was made that the time bar set out in Article 3, rule 6 of the Hague Rules for the enforcement of the charterer's damages claim had expired, with the result that the charterer's claim had ceased to exist as distinct from being merely unenforceable. Lord Wilberforce in the leading judgment said that a claim which had ceased to exist could not be introduced into legal proceedings as a set-off.[183] That was so notwithstanding that the charterers had asserted their claim within the limitation period by deducting the amount of the claim from the freight. Their problem was that they had not taken the extra step of commencing a suit during the period so as to preserve the claim. Therefore, any formerly existing right of equitable set-off that they otherwise may have had was lost. A necessary consequence of that view is that a set-off had not already taken effect as an automatic extinction of the liabilities.

4.32   Philip Wood has presented a different analysis of the substantive nature of the defence.[184] Essentially, his analysis has two aspects. The first is that an equitable set-off (or, as he terms it, a transaction set-off) is a 'self-help' remedy, by which it is meant that it entitles the debtor to 'exercise' or 'declare' the set-off so as to bring about a discharge or payment of the cross-demands.[185] The second is that, if the debtor does not exercise the right in this manner, he may rely on the set-off as a defence in judicial proceedings, in which case the judgment for a set-off has a 'retroactive' effect to the date that the debtor's cross-claim accrued.[186] Taking the second point first, it is not necessary to have recourse to an artificial notion of retroactivity of the judgment. The substantive nature of the defence in the period before the demands have been extinguished by judgment or by agreement is adequately explained on the basis outlined above. In so far as the concept of 'self-help' is concerned, the *Aries Tanker* case provides authority for the view that a right of equitable set-off does not entitle the debtor himself to bring about a discharge of the cross-demands by setting them against each other. The charterers in that case had deducted the amount of their claim from the freight payable and tendered the balance before the expiration of the limitation period. The owners on the other hand made it clear that they did not accept the validity of the deduction.[187] Lord

---

[182]   [1989] 1 AC 1056, 1103. See also Mustill LJ in the Court of Appeal, at 1071.

[183]   Compare Lord Denning's reference to the *Aries Tanker* case in *Federal Commerce & Navigation Co Ltd v Molena Alpha Inc* [1978] 1 QB 927, 973–974, which is difficult to follow.

[184]   See generally Wood, *English and International Set-off* (1989) 111–12.

[185]   Wood, *English and International Set-off* (1989) 112 para 4–25, 663 para 11–24 (in the context of foreign currency claims) 784 para 14–56, 894 para 16–125, and 895 para 16–128. See also McCracken, *The Banker's Remedy of Set-off* (2nd edn, 1998), 120–1, 136, and Goode, *Principles of Corporate Insolvency Law* (2nd edn, 1997), 175–6. In *BICC plc v Burndy Corporation* [1985] 1 Ch 232, 254–255 Kerr LJ suggested that Burndy could have acted unilaterally to bring about a set-off so as to extinguish BICC's claim. However the case concerned legal set-off under the Statutes of Set-off (see Dillon LJ at 247 and Kerr LJ at 256 and 259), and presumably the comment was intended to apply in that context. It would not be correct in that context, however. See para 2.39 above.

[186]   Wood, *English and International Set-off* (1989) 112, cross-referring to para 2–192 *et seq*.

[187]   See [1977] 1 WLR 185, 187, *per* Lord Wilberforce.

Wilberforce (in a judgment with which Viscount Dilhorne, Lord Simon of Glaisdale, and Lord Edmund-Davies agreed[188]) rejected the argument that the charterer's action brought about a set-off. He said that:[189] 'The deduction of $30,000, unaccepted by the respondents, conferred no legal rights, and could not alter the legal position.' This was in the context of the primary ground for the decision in the *Aries Tanker* case, that a claim that has ceased to exist could not be relied on by way of set-off. The fact that the charterers had asserted their claim within the limitation period and purported to make a deduction did not affect his Lordship's view. Even if it were possible to have a set-off against a claim for freight, the unilateral deduction and the assertion of a right to make it were regarded as insufficient to bring about a cancellation of the cross-demands. That conclusion is also consistent with a comment earlier made by Megarry J in *Samuel Keller (Holdings) Ltd v Martins Bank Ltd.*[190] In response to an argument that a mortgagor's indebtedness to the mortgagee had been reduced as a result of the appropriation to it by the mortgagor of a damages claim available against the mortgagee, Megarry J said that 'the concept that the appropriation of an unliquidated claim to a mortgage debt by the mortgagor will effect a discharge nisi of that debt seems both novel and awkward'.[191] Admittedly, Robert Goff J in *The Kostas Melas*[192] described equitable set-off as a self-help remedy. However, he appears to have used that expression merely in the sense that the debtor was entitled to withhold payment of the debt to the extent of the equitable set-off, which accords with the view that, while the circumstances which support an equitable set-off exist, it is unconscionable for the creditor to regard the debtor as being indebted. It does not require a conclusion that the debtor's equitable right is such as to entitle him to act unilaterally to extinguish the cross-demands at law.

Sim v Rotherham Metropolitan BC[193] is susceptible to a similar explanation. A local **4.33** authority made a deduction from a teacher's salary because of a breach of contract by the teacher in failing to comply with a request to perform certain duties. The teacher issued a writ claiming payment of the amount of the deduction, and also

---

188 See also *per* Lord Salmon at [1977] 1 WLR 185, 196.
189 [1977] 1 WLR 185, 188.
190 [1971] 1 WLR 43.
191 [1971] 1 WLR 43, 47. In the Court of Appeal Russell LJ (at 51) agreed with that view. See also *Inglis v Commonwealth Trading Bank* (1972) 126 CLR 161, 165; *Mobil Oil Co Ltd v Rawlinson* (1981) 43 P & CR 221, 226; *Ashley Guarantee plc v Zacaria* [1993] 1 WLR 62, 69, 70. While Megarry J in *Samuel Keller* did not mention equitable set-off, the judgment of Russell LJ in the Court of Appeal suggests that he recognized that the cross-claim in that case would have been available by way of defence to an action for payment of the mortgage debt, and his approval of Megarry J's comment should be considered with that in mind. See the reference (at 49) to unconditional leave to defend, and also (at 49 and 51) to the earlier Court of Appeal decision in *Morgan & Son Ltd v S Martin Johnson & Co Ltd* [1949] 1 KB, 107, which was concerned with equitable set-off.
192 *SL Sethia Liners Ltd v Naviagro Maritime Corporation (The Kostas Melas)* [1981] 1 Lloyd's Rep 18, 26.
193 [1987] 1 Ch 216.

seeking a declaration that the local authority was not entitled to make a deduction from her salary. It was argued that, even if the teacher were in breach of contract, the only remedy of the local authority was to bring a separate action. Scott J rejected that view. He held that the teacher's failure to act constituted a breach, and that the resulting damages cross-claim gave rise to an equitable set-off which justified the deduction. The local authority had counterclaimed for various declarations, including that it was entitled to make the deduction,[194] and Scott J at the end of his judgment indicated that he was prepared to make the declarations sought by the local authority, subject to hearing counsel as to their form.[195] A declaration to the effect that the local authority was entitled to make a deduction may suggest that the local authority could act unilaterally to extinguish the cross-claims to the extent of the set-off. However that proposition was not suggested in the judgment. Scott J said that the cross-claim impeached the plaintiff's claim for salary, so that she could not recover her salary without taking into account the loss to the local authority.[196] The declaration was simply a recognition that it was unjust for the plaintiff to regard the local authority as being indebted to the extent of the deduction, and that as a matter of equity the local authority was entitled to tender the reduced amount. The declaration did not deal with the existence or otherwise of the common law claims giving rise to the equitable set-off at the time of a deduction.

Some problems

4.34   The debtor in most cases would be adequately protected by this analysis in terms of unconscionability. For example, the point is made below that the debtor would not be adversely affected by the expiration of the usual form of limitation period, which merely renders the cross-action unenforceable. He would, however, be at risk in a case such as *Aries Tanker*, where the debtor's cross-claim has a shorter limitation period than the creditor's claim, and the effect of the expiration of the period is to *extinguish* the cross-claim. In such a case the debtor would be well-advised to commence a suit so as to preserve the position, unless representations by the creditor would give rise to an estoppel so as to preclude him from relying on the time bar in any event. In substance that was the view of Lord Wilberforce in the *Aries Tanker* case.[197] A similar difficulty may arise when an equitable set-off is available to a debtor, and the creditor assigns the debt to a third party. The third-party assignee should take subject to the set-off in accordance with normal principles.[198] Consider, however, that the assignor becomes bankrupt. Because of the

---

[194]   For the declarations sought by the local authority, see the report of *Sim v Rotherham* at [1986] 3 All ER 387, 389.
[195]   [1987] 1 Ch 216, 263.
[196]   [1987] 1 Ch 216, 261–262.
[197]   [1977] 1 WLR 185, 189.
[198]   See para 17.22 below.

assignment the debt would no longer be an asset of the estate, and accordingly a set-off would not be available under the insolvency set-off section.[199] Normally this would not concern the debtor if he can still assert an equitable set-off against the assignee. But what if the assignee does not proceed against the debtor until after the assignor's discharge from bankruptcy? In that circumstance, Wood would appear to be correct in his view that the set-off would be lost.[200] The discharge would release the assignor from liability to the debtor,[201] in which case *Aries Tanker* suggests that the debtor would no longer have a right of set-off which he could assert against the assignee. The problem is not confined to equitable set-off. It may also apply in relation to the principle in *Cherry v Boultbee*,[202] as well as set-off under the Statutes of Set-off.[203] This seems an unfair result. It is justifiable in the case of set-off under the Statutes, which in any event is only a procedural defence,[204] but equitable set-off is substantive. At least in the *Aries Tanker* case the charterers could have preserved their position by commencing a suit within the limitation period, though that mechanism would not be available when an assignor has become bankrupt. One possibility would be to permit a debtor faced with this situation to apply before the discharge for a declaration[205] and a permanent injunction to restrain an action by the assignee on the assigned debt, although this is unsupported by authority. Moreover, an injunction operates *in personam*, and the debtor would require protection against the possibility of a further assignment by the assignee.

Wood has also expressed a concern in relation to the situation in which a trustee **4.35** in his capacity as such enters into a transaction with a third party pursuant to which the trustee incurs a debt, though a cross-claim for damages is available against the third party which is sufficiently closely connected to give rise to an equitable set-off.[206] While the trustee is personally liable for the debt, and the damages claim is an asset of the estate held on trust for the beneficiaries, the apparent lack of mutuality would not be a sufficient ground for denying an equitable set-off.[207] The situation posited by Wood is that the set-off is not 'declared' before the bankruptcy of the trustee or the third party. The concern is that the damages

---

[199] See para 11.06 below.
[200] Wood, *English and International Set-off* (1989) 894–5.
[201] Insolvency Act 1986, s 281.
[202] See para 14.18 above.
[203] See para 17.29 below.
[204] See paras 2.33–2.48 above.
[205] See eg *Sim v Rotherham Metropolitan BC* [1987] 1 Ch 216 (para 4.33 above), and in Australia *P Rowe Graphics Pty Ltd v Scanagraphix Pty Ltd* (NSW SC, Young J, 6 September 1988). On the other hand, Young J doubted that a similar declaration would be available in the case of a procedural defence such as that conferred by the Statutes of Set-off. In that situation, the defendant would be required to wait until he is sued before the right of set-off could be given effect. See also the discussion of *Parker v Jackson* [1936] 2 All ER 281 in paras 2.42–2.47 above.
[206] Wood, *English and International Set-off* (1989) 784.
[207] *Murphy v Zamonex Pty Ltd* (1993) 31 NSWLR 439. See para 17.90 below.

claim and the debt in such a case would have retained their separate identities, and accordingly they may not be available for a set-off under the insolvency set-off section because of lack of mutuality. However this should not present a problem if equitable set-off is analysed in the manner suggested above. If the cross-demands are sufficiently closely connected, the third party's title to the debt would be impeached such that it would be unconscionable for the third party to regard the trustee as a debtor, and this should continue to apply during the third party's bankruptcy or liquidation.[208] Further, while the leave of the court is required for the commencement of proceedings against a bankrupt or a company after a winding-up order has been made against it,[209] leave should be available when an injunction is sought to restrain the taking of action which is inconsistent with the substantive nature of the defence of equitable set-off. A similar result should follow in the converse situation in which the third party incurs the debt to the trustee but at the same time has a cross-claim available as an equitable set-off, and the trustee becomes insolvent. The third party should still retain his equitable set-off.[210]

Right to take action consequent upon default

4.36 The characterization of the defence as substantive can have important consequences. For example, a contract may entitle one party to take a particular course of action if the other party defaults in making a payment pursuant to the contract. If the other party indeed fails to pay but nevertheless has available a substantive defence of equitable set-off, the first party could not treat that other party as having defaulted,[211] and accordingly could not take the action which is available upon default.[212] The point is illustrated by *Federal Commerce and Navigation Co Ltd v*

---

[208] There is nevertheless authority to the contrary. See paras 6.16–6.20 below.

[209] Insolvency Act 1986, s 130(2) for company liquidation, and for bankruptcy s 285(3).

[210] Compare Wood, *English and International Set-off* (1989) 1055.

[211] In addition to the cases referred to below, see *Roadshow Entertainment Pty Ltd v (ACN 053 006 269) Pty Ltd* (1997) 42 NSWLR 462, 481. *Quaere* whether indeed it was correct to say that Roadshow was entitled, by virtue of equitable set-off, to withhold the payment due by it on 31 October 1993, given that the repudiation by CEL/Vision that led to the rescission did not occur until late November or early December when the receiver sold the business. While the New South Wales Court of Appeal accepted that there had been an anticipatory breach of contract by CEL/Vision by early October (see at 480–1), in order to be able to sue for damages for anticipatory breach there must have been an acceptance of the repudiation and thus a termination. See *Ogle v Comboyuro Investments Pty Ltd* (1976) 136 CLR 444, 450; *Johnstone v Milling* (1886) 16 QBD 460, 467. But termination did not occur until 6 December. The *Roadshow Entertainment* case should be compared to *Sloan Stanley Estate Trustees v Barribal* [1994] 2 EGLR 8, in which the Court of Appeal held that an equitable set-off was not available in respect of a cross-demand that was still contingent. Indeed, the awarding of interest to CEL/Vision in the *Roadshow Entertainment* case (see at 490) seems inconsistent with the view that Roadshow was entitled to withhold payment on the basis of an equitable set-off. See para 4.42 below in relation to interest.

[212] See Lord Denning in *Federal Commerce & Navigation Co Ltd v Molena Alpha Inc* [1978] 1 QB 927, 974, referred to with approval by Dillon LJ in *BICC plc v Burndy Corp* [1985] 1 Ch 232, 248–249. In *Ashley Guarantee plc v Zacaria* [1993] 1 WLR 62, 68 Nourse LJ agreed with counsel's

Molena Alpha Inc.[213] The Court of Appeal[214] held that a charterer of a vessel on a time charter has a right of equitable set-off entitling it to make a deduction[215] from the hire otherwise stipulated in the charter if the owner through its neglect or default has deprived the charterer of the use of the vessel, or has otherwise hindered or prejudiced the charterer's use, for example through a breach of a speed warranty.[216] The right arises on the due date for payment, and it does not merely provide a defence to an action at law for the payment of hire.[217] A charterer possessed of the right, and who pays less than the sum stipulated in the contract, is not considered to be in breach of contract. Therefore, when the time charter contains the usual provision whereby the owner can withdraw the vessel in the event of non-payment of hire, the charterer can tender a reduced amount in consequence of the cross-demand without bringing into existence the right of withdrawal.[218] If the owner does not accept the tender, it acts at its peril. It will be liable in damages if it withdraws the vessel. If on the other hand the defence were procedural, rather than substantive, the owner would have been entitled to withdraw the vessel because, until there had been a judgment for a set-off, the charterer would be regarded as having defaulted in payment. The same analysis may apply when a landlord asserts a right to re-take possession of the premises because of the tenant's failure to pay rent.[219] If an equitable set-off is available, the tenant may say that there was no such failure upon which the landlord can rely.[220] Similarly, when a

---

submission that if an equitable set-off was available in that case the company would not have defaulted in any of its obligations.

[213] [1978] 1 QB 927, affirmed on other grounds [1979] AC 757. When a contract entitles one party to terminate the contract in the event of a failure by the other party to pay any sums payable by it to the first party, it has been held in Victoria that there will not have been a failure by the second party to pay sums payable to the first party if the second party has an equitable set-off. See *Auspac Trade International Pty Ltd v Victorian Dairy Industry Authority* (Vic SC, Byrne J, 30 June 1993, at pp 67–71). Byrne J's observations on set-off were affirmed on appeal (22 February 1994, at pp 38 and 39).

[214] Lord Denning MR and Goff LJ, Cumming-Bruce LJ dissenting on the question whether there may be a set-off against hire.

[215] While the right in question was described as a right of deduction, the courts on other occasions have been reluctant to accept that 'deduction' describes equitable set-off. See eg *Connaught Restaurants Ltd v Indoor Leisure Ltd* [1994] 1 WLR 501, and generally paras 5.82–5.86 below.

[216] See [1978] 1 QB 927, 976, *per* Lord Denning MR, 981, *per* Goff LJ. Set-off in the context of charterparties is considered in paras 5.02–5.24 below.

[217] See also *Compania Sud Americana de Vapores v Shipmair BV (The Teno)* [1977] 2 Lloyd's Rep 289, 294 (explaining *Steelwood Carriers Inc v Evimeria Compania Naviera SA (The Agios Giorgis)* [1976] 2 Lloyd's Rep 192); *Santiren Shipping Ltd v Unimarine SA (The Chrysovalandou-Dyo)* [1981] 1 Lloyd's Rep 159; *SL Sethia Liners Ltd v Naviagro Maritime Corporation (The Kostas Melas)* [1981] 1 Lloyd's Rep 18, 26–27.

[218] See Lord Denning and Goff LJ at [1978] 1 QB 927, 974, 982. A similar analysis may apply when a shipowner claims to exercise a lien in the event of non-payment of hire. See *Santiren Shipping Ltd v Unimarine SA (The Chrysovalandou-Dyo)* [1981] 1 Lloyd's Rep 159.

[219] See also para 5.61 below in relation to a landlord's right to levy distress for non-payment of rent.

[220] *Federal Commerce & Navigation Co Ltd v Molena Alpha Inc* [1978] 1 QB 927, 974; *Televantos v McCulloch* [1991] 1 EGLR 123; *Tomlinson v Cut Price Deli Ltd* (1992) 38 FCR 490, 494–495;

debt is payable by instalments, and the contract provides that, in the event of a default in payment of one instalment the creditor may accelerate the debt so that the full amount is presently payable, there would not be a default for the purpose of the right to accelerate if the debtor is entitled to an equitable set-off in relation to the instalment which is otherwise due.[221]

4.37 In a case in Australia,[222] a bank provided a foreign currency facility to a customer on terms that, if the Australian dollar equivalent of the moneys from time to time 'owing to the bank' exceeded a certain amount, the bank could call for further security. The Full Court of the Federal Court[223] said that there was a serious question to be tried as to whether a cross-claim by the customer relating to the grant and management of the foreign currency facility gave rise to an equitable set-off, so as to call in question whether the amount 'owing to the bank' exceeded the stipulated level, and therefore to impeach the bank's right to call for further security. A lease may give an option to the tenant to renew the lease for a further term if it has complied with its obligations under the lease, including in the payment of rent. In a case in Queensland, the tenants admittedly had not tendered the rent stipulated in the lease. But since they had an equitable set-off, it was held that they had not breached the payment obligation and accordingly they were entitled to exercise the option.[224] This was the converse of the other instances referred to above, in that 'debtors' had to show that they were not in default before they could exercise a right (ie renew the lease), rather than that a right of a creditor to take a particular course of action depended upon whether the debtor had defaulted, though the principle nevertheless is the same.

MEK Nominees Pty Ltd v Billboard Entertainments Pty Ltd (1993) V Conv R 54–468. See also *British Anzani (Felixstowe) Ltd v International Marine Management (UK) Ltd* [1980] 1 QB 137; *BICC plc v Burndy Corp* [1985] 1 Ch 232, 249; *Connaught Restaurants Ltd v Indoor Leisure Ltd* [1994] 1 WLR 501; *Liangis Investments Pty Ltd v Daplyn Pty Ltd* (1994) 117 FLR 28, 36. For analogous situations in Australia, see *Novamaze Pty Ltd v Cut Price Deli Pty Ltd* (1995) 128 ALR 540, 544 (franchisor's contractual right to re-take possession consequent upon default by the franchisee), and *Parraville Pty Ltd v Madden Woods Pty Ltd* (Vic SC, Coldrey J, 2 April 1997) (vendor's right to possession following default in payment by the purchaser). Compare *Hazcor Pty Ltd v Kirwanon Pty Ltd* (1995) 12 WAR 62 and *Star Rider Ltd v Inntreprenneur Pub Co* [1998] 1 EGLR 53, in which a defence of equitable set-off was not made out. Note that different principles may apply in relation to a claim for possession by a mortgagee. See paras 4,89–4.107 below.

[221] This was assumed in *Marubeni Corp v Sea Containers Ltd* (QBD, Waller J, 17 May 1995), although it was held that the contract excluded the right to rely on an equitable set-off. Depending on the construction of the contract, a different result may follow in the case of a procedural defence of set-off under the Statutes of Set-off. See the discussion of *Shipton v Casson* (1826) 5 B & C 378, 108 ER 141 in para 2.41 above.

[222] *Westpac Banking Corp v Eltran Pty Ltd* (1987) 14 FCR 541.

[223] Fox and Burchett JJ, Northrop J dissenting.

[224] *Knockholt Pty Ltd v Graff* [1975] Qd R 88.

Estimating the value of the cross-claim

Since the cross-demand in these cases usually is for an unliquidated sum, a person **4.38**
asserting a right to an equitable set-off may have to make an estimate of the value
of his damages claim when the date arrives for payment of the sum stipulated in
the contract. For example, a charterer of a vessel may not be in a position to calculate with precision the value of a cross-demand available to it against the owner
for breach of a speed warranty when the next payment of hire becomes due. Goff
LJ in the *Federal Commerce* case[225] suggested that the charterer acts at its peril if it
pays less than the amount otherwise required by the contract. If the charterer is
wrong the owner is justified in withdrawing the vessel for non-payment of hire.
Lord Denning on the other hand considered that the charterer would not be in
default if it has quantified the loss by a reasonable assessment made in good
faith,[226] and this approach has since been favoured in other cases.[227]

Statute of limitation

The substantive nature of the defence of equitable set-off may assume importance **4.39**
in the case of a statute of limitation. The usual form of statute of limitation preserves the existence of the right but takes away the remedy of enforcing the right
by action at law.[228] Since the Statutes of Set-off merely perform a procedural function, a defence of set-off under the Statutes may only be based upon a debt that is
enforceable by action. Therefore, a debt owing by the plaintiff which is unenforceable as a result of the expiration of a limitation period would not give rise to
a defence under the Statutes.[229] Equitable set-off on the other hand is a substantive defence which does not require an order of the court for its enforcement.[230] As
a consequence, an equitable set-off may be asserted notwithstanding that the
cross-demand upon which it is based is no longer enforceable by action because of
the expiration of a limitation period.[231] Indeed, that approach has been adopted in

---

[225] [1978] 1 QB 927, 982.

[226] [1978] 1 QB 927, 975.

[227] *SL Sethia Liners Ltd v Naviagro Maritime Corporation (The Kostas Melas)* [1981] 1 Lloyd's
Rep 18, 26–27; *Santiren Shipping Ltd v Unimarine SA (The Chrysovalandou-Dyo)* [1981] 1 Lloyd's
Rep 159, 163–164. See also *Gilbert-Ash (Northern) Ltd v Modern Engineering (Bristol) Ltd* [1989]
AC 689, 712 in the context of building contracts ('amounts bona fide claimed'). Compare *Steelwood
Carriers Inc v Evimeria Compania Naviera SA (The Agios Giorgis)* [1976] 2 Lloyd's Rep 192.

[228] For example, the Limitation Act 1980, ss 2 and 5, which deal respectively with claims in tort
and contract, each stipulate that 'An action . . . shall not be brought' after the expiration of six years
from the date on which the cause of action accrued.

[229] See para 2.49 above.

[230] *SL Sethia Liners Ltd v Naviagro Maritime Corporation (The Kostas Melas)* [1981] 1 Lloyd's
Rep 18, 26.

[231] See Lord Denning in *Henriksens Rederi A/S v THZ Rolimpex (The Brede)* [1974] 1 QB 233,
245–246, 249 (though compare Cairns and Roskill LJJ at 254 and 264), and again in *Federal
Commerce v Molena* [1978] 1 QB 927, 973–974. See also *Sidney Raper Pty Ltd v Commonwealth
Trading Bank of Australia* [1975] 2 NSWLR 227, 236–240, *per* Moffitt P (though compare Glass

circumstances where an action brought on the cross-demand previously had been struck out for want of prosecution.[232] Furthermore, the availability of the defence should not be affected by section 35 (1) and (2) of the Limitation Act 1980, according to which a claim by way of set-off or counterclaim is deemed to be a separate action and to have been commenced on the same date as the original action. Unlike the procedural defence of set-off under the Statutes of Set-off, an equitable set-off does not require an action at law before it can be invoked. For that reason, section 35 would appear not to be relevant to equitable set-off, but would refer only to set-off under the Statutes.[233]

4.40 When questions of equitable set-off arise in relation to time bars, the conclusion that the availability of the defence survives the expiration of a limitation period assumes that the statute of limitation in question merely takes away the remedy without affecting the existence of the underlying right. If however the right itself is extinguished,[234] the circumstances necessary to support an equitable set-off would no longer exist, and the debtor would not be successful in an application for an equitable set-off as a defence to an action brought against him for payment of the debt. *Aries Tanker Corp v Total Transport Ltd*[235] illustrates that proposition.

JA at 255–256, which is difficult to follow); *AMP v Specialist Funding Consultants Pty Ltd* (1991) 24 NSWLR 326, 331–332; *Westdeutsche Landesbank v Islington BC* [1994] 4 All ER 890, 944–945 (Hobhouse J); *Philip Collins Ltd v Davis* [2000] 3 All ER 808, 831. There is also support for this proposition in the judgment of Lord Salmon in *Aries Tanker Corp v Total Transport Ltd* [1977] 1 WLR 185, 196–197 (on the assumption that English law permitted deductions from freight by way of equitable set-off). For the contrary view, see *NV Bureau Wijsmuller v The Owners of the MV Tojo Maru (The Tojo Maru)* [1970] P 21, 48; *Renner v Racz* (1971) 22 DLR (3d) 443. On the same principle a possessory lien may be exercised in respect of a statute barred debt, because the right to exercise the lien is not dependent upon an action at law. See for example *Spears v Hartly* (1800) 3 Esp 81, 170 ER 545 and *Higgins v Scott* (1831) 2 B & Ad 413, 109 ER 1196. See also the discussion of unenforceable claims in the context of the rule in *Cherry v Boultbee* (1839) 4 My & Cr 442, 41 ER 171 in paras 14.15–14.18 below. Compare *Strachan v Marriott* [1995] 3 NZLR 272, 291–292 in relation to the Property Law Act 1952 (NZ), s 92(6).

[232] *Filross Securities Ltd v Midgeley* [1998] 3 EGLR 43.

[233] See Lord Denning M.R. in *Henriksens Rederi A/S v THZ Rolimpex (The Brede)* [1974] 1 QB 233, 246 (though compare Cairns and Roskill LJJ at 254 and 264), and Hobhouse J at first instance in *Westdeutsche Landesbank v Islington BC* [1994] 4 All ER 890, 943, whose views were followed by the Court of Appeal in *Filross Securities Ltd v Midgeley* [1998] 3 EGLR 43 and by Jonathan Parker J in *Philip Collins Ltd v Davis* [2000] 3 All ER 808, 831. Compare the Convention on the Contract for the International Carriage of Goods by Road (CMR), Art 32(4), which stipulates that: 'A right of action which has become barred by lapse of time may not be exercised by way of counter claim or set-off.' *Impex Transport Aktieselskabet v A G Thames Holdings Ltd* [1981] 2 Lloyd's Rep 566 supports the view that this encompasses equitable set-off, but it was held subsequently in *R H & D International Ltd v IAS Animal Air Services Ltd* [1984] 1 WLR 573 that freight payable under a contract for the carriage of goods by road cannot be reduced by equitable set-off in any event. See para 5.06 below.

[234] See, for example, the Hague Rules, Art 3, r 6, which was in issue in *Aries Tanker Corp v Total Transport Ltd* [1977] 1 WLR 185. See also the Limitation Act 1969 (NSW), s 63, but note the effect of s 68A.

[235] [1977] 1 WLR 185. See para 4.31 above.

Arbitration and foreign jurisdiction clauses

The distinction between a substantive and a procedural defence may also be im- **4.41**
portant when a cross-demand asserted as a set-off is subject to an arbitration
clause or a foreign jurisdiction clause to which the court would give effect. In an
application by a claimant for summary judgment, leave to defend will not be
granted when a procedural defence of set-off is asserted under the Statutes of
Set-off, if the court in the claimant's action would refuse to try the merits of the
cross-claim because of the arbitration or foreign jurisdiction clause applicable to
the cross-claim. There is no such difficulty however when a substantive defence of
equitable set-off is in issue which impugns the claimant's title to sue.[236]

Interest

Consider the case of an interest-bearing debt. If the debtor has a valid claim for an **4.42**
equitable set-off, the principal sum upon which interest is payable is reduced to
the extent of the value of the cross-demand during the period while circumstances
exist which support an equitable set-off.[237] This is indicative of a substantive defence, as opposed to the form of procedural defence available under the Statutes
of Set-off.

Winding-up petition

If an equitable set-off is available to the debtor, the creditor will be restrained from **4.43**
presenting a winding-up petition because of failure to pay, given that the set-off
provides a substantive defence to the debtor.[238]

E. Discretion

A court of equity will only provide relief by way of set-off if the person claiming **4.44**
relief can show some equitable ground for being protected from his adversary's demand.[239] Therefore, an equitable set-off may be denied, notwithstanding that the

---

[236] *Aectra Refining and Marketing Inc v Exmar NV* [1994] 1 WLR 1634, 1649–1650; *Glencore Grain Ltd v Agros Trading Co* [1999] 2 Lloyd's Rep 410, 416–417; *Bim Kemi AB v Blackburn Chemicals Ltd* [2001] 2 Lloyd's Rep 93, 96 para 9.

[237] *Connaught Restaurants Ltd v Indoor Leisure Ltd* [1994] 1 WLR 501; *Newman v Cook* [1963] VR 659 (particularly the judgment of Hudson J at 676–677). See also *Barnett v Peter Cox Group Ltd* (1995) 45 Con LR 131. In *Wallis v Bastard* (1853) 4 De G M & G 251, 43 ER 503 the court found an implied agreement for a set-off so that interest was only payable on the balance. Compare *Axel Johnson Petroleum AB v MG Mineral Group AG* [1992] 1 WLR 270, 275 with respect to a counter-claim. Compare also the order made in *Roadshow Entertainment Pty Ltd v (ACN 053 006 289) Pty Ltd* (1997) 42 NSWLR 462, 490 in relation to interest under the Supreme Court Act (NSW).

[238] *McDonald's Restaurants Ltd v Urbandivide Co Ltd* [1994] BCLC 306. Compare *TSB Bank plc v Platts* [1998] 2 BCLC 1, 8–12.

[239] *Hanak v Green* [1958] 2 QB 9, 18–19. See para 4.02 above.

demands are otherwise sufficiently closely connected, if in the circumstances it would be unjust that a set-off should occur. Thus, the conduct of the parties may be relevant to the question of the availability of equitable relief by way of set-off.[240] The courts have given little guidance as to the circumstances in which this concept may apply, but in one case in Australia an equitable set-off was denied even though the claims were closely connected because the cross-claimant had failed to investigate, quantify or press his claim.[241]

4.45   If a charge granted by a company is void as against an administrator or a liquidator for non-registration under the Companies Act 1985, section 395, and the chargee is liable for damages for conversion as a result of a wrongful dealing with the property the subject of the void charge, the House of Lords in *Smith v Bridgend County BC*[242] held that the chargee could not set off in equity its claim against the company arising out of the transaction which gave rise to the charge against its damages liability. If a set-off were available, it would allow the chargee to exercise the very right which it could have exercised if the charge had been registered. Parliament has said that the charge is void if it is not registered, and in that circumstance equity would not intervene to protect the chargee from its failure to comply with the statute. Further, if a creditor is holding an asset belonging to the debtor, but without the benefit of a lien or other security, the creditor could not claim to retain the asset by way of a set-off against the debt,[243] in which case Lord Hoffmann said that the creditor could not improve his position in equity by wrongfully converting the property and attempting to set off the resulting damages liability.[244]

4.46   An equitable set-off may be denied if the quantum of the cross-claim is highly speculative,[245] or if the cross-claim depends upon the outcome of the taking of a long and complicated account,[246] or if the determination of the cross-claim would otherwise involve considerable delay such that the claimant would not be ad-

---

[240] *Galambos & Son Pty Ltd v McIntyre* (1974) 5 ACTR 10, 26; *Sydmar Pty Ltd v Statewise Developments Pty Ltd* (1987) 73 ALR 289, 296; *AMP v Specialist Funding Consultants Pty Ltd* (1991) 24 NSWLR 326, 329; *AWA Ltd v Exicom Australia Pty Ltd* (1990) 19 NSWLR 705, 712; *Walker v Department of Social Security* (1995) 56 FCR 354, 365. See also *Televantos v McCulloch* [1991] EGLR 123, in which it was argued that the defendant should be precluded from asserting an equitable set-off because of her conduct, though it was held that the conduct in question was not sufficient to have that effect.

[241] *APM Wood Products Pty Ltd v Kimberley Homes Pty Ltd* (NSW SC, Cole J, 17 February 1989), referred to in *AWA Ltd v Exicom Australia Pty Ltd* (1990) 19 NSWLR 705, 712.

[242] [2002] 1 AC 336, 351 para 36, *per* Lord Hoffmann, 360 para 76, *per* Lord Scott of Foscote.

[243] See para 3.02 above.

[244] [2001] 3 WLR 1347, 1358 para 36.

[245] *Star Rider Ltd v Inntreprenneur Pub Co* [1983] 1 EGLR 53, 56. See also *Abignano v Wenkart* (1998) 9 BPR 16,765, 16,774.

[246] *Rawson v Samuel* (1841) Cr & Ph 161, 41 ER 451, and see also *General Credits (Finance) Pty Ltd v Stoyakovich* [1975] Qd R 352.

equately compensated for being kept from his money for this period,[247] although in that circumstance interest may be an adequate remedy if it turns out that some or all of the claimant's claim is not reduced by a set-off.[248] Alternatively, terms may be imposed as a condition of equitable relief.[249] Thus, a defendant may be given leave to defend, or a claimant may be restrained from exercising a right consequent upon non-payment, only on condition that the defendant pays all or part of the claimant's claim into court, or provides some other acceptable form of security pending the determination of the cross-claim.[250] This has arisen particularly in the context of mortgages, where a mortgagor has sought to restrain the mortgagee from exercising his security rights consequent upon default on the basis of an alleged equitable set-off.[251]

If the claims are otherwise sufficiently closely connected, it is not necessary that **4.47** the defendant should have commenced proceedings against the claimant on the cross-claim.[252] Furthermore, in contrast to the position under the Statutes of Set-off,[253] a defendant will not be precluded from raising a cross-claim as a defence by way of equitable set-off merely because the parties had agreed that the cross-claim should be the subject of arbitration, or that it should be determined by the courts of a foreign jurisdiction.[254] Therefore, in an application by the claimant for summary judgment, the defendant in such a case may be granted leave to defend. Indeed, in the case of the usual arbitration agreement which provides for all 'disputes' to be referred to arbitration, the availability of an equitable set-off would mean that the claimant's claim is also in dispute, so that both the claim and the cross-claim must be referred.[255] This is a consequence of the substantive nature of the defence.[256]

---

[247] *Best v Hill* (1872) LR 8 CP 10, 15; *Roadshow Entertainment Pty Ltd v (ACN 053 006 269) Pty Ltd* (1997) 42 NSWLR 462, 489. See also *Rawson v Samuel* (1841) Cr & Ph 161, 179, 41 ER 451, 458; *Abignano v Wenkart* (1998) 9 BPR 16,765, 16,774.

[248] *Best v Hill* (1872) LR 8 CP 10, 15; *Roadshow Entertainment Pty Ltd v (ACN 053 006 269) Pty Ltd* (1997) 42 NSWLR 462, 489.

[249] *Roadshow Entertainment Pty Ltd v (ACN 053 006 269) Pty Ltd* (1997) 42 NSWLR 462, 489.

[250] In addition to the mortgage cases referred to below, see *General Credits (Finance) Pty Ltd v Stoyakovich* [1975] Qd R 352; *Tomlinson v Cut Price Deli Pty Ltd* (1992) 38 FCR 490. See also *Atterbury v Jarvie* (1857) 2 H & N 114, 121, 157 ER 47, 50, *per* Bramwell B, and *Gale v Luttrell* (1826) 1 Y & J 180, 195, 148 ER 636, 642, *per* Alexander CB.

[251] See paras 4.94–4.107 below.

[252] *McDonald's Restaurants Ltd v Urbandivide Co Ltd* [1994] 1 BCLC 306.

[253] See para 2.52 above.

[254] *Aectra Refining and Marketing Inc v Exmar NV* [1994] 1 WLR 1634, 1649, referring to *Gilbert-Ash (Northern) Ltd v Modern Engineering (Bristol) Ltd* [1974] AC 689 (esp at 720, 726). See also *Glencore Grain Ltd v Agros Trading Co* [1999] 2 Lloyd's Rep 410, 416–417.

[255] See eg *Federal Commerce & Navigation Co Ltd v Molena Alpha Inc.* [1978] 1 QB 927, 974, and generally para 1.08 above.

[256] See paras 4.29–4.43 above.

F. Mutuality

4.48 In *The Evelpidis Era*,[257] Mocatta J accepted as correct a submission by counsel that an equitable set-off where different parties are involved in the respective claims is 'a creature unknown to the law'. That statement is not accurate however, because, unlike set-off under both the Statutes of Set-off and the set-off section in the insolvency legislation, mutuality is not a strict requirement of equitable set-off.[258] There are indeed a number of instances where a court of equity considered that, because of special circumstances, it was appropriate that a set-off should occur despite the absence of mutuality. In *Ex parte Hanson*[259] one of two joint debtors on a bond given as security for a debt had only joined in the bond as a surety. It was held that the person who was the principal debtor could employ the joint debt in a set-off against a separate claim that he had against the creditor, despite the fact that a joint debt and a separate claim are not mutual.[260] *Hamp v Jones*[261] was a similar case. A judgment had been obtained against both Hamp and his bailiff for damages for wrongful distress. In addition, Hamp had a separate claim against the judgment creditor. Because the demands were not mutual they could not be set off at law. Hamp however had agreed to indemnify the bailiff on the judgment. Since Hamp was the party who would bear the ultimate burden of the judgment, it was held that he could set it off against his separate claim. Another example is *Vuillamy v Noble*.[262] Bankers had fraudulently sold a customer's property and applied the proceeds to their own use. The customer was indebted to the bank jointly with another person, and Lord Eldon allowed the customer to set off his separate claim arising from fraud against the joint debt. However, while those cases demonstrate that mutuality is not an absolute prerequisite to an equitable set-off, usually it would not be just or equitable that a set-off occur unless the same parties are beneficially interested in the respective claims.[263] Usually it is not just that a claim by A against B be set off against a liability of A to C, because this

---

[257] *First National Bank of Chicago v The West of England Shipowners Mutual Protection and Indemnity Association (Luxembourg) (The Evelpidis Era)* [1981] 1 Lloyd's Rep 54, 67.

[258] *Sidney Raper Pty Ltd v Commonwealth Bank of Australia* [1975] 2 NSWLR 227, 255; *CIBC v Tuckerr Industries Inc* (1983) 149 DLR (3d) 172, 175; *Coopers & Lybrand Ltd v Lumberland Building Materials Ltd* (1983) 150 DLR (3d) 411, 416; *Telford v Holt* (1987) 41 DLR (4th) 385, 394; *Westmex Operations Pty Ltd (in liq) v Westmex Ltd (in liq)* (1992) 8 ACSR 146, 153 (affirmed (1993) 12 ACLC 106); *Murphy v Zamonex Pty Ltd* (1993) 31 NSWLR 439, 464 (see para 17.90 below); *Walker v Department of Social Security* (1995) 56 FCR 354, 367. See also *Sovereign Life Assurance Co v Dodd* [1892] 2 QB 573, *Baillie v Edwards* (1848) 2 HLC 74, 9 ER 1020 and *Clarkson v Smith and Goldberg* [1926] 1 DLR 509, discussed in paras 6.18, 6.19 and 12.39 below.

[259] (1811) 18 Ves Jun 232, 34 ER 305.

[260] See ch 12 below.

[261] (1840) 9 LJ Ch 258.

[262] (1817) 3 Mer 593, 36 ER 228. See also *Ex parte Stephens* (1805) 11 Ves Jun 24, 32 ER 996 (joint and several debt), though note the explanation of that case in *Re Bank of Credit and Commerce International SA (No 8)* [1996] Ch 245, 265–270, which is criticized in paras 12.26–12.37 below.

[263] See eg *Savory Holdings Ltd v Royal Oak Mall Ltd* [1992] 1 NZLR 12, 14.

would involve using C's asset to satisfy B's debt. This includes the situation in which C is a wholly-owned subsidiary of B, if there is no agency relationship between those companies.[264]

Consider that A is induced to enter into a contract with C as a result of misrepresentations by B, such that A becomes indebted to C under the contract but has a damages claim against B. In the absence of special circumstances which would justify equitable intervention, those facts would not give rise to an equitable set-off. But if C subsequently should assign A's indebtedness under the contract to B, an equitable set-off may become available to A at that point, based on B's initial misrepresentations inducing the contract, so as to impeach B's right to enforce the assigned debt against A.[265] **4.49**

Guarantees and related parties

In the situation in which A has a claim against B and A is liable to C, if A becomes **4.50** insolvent, and B and C are related, it may well be to the advantage of B and C that there should be a set-off. However, the fact that one of the parties to a dealing has become insolvent on its own does not give rise to an equity sufficient to support an equitable set-off. Lord Cottenham emphasized this point in *Rawson v Samuel*.[266] If a set-off is to occur, the facts should support an equitable set-off irrespective of A's insolvency. The decision of Brownie J in the New South Wales Supreme Court in *Bank of New Zealand v Harry M Miller & Co Ltd*,[267] should be considered in light of that proposition. A lender entered into a loan agreement with the defendant debtor, as security for which a number of guarantees were obtained. Pursuant to the deed of guarantee, the guarantors promised to deposit their surplus funds with the lender on interest bearing deposits, and the lender was authorized on the happening of an event of default to appropriate the money so deposited in reduction of the debtor's debt arising from the loan. Subsequently the lender assigned both the debt and the benefit of the guarantees to the plaintiff. However, the deposits made by the guarantors remained with the lender. The amount paid by the plaintiff assignee for the assignment was the sum calculated as the principal debt then outstanding together with accrued interest, and no deduction was made for the deposits. The lender went into liquidation and, after that, the assignee brought this action against the debtor claiming the amount outstanding and interest. The debtor asserted as a defence an entitlement to an equitable set-off in respect of the amounts deposited with the lender by the guarantors.

---

[264] *Fuller v Happy Shopper Markets Ltd* [2001] 1 WLR 1681, 1686 para 11 (HSM being a wholly-owned subsidiary of N & P). See also *Hamilton Ice Arena Ltd v Perry Developmets Ltd* [2002] 1 NZLR 309 (claim against company and cross-claim by shareholders).

[265] *Horrobin v Australia & New Zealand Banking Group Ltd* (1996) 40 NSWLR 89, 100, and see also *Ling v Commonwealth* (1996) 68 FCR 180, 190–191.

[266] (1841) Cr & Ph 161, 175, 41 ER 451, 457.

[267] (1992) 26 NSWLR 48.

Brownie J held that the defence was available. He analysed the situation in two parts. First, he considered the position that would have applied if the deposits had been made by the debtor itself rather than by the guarantors. In such a case, if the lender had sued the debtor, his Honour said that there would have been available to the debtor a substantive defence by way of equitable set-off to the extent of the deposits made, since the cross-claim in respect of the deposits raised an equity which impeached, or was essentially bound up with or went to the root of, the lender's title to the claim against the debtor, and it flowed out of and was inseparably connected with the dealing and the transactions which gave rise to the lender's claim. Further, his Honour said that an assignee would have taken subject to this equity available against the lender/assignor.[268] In fact, the guarantors rather than the debtor had made the deposits, and his Honour then considered whether this made any difference to the result. He concluded that it did not. Admittedly there was a lack of mutuality, since the lender had a claim against the debtor but was subject to a cross-claim from the guarantors in respect of the deposits, though, as his Honour noted, mutuality is not an essential requirement of an equitable set-off. The important point was that the lender had agreed to advance the money to the debtor upon terms which included the taking of the guarantee and the guarantors agreeing to deposit and keep deposited their surplus funds, with a right in the lender upon the happening of an event of default to appropriate those funds towards satisfaction of the debt owing by the debtor. The deposits were said to be inseparably connected with the obligations arising out of the loan agreement. Accordingly, Brownie J concluded that an equitable set-off was available to the debtor and the guarantors in respect of the deposits,[269] notwithstanding the lack of mutuality,[270] and the assignee took subject to this equity.

4.51 Was it appropriate to allow an equitable set-off in the *Harry M Miller* case when different parties were involved in the claims, notwithstanding that the claims arose out of and were inseparably connected with the same transaction? In *Lord v Direct Acceptance Corp Ltd*[271] the New South Wales Court of Appeal expressed 'considerable doubt' as to the correctness of Brownie J's decision.[272] The substance of the agreement in the *Harry M Miller* case was that the debtor was primarily liable to discharge the debt, though the lender could apply the deposits in satisfaction of the debt if default occurred. The lender was authorized to apply the

---

[268] See paras 17.22–17.27 below.

[269] Brownie J acknowledged ((1992) 26 NSWLR 48, 56) that some adjustment may have had to be made as between the debtor and the guarantors, but he said that the question did not arise for decision in the proceedings before him.

[270] Because of the assignment, and the consequent lack of mutuality, the insolvency set-off section did not apply, and for this reason the case is distinguishable from *M S Fashions Ltd v Bank of Credit and Commerce International* [1993] Ch 425. See para 12.23 below.

[271] (1993) 32 NSWLR 362.

[272] (1993) 32 NSWLR 362, 371.

deposits, but it was not required to do so. It had a discretion in that regard. If it did not do so, the deposits would be repaid to the guarantors if and when the principal debt was repaid. On the other hand, the effect of allowing an equitable set-off to the principal debtor in relation to the deposits was to override the agreement between the parties, by requiring the application of the deposits against the debt and making the guarantors primarily liable to the extent of their deposits. As Sheller JA noted in delivering the judgment of the Court of Appeal, there was no equity in that result.[273] The English Court of Appeal expressed a similar sentiment in *Re Bank of Credit and Commerce International SA (No 8)*[274] in the context of insolvency set-off, commenting that to allow the principal debtor to compel the creditor to look to the surety rather than to his own personal liability (or vice versa) would invert the ordinary rule of priorities between the creditor, the surety and the principal debtor.[275] As it turned out, because of the insolvency of the lender and the assignment of the loan, a set-off would have benefited the guarantors in the *Harry M Miller* case, since the guarantors and the debtor were closely associated, and it was not in their interests that the debtor should be liable to pay the principal debt in full and that the guarantors be confined to a dividend in respect of their deposits. Nevertheless, the mere fact of insolvency is not a sufficient justification for allowing an equitable set-off.[276] If the intention was that the guarantors should be primarily liable to the extent of their deposits, that should have been made clear in the agreement.

A deposit as security, where the depositor is not personally liable

The facts in issue in *Lord v Direct Acceptance* were similar to those in the *Harry M* **4.52**
Miller case, though the case differed in that the person providing the deposit as security for the loan to the borrower had not assumed a personal liability, whether as guarantor or by agreeing to be jointly and severally liable. Direct Acceptance lent money to Bonnie Breck Pty Ltd secured by a guarantee given by the appellant. In addition, another company associated with the appellant, Me and Angus Pty Ltd, placed a sum on deposit with Direct Acceptance, on terms that it could not be withdrawn until the principal debt was repaid in full, and Direct Acceptance was authorized in its discretion to set off and appropriate the deposit in total or partial satisfaction of the principal debt. Me and Angus however was not personally liable for the debt, Direct Acceptance's rights as against that company being confined to the deposit. When Bonnie Breck defaulted in repayment of the loan Direct Acceptance sued the appellant on the guarantee, whereupon the appellant

---

[273] See the discussion at (1993) 32 NSWLR 362, 369.
[274] [1996] Ch 245, 256. See para 4.53 below.
[275] In the context of insolvency set-off, compare the situation in which the surety contracted on the basis of being a principal debtor. See *M S Fashions Ltd v Bank of Credit and Commerce International* [1993] Ch 425, for which see para 12.23 below.
[276] *Rawson v Samuel* (1841) Cr & Ph 161, 175, 41 ER 451, 457.

asserted that the deposit should be set off against the debt so as to reduce his liability as guarantor. The impetus for this was that Direct Acceptance was in liquidation so that, if the deposit was not applied against the loan, the appellant would be liable for the full amount of the debt under the guarantee, and Me and Angus would be confined to a proof in the liquidation in respect of the deposit. The New South Wales Court of Appeal held that there was no set-off. In the first place, there was nothing in the terms of the contract governing the deposit which required Direct Acceptance to apply the deposit in reduction of the debt. On the contrary, the deposit was expressed not to be repayable until the loan was repaid, and the right to set off the deposit was given to Direct Acceptance 'in its absolute discretion'. Nor did the insolvency set-off section apply, since the demands were not mutual.[277] While Me and Angus was a creditor of Direct Acceptance in relation to the deposit, it was not liable to Direct Acceptance, so that it was not a case of cross-demands which could be set against each other to produce a balance.[278] Moreover, for the reason noted above in relation to the *Harry M Miller* case, it was not an appropriate case for an equitable set-off. Sheller JA said that he had difficulty in discerning a basis for saying that Direct Acceptance's title to demand payment from the appellant guarantor was impeached because of a debt owing by Direct Acceptance to a third party representing moneys deposited to secure repayment of the principal debt, when the agreement stated that Direct Acceptance was not required to repay the deposit unless and until the principal debt was paid in full.[279] To allow a set-off would override the terms on which the moneys were deposited and make the depositor primarily liable to discharge the debt.[280] In support of an equitable set-off the appellant relied on the *Harry M Miller* case, though the Court of Appeal doubted the correctness of that decision.[281] In any event, the *Harry M Miller* case was distinguishable because, unlike the depositors in that case, the depositor in *Lord v Direct Acceptance* had not assumed a personal liability for the debt which could be the subject of a set-off against the deposit.[282]

4.53 In England, circumstances similar to those in *Lord v Direct Acceptance* later arose for consideration in *Re Bank of Credit and Commerce International SA (No 8)*.[283] A bank lent money to a customer secured by a deposit made by a third party which was 'charged' with repayment of the loan, though without the third party having provided a guarantee or other personal covenant as to repayment. The bank subsequently went into liquidation. The liquidator declined to apply the deposit against the loan, preferring to proceed against the customer and to confine the

---

[277] See ch 11 below.
[278] (1993) 32 NSWLR 362, 373.
[279] (1993) 32 NSWLR 362, 367–368.
[280] (1993) 32 NSWLR 362, 369, 371.
[281] (1993) 32 NSWLR 362, 371.
[282] (1993) 32 NSWLR 362, 369.
[283] [1998] AC 214, affirming [1996] Ch 245, CA.

depositor to a proof in the liquidation. The House of Lords held that there was a lack of mutuality which prevented a set-off under the insolvency set-off section.[284] Equitable set-off was not in issue before their Lordships, but it was considered by the Court of Appeal, which rejected an argument that an equitable set-off was available in that case in circumstances that were outside the scope of the insolvency set-off section.[285] The better view is that equitable set-off is not confined by the insolvency section, and that in an appropriate case an equitable set-off may be available in bankruptcy or company liquidation in circumstances where the statutory right does not apply.[286] Nevertheless, consistent with the view earlier expressed by the New South Wales Court of Appeal in *Lord v Direct Acceptance Corp*, the decision in *BCCI (No 8)* not to allow an equitable set-off would seem correct.

In a case such as *BCCI (No 8)*, it has been suggested that it may be possible to support an equitable set-off on the basis of the decision of the House of Lords in 1848 in *Baillie v Edwards*.[287] In that case, Baillie had a life interest in an estate in Jamaica. Innes had made advances in respect of the estate to the extent of some £8,000, on terms that Baillie should not be personally liable for them but that Innes would look only to the estate for repayment. Innes accordingly had a charge or lien on the estate for that amount. In addition, Innes was indebted to Baillie personally in the amount of £11,884. Baillie instituted a suit in equity against Innes seeking redemption of the estate. Innes became bankrupt, whereupon his assignees in bankruptcy were joined as defendants. The House of Lords held that Baillie was entitled to have Innes' claim against the estate for £8,000 paid and satisfied by the application of a sufficient part of the £11,884 due from Innes to Baillie,[288] and on that basis Baillie was entitled to have the estate restored to him. The result could not have been supported on the strict legal principles of set-off of mutual debts and demands, since there was not mutuality. While Innes was indebted to Baillie personally, Innes' claim was against the estate.[289] Rather, counsel for Baillie justified it on the ground that it was in the nature of an equitable set-off.[290] He argued successfully in the House of Lords that Baillie was entitled to say that, although he was not personally liable in respect of Innes' charges against the estate, he could require that the charges be paid out of the moneys that Innes owed him.[291] Based on that

4.54

---

[284] See also *Lord v Direct Acceptance* (1993) 32 NSWLR 362 (above), and para 12.38 below.

[285] [1996] Ch 245, 265–270. Compare *Clarkson v Smith and Goldberg* [1926] 1 DLR 509. See para 12.39 below

[286] There is nevertheless authority to the contrary. See paras 6.16–6.20 below.

[287] (1848) 2 HLC 74, 9 ER 1020. See Berg, 'Liquidation Set-off: The Mutuality Principle and Security over Bank Balances' [1996] LMCLQ 176.

[288] See the terms of the order at (1848) 2 HLC 74, 86–87, 9 ER 1020, 1025.

[289] Lord Lyndhurst earlier had emphasized lack of mutuality as a reason for disallowing a set-off, his Lordship's decision to that effect being the subject of a successful appeal to the House of Lords in this proceeding. See *Baillie v Innes* (1845) 14 LJ Ch 341, 343.

[290] (1848) 2 HLC 74, 79, 9 ER 1020, 1022.

[291] See Bethell's argument at (1848) 2 HLC 74, 78–79, 9 ER 1020, 1022.

decision, it has been suggested that the depositor in *BCCI (No 8)*, although not personally liable for the borrower's debt, similarly may have been entitled to require BCCI's liquidators to satisfy the debt out of the sum which BCCI owed to the depositor, and to assign to him their claim against the Borrower. *Baillie v Edwards* would not appear to justify that result, however. In the first place, *Baillie v Edwards* was concerned with the redemption of an estate and the determination of the amount required to be paid in order to take the estate free of an equitable lien. The point in issue in *BCCI (No 8)*, on the other hand, was not the redemption of the deposit charged in favour of the bank, but rather whether the deposit should be applied in a particular way. Further, pursuant to the agreement governing the deposit in *BCCI (No 8)*, the depositor had limited its rights in relation to the deposit by charging it in favour of the bank. The bank was not obliged to release the deposit until the principal debt was paid in full, and it was empowered, but not obliged, to apply the deposit in reduction of the debt. In contrast, Baillie's rights in relation to the money owing to him by Innes were not limited.

G. The Same Contract

4.55   Lord Cottenham emphasized in *Rawson v Samuel*[292] that it is not sufficient for an equitable set-off that both demands arose out of the same contract, a view that the courts generally have continued to espouse.[293] Equally, though, it is not an essential requirement of an equitable set-off that the claim and the cross-claim should have originated in the same contract,[294] notwithstanding occasional statements

---

[292] (1841) Cr & Ph 161, 178, 41 ER 451, 458.

[293] *Government of Newfoundland v Newfoundland Railway Co* (1888) 13 App Cos 199, 212; *Covino v Bandag Manufacturing Pty Ltd* [1983] 1 NSWLR 237, 238; *Atlantic Lines & Navigation Co Inc v The Ship 'Didymi' (The Didymi)* [1988] 1 Lloyd's Rep 97; *Bank of Boston Connecticut v European Grain and Shipping Ltd* [1989] 1 AC 1056, 1102; *Grant v NZMC Ltd* [1989] 1 NZLR 8, 13; *AWA Ltd v Exicom Australia Pty Ltd* (1990) 19 NSWLR 705, 712; *Lambert Pty Ltd v Papadatos Pty Ltd* (1991) 5 ACSR 468, 470; *Westwind Air Charter Pty Ltd v Hawker De Havilland Ltd* (1990) 3 WAR 71. Compare *Westacott v Bevan* [1891] 1 QB 774, 780; *Parsons v Sovereign Bank of Canada* [1913] AC 160, 166, PC; *R M Douglas Construction Ltd v Bass Leisure Ltd* (1990) 53 BLR 119, 133. Compare also *Roadshow Entertainment Pty Ltd v (ACN 053 006 269) Pty Ltd* (1997) 42 NSWLR 462, 482, although the comment regarding an assignee taking subject to unliquidated cross-claims arising out of the same contract should be considered in the context of a proposition that has found favour in Australia, that an assignee (including a secured creditor under a crystallized floating charge) may take subject to a counterclaim available to the debtor against the assignor which arises out of the same contract as the assigned debt, whether or not it would have given rise to an equitable set-off as between the assignor and the debtor. See the discussion of *Roadshow Entertainment* in para 4.27 above.

[294] *Galambos & Son Pty Ltd v McIntyre* (1974) 5 ACTR 10, 26; *The Angelic Grace* [1980] 1 Lloyd's Rep 288; *British Anzani (Felixstowe) Ltd v International Marine Management (UK) Ltd* [1980] 1 QB 137; *Banco Central SA v Lingoss & Falce Ltd (The Raven)* [1980] 2 Lloyd's Rep 266, 272; *Coba Industries Ltd v Millie's Holdings (Canada) Ltd* [1985] 6 WWR 14; *Grant v NZMC Ltd* [1989] 1 NZLR 8; *National Westminster Bank plc v Skelton* [1993] 1 WLR 72, 76; *Bim Kemi AB v Blackburn Chemicals Ltd* [2001] 2 Lloyd's Rep 93, 100 paras 29 and 30. See also *Melville v Grapelodge Developments Ltd* (1978) 39 P & C R 179. In *Hanak v Green* [1958] 2 QB 9, 31 Sellers

that may suggest the contrary.[295] The crucial question, according to the formulation approved by the House of Lords in the *Bank of Boston* case,[296] is whether the cross-claim is inseparably connected with the transaction that gave rise to the claim, or alternatively, in the traditional formulation, whether the claims are so closely connected that the title of the claimant to prosecute his demand is impeached. While the fact that the claim and the cross-claim each arose under different contracts is a factor to be considered in relation to the question whether there is a sufficient connection, it is not conclusive. An example is *Bim Kemi AB v Blackburn Chemicals Ltd*,[297] to which reference was made earlier.[298] Another example is *The Angelic Grace*.[299] The owners of a vessel had let the vessel under three consecutive charterparties to the same charterers. When the vessel was redelivered after the expiration of the third charter it contained a large quantity of bunkers for which the owners were liable to reimburse the charterers. However the owners had a cross-claim for stevedore damage occurring during the currency of both the second and the third charterparties for which the charterers were liable under the terms of the charterparties. Lord Denning and Waller LJ considered that the claim and cross-claim under the charters were so closely connected that it would be a case for equitable set-off. The three charterparties in this case involved the same vessel being chartered to the same charterers over a continuous period. In effect they were all a part of the same transaction. The decision illustrates the difference between the modern and the traditional approaches to equitable set-off. While the cross-claim for stevedore damage could be said to have been inseparably connected with the same transaction which gave rise to the claim, it is not easy to see how one claim could be said to be impeached by the other within Lord Cottenham's traditional formulation in *Rawson v Samuel*.[300] Nevertheless, the

LJ considered that a set-off could proceed where the cross-claim was 'closely associated with and incidental to the contract'. In *Telford v Holt* (1987) 41 DLR (4th) 385, 401 the Canadian Supreme Court said that the debts in that case could only be set off if they arose out of the same contract or closely related contracts.

[295] See eg *Provident Finance Corp Pty Ltd v Hammond* [1978] VR 312, 321.

[296] [1989] 1 AC 1056. See para 4.15 above.

[297] [2001] 2 Lloyd's Rep 93.

[298] See para 4.19 above.

[299] *Japan Line Ltd v Aggeliki Charis Compania SA (The Angelic Grace)* [1980] 1 Lloyd's Rep 288. See also *Parsons v Sovereign Bank of Canada* [1913] AC 160; *Kaps Transport Ltd v McGregor Telephone & Power Construction Co Ltd* (1970) 73 WWR 549 (in which the set-off claimed in respect of the damage to the appellant's equipment does not appear to have been confined to the claim for the price of the trucking services relating to the particular contract for the carriage of that equipment); *John Dee Group Ltd v WMH (21) Ltd* [1997] BCC 518, 531 (referring to *Business Computers Ltd v Anglo-African Leasing Ltd* [1977] 1 WLR 578, 585).

[300] Stone J in the Canadian Federal Court of Appeal in *Atlantic Lines & Navigation Co Inc v The Ship 'Didymi' (The Didymi)* [1988] 1 Lloyd's Rep 97, 105 appears not to have been entirely comfortable with the view that *The Angelic Grace* was an appropriate case for an equitable set-off.

principle that in appropriate circumstances claims under separate contracts can give rise to an equitable set-off would seem to be correct.

4.56   If on the other hand separate contracts in truth each involve separate transactions, a set off generally should not be allowed.[301] This brings into question *Bankes v Jarvis*.[302] The plaintiff's son bought a veterinary surgeon's practice from the defendant. The defendant was lessee of a house used in connection with the practice, and at the time of the sale he also assigned the lease to the plaintiff's son, who covenanted to pay the rent and perform the covenants in the lease and also to indemnify the defendant against all claims arising thereunder. Some six years later the plaintiff's son left the country, having given the plaintiff authority to sell the practice. The plaintiff then sold it back to the defendant. When the plaintiff sued for the balance of the purchase price the defendant sought to set off a cross-claim for damages against the plaintiff's son for breach of the covenant to indemnify against claims arising under the lease. It was held that, if the son instead had been the party suing, the defendant would have been entitled to the set-off, and that the plaintiff suing as a trustee accordingly should also be subject to this defence.[303] Though Morris LJ later commented in *Hanak v Green*[304] that this 'conclusion seems to me to be clearly correct and obviously fair', the transactions appear to have been totally separate and distinct, and it is not at all clear what the justification for a set-off was.[305]

H. Creditor's Conduct Affecting Debtor's Ability to Pay

4.57   It is sometimes asserted that a creditor's own conduct is the cause of the debtor's inability to pay, and that the resulting cross-claim against the creditor accordingly should be set off against the debt.

---

[301]   See in this regard *Minshull v Oakes* (1858) 2 H & N 793, 157 ER 327; *Indrisie v General Credits Ltd* [1985] VR 251, 254; *Peninsular and Oriental Steam Navigation Co v Youell* [1997] 2 Lloyd's Rep 136. See also the fact situation considered by Isaacs J in *Tooth v Brisbane City Council* (1928) 41 CLR 212, 223–224. A claim for an indemnity under a policy of insurance and a cross-claim for premiums due on other policies covering other subject-matters are not sufficiently connected for an equitable set-off. See *E Pellas & Co v Neptune Marine Insurance Co* (1879) 5 CPD 34, and also *Baker v Adam* (1910) 15 Com Cas 227.

[302]   [1903] 1 KB 549.

[303]   Wills J in his judgment ([1903] 1 KB 549, 552) said that he had some difficulty in seeing how the plaintiff even had standing to sue in this case, though he declined to express a decided opinion on the point.

[304]   [1958] 2 QB 9, 24.

[305]   Channell J in *Bankes v Jarvis* [1903] 1 KB 549, 553 said that 'the Judicature Act, and more especially the rules, distinctly put an unliquidated claim on the same footing as a liquidated claim for the purpose of set-off'. This is clearly incorrect (see *McDonnell & East Ltd v McCregor* (1936) 56 CLR 50, 61–62; *Galambos & Son Pty Ltd v McIntyre* (1974) 5 ACTR 10, 19), and it may detract from the weight which otherwise would be attached to his Lordship's judgment.

An early instance is *Beasley v Darcy*.[306] A landlord brought an action for ejectment **4.58** against the tenant for non-payment of rent. The tenant however had a claim for damages against the landlord for cutting down timber on the demised land. The House of Lords affirmed a decree granting relief from forfeiture to the tenant, on paying what was due for rent after deducting the damages. The set-off in this case has been explained on the ground that the landlord's trespass resulted in a loss of the produce of the land to the tenant, thereby rendering the land of less value and affecting the tenant's ability to get rent out of it.[307]

It should not suffice for an equitable set-off that the creditor's own conduct af- **4.59** fected the debtor's ability to pay the debt.[308] There must be a connection between the demands. In *Beasley v Darcy*, it may be inferred that the rent was set on the basis that the land in question was income-producing, so that the rent was to come out of the land. There was a clear connection between the claim for rent and the cross-claim in respect of the landlord's actions which reduced the tenant's ability to pay rent. There was also a sufficient connection in *Popular Homes Ltd v Circuit Developments Ltd*.[309] The plaintiff, a building contractor, bought some land from the defendant with the intention of building some town houses on it, the unpaid price being secured by a mortgage in favour of the defendant. As part of the consideration for the purchase, the defendant also agreed to provide development finance so as to enable the plaintiff to complete the construction. The defendant defaulted in its obligation to provide the finance, as a result of which the plaintiff was unable to complete the project and to repay the mortgage debt. Barker J in the New Zealand Supreme Court held that the plaintiff's resulting damages claim could be set off against the debt. The cross-claims were based on the same contract, and moreover the defendant's default was a direct cause of the plaintiff's inability to repay. Similarly, in *Doherty v Murphy*[310] a financier agreed to provide finance for the purpose of a property development. The financier however was unable to make all the required payments, as a result of which work ceased on the project. The borrower was unable to sell any part of the uncompleted development, and was unable to repay the amount outstanding to the financier.[311] In a summary judgment application, the Appeal Division of the Supreme Court of Victoria held that the circumstances showed an arguable defence of equitable set-off.

---

[306] (1800) 2 Sch & Lef 403n. See the discussion of the case in *British Anzani (Felixstowe) Ltd v International Marine Management (UK) Ltd* [1980] 1 QB 137, 149–151.

[307] See Lord Redesdale in *O'Mahony v Dickson* (1805) 2 Sch & Lef 400, 412–413, and Bramwell B in *Stimson v Hall* (1857) 1 H & N 831, 835–836, 156 ER 1436, 1438.

[308] In Australia, see *Van Leeuwen v Bank of Western Australia Ltd* [2001] FCA 1826 at para 14. See also *Hamilton Ice Arena Ltd v Perry Developments Ltd* [2002] 1 NZLR 309, 318, 319.

[309] [1979] 2 NZLR 642.

[310] [1996] 2 VR 553.

[311] See [1996] 2 VR 553, 559–560.

4.60 Those cases should be compared to *United Dominions Corp Ltd v Jaybe Homes Pty Ltd*.[312] A vendor of land had agreed to provide finance to the purchaser to enable the purchaser to erect houses on the land for the purpose of sale. When the vendor defaulted in its obligation to provide the finance, Andrews J in the Queensland Supreme Court held that the resulting damages claim did not provide the purchaser with a defence to the vendor's claim for payment of the price. The agreement to provide finance was entered into after the agreement for the sale and purchase of the land, and in truth it was a separate transaction.[313] The circumstances in issue in *Cunningham v National Australia Bank Ltd*[314] similarly were insufficient to support an equitable set-off. Customers of a bank requested the bank to obtain a credit check on a company with whom they were proposing to do business. The bank obtained a favourable report and advised the customers, who entered into a contract with the company. Shortly after making the contract, the customers borrowed from the bank in order to acquire plant for the purpose of carrying out the contract. Subsequently the company failed, as a result of which the customers lost the benefit of the contract and were unable to repay the bank. They argued that they had a claim in damages against the bank for negligence and for misleading or deceptive conduct[315] in relation to the credit check, which should be set off against the outstanding loan. Jenkinson J in the Federal Court of Australia disagreed. It was not sufficient that the customers, to the knowledge of the bank, intended to discharge the loan with funds expected to be obtained from carrying out the contract. The subject of the loan had not been raised between the customer and the bank before the customers entered into the contract with the company, and it was not alleged that the bank's conduct induced the making of the contract of loan. The bank's title to sue on the loan therefore was not impeached by the cross-claim.

4.61 A debtor's inability to pay the debt may be due simply to the creditor's insolvency, in that the creditor is unable to pay an amount that it in turn owes to the debtor on a cross-claim. Insolvency without more, however, is not sufficient to give rise to an equitable set-off.[316]

I. Repudiation of a Contract

4.62 If a person suing for payment of a sum due under a contract has repudiated the contract, the resulting liability for damages ordinarily can be set off in equity

---

[312] [1978] Qd R 111.

[313] Similarly, in *Indrisie v General Credits Ltd* [1985] VR 251, 253–254, the principal debtor's cross-claim for damages for breach of the agreement to lend money was regarded as a separate transaction from that upon which the principal debtor was liable.

[314] (1987) 15 FCR 495.

[315] Contrary to the Trade Practices Act 1974 (Cth), s 52.

[316] *Rawson v Samuel* (1841) Cr & Ph 161, 175, 41 ER 451, 457.

against the claim for payment. This occurred in *Government of Newfoundland v Newfoundland Railway Co,*[317] where a contract for the construction of a railway line was repudiated by the contractor before completion, and the contractor's claim for payment in respect of the completed part was met by a cross-claim for damages arising from the repudiation.

Contracts requiring periodic performance

This may also apply in the situation in which a single contract requires perfor-   **4.63**
mance on a periodic basis. A damages claim arising from a repudiation of the contract may give rise to an equitable set-off against a claim for payments due under
the contract. In *Parsons v Sovereign Bank of Canada*[318] a company which operated
a paper mill had entered into various contracts with the appellant. Each contract
was for the periodic supply of quantities of paper, and each extended over a considerable period. During the currency of the contracts receivers were appointed by
the court to the company. After the appointment the appellant continued to send
orders for paper pursuant to the contracts, which the receivers duly accepted and
satisfied. Subsequently the receivers notified the appellant that they would not execute any more orders under the existing contracts, thereby repudiating the contracts. The appellant was then sued for the price of paper delivered to it. The Privy
Council[319] held that the amount sued for was due under the old contracts with the
company, rather than under new contracts made with the receivers. Further, the
company was responsible for the repudiation, and so the appellant was permitted
to set off its damages cross-claim arising from the breach. The set-off was allowed
notwithstanding that the orders in respect of which payment was sought had been
carried out, by the delivery of paper to the appellant. The judgment is open to criticism, in that it was assumed that it was sufficient for an equitable set-off that the
cross-claim for damages arose under the same contract as the claim for payment,[320]
whereas the courts on other occasions have emphasized that this is not sufficient.[321] Furthermore, it does not appear that the set-off against the debt for the
price of paper delivered was confined to the damages for the repudiation of the
particular contract pursuant to which the delivery occurred, or at least there was
no attempt to break down the claims in that manner. Nevertheless, the authority
of the *Parsons* case has not been questioned.[322]

---

[317] (1888) 13 App Cas 199.

[318] [1913] AC 160.

[319] Viscount Haldane, Lord MacNaghten, Lord Atkinson and Lord Shaw of Dunfermline.

[320] [1913] AC 160, 166.

[321] See para 4.55 above.

[322] The *Parsons* case was followed and applied by the New South Wales Court of Appeal in the context of a repudiation in *Roadshow Entertainment Pty Ltd v (ACN 053 006 269) Pty Ltd* (1997) 42 NSWLR 462, 483–484. The judgment is difficult to follow, *sed quaere* whether this was a case of a true equitable set-off, or alternatively an example of a proposition that has been put forward in Australia, that an assignee (including a secured creditor under a crystallized floating charge) takes

Repudiation of an overriding agreement

4.64 The *Parsons* case concerned a number of contracts, each for the periodic supply of goods, and the Privy Council in allowing a set-off emphasized the fact that the debts for the price and the damages claims for repudiation related to the original contracts. Alternatively, separate contracts may be entered into in the course of a trading relationship, but each contract is subject to an overriding agreement between the parties. If the overriding agreement is repudiated, may the resulting damages claim be set off against an indebtedness for the price of goods sold pursuant to the separate contracts? The question of set-off in this context has been the subject of two recent cases.

4.65 In *Dole Dried Fruit and Nut Co v Trustin Kerwood Ltd*,[323] the plaintiffs had appointed the defendants as their exclusive agent for importing the plaintiffs' goods into and distributing the goods in England. Subsequently the plaintiffs purported to terminate the agency agreement without notice, and proceeded to sue the defendants for the price of goods sold and delivered under a series of sale contracts. The defendants sought to set off their damages claim against the plaintiffs arising from the repudiation of the agency agreement. Lloyd LJ (with whom Beldam LJ concurred) said that the whole purpose and intent of the agency agreement was that the parties should enter into contracts for the purchase and sale of the plaintiff's goods, and therefore the sale contracts were concluded in fulfilment of the agency agreement. In those circumstances he was of the view, applying Lord Denning's formulation in *Federal Commerce v Molena*,[324] that the claims were sufficiently closely connected to make it unjust to allow the plaintiffs to claim the price of goods sold and delivered without taking into account the cross-claim.

4.66 The *Dole Dried Fruit* case should be compared to the later decision of the Court of Appeal in *Esso Petroleum Co Ltd v Milton*.[325] Esso was suing for the price of nine deliveries of petrol made to the defendant, who occupied and managed two petrol service stations under a licence agreement with Esso. Under the licence agreement, Esso agreed to sell to the defendant, and the defendant agreed to buy from Esso, his entire requirements for petrol. The sales took place in fulfilment of the licence agreement, and in that sense the licence agreement was similar to the agency agreement in the *Dole Dried Fruit* case. However a differently constituted

---

subject to a counterclaim available to the debtor against the assignor which arises out of the same contract as the assigned debt, whether or not it would have given rise to an equitable set-off as between the assignor and the debtor. See the discussion of *Roadshow Entertainment* in para 4.27 above. The *Parsons* case similarly was concerned with an assignment, the receivers having assigned the amounts due from the appellant to the Sovereign Bank of Canada. It was not suggested however that the assignment affected the availability of the set-off.

[323] [1990] 2 Lloyd's Rep 309.
[324] [1978] 1 QB 927, 974–975. See para 4.12 above.
[325] [1997] 1 WLR 938.

Court of Appeal[326] in *Esso v Milton* held that an equitable set-off was not available
to the defendant in respect of a cross-claim for damages for loss of future profit
(and for other future losses) as a result of an alleged repudiation by Esso of the licence agreement, the reason being that that there was an insufficient connection
between the cross-demands. Simon Brown LJ, with whom Sir John Balcombe
agreed on this point, commented:[327]

> At the point when those deliveries were made, there was no cross-claim at all in ex-
> istence and no loss yet suffered by the defendant. No case has been cited to us in
> which payment of a debt presently due has been required to await the resolution of
> a cross-claim for future losses. The mere fact that both claim and counterclaim arise
> out of a single trading relationship between the parties is in my judgment wholly
> insufficient to supply the close link necessary to support an equitable set-off.

The fact that no loss had been suffered at the date of delivery should not have been
a sufficient reason to preclude an equitable set-off. Rather, the comment should
be considered in the context that there was no connection between the claims
other than that they arose out of a single trading relationship, which was thought
to be insufficient to found an equitable set-off.

The similarity between the *Dole Dried Fruit* case and *Esso v Milton* is evident, and   **4.67**
in both cases reference was made to Lord Denning's judgment in *Federal
Commerce v Molena*. The results were different, however. In *Esso v Milton* the
losses sought to be set off were future losses, whereas in the *Dole Dried Fruit* case
the report refers simply to a damages claim arising from the repudiation of the
agency agreement, without identifying precisely the nature of the damages sought
to be set off. It may be assumed, however, that the damages for repudiation would
have included future loss. In concluding that the claims in *Esso v Milton* were insufficiently connected, Simon Brown LJ also emphasized that the deliveries of
petrol were to be converted immediately into cash through forecourt sales, so that,
as he said, even less reason existed for the defendant to postpone the discharge of
his debt until after the cross-claim was litigated.[328] That point may not have had
the same cogency in the *Dole Dried Fruit* case. Nevertheless the tenor of Simon
Brown LJ's judgment suggests a more rigorous approach to the question of set-off
than that evident in the earlier decision. While there was a connection between
the demands in the *Dole Dried Fruit* case, in the sense described by Lloyd LJ,[329]
that connection, as the Court of Appeal later observed in *Peninsular and Oriental
Steam Navigation Co v Youell*,[330] would not appear to have been such as to give rise
to an impeachment of the plaintiff's title to sue. More recently, however, the

---

[326] Simon Brown and Thorpe LJJ, and Sir John Balcombe.
[327] [1997] 1 WLR 938, 951.
[328] [1997] 1 WLR 938, 951–952.
[329] See above.
[330] [1997] 2 Lloyd's Rep 136, 144, *per* Potter LJ, with whom Mummery and Nourse LJJ agreed.

Court of Appeal referred to the *Dole Dried Fruit* case with evident approval in *Bim Kemi AB v Blackburn Chemicals Ltd*,[331] the Court of Appeal in that case recognizing an equitable set-off in circumstances where the connection between the demands was described as 'less close' than that in the *Dole Dried Fruit* case.[332] Potter LJ, in delivering the judgment of the Court in *Bim Kemi*, commented that the formulation approved by the House of Lords in the *Bank of Boston* case[333] 'is apt to cover a situation where there are claims and cross-claims for damages in respect of different but closely connected contracts arising out of a long-standing trading relationship which is terminated'.[334] He went on to comment that this situation would not *per se* establish the requisite connection for an equitable set-off, but where it applies he said that in an appropriate case it may be manifestly unjust to allow one claim to be enforced without taking account of the other. The *Dole Dried Fruit* and *Bim Kemi* cases illustrate the tendency of English courts in recent times to adopt a more expansive view of the scope of equitable set-off.

J. Misrepresentation, Fraud, and Misleading or Deceptive Conduct

Misrepresentation inducing a contract

4.68 A question in respect of which there are conflicting views is whether a claim in tort for damages for fraudulent misrepresentation inducing a contract may be brought into account in an action for payment of a sum of money owing under the contract. Typically this may arise where the vendor of a business is suing for the price and the purchaser has a cross-claim for damages for fraud inducing the contract.

4.69 It has been held in the context of assignments of debts that an assignee does not take subject to a cross-claim for fraud inducing the contract under which the debt arose, the reason being, it is said, that this is not a claim arising under the contract, or for breach of the contract, but is a claim *dehors* the contract.[335] Since an assignee takes subject to rights of set-off available to the debtor against the assignor, but not mere counterclaims,[336] those cases may suggest that the damages claim similarly would not give rise to an equitable set-off in an action between the original

---

[331] [2001] 2 Lloyd's Rep 93, *per* Potter, Sedley and Jonathan Parker LJJ. See paras 4.19 and 4.20 above.

[332] [2001] 2 Lloyd's Rep 93, 102 para 37.

[333] See para 4.15 above.

[334] [2001] 2 Lloyd's Rep 93, 100 para 30.

[335] *Stoddart v Union Trust, Ltd* [1912] 1 KB 181; *Cummings v Johnson* (1913) 4 WWR 543; *Provident Finance Corporation Pty Ltd v Hammond* [1978] VR 312. See also *Birchal v Birch, Crisp & Co* [1913] 2 Ch 375, 379.

[336] A different view has been expressed in Australia. See para 17.05 below.

parties. There are two difficulties with that view, however.[337] The first is that it is contrary to the principle applied in bankruptcy, that a claim for damages for misrepresentation inducing a contract is not a mere personal tort but rather is a breach of the obligation arising under the contract, so that, even before the insolvency legislation was amended in 1986 to allow claims in tort to be proved in a bankruptcy, it could be employed in a set-off.[338] The second is that in any event it is not a prerequisite to an equitable set-off that the demands should have arisen under the same contract.[339] The better view is that a cross-claim available to a purchaser against the vendor for fraud inducing the purchaser to enter into the contract is capable of being set off in an action brought by the vendor for the price. While this has been rejected in New Zealand,[340] there is support for it in Australia.[341] To adopt the test approved by the House of Lords in the *Bank of Boston* case,[342] the cross-claim for damages would be inseparably connected with the transaction that gave rise to the claim.[343] The traditional impeachment tested espoused by Lord Cottenham in *Rawson v Samuel* would also appear to be satisfied. If the fraud induced the purchaser to enter into the contract, the purchaser in the absence of fraud presumably would not have contracted, in which case he would not have breached any contractual obligation to the vendor to tender a sum of money as payment of a purchase price. On this analysis it can be said that the vendor's own conduct contributed to the existence of the purchaser's liability to him, so as to impeach the vendor's title to his demand.[344] The argument for a set-off would be even stronger if the statements giving rise to the fraud also constitute a term of the contract.[345] Furthermore, for a set-off to occur it would not be

---

[337] In *Banco Santander SA v Bayfern Ltd* [2001] 1 All ER (Comm) 776 Waller LJ (at 780) noted that *Stoddart v Union Trust* [1912] 1 KB 181 has been criticized.

[338] *Jack v Kipping* (1882) 9 QBD 113; *Tilley v Bowman Ltd* [1910] 1 KB 745. In New South Wales, McLelland CJ in Eq in *Re NIAA Corp Ltd (in liq)* (NSW SC, 2 December 1994) questioned whether the claim in *Jack v Kipping* indeed was provable, and whether the insolvency set-off section therefore applied. Rather, he suggested that the set-off may have been an equitable set-off. Subsequently Charles JA in the Victorian Court of Appeal referred to that view in terms suggesting approval in *Aliferis v Kyriacou* (2000) 1 VR 447, 463 para 48. On the other hand, the High Court of Australia in *Gye v McIntyre* (1991) 171 CLR 609, 630–631 accepted *Jack v Kipping* as an authority on insolvency set-off. For the current position in bankruptcy and company liquidation in relation to claims in tort, see paras 8.44–8.47 below.

[339] See para 4.55 above.

[340] *Wilsons (NZ) Portland Cement Ltd v Gatx-Fuller Australasia Pty Ltd (No 2)* [1985] 2 NZLR 33 (in particular at 37–38).

[341] *Petersville Ltd v Rosgrae Distributors Pty Ltd* (1975) 11 SASR 433; *Altarama Ltd v Camp* (1980) 5 ACLR 513, 519–520; *AMP v Specialist Funding Consultants Pty Ltd* (1991) 24 NSWLR 326; *Tomlinson v Cut Price Deli Pty Ltd* (1992) 38 FCR 490, 494; *Re Kleiss, ex p Kleiss v Capt'n Snooze Pty Ltd* (1996) 61 FCR 436, 441. See also paras 4.74–4.77 below in relation to the Trade Practices Act 1974 (Cth), s 52. Compare *Provident Finance Corporation Pty Ltd v Hammond* [1978] VR 312, 318.

[342] [1989] 1 AC 1056. See para 4.15 above.

[343] See *Altarama Ltd v Camp* (1980) 5 ACLR 513, 519–520.

[344] See *Piggott v Williams* (1821) 6 Madd 95, 56 ER 1027, and para 4.04 above.

[345] As in *Sun Candies Pty Ltd v Polites* [1939] VLR 132.

necessary that the person who induced the contract was a party to it, if the benefit of the contract has since been transferred to that person.[346]

4.70 A party may have been induced to enter into a contract by a false representation that was not fraudulent, though the same principle should apply as for fraudulent misrepresentation. A resulting damages claims should be able to be employed in a set-off against a claim on the contract, the important point being that the party would not have entered into the contract but for the false representation.[347] This should also apply where the representation was contained in a collateral contract.[348] It should be the fact of the inducement, not the nature of the misrepresentation, that gives rise to the impeachment of title.

Fraudulent claim on a contract

4.71 The discussion in the preceding section concerned fraud inducing a contract. It should be compared to *Etablissement Esefka International Anstalt v Central Bank of Nigeria*,[349] in which the question instead related to an alleged fraudulent claim on a contract. The plaintiff made a claim on letters of credit issued by the defendant in respect of demurrage. Prior to the action the plaintiff had been paid various sums of money on the same letters of credit in respect of demurrage when there was evidence to suggest that the shipments in question had never taken place. As a result, the defendant appeared to have a cross-claim to recover this as money paid under a mistake of fact. In an application for a Mareva injunction, Lord Denning said that all the claims on the letter of credit should be considered as part of the one transaction, and that the cross-claim was so closely connected with the instant claim that it could well be a case for an equitable set-off.[350]

4.72 *Etablissement Esefka* should be compared to *Walker v Department of Social Security*,[351] a decision of the Federal Court of Australia. The Department had paid the appellant a sum by way of sickness benefits as a result of various fraudulent claims made by him. Subsequently he made a further claim for benefits, to which he was entitled. The Department said that the appellant's entitlement should be

---

[346] *Horrobin v Australia & New Zealand Banking Group Ltd* (1996) 40 NSWLR 89, 100.

[347] *Aquaflite Ltd v Jaymar International Freight Consultants Ltd* [1980] 1 Lloyd's Rep 36. See also *Box v Midland Bank Ltd* [1981] 1 Lloyd's Rep 434 (customer of a bank induced to draw on an overdraft as a result of negligent advice by a manager of the bank that further facilities would be made available).

[348] *Grant v NZMC Ltd* [1989] 1 NZLR 8. See also *British Anzani (Felixstowe) Ltd v International Marine Management (UK) Ltd* [1980] 1 QB 137.

[349] [1979] 1 Lloyd's Rep 445. See also *Black King Shipping Corp v Massie (The Litsion Pride)* [1985] 1 Lloyd's Rep 437, 518–519.

[350] Compare *Attorney-General v McLeod* (1893) 14 NSWLR 121, in which a plea of cross-action, pursuant to the Common Law Procedure Act 1857 (NSW), for breach of contract in an action for damages for fraud was held to be bad, on the ground that the cause of action could not be said to have arisen out of the same subject-matter as the plaintiff's claim.

[351] (1995) 56 FCR 354.

applied to meet the overpayment. The Full Court of the Federal Court[352] held that this was not justified on the basis of equitable set-off, since the Department was unable to point to an equity of the type necessary to sustain the defence.[353] The *Etablissement Esefka* case was not referred to, but the cases differed in that, in the *Walker* case, the claims were not derived from a single transaction or contract with the Department, but were separate.

In any event, the question whether the circumstances in the *Etablissement Esefka* **4.73** case gave rise to an equitable set-off may well have been unnecessary. The cross-claims would appear to have constituted mutual debts giving rise to a defence of set-off under the Statutes of Set-off,[354] in which case it would not have been necessary to show any connection between them.

Misleading or deceptive conduct in Australia

In Australia, section 52 of the Trade Practices Act 1974 (Cth) provides that: 'A **4.74** corporation shall not, in trade or commerce, engage in conduct that is misleading or deceptive or is likely to mislead or deceive.' A question of interest to Australian lawyers is whether a claim arising as a result of a contravention of s 52 is capable of being employed defensively as an equitable set-off.[355]

In *Bank of New Zealand v Spedley Securities Ltd*[356] the New South Wales Court of **4.75** Appeal held that conduct which was prohibited by section 52 could not be relied on as a defence in proceedings to establish a constructive trust. Kirby P in his judgment endorsed earlier authority to the effect that section 52 on its own does not give rise to a duty which is enforceable at law.[357] Rather, the section is regarded as describing a 'norm of conduct' which 'should not be interpreted according to

---

[352] *Per* Cooper and Spender JJ, Drummond J dissenting.

[353] (1995) 56 FCR 354, 375. Moreover, there was no set-off under the Statutes of Set-off, since the appellant's entitlement was not a debt for the purpose of the Statutes. See at 373–374 Drummond J dissented. He regarded the appellant's conduct in procuring the earlier payments by fraud as sufficient, when added to the connection that both lots of claims involved the disbursement of moneys from the consolidated revenue, as to make it unjust to allow recovery without bringing into account his liability.

[354] Certainly a sum specified in a shipping contract as being payable by way of demurrage is regarded as constituting liquidated damages (see *President of India v Lips Maritime Corp* [1988] 1 AC 395), so that a claim for demurrage may be the subject of a set-off under the Statutes. See *Axel Johnson Petroleum AB v MG Mineral Group AG* [1992] 1 WLR 270.

[355] Compare *Westco Motors (Distributors) Pty Ltd v Palmer* [1979] 2 NSWLR 93. The claim in that case related to the price payable for goods sold and delivered, and the cross-claim was for damages under the Trade Practices Act consequent upon allegations of restraint of trade, misuse of market power and resale price maintenance. Sheppard J (at 98–99) considered that the claims were insufficiently connected to give rise to an equitable set-off.

[356] (1992) 27 NSWLR 91.

[357] See eg *State of Western Australia v Wardley Australia Ltd* (1991) 30 FCR 245, 256–257, referring to *Tobacco Institute of Australia Ltd v Australian Federation of Consumer Organisations Inc* (1988) 19 FCR 469. See also Toohey J on appeal in the High Court in *Wardley* (1992) 175 CLR 514, 551.

established principles of liability under the general law and which, since it may be offended by acts both honest and reasonable . . . , is morally neutral'.[358] If the 'norm of conduct' specified in section 52 is not complied with, sanctions are provided elsewhere in the Act. In particular, section 82 provides that a person who suffers loss by the conduct of another person which contravenes section 52 may recover the amount of the loss 'by action against that other person'. Section 82, it has been said, is a provision which creates both right and remedy.[359] In the *Spedley Securities* case, however, a claim for relief under section 82 had not been made.[360] It was simply argued that conduct which contravened section 52 gave rise to a defence, an argument that the Court of Appeal rejected.[361]

4.76 The position would appear to be different if a cross-claim has been mounted under section 82. In the *Spedley Securities* case, Hope A-JA accepted the proposition that: 's 52 of the Trade Practices Act cannot be pleaded by way of defence, *absent a claim for relief under s 82 or s 87 of the Act . . .*'.[362] Kirby P on the other hand commented in relation to section 82 that, 'the words of that section are not apt to support a defence',[363] which might be thought to suggest that a section 82 claim cannot be used defensively by way of set-off. In other cases however it has been assumed that a cross-claim for damages under section 82, based upon a contravention of the 'norm of conduct' described in section 52, can be relied on as an equitable set-off.[364]

4.77 The relationship between the claims in any event must be sufficiently close to give rise to an equitable set-off. A cross-claim based on section 52 generally would not

---

[358] *Commonwealth Bank of Australia v Mehta* (1991) 23 NSWLR 84, 88, *per* Samuels JA.

[359] *State of Western Australia v Wardley Australia Ltd* (1991) 30 FCR 245, 257.

[360] This was emphasized by Cole J at first instance. See *Spedley Securities Ltd v Bank of New Zealand* (1991) 13 ATPR 41–143 at p 53,066.

[361] Disapproving of *Australian Mutual Provident Society v Specialist Funding Consultants Pty Ltd* (1991) 24 NSWLR 326. See also *Drabsch v Switzerland and General Insurance Co Ltd* (NSW SC, Santow J, 28 February 1996, at p 42).

[362] (1992) 27 NSWLR 91, 109 (emphasis added), referring to *State of Western Australia v Wardley Australia Ltd* (1991) 30 FCR 245, 256–257. See also Cole J at first instance (1991) 13 ATPR 41–143 at p 53,066.

[363] (1992) 27 NSWLR 91, 99.

[364] *Walker v Department of Social Security* (1995) 56 FCR 354, 367; *Doherty v Murphy* [1996] 2 VR 553, 565; *Re Kleiss, ex p Kleiss v Capt'n Snooze Pty Ltd* (1996) 61 FCR 436. See also *Westpac Banking Corp v Eltran Pty Ltd* (1987) 14 FCR 541 (and subsequent proceedings: *Eltran Pty Ltd v Westpac Banking Corp* (1988) 32 FCR 195, 204); *Glass & Co Pty Ltd v Soonhock* (1996) 18 ATPR 41–453 (esp at p 41,567); *John Shearer Ltd v Gehl Co* (1995) 60 FCR 136, 142. This was also assumed in *Murphy v Zamonex Pty Ltd* (1993) 31 NSWLR 439, 463 and *Tomlinson v Cut Price Deli Pty Ltd* (1992) 38 FCR 490, although in these cases reliance was placed on *Australian Mutual Provident Society v Specialist Funding Consultants Pty Ltd* (1991) 24 NSWLR 326, which was disapproved by the Court of Appeal in *Bank of New Zealand v Spedley Securities* (1992) 27 NSWLR 91. Since a breach of s 52 cannot be pleaded by way of defence in the absence of a claim for relief under the Trade Practices Act, if the claim for relief is time-barred a defence would not be available. See Cole J at first instance in *Spedley Securities Ltd v Bank of New Zealand* (1991) 13 ATPR 41–143 at p 53,066, and Kirby P on appeal (1992) 27 NSWLR 91, 99–100.

be regarded as impeaching the plaintiff's title to sue if the representation giving rise to the section 52 claim did not induce the contract being sued upon by the plaintiff.[365]

K. Limitation on Liability

It may be that the liability of one of the parties is limited by contract or statute to a certain amount. In such a case the principle is that the liability is first limited and a set-off may then take place against this limited sum, rather than that the two demands are first set against each other at their full face value with the limitation rule then being applied to the balance.[366] That approach should be compared to the rule applied in admiralty law in the event of a collision at sea, that a balance should be struck before the limit is applied.[367]   **4.78**

L. Periodic Payments

Sometimes a contract imposes an obligation on one party to make periodic payments to another,[368] for example a tenant's obligation to pay rent to the landlord under a periodic tenancy,[369] or a time charterer's obligation to pay hire to the owner of the vessel. The question may arise whether a set-off based upon a damages claim for breach of contract would be confined to the payment obligation that relates to the particular period in which the breach occurred, or whether the damages claim may be employed in a set-off against payment obligations that accrue in respect of other periods.   **4.79**

In *Government of Newfoundland v Newfoundland Railway Co*[370] the Privy Council held that a claim for damages against a contractor for failure to complete a railway line could be set off against the contractor's entitlement to an annual subsidy for each five-mile section of the track that had been completed. In this case the failure to complete went to the value of what previously had been performed. In the context of a time charter of a ship, on the other hand, there is authority for the view   **4.80**

---

[365] *Cunningham v National Australia Bank Ltd* (1987) 15 FCR 495.

[366] *NV Bureau Wijsmuller v The Owners of the MV Tojo Maru (The Tojo Maru)* [1970] P 21, 48, 67–68, 75.

[367] For a discussion on the practice of the courts in these cases, see *Stoomvaart Maatschappy Nederland v Peninsular and Oriental Steam Navigation Co (The Khedive)* (1882) 7 App Cas 659. As Lord Selborne noted (at 806–807), the admiralty rule operates independently of any principle of set-off.

[368] Compare *Peninsular and Oriental Steam Navigation Co v Youell* [1997] 2 Lloyd's Rep 136 (see para 4.18 above), in which there were different contracts relating to different periods.

[369] See Waite, 'Disrepair and Set-off of Damages Against Rent: The Implications of British Anzani' [1983] The Conveyancer 373, 381–2.

[370] (1888) 13 App Cas 199.

that, if the shipowner breached the contract during one or more periods, but in subsequent periods the contract was properly performed, the charterer cannot set off the damages claim against the obligation to pay the hire applicable to those later periods.[371] In *The Aditya Vaibhav*[372] charterers alleged that, in breach of the charter, the owners failed to perform their hold-cleaning obligations,[373] which resulted in the vessel being delayed at port for about fourteen days. The charterers suffered consequential loss and expense as a result of the vessel not being available for service, which they deducted in part from the hire due during the fourteen-day period. They then submitted that they could set off the remainder of the damages claim against subsequent payments of hire. Saville J held that the damages claim did not impeach the owners' entitlement to hire for periods during which they had actually performed the services contracted for, so that a set-off was not available in respect of the remainder of the damages. This accords with Parker J's explanation in *The Teno*[374] of the rationale for allowing an equitable set-off against a claim for hire under a time charter, that 'it would be grossly unjust to allow an owner to recover hire in respect of a period during which he had, in breach of contract, failed to provide that for which the hire was payable'. Nevertheless it seems an unduly strict approach. The charterparty is a single contract, and the choice of periods of hire to an extent is arbitrary. Yet the shorter the period, the more limited the scope for a set-off.

4.81 A time charter usually provides for payment of hire in advance at the commencement of each period. If during the period there is a breach of contract which has the effect of depriving the payer of part of the consideration for which the advance payment was made, it would be too late for a set-off to occur against the pre-paid consideration for that period. Instead, a set-off may occur against the amount due in respect of the next period, even though the contract may have been performed properly during that period.[375]

4.82 *The Aditya Vaibhav* concerned a time charter of a ship, and it may be restricted to that context. It has been said, for example, that it does not apply to rent payable

---

[371] Compare *Japan Line Ltd v Aggeliki Charis Compania Maritima SA (The Angelic Grace)* [1980] 1 Lloyd's Rep 288, which concerned successive charters.

[372] *Century Textiles and Industry Ltd v Tomoe Shipping Co (Singapore) Pte Ltd (The Aditya Vaibhav)* [1991] 1 Lloyd's Rep 573.

[373] At the subsequent trial the charterers failed to prove this allegation. See *Century Textiles and Industry Ltd v Tomoe Shipping Co (Singapore) Pte Ltd (The Aditya Vaibhav)* [1993] 1 Lloyd's Rep 63.

[374] *Compania Sud Americana de Vapores v Shipmair BV (The Teno)* [1977] 2 Lloyd's Rep 289, 296. See also *Atlantic Lines & Navigation Co Inc v The Ship 'Didymi' (The Didymi)* [1988] 1 Lloyd's Rep 97, 110, Canadian Federal Court of Appeal. This is also consistent with Lord Denning's comments in *Federal Commerce & Navigation Co Ltd v Molena Alpha Inc* [1978] 1 QB 927, 975, 976 to the effect that the charterer had been deprived of part of the consideration for which hire had been paid in advance.

[375] *Federal Commerce & Navigation Co Ltd v Molena Alpha Inc* [1978] 1 QB 927, 975–976.

periodically under a lease. In *Courage Ltd v Crehan*[376] it was argued that, if a tenant in an action for payment of rent has a cross-claim in damages against the landlord, the cross-claim will only give rise to a set-off if it arises in respect of the same period of time as that for which the claim for rent was made. The Court of Appeal, while acknowledging the decision in *The Aditya Vaibhav* in relation to a time charter, nevertheless rejected the suggestion that any such temporal limitation should be introduced in the case of a lease of land.[377] This is also suggested by *Melville v Grapelodge Developments Ltd.*[378] A prospective tenant went into occupation of the premises, at the outset rent free. Protracted negotiations then took place concerning the condition of the premises. It was agreed that, if the tenant signed a lease, the landlord would carry out repairs as soon as possible. The first quarter's rent became due a few days later. When the landlord failed to carry out the repairs, Neill J held that the tenant could set off the resulting damages claim against unpaid rent, including the first quarter's rent, even though there was no determination that the landlord was in breach of the repair obligation by failing to have the repairs completed during the first quarter.[379]

If a breach of contract constituted a repudiation of the contract, which was ac- **4.83**
cepted so as to result in the termination of the contract, the resulting damages claim ordinarily could be set off against sums previously due to the repudiating party under the contract,[380] including in relation to prior periods.

M. Mortgages

(1) The Scope of Equitable Set-off

The right to an equitable set-off against a mortgage debt has been recognized in a **4.84**
number of circumstances, including where the mortgagee is liable to the mortgagor for failure to renew the insurance on the mortgaged property,[381] where the mortgagee's title to sue for the debt is impeached as a result of a sale of the mortgaged property at an undervalue,[382] where the mortgagee in selling the mortgaged

---

[376] [1999] 2 EGLR 145.

[377] See the discussion at [1999] 2 EGLR 145, 156.

[378] (1978) 39 P & CR 179.

[379] The first quarter commenced on 25 March 1977. Neill J was prepared to accept (at (1979) 39 P & CR 179, 185–186) that the landlord was obliged to *commence* the work by 21 June, but that would not have required completion by the end of the quarter, on 25 June. Nor was there a specific finding, or indeed an assumption made, that work did not commence by 21 June, which suggests that it was not regarded as significant to the question of set-off. There was simply a concession for the purpose of the case (at 184) that 'no sufficient repairs' were carried out in fulfilment of the repair obligation.

[380] *Parsons v Sovereign Bank of Canada* [1913] AC 160. See paras 4.62–4.63 above.

[381] *Campbell v Canadian Co-operative Investment Co* (1906) 16 Man LR 464.

[382] *General Credits (Finance) Pty Ltd v Stoyakovich* [1975] Qd R 352, 355 (leave to defend granted subject to conditions); *TSB Bank plc v Platts* [1998] 2 BCLC 1, 9–10. Compare *Continental*

property breached its duty to take reasonable steps to obtain the best price by failing to preserve the property,[383] and where the mortgagee is liable in damages to the mortgagor for breach of contract in not providing further finance to the mortgagor for the purpose of a development on the mortgaged land, with the result that the mortgagor was unable to complete the development and consequently to repay the debt.[384]

Mortgage to secure the unpaid price of property sold

4.85   Alternatively, the issue may arise in the context of a contract for the sale of property which stipulates for a mortgage or other form of security to secure payment of the unpaid balance of the purchase price. A purchaser being sued for the price generally could set off in that action a cross-claim for damages for breach of warranty in the contract of sale directly affecting the value of the property, and the right to a set-off should not be lost simply because the debt is secured by a mortgage.[385] Further, as a matter of principle it should not matter that the action for payment is brought on a covenant to pay contained in the mortgage, rather than upon the original contract. While the damages cross-claim in this situation admittedly would arise under a different contract to that pursuant to which the action is brought for payment, it is not an essential requirement of an equitable set-off that the same contract should be the source of both demands.[386] The mortgage is part of the same transaction as the contract of sale.[387] Its purpose is to secure payment of the price, and if the purchaser would have had a set-off in an action brought against him on the contract of sale the amount outstanding secured by the mortgage similarly should be regarded as reduced *pro tanto*.[388] This is consistent with the substantive nature of this form of set-off.[389]

4.86   In Victoria, Lush J reached a different conclusion in *Provident Finance Corporation Pty Ltd v Hammond*.[390] The purchaser of a business had agreed to pay

---

Illinois National Bank & Trust Co of Chicago v Papanicolaou [1986] 2 Lloyd's Rep 441, in which the contract excluded set-offs.

[383] *National Australia Bank Ltd v Jenkins* (1999) V ConvR 54–601 at p 67,217 (appeal dismissed (1999) V ConvR 54–602).

[384] *Popular Homes Ltd v Circuit Developments Ltd* [1979] 2 NZLR 642. See also *Doherty v Murphy* [1996] 2 VR 553 (in particular, the explanation given for the default at 560). Compare *United Dominions Corp Ltd v Jaybe Homes Pty Ltd* [1978] Qd R 111, in which the agreement to provide finance was not part of the same transaction as the debt sued upon.

[385] *Altarama Ltd v Camp* (1980) ACLR 513; *Newman v Cook* [1963] VR 659 (in particular, the judgment of Hudson J in relation to equitable set-off). Compare *Indrisie v General Credits Ltd* [1985] VR 251, 254.

[386] See para 4.55 above.

[387] *Altarama Ltd v Camp* (1980) 5 ACLR 513, 520. See also *Popular Homes Ltd v Circuit Developments Ltd* [1979] 2 NZLR 642, 658.

[388] See the discussion in *Newman v Cook* [1963] VR 659.

[389] See paras 4.29–4.43 above.

[390] [1978] VR 312.

the unpaid balance of the price in a number of instalments, and signed a bill of sale for the outstanding amount. The vendor then assigned the bill of sale to the plaintiff. When the plaintiff sued on the bill for payment, it was held that the purchaser could not set off a damages claim available against the vendor for breach of warranty and for fraudulent misrepresentation inducing the contract.[391] The basis of any set-off would have been the principle that an assignee takes subject to equities, which include rights of set-off available to the debtor against the assignor.[392] Lush J justified the conclusion that there was no set-off on the ground that a debtor may not set up against an assignee (and therefore also against the assignor) a claim for damages under a contract other than that assigned. But equitable set-off does not require a single contract as the source of the cross-demands, and if the claims are otherwise sufficiently closely connected to give rise to a set-off as between the assignor and the debtor, the set-off ordinarily should be available as against the assignee.[393] Lush J also sought to explain the result on another ground. He said that one of the objects of the contract of sale in providing for the execution of a bill of sale was to give the debt and the security aspects of the contract a separate existence. That had as a consequence that a separate document was brought into existence, in the form of the bill of sale, which in the ordinary course of business was transferable. From that he inferred that the rights embodied in the bill of sale were not intended to be 'intertwined' with the various other rights and obligations in the contract of sale.[394] That inference is debatable, however. Often it would simply be as a matter of convenience, and prevailing commercial practice, that separate contracts are used.

Payment of the price by way of a loan from the vendor

Sometimes a different arrangement is adopted. Instead of the mortgage securing **4.87** the unpaid price, the price is satisfied by means of a loan from the vendor, and it is the repayment of this loan which is secured by a mortgage. In such a case, the Privy Council in *Bow, McLachlan & Co Ltd v Ship 'Camosun'*[395] considered that a damages claim for breach of warranty will not provide the purchaser with a defence to an action to enforce the mortgage debt, either on the basis of equitable set-off or the common law defence of abatement,[396] since the sale and the loan secured by the mortgage are separate contracts.[397] Their Lordships' view on this point was obiter,[398] but it nevertheless has been regarded as correct by Australian

---

[391] See paras 4.68–4.70 above.
[392] See ch 17 below.
[393] See para 17.22 below.
[394] [1978] VR 312, 321.
[395] [1909] AC 597.
[396] See paras 2.87–2.97 below.
[397] [1909] AC 597, 612–613.
[398] The case was decided on the ground that the Exchequer Court of Canada in Admiralty was not possessed of a general common law jurisdiction to enforce the damages cross-claim.

courts.[399] The loan, and the security for it, is considered to be a separate transaction from the sale.[400] A comment in the judgment of the Court of Appeal in *Samuel Keller (Holdings) Ltd v Martins Bank Ltd*[401] suggests the contrary view. A purchaser bought all the issued shares in a company, the vendor providing a loan to the purchaser to pay part of the price, with the loan being secured by a mortgage over property. The vendor sued for payment, whereupon the purchaser was granted unconditional leave to defend on the basis of a counterclaim for unliquidated damages for breach of warranties and conditions in the sale of shares agreement. The case then proceeded on another issue,[402] but Russell LJ, in delivering the Court of Appeal's judgment in the case, commented in passing that the grant of unconditional leave to defend seemed to have been in accordance with *Morgan & Son Ltd v S Martin Johnson & Co Ltd*,[403] which at the time was a leading authority on equitable set-off. In other words, the Court of Appeal seems to have been of the opinion that the cross-claim for damages provided an arguable defence of equitable set-off to the action for payment, notwithstanding that the case was one involving a loan to pay the price.[404] The point was not the subject of detailed discussion, however, and the *Bow, MacLachlan* case was not referred to. The effect of the arrangement in these cases is to separate the payment obligation from the sale, and on that basis the view of the Privy Council is to be preferred.

(2) *Enforcing Rights Under the Mortgage*

4.88   The position is more complex when the mortgagee is not suing for the debt, but rather is seeking to enforce his rights as mortgagee. In considering this issue, a distinction may be drawn between a claim by a legal mortgagee for possession of the mortgaged premises, and the exercise of other rights by a mortgagee which depend upon default, for example the exercise of a power of sale.

(3) *Claim for Possession, where Possession does not Depend on Default*

4.89   In the absence of a contractual or a statutory provision to the contrary, the right of a legal mortgagee in England to possession of the premises is independent of any question of default.[405] He 'may go into possession before the ink is dry on the

---

[399] *Newman v Cook* [1963] VR 659, 675–676; *Altarama Ltd v Camp* (1980) 5 ACLR 510, 520.

[400] Compare *Altarama Ltd v Camp* (1980) 5 ACLR 513, 520.

[401] [1971] 1 WLR 43.

[402] See para 4.96 below.

[403] [1949] 1 KB 107.

[404] In *Parry v Grace* [1981] 2 NZLR 273, 278–279, the *Samuel Keller* case (n 401 above) was discussed in terms suggesting that the Court of Appeal was of the view that the facts did not give rise to an equitable set-off. However, the passage in *Samuel Keller* (at [1971] 1 WLR 43, 51) to which reference was made was concerned with a different issue, as to whether the mortgagee could be kept out of its rights as mortgagee on the basis of a cross-claim available to the mortgagor. See paras 4.88–4.107 below.

[405] This is also the case in Australia in relation to an old title mortgage of land. See *Ex parte Jackson; Re Australasian Catholic Assurance Co Ltd* (1941) 41 SR (NSW) 285, 289. It should be

mortgage unless there is something in the contract, express or by implication, whereby he has contracted himself out of that right'.[406] This is a consequence of the mortgagee's legal estate.[407]

In *Birmingham Citizens Permanent Building Society v Caunt*[408] Russell J said that **4.90** the court has no jurisdiction to decline to order possession in favour of the mortgagee unless the mortgagor pays the full principal, interest and costs secured by the mortgage,[409] the 'sole exception' being that the application may be adjourned for a short time to afford to the mortgagor a chance of paying off the mortgagee in full. He emphasized, however, that the application should not be adjourned if there is no reasonable prospect of payment occurring.[410] Consistent with that strict approach, the courts have held that a mortgagee should not be denied possession of the premises on the ground that the mortgagor has a counterclaim against the mortgagee for an amount in excess of the mortgage debt,[411] and this has also been held to apply when there is a cross-claim which would give rise to an equitable set-off in an action to enforce the debt.[412] Nor does it make any difference that the mortgagor is willing to pay into court the difference between the amount owing under the mortgage and the estimate of the sum sought to be set off.[413] An equitable set-off is a substantive defence, in that it is unconscionable for a creditor against whom the defence may be asserted to regard the debtor as being in default to the extent of the set-off while circumstances exist which support an equitable set-off.[414] Nevertheless, until the debt is paid, including by judgment for a set-off, so that the mortgagor is entitled to redemption, the principle by which the mortgagee as the party with the legal estate has the right to possession still applies.[415]

---

compared to a mortgage under the Torrens system, where the mortgagor is entitled to possession until default. See Sykes and Walker, *The Law of Securities* (5th edn, 1993) 248.

[406] *Four-Maids Ltd v Dudley Marshall (Properties) Ltd* [1957] 1 Ch 317, 320, per Harman J.

[407] The same principle applies where a legal mortgage of land is created by a charge by deed expressed to be by way of legal mortgage. See the Law of Property Act 1925, s 87(1), and *Four-Maids Ltd v Dudley Marshall (Properties) Ltd* [1957] 1 Ch 317, 320.

[408] [1962] 1 Ch 883.

[409] [1962] 1 Ch 883, 891.

[410] [1962] 1 Ch 883, 912.

[411] *Mobil Oil Co Ltd v Rawlinson* (1981) 43 P & C R 221, 226; *Citibank Trust Ltd v Ayivor* [1987] 1 WLR 1157.

[412] *Mobil Oil Co Ltd v Rawlinson* (1981) 43 P & C R 221; *National Westminster Bank plc v Skelton* [1993] 1 WLR 72 (esp at 78); *Ashley Guarantee plc v Zacaria* [1993] 1 WLR 62, 66–67, 70. See also *TSB Bank plc v Platts* [1998] BCLC 1, 10.

[413] *Mobil Oil Co Ltd v Rawlinson* (1981) 43 P & C R 221. Indeed, Nourse J said (at 227) that payment of the full amount secured into court will not suffice to prevent the mortgagee obtaining possession. Payment must be made to the mortgagee himself.

[414] See para 4.30 above.

[415] Compare *National Westminster Bank plc v Gaskin* [1998] EWCA Civ 1449, although the terms of the mortgage are not set out in the judgment, in particular as to whether the mortgagee's right to possession was limited to the case of default. See paras 4.94–4.107 below.

4.91   Slade LJ re-affirmed the general principle in *National Westminster Bank plc v Skelton*,[416] but he left open the question whether it would apply where the mortgagor 'establishes that he has a claim to a quantified sum by way of equitable set-off'.[417] He said that: 'Possibly such a claim might have the effect of actually discharging the mortgage debt.'[418] An equitable set-off does not operate as an automatic extinction of cross-demands, although because of the substantive nature of the defence its effect in equity is similar to a discharge to the extent of the set-off.[419] But given that the availability of an equitable set-off is not dependant upon whether the cross-demand is liquidated or unliquidated, it is difficult to see why a cross-claim for a 'quantified sum' should be treated differently to a damages cross-claim available by way of equitable set-off, if it can be established that the damages payable would exceed the mortgage debt.[420]

4.92   The view that a mortgagee is entitled to possession notwithstanding that an action to enforce the mortgage debt could be met by an equitable set-off also applies when the mortgage was given by a third party as surety for the debt secured by the mortgage,[421] and, *a fortiori*, when the third party had agreed that the mortgage should apply as if the third party was primarily liable for the debt.[422]

4.93   The Administration of Justice Act 1970, section 36[423] has provided some relief to mortgagors in the face of applications by mortgagees for possession when the

---

[416] [1993] 1 WLR 72.

[417] [1993] 1 WLR 72, 78. Nourse LJ noted this reservation in *Ashley Guarantee plc v Zacaria* [1993] 1 WLR 62, 66, and see also *Murphy v Abi-Saab* (1995) 37 NSWLR 280, 289.

[418] [1993] 1 WLR 72, 78. It appears that the principal debtor in the *Skelton* case was in liquidation (see [1993] 1 WLR 72, 78, 80), in which case *quaere* why there was not an automatic set-off under the insolvency set-off section upon the occurrence of the liquidation (see paras 6.79–6.103 below) so as to discharge the principal debt to the extent of the set-off at that date.

[419] See paras 4.29–4.43 above. The point was noted, but not discussed, in *Ashley Guarantee plc v Zacaria* [1993] 1 WLR 62, 66.

[420] Ralph Gibson LJ in *Ashley Guarantee plc v Zacaria* [1993] 1 WLR 62, 70–71, while not doubting Slade LJ's judgment in *National Westminster v Skelton*, nevertheless commented, in the context of a mortgage given by a surety, that: 'it is to me an arresting concept that a mortgagor, who is a guarantor of the debt of the principal debtor . . . could be required to give possession of his home despite the existence of unliquidated claims which are admitted or shown to be likely to succeed, in an amount which would either exceed the sum due from the principal debtor or be such as, when established, to enable the principal debtor or the mortgagor to pay in full. It might possibly, in a particular case, be that an implied term could be held to have arisen which would exclude the immediate right to possession, but it is obvious that there are difficulties against such an implication in most ordinary cases'.

[421] *Ashley Guarantee plc v Zacaria* [1993] 1 WLR 62, 69. In the *Ashley Guarantee* case, however, the mortgagee's right to possession was expressed in the mortgage instrument to depend upon 'default' by the principal debtor. See para 4.101 below.

[422] *National Westminster Bank plc v Skelton* [1993] 1 WLR 72 (esp at 79–80). In *Ashley Guarantee plc v Zacaria* [1993] 1 WLR 62, 69 Nourse LJ said that he could 'see no distinction in principle between a case where the mortgagor is the principal debtor of the mortgagee and one where he is only a guarantor. In each case the mortgagee has, as an incident of his estate in the land, a right to possession of the mortgaged property'.

[423] As amended by the Administration of Justice Act 1973, s 8.

mortgaged property is a dwelling-house. Section 36 provides that where, in an application for possession of a dwelling-house, it appears to the court that the mortgagor is likely to be able within a reasonable period to pay any sums due under the mortgage or to remedy any other default, the court may adjourn the proceedings or postpone the date for delivery of possession for such period as it thinks reasonable. In *Citibank Trust Ltd v Ayivor*[424] Mervyn Davies J suggested that, in determining whether the mortgagor is likely to be able to pay the sums due within a reasonable time, it may be an inadmissible consideration to take into account that the mortgagor may succeed on a cross-claim, since this might nullify or circumvent the general rule that the existence of a cross-claim does not prevent the mortgagee from taking possession. Indeed, it has been said that, for section 36 to apply, the court must be able to fix a period ending with some specified or ascertainable date during which it is likely that payment will be made,[425] and it may be difficult to do this when reliance is placed on the fruits of an unlitigated cross-claim as the source of the repayment. Notwithstanding that view, in *Ashley Guarantee plc v Zacaria*[426] Ralph Gibson LJ noted the possibility that a stay under section 36 pending trial of the cross-claim may be appropriate if the existence and the prospects of success of the cross-claim could, in all the circumstances, be regarded as enabling the sum due to be paid within a reasonable period, and Woolf LJ also countenanced that possibility in his judgment.[427]

(4) Remedies Dependent Upon Default

Alternatively, the remedy sought to be exercised by the mortgagee may depend upon default, as, for example, the exercise of a power of sale, or a claim to possession of the premises in circumstances where either the mortgage limits the mortgagee's right to possession to the occurrence of a default by the mortgagor[428] or, as in Australia in relation to land under the Torrens system, where this is the position that applies in any event.[429] **4.94**

Restraining the exercise of a power of sale

In the case of a power of sale, it is commonly said that a mortgagee generally will not be restrained by an interlocutory injunction from exercising the power unless the amount which the mortgagee claims is due to him is paid into court, or some **4.95**

---

[424] [1987] 1 WLR 1157, 1163–1164.
[425] *Royal Trust Co of Canada v Markham* [1975] 1 WLR 1416; *Bristol & West Building Society v Ellis and Ellis* (1996) 73 P & CR 158.
[426] [1993] 1 WLR 62, 71.
[427] [1993] 1 WLR 62, 71.
[428] The courts will not readily imply such a restriction in the mortgage. See *National Westminster Bank plc v Skelton* [1993] 1 WLR 72, 77.
[429] Sykes and Walker, *The Law of Securities* (5th edn, 1993) 248.

other compensatory form of security is provided.[430] The basis of the principle is said to be the precept that he who seeks equity must do equity.[431] The rule is subject to a number of exceptions,[432] but in Australia the High Court held in *Inglis v Commonwealth Trading Bank of Australia*[433] that it applies in the situation in which a mortgagor has an unlitigated cross-claim which, if established, would exceed the debt secured by the mortgage. The mortgagee will not be restrained from exercising a power of sale on the basis of the cross-claim in the absence of a payment into court or the provision of some other form of security such as a banker's bond. Neither the judgment of Walsh J, nor that of Barwick CJ on appeal, referred specifically to the question whether the cross-claim in issue in that case gave rise to an equitable set-off. Indeed, set-off was not mentioned in the judgments,[434] and nor did Walsh J suggest that there was any connection between the circumstances out of which the mortgagor's claim for damages arose and the circumstances surrounding the grant of the mortgage.[435] On the other hand, Walsh J referred to some well-known authorities on equitable set-off,[436] and it has been accepted in subsequent cases in Australia that the *Inglis* case applies in that context.[437]

---

[430] *Fisher and Lightwood's Law of Mortgage* (11th edn, 2002) 576 para 20.36; Cousins, *The Law of Mortgages* (1989) 243; *Warner v Jacob* (1882) 20 Ch D 220, 224; *Hill v Kirkwood* (1880) 28 WR 358; *Inglis v Commonwealth Trading Bank of Australia* (1972) 126 CLR 161, 164; *Murphy v Abi-Saab* (1975) 37 NSWLR 280, 289; Bryson, 'Restraining Sales by Mortgagees and a Curial Myth' (1993) 11 Australian Bar Review 1. Compare *Rottenberg v Monjack* [1993] BCLC 374. It has been said that the requirement to pay into court applies only in the case of interlocutory injunctions, and not to claims for final relief. See *ANZ Banking Group Ltd v Comer* (1993) 5 BPR 11,748, 11,753, NSW SC, *per* Young J referring to *Hill v Kirkwood* (1880) 28 WR 358, 359–360 and *Harvey v McWatters* (1948) 49 SR (NSW) 173, 177; *Brutan Investments Pty Ltd v Underwriting and Insurance Ltd* (1980) 39 ACTR 47, 55; *Mediservices International Pty Ltd v Stocks & Realty (Security Finance) Pty Ltd* [1982] 1 NSWLR 516, 525; Fisher and Lightwood, *op cit* 576 n 13.

[431] *Town & Country Sport Resorts (Holdings) Pty Ltd v Partnership Pacific Ltd* (1988) 20 FCR 540, 545. *Clarke v Japan Machines (Australia) Pty Ltd (No 2)* [1984] 1 Qd R 421, 422.

[432] See generally *Fisher and Lightwood's Law of Mortgage* (11th edn, 2002) 576 para 20.36, and in Australia, Bryson, 'Restraining Sales by Mortgagees and a Curial Myth' (1993) 11 Australian Bar Review 1.

[433] (1972) 126 CLR 161. The judgment of Walsh J was affirmed on appeal (at 168) by the Full Court of the High Court, *per* Barwick CJ, Menzies and Gibbs JJ.

[434] Set-off is referred to in the headnote, however.

[435] This point has been made in later cases. See *Cunningham v National Australia Bank Ltd* (1987) 15 FCR 495, 499; *Eltran Pty Ltd v Westpac Banking Corp* (1988) 32 FCR 195, 203.

[436] *Rawson v Samuel* (1841) Cr & Ph 161, 41 ER 451 and *Morgan & Son Ltd v S Martin Johnson & Co Ltd* [1949] 1 KB 107.

[437] *Altarama Ltd v Camp* (1980) 5 ACLR 513, 518; *Glandore Pty Ltd v Elders Finance and Investment Co Ltd* (1984) 4 FCR 130, 133, 135; *Graham v Commonwealth Bank of Australia* (1988) 10 ATPR 40–908 at p 49,757; *Nicholas John Holdings Pty Ltd v ANZ Banking Group Ltd* [1992] 2 VR 715, 728; *Murphy v Abi-Saab* (1995) 37 NSWLR 280, 289; *Latrobe Capital and Mortgage Corp Ltd v Mt Eliza Mews Pty Ltd* [2001] VSC 464. See also *Kennedy v General Credits Ltd* (1982) 2 BPR 9456 at p 9464 (though in that case the set-off was characterized as procedural and not substantive). In *Murphy v Abi-Saab* the New South Wales Court of Appeal referred to *National Westminster Bank plc v Skelton* [1993] 1 WLR 72 as supporting that proposition. The *Skelton* case, however, turned on a different principle, that a mortgagee in England is entitled by virtue of his legal estate to go into possession, whether or not there has been default, unless the mortgagee has contracted

Walsh J in the *Inglis* case was influenced particularly by the decision of Megarry J, **4.96**
and of the Court of Appeal on appeal, in *Samuel Keller v Martins Bank*.[438] In the
Samuel Keller case, a second mortgagee held a surplus after satisfying the debt due
to it from the proceeds of sale of the mortgaged property. A third mortgagee
sought to have the balance paid to it. The mortgagor however said that it had a
damages claim against the third mortgagee exceeding the mortgage debt and that,
until this could be litigated, the surplus should be paid into court. The judgment
of the Court of Appeal was delivered by Russell LJ.[439] He seems to have accepted
that the cross-claim would have provided grounds for a set-off in an action for
payment of the mortgage debt,[440] though he nonetheless held that the proceeds
should be paid to the third mortgagee rather than into court. The *Inglis* and
Samuel Keller cases differed in that, unlike the exercise of the power of sale by the
mortgagee in *Inglis*, the third mortgagee's right to the surplus in *Samuel Keller* was
not dependent upon default.[441] Nor was the *Samuel Keller* case concerned with an
interlocutory injunction. On the other hand, Russell LJ noted a concession from
counsel, which his Lordship also seems to have accepted, that the court would not
prevent a mortgagee from exercising a power of sale when the mortgage was created as a result of the same contract that gave rise to the unliquidated cross-
claim.[442] The way in which the proposition was expressed would not necessarily
extend to equitable set-off, since it is not sufficient for an equitable set-off that the
claims originated in the same contract,[443] and the circumstances in issue indeed
were a step removed from that. Nevertheless, it should be considered in the context of his Lordship's evident view that the circumstances would have provided an
arguable basis for an equitable set-off, sufficient for unconditional leave to defend,
in an action for payment.[444] To that extent, the *Samuel Keller* case also provides
support for the view that a mortgagee will not be restrained from exercising a
power of sale because of an equitable set-off that would have been available to the
mortgagor in an action for payment of the mortgage debt.

---

himself out of that right. See para 4.89 above. In New Zealand, see *Parry v Grace* [1981] 2 NZLR
273, 278, 280, in which Thorp J, without deciding the point, seemed inclined to accept that an unlitigated cross-claim which, if successful, would give rise to an equitable set-off would not be a sufficient ground for restraining the mortgagee in the absence of payment into court.

[438] [1971] 1 WLR 43.

[439] Edmund Davies and Cross LJJ concurring.

[440] See the reference in Russell LJ's judgment ([1971] 1 WLR 43, 49) to unconditional leave to
defend, and also (at 49 and 51) to the earlier Court of Appeal decision in *Morgan & Son Ltd v S
Martin Johnson & Co Ltd* [1949] 1 KB 107, which was concerned with equitable set-off.

[441] The mortgagee's claim in the *Samuel Keller* case has been equated with a claim for possession
of the mortgaged property (for which see above). See *TSB Bank plc v Platts* [1998] 2 BCLC 1, 10. A
mortgagee who has a surplus after the exercise of a power of sale holds the surplus subject to a constructive trust in favour of a subsequent mortgagee. See *Banner v Berridge* (1881) 18 Ch D 254.

[442] [1971] 1 WLR 43, 50–51.

[443] See para 4.55 above.

[444] See above.

4.97 But notwithstanding those cases, in the usual case where a power of sale is expressed to be exercisable only in the event of a 'default' in payment, there is much to be said for the view that the principle requiring payment into court should not apply where the mortgagor is seeking to restrain the exercise of a power of sale on the basis of an equitable set-off equal to or exceeding the mortgage debt,[445] at least where the strength of the cross-claim and the availability of a set-off are sufficiently clear.[445a] A 'default' in this context should be taken as referring to a failure to pay in circumstances where there is a legal obligation to do so.[446] An equitable set-off does not operate as an automatic cancellation of cross-demands,[447] and in the situation posited there will have been a failure by the mortgagor to pay. On the other hand, because of the equitable set-off, the mortgagor is not required to pay, and because of the substantive nature of the defence[448] the mortgagee is not permitted in equity to treat the mortgagor as having failed to pay. The mortgagee, therefore, should not be permitted to assert that there has been default in payment, so as to be able to rely on the condition for the exercise of the power. It has been suggested that the 'payment in' rule does not apply where the matter in dispute relates to whether the power of sale has arisen;[449] the mortgagee may be restrained by injunction in that circumstance from exercising the power without the mortgagor being required to bring the money into court.[450] The same principle should apply in the situation in which the mortgagee's right to sell is impeached by a clearly arguable equitable set-off.

4.98 In Victoria[451] Hedigan J contemplated the possibility, although without deciding, that a cross-claim available by way of equitable set-off could be relevant in determining the amount that might be required to be brought into court, depending

---

[445] Compare *Atkinson v Hastings Deering (Queensland) Pty Ltd* (1985) 6 FCR 331, 333.

[445a] See also paras 4.100 and 4.101 below in relation to foreclosure and possession.

[446] *The Oxford English Dictionary* defines 'default', inter alia, as a 'failure to perform some legal requirement or obligation'.

[447] See para 4.30 above.

[448] See paras 4.29–4.43 above.

[449] *Fisher and Lightwood's Law of Mortgage* (11th edn, 2002) 576 para 20.36; *Halsbury's Laws of England* (4th edn, 1999) vol 32, 315–16 para 658; *Allfox Building Pty Ltd v Bank of Melbourne Ltd* (1992) NSW ConvR 55–634 at p 59,627. This includes a failure to give a proper statutory notice as a pre-condition to the exercise of a power of sale. See *Mediservices International Pty Ltd v Stocks & Realty (Security Finance) Pty Ltd* [1982] 1 NSWLR 516; *Atkinson v Hastings Deering (Queensland) Ltd* (1985) 6 FCR 331; *National Australia Bank Ltd v Zollo* (1992) 59 SASR 76.

[450] In Australia the principle has been expressed in terms that, where the matter in dispute is whether the power of sale has arisen at all, the terms as to payment into court may be moulded so as to require payment in of so much only as will suffice to give adequate protection to the mortgagee, depending on what the justice of the case requires. See *Harvey v McWatters* (1948) 49 SR (NSW) 173; *Glandore Pty Ltd v Elders Finance and Investment Co Ltd* (1984) 4 FCR 130 (in which there was an allegation of misleading or deceptive conduct against the mortgagee contrary to the Trade Practices Act 1974 (Cth), s 52, and the relief sought included an order varying the terms of the loan agreement); *Nicholas John Holdings Pty Ltd v ANZ Banking Group Ltd* [1992] 2 VR 715, 728–729.

[451] *Nicholas John Holdings Pty Ltd v ANZ Banking Group Ltd* [1992] 2 VR 715, 728.

on the strength of the evidence and the estimation of the possible damages.[452] He also contemplated that the availability of an equitable set-off could be capable of forming one of the matters to be taken into account in weighing the balance of convenience for the purpose of an application for an interlocutory injunction. Nevertheless, he went on to say that: 'an examination of the cases does not justify an easy departure from the *Inglis* principle'.[453] There have been other judicial statements in Australia which suggest that relief may be granted to a mortgagor free of the condition that the amount secured be paid into court if the mortgagor's cross-claim is sufficiently connected with the mortgage so as to give rise to an equitable set-off.[454] The statements admittedly were made in the context of an application for an injunction under section 80 of the Trade Practices Act 1974 (Cth), and it has been said that the injunctive power under the Trade Practices Act is not necessarily confined by principles observed in courts of equity in their traditional jurisdiction, and that the court may grant interlocutory or final injunctive relief under the Act that does not correspond with what would follow from the application of the traditional rules.[455] There are also other cases concerned with cross-claims under the Trade Practices Act in which it was assumed that the principle in the *Inglis* case extends to set-off.[456] Nevertheless, the statements in question reflect what has been described as the 'lack of enthusiasm' for the rule applied in the *Inglis* case,[457] and the 'judicial uneasiness' as to its operation.[458]

In any event, where a mortgagor has a cross-claim over-topping the mortgage **4.99** debt, the mortgagee would not be permitted to exercise a power of sale if the cross-claim has been liquidated and an equitable set-off in respect of it has been established by the court. This occurred in Victoria, in *Newman v Cook*.[459] In that case, a vendor's application for a declaration that he was entitled to exercise a power of sale pursuant to a mortgage given as security for the unpaid part of the purchase

---

[452] Compare *Altarama Ltd v Camp* (1980) 5 ACLR 513, 518, where McLelland J in invoking the *Inglis* principle commented that it was not known whether the mortgagor would succeed in establishing an entitlement to damages against the mortgagee, or if so in what amount.

[453] [1992] 2 VR 715, 728.

[454] *Cunningham v National Australia Bank Ltd* (1987) 15 FCR 495, 500–501, referred to with approval in *Eltran Pty Ltd v Westpac Banking Corporation* (1988) 32 FCR 195, 204. See also *Australian Natives' Association Friendly Society v Peball Pty Ltd* (1993) V Conv R 54–482 at pp 65,612–65,613; *Rawcliffe v Custom Credit Corporation* (1994) 16 ATPR 41–292 at p 41,923; *Swift v Westpac Banking Corp* (1995) 17 ATPR 41–401 at p 40,431. It would be necessary to show that the cross-claim is clearly arguable. See *Town & Country Sport Resorts (Holdings) Pty Ltd v Partnership Pacific Ltd* (1988) 20 FCR 540, 545; *Swift v Westpac Banking Corp* at p 40,431.

[455] *Town & Country Sport Resorts (Holdings) Pty Ltd v Partnership Pacific Ltd* (1988) 20 FCR 540, 545, *per* Davies, Gummow and Lee JJ, and see also *ANZ Banking Group Ltd v Comer* (1993) 5 BPR 11,748, 11,753, NSW SC, *per* Young J.

[456] *Glandore Pty Ltd v Elders Finance and Investment Co Ltd* (1984) 4 FCR 130, 133; *Graham v Commonwealth Bank of Australia* (1988) 10 ATPR 40–908 at p 49,757.

[457] *Atkinson v Hastings Deering (Queensland) Pty Ltd* (1985) 6 FCR 331, 333.

[458] *Angelatos v National Australia Bank* (1994) 51 FCR 574, 581.

[459] [1963] VR 659.

price took the form of a counterclaim in the purchaser's action for damages for breach of contract. The Full Court[460] was in a position to declare that the damages claim should be brought into an account with the price on the basis of common law abatement,[461] and also, according to Hudson J, by way of equitable set-off, so that to that extent the price was paid.

Restraining other remedies dependent upon default

4.100 The payment rule is often expressed generally, in terms not confined to the exercise of a power of sale, but rather in terms that a mortgagee will not be restrained by interlocutory injunction from exercising his rights under the mortgage instrument unless the amount owing is paid into court.[462] Indeed, the point has been made that the requirement imposed by the courts in relation to an attempt to restrain the exercise of a power of sale seems merely to have continued earlier practices adopted where mortgagors sought to restrain the exercise of other remedies of mortgagees, such as the enforcement of bonds and covenants or an action for foreclosure.[463] Thus, the payment in rule has been invoked in the context of an attempt to stay a foreclosure action.[464] On the other hand, it is the practice to give a mortgagor a period of time after the foreclosure order nisi (usually six months) in which to pay the debt before the order is made absolute. That period may then be enlarged, or the foreclosure may be reopened.[465] Consistent with that indulgence to mortgagors, there is authority for the view that an equitable set-off may be pleaded as a defence to an action for foreclosure.[466] In *Piggott v Williams*,[467] a deci-

---

[460] Herring CJ, Dean and Hudson JJ.

[461] See paras 2.87–2.97 above.

[462] See eg *Inglis v Commonwealth Trading Bank* (1971) 126 CLR 161, 164, *per* Walsh J, 169, *per* Barwick CJ; *Glandore Pty Ltd v Elders Finance and Investment Co Ltd* (1984) 4 FCR 130, 133; *Murphy v Abi-Saab* (1995) 37 NSWLR 280, 289.

[463] See Bryson, 'Restraining Sales by Mortgagees and a Curial Myth' (1993) 11 Australian Bar Review 1, 11–12, referring to Faucett J in *Bank of New South Wales v Tyson* (1871) 11 SCR (NSW) (Eq) 1, 20 *et seq*.

[464] *Paynter v Carew* (1854) Kay App 36, 39, 69 ER 331, 333; *Bank of New South Wales v Tyson* (1871) 11 SCR (NSW) (Eq) 1, 20–22. For examples of payments into court in foreclosure actions, see *Jones v Tinney* (1845) Kay App 45, 69 ER 336 and *Challie v Gwynne* (1846) Kay App 46, 69 ER 337. See also the order made by Wigram VC in *Dodd v Lydall* (1842) 1 Hare 333, 66 ER 1060. The set-off in issue in *Dodd v Lydall* appears to have been an equitable set-off based upon equity acting by analogy with the Statutes. See generally, as to that form of set-off, para 3.06 above.

[465] See *Fisher and Lightwood's Law of Mortgage* (11th edn, 2002), 626–30, 640–2.

[466] In addition to the cases discussed below, see *Dodd v Lydall* (1841) 1 Hare 333, 66 ER 1060. Wigram VC in that case said that he would not suspend a decree of foreclosure because of a crossclaim by the mortgagor for an account of amounts due from the mortgagee in his capacity as trustee of a trust in which the mortgagor was beneficially interested. In doing so he emphasized that the mortgage and the trust accounts had no original or necessary connection with each other, though the tenor of his judgment suggests that, if that had not been the case, he would not have made the decree. In any event, the Vice Chancellor said that he would suspend the decree until the trust account could be taken if the amount of the mortgage debt was paid into court.

[467] (1821) 6 Madd 95, 56 ER 1027.

sion of Sir John Leach VC in 1821, a solicitor failed in an application for an order for foreclosure of an estate pledged as security for costs, because of an allegation by the client that the costs claimed would not have been incurred were it not for the solicitor's own negligence. The Vice Chancellor said that, taking the matter alleged to be true, the client had a clear title to restrain the solicitor from proceeding to enforce his security and leaving the client's demand for damages unsatisfied. In the *Inglis* case,[468] Walsh J sought to explain *Piggott v Williams* on the ground that the client's allegation in that case went to the question whether the debt which the security was intended to secure had ever been incurred at all. It is true that the client's cross-bill alleged that nothing was due to the solicitor. Nevertheless, Sir John Leach referred to the client's 'demand for damages', and commented that the facts alleged, if true, disclosed 'a clear case of equitable set-off'.[469] He said that the course which the cause would probably take would be to retain the solicitor's bill until an action for damages were tried. The Vice Chancellor in truth proceeded on the basis that there were cross-demands operating by way of equitable set-off. More recently, the British Columbia Court of Appeal in *Coba Industries Ltd v Millie's Holdings (Canada) Ltd*[470] refused foreclosure on the basis of an equitable set-off available to the mortgagor. In cases of foreclosure, where it is the practice in any event to give the mortgagor time to pay, there is not the same urgency that may exist in relation to the exercise of a power of sale, in circumstances where a delay in selling may adversely affect the price obtainable for the property in the short term. For that reason, it is suggested that the courts should favour the approach adopted in *Piggott v Williams* and the *Coba Industries* case, notwithstanding Walsh J's comments in the *Inglis* case.

Action for possession, where possession depends upon default

The preceding discussion related to the position in equity. In Australia, where a mortgagee's right to possession of land under the Torrens system depends on default,[471] it has been suggested that the equitable requirement to pay money into court in an application for an interlocutory injunction does not apply where a mortgagor is seeking instead to defend a common law action for possession of the mortgaged land, though it has also been said that the judge in such a case has a discretion to require payment.[472] In England, comments in the Court of Appeal in

4.101

---

[468] (1972) 126 CLR 161, 167.

[469] (1821) 6 Madd 95, 56 ER 1027.

[470] [1985] 6 WWR 14.

[471] *Fisher and Lightwood's Law of Mortgage* (Australian edn, 1995) 377 *et seq*. Compare the case of an old title mortgage, in which the mortgagee is entitled to possession by virtue of the legal estate, and irrespective of default, unless the contract provides otherwise. See *Ex parte Jackson, re Australasian Catholic Assurance Co Ltd* (1941) 41 SR (NSW) 285, 289, and para 4.89 above.

[472] *Murphy v Abi-Saab* (1995) 37 NSWLR 280, 289, NSW CA, referring to *ANZ Banking Group Ltd v Comer* (1993) 5 BPR 11,748, 11,753–11,754, NSW SC *per* Young J. See also *Long Leys Co Pty Ltd v Silkdale Pty Ltd* (1991) 5 BPR 11,512, 11,519–11,520, where the New South Wales

Ashley Guarantee plc v Zacaria[473] suggest that an equitable set-off exceeding the mortgage debt may provide a defence to an action for possession in circumstances where possession depends upon default, without the imposition of a requirement of payment into court.[474] The plaintiff in that case had lent money to a company, repayment of which was secured by a mortgage given by the defendant. The mortgage contained a provision to the effect that the plaintiff could exercise its rights and remedies over the mortgaged property only in the event of default by the company. The plaintiff sought possession of the property consequent upon a default in repayment of the loan. The defendant argued that the company had a cross-claim against the plaintiff which gave it a right of equitable set-off, and that, because of the set-off, the company had not defaulted in any of its obligations to the plaintiff. Accordingly, it was said that the plaintiff was not entitled to possession under the mortgage. The argument failed because, as Nourse LJ pointed out, the cross-claim did not come anywhere near the amount of the company's debt to the plaintiff.[475] But if it had exceeded the debt, he indicated that he would have been prepared to accept the argument.[476] Similarly, Woolf LJ suggested that possession would have been refused if a set-off had been available for a sum greater than the mortgage debt.[477] Neither of their Lordships indicated that this would have been subject to payment in.[478]

4.102 The view that a common law action for possession is not subject to a strict 'payment in' rule is relevant when the subject of the dispute is the amount of the debt secured by the mortgage.[479] But when a mortgagor is asserting an equitable defence of set-off, it would be difficult from a historical perspective to justify a distinction between, on the one hand, an application to a court of equity for an

---

Court of Appeal assumed that equitable set-off provided a defence. Compare *Fisher and Lightwood's Law of Mortgage* (Australian edn, 1995) 392 para 19.11, where it is suggested that there is no room, in a common law action for possession, for the rule of equity requiring payment into court before the court will listen to the mortgagor's defence. Compare also *Indrisie v General Credits* (1984) 5 FCR 582, in which an injunction was sought to restrain a mortgagee from executing a judgment obtained for possession, as opposed to the mortgagor defending a common law action for possession. In that circumstance, the 'payment in' rule was regarded as applicable: see at 587–588. Similarly, the 'payment in' rule may apply where an injunction is sought to prevent the mortgagee remaining in possession. See *Harvey v McWatters* (1948) 49 SR (NSW) 173, 177, referring to *Hill v Kirkwood* (1880) 28 WR 358.

[473] [1993] 1 WLR 62.
[474] See also *National Westminster Bank plc v Gaskin* [1998] EWCA Civ 1449.
[475] See also *Murphy v Abi-Saab* (1995) 37 NSWLR 280, 290.
[476] [1993] 1 WLR 62, 68. Compare however Nourse LJ's comments at 69. *Quaere* whether the cross-claim must be admitted or be shown to be likely to succeed. See Ralph Gibson LJ at 70.
[477] [1993] 1 WLR 62, 71.
[478] In Australia, Professor O'Donovan has suggested (*Company Receivers and Administrators* (2nd edn, looseleaf) 8293 [18.565]) that the 'payment in' rule in any event may not apply if the mortgagee has caused damage to the secured property before going into possession, so that the mortgagor's ability to service the secured debt is impaired. This suggestion is based on *Beasley v Darcy* (1800) 2 Sch & Lef 403n, which concerned possession as between landlord and tenant.
[479] As in *ANZ Banking Group Ltd v Comer* (1993) 5 BPR 11,748.

injunction to restrain a mortgagee from exercising rights under the mortgage instrument, and on the other a defence to a common law action for possession,
given that before the Judicature Acts the mortgagor's equitable set-off would have
been given effect in any event by means of an injunction to restrain the
common law proceeding.[480] Having said that, the approach suggested by the dicta
in the *Ashley Guarantee* case would seem correct, based on the construction of the
contract. The mortgagee in the *Ashley Guarantee* case was only entitled to possession in the event of a default. In that circumstance, the point made above in relation to a power of sale should apply equally here.[481] In other words, an entitlement
to an equitable set-off equal to or exceeding the debt should preclude the mortgagee from asserting that there has been a 'default', in the sense of a failure to pay
a sum where there was a legal obligation to do so, so that the mortgagee should not
be able to assert that the contractual condition circumscribing the mortgagee's
right to possession has been satisfied.

Similarly in Australia a mortgagee of land under the Torrens system is only   **4.103**
entitled to go into possession upon 'default' in payment by the mortgagor.[482] If
the mortgagor has an equitable set-off exceeding the debt, the mortgagee should
not be in a position to assert that there has been a default in payment, so as to
establish the element necessary to support the mortgagee's statutory claim for
possession.[483]

In any event, if the mortgagor has an arguable cross-claim against the mortgagee   **4.104**
for fraudulent misrepresentation, in circumstances where it is said that the giving
of the mortgage itself was induced by fraud, the mortgagee will not be entitled to
summary judgment to recover possession, and the 'payment in' rule will not
apply.[484]

---

[480] See para 3.01 above. Before the Judicature Acts, the payment principle applied when an injunction was sought to restrain ejectment proceedings by a mortgagee. See *Booth v Booth* (1742) 2
Atk 343, 26 ER 609.

[481] See para 4.97 above.

[482] See, eg, the Transfer of Land Act 1958, s 78(1), and the Real Property Act 1900 (NSW), s 60.

[483] *Fisher and Lightwood's Law of Mortgage* (Australian edn, 1995) 395–398, and see also the
qualification to the statement of principle by Tadgell J in *MEK Nominees Pty Ltd v Billboard
Entertainments Pty Ltd* (1993) V ConvR 54–468 at p 65,469, in terms of a statute which cuts down
the mortgagee's right to possession. In the case of a Torrens mortgage, the mortgagee's right to possession is indeed cut down by statute, by the imposition of a requirement of showing default by the
mortgagor. Compare the comments of Sheller JA in *Horrobin v Australia & New Zealand Banking
Group Ltd* (1996) 40 NSWLR 89, 100, which were of a general nature and not specifically directed
to the case of a Torrens mortgage. His Honour referred to *National Westminster v Skelton* [1993] 1
WLR 72, 78, which concerned a mortgage in England where the mortgagee was entitled to possession by virtue of its legal estate without the necessity of showing default. The court nevertheless may
have a discretion to require payment in. See *Murphy v Abi-Saab* (1995) 37 NSWLR 280, 289,
though compare *Fisher and Lightwood's Law of Mortgage* (Australian edn, 1995) 392.

[484] *Horrobin v Australia & New Zealand Banking Group Ltd* (1996) 40 NSWLR 89 (in particular the judgment of Sheller JA at 100). Compare *Radin v Commonwealth Bank of Australia* (Federal

4.105 In the *Ashley Guarantee* case, the defendant was a surety for the debts of the company, and the right to possession under the mortgage was contingent upon default by the company. Nourse and Woolf LJJ were of the view that, if the company's cross-claim against the plaintiff had exceeded the debt secured by the mortgage, and that cross-claim was available to the company by way of equitable set-off, the defendant would have had a defence to the claim for possession pursuant to the mortgage. That view should be compared to *Indrisie v General Credits Ltd,*[485] in which the Supreme Court of Victoria considered that, even if the principal debtor's cross-claim in that case gave rise to an equitable set-off,[486] it would not have assisted the surety in resisting the creditor's claim for possession of the property mortgaged by the surety.[487] In the *Indrisie* case, however, the court seems to have proceeded on the incorrect assumption that the surety in these cases is seeking to employ the principal's claim in a set-off against the surety's own liability under the guarantee, rather than that the surety is asserting that the principal has a defence as against the creditor, and that the surety is also entitled to rely on that defence as against the creditor.[488] For that reason, the views of Nourse and Woolf LJJ should be preferred.[489]

Statutes of Set-off

4.106 The above discussion concerned equitable set-off. A different question is whether the court on the application of the mortgagor will order that an independent cross-debt owing to the mortgagor be set off against the mortgage debt under the Statutes of Set-off, so as to allow the mortgagor to redeem. This was considered earlier in the context of a discussion of *Parker v Jackson.*[490]

Rent payable to a mortgagee in possession

4.107 The question sometimes arises as to whether a mortgagee in possession who is entitled to rent payable by a tenant takes subject to an equitable set-off that otherwise would have been available to the tenant as against the mortgagor. This issue is considered later.[491]

Court of Australia, Lindgren J, 25 March 1998), in which the bank's alleged fraud did not relate to the giving of the mortgage.

[485] [1985] VR 251, 254.

[486] In fact, the Supreme Court in the *Indrisie* case was of the view that the circumstances did not give rise to an equitable set-off. See [1985] VR 251, 253–254.

[487] Under the Transfer of Land Act 1958 (Vic), s 78, a mortgagee is only entitled to possession in the event of default.

[488] See para 18.22 below.

[489] The High Court refused special leave to appeal from the decision in the *Indrisie* case (see [1985] VR 251, 254), but the reason for the refusal is not clear.

[490] [1936] 2 All ER 281, for which see para 2.42 above.

[491] See paras 17.59–17.70 below.

5

SET-OFF BETWEEN SOLVENT PARTIES: VARIOUS ASPECTS

This chapter considers various aspects of set-off between parties neither of whom **5.01** is bankrupt or is a company in liquidation.

A. Charterparties and Bills of Lading

(1) Equitable Set-off

Questions of set-off in the context of charterparties have been the subject of **5.02** particular attention in recent years.[1] In that regard the courts have drawn a

---

[1] See Rose, 'Deductions From Freight and Hire under English Law' [1982] Lloyd's Maritime and Commercial Law Quarterly 33. In *Japan Line Ltd v Aggeliki Charis Compania Maritime SA (The Angelic Grace)* [1980] 1 Lloyd's Rep 288 the Court of Appeal, Lord Denning MR and Waller LJ held that a shipowner's liability to reimburse charterers for a quantity of bunkers remaining on the vessel at the expiration of the charter could be set off against the owner's cross-claim for stevedore damage. In *Exmar BV v National Iranian Tanker Co (The Trade Fortitude)* [1992] 1 Lloyd's Rep

distinction between, on the one hand, freight payable under a voyage charter or a bill of lading, and on the other hire payable under a time charter or a charter by demise.[2] In the former case equitable set-off generally is not available, whereas it may apply in the latter.

Freight

5.03 At common law, the defendant in an action for payment of the price of goods sold with a warranty, or of work to be performed according to a contract, in some cases can deduct the amount of any damage sustained by reason of a breach of warranty or contract by the claimant. This is not by way of set-off, but rather it is a means by which the defendant can defend himself by showing how much less the subject-matter of the contract is worth as a result of the claimant's breach. This principle, known as abatement, or the rule in *Mondel v Steel*,[3] was considered earlier.[4] However the right to abate does not apply to every contract for work and labour. It was established early in the nineteenth century[5] that, in the case of a contract for the carriage of goods by sea, a bill of lading holder or a voyage charterer cannot make a deduction from the freight payable[6] except to the extent specifically allowed by the contract.[7] As a consequence of this exception,[8] a defence of abatement has failed in cases involving damage done to the goods being shipped,[9] short delivery,[10] and delay.[11]

169, arbitrators had decided that a charterer's cross-claim in respect of cargo shortages could be set off against the owner's claim for demurrage. Judge Diamond QC in the Commercial Court (at 178–179) found it unnecessary to decide if the arbitrators were correct on this point, though (at least on the traditional impeachment test) the claims seem insufficiently connected to give rise to an equitable set-off.

[2] For a discussion of the difference between the modern form of time charter and a charter by demise, see *Sea and Land Securities Ltd v William Dickinson and Co Ltd* [1942] 2 KB 65, 69, *per* McKinnon LJ.

[3] (1841) 8 M & W 858, 151 ER 1288.

[4] See paras 2.87–2.97 above.

[5] *Bornmann v Tooke* (1808) 1 Camp 376, 170 ER 991; *Sheels v Davies* (1814) 4 Camp 119, 171 ER 39, subsequent proceedings *sub nom Shields v Davis* (1815) 6 Taunt 65, 128 ER 957.

[6] In addition to the cases cited below, see *Mondel v Steel* (1841) 8 M & W 858, 871, 151 ER 1288, 1293; *Kish v Charles Taylor, Sons & Co* [1912] AC 604, 616; *St John Shipping Corp v Joseph Rank Ltd* [1957] 1 QB 267, 291.

[7] As eg in *Lakeport Navigation Co Panama SA v Anonima Petroli Italiana SpA (The Olympic Brilliance)* [1982] 2 Lloyd's Rep 205.

[8] Strictly, the rule prohibiting deductions from freight is an application of the rule which was in force generally before the common law courts developed the defence of abatement. See *Aries Tanker Corp v Total Transport Ltd* [1977] 1 WLR 185, 192–193. Nevertheless, to the extent that the allowance of an abatement in a contract for work and labour has now become the general rule, the freight rule may be regarded as the exception.

[9] *Davidson v Gwynne* (1810) 12 East 381, 104 ER 149; *Sheels v Davies* (1814) 4 Camp 119, 171 ER 39; *Garrett v Melhuish* (1858) 33 LTOS 25; *Dakin v Oxley* (1864) 15 CB(NS) 646, 143 ER 938; *Hoenig v Isaacs* [1952] 2 All ER 176, 178; *Henriksens Rederi A/S v THZ Rolimpex (The Brede)* [1974] 1 QB 233. Compare *Bellamy v Russell* (1681) 2 Show KB 167, 89 ER 865, in which the Court of King's Bench indicated that a merchant could retain the freight otherwise payable under a charter-

It is unclear whether the rule against deductions from freight originally was **5.04**
thought to extend to the equitable defence of set-off as well as the common law
defence. In *Stimson v Hall*[12] a lighterman brought an action against a goods owner
for freight owing for the conveyance of the goods. The goods owner alleged that
other goods had been lost as a result of the negligence of the lighterman,[13] and said
that his cross-claim for damages for the loss of those goods gave rise to an equitable
defence to the claim. While the Court of Exchequer rejected this contention on
the ground that the facts failed to disclose a natural equity sufficient to ground a
set-off, there is nothing in the judgments or in the arguments of counsel to suggest that an equitable set-off was considered not to be available in any event
against a claim for freight. The courts have since accepted, however, that equitable
set-off is indeed subject to the same restriction as for common law abatement with
respect to the payment of freight.[14] It is not confined to cases of short or damaged
delivery of cargo or delay in its delivery, but applies to any damages claim available
to the charterer or bill of lading holder.[15] In *Bank of Boston Connecticut v European*

---

party as compensation for damage caused to the goods by the fault of the master. This was not based
upon a defence of abatement or set-off, but rather upon a custom of merchants which the court said
permitted a deduction.

[10] *Aries Tanker Corp v Total Transport Ltd* [1977] 1 WLR 185 (in which freight was to be calcu-
lated according to the *intaken* quantity of cargo rather than the quantity delivered, for which see
Dakin v Oxley (1864) 15 CB(NS) 646, 664–665, 143 ER 938, 946). See also *Blanchet v Powell's
Llantivit Collieries Co Ltd* (1874) LR 9 Ex 74. *A fortiori* there may not be a deduction in respect of
the value of missing goods against the freight due upon other goods actually delivered. See *Meyer v
Dresser* (1864) 16 CB(NS) 646, 143 ER 1280.

[11] *A/S Gunnstein & Co v K/S Jensen, Krebs and Nielsen (The Alfa Nord)* [1977] 2 Lloyd's Rep 434.
See also *Bornmann v Tooke* (1808) 1 Camp 376, 170 ER 991; *R H & D International Ltd v IAS
Animal Air Services Ltd* [1984] 1 WLR 573.

[12] (1857) 1 H & N 831, 156 ER 1436, 5 WR 367.

[13] The plaintiff's claim for freight apparently was not in respect of the goods alleged to have been
lost. This appears more clearly from the report of the case at 5 WR 367. Watson B commented (at
368) that he was not certain how equity would have dealt with the matter in a case in which there
was a demand for freight and the goods in respect of which the freight was claimed were damaged
by the shipowner or carrier.

[14] *Cleobulos Shipping Co Ltd v Intertanker Ltd (The Cleon)* [1983] 1 Lloyd's Rep 586; *Elena
Shipping Ltd v Aidenfield Ltd (The Elena)* [1986] 1 Lloyd's Rep 425; *Bank of Boston Connecticut v
European Grain and Shipping Ltd* [1989] 1 AC 1056; *Protank Shipping Inc v Total Transport Corp
(The Protank Orinoco)* [1997] 2 Lloyd's Rep 42, 44. See also *Henriksens Rederi A/S v THZ Rolimpex
(The Brede)* [1974] 1 QB 233; *Aries Tanker Corp v Total Transport Ltd* [1977] 1 WLR 185, 193,
195; *Compania Sud Americana de Vapores v Shipmair BV (The Teno)* [1977] 2 Lloyd's Rep 289, 293;
A/S Gunnstein & Co K/S v Jensen, Krebs and Nielsen (The Alfa Nord) [1977] 2 Lloyd's Rep 434; *Nova
(Jersey) Knit Ltd v Kammgarn Spinnerei GmbH* [1977] 1 WLR 713, 721. Compare Stephenson LJ
in *James & Co Scheepvaart en Handelmij BV v Chinecrest Ltd* [1979] 1 Lloyd's Rep 126, 129 ('unless
you can find an equity sufficient to override that long-standing rule of common law').

[15] Thus, Roskill LJ in *A/S Gunnstein & Co K/S v Jensen, Krebs and Nielsen (The Alfa Nord)* [1977]
2 Lloyd's Rep 434, 436 referred to 'the well-established principle that there is no right of set-off for
claims for damages for breach of charter, whether for loss of or damage to goods or for alleged failure to prosecute a voyage with reasonable dispatch or otherwise, against a claim for freight'. See also
Exmar BV v National Iranian Tanker Co (The Trade Fortitude) [1992] 1 Lloyd's Rep 169, 177 ('no
deductions are possible').

Grain and Shipping Ltd[16] the House of Lords confirmed that the restriction also extends to the situation in which the voyage was never completed as a result of the shipowner's wrongful repudiation of the charterparty, where the right to freight had accrued under the charterparty before it was terminated by acceptance of the repudiation.[17] Moreover, it applies equally to advance freight and to freight payable on delivery of the goods at the port of discharge.[18] It has also been held to extend to a claim for additional freight, in circumstances where additional freight became payable because of the owner's own breach of contract.[19]

5.05 This principle precluding deductions is not limited to the situation in which a shipowner is suing a voyage charterer or a bill of lading holder for freight. An agent who collects freight on behalf of the shipowner or charterer must account for the freight without deduction or set-off.[20] Similarly a freight forwarder who arranges carriage as agent for a goods owner, and who pays the cost of carriage on behalf of the owner, is entitled to be reimbursed without a set-off in respect of an allegation of breach of duty as agent.[21] The principle is also relevant when the right to freight has been assigned. The assignee is entitled to the freight undiminished by an equitable set-off.[22]

5.06 Nor is the principle confined to shipping. Contracts for the carriage of goods by road pursuant to the Convention on the Contract for the International Carriage of Goods by Road (CMR) are subject to the rule,[23] even though Articles 32 and 36

---

[16] [1989] 1 AC 1056.

[17] Compare Lord Simon of Glaisdale in *Aries Tanker Corp v Total Transport Ltd* [1977] 1 WLR 185, 193, whose comments were explained in *Bank of Boston Connecticut v Europan Grain and Shipping Ltd* [1989] 1 AC 1056, 1104–1105. In the *Bank of Boston* case the bills of lading were signed on 14 July 1982, the charterparty provided that the freight was deemed to be earned on the signing of the bills of lading, and the charterparty was terminated as a result of acceptance of the owner's repudiation on 22 July. Since the right to freight had accrued before acceptance of the repudiation, it was unaffected by the termination. See [1989] 1 AC 1056, 1098–1099. On the other hand, there may be a total failure of consideration which prevents freight becoming payable. See *Bank of Boston* at 1105, and *Britannia Distribution Co Ltd v Factor Pace Ltd* [1998] 2 Lloyd's Rep 420, 423.

[18] *Bank of Boston Connecticut v European Grain and Shipping Ltd* [1989] 1 AC 1056, 1100.

[19] *Cleobulos Shipping Co Ltd v Intertanker Ltd (The Cleon)* [1983] 1 Lloyd's Rep 586. However the rule does not apply to diversion expenses. See *Re Bayoil SA* Re [1999] 1 WLR 147, 149–150.

[20] *James & Co Scheepvaart en Handelmij BV v Chinecrest Ltd* [1979] 1 Lloyd's Rep 126; *Opal Maritime Agencies Pty Ltd v Baltic Shipping Co* (1998) 158 ALR 416. *Aliter* if there is an agreement for a set-off. *See Opal Maritime Agencies Pty Ltd v 'Skulptor Konenkov'* (2000) 98 FCR 519, 562 *et seq*. The decision in *Samuel v West Hartlepool Steam Navigation Co* (1906) 11 Com Cas 115, (1907) 12 Com Cas 203, in so far as it allowed a set-off of the damages claim, seems contrary to this principle and is difficult to support. See *Colonial Bank v European Grain & Shipping Ltd (The Dominique)* [1987] 1 Lloyd's Rep 239, 256–257, where Hobhouse J nevertheless left open the question whether the decision could stand together with the *Chinecrest* case (above). Compare also *Wehner v Dene Steam Shipping Co* [1905] 2 KB 92, for which see para 5.23 below.

[21] *Britannia Distribution Co Ltd v Factor Pace Ltd* [1998] 2 Lloyd's Rep 420.

[22] *Bank of Boston Connecticut v European Grain and Shipping Ltd* [1989] 1 AC 1056; *Britannia Distribution Co Ltd v Factor Pace Ltd* [1998] 2 Lloyd's Rep 420, 423.

[23] *R H & D International Ltd v IAS Animal Air Services Ltd* [1984] 1 WLR 573, following six unreported cases to the same effect. See also *Britannia Distribution Co Ltd v Factor Pace Ltd* [1998] 2

of the Schedule to the Convention seem to contemplate that set-offs are possible. Further, it has been held, although with reluctance, that the principle is equally applicable to a domestic contract for carriage by land.[24] It probably would also apply to a contract for carriage of goods by air.[25]

The House of Lords in the *Bank of Boston* case[26] also warned that the rules of procedure should not be used to bring about a result contrary to the principle. Lord Brandon of Oakbrook, who delivered the judgment of their Lordships, rejected an argument that the court could try both the claim and the counterclaim and then make an order pursuant to the former RSC O 15 r 2(4). The rule provided that: 'Where a defendant establishes a counterclaim against the claim of a plaintiff and there is a balance in favour of one of the parties, the court may give judgment for the balance . . .' He said that to utilize the rule for that purpose would constitute a wrong exercise of the court's discretion. Similarly, a cross-claim available to a charterer ordinarily does not constitute a ground for staying execution on a judgment obtained against the charterer for payment of freight.[27]   **5.07**

While freight must be paid without deduction in respect of a damages cross-claim, Judge Diamond QC sitting in the Commercial Court suggested that, in the case of an arbitration, when an arbitrator is called upon to exercise his discretion to make an interim award in respect of freight, he may make it a condition of the issue of the interim award that the owner provide reasonable security for the charterer's cross-claim. He also suggested that there 'may perhaps' be exeptional cases where an arbitrator in the exercise of his discretion may find a valid reason for refusing to issue an interim award in respect of a claim for freight, but conceded that those cases would be rare.[28]   **5.08**

On the other hand, the freight rule does not apply when a shipowner has presented a petition to wind up a company for non-payment of freight, and the company has a genuine and serious cross-claim against the petitioner. If the amount of   **5.09**

Lloyd's Rep 420. Compare *Impex Transport Aktieselskabet v AG Thames Holdings Ltd* [1981] 2 Lloyd's Rep 566, in which Robert Goff J seemed to assume that a set-off is possible in contracts for the carriage of goods by road, though in the particular case it was denied on other grounds.

[24] *United Carriers Ltd v Heritage Food Group (UK) Ltd* [1996] 1 WLR 371, *per* May J.

[25] This seems to have been accepted in *Britannia Distribution Co Ltd v Factor Pace Ltd* [1998] 2 Lloyd's Rep 420, 422.

[26] [1989] 1 AC 1056, 1109.

[27] *Cleobulos Shipping Co Ltd v Intertanker Ltd (The Cleon)* [1983] 1 Lloyd's Rep 586; *Colonial Bank v European Grain & Shipping Ltd (The Dominique)* [1987] 1 Lloyd's Rep 239, 257–258. See also *Sherborne v Siffkin* (1811) 3 Taunt 525, 128 ER 208, in which the court refused to order that the freight be paid into court to be applied towards payment of any damages that may be awarded for damage to cargo. Compare *Halsbury's Laws of England* (4th edn, 1999) vol 42, 246 para 413. In *James & Co Scheepvaarten en Hendelmij BV v Chinecrest Ltd* [1979] 1 Lloyd's Rep 126 a stay was granted on condition that the amount of the freight be paid into court, though in that case there was an unresolved issue as to the terms of the contract.

[28] *Exmar BV v National Iranian Tanker Co (The Trade Fortitude)* [1992] 1 Lloyd's Rep 169, 177.

the cross-claim exceeds the debt to the shipowner, the court may dismiss or stay the petition unless there are special circumstances which make it inappropriate for the petition to be dismissed or stayed.[29]

Hire under a time charter

5.10 Different considerations apply to hire payable under a time charter.[30] Admittedly in *Russell v Pellegrini*[31] the Court of Queen's Bench assumed, after a concession by counsel to that effect, that a cross-claim for damages for breach of an implied warranty of seaworthiness could not be set off against a claim for hire,[32] while more recently Donaldson J apparently applied the freight rule in that context in two unreported decisions on interlocutory applications,[33] and later in *Seven Seas Transportation Ltd v Atlantic Shipping Co SA*.[34] Subsequently, however, Parker J in *The Teno*[35] followed an unreported decision of Ackner J to the contrary,[36] and held that the rule by which freight must be paid without deduction does not extend to hire. Parker J's judgment received the approval of the Court of Appeal in *Federal Commerce & Navigation Co Ltd v Molena Alpha Inc*,[37] and the principle has since become accepted.[38] It applies in the case of a charter by demise (sometimes called a bareboat charter),[39] as well as when a time charter is expressed to be for

---

[29] *Re Bayoil SA* [1999] 1 WLR 147. See also para 5.33 below in relation to cheques and bills of exchange. Notwithstanding the reference to inability to litigate in *Re Bayoil*, the better view is that delay in litigating the cross-claim is not fatal. See *Hurst v Bennett* [2001] EWCA Civ 182, at paras 9 and 19 and *Montgomery v Wanda Modes Ltd* [2002] 1 BCLC 289, 297–298, each referring to *Re A Debtor (No 87 of 1999)* The Times Law Reports, 14 February 2000.

[30] For the position in relation to interim awards in arbitrations, see *Exmar BV v National Iranian Tanker Co (The Trade Fortitude)* [1992] 1 Lloyd's Rep 169, 177.

[31] (1856) 26 LJQB 75, 6 El & Bl 1020, 119 ER 1144.

[32] See also, and compare, *Daunt v Lazard* (1858) 27 LJ Ex 399. For a discussion of these cases, see *Compania Sud Americana de Vapores v Shipmair BV (The Teno)* [1977] 2 Lloyd's Rep 289, 295.

[33] Parker J referred to the decisions in *Compania Sud Americana de Vapores v Shipmair BV (The Teno)* [1977] 2 Lloyd's Rep 289, 293.

[34] [1975] 2 Lloyd's Rep 188. See also *Steelwood Carriers Inc v Evimeria Compania Naviera SA (The Agios Giorgis)* [1976] 2 Lloyd's Rep 192, 201.

[35] *Compania Sud Americana de Vapores v Shipmair BV (The Teno)* [1977] 2 Lloyd's Rep 289.

[36] *Naxos Shipping Corp v Thegra Shipping Co NV (The Corfu Island)* (1973). Parker J also referred to a number of statements in other cases as constituting authorities in support of the proposition that there may be a set-off against hire. See *Sea and Land Securities Ltd v William Dickinson and Co Ltd* [1942] 1 KB 286, 298; *Halcyon Steamship Co Ltd v Continental Grain Supply* (1943) 75 Ll L Rep 80, 84; *Nippon Yusen Kaisha v Acme Shipping Corp (The Charalambos N Pateras)* [1971] 2 Lloyd's Rep 42, 48. For a discussion of these cases, see Rose, 'Deductions From Freight and Hire under English Law' [1982] Lloyd's Maritime and Commercial Law Quarterly 33, 43–8.

[37] [1978] 1 QB 927, the result of which was affirmed by the House of Lords [1979] AC 757 on other grounds.

[38] In addition to the cases cited below, see *SL Sethia Liners Ltd v Naviagro Maritime Corp (The Kostas Melas)* [1981] 1 Lloyd's Rep 18.

[39] See *Banco Central SA v Lingoss & Falce Ltd (The Raven)* [1980] 2 Lloyd's Rep 266 (esp at 273). For the difference between the modern form of time charter and a charter by demise, see *Sea and Land Securities Ltd v William Dickinson and Co Ltd* [1942] 2 KB 65, 69, *per* McKinnon LJ.

the period of a particular voyage,[40] so that in substance it resembles a voyage charter.[41]

This right to an equitable set-off against a claim for hire is not confined to cases in which there has been a total withdrawal of the vessel for a specified time.[42] A set-off against hire may take place when the master has wrongfully refused to load a full cargo,[43] and when a speed warranty has been breached.[44] An equitable set-off may also be available when the owners have failed to perform their hold-cleaning obligations resulting in a delay to the vessel at port,[45] and when the vessel had to proceed to another port to discharge the cargo because of contamination which was caused by the owners' breach of the charterparty.[46] A time charterparty may contain a clause to the effect that the owner must 'provide and pay for all provisions and wages . . . for insurance of the vessel, for all deck and engine-room stores including lub oil, galley oil, and fresh water'. If the owner fails to make the payments and the charterer, in order to ensure the vessel's availability and use, instead expends the money, the charterer's damages claim against the owner for breach of the clause may be employed in a set-off against hire.[47]

5.11

It is not every cross-claim that can be set off. In *Federal Commerce v Molena*[48] Lord Denning suggested that the right of deduction should be limited to cases where the owner through his neglect or default has either deprived the charterer of the use of the vessel or has hindered or prejudiced the charterer's use.[49] For example, both he and Lord Goff said that a deduction would not be available when the cross-claim arises merely from damage to cargo. Similarly, a charterer may not set off the estimated value of bunkers remaining on redelivery of the vessel, unless the

5.12

---

[40] *SL Sethia Liners Ltd v Naviagro Maritime Corp (The Kostas Melas)* [1981] 1 Lloyd's Rep 18; *Santiren Shipping Ltd v Unimarine SA (The Chrysovalandou-Dyo)* [1981] 1 Lloyd's Rep 159.

[41] See the discussion in *Carver's Carriage by Sea* (13th edn, 1982) vol 1, 472–4.

[42] *Compania Sud Americana de Vapores v Shipmair BV (The Teno)* [1977] 2 Lloyd's Rep 289, 297.

[43] *Compania Sud Americana de Vapores v Shipmair BV (The Teno)* [1977] 2 Lloyd's Rep 289, 297.

[44] *The Corfu Island* (1973), unreported decision of Ackner J. See also *Marbienes Compania Naviera SA v Ferrostal AG (The Democritos)* [1975] 1 Lloyd's Rep 386, 402; *Federal Commerce & Navigation Co Ltd v Molena Alpha Inc* [1978] 1 QB 927; *Santiren Shipping Ltd v Unimarine SA (The Chrysovalandou-Dyo)* [1981] 1 Lloyd's Rep 159.

[45] Compare *Century Textiles and Industry Ltd v Tomoe Shipping Co (Singapore) Pte Ltd (The Aditya Vaibhav)* [1991] 1 Lloyd's Rep 573.

[46] *Stargos SpA v Petredec Ltd (The Sargasso)* [1994] 1 Lloyd's Rep 412, 426–427.

[47] *Banco Central SA v Lingoss & Falce Ltd (The Raven)* [1980] 2 Lloyd's Rep 266, 273.

[48] [1978] 1 QB 927, 976, 981, following Parker J in *Compania Sud Americana de Vapores v Shipmair BV (The Teno)* [1977] 2 Lloyd's Rep 289, 297. See also *Atlantic Lines & Navigation Co Inc v The Ship 'Didymi'(The Didymi)* [1988] 1 Lloyd's Rep 97, 104, Canadian Federal Court of Appeal.

[49] Lord Goff also said that equitable set-off can arise where the owner through his neglect or default deprives the charterer of the use of the vessel or hinders or prejudices that use, though without saying that the scope of the set-off is limited to those circumstances. See [1978] 1 QB 927, 981.

charterparty specifically sanctions a deduction.[50] The principle is illustrated by *The Leon*.[51] The charterers alleged three breaches by the owners: (1) that the master had failed to keep full and accurate logs of the fuel consumption; (2) that the master had procured that invoices which did not represent the fuel actually taken on board should be sent to and paid for by the charterers; (3) that the owners had breached their duty as bailees of the bunkers to use them during the charterparty in accordance with the charterer's orders. It was held that none of the breaches affected the use of the vessel, and that consequently they did not give rise to a set-off against hire. Hobhouse J in his judgment emphasized however that there was nothing to show 'overriding fraud' on the part of the owners. If there had been, he suggested that the result may have been different.[52]

5.13 Lord Denning's later judgment in *The Aliakmon Progress*[53] suggested a narrower scope to the set-off than that described in *Federal Commerce v Molena*. A vessel the subject of a time charter sustained damage while attempting to berth at a port in Iceland. Temporary repairs were effected there, and the vessel then sailed to Antwerp, where permanent repairs were undertaken. Owing to the resulting delay the vessel lost an anticipated cargo at Antwerp and had to wait some thirty-nine days for a new cargo. Lord Denning, with whom Geoffrey Lane LJ agreed, doubted that the loss sustained by the charterers constituted a ground for equitable set-off. He cited *Federal Commerce v Molena* as authority for the proposition that equitable set-off is only available against a claim for hire 'where the charterers have been deprived of the use of the ship by the fault of the owner'.[54] He said that, in the case before him, the charterers in fact did have the use of the ship but could not get a cargo. There was no mention of whether a set-off may arise when the shipowner merely prejudiced the charterer in the use of the vessel, and there was no discussion of whether in the instant case there had been any such prejudice. Subsequently however the courts have reiterated that prejudice in the use of the vessel not amounting to total deprivation may ground a set-off.[55]

5.14 Counsel in *The Leon*[56] attacked the proposition that equitable set-off in the context of time charters should be limited to cases in which the charterer has been deprived of or prejudiced in the use of the vessel. Rather, it was suggested that the allowance or otherwise of a set-off should be determined by reference to whether

---

[50] *Tropwind AG v Jade Enterprises Ltd (The Tropwind)* [1981] 1 Lloyd's Rep 45, 48. Compare *Aurora Borealis Compania Armadora SA v Marine Midland Bank NA (The Maistros)* [1984] 1 Lloyd's Rep 646, in which there was an agreement for a set-off.

[51] *Leon Corp v Atlantic Lines and Navigation Co Inc (The Leon)* [1985] 2 Lloyd's Rep 470.

[52] [1985] 2 Lloyd's Rep 470, 476.

[53] *Aliakmon Maritime Corp v Trans Ocean Continental Shipping Ltd (The Aliakmon Progress)* [1978] 2 Lloyd's Rep 499.

[54] [1978] 2 Lloyd's Rep 499, 501.

[55] *Banco Central SA v Lingoss & Falce Ltd (The Raven)* [1980] 2 Lloyd's Rep 266, 273; *Leon Corp v Atlantic Lines and Navigation Co Inc (The Leon)* [1985] 2 Lloyd's Rep 470, 475.

[56] *Leon Corp v Atlantic Lines and Navigation Co Inc (The Leon)* [1985] 2 Lloyd's Rep 470.

it would be unfair in the particular case to allow the owner to sue for hire without giving credit for the cross-demand. Hobhouse J however declined to depart from the statements of the ambit of the set-off by Lord Denning and Goff LJ in *Federal Commerce v Molena*, and emphasized that the relevant principle is set out in Lord Cottenham's judgment in *Rawson v Samuel*,[57] that the equity of the bill must impeach the title to the legal demand. In the case of a time charter, hire is paid for the right to use the vessel for a specified period of time, irrespective of whether the charterer chooses to use it for carrying cargo or instead lays it up out of use. The hire is required to be paid in advance, and failure to make punctual payment gives the owner the right to withdraw the vessel. In those circumstances, Hobhouse J said that it is not a coincidence that, in cases where the right to an equitable set-off was upheld, the cross-claim involved something which could be identified as depriving the charterer of the use of the vessel or which prejudiced or hindered that use, because, in the context of a time charter contract and a claim for time charter hire, it is that type of cross-claim which has the requisite effect of impeaching the plaintiff's demand.[58]

In a case where hire is payable periodically under a time charter, the charterer may **5.15** have been prejudiced in the use of the vessel only in certain defined periods. In other periods the vessel in fact may have been made available in accordance with the contract. If the charterer's damages claim in such a case exceeds the amount of hire owing for the periods during which the use of the vessel was prejudiced, the charterer may wish to set off the excess against payments of hire relating to other periods. The question whether this is permissible was considered earlier.[59]

The justification for the freight rule

Given that there is this distinction between freight and hire as regards equitable set- **5.16** off, the question arises whether there is any justification for it. It has been suggested that the original justification for the freight rule may have been based upon cash flow considerations, in that the master would require the freight to be paid in full at the end of the voyage in order to pay off his crew, and to refit and victual his ship. Communications in those days were slow, and the master could not wait a long time for funds to be remitted to him.[60] Yet, in the context of building contracts, the courts have said that cash flow considerations are no longer regarded as a sufficient

---

[57] (1841) Cr & Ph 161, 41 ER 451.
[58] [1985] 2 Lloyd's Rep 470, 475.
[59] See paras 4.79–4.83 above.
[60] See Goff LJ in *Federal Commerce & Navigation Co Ltd v Molena Alpha Inc* [1978] 1 QB 927, 983. See also *Henriksens Rederi A/S v THZ Rolimpex (The Brede)* [1974] 1 QB 233, 263. Thus, Willes J commented in *Meyer v Dresser* (1864) 16 CB(NS) 646, 663, 143 ER 1280, 1287 that it would have been inconvenient for a vessel to be delayed while disputes as to the amount of freight were being settled. See also *Dakin v Oxley* (1864) 15 CB(NS) 646, 667, 143 ER 938, 946–947, *per* Willes J.

reason for denying a set-off.[61] On the other hand, Lord Wilberforce has expressed doubts as to whether the freight rule indeed is anything other than an arbitrary rule, 'in the sense that no very clear justification for it has ever been stated and perhaps also in the sense that the law might just, or almost, as well have settled for a rule to the opposite effect'.[62] Despite this he concluded that the rule is too well established to be departed from now.[63] There are, nevertheless, dicta to the effect that it should not be extended,[64] and the attitude of the courts has been that voyage and time charters are sufficiently dissimilar in their operation to justify the application in the case of hire of the general rule permitting deductions, rather than having resort to the exception precluding deductions found in the freight rule. Thus, Lord Denning in justifying the distinction noted that freight is the sum payable for the carriage of goods from one place to another, while hire is paid for the right to use the vessel for a specified period of time irrespective of whether or not the charterer chooses to use it for carrying cargo.[65] But even this as a basis for treating them differently becomes blurred when a time charter is for the period of a particular trip.[66]

(2) The Statutes of Set-off

5.17 A question in respect of which conflicting opinions have been expressed is whether the principle which precludes a defence of equitable set-off against a claim for freight also extends to the defence provided by the Statutes of Set-off in the case of mutual debts.[67]

---

[61] *Gilbert-Ash (Northern) Ltd v Modern Engineering (Bristol) Ltd* [1974] AC 689, 707, 718; *Mottram Consultants Ltd v Bernard Sunley & Sons Ltd* [1975] 2 Lloyd's Rep 197, 214. See the discussion of building contracts in para 5.49 below. See also *Federal Commerce & Navigation Co Ltd v Molena Alpha Inc* [1978] 1 QB 927, 983, 986.

[62] *Aries Tanker Corp v Total Transport Ltd* [1977] 1 WLR 185, 190. Similarly Lord Simon of Glaisdale said (at 193) that 'there is no question of high legal policy involved at all'. See also *Dole Dried Fruit and Nut Co v Trustin Kerwood Ltd* [1990] 2 Lloyd's Rep 309, 310. Compare Lord Salmon in *Aries Tanker* (at 195), who suggested that the incidence of insurance cover in respect of freight may be based upon the rule. See also, with respect to insurance, *Henriksens Rederi A/S v THZ Rolimpex (The Brede)* [1974] 1 QB 233, 244, 263.

[63] Similarly, Lord Brandon in the House of Lords in *Bank of Boston Connecticut v European Grain and Shipping Ltd* [1989] 1 AC 1056, 1100 accepted that, whatever its merits or demerits, the rule is not open to challenge.

[64] *Seven Seas Transportation Ltd v Atlantic Shipping Co SA* [1975] 2 Lloyd's Rep 188, 191; *Federal Commerce & Navigation Co Ltd v Molena Alpha Inc* [1978] 1 QB 927, 982. Notwithstanding those dicta, the freight rule has been extended to contracts for the carriage of goods by road. See para 5.06 above.

[65] *Federal Commerce & Navigation Co Ltd v Molena Alpha Inc* [1978] 1 QB 927, 973.

[66] See eg *SL Sethia Liners Ltd v Naviagro Maritime Corporation (The Kostas Melas)* [1981] 1 Lloyd's Rep 18 and *Santiren Shipping Ltd v Unimarine SA (The Chrysovalandou-Dyo)* [1981] 1 Lloyd's Rep 159, and generally the discussion in *Carver's Carriage by Sea* (13th edn, 1982) vol 1, 472–4. Note however Steyn J's justification of the distinction in *Itex Itagrani Export SA v Care Shipping Corp (The Cebu) (No 2)* [1990] 2 Lloyd's Rep 316, 320.

[67] There is no reason why a set-off under the Statutes should not be available against a claim for hire under a time charter, given that it is susceptible to an equitable set-off. This was assumed to be the case in *Aectra Refining and Marketing Inc v Exmar NV* [1994] 1 WLR 1634.

The cases favour the view that the freight rule does not apply in this context.[68] In   **5.18**
Wilson v Gabriel[69] the defendant in an action for payment of freight pleaded set-off as a defence, based upon an unconnected debt owing by the plaintiff. The plaintiff replied, on equitable grounds,[70] that when the freight was in the course of being earned he had assigned it for value to a third party, and that the plaintiff brought this action as trustee for the third party. The Court of Queen's Bench[71] held that this did not to constitute an answer to the plea, the defendant not having been notified of the assignment before the mutual debts arose.[72] Cockburn CJ (with whom Wightman J concurred) and Blackburn J each accepted that the defendant was entitled to a set-off at law against the liability for freight, and that the set-off was not affected by the assignment. Moreover this was after the courts had adopted the principle that the common law defence of abatement does not extend to freight,[73] so that the statutory defence evidently was thought to be subject to different considerations. More recently, Hirst J adopted the contrary view in *The Khian Captain (No 2)*.[74] He held that set-off under the Statutes is subject to the freight rule, and suggested that *Wilson v Gabriel* was impliedly overruled by the House of Lords in *Aries Tanker Corp v Total Transport Ltd*.[75] The issue in the *Aries Tanker* case, however, was whether a damages claim in respect of cargo could be applied in reduction of a liability for freight either on the basis of equitable set-off or common law abatement. The House of Lords held that those defences did not apply. The statutory defence of set-off was not in issue, and nor was it considered. Subsequently Hobhouse J at first instance in the *Bank of Boston* case[76] disagreed with Hirst J. He accepted that a freight debt and another debt can be set off under the Statutes, and that *Wilson v Gabriel* was not overruled by the *Aries Tanker* case.

---

[68]   See also *Jones v Moore* (1841) 4 Y & C Ex 351, 160 ER 1041. Compare *Isberg v Bowden* (1853) 8 Ex 852, 155 ER 1599, though in that case the action for freight was brought by the master rather than by the owner of the vessel. It was held that a debt owing by the owner could not be set off, but this was on the basis of a perceived lack of mutuality. There is nothing in the judgments, or indeed in the arguments of counsel, to suggest that it was thought that an action for freight was not susceptible in any event to a defence of set-off under the Statutes.

[69]   (1863) 4 B & S 243, 122 ER 450.

[70]   *Wilson v Gabriel* was decided at common law before the Judicature Acts fused the courts of law and equity, but the Common Law Procedure Act 1854, ss 83–86 allowed equitable defences to be pleaded in the common law courts.

[71]   Cockburn CJ, Wightman and Blackburn JJ.

[72]   (1863) 4 B & S 243, 248, 122 ER 450, 452–453, *per* Blackburn J. See para 17.10 below.

[73]   *Sheels v Davies* (1814) 4 Camp 119, 171 ER 39; *Mondel v Steel* (1841) 8 M & W 858, 871, 151 ER 1288, 1293.

[74]   *Freedom Maritime Corp v International Bulk Carriers SA (The Khian Captain) (No 2)* [1986] 1 Lloyd's Rep 429.

[75]   [1977] 1 WLR 185.

[76]   *Sub nom Colonial Bank v European Grain & Shipping Ltd (The Dominique)* [1987] 1 Lloyd's Rep 239, 250–251.

5.19 Apart from *The Khian Captain*, it is difficult to find authority for the proposition that the Statutes do not apply in this context.[77] Two cases which have been said to support that view[78] are explicable on other grounds.

5.20 In *Weguellin v Cellier*[79] the consignees of cargo had a claim against the shipowner as a result of accepting six-month bills at the request of the shipowner. The shipowner assigned the freight payable by way of security to the respondents, who then brought the present action seeking a declaration that they were entitled to be paid the freight. However the consignees, having honoured the bills, had a claim against the shipowner, and argued that this gave rise to a set-off against the liability for freight and that the respondents as assignees took subject to the set-off. It is apparent that any right of set-off would have arisen under the Statutes, based upon mutual debts, given that the demands would not have been sufficiently closely connected to give rise to an equitable set-off. While Lord Chelmsford held that there was no such set-off which would defeat the respondent's right to the freight, this was not because of a general principle that a claim for freight is not susceptible to a defence of set-off under the Statutes. In the first place, as counsel for the respondents argued, the bills did not mature until after the consignees received notice of the assignment, so that at the date of notice there was no accrued debt owing by the shipowner. An assignee does not take subject to a cross-debt which arises after notice, albeit as a result of a prior contract.[80] But even apart from that, the Statutes of Set-off only provided a procedural defence to an action for payment of a debt, and until a judgment for a set-off is obtained separate and distinct debts remain in existence.[81] In *Weguellin v Cellier*, when the goods arrived at the port of discharge the respondents put a stop on them. They had a lien and, as Lord Chelmsford pointed out, the consignees could not have obtained the cargo without payment of the freight, and the master of the ship would have been bound to insist upon payment before delivery.[82] Because of the procedural nature of the defence, the consignees could not have acted unilaterally to bring about a set-off so as to obtain the release of goods the subject of the lien. The circum-

---

[77] In *Opal Maritime Agencies Pty Ltd v Baltic Shipping Co* (1998) 158 ALR 416 the cross-claim of the agent which had collected freight was for liquidated amounts, in the form of fees and disbursements. Tamberlin J in the Federal Court of Australia held that the non-deduction rule applied, so that that agent had to account for the freight without a set-off. In coming to that conclusion his Honour considered only cases concerned with equitable set-off. The possible application of the Statutes of Set-off was not countenanced. However the case was decided in New South Wales, where the Statutes of Set-off have been abolished. See para 2.56 above.

[78] Wood, *English and International Set-off* (1989) 707.

[79] (1873) LR 6 HL 286, 42 LJ Ch 758.

[80] *Watson v Mid Wales Railway Co* (1867) LR 2 CP 593. See para 17.12 below.

[81] See paras 2.33–2.48 above.

[82] Compare *Campbell v Thompson* (1816) 1 Stark 490, 171 ER 539, in which it was accepted that an assignee of freight was not entitled to refuse to allow delivery of the cargo unless freight was paid without deduction, though Dr Lushington doubted the authority of that case in *The Salacia* (1862) Lush 578, 167 ER 263.

stances in *Weguellin v Cellier* were different, in that the consignees after some correspondence had paid the amount of the freight to the dock company holding the goods so as to obtain their release, and the respondents then filed a bill seeking a declaration that the freight in the hands of the dock company should be applied towards payment of what was due to them by the shipowner.[83] But it was still not a case of set-off under the Statutes, because it was not an action against the consignees for payment.

The second case, *Tanner v Phillips*,[84] similarly may be explained on other grounds. **5.21** The plaintiff was mortgagee of a ship, and as further security held a mortgage of freight. The ship was chartered to the defendant. The charterparty provided that the defendant could make advances not exceeding £150 to the master as agent for the mortgagor/owner on account of freight, though other advances in excess of that amount were made. Before the cargo was unloaded and freight became due, the mortgagee took possession. When the freight later became payable the mortgagee sued the defendant for payment, and it was held that the defendant could not set off the excess advances. This was so notwithstanding that the advances were made before the defendant had notice of the mortgage, whereas ordinarily, if there are mutual debts in existence before notice of an assignment, the assignee takes subject to a right of set-off under the Statutes.[85] However the mortgagee's entitlement to freight in *Tanner v Phillips* was not based upon an assignment of a debt. Rather, the mortgagee claimed payment of freight as mortgagee in possession. The mortgagee became entitled in his own right to freight which the ship was in the course of earning. As Lord Cairns pointed out in *Keith v Burrows*,[86] the right of a mortgagee in possession to freight in the course of being earned does not arise by virtue of any contract or antecedent right, but rather it is payable to the mortgagee once he goes into possession because the mortgagee is then regarded as the master or owner of the ship.[87] His right depends on property, not on contract.[88] *Tanner v Phillips* therefore was not a case in which there were mutual debts between the mortgagor and the charterer which would have given rise to a set-off available against the mortgagee, were it not for a supposed principle that there may not be a set-off under the Statutes against a claim for freight. Rather, mutuality for the purpose of the Statutes was lacking, in that, on the one hand, the

---

[83] This appears more clearly from the report at (1873) 42 LJ Ch 758, 760.

[84] (1872) 42 LJ Ch 125.

[85] See paras 17.10–17.12 below.

[86] (1877) 2 App Cas 636, 646. See also *Kerswill v Bishop* (1832) 2 C & J 529, 149 ER 224; *Japp v Campbell* (1888) 57 LJQB 79; *Wilson v Wilson* (1872) LR 14 Eq 32 (mortgagee's right to freight has priority over an earlier assignment of freight of which the mortgagee did not have notice).

[87] In the same way, when there is a sale of a ship the right to freight in the course of being earned passes to the purchaser. See eg *Morrison v Parsons* (1810) 2 Taunt 407, 127 ER 1136. As Lord Ellenborough remarked in *Case v Davidson* (1816) 5 M & S 79, 82, 105 ER 980, 981, 'freight follows, as an incident, the property in the ship'.

[88] *Rusden v Pope* (1868) LR 3 Ex 269, 276–277.

charterer had a claim against the mortgagor for the excess advances and, on the other, the mortgagee in his own right was entitled to the freight from the charterer.[89]

5.22 The better view is that the freight rule, which precludes an equitable set-off or a common law defence of abatement against a claim for freight, does not extend to the Statutes of Set-off. In the case of the Statutes, the right is statutory in origin, and the Statutes specifically allowed a set-off in the case of mutual debts. While the Statutes themselves have been repealed, the repealing legislation preserved the right of set-off conferred by the Statutes.[90] The proper approach in the case of a statutory-based defence is to interpret the legislation, and there is nothing in the language of the Statutes to suggest that there is an exception in the case of an action for freight.

(3) Bill of Lading Freight When the Vessel is Chartered

5.23 When a ship has been chartered, and the master signs bills of lading with third-party shippers for the carriage of goods, the question whether the shipowner or the charterer is entitled to the bill of lading freight depends upon whether the master signed as agent for the shipowner or the charterer. If the charter is by demise the contract will be with the charterer, but in other cases the question will depend upon the documents and circumstances of the particular case.[91] When the contract is with the shipowner, he can sue the shipper for freight. If the charterer nevertheless has appointed an agent to collect the freight, and the shipowner gives notice to the agent before the freight has been received requiring the freight to be paid to him rather than the charterer, the shipowner can sue the agent for the freight as money had and received.[92] Any expenses incurred by the agent in carrying out the charterer's instructions cannot be set off by the agent,[93] since mutuality for the purpose of the Statutes of Set-off is lacking. If on the other hand the owner as the contracting party is paid the bill of lading freight, he is only entitled to retain an amount equal to the hire or freight then unpaid under the charterparty. The surplus must be paid to the charterer. Channell J decided this in *Wehner v Dene Steam Shipping Co*.[94] The reason is not that the owner is liable to the charterer for the bill of lading freight received and the charterer is liable for hire or freight under the charterparty, and that these obligations are set off.[95] It is not a

---

[89] See para 17.71 below.
[90] See para 2.06 above.
[91] *Samuel v West Hartlepool Steam Navigation Co* (1906) 11 Com Cas 115, 125–126.
[92] *Molthes Rederi Aktieselskabet v Ellerman's Wilson Line Ltd* [1927] 1 KB 710, 715–716. Greer J left open the question whether the agent similarly could be sued in respect of freight received before notice from the shipowner.
[93] *Molthes Rederi v Ellerman's Wilson Line* [1927] 1 KB 710.
[94] [1905] 2 KB 92.
[95] Compare Wood, *English and International Set-off* (1989) 705, 978–9.

case of cross-demands at all. Rather, the owner had contracted by the charterparty that he would be satisfied with the payment of the freight or hire specified in the charterparty for the use of the ship, and accordingly if the owner receives the bill of lading freight it is part of their contract that he will account for any surplus to the charterer.[96]

When the contract is with the charterer rather than the shipowner, the shipowner **5.24** may have reserved a lien on sub-freights, entitling the shipowner to require payment to him of the bill of lading freight that is otherwise due to the charterer.[97] The lien can only be exercised before the freight has been paid to the charterer or his agent.[98] Moreover, it can only be exercised in respect of sums due to the shipowner at the time that the demand for payment is made pursuant to the lien.[99] The lien does not confer a proprietary interest in the freight, but rather it is merely a personal right to intercept freight before it is paid. It is analogous to a right of stoppage in transitu.[100] The lien therefore would be subject to a right of set-off available to the shipper against the charterer, including under the Statutes in the case of mutual debts, since the set-off would have the effect that nothing would be paid to the extent of the set-off which could be intercepted.

B. Negotiable Instruments, Letters of Credit, and Direct Debits

(1) Negotiable Instruments—Equitable Set-off

An unliquidated cross-demand generally cannot be employed as an equitable **5.25** set-off in an action to enforce payment of a bill of exchange or other negotiable instrument.[101] The House of Lords affirmed the principle in *Nova (Jersey) Knit Ltd v Kammgarn Spinnerei GmbH*,[102] and it is also accepted in

---

[96] *Wehner v Dene Steam Shipping Co* [1905] 2 KB 92, 99, explained in *Molthes Rederi v Ellerman's Wilson Line* [1927] 1 KB 710. See also *Tradigrain SA v King Diamond Shipping SA (The Spiros C)* [2000] 2 Lloyd's Rep 319, 328; *Carver's Carriage by Sea* (13th edn, 1982) vol 2, 1225–6 para 1744.

[97] See generally *Carver's Carriage by Sea* (13th edn, 1982) vol 2, 1395 para 2013.

[98] *Tagart, Beaton & Co v Fisher & Sons* [1903] 1 KB 391.

[99] *Wehner v Dene Steam Shipping Co* [1905] 2 KB 92.

[100] *Agnew v Commissioner of Inland Revenue* [2001] 2 AC 710, 727–728 paras 39–41.

[101] This includes a cheque. See *Finch Motors Ltd v Quin* [1980] 2 NZLR 513, 516.

[102] [1977] 1 WLR 713. See also *Morgan v Richardson* (1806) 7 East 482n, 170 ER 868; *Tye v Gwynne* (1810) 2 Camp 346, 170 ER 1179; *Solomon v Turner* (1815) 1 Stark 51, 171 ER 398; *Day v Nix* (1824) 2 LJOSCP 133; *Obbard v Betham* (1830) M & M 483, 173 ER 1232; *Glennie v Imri* (1839) 3 Y & C Ex 436, 160 ER 773; *Trickey v Larne* (1840) 6 M & W 278, 151 ER 414; *Sully v Frean* (1854) 10 Ex 535, 156 ER 551; *Warwick v Nairn* (1855) 10 Ex 762, 156 ER 648; *Jackson v Murphy* (1886) 4 TLR 92n; *Bow, McLachlan & Co Ltd v Ship 'Camosun'* [1909] AC 597, 612; *James Lamont & Co Ltd v Hyland Ltd* [1950] 1 KB 585; *Montecchi v Shimco (UK) Ltd* [1979] 1 WLR 1180, 1183; *Montebianco Industrie Tessili SpA v Carlyle Mills (London) Ltd* [1981] 1 Lloyd's Rep 509; *Case Poclain Corp Ltd v Jones* [1986] ECC 569. Compare the uncertainty of the Court of Appeal in *Oscar Harris, Son & Co v Vallarman & Co* [1940] 1 All ER 185, and the decision in *Court*

Australia[103] and New Zealand.[104] The principle applies whether the parties are immediate or remote,[105] and whether the cross-demand arose out of the transaction in respect of which the instrument was given or, *a fortiori*, in any other way.[106]

5.26   The principle typically is invoked when a cheque is given as payment for the price of goods sold, and the vendor has breached a term in the contract which amounts to a partial failure of consideration[107] so as to give rise to a claim against him for unliquidated damages. The breach does not provide the purchaser with a defence to an action by the vendor for payment of the cheque. This is sometimes explained on the ground that the cheque is a separate contract from the contract of sale, although it is not an essential requirement of an equitable set-off that the claim

---

v Sheen (1891) 7 TLR 556 (the report of which is criticized in *James Lamont v Hyland* [1950] 1 KB 585, 592). Compare also the statement by Thesiger LJ in *Anglo-Italian Bank v Wells* (1878) 38 LT 197, 201, though note the more cautious approach of Jessel MR at 199. The view of the Master of the Rolls was preferred in *James Lamont v Hyland* [1950] 1 KB 585, 592–593. The principle continues to apply under the Civil Procedure Rules 1998. See *Safa Ltd v Banque du Caire* [2000] 2 Lloyd's Rep 600, 605, 606, 610, and also *Balfour Beatty Civil Engineering v Technical & General Guarantee Co Ltd* (1999) 68 Con LR 180, 190 in relation to fraud.

[103]   *Eversure Textiles Manufacturing Co Ltd v Webb* [1978] Qd R 347; *K D Morris & Sons Ltd v Bank of Queensland* (1980) 30 ALR 321, 350; *Rigg v Commonwealth Bank of Australia* (1989) 97 FLR 261, 267–268. See also the discussion in, and compare, *John Shearer Ltd v Gehl Co* (1995) 60 FCR 136 (application to set aside a statutory demand, for which see para 5.33 below). In Victoria it has been held that the principle under discussion applies when the claim on the bill is brought pursuant to the summary procedure set out in the Instruments Act 1958 (Vic). See *Mobil Oil Australia Ltd v Caulfield Tyre Service Pty Ltd* [1984] VR 440. Compare *Graham v Seagoe* [1964] 2 Lloyd's Rep 564, in which an action on promissory notes given in connection with the sale of a boat was stayed while disputes as to the condition of a boat were referred to arbitration. However, the court concerned itself only with the construction of the particular arbitration clause, and no mention was made of the principle under discussion. Compare also Moffitt P and Glass JA in *Sidney Raper Pty Ltd v Commonwealth Trading Bank* [1975] 2 NSWLR 227, 238–239, 255, who seemed to accept that a claim on a bank cheque could be the subject of an equitable set-off. This aspect of their judgment is unlikely to be followed, though a set-off may have been available in any event in that case on the basis of equity acting by analogy with the Statutes of Set-off. See the discussion of the Statutes in paras 5.35–5.40 below. In New South Wales, the Common Law Procedure Act 1899, s 79 formerly provided that matters which were the subject of a cross-action between the parties could by leave of a judge be pleaded by way of set-off. The courts accepted that s 79 permitted a damages claim to be pleaded by way of set-off against a claim on a promissory note if the demands arose out of the same transaction. See eg *Karbowsky v Redaelli* (1914) 31 WN(NSW) 80; *Richardson v Hill* (1922) 22 SR(NSW) 326. The requirement that the demands should have originated in the same transaction followed from a requirement that the courts held was inherent in s 79 and applied generally. See eg *Assets & General Finance Co v Crick* (1911) 28 WN(NSW) 91; *Austral Bronze Co Ltd v Sleigh* (1916) 34 WN(NSW) 143. For a discussion of s 79, see Russell, 'Defences by Way of Set-off, Counterclaim and Cross Action' (1928) 2 Australian Law Journal 80. Section 79 was repealed by the Supreme Court Act 1970, and so these cases would no longer apply.

[104]   *Finch Motors Ltd v Quin* [1980] 2 NZLR 513; *International Ore & Fertilizer Corporation v East Coast Fertilizer Co Ltd* [1987] 1 NZLR 9. *Union Bank of Australia v Williams* (1892) 11 NZLR 65 would no longer appear to be good law.

[105]   For remote parties see eg *All Trades Distributors Ltd v Agencies Kaufman Ltd* (1969) 113 Sol Jo 995, 996; *Brown, Shipley & Co Ltd v Alicia Hosiery Ltd* [1966] 1 Lloyd's Rep 668.

[106]   *Cebora SNC v SIP (Industrial Products) Ltd* [1976] 1 Lloyd's Rep 271, 278–279; *Buying Systems (Aust) Pty Ltd v Tien Mah Litho Printing Co Ltd* (1986) 5 NSWLR 317, 328.

[107]   Compare total failure of consideration. See para 5.31 below.

and the cross-claim should have originated in the same contract.[108] The cheque has also been described as constituting a separate transaction from the sale,[109] and indeed in the case of letters of credit in sale transactions this principle has been expressly incorporated in the Uniform Customs and Practice for Documentary Credits.[110] But the most commonly accepted explanation is that the rule precluding a defence of equitable set-off is based upon a policy consideration, that a cheque or bill of exchange given as payment is considered to be equivalent to cash, albeit with payment deferred, and if an unliquidated cross-demand could provide a defence to an action on the instrument there would be a substantial inroad upon this commercial principle.[111]

Stays of execution are subject to a similar restriction. A defendant in an application for summary judgment who asserts a counterclaim not amounting to a set-off ordinarily would not be granted leave to defend. On the other hand, the court in its discretion may order a stay of execution[112] on the claimant's judgment until the defendant's cross-action has been tried,[113] so that if the defendant succeeds in the cross-action execution would only issue for the balance of the two claims. However a different practice applies when the claimant's claim is on a cheque or bill of exchange. The fact that the defendant in an action to enforce payment of a cheque asserts a counterclaim for unliquidated damages is not usually regarded as a ground for staying execution.[114] This is not an inflexible principle, however, because it is said that the court may grant a stay if there are exceptional circumstances.[115] But while the existence of this exception is generally recognized, the **5.27**

---

[108] See para 4.55 above.

[109] *Eversure Textiles Manufacturing Co Ltd v Webb* [1978] Qd R 347, 348–349. Compare *Montecchi v Shimco (UK) Ltd* [1979] 1 WLR 1180, 1183.

[110] The Uniform Customs and Practice, Art 3(a) provides that: 'Credits, by their nature, are separate transactions from the sales or other contract(s) on which they may be based . . .' See paras 5.42–5.47 below in relation to letters of credit.

[111] *Nova (Jersey) Knit Ltd v Kammgarn Spinnerei GmbH* [1977] 1 WLR 713, 721, *per* Lord Wilberforce, 722, *per* Viscount Dilhorne. See also *Fielding & Platt Ltd v Najjar* [1969] 1 WLR 357, 361; *Montecchi v Shimco (UK) Ltd* [1979] 1 WLR 1180, 1183.

[112] Formerly pursuant to RSC O 14 r 3(2). See now CPR rr 3.1(3) and 24.6, and para 5.1 of the Practice Direction supplementing CPR Part 24. See generally *Civil Procedure* (Autumn 2001) vol 1, paras 24.2.6 and 24.6.3.

[113] See eg *Mottram Consultants Ltd v Bernard Sunley & Sons Ltd* [1975] 2 Lloyd's Rep 197, 214, and para 1.05 above.

[114] *Brown, Shipley & Co Ltd v Alicia Hosiery Ltd* [1966] 1 Lloyd's Rep 668; *Cebora SNC v SIP (Industrial Products) Ltd* [1976] 1 Lloyd's Rep 271; *Walek & Co K G v Seafield Gentex Ltd* [1978] IR 167; *Montecchi v Shimco (UK) Ltd* [1979] 1 WLR 1180, 1183; *Montebianco Industrie Tessili SpA v Carlyle Mills (London) Ltd* [1981] 1 Lloyd's Rep 509. In Queensland, compare *Hoe and Bickley v Baulch* [1951] QWN 14.

[115] *Brown, Shipley & Co Ltd v Alicia Hosiery Ltd* [1966] 1 Lloyd's Rep 668, 669; *Mottram Consultants Ltd v Bernard Sunley & Sons Ltd* [1975] 2 Lloyd's Rep 197, 214; *Eversure Textiles Manufacturing Co Ltd v Webb* [1978] Qd R 347, 350–351; *Continental Illinois National Bank and Trust Co of Chicago v Papanicolaou* [1986] 2 Lloyd's Rep 441, 445; *Thoni GmbH v RTP Equipment Ltd* [1979] 2 Lloyd's Rep 282, 284, 285; *Case Poclain Corp Ltd v Jones* [1986] ECC 569, 573; *Safa Ltd v Banque du Caire* [2000] 2 Lloyd's Rep 600, 605. See also *Begley Industries Ltd v Cramp* [1977]

courts have been reluctant to recognize 'exceptional circumstances' which may detract from the principle that cheques and bills of exchange should be treated as cash.[116] Indeed, in *Nova (Jersey) Knit Ltd v Kammgarn Spinnerei GmbH*[117] Viscount Dilhorne said that it would 'seldom, if ever'[118] be right to allow a cross-claim to operate as a bar to execution, while Lord Russell of Killowen said that an unliquidated cross-demand is not available as a counterclaim in an action on a bill of exchange without referring to an exception of 'exceptional circumstances' in relation to a stay.[119] Certainly it is not sufficient for a stay that there is a counterclaim which is likely to succeed,[120] or that the claim on the cheque and the cross-action for unliquidated damages are part of the same transaction.[121]

5.28 A stay nevertheless was ordered in *Barclays Bank Ltd v Aschaffenburger Zellstoffwerke AG*.[122] A German acceptor of bills of exchange had a cross-claim against the English drawer that was the subject of an arbitration to be held in Copenhagen. Judgment was given against the acceptor on the bills, but the Court of Appeal stayed execution until the result of the arbitration was known.[123] The reason for the stay is not altogether clear, although it appears from the judgment

---

2 NZLR 207, 213; *John Shearer Ltd v Gehl Co* (1995) 60 FCR 136, 141, and Lord Salmon in his dissenting judgment in *Nova (Jersey) Knit Ltd v Kammgarn Spinnerei GmbH* [1977] 1 WLR 713, 726. The discretion should be available whether or not the counterclaim arises directly out of the transaction in respect of which the bills were given. See *Cebora SNC v SIP (Industrial Products) Ltd* [1976] 1 Lloyd's Rep 271, 275 (referring to *James Lamont v Hyland* [1950] 1 KB 585).

[116] In *Cebora SNC v SIP (Industrial Products) Ltd* [1976] 1 Lloyd's Rep 271, 279 Sir Eric Sachs warned that 'the Courts should be really careful not to whittle away the rule of practice by introducing unnecessary exceptions to it under the influence of sympathy-evoking stories, and should have due regard to the maxim that hard cases can make bad law. Indeed, in these days of increasing international interdependence and increasing need to foster liquidity of resources, the rule may be said to be of special import to the business community. Pleas to leave in Court large sums to deteriorate in value while official referee scale proceedings are fought out may well to that community seem rather divorced from business realities, and should perhaps be examined with considerable caution.'

[117] [1977] 1 WLR 713.

[118] [1977] 1 WLR 713, 722.

[119] [1977] 1 WLR 713, 732. See also *Associated Bulk Carriers Ltd v Koch Shipping Inc (The Fuohsan Maru)* [1978] 1 Lloyd's Rep 24, 28; *Exmar BV v National Iranian Tanker Co (The Trade Fortitude)* [1992] 1 Lloyd's Rep 169, 177.

[120] *Cebora SNC v SIP (Industrial Products) Ltd* [1976] 1 Lloyd's Rep 271, 277; *Continental Illinois National Bank and Trust Co of Chicago v Papanicolaou* [1986] 2 Lloyd's Rep 441, 445.

[121] *Walek & Co K G v Seafield Gentex Ltd* [1978] IR 167.

[122] [1967] 1 Lloyd's Rep 387. In *Eversure Textiles Manufacturing Co Ltd v Webb* [1978] Qd R 347, 350–351 Connolly J contemplated that, if a bill of exchange constituted the consideration for the purchase of goods which were acquired by the defendant for resale to third parties, the defendant 'might at least have an argument' in support of a stay if the plaintiff had acted in some manner which made it difficult for the defendant to sell the goods. Nevertheless he went on to comment that it was 'extremely doubtful' whether in principle this should lead to a stay.

[123] The drawer had indorsed the bills to the plaintiff bank. When the plaintiff sued on the bills the acceptor sought leave to defend, alleging that it had a set-off and cross-claim against the drawer which it could assert against the plaintiff because the plaintiff was either an agent for collection on behalf of the drawer or alternatively it was a trustee for the drawer.

of Harman LJ[124] that the German acceptor had argued that there may have been some difficulty in obtaining payment if it succeeded. The case received a mixed reception when the Court of Appeal later considered it in *Cebora SNC v SIP (Industrial Products) Ltd.*[125] Buckley LJ said that it should be regarded as turning on its own particular facts. Stephenson LJ was more positive. He said that he was 'not surprised'[126] that a stay was granted in the circumstances of the case. Sir Eric Sachs on the other hand was critical of the decision. He noted that the report of the case, 'perhaps wisely',[127] had not been included in the Law Reports or the All England Reports, and suggested that it was out of line with other authorities. However a judge ordered a stay in similar circumstances in *Montecchi v Shimco (UK) Ltd.*[128] The plaintiff was an Italian businessman who had sold some goods to the defendant English company. The goods were paid for by bill of exchange drawn by the defendant. The defendant alleged that the goods were defective, and refused to honour the bill. The plaintiff then sought, and obtained, summary judgment for the amount of the bill, although execution was stayed until after the hearing of the counterclaim on condition that the defendant pay the amount of the judgment into a joint account or into court. In addition, the judge granted a Mareva injunction restraining the plaintiff from dealing in any way with or disposing of the proceeds of the judgment. The Court of Appeal upheld an appeal by the plaintiff against the order, principally on the ground that a Mareva injunction was inappropriate because there was no evidence that the plaintiff would attempt to avoid enforcement of a judgment obtained against him on the cross-action. In delivering the judgment of the Court,[129] Bridge LJ emphasized that it is not sufficient for a stay that the plaintiff suing on the bill, and against whom there is a cross-claim for damages, is foreign.[130] This particularly would be the case if the claimant has a substantial business in its own country.[131] On the other hand, Bridge LJ said that he should not be taken as saying that in no circumstances whatever could an injunction be granted to restrain a plaintiff from dealing with the fruits of a judgment in a case such as that before him.

The size of the paid up capital of a foreign company is regarded as of little signif- **5.29**
icance,[132] while Sir Eric Sachs in *Cebora SNC v SIP (Industrial Products) Ltd*[133]

---

[124] [1967] 1 Lloyd's Rep 387, 389.
[125] [1976] 1 Lloyd's Rep 271.
[126] [1976] 1 Lloyd's Rep 271, 278.
[127] [1976] 1 Lloyd's Rep 271, 279.
[128] [1979] 1 WLR 1180.
[129] Bridge, Geoffrey Lane and Roskill LJJ.
[130] See also *Cebora SNC v SIP (Industrial Products) Ltd* [1976] 1 Lloyd's Rep 271, followed and applied in *Walek & Co KG v Seafield Gentex Ltd* [1978] IR 167.
[131] *Cebora SNC v SIP (Industrial Products) Ltd* [1976] 1 Lloyd's Rep 271, 280.
[132] *Cebora SNC v SIP (Industrial Products) Ltd* [1976] 1 Lloyd's Rep 271, 277.
[133] [1976] 1 Lloyd's Rep 271, 279.

rejected a submission that it is material to inquire into the virtues or defects of legal procedures in the country of a foreign plaintiff to which recourse may be necessary to enforce any judgment obtained on a cross-action. It has been suggested that a stay may be granted if there are 'real grounds' for supposing that the foreign plaintiff would not be likely to meet the counterclaim.[134] If Sir Eric Sachs was correct in the *Cebora* case in saying that it is not relevant to inquire into defects of the legal procedures of the plaintiff's country, it is difficult to see what could give rise to 'real grounds' for supposing that the counterclaim would not be met other than issues relating to the solvency of the claimant. But that circumstance should be just as relevant in the case of an English plaintiff. In *Continental Illinois National Bank and Trust Co of Chicago v Papanicolaou*[135] Parker LJ suggested, in the context of a guarantee given in circumstances such that it was the equivalent of a letter of credit, and which attracts a similar principle to that applicable to bills of exchange,[136] that it 'might be' that a stay would be granted if there was a counterclaim which was likely to succeed, coupled with cogent evidence that the holder of the guarantee, if paid, would be unable to meet a judgment on the counterclaim. Even in those circumstances, however, it is suggested that the courts would be reluctant to grant a stay. For example, it has been held that it is not sufficient for a stay that the claimant on the cheque is a company in administration.[136a]

5.30 The concept of exceptional circumstances is usually referred to in the context of a stay of execution, but there is authority suggesting that it may also be invoked in relation to the primary question, whether the holder of the instrument is entitled to judgment.[137] In *Barclays Bank v Aschaffenburger*[138] Lord Denning said that, while the holder of a bill of exchange ordinarily is entitled to judgment notwithstanding a cross-claim for damages available against him, there may be exceptions to the rule,[139] and similarly Salmon LJ indicated that the rule is not invariable.[140] It is noticeable however that a stay of execution was granted to the defendant in that case, as opposed to a judgment recognizing that there was a defence to the extent of the cross-claim. Subsequently, in *Brown, Shipley & Co Ltd v Alicia Hosiery*

---

[134] See Stephenson LJ in *Montebianco Industrie Tessile SpA v Carlyle Mills (London) Ltd* [1981] 1 Lloyd's Rep 509, 512, referring to *Cebora SNC v SIP (Industrial Products) Ltd* [1976] 1 Lloyd's Rep 271 ('In that case also comment was made on the need to have real grounds for supposing that the Italian company would not be likely to meet any counterclaim that was made').

[135] [1986] 2 Lloyd's Rep 441, 445.

[136] See para 5.42 below.

[136a] *Isovel Contracts Ltd v ABB Building Technologies Ltd* [2002] 1 BCLC 390.

[137] In addition to the cases referred to below, see *Newman v Lever* (1887) 4 TLR 91, 92; *Safa Ltd v Banque du Caire* [2000] 2 Lloyd's Rep 600, 606. In *Finch Motors Ltd v Quin* [1980] 2 NZLR 513, 516 it is unclear whether the reference to 'exceptional circumstances' was in the context of a stay of execution or leave to defend on the basis of a set-off. A similar comment may be made in respect of *John Shearer Ltd v Gehl Co* (1995) 60 FCR 136, 141.

[138] [1967] 1 Lloyd's Rep 387.

[139] [1967] 1 Lloyd's Rep 387, 388.

[140] [1967] 1 Lloyd's Rep 387, 391.

Ltd,[141] Lord Denning once again expressed the principle in terms that 'in the ordinary way' judgment should be given upon a bill notwithstanding a cross-claim, although the discussion later in his judgment concerned the possibility that the court in its discretion may grant a stay of execution, and indeed the availability of a stay was the issue in the case. In *Saga of Bond Street Ltd v Avalon Promotions Ltd*[142] the defendant against whom judgment had been given on a bill succeeded in an application to set aside the judgment because of a breach of contract by the plaintiff. In later cases however the courts have sought to distinguish the case (albeit unsatisfactorily),[143] and it is doubtful if it would now be followed.[144]

Circumstances which may provide a defence

The preceding discussion concerned the situation in which the unliquidated **5.31** cross-demand either is unrelated to the transaction for which the bill of exchange or cheque constituted consideration or, if it arose out of the same transaction as the instrument, it merely gives rise to a case of partial failure of consideration. On the other hand, an acceptor of a bill of exchange has a defence to a claim brought against him by the drawer if his acceptance was procured by fraud, invalidity, or for a consideration which has totally failed.[145] Therefore, if there has been a total failure of the consideration for which the bill was given,[146] the acceptor has a defence.[147] Similarly, fraud in relation to the transaction in respect of which the bill constituted payment or security may provide a defence to an action on the bill by

---

[141] [1966] 1 Lloyd's Rep 668, 669.

[142] [1972] 2 QB 325.

[143] See *Cebora SNC v SIP (Industrial Products) Ltd* [1976] 1 Lloyd's Rep 271, 279, in which Sir Eric Sachs said that *Saga of Bond Street* 'was a case extremely close to a total failure of consideration', and *Eversure Textiles Manufacturing Ltd v Webb* [1978] Qd R 347, 349.

[144] In *Anglo-Italian Bank v Wells* (1878) 38 LT 197, 199, Jessel MR said that he could not imagine a case which would justify allowing an equitable set-off against a claim on promissory notes. See also *Isovel Contracts Ltd v ABB Building Technologies Ltd* [2002] 1 BCLC 390, 398.

[145] See *Churchill & Sim v Goddard* [1937] 1 KB 92, 109; *Nova (Jersey) Knit Ltd v Kammgarn Spinnerei GmbH* [1977] 1 WLR 713, 721, 722, 726.

[146] Compare *Fielding & Platt Ltd v Najjar* [1969] 1 WLR 357. *Quaere* if it is sufficient if it is a case 'extremely close to a total failure of consideration'. See Sir Eric Sachs in *Cebora SNC v SIP (Industrial Products) Ltd* [1976] 1 Lloyd's Rep 271, 279 (distinguishing the *Saga of Bond Street* case [1972] 2 QB 325).

[147] *Obbard v Betham* (1830) M & M 483, 485, 173 ER 1232; *Glennie v Imri* (1839) 3 Y & C Ex 436, 443, 160 ER 773, 776; *Trickey v Larne* (1840) 6 M & W 278, 280, 151 ER 414, 415; *Bow, McLachlan & Co Ltd v Ship 'Camosun'* [1909] AC 597, 612; *James Lamont & Co Ltd v Hyland Ltd* [1950] 1 KB 585, 592; *Cebora SNC v SIP (Industrial Products) Ltd* [1976] 1 Lloyd's Rep 271, 279; *Nova (Jersey) Knit Ltd v Kammgarn Spinnerei GmbH* [1977] 1 WLR 713, 732–733; *Finch Motors Ltd v Quin* [1980] 2 NZLR 513; *Montebianco Industrie Tessili SpA v Carlyle Mills (London) Ltd* [1981] 1 Lloyds Rep 509, 511; *International Ore & Fertilizer Corp v East Coast Fertilizer Co Ltd* [1987] 1 NZLR 9. In *All Trades Distributors Ltd v Agencies Kaufman Ltd* (1969) 113 Sol Jo 995 there was a thin, but at least arguable, case of total failure of consideration. Conditional leave to defend was granted, the condition being that the money due on the bill should be brought into court.

the drawer,[148] while it has been held in Australia that the principle under discussion does not apply where the cross-claim is to have the bill set aside or treated as a nullity pursuant to the Trade Practices Act 1974 (Cth), section 87.[149] In addition, the Full Court of the Federal Court has suggested that the rule might not apply where the bill was obtained as a result of conduct that was misleading or deceptive in breach of section 52 of the Trade Practices Act.[150]

Debt on a negotiable instrument pleaded as a defence

5.32 The principle precluding an equitable set-off against a claim on a cheque or similar instrument should not apply in the converse situation in which the holder is seeking to employ the the debt on the instrument in a set-off. In *Williams v Davies*[151] Sir Lancelot Shadwell permitted a person who had obtained judgment on some promissory notes to set off the judgment against a damages liability to the maker of the notes. While the case has been criticized on the ground that the cross-demands were not sufficiently closely connected to give rise to an equitable set-off,[152] it nevertheless suggests that a claim on a negotiable instrument may be employed defensively in a set-off.

Setting aside a statutory demand

5.33 Further, the existence of a cross-demand may provide a ground for setting aside a statutory demand served under section 268 of the Insolvency Act 1986 as a prelude to a bankruptcy petition based upon non-payment of a cheque. Pursuant to the Insolvency Rules 1986, rule 6.5(4)(a), the court may grant an application for an order setting aside a statutory demand if the debtor appears to have a 'counterclaim, set-off or cross demand' which equals or exceeds the amount of the debt. 'Cross-demand' has a wider meaning than the technical terms 'set-off' and 'counterclaim'.[153] The fact that the damages cross-claim would not have given rise to a defence to a claim on the cheque, and would not have constituted grounds for a

---

[148] *Brown v Trynor* (1980) 109 DLR (3d) 312. See also *Ledger v Ewer* (1794) Peake 283, 170 ER 157; *Fleming v Simpson* (1806) 1 Camp 40n, 170 ER 868; *Solomon v Turner* (1815) 1 Stark 51, 171 ER 398; *Glennie v Imri* (1839) 3 Y & C Ex 436, 443, 160 ER 773, 776; *John Shearer Ltd v Gehl Co* (1995) 60 FCR 136, 142; *Solo Industries UK Ltd v Canara Bank* [2001] 1 WLR 1800, 1815 para 38. See also *Ex parte Stephens* (1805) 11 Ves Jun 24, 32 ER 996 in which the set-off was an equitable set-off. Fraud also may be raised against a remote party who is not a holder in due course. See the Bills of Exchange Act 1882, ss 29(2) and 38.

[149] *Ferro Corp (Aust) Pty Ltd v International Pools Aust Pty Ltd* (1993) 30 NSWLR 539; *John Shearer Ltd v Gehl Co* (1995) 60 FCR 136, 142. This should also be the case where relief is sought under the Contracts Review Act 1980 (NSW) to strike down a bill of exchange or otherwise to fashion appropriate relief. See *Ferro Corp* at 541.

[150] *John Shearer Ltd v Gehl Co* (1995) 60 FCR 136, 142.

[151] (1829) 2 Sim 461, 57 ER 860.

[152] *Rawson v Samuel* (1841) Cr & Ph 161, 178, 179, 41 ER 451, 458. See para 4.04 above.

[153] *Re A Bankruptcy Notice* [1934] 1 Ch 431, 438; *John Shearer Ltd v Gehl Co* (1995) 60 FCR 136, 142.

stay of execution on a judgment on the cheque, does not mean that it is not a cross-demand for the purpose of rule 6.5(4)(a).[154] A similar principle applies in the case of a petition to wind up a company for failure to pay a cheque or other instrument. If the company has a genuine and serious cross-claim in an amount which exceeds the debt to the petitioner, the petition may be dismissed or stayed unless there are special circumstances which make it inappropriate to do so.[155]

Insolvency set-off

Similarly, a claim on a cheque or other instrument may be the subject of a mandatory set-off under the insolvency legislation in the event of a bankruptcy or a liquidation of the party liable on the instrument, provided that the other requirements of the insolvency set-off section are satisfied.[156]   **5.34**

(2) Negotiable Instruments—Statutes of Set-off

While it is now settled that an equitable set-off based upon a cross-claim for damages is not available as a defence to an action on a bill of exchange or other negotiable instrument, save in exceptional circumstances, there are conflicting views in relation to the availability of a set-off under the Statutes of Set-off in the case of mutual debts. It is sometimes suggested that the principle which precludes an equitable set-off in respect of an unliquidated cross-demand also applies to the Statutes, so that generally the drawer of a cheque or the acceptor of a bill being sued for payment cannot raise as a defence an independent debt owing by the holder. There is one situation in which it is recognized that a set-off may arise under the Statutes, and that is when a cheque or other instrument is given as payment for goods sold or services performed and there is a liquidated cross-demand arising from a partial failure of consideration.[157] But if the cross-debt is not connected in that way, it has been suggested that it cannot be set off.[158] This view is   **5.35**

---

[154] *Hofer v Strawson* [1999] 2 BCLC 336. In Australia, see *John Shearer Ltd v Gehl Co* (1995) 60 FCR 136, distinguishing *Buying Systems (Aust) Pty Ltd v Tien Mah Litho Printing Co (Pte) Ltd* (1986) 5 NSWLR 317. See also *Equuscorp Pty Ltd v Perpetual Trustees WA Ltd* (1997) 24 ACSR 194, 203 in relation to a letter of credit (appeal dismissed (1997) 25 ACSR 675).

[155] *Hofer v Strawson* [1999] 2 BCLC 336, 341–342, referring to *Re Bayoil SA* [1999] 1 WLR 147. *Quaere* whether delay in litigating the cross-claim affects the position. See n 29 above. In Australia, see *John Shearer Ltd v Gehl Co* (1995) 60 FCR 136.

[156] *Willment Brothers Ltd v North West Thames Regional Health Authority* (1984) 26 BLR 51; *Isovel Contracts Ltd v ABB Building Technologies Ltd* [2002] 1 BCLC 390, 398. See also *John Shearer Ltd v Gehl Co* (1995) 60 FCR 136, 143.

[157] *Agra & Masterman's Bank v Leighton* (1866) LR 2 Ex 56, 65; *Nova (Jersey) Knit Ltd v Kammgarn Spinnerei GmbH* [1977] 1 WLR 713, 720, 732–733; *Safa Ltd v Banque du Caire* [2000] 2 Lloyd's Rep 600, 605; *Isovel Contracts Ltd v ABB Building Technologies Ltd* [2002] 1 BCLC 390, 396–398. See also *Eversure Textiles Manufacturers Co Ltd v Webb* [1978] Qd R 347, 349.

[158] See eg Wood, *English and International Set-off* (1989) 700–701. In addition to *Cebora SNC v SIP (Industrial Products) Ltd* [1976] 1 Lloyd's Rep 271, 278 (see below), Wood has referred to the cross-claim for commissions in *Eversure Textiles Manufacturing Co Ltd v Webb* [1978] Qd R

said to be supported by a comment by Sir Eric Sachs in *Cebora SNC v SIP (Industrial Products) Ltd,*[159] which has been referred to by the courts on other occasions with evident approval.[160] Sir Eric Sachs remarked that the courts will refuse to regard as a defence to a claim on a bill of exchange 'any set off, *legal or equitable,* or any counterclaim, whether arising on the particular transaction upon which the bill of exchange came into existence, or, a fortiori, arising in any other way'.[161] There are four points to note in relation to this comment. The first is that, in so far as it extended to legal set-offs, it was obiter. The second is that the reference to 'legal' set-off may have had in contemplation the common law cases which have held that the principle of abatement[162] does not apply when the price had been paid by way of bill of exchange, as opposed to the form of set-off conferred by the Statutes of Set-off in the case of mutual debts.[163] The third is that the decision of the House of Lords in *Nova (Jersey) Knit Ltd v Kammgarn Spinnerei GmbH*[164] does not require the conclusion that the Statutes have a limited operation in the case of bills of exchange. The *Nova (Jersey) Knit* case concerned equitable set-off, not the statutory defence.[165] The fourth point is that, if Sir Eric Sachs did intend to refer to the Statutes, it is not an accurate statement of the traditionally accepted position. The right of set-off in the case of mutual debts was not developed as an equitable or a common law doctrine, but rather it is statutory in origin. In the case of a defence conferred by statute, the proper approach is to examine the words of the relevant legislation, and the Statutes of Set-off simply stipulated that a set-off could occur in the case of mutual debts. There is nothing

---

347. However Connolly J commented in that case (at 348) that the claims for commission were not clearly raised against the plaintiff.

[159] [1976] 1 Lloyd's Rep 271.

[160] *Begley Industries Ltd v Cramp* [1977] 2 NZLR 207, 212–213; *Buying Systems (Aust) Pty Ltd v Tien Mah Litho Printing Co Ltd* (1986) 5 NSWLR 317, 327–328; *Re Julius Harper Ltd* [1983] NZLR 215, 224; *Finch Motors Ltd v Quin* [1980] 2 NZLR 513, 516; *Halsbury's Laws of England* (4th edn, 1992) vol 4(1), 246 para 497. In *Power Curber International Ltd v National Bank of Kuwait* [1981] 1 WLR 1233, 1241 Lord Denning MR said that 'No set-off or counterclaim is allowed to detract from' the principle that a bill is equivalent to cash, though this comment was made in the context of a bill given for the price of goods, and his Lordship may have had in mind a damages claim arising out of the underlying contract.

[161] [1976] 1 Lloyd's Rep 271, 278 (emphasis added).

[162] See paras 2.87–2.97 above.

[163] In *Bank of Boston Connecticut v European Grain & Shipping Ltd* [1989] 1 AC 1056, 1105 Lord Brandon would appear to have used the expression 'legal set-off' in the sense of a claim for an abatement (though in the context of freight payable under a charterparty).

[164] [1977] 1 WLR 713.

[165] Lord Wilberforce commented in *Nova (Jersey) Knit* [1977] 1 WLR 713, 720 that: 'As between the immediate parties, a partial failure of consideration may be relied upon as a pro tanto defence, but only when the amount involved is ascertained and liquidated.' The emphasis however was on confining the set-off to the case of liquidated debts, in other words set-off under the Statutes, rather than to immediate parties where there was a partial failure of consideration. The case concerned bills of exchange given as payment for goods where the parties to the action were immediate parties to the bills, and the dictum should be considered in that context. The same point may be made in relation to Lord Russell of Killowen's comments at 732–733.

in them to suggest that they were not intended to apply when the plaintiff is suing on a cheque or other instrument.

At least since the latter half of the eighteenth century the courts have recognized **5.36** that an independent cross-debt may be set off under the Statutes against a claim on a negotiable instrument.[166] In *Baskerville v Brown*[167] Lord Mansfield accepted that Baskerville could have pleaded the debt owing to him as a defence in Brown's action against him on the promissory note, and Lord Kenyon allowed a set-off in a similar situation in *Lechmere v Hawkins*.[168] In 1812 the Court of King's Bench in *Wake v Tinkler*[169] did not dispute that a set-off under the Statutes was available in principle against a claim on a promissory note, although a set-off was denied on another ground. The availability of a set-off is also supported by the line of cases which developed in the middle of the nineteenth century dealing with overdue bills and promissory notes.[170] The cases established the proposition that, when the indorsee of an overdue bill sues the acceptor, he does not take subject to a set-off under the Statutes in respect of an unconnected cross-debt owing to the acceptor by an earlier holder.[171] Nevertheless it was assumed that a set-off would have been available if the prior holder himself had sued. For example, in *Burrough v Moss*[172] the defendant gave a promissory note to a married woman. According to the then applicable law, this entitled her husband (one Fearn) to treat it as his own property. Fearn himself was indebted to the defendant on an unrelated matter. After the note became due, Fearn indorsed it to the plaintiff. When the plaintiff sued the defendant on the note, the defendant sought to set off Fearn's indebtedness to him. It was held that a set-off was not available against the plaintiff as indorsee. On the other hand, Bayley J considered that one of the consequences of Fearn treating the note as his own 'would be, to let in by way of set-off to any claim by him, any debts due from him',[173] and he said that: 'As to the other sum of 28*l* due from Fearn alone . . . it might have been set off had Fearn sued on the note.'[174] That

---

[166] In addition to the cases cited below, see *L D Nathan & Co Ltd v Vista Travel Ltd* [1973] 1 NZLR 233, which may have been correctly decided on the basis of a set-off under the Statutes, though compare *Finch Motors Ltd v Quin* [1980] 2 NZLR 513, 516 and *International Ore & Fertilizer Corp v East Coast Fertilizer Co Ltd* [1987] 1 NZLR 9, 15. This also may explain *Murphy v Glass* (1869) LR 2 PC 408, where the cross-claim had been the subject of an award by an arbitrator.

[167] (1761) 2 Burr 1229, 97 ER 804.

[168] (1798) 2 Esp 626, 170 ER 477. See also *Ord v Ruspini* (1797) 2 Esp 569, 170 ER 458.

[169] (1812) 16 East 36, 104 ER 1002.

[170] The relevant cases are *Burrough v Moss* (1830) 10 B & C 558, 109 ER 558; *Stein v Yglesias* (1834) 1 Cr M & R 565, 149 ER 1205; *Whitehead v Walker* (1842) 10 M & W 696, 152 ER 652; *Oulds v Harrison* (1854) 10 Ex 572, 156 ER 566; *Re Overend Gurney, ex p Swan* (1868) LR 6 Eq 344.

[171] See paras 17.56–17.58 below. Compare *Holmes v Kidd* (1858) 3 H & N 891, 157 ER 729, in which there was an agreement for a set-off which constituted an equity attaching to the bill, as opposed to merely a personal equity.

[172] (1830) 10 B & C 558, 109 ER 558.

[173] (1830) 10 B & C 558, 562, 109 ER 558, 559.

[174] (1830) 10 B & C 558, 562, 109 ER 558, 560.

also accords with views expressed by counsel for both parties during argument. *Oulds v Harrison*[175] was a similar case. In the course of giving the judgment of the Court of Exchequer, Parke B asked:[176]

> [W]hat is the effect of an indorsement of an overdue bill under the circumstances mentioned in the plea? These though inaccurately stated, we think, amount to an averment, that both the indorser and indorsee, knowing that *there was a debt due to the defendant, which would be set off if the action should be brought by the indorser against the defendant*, in order to defeat that set-off, and fraudulently, so far as that was a fraud but no further, agreed that the bill should be indorsed, and it was therefore indorsed, without value, to the plaintiff.

It was held that the circumstances referred to did not prevent the application of the principle that an indorsee of an overdue note takes free from rights of set-off available against the indorser. Parke B nevertheless recognized that, if the indorser instead had been the party suing on the bill, he could have been met by a set-off under the Statutes in respect of the debt that he owed to the acceptor. Nor is there anything in the report to suggest that the indorser's debt to the acceptor was connected with the transaction in respect of which the bill was given. These cases were decided after some of the early cases which had established that a claim on a bill of exchange given as payment of the price of goods sold and delivered cannot be met by a defence based upon a cross-claim for damages for a defect in the goods,[177] and it may be assumed that the judges were aware of those earlier cases.

5.37   There are instances in Victoria in which the courts have held that a debt arising otherwise than as a result of a partial failure of consideration could be set off under the Statutes against a claim on a negotiable instrument. One such case is *Ingleton v Coates*,[178] a decision of Madden CJ, in which the debt sought to be set off originated in a loan made to the person to whom the promissory note being sued upon had been indorsed, the debt on the loan having been assigned to the maker of the promissory note. In *Mobil Oil Australia Ltd v Caulfield Tyre Service Pty Ltd*[179] Young CJ, having quoted the passage from the judgment of Sir Eric Sachs in the *Cebora* case referred to above, suggested that the decision in *Ingleton v Coates* to allow the maker leave to defend may need to be reconsidered,[180] though the better view is that it was correct. Two other Victorian cases support that view. The first is *Nisbet v Cox*,[181] which concerned a set of bills. The report only takes the form of a short note, but it appears to have been accepted that a set-off under the Statutes

---

[175] (1854) 10 Ex 572, 156 ER 566.
[176] (1854) 10 Ex 572, 579, 156 ER 566, 569 (emphasis added).
[177] See, for example, *Morgan v Richardson* 1 Camp 40n, 170 ER 868; *Tye v Gwynne* (1810) 2 Camp 346, 170 ER 1179; *Day v Nix* (1824) 2 LJOSCP 133; *Obbard v Betham* (1830) M & M 483, 173 ER 1232; *Glennie v Imri* (1839) 2 Y & C Ex 436, 160 ER 773.
[178] (1896) 2 ALR 154.
[179] [1984] VR 440.
[180] [1984] VR 440, 443.
[181] (1873) 4 AJR 115.

was available once the last bill became due. The report simply states that a debt was alleged to be due from the plaintiff to the defendant acceptor. The nature of the debt is not mentioned, and presumably it was not regarded as significant. The second case is *Woodroffe v Moss*.[182] The defendant in an action brought against him on a cheque pleaded by way of defence that the plaintiffs had been his agents for the sale of some goods, and in breach of their duty as agents themselves purchased the goods and sold them on their own account at enhanced prices without accounting for the difference in price. The Full Court of the Victorian Supreme Court held that this could be pleaded as a defence of set-off. It has been suggested that the case turned on the circumstance that it involved delinquency by a fiduciary.[183] However that point was not emphasized in argument or in any of the judgments. The whole discussion centred on whether the claim against the plaintiff was liquidated. It was held that it was. Therefore, a set-off was allowed under the Statutes.

Furthermore, in *Hongkong and Shanghai Banking Corp v Kloeckner & Co AG*[184] **5.38** Hirst J accepted as 'well settled' a general statement by counsel to the effect that a set-off is permissible against a claim on a bill of exchange when the cross-claim is liquidated though not when it is unliquidated.[185]

The case of freight payable to a shipowner provides an analogy.[186] The position in **5.39** relation to freight is similar to that applicable to bills of exchange, in that neither equitable set-off nor the common law defence of abatement may be asserted in answer to a claim for freight. But there is also authority in that context for the proposition that the principle which precludes those defences does not affect the application of the Statutes of Set-off when the case involves mutual debts.[187]

Nevertheless recent comments in the Court of Appeal support the more restrictive **5.40** view. In *Safa Ltd v Banque du Caire*[188] Waller LJ, in a judgment with which Lady Justice Hale and Lord Justice Schiemann agreed, said in the context of bills of exchange that set-off is '*only* available between immediate parties in relation to

---

182 [1915] VLR 237.
183 Wood, *English and International Set-off* (1989) 700.
184 [1990] 2 QB 514.
185 [1990] 2 QB 514, 524. *Kloeckner* concerned a letter of credit, which is regarded as similar to a bill of exchange: see below. The beneficiary sought summary judgment against the bank on the letter. The bank asserted a set-off in respect of a liquidated sum owing to it by the beneficiary. Hirst J allowed the set-off, although he emphasized that it was a 'striking feature' that the debt to the bank arose out of the same transaction as the letter. Nevertheless he went on to say (at 526) that this was an *additional* circumstance for allowing a set-off. The Statutes of Set-off themselves do not require that the cross-debts should be connected in any way, and the better view is that the set-off in *Kloeckner* was not dependent upon the connection to which Hirst J referred.
186 See paras 5.02–5.24 above.
187 See paras 5.17–5.22 above.
188 [2000] 2 Lloyd's Rep 600.

liquidated sums'.[189] This was not expressly limited to the case of a partial failure of consideration, although the discussion earlier in the judgment[190] suggests that he also had in mind that limitation. Thus, Mance LJ, in delivering the judgment of the Court of Appeal[191] in *Solo Industries UK Ltd v Canara Bank*,[192] later referred to Waller LJ in the *Safa* case as having cited 'the principles governing bills of exchange, according to which set-off is not admissible, other than between immediate parties in cases of partial failure of consideration when the amount involved is both ascertained and liquidated . . .'. However the justification for restricting the defence to immediate parties and to cases of partial failure of consideration remains unclear. When a bill of exchange is issued by reference to an underlying transaction,[193] and there has been a partial failure of consideration where the amount involved is liquidated and ascertained,[194] the case is one of mutual debts, and therefore the Statutes of Set-off prima facie apply. But the Statutes do not require any connection between the debts the subject of the set-off,[195] and so the connection or otherwise between the debt sought to be set off and the transaction that gave rise to the instrument should not be relevant to the question whether the Statutes apply. For the same reason it should not matter whether the parties are immediate or remote. The comments in the *Safa* and *Solo Industries* cases were obiter, and the point was not subjected to detailed analysis. In view of the earlier authorities suggesting that the defence is not so restricted, and in view of the language of the Statutes of Set-off themselves, the comments should not be regarded as having settled the issue.

(3) Statutes of Set-off—Set-off Against a Subsequent Holder

5.41 If, as suggested, a set-off under the Statutes of Set-off may be asserted against a claim on a bill of exchange or other negotiable instrument, the further question may arise whether a subsequent holder of a bill takes subject to a right of set-off that would have been available against the prior holder under the Statutes if the prior holder had sued on the bill. If the subsequent holder is a holder in due course, he takes free from personal defences between prior parties, which include rights of set-off. This is a long-standing principle which has been codified in the Bills of Exchange Act 1882, section 38(2). On the other hand, section 38(2) does not state what happens when the subsequent holder is not a holder in due course, and opinions differ amongst text-writers as to whether a subsequent holder in

---

[189] [2000] 2 Lloyd's Rep 600, 606 (emphasis added).
[190] [2000] 2 Lloyd's Rep 600, 605.
[191] Potter and Mance LJJ, and Sir Martin Nourse.
[192] [2001] 1 WLR 1800, 1810 para 22.
[193] See *Safa Ltd v Banque du Caire* [2000] 2 Lloyd's Rep 600, 605.
[194] See para 5.35 above.
[195] See para 2.14 above.

such a case is bound by rights of set-off between prior parties.[196] The issue is dealt with later.[197] The better view is that he is not bound, even if he is a mere holder who has not given value.

(4) Letters of Credit

Letters of credit generally are treated in a similar manner to cheques and bills of exchange. An irrevocable letter of credit is regarded in mercantile practice as being the equivalent of cash in hand.[198] In the absence of fraud it must be paid regardless of any cross-claim available to the person at whose request the letter was issued against the holder, even if the cross-claim arose out of the transaction on which the letter was based.[199] This is also the case for performance bonds and bank guarantees when they are given in circumstances such that they are equivalent to letters of credit.[200]   **5.42**

A transaction involving a letter of credit typically differs from a transaction in which a cheque or bill of exchange is given. A cheque or a bill is often given as payment for the price of goods or services. In that situation the person liable on the instrument is commonly a party to the transaction which gave rise to the instrument. A letter of credit also may be given in order to effect payment to the seller of goods, but it would be rare for the issuer of the letter of credit, typically a bank, to be involved in the underlying transaction. But what if, in a rare case, the bank is involved in the transaction?   **5.43**

In *Power Curber International Ltd v National Bank of Kuwait SAK*[201] goods had been sold on terms that they were to be paid for by letter of credit issued by the defendant bank. In the course of his judgment Lord Denning commented that: 'A   **5.44**

---

[196] For the view that a subsequent holder who is not a holder in due course takes subject to rights of set-off available between prior parties, see Wood, *English and International Set-off* (1989) 901, and Goode, *Commercial Law* (2nd edn, 1995), 563–4. See also *Paget's Law of Banking* (11th edn, 1996) 414. For the contrary (and preferred) view, see Crawford and Falconbridge, *Banking and Bills of Exchange* (8th edn, 1986) vol 2, 1524 *et seq* and *Chitty on Contracts* (28th edn, 1999) vol 2, 214 para 34–097. See also *Chalmers and Guest on Bills of Exchange* (15th edn, 1998) 246 para 762 in relation to a holder for value. *Byles on Bills of Exchange and Cheques* (27th edn, 2002) 231 also appears to support this view in relation to set-off of unconnected cross-debts under the Statutes of Set-off.

[197] See paras 17.56–17.58 below.

[198] *Intraco Ltd v Notis Shipping Corp (The Bhoja Trader)* [1981] 2 Lloyd's Rep 256, 257; *Power Curber International Ltd v National Bank of Kuwait SAK* [1981] 1 WLR 1233, 1241, 1243; *Solo Industries UK Ltd v Canara Bank* [2001] 1 WLR 1800, 1812 para 31.

[199] *Power Curber International Ltd v National Bank of Kuwait SAK* [1981] 1 WLR 1233, 1241, 1243; *Hongkong and Shanghai Banking Corp v Kloeckner & Co AG* [1990] 2 QB 514, 521–522; *Safa Ltd v Banque du Caire* [2000] 2 Lloyd's Rep 600, 605.

[200] *Intraco Ltd v Notis Shipping Corp (The Bhoja Trader)* [1981] 2 Lloyd's Rep 256; *Balfour Beatty Civil Engineering v Technical & General Guarantee Co Ltd* (1999) 68 Con LR 180, 189. See also *Continental Illinois National Bank and Trust Co of Chicago v Papanicolaou* [1986] 2 Lloyd's Rep 441, 445; *Sim v Rotherdam Metropolitan BC* [1987] 1 Ch 216, 259; *Solo Industries UK Ltd v Canara Bank* [2001] 1 WLR 1800 (performance bond).

[201] [1981] 1 WLR 1233, 1241.

letter of credit is like a bill of exchange given for the price of goods. It ranks as cash and must be honoured. No set-off or counterclaim is allowed to detract from it . . .' Later, Hirst J in *Hongkong and Shanghai Banking Corporation v Kloeckner & Co AG*[202] said of that statement that it must be interpreted as meaning a set-off or counterclaim by the buyer against the seller, and not one by the bank against the seller, the latter situation not being under consideration in the *Power Curber* case. In the *Kloeckner* case a bank had issued a standby letter of credit in relation to transactions in which the bank itself was involved. The transactions involved back-to-back sales, and the beneficiary of the letter of credit in turn had given a payment undertaking to the bank. One of the questions was whether the bank could set off its claim on the payment undertaking against its liability on the letter of credit. Hirst J said that the case before him had two striking features. The first was that the bank's claim arose out of the banking transactions which gave rise to the letter of credit, and the second was that the set-off in issue was a 'liquidated set-off'. In those circumstances he concluded that the case in favour of a set-off was overwhelming.

5.45 Subsequently the issue received the attention of the Court of Appeal in *Safa Ltd v Banque du Caire*.[203] A bank had given a letter of credit to an insurance broker, the purpose of the letter of credit being to cover the premium payable to an insurance company which was to provide a financial insurance guarantee to the bank in relation to a facility to be provided by the bank to a third party. The broker made a claim on the letter of credit which the bank alleged was fraudulent. After a review of the authorities, including *Kloeckner*, Waller LJ formulated a number of propositions:[204]

1. The principle that letters of credit must be treated as cash is an important one, and must be maintained.
2. It is however unusual for a bank which has opened a letter of credit to be involved in the related transaction to the extent this bank was.
3. When a bank is involved in the related transaction it may be unjust for that bank to be forced to pay on a summary judgment where it has a real prospect of succeeding by reference to a claim on the underlying transaction, and particularly if that claim is a liquidated claim, the Court should not give summary judgment either because a set-off has a reasonable prospect of success or because there is a compelling reason to have a trial of the letter of credit issue.
4. If a bank can establish a claim with a real propect of success, either that the demand was fraudulent even if it had not clear evidence of fraud at the time of demand, or that there was a misrepresentation by the beneficiary directed at persuading the bank to enter into the letter of credit, it may also be unjust to enter summary judgment against the bank either because the bank has a reason-

---

[202] [1990] 2 QB 514, 525–526.
[203] [2000] 2 Lloyd's Rep 600.
[204] [2000] 2 Lloyd's Rep 600, 608.

able prospect of succeeding in a defence of set-off or because there is a compelling reason for a trial of the letter of credit issue.

In his third proposition, dealing with the situation in which the bank is involved in the underlying transaction, Waller LJ referred to a case in which the bank's claim is liquidated. But he seems to have regarded that factor as an additional reason for refusing summary judgment to the beneficiary of the letter of credit, as opposed to constituting a necessary element. He said that a set-off may be available, and the court therefore should not give summary judgment, if the bank has a claim on the underlying trasaction which has a real prospect of success,[205] and he continued that this *particularly* should be the case if the bank's claim is liquidated. This leaves open the possibility that the bank's claim in some cases may be unliquidated, though presumably subject to a requirement that the cross-claims must be sufficiently connected to give rise to an equitable set-off. Later Mance LJ in *Solo Industries UK Ltd v Canara Bank*,[206] after referring to the propositions in the *Safa* case, commented that he agreed that 'special considerations arise in circumstances such as those in the *Safa* case itself, where the beneficiary and bank are both intimately involved in a wider underlying transaction'. In the *Safa* case, Waller LJ said that if the bank in that case paid under the letter of credit it would have been entitled to immediate reimbursement from the broker. The claim would be for a liquidated sum, and he said that the connection between the claims would be such that a set-off would be allowed if the bank's claim were established.[207] Any such set-off would not have been based on the Statutes of Set-off. For the Statutes to apply, there must be mutual debts. However the bank's right to reimbursement would only have crystallized into a debt after the bank had paid under the letter of credit. But at that point there would no longer have been a debt owing by the bank. There would not therefore have been mutual debts, so that the set-off could not have been based on the Statutes. It could only have been an equitable set-off arising from the closeness of the connection of the claims, and equity has never regarded the distinction between liquidated and unliquidated claims as critical to the question whether the equitable defence should apply.

This view would give rise to a problem, however. If a bank which has issued a letter of credit is entitled to assert a set-off when it has a claim against the beneficiary arising out of the underlying transaction in respect of which the letter of credit was given, so as to justify refusing summary judgment to the beneficiary of the letter, and if that may apply also when the bank's claim is unliquidated, the letter of **5.46**

---

[205] CPR r 24.2.

[206] [2001] 1 WLR 1800, 1811 paras 27–28.

[207] See also the analogous circumstances in *Ralston v South Greta Colliery Co* (1912) 13 SR (NSW) 6, for which see para 4.08 above. Waller LJ referred to the defence as a set-off, but another possibility in the circumstances may have been a defence of circuity of action, as discussed in *Aktieselskabet Ocean v B Harding and Sons Ltd* [1928] 2 KB 371, 384–385 and *Co-operative Retail Services Ltd v Taylor Young Partnership* [2000] BLR 461, 474–475.

credit cases would depart from the principle applicable in the case of cheques and bills of exchange. In the case of a cheque or a bill of exchange given as payment of the price of goods sold or services performed, it is established that the fact that the drawer of the cheque or the acceptor of the bill may have a damages claim against the other party arising out of the underlying transaction is not sufficient to give rise to a set-off.[208] The generality of the third proposition in the *Safa* case therefore may require reconsideration. In the *Safa* case there were allegations of fraud. Fraud was the subject of the fourth proposition put forward by Waller LJ, but, as Mance LJ later remarked, this appears to have been an independent point and it is not clear that the case was decided by reference to it.[209] In order to preserve the analogy with bills of exchange,[210] the *Safa* case should be regarded as turning on its peculiar facts, in particular the allegation of fraud. Furthermore, in so far as the third proposition is to be regarded as an independent principle, it should be confined to liquidated claims, so as to accommodate set-off under the Statutes of Set-off. This reflects the circumstances in issue in the *Kloeckner* case, but it is not clear nevertheless why the availability of the statutory defence should be limited to a claim arising out of the underlying transaction.[211]

5.47 In his fourth point in the *Safa* case, Waller LJ referred to a fraudulent claim on a letter of credit and to a situation in which there was misrepresentation inducing the bank to enter into the letter of credit. In both cases he suggested that it would suffice in a summary judgment application for the bank to establish a claim with a real propect of success. Subsequently the Court of Appeal in *Solo Industries UK Ltd v Canara Bank*[212] declined to accept that view. Mance LJ in delivering the judgment of the Court drew a distinction between fraud going to the validity of the instrument itself, and a fraudulent demand under the instrument. In the former case he said that the bank may be granted leave to defend in a summary judgment application if it can show that it has a real prospect of successfully defending the claim.[213] A higher standard applies however in the case of a fraudulent demand. If the bank paid under a fraudulent demand, it would have a cause of action against the beneficiary for fraudulent misrepresentation.[214] That cause of action may provide a defence to the bank, but in order to justify leave to defend the fraud must be established, or clear. It is not sufficient that the defence has a real

---

[208] See para 5.25 above.

[209] *Solo Industries UK Ltd v Canara Bank* [2001] 1 WLR 1800, 1811–1812 para 28. Waller LJ in *Safa* (n 203 above) seems to have referred to fraud as an alternative ground for the decision in that case. See [2000] 2 Lloyd's Rep 600, 609–610.

[210] See *Solo Industries UK Ltd v Canara Bank* [2001] 1 WLR 1800, 1815 para 38.

[211] See paras 5.35–5.40 above in relation to the Statutes of Set-off.

[212] [2001] 1 WLR 1800.

[213] CPR r 24.2.

[214] *Balfour Beatty Civil Engineering v Technical & General Guarantee Co Ltd* (1999) 68 Con LR 180, 189.

prospect of success. Short of established fraud, a bank normally would not be allowed to raise an alleged impropriety affecting the demand as a defence.

(5) Direct Debit

In *Esso Petroleum Co Ltd v Milton*[215] the Court of Appeal held that the principle **5.48**
applicable to cheques extends also to a direct debit arrangement. The case concerned a purchaser of goods who had authorized payment by way of a direct debit
to his bank account, but cancelled the bank's mandate to debit the account after
the goods were delivered. The majority (Thorpe LJ and Sir John Balcombe,
Simon Brown LJ dissenting on this point) considered that the vendor was entitled
to summary judgment for the amount otherwise admitted to be due, and the purchaser was not granted leave to defend on the basis of an unliquidated damages
cross-claim. This conclusion was justified by reference to a perception that in
modern commercial practice a direct debit is treated in the same way as payment
by cheque and, as such, as being the equivalent of cash.[216] There is nevertheless
much force in Professor Tettenborn's criticism of the decision,[217] which expands
on the dissenting judgment of Simon Brown LJ on this issue.[218] A direct debit
arrangement in truth differs in an important respect from payment by cheque or
bill of exchange. When a cheque is given as payment for goods or services supplied, the vendor does not sue for the price on the underlying contract, but rather
on the cheque. On the other hand, when a direct debit arrangement is cancelled,
the vendor's action is for the price pursuant to the original contract. Unlike a
cheque, a direct debit arrangement does not confer any rights upon the vendor
which are independent of the original contract. Subsequently a differently constituted Court of Appeal in *Courage Ltd v Crehan*[219] followed the *Milton* case in the
context of a commercial lease. In giving the Court's judgment Morritt LJ said that
he was bound by the *Milton* case, and he declined to express a view on the merits
of the decision.[220]

C. Building Contracts

A cross-claim for damages for delay or for bad workmanship is capable in **5.49**
principle[221] of being employed in a set-off against an amount due for work

---

[215] [1997] 1 WLR 938. Compare *Star Rider Ltd v Inntreprenneur Ltd* [1998] 1 EGLR 53, 55–56.
[216] See Sir John Balcombe at [1997] 1 WLR 938, 954, and Thorpe LJ at 952–953.
[217] Tettenborn, Note (1997) 113 LQR 374.
[218] [1997] 1 WLR 938, 947–948.
[219] [1999] 2 EGLR 145 (Morritt, Schiemann and Mance LJJ). See also *Gibbs Mew plc v Gemmell*
[1999] 1 EGLR 43, 50, *per* Peter Gibson, Schiemann and Mantell LJJ.
[220] [1999] EGLR 145, 157.
[221] Subject to the Housing Grants, Construction and Regeneration Act 1996, s 111. See below.

performed under a building contract.[222] At one time it was thought that a set-off was not available in cases in which the price was to be paid by instalment on the certificate of an architect or engineer, or some other such person. In a series of cases, commencing in 1971 with the Court of Appeal decision in *Dawnays Ltd v F G Minter Ltd*,[223] it was held that a certificate issued in respect of the work done to date by a contractor or a subcontractor under a building contract was to be regarded as equivalent to cash, and therefore the debt due under the certificate had to be paid save only for deductions permitted by the contract. A claim on the certificate by the contractor against the employer, or by a subcontractor against the contractor, could not be met by a set-off or a counterclaim in respect of an unliquidated cross-demand. Nor would the existence of the unliquidated cross-demand provide a ground for a stay of an action on the certificate pending arbitration. Provisions in the contract permitting certain deductions or set-offs were interpreted as referring only to liquidated ascertained sums which were established or admitted as being due.[224] Unliquidated cross-demands had to be prosecuted separately. The impetus for these decisions was cash flow. It was said that, if the contractor or subcontractor failed to receive the money stipulated in the certificate, it might not be in a position to complete the contract works. The contracts in question therefore were construed so as to give effect to the presumed intention of the parties that cash flow should be preserved.[225] However, *Dawnays v Minter* and the cases following it were the subject of trenchant criticism by one

---

[222] For examples of cases concerned with delay, see *Young v Kitchin* (1878) 3 Ex D 127; *Mitchell v Purnell Motors Pty Ltd* [1961] NSWLR 165; *Rapid Building Group Ltd v Ealing Family Housing Association Ltd* (1984) 29 BLR 5; *Archital Luxfer Ltd v A J Dunning & Sons (Weyhill) Ltd* (1987) 47 BLR 1; *M L Paynter Ltd v Ben Candy Investments Ltd* [1987] 1 NZLR 257. See also *Galambos & Sons Pty Ltd v McIntyre* (1974) 5 ACTR 10; *R M Douglas Construction Ltd v Bass Leisure Ltd* (1990) 53 BLR 119. In an action by an employer arising out of a delay in completion, a cross-claim available to the contractor against the employer for hindering or preventing the contractor's performance of the contract may give rise to an equitable set-off. See *Rosehaugh Stanhope (Broadgate Phase 6) plc v Redpath Dorman Long Ltd* (1990) 50 BLR 75; *Beaufort House Development Ltd v Zimmcor (International) Inc* (1990) 50 BLR 91. See also *Hanak v Green* [1958] 2 QB 9. For cases concerned with bad workmanship, see eg *Mitchell v Purnell Motors Pty Ltd*; *Galambos & Son Pty Ltd v McIntyre*; *Acsim (Southern) Ltd v Danish Contracting and Development Co Ltd* (1989) 47 BLR 55 (equitable set-off restricted by contract). See also *Lowe v Holme* (1883) 10 QBD 286; *Hanak v Green*.
[223] [1971] 1 WLR 1205. See also *Frederick Mark Ltd v Schield* [1972] 1 Lloyd's Rep 9; *GKN Foundations Ltd v Wandsworth London Borough Council* [1972] 1 Lloyd's Rep 528; *John Thompson Horseley Bridge Ltd v Wellingborough Steel & Construction Co Ltd* (1972) 1 BLR 69; *Token Construction Co Ltd v Naviewland Properties Ltd* (1972) 2 BLR 1; *Carter Horseley (Engineers) Ltd and John Thompson Horseley Bridge Ltd v Dawnays Ltd* (1972) 2 BLR 8.
[224] See eg *Algrey Contractors Ltd v Tenth Moat Housing Society Ltd* [1973] 1 Lloyd's Rep 369 (liquidated damages clause).
[225] Curiously, the courts also denied a right of deduction when the claim for payment was on the final certificate or the contract works in any event were completed, even though the case would not have been one in which the funds were required in order to finance the completion of the contract works. See *GKN Foundations Ltd v Wandsworth LBC* [1972] 1 Lloyd's Rep 528; *Token Construction Co Ltd v Naviewland Properties Ltd* (1972) 2 BLR 1; *Carter Horseley (Engineers) Ltd v Dawnays Ltd* (1972) 2 BLR 8. See the discussion of these cases in Wallace, 'Set Back to Set-off' (1973) 89 LQR 36, 54–56, 58–59, 59–60.

commentator,[226] and it was overruled some two years later by the House of Lords in *Gilbert-Ash (Northern) Ltd v Modern Engineering (Bristol) Ltd.*[227] The House of Lords held that there is no presumption in building cases in which the price is to be paid by instalment on certificate that the parties intend that the ordinary defences of set-off and abatement[228] should not apply. The perceived desirability of facilitating cash flow was not considered to be something unique to the building industry, and it was not regarded as a sufficient justification for ousting those rights.[229]

Housing Grants, Construction and Regeneration Act 1996

The right to assert a set-off or an abatement in this context is now subject to section 111(1) of the Housing Grants, Construction and Regeneration Act 1996. Section 111 prohibits a party to a construction contract[230] from withholding payment of a 'sum due under the contract' unless he has given an effective notice of intention to withhold payment pursuant to the Act. This has been held to extend to both equitable set-off[231] and abatement,[232] where the sum claimed is otherwise payable in accordance with the terms of the contract.[233] On one view this is a surprising conclusion, because for section 111(1) to apply there must be a 'sum due', whereas if an equitable set-off is available there is nothing due, so far as equity is concerned, to the extent of the set-off.[234] Similarly nothing is due when there is a

5.50

---

[226] Wallace, 'Set Back to Set-off' (1973) 89 LQR 36.

[227] [1974] AC 689, discussed in Wallace, 'Set Fair for Set-off' (1974) 90 LQR 21. See also *Mottram Consultants Ltd v Bernard Sunley & Sons Ltd* [1975] 2 Lloyd's Rep 197 (discussed below) and *M L Paynter Ltd v Ben Candy Investments Ltd* [1987] 1 NZLR 257. *Gilbert-Ash* has been followed in Scotland. See *Redpath Dorman Long Ltd v Cummins Engine Co Ltd* [1981] SC 370. See also, in Ireland, *P J Hegarty & Sons Ltd v Royal Liver Friendly Society* [1985] IR 524. In New Zealand, compare *Savory Holdings Ltd v Royal Oak Mall Ltd* [1992] 1 NZLR 12, 27, where Smellie J said that the particular circumstances of that case distinguished it from *Gilbert-Ash*, so as to disentitle the employer from relying on an equitable set-off in order to defeat a claim for summary judgment. The circumstances were that the moneys had been certified as owing almost a year before, further substantial sums were likely to be certified in due course, and the amount certified was merely 'provisional' and there was an ample margin for adjustment. The New Zealand Court of Appeal referred to Smellie J's judgment with evident approval in *Hempseed v Durham Developments Ltd* [1998] 3 NZLR 265, 269.

[228] See paras 2.87–2.97 above.

[229] See Viscount Dilhorne and Lord Diplock [1974] AC 689, 707, 718. See also *Mottram Consultants Ltd v Bernard Sunley & Sons Ltd* [1975] 2 Lloyd's Rep 197, 214; *Compania Sud Americana de Vapores v Shipmair BV (The Teno)* [1977] 2 Lloyd's Rep 289, 293–294; *Federal Commerce & Navigation Co Ltd v Molena Alpha Inc* [1978] 1 QB 927, 983, 986.

[230] Defined in s 104.

[231] *VHE Construction plc v RBSTB Trust Co Ltd* [2000] BLR 187, 192 para 36, 196–197 para 66; *Northern Developments (Cumbria) Ltd v J & J Nichol* [2000] BLR 158, 164 paras 29–31; *Solland International Ltd v Daraydan Holdings Ltd* [2002] EWHC 220 (TCC).

[232] *Whiteways Contractors (Sussex) Ltd v Impresa Castelli Construction UK Ltd* (2000) 75 Con LR 92, 99–100 para 32.

[233] Compare *SL Timber Systems Ltd v Carillion Construction Ltd* [2001] BLR 516.

[234] See paras 4.29–4.43 above.

defence of abatement. Nevertheless the adoption of that analysis to a considerable extent would denude the provision of effect, and the courts are likely to adhere to the view that section 111(1) extends to defences of equitable set-off and abatement.[235] If therefore an adjudicator appointed under a procedure complying with s 108 of the Act decides that an amount is due to a contractor, the employer, having failed to give an effective notice, ordinarily cannot resist an application by the contractor for summary judgment for the sum awarded on the basis of a set-off.[236] On the other hand, an adjudicator must still value the contractor's claim for payment in accordance with the contract. Therefore the absence of a notice might not preclude an adjudicator from taking defects into account in order to ascertain the amount which is contractually due, for example where the contractor is only entitled to be paid for the value of work properly performed.[237]

Excluding equitable set-off and abatement by contract

5.51 The parties may choose to exclude the defences by agreement. In the context of building contracts, it should be borne in mind however that a cross-claim for damages for defective workmanship can give rise not only to an equitable set-off but also to the common law defence of abatement.[238] Therefore, if it is intended that the contract sum should be paid in full without reduction for a cross-claim arising out of defects, care must be taken to negative both defences. In *Acsim (Southern) Ltd v Danish Contracting and Development Co Ltd*[239] the contract provided that Danish Contracting ('Dancon') could set off against any moneys otherwise due to Acsim as contractor the amount of any cross-claim which Dancon had for loss suffered as a result of a breach by Acsim, but only if the cross-claim was quantified and notified to Acsim within a specified time limit. The contract went on to provide that this fully set out the rights of the parties in respect of set-off. The Court of Appeal considered that the contract was effective to prevent a cross-claim for damages for bad workmanship that was quantified outside the required period from being employed as an equitable set-off. On the other hand there were not sufficiently clear and express words to exclude the common law defence of

---

[235] See also *Keating on Building Contracts* (7th edn, 2001) 462–3.

[236] *Solland International Ltd v Daraydan Holdings Ltd* [2002] EWHC 220 (TCC) at para 30. *Aliter* if the contractor is in insolvent liquidation. See *Bouygues (UK) Ltd v Dahl-Jensen (UK) Ltd* [2000] BLR 522. In relation to insolvency other than liquidation, see *Rainford House Ltd v Cadogan Ltd* [2001] BLR 416 (administrative receivership), and compare *SL Timber Systems v Carillion Construction Ltd* [2001] BLR 516.

[237] *SL Timber Systems Ltd v Carillion Construction Ltd* [2001] BLR 516 (including the commentary at 518), and see *Whiteways Contractors (Sussex) Ltd v Impresa Castelli Construction UK Ltd* (2000) 75 Con LR 92, 100 para 32. The Court of Appeal left the question open in *C & B Scene Concept Design Ltd v Isobars Ltd* [2002] EWCA Civ 46 at paras 17 and 19, and see also *Solland International Ltd v Daraydan Holdings Ltd* [2002] EWHC 220 (TCC) at paras 24 & 33.

[238] See paras 2.87–2.97 above.

[239] (1989) 47 BLR 55. See also, and compare, *Mellowes Archital Ltd v Bell Projects Ltd* (1997) 87 BLR 26 (damages for delay not within the common law principle of abatement).

abatement.[240] The subject of the cross-claim was not being raised as a set-off as such. Rather, pursuant to the common law principle, Dancon was defending itself by showing that, by reason of Acsim's breaches of contract, the value of the work done was less than the sum claimed. This defence was not precluded by the contract.

5.52 The question whether the parties have agreed to exclude the defences is one of interpretation of the contract, and in that regard it is often said that the intention to exclude them must be evidenced by clear express words, or at least there must be a clear implication in the contract that they are not to apply. This issue is addressed below.[241]

D. Contracts of Employment

Failure to work

5.53 An employee may have refused to work in accordance with the contract of employment for part of a period in respect of which he is making a claim for wages. The analysis in such a case is not that the employee has a prima facie entitlement to wages for that period but subject to a set-off available to the employer, to the extent of a proportion of the wages equal to the proportion of the period during which the employee refused to work.[242] Rather, the employee fails at the first hurdle, in that he is not entitled to wages to the extent that he was not ready and willing to perform the services required by the contract.[243]

Claim for damages

5.54 Alternatively an employer may have suffered loss as a result of the actions of an employee which give rise to a claim in damages against the employee. There is authority which supports the availability of an equitable set-off in that circumstance,[244] although it has been said that the principles upon which an equitable

---

[240] Compare *Skipskredittforeningen v Emperor Navigation* [1998] 1 Lloyd's Rep 66, 78–79, *per* Mance J.

[241] See paras 5.78–5.118 below.

[242] Compare *Sim v Rotherham Metropolitan BC* [1987] 1 Ch 216.

[243] *Miles v Wakefield Metropolitan DC* [1987] 1 AC 539; *Wiluszynski v Tower Hamlets LBC* [1989] ICR 493. However, as Lord Oliver of Aylmerton noted in the *Miles* case (at 571), this would be subject to an implied term exonerating the employee from inability to perform in certain circumstances, eg illness.

[244] *Sim v Rotherham Metropolitan BC* [1987] 1 Ch 216, and see also *Sagar v H Ridehalgh and Son, Ltd* [1931] 1 Ch 310; *New Centurion Trust v Welch* [1990] ICR 383. In *Miles v Wakefield Metropolitan DC* [1987] 1 AC 539, 570 Lord Oliver of Aylmerton left open the possibility of a set-off in this situation. An employee sued by his employer for money had and received may set off a claim for arrears of wages under the Statutes of Set-off. See *East Anglian Railway Co v Lythgoe* (1851) 10 CB 726, 138 ER 287.

set-off can be effective in a claim for wages are extremely limited, and that it would depend upon a careful analysis of the nature of the breach relative to the nature of the employee's contractual claim.[245] The Employment Rights Act 1996, section 13 prohibits an employer from making a deduction from wages except in certain defined circumstances,[246] but prima facie this would not seem to preclude an equitable set-off. Equitable set-off is a substantive defence,[247] and if the defence is available it would not be a case of the employer making a deduction from wages to which the employee was entitled. Rather, the set-off would render it unconscionable for the employee to regard the employer as being liable to pay wages to the extent of the cross-claim,[248] so as to impugn the employee's right to claim wages. Similarly, a stipulation in a contract that a payment is to be made 'without any deduction' has been held in other contexts not to be effective to exclude an equitable set-off.[249] Nevertheless, the point may be made that this seems inconsistent with the legislative intent in enacting a provision such as section 13, and in Australia it has been doubted whether an equitable set-off is available against a claim for wages in the face of a statute to that effect.[250]

Insolvency set-off

5.55 In any event, if the employer becomes bankrupt or goes into liquidation, cross-demands between the employer and the employee, including a cross-demand in relation to wages, prima facie would come within the ambit of the insolvency set-off section.[251] The prevailing view of insolvency set-off is that it is automatic and self-executing,[252] and provided that the requirements of the section are satisfied a set-off should occur at the date of the bankruptcy or liquidation by force of law.[253] It would not be a case of the employer making a deduction from wages.

---

[245] *New Centurion Trust v Welch* [1990] ICR 383, 386, EAT.

[246] The prohibition extends to an attempt by an employer to set off a sum which is otherwise recoverable by the employer from the employee as a mistaken payment. See *Re A Company (No 005174 of 1999)* [2000] 1 WLR 502.

[247] See paras 4.29–4.43 above.

[248] See para 4.30 above.

[249] See paras 5.82–5.86 below.

[250] Macken, McCarry and Sappideen, *The Law of Employment* (4th edn, 1997) 291–2; *Conti Sheffield Real Estate v Brailey* (1992) 48 IR 1, 7, WA Industrial Relations Commission.

[251] For bankruptcy see the Insolvency Act 1986, s 323, and for company liquidation the Insolvency Rules 1986, r 4.90. See generally ch 6 below.

[252] See paras 6.79–6.103 below.

[253] *Secretary of State for Employment v Wilson* [1996] IRLR 330, EAT. Similarly a cross-demand available to an employer against an employee should be able to provide a ground for setting aside a statutory demand served on the employer for non-payment of wages as a prelude to a bankruptcy petition. In Victoria, see *Lighting Sciences Australasia Pty Ltd v Southgate* (1997) 15 ACLC 632 (statutory demand served on company).

E. Landlord and Tenant

At one time it was thought that special considerations applied to a landlord's claim **5.56**
for rent, so that a tenant could not raise an unliquidated cross-claim against the
landlord, for example for breach of an obligation to repair, as a defence to an action by the landlord against the tenant for payment of arrears of rent.[254] Whether
indeed that view ever had a solid foundation in equity may be doubted. Thus, in
Beasley v Darcy[255] a landlord had served the tenant with an ejectment for non-
payment of rent and duly recovered possession, but the tenant obtained an injunction restoring him to possession on the basis of a cross-claim in damages
against the landlord for damage suffered as a result of timber on the demised land
being cut down and carried away.[256] But whatever the position was formerly, a tenant's liability to pay rent is not now regarded as being different in kind to other
forms of indebtedness as regards set-off, so that an equitable set-off may proceed
if the tenant's cross-demand is sufficiently closely connected with his liability to
pay rent.[257] The principle was confirmed in *British Anzani (Felixstowe) Ltd v
International Marine Management (UK) Ltd.*[258] The plaintiff had a leasehold interest in a plot of land. It agreed with the defendant that it would construct a warehouse on part of the land, after which it would grant an underlease to the

---

[254] *Hart v Rogers* [1916] 1 KB 646; *Fong v Cilli* (1968) 11 FLR 495; *Galambos & Son Pty Ltd v
McIntyre* (1974) 5 ACTR 10, 24–25; *Chatfield v Elmstone Resthouse Ltd* [1975] 2 NZLR 269;
Knockholt Pty Ltd v Graff [1975] Qd R 88, 91; *Halsbury's Laws of England* (3rd edn, 1960) vol 34,
406–7, para 705. See also the reference to rent in *Bim Kemi AB v Blackburn Chemicals Ltd* [2001] 2
Lloyd's Rep 93, 102 para 38, and *A B Contractors Ltd v Flaherty Brothers Ltd* (1978) 16 BLR 8, 12
in relation to a stay of execution. In *Taylor v Webb* [1937] 2 KB 283, du Parcq J held that the landlord in that case was not absolved from his obligation to repair because of the tenant's non-payment
of rent. Scrutton J in *Hart v Rogers* was influenced by *Surplice v Farnsworth* (1844) 7 Man & G 576,
135 ER 232, but in truth questions of equitable set-off were not considered in that case.
[255] (1800) 2 Sch & Lef 403n, explained in *Rawson v Samuel* (1841) Cr & Ph 161, 179, 41 ER
451, 458–459 and *South Eastern Railway Co v Brogden* (1850) 3 Mac & G 8, 24–25, 42 ER 163,
170.
[256] See also *O'Connor v Spaight* (1804) 1 Sch & Lef 305 (explained in *Rawson v Samuel* (1841)
Cr & Ph 161, 179, 41 ER 451, 458–459), in which Lord Redesdale granted an injunction to restrain an action for ejectment so that an account could be taken of the various dealings between the
landlord and the tenant, the justification for equitable relief being that the account was too complicated to be taken at law. Compare *O'Mahony v Dickson* (1805) 2 Sch & Lef 400.
[257] In addition to the cases referred to below, see *Melville v Grapelodge Developments Ltd* (1978)
39 P & CR 179; *BICC plc v Burndy Corp* [1985] 1 Ch 232, 249; *Lambert Pty Ltd v Papadatos Pty
Ltd* (1991) 5 ACSR 468, 471; *Gibb Australia Pty Ltd v Cremor Pty Ltd* (1992) 108 FLR 129; *MEK
Nominees Pty Ltd v Billboard Entertainments Pty Ltd* (1993) V Conv R 54–468; *Televantos v
McCulloch* [1991] 1 EGLR 123; *Connaught Restaurants Ltd v Indoor Leisure Ltd* [1994] 1 WLR 501;
Liangis Investments Pty Ltd v Daplyn Pty Ltd (1994) 117 FLR 28, 36. See also *Filross Securities Ltd v
Midgeley* [1998] 3 EGLR 43 (service charge payable as additional rent). In *Coba Industries Ltd v
Millie's Holdings (Canada) Ltd* [1985] 6 WWR 14 a cross-claim for damages for repudiating a lease
was held to give rise to an equitable set-off.
[258] [1980] 1 QB 137. In Australia, see *Bennett v Excelsior Land, Investment and Building Co Ltd*
(1893) 14 NSWR (Eq) 179, 185.

defendant. Under the terms of the agreement, the plaintiff was obliged to make good any defects which appeared in the floor of the warehouse. The building was completed and a sub-lease entered into. The plaintiff subsequently sued the defendant for arrears of rent, whereupon the defendant raised as a defence a cross-demand against the plaintiff for breach of the agreement to repair defects in the floor. Forbes J held that there was a sufficiently close connection between the demands to give rise to an equitable set-off, notwithstanding that the cross-demand did not arise out of the lease itself, but rather pursuant to the original agreement.[259]

5.57   Equitable set-off against rent is not limited to breach of a covenant to repair or other similar undertaking.[260] For example, equitable set-off has been held to apply when a landlord breached a covenant for quiet enjoyment,[261] when a home loss payment was payable to a tenant under the Land Compensation Act 1973,[262] and, in New Zealand, when tenants were induced to enter into the lease by a collateral contract with the lessor pursuant to which the lessor agreed to refer business to the tenants, and the lessor breached that agreement.[263] On the other hand, when the tenant of a public house was sued for arrears of rent, and the lease contained a 'beer tie'[264] that infringed Article 85 of the EC Treaty, the Court of Appeal considered that any liability for damages that may have resulted from the infringement would not have been sufficiently connected with the obligation to pay rent so as to give rise to an equitable set-off.[265]

[259] See also *Melville v Grapelodge Developments Ltd* (1978) 39 P & CR 179 (covenant to repair contained in a separate letter), and *Grant v NZMC Ltd* [1989] 1 NZLR 8 (collateral contract). Compare *Hamilton Ice Arena Ltd v Perry Developments Ltd* [2002] 1 NZLR 309, in which the demands were insufficiently connected.

[260] In addition to *British Anzani*, see *Melville v Grapelodge Developments Ltd* (1978) 39 P & CR 179; *Re Partnership Pacific Securities Ltd* [1994] 1 Qd R 410, 421–424 (breach of covenant relating to refurbishment of the premises); *Filross Securities Ltd v Midgeley* [1998] 3 EGLR 43. In Australia see *Knockholt Pty Ltd v Graff* [1975] Qd R 88, which is explained in Weir, 'A Tenant's Right of Set-off' (1994) 68 Australian Law Journal 857, 863–5, and *Mirvac Hotels Pty Ltd v 333 Collins St. Pty Ltd* (Vic SC, Byrne J, 20 December 1994). In *Sloan Stanley Estate Trustees v Barribal* [1994] 2 EGLR 8, Balcombe LJ (at 11) was prepared to accept that a tenant's right to be reimbursed by the landlord for a rate paid under the Land Drainage Act 1976 could be the subject of an equitable set-off against rent. See also the formulation adopted in *Hamilton Ice Arena Ltd v Perry Developments Ltd* [2002] 1 NZLR 309, 318–319.

[261] *Connaught Restaurants Ltd v Indoor Leisure Ltd* [1994] 1 WLR 501; *MEK Nominees Pty Ltd v Billboard Entertainments Pty Ltd* (1993) V Conv R 54–468; *Liangis Investments Pty Ltd v Daplyn Pty Ltd* (1994) 117 FLR 28, 36; *Filross Securities Ltd v Midgeley* [1998] 3 EGLR 43.

[262] *Khan v Islington LBC* [1999] EWCA Civ 1546.

[263] *Grant v NZMC Ltd* [1989] 1 NZLR 8, referred to in *Courage Ltd v Crehan* [1999] 2 EGLR 145, 146.

[264] Pursuant to the tie, the tenant had to purchase all or most of its beer for sale in the premises from the landlord or a brewer nominated by the landlord at prices prescribed by the supplier.

[265] *Courage Ltd v Crehan* [1999] 2 EGLR 145, following *Star Rider Ltd v Inntrepenneur Pub Co* [1998] 1 EGLR 53 and *Gibbs Mew plc v Gemmell* [1999] 1 EGLR 43, CA. In *Star Rider* Blackburne J (at 56) said that the infringement did not prejudice or hinder the tenant's physical use and occupation of the premises, much less affect the physical condition of the premises. He said that at most it affected the extent to which the tenant was able to derive profit from the use of the premises, which he considered was insufficient to support an equitable set-off. However there may be cases where

In *Star Rider Ltd v Inntreprenneur Pub Co*[266] Blackburne J referred to a submission **5.58**
by counsel to the effect that equitable set-off against rent is confined to a claim
which relates to the quality of occupation of the demised premises. Blackburne J
said that he was unwilling to attempt a definition of what must be established in
order to give rise to an equitable set-off, but he said that he would ordinarily expect the cross-claim to be of that nature. A similar limitation has been suggested
in the case of a time charter of a ship, that equitable set-off is confined to the case
where the shipowner has wrongly deprived the charterer of the use of the ship or
has prejudiced him in the use of it.[267] Subsequently, however, the Court of Appeal
in *Courage Ltd v Crehan*[268] rejected the proposition that equitable set-off against
rent is limited to claims affecting the tenant's physical use or occupation of the
premises,[269] commenting that, while the connection referred to is likely to be sufficient, it should not in all cases be necessary. For example, if the lease requires the
tenant to carry on a particular business, the Court of Appeal could see no reason
why cross-claims arising out of the conduct of the business should not be set off
against rent. The point is also illustrated by the later decision of the Court of
Appeal in *Fuller v Happy Shopper Markets Ltd*,[270] in which a tenant liable for
unpaid rent was allowed an equitable set-off in respect of a claim for earlier overpayments of rent under the lease.[271]

The preceding discussion relates to equitable set-off of unliquidated cross- **5.59**
demands. If the tenant's cross-demand is for a liquidated sum, a set-off against
a claim for rent may proceed on the basis of mutual debts under the Statutes of
Set-off.[272]

---

the fact that the circumstances giving rise to the cross-claim affect the profit that may be derived
from the premises would give rise to an equitable set-off. This may be the case, for example, if the
circumstances affected the tenant's ability to pay rent. See the explanation of *Beasley v Darcy* (1805)
2 Sch & Lef 403n in *O'Mahony v Dickson* (1805) 2 Sch & Lef 400, 412 and in *Stimson v Hall* (1857)
1 H & N 831, 835–836, 156 ER 1436, 1438.

[266] [1998] 1 EGLR 53.
[267] *Federal Commerce & Navigation Co Ltd v Molena Alpha Inc* [1978] 1 QB 927, 976, *per* Lord
Denning. See para 5.12 above.
[268] [1999] 2 EGLR 145, 156.
[269] Referring to *Grant v NZMC Ltd* [1989] 1 NZLR 8 (see above).
[270] [2001] 1 WLR 1681. See also *Philip Collins Ltd v Davis* [2000] 3 All ER 808, 831 (overpayment of royalties). Compare *Unchained Growth III plc v Granby Village (Manchester) Management
Co Ltd* [2000] 1 WLR 739 (overpayment of service charge to a management company), in which
set-off had been excluded by contract.
[271] Compare *Ory & Ory v Betamore Pty Ltd* (1993) 60 SASR 393, where the unpaid rent was
claimed by a mortgagee in possession, as opposed to the landlord/mortgagor who was the recipient
of the overpayment. See paras 17.59–17.70 below.
[272] *Gower v Hunt* (1734) Barnes 290, 291, 94 ER 920; *Brown v Holyoak* (1734), referred to in
Hutchison v Sturges (1741) Willes 261, 263, 125 ER 1163, 1164; *Cleghorn v Durrant* (1858) 31
LTOS 235. See also *Hamp v Jones* (1840) 9 LJ Ch 258 (cross-demand for rent set off against judgment obtained by tenant against landlord). Compare *Samways v Eldsley* (1676) 2 Mod 73, 86 ER
949, which was decided before the enactment of the Statutes of Set-off.

Forfeiture for non-payment of rent

5.60   Equitable set-off and the right of set-off conferred by the Statutes of Set-off differ in an important respect. Equitable set-off is a substantive defence which may be set up by a person as an immediate answer to liability.[273] The Statutes, on the other hand, only provided a procedural defence, in the sense that prior to judgment for a set-off the rights and obligations consequent upon being a creditor or a debtor still attach.[274] This distinction may be important in the context of forfeiture for non-payment of rent. Because equitable set-off is a substantive defence, a landlord is not entitled to regard a tenant possessed of this form of set-off as being indebted for rent to the extent of the set-off. As a result the landlord would not be justified in asserting forfeiture, and the tenant would have a defence to an action for possession.[275] Given, however, that the defence under the Statutes is merely procedural, in the sense noted earlier,[276] a landlord would be entitled to assert that a tenant relying on this defence nevertheless still has a liability for unpaid rent, and therefore under the contract the landlord has a ground for forfeiting the lease. It would then be a matter for the court in its discretion to consider whether relief from forfeiture is appropriate in the circumstances.[277]

Distress

5.61   Traditionally a right of set-off under the Statutes has not been regarded as a ground sufficient to protect a tenant against a landlord levying distress for rent.[278] The Statutes only provided a procedural defence to an action at law, whereas distress is a form of self-help remedy to which a landlord is entitled without recourse to legal process. Equitable set-off, on the other hand, is a substantive defence which may be set up independently of an order of the court,[279] in the sense that the circumstances render it unconscionable for a creditor to regard the debtor as being in default to the extent of the set-off.[280] Therefore, when a tenant is possessed of a

---

[273]   See paras 4.29–4.43 above.

[274]   See paras 2.33–2.48 above.

[275]   See eg *Televantos v McCulloch* [1991] 1 EGLR 123, and also *Beasley v Darcy* (1800) 2 Sch & Lef 403n (above).

[276]   See paras 2.33–2.40 above.

[277]   See generally, with respect to forfeiture for non-payment of rent, the Supreme Court Act 1981, s 38(1), and *Belgravia Insurance Co Ltd v Meah* [1964] 1 QB 436, 443.

[278]   *Absolon v Knight* (1743) Barnes 450, 94 ER 998; *Townrow v Benson* (1818) 3 Madd 203, 56 ER 484. See also *Sapsford v Fletcher* (1792) 4 TR 511, 512–513, 514, 100 ER 1147, 1148, 1149; *Andrew v Hancock* (1819) 1 Brod & B 37, 43, 46, 47, 129 ER 637, 639–641; *Willson v Davenport* (1833) 5 Car & P 531, 172 ER 1085; *Pratt v Keith* (1864) 33 LJ Ch 528; *British Anzani (Felixstowe) Ltd v International Marine Management (UK) Ltd* [1980] 1 QB 137, 149. Distress for rent has been abolished in some jurisdictions. See eg the Landlord and Tenant Act 1958 (Vic), s 12, and Sykes and Walker, *The Law of Securities* (5th edn, 1993) 285–8.

[279]   See *SL Sethia Liners Ltd v Naviagro Maritime Corporation (The Kostas Melas)* [1981] 1 Lloyd's Rep 18, 26.

[280]   See para 4.30 above.

cross-claim that gives rise to an equitable set-off, the landlord should not be permitted to assert that the tenant is in arrears in payment of rent so as to entitle the landlord to distrain for non-payment. Consistent with that view, the Court of Appeal in *Eller v Grovecrest Investments Ltd*[281] granted an injunction to a tenant to restrain the landlord from proceeding with distraint against the tenant's goods because of an equitable set-off. However, neither Hoffmann LJ[282] nor Neill LJ in their respective judgments in the *Eller* case emphasized the substantive nature of the defence, and there are indications that they would have been sympathetic to the view that the availability of a procedural defence of set-off under the Statutes should have the same effect. Thus, Neill LJ said that he could:

> see no reason to distinguish between the position of a landlord who is asserting his rights in respect of arrears of rent by a claim for possession or by an action in debt, on the one hand, and that of a landlord who is asserting identical rights, but who is availing himself of the remedy of distress. In both cases the proper question to be determined is, looking at the state of account between the parties in the light of their rights under the lease, is any sum due to the landlord.[283]

Similarly Hoffmann LJ said that: 'It is contrary to principle that a landlord should be able to recover more by distress than he can by action.'[284] This reasoning would appear to be equally applicable when a tenant has a defence under the Statutes to an action for payment of rent. Indeed, Hoffmann LJ concluded his judgment by commenting that 'this court is free to hold that set-off is available against a claim to levy distress',[285] without drawing a distinction between the various forms of set-off. In his later judgment in *Aectra Refining and Marketing Inc v Exmar NV*,[286] however, Hoffmann LJ appeared to distinguish between equitable set-off and set-off under the Statutes in this context, so as, apparently, to reassert the traditional position in relation to the Statutes. More recently, Lightman J affirmed that view in *Fuller v Happy Shopper Markets Ltd.*[287]

---

[281] [1995] QB 272. See also *Fuller v Happy Shopper Markets Ltd* [2001] 1 WLR 1681. Compare *Halsbury's Laws of England* (4th edn reissue, 1994) vol 27(1), 224 para 234, and the earlier comments of Neill LJ (one of the judges in the Court of Appeal in *Eller*) in *Connaught Restaurants Ltd v Indoor Leisure Ltd* [1994] 1 WLR 501, 511. Note also *Townrow v Benson* (1818) 3 Madd 203, 56 ER 484, in which Sir John Leach said that a court of equity would follow the law in relation to the principle that a set-off does not defeat an entitlement to levy distress, though that was in the context of whether equity would grant an injunction to restrain the landlord from levying distress on the basis of a set-off under the Statutes, as opposed to whether the substantive form of equitable set-off under discussion is subject to the same principle.

[282] Waite LJ agreed with Hoffmann LJ's judgment.

[283] [1995] QB 272, 280.

[284] [1995] QB 272, 278.

[285] [1995] QB 272, 278.

[286] [1994] 1 WLR 1634, 1650.

[287] [2001] 1 WLR 1681.

Payment by a sub-tenant to the superior landlord

5.62 Whatever the position in relation to a landlord's right to levy distress where the tenant is entitled to a set-off under the Statutes, it is necessary to distinguish the cases which have held that, where a sub-tenant is compelled by the superior landlord to pay a sum owing by the sub-tenant's immediate landlord for unpaid rent or other like charges, to the extent of the payment the immediate landlord cannot levy distress for unpaid rent.[288] The principle applies where the sub-tenant's payment was such as to give rise to a right of action against the immediate landlord for money paid to his use,[289] but the sub-tenant's right nevertheless is not characterized as a set-off.[290] When a sub-tenant is compelled to make a payment to the superior landlord which ought to have been made by the immediate landlord, the sub-tenant is considered as having been authorized by the immediate landlord to apply rent which is either due or accruing due to him in this manner.[291] Accordingly, the basis upon which the sub-tenant impugns a subsequent attempt by the immediate landlord to distrain for unpaid rent is that the rent alleged to be outstanding in fact has been paid.[292]

Recoupment

5.63 A principle which is analogous to, but which nevertheless is distinct from, set-off may apply where leased premises have fallen into disrepair and responsibility for the repairs is on the landlord. In such a case, the tenant may expend money in executing the repairs and recoup himself from future payments of rent or from arrears of rent.[293] This is not bound up with technical rules of set-off, but rather it is an ancient common law right of recoupment which entitles the tenant to treat the amount expended on repairs as payment of rent.[294] As early as 1591 Gawdy J in

---

[288] See eg *Sapsford v Fletcher* (1792) 4 TR 511, 100 ER 1147, and *Carter v Carter* (1829) 5 Bing 406, 130 ER 1118. A similar principle applies when a tenant pays sums owing by his landlord to a rent chargee with a power to distrain or to a mortgagee. See *Taylor v Zamira* (1816) 6 Taunt 524, 128 ER 1138 (rent charge); *Johnson v Jones* (1839) 9 Ad & E 809, 112 ER 1421 (mortgage). See also *Doe v Hare* (1833) 2 C & M 145, 149 ER 709 (claim for mesne profits), and generally *Graham v Allsopp* (1848) 3 Ex 186, 198, 154 ER 809, 814. Compare *Boodle v Cambell* (1844) 7 Man & G 386, 135 ER 161.

[289] *Graham v Allsopp* (1848) 3 Ex 186, 198, 199, 154 ER 809, 814–815.

[290] Compare Wood, *English and International Set-off* (1989) 130.

[291] *Graham v Allsopp* (1848) 3 Ex 186, 198, 154 ER 809, 814; *Jones v Morris* (1849) 3 Ex 742, 747, 154 ER 1044, 1046–1047.

[292] *Sapsford v Fletcher* (1792) 4 TR 511, 100 ER 1147; *Graham v Allsopp* (1848) 3 Ex 186, 198, 154 ER 809, 814; *Jones v Morris* (1849) 3 Ex 742, 154 ER 1044.

[293] See generally Rank, 'Repairs in Lieu of Rent' (1976) 40 Conv (NS) 196; Waite, 'Repairs and Deduction from Rent' [1981] The Conveyancer 199. The money must be expended. A tenant is not justified in withholding rent in an effort to compel the landlord to address his grievances. See *Camden Nominees Ltd v Forcey* [1940] 1 Ch 352. *Quaere* whether recoupment is confined to rent, or whether it extends to other moneys payable to a landlord, such as an obligation to pay outgoings. See *Batiste v Lenin* [2002] NSUSC 233 at para 102.

[294] *Connaught Restaurants Ltd v Indoor Leisure Ltd* [1994] 1 WLR 501, 507, *per* Waite LJ, 511, *per* Neill LJ, referring to *Lee-Parker v Izzet* [1971] 1 WLR 1688, 1693, *per* Goff J. See also para 17.68 below.

Taylor v Beal[295] is reported to have said[296] that 'the law giveth this liberty to the lessee to expend the rent in reparations, for he shall be otherwise at great mischief, for the house may fall upon his head before it be repaired; and therefore the law alloweth him to repair it, and recoupe the rent'.[297] There is surprisingly little case law on this right, but its existence seems to have been accepted in 1795 in *Waters v Weigall*.[298] The tenant in that case had covenanted to keep the premises in repair 'accidents by fire and tempest excepted'. The house was damaged by tempest and, being in want of emergency repairs, the tenant repaired it himself in order to prevent further mischief.[299] The landlord refused to allow the tenant to deduct the cost of repairs from the rent, and brought an action for payment of rent. The tenant then filed a bill in the equity side of the Exchequer seeking relief in the form of a right to retain the amount of the repairs out of the rent. It appears from the report of the argument in support of the bill that the tenant proceeded in equity because there was no express covenant in the lease that the landlord was liable to repair in the case that happened, and it was thought that consequently the tenant did not have a cross-claim at law against the landlord.[300] For that reason MacDonald CB held that the tenant similarly was not entitled to relief from equity. Nevertheless, it seems clear that in the opinion of the Chief Baron a right of recoupment would have been available if the landlord had been bound to repair in consequence of the accident that happened.[301]

The next reported occasion on which it appears that English courts were called **5.64** upon to consider the right of recoupment was in 1971, in *Lee-Parker v Izzet*.[302]

---

[295] (1591) Cro Eliz 222, 78 ER 478.

[296] Citing three cases from the Year Books, for which see Waite, 'Repairs and Deduction from Rent' [1981] The Conveyancer 199, 200–1.

[297] Clench J apparently agreed with the proposition that the tenant 'might well expend the rent in reparations', though he found against the tenant on a point of pleading. Fenner J on the other hand said that the tenant had to bring a separate action.

[298] (1795) 2 Anst 575, 145 ER 971.

[299] It appears from the report of the subsequent proceedings at law in *Weigall v Waters* (1795) 6 TR 488, 101 ER 663 that 'a violent tempest arose and threw down with great force and violence a stack of chimneys belonging to the house on the roof of the house . . . and damaged the house so much that it would soon have become uninhabitable, if he [the tenant] had not immediately repaired it'.

[300] See the subsequent proceedings at law in *Weigall v Waters* (1795) 6 TR 488, 101 ER 663.

[301] MacDonald CB referred in his judgment ((1795) 2 Anst 575, 576, 145 ER 971) to a right of 'set-off' against the demand for rent. However, the claim of the tenant appears to have been that he should be allowed to recoup or 'retain' his expenses from the rent otherwise payable to the landlord, rather than that a cross-demand constituted a defence to the landlord's demand for rent. The question appears to have been one concerning recoupment, or payment, rather than set-off.

[302] [1971] 1 WLR 1688. See also *British Anzani (Felixstowe) Ltd v International Marine Management (UK) Ltd* [1980] 1 QB 137, 146–149, and in Australia *Knockholt Pty Ltd v Graff* [1975] Qd R 88. Compare *Batiste v Lenin* [2002] NSWSC 233 at paras 102–105. The common law right of recoupment did not apply in *British Anzani* given that the tenants had not expended any money on repairs. However they were entitled to an equitable set-off against the obligation to pay rent because of a cross-demand against the landlord for breach of the repair obligation. See also *Melville v Grapelodge Developments Ltd* (1978) 39 P & CR 179.

Goff J in that case granted a declaration to tenants to the effect that, in so far as repairs carried out by the tenants were within the express or implied repairing covenants of the landlord, including those imported by section 32(1) of the Housing Act 1961,[303] they were entitled to deduct[304] the proper cost from future payments of rent, and moreover to the extent of such proper costs they were not liable to be sued for the rent. Further, if a tenant with a right of recoupment has, to the extent of the sum expended, a defence to a claim for rent, the availability of the right should also provide an answer to a claim to distrain,[305] on the ground that the rent has been paid.[306] Subsequently Megarry VC held in *Asco Developments Ltd v Gordon*[307] that a right of recoupment is available not only against future rent but also against arrears of rent.

5.65 A landlord must have information as to the existence of a defect in the premises before an obligation arises to carry out works of repair.[308] The landlord's obligation is to effect the repairs within a reasonable time of receiving notice.[309] Consistent with that proposition, it has been said that the landlord must have notice of want of repair before the right of recoupment can be exercised.[310] This may give rise to difficulty in a situation in which the damage is such that emergency repairs are necessary in order to prevent the premises sustaining further damage. There is much to be said for the view that, in cases of emergency, the tenant should be able to effect repairs and recoup the expense from rent despite the absence of prior notice to the landlord.[311]

5.66 Forbes J in *British Anzani (Felixstowe) Ltd v International Marine Management (UK) Ltd*[312] suggested a limitation on the right of recoupment, and that is that it must not be based upon a sum which is regarded as unliquidated damages. By this he meant that it must be in respect of a sum certain which has actually been paid, and of which, in addition, the quantum has either been acknowledged by the

---

[303] See now the Landlord and Tenant Act 1985, s 11.

[304] In truth, 'deduct' seems an inaccurate description of the right. See para 5.85 below.

[305] In some jurisdictions, distress for rent has been abolished. See eg, in Victoria, the Landlord and Tenant Act 1958, s 12.

[306] There have been suggestions to this effect. See *Connaught Restaurants Ltd v Indoor Leisure Ltd* [1994] 1 WLR 501, 511; *Lee-Parker v Izzet* [1971] 1 WLR 1688, 1692–1693. See also para 17.68 below.

[307] (1978) 248 EG 683.

[308] *O'Brien v Robinson* [1973] AC 912, 928.

[309] *Chatfield v Elmstone Resthouse Ltd* [1975] 2 NZLR 269; *Andrews v Brewer* [1997] EWCA Civ 1029.

[310] *Lee-Parker v Izzet* [1971] 1 WLR 1688, 1693; *British Anzani (Felixstowe) Ltd v International Marine Management (UK) Ltd* [1980] 1 QB 137, 147–148; *Andrews v Brewer* [1997] EWCA Civ 1029.

[311] Waite, 'Repairs and Deduction from Rent' [1981] The Conveyancer 199, 203–4, and see also the headnote to *Waters v Weigall* (1795) 2 Anst 575, 145 ER 971. Waite also suggested that, if the landlord has disappeared so that notice of disrepair is not possible, a tenant effecting repairs should not be deprived of a right of recoupment in respect of the expenditure incurred.

[312] [1980] 1 QB 137, 148.

landlord or in some other way it can no longer be disputed by him. The better view however is that there is no such limitation, and that, as long as the expenditure was properly incurred by the tenant,[313] it makes no difference that the quantum is disputed by the landlord.[314] Forbes J based his suggested limitation upon the judgment of Lord Kenyon CJ in *Weigall v Waters*.[315] *Weigall v Waters* was decided at common law, and was in respect of the same situation considered in the earlier proceedings in equity referred to above in *Waters v Weigall*. The landlord was suing for rent, and the tenant sought to set off his expenditure incurred in effecting the repairs. Lord Kenyon held against a set-off, inter alia on the ground that, if the landlord indeed was liable to repair the premises, the defendant's cross-demand would have had to be assessed by a jury and consequently it was for unliquidated damages. However it is important to note that the only defence pleaded by the defendant was set-off, and a prerequisite to a set-off in an action at law under the Statutes of Set-off was mutual debts. The defendant had not pleaded the alternative defence that he was entitled to recoup his expenditure from rent, and that this recoupment constituted payment of the rent.

F. Specific Performance

The question sometimes arises whether a right of set-off constitutes a defence to a **5.67** claim for specific performance of a contract. In *Phipps v Child*[316] the plaintiff and the defendant agreed that the defendant would purchase the plaintiff's interest in a colliery. The defendant failed to complete the purchase in accordance with the contract, whereupon the plaintiff sought an order for specific performance. The defendant argued that, as a result of dealings between the parties, the plaintiff was liable to him for a sum of money which should be set off against the purchase money. Sir Richard Kindersley VC rejected the defence, commenting: 'There may be a right in the Defendant to bring an action against the Plaintiff. But, if there is such a right, that is not a reason for non-performance of the contract.'[317] However the decision, and the Vice Chancellor's comments, should be considered in the context that the monetary cross-demands in issue appear not to have been such as would have given rise to a set-off in an action for the price.[318]

---

[313] *Lee-Parker v Izzet* [1971] 1 WLR 1688, 1693; *Connaught Restaurants Ltd v Indoor Leisure Ltd* [1994] 1 WLR 501, 511.

[314] See Waite, 'Repairs and Deduction from Rent' [1981] The Conveyancer 199, 205–7, citing *Mason v Kerver* (1387) YB Barr, 11 Ri 2 f 242.

[315] (1795) 6 TR 488, 101 ER 663.

[316] (1857) 3 Drewry 709, 61 ER 1074.

[317] (1857) 3 Drewry 709, 715, 61 ER 1074, 1076.

[318] See Spry, *Equitable Remedies* (6th edn, 2001) 177, and also *BICC plc v Burndy Corp* [1985] 1 Ch 232, 250, 257. The defendant's cross-demand appears to have been for an unliquidated sum, in which case a set-off would not have been available under the Statutes of Set-off. Moreover, there does not appear to have been a sufficient connection between the cross-demands to support an equitable set-off.

5.68 This question of the availability of set-off as a defence to a claim for specific performance came before the Court of Appeal in *BICC plc v Burndy Corp.*[319] The
plaintiff and the defendant had traded together for a number of years in a joint enterprise. They decided to dissolve the relationship, and accordingly entered into a
number of agreements. One agreement provided for the continued sale of goods by
the defendant to the plaintiff. According to a second agreement the plaintiff was to
be responsible for the processing and maintenance of the joint rights, while the defendant was liable to reimburse the plaintiff for half of any expenses thereby incurred. This second agreement further provided that, if either of the parties failed
to fulfil its obligations under the agreement, the party not in default could require
the party in default to assign to it all the interests possessed by the party in default
in the joint rights. The plaintiff incurred expenses in relation to a number of joint
rights and duly invoiced the defendant for half of that sum. When the defendant
failed to make reimbursement within the stipulated time the plaintiff claimed that,
in accordance with the second agreement, it was entitled to an assignment of the
defendant's interests in the joint rights, and brought an action seeking specific performance of the agreement. As a defence the defendant argued that it had a right to
set off against the sums owing by it the sums due to it from the plaintiff under the
first agreement for the sale of goods. The form of set-off considered to be in issue
was the right to set off mutual debts under the Statutes of Set-off.[320] It was not regarded as a case of equitable set-off. Dillon LJ, with whom Ackner LJ concurred,
considered that statutory and equitable set-off both constitute a good defence to a
claim for specific performance. That view would seem correct with respect to equitable set-off. Equitable set-off operates as a substantive defence which may be invoked independently of an order of the court.[321] If a person has a money obligation
under a contract but also has a cross-demand which is sufficiently closely connected to give rise to an equitable set-off, the other party to the contract could not
in good conscience regard the first person as being indebted to the extent of the
value of the cross-demand, in which case that other party should hardly be entitled
to an order for specific performance when the right to the equitable relief sought
depends upon a recognition of the existence of that very debt. However this explanation would not extend to the Statutes of Set-off. [322] Unlike equitable set-off, the
defence provided by the Statutes is procedural, in that the set-off depends for its
effect upon a judgment. Prior to judgment for a set-off each of the parties is still indebted to the other, and the rights consequent upon being a creditor still attach, as
do the obligations and liabilities concequent upon being a debtor.[323]

---

[319] [1985] 1 Ch 232.
[320] See [1985] 1 Ch 232, 245, 249, 259.
[321] *SL Sethia Liners Ltd v Naviagro Maritime Corp (The Kostas Melas)* [1981] 1 Lloyd's Rep 18,
26. See paras 4.29–4.43 above.
[322] Compare Dillon LJ at [1985] 1 Ch 232, 251.
[323] See paras 2.33–2.48 above.

The third member of the Court of Appeal, Kerr LJ, similarly refused to grant spe-   **5.69**
cific performance, though he adopted a different approach. In his Lordship's
opinion the existence of a right of set-off, whether legal or equitable, does not *per
se* provide a defence to a claim for specific performance, though it does constitute
a factor relevant to the exercise of the court's discretion in determining whether to
grant the relief sought.[324] The difficulty with this view, in so far as it applies to
equitable set-off, is that, if indeed the cross-demands are such that an equitable
set-off would be available, it is not easy to see how a court could ever grant an order
for specific performance without detracting from the substantive nature of the defence. On the other hand, there is much to commend Kerr LJ's analysis in relation
to the availability of a statutory right of set-off upon an application for an order
for specific performance. The better view is that it constitutes a factor which,
along with the other relevant circumstances, the court should take into consideration in the exercise of its discretion. In the instant case Kerr LJ noted that the
conduct of the plaintiff throughout the negotiations between the parties had been
inconsistent with the applicability of the agreement for an assignment, which it
suddenly sought to impose without any warning.[325] This factor, when combined
with the defendant's claim for a set-off under the Statutes, led Kerr LJ to conclude
that an order for specific performance was inappropriate.

In *BICC v Burndy*, set-off was raised as a defence to an application for an order for   **5.70**
specific performance. Alternatively, the applicant for the order may assert a set-off.
This could arise where the applicant's obligation under the contract is to pay
money. In order to obtain specific performance the applicant must show that he is
ready and willing to perform his own obligation, but because of an equitable set-
off he may assert that he need only tender a reduced amount, after taking into
account the set-off, in order to satisfy that requirement. This issue is considered
below.[326]

Consider that a vendor has entered into a contract to sell land to a purchaser, who   **5.71**
happens to be separately indebted to the vendor, but that the vendor becomes
bankrupt before conveyance. In *Re Taylor, ex p Norvell*[327] the Court of Appeal[328]
held that the purchaser in such a case is entitled to specific performance of the contract on terms that the purchase price should be reduced to the extent of a set-off
available to the purchaser against the price pursuant to the set-off section in the
insolvency legislation.[329] Buckley LJ in his judgment[330] noted that title had been

---

[324] See also *Handley Page Ltd v Commissioners of Customs and Excise and Rockwell Machine Tool
Company Ltd* [1970] 2 Lloyd's Rep 459 (in particular at 466).
[325] [1985] 1 Ch 232, 253.
[326] See para 5.72 below.
[327] [1910] 1 KB 562.
[328] *Per* Cozens-Hardy MR and Buckley LJ, Fletcher Moulton LJ dissenting.
[329] See ch 6 below.
[330] [1910] 1 KB 562, 580.

accepted before the bankruptcy, so that, when the bankruptcy occurred, there was nothing to be done but for the purchaser to pay the money and the vendor to execute the conveyance. Cozens Hardy MR however expressed the preferred view,[331] that it was not material when title was accepted as long as a good title had in fact been made. A similar principle should apply when the vendor is not bankrupt or in liquidation, so that the insolvency set-off section is not applicable, but the purchaser has a cross-action which is available as an equitable set-off.[332]

G. Set-off as a Sword

5.72 It is sometimes said that set-off is a shield, not a sword,[333] an aphorism that Meagher, Gummow and Lehane in Australia have suggested has the same meaning in this context as it has in the case of equitable estoppel. In other words, it is capable of being used offensively, but whether or not it can be used offensively it is also capable of being pleaded as a ground for absolution.[334] When a substantive defence of equitable set-off is in issue,[335] there is no reason why in an appropriate case it should not be capable of being used offensively. For example, an applicant for a decree of specific performance must show that he is ready and willing to perform his own essential obligations under the contract. If this involves the payment of money, he should be entitled to assert that the liability in question is reduced because of an equitable set-off available against the defendant. In that regard, in contracts for the sale of land where there is a deficiency in the quantity or quality of the estate agreed to be transferred, for example, because the vendor does not have title to part of the land,[336] or because his title is different to that which he represented,[337] or because the property has deteriorated as a result of the vendor's neglect between the date of the contract and the date the purchaser obtains possession,[338] courts of equity for a long time have allowed the purchaser to obtain

---

[331] [1910] 1 KB 562, 572.

[332] Compare *King v Poggioli* (1923) 32 CLR 222 (esp Starke J at 248), in which equitable set-off was not considered. See *Eagle Star Nominees Ltd v Merril* [1982] VR 557, 560.

[333] See eg *Commercial Factors Ltd v Maxwell Printing Ltd* [1994] 1 NZLR 724, 735 and, in the context of the Statutes of Set-off, *Stooke v Taylor* (1880) 5 QBD 569, 575 and *Galambos & Son Pty Ltd v McIntyre* (1974) 5 ACTR 10, 18. In Australia, set-off has been described as a 'defensive equity'. See *Giumelli v Giumelli* (1999) 196 CLR 101, 113, referring to Deane J in *The Commonwealth v Verwayen* (1990) 170 CLR 394, 435.

[334] Meagher, Gummow and Lehane, *Equity Doctrines and Remedies* (3rd edn, 1992) 810. See eg the discussion of equitable estoppel in Treitel, *The Law of Contract* (10th edn, 1999) 107.

[335] See paras 4.29–4.43 above.

[336] See eg *Western v Russell* (1814) 3 V & B 187, 35 ER 450; *Jones v Evans* (1848) 17 LJ Ch 469; *Hooper v Smart* (1874) LR 18 Eq 683.

[337] See eg *Mortlock v Buller* (1804) 10 Ves Jun 292, 315–316, 32 ER 857, 866; *Nelthorpe v Holgate* (1844) 1 Coll 203, 63 ER 384; *Barnes v Wood* (1869) LR 8 Eq 424.

[338] *Phillips v Silvester* (1872) LR 8 Ch App 173, and see also *Clarke v Ramuz* [1891] 2 QB 456, 461–462. It has been suggested in New South Wales that this covers also questions of interest for

specific performance of the contract to the extent of the vendor's ability to comply with it, with an abatement in the price by way of compensation for the deficiency. This right was developed independently of the principle of equitable set-off. While it does not apply where there is a breach of contract by the vendor which does not have the effect of lessening the value of the property as such,[339] the better view is that the purchaser in such a case nevertheless should be in a similar position in an application for specific performance if the cross-claim would give rise to a substantive defence of equitable set-off against the liability for the price, in that the purchaser should only be required to show that he is ready and willing to pay the price as reduced by the set-off.[340]

Statutes of Set-off

It is more difficult, however, to see how the availability of a right of set-off under the Statutes of Set-off could be used offensively. The nature of this defence is such that it has a procedural operation,[341] in the sense that the Statutes only authorize a set-off if it is pleaded as a defence to an action for payment of a debt. Until such time as judgment for a set-off is obtained, each of the parties has the rights and obligations of creditor and debtor in relation to the cross-debts. Therefore, if in the example referred to the applicant seeking specific performance merely tenders the balance after deducting a separate debt owing to him by the defendant, he will not have shown that he is ready and willing to perform his own obligation.   **5.73**

H. Foreign Currencies

It may be that one or both of the claims in a proposed set-off is in a foreign currency. The question of how a set-off should proceed is considered, first, in the context of the Statutes of Set-off, and then in relation to equitable set-off.   **5.74**

Statutes of Set-off

Until comparatively recently it was a settled principle of English law that, when a foreign currency obligation was enforced in an English court, any judgment for the plaintiff had to be in sterling measured at the rate of exchange prevailing at the date when the obligation became due and payable.[342] However in 1975 the House   **5.75**

---

delay and costs of ensuring vacant possession as promised by the vendor. See *Goodger v Ayre* (1988) 88 FLR 188, 190, *per* Young J.

[339] *King v Poggioli* (1923) 32 CLR 222; *Rutherford v Acton-Adams* [1915] AC 866, 870; *Batey v Gifford* (1997) 42 NSWLR 710, 718; *Re Mujaj* [1998] 2 Qd R 152.

[340] See the comments of Tadgell J in *Eagle Star Nominees Ltd v Merril* [1982] VR 557, 560 in relation to *King v Poggioli* (1923) 32 CLR 222, in which equitable set-off was not considered.

[341] See paras 2.33–2.48 above.

[342] *Re United Railways of Havana and Regla Warehouses Ltd* [1961] AC 1007.

of Lords held in *Miliangos v George Frank (Textiles) Ltd* [343] that this restriction no longer applies. An English court may give judgment for a sum of money expressed in a foreign currency and, if the defendant fails to tender payment in that currency, execution may issue for the sterling equivalent. Conversion for this purpose theoretically should take place at the rate prevailing at the date of actual payment. [344] But, as Lord Fraser of Tullybelton pointed out, [345] theory must yield to practical necessity to the extent that, if the judgment has to be enforced in England, it must be converted before enforcement. Accordingly, the date of conversion was said to be the date that the court authorizes enforcement of the judgment in sterling. [346]

5.76 The effect of this development upon the right of set-off has yet to be determined. The Law Commission in its report on *Private International Law Foreign Money Liabilities* [347] suggested that a right of set-off should not be available in an action when different currencies are involved. Each party should obtain judgment for the amount of his claim expressed in the appropriate currency, though, as a qualification, it suggested that neither judgment should be enforceable without the other judgment being taken into account. The difficulty with this proposal is that it may have the effect of making the parties to mutual debts vulnerable to an assignment or other intervening third-party interest. If one of the claims is assigned, the debtor on that claim would not have a right of set-off available as a defence to an action brought by the assignor which he could assert against the assignee. [348] The recommendation that the judgments themselves should be capable of being set off at the date of enforcement may not assist in this situation, since an assignee only takes subject to prior equities, or defences. A right of set-off that only accrues upon the enforcement of a judgment could not be classed as a defence. Nor, on one view, would it be a *prior* equity. An alternative, and the preferable, approach is to convert the foreign currency into sterling at the rate prevailing at the date of judgment for a set-off. If both demands are in foreign currencies, the currency of the lesser debt should be converted into the currency of the greater debt at the date of judgment, and a set-off should then be effected. [349] This is consistent with the

---

[343] [1976] AC 443. See also the earlier Court of Appeal decision in *Schorsch Meier GmbH v Hennin* [1975] 1 QB 416.

[344] Alternatively, it has been said in Victoria that, where the plaintiff so elects, it is open to the court to give judgment converted into domestic currency at the date of judgment, with interest to be calculated at the rate applicable in the country of the foreign currency. See *Vlasons Shipping Inc v Neuchatel Swiss General Insurance Co Ltd (No 2)* [1998] VSC 135 (Byrne J).

[345] [1976] AC 443, 501.

[346] [1976] AC 443, 468–469, *per* Lord Wilberforce, 497–498, *per* Lord Cross, 501, *per* Lord Edmund-Davies, 501, *per* Lord Fraser.

[347] *Report on Private International Law Foreign Money Liabilities* (Cmnd 9064, 1983), 32–5.

[348] See paras 17.05–17.09 below.

[349] See Brandon J at first instance in *The Despina R* [1978] 1 QB 396, 414–415 in the context of a 'both to blame' collision under Admiralty law, and also *The Transoceanica Francesca* [1987] 2 Lloyd's Rep 155.

Miliangos principle, since the set-off effectively constitutes payment and, to the extent of the set-off, conversion accordingly takes place at the time of payment. Once the balance is struck in this manner, if the currency of the balance is not sterling and payment is not forthcoming in that currency, it should be converted into sterling at the date that leave is given to enforce the judgment, in accordance with the *Miliangos* case.

Equitable set-off

Equitable set-off differs from set-off under the Statutes of Set-off in that it pro- **5.77** vides a substantive rather than a procedural defence.[350] This does not mean that it operates as an automatic extinction of cross-demands prior to judgment for a set-off. Rather, the notion that the defence is substantive means that it is unconscionable for the creditor to regard the debtor as being indebted to the extent of the cross-demand even before judgment. The question of foreign currency claims in the context of equitable set-off has yet to be considered by the courts, although the following is consistent with the true nature of the defence. When an equitable set-off is pleaded as a defence to an action and one or both of the demands is in a foreign currency, the principle should be the same as for the Statutes of Set-off, so that conversion should take place by reference to the rate applicable at the date of judgment for a set-off. However, the creditor's conscience is affected even before judgment, so that to the extent of the defence the creditor is not permitted to treat the debtor as having defaulted in payment. In the determination at any point in time prior to judgment whether the debtor has defaulted, and whether the creditor can take action on the basis that a default has occurred,[351] regard should be had to the exchange rate at that time.[352]

I. Contracting Out of Set-off

(1) Equitable Set-off and Common Law Abatement

It may be important for cash flow reasons that a party should receive payment in **5.78** full under a contract so that, if the other party has a cross-claim which otherwise would give rise to an equitable set-off or a common law defence of abatement, that other party should not be entitled to rely upon it as a justification for tendering a reduced amount, but should be required to seek his remedy instead in separate proceedings. There is no ground of public policy which would preclude the

---

[350] See paras 4.29–4.43 above.
[351] See eg the circumstances referred to in paras 4.36 and 4.37 above.
[352] Compare Wood, *English and International Set-off* (1989) 663 para 11–24, 664–5 para 11–28, and 665 para 11–29. However, Wood has adopted a different analysis of the substantive nature of equitable set-off (see para 4.32 above), and his view of foreign currency conversions should be considered with that in mind.

parties from agreeing to exclude defences of equitable set-off and abatement,[353] including in relation to a cross-claim based on fraud.[354]

5.79 Different views have been expressed as to the approach to be adopted in relation to clauses in contracts which, it is asserted, operate to exclude or restrict defences of set-off and abatement. On the one hand, Lord Diplock in *Gilbert-Ash (Northern) Ltd v Modern Engineering (Bristol) Ltd*[355] said that there is a presumption that the defences are not excluded, and that clear words are required to rebut the presumption:

> It is, of course, open to parties to a contract for sale of goods or for work and labour or for both to exclude by express agreement a remedy for its breach which would otherwise arise by operation of law or such remedy may be excluded by usage binding upon the parties . . . But in construing such a contract one starts with the presumption that neither party intends to abandon any remedies for its breach arising by operation of law, and clear express words must be used in order to rebut this presumption.[356]

Lord Morris, on the other hand, adopted a more even-handed attitude. In his opinion it depends simply and solely upon the interpretation of the contract,[357] an approach that was reflected also in the judgment of Lord Cross of Chelsea (with whom Lord Hodson and Lord Wilberforce agreed) a year later in *Mottram Consultants Ltd v Bernard Sunley & Sons Ltd.*[358] Lord Cross considered that 'one should approach each case without any "parti pris" in favour or against the existence of a right of set-off . . .'. While there is support for that view,[359] the tendency in subsequent cases, however, has been to refer to Lord Diplock's judgment as setting out the relevant principle. In other words, it is said that there is a presumption that the parties to a contract do not intend to give up rights of set-off and

---

[353] *Coca-Cola Financial Corp v Finsat International Ltd* [1998] QB 43; *Morrison Knudsen Corp of Australia Ltd v Australian National Railways Commission* (1996) 22 ACSR 262, 267; *Society of Lloyd's v Fraser* [1999] Lloyd's Rep IR 156, 171. In New Zealand, see *Liapis v Vasey* (1989) 4 NZCLC 64,959. The Court of Appeal in *Coca-Cola v Finsat* (at 52) also rejected an argument that contracting out of set-off rights is contrary to the Supreme Court Act 1981, s 49(2), which preserves the power of the Court of Appeal and the High Court to stay any proceedings.

[354] *Society of Lloyd's v Leighs* [1997] 6 Re LR 289; *WRM Group Ltd v Wood* [1997] EWCA Civ 2802.

[355] [1974] AC 689.

[356] [1974] AC 689, 717. Later in his judgment Lord Diplock commented (at 718): 'So when one is concerned with a building contract one starts with the presumption that each party is to be entitled to all those remedies for its breach as would arise by operation of law, including the remedy of setting up a breach of warranty in diminution or extinction of the price of material supplied or work executed under the contract. To rebut that presumption one must be able to find in the contract clear unequivocal words in which the parties have expressed their agreement that this remedy shall not be available in respect of breaches of that particular contract.'

[357] [1974] AC 689, 702. See also Lord Reid at 699.

[358] [1975] 2 Lloyd's Rep 197, 205.

[359] In Australia, see *Triden Contractors Pty Ltd v Belvista Pty Ltd* (1986) 3 BCL 203, 215; *Algons Engineering Pty Ltd v Abigroup Contractors Pty Ltd* (1997) 14 BCL 215, 222 (referring to *Gilbert-Ash* (n 355 above)); *Daewoo Australia Pty Ltd v Porter Crane Imports Pty Ltd* [2000] QSC 050 at para 17.

abatement otherwise available at law in the event of a breach by the other,[360] and if they intend to exclude those rights they must use clear words.[361] Clauses which expressly refer to set-off have been held to be effective to exclude the defence,[362] but it is not necessary that the clause should be drafted in that manner. The defence may also be excluded if there is a clear implication to that effect.[363]

---

[360] *Federal Commerce & Navigation Co Ltd v Molena Alpha Inc* [1978] 1 QB 927, 988; *BICC plc v Burndy Corp* [1985] 1 Ch 232, 248; *Acsim (Southern) Ltd v Danish Contracting & Development Co Ltd* (1989) 47 BLR 55, 69–70; *Rosehaugh Stanhope (Broadgate Phase 6) plc v Redpath Dorman Long Ltd* (1990) 50 BLR 75, 84; *Connaught Restaurants Ltd v Indoor Leisure Ltd* [1994] 1 WLR 501, 505; *Re Partnership Pacific Securities Ltd* [1994] 1 Qd R 410, 424–425; *Marubeni Corp v Sea Containers Ltd* (Queen's Bench Division, Waller J, 17 May 1995); *Melbourne Glass Pty Ltd v Coby Constructions Pty Ltd* (1997) 14 BCL 409, 415, Vic SC, *per* Gillard J. See also *Morrison Knudsen Corp of Australia Ltd v Australian National Railways Commission* (1996) 22 ACSR 262, 267–268; *Esso Petroleum Co Ltd v Milton* [1997] 1 WLR 938, 948; *Beaufort Development (NI) Ltd v Gilbert-Ash NI Ltd* [1999] 1 AC 266, 279, 286–287; *Parsons Plastics (Research and Development) Ltd v Purac Ltd* [2002] EWCA Civ 459 at para 12. Compare Lloyd LJ in *NEI Thompson Ltd v Wimpey Construction UK Ltd* (1987) 39 BLR 70, 73, who expressed the principle instead in terms of a 'prima facie' entitlement to an equitable set-off or a common law defence of abatement.

[361] In addition to the cases referred to above in relation to the presumption, see *Compania Sud Americana de Vapores v Shipmair BV (The Teno)* [1977] 2 Lloyd's Rep 289, 293; *Redpath Dorman Long Ltd v Cummins Engine Co Ltd* [1981] SC 370, 374 (Scotland); *Wilson's (NZ) Portland Cement Ltd v Gatx-Fuller Australasia Pty Ltd (No 2)* [1985] 2 NZLR 33, 39; *C M Pillings & Co Ltd v Kent Investments Ltd* (1985) 30 BLR 80, 92–93; *Construction Services Civil Pty Ltd v J & N Allen Enterprises Pty Ltd* (1985) 1 BCL 363, 367–368 (White J, South Australian SC); *Nile Co for the Export of Agricultural Crops v H & J M Bennett (Commodities) Ltd* [1986] 1 Lloyd's Rep 555, 588; *Marubeni Corp v Sea Containers Ltd* (QBD, Waller J, 17 May 1995); *John Dee Group Ltd v WMH (21) Ltd* [1997] BCC 518, 521, 527 (decision affirmed [1998] BCC 972); *WRM Group Ltd v Wood* [1997] EWCA Civ 2802 at para 9 ('clear and unambiguous language'); *Liberty Mutual Insurance Co (UK) Ltd v HSBC Bank Plc* [2002] EWCA Civ 691 at para 56. See also *NEI Thompson Ltd v Wimpey Construction UK Ltd* (1987) 39 BLR 70, 72–73.

[362] See eg *Continental Illinois National Bank & Trust Co of Chicago v Papanicolaou* [1986] 2 Lloyd's Rep 441 ('All payments . . . shall be made without set-off or counterclaim and without deductions or withholdings whatsoever'); *Coca-Cola Financial Corp v Finsat International Ltd* [1998] QB 43 ('free and clear of any right of set-off or counterclaim or any withholding or deduction whatsoever'); *Daewoo Australia Pty Ltd v Porter Crane Imports Pty Ltd* [2000] QSC 050 ('free of any set-off or counterclaim and without deduction or withholding'). See also, in relation to the Statutes of Set-off, *Hongkong & Shanghai Banking Corp v Kloeckner & Co AG* [1990] 2 QB 514 ('irrevocably undertake to make payment in full . . . without any discount, deduction, offset, or counterclaim whatsoever on the due date'). Compare *Esso Petroleum Co Ltd v Milton* [1997] 1 WLR 938. The clause in that case stated that: 'The Licensee agrees that he will not for any reasons withhold payment of any amount properly due to Esso . . .' Sir John Balcombe commented (at 954) that in his opinion the clause in its terms would have been sufficient to exclude an equitable set-off, were it not for the Unfair Contract Terms Act 1977 (see paras 5.94–5.100 below). Simon Brown LJ on the other hand (at p 949) considered, on balance, that it was not sufficiently clear to exclude the defence, apparently for the reason given by counsel, that the use of the words 'properly due' begged the very question in issue. This seems the preferred view.

[363] *Gilbert-Ash (Northern) Ltd v Modern Engineering (Bristol) Ltd* [1974] AC 689, 723, *per* Lord Salmon; *Grant v NZMC Ltd* [1989] 1 NZLR 8, 13; *Connaught Restaurants Ltd v Indoor Leisure Ltd* [1994] 1 WLR 501, 505; *Sonat Offshore SA v Amerada Hess Development Ltd* (1987) 39 BLR 1, 22 ('express term or necessary intention'). See also *Marubeni Corp v Sea Containers Ltd* (QBD, Waller J, 17 May 1995), discussed in para 5.83 below. In *Nile Co for the Export of Agricultural Crops v H & J M Bennett (Commodities) Ltd* [1986] 1 Lloyd's Rep 555 a contract of sale provided that, if the consignment arrived in bad condition, the purchaser had to advise the seller immediately so that the

5.80 There was no such clear implication in *BOC Group plc v Centeon LLC*,[364] and the Court of Appeal therefore held that the contract did not exclude set-offs. Evans LJ, with whom Brooke LJ agreed, framed the relevant question in terms whether the clause in that case provided 'with sufficient clarity' that the purchaser was to pay the price regardless of any cross-claim that it may have had, and he emphasized that the court should take account of all the surrounding circumstances.[365] He regarded this as consistent with the approach advocated by Lord Hoffmann in relation to the interpretation of contractual documents in *Investors Compensation Scheme Ltd v West Bromwich Building Society*.[366] *BOC v Centeon* concerned the sale of a research and development company, Delta Biotechnology Ltd. The sale agreement provided for the payment of the price by way of instalments, and the present action was for payment of one of the instalments. The purchaser asserted a set-off in respect of cross-claims for damages for breach of the agreement and misrepresentation, but the vendor responded that set-off was precluded by the terms of clause 2.7 of the agreement. The clause provided that the purchaser's payment obligation was:

> absolute and unconditional and *shall not be affected by* any transfer of any of the equity interest in Delta, the transfer of any or all of Delta's assets or business, the dissolution of Delta, the termination of the business of Delta (or any part thereof), the success or failure of any research projects undertaken by Delta, the future commercialization or otherwise of any products, Delta's future business prospects or technological or technical successes *or by any other matter whatsover*.[367]

The vendor sought to justify its argument that set-off was excluded by reference to the inclusion of 'whatsoever', which, it said, is a word of the widest possible import.[368] The difficulty with the argument was that the other matters listed were all concerned with the subsequent fate of Delta and its project, and the general words that followed the list were capable of referring to other factors concerned with the future progress of the venture. The word 'whatsoever' therefore was ambivalent. Moreover the parties were legally represented during the negotiation of the contract, and so they were aware of their legal rights. In that context the question was, what words might they have used to make their meaning clear if they had

---

seller could send a representative to inspect the goods, and in addition the purchaser had to provide its own survey report to the seller. The purchaser could then 'deduct the landed value of the damaged goods from the FOB amount drawn by the [seller] and only the balance will then be payable against the documents'. Evans J held (at 588–589) that the purchaser's failure to comply with the procedure did not preclude the purchaser from later claiming damages for damage to the goods, but it did preclude the purchaser from relying upon its claim by way of defence to its liability for the price.

[364] [1999] 1 All ER (Comm) 970.

[365] [1999] 1 All ER (Comm) 970, 979–980.

[366] [1998] 1 WLR 896, 912–913.

[367] Emphasis added.

[368] Referring to *Smith v New South Wales Switchgear Co Ltd* [1978] 1 WLR 165, 178, *per* Lord Keith of Kinkel. See also the cases to which Rix J referred at first instance in *BOC Group plc v Centeon LLC* [1999] 1 All ER (Comm) 53, 61–62.

intended to exclude set-off? Evans LJ regarded the absence of words such as 'deduction', 'withholding' or 'payment in full' as an 'eloquent silence' in that regard. In the circumstances, he considered that the clause did not provide with sufficient clarity that the right to invoke the defence was excluded.

Evans LJ in *BOC v Centeon* discussed the issue without recourse to the label 'presumption', and indeed he exhibited a degree of hesitancy in adopting that term.[369] However, the relevant passage in Lord Diplock's judgment in the *Gilbert-Ash* case has since been cited with evident approval in the House of Lords,[370] and 'presumption' would seem to be accepted as an accurate description of the approach to be adopted in these cases. **5.81**

Payment 'without deduction'

Contracts often provide that money is to be paid 'without deduction', which in- **5.82**
vites the question whether those words are apt to exclude defences of equitable set-off and abatement. The issue came before the Court of Appeal in *Connaught Restaurants Ltd v Indoor Leisure Ltd*.[371] In dispute was a lease which provided that rent was to be paid 'without any deduction'. The word 'deduction' is sometimes used by the courts to describe the result which follows when a right of set-off is exercised,[372] and indeed Lord Salmon in the *Gilbert-Ash* case[373] rejected the view that it does not describe the process of set-off in the case of a contract for the sale of goods where the purchaser sets up a cross-claim for damages under the contract in extinction of the purchase price. However in the *Connaught Restaurants* case Waite LJ considered that the term was ambiguous. He said that 'deduction' may be used in its strict sense to describe the ordinary process of subtraction, in other words the action of taking something away, or it may be used in a broader sense to describe the result which follows when one claim is set against another and a balance is struck. The process of subtraction may encompass contractual or statutory deductions, where the contract or the statute authorizes a subtraction from rent.[374] But because clear words are needed to exclude the remedy of equitable set-off, he thought that 'deduction' in the lease before him was insufficiently clear

---

[369] After referring to Lord Diplock's judgment in *Gilbert-Ash*, Evans LJ continued with the comment, 'Whether there is such a presumption or not . . .'. See [1999] 1 All ER (Comm) 970, 979.

[370] *Beaufort Developments (NI) Ltd v Gilbert-Ash NI Ltd* [1999] 1 AC 266, 279, *per* Lord Hoffmann, 286–287, *per* Lord Hope of Craighead; *Stocznia Gdanska SA v Latvian Shipping Co* [1998] 1 WLR 574, 585, *per* Lord Goff of Chieveley. In Australia, see *Concut Pty Ltd v Worrell* (2000) 75 ALJR 312, 317.

[371] [1994] 1 WLR 501, referred to in *Esso Petroleum Co v Milton* [1997] 1 WLR 938, 948.

[372] See eg *Hanak v Green* [1958] 2 QB 9, 26; *Gilbert-Ash (Northern) Ltd v Modern Engineering (Bristol) Ltd* [1974] AC 689, 726; *Federal Commerce & Navigation Co Ltd v Molena Alpha Inc* [1978] 1 QB 927, 974, 975; *SL Sethia Liners Ltd v Naviagro Maritime Corp (The Kostas Melas)* [1981] 1 Lloyd's Rep 18, 26.

[373] [1974] AC 689, 726.

[374] Various statutory provisions which empowered a tenant to make deductions from rent were noted at [1994] 1 WLR 501, 509, 511.

to achieve that result.[375] In a short judgment Neill LJ agreed with Waite LJ's reasons, and Simon Brown LJ agreed with both judgments. The Court of Appeal followed an earlier decision of the New Zealand Court of Appeal,[376] which held that 'deduction' does not in its natural sense embrace a set-off. This view similarly has been adopted in Australia,[377] though there is also support there for the contrary view.[377a] The *Connaught* case is consistent with a similar opinion expressed in relation to a stipulation in a time charter of a ship that hire was to be paid 'without discount'.[378]

5.83 While Waite LJ considered that the expression 'without any deduction' in the case before him was insufficient to exclude equitable set-off, he nevertheless contemplated that there may be instances where the context suggests by implication that the words were intended to have that effect.[379] One such case is *Marubeni Corp v Sea Containers Ltd*.[380] It concerned a sale of containers by Marubeni to Sea Containers. The contract provided for payment of the price by instalments on the nominated due dates 'without any deductions or withholdings whatsoever'. There were defects in some of the containers, and Sea Containers sought to 'deduct' by way of equitable set-off from an instalment of the price an amount corresponding to the damages flowing from the defects. Waller J accepted that neither 'deduction' nor 'withholding' is a term of art, and they could not be described as clear words. The question nevertheless was one of construction in the context of the contract as a whole, and looking at the contract as a whole he held that the purported 'deduction' in respect of an equitable set-off was precluded by the exclusion of deductions and withholdings. In the first place, he said that the court has to find some meaning for the words and, in contrast to the *Connaught Restaurants* case, it was difficult in this case to see to what else they could apply.

---

[375] See also Waite, 'Disrepair and Set-off of Damages Against Rent' [1983] The Conveyancer 373, 389. Waite LJ declined to follow *Famous Army Stores v Meehan* [1993] EGLR 73, in which Steyn J adopted a contrary view. *Quaere* whether the expression 'free and clear from any . . . deduction on any account whatsoever' would encompass a common law defence of abatement. See *Society of Lloyd's v Leighs* [1997] 6 Re LR 289, 298, CA.

[376] *Grant v NZMC Ltd* [1989] 1 NZLR 8.

[377] *Re Partnership Pacific Securities Ltd* [1994] 1 Qd R 410, not following *Citibank Pty Ltd v Simon Fredericks Pty Ltd* [1993] 2 VR 168, 175. *Partnership Pacific* was referred to without adverse comment in *Morrison Knudsen Corp of Australia Ltd v Australian National Railways Commission* (1996) 22 ACSR 262, 267–268.

[377a] In addition to *Citibank v Simon Fredericks* (see n 377 above), see *Batiste v Lenin* [2002] NSWSC 233 at paras 94–105, though Bryson J did not refer to the *Connaught* case or the *Partnership Pacific Securities* case. *Debonair Nominees Pty Ltd v J & K Berry Nominees Pty Ltd* (2000) 77 SASR 261, to which Bryson J referred, did not canvas equitable set-off. See also however, in the context of guarantees, *Langford Concrete Pty Ltd v Finlay* [1978] 1 NSWLR 14, 17; *Australia and New Zealand Banking Group Ltd v Harvey* (1994) 16 ATPR 46–132 at p 53, 643; *Commonwealth Development Bank v Windermere Pastoral Co Pty Ltd* [1999] NSWSC [52]–[57].

[378] *Compania Sud Americana de Vapores v Shipmair BV (The Teno)* [1977] 2 Lloyd's Rep 289.

[379] [1994] 1 WLR 501, 510.

[380] QBD, Waller J, 17 May 1995.

Moreover, the price was to be paid over a substantial period of nine years after delivery. Marubeni, therefore, in substance was providing finance, and it was likely that a finance party would insist that instalments should be paid without deducting for a cross-claim arising from a breach of warranty. In that respect he considered that the context was different from a building contract or a lease or a charter of a ship. Furthermore, the contract provided for a bank guarantee to secure payment of some of the instalments. If a claim were made against the bank on the guarantee Sea Containers could not have exercised a right of set-off, and it would produce consistency in the contract if the same position were held to apply in relation to other instalments not secured by a bank guarantee.

In *BOC v Centeon*,[381] Evans LJ referred to 'payment in full without deduction or **5.84** withholding of any sort' as being familiar words in the context of agreements which purport to exclude rights of set-off. If 'deduction' or 'withholding' is insufficiently precise to exclude set-off, the addition of 'of any sort' would hardly add the necessary clarity.[382] It may also be queried whether 'payment in full' would overcome the perceived difficulty. It begs the question as to what constitutes 'payment in full', in circumstances where there is an equitable defence of set-off which renders it unconscionable for the creditor to regard the debtor as being indebted to the extent of the set-off.[383] Evans LJ also emphasized however that there is not necessarily a magic formula, and where the parties do not expressly refer to set-off one should have regard to the surrounding circumstances of the case.[384]

As in the case of equitable set-off, a stipulation in a lease that rent is to be paid **5.85** without deduction ordinarily should not extend to the right of recoupment considered by Goff J in *Lee-Parker v Izzet*.[385] This right of recoupment may apply where leased premises have fallen into disrepair, and the tenant expends money in executing the repairs in circumstances where responsibility for the repairs is on the landlord. The tenant in such a case may recoup the cost from future payments of rent or from arrears of rent. Goff J admittedly referred in his order to the right of the tenant to 'deduct' the cost of repairs from future payments of rent,[386] although that may have been for the sake of brevity.[387] The exercise of the right does not involve a deduction from rent otherwise due, but rather the tenant is entitled to treat

---

[381] [1999] 1 All ER (Comm) 970, 980.

[382] As Waite LJ remarked in *Connaught Restaurants Ltd v Indoor Leisure Ltd* [1994] 1 WLR 501, 510: 'Added words of exception or qualification are relevant to the construction of [a phrase such as "without any deduction"], but they too are subject to the general requirement of clarity and will only be effective to displace the lessee's right of equitable set-off if their effect is to create a clear context for exclusion.'

[383] See para 4.30 above.

[384] [1999] 1 All ER (Comm) 970, 979–980.

[385] [1971] 1 WLR 1688. See para 5.64 above.

[386] [1971] 1 WLR 1688, 1695.

[387] *Connaught Restaurants Ltd v Indoor Leisure Ltd* [1994] 1 WLR 501, 507, *per* Waite LJ.

the amount expended on repairs as a payment of rent.[388] Accordingly, the stipulation for payment 'without deduction' should not be relevant.[389]

5.86 A contract may include a provision to the effect that one party must pay 'all sums immediately when due, without deduction or set-off'. It is unlikely that a contract in those terms would be effective to preclude an equitable set-off in relation to a damages cross-claim which is inseparably connected with a debt the subject of the plaintiff's claim, because the substantive nature of the set-off[390] would mean that the plaintiff could not assert that the debt is 'due' for the purpose of the clause.[391] The same reasoning would not apply however in the case of the Statutes of Set-off. The statutory form of set-off has a procedural operation in that, prior to judgment for a set-off, the rights consequent upon being a creditor still attach, as do the obligations and liabilities consequent upon being a debtor.[392] The availability of the set-off would not mean that the debt to the plaintiff is not due.

The effect of specifying some deductions

5.87 Because of the need for clear words to exclude equitable set-off, the fact that a contract makes provision for certain specified deductions from contract payments is not regarded in England as sufficient to give rise to an implication that a right of set-off in respect of other sums is excluded,[393] though there is authority in Australia which suggests the contrary.[394] The contract may go further,

---

[388] *Connaught Restaurants Ltd v Indoor Leisure Ltd* [1994] 1 WLR 501, 507, *per* Waite LJ, 511, *per* Neill LJ. See para 17.68 below.

[389] *Connaught Restaurants Ltd v Indoor Leisure Ltd* [1994] 1 WLR 501, 507 (disapproving of the contrary opinion expressed by the New Zealand Court of Appeal in *Grant v NZMC Ltd* [1989] 1 NZLR 8, 13), and see also Waite, 'Repairs and Deduction From Rent' [1981] The Conveyancer 199, 210–211. Compare *Batiste v Lenin* [2002] NSUSC 233 at paras 102–105, though the *Connaught* case was not referred to.

[390] See paras 4.29–4.43 above.

[391] This was the view of Mr Geoffrey Brice QC sitting as a Deputy High Court Judge in *Schenkers Ltd v Overland Shoes Ltd* [1998] 1 Lloyd's Rep 498, 502–503 (decision affirmed by the Court of Appeal (at 504 *et seq*) without reference to this point). Compare *Star Rider Ltd v Inntreprenneur Pub Co* [1998] 1 EGLR 53, 55 in relation to a clause requiring payment of rent 'without deduction or set-off whatsoever', but without being limited by 'due'. See also, in relation to similar clauses, *Electricity Supply Nominees Ltd v IAF Group Ltd* [1993] 1 WLR 1059 and *Unchained Growth III plc v Granby Village (Manchester) Management Co Ltd* [2000] 1 WLR 739.

[392] See para 2.33 above.

[393] *Compania Sud Americana de Vapores v Shipmair BV (The Teno)* [1977] 2 Lloyd's Rep 289, 292–293; *Federal Commerce & Navigation Co Ltd v Molena Alpha Inc* [1978] 1 QB 927, 988; *Acsim (Southern) Ltd v Danish Contracting and Development Co Ltd* (1989) 47 BLR 55, 69–70. See also *Redpath Dorman Long Ltd v Cummins Engine Co Ltd* [1981] SC 370 (Scotland); *Ellis Tylin Ltd v Co-operative Retail Services Ltd* [1999] BLR 205, 220–221.

[394] *Melbourne Glass Pty Ltd v Coby Construction Pty Ltd* (1997) 14 BCL 409, 417; *Novawest Contracting Pty Ltd v Taras Nominees Pty Ltd,* [1998] VSC 205 at [103] and [104]. See also *Re Concrete Constructions Group Pty Ltd* [1997] 1 Qd R 6, 13. But there are also Australian cases which support the English approach. See *Hyder Consulting (Victoria) Pty Ltd v Transfield Pty Ltd* (2000) 17 BCL 129 (a provision in a contract to the effect that a debt due under the agreement may be deducted from any moneys payable by the creditor to the debtor would not preclude defences of

however, and stipulate that payments are to be made 'less only' a list of specified deductions.

In *Mottram Consultants Ltd v Bernard Sunley & Sons Ltd*[395] a building contract **5.88** provided that the employer was to pay the amount specified in an architect's certificate 'less only' retention money and any sum previously paid. The printed form which the parties used originally provided for a third item, being any amount which the employer was entitled to deduct from or set off against any money due to the contractor by virtue of any breach of the contract by the contractor. However, the third item had been deleted. Lord Cross (with whom Lord Hodson and Lord Wilberforce agreed) said that: 'When the parties use a printed form and delete parts of it one can, in my opinion, pay regard to what has been deleted as part of the surrounding circumstances in the light of which one must construe what they have chosen to leave in.'[396] He said that the fact that the parties had deleted the third item showed that they had turned their minds to the questions of deductions under the common law principle of abatement, and had decided that no such deductions should be allowed.[397] That reasoning would apply equally to equitable set-off. [398]

Mottram v Sunley was complicated by the deletion. That factor was not present in **5.89** relation to the clause in a standard RIBA building contract[399] considered earlier in the *Gilbert-Ash* case.[400] The clause appeared in the main contract, between the employer and the contractor, though it dealt with the contractor's obligation to pay the sub-contractor. It provided that the contractor had to pay the sub-contractor the amount stated in a certificate less only a list of a specified deductions. Lord Diplock said that this did not seem to him to be strong enough to amount to an undertaking by the contractor to the employer that the contractor would not rely

---

set-off or abatement in respect of other claims against the debtor) and *Leighton Contractors Pty Ltd v East Gippsland Catchment Management Authority* (2000) 17 BCL 35, 40 [21]–[24] (contractual set-off right in relation to quantified amounts did not preclude an equitable set-off in relation to an unquantified claim).

[395] [1975] 2 Lloyd's Rep 197.

[396] [1975] 2 Lloyd's Rep 197, 209.

[397] In Australia, see also *Melbourne Glass Pty Ltd v Coby Constructions Pty Ltd* (1997) 14 BCL 409, 413, referring to *Codelfa Construction Pty Ltd v State Rail Authority of NSW* (1982) 149 CLR 337, 352–353. Lord Cross' comment on abatement was obiter. The case concerned overpayments said to have been made by the employer, which the employer sought to deduct from subsequent payments sought by the contractor, including on the basis of a cross-claim against the contractor for negligence and breach of an implied term in paying out sums which had not been incurred in accordance with the contract.

[398] This is suggested by Lord Cross' discussion at [1975] 2 Lloyd's Rep 197, 209–210. See also Lord Morris (at 204) and Lord Salmon (at 212–213) in their dissenting judgments, who both indicated that they were prepared to assume that the condition precluded a set-off, though neither expressed a concluded view on the subject. Moreover Lord Salmon, in deciding that leave to defend should be granted, went on to refer (at 214, and see also at 212) to authorities on equitable set-off.

[399] Clause 27(b) of the RIBA Local Authorities (with Quantities) 1963 edition.

[400] [1974] AC 689, 721.

on a common law defence of abatement in an action by a sub-contractor for payment. He considered that it was directed simply at calculating the amount of the instalment due to the sub-contractor, and not to defences available to the contractor if sued by the sub-contractor for payment.[401] While those comments were expressed in the context of a defence of abatement, the view that Lord Diplock also expressed in his judgment, that clear words are required in order to rebut the presumption that neither party to a contract intends to abandon any remedies for its breach arising by operation of law, suggests that he would have regarded the provision similarly as being ineffective to preclude a defence of equitable set-off.[402] As Mr Duncan Wallace commented in a note on the *Mottram v Sunley* case:

> the right of set-off is so fundamental, and the potential injustices and anomalies of departing from it so great, that the mere use of the words 'less only' when referring to certain inevitable deductions required by the scheme of the contract (prior payment, retention money, and so on) should not be construed as intending to apply to and exclude other contingent situations which might justify a deduction under the general principles of law relating to defence, set-off, or counterclaim.[403]

With respect, there is much to commend that view.

Stay of execution

5.90 If there is an effective agreement excluding rights of equitable set-off, ordinarily this would not only preclude the defendant from being able to defend a claim for payment on the basis of a cross-claim, but in addition in a summary judgment application the court usually would regard it as inappropriate to order a stay of execution pending adjudication on the cross-claim.[404] As the Court of Appeal noted in *Continental Illinois National Bank and Trust Co of Chicago v Papanicolaou*[405]

---

[401] Lord Salmon (at [1974] AC 689, 726) agreed with Lord Diplock's analysis of clause 27. See also Viscount Dilhorne in *Gilbert-Ash* [1974] AC 689, 709, referring to the provisions of the main contract relating to payment by the contractor to a sub-contractor (for which see 707–708).

[402] See in that regard Viscount Dilhorne at [1974] AC 689, 709.

[403] Note (1975) 91 LQR 471, 474–475.

[404] In addition to *Continental Illinois National Bank & Trust Co of Chicago v Papanicolaou* [1986] 2 Lloyd's Rep 441 (below), see *Mottram Consultants Ltd v Bernard Sunley & Sons Ltd* [1975] 2 Lloyd's Rep 197, 210 (in which the contract was interpreted as having excluded the defence of abatement); *BWP (Architectural) Ltd v Beaver Building Systems Ltd* (1988) 42 BLR 86; *Skipskredittforeningen v Emperor Navigation* [1998] 1 Lloyd's Rep 66, 79; *Coca-Cola Financial Corp v Finsat International Ltd* [1998] QB 43, 53. See also *John Dee Group Ltd v WMH (21) Ltd* [1988] BCC 972, 976 (in which it was regarded as relevant that the plaintiff had charged its assets, including the claim against the defendant, to a third party). In Australia, see *L U Simon Builders Pty Ltd v H D Fowles* [1992] 2 VR 189, 196; *John Holland Construction and Engineering Pty Ltd v Majorca Projects Pty Ltd* (Vic CA, 27 July 1995). Compare *Stewart Gill Ltd v Horatio Myer & Co Ltd* [1992] 1 QB 600, 604, where Lord Donaldson of Lymington MR contemplated that a stay of execution could be ordered, and *Hegarty & Sons Ltd v Royal Liver Friendly Society* [1985] IR 524, 531, in which Murphy J indicated that, if he had reached the conclusion in that case that the right of set-off had been excluded, he would have stayed execution.

[405] [1986] 2 Lloyd's Rep 441.

when it allowed an appeal against an order granting a stay in this situation, the contrary conclusion would negate the very purpose of inserting a provision excluding rights of set-off, the purpose being to prevent a situation arising in which the creditor is kept waiting for payment. Admittedly the contract in that case specifically stated that the debt should be paid without counterclaim as well as set-off, though Parker LJ's analysis suggests that the same result would have followed if the contract had only excluded set-off. The court nevertheless has a discretion to grant a stay, and his Lordship postulated that a stay may be granted in exceptional circumstances notwithstanding the exclusion.[406] In that regard he said that it would not be enough that the defendant has a counterclaim which is likely to succeed, though he contemplated that it might suffice if there is such a counterclaim coupled with cogent evidence that the plaintiff would, if paid, be unable to meet a judgment on the counterclaim.[407] But in the absence of special circumstances, execution on a judgment should not be stayed pending determination of a cross-claim if the contract has excluded defences of set-off.

Negligence claims

The Court of Appeal in the *Continental Illinois* case also noted that a clause which **5.91** excludes rights of set-off is not subject to the same rule of construction applicable to exclusion of liability clauses in relation to claims for negligence.[408] In order to be effective to exclude liability it is usually necessary that the clause should refer specifically to negligence, or use a sufficiently wide term such as 'whatsoever'.[409] It is not necessary, however, that similar terminology be employed in order to exclude an equitable set-off based upon a cross-claim for negligence. The clauses serve different functions. An exclusion clause purports to exclude liability altogether, whereas a clause excluding set-off does not touch liability. The debtor can still prosecute the cross-claim to judgment, but in a separate action.

Arbitration clauses

While conceding that comments by Lord Salmon in the *Gilbert-Ash* case[410] were **5.92** against his view, Wood has suggested that a party to a contract might perhaps be taken to have agreed to exclude equitable set-off in relation to a disputed

---

[406] See also RSC O 47 r 1(a) ('special circumstances').

[407] [1986] 2 Lloyd's Rep 441, 445.

[408] [1986] 2 Lloyd's Rep 441, 443–444. In *Society of Lloyd's v Leighs* [1997] 6 Re LR 289, 297 the Court of Appeal was 'far from persuaded' that a clause excluding rights of set-off should be treated as an exceptions clause. See also *WRM Group Ltd v Wood* [1997] EWCA Civ 2802 at para 10; *Sinochem International Oil (London) Co Ltd v Mobil Sales and Supply Corp* [2000] 1 All ER (Comm) 474, 483.

[409] See *Continental Illinois National Bank & Trust Co of Chicago v Papanicolaou* [1986] 2 Lloyd's Rep 441, 444, and generally Treitel, *The Law of Contract* (10th edn, 1999) 203–5.

[410] [1974] AC 689, 726. See also Lord Diplock at 720, and *Aectra Refining and Marketing Inc v Exmar NV* [1994] 1 WLR 1634, 1649, *per* Hoffmann LJ.

cross-claim if he has agreed to submit disputes to arbitration, and no arbitration has been held.[411] Whether this is the case would depend upon the terms of the particular arbitration clause, but the usual clause providing for disputes to be referred to arbitration ordinarily should not require the debtor to pay in full if a cross-demand available as an equitable set-off has not been arbitrated. Indeed, the availability of an equitable set-off would mean that the debt is also in dispute, so that both the debt and the cross-claim should be referred.[412] This is a consequence of the substantive nature of the defence.[413]

Conclusive evidence certificate

5.93   A contract may provide that a certificate from an authorized officer of one of the parties as to the amount owing to that party by the other shall be conclusive evidence of the amount owing. Conclusive evidence clauses are not contrary to public policy, and the courts will give effect to them in the absence of some factor such as fraud.[414] On the other hand, subject to the terms of the parties' agreement, a conclusive evidence certificate ordinarily should not have the effect of precluding recourse to an equitable set-off,[415] which admits the existence of the debt, in the sense that an equitable set-off does not operate as an automatic extinction of cross-demands, but renders it unconscionable for the creditor to regard the debtor as being indebted.[416]

(2) Unfair Contract Terms Act 1977

5.94   The Unfair Contract Terms Act 1977 prohibits in certain situations contract terms which exclude or restrict liability in relation to a claim for negligence or breach of contract, except, in some cases, in so far as the term satisfies a requirement of reasonableness. In particular, the prohibition may apply, subject to the reasonableness requirement, in the situation in which one party's written standard terms of business are used.[417] The reference to excluding or restricting liability is expressed in s 13(1)(b) to encompass also excluding or restricting any right or remedy in respect of the liability. In *Stewart Gill Ltd v Horatio Myer & Co Ltd*[418]

---

[411]   Wood, *English and International Set-off* (1989) 691. The authority principally relied on by Wood, *Cuddy v Cameron* (1911) 1 WWR 35, was concerned with a contractual right of deduction rather than equitable set-off, and in any event it was ultimately reversed on appeal by the Privy Council in *Cameron v Cuddy* [1914] AC 651.

[412]   See eg *Federal Commerce & Navigation Co Ltd v Molena Alpha Inc* [1978] 1 QB 927, 974, and para 1.08 above.

[413]   See paras 4.29–4.43 above.

[414]   *Dobbs v National Bank of Australasia Ltd* (1935) 53 CLR 643; *Bache & Co (London) Ltd v Banque Vernes et Commerciale de Paris SA* [1973] 2 Lloyd's Rep 437.

[415]   *Long Leys Co Pty Ltd v Silkdale Pty Ltd* (1991) 5 BPR 11,512, 11,520, NSW CA; *Shomat Pty Ltd v Rubinstein* (1995) 124 FLR 284, 290, NSW SC, *per* Young J.

[416]   See para 4.30 above.

[417]   See s 3(1).

[418]   [1992] 1 QB 600.

the Court of Appeal held that this extended to a term in a standard contract which purported to exclude a right to raise a cross-claim for negligence or breach of contract by way of set-off.[419]

The Act contains an exemption, in Schedule 1, paragraph 1(b), in the case of a **5.95** contract so far as it relates to the creation or transfer of an interest in land. In *Electricity Supply Nominees Ltd v IAF Group Ltd*[420] Mr Hamilton QC, sitting as a deputy High Court judge, held that a term in a lease, by which rent was to be paid 'without any deduction or set-off whatsoever', was an integral part of the creation of the lease, and therefore it was a provision which related to the creation of an interest in land for the purpose of the exemption. The decision has since been followed,[421] and indeed it has been extended to the case of an obligation in a standard form of lease to pay a service fee to a management company charged with responsibility for the maintenance and management of the demised property.[422]

The test for determining reasonableness is laid down in section 11(1) of the Act. **5.96** The term in question must have been a fair and reasonable one to be included in the contract having regard to the circumstances which were, or ought reasonably to have been, known to or in the contemplation of the parties when the contract was made. In relation to contracts covered by sections 6 and 7 of the Act, which deal with sales and hire purchase and miscellaneous contracts under which goods pass, section 11(2) goes on to provide that, for the purpose of determining whether a term in the contract satisfies the requirement of reasonableness, regard is to be had in particular to the various matters set out in Schedule 2. The guidelines in Schedule 2 are also regarded as relevant to the determination of 'reasonableness' in other contexts.[423]

Section 11(1) stipulates that reasonableness is to be determined by reference to the **5.97** circumstances when the contract was made. The parties therefore must be able to judge at that time whether a term is reasonable. Moreover, the Court of Appeal in the *Stewart Gill* case emphasized that the term as a whole must be looked at, and

---

[419] Lord Donaldson of Lymington MR also referred to s 13(1)(c), to the effect that excluding or restricting liability includes also excluding or restricting rules of procedure. His Lordship said (at [1992] 1 QB 600, 606) that a clause which excludes or restricts set-off operates to exclude or restrict the procedural rules as to set-off, and on that ground also the clause is within the scope of the Act. The point may be made that set-off, even under the Statues of Set-off, is not wholly procedural. See paras 2.35–2.38 above. But to the extent that it does have procedural aspects, s 13(1)(c) would appear to apply.

[420] [1993] 1 WLR 1059.

[421] *Star Rider Ltd v Inntrepprenneur Pub Co* [1998] 1 EGLR 53 (licence fee payable under an agreement to grant a lease); *Unchained Growth III plc v Granby Village (Manchester) Management Co Ltd* [2000] 1 WLR 739, CA.

[422] *Unchained Growth III plc v Granby Village (Manchester) Management Co Ltd* [2000] 1 WLR 739.

[423] *Stewart Gill Ltd v Horatio Myer & Co Ltd* [1992] 1 QB 600, 608; *Schenkers Ltd v Overland Shoes Ltd* [1998] 1 Lloyd's Rep 498, 505.

not merely the part of it upon which reliance is sought to be placed when the issue ultimately arises.[424] In issue in the *Stewart Gill* case was the following clause: 'The customer shall not be entitled to withhold payment of any amount due to the company under the contract by reason of any payment credit set off counterclaim allegation of incorrect or defective goods or for any other reason whatsoever which the customer may allege excuses him from performing his obligations hereunder.' Lord Donaldson of Lymington MR and Stuart-Smith LJ[425] considered that it was unreasonable that the defendant should not be entitled to withhold payment to the plaintiff of any amount due under the contract by reason of a 'credit' owing by the plaintiff to the defendant, or a 'payment' made by the defendant to the plaintiff, which Lord Donaldson interpreted as having in contemplation an overpayment under another contract.[426] Stuart-Smith LJ noted that the concluding words of the clause were unlimited, and would extend to a defence based on fraud. The clause as a whole therefore was unreasonable, notwithstanding that it was not sought to rely on those particular aspects of it in this case, but simply on the exclusion in relation to set-offs.

5.98 The clause in issue in *Esso Petroleum Co Ltd v Milton*[427] similarly was thought to be unreasonably wide for the purpose of the Unfair Contract Terms Act.[428] The clause was in a licence agreement between Esso (as licensor) and a person who occupied and managed a service station the subject of the licence. The clause provided: 'The licensee agrees that he will not for any reasons withhold payment of any amount properly due to Esso under this licence whatsoever . . .' The objectionable aspect of this, in the opinion of Simon Brown LJ,[429] was that it would have precluded deductions for credits which could have been due and owing from Esso to the licensee, in circumstances where the licence agreement contemplated that credits could accrue in favour of the licensee.

5.99 Notwithstanding the rigorous attitude to the question of reasonableness suggested by those cases, Mance J adopted a commercially sensible approach to the issue in *Skipskredittforeningen v Emperor Navigation*.[430] In the *Stewart Gill* case the Court of Appeal said that reasonableness is to be determined by reference to the clause as a whole, and not simply in relation to the point currently in issue. Mance J warned nevertheless that the courts 'should not be too ready to focus on remote

---

[424] [1992] 1 QB 600, 606–607, 608–609. See also *Skipskredittforeningen v Emperor Navigation* [1998] 1 Lloyd's Rep 66, 75; *Schenkers Ltd v Overland Shoes Ltd* [1998] 1 Lloyd's Rep 498, 506. Compare *Messer UK Ltd v Thomas Hardy Packaging Ltd* [2002] EWCA Civ 549 at para 26.

[425] Balcombe LJ agreeing with both judgments.

[426] [1992] 1 QB 600, 606.

[427] [1997] 1 WLR 938.

[428] See also *Fastframe Ltd v Lohinski* (Court of Appeal, 3 March 1993), discussed in Adams, ' "No Deduction or Set-off" Clauses' (1994) 57 MLR 960.

[429] [1997] 1 WLR 938, 949, and see also Sir John Balcombe at 954.

[430] [1998] 1 Lloyd's Rep 66. See also *WRM Group Ltd v Wood* [1997] EWCA Civ 2802 at para 26.

possibilities or to accept arguments that a clause fails the test by reference to relatively uncommon or unlikely situations'.[431] In particular, he noted that the clause before the Court of Appeal in the *Stewart Gill* case contained express provisions which were so wide and obviously unacceptable as to invite overall rejection of the clause. That was not the case, however, in the *Emperor Navigation* case. The plaintiff had advanced a loan to the defendant. The loan agreement provided, inter alia: 'All payments to be made by or on behalf of the Borrowers pursuant to this Agreement . . . shall be made (a) without set-off, counterclaim or condition whatsoever and (b) free and clear of, and without deduction for or on account of, any present or future Taxes . . .' Mance J considered that the clause was not unreasonable in the context of the loan agreement; on the contrary it was 'generally familiar, sensible and understandable'.[432] While on its face it would have precluded a set-off in respect of a cross-claim for fraud, he said that the possibility of fraud by the lender is unlikely to have played any significant part in either party's thinking when they entered into the loan agreement. The practical reality was that the parties could not be taken as having envisaged it as likely that there would be a call to invoke the clause in relation to fraud. The clause was not, therefore, unreasonable when the loan agreement was entered into.

A clause precluding set-offs was also held to be reasonable in *Schenkers Ltd v* **5.100** *Overland Shoes Ltd*.[433] The plaintiffs were freight forwarders who were seeking to recover the cost of freight and ancillary charges in relation to the importation of goods for the defendants. The defendants asserted that they had a cross-claim against the plaintiffs for failure to reclaim VAT on goods that had come through Portugal, and that this could be set off against the plaintiffs' claim. The plaintiffs were members of the British International Freight Association ('BIFA'), and their contract with the defendant incorporated the BIFA standard trading conditions, which required the customer to pay all sums immediately when due, 'without deduction or deferment on account of any claim, counterclaim or set-off'. The Court of Appeal rejected the defendants' argument that the clause was unreasonable for the purpose of the Unfair Contract Terms Act. The clause was in common use and was well-known in the trade. It was in standard conditions which had been adopted following comprehensive discussions with various interested and representative bodies, and it was thought to represent a general view as to what was reasonable in the trade concerned. There was no significant inequality of bargaining power between the parties, and in that circumstance the custom of the trade was an important factor. Another factor, which in itself nevertheless was said not to be conclusive, was that the plaintiffs would incur substantial disbursements in the course of their business on behalf of customers. The point was also made

---

[431] [1998] 1 Lloyd's Rep 66, 75–76.
[432] [1998] 1 Lloyd's Rep 66, 76.
[433] [1998] 1 Lloyd's Rep 498.

that the clause did not purport to exclude or limit the plaintiffs' contractual liability, but aimed to achieve the 'different and lesser objective' of making it necessary for the defendant to sue the plaintiffs separately for breach of contract.[434]

(3) Misrepresentation Act 1967

5.101 The Misrepresentation Act 1967, s 3 in substance provides that, if a contract contains a term which would exclude or restrict any liability for misrepresentation to which a party may be subject, or any remedy available to another party to the contract by reason of that misrepresentation, the term is of no effect except in so far as it satisfies the requirement of reasonableness as stated in section 11(1) of the Unfair Contracts Terms Act 1977. A clause in a contract which excludes a set-off in respect of a cross-claim for damages for misrepresentation is regarded as a term which excludes a remedy available 'by reason of such misrepresentation', and as such it is of no effect unless it satisfies the same test of reasonableness applicable in the case of the Unfair Contract Terms Act.[435]

(4) Building and Construction Contracts[436]

5.102 Building and construction contracts have been a prime source of litigation in relation to attempts to exclude defences of set-off and abatement. Typically the issue arises when a certificate is presented by an architect or an engineer requiring a progress payment by the employer to the contractor, or by the contractor to a subcontractor, and the employer or the contractor refuses to pay because of allegations of bad workmanship or delay.[437] Summary judgment is then sought for the amount of the certificate. The question is whether leave to defend should be given on the basis of the cross-claim, or whether the contract has excluded defences of set-off and abatement so that the amount of the certificate must be paid with the cross-claim being litigated or arbitrated later. The determination of that question can be crucial to the parties' cash flow.[438]

---

[434] [1998] 1 Lloyd's Rep 498, 507, *per* Pill LJ, and see also *per* Thorpe LJ at 508.

[435] *Skipskredittforeningen v Emperor Navigation* [1998] 1 Lloyd's Rep 66; *WRM Group Ltd v Wood* [1997] EWCA Civ 2802. Mance J in *Skipskredittforeningen v Emperor Navigation* declined to follow *Society of Lloyd's v Wilkinson (No 2)* (1997) 6 Re LR 214, in which Colman J expressed the contrary view, Mance J noting (at [1998] 1 Lloyd's Rep 66, 74–5) that the decision in *Stewart Gill* was not cited to Colman J in this connection. After Mance J's judgment, the Court of Appeal on appeal affirmed the decision of Colman J, though the Misrepresentation Act point does not appear to have been argued before their Lordships. See *Society of Lloyd's v Leighs* [1997] 6 Re LR 289.

[436] See paras 5.49–5.52 above.

[437] Note also the effect of the Housing Grants, Construction and Regeneration Act 1996, s 111. See para 5.50 above.

[438] The Privy Council has described cash flow as 'the life blood of a business'. See *Agnew v Commissioner of Inland Revenue* [2001] 2 AC 710, 717 para 7. See also *Modern Engineering (Bristol) Ltd v Gilbert-Ash (Northern) Ltd* (1973) 71 LGR 162, 167, CA in relation to the construction industry.

In *Gilbert-Ash (Northern) Ltd v Modern Engineering (Bristol) Ltd*[439] the House of **5.103**
Lords rejected the proposition that the Court of Appeal had developed in cases
such as *Dawnays Ltd v F G Minter Ltd*,[440] that a certificate issued under a building
contract is to be regarded as equivalent to cash, and that therefore the debt due
under the certificate has to be paid save only for deductions permitted by the contract. On the other hand, the parties may choose to exclude defences of equitable
set-off and common law abatement. In the *Gilbert-Ash* case[441] Lord Diplock said
that there is a presumption that the parties to a contract do not intend to give up
remedies for its breach that otherwise would arise by operation of law. This applies
to rights of set-off and abatement. In order to rebut the presumption there must be
clear words, or at least a clear implication, to that effect.[442] Following the *Gilbert-
Ash* case, various attempts have been made by draftsmen of standard-form contracts to exclude or restrict rights of set-off and abatement in relation to interim
certificates. It is not proposed to consider these in detail. They are referred to in
specialist texts on building contracts.[443] The point is made in *Hudson's Building and
Engineering Contracts*[444] however that, when the constraints of the express wording
have permitted, English courts have not been slow to re-affirm the *Gilbert-Ash*
principle. *Acsim (Southern) Ltd v Danish Contracting & Development Co Ltd*[445]
illustrates that proposition. A building contract included a term to the effect that
Danish Contracting ('Dancon') could set off against any moneys otherwise due to
Acsim as contractor the amount of any claim for loss, provided the claim had been
quantified and notified to Acsim within a specified period. The contract went on
to provide that this fully set out the rights of the parties in respect of set-off. While
the Court of Appeal held that the contract was effective to prevent a cross-claim for
damages for bad workmanship that was quantified outside the period from being
employed as an equitable set-off, there were not sufficiently clear words to exclude
the common law defence of abatement.[446] The subject of the cross-claim was not
being raised as a set-off as such. Rather, Dancon was defending itself by showing
that, by reason of Acsim's breaches of contract, the value of the work was less than
the sum claimed.[447] This defence was not prohibited by the contract.

---

[439] [1974] AC 689.

[440] [1971] 1 WLR 1205. See para 5.49 above.

[441] *Gilbert-Ash (Northern) Ltd v Modern Engineering (Bristol) Ltd* [1974] AC 689, 717.

[442] See Lord Salmon in *Gilbert-Ash (Northern) Ltd v Modern Engineering (Bristol) Ltd* [1974] AC
689, 723.

[443] See eg *Hudson's Building and Engineering Contracts* (11th edn, 1995) vol 1, 856–60, and the
cases referred to in *Keating on Building Contracts* (7th edn, 2001) 574.

[444] *Hudson's Building and Engineering Contracts* (11th edn, 1995) vol 1, 858.

[445] (1989) 47 BLR 55.

[446] (1989) 47 BLR 55, 72. See also, and compare, *Mellowes Archital Ltd v Bell Projects Ltd* (1997)
87 BLR 26 (damages for delay not within the common law principle of abatement). Compare also,
in a different context, *Skipskredittforeningen v Emperor Navigation* [1998] 1 Lloyd's Rep 66, 78–79.

[447] See para 2.87 above.

Australia

5.104 In Australia, the courts generally have shown a greater preparedness than those in England to interpret building and construction contracts as excluding the defences in relation to interim or progress certificates.[448] While the cases were not all concerned with the same form of contract, a number of factors have been emphasized as indicating an intention that interim or progress certificates were to be paid without deductions for cross-claims.[449] Of particular significance have been the terms of the payment clause. For example, clause 42.1 of the Australian General Conditions of Contract AS 2124–1992 provided that the employer 'shall pay . . . an amount not less than the amount shown in the certificate as due to the contractor . . .'. The obligation was expressed in terms of paying the amount shown in the certificate, as opposed to the amount due to the contractor, and, considered in conjunction with other relevant factors mentioned below, it has been interpreted as requiring payment of the amount shown in the certificate without a deduction for liquidated damages payable by the contractor for delay.[450] The same interpretation has been adopted in other cases in Australia where the payment clause was expressed in similar terms.[451]

5.105 Courts in Australia have referred to other aspects of building contracts as supporting that view. In one case, it was regarded as persuasive that the clause dealing with payment of progress certificates made no provision for the situation in which the proprietor disputed the whole or part of the certificate, although it was expressly dealt with in relation to the final certificate, in that the obligation to pay only extended to the amount that was not in dispute.[452] Similarly, it has been said to be relevant that the contract provides a scheme for making deductions in

---

[448] In addition to the cases referred to below, see *John Holland Construction and Engineering Pty Ltd v Majorca Projects Pty Ltd* (Vic SC, Hansen J, 27 July 1995). See also in New Zealand *Hempseed v Durham Developments Ltd* [1998] 3 NZLR 265, 269. For cases in which an intention to exclude defences of set-off and abatement was not found, see *Construction Services Civil Pty Ltd v J & N Allen Enterprises Pty Ltd* (1985) 1 BCL 363; *Melbourne Glass Pty Ltd v Coby Constructions Pty Ltd* (1997) 14 BCL 409; *Dames & Moore Pty Ltd v Jovista Pty Ltd* (1998) 14 BCL 421.

[449] In *Melbourne Glass Pty Ltd v Coby Constructions Pty Ltd* (1997) 14 BCL 409, 417, Gillard J said that two substantial factors which have influenced the courts in Australia to exclude the defence of set-off in building contracts are, first, the presence of a detailed scheme allowing for deductions, and, second, a dispute resolution procedure which obliges the works to continue even though the parties have commenced some form of litigation. See below.

[450] *Re Concrete Constructions Group Pty Ltd* [1997] 1 Qd R 6; *Novawest Contracting Pty Ltd v Taras Nominees Pty Ltd* [1998] VSC 205.

[451] *Algons Engineering Pty Ltd v Abigroup Contractors Pty Ltd* (1997) 14 BCL 215; *Minson Nacap Pty Ltd v Aquatec Maxcon Pty Ltd* [2000] VSC 402; *L U Simon Builders Pty Ltd v H D Fowles* [1992] 2 VR 189; *Sabemo Pty Ltd v de Groot* (1991) 8 BCL 132. Compare *Dames & Moore Pty Ltd v Jovista Pty Ltd* [1998] WASC 157.

[452] *L U Simon Builders Pty Ltd v H D Fowles* [1992] 2 VR 189, 192–193. See also *Sabemo Pty Ltd v de Groot* (1991) 8 BCL 132, 143. On that view, the contract had the effect of deferring the right to a set-off until the final claim for payment under the contract. See *Algons Engineering Pty Ltd v Abigroup Contractors Pty Ltd* (1997) 14 BCL 215, 230, 231.

respect of defects and for delay.[453] In the case of defects, the contract in issue provided that the employer could employ others to rectify defects if the contractor failed to do so, and the employer could then recover the cost from moneys payable to the contractor. In the case of delay, the contract enabled the employer to deduct liquidated damages from progress certificates issued after practical completion. Courts in Australia have also had regard to a clause entitling the contractor to suspend or terminate the contract in the event of a failure to pay by the proprietor. It has been said that it would be curious if the proprietor could refuse to pay because of a cross-claim when the contractor is entitled to terminate in the event of non-payment.[454] In that regard the point has been made that the contractor would not know whether it could act where the proprietor is raising a cross-claim until a decision was made on the dispute. Until that occurred, it would not be possible to determine whether the proprietor had 'failed to pay', and the power given to the contractor in practice would be rendered worthless.[455] Reference has also been made to arbitration clauses. The presence of an arbitration clause in relation to disputes on its own should not suffice to exclude defences of set-off and abatement.[456] Nevertheless it has been suggested that the clause may indicate an intention to that effect if the clause requires disputes to be referred to arbitration, and also requires the contractor to continue to perform and execute the works pending resolution of the dispute. It has been said that, unless the contractor continues to receive progress payments, it may not be able to execute the works, and that the entitlement to progress payments should be regarded as the *quid pro quo* for the obligation to continue working while the parties are in dispute.[457]

In so far as a payment clause may be expressed in terms such those set out in the **5.106** Australian General Conditions of Contract AS 2124–1992 (above), it nevertheless is the case that the amount shown in the certificate was intended to be the

---

[453] See *L U Simon Builders Pty Ltd v H D Fowles* [1992] 2 VR 189, 194.

[454] *Triden Contractors Pty Ltd v Belvista Pty Ltd* (1986) 3 BCL 203, 215–216. On the other hand, this was not regarded as significant in *Construction Services Civil Pty Ltd v J & N Allen Enterprises Pty Ltd* (1985) 1 BCL 363, 369.

[455] *L U Simon Builders Pty Ltd v H D Fowles* [1992] 2 VR 189, 193, referring to *Sabemo Pty Ltd v de Groot* (1991) 8 BCL 132, 143.

[456] See para 5.92 above.

[457] *L U Simon Builders Pty Ltd v H D Fowles* [1992] 2 VR 189, 193. See also *Sabemo Pty Ltd v de Groot* (1991) 8 BCL 132, 143; *Algons Engineering Pty Ltd v Abigroup Contractors Pty Ltd* (1997) 14 BCL 215, 220, 224; *Melbourne Glass Pty Ltd v Coby Constructions Pty Ltd* (1997) 14 BCL 409, 417; *Novawest Contracting Pty Ltd v Taras Nominees Pty Ltd* [1998] VSC 205 at [96]. In *G Hawkins & Sons Pty Ltd v Cable Belt (Australia) Pty Ltd* (1984) 2 BCL 246 an employer's claims against a contractor for delay and bad workmanship were the subject of an arbitration, which was proceeding. The contract provided that any payment due to the contractor was not to be withheld on account of arbitration proceedings unless authorized by the contractor or required by the arbitrator. Rogers J in the New South Wales Supreme Court held that the employer was required to pay retention moneys due to the contractor, and that the clause precluded any right to withhold payment on the basis of equitable set-off.

amount "due" to the contractor,[458] and when a substantive defence of equitable set-off is available courts of equity proceed on the basis that nothing is due to the creditor to the extent of the set-off.[459] It is unlikely that an English court applying the presumption to which Lord Diplock referred in the *Gilbert-Ash* case[460] would regard a clause in those terms as sufficiently clear to show that the parties intended to exclude their ordinary rights of set-off and abatement. Thus, it is doubted in *Hudson's Building and Engineering Contracts* whether some of the Australian cases in truth are consistent with the *Gilbert-Ash* case,[461] and the point may be made that some of the reasons given by Australian courts for denying a set-off do not seem persuasive in the light of the views expressed in the House of Lords. In the *Gilbert-Ash* case the main contract between the employer and the contractor was in the form issued by the RIBA for Local Authorities 1963 Edition (December 1967 issue).[462] Viscount Dilhorne said that there was no ground for inferring that the contract excluded reliance by the employer on his common law and equitable rights of set-off if sued,[463] and that was also the view of Lord Salmon.[464] Lord Diplock expressed a similar opinion in relation to the common law defence of abatement.[465] One of the features of the RIBA contract was that it entitled the contractor to terminate the contract in the event that the employer failed to pay the amount due on a certificate.[466] In Australia a clause in those terms has been regarded as a factor indicating that defences of equitable set-off and abatement have been excluded in relation to progress certificates,[467] whereas it did not affect the views expressed in the *Gilbert-Ash* case that the defences applied in that case.[468] A similar issue has arisen in the context of a time charter of a ship. The charterparty

---

[458] Thus, clause 42.1 of AS 2124–1992 required the contractor to 'deliver to the Superintendent claims for payment supported by evidence of the amount due to the Contractor . . .'.

[459] See para 4.30 above.

[460] See para 5.79 above.

[461] *Hudson's Building and Engineering Contracts* (11th edn, 1995) vol 1, 730 n 23, 856 and 860–1, referring to *Triden Contractors Pty Ltd v Belvista Pty Ltd* (1986) 3 BCL 203, *Sabemo Pty Ltd v de Groot* (1991) 8 BCL 132 and *L U Simon Builders Ltd v H D Fowles* [1992] 2 VR 189.

[462] See [1974] AC 689, 696. The contract immediately in issue was a contract between the contractor and a sub-contractor, but the contract between those parties incorporated the parts of the main contract that were applicable to the works.

[463] [1974] AC 689, 707, 709–710. The sub-contract in fact gave an express right of deduction, but Viscount Dilhorne (at 712) said that, even if that had not been the case, it similarly would not have excluded common law and equitable rights of set-off.

[464] [1974] AC 689, 726–727.

[465] [1974] AC 689, 720.

[466] See clause 26(1), the terms of which are set out in Keating, *Law and Practice of Building Contracts* (3rd edn, 1969) 370. The form set out in Keating is the July 1968 revision, as opposed to the December 1967 issue which was the subject of *Gilbert-Ash*, though the differences between the two forms are not material. See the history of the amendments to the 1963 edition in Keating, *Law and Practice of Building Contracts* 295–6.

[467] See para 5.105 above.

[468] See in particular Viscount Dilhorne at [1974] AC 689, 709, who was influenced by the presence of other clauses which conferred express rights of deduction in certain specified circumstances.

usually gives the owner the right to determine the charter in the event of non-payment of hire, and it has been said that the power of determination is not sufficient to exclude equitable set-off in favour of the charterer in relation to breaches of the charterparty by the owner.[469] If the charterer asserts a cross-claim which, if established, would give rise to an equitable set-off, the owner would act at its peril if it nevertheless determined the charterparty for non-payment. If it should turn out that the deduction was justified, the owner's purported determination would constitute a repudiation.[470]

Another factor emphasized in Australia is the presence of a clause permitting the employer to deduct liquidated damages for delay from progress certificates issued after practical completion.[471] However, the RIBA contract the subject of consideration in the *Gilbert-Ash* case contained a similar provision,[472] so that it would seem that in the *Gilbert-Ash* case the presence of that clause was not regarded as having militated against the employer's right to set up defences of set-off and abatement against the contractor in relation to a cross-claim for delay. Furthermore, the fact that the contract gives a remedy in relation to defects, in that the employer may employ someone else to rectify defects if the contractor has failed to do so and to deduct the cost from progress payments,[473] seems insufficient to give rise to a clear implication that the contract excludes reliance by the employer on equitable and common law rights of set-off and abatement in other circumstances.[474] **5.107**

Courts in Australia have referred to other factors as supporting a conclusion that particular building contracts have excluded rights of set-off and abatement. For example, reference has been made in that context to a provision to the effect that an interim payment was not to prejudice the right of either party to dispute whether the amount paid was properly due and payable, and that payment was not evidence of the value of the work or an admission that the work had been executed satisfactorily, but was to be a payment on account only.[475] However the **5.108**

---

[469] *Federal Commerce & Navigation Co Ltd v Molena Alpha Inc* [1978] 1 QB 927, 981, 988–989, *per* Goff LJ.

[470] *Federal Commerce & Navigation Co Ltd v Molena Alpha Inc* [1978] 1 QB 927, 981. The cases favour the view that the charterer will not be in default in making a deduction from hire payments if the amount of the loss has been quantified by a reasonable assessment made in good faith. See para 4.38 above.

[471] See para 5.105 above.

[472] See clause 22, the terms of which are set out in Keating, *Law and Practice of Building Contracts* (3rd edn, 1969) 352.

[473] This has been regarded as a relevant factor in Australia. See para 5.105 above.

[474] See also Viscount Dilhorne in *Gilbert-Ash (Northern) Ltd v Modern Engineering (Bristol) Ltd* [1974] AC 689, 707, 710 in relation to clauses 2(1) & 6 of the RIBA contract, and also Lord Diplock at 719.

[475] *Novawest Contracting Pty Ltd v Taras Nominees Pty Ltd* [1998] VSC 205 at paras 96–99. See also *Algons Engineering Pty Ltd v Abigroup Contractors Pty Ltd* (1997) 14 BCL 215, 219, 227; *Leighton Contractors Pty Ltd v East Gippsland Catchment Management Authority* (2000) 17 BCL 35, 38 [11].

sub-contract in the *Gilbert-Ash* case had a similar clause,[476] and moreover it simply reflects the effect which is usually ascribed to interim certificates.[477] The presence of an express clause in the contract allowing the principal to make certain deductions has also been regarded as a factor suggesting that other rights of set-off and abatement have been excluded.[478] It is difficult however to reconcile that proposition with the view adopted by English courts, that the fact that a contract makes provision for certain specified deductions does not give rise to an implication that a right of set-off in respect of other sums has been excluded.[479]

5.109 Australian courts have also emphasized the presence of an arbitration clause which requires disputes to be referred to arbitration, and which also requires the contractor to continue to execute the works pending resolution of the dispute. The point has been made in relation to a clause in that form that, if the contractor is not paid, it may not be able to complete the works, so that the entitlement to progress payments should be regarded as the *quid pro quo* for the obligation to continue.[480] One may query however the significance of the stipulation that the contractor must continue with the work. The stipulation that the work must continue on one view simply reflects the position that would apply if defences of equitable set-off and abatement were available against a claim on a progress certificate. If in a summary judgment application by a contractor for payment of the amount certified the court was satisfied that there was a bona fide cross-claim which, if established, would give rise to a set-off or an abatement, the contractor would not obtain immediate payment to the extent of the cross-claim. Furthermore, the contractor would have to continue work unless it was prepared to take the risk that the cross-claim would not be made out. If the contractor ceased work and the cross-claim ultimately was established, its conduct would have constituted a breach of the contract.[481] The stipulation adds certainty to the question of what happens in the event of a dispute. It is debateable however whether it gives rise to a clear implication that the parties had intended to exclude defences of set-off and abatement in relation to progress certificates, for the purpose of rebutting the presumption referred to in the *Gilbert-Ash* case.[482]

---

[476] See clause 14 of the sub-contract, the terms of which are set out at [1974] AC 689, 697. While the sub-contract expressly conferred a right of deduction, Viscount Dilhorne (at 712) commented that, even in the absence of that provision, the sub-contract would not have excluded the contractor's common law and equitable rights of set-off.

[477] See *Hudson's Building and Engineering Contracts* (11th edn, 1995) vol 1, 849–51, and *Re Concrete Constructions Group Pty Ltd* [1997] 1 Qd R 6, 12.

[478] *Melbourne Glass Pty Ltd v Coby Constructions Pty Ltd* (1997) 14 BCL 409, 417; *Novawest Contracting Pty Ltd v Taras Nominees Pty Ltd* [1998] VSC 205 at paras 101–103. See also *Re Concrete Constructions Group Pty Ltd* [1997] 1 Qd R 6, 13.

[479] See para 5.87 above.

[480] See para 5.105 above.

[481] See the discussion in *Federal Commerce & Navigation Co Ltd v Molena Alpha Inc* [1978] 1 QB 927, 975, and also para 4.38 above.

[482] See para 5.79 above.

(5) Statutes of Set-off

The set-off section in the insolvency legislation[483] is considered to be mandatory **5.110** in its operation, so that it is not possible to contract out of its terms.[484] This has been justified on two grounds. The first is the mandatory language used in the section, which provides that an account 'shall be taken' in the stated circumstances. The second is based upon a perceived policy consideration,[485] that the insolvency set-off section relates to a matter in which the public have an interest. According to this view, the section was not enacted for the benefit of a particular person or persons, but rather it is a part of a code of procedure dealing with the administration of the estate of a bankrupt or a company in liquidation. Neither of these grounds apply however to the right of set-off conferred by the Statutes of Set-off. In the first place, the Statutes provided that mutual debts 'may', as opposed to 'shall', be set off.[486] Moreover, the occurrence of a set-off under the Statutes would not appear to be a matter in which the public have an interest. Rather, the right was introduced by the Statutes for the benefit of defendants.[487] Consistent with that view, a defendant is not obliged to raise a cross-debt as a defence under the Statutes,[488] but may bring separate proceedings in respect of it, though in such a case he could be penalized in relation to costs.[489] Prima facie, then, the maxim '*quilibet potest renunciare juri pro se introducto*'[490] should apply, so that it should be possible to renounce the right to invoke the defence. There is nevertheless early authority to the contrary.[491] In *Lechmere v Hawkins*[492] the defendant had promised to repay money borrowed from the plaintiff without taking any notice of a debt due to him from the plaintiff, and without setting one demand against

---

[483] Insolvency Act 1986, s 323 and, for company liquidation, the Insolvency Rules 1986, r 4.90. See generally ch 6.

[484] See paras 6.71–6.78 below.

[485] See Lord Simon of Glaisdale in *National Westminster Bank Ltd v Halesowen Presswork & Assemblies Ltd* [1972] AC 785, 808–809, and Vinelott J in *Re Maxwell Communications Corp plc (No 2)* [1993] 1 WLR 1402, 1411. For a criticism of this view, see para 6.72 below.

[486] See (1729) 2 Geo II, c 22, s 13, and (1735) 8 Geo II, c 24, s 5.

[487] *Davis v Hedges* (1871) LR 6 QB 687, 690.

[488] See eg *Green v Law* (1805) 2 Smith KB 668; *Laing v Chatham* (1808) 1 Camp 252, 170 ER 947; *Jenner v Morris* (1861) 3 De G F & J 45, 54, 45 ER 795, 798; *Davis v Hedges* (1871) LR 6 QB 687, 690. In *Coca-Cola Financial Corp v Finsat International Ltd* [1998] QB 43, 52 Neill LJ noted that, under the Statutes of Set-off, there was no obligation for a solvent debtor to exercise his right of set-off.

[489] See *Green v Law* (1805) 2 Smith KB 668.

[490] Anyone may, at his pleasure, renounce the benefit of a stipulation or other right introduced entirely in his own favour. See *Broom's Legal Maxims* (10th edn, 1939) 477.

[491] The cases are discussed by Farrar, 'Contracting Out of Set-off' (1970) 120 New Law Journal 771. Professor Farrar rightly pointed out that *Skyring v Greenwood* (1825) 4 B & C 281, 107 ER 1064 was a case in which the debt itself, as opposed to a right of set-off, had been waived. *Quaere* whether this would explain *Baker v Langhorn* (1816) 6 Taunt 519, 128 ER 1136, in which the broker was claiming payment of a loss as agent for the insured rather than for himself, though in any event the case was concerned with bankruptcy set-off as opposed to the Statutes of Set-off.

[492] (1798) 2 Esp 626, 170 ER 477.

the other. Lord Kenyon said that this was an honorary obligation only, and that the defendant could not be compelled to abide by it when the Statutes themselves conferred upon him the right to set one demand against the other. That decision subsequently was followed by Lord Erskine in *Taylor v Okey*.[493] There are also cases in which a purchaser of goods was allowed a set-off in an action for the price even though he had agreed to pay in ready money,[494] an agreement which would appear to be inconsistent with payment by way of set-off.[495] This is no longer the prevailing view, however.[496] In *Hongkong and Shanghai Banking Corp v Kloeckner & Co AG*[497] Hirst J held that a person can contract out of the right of set-off, a view which was shared by Dillon LJ in *BICC plc v Burndy Corp*,[498] and which was affirmed by the Court of Appeal in *Coca-Cola Financial Corp v Finsat International Ltd*.[499] The New South Wales Supreme Court came to the same conclusion in *Stephen v Doyle*,[500] and it is also supported by some cases in which the courts have given effect to a term of a contract between a debtor and a creditor by which the debtor agreed that he would not invoke against an assignee of his debt any right of set-off otherwise available to him against the creditor/assignor.[501]

Clear words

5.111 In the context of equitable set-off and common law abatement, the courts have said that there is a presumption that neither party to a contract intends to abandon any remedies for its breach arising by operation of law, and that accordingly there must be clear words to exclude a set-off or a defence of abatement.[502] In *BICC plc v Burndy Corp*[503] Dillon LJ commented that this applies 'equally, if not *a fortiori*', to set-off under the Statutes.

5.112 As in the case of equitable set-off, it should not necessary that the agreement should refer specifically set-off in order to exclude the defence. The defence may

---

[493] (1806) 13 Ves Jun 180, 33 ER 263.

[494] *Eland v Karr* (1801) 1 East 375, 102 ER 145; *Cornforth v Rivett* (1814) 2 M & S 510, 105 ER 471. See also *M'Gillivray v Simson* (1826) 5 LJOSKB 53.

[495] *Brandao v Barnett* (1846) 12 Cl & Fin 787, 808, 8 ER 1622, 1630, *per* Lord Campbell.

[496] In addition to the cases referred to below, see *Hoverd Industries Ltd v Supercool Refrigeration and Air Conditioning (1991) Ltd* [1995] 3 NZLR 577, 588, in which there was a clear implication that set-off was to be excluded. See para 5.112 below.

[497] [1990] 2 QB 514.

[498] [1985] 1 Ch 232, 248.

[499] [1998] QB 43.

[500] (1882) 3 NSWR (Eq) 1. See also *Morrison Knudsen Corp of Australia Ltd v Australian National Railways Commission* (1996) 22 ACSR 262, 267, Federal Court of Australia, *per* Mansfield J.

[501] See eg *Re Blakely Ordnance Co, ex p New Zealand Banking Corp* (1867) LR 3 Ch App 154 and *Re Goy & Co Ltd (Farmer v Goy & Co Ltd)* [1900] 2 Ch 149, 154, and generally para 17.33 below.

[502] See para 5.79 above.

[503] [1985] 1 Ch 232, 248.

also be excluded if there is a clear implication to that effect.[504] In a case in New Zealand, B owed a debt to A, and A had issued redeemable preference shares to C, B and C being related companies, and the parties had agreed that B was not required to make repayments of the debt unless there was simultaneously a redemption by A of a corresponding amount of preference shares. The New Zealand Court of Appeal considered that the agreement showed a clear intention to tie the repayments of the debt by B to payments by A for redemption of shares, so as to preclude a set-off of B's debt against a separate debt owing by A to B.[505]

Waiver

Given that it is possible to contract out of this statutory right of set-off, in an **5.113** appropriate case the right may be held to have been waived.[506]

Second ranking security, and subordination

A creditor may have agreed that security given for the debt is to be second ranking **5.114** after security given by the debtor to another creditor. Ordinarily this would not be regarded as an agreement by the first creditor not to set off the debt owing to him until the prior ranking secured creditor has been paid. The agreement goes to the ranking of the security, not to the payment of the debts.[507] It should be compared to an agreement by a creditor to subordinate his debt in point of payment to another creditor's debt. In such a case the first creditor may not employ the subordinated debt in a set-off.[508] This may be justified on the basis of an implied agreement to that effect arising from the subordination,[509] though it should also follow from the principle that set-off under the Statutes requires that both debts be due and payable.[510] Until the other creditor's debt has been paid, the subordinated debt is not payable.

Agreement not to assign

An agreement by a creditor not to assign the debt to a third party ordinarily would **5.115** not be interpreted as precluding the creditor from employing the debt in a set-off. *Gathercole v Smith*[511] may seem contrary to that view. A statute which provided

---

[504] See para 5.79 above.

[505] *Hoverd Industries Ltd v Supercool Refrigeration and Air Conditioning* (1991) Ltd [1995] 3 NZLR 577, 586, 588.

[506] See *Baker v Langhorn* (1816) 6 Taunt 519, 128 ER 1136. Compare *Moore v Jervis* (1845) 2 Coll 60, 63 ER 637. *Skyring v Greenwood* (1825) 4 B & C 281, 107 ER 1064 was a case in which the debt itself, as opposed to a right of set-off, was waived. See Farrar, 'Contracting Out of Set-off' (1970) 120 New Law Journal 771, 772.

[507] *Edward Nelson & Co Ltd v Faber & Co* [1903] 2 KB 367, 377.

[508] *H Wilkins & Elkington Ltd v Milton* (1916) 32 TLR 618.

[509] See Wood, *English and International Set-off* (1989) 690.

[510] See para 2.29 above.

[511] (1881) 17 Ch D 1 (and see further proceedings at (1881) 7 QBD 626).

that a pension payable to a retired incumbent of a benefice was not transferable was interpreted as also precluding a set-off against it. However the decision should be regarded as turning on the object of the legislation, to provide for the maintenance of retired clergy. The object would have been defeated if the pension were to be reduced or extinguished by a set-off.

Estoppel, and credit notes

5.116 When a contract provides for payments under it to be made without set-off, the fact that the parties in the past have settled their debts by tendering a net amount on its own should not suffice to give rise to an estoppel so as to preclude reliance by the creditor on the clause. Often it would simply mean that, while the parties appeared to be solvent and their relationship was continuing on a satisfactory basis, there was no point in each of them tendering a separate payment. In the absence of an agreement or a clearly expressed understanding that this was intended to alter their contractual rights, it should not preclude the creditor from insisting on its strict legal rights in the future.[512] Further, when a creditor has issued a credit note to the debtor pursuant to a contract which contains a clause precluding set-offs, it would be a question of construction as to whether the credit note was intended to operate by way of a set-off against future contract payments. It may simply be an acknowledgement of indebtedness by the creditor which, in accordance with the contract, cannot be utilized by the debtor in a set-off.[513]

Payment in advance

5.117 Consider the case of a payment in advance under a contract. The payment may operate as a prepayment of a debt, in which case the question of set-off would not arise in relation to the debt the subject of the prepayment, or alternatively it may constitute a security for future debts generally, in which case the question whether the debtor (as opposed to the creditor) can bring it into account in an action for payment of one such debt would depend on the terms of the contract.[514]

(6) Company under Administration

5.118 In Australia, Mansfield J in the Federal Court, when faced with a clause which clearly and unambiguously excluded rights of set-off, declined to interpret it so as to permit a set-off when an administrator was appointed to the plaintiff pursuant to Part 5.3A of the Corporations Law,[515] notwithstanding that the statutory

---

[512] *John Dee Group Ltd v WMH (21) Ltd* [1997] BCC 518, 525–526 (decision affirmed [1998] BCC 972).

[513] *John Dee Group Ltd v WMH (21) Ltd* [1998] BCC 972.

[514] *John Dee Group Ltd v WMH (21) Ltd* [1998] BCC 972, 975–976, CA, affirming [1997] BCC 518.

[515] Now the Corporations Act 2001 (Cth).

moratorium consequent upon the appointment[516] meant that the plaintiff under administration was entitled to payment of the debts owing to it though it could not be sued for the debts which it owed.[517]

J. Failure to Plead Set-off in the Plaintiff's Action

Introduction

Consider that A is suing B for payment of a debt or other money sum, and B has **5.119** a cross-claim against A which is available as a defence by way of set-off, though B does not rely on it as a defence. In that circumstance, if A obtains judgment on the claim, can B then enforce the cross-claim in a later action against A?

In *Henderson v Henderson*[518] Sir James Wigram VC formulated the relevant prin- **5.120** ciple in the following terms:

> [W]here a given matter becomes the subject of litigation in, and of adjudication by, a Court of competent jurisdiction, the Court requires the parties to that litigation to bring forward their whole case, and will not (except under special circumstances) permit the same parties to open the same subject of litigation in respect of matter which might have been brought forward as part of the subject in contest, but which was not brought forward, only because they have, from negligence, inadvertence, or even accident, omitted part of their case. The plea of *res judicata* applies, except in special cases, not only to points upon which the Court was actually required by the parties to form an opinion and pronounce a judgment, but to every point which properly belonged to the subject of litigation, and which the parties, exercising reasonable diligence, might have brought forward at the time.

The principle has been described variously as an extended doctrine of res judicata,[519] or as res judicata in its wider sense,[520] or as an estoppel,[521] and is based on abuse of process.[522]

---

[516] Corporations Law, s 440D.

[517] *Morrison Knudsen Corporation of Australia Ltd v Australian National Railways Commission* (1996) 22 ACSR 262.

[518] (1843) 3 Hare 100, 115, 67 ER 313, 319. This has since been affirmed by the courts on numerous occasions. See eg *Hoystead v Commissioner of Taxation* [1926] AC 155, 170, PC; *Yat Tung Investment Co Ltd v Dao Heng Bank Ltd* [1975] AC 581, 590, PC; *Brisbane City Council v Attorney-General* [1979] AC 411, 425, PC; *Port of Melbourne Authority v Anshun Pty Ltd* (1981) 147 CLR 589, HCA.

[519] Spencer Bower, Turner and Handley, *The Doctrine of Res Judicata* (3rd edn, 1996), 251 para 443.

[520] *Brisbane City Council v Attorney-General* [1979] AC 411, 425.

[521] See eg *Port of Melbourne Authority v Anshun* (1981) 147 CLR 589, 602, 604.

[522] *Brisbane City Council v Attorney-General* [1979] AC 411, 425; *Barrow v Bankside Agency Ltd* [1996] 1 WLR 257, 263; *Johnson v Gore Wood & Co* [2002] 2 AC 1. In Australia, Gibbs CJ and Mason and Aickin JJ in their joint judgment in *Port of Melbourne Authority v Anshun Pty Ltd* (1981) 147 CLR 589, 602 nevertheless said that 'the abuse of process test is not one of great utility', and proceeded to formulate a principle based on unreasonableness. See para 5.123 below.

5.121   The scope of the doctrine has been expressed in various terms. In *Greenhalgh v Mallard*[523] Somervell LJ said that it 'covers issues or facts which are so clearly part of the subject-matter of the [original] litigation and so clearly could have been raised that it would be an abuse of the process of the court to allow a new proceeding to be started in respect of them'. Subsequently the Privy Council in *Yat Tung Investment Co Ltd v Dao Heng Bank Ltd*[524] adopted a wider formulation, commenting that it would be 'an abuse of process to raise in subsequent proceedings matters which could and therefore should have been litigated in earlier proceedings'. In other words, if the matter could have been raised in earlier proceedings, it should have been, and failure to do so may result in the doctrine being invoked where there is an attempt to raise the matter in later proceedings. On the other hand, while Wigram VC in *Henderson v Henderson* said that 'negligence, inadvertence, or even accident' would not justify the failure to bring forward the matter in the earlier litigation, he also recognized that it may be excused in special circumstances. For example, it has been said that it would be a special circumstance if the party seeking to litigate the matter at a later date was unaware, and could not reasonably have been expected to be aware, of the circumstances attending that matter at the time of the earlier litigation.[525]

5.122   Recently the House of Lords considered the issue in *Johnson v Gore Wood & Co*,[526] and in doing so signalled a flexible approach to the application of the principle. Lord Bingham of Cornhill[527] rejected the *Yat Tung* approach, commenting that it would be wrong to hold that, because a matter could have been raised in earlier proceedings, it should have been, so as to render the raising of it in later proceedings necessarily abusive.[528] He criticized that approach as too dogmatic, and said that the question calls for:

---

[523]   [1947] 2 All ER 255, 257, referred to in *Johnson v Gore Wood & Co* [2002] 2 AC 1, 23. Similarly, Colman J said in *Stocznia Gdanska SA v Latvian Shipping Co* [1997] 2 Lloyd's Rep 228, 239 that: 'One must therefore look to the subject-matter of the new proceedings and compare it with that of the original proceedings. If the issues raised in the later proceedings ought properly to have been raised in the earlier proceedings because they arose from the same subject-matter, the Court will treat the subsequent attempt to raise the issues as an abuse of process, unless there are special circumstances.'

[524]   [1975] AC 581, 590. See also *Republic of India v India Steamship Co Ltd* [1993] AC 410, 417, reversing [1992] 1 Lloyd's Rep 124.

[525]   *Yat Tung Investment Co Ltd v Dao Heng Bank Ltd* [1975] AC 581, 590; *Ling v Commonwealth* (1996) 68 FCR 180, 195 (where however it was suggested that this is a situation in which the rule would not apply at all as opposed to a special circumstance requiring the non-application of the rule). See also *Arnold v National Westminster Bank plc* [1991] 2 AC 93 (change in the interpretation of the law); *C (A Minor) v Hackney LBC* [1996] 1 WLR 789, 792. It has been doubted whether *Arnold v National Westminster* is good law in Australia. See *Linsley v Petrie* [1998] 1 VR 427, 441, referring to *O'Toole v Charles David Pty Ltd* (1991) 171 CLR 232, 258.

[526]   [2002] 2 AC 1. See also *Gairy v Attorney General of Grenada* [2002] 1 AC 167, 181 paras 26 and 27, PC.

[527]   [2002] 2 AC 1, 31. Lord Goff of Chieveley, Lord Cooke of Thorndon and Lord Hutton agreed with Lord Bingham's judgment on this point.

[528]   See also Lord Millett at [2002] 2 AC 1, 59–60.

a broad, merits-based judgment which takes account of the public and private interests involved and also takes account of all the facts of the case, focusing attention on the crucial question whether, in all the circumstances, a party is misusing or abusing the process of the court by seeking to raise before it the issue which could have been raised before. As one cannot comprehensively list all possible forms of abuse, so one cannot formulate any hard and fast rule to determine whether, on given facts, abuse is to be found or not.

Lord Bingham went on to reject the approach that hitherto had been adopted, of asking whether the conduct is an abuse and then, if it is, asking whether the abuse is excused or justified by special circumstances. Rather, he suggested that the question should be framed simply in terms whether in all the circumstances the party's conduct is an abuse. In that regard, he said that there would rarely be a finding of abuse unless the later proceeding involves what the court regards as unjust harassment of a party.

Australia

The *Yat Tung* formulation has also been criticized in Australia. In a joint judgment **5.123** in the High Court in *Port of Melbourne Authority v Anshun Pty Ltd*,[529] Gibbs CJ, Mason and Aickin JJ said that in the *Yat Tung* case the adoption of the *Henderson v Henderson* principle 'was taken too far'.[530] Instead, they proposed a test based on reasonableness. In other words, was the matter now sought to be raised so relevant to the subject-matter of the former proceeding that it is reasonable to expect that it would have been raised in that proceeding?

> In this situation we would prefer to say that there will be no estoppel unless it appears that the matter relied upon as a defence in the second action was so relevant to the subject matter of the first action that it would have been unreasonable not to rely on it. Generally speaking, it would be unreasonable not to plead a defence if, having regard to the nature of the plaintiff's claim, and its subject matter it would be expected that the defendant would raise the defence and thereby enable the relevant issues to be determined in the one proceeding.[531]

Statutes of Set-off

Consider the case of a creditor who failed to assert the debt being sued upon as a **5.124** defence under the Statutes of Set-off[532] in an earlier action brought against him by the debtor in relation to another debt.

---

[529] (1981) 147 CLR 589.

[530] (1981) 147 CLR 589, 601–602.

[531] (1981) 147 CLR 587, 602. It has been questioned whether the notion of relevance indeed is helpful when the issue concerns a failure to advance a claim which might have been raised in an earlier proceeding, as opposed to a defence. See *Gibbs v Kinna* [1999] 2 VR 19, 27, referring to *Boles v Esanda Finance Corp Ltd* (1989) 18 NSWLR 666, 674.

[532] See ch 2 above.

5.125   The Statutes do not require that there be any connection between the debts. They may be totally unconnected, both as to their subject-matter and the circumstances relating to their creation. According to the formulation approved in the *Yat Tung* case, the absence of a connection would not matter. The cross-debt 'could and therefore should' have been litigated in the original proceeding as a defence, a view that is also consistent with statements suggesting that all defences should be brought forward.[533] The *Yat Tung* formulation is no longer current, however.[534] If the debts exhibit no commonality of issues or facts, and they relate to different subject-matters, enforcing the debt in a later action should not constitute unjust harassment of the debtor, in which case it should not be an abuse of process to enforce it separately.[535] Similarly, in Australia it should not be regarded as unreasonable in those circumstances to sue for it separately, for the purpose of the test set out in the *Anshun* case. This indeed reflects the position that has been adopted in the cases. The courts have said that a defendant is not obliged to raise a cross-debt as a defence under the Statutes, but is entitled to bring separate proceedings in respect of it,[536] though he may be penalized in relation to costs if he adopts that course of action.[537]

5.126   Separate judgments on the debts would not result in conflicting or contradictory judgments, so that the concern expressed in that regard in other contexts[538] would

---

[533]   See eg *Ord v Ord* [1923] 2 KB 432, 439, 443; *Ling v Commonwealth* (1996) 68 FCR 180, 182.

[534]   See above.

[535]   *Johnson v Gore Wood & Co* [2002] 2 AC 1, 31.

[536]   *Green v Law* (1805) 2 Smith KB 668; *Jenner v Morris* (1861) 3 De G F & J 45, 53–54, 45 ER 795, 798, *per* Lord Campbell; *Davis v Hedges* (1871) LR 6 QB 687, 690; *Bank of Ireland v Martin* [1937] IR 189, 206. See also *Laing v Chatham* (1808) 1 Camp 252, 170 ER 947 and *Baskerville v Brown* (1761) 2 Burr 1229, 97 ER 804. In *Coca-Cola Financial Corp v Finsat International Ltd* [1998] QB 43, 52 Neill LJ (with whose judgment Morritt and Hutchison LJJ agreed) noted that, under the Statutes of Set-off, there was no obligation for a solvent debtor to exercise his right of set-off. Thus, in *Port of Melbourne Authority v Anshun* (1981) 147 CLR 589 it was not sufficient that the indemnity gave rise to a defence. Rather, the High Court emphasized (at 604) the additional elements that the indemnity was closely connected with the subject-matter of the first action, and that, if it could be the subject of separate proceedings, it would give rise to a conflicting judgment. Compare Hobhouse LJ in *Escudier v Lloyd's Bank plc* [1996] EWCA Civ 1131 at para 3, who left open the question of the application of the *Henderson v Henderson* estoppel in the case of legal set-off.

[537]   This was contemplated in *Green v Law* (1805) 2 Smith KB 668.

[538]   *Caird v Moss* (1886) 33 Ch D 22, 35–36; *Re Konigsberg* [1949] Ch 348, 360–361; *Port of Melbourne Authority v Anshun Pty Ltd* (1981) 147 CLR 589, 596, 603–604; *Republic of India v India Steamship Co Ltd (The Indian Grace)* [1992] 1 Lloyd's Rep 124, 133 (Leggatt LJ, referred to in subsequent proceedings [1996] 2 Lloyd's Rep 12, 24). Thus, a factor that influenced the Australian High Court in *Anshun* to apply *Henderson v Henderson* was that the indemnity which the Authority sought to litigate in the later action would have impugned Anshun's entitlement to contribution that was the subject of the order in the first action. Accordingly, there could have been contradictory judgments if the second action proceeded. See the discussion at 596 and 603–604. Further, while the Authority claimed contribution on one basis in the first action, in the second action it was seeking indemnity from the same person on a different basis. See *Triantafillidis v National Australia Bank* (1995) V ConvR 54–536 at p 66,371.

not apply. A set-off under the Statutes does not occur until judgment for a set-off. Prior to judgment the debts retain their separate identities.[539] Therefore, the fact that a defendant may obtain judgment in a later proceeding on a debt owing to him by the claimant in an earlier action would not contradict the judgment that the claimant earlier had obtained on a debt owing to him by the defendant. There may be contradictory judgments if the judgment in the first action determined that there was no set-off,[540] or if it was for the taking of an account which in its terms would have extended to the debt sought to be agitated in the second action,[541] but in the ordinary case, where the judgment in the first action related simply to payment of a debt, and this is also the effect of the judgment sought in the second action in relation to an unrelated cross-debt, there would not be any element of contradiction. Nor, if the debt to the defendant had been pleaded in the original action, would it have obviated the necessity to inquire into and establish the claimant's claim.[542]

Common law abatement

At common law, a defendant being sued for the price of goods sold with a warranty, or of work to be performed according to a contract, can plead in that action by way of defence circumstances which constitute a breach of the warranty or of the contract, and which show a diminution in the value of the subject-matter of the contract.[543] This is not in the way of pleading a cross-claim as a set-off. Rather, the defendant is permitted to defend himself by showing how much less the subject of the contract was worth by reason of the breach, and to obtain an abatement of the price accordingly.[544]   **5.127**

There is long-standing authority for the view that the purchaser need not rely on the circumstances giving rise to the breach as a defence to an action for the price, but that those circumstances instead can form the basis of a later action. Indeed, in the case of a sale of goods this is reflected in section 53 of the Sale of Goods Act   **5.128**

---

[539] See para 2.33 above.

[540] *Johnson v Durant* (1831) 2 B & Ad 925, 109 ER 1386. If the first action resulted in a judgment for a set-off, a later action obviously could not be brought on the cross-claim. See *Hennell v Fairlamb* (1800) 3 Esp 104, 170 ER 554. Lord Kenyon held in *Hennell v Fairlamb* that, to the extent that the cross-claim exceeded the amount of the plaintiff's claim in the first action, and therefore of the set-off, the surplus could be sued for separately. However, that was before the Judicature Acts introduced a right of counterclaim. It is likely that *Henderson v Henderson* would now preclude a second action where the surplus was not the subject of a counterclaim in the first action.

[541] See *Henderson v Henderson* (1843) 3 Hare 100, 67 ER 313 (explained in Handley, 'Anshun Today' (1997) 71 Australian Law Journal 934, 936–7, and Spencer Bower, Turner and Handley, *The Doctrine of Res Judicata* (3rd edn, 1996) 444, 452), and *Public Trustee v Kenward* [1967] 1 WLR 1062.

[542] Compare *Port of Melbourne Authority v Anshun Pty Ltd* (1981) 147 CLR 589, 604.

[543] See paras 2.87–2.97 above.

[544] *Mondel v Steel* (1841) 8 M & W 858, 871–872, 151 ER 1288, 1293–1294.

1979. The principle was established in *Davis v Hedges*,[545] a decision of the Court of Queen's Bench handed down some twenty-eight years after *Henderson v Henderson*, though without reference to that case. In issue was a claim for damages for the improper performance of work agreed to be done by the defendant for the plaintiff. The defendant argued that he had previously sued for the price and had recovered the whole amount, and that, not having complained of the defective performance on that occasion, the plaintiff was precluded from bringing this action. The defence was rejected, Hannen and Blackburn JJ declining to follow an opinion earlier expressed by Lord Ellenborough in *Fisher v Samuda*,[546] that the defence should be made out in the original action.

5.129 In *Davis v Hedges* the action for the price was settled without having proceeded to judgment, whereas Wigram VC in his statement of the principle in *Henderson v Henderson* referred to the earlier action as having been the subject of an adjudication by a court of competent jurisdiction.[547] It is now accepted, however, that the fact that the first action was settled prior to judgment does not preclude the application of the *Henderson v Henderson* principle,[548] and in any event that aspect of *Davis v Hedges* has not been emphasized in subsequent discussions of the case. *Davis v Hedges* has been accepted as authority for a general proposition that a purchaser of goods or of work and labour is not obliged to set up as a defence a cross-claim relating to a breach of warranty or contract which diminishes the value of the subject-matter of the contract, but can pay the agreed price and bring a separate action of his own.[549] It has not been suggested that a different principle may apply when an action for the price proceeded to judgment without the defence having been pleaded. Indeed, the opposite has been stated.[550] Moreover, *Davis v Hedges* has continued to be accepted notwithstanding that the main reason given by Hannen J for not following the contrary view expressed earlier by Lord

---

[545] (1871) LR 6 QB 687, 25 LT 155.

[546] (1808) 1 Camp 190, 191, 170 ER 925.

[547] (1843) 3 Hare 100, 115, 67 ER 313, 319. See also *Dallal v Bank Mellat* [1986] 1 QB 441, 454–455, *per* Hobhouse J. This applies to res judicata generally. See *Thoday v Thoday* [1964] P 181, 197–198.

[548] *Johnson v Gore Wood & Co* [2002] 2 AC 1, 32–33. Compare *Hoppe v Titman* [1996] 1 WLR 841 (referring to *A Martin French v Kingswood Hill Ltd* [1961] 1 QB 96) and *Rigge v Burbidge* (1846) 15 M & W 598, 153 ER 988.

[549] *Caird v Moss* (1886) 33 Ch D 22, 34, *per* Cotton LJ, 35, *per* Lindley LJ; *Healing (Sales) Pty Ltd v Inglis Electrix Pty Ltd* (1968) 121 CLR 584, 593, 601, 615; *Henriksens Rederi A/S v THZ Rolimpex (The Brede)* [1974] 1 QB 233, 248; *Langford Concrete Pty Ltd v Finlay* [1978] 1 NSWLR 14, 18; *Port of Melbourne Authority v Anshun Pty Ltd* (1981) 147 CLR 589, 600; *Bellowes Archital Ltd v Bell Projects Ltd* (1997) 87 BLR 31, 35; Spencer Bower, Turner and Handley, *The Doctrine of Res Judicata* (3rd edn, 1996) 97 para 192, 264 para 452; *Benjamin's Sale of Goods* (5th edn, 1997) 932 para 17–047.

[550] See Lindley LJ in *Caird v Moss* (1886) 33 Ch D 22, 35 (who seems to have assumed that the plaintiff in *Davis v Hedges* had obtained a judgment in the first action); Spencer Bower, Turner and Handley, *The Doctrine of Res Judicata* (3rd edn, 1996) 97 para 192, 264 para 452; *Benjamin's Sale of Goods* (5th edn, 1997) 932, para 17-047.

Ellenborough in *Fisher v Samuda*[551] has ceased to be relevant after the Judicature Acts.[552] Hannen J said[553] that the effect of Lord Ellenborough's opinion would be that part of the damages recoverable by the buyer of goods or of work and labour, to the extent that they represented a depreciation in the value of the subject matter of the contract, could be pleaded as a defence to an action for the price, but that other consequential damages recoverable by the buyer could not,[554] thereby complicating and increasing litigation. Since the Judicature Acts, however, it has been possible to include a claim for consequential damages by way of a counter-claim in the plaintiff's action, and in any event a claim for consequential damages could be the subject of a separate defence of equitable set-off in the action.

Equitable set-off

Alternatively, the question may concern the availability of an equitable set-off, **5.130** in circumstances where a debtor suffered judgment on the debt and later seeks to enforce an unliquidated damages claim against the creditor which could have provided a defence in equity to the action on the debt if it had been so asserted. Equitable set-off differs from set-off under the Statutes in that the cross-demands generally must be connected. The traditional formulation is that the defendant's cross-demand must be sufficiently closely connected with the plaintiff's claim such that the plaintiff's title to sue is impeached.[555]

When it is sought to litigate in a later action a cross-claim that would have given **5.131** rise to a defence of equitable set-off if pleaded in an earlier action to enforce a debt, a judgment on the cross-claim in the later action would not contradict the earlier judgment for payment of the debt.[556] Equitable set-off, unlike set-off under the Statutes of Set-off, admittedly is regarded as a substantive defence. But this does not mean that it takes effect as an automatic extinction of the cross-demands to the extent of the set-off. If that were the case, judgment in a later action on the cross-claim would contradict the earlier judgment. Rather, the substantive nature of the defence means that, prior to judgment for a set-off, the unpaid creditor's conscience is affected in equity such that he is not entitled to treat the debtor as being in default to the extent of the cross-demand, notwithstanding that the cross-demands still exist at common law.[557] If the question of unconscionability in

---

[551] (1808) 1 Camp 190, 191, 170 ER 925. See above.

[552] See *Port of Melbourne Authority v Anshun Pty Ltd* (1981) 147 CLR 589, 601.

[553] (1871) LR 6 QB 687, 691.

[554] The defence of abatement only applies to the extent that the value of the goods or the work and labour the subject of the contract has been reduced as a result of the breach of warranty or con-tract. Other claims for consequential damage are not within the principle. See para 2.90 above.

[555] See para 4.02 above.

[556] *Aliter* if the present claimant earlier had failed to establish the claim when he unsuccessfully asserted it as an equitable set-off in a summary judgment application brought against him by the present defendant. See *Escudier v Lloyd's Bank plc* [1996] EWCA Civ 1131.

[557] See para 4.30 above.

equity has not been raised, the simple fact of separate judgments on the common law claims should not show any inconsistency.[558]

5.132 The question remains whether it would be an abuse of process for the purpose of the *Henderson v Henderson* principle to bring a separate action on the cross-claim, rather than raising it as a defence in earlier proceedings. In *Escudier v Lloyd's Bank plc*[559] Hobhouse LJ, with whom Peter Gibson LJ agreed, accepted that a defendant who is sued in debt is not under any obligation to raise an equitable set-off,[560] and Simon Brown LJ expressed a similar opinion in relation to the circumstances in issue in that case.[561] Views to a similar effect have been expressed on other occasions.[562] Indeed, the contrary view would sit uncomfortably with the position that the courts to date have accepted in relation to the common law defence of abatement,[563] and it would be difficult to offer a rational explanation for treating the common law and the equitable defences differently.

5.133 The position in Australia is more complex. There is authority in that country which suggests that the *Henderson v Henderson* principle may apply in the case of closely connected cross-claims, on the basis of the principle as formulated by the High Court in *Port of Melbourne Authority v Anshun*,[564] and there is also support for that view in Canada.[565]

5.134 In the *Anshun* case[566] Gibbs CJ, Mason and Aickin JJ warned that: 'To require that the defendant always raise his cross-claim or set-off at the first available time could cause great inconvenience.' Subsequently, in *Tanning Research Laboratories Inc v O'Brien*,[567] Brennan and Dawson JJ said that a plaintiff could not be precluded

---

[558] See *Murphy v Abi-Saab* (1995) 37 NSWLR 280, 290–291. In *Triantafillidis v National Australia Bank* (1995) V ConvR 54–536 at p 66,370, the later damages claim against the mortgagee for negligence, fraud and misleading or deceptive conduct in relation to the mortgage transaction was not regarded as inconsistent with the earlier judgment for possession in favour of the mortgagee, where the judgment for possession was founded upon default in the mortgage payments. There may however be cases where the circumstances would show conflicting judgments. An example mentioned by Handley JA is where the first judgment in favour of the creditor involved the taking of an account, for example for the balance due under the mortgage. The account would be regarded as covering all debit and credit items that could have been brought forward, and a subsequent action on a cross-claim that would have been admissible as an item in that account accordingly would be inconsistent with the earlier judgment. See Handley, 'Anshun Today' (1997) 71 Australian Law Journal 934, 937–8, and also his discussion of *Yat Tung* in Spencer Bower, Turner and Handley, *The Doctrine of Res Judicata* (3rd edn, 1996) 446–7.
[559] [1996] EWCA Civ 1131.
[560] [1996] EWCA Civ 1131 at para 3.
[561] [1996] EWCA Civ 1131 at para 56.
[562] *Mullen v Conoco Ltd* [1998] QB 382, 397; *Specialist Group International Ltd v Deakin* [2001] EWCA Civ 777 at paras 14–15 and 25. Compare *Ron Jones (Burton-on-Trent) Ltd v Hall* [1998] EWHC Technology 328 (arbitration).
[563] See paras 5.127–5.129 above.
[564] See para 5.123 above.
[565] *420093 BC Ltd v Bank of Montreal* (1995) 128 DLR (4th) 488, Alberta CA.
[566] (1981) 147 CLR 589, 600.
[567] (1990) 169 CLR 332, 346.

from taking proceedings in respect of a cause of action merely because he could have counterclaimed on that cause of action in an earlier proceeding in which the opposite party sued him, except in a case where the relief claimed in the second proceeding is inconsistent with the judgment in the first. That view was qualified however by the Full Court of the Federal Court in *Bryant v Commonwealth Bank of Australia*,[568] their Honours suggesting that, in making that comment in *Tanning Research Laboratories v O'Brien*, Brennan and Dawson JJ may have had in mind a situation, such as that before them in that case, where the cross-claim depended on facts remote from those in the principal claim. In that circumstance, there is no policy justification for forcing a defendant to litigate his own claim as a cross-claim rather than as a principal claim in a separate action. But where a defendant's cross-claim is intimately connected with the plaintiff's claim, in the sense that each arises substantially out of the same matters of fact, the Full Court in the *Bryant* case considered that the claims should be litigated at the one time,[569] so as to minimize costs and avoid the possibility of inconsistent judgments.[570]

Subsequently Wilcox J, who was one of the judges in the *Bryant v Commonwealth Bank* case, offered a refinement on the views expressed in that case. He pointed out in *Ling v Commonwealth*[571] that some cross-claims overlap the facts of the principal claim but also involve additional facts. In such a case, a question of degree arises. He emphasized that it would be wrong to say that the principle in *Henderson v Henderson* is excluded where there are additional facts. But where the additional facts are substantial, he suggested that it may be appropriate to accept the reasonableness of separate proceedings. **5.135**

---

[568] (1995) 57 FCR 287, 297–298, *per* Beaumont, Wilcox and Moore JJ. Compare also *Yat Tung Investment Co Ltd v Dao Heng Bank Ltd* [1975] AC 581, 589 in relation to the possibility of a counterclaim (though note the explanation for the case offered by Handley, 'Anshun Today' (1997) 71 Australian Law Journal 934, 937), and also compare Buckley J's qualified comment in *Public Trustee v Kenward* [1967] 1 WLR 1062, 1067 in relation to a 'counterclaim . . . relating to some quite different cause of action . . .').

[569] In Australia, see also *Ling v Commonwealth* (1996) 68 FCR 180 (though in the circumstances of that case it was held that it was not unreasonable to commence separate proceedings), *McFarlane v Eastern Pastoral Co Pty Ltd* (Vic SC, Beach J, 10 Nov 1998), and *Ryan v Hanson* (2000) 49 NSWLR 184, 194–195. In the New South Wales Court of Appeal in *O'Brien v Tanning Research Laboratories Inc* (1988) 14 NSWLR 601, 613, Kirby P referred to 'a cross or counter-claim which was so relevant to the subject matter of the litigation that it would have been unreasonable not to plead it'.

[570] In the *Bryant* case, the Commonwealth Bank had obtained judgment against the appellant on a claim for payment of an amount owing under guarantees and for possession of premises mortgaged to the bank, and the appellant sought in the present action to sue the bank on representations alleged to have been made by the bank and upon which he relied in executing the guarantees, as well as for breaches of various duties by the bank in relation to the obtaining of the guarantees and the mortgages. Since the matters sought to be raised by the appellant in the claim against the bank were all matters connected with the claims formerly prosecuted by the bank against the appellant, the principle in *Henderson v Henderson* was held to apply.

[571] (1996) 68 FCR 180, 183.

5.136 In relation to the common law defence of abatement, Hannen J in *Davis v Hedges*[572] noted that the extent to which the breach of warranty or contract may afford a defence may be uncertain at the date that the plaintiff issues a writ for payment of the price, and it may take some time to ascertain to what amount the value of the subject-matter of the contract is diminished by the plaintiff's default. This is a valid consideration[573] which may apply equally to equitable set-off. It may provide a justification in Australia for not pleading a damages cross-claim by way of a defence of set-off in the original action.

Default judgments

5.137 The Privy Council in *Kok Hoong v Leong Cheong Kwen Mines Ltd*[574] said that 'it would be wrong to apply the full vigour' of the principle in *Henderson v Henderson* where the judgment was a default judgment, so that it was not contested. Rather, it is said that a default judgment gives rise to an estoppel only for what must 'necessarily and with complete precision' have been determined by the judgment.[575] Ordinarily this should not preclude an action on a cross-claim which is not inconsistent with the earlier judgment.[576]

Dismissal of counterclaim for want of prosecution

5.138 The dismissal of a defendant's counterclaim for want of prosecution does not preclude the defendant from employing it defensively as a set-off against the claimant's claim. The dismissal nevertheless would affect the defendant if the cross-claim exceeds the claimant's claim, since the defendant would not be able to recover the excess by way of a counterclaim.[577]

K. Criticisms of the State of the Law of Set-off

5.139 Before insolvency, a set-off may occur at law under the Statutes of Set-off when there are mutual liquidated debts, even if they are unconnected, and a set-off may occur in equity in relation to claims which are sufficiently connected, even if they are unliquidated, but there may not be a set-off of claims if one or both is unliquidated and they are unconnected. This has been described as unsatisfactory and

---

[572] (1871) LR 6 QB 687, 690–691.

[573] See *Port of Melbourne Authority v Anshun Pty Ltd* (1981) 147 CLR 589, 600–601.

[574] [1964] AC 993, 1011. See also *Arnold v National Westminster Bank plc* [1991] 2 AC 93, 107.

[575] *Kok Hoong v Leong Cheong Kwen Mines Ltd* [1964] AC 993, 1012, referring to Lord Maugham in *New Brunswick Railway Co v British and French Trust Corp Ltd* [1939] AC 1, 21; *Carl Zeiss Stiftung v Rayner & Keeler Ltd* [1967] AC 853, 946 (Lord Upjohn); *Mullen v Conoco Ltd* [1998] QB 382, 389. Compare *Triantafillidis v National Australia Bank* (1995) V ConvR 54–536 at p 66,371.

[576] See *Mullen v Conoco Ltd* [1998] QB 382.

[577] *Owen v Pugh* [1995] 3 All ER 345, 351–352.

lacking logic and sense.[578] Yet, on other occasions the courts have commented adversely on suggestions that it should be possible for a cross-claim for libel to be set off against an action for goods sold and delivered,[579] or that, if A sues B for damages for breaking his leg, B should be able to set up as a defence a claim against A as the acceptor of a bill of exchange.[580] Is it then really the case that the law of set-off is in an unsatisfactory state?

Consider set-off under the Statutes of Set-off. For this form of set-off both demands must be for liquidated amounts.[581] In that situation the net position should have been apparent to the claimant, and he therefore should have taken it into account in considering whether to sue.[582] It would be difficult in that circumstance to question the availability of a defence. The same cannot always be said when one or both of the claims is unliquidated, but when the defendant's unliquidated cross-claim is closely connected with the plaintiff's claim, so that, in the language of Lord Cottenham in *Rawson v Samuel*,[583] the plaintiff's title to sue is impeached, the justice of a set-off is also apparent. The outstanding question is whether the defence should be extended to include an unconnected damages claim. In considering this question, it should be appreciated that an expansion in the scope of the defence could have important consequences. **5.140**

In the first place it could adversely affect the rights and interests of third parties. For example, an assignee of a debt takes subject to any defences, including rights of set-off, available to the debtor against the assignor before the debtor had notice of the assignment.[584] An expansion in the scope of the defence of set-off accordingly may reduce the value of the assigned debt in the hands of the assignee, even though the assignee may have provided full consideration for the assignment, and **5.141**

---

[578] *Axel Johnson Petroleum AB v MG Mineral Group AG* [1992] 1 WLR 270, 274, *per* Leggatt LJ, 275–276, *per* Staughton LJ. See also *B Hargreaves Ltd v Action 2000 Ltd* [1993] BCLC 1111, 1116, *per* Nolan LJ.

[579] *Stooke v Taylor* (1880) 5 QBD 569, 591–592, *per* Manisty J.

[580] *Pellas v Neptune Marine Insurance Co* (1879) 5 CPD 34, 41, *per* Bramwell LJ, with whom Brett and Cotton LJJ agreed, referred to in *McDonnell & East Ltd v McGregor* (1936) 56 CLR 50, 59, *per* Dixon J.

[581] See para 2.14 above.

[582] *Stooke v Taylor* (1880) 5 QBD 569, 576, 586; *Hanak v Green* [1958] 2 QB 9, 23; *BICC plc v Burndy Corp* [1985] 1 Ch 232, 248, 249.

[583] (1841) Cr & Ph 161.

[584] See ch 17 below. In Australia it has been suggested that an assignee of a debt may take subject to an unliquidated cross-demand available to the debtor against the assignor, notwithstanding that it would not have given rise to a defence as between those parties, if it arose out of the same contract as the assigned debt. See para 17.05 below. The point is that it is not sufficient for an equitable set-off that the cross-demands arose out of the same contract. See para 4.55 above. The proposition inherent in the Australian view, that an assignee could take subject to a cross-demand that is not available as a set-off against an assignor, was rejected by the House of Lords in *Bank of Boston Connecticut v European Grain and Shipping Ltd* [1989] 1 AC 1056, 1105–1106, 1109–1111, and it seems incorrect.

may not have been aware at the time of the assignment of the existence of an un-related damages claim available to the debtor against the assignor.

5.142 Third parties in other contexts could be affected. Thus a secured creditor may have a fixed charge over a debt owing to the chargor but the chargor itself is liable to the debtor.[585] The creditor would take subject to a defence of set-off available to the debtor against the chargor before the debtor had notice of the security, but under the law as it now stands the creditor would not be bound by an unrelated damages cross-claim that would not constitute a defence as between the chargor and the debtor. The issue could also arise in the context of subrogation,[586] for ex-ample in the case of a subrogated insurer, where the insurer is subrogated to its in-sured's claim against a third party, but the third party has a cross-claim against the insured. A subrogated insurer takes subject to defences available to the third party against the insured,[587] which should include defences of set-off. Similarly, the issue is relevant to a judgment creditor who is seeking to attach a debt owing by a third party to the judgment debtor by way of a garnishee order. The judgment creditor would take subject to any defence of set-off available to the third party against the judgment debtor before service of the order nisi.[588] An analogous principle applies when an undisclosed principal sues for payment of a debt arising on a contract en-tered into by the agent. The principal may be met by a defence of set-off that arose before the debtor had notice of the agency.[589]

5.143 Set-off also affects cash flow,[590] and an extension in the ambit of the defence could adversely affect a business which is sensitive to cash flow, such as in the construc-tion industry. Indeed, the Privy Council recently referred to cash flow as 'the life blood of business',[591] and in a shipping case Robert Goff J described it as 'a matter of considerable, sometimes crucial, importance'.[592] The problem is that, if a debtor being sued for a debt has an arguable defence, the creditor ordinarily

---

[585] See paras 17.73–17.87 below.

[586] See paras 17.119–17.122 below.

[587] *Sydney Turf Club v Crowley* [1971] 1 NSWLR 724, 734, *per* Mason JA ('When an insurer is subrogated to the rights of the insured against a third party . . . [the action] is brought in the name of the insured and it is subject to all the defences which would be available if the action had been brought by the insured for his own benefit'), and see Derham, *Subrogation in Insurance Law* (1985) 122–3.

[588] See *Bishop v Woinarski* (1875) 1 VLR (L) 31; *Tapp v Jones* (1875) LR 10 QB 591, 593. See generally paras 17.104–17.112 below.

[589] See eg *Turner v Thomas* (1871) LR 6 CP 610, 613, *per* Willes J ('Where the factor sells in his own name to a third party who buys without notice that he is dealing with an agent, the latter . . . may set up against the concealed principal any defence which he may have against the factor'), and generally paras 13.71–13.91 below.

[590] *Stein v Blake* [1996] AC 243, 251.

[591] *Agnew v Commissioner of Inland Revenue* [2001] 2 AC 710, 712 para 7.

[592] *SL Sethia Liners Ltd v Naviagro Maritime Corporation (The Kostas Melas)* [1981] 1 Lloyd's Rep 18, 26. See also *Modern Engineering (Bristol) Ltd v Gilbert-Ash (Northern) Ltd* (1973) 71 LGR 162, 167, CA in relation to the construction industry.

would not be able to obtain prompt payment through the summary judgment procedure.[593]

Consider, for example, that a sub-contractor has completed a job, and it is not **5.144** disputed that the work was completed in accordance with the contract, so that the sub-contractor is otherwise entitled to payment by the contractor. However, the contractor alleges that the sub-contractor was negligent in relation to another project that is not connected with the present claim for payment, or the contractor asserts some other damages claim against the sub-contractor that is unrelated to the sub-contractor's claim, for example for defamation. If the defence of set-off were expanded to include unconnected damages cross-claims, and the contractor has a real prospect of succeeding on the cross-claim,[594] the availability of the defence ordinarily would preclude the sub-contractor from being able to obtain summary judgment for payment of the otherwise admitted debt.[595] The sub-contractor could be kept out of its money, with the result that it may not be able to pay suppliers, or pay wages, or service bank loans, until the determination of what may be a protracted and an uncertain action for damages. But, in the interim, suppliers could deny the sub-contractor credit or employees could leave because they have not been paid, or the sub-contractor could default under its bank facilities, which in turn could result in the failure of the business.

Indeed, a claimant could be denied summary judgment even though it has insur- **5.145** ance covering it for liability on an unrelated damages cross-claim asserted against it. The defendant could sit back until the determination of the damages cross-claim, and use it in order to resist the claimant's demand for payment, even though the defendant is assured of payment in any event because of insurance, and notwithstanding that the claimant requires cash flow to support its business.

This discussion is subject to three qualifications. **5.146**

The first is that, if a cross-claim does not amount to a defence, the court in giving **5.147** summary judgment on the claim has a discretion to order a stay on enforcement pending trial of the counterclaim.[596] An order to that effect would still deny the claimant cash flow from the judgment. However in a particular case the court may regard a stay as inappropriate. Under former rules of court, the question whether enforcement of a judgment should be stayed depended on such factors as whether the counterclaim arose out of a separate and distinct transaction or whether there

---

[593] CPR Part 24.

[594] Under CPR r 24.2(a)(ii) the court may give summary judgment against a defendant if it considers that the defendant has no real prospect of successfully defending the claim.

[595] Andrews, 'The Proper Limits of Set-off' [1992] Cambridge Law Journal 239. This should also apply under the new Civil Procedure Rules 1998. See para 1.05 above.

[596] See CPR rr 3.1(3) and 24.6, and para 5.1 of the Practice Direction supplementing CPR Part 24. See generally *Civil Procedure* (Autumn 2001) vol 1, paras 24.2.6 and 24.6.3.

was a connection between the claims, the strength of the counterclaim and the ability of the plaintiff to satisfy any judgment on the counterclaim.[597] The court could also take into account the needs of the parties for cash.[598] In *A B Contractors Ltd v Flaherty Brothers Ltd*[599] a sub-contractor obtained judgment for payment of an amount owing for work completed at one site, and the contractor sought a stay of execution pending trial of a counterclaim for damages arising out of a separate and distinct contract at a different site. The Court of Appeal[600] held that the circumstances did not justify a stay. Cumming-Bruce LJ delivered the leading judgment. He posed the question in terms whether it was 'fair and reasonable to keep the plaintiffs out of their money on a judgment which they have obtained . . .'.[601] In the circumstances, where there was no connection between the contracts, he said that it was not just and equitable for the plaintiffs to be kept out of their money. It has been suggested that, under the new Civil Procedure Rules 1998, the courts may be prepared to grant summary judgment and a delay on enforcement more frequently than hitherto.[602] However the factors to which the courts formerly had regard should still be relevant to the determination of whether a stay should be granted.

5.148 The second qualification is that the contractor would be entitled to leave to defend if it is owed an unrelated debt, because the case would then be one of mutual debts giving rise to a defence of set-off under the Statutes of Set-off. Often however an action for payment of a debt is more straightforward than a damages claim, so that the period during which the sub-contractor is kept out of its money while the cross-debt is determined would not be as significant. Moreover, when both demands are for liquidated debts, it can be said that the existence and amount of the set-off should have been apparent to the plaintiff, who should have

---

[597] *A B Contractors Ltd v Flaherty Brothers Ltd* (1978) 16 BLR 8, CA; *Drake and Fletcher Ltd v Batchelor* (1986) 83 LS Gaz 1232, *per* Sir Neil Lawson; *State Bank of Victoria v Parry* [1989] WAR 240, 246. See also *Aectra Refining and Manufacturing Inc v Exmar NV* [1994] 1 WLR 1634, 1652, and the discussion in *The Supreme Court Practice* (1999) vol 1, para 14/4/14 pp 178–9 in relation to the former rules of court. For instances in which a stay was denied, see eg *Anglian Building Products Ltd v W & C French (Construction) Ltd* (1972) 16 BLR 1, and *Century Textiles and Industry Ltd v Tomoe Shipping Co (Singapore) Pte Ltd (The Aditya Vaibhav)* [1991] 1 Lloyd's Rep 573. Compare Dillon LJ in *Schofield v Church Army* [1986] 1 WLR 1328, 1334–1335, who said that a summary judgment 'ought to be stayed' until after the trial of a counterclaim if the counterclaim is not frivolous, and see also Croom Johnson LJ at 1337. Compare also Smith J in *L U Simon Builders Pty Ltd v H D Fowles* [1992] 2 VR 189, 196, although that was in the context of a cross-claim that was closely connected with the plaintiff's claim.

[598] *Aectra Refining and Manufacturing Inc v Exmar NV* [1994] 1 WLR 1634, 1652.

[599] (1978) 16 BLR 8. See also *Anglian Building Products Ltd v W & C French (Construction) Ltd* (1972) 16 BLR 1.

[600] Stephenson, Geoffrey Lane and Cumming-Bruce LJJ

[601] (1978) 16 BLR 8, 12. Geoffrey Lane and Stephenson LJJ agreed with Cumming-Bruce LJ's judgment.

[602] *Civil Procedure* (Autumn 2001) vol 1, para 24.2.6.

given credit for it in his action.[603] That consideration would not apply with the same force when one or both of the demands requires an assessment of damages.

The third qualification is that, if the damages claim arises from defects in the work **5.149** the subject of the sub-contractor's claim for payment, the contractor ordinarily would be entitled to an equitable set-off, or alternatively a defence under the common law principle of abatement.[604] But in that circumstance there is nothing inequitable in the contractor withholding payment pending the determination of the damages claim, since it goes to the question of the true value of the work performed for which payment is sought. It is in the situation in which an unrelated cross-claim for damages could be used to keep the sub-contractor out of its money that an extended defence could operate harshly.

Because of these considerations, it is suggested that it is undesirable to extend the **5.150** defence of set-off to encompass unrelated damages cross-claims.[605] But this does not mean that there is no scope for reform.

There have been occasions where the question whether a cross-claim gives rise to **5.151** a set-off or a counterclaim has resulted in time-consuming debate in the courts for no purpose other than for the determination of costs. A defendant generally is in a better position in relation to costs if he has a defence of set-off than in the case of a mere counterclaim. A defence ordinarily results in an order for costs in favour of the defendant, as having successfully defended the claim, whereas in the event of a successful claim and counterclaim the defendant ordinarily is entitled to a costs order in relation to the counterclaim but will have to pay the claimant's costs in relation to the claim.[606] Costs are within the court's discretion, and the circumstances of the case may warrant a different order, but this represents the prima facie position. It would seem an unproductive use of the courts time to determine whether a cross-claim gives rise to a set-off or a counterclaim simply for the purpose of deciding costs. Morris LJ's judgment in *Hanak v Green*[607] reflects this sentiment: 'So it has come about that we have heard a learned debate, rich in academic interest, but, save so far as costs are affected, barren of practical consequence, on the subject as to whether certain claims could be proudly marshalled as set-off or could only be modestly deployed as counterclaim.'

An extension in the ambit of the defence to include unconnected damages cross- **5.152** claims would remedy this perceived problem. But it could have other results that are not as easy to justify. In particular, it would affect the interests of third parties,

---

[603] See para 5.140 above.

[604] See paras 2.87–2.97 above.

[605] This was also the view of the New South Wales Law Reform Commission in its report on 'Set-off', No 94, February 2000, paras 4.10–4.13, 5.10–5.12.

[606] See para 1.06 above.

[607] [1958] 2 QB 9, 16.

for example assignees for value, and it would affect legitimate business requirements for cash flow. With that in mind, there is another way of dealing with the issue, and that is by way of the order for costs. Where a defendant in an action for payment of a debt or damages succeeds in establishing a cross-claim for payment of a debt or damages, in appropriate cases costs could be awarded as if the defendant had succeeded in defending the claim to the extent of the cross-claim, whether or not that was the case. The advantage of this approach is that it would not affect third parties, whose position would still depend on whether the cross-claim gives rise to a defence, but at the same time it would avoid arid debates as to the distinction between set-off and counterclaim where the only consequence is in relation to costs. Under the new CPR r 44.3 the principle that 'costs follow the event' is still the general rule, but the rule also emphasizes that the court can make a different order.[608]

5.153 In *Axel Johnson Petroleum AB v M G Mineral Group AG*.[609] Leggatt and Staughton LJJ also questioned the utility of the distinction in the context of the right to summary judgment. In other words, should the question whether a defendant can resist an application for summary judgment on the basis of a cross-claim depend on the technical question whether the defendant has a defence of set-off or a counterclaim? In truth, though, the case for reform in this area is not compelling. Indeed, the point was made above that the notion that any monetary cross-claim can be utilized by way of defence, and that therefore it should be sufficient to defeat an application for summary judgment on a claim for payment of an admitted debt to the extent of the cross-claim, could operate harshly where cash flow is essential for the on-going operation of a business. As mentioned above also, a defendant with a cross-claim not amounting to a defence is not without a remedy, because the court in giving judgment for the claimant on the claim can order a stay of execution pending trial of the counterclaim. Whether the court will order a stay is a matter of discretion. The degree of connection between the claim and counterclaim, the strength of the counterclaim, and the ability of the claimant to satisfy any judgment on the counterclaim are considerations that the court will take into account in the exercise of its discretion.[610] In cases where there is no set-off, Staughton LJ commented in the *Axel Johnson* case[611] that the grant of a stay pending the trial of a counterclaim 'has generally been sufficient to safeguard the defendant's cashflow when justice requires that result, and not if the defendant does not deserve indulgence'. He therefore concluded that 'perhaps, we can continue to tolerate the law as it stands'.

---

[608] See the discussion of CPR r 44.3 in *AEI Rediffusion Music Ltd v Phonographic Performance Ltd* [1999] 1 WLR 1507, 1522–1523.
[609] [1992] 1 WLR 270.
[610] See para 5.147 above.
[611] [1992] 1 WLR 270, 276.

6

SET-OFF IN BANKRUPTCY AND COMPANY LIQUIDATION

A. The Scope of the Set-off

The principal source of rights of set-off in the event of a bankruptcy is the **6.01** Insolvency Act 1986, s 323,[1] which provides that:

(1) This section applies where before the commencement of the bankruptcy there have been mutual credits, mutual debts or other mutual dealings between the bankrupt and any creditor of the bankrupt proving or claiming to prove for a bankruptcy debt.

(2) An account shall be taken of what is due from each party to the other in respect of the mutual dealings and the sums due from one party shall be set off against the sums due from the other.

---

[1] The corresponding provision in Australia is the Bankruptcy Act 1966 (Cth), s 86.

(3) Sums due from the bankrupt to another party shall not be included in the account taken under subsection (2) if that other party had notice at the time they became due that a bankruptcy petition relating to the bankrupt was pending.

(4) Only the balance (if any) of the account taken under subsection (2) is provable as a bankruptcy debt or, as the case may be, to be paid to the trustee as part of the bankrupt's estate.

6.02 For company liquidation, there is a similar provision in the Insolvency Rules 1986, r 4.90.[2] Set-off in bankruptcy and company liquidation is referred to collectively in this book as insolvency set-off.

6.03 The existence of a right of set-off may be crucial in circumstances where a bankrupt and a creditor have had prior mutual dealings giving rise to cross-demands. In the absence of a set-off, the creditor would be obliged to pay the full amount of his debt to the trustee in bankruptcy, and would be confined to proving with the other creditors for the amount for which the bankrupt is indebted to him. If on the other hand the requirements of the set-off section (or, as it is sometimes called, the mutual credit provision) are satisfied, only the balance remaining after deducting one claim from the other is payable. Therefore, if the bankrupt's claim against the creditor exceeds the creditor's claim against the bankrupt, the creditor in effect obtains payment in full for his claim in the form of a deduction from his liability, and he is only required to pay the balance to the trustee. Alternatively, if the creditor's claim is the greater, he receives payment in full to the extent of his liability to the bankrupt, and he need only prove for the balance.

6.04 Notwithstanding the reference in subsection (1) to a 'creditor of the bankrupt proving or claiming to prove for a bankruptcy debt', it is not necessary that the creditor should have lodged, or attempted to lodge, a proof in the bankruptcy as a prerequisite to invoking the section. In *Stein v Blake*[3] the House of Lords held that the insolvency set-off section takes effect automatically upon the occurrence of the bankruptcy.[4] Therefore to the extent of the set-off there is nothing that can be proved. Lord Hoffmann in delivering the judgment of the Law Lords said that the words in subsection (1) should be construed to mean a 'creditor of the bankrupt who (apart from section 323) would have been entitled to prove for a bankruptcy debt'.[5]

---

[2] In Australia, see the Corporations Act 2001 (Cth), s 553C. For set-off in company liquidation, see para 6.06 below.

[3] [1996] AC 243.

[4] See para 6.79 *ff* below.

[5] [1996] AC 243, 253. See also *Re Bank of Credit and Commerce International SA (No 8)* [1998] AC 214, 228. In Australia, a similar meaning has been ascribed to the expression, 'a person claiming to prove a debt in the bankruptcy', in the Bankruptcy Act 1966 (Cth), s 86, and also the expression 'a person who wants to have a debt or claim admitted against the company', in the Corporations Act 2001 (Cth), s 553C. See *Gye v McIntyre* (1991) 171 CLR 609, 621; *G M & A M Pearce and Co Pty Ltd v RGM Australia Pty Ltd* [1998] 4 VR 888, 890, 899. See also *Handberg v Smarter Way (Aust) Pty Ltd* (2002) 20 ACLC 856, 868.

The mutual credit provision applies in the event of a bankruptcy or a company **6.05**
liquidation, including when an insolvent partnership is wound up in accordance
with the Insolvent Partnerships Order 1994.[6] It also applies in the winding up of
a limited liability partnership incorporated under the Limited Liability
Partnerships Act 2000.[7] It does not apply however to an individual voluntary
arrangement under Part VIII of the Insolvency Act, or to an arrangement under
the Deeds of Arrangements Act 1914,[8] unless it has been expressly incorporated
into the deed itself.[9]

B. Companies

The set-off section in company liquidation

Prior to the enactment of the Supreme Court of Judicature Act 1875, the insol- **6.06**
vency set-off section in the bankruptcy legislation did not apply to company
liquidation. There were instances of set-offs being enforced in liquidations,[10] but
the set-offs in those cases were founded upon the right of set-off conferred by the
Statutes of Set-off in the case of mutual debts,[11] as opposed to the bankruptcy section. In a number of respects, however, the courts appear to have departed from
orthodoxy in allowing a set-off. The Statutes only operated as a procedural defence to an action at law to obtain payment of a debt.[12] Prima facie they should not
have justified a set-off in the context of a proof lodged in the liquidation.[13]
Nevertheless a set-off was allowed in that context.[14] Moreover, the application of

---

[6] See para 12.05 below. In Australia, a partnership, association or other body that consists of
more than five members may be wound up under the Corporations Act 2001 (Cth) as a Part 5.7
body, in which case the set-off section (s 553C) applies. See s 583.
[7] See the Limited Liability Partnerships Regulations 2001, regs 5 & 10 (SI 2001/1090).
[8] In Australia, compare ss 231, 237 and 243 of the Bankruptcy Act 1966 (Cth) dealing with
deeds of assignment, deeds of arrangement and compositions, each of which specifically imports the
right of set-off in s 86. In relation to compositions, see *Gye v McIntyre* (1991) 171 CLR 609; *Re
Dingle, Westpac Banking Corp v Worrall* (1993) 47 FCR 478.
[9] See *Re E J Casse, ex p G H Robinson v The Trustee* [1937] 1 Ch 405; *Re Rissik* [1936] 1 Ch 68.
See also *Baker v Lloyd's Bank Ltd* [1920] 2 KB 322, although compare *Baker v Adam* (1910) 15 Com
Cas 227. Compare also the concession made by counsel in *Re Fenton, ex p Fenton Textile Association
Ltd* [1931] 1 Ch 85, 97. The set-off in *Re Fenton* may be explained on the ground that it resulted
from the liquidation of the company proving under the deed, rather than from the deed itself. See
eg Lord Hanworth MR at 105, and Romer LJ at 120, but compare Lawrence LJ at 111.
[10] See eg *Re Agra and Masterman's Bank, Anderson's Case* (1866) LR 3 Eq 337; *Smith, Fleming &
Co's Case* (1866) LR 1 Ch App 538; *Re South Blackpool Hotel Co, ex p James* (1869) LR 8 Eq 225; *Re
Progress Assurance Co, ex p Bates* (1870) 22 LT 430; *Sankey Brook Coal Co Ltd v Marsh* (1871) LR 6
Ex 185.
[11] *Brighton Arcade Co Ltd v Dowling* (1868) LR 3 CP 175, 182, 184; *Ex parte Price, Re Lankester*
(1875) LR 10 Ch App 648, 650.
[12] See para 2.33 above.
[13] *Ex parte Price* (1875) LR 10 Ch App 648, 650; *Re Daintrey* [1900] 1 QB 546, 547–548.
[14] *Re South Blackpool Hotel Co ex p James* (1869) LR 8 Eq 225. See also *Re China Steamship Co,
ex p MacKenzie* (1869) LR 7 Eq 240 (set-off against an assignee), and para 17.31 below.

the Statutes when the set-off was asserted as a defence to an action brought by the liquidator in a compulsory liquidation is not free from difficulty. The debt sought to be set off should have been recoverable by action against the company.[15] But after a winding-up order an action could not have been brought against the company without the leave of the court.[16]

6.07 The Supreme Court of Judicature Act 1875, section 10, incorporated the rules of bankruptcy 'as to debts and liabilities provable' into the law of company liquidation whenever the assets of the company were insufficient for the payment of its debts and liabilities and the costs of the winding up, and it was confirmed by the House of Lords in 1884 that the incorporation included the set-off section.[17] Formerly this set-off was considered to be applicable to any company in liquidation unless and until it was shown that the company's assets were sufficient to pay all the company's debts in full, together with costs of the winding up.[18] This is no longer the case in England, however. Rule 4.90 of the Insolvency Rules 1986, which sets out the mutual credit provision in the event of a company liquidation in terms similar to the bankruptcy section, applies in the case of every company liquidation, compulsory or voluntary, irrespective of the solvency or otherwise of the company.[19] In Australia, on the other hand, the corresponding provision, section 553C of the Corporations Act 2001 (Cth),[20] applies only to insolvent companies.[21]

Administration and company arrangements

6.08 In England, the set-off section in the insolvency legislation only applies to a company which is in liquidation. It does not apply to a company which is subject to an administration order,[21a] or to a company voluntary arrangement under Part 1 of

---

[15] See para 2.49 above.

[16] See eg the Companies Act 1862, s 87, and now the Insolvency Act 1986, s 130(2).

[17] *Mersey Steel and Iron Co v Naylor, Benzon & Co* (1884) 9 App Cas 434, 437–438. See also *Bank of Credit and Commerce International SA (No 8)* [1996] Ch 245, 256, CA.

[18] *Fryer v Ewart* [1902] AC 187, 192; *Re Pink, Elvin v Nightingale* [1927] 1 Ch 237, 241; *Re Rolls-Royce Co Ltd* [1974] 1 WLR 1584, 1590. See also *Re Fine Industrial Commodities Ltd* [1956] 1 Ch 256. It was held in *Re Canada Cycle and Motor Agency (Queensland) Ltd* [1931] St R Qd 281 (and see also *Page v Commonwealth Life Assurance Society Ltd* (1935) 36 SR (NSW) 85, 89) that this applied also to voluntary liquidation, but compare *Gerard v Worth of Paris, Ltd* [1936] 2 All ER 95 in relation to a members' voluntary winding up.

[19] This is the effect of r 4.90, combined with sub-rules 4.1(1)(c) and (4).

[20] In *Re Parker* (1997) 80 FCR 1, 7 Mansfield J said of s 553C that it 'amounts to an adoption of the concepts underlying s 86 of the Bankruptcy Act in terms more appropriate to corporations'. See also *G M & A M Pearce and Co Pty Ltd v RGM Australia Pty Ltd* [1998] 4 VR 888, 899.

[21] A company is insolvent if it is unable to pay all its debts as and when they become due and payable. See the Corporations Act 2001 (Cth), s 95A. Section 553C also applies in the winding up of a 'Part 5.7 body' under the Corporations Act 2001 (Cth). See s 583. A Part 5.7 body is defined in s 9 as including various entities such as a foreign company, and a partnership, association or other body that consists of more than five members.

[21a] *Isovel Contracts Ltd v ABB Building Technologies Ltd* [2002] 1 BCLC 390.

the Insolvency Act.[22] Rights of set-off in those circumstances are determined instead by reference to the forms of set-off available as between solvent parties.[23] This is also the case in Australia in relation to an administration under Part 5.3A of the Corporations Act 2001 (Cth).[24] On the other hand, the set-off available under the Corporations Act 2001 (Cth), s 553C in the case of a company liquidation is incorporated, by Schedule 8A, clause 8 of the Corporations Regulations, into a deed of company arrangement which is entered into pursuant to Division 10 of Part 5.3A of the Act, unless the deed provides otherwise.[25]

While an administration order remains in force in relation to a company, **6.09** s 11(3)(d) of the Insolvency Act provides that a creditor may not commence proceedings or issue execution or other legal process against the company or its property except with the consent of the administrator or the leave of the court.[26] This should not prevent a creditor from relying on a substantive defence of equitable set-off,[27] or preclude a bank from asserting a combination of accounts.[28] Nor should it prevent a creditor from exercising a contractual right of set-off. None of

---

[22] Nor does the section apply to a moratorium under the Insolvency Act 1986, s 1A.

[23] See below.

[24] *Morrison Knudsen Corp of Australia Ltd v Australian National Railways Commission* (1996) 22 ACSR 262, 266, 268.

[25] Corporations Act 2001 (Cth), s 444A(5), and the Corporations Regulations 2001, reg 5.3A.06. For the application off s 553C in the case of a deed of company arrangement, see *G M & A M Pearce and Co Pty Ltd v RGM Australia Pty Ltd* [1998] 4 VR 888; *Handberg v Smarter Way (Aust) Pty Ltd* (2002) 20 ACLC 856. See also *Winterton Constructions Pty Ltd v M A Coleman Joinery Co Pty Ltd* (1996) 20 ACSR 671; *Meehan v Stockmans Australian Café (Holdings) Pty Ltd* (1996) 22 ACSR 123. It seems to have been assumed in *Winterton Constructions* at 674–676 that set-off under the deed had a procedural operation, in that it depended upon the creditor's claim being dealt with under the deed, whereas it is now accepted that insolvency set-off operates automatically. See para 6.79 *ff* below, and *Pearce v RGM Australia*. If s 553C has been excluded from a deed, creditors who are also debtors should not have the benefit of a set-off unless rights of set-off are dealt with in other provisions of the deed, or in any event a right of set-off is available under the Statutes of Set-off or by way of equitable set-off. In the case of the Statutes of Set-off, however, the statutory moratorium on proceedings against the company by a person bound by the deed save with the leave of the court (see s 444E) should preclude a set-off as a defence to an action to enforce payment of a debt owing to the company unless leave has been obtained. See paras 2.49–2.51 above. Even when the Corporations Regulations, Sch 8A, cl 8 has been excluded, the courts have been prepared to find that s 553C applies. See *Central Data Networks Pty Ltd v Global Diagnostics Ltd* (1998) 84 FCR 304, 320–321; *Metal Manufacturers Ltd v Hall* (2002) 41 ACSR 466.

[26] See also the Insolvency Act, s 252(2) in the situation in which an interim order has been made under Part VIII in relation to an individual voluntary arrangement. Similar principles apply in Australia when a company is the subject of an administration order, and also in the case of a deed of company arrangement. See the Corporations Act 2001 (Cth), ss 440D and 440F in relation to administration and, for deeds of company arrangement, s 444E(3).

[27] For the substantive nature of equitable set-off, see paras 4.29–4.43 above.

[28] See ch 15 below. This was assumed in *Cinema Plus Ltd v ANZ Banking Group Ltd* (2000) 49 NSWLR 513, 543–544 para 116, *per* Sheller JA, 550 para 145, *per* Giles JA.

these involve the commencement of proceedings or other legal process.[29] On the other hand, section 11(3)(c) also prohibits any steps being taken to enforce a security over the company's property.[30] Whether this would extend to the exercise of a contractual right of set-off would depend on whether the agreement takes effect as a charge. This question is considered later.[31]

6.10 Different considerations apply to the procedural defence of set-off available under the Statutes of Set-off. It is a requirement of this form of set-off that the debt sought to be set off be enforceable by action,[32] and that requirement would not be satisfied in relation to a debt owing by a company the subject of an administration order unless the consent of the administrator or the leave of the court has been obtained. The debt therefore should not be able to be employed defensively in a set-off under the Statutes in the absence of consent or leave.[33]

C. The Rationale for Insolvency Set-off

6.11 The right of set-off in insolvency has received almost universal approbation in English law. Its operation has been steadily enlarged since 1705,[34] while the courts

---

[29] See generally the discussion of 'proceedings' in *Re Olympia and York Canary Wharf Ltd* [1993] BCLC 453. In Australia, the Corporations Act 2001 (Cth), s 437D applies where a person enters into, on behalf of a company under administration, a transaction or dealing affecting property of the company. The transaction is void unless the administrator or the court consented to it. However, this does not affect the exercise of a contractual right of set-off by a creditor of the company, since the creditor in exercising the right does not do so on behalf of the company. See *Cinema Plus Ltd v ANZ Banking Group Ltd* (2000) 49 NSWLR 513 and, in a different context, *Osborne Computer Corp Pty Ltd v Airroad Distribution Pty Ltd* (1995) 17 ACSR 614.

[30] See also s 10(1)(b) with respect to the period between the presentation of the petition for an administration order and the making of the order or the dismissal of the petition. In Australia there is a similar provision in the Corporations Act 2001 (Cth), s 440B, and see also s 444F(2) in relation to the situation in which it has been proposed that the company execute a deed of company arrangement or the company has executed the deed. There is however an exception in Australia in relation to security which is over all or substantially all of the company's property. See s 441A.

[31] See paras 16.78–16.91 below. In Australia, an administrator is entitled to be indemnified out of the company's property for debts for which the administrator is liable and for his or her remuneration, and as security for the right of indemnity the administrator has a lien on the company's property. See the Corporations Act 2001 (Cth), ss 443D and 443F. In *Cinema Plus Ltd v ANZ Banking Group Ltd* (2000) 49 NSWLR 513 the New South Wales Court of Appeal held that, where the company has a bank account in credit, a contractual right of set-off held by the bank is not affected by the administration, although the exercise of the right is subject to the administrator's right to be indemnified out of the account in respect of debts and remuneration incurred before the set-off is effected. See paras 16.21–16.24 below.

[32] See para 2.49 above.

[33] For the contrary view, see Wood, *English and International Set-off* (1989) 277. Compare also *Morrison Knudsen Corp of Australia Ltd v Australian National Railways Commission* (1996) 22 ACSR 262, in which Mansfield J decided the case on the basis that rights of set-off had been excluded by agreement.

[34] See paras 6.25–6.30 below.

have said that it should be supported and given the widest possible scope.[35] It is designed to ameliorate a perceived injustice, that a person should have to pay the full amount of his liability to a bankrupt and at the same time be confined to receiving a dividend for what the bankrupt owes him.[36] But it should also be borne in mind that the effect of a set-off is to prefer one creditor over the general body of creditors,[37] and that consequently it operates against the policy favouring equal treatment of creditors. That being the case, it is perhaps surprising that the rationale for the existence of the right has not been questioned to any great extent, and that Lord Mansfield's aphorism: 'Natural equity says, that cross demands should compensate each other, by deducting the less sum from the greater',[38] has been accepted almost without reservation. While admittedly it may seem harsh that a creditor of the bankrupt should only receive a dividend for what the bankrupt owes him and at the same time be required to pay the full value of what he owes to the bankrupt, other creditors similarly are disadvantaged by being confined to a rateable dividend for the debts owing to them. It is debatable whether the justice in favour of setting off cross-demands is always so great that the assets available for distribution amongst the general body of creditors should be depleted in favour of a single creditor with a set-off entitlement, with the consequent reduction in the dividend payable generally. Consider, for example, that A has accepted a bill of exchange drawn in favour of C. A also happens to be a creditor of B. If B becomes bankrupt, the result would be that A would only be entitled to a dividend for the amount owing by B, and at the same time would be liable to pay the full amount of the bill to C. Assume however that, unknown to A, C had negotiated the bill to B before the bankruptcy. There would then be a situation of mutual credit between A and B which may result in a set-off in favour of A. As far as A is concerned, however, the negotiation of the bill to B was entirely fortuitous, and yet it may still have the result of improving his overall position by effectively enabling him to obtain the full value of his claim against B to the extent of the set-off rather than just a dividend. In that circumstance, it hardly seems just that A should be favoured with a set-off at the expense of the other creditors. Parke B said in

---

[35] See *Peat v Jones & Co* (1881) 8 QBD 147, 150, *per* Cotton LJ; *Mersey Steel and Iron Co v Naylor, Benzon & Co* (1882) 9 QBD 648, 660–661; *The Eberle's Hotels and Restaurant Co Ltd v E Jonas & Brothers* (1887) 18 QBD 459, 465; *Day & Dent Constructions Pty Ltd v North Australian Properties Pty Ltd* (1982) 150 CLR 85, 108; *Gye v McIntyre* (1991) 171 CLR 609, 619. Compare Chambré J's warning in *Ouchterlony v Easterby* (1813) 4 Taunt 888, 893, 128 ER 582, 583, that 'we ought to be particularly cautious how we admit these things to be mutual credits; for it may lead, if abused, to great mischief'.

[36] *National Westminster Bank Ltd v Halesowen Presswork & Assemblies Ltd* [1972] AC 785, 813; *Day & Dent Constructions Pty Ltd v North Australian Properties Pty Ltd* (1982) 150 CLR 85, 95, 107.

[37] *Re Bank of Credit and Commerce International SA (No 8)* [1996] Ch 245, 256, CA.

[38] *Green v Farmer* (1768) 4 Burr 2214, 2220, 98 ER 154, 157. The justice or equity of set-off has been mentioned on other occasions. See for example *Ex parte Flint* (1818) 1 Swans 30, 34, 36 ER 285, 287; *Forster v Wilson* (1843) 12 M & W 191, 203–204, 152 ER 1165, 1171.

Forster v Wilson[39] that the object of the mutual credit provision is 'to do substantial justice between the parties'.[40] But as Phillips J remarked in the Supreme Court of Victoria, justice must extend also to the unsecured creditors.[41]

6.12   There is an alternative justification for the right of set-off, and that is that it enhances the provision of credit and generally acts as a stimulus to trade and commerce. If an enterprise wishes to raise cash, or does not wish to pay for goods or services immediately, but is otherwise reasonably sound, the possibility of a set-off in a bankruptcy or winding up may encourage other parties to deal with it, or to deal in negotiable securities upon which the enterprise is liable. In other words, the possibility of a set-off may be perceived as a form of security,[42] and while it is not a security in the strict sense of the word, it may give a degree of confidence to parties dealing with each other.[43] In any particular case, however, it could only be said that there may have been reliance on the security offered by a set-off if the party claiming the benefit of the set-off was aware, at the time of transacting the later of the two dealings upon which the set-off is sought to be based, of the possibility of there being cross-demands. Unless this were the case, the possibility of a set-off could hardly have influenced his decision to deal with the bankrupt, in which case it is questionable whether indeed there is any justification for preferring him over the other creditors by means of a set-off. It is difficult, then, to see why a set-off should be allowed in the situation posited above, where the bankrupt's right to sue the creditor only came into existence as a result of a transaction with a third party unknown to the creditor after the creditor had entered into the dealing upon which his own claim against the bankrupt is based. The conferral of a set-off effectively constitutes a windfall in comparison to what he would otherwise have expected to be his overall financial position.

---

[39]   (1843) 12 M & W 191, 203–204, 152 ER 1165, 1171.

[40]   This has been repeated on numerous occasions. See eg *Ex parte Cleland, re Davies* (1867) LR 2 Ch App 808, 813; *Re City Life Assurance Co Ltd, Stephenson's Case* [1926] 1 Ch 191, 216; *Re D H Curtis (Builders) Ltd* [1978] 1 Ch 162, 173; *Re Cushla Ltd* [1979] 3 All ER 415, 421; *Re Unit 2 Windows Ltd* [1985] 1 WLR 1383, 1387; *Gye v McIntyre* (1990) 171 CLR 609, 618; *Stein v Blake* [1994] Ch 16, 22, CA; *G M & A M Pearce and Co Pty Ltd v RGM Australia Pty Ltd* [1998] 4 VR 888, 900.

[41]   *Lloyds Bank NZA Ltd v National Safety Council* [1993] 2 VR 506, 513.

[42]   Thus, Vaughan Williams J in *Re Washington Diamond Mining Co* [1893] 3 Ch 95, 104 referred to 'the security, by way of set-off'. Similarly Lord Hoffmann in *Stein v Blake* [1996] AC 243, 251 commented that bankruptcy set-off enables a creditor 'to use his indebtedness to the bankrupt as a form of security'.

[43]   Indeed, in the United States Supreme Court Lamar J warned that in some situations the abolition of set-off could 'interfere with the course of business as to produce evils of serious and far reaching consequence'. See *Studley v Boylston National Bank of Boston* (1913) 229 US 523, 529.

D. The Statutes of Set-off, Equitable Set-off and Counterclaim in Bankruptcy

Counterclaim

Counterclaim, when used in contra-distinction to set-off, has no application after **6.13** the occurrence of a bankruptcy or the commencement of a liquidation.[44] A debtor of the bankrupt who has a claim against the bankrupt's estate is remitted to a proof in respect of his claim unless he has a right of set-off.

Statutes of Set-off

Similarly, the Insolvency Act 1986 and the Insolvency Rules made pursuant to it **6.14** provide the sole statutory right of set-off available as a defence to an action brought by a bankrupt's trustee or the liquidator of a company for payment of a sum owing to the bankrupt or the company.[45] The Statutes of Set-off (including where equity would otherwise act by analogy with the Statutes) would not apply in that context. This has not always been the prevailing view. In the eighteenth century, defendants in actions at law instituted by assignees in bankruptcy for the recovery of a debt commonly would base their argument for a set-off upon both the Statutes of Set-off and the bankruptcy section.[46] The Statutes of Set-off were said to apply on the ground that 'the assignees are the bankrupt'.[47] According to Professor Christian,[48] it was only after 1786, when Buller J in *Grove v Dubois*[49] confirmed that the bankruptcy section provided a defence to such an action, that pleaders began to rely solely on the bankruptcy provision. That early view as to the relevance of the Statutes would not be followed today, however. If, for example, a person against whom a bankruptcy petition was pending incurred a debt to someone who was already indebted to him, the second person would not have the benefit of a set-off under section 323 of the Insolvency Act if at the time that sums became due to him he had notice that the petition was pending.[50] Nor could he

---

[44] *Peat v Jones & Co* (1881) 8 QBD 147, 150. See also, in the context of company liquidation, *Government Security Investment Co v Dempsey* (1880) 50 LJQB 199; *Langley Constructions (Brixham) Ltd v Wells* [1969] 1 WLR 503.

[45] See *Day & Dent Constructions Pty Ltd v North Australian Properties Pty Ltd* (1981) 34 ALR 595, 599, 601 (Federal Court of Australia); *Re Daintrey* [1900] 1 QB 546, 548, 567. See also *McIntyre v Perkes* (1990) 22 FCR 260, 271, Federal Court of Australia. Compare the comments of Lord Esher MR in *Sovereign Life Assurance Co v Dodd* [1892] 2 QB 573, 577–578.

[46] See eg *Ridout v Brough* (1774) 1 Cowp 133, 98 ER 1006.

[47] *Ridout v Brough* (1774) 1 Cowp 133, 135, 98 ER 1006, 1008. See also *Freeman v Lomas* (1851) 9 Hare 109, 115, 68 ER 435, 438; *McIntyre v Perkes* (1990) 22 FCR 260, 271, Federal Court of Australia.

[48] Christian, *Bankrupt Law* (2nd edn, 1818) vol 1, 504–5.

[49] (1786) 1 TR 112, 99 ER 1002.

[50] See the Insolvency Act, s 323(3), and generally paras 6.49–6.64 below.

avoid that result by pleading a set-off under the Statutes of Set-off and arguing that the trustee in bankruptcy took subject to the equity.

6.15 This is not to suggest that that the right to set off mutual debts under the Statutes of Set-off has no application to bankruptcies and company liquidations. When it is said that an assignee of a debt takes subject to rights of set-off available to the debtor against the assignor, it is meant rights of set-off which could have provided a defence to an action brought against the debtor by a solvent assignor, including pursuant to the Statutes. If the assignor has become bankrupt or is a company in liquidation the debtor cannot have recourse to the wider right of set-off provided by the insolvency legislation.[51]

Equitable set-off

6.16 On the other hand, in principle there should not be any such restriction in relation to a substantive defence of equitable set-off.[52] Unlike insolvency set-off, mutuality is not necessary in all cases for equitable set-off.[53] If in an exceptional case an equitable set-off is available notwithstanding the absence of mutuality, the right to rely on it should not be lost on the ground that the person against whom it is asserted is bankrupt or is in liquidation.[54] The traditional ground for an equitable set-off is impeachment of title.[55] If a debtor's title to sue was impeached before bankruptcy, so should the title of the debtor's trustee in bankruptcy, given that the trustee steps into the shoes of the debtor and takes the debtor's property subject to all clogs and fetters affecting it in the hands of the debtor.[56] The same reasoning should apply in company liquidation.[57]

---

[51] See eg *Re Asphaltic Wood Pavement Co. Lee & Chapman's Case* (1885) 30 Ch D 216, 225, and para 17.28 below.

[52] Compare *Provincial Bill Posting Co v Low Moor Iron Co* [1909] 2 KB 344, in which a counterclaim, or a set-off of judgments (see paras 2.78–2.86 above), was in issue, as opposed to an equitable set-off of cross-demands.

[53] See paras 4.48–4.54 below.

[54] In addition to the cases referred to below, see *Clarkson v Smith and Goldberg* [1926] 1 DLR 509 (see para 12.39 below), and also the note to the report of *Jeffs v Wood* (1723) 2 P Wms 128, 130, 24 ER 668, 669. The proposition is also consistent with Lord Loughborough's judgment in *Ex parte Quintin* (1796) 3 Ves Jun 248, 30 ER 994. *Quintin* effectively was overruled by Lord Eldon in *Ex parte Twogood* (1805) 11 Ves Jun 517, 32 ER 1189, not on the ground that a set-off was not available in equity in circumstances going beyond the bankruptcy set-off section, but rather because of the consequences of allowing a set-off in the circumstances in issue. See para 12.20 below. Compare however *Day & Dent Constructions Pty Ltd v North Australian Properties Pty Ltd* (1981) 34 ALR 595, 636–637, Federal Court of Australia, and also *McIntyre v Perkes* (1990) 22 FCR 260, 271 wherein Gummow and von Doussa JJ left the question open.

[55] See para 4.02 above.

[56] See Jenkins LJ in *Bradley-Hole v Cusen* [1953] 1 QB 300, 306.

[57] See generally Goode, *Principles of Corporate Insolvency Law* (2nd edn, 1997) 56–7 and *Attorney-General v McMillan & Lockwood* [1991] 1 NZLR 53, 65. However Professor Goode (see at 57 and 177) regarded the pre-liquidation right of set-off as an exception to the general principle that a liquidator takes subject to equities.

In New South Wales, Young J in *Re Trivan Pty Ltd*[58] considered that the equitable **6.17** doctrine of set-off is not completely displaced by the insolvency set-off section, and that also seems to have been assumed by the New South Wales Court of Appeal in *Westmex Operations Pty Ltd v Westmex Ltd*,[59] which contemplated that there could have been a set-off in the liquidations in that case either on the basis of equitable set-off or pursuant to the insolvency section.[60] English cases also support that view. Thus, equitable set-off has been allowed in bankruptcy where fraud was involved, notwithstanding an absence of mutuality.[61] Further, in *Ex parte Hanson*[62] a set-off was permitted in a bankruptcy in circumstances where a surety had been made jointly liable with the principal debtor. Since the joint liability was no more than a form of security for the principal debtor's debt, Lord Eldon said that upon equitable considerations the principal debtor should be allowed to set off the debt in the creditor's bankruptcy against a separate debt owing to him by the creditor, even though the demands strictly were not mutual.[63]

It was also assumed in *Sovereign Life Assurance Co v Dodd*[64] that equitable set-off **6.18** could apply in company liquidation. An insured had assigned a policy of insurance back to the insurance company as security for loans made by the company. Subsequently the company went into liquidation. The company by its liquidator sued to recover the loans, whereupon the defendant sought to set off a claim that he had on the policy. The liquidator argued that, because the insured had assigned the policy back to the company, the insured could not employ the claim on the

---

[58] (1996) 134 FLR 368, 373.

[59] (1994) 12 ACLC 106.

[60] Similarly the New South Wales Court of Appeal in *Lord v Direct Acceptance Corp Ltd* (1993) 32 NSWLR 362 considered the possibility of equitable set-off as well as insolvency set-off in the liquidation of Direct Acceptance, but held that the facts in issue supported neither form of set-off. See also *Signature Resorts Pty Ltd v DHD Constructions Pty Ltd* (1995) 18 ACSR 627, 634–635. In relation to a deed of company arrangement, see *Metal Manufacturers Ltd v Hall* (2002) 41 ACSR 466. In *Re NIAA Corp Ltd (in liq)* (NSW SC, 2 December 1994) McLelland CJ in Eq questioned whether *Jack v Kipping* (1882) 9 QBD 113 was correct in so far as it held that a claim for damages for misrepresentation inducing a contract was provable in the representor's bankruptcy and therefore could be the subject of a set-off under the insolvency set-off section. See para 8.45 above. Rather, he suggested that the decision should properly be treated as illustrating the availability of equitable set-off (see paras 4.68–4.70 above). Subsequently in *Aliferis v Kyriacou* (2000) 1 VR 447, 463 para 48 Charles JA referred to McLelland CJ in Eq's comments without criticism. Those comments pre-suppose that equitable set-off may be available in bankruptcy in circumstances where the insolvency set-off section does not apply.

[61] *Vuillamy v Noble* (1817) 3 Mer 593, 36 ER 228, *per* Lord Eldon. See also *Ex parte Stephens* (1805) 11 Ves Jun 24, 27, 32 ER 996, 997, which is explained in paras 12.27–12.36 below.

[62] (1811) 18 Ves Jun 232, 34 ER 305, affirming (1806) 12 Ves Jun 346, 33 ER 131. In *Addis v Knight* (1817) 2 Mer 117, 121, 35 ER 885, 887 Sir William Grant said of *Ex parte Hanson* and *Ex parte Stephens* (1805) 11 Ves Jun 24, 32 ER 996 that they 'establish that, under certain circumstances, there may be a set-off in Equity when there can be none at Law'.

[63] Lord Eldon's later comments in *Ex parte Blagden* (1815) 19 Ves Jun 465, 467, 34 ER 589, 589–590 also suggest that set-off in equity was not thought to be limited by the statute relating to mutual credit.

[64] [1892] 2 QB 573, affirming [1892] 1 QB 405.

policy in a set-off in the liquidation.[65] However Bowen LJ in the Court of Appeal accepted that, even if the assignment otherwise would have prevented a set-off, there was in any event a set-off in equity, and Kay LJ also considered that that was probably the case.[66]

6.19   Consider also the situation in which A as a result of the expenditure of money in respect of B's land is entitled to an equitable charge or lien on the land, but A happens also to be personally indebted to B. In that circumstance, there is authority for the view that B may set off the debt owing to him against the sum secured on the land, so that the amount that B must pay in order to take the land free of the charge is the amount secured less the separate debt owing to him.[67] In *Baillie v Edwards*[68] this occurred in circumstances where A was bankrupt, even though there was a lack of mutuality. While A was indebted to B, A's claim was not against B but rather it was against the land. Indeed, Lord Lyndhurst earlier had emphasized lack of mutuality as a reason for disallowing a set-off,[69] his Lordship's decision to that effect being the subject of a successful appeal to the House of Lords in this proceeding. Further, Bethell[70] in his argument in favour of the set-off in the House of Lords acknowledged that it could not be supported on the strict legal principles of set-off in respect of mutual debts and demands, but instead described it as being in the nature of an equitable set-off.[71]

6.20   On the other hand, Bigham J said in *Re Daintrey*[72] that the law regulating the adjustment of cross-claims between a bankrupt and his creditor is to be found exclusively in the bankruptcy set-off section. Further, the Court of Appeal in *Brown v Cork*[73] accepted without demur the proposition that 'there is, in bankruptcy at any rate, no equity outside the [set-off] section'. Opinions to a similar effect have been expressed in Australia and New Zealand.[74] More recently, the Court of

---

[65] See the argument at first instance [1892] 1 QB 405, 408, and the discussion of charge-backs and mutuality in paras 16.68–16.73 below.

[66] [1892] 2 QB 573, 582, per Bowen LJ, 584–585 per Kay LJ. See also para 16.72 below.

[67] *Baillie v Edwards* (1848) 2 HLC 74, 9 ER 1020; *Unity Joint Stock Mutual Banking Association v King* (1858) 25 Beav 72, 79–80, 53 ER 563, 566. See also paras 3.04 & 4.54 above.

[68] (1848) 2 HLC 74, 9 ER 1020. I acknowledge my debt to Alan Berg's discussion of *Baillie v Edwards* in his article, 'Liquidation Set-off: The Mutuality Principle and Security over Bank Balances' [1996] LMCLQ 176, 177–178.

[69] *Baillie v Innes* (1845) 14 LJ Ch 341, 343.

[70] Presumably Richard Bethell, later Lord Westbury LC. See Berg, 'Liquidation Set-off: The Mutuality Principle and Security over Bank Balances' [1996] LMCLQ 176, 178 note 16, and also Holdsworth, *A History of English Law* (1966) vol 16, 70 *et seq*

[71] (1848) 2 HLC 74, 79, 9 ER 1020, 1022.

[72] [1900] 1 QB 546, 567.

[73] [1985] BCLC 363, 376, referring to *Re A Debtor (No 66 of 1955)* [1956] 1 WLR 1226, 1236, *per* Lord Everted MR.

[74] *Day & Dent Constructions Pty Ltd v North Australian Properties Pty Ltd* (1981) 34 ALR 595, 599, 601, 636–637, Federal Court; *Paganini v The Official Assignee* (NZ CA, CA308/98, 22 March 1999 at para 10) ('no claim for set off can be made outside the legislation').

Appeal in *Re Bank of Credit and Commerce International SA (No 8)*[75] rejected an argument that an equitable set-off was available in that case in circumstances that were outside the operation of the insolvency set-off section, and concluded that two cases[76] said to support the existence of an equitable right of set-off in bankruptcy that was wider than the statutory right in fact were not authority for that proposition.[77] However, the discussion was confined to an examination of the two cases in question, and moreover the conclusion seems correct that the circumstances in issue in *Re BCCI (No 8)* were not such as to support an equitable set-off.[78] In light of earlier authority, the views expressed in these cases should not be taken as having settled the question of the availability generally of equitable set-offs in bankruptcy and company liquidation.

E. Early Development, and the Influence of Equity

The insolvency set-off section has a long ancestry which can be traced back to the original mutual credit provision enacted in 1705 by the statute 4 & 5 Anne, c 17. But even before then accounts between merchants used to be balanced when one became bankrupt, and indeed the judgment of Flemming CJ in *Powel v Stuff and Timewell*[79] suggests that the practice had been adopted as early as 1612. The case involved an application of section 13 of the statute (1603) 1 Jac, c 15, which empowered the commissioners appointed in a bankruptcy to assign to a creditor of the bankrupt a debt owing to the bankrupt by a third party. The creditor could then

6.21

---

[75] [1996] Ch 245, 269–270, *per* Rose, Saville and Millett LJJ.

[76] *Ex parte Stephens* (1805) 11 Ves Jun 24, 32 ER 996, and *Jones v Mossop* (1844) 3 Hare 568, 67 ER 506.

[77] In relation to *Ex parte Stephens* (1805) 11 Ves Jun 24, 32 ER 996, Lord Eldon's judgment (at 27) (and see also *Ex parte Blagden* (1815) 19 Ves Jun 465, 467, 34 ER 589, 589–590) indeed suggests that he was of the view that there may be a set-off in equity where it is not available under the statute relating to mutual credit. The Court of Appeal in *Re BCCI (No 8)* [1996] Ch 245, 266, 269, on the other hand, said that *Ex parte Stephens* is 'no authority for the existence of any equitable right of set-off in bankruptcy wider than the statutory right'. However, the statement in Lord Eldon's judgment in *Ex parte Stephens* (at 27) to which the Court of Appeal referred in *BCCI (No 8)* (at 266), that 'as to mutual debt and credit, equity must make the same construction as the law . . .', should be read subject to the qualification that preceded it, that '*where the court does not find a natural equity, going beyond the statute* the construction of the law is the same in equity as at law . . .'. (emphasis added) Lord Eldon went on to comment (at 27) that: 'the contract was entered into by Miss Stephens in ignorance; and, if not, I should make the same construction . . .'. In other words, if Miss Stephens had not entered into the contract in ignorance of her right, equity would have given the 'same construction', which referred to the statute relating to mutual debt and credit. But since she had entered into the contract in ignorance of her right, equity was not bound by the construction otherwise applicable to the statute. See the explanation of *Ex parte Stephens* in paras 12.27–12.36 below.

[78] See para 6.20 above.

[79] (1612) 2 Bulst 26, 80 ER 930.

institute proceedings in his own name to recover the debt.[80] The present case concerned such an action. The Chief Justice in the course of his judgment is reported as having commented that, 'if the plaintiff had been in debt, in as great a sum as the bankrupt was indebted unto him, and yet his debt assigned, this assignment had not been good'.[81] By 1675, the right to a balanced account in bankruptcy appears to have been accepted. In that year North CJ is reported as having said that:[82]

> If there are accounts between two merchants, and one of them become bankrupt, the course is not to make the other, who perhaps upon stating the accounts is found indebted to the bankrupt, to pay the whole that originally was entrusted to him, and to put him for the recovery of what the bankrupt owes him, into the same condition with the rest of the creditors; but to make him pay that only which appears due to the bankrupt on the foot of the account; otherwise it will be for accounts betwixt them after the time of the other's becoming bankrupt, if any such were.

Similarly, in 1689 reference was made in the judgment in *Chapman v Derby*[83] to an earlier judgment of Sir Matthew Hale CJ, in which the Chief Justice commented to the effect that, where there were dealings on account, a man should not be charged with the account on the credit side and be put to come in as a creditor for the debt owing to himself, but should only answer to the bankrupt's estate for the balance of the account.

Competing explanations

There are two competing explanations as to how the right to a balanced account in bankruptcy developed before the enactment of the first mutual credit provision **6.22** in 1705.[84] The first is that it may have originated as a principle of equity. This appears to have been the view of Lord Eldon,[85] of Fletcher Moulton LJ,[86] and pos-

---

[80] It appears that the commissioners acting pursuant to this provision would sometimes assign the debts to creditors as payment of their dividends, although the usual practice was to make an assignment to one or more creditors who would then recover the debts as trustees for the creditors as a whole. See Goodinge, *The Law Against Bankrupts* (2nd edn, 1701), 147–8, and also Christian, *Bankrupt Law* (2nd edn, 1818) vol 1, 469–70, 499–500. It was not until 1706 that s 4 of the statute 5 & 6 Anne, c 22 empowered the creditors of the bankrupt to choose the assignees to whom the commissioners were required to assign all the bankrupt's estate and effects. These assignees were obliged by s 33 of (1732) 5 Geo II, c 30 to make a distribution to the creditors, and to account to the commissioners for their receipts and for their payments concerning the bankrupt's estate. A further modification occurred in 1831, when a number of official assignees were appointed from the ranks of merchants, brokers, accountants, and traders. An official assignee had to be one of the assignees of the bankrupt's estates and effects in every bankruptcy. See (1831) 1 & 2 Will IV, c 56, s 22. Eventually the office of assignee was replaced by that of trustee by the Bankruptcy Act 1869.

[81] (1612) 2 Bulst 26, 80 ER 930.

[82] *Anon* (1675) 1 Mod 215, 86 ER 837.

[83] (1689) 2 Vern 117, 23 ER 684.

[84] See also *Gye v Davies* (1995) 37 NSWLR 421, 425.

[85] *Ex parte Stephens* (1805) 11 Ves Jun 24, 27, 32 ER 996, 997. See also *Bacon's Abridgement of the Law* (7th edn, 1832) vol 1, 652; Houlden and Morawetz, *Bankruptcy Law of Canada* (1960) 160.

[86] *Lister v Hooson* [1908] 1 KB 174, 178.

sibly also of Sir George Turner.[87] Professor Christian[88] on the other hand argued that it had a statutory basis. The law of bankruptcy in force during the seventeenth century was set out primarily in an Elizabethan statute, (1570) 13 Eliz, c 7. The commissioners in bankruptcy were required by section 2 of the Act to pay 'to every of the said creditors a portion, rate and rate like, according to the quantity of his or their debts'. Christian suggested that quantity of the creditor's debt was taken to mean any balance due to him.[89] The early cases referred to above support that explanation, and it should be preferred over the view that a right of set-off in bankruptcy was developed in equity.[90]

An important point to note is that both North and Hale were common law **6.23** judges. This by itself is not conclusive, because they may have been enunciating a principle that had been adopted by the commissioners as a result of the influence of the Chancellor. However, there are two arguments which detract from that explanation. The first is the apparent lack of Chancery cases reported from this period in which a right of set-off was enforced in a bankruptcy.[91] It is true that, towards the end of the seventeenth century, equity was beginning to enforce set-offs in actions at law by restraining the plaintiff at law from proceeding with his claim unless he gave credit to the defendant for his cross-demand.[92] Those cases however were not concerned with bankruptcies, and indeed there is evidence to suggest

---

[87] See *Freeman v Lomas* (1851) 9 Hare 109, 112–113, 68 ER 435, 436–437. It is not clear however whether Sir George Turner was referring to bankruptcy set-off.

[88] See Christian, *Bankrupt Law* (2nd edn, 1818) vol 1, 499–500. Christian was the first Downing Professor of the Laws of England at Cambridge, but according to Holdsworth he was not well regarded by his contemporaries. Indeed, Holdsworth tells us that it had been said of Christian upon his death that he died in 'the full vigour of his incapacity'. See Holdsworth, *A History of English Law* (1952) vol 13, 480–1. Whether Christian deserved that harsh judgment is debatable. For example Maddock, in his *Principles and Practice of the High Court of Chancery* (3rd edn, 1837) vol 2, 786 n described Christian's *Bankrupt Law* as 'a work, profound, original and useful. No book so strikingly exhibits the fallibility of judges'. For a discussion of Christian's contribution to the law, see Hoffheimer, 'The Common Law of Edward Christian' [1994] Cambridge Law Journal 140.

[89] Therefore when the commissioners, acting pursuant to (1603) 1 Jac 1, c 15, s 13, assigned the debts owing to the bankrupt to one creditor as trustee for the creditors as a whole, the accounts between the bankrupt and his creditors would already have been balanced. See Christian, *Bankrupt Law* (2nd edn, 1818) vol 1, 499–500.

[90] See also *Gye v Davies* (1995) 37 NSWLR 421, 425.

[91] Compare *Peters v Soame* (1701) 2 Vern 428, 23 ER 874. In that case the Lord Keeper, Sir Nathan Wright, said that the assignee of a debt should take subject to a right of set-off that the debtor could have asserted in an action brought against him by the assignor, who had become bankrupt. The bankruptcy however appears to have been incidental to the main question of the effect of an assignment, which was within the exclusive jurisdiction of equity. It seems that the fact of the assignor's bankruptcy prevented the assignee from bringing an action at law against the debtor in the assignor's name (compare subsequently *Winch v Keeley* (1787) 1 TR 619, 99 ER 1284), and so the assignee had to bring this bill in equity in order to obtain payment.

[92] See para 3.01 above.

that equity was encouraged to advance its jurisdiction in this area because of the fact that such a practice already existed in bankruptcy.[93]

6.24 There is a second reason for doubting that the Chancellor may have originated the early practice of balancing accounts. This arises from an examination of the development of the Chancellor's jurisdiction in matters of bankruptcy. In particular, it brings into question the assertion made by Fletcher Moulton LJ in *Lister v Hooson*,[94] that 'the jurisdiction in bankruptcy was from the first an equitable jurisdiction'. What he meant by that statement is not clear. The jurisdiction and power of the commissioners over the person and property of the bankrupt arose by force of an Act of Parliament, and presumably his Lordship meant that the exercise of those powers was controlled and influenced by the Chancellor. In fact, this is not an accurate description of what appears to have happened. Section 2 of the statute 13 Eliz, c 7 empowered the Lord Chancellor to commission 'wise and honest discreet persons' in each case to conduct bankruptcy proceedings. This was the only power conferred on the Chancellor by the statute, and initially it seems to have represented the extent of the Chancellor's involvement in bankruptcy. Cooper explained in 1828[95] that, while the Chancellor would act to prevent unfair dealing or abuse of power by the commissioners he had appointed,[96] he did not exercise an extensive jurisdiction in matters of bankruptcy in the early years of the operation of the legislation. The common law courts from early times had reserved the right to review a finding by the commissioners that a person was bankrupt.[97] Moreover, when the Elizabethan bankruptcy legislation was first enacted, commissioners acting in bankruptcy proceedings often applied to the common law judges, rather than to the Chancellor, for advice as to how they should exercise the extensive powers conferred upon them.[98] It was only in 1676[99] that the

---

[93] In *Arnold v Richardson* (1699) 1 Eq Ca Abr 8, 21 ER 833 the Master of the Rolls, Sir John Trevor, ordered that the plaintiff in an action at law should reduce his claim to the extent that he was indebted to the defendant, commenting that if the plaintiff at law had been bankrupt, the commissioners would have allowed a discount. Indeed, it is noticeable that when the court in *Chapman v Derby* (1689) 2 Vern 117, 23 ER 684 was considering whether to sanction a set-off, it saw fit to refer to a judgment of Hale, a common law judge, for the proposition that accounts may be balanced in bankruptcy.

[94] [1908] 1 KB 174, 178.

[95] *Cooper's Parliamentary Proceedings* (1828), 242–5. Holdsworth referred extensively to this section of Cooper's book. See Holdsworth, *A History of English Law* (7th edn, 1956) vol 1, 470–3.

[96] See eg *Wood v Hayes* (1606–7) Tothill 62, 21 ER 125.

[97] See *Dr Bonham's Case* (1609) 8 Co Rep 113b, 121a, 77 ER 646, 657, in which Coke CJ said that the commissioner's decision was traversable in an action for false imprisonment. It seems from *Bacon's Abridgement of the Law* (7th edn, 1832) vol 1, 526–7 that the common law courts continued as the proper forum for determining questions relating to the construction of the bankruptcy legislation, so that if a bankruptcy was denied the Chancellor usually ordered the issue to be tried in a court of law.

[98] See *Cooper's Parliamentary Proceedings* (1828) 246, and also Yale, *Lord Nottingham's Chancery Cases* vol 1, 73 *Selden Society* (1957) cxv. Neither of those writers has cited any instances in which this happened, although four cases are mentioned in Christian, *Bankrupt Law* (2nd edn, 1818) vol

Chancellor was prepared for the first time to review a decision made by the commissioners, in that case whether a creditor ought to be admitted to proof.[100] It appears from the report of the decision that Lord Nottingham's initial reaction was not to interfere, but to 'leave it to the Course the Statute hath provided'.[101] Ultimately however he changed his mind and ordered that the creditor's debt should be admitted.[102] Thus it was only in the last quarter of the seventeenth century that it can be said that the Chancellor began to exercise any great influence over bankruptcy law,[103] and indeed it was not until Lord Hardwicke's time that the jurisdiction flourished.[104] The Chancellor does not appear to have been active in

---

2, 8–10. In *Anon* (1583) Cro Eliz 13, 78 ER 279 the Common Pleas was asked to determine whether a person who had kept his house in order to avoid arrest had committed an act of bankruptcy. In *Osborne and Bradshaw v Churchman* (1606) Cro Jac 127, 79 ER 111 the King's Bench ruled that a surety who paid the debt was a creditor of the principal debtor within the terms of the bankruptcy legislation. In the first volume of Brownlow and Goldsborough's report of cases in the Common Pleas, there is a reference at p 47 (123 ER 656) to a case decided in 1612, in which 'The Court was moved, to know whether the wife of a bankrupt can be examined by the commissioners upon the Statute of Bankrupt; and they were of the opinion she could not be examined.' Finally, the Common Pleas was asked upon motion in *Ruggles Case* (1619) Hutton 37, 123 ER 1084 to advise on the procedure to be adopted in distributing the estate of the bankrupt.

[99] See *Anon* (1676) 1 Chan Cas 275, 22 ER 798.

[100] See Yale, *Lord Nottingham's Chancery Cases* vol 1, 73 *Selden Society* (1957) cxv–cxvi. It seems that, as the influence of the Chancellor over bankruptcy law developed, this remained the most extensive part of his jurisdiction, ie deciding whether to order the commissioners to admit the proof of a debt which they had rejected, or to expunge the proof of a debt which they had admitted. See Christian, *Bankrupt Law* (2nd edn, 1818) vol 2, 11. Yale has pointed out that there were earlier instances in which decrees had been made by the Chancellor in matters concerning bankruptcy. However, the issue of bankruptcy in those cases arose as an incident to a question involving an established area of equitable jurisdiction, for example a bill for an account and for redemption of a mortgage, or a bill for discovery. See Yale, *op cit*, cxvi–cxx.

[101] (1676) 1 Chan Cas 275, 22 ER 798.

[102] There is a passage in the fourth part of Coke's *Institutes* which suggests that little recourse was had to the Chancellor in matters of bankruptcy during the earlier part of the seventeenth century. Coke commented that the commissioners 'are subject to the action of the party grieved, for he hath no other remedy'. Presumably he meant by this an action at law, while the only authority of the Chancellor mentioned was the power to grant the commission. See *Coke's Institutes* (1648) 277.

[103] See Holdsworth, *A History of English Law* (2nd edn, 1937) vol 8, 241–3. The Chancellor decided a number of issues in the next few decades, particularly in relation to the bankruptcy of partnerships, the distribution of the bankrupt's estate, and the effect of a bankruptcy upon equitable interests.

[104] See Yale, *Lord Nottingham's Chancery Cases* vol 1, 73 *Selden Society* (1957) cxv. The bankruptcy legislation of the first two decades of the eighteenth century conferred a number of discreet powers upon the Chancellor. Included amongst them was the power to remove the assignees if petitioned by creditors and to make such order as he thought just and reasonable, for example that a new assignment be made (see (1718) 5 Geo 1, c 24, s 23), while s 25 of that Act allowed the Chancellor in some cases to supersede the commission. See also the statutes (1705) 4 & 5 Anne, c 17; (1706) 5 & 6 Anne, c 22, and (1718) 5 Geo 1, c 24. However the legislation did not confer a general jurisdiction in the Chancellor over matters in bankruptcy. Lord Eldon thought that the bankruptcy legislation was framed with the general authority of the Chancellor in mind, and that, if the legislation was silent as to the means of giving effect to its provisions, the Chancellor had a general jurisdiction to act to attain the objects of the commission. See *Anon* (1808) 14 Ves Jun 449, 451, 33 ER 593 and also Henley, *A Digest of the Bankrupt Law* (3rd edn, 1832) 451–2. Professor

matters of bankruptcy when North and Hale mentioned the right to a balanced account,[105] and it is unlikely that the Chancellor was influential in its development.

F. The Development of the Set-off Section

6.25   A set-off section was first incorporated into the bankruptcy legislation in 1705.[106] Section 11 of the statute (1705) 4 & 5 Anne, c 17[107] provided:

> Where there shall appear to the commissioners or the major part of them that there hath been mutual credit given between such person or persons against whom such commission shall issue forth and any person or persons who shall be debtor or debtors to such person or persons and due proof thereof made and that the accounts are open and unbalanced that then it shall be lawful for the commissioners in the said commission named or the major part of them or the assignee or assignees of such commission to adjust the said account and to take the balance due in full discharge thereof and the person debtor to such bankrupt shall not be compelled or obliged to pay more than shall appear to be due on such balance.

This section has formed the foundation of the modern right of set-off in bankruptcy, although subsequent amendments have considerably enlarged the scope of its operation. The language of the provision was simplified in 1718,[108] while in

---

Christian expressed a different view. He argued that the Chancellor's authority in matters over which he had not been given express jurisdiction was recommendatory only, but was enforceable by means of his control over the appointment of commissioners. The power and authority of the commissioners was conferred by an Act of Parliament, and for that reason Christian said that they were not bound to obey the Chancellor. They depended upon him, however, for their appointment as commissioners, and failure to follow his directions could have resulted in the Chancellor renewing the commission under (1732) 5 Geo II, c 30, s 45 with other more compliant persons being appointed. See Christian, *Bankrupt Law* (2nd edn, 1818) vol 2, 6–24. In any event, there is probably some truth in Cooper's assertion that equity usurped jurisdiction in this area, possibly because of the immense fees and the control of patronage that went with it. See *Cooper's Parliamentary Proceedings* (1828), 251–2.

[105] North CJ made his statement in 1675, while the judgment of Lord Hale referred to in *Chapman v Derby* could not have been delivered later than 1676, when he retired as Chief Justice of the King's Bench.

[106] Contrary to Sir George Jessel MR's assertion in *Peat v Jones & Co* (1881) 8 QBD 147, 149, that the enactment as to 'mutual credits' appeared in (1732) 5 Geo II, c 30.

[107] It was not until 1797 that the mutual credit provision in the bankruptcy legislation was made permanent. Until then, it was to be found in a number of temporary statutes, the operation of each of which was continued, with occasional amendment, by a subsequent enactment. The 1705 Act was to remain in force for only three years (see s 17), although it was continued *in toto* by (1708) 7 Anne, c 25, and then by (1716) 3 Geo I, c 12.

[108] See (1718) 5 Geo 1, c 24, which was continued by (1724) II Geo I, c 29, and by (1726) 13 Geo I, c 27. The words 'assignee or assignees' were omitted from the 1718 legislation, so that apparently only the commissioners were empowered to balance the accounts. However those words were reintroduced in 1732.

1732[109] the ambit of the right was expressed in terms of mutual credit and mutual debts, rather than simply mutual credit.[110]

It was a feature of the early legislation that there could only be a set-off if the mu-   **6.26**
tual debts or mutual credit existed 'at any time such person became bankrupt',[111]
by which was meant when an act of bankruptcy was committed.[112] In 1806 however the legislation was amended so as to offer some protection in the event that the person giving credit to the bankrupt was not aware of the commission of an act of bankruptcy.[113] Subject to two qualifications, section 3 of the statute (1806) 46 Geo III, c 135 allowed one debt or demand to be set against another notwithstanding that a prior act of bankruptcy had been committed by the bankrupt before the credit was given to him or a debt was contracted by him. The qualifications were that the section only applied when the credit was given to the bankrupt at least two calendar months before the date of the commission,[114] and moreover the person claiming the set-off must not have had notice of an act of bankruptcy committed by the bankrupt at the time of giving credit or notice that he was insolvent or had stopped payment. On the other hand, the issuing of the commission was deemed to constitute notice of an act of bankruptcy.

In 1825 the various statutes which up until then had set out the law of bankruptcy   **6.27**
were repealed and replaced by a consolidating statute 6 Geo IV, c 16.[115] The new mutual credit provision was set out in section 50 of the Act, and it contained a number of amendments to the pre-existing law. In particular, there was a further liberalization of the right to a set-off in the event of credit being given to, or a debt contracted by, the bankrupt after the commission of a secret act of bankruptcy.

---

[109] See 5 Geo II, c 30, s 28.

[110] Apart from this, there were only minor differences between the language of the 1718 and the 1732 set-off sections, although the latter did bring assignees back within the scope of the right. The Act of 1732 was only to remain in force for a period of three years (see s 49), but its operation was continued by the following statutes: (1736) 9 Geo II, c 18; (1743) 16 Geo II, c 27; (1751) 24 Geo II, c 57; (1758) 31 Geo II, c 35; (1763) 4 Geo III, c 36; (1772) 12 Geo III, c 47; (1776) 16 Geo III, c 54; (1781) 21 Geo III, c 29; (1786) 26 Geo III, c 80; (1788) 28 Geo III, c 24, and by (1794) 34 Geo III, c 57. It was made perpetual in 1797 by 37 Geo III, c 124.

[111] See s 28 of (1732) 5 Geo II, c 30. This notion first appeared in the statute (1718) 5 Geo I, c 24, which required that there should have been 'mutual credit given by the bankrupt and any other person at any time before the person against whom such commission is or shall be awarded became bankrupt'.

[112] See *Bamford v Burrell* (1799) 2 Bos & Pul 1, 126 ER 1120. Acts of bankruptcy were a series of defined acts the commission of any one of which constituted a statutory recognition of insolvency. A person must have committed an act of bankruptcy before he could be made bankrupt. The concept of the act of bankruptcy has been abolished in the Insolvency Act 1986, the sole ground for bankruptcy proceedings now being inability to pay debts.

[113] See eg *Dickson v Cass* (1830) 1 B & Ad 343, 358–359, 109 ER 814, 820, *per* Parke J.

[114] The date of the commission was the date upon which it was sealed and issued by the Chancellor. See Christian, *Bankrupt Law* (2nd edn, 1818) vol 1, 457–9.

[115] In fact an earlier bankruptcy consolidation Act (5 Geo IV, c 98) had been enacted the previous year, but it was repealed by 6 Geo IV, c 16 the day after it was due to take effect.

The proviso in (1806) 46 Geo III, c 135, s 3, that the credit must have been given at least two calendar months before the date of the commission in bankruptcy, was deleted,[116] while the second proviso was amended so that only notice of a prior act of bankruptcy would invoke the principle that the right of set-off should have existed at the time of the act of the bankruptcy. Notice of the fact that the debtor was insolvent or had stopped payment was no longer sufficient. Further, the issuing of a commission in bankruptcy was no longer deemed to be notice of a prior act of bankruptcy. The legislation also provided that every debt or demand made provable by the Act could be the subject of a set-off against the bankrupt's estate. The idea that all provable debts could be the subject of a set-off was not new.[117] However, the insertion of this principle into the 1825 mutual credit provision ensured that contingent debts could be set off, since it was only as a result of section 56 of (1825) 6 Geo IV, c 16 that contingent debts became provable.

6.28 The terms of the 1825 set-off section remained essentially unaltered when the law of bankruptcy once again was consolidated in 1849,[118] the only difference being that the creation in 1831 of a separate Court of Bankruptcy with jurisdiction over all matters in bankruptcy[119] meant that the court, rather than the commissioners, was to control the balancing of the accounts.

6.29 When another consolidation took place in 1869,[120] the ambit of the right of set-off was extended from mutual credit and mutual debts to cover also mutual dealings. The proviso relating to notice of an act of bankruptcy was also amended. Whereas it had been a prerequisite to the operation of the previous sections that the person claiming the benefit of the set-off should not have given credit to the bankrupt after notice of an act of bankruptcy, the new section stipulated that the notice had to be of an act of bankruptcy that was available against the bankrupt for adjudication. This referred to section 6 of the Act, and required that the act of bankruptcy must have occurred within six months of the presentation of the petition.[121] In addition, the legislation no longer specifically provided that every debt or demand which was provable against the estate of the bankrupt could also be the subject of a set-off, although this omission was of little consequence because the courts in any event continued to emphasize that notion.[122] The 1869 mutual credit provision was, with one exception, virtually identical to the set-off section in the 1914 legislation. The 1869 Act stipulated that the mutual dealings

---

[116] Therefore the account could be taken down to the issuing of the commission, rather than two months before. See Babington, *The Law of Set-off and Mutual Credit* (1827) 118, and also Henley, *A Digest of the Bankrupt Law* (3rd edn, 1832) 187.

[117] See eg Christian, *Bankrupt Law* (2nd edn, 1818) vol 1, 509.

[118] See the Bankrupt Law Consolidation Act 1849, s 171.

[119] See (1831) 1 & 2 Will IV, c 56.

[120] See the Bankruptcy Act 1869, s 39.

[121] Compare the Bankruptcy Act 1914, s 4(1)(c), which specified a three-month period.

[122] See paras 7.15–7.17 below.

had to be between a 'bankrupt and any other person proving or claiming to prove a debt under his bankruptcy'. However, in the Bankruptcy Act 1883, section 38,[123] which was similar to the Bankruptcy Act 1914, section 31, the language was altered so that the mutual dealings had to be 'between a debtor against whom a receiving order shall be made under this Act, and any other person proving or claiming to prove a debt under such receiving order'. The concept of the receiving order was introduced in the 1883 Act[124] as a step between the presentation of the petition and the adjudication of bankruptcy. It served to stay all actions against the debtor, and also to vest the possession and control of the debtor's property in an official receiver,[125] while the creditors considered whether any proposals for a composition or scheme of arrangement should be accepted, or whether it was expedient for the debtor to be adjudged bankrupt.

The concept of the receiving order was discarded in the Insolvency Act 1986. **6.30**
Reference to it therefore was deleted from the set-off section (section 323), which is drafted in terms of sanctioning a set-off in the event of 'mutual dealings between the bankrupt and any creditor of the bankrupt proving or claiming to prove for a bankruptcy debt'. It has been said of the current section that it was recast in a simpler and more modern form than its predecessor, but that it was not intended to alter the substantive scope or effect of the earlier section.[126]

G. The Relevant Date for Determining Rights of Set-off

(1) The General Principle

England

The right of set-off essentially is an aspect of the rules regulating the proof of **6.31**
debts,[127] and it has generally been the case in the past that the date which defined the accounts to be balanced was the same as that which determined what claims could be proved in the bankruptcy.[128] The Insolvency Act 1986 conforms with the

---

[123] The Bankruptcy Act 1883 repealed the Bankruptcy Act 1869, and amended and consolidated the law of bankruptcy.

[124] Bankruptcy Act 1883, ss 5–14, and also the Bankruptcy Act 1914, s 7.

[125] See the Bankruptcy Act 1914, s 7.

[126] *Bank of Credit and Commerce International SA (No 8)* [1996] Ch 245, 256, CA.

[127] See *Mersey Steel and Iron Co Ltd v Naylor, Benzon & Co* (1884) 9 App Cas 434, 437–438; *Re Northside Properties Pty Ltd and the Companies Act* [1971] 2 NSWLR 320, 323; *Re Bank of Credit and Commerce International SA (No 8)* [1996] Ch 245, 256, CA.

[128] Before the amendment of the 1732 Act in 1806, the date of the act of bankruptcy applied to both proof and set-off. See eg *Bamford v Burrell* (1799) 2 Bos & Pul 1, 7, 126 ER 1120, 1123–1124 for proof of debts, and *Collins v Jones* (1830) 10 B & C 777, 780, 109 ER 638, 639 for set-off. Under the 1825 consolidation the date of the issuing of the commission, and after 1831 of the fiat, was applied in both instances. See s 47 of (1825) 6 Geo IV, c 16 for the proof of debts, and for set-off *Collins v Jones* at 780–781, 639. However, the dates did not always coincide when Parliament acted

general approach, since the 'commencement of the bankruptcy' is expressed to constitute the relevant date in both cases.[129] This refers to the day of the bankruptcy order,[130] as opposed to the date of the petition.[131]

6.32   In the case of a company liquidation, both the right of proof and the right of a set-off are determined by reference to when the company goes into liquidation.[132] A company goes into liquidation if it passes a resolution for a voluntary winding up, or if an order is made for its winding up by the court at a time when it has not already gone into liquidation by passing such a resolution.[133]

6.33   The positions in bankruptcy and company liquidation differ in a curious respect. In bankruptcy, the dividing line is expressed in terms of a particular day, being the day of the bankruptcy order. In company liquidation, on the other hand, the reference point is when the company goes into liquidation, which seems to contemplate a time of the day.

---

in 1806 to ameliorate the harsh consequences under the 1732 Act of a secret act of bankruptcy. Section 2 of the statute (1806) 46 Geo III, c 135 allowed debts contracted before the issuing of the commission to be proved if the creditor did not have notice of a prior act of bankruptcy, while for set-off s 3 only provided relief when credit was given to the bankrupt at least two calendar months before the issuing of the commission. It is difficult to ascertain the position under the 1849 and 1869 Acts. Section 165 of the Bankrupt Law Consolidation Act 1849 allowed a creditor to prove any debt or demand contracted before the filing of the petition, and similarly it was accepted in Doria and Macrae *The Law and Practice of Bankruptcy* (1863) vol 2, 804–5 that this date applied to set-off. On the other hand, in *Astley v Gurney* (1869) LR 4 CP 714 the report only refers to the date of the adjudication, not the date of the petition, and the former may have been regarded as the relevant date for the purpose of set-off. The Bankruptcy Act 1869, s 31 differed from its 1849 predecessor in relation to the proof of debts, in that it allowed claims to which the bankrupt was subject at the date of the adjudication order to be proved, although in 1874 Doria had not changed his opinion that the existence of a right of set-off should be ascertained as at the date of the petition. See Doria, *The Law and Practice of Bankruptcy* (1874) 679. The 1883 and 1914 Acts both conformed with the general rule, since the date of the receiving order in each case determined questions relating to both proof and set-off. See *Re Daintrey* [1900] 1 QB 546.

[129]   See s 323 for set-off, and, for proof, the definition of 'bankrupt debt' in s 382. In Australia the date of the sequestration order is the relevant date in bankruptcies. See *Hiley v The Peoples Prudential Assurance Co Ltd* (1938) 60 CLR 468, 487.

[130]   See the Insolvency Act 1986, s 278.

[131]   See also, with respect to proof of debts, the Insolvency Rules 1986, rr 6.98(1)(b), 6.111–6.114.

[132]   See the Insolvency Rules 1986, r 13.12 with respect to proof of debts, and for set-off r 4.90.

[133]   See the Insolvency Act 1986, s 247(2). Pursuant to s 247(3), the reference to a resolution for voluntary winding up includes a resolution deemed to occur by virtue of an order made following conversion of a voluntary arrangement or administration into winding up under Article 37 of the Council Regulation (EC) No 1346/2000. Section 247(2) should be distinguished from s 129 dealing with the commencement of the winding up. While s 247(2) is not specifically expressed to apply to r 4.90 of the Insolvency Rules, its application in that context would be consistent with the approach which the courts generally have adopted in the past. See *Re Fenton* [1931] 1 Ch 85, 105; *Barclays Bank Ltd v TOSG Trust Fund Ltd* [1984] BCLC 1, 25; *Re Charge Card Services Ltd* [1987] 1 Ch 150, 177; *M S Fashions Ltd v Bank of Credit and Commerce International SA* [1993] Ch 425, 446. Compare *Re City Equitable Fire Insurance Co Ltd* [1930] 2 Ch 293, 310 and *Re Dynamics Corp of America* [1976] 1 WLR 757, 769, which supported the date of the petition rather than the date of the winding-up order.

Australia—bankruptcy

In Australia, the date of the bankruptcy determines the availability of both rights   **6.34**
of proof and rights of set-off in bankruptcy.[134]

Australia—company liquidation, administration, and deeds of company arrangement

In company liquidation,[135] the provable debts are determined by reference to 'the   **6.35**
relevant date',[136] which is defined in the Corporations Act 2001 (Cth) as the day
that the winding-up is taken to have begun.[137] This in turn refers to the day of the
winding-up order or the day on which a resolution was passed for a winding up,
but if the company immediately before the winding up was under administration
or was subject to a deed of company arrangement, it is the day on which the administration began.[138] The date is modified in relation to proof of debts by sections 553(1A) and 553(1B) of the Corporations Act, to accommodate the
situation in which the circumstances giving rise to a claim against the company
occurred at a time when the company was under a deed of company arrangement,
and the company was under the deed immediately before the resolution or the
court order for a winding up. In that case, the claim is admissible to proof against
the company and, for the purpose of applying the sections in Part 5.6, Division 6
of the Act (dealing with proof and ranking of claims), the relevant date for the
claim is the date on which the deed terminates.

The concept of 'the relevant date' has not been specifically incorporated into sec-   **6.36**
tion 553C of the Corporations Act dealing with mutual credit and set-off.
Traditionally, the question whether there are mutual debts, mutual credits or
other mutual dealings between a company in liquidation and a creditor so as to
qualify for a set-off has been said to be determined by reference to the date of the
liquidation.[139] In a voluntary liquidation this has been taken as referring to the
date of the resolution, while in a court-ordered winding up the weight of authority has favoured the view that it means the date of the order.[140] The authorities in

---

[134] See, for proof of debts, the Bankruptcy Act 1966 (Cth), s 82(1) and, for set-off, *Gye v McIntyre* (1991) 171 CLR 609, 619–620. When a debtor is made bankrupt on a creditor's petition, the date of the bankruptcy is the date of the sequestration order. See the definition of 'the date of the bankruptcy' in s 5.

[135] The insolvency set-off section may also be incorporated into a deed of company arrangement. See para 6.08 above and para 6.44 below.

[136] See the Corporations Act 2001 (Cth), s 553(1).

[137] See s 9.

[138] Corporations Act 2001 (Cth), ss 513A-513C.

[139] *Day & Dent Constructions Pty Ltd v North Australian Properties Pty Ltd* (1982) 150 CLR 85, 98.

[140] See Street J in *Re Northside Properties Pty Ltd and the Companies Act* [1971] 2 NSWLR 320, 323 (decision affirmed [1972] 2 NSWLR 573), whose view was accepted by Mason J in *Day and*

question however pre-dated the inclusion in the Corporations legislation of both the definition of 'the relevant date' and the concept of company administration. In *Re Parker*,[140a] Mansfield J held that the determination of set-off entitlements should also now take place by reference to 'the relevant date', so that when, as in that case, liquidation follows immediately after an administration, the date for determining whether there are mutual credits, mutual debts or other mutual dealings is the day on which the administration began.[141]

6.37   Three points may be made in relation to the situation in which there was a prior administration. In the first place, if a debt incurred by a company while under administration is not provable in a subsequent liquidation, the debt similarly could not be employed in a set-off, since the set-off section requires that the creditor's claim be provable. Therefore, at least to that extent, the concept of 'the relevant date' must apply to set-off. Second, in relation to the claim on the other side of the account, being a claim accruing to the company while under administration, the same result often would follow whether the determinative date is the day the administration began or the date of the winding-up order.[142] This is because of the qualification to the set-off section in section 553C(2) of the Corporations Act, which provides that a creditor is not entitled to claim a set-off if at the time of giving credit to or receiving credit from the company the creditor had notice of the fact that the company was insolvent.[143] The board of a company may resolve to appoint an administrator if in the opinion of the directors the company is insolvent, or it is likely to become insolvent at some future time.[144] It is not necessary that the company be insolvent at the time of the appointment, and so bare knowledge of the appointment by itself would not seem to constitute notice of the fact that the company was insolvent.[145] However other circumstances combined with the appointment may provide notice of present insolvency,[146] in which case any debt that the creditor subsequently incurred to the company could not be set off in a

---

Dent Constructions Pty Ltd v North Australian Properties Pty Ltd (1982) 150 CLR 85, 98–99. Compare the opinions of Barwick CJ and Taylor J in *Motor Inns Co Pty Ltd v Liberty Insurance Ltd* (1967) 116 CLR 177, that one should look to the date of the presentation of the petition in order to ascertain the rights of the creditors.

[140a] (1997) 80 FCR 1.

[141] See in particular at (1997) 80 FCR 1, 15–16. See also *Silberman v One Tel Ltd* [2001] NSWSC 895.

[142] Or, as the case may be, the resolution for a winding up.

[143] See generally paras 6.49 *ff* below.

[144] Corporations Act 2001 (Cth), s 436A(1).

[145] Compare the Australian Law Reform Commission Report No 45, *General Insolvency Inquiry* (1988) ('the Harmer Report'), which recommended (in para 819) that a person should not have a right of set-off if at the time of a transaction occurring within six months of the winding up the person had reason to suspect that the company was unable to pay its debts. That recommendation is not reflected in the more stringent requirement in s 553C(2), that the person must have had notice of the fact that the company was insolvent.

[146] For example, insolvency may be disclosed in the report provided to creditors pursuant to the Corporations Act, s 439A(4).

subsequent liquidation whether the date for determining set-offs is the date of the liquidation or the date of the administration. The third point is that a creditor often would not be disadvantaged by being unable to prove a debt incurred by the company after an administrator has been appointed,[147] and therefore being denied a set-off in respect of it. This is because an administrator is personally liable for debts incurred in the exercise of his functions and powers for services rendered, or for goods bought or property hired, leased, used or occupied.[148] In those circumstances the creditor can sue the administrator personally. Moreover, expenses incurred by an administrator in preserving, realizing or getting in property of the company or carrying on the company's business have priority of payment in a liquidation.[149] If the creditor would be paid in full in any event, he would not need a set-off. For those reasons, the question whether the availability of a set-off is determined by reference to the date that the administration began, or the date of the winding-up order or the resolution for a voluntary winding up, often would not be significant.

The question was important however in *Re Parker*.[150] The creditors of a company **6.38** under administration resolved that it be wound up. The company had a holding company, and it was alleged that there were cross-debts between them. The holding company had given a floating charge over all its assets to a secured creditor, which included debts owing to the holding company. Because of the charge, nothing would be available for the holding company's unsecured creditors. The charge crystallized after the commencement of the subsidiary's administration and before the resolution for its winding up. Mansfield J was asked to determine whether, in those circumstances, there could be a set-off in the subsidiary's liquidation. One of the issues was the date for determining rights of set-off. If the date was the date of the winding up, the crystallized charge would have had the effect of destroying mutuality as between the subsidiary and the holding company in relation to the debts.[151] The secured creditor therefore would have obtained the benefit of the holding company's claim against the subsidiary without reduction for a set-off.[152] However Mansfield J held that the appropriate date was the same as that fixed for determining what debts were provable in the winding up, being the date that the administration began. He accepted that there were mutual debts for the

---

[147] When performing a function or exercising a power as administrator of a company the administrator acts as the company's agent. See the Corporations Act 2001 (Cth), s 437B.
[148] Corporations Act 2001 (Cth), s 443A.
[149] Corporations Act 2001 (Cth), s 556(1).
[150] (1997) 80 FCR 1.
[151] See para 11.33 below.
[152] The holding company's liability to the subsidiary was founded upon an allegation of insolvent trading pursuant to the Corporations Act 2001 (Cth), s 588W. Since the liability had not vested at the date of crystallization of the charge, it was not a case of existing mutual debts at the date of crystallization giving rise to a defence of set-off under the Statutes of Set-off to which the secured creditor as an equitable assignee took subject. See paras 17.12 and 17.76 below.

purpose of the insolvency set-off section at that date,[153] and therefore the secured creditor took subject to the prior set-off entitlement.

6.39 The approach adopted in *Re Parker* would become complicated in the situation in which an administration is followed by a deed of company arrangement before the company goes into liquidation. The day on which the administration began is still defined as the relevant date, but special provision is made in section 553(1A) for the situation in which the circumstances giving rise to a debt or claim against the company occurred while the company was under the deed. The debt may be proved in the liquidation, and section 553(1B) provides that, for the purpose of applying the other sections of Part 5.6, Division 6 dealing with proof and ranking of claims, the relevant date for that debt is the date on which the deed terminates. If a debt is provable under section 553(1A) it would ordinarily be regarded as capable of being included in a set-off,[154] so that the view expressed in *Re Parker* would have to be qualified to accommodate a set-off in relation to debts coming within the ambit of section 553(1A).[155] Presumably there could be two relevant dates for determining rights of set-off. Once a company goes into administration the day on which the administration began would constitute a relevant date for the purpose of a subsequent liquidation. But if the administration was followed by a deed of company arrangement before the liquidation, the date on which the deed terminated would constitute a second relevant date for debts of the company arising out of circumstances occurring while the company was under the deed. In either case, however, a debt of the company which arose out of circumstances that occurred while the company was under administration and before the deed would not be provable, in which case it could not be set off under section 553C.

---

[153] See the discussion at (1997) 80 FCR 1, 11–12. The view that a claim against a holding company under s 588W of the Corporations Act 2001 (Cth) for compensation for loss resulting from insolvent trading can be the subject of a set-off is criticized in paras 13.20–13.26 below.

[154] Note however the decision in paras 7.15–7.17 below. This is subject to s 553C(2) of the Corporations Act 2001 (Cth), which provides that a person is not entitled to claim the benefit of a set-off in a company's liquidation if at the time of giving credit to or receiving credit from the company the person had notice of the fact that the company was insolvent. See generally paras 6.49–6.64 below. However, when an insolvent company enters into a deed of company arrangement, the terms of the deed may be such that the company is no longer insolvent, in that, if it complies with the deed, it could pay its debts as and when they fall due. The deed may permit the creditors to terminate it and resolve to wind the company up if the administrator determines that it is no longer practicable or desirable to continue to carry on the company's business. See the Corporations Regulations, Schedule 8A, clause 3 of which applies to a deed of company arrangement unless it has been excluded. See the Corporations Act, s 444A(5), and the Corporations Regulations, reg 5.3A.06. But, depending on the term of the deed, the fact that a person dealing with a company is aware that the company has executed a deed of company arrangement may not have the consequence in a subsequent liquidation that the person had notice at the time of the dealing that the company was insolvent.

[155] The liquidation in *Re Parker* (n 141 above) occurred before ss 553(1A) and 553(1B) were inserted into the Corporations legislation, by the Corporations Law Amendment Act 1997 (Cth).

But how would this work for the claim on the other side of the account which it is   **6.40**
sought to include in a set-off, being the company's claim against the creditor? If
the company's claim arose before the day on which the administration began, and
the administration was followed by a deed of company arrangement before the
liquidation, the claim should be capable of being included in a set-off against a
provable debt whether that provable debt relates to the first or the second relevant
date.[156] Further, if the company's claim against the creditor arose while the company was under the deed, it should be capable of being included in a set-off against
a provable debt arising in that period.[157] But what about a claim which accrued to
the company before the deed, while the company was under administration?
Once a debt of the company which arises out of circumstances occurring during
the period of a deed of company arrangement becomes provable under section
553(1A), so that pursuant to section 553(1B) the relevant date for that debt is the
date that the deed terminates, there is nothing in section 553C to suggest that a
set-off in respect of that debt should be limited to cross-debts which similarly accrued to the company during that period. A person dealing with a company during the period of the administration may have notice of insolvency so as to
preclude a set-off under section 553C(2),[158] but apart from that there is nothing
in section 553C which would exclude a set-off in relation to a claim which accrued to the company before the deed and while it was under administration. A
limitation to that effect would not follow from the concept of mutuality, because
mutuality does not require that there should be a temporal or other connection
between the claims the subject of a set-off.[159] As the High Court observed in *Gye
v McIntyre*,[160] the word 'mutual' conveys the notion of reciprocity rather than of
correspondence. If then *Re Parker* is followed, and if administration is followed by
a deed of company arrangement before liquidation, it would appear that a claim
possessed by the company which arose out of circumstances occurring before the
deed and while the company was under administration would be treated differently for the purpose of set-off than a claim against the company which arose out
of circumstances occurring in the same period.[161] Moreover, while it was held in
Re Parker that a floating charge held by a third party over the company's assets
which crystallized during the period of the administration is subject to a set-off
determined as at the date the administration began, the charge nevertheless
should preclude a set-off in relation to a provable debt which was incurred while
the company was under the deed. This is because crystallization would destroy

---

[156] The deed itself may have incorporated the insolvency set-of section. See para 6.44 below.
[157] Subject to a set-off being excluded under the Corporations Act 2001 (Cth), s 553C(2) because of notice of insolvency. But see n 154 above.
[158] See para 6.37 above.
[159] See para 11.01 below.
[160] (1991) 171 CLR 609, 623.
[161] See para 6.39 above.

mutuality for the purpose of a set-off determined as at the date that the deed terminated,[162] the date of termination being the relevant date for that debt.[163]

6.41   The *Re Parker* approach would be artificial in the common situation in which an administrator carries on the company's business during the administration,[164] the object of administration being to maximize the chances of the company, or as much of its business as possible, continuing in existence.[165] Consider, for example, the case of a company which has a credit balance on a current account with its bank on the day that an administrator is appointed.[166] At the same time the company has a contingent liability to indemnify the bank, for example in relation to letters of credit which the bank has issued at its request. Subsequently the company goes into liquidation, and the bank is called upon to honour the letters of credit. The bank has a provable debt in the liquidation for its right of indemnity from the company, the amount of which is to be valued as at the day of the appointment of the administrator.[167] On that day there were mutual dealings between the bank and the company, which could be the subject of a set-off.[168] But what if during the administration the administrator drew on the current account in the course of carrying on the company's business? The drawings would have reduced the credit balance, but a set-off entitlement determined as at the date of the administrator's appointment would not take them into account. Alternatively, the administrator after his appointment may have closed the account, and transferred the credit funds to an account with another bank. It would make little sense in that situation to talk of determining the set-off rights of the first bank in the liquidation as at the date that the administration began. The point is that the account remained an operating bank account notwithstanding the administration, and the company through the administrator[169] was entitled to deal with the funds on deposit.

6.42   This raises another point. The prevailing view as to the operation of the insolvency set-off section is that a set-off occurs automatically, and it is not the subject of a procedural step of taking an account in the liquidation.[170] The question of the automatic nature of insolvency set-off was not specifically addressed in *Re Parker*, but the decision suggests that the set-off in that case was regarded as having occurred at the date of commencement of the administration, as opposed to the date

---

[162]   See para 11.33 below.

[163]   Corporations Act 2001 (Cth), s 553(1B).

[164]   Pursuant to the Corporations Act 2001 (Cth), s 437A(1)(b).

[165]   Corporations Act 2001 (Cth), s 435A.

[166]   As in *Cinema Plus Ltd v Australia and New Zealand Banking Group Ltd* (2000) 49 NSWLR 513.

[167]   Corporations Act 2001 (Cth), s 554A.

[168]   The bank's contingent claim for an indemnity could be the subject of a set-off. See paras 8.07–8.26 below.

[169]   See the Corporations Act 2001 (Cth), s 437D.

[170]   See paras 6.79–6.103 below.

of the liquidation.[171] It was not simply a matter of looking at the date of commencement of the administration in order to determine which claims could be included in a set-off, which set-off did not occur until the liquidation. In *Re Parker* a floating charge over the holding company's assets crystallized after the appointment of administrators to the subsidiary and before the subsidiary's winding up, and Mansfield J held that the chargee took subject to a set-off under section 553C determined as at the date of commencement of the administration. Section 553C provides that, 'an account is to be taken of what is due from the one party to the other in respect of those mutual dealings', and 'the sum due from the one party is to be set off against any sum due from the other party'. The 'one party' and 'the other' are the parties to the set-off, and the use of the present tense ('is due') suggests that there should be mutuality when the set-off occurs.[172] If it was thought in *Re Parker* that a set-off, if available, would have taken place on the date of the liquidation, there should not in fact have been a set-off in that case. Mutuality in insolvency set-off is determined by reference to equitable interests,[173] but crystallization of the charge before liquidation would have had the consequence that there was not mutuality in equity when the liquidation occurred.[174] In equity, the subsidiary's debt was due to the secured creditor rather than to the holding company. Therefore the decision to allow a set-off would seem to have been on the basis that a set-off was thought of as having occurred before crystallization, at the date of the administration, when there was mutuality. It would be a curious notion, however, if a set-off in a liquidation were regarded as having taken place retrospectively at the date of commencement of a prior administration, when the company's business was still operating and it continued to operate during the period of the administration. Consider for example the situation posited above, where a company's current account with its bank had a credit balance when an administrator was appointed, and the company and the bank had entered into a dealing before the administration, for example the issue by the bank of a letter of credit at the request of the company, which later gave rise to a claim by the bank against the company. If a set-off in a subsequent liquidation were thought of as having occurred at the date the administration began, where would that leave drawings on the account after the commencement of the administration, including where the administrator transferred the funds to another account?[175] Looking at the matter retrospectively, the conclusion would be that, to the extent of the bank's claim against the company, the current account was not in credit when the

---

[171] See also *Silberman v One Tel Ltd* [2001] NSWSC 895 at para 23.

[172] In adopting the automatic theory in *Stein v Blake* [1996] AC 243, the House of Lords (at 255–256) rejected the application of a notion of 'taking subject to equities' in the context of insolvency set-off.

[173] See paras 11.04–11.07 below.

[174] See para 11.33 below.

[175] See para 6.41 above.

administrator was appointed because the account was the subject of a set-off as at that date. If there was no credit balance, the administrator should not have been entitled to draw on the account.

6.43   Moreover, if the set-off were taken to have occurred retrospectively on the date of the administrator's appointment, the administrator could be adversely affected in relation to his lien on the company's assets. An administrator is personally liable for certain debts incurred in the performance of his functions or powers.[176] On the other hand, the administrator is entitled to be indemnified out of the company's property for debts for which he is liable and also for remuneration,[177] the right of indemnity being secured by a lien on the company's property.[178] An administrator may look upon a credit balance on the company's bank account as an asset against which he is entitled to exercise the right of indemnity, and on the faith of that assumption he may incur debts for which he is personally liable.[179] But if the company goes into liquidation while the debts are still outstanding, and the bank has a claim against the company, for example in relation to letters of credit issued before the administration which the bank was later called upon to honour, the application of the automatic theory of insolvency set-off as at the date of commencement of the administration would mean that, because of the liquidation, the company's asset against which the administrator incurred the debts would have disappeared in a set-off determined retrospectively when the administration began. The administrator therefore would be personally liable for the debts without a valuable right of indemnity from the account. If on the other hand set-offs are regarded as occurring at the date of the liquidation, albeit that the provable debt necessary for the set-off is determined as at the commencement of the administration,[180] the administrator's lien on the account in credit would destroy mutuality in the liquidation as between the account and the company's liability to the bank. To the extent of the lien there would not be a set-off,[181] and the administrator therefore would not be prevented by the liquidation from exercising the lien against the account.

6.44   The evident view in *Re Parker* as to the operation of the set-off nevertheless is consistent with views expressed in the Victorian Court of Appeal in *G M & A M Pearce and Co Pty Ltd v RGM Australia Pty Ltd*[182] in the context of a deed of company arrangement that was not followed by a liquidation. The deed in that case

---

[176] Corporations Act 2001 (Cth), s 443A.
[177] Corporations Act 2001 (Cth), s 443D.
[178] Corporations Act 2001 (Cth), s 443F.
[179] See eg *Cinema Plus Ltd v Australia and New Zealand Banking Group Ltd* (2000) 49 NSWLR 513.
[180] See para 6.37 above.
[181] See paras 11.25–11.36 below.
[182] [1998] 4 VR 888.

incorporated the insolvency set-off section applicable in company liquidation.[18]
In accordance with section 444A(4)(i) of the Corporations Law,[184] the deed spe
cified that the admissible claims under the deed were those which arose on or before the date of the appointment of the administrator to the company. The Court
of Appeal held that a set-off occurred automatically under the deed, so that it was
not necessary for a debtor to the company who also had a claim against the company to make a claim under the deed in order to obtain a set-off. The date that the
set-off occurred, accepting an automatic operation, was not in issue, but it was assumed that it would have taken place when the administration began,[185] as opposed to when the deed was executed. At least in the case of a deed of company
arrangement, however, the Corporations Act does not require that the insolvency
set-off section be incorporated into the deed,[186] so that the parties may have some
control over its operation.[187] This is not so in a company liquidation, given that
the section is mandatory in a liquidation and cannot be contracted out of.[188]

In the circumstances in issue in *Re Parker*, an alternative view is that the date for **6.45**
determining the availability of a set-off should remain the date of the liquidation,
given that the concept of 'the relevant date' has not been specifically incorporated
into s 553C. On the other hand there still has to be a provable debt, and the determination whether there is a provable debt would take place by reference to 'the
relevant date', including as modified by section 553(1B) when the company was
under a deed of company arrangement before the liquidation. This alternative
view would have the consequence that the company's claim against the creditor
and the provable debt owing by the company would be treated differently for the
purpose of a set-off, but that may also happen in some circumstances on the *Re
Parker* approach.[189] It would also mean that the date for determining set-offs and
the date for determining the provable debts would not coincide, which would represent a departure from the approach generally adopted in the past.[190] There

---

[183] See para 6.08 above.
[184] See now the Corporations Act 2001 (Cth), s 444A(4)(i).
[185] See Callaway JA at [1998] 4 VR 888, 891 (23 May 1994 being the date that the directors resolved to appoint an administrator), with whom Batt JA at 900 agreed. This view is also consistent
with clause 7(d) of the prescribed provisions in Schedule 8A of the Corporations Regulations. See
also *Handberg v Smarter Way (Aust) Pty Ltd* (2002) 20 ACLC 856, 862, 864, 867.
[186] *G M & A M Pearce and Co Pty Ltd v RGM Australia Pty Ltd* [1998] 4 VR 888, 891, *per*
Callaway JA, and see also Batt JA at 897. The insolvency set-off section (s 553C) applies if the deed
does not exclude the prescribed provisions in Schedule 8A of the Corporations Regulations. See the
Corporations Act 2001 (Cth), s 444A(5), and Schedule 8A, cl 8. Compare *Central Data Networks
Pty Ltd v Global Diagnostics Ltd* (1998) 84 FCR 304, 320–321.
[187] This is subject to the question whether the omission of the insolvency set-off section from the
deed may provide grounds for setting it aside, as being unfairly prejudicial to or unfairly discrim-
inatory against one of more creditors. See the Corporations Act 2001 (Cth), s 445D(1)(f). Compare
Central Data Networks Pty Ltd v Global Diagnostics Ltd (1998) 84 FCR 304, 320–321.
[188] See paras 6.71–6.72 below.
[189] See paras 6.39 and 6.40 above.
[190] See para 6.31 above.

would still nevertheless be a connection because of the requirement that there be a provable debt, and in any event it has not always been the case in the past that the dates coincided.[191] This view would avoid the difficulties which may follow from the *Parker* approach.

(2) Claims Accruing Subsequent to the Relevant Date

6.46   Once a particular date is fixed for determining the existence of a set-off, the acquisition of a right or a liability after that date, when it is not the result of a prior dealing between the parties,[192] or it is not a natural result of a prior transaction so as to come within the concept of giving credit,[193] will not result in a set-off.[194] Thus, a sale of goods by a liquidator in the course of winding up the company will not entitle the purchaser to employ his liability for the price in a set-off against a provable debt owing to him by the company.[195] An amount paid by a director of a company after the commencement of the company's liquidation in order to settle an action that had been commenced against both the director and the company similarly has been held not to be available as a set-off in the liquidation,[196] and a set-off cannot be based upon an assignment of the benefit of a proof of debt lodged by someone else.[197] On the same principle, save for the exception relating to a temporary suspension of mutuality,[198] a set-off may not be based upon an assignment of a debt or a dealing with a negotiable instrument that only took place

---

[191] This was the position when Parliament intervened in 1806 to ameliorate the harsh consequences of a secret act of bankruptcy under the early bankruptcy Act (1732) 5 Geo II, c 30. Section 2 of the statute (1806) 46 Geo III, c 135 allowed debts contracted before the issuing of the commission to be proved if the creditor did not have notice of a prior act of bankruptcy, but s 3 only provided relief in the case of set-off when credit was given to the bankrupt at least two calendar months before the issuing of the commission. See para 6.26 and n 128 above.

[192] See ch 7 below.

[193] See para 7.04 below.

[194] In addition to the cases referred to below, see *Glennie v Edmunds* (1813) 4 Taunt 775, 128 ER 536; *Re Henley, Thurgood & Co* (1863) 11 WR 1021; *Sankey Brook Coal Co Ltd v Marsh* (1871) LR 6 Ex 185; *Re the United Ports and General Insurance Co, ex p The Etna Insurance Co* (1877) 46 LJ Ch 403; *Re Milan Tramways Co, ex p Theys* (1884) 24 Ch D 587; *Re Gunson (A Bankrupt), ex p Official Receiver* [1966] NZLR 187. See also *Re Buchanan Enterprises Pty Ltd* (1982) 7 ACLR 407 (no equitable set-off). Given the inclusion of the mutual dealings head in the set-off section in 1869, *quaere* whether *Graham v Allsopp* (1848) 3 Ex 186, 154 ER 809 would now be followed in relation to the claim for a set-off against the rent due before the immediate landlord's bankruptcy. This is because the payment by the lessee after the bankruptcy to the superior landlord as a result of the distress levied pursuant to the lease not taken up by the assignees in bankruptcy nevertheless arose out of a prior dealing, in the form of that lease.

[195] *Hiley v The Peoples Prudential Assurance Co Ltd* (1938) 60 CLR 468, 496; *Re Kidsgrove Steel, Iron, and Coal Co* (1894) 38 Sol Jo 252. See also *Re Henley, Thurgood, & Co* (1863) 11 WR 1021. *Quaere* if this would apply if assets are purchased from a company in liquidation pursuant to a prior option. See paras 13.53–13.57 below.

[196] *Re Buchanan Enterprises Pty Ltd* (1982) 7 ACLR 407.

[197] *Re Gill, ex p Official Receiver* (1964) 6 FLR 273, 276.

[198] See para 6.65 below.

after the relevant date.[199] A debt or a negotiable instrument admittedly may be proved even though it may have been acquired from another party after the cut-off date for determining rights of proof.[200] However, the proof in that case should not be lodged by the subsequent holder, but rather by the holder at the relevant date as trustee for the latter.[201] The subsequent holder would take subject to any set-off that may have been available as between the bankrupt and the holder at that date.[202]

Receipt of money by an agent after the principal's bankruptcy

If a person appointed as an agent receives the principal's money after the principal **6.47** has become bankrupt, he could not ordinarily employ his liability to account in a set-off because the bankruptcy would have terminated the agency. Accordingly, a claim of mutual credit or mutual dealings based upon an expectation of the continuance of the agency could not be supported.[203] This is in addition to any difficulty that may arise from the possibility that the agent may have received the moneys impressed with a trust.[204]

Unaware of the bankruptcy

It has been suggested that a claim arising after the relevant date, and not related to **6.48** a dealing entered into before that date, may be employed in a set-off if the fact of the bankruptcy was unknown to the other party.[205] The only instance in which this has actually occurred is *Billon v Hyde*,[206] but the facts in issue were exceptional. The case concerned the old doctrine of relation back, and an attempt by Lord Hardwicke to use set-off as a means of bringing about a result consistent with a statute[207] which had been enacted in order to ameliorate the harshness of the doctrine, but which had not come into force when the dealings before him occurred. In *Kinder v Butterworth*,[208] claims entered into after the relevant date in ignorance

---

[199] *Marsh v Chambers* (1749) 2 Str 1234, 93 ER 1152; *Dickson v Evans* (1794) 6 TR 57, 101 ER 433; *Sempill v The Oriental Bank* (1868) 7 SCR (NSW) 68; *Middleton v Pollock, ex p Nugee* (1875) LR 20 Eq 29 (assignment of debt); *Re Gillespie, ex p Reid & Sons* (1885) 14 QBD 963. See also *McColl's Wholesale Pty Ltd v State Bank of NSW* [1984] 3 NSWLR 365, 381.

[200] *Ex parte Deey* (1796) 2 Cox 423, 30 ER 196; *Ex parte Atkins, Re Atkins* (1820) Buck 479; *Ex parte Rogers, Re Bowles* (1820) Buck 490.

[201] *Ex parte Dickenson, Re Gibson* (1832) 2 Deac & Ch 520.

[202] *Ex parte Deey* (1796) 2 Cox 423, 424, 30 ER 196. This would follow from the automatic nature of insolvency set-off. See paras 6.79–6.103 below.

[203] *Elgood v Harris* [1896] 2 QB 491, 495. In Australia compare *Re Clune* (1988) 14 ACLR 261, 267–268.

[204] See ch 10 below.

[205] *Re Gill, ex p Official Receiver* (1964) 6 FLR 273, 276. See also *Re Clements* (1931) 7 ABC 255, 268.

[206] (1749) 1 Ves Sen 326, 27 ER 1061.

[207] (1746) 19 Geo II, c 32.

[208] (1826) 6 B & C 42, 108 ER 369.

of the bankruptcy were not allowed to be set-off,[209] and moreover the contrary conclusion would seem to conflict with judicial opinions to the effect that the question whether there is a set-off cannot be varied by transactions entered into subsequent to the relevant date.[210]

H. Qualification to the Set-off Section

(1) The Scope of the Qualification

6.49 Although in England the claims which may be brought into an account in a bankruptcy generally are determined by reference to the date of the bankruptcy order, this is subject to the qualification in the Insolvency Act 1986, section 323(3), that: 'Sums due from the bankrupt to another party shall not be included in the account . . . if that other party had notice at the time they became due that a bankruptcy petition relating to the bankrupt was pending.'[211] A petition is pending if the petition has been presented but as yet a bankruptcy order has not been made consequent upon it.[212] The onus should be on the trustee in bankruptcy (or liquidator) to establish the requisite notice.[213]

Bankruptcy in Australia

6.50 In Australia, the equivalent concept in bankruptcy is notice of an available act of bankruptcy at the time of giving or receiving credit.[214] An available act of bankruptcy is an act of bankruptcy committed within six months of the presentation of the petition,[215] while notice of the act has been said to mean such knowledge of the act and its attendant circumstances, conditions and consequences as are necessary to make it an act of bankruptcy.[216]

---

[209] Compare the headnote to *Re Gillespie, ex p Reid & Sons* (1885) 14 QBD 963, although Cave J in his judgment seems to have been referring to notice of an act of bankruptcy.

[210] See *Dickson v Evans* (1794) 6 TR 57, 59, 101 ER 433, 434; *Re Milan Tramways Co ex p Theys* (1884) 25 Ch D 587, 591; *Savage v Thompson* (1903) 29 VLR 436, 440.

[211] In the case of an assignment, 'due' in s 323(3) should refer to the time that the sum became due to the assignee. See para 6.58 below.

[212] See eg the Insolvency Act 1986, s 285.

[213] In Australia, see *Thomas v Hatzipetros* (1997) 24 ACSR 286, 290.

[214] Bankruptcy Act 1966 (Cth), s 86(2). For the meaning of 'credit', see paras 7.01–7.06 below. In the case of an assignment, the 'time of giving credit' for the purpose of s 86(2) is the time when the assignment became effective. See *Southern Cross Construction Ltd (In Liq) v Southern Cross Club Ltd* [1973] 1 NZLR 708, and also *Citizens Investments Pty Ltd v Murphy* (1994) 14 ACSR 575, 579.

[215] See the Bankruptcy Act 1966 (Cth), ss 5 and 44(1)(c).

[216] *Central Brake Service (Sydney) Pty Ltd v Central Brake Service (Newcastle) Pty Ltd* (1992) 27 NSWLR 406, 412 (NSW CA), referring to *Re Hardman* (1932) 4 ABC 207, 212.

Company liquidation

In so far as company liquidation is concerned, r 4.90(3) of the English Insolvency **6.51** Rules 1986 is similar, but not identical, to the qualification applicable in bankruptcy. Sums due from the company may not be included in the account if the other party had notice at the time they became due that a meeting of creditors had been summoned under section 98 of the Act, or that a petition for the winding up of the company was pending. A petition is filed in a court-ordered winding up, and a section 98 meeting takes place in a creditors' voluntary winding up. A creditors' voluntary winding up should be distinguished from a members' voluntary winding up. Briefly, a voluntary winding up may proceed as a members' voluntary winding up if the directors made a statutory declaration within the five-week period immediately preceding the date of the passing of the resolution for winding up to the effect that in their opinion the company would be able to pay its debts in full together with interest.[217] A creditors' voluntary winding up is a voluntary winding up in which the directors failed to make such a declaration. The proviso to the mutual credit provision applies in the case of a creditors', but not a members', voluntary winding up. A different principle applies in the case of an insurance company[218] in liquidation, when it had been subject to a prior administration order. In that circumstance, Article 5 of the Financial Services and Markets Act 2000 (Administration Orders Relating to Insurers) Order 2002[219] provides that sums due from the insuer to another party are not to be included in a set-off under rule 4.90 of the Insolvency Rules if, at the time they became due, a petition had been presented to the court under section 9 of the Insolvency Act 1986 for an administration order in relation to the insurer. This is not expressed to depend upon notice of the petition.

Effect of the qualification

The qualification has the effect of discouraging dealings in debts owing by the **6.52** bankrupt or the company, as the case may be, in a way that would negate the principle of a pari passu distribution of the bankrupt's or the company's property. A person who buys a debt at a discount is entitled to base a claim for a set-off upon the full face value of the debt.[220] Therefore, in the absence of a provision such as section 323(3), a creditor who otherwise would only receive a dividend could sell the debt at a discount to a person who himself is indebted to the insolvent party, and who could obtain the full value of the assigned debt by means of a set-off in

---

[217] See the Insolvency Act 1986, ss 89 and 90.

[218] As defined in the Financial Services and Markets Act 2000 (Insolvency) (Definition of 'Insurer') Order 2001 (SI 2001/2634).

[219] SI 2002/1242.

[220] *Stonehouse v Read* (1825) 3 B & C 669, 107 ER 881. Similarly, in the absence of fraud in the inception or preparation of a bill of exchange, a discounter is entitled to prove for its face value. See *Re Gomersall* (1875) 1 Ch D. 137, 146–147.

the ensuing bankruptcy.[221] The qualification seems unduly narrow, however. Other than in the case of an insurance company in liquidation that was subject to a prior administration order,[222] it operates as from the date of notice of the presentation of the petition or, in a creditors' voluntary winding up, the summoning of a meeting under section 98, and yet it may be evident well before then that bankruptcy or liquidation is likely. In such a case it seems that a debt assigned before the petition or the section 98 meeting may be able to be employed in a set-off, even though the very purpose of the assignment may have been to obtain the full value of the debt in a subsequent bankruptcy or liquidation rather than just a dividend. The Cork Committee in its report on the reform of insolvency law originally recommended that the qualification should be framed in terms of notice of inability to pay debts,[223] an approach that essentially has been adopted in Australia in relation to company liquidation. The qualification in section 553C(2) of the Corporations Act 2001 (Cth) applies where the creditor, at the time of giving or receiving credit, had notice of the fact that the company was insolvent,[224] and insolvent is defined in section 95A in terms of inability to pay debts as and when they become due and payable. It is not clear why the Cork Committee's recommendation was not adopted in the Insolvency Act.

Other differences beween the English and the Australian provisions

6.53 There are other differences between the English and the Australian provisions. The English provision only refers to sums due *from* the bankrupt or the company in liquidation, whereas the qualification in the Australian legislation covers both sides of the account.[225] Further, the qualification in England is expressed simply in

---

[221] See *Gye v McIntyre* (1991) 171 CLR 609, 619.

[222] See para 6.51 above.

[223] *Cork Committee Report on Insolvency Law and Practice* (Cmnd 8558, 1982) 127, 307.

[224] Section 553C(2) should be compared to the Corporations Act 2001 (Cth), s 588FG, which provides a defence to a claim to set aside a transaction in a liquidation as an unfair preference, an uncommercial transaction or an unfair loan, if the person the subject of the application 'had no reasonable grounds for suspecting that the company was insolvent'. It should also be compared to the recommendation of the Australian Law Reform Commission in its Report No 45, *General Insolvency Inquiry* (1988) ('the Harmer Report') para 819, that a person should not have a right of set-off if at the time of the transaction the person had reason to suspect that the company was unable to pay its debts. That recommendation is not reflected in 553C(2), which refers instead to the person having 'notice of the fact that the company was insolvent'. This would include wilfully shutting one's eyes to the obvious. See *English and Scottish Mercantile Investment Co v Brunton* [1892] 2 QB 700, 707–708. Bare knowledge of the appointment of an administrator to a company under Part 5.3A of the Corporations Act on its own would not seem to constitute notice of the fact that the company is insolvent for the purpose of s 553C(2), since the ground for the appointment could be the directors' belief that the company is likely to become insolvent at some future time. See s 436A, and para 6.37 above. However this should not be significant if *Re Parker* (1997) 80 FCR 1 is followed, save perhaps where administration is followed by a deed of company arrangement before liquidation. See paras 6.36–6.45 above. See also n 154 above in relation to notice of a deed of company arrangement.

[225] See para 6.59 below.

terms that sums due from the bankrupt (or the company) to the other party shall not be included in the account if that other party had the requisite notice at the time that those sums became due. It draws no distinction between which of the parties is asserting the set-off. The English provision should be compared to the corresponding provision in the Australian legislation, which is drafted in terms that '[a] person is not entitled under this section to claim the benefit of a set-off' if at the time of giving credit[226] to the bankrupt or the company, or at the time of receiving credit, 'he or she' (in the case of bankruptcy) or 'the person' (in company liquidation) had the requisite notice. This assumes that the creditor of the bankrupt or the company is the party 'claiming' a set-off, which usually is the case. The creditor wants a set-off so that he would not be confined to receiving a dividend in the bankruptcy or the liquidation, and at the same time be obliged to pay the full value of the cross-claim against him. But what if in an exceptional case, such as occurred in *Re Parker*,[227] the trustee in bankruptcy or the liquidator is the party arguing for a set-off, and the creditor is opposing it? On the face of the Australian legislation the creditor's notice of an act of bankruptcy or of insolvency would not preclude a set-off, because the creditor is not claiming the benefit of a set-off.[228] The difficulty with that analysis is the prevailing view as to the nature of insolvency set-off, that it takes effect automatically by force of the operation of the section.[229] It seems contrary to that view that the question whether there is a set-off should depend upon which of the parties is claiming it. But notwithstanding that objection, it is suggested that the words used in the qualification in the Australian section should be given their ordinary meaning. The evident purpose of the qualification is to prevent a creditor being able to deal in an insolvent's debts so as to defeat the requirement of a *pari passu* distribution in the event of a subsequent bankruptcy or liquidation, by obtaining the full value of a provable debt by way of a set-off rather then being confined to a dividend.[230] But if the creditor is not claiming a set-off, that would not be an issue. As a matter of policy there is no reason why the qualification should be invoked to prevent a set-off, based upon the creditor's notice, when the set-off is sought, not by that party, but by the trustee in bankruptcy or the liquidator.

---

[226] For the meaning of 'credit', see paras 7.01–7.06 below.

[227] (1997) 80 FCR 1. A creditor lodged a proof of debt in the liquidation of a company in circumstances where the liquidator asserted a cross-claim against the creditor. The problem was that the creditor had charged all its assets in favour of a bank, so that it had no assets with which to satisfy the cross-claim. Therefore, the liquidator was the party asserting a set-off, so as to prevent a situation arising in which a dividend would have to be paid on the provable debt and at the same time nothing would be recoverable by the company in liquidation in respect of the cross-claim.

[228] See Duns, Note (1998) 6 Insolvency Law Journal 4, 5. While there was some discussion of the question of notice in *Re Parker* (1997) 80 FCR 1, 8, with respect it is not particularly clear.

[229] See paras 6.79–6.103 below.

[230] *Gye v McIntyre* (1991) 171 CLR 609, 619. See para 6.52 above.

(2) The Meaning of 'Due', and the Time of Giving Credit

6.54 A critical question in relation to section 323(3), as well as rule 4.90(3) in company liquidation, is the meaning of 'due'. Sums due from the bankrupt cannot be included in a set-off if the creditor had notice at the time they 'became due' that a bankruptcy petition was pending. If 'due' were interpreted as meaning 'due and payable', the qualification in many cases would operate to deny a set off in respect of a debt which was contracted by the debtor well before insolvency but which only became payable after the presentation of the petition. That result would have little merit and, in order to avoid it, it is suggested that the courts would readily interpret 'due' in this context as extending to a debt which is owing but not presently payable. If at the time that the liability was incurred the creditor did not have notice of a bankruptcy petition, it should not matter that a petition is presented before the due date for payment.

6.55 But even that approach is not without difficulty. It would not provide a solution in the situation in which a person incurs a contingent liability while solvent and the liability vests after presentation of a petition against him. Until the liability vests nothing is owing so that, even if 'due' were interpreted as meaning 'owing' rather than merely 'payable', the liability in question could not be set off. Yet it is difficult to see why a set-off would be objectionable in that situation.

6.56 The reference to sums becoming due in section 323(3) should be taken as referring to the time that a contract was entered into out of which a liability subsequently arose, as opposed to the time that the liability actually vested pursuant to the contract.[231] As long as the creditor did not have notice at the time of entering into the contract, any liability of the debtor that arises subsequently out of the contract should not be precluded from being employed in a set-off merely on the ground that a bankruptcy petition was presented before the liability vested. In essence this appears to have been the position under earlier bankruptcy legislation, where the qualification was drafted in terms whether the creditor had notice of an available act of bankruptcy at the time that credit was given to the debtor,[232] and it remains the position in Australia, where the set-off section is still drafted in that manner. Thus, when it was held in the nineteenth century that an accommodation acceptor or indorser of a bill of exchange could employ his claim for an indemnity in a set-off in the drawer's bankruptcy, the pleadings were framed in terms that the acceptor or indorser gave credit for the purpose of the qualification when he accepted or indorsed the bill, as opposed to when his claim for an in-

---

[231] This was the view of Sir John Jarvis QC, sitting as a deputy judge in the Chancery Division, in *Ashurst v Coe* The Times Law Reports, 25 March 1999.

[232] See eg the Bankruptcy Act 1914, s 31.

demnity subsequently vested by payment.[233] More recently in New South Wales,[234] a creditor of a company purchased goods from the company after the commencement of the company's liquidation but pursuant to a prior contract, and in determining whether the resulting liability to the company[235] could be employed in a set-off Hodgson J considered that the qualification to the set-off section should be applied on the basis that credit was given when the contract was entered into, as opposed to when the sale occurred. Similarly in Victoria Hayne J held, in the case of a licence fee payable periodically, that credit was given when the transaction was entered into which gave rise to the fee, rather than on each occasion when an instalment of the licence fee became payable.[236]

This suggested interpretation of 'due' in section 323(3) may be criticized on the **6.57** ground that 'due' normally is not regarded as including an amount that is only contingently due.[237] Moreover, it would have the consequence that a different meaning would be ascribed to 'due' in section 323(3) than in section 323(2). Subsection (2) provides that an account shall be taken of what is 'due' from each party to the other. In the case of a debt owing by a bankrupt which is still contingent, this should extend to a valuation made by the trustee in bankruptcy pursuant to the Insolvency Act 1986,[238] but when a bankrupt is a contingent creditor the claim, while it remains contingent, is not 'due' for the purpose of a set-off.[239] There is a presumption that when a word is repeated in the same section it has the same meaning, but it has been emphasized that this is only a presumption,[240] and that it yields to the requirements of the context.[241] In the present case, unless the word 'due' where it appears in the qualification is interpreted in the manner suggested, a contingent liability of a bankrupt would seldom be able to be employed in a set-off if the contingency occurs after the occurrence of the bankruptcy, even though the weight of authority now favours the view that a contingent debt in

---

[233] *Hulme v Muggleston* (1837) 3 M & W 30, 150 ER 1043; *Russell v Bell* (1841) 8 M & W 277, 151 ER 1042; *Bittleston v Timmis* (1845) 1 CB 389, 135 ER 591. The set-off section in issue in those cases was s 50 of (1825) 6 Geo IV, c 16, which provided that the creditor claiming the benefit of a set-off must not have had 'when such credit was given, notice of an act of bankruptcy by such bankrupt committed'.

[234] *Shirlaw v Lewis* (1993) 10 ACSR 288, 295–296.

[235] Hodgson J held that the sale constituted a void disposition pursuant to the Corporations Law, s 468, so that it was not a question of setting off the price. He nevertheless considered the issue of set-off on the assumption that the creditor was liable on the basis of unjust enrichment, or possibly in conversion.

[236] *Old Style Confections Pty Ltd v Microbyte Investments Pty Ltd* [1995] 2 VR 457, 464. The provision in issue was the Corporations Law, s 553C(2).

[237] *Merritt Cairns Constructions Pty Ltd v Wulguru Heights Pty Ltd* [1995] 2 Qd R 521, 526; *Ex parte Kemp, Re Fastnedge* (1874) LR 9 Ch App 383.

[238] See para 8.26 below.

[239] See para 8.27 below.

[240] *Littlewoods Mail Order Stores Ltd v Inland Revenue Commissioners* [1963] AC 135, 159, *per* Lord Reid.

[241] *Madras Electricity Supply Corp Ld v Boarland (Inspector of Taxes)* [1955] AC 667, 685.

principle is capable of being the subject of a set-off.[242] Indeed, the bankruptcy legislation of 1825 and 1849 in each case stipulated that a proof could be lodged in respect of a debt which was still contingent at the time of the bankruptcy,[243] and it also specifically provided that all provable debts could be set off.[244] As Sir George Jessel MR once remarked, the whole tendency of the history of the bankruptcy legislation has been to extend the principle upon which the right of set-off is based,[245] and it would be strange if in this context it has been narrowed. The courts have emphasized that the right of set-off should be given the widest possible scope,[246] which suggests that they would lean towards an interpretation of 'due' in section 323(3) that would not restrict the availability of the right in comparison with the previously accepted position, in the absence of a compelling policy reason for doing so. Nevertheless, the uncertainty surrounding the meaning of section 323(3) is unsatisfactory, and it would be appropriate for Parliament to clarify the position.

Assignment of a debt

6.58 Consider that a debt is assigned before the bankruptcy or liquidation of the debtor. The qualification to the set-off section provides that a sum due from the bankrupt or the company to another party cannot be included in an account if that other party had the requisite notice at the time that the sums became 'due'. This should refer to the time that sums became due to the person asserting the right to the set-off, ie the assignee.[247] If the assignee did not have notice at the time that sums first became due on the assigned debt to the assignor, but he did at the time of the assignment itself, he should not be entitled to employ the debt in a set-off.

Australia

6.59 A noticeable feature of section 323(3), and of rule 4.90(3) in company liquidation, is that it only prevents a set-off in relation to sums due *from* the bankrupt after notice of the petition. It does not apply when sums become due *to* the bank-

---

[242] See paras 8.14–8.21 below.

[243] See (1825) 6 Geo IV, c 16, s 56, and the Bankrupt Law Consolidation Act 1849, s 177.

[244] See (1825) 6 Geo IV, c 16, s 50, and the Bankrupt Law Consolidation Act 1849, s 171.

[245] *Peat v Jones & Co* (1881) 8 QBD 147, 149. See also *Re Fenton, ex p Fenton Textile Association Ltd* [1931] 1 Ch 85, 107, *per* Lord Hanworth MR.

[246] *Eberle's Hotels and Restaurant Co Ltd v E Jonas & Brothers* (1887) 18 QBD 459, 465; *Day & Dent Constructions Pty Ltd v North Australian Properties Pty Ltd* (1982) 150 CLR 85, 108; *Gye v McIntyre* (1991) 171 CLR 609, 619; *Central Brake Service (Sydney) Pty Ltd v Central Brake Service (Newcastle) Pty Ltd* (1992) 27 NSWLR 406, 411. See also *Peat v Jones & Co* (1881) 8 QBD 147, 150, *per* Cotton LJ; *Mersey Steel and Iron Co v Naylor, Benzon & Co* (1882) 9 QBD 648, 660–661.

[247] Shea, 'Further Reflections on Statutory Set-off' (1987) 3 Journal of International Banking Law 183, 184. See also *Southern Cross Construction Ltd v Southern Cross Club Ltd* [1973] 1 NZLR 708; *Citizens Investments Pty Ltd v Murphy* (1994) 14 ACSR 575, 579.

rupt after notice. In Australia, on the other hand, the qualification to the insolvency set-off section[248] covers both sides of the account. Moreover, it is drafted in terms similar to the provision formerly applicable in England,[249] in that it refers to credit being given[250] rather than sums becoming due. Therefore the difficulties that may arise in England from the use of the word 'due' would not apply. In bankruptcy a creditor is not entitled to claim the benefit of a set-off if at the time of giving credit to the person who became bankrupt or at the time of receiving credit from that person he had notice of an available act of bankruptcy. Similarly, in company liquidation section 553C(2) of the Corporations Act 2001 (Cth) prohibits a set-off if at the time of receiving or giving credit the person had notice of the fact that the company was insolvent.[251]

(3) Assignment of a Debt as a Preference

Because the qualification to the set-off section in the Insolvency Act 1986, section 323 only applies after notice of a pending petition,[252] it would seem that a person who takes an assignment of a debt after notice of the debtor's insolvency but before notice of a pending petition would not be precluded by the qualification from employing the debt in a set-off, even though in the absence of a set-off a repayment of the debt may have been voidable as a preference. *Watts v Christie*[253] suggests that a set-off may not be available in this situation, but there are difficulties with Lord Langdale's judgment. **6.60**

In *Watts v Christie* a partnership consisting of A and B was indebted to a firm of bankers, while the bank was separately indebted to A on an account in credit. After the partners became aware of the bankers' insolvency they entered into an agreement by which A purported to assign the credit account to the partnership. The assignment was an equitable assignment, since the ability to assign at law only arose later with the enactment of the Judicature Acts.[254] The partners gave notice of the assignment to the banking firm, and directed that the balance on the account be applied in reduction of the partners' joint indebtedness. The direction was not complied with, however. The banking firm became bankrupt, and their assignees in bankruptcy sued the partners on their joint debt, whereupon the partners filed a bill for an injunction to restrain the action on the ground that the **6.61**

---

[248] Bankruptcy Act 1966 (Cth), s 86(2), and for companies the Corporations Act 2001 (Cth), s 553C(2).

[249] See the Bankruptcy Act 1914, s 31.

[250] The better view is that this does not encompass a damages claim. See paras 7.05 and 7.06 below, although compare *Gye v McIntyre* (1991) 171 CLR 609, 624–625.

[251] See eg *Citizens Investments Pty Ltd v Murphy* (1994) 14 ACSR 575 (assignment of a debt), distinguishing *Re Moseley Green Coal and Coke Co Barrett's Case (No 2)* (1865) 4 De G J & S 756, 46 ER 1116 on the ground that the assignment in that case was pursuant to a prior arrangement.

[252] See para 6.49 *ff* above.

[253] (1849) 11 Beav 546, 50 ER 928.

[254] See para 17.04 below.

279

assigned debt should be set off against their joint debt. If A instead had withdrawn the credit balance in order to pay off the partnership debt, the payment to A would have constituted a preference, since A had notice of the bank's insolvency. The purpose of the assignment evidently was to avoid that result, by bringing about a situation in which the partners' joint liability could be set off against a joint asset in the form of the credit account assigned to them.[255] Under the bankruptcy legislation then in force, the qualification to the set-off section was drafted in terms of notice of an act of bankruptcy,[256] whereas, while the assignment in *Watts v Christie* occurred after notice of insolvency, an act of bankruptcy as yet had not taken place. The qualification therefore was not applicable. Despite this, it was held that a set-off was not available. Lord Langdale in his judgment concentrated on the direction to the bank to apply A's credit balance in reduction of the joint debt.[257] Since this occurred after notice of insolvency, he said that an application of the credit balance in accordance with the direction would have constituted a preference. It is not clear, however, why the case was decided only in terms of the direction as opposed to the assignment itself. It is now recognized that a direction to pay, or indeed notice to the debtor, is not a necessary requirement of an equitable assignment.[258] Notice is desirable for the purpose of preserving the assignee's priority in accordance with the rule in *Dearle v Hall*,[259] and to ensure that the debtor cannot discharge the debt by payment to the assignor.[260] But the failure to give notice does not mean that the assignment itself is ineffective. If in a case such as *Watts v Christie* there has been a valid assignment, whether legal or equitable, in the language of the current set-off section it is difficult to see why the fact that a payment by the debtor at the time of the assignment would have constituted a preference should affect the argument for a set-off.

6.62 It has been suggested that an assignment in that circumstance nevertheless could constitute a preference if the insolvent debtor was involved in it with a preferential motive, for example where the debtor consented to the assignment pursuant to a provision in the contract which required the debtor's consent.[261] Whether the giving of consent is a preference would depend on the circumstances. The preference section is expressed to apply where a person does something or suffers some-

---

[255] In the absence of an effective assignment a set-off would not have been available, since A's separate demand and the partners' joint liability would not have been mutual for the purpose of the set-off section. See para 12.02 below.

[256] See (1825) 6 Geo IV, c 16, s 50.

[257] This accords with the argument of counsel for the partners, which was presented in terms that the direction to transfer operated as an equitable transfer of the separate debt to the partners. See (1849) 11 Beav 546, 548, 50 ER 928, 929.

[258] *Re Patrick, Bills v Tatham* [1891] 1 Ch 82.

[259] (1823) 3 Russ 1, 38 ER 475.

[260] Compare *Brice v Bannister* (1878) 3 QBD 569.

[261] Wood, *English and International Set-off* (1989) 358, 371–2. The courts will give effect to a stipulation in a contract that the benefit of the contact is not assignable save with the consent of the other party. See *Linden Gardens Trust Ltd v Lenesta Sludge Disposals Ltd* [1994] 1 AC 85.

thing to be done in favour of a creditor,[262] by which is meant someone who, but for the payment or other transaction being impugned, would share in the distribution of the assets.[263] Further, the person must have been influenced by a desire to improve the position of the creditor.[264] In the assignment under discussion there are two parties to consider, the assignor and the assignee. If the debtor in consenting to the assignment was influenced by a desire to improve the position of the assignor, for example because the consideration for the assignment was greater than what the assignor otherwise would have received in the bankruptcy or liquidation, the giving of the consent may be a preference. But if the debtor was influenced only by a desire to benefit the assignee, for example because the consideration payable by the assignee for the debt was less than the benefit that would accrue to him by being able to set off the full value of the assigned debt against his liability to the debtor, it is doubtful whether the debtor's consent would be a preference. The assignee is not a person who, apart from the transaction in question, would have shared in the administration of the estate. Before the assignment the assignee was a debtor, not a creditor.

Re Land Development Association. Kent's Case,[265] while it may appear to be relevant, **6.63** should be considered in the context of the facts in issue. A shareholder who held partly paid shares in a company, and who therefore had a contingent liability to contribute the unpaid amount, took an assignment of a debt owing by the company to a third party. The company resolved that the seal of the company be affixed to the assignment.[266] The shareholder on the same day wrote to the directors requesting them to transfer from the amount due on the debt a sum sufficient to pay up his shares, and the directors that same day passed a resolution to that effect. The arrangement was struck down as giving the shareholder a preference in the company's subsequent liquidation. The critical point however is that one of the debts was for an amount unpaid on shares, and therefore it could not have been employed in a set-off in the liquidation.[267] Were it not for the directors' action in applying the debt against the unpaid capital, the shareholder would have been obliged to pay the unpaid capital and would only have received a dividend in the liquidation on the assigned debt. It is apparent then that the arrangement with the company prior to its liquidation resulted in the shareholder receiving a preference.[268] The preference was not the assignment however, or the company's

---

[262] See the Insolvency Act 1986, ss 239(4)(a) and 340(3)(a).

[263] *Re Paine, ex p Read* [1897] 1 QB 122, 123–124, and see generally the discussion in *Re Blackpool Motor Car Co Ltd* [1901] 1 Ch 77.

[264] See the Insolvency Act 1986, ss 239(5) and 340(4).

[265] (1888) 39 Ch D 259, referred to in Wood, *English and International Set-off* (1989) 371–2.

[266] *Quaere* what the significance of this was, although it appears from the judgment of Fry LJ ((1888) 39 Ch D 259, 267) that it may have been done in order to fix the amount of one of the instalments of the debt.

[267] See paras 8.50–8.62 below.

[268] See also *Re Washington Diamond Mining Co* [1893] 3 Ch 95, and para 13.10 below.

consent to it, but rather the company's act in setting off the debt against the liability for unpaid capital. The event constituting the preference therefore took effect in favour of a person who at the time was a creditor. On the other hand, where the issue is whether the giving of consent required for an assignment can constitute a preference in relation to the assignee, the giving of the consent, in so far as the assignee is concerned, would not have the effect of preferring an existing creditor because, even if consent is a prerequisite to the validity of the assignment, the assignee was not a creditor before the consent was given.

6.64 While this appears to be the effect of the preference and set-off sections, it is not a felicitous result. The qualification to the set-off section should be amended to reflect the Cork Committee's original recommendation, that it be framed in terms of notice of inability to pay debts.[269]

I. Temporary Suspension of Mutual Credit

6.65 For the insolvency set-off section to apply there must have been mutual credit, mutual debts, or other mutual dealings 'before' the commencement of the bankruptcy or the liquidation.[270] Therefore some time before the bankruptcy or the liquidation there must have been mutuality. It is not necessary however that mutuality be present at the date of the bankruptcy or the liquidation, if it is merely in suspense at that time.[271] In *Bolland v Nash*[272] a creditor of some debtors had accepted a bill of exchange, and the bill having come into the hands of the debtors it was indorsed by them before their bankruptcy to a third person. After the bankruptcy the creditor dishonoured the bill, and the bill was returned to the bankrupts as indorsers. It was held that the creditor could set off his liability on the bill against the debt owing to him by the bankrupts, even though at the date of the bankruptcy the bill was in the hands of the third party, so that at that date there was not mutual credit as between the creditor and the bankrupts. Conversely, in *Collins v Jones*[273] it was the bankrupt acceptor who dishonoured a bill, and a

---

[269] See para 6.52 above.

[270] Insolvency Act 1986, s 323(1), and for company liquidation the Insolvency Rules 1986, r 4.90(1). This is also the effect of the Australian legislation, which applies where there 'have been' mutual credits, mutual debts or other mutual dealings. See the Bankruptcy Act 1966 (Cth), s 86(1) and the Corporations Act 2001 (Cth), s 553C(1). See also *Bolland v Nash* (1828) 8 B & C 105, 109, 108 ER 982, 984 and *Collins v Jones* (1830) 10 B & C 777, 781, 109 ER 638, 639–640.

[271] This is also the case for the proof of debts. See for example *Joseph v Orme* (1806) 2 Bos & Pul (NR) 180, 127 ER 593, where the indorser had been obliged to take up the bill again after the acceptor's bankruptcy, but compare *Ex parte Isbester* (1810) 1 Rose 20.

[272] (1828) 8 B & C 105, 108 ER 982. Selwyn LJ in *Re Anglo-Greek Steam Navigation and Trading Co* (1869) LR 4 Ch App 174 followed *Bolland v Nash* as an alternative ground for his decision. See also *Ex parte Banes, re the Royal British Bank* (1857) 28 LTOS 296.

[273] (1830) 10 B & C 777, 109 ER 638. See also *Ex parte Hastie and Hutchinson, re Alexander and Co* (1850) 1 Fonbl 59, 14 LTOS 402; *McKinnon v Armstrong Brothers & Co* (1877) 2 App Cas 531;

debtor of the bankrupt who had indorsed it prior to the bankruptcy was forced to take it up again as indorser after the bankruptcy. Once again, it was held that the debtor could set off the claim on the bill against the debt that he owed to the bankrupt acceptor, despite the absence of mutual credit between the parties when the bankruptcy occurred. This can also apply when a creditor assigns the debt by way of security to a third party. If the security is redeemed after the bankruptcy of either the creditor or the debtor, so that the debt comes back to the creditor, the debt can be the subject of a set-off as between them.[274] The important point in these cases is that the debt was taken up again as a result of a prior obligation,[275] or a prior right of redemption. Unless this limitation is imposed, a debtor of the bankrupt would be able to buy up at a discount any liabilities of the bankrupt that had passed through his hands, and yet be able to obtain the full value of those liabilities by means of a set-off.[276] This would be unfair to the general body of creditors, and the courts have emphasized that the buying up of liabilities in order to obtain rights of set-off should not be encouraged.[277]

The essence of a set-off on this ground is that there was merely a temporary suspension of mutual credit. If there never was mutuality prior to the relevant date, the person upon acquiring the debt could not employ it in a set-off. This may be the case, for example, when a person had contracted with a creditor to take an assignment of the debt upon the occurrence of an event which occurred after the relevant date for determining rights of set-off in the debtor's bankruptcy. Even though the debt was acquired pursuant to a pre-existing obligation, there never was mutuality prior to the relevant date so as to entitle the person to employ the debt in a set-off in the debtor's bankruptcy. **6.66**

Hiley v The Peoples Prudential Assurance Co Ltd (1938) 60 CLR 468, 501. A similar principle applies in the context of receivership. See *Handley Page Ltd v Commissioners of Customs and Exercise and Rockwell Machine Tool Co Ltd* [1970] 2 Lloyd's Rep 459.

[274] See *Hiley v The Peoples Prudential Assurance Co Ltd* (1938) 60 CLR 468, where the debt in question was redeemed as part of a compromise rather than by payment to the assignee of the secured amount. *Re City Life Assurance Co Ltd, Stephenson's Case* [1926] 1 Ch 191, 214 was distinguished on the ground that the mortgages in that case had not been redeemed.

[275] See *Collins v Jones* (1830) 10 B & C 777, 782, 109 ER 638, 640, and also Robson, *The Law of Bankruptcy* (7th edn, 1894) 367. Compare *Ex parte Isbester* (1810) 1 Rose 20 in the context of proof of debts.

[276] In the absence of fraud in the inception or preparation of a bill of exchange, a discounter is entitled to prove for its full value. See *Re Gomersall* (1875) 1 Ch D 137, 146–7, *per* Baggallay JA. In *Stonehouse v Read* (1825) 3 B & C 669, 107 ER 881 an accommodation acceptor of various bills had entered into a composition with the holders of the bills, so that the bills were delivered up to him upon payment of a sum less than their full face value. Since the composition had been effected solely for the relief of the acceptor, and not for the drawer, the acceptor was entitled to a set-off in the drawer's bankruptcy to the extent of the full face value of the bills.

[277] *Re Moseley Green Coal and Coke Co Ltd, Barrett's Case* (No 2) (1865) 4 De G J & S 756, 760, 46 ER 1116, 1118; *Day & Dent Constructions Pty Ltd v North Australian Properties Pty Ltd* (1982) 150 CLR 85, 95.

6.67 The insolvency set-off section applies in the case of mutual debts or credits, or claims arising out of mutual dealings. It is not necessary that the claims should have arisen out of dealings between the parties if there are mutual debts.[278] For example, one of the debts the subject of a proposed set-off may have been acquired by the party asserting it in a set-off by way of an assignment from a third person, or, if one of the debts is a claim on a negotiable instrument, the instrument may have been negotiated by a third person to the party asserting it in a set-off. In neither case is the debt the result of a dealing between the parties to the set-off, but a set-off nevertheless may proceed.[279] In considering the question of suspension of mutuality, the distinction between mutuality of debts and mutuality of dealings may be important in some cases. Consider that a creditor before its liquidation had assigned the debt by way of security to a third party, and the liquidator redeemed the security after the liquidation. In addition, the creditor is separately indebted to the debtor. If the creditor incurred the debt before the assignment, there will have been mutuality of debts before the liquidation, and the case will be one of suspension of mutuality so as to permit a set-off on that ground.[280] But if the creditor became indebted to the debtor *after* the assignment, there never will have been mutuality of debts. Mutuality in insolvency set-off is determined by reference to equitable interests.[281] The debtor in this situation is the beneficial owner of the claim against the creditor, but at the time when the creditor became liable to the debtor the debt on the other side of the account had already been assigned. That assignment would have prevented mutuality in equity arising before the liquidation in relation to the debts.[282] The absence of prior mutuality in equity in relation to the debts should not preclude a set-off, however, if the debts arose out of dealings between the debtor and the creditor before the liquidation. A set-off may then be supported on the basis of prior mutual dealings before the liquidation. As Dixon J remarked in the Australian High Court in *Hiley v Peoples Prudential Assurance Co Ltd*:[283] 'It is enough that at the commencement of the winding up mutual dealings exist which involve rights and obligations whether absolute or contingent of such a nature that afterwards in the events that happen they mature or develop into pecuniary demands capable of set off.' The important point in relation to the debt assigned by way of security is that the redemption after the liquidation involved the enforcement of rights subsisting at the date of the liquidation, and involved no new and independent transaction.[284]

---

[278] See paras 7.10–7.13 below.

[279] See para 7.11 below.

[280] See para 6.65 above.

[281] See paras 11.04–11.07 below.

[282] See para 11.04 below, and *Re City Life Assurance Co Stephenson's Case* [1926] 1 Ch 191, 214, as explained by Dixon J in *Hiley v Peoples Prudential Assurance Co Ltd* (1938) 60 CLR 468, 501–505, and see also Rich J at 488.

[283] (1938) 60 CLR 468, 497.

[284] See Dixon J in *Hiley v Peoples Prudential Assurance Co Ltd* (1938) 60 CLR 468, 499, and also Rich J at 487.

J. The Necessity for Cross-Demands

Set-off in bankruptcy and company liquidation depends upon the existence of **6.68** cross-demands between the parties to the proposed set-off. Consider, for example, that a bank has made a loan to a customer on the security of a deposit provided by a third party. If the third party has not assumed a personal liability in respect of the customer's debt, whether on the basis of a joint or a joint and several liability or as a guarantor, the case would not be one of mutual cross-demands between the bank and the third party. Nor, if the bank has gone into liquidation, could the bank's claim against the customer be set off against its liability to the third party on the deposit, because the requirement of mutuality would be lacking.[285] The liquidator in such a case could sue the customer on the loan and confine the third party to a proof in the liquidation in respect of the deposit,[286] subject, however, to any contractual limitation on the right to recover all or part of the deposit until repayment of the loan in full.[287]

K. Enforceable Demands

A creditor may not prove in a bankruptcy or a company liquidation for a debt **6.69** which is unenforceable, for example because of the expiration of a limitation period.[288] Further, because the insolvency set-off section only applies when the creditor has a provable debt,[289] this unenforceable debt similarly could not be the subject of a set-off.[290] Consider, however, that it is a debt on the other side of the account, being a debt owing to the bankrupt or to the company, which is unenforceable. Prima facie there is nothing in the language of the insolvency set-off section which suggests that the debt may not be set off. While the debt may not be enforceable, it is still an existing debt. If the person liable on the debt in turn has a provable claim against the bankrupt or the company, it may be said that there are mutual debts which, according to the set-off section, must be set against each other. The creditor would regard this as unfair, however. In the absence of a set-off, he would have been entitled to receive a dividend on the provable debt, and at the same time he could not have been sued on his unenforceable liability. The effect of setting off the unenforceable liability against the provable debt would be to

---

[285] See para 12.38 below.

[286] *Lord v Direct Acceptance Corporation Ltd* (1993) 32 NSWLR 362; *Re Bank of Credit and Commerce International SA (No 8)* [1998] AC 214.

[287] See the discussion in *Re Bank of Credit and Commerce International SA (No 8)* [1996] Ch 245, 262–263, CA.

[288] *Ex parte Dewdney* (1809) 15 Ves Jun 479, 33 ER 836.

[289] See the Insolvency Act, s 323(1), and the Insolvency Rules, r 4.90(1).

[290] *Pott v Clegg* (1847) 16 M & W 321, 153 ER 1212.

deprive him of the dividend that he otherwise would have received. The courts therefore may incline against that result on the ground that the purpose of the set-off section is to do substantial justice between the parties,[291] and a set-off in that situation would hardly be just. [292]

6.70 The prevailing view of the operation of the insolvency set-off section is that it is self-executing and takes effect automatically on the date of the bankruptcy or the liquidation.[293] The cross-demands are set against each other and to the extent of the set-off they are extinguished as at that date. This should have the consequence that the question whether a limitation period has expired for the purpose of ascertaining set-off entitlements should also be determined by reference to that date.[294]

L. Insolvency Set-off is Mandatory

Contracting out of insolvency set-off

6.71 In *National Westminster Bank Ltd v Halesowen Presswork & Assemblies Ltd*[295] the House of Lords[296] held that the set-off section in the insolvency legislation is mandatory in its operation, so that the parties to mutual dealings cannot contract out of its terms.[297] It re-affirmed that view in *Stein v Blake*,[298] and it has also been followed in Australia[299] and New Zealand.[300] If it is not possible to contract out of the terms of the set-off section, it should not be possible to waive the operation of the section,[301] and nor could the creditor be estopped by his conduct from asserting a set-off.[302] Nevertheless, while Lord Kilbrandon in the *Halesowen* case agreed

---

[291] *Forster v Wilson* (1843) 12 M & W 191, 203–204, 152 ER 1165, 1171.

[292] In New South Wales, Sheller JA quoted the corresponding passage in the second edition of this book in *Centurian Constructions Pty Ltd v Beca Developments Pty Ltd* [1999] NSWCA 457 at para 27.

[293] See para 6.79 *ff* below.

[294] Compare *Centurian Constructions Pty Ltd v Beca Developments Pty Ltd* [1999] NSWCA 457. Given that Beca was wound up in April 1992, which was within the limitation period for Centurian's claim, it should not have mattered that the limitation period for Centurian's claim had expired when Beca commenced proceedings.

[295] [1972] AC 785.

[296] *Per* Viscount Dilhorne, Lord Simon of Glaisdale, and Lord Kilbrandon; Lord Cross of Chelsea dissenting.

[297] This may not be the case in Ireland. See Breslin, 'Set-off under Irish Law' (1997) 18 Company Lawyer 198, 200. For a criticism of the mandatory principle, see Berg, 'Contracting Out of Set-off in a Winding Up' [1996] LMCLQ 49.

[298] [1996] AC 243, 254, 255. See also *Re ILG Travel Ltd* [1995] 2 BCLC 128, 160.

[299] *Re Paddington Town Hall Centre Ltd* (1979) 41 FLR 239. In *Gye v McIntyre* (1991) 171 CLR 609, 622 the High Court described this as 'the traditional and better view'.

[300] *Rendell v Doors and Doors Ltd* [1975] 2 NZLR 191.

[301] *Re Cushla Ltd* [1979] 3 All ER 415, 423.

[302] *Re Paddington Town Hall Centre Ltd* (1979) 41 FLR 239. Compare *Hunter v The Official Assignee of Bispham* (1898) 17 NZLR 175.

with the view that the terms of the set-off section are mandatory, he expressed reservation about the desirability of preserving the rule.[303] Subsequently the Cork Committee reiterated his Lordship's call for legislative intervention in this area, and recommended that the *Halesowen* case be reversed.[304] As a result of the decision in that case, whenever a company which is indebted to a bank attempts to realize its assets for the benefit of its creditors generally, or to arrange a moratorium, if properly advised it should open a new account with a different bank in order to ensure that future credits do not solely benefit the first bank in the event of the company's winding up in the form of a set-off against the debt. It would not be sufficient for the first bank to agree not to assert a set-off. In the opinion of the Cork Committee this is an unnecessary and an undesirable complication. It is difficult to see any convincing reason why a creditor who otherwise would be benefited by a set-off should not be permitted to renounce that benefit, with a consequent increase in the value of the assets available for distribution generally, and it is unfortunate that the Cork proposal has not been included in the Insolvency Act.

In the *Halesowen* case, Lord Simon of Glaisdale[305] justified their Lordship's view **6.72** on two grounds. The first is the mandatory nature of the language of the set-off section. The section provides that an account 'shall' be taken, and that the sums due on each side of the account 'shall' be set-off.[306] But, in addition, he supported the decision on the basis of a policy consideration, that the set-off section appears in a part of the insolvency legislation which lays down a procedure for a proper and orderly administration of a bankrupt's estate, and that this is a matter in which the commercial community has an interest. In truth, it is not clear why the setting off of cross-demands should be regarded as necessary for a proper and orderly administration of the estate. In *Re Maxwell Communications Corp plc (No 2)*[307] Vinelott J suggested a reason. He postulated that, if a creditor could waive his set-off, he might then prove in the bankruptcy and leave it to the trustee to recover the debt due to the estate in proceedings that might be protracted and expensive, and which might not result in the recovery of the full amount of the

---

[303] His Lordship said that 'such a rule . . . may be expected to form a serious embarrassment to those wishing to adopt the beneficial course of agreeing to moratoria for the assistance of a business in financial difficulties'. ([1972] AC 785, 824).

[304] *Cork Committee Report*, 305–306. If this recommendation were adopted, any agreement would have to be such that it was intended to survive bankruptcy or winding up proceedings. Compare *Victoria Products Ltd v Tosh and Co Ltd* (1940) 165 LT 78; *Ex parte Fletcher, Re Vaughan* (1877) 6 Ch D 350; *National Westminster Bank Ltd v Halesowen Presswork & Assemblies Ltd* [1972] AC 785.

[305] [1972] AC 785, 808–809. See also Viscount Dilhorne at 805, and Lord Kilbrandon at 824.

[306] Compare the New Zealand legislation considered in *Rendell v Doors and Doors Ltd* [1975] 2 NZLR 191, which provided that a debt 'may' be set off, although Chilwell J nevertheless followed the *Halesowen* case and held that the section is mandatory.

[307] [1993] 1 WLR 1402, 1411. See also *Stotter v Ararimu Holdings Ltd* [1994] 2 NZLR 655, 660.

debt. Vinelott J said that in the meantime the distribution of the insolvent estate might be held up, and a question might arise whether the creditor would be entitled to a dividend while proceedings to recover the debt due from him were on foot. This last comment is the key to the issue. If indeed it were possible to contract out of the right of set-off, and a creditor did so, the rule in *Cherry v Boultbee*[308] should apply so that, when the creditor later sought to participate in the fund represented by the insolvent's estate by claiming a dividend, he would be told that he already had an asset of the estate, in the form of his own indebtedness, which should be appropriated as satisfaction of the right to the dividend.[309] Vinelott J was concerned that the trustee in bankruptcy or the liquidator may have to undertake protracted and expensive legislation. If the purpose of the litigation was to establish the creditor's liability, in circumstances where the creditor was denying that he was liable and at the same time was claiming a dividend on the bankrupt's or the company's liability to him, presumably that would have to be undertaken in any event before a set-off could be accepted. If however his Lordship had in mind proceedings merely to enforce an otherwise admitted liability, the application of *Cherry v Boultbee* should obviate that concern. The adoption of a rule that a creditor can renounce the benefit of a set-off that otherwise may be available to him in the insolvency of the debtor would have the effect of increasing the estate available for distribution to the other creditors, and it is difficult to see what policy ground there is which is sufficient to override this benefit.

Agreement not to prove

6.73 While it appears settled that the parties to mutual dealings cannot contract out of the insolvency set-off section, a creditor may agree not to prove for his debt in the debtor's bankruptcy or liquidation. In such a case there would not be a creditor proving or claiming to prove for a debt, so that the prerequisite to the operation of the set-off section to that effect in section 323(1) of the Insolvency Act and rule 4.90(1) of the Insolvency Rules would not be satisfied.[310] By this method a creditor can renounce a right of set-off, but at a cost. The creditor gives up not only the set-off but also the right to a dividend on the debt owing to him.

Subordinated debt

6.74 It is a basic principle of insolvency law that the debts of a bankrupt or a company in liquidation (other than preferential and secured debts) must be paid *pari*

---

[308] (1839) 4 My & Cr 442, 41 ER 171. See ch 14 below.

[309] Williams J in *Fused Electrics Pty Ltd v Donald* [1995] 2 Qd R 7 doubted that *Cherry v Boultbee* applies in the context of a company liquidation, but the cases suggest otherwise. See para 14.07 below.

[310] *Kitchen's Trustee v Madders* [1950] 1 Ch 134, and see also *Re Bank of Credit and Commerce International SA (No 8)* [1996] Ch 245, 256, CA.

passu,[311] but recent case law suggests that this does not render subordination agreements ineffective. Pursuant to a subordination agreement, a creditor agrees that a debt owing to him is to be subordinated, or postponed, to debts owing to other unsubordinated creditors, so that the subordinated creditor is not to be paid anything until the unsubordinated creditors have been paid in full. One method of effectively subordinating a debt is for the creditor to agree to hold the debt or its proceeds on trust for other creditors,[312] or to assign the benefit of the debt to those creditors, so that they obtain the benefit of the debt in question.[313] In *Re Maxwell Communications Corp plc (No 2)*[314] however Vinelott J held that a simple contractual subordination, without a trust or an assignment, similarly is effective in the insolvency of the debtor. Courts in Australia have expressed similar views,[315] and moreover subordination now has statutory approval in Australia in certain defined circumstances pursuant to section 563C of the Corporations Act 2001 (Cth).[316] Subordination has also been upheld in New Zealand.[317] It has been suggested[318] that contractual subordination does not infringe the requirement of a

---

[311] See the Insolvency Act 1986, s 107 for voluntary winding up. The same principle applies to compulsory liquidations. See the Insolvency Rules, r 4.181 and *Webb v Smith* (1872) LR 5 HL 711, 735. For bankruptcies see the Insolvency Act, s 328(3)

[312] The distinction between a trust of a debt and a trust of the proceeds of a debt when received may be important in relation to set-off. In the former case a declaration of trust by the subordinated creditor would mean that mutuality would be lacking between the subordinated debt and a separate debt owing by the subordinated creditor to the debtor. If, however, the trust only attaches to the proceeds of the debt once received, the subordinated creditor would still have the equitable title to the debt itself, so that there would be mutuality in relation to the debt and the subordinated creditor's separate indebtedness. As Lord Templeman remarked in *Barclays Bank Ltd v TOSG Trust Fund Ltd* [1984] 1 AC 626, 674 (although in another context), equity does not overlook the distinction between a debt and a dividend on a debt. Before bankruptcy or liquidation, the question of a set-off under the Statutes of Set-off may depend, not only on whether the subordination agreement has given rise to a trust of the debt, but also whether the debt is enforceable at that time. See *Atlantic Acceptance Corporation Ltd v Burns & Dutton Construction (1962) Ltd* (1970) 14 DLR (3d) 175.

[313] See *Re Maxwell Communications Corp plc (No 2)* [1993] 1 WLR 1402, 1404–1405, 1416, referring to *Re British and Commonwealth Holdings plc (No 3)* [1992] 1 WLR 672.

[314] [1993] 1 WLR 1402. See also *Cheah v Equiticorp Finance Group Ltd* [1992] 1 AC 472, 477, PC.

[315] *Horne v Chester and Fein Property Developments Pty Ltd* [1987] VR 913; *Re NIAA Corp Ltd* (1993) 33 NSWLR 344; *United States Trust Co of New York v Australia and New Zealand Banking Group Ltd* (1995) 37 NSWLR 131. Compare *TBGL Enterprises Ltd v Belcap Enterprises Pty Ltd* (1995) 14 ACLC 205.

[316] The Corporations Act 2001 (Cth), s 563C(1) provides that nothing in Division 6 of Part 5.6, dealing with proof and ranking of claims, renders a debt subordination by a company unlawful or unenforceable, except so far as it would disadvantage a creditor who was not a party to, or otherwise concerned in, the debt subordination. Debt subordination is then defined in subsection (2) for the purpose of that provision, in terms of an agreement or declaration by a creditor of a company to the effect that, in specified circumstances, a specified debt that the company owes the creditor, or a specified part of the debt, will not be repaid until other specified debts that the company owes are repaid to a specified extent.

[317] *Stotter v Ararimu Holdings Ltd* [1994] 2 NZLR 655, referring to the Companies Act 1993 (NZ), s 313(3).

[318] See Southwell J in the Victorian Supreme Court in *Horne v Chester and Fein Property Developments Pty Ltd* [1987] VR 913.

pari passu distribution because it does not lessen the rights of creditors who are not a party to it, although that explanation has been doubted.[319]

6.75 If contractual subordination is effective, it is apparent that the effect of the subordination would be defeated if the creditor could set off the subordinated debt against a separate debt owing to him by the debtor in the latter's bankruptcy or liquidation. There is no authority directly on point, but the better view is that the subordinated creditor's debt would not be the subject of a set-off.[320] This may be justified on either of two grounds. The first is that an agreement for subordination of a debt may be interpreted as importing an intention that, until the debts of the unsubordinated creditors have been paid in full, the subordinated creditor's debt is not provable. If the debt is not provable, it cannot be set off, since it is a prerequisite to the operation of the set-off section that there be a creditor 'proving or claiming to prove' for a debt.[321] Thus, Vinelott J in *Re Maxwell Communications*,[322] while not expressly equating subordination with a waiver by a creditor of his right to prove save to the extent of any surplus assets remaining after other unsecured creditors have been paid, nevertheless had recourse to that concept as support for the validity of subordination. Alternatively, the agreement to postpone may be regarded as having the consequence that, until the unsubordinated creditors have been paid in full, nothing is to be regarded as due to the subordinated creditor for the purpose of the administration of the insolvent estate, including by way of dividend.[323] The set-off section provides that 'the sums due

---

[319] See Goode, *Legal Problems of Credit and Security* (2nd edn, 1988) 96.

[320] The Partnership Act 1890, s 3 provides that, if a person lends money in return for a share of profits in a business, and the borrower becomes bankrupt, the lender shall not be entitled to 'recover' anything in respect of the loan until the claims of the other creditors of the borrower have been satisfied. In *Ex parte Sheil, re Longeran* (1877) 4 Ch D 789, 791 James LJ suggested during argument that a similar provision in the Partnership Law Amendment Act 1865 would not have prevented the lender from setting off his claim on the loan against a separate indebtedness to the borrower. This conclusion however turned on the meaning of 'recover' in the legislation. A set-off was thought not to be prohibited because it does not involve any form of recovery. Accordingly, James LJ's comment is not an authority against the view expressed in the text in relation to set-off against subordinated debt generally. In *Atlantic Acceptance Corp Ltd v Burns & Dutton Construction (1962) Ltd* (1970) 14 DLR (3d) 175 it was held that a subordinated debt could not be set off, but that case concerned a claim for a set-off under the Statutes of Set-off where the debtor was not in liquidation. The debt could not be the subject of a set-off under the Statutes because according to its terms it was unenforceable at that time. See para 2.49 above.

[321] See the Insolvency Act 1986, s 323(1), and for companies the Insolvency Rules 1986, r 4.90(1).

[322] [1993] 1 WLR 1402, 1411–1412.

[323] Compare the discussion in *Gore-Browne on Companies* (44th edn, looseleaf, supplement 33) vol 1, §17.6.4, p 17.038. Contractual subordination is sometimes explained on the basis that the subordinated debt is subject to a contingency, the contingency being that the unsubordinated debts have been paid in full. Accordingly, if the debtor's assets are insufficient to pay the unsubordinated creditors' claims in full, the value of the subordinated debt would be nil for the purpose of proof. See eg in Australia *United States Trust Co of New York v Australia & New Zealand Banking Group Ltd* (1993) 11 ACLC 707, 711; *Re NIAA Corp Ltd* (1993) 33 NSWLR 344, 358. However, Vinelott J in *Re Maxwell Communications* [1993] 1 WLR 1402, 1418 doubted that a subordinated debt is

from one party shall be set off against the sums due from the other'.[324] If there is nothing due, there is nothing that can be set off.

It may transpire that the debtor's estate is in a position to pay something to the **6.76** subordinated creditor after payment in full of the unsubordinated creditors' debts. In such a case the subordinated debt should be capable of being employed in a set-off, because there is a debt which is then 'due' to the subordinated creditor. But this should only occur if the debtor's estate is sufficient to pay the unsubordinated creditors without taking into account the asset of the estate represented by the claim against the subordinated creditor, because this asset would disappear if the subordinated creditor could utilize it in a set-off.

The Insolvency Act 1986, section 74(2)(f) provides that a sum due to a member **6.77** of a company in his character of a member,[325] by way of dividends profits or otherwise, is not deemed to be a debt of the company payable to that member in a case of competition between himself and external creditors, although it may be taken into account for the purpose of the final adjustment of the rights of contributories among themselves. The section effects a statutory subordination, so that the sum due should not be able to be employed by the member in a set-off against a separate liability owing to the company where this would operate to the detriment of the external creditors. In Australia a similar provision appears in section 563A of the Corporations Act 2001 (Cth), according to which payment of a debt owed by a company to a member in that capacity is to be 'postponed' to other creditors.[326]

Ancillary liquidation

When a foreign company is in liquidation in the country of its incorporation and **6.78** there is an ancillary winding up in England, the set-off conferred by rule 4.90 of

---

accurately described as a contingent liability. The contingent theory does not adequately reflect the intended effect of subordination in all cases. Consider that the value of the debtor's assets exceeds the amount of the unsubordinated debts, but is less than the aggregate of the subordinated and the unsubordinated debts. According to the contingent theory, the trustee in bankruptcy or the liquidator would be required to value the subordinated debt. In the situation posited, the subordinated debt would have a value, because there are assets available to pay part of it after satisfying the unsubordinated debts. The difficulty is that, once a value is put upon the subordinated debt, that value under normal principles would be provable and would rank *pari passu* with the unsubordinated debts. But that would be contrary to the intended effect of the subordination.

[324] See the Insolvency Act 1986, s 323(2), and for companies the Insolvency Rules 1986, r 4.90(2).

[325] For a discussion of that expression, see *Soden v British and Commonwealth Holdings plc* [1998] AC 298. See also Hogan, 'Set-off, Members' Rights and Winding Up' (1998) 19 Company Lawyer 16.

[326] See also the Corporations Act 2001 (Cth), s 553A, which provides that a debt due by a company to a person in the person's capacity as a member, whether by way of dividends, profits or otherwise, is not admissible to proof unless the person has paid all amounts for which the person is liable as a member.

the Insolvency Rules 1986, being a substantive rule of English law,[327] must under English law be given effect in the English winding up. The court does not have a discretion to disapply it, notwithstanding that the law of the principal liquidation does not recognize a similar set-off.[328] This reflects the mandatory nature of the set-off. It also accords with the position under the European Union Regulation on Insolvency,[329] which came into force on 31 May 2002.[330] Pursuant to Article 4 of the Regulation, the law of the State within whose territory insolvency proceedings are opened determines the question of set-off.[331]

M. The Nature of Insolvency Set-off

(1) Automatic or Procedural?

6.79 A fundamental issue in relation to the set-off section in the insolvency legislation is whether it operates automatically upon the occurrence of a bankruptcy or a liquidation so as to bring about an extinguishment of the claims at that date to the extent of the set-off, or whether the section is procedural in its operation, in the sense that it requires the taking of an account at some stage during the bankruptcy or liquidation and, until that occurs, the demands retain their separate identities. In that regard, the commencement of the bankruptcy or, as the case may be, the time when the company goes into liquidation, generally is the point for determining what mutual debts, credits and dealings can be brought into an account.[332] But it does not necessarily follow that this is also the time when the demands are actually set against each other to produce a balance.

6.80 The key provision in the insolvency set-off section is the stipulation that: 'An account shall be taken of what is due from each party to the other in respect of the

---

[327] *Re Bank of Credit and Commerce International SA (No 10)* [1997] Ch 213, 246, referring to *Stein v Blake* [1996] AC 243. Compare *Macfarlane v Norris* (1862) 2 B & S 783, 792, 121 ER 1263, 1266.

[328] *Re Bank of Credit and Commerce International SA (No 10)* [1997] Ch 213. See Smart, "International Insolvency: Banks and Set-off" (1999) 1 Journal of International Banking and Financial Law 10.

[329] General Regulation (EC) No 1346/2000 of May 29, 2000 on insolvency proceedings.

[330] See Article 47.

[331] See Lightman and Moss, *The Law of Receivers and Administrators of Companies* (3rd edn, 2000) 542–4, and generally ch 26. In addition, Article 6 provides that the opening of insolvency proceedings does not affect the right of a creditor to demand a set-off against a claim by the debtor if a set-off is permitted under the law of the insolvent debtor's claim. Lightman and Moss makes the point (at 544) that, if a company is being wound up in another member state, and the insolvent company's claim against a creditor is governed by English law, it is doubtful whether Article 6 would have the effect of permitting a set-off under the Insolvency Rules 1986, r 4.90, because for r 4.90 to apply there must be a liquidation under English law. Article 6 would seem to contemplate instead rights of set-off before insolvency, in other words pursuant to the Statutes of Set-off and in accordance with the principles applicable to equitable set-off.

[332] *Ellis & Company's Trustee v Dixon-Johnson* [1924] 1 Ch 342, 356. See paras 6.31–6.45 above.

mutual dealings and the sums due from one party shall be set off against the sums due from the other.' On its face this may be thought to support a procedural operation, given that it appears to require the taking of an account of amounts which are due at the date of the account. The account could be taken in a bankruptcy either by the trustee in bankruptcy or by the court in proceedings before it. This interpretation would not mean that the trustee would have a discretion as to whether a set-off should occur,[333] and nor would it be inconsistent with the view that set-off in insolvency cannot be contracted out of,[334] particularly given that Lord Simon of Glaisdale who, as one of the majority in the *Halesowen* case[335] held that contracting out is not possible, nevertheless regarded the section as prescribing a course of procedure.[336] In other words, he said that it lays down a 'code of procedure'[337] which must be followed regardless of any agreement to the contrary.[338] The procedural view is consistent with views expressed in a long line of cases,[339] and in 1993 it was approved by the Court of Appeal in *Stein v Blake*.[340]

---

[333] A creditor could request the trustee to take an account and, if the trustee refused, or the creditor was otherwise dissatisfied with the result, the creditor could ask the court to review the decision under the Insolvency Act 1986, s 303. See *Stein v Blake* [1994] Ch 16, 29, CA.

[334] See para 6.71 above.

[335] [1972] AC 785.

[336] [1972] AC 785, 808. This is also consistent with Lord Simon's reference (at 808) to 'the imposition of a duty on a public officer'. The officer that he had in mind presumably was a trustee in bankruptcy, with the duty being the taking of an account. The comment would hardly have been apt if a set-off was thought to occur automatically. Viscount Dilhorne referred (at 305) to the set-off section as 'prescribing the course to be followed in the administration of the bankrupt's property.'

[337] [1972] AC 785, 809.

[338] Similarly, while Hallett J in *Victoria Products Ltd v Tosh & Co* (1940) 165 LT 78, 80 agreed that the set-off section cannot be contracted out of, he nevertheless described it in terms of laying down a 'process'.

[339] In *Sovereign Life Assurance Co v Dodd* [1892] 2 QB 573 Lord Esher MR apparently considered (see esp at 578) that the cross-demands in issue in that case were still subsisting at the date of the liquidator's action, which accords with his earlier dictum (as Brett J) in *New Quebrada Co Ltd v Carr* (1869) LR 4 CP 651, 653–654, that the set-off section does not extinguish mutual debts. In a similar vein, Rich J in the Australian High Court in *Hiley v The Peoples Prudential Assurance Co Ltd* (1938) 60 CLR 468, 487 referred with evident approval to Bigham J's description of the operation of the set-off section in *Re Daintrey* [1900] 1 QB 546, 568 in terms that, 'the account which the section of the Act directed should be taken is to be taken when the claim on the one side or the other is presented'. This suggests that an account is required to be taken in respect of subsisting cross-demands. See also Romer LJ at 574 ('It is quite sufficient if the account can be taken when the set-off arises'). Wright J in that case noted (at 552) that Lord Selborne in *Ex parte Barnett, Re Deveze* (1874) LR 9 Ch App 293, 295 seemed to have considered that a set-off took effect at the time that the creditor came in to prove. Indeed, Lord Selborne was a member of the House of Lords in *Mersey Steel and Iron Co v Naylor, Benzon & Co* (1874) 9 App Cas. 434 when it affirmed an order made by the Court of Appeal ((1882) 9 QBD 648, 672) in an action brought by a liquidator for payment of a debt, to the effect that 'the defendants are entitled to set-off against the 1713*l admitted to be due* to the plaintiffs such damages as they the defendants may have sustained' (emphasis added). This contemplated that there was still an amount due to the plaintiffs at the time of the action, notwithstanding the availability of a set-off, and that it was the order of the court itself which brought about the set-off. See also Lord Selborne in *Re Milan Tramways Co, ex p Theys* (1884) 25 Ch D 587, 591.

cont./

6.81   It is difficult on the other hand to find clear evidence of the automatic extinguish-ment theory before 1984,[341] when it was adopted by Neill J in *Farley v Housing and Commercial Developments Ltd*.[342] After that judgment, however, it gained rapid support. It received the approval of the High Court of Australia in *Gye v McIntyre*,[343] and it was also accepted by Hoffmann LJ in the Chancery Division, as well as by the Court of Appeal on appeal, in *M S Fashions Ltd v Bank of Credit and Commerce International SA*.[344] *M S Fashions* concerned a bank which had pro-vided an advance to a customer secured by both a guarantee and a cash deposit by the guarantor. The bank went into liquidation and the liquidator, instead of pro-ceeding against the guarantor, made a demand on the debtor, and said that the guarantor should be confined to a proof in the liquidation in respect of the de-posit. The Court of Appeal held that there was a set-off as between the guarantor and the bank which had the effect of automatically satisfying the guarantor's li-ability to the bank, and since the guarantor had paid the debt by means of the set-off the customer could no longer be sued.[345] Following the conflicting decisions by differently constituted Courts of Appeal in the *M S Fashions* case and *Stein v Blake*, the issue came before the House of Lords by way of an appeal in *Stein v Blake*.[346] Their Lordships[347] unanimously held that the automatic extinguishment theory provides the correct analysis of the operation of the insolvency set-off section, and rejected the argument that the section has a procedural operation. Subsequently the House of Lords re-affirmed that view in *Re Bank of Credit and Commerce International SA (No 8)*,[348] and it is now firmly established.[349]

On another occasion Kay LJ referred to a 'right of set-off after the bankruptcy'. See *Re Washington Diamond Mining Co* [1893] 3 Ch 95, 113. More recently, see *Re Bank of Credit and Commerce International SA (No 8)* [1995] Ch 46, 63–64, *per* Rattee J; *Day & Dent Constructions Pty Ltd v North Australian Properties Pty Ltd* (1982) 150 CLR 85, 109 *per* Murphy J; *McIntyre v Perkes* (1990) 22 FCR 260, 270, *per* Gummow and von Doussa JJ; *Re Capel, ex p Marac Finance Australia Ltd v Capel* (1994) 48 FCR 195.

[340]   [1994] Ch 16.

[341]   An exception is Wright J's comment in passing in *Watkins v Lindsay and Co* (1898) 67 LJQB 362, 364, that set-off in bankruptcy is automatic. In *Ex parte Barnett, re Deveze* (1874) LR 9 Ch App 293, 297 Mellish LJ said in relation to the insolvency set-off section that, 'I doubt whether it does not affect it even before either party comes in to prove; but, at any rate, when the party does come in to prove, the statute sets the one debt against the other, and that is equivalent to payment'.

[342]   (1984) 26 BLR 66.

[343]   (1991) 171 CLR 609, 622.

[344]   [1993] Ch 425.

[345]   Why was a set-off available as between the guarantor and the bank? See the discussion of the case in para 12.23 below.

[346]   [1996] AC 243.

[347]   Lord Keith of Kinkel, Lord Ackner, Lord Lloyd of Berwick, Lord Nicholls of Birkenhead, and Lord Hoffmann.

[348]   [1998] AC 214, 223.

[349]   See eg *Manson v Smith* [1997] 2 BCLC 161, 164, *per* Millett LJ; *Re Bank of Credit and Commerce International SA (No 10)* [1997] Ch 213, 226, 236, *per* Sir Richard Scott VC; *Craig v Humberclyde Industrial Finance Group Ltd* [1999] 1 WLR 129; *Bank of Credit and Commerce*

The issue in *Stein v Blake* was whether a trustee in bankruptcy could assign a debt **6.82** owing to the bankrupt when the debtor had a cross-claim available for a set-off. The Court of Appeal held that the debt could be assigned. The set-off section was regarded as being procedural in its operation, so that it did not of itself extinguish the mutual debts. For the debts to be extinguished an account had to be taken,[350] either by the trustee in bankruptcy or by the court. Since this had not occurred at the date of the assignment, it was held that the separate debts retained their separate identities and therefore they could be assigned. This did not mean that the defendant lost the benefit of the set-off otherwise available in the bankruptcy. Because the assignment occurred after the bankruptcy, the assignee would still have taken subject to an equity in the form of the defendant's right of set-off under the insolvency legislation. On appeal the House of Lords rejected the Court of Appeal's analysis.[351] The judgment of the Law Lords was delivered by Lord Hoffmann, who also had delivered the judgment in the Chancery Division in the *M S Fashions* case. His view on the point had not changed. He said that insolvency set-off 'is self-executing and takes effect on the bankruptcy date'.[352] Its operation does not depend upon any procedural step, but rather it 'results, as of the bankruptcy date, in only a net balance being owing',[353] so that at that date the cross-claims cease to exist as separate choses in action. Accordingly, it was not possible for a trustee in bankruptcy to assign the debt owing to the bankrupt to the extent that it had already been extinguished by a set-off.[354]

The notion of an automatic cancellation of cross-demands on the date of the **6.83** bankruptcy or liquidation may be inconvenient when a trustee in bankruptcy is proposing to assign a debt owing to the bankrupt. Neither the trustee nor the

---

International (Overseas) Ltd v Habib Bank Ltd [1999] 1 WLR 42; *Bouygues (UK) Ltd v Dahl-Jensen (UK) Ltd* [2000] BLR 522, 528, CA.

[350] See Staughton LJ at [1994] Ch 16, 29.

[351] [1996] AC 243. In particular, the House of Lords rejected (at 255–256) the application of the notion of 'taking subject to equities' in this context.

[352] [1996] AC 243, 256. In *Re Bank of Credit and Commerce International SA (No 8)* [1996] Ch 245, 255 the Court of Appeal, *per* Rose, Saville, and Millett LJ described insolvency set-off as 'mandatory, automatic and immediate on the bankruptcy or liquidation taking place'. On appeal in the House of Lords in that case [1998] AC 214, 223, Lord Hoffmann commented: 'When the conditions of [the Insolvency Rules 1986, r 4.90] are satisfied, a set-off is treated as having taken place automatically on the bankruptcy date.'

[353] [1996] AC 243, 255.

[354] See also *Craig v Humberclyde Industrial Finance Group Ltd* [1999] 1 WLR 129. The House of Lords in *Stein v Blake* went on to hold that the trustee nevertheless could assign any claim for the net balance owing to the estate after taking into account the set-off, and that as a matter of construction the assignment of the claim in that case also carried the right to the balance after deducting the cross-claim. See [1996] AC 243, 258–259. In *Citicorp Australia Ltd v Official Trustee in Bankruptcy* (1996) 71 FCR 550, 567–568 the Full Court of the Federal Court rejected an argument that there could be no assignment where it was not possible on the evidence available to the trustee or the court to conclude that the net balance after any set-off was in favour of the bankrupt. Rather, the merits and the quantum of the claim and cross-claim could be litigated, and that litigation would determine whether there was a balance one way or the other.

bankrupt may be aware that the debtor has a cross-claim extinguishing the debt, for example where the debtor before the bankruptcy had taken an assignment of a debt owing by the bankrupt to a third party. Under the automatic theory the debtor need not do anything. There would not be any incentive for him to notify the trustee of the set-off, or indeed to respond to inquiries, since a set-off would have occurred automatically. It may not be until some time later, when the debt assigned by the trustee matures and the assignee seeks payment, that the set-off comes to light. If on the other hand the set-off were procedural in its operation, it is more likely that the debtor would have informed the trustee of the set-off enti-tlement, in which case the trustee could have tempered his dealings with the pro-posed assignee accordingly. In other respects, however, the notion of an automatic cancellation of cross-demands at the date of the bankruptcy or liquidation is a convenient result. For example, when an interest-bearing debt is owing to a bank-rupt, it prevents an argument that interest continues to run until the account is taken.[355] Furthermore, when a trustee in bankruptcy assigns a debt owing to the bankrupt, and the debtor has a cross-claim available as a set-off, the set-off would have occurred automatically, and the assignee would be bound by it. It would not be necessary for the debtor to insist that the trustee take an account, so as to pre-vent a situation arising whereby the assignee could take free of the set-off if the bankrupt is discharged from bankruptcy, and as a result is released from his liabil-ity to the debtor, before a set-off has occurred.[356] From this perspective *Stein v Blake* is a welcome development. Nevertheless, the automatic theory raises a number of questions.

Pleading set-off as a defence to an action by a trustee in bankruptcy

6.84 A trustee in bankruptcy may sue for a debt owing to the estate, and the defendant may plead as a defence a set-off under the insolvency legislation. The House of Lords in *Stein v Blake* said that this does not mean that separate claims exist until the court has decided the issue. Rather, their Lordships considered that the litiga-tion is merely part of a process of retrospective calculation, from which it will ap-pear that from the date of the bankruptcy the only chose in action that continued to exist was a claim for the balance.[357] However, this is not the way that the issue

---

[355] See para 6.108 below.

[356] See *Farley v Housing and Commercial Developments Ltd* (1984) 26 BLR 66. In Australia, com-pare *Re Capel, ex p Marac Finance Australia Ltd v Capel* (1994) 48 FCR 195. See paras 6.101–6.103 below. Compare also *Edmonds Judd v Official Assignee* [1999] NZCA 283, in which it was assumed that the discharge from the bankruptcy affected the creditor's right to assert the set-off. The credi-tor had recieved a dividend, but see para 6.112 below.

[357] [1996] AC 243, 255. Compare Bigham J in *Re Daintrey* [1900] 1 QB 546, 568, who equated the stipulation in the 1883 bankruptcy set-off section (Bankruptcy Act 1883, s 38) that there should be a person 'proving or claiming to prove a debt under such receiving order' with the notion that there should be a person 'having a right to prove a debt in the bankruptcy proceedings initiated by the receiving order'.

appears to have been regarded historically. From early days, the defendant in an action brought against him by assignees in bankruptcy who wished to defend the action on the basis of a set-off would not deny that he was liable to the bankrupt because of a set-off that had already occurred at the date of the bankruptcy. Rather, he would plead that the bankrupt 'was, *and still is*, indebted to the defendant'.[358] A similar form of pleading is to be found in successive editions of Bullen and Leake.[359] This suggests that the cross-demands were regarded as still retaining their separate identities at the date of the action, which of course was after the bankruptcy. Indeed, when the Court of Appeal in 1881[360] confirmed that insolvency set-off could be relied on as a defence to an action at law brought by a trustee in bankruptcy for payment of a debt owing to the bankrupt,[361] Sir George Jessel explained this on the ground that, while the bankruptcy legislation contemplated a set-off occurring in the Bankruptcy Court, the common law courts considered that it was within 'the equity of the statute' that it should also provide a defence to a trustee's action.[362] If however the bankruptcy legislation were regarded as bringing about an automatic extinguishment of cross-demands upon the occurrence of a bankruptcy, it would hardly have been necessary for the common law courts to have recourse to that concept.

When considering nineteenth century cases, it should therefore be appreciated **6.85** that insolvency set-off at the time was not thought of as operating automatically at the date of the bankruptcy. Attempts to explain the cases by reference to the automatic theory would be founded upon a false premise.[363]

---

[358] See eg *Hulme v Muggleston* (1837) 3 M & W 30, 31, 150 ER 1043, 1044; *Russell v Bell* (1841) 8 M & W 277, 278, 151 ER 1042, 1043; *Bittleston v Timmis* (1845) 1 CB 389, 391, 135 ER 591, 592. See also *West v Baker* (1875) 1 Ex D 44, 45. In *Gibson v Bell* (1835) 1 Bing NC 743, 131 ER 1303 the defendant pleaded (at 746, 1305) that 'the said sum of money still remained unpaid and unsatisfied to the Defendant.'

[359] In the second edition of Bullen and Leake, *Precedents of Pleading* in 1863, the plea was set out (at 580) in terms that a debt owing by the bankrupt 'at the commencement of this suit was and still is due to the defendant'. The substance of the plea was repeated in subsequent editions, save for the 13th edition in 1990, where the set-off was pleaded instead (at 1420–1) in terms that: 'there is due from the plaintiff to the defendant the sum of £. The defendant is entitled to set off such sum against the plaintiff's claim under section 323 of the Insolvency Act 1986.' That revised form of plea also suggests a procedural operation to the set-off section. In the most recent edition (*Bullen and Leake and Jacob's Precedents of Pleadings* (14th edn, 2001)), the pleading for insolvency set-off has been omitted.

[360] *Peat v Jones & Co* (1881) 8 QBD 147.

[361] In the case of company liquidation, see eg *Mersey Steel and Iron Co v Naylor, Benzon & Co* (1884) 9 App Cas 434.

[362] (1881) 8 QBD 147, 149. See also *Mersey Steel and Iron Co v Naylor, Benzon & Co* (1882) 9 QBD 648, 664; *McIntyre v Perkes* (1990) 22 FCR 260, 270–271, Federal Court. For a discussion of the concept of the equity of a statute, see *Nelson v Nelson* (1995) 184 CLR 538, 552–554.

[363] The Court of Appeal failed to appreciate this in *Re Bank of Credit and Commerce International SA (No 8)* [1996] Ch 245, 265–269 when it sought to reconcile Lord Eldon's decision in *Ex parte Stephens* (1805) 11 Ves Jun 24, 32 ER 996 with the automatic theory. This led the Court of Appeal to suggest that discharge of a surety by way of set-off may not discharge the principal debtor. See paras 12.26–12.36 below.

Contingent debts and claims

6.86 The set-off section stipulates that 'the sums due from one party shall be set off against the sums due from the other'. There must then be a sum 'due' on each side of the account when the set-off occurs, which, according to the House of Lords in *Stein v Blake*, is the date of the bankruptcy. The requirement of a sum due would be satisfied in relation to a claim which has accrued and which is presently payable at that date. It would also be satisfied in relation to a debt which is presently existing but which is expressed not to be payable until a future date. It would be appropriate in that regard to interpret 'due' as including 'owing, although not payable until some future date'.[364] It may also be accepted that 'due' would encompass a liability which has accrued but which remains to be quantified.[365] Consider, however, a debt or liability which is still contingent at the date of the bankruptcy.

6.87 It is clear that the fact that a debt or liability is still contingent at the date of the bankruptcy does not suffice to exclude it from the operation of the set-off section.[366] This cannot be explained however simply by interpreting 'due', in the stipulation 'the sums due from the one party shall be set off against the sums due from the other', as including contingent debts. 'Due' is not usually interpreted as extending to such debts.[367] Moreover, if indeed it were simply a case of saying that 'due' includes 'contingently due', that should apply to both sides of the account, which would have as a consequence that a contingent debt owing *to* a bankrupt in respect of which the contingency has not occurred could be included in a set-off. Yet, it has been accepted, including by Hoffmann LJ (as he then was) in *M S Fashions Ltd v Bank of Credit and Commerce International SA*,[368] that a contingent claim possessed by a bankrupt cannot be the subject of a set-off until the contingency occurs and the claim vests.[369] How, then, do contingent debts fit in with the automatic theory of insolvency set-off approved by the House of Lords?

6.88 Consider first that the subject of a set-off is a contingent debt owing by the bankrupt. The fact that the liability is contingent at the date of the bankruptcy is not inconsistent with the automatic extinguishment theory. Debts must be proved according to their value as at the date of the bankruptcy. If a liability of the bankrupt

---

[364] *Clyne v Deputy Commissioner of Taxation* (1981) 150 CLR 1, 8.

[365] See eg *Gye v McIntyre* (1991) 171 CLR 609. See also Malins VC in *Booth v Hutchinson* (1872) LR 15 Eq 30, 34 in the context of the judgment for damages for £50 given after the deed of assignment in relation to the prior breach.

[366] See paras 8.14–8.26 (contingent debt owing by the insolvent) and paras 8.27–8.37 (contingent debt owing to the insolvent) below.

[367] *Merritt Cairns Constructions Pty Ltd v Wulguru Heights Pty Ltd* [1995] 2 Qd R 521, 526; *Ex parte Kemp, Re Fastnedge* (1874) LR 9 Ch App 383.

[368] [1993] Ch 425, 435. See also *Re Bank of Credit and Commerce International SA (No 8)* [1998] AC 214, 224, *per* Lord Hoffmann.

[369] See para 8.27 below.

is contingent, the trustee must estimate its value as at that date, and that value may be proved in the bankruptcy.[370] This provable valuation is treated as the amount due for the purpose of the administration of the bankruptcy, including in relation to the set-off section.

The position is different, when the contingency is on the other side of the account, in other words when the bankrupt is possessed of a contingent claim. In contrast to the case of a bankrupt's contingent liabilities, there is no mechanism in the Insolvency Act for a trustee or the court to value the bankrupt's contingent claims. If the contingency occurs after the bankruptcy, the claim should ordinarily be capable of being employed in a set-off.[371] But given that there is no power in the insolvency legislation to put a value on the contingent claim as at the date of the bankruptcy, it seems difficult to say that anything is 'due' in respect of it as at that date. **6.89**

Hindsight and estimation

In *Stein v Blake*[372] Lord Hoffmann sought to explain the position with respect to contingencies by reference to two 'techniques'. **6.90**

> How does the law deal with the conundrum of having to set off, as of the bankruptcy date, 'sums due' which may not yet be due or which may become owing upon contingencies which have not yet occurred. It employs two techniques. The first is to take into account everything which has actually happened between the bankruptcy date and the moment when it becomes necessary to ascertain what, on that date, was the state of account between the creditor and the bankrupt. If by that time the contingency has occurred and the claim has been quantified, then that is the amount which is treated as having been due at the bankruptcy date . . .
>
> But the winding up of the estate of a bankrupt or an insolvent company cannot always wait until all possible contingencies have happened and all the actual or potential liabilities which existed at the bankruptcy date have been quantified. Therefore the law adopts a second technique, which is to make an estimation of the value of the claim.

Later he remarked that ' "due" merely means treated as having been owing at the bankruptcy date with the benefit of the hindsight and, if necessary, estimation prescribed by the bankruptcy law.'[373]

---

[370] See the Insolvency Act 1986, s 322 and, for company liquidation, the Insolvency Rules 1986, r 4.86.

[371] See paras 8.28–8.35 below.

[372] [1996] AC 243, 252.

[373] [1996] AC 243, 256. Similarly, the Court of Appeal in *Re Bank of Credit and Commerce International SA (No 8)* [1996] Ch 245, 269 commented that: 'it is now settled that the set-off operates automatically upon the date of bankruptcy, and that the hindsight principle enables debts to be treated as owing or not on that date with the benefit of hindsight . . .'.

The difficulty with hindsight

6.91 While the application of the hindsight principle is not open to question in the case of a contingent liability of a bankrupt, the same cannot be said where the issue concerns a *claim* of a bankrupt that was contingent at the relevant date,[374] given that the power of estimation does not apply in that context.[375] In that regard, it should be appreciated the first technique of hindsight is not independent of the second technique of estimation. Consider the application of the techniques when a bankrupt's contingent liability is in issue. In such a case, a subsequent occurrence of the contingency may be taken into account for the purpose of proof and of set-off, although it has been emphasized that this is not because the happening of the contingency is accelerated so as to fix the amount of the claim on the basis of the contingency having occurred at the date of the bankruptcy.[376] It is not a matter of deeming a state of affairs to have existed at the bankruptcy date that in fact did not exist. That accords with the ordinary meaning of 'hindsight', that one sees what has happened after the event.[377] Rather, the insolvency legislation has provided in the case of a contingent liability that a sum is to be regarded as due for the purpose of the administration of the bankruptcy, in the form of the value which the trustee must put on a it.[378] This has been interpreted as requiring a valuation as at the date of the bankruptcy,[379] and in taking into account a subsequent occurrence of the contingency the trustee is merely using all the available evidence to ascertain what, with hindsight, was *as a matter of fact* the true value of the liability as at that date.[380] The position is entirely different, however, when a bankrupt's *claim* was still subject to a contingency when the bankruptcy occurred. In such a case there is no question of a valuation as at the date of the bankruptcy, because there is no machinery in the insolvency legislation for a trustee or the court to put a value on it

---

[374] The ensuing discussion is also relevant to Lord Hoffmann's earlier discussion of contingent claims in the *M S Fashions* case [1993] Ch 425, 435.

[375] *Sovereign Life Assurance Co v Dodd* [1892] 2 QB 573, to which Lord Hoffmann referred in his judgment ([1996] AC 243, 252), concerned a contingent liability of a company in liquidation, rather than a contingent claim. The full matured value of the policies was allowed to be set off, because that was the provable value. In other words, this was an aspect of the second technique, which only applies to a contingent liability owing by a bankrupt, and not to a contingent claim.

[376] *Ellis & Company's Trustee v Dixon-Johnson* [1924] 1 Ch 342, 356–357, *per* P O Lawrence J. This has since been regarded as a correct statement of the principle. See *Re Dynamics Corp of America* [1976] 1 WLR 757, 768, *per* Oliver J; *Re Hurren* [1983] 1 WLR 183, 189, *per* Walton J.

[377] 'Hindsight' is defined in *The Oxford English Dictionary* (2nd edn, 1989) vol VII, 244 as: 'Seeing what has happened, and what ought to have been done, after the event; perception gained by looking backward.'

[378] A similar principle applies in a company liquidation. See the Insolvency Rules 1986, r 4.86.

[379] *Ellis & Company's Trustee v Dixon-Johnson* [1924] 1 Ch 342, 356–357 (date of the receiving order under the Bankruptcy Act 1914); *Re Dynamics Corporation of America* [1976] 1 WLR 757, 767 (winding up).

[380] *Ellis & Company's Trustee v Dixon-Johnson* [1924] 1 Ch 342, 356–357; *Re Dynamics Corp of America* [1976] 1 WLR 757, 767–768; *Re Hurren* [1982] 3 All ER 982, 987. See also *Transit Casualty Co v Policyholders Protection Board* [1992] 2 Lloyd's Rep 358, 359, 361.

as at that date.[381] If there is no basis for valuing it as at the date of the bankruptcy, then, unlike a contingent liability of the bankrupt, there is no justification for saying that there was an amount then 'due' for the purpose of the administration of the bankrupt's estate. The set-off section provides that 'the sums due from one party shall be set off against the sums due from the other'. The fundamental point is that it only contemplates a set-off occurring against a sum which is then due,[382] and it seems difficult to assert that a sum was due to the bankrupt at the date of the bankruptcy for the purpose of an automatic set-off occurring at that date if the claim in question was still subject to a contingency.

For example, there have been cases in which property was deposited with a person **6.92** with authority to sell, and the sale did not occur until after the depositor's bankruptcy,[383] or a policy of insurance was deposited by an insured with a broker with authority to collect the insurance money in the event of a loss, and the loss occurred and the proceeds were received after the insured had become bankrupt.[384] In each case it was held that the claim brought by the assignees or the trustee in bankruptcy of the depositor could be the subject of a set-off. But until the sale occurred, or the insurance proceeds were received in respect of the loss occurring after the bankruptcy, there hardly seems to have been any sum which could be described as 'due' to the bankrupt. Moreover, since the question concerned a contingent claim possessed by a bankrupt, as opposed to a contingent liability, there was no question of the contingent claim being valued as at the date of the bankruptcy for the purpose of the administration of the estate.[385] In truth, until the relevant event occurred, there was nothing due.[386] Consider also *Graham v Russell.*[387] An underwriter was allowed to set off his liability on a policy in the insured's bankruptcy, even though the loss occurred after the bankruptcy.[388] But if there was no loss at the date of the bankruptcy, on what basis could it be said that there was then a sum due from the underwriter to the bankrupt insured for the purpose of a set-off occurring at that date? In *Lee & Chapman's Case*[389] a company had contracted with the Commissioners of Sewers to pave a street. The company went

---

[381] *Re Daintrey* [1900] 1 QB 546, 557, 565, 573.

[382] The question, according to Lawrence LJ in *Re Fenton* [1931] 1 Ch 85, 113, is whether 'there was any sum due . . . when the right to set off was claimed . . .'.

[383] *Palmer v Day & Sons* [1895] 2 QB 618; *French v Fenn* (1783) 3 Dougl 257, 99 ER 642. See also *Astley v Gurney* (1869) LR 4 CP 714.

[384] *Olive v Smith* (1813) 5 Taunt 56, 128 ER 607. See also *Parker v Carter* (1788), unreported but noted in Cooke, *The Bankrupt Laws* (8th edn, 1823) vol 1, 578.

[385] The right to obtain a valuation of a contingent debt and to prove in respect of that amount was introduced by the statute (1825) 6 Geo IV, c 16, s 56.

[386] See also *Booth v Hutchinson* (1872) LR 15 Eq 30, 35 with respect to rent accruing to a bankrupt landlord after the bankruptcy.

[387] (1816) 5 M & S 498, 105 ER 1133.

[388] The court declined to follow *Glennie v Edmunds* (1813) 4 Taunt 775, 128 ER 536. Compare also *Ex parte Blagden* (1815) 19 Ves Jun 465, 34 ER 589.

[389] (1885) 30 Ch D 216.

into liquidation before completion of the works, but the liquidator subsequently completed them and claimed the price. The Court of Appeal held that the Commissioners were entitled to a set-off under the Bankruptcy Act 1869 in respect of a damages claim that they had against the company. Once again, however, it would be difficult to argue that the price was due to the company at the date of the liquidation, given that the works had not then been completed. Indeed, Brett MR referred in his judgment to 'a right of set-off as between the company in liquidation and these Commissioners accruing *after* the winding-up'.[390]

6.93 Admittedly the set-off section in issue in some of those cases did not specifically provide that the debts to be set off had to be 'due'. [391] The section was not drafted in this manner until the 1869 Act, which was similar to the current provision. It has never been suggested, however, that the 1869 Act had the effect of narrowing the scope of insolvency set-off, which would have been the consequence if those early cases were not good law after that Act.[392] On the contrary, as Sir George Jessel MR remarked in the context of a discussion of the 1869 Act, the whole tendency of the history of the insolvency legislation has been to extend the principle upon which the right of set-off is founded.[393]

6.94 The problem comes even more sharply into focus if one considers the cases dealing with a temporary suspension of mutual credit,[394] such as *Bolland v Nash*.[395] In *Bolland v Nash* a bill of exchange had been accepted by a creditor of some debtors and, having come into the hands of the debtors, it was indorsed by them before their bankruptcy to a third party. After the bankruptcy the bill was dishonoured

---

[390] (1885) 30 Ch D 216, 222 (emphasis added).

[391] Prior to the 1869 Act the set-off section in force was s 171 of the Bankrupt Law Consolidation Act 1849, which provided that, where there was mutual credit between a bankrupt and another person, 'the court shall state the account between them, and one debt or demand may be set against another . . .'. The set-off section in the previous 1825 Act (6 Geo IV, c 16, s 50) was expressed in similar terms, although referring to the commissioners rather than the court. The House of Lords in *Stein v Blake* [1996] AC 243, 257 noted the reference to 'may' in the 1849 Act, and suggested that, because of this, the self-executing nature of the set-off may not have been as fully apparent then as it is today. On the contrary, one would have thought that the stipulation that 'the court shall state the account' indicates a procedural operation.

[392] Nor, apparently, did text-writers at the time attach any great consequence to the change in the wording of the section. Thus, Robson in his *Treatise on the Law of Bankruptcy* (3rd edn, 1876) 330 commented in relation to the 1869 Act that, apart from the expansion in the scope of the set-off section by the introduction of mutual dealings as forming a ground of set-off, and some other 'verbal variations' from the old clause, the principles and practice relating to set-off did not appear to have been substantially altered by the new provision, and a similar view was expressed in the first edition of *Williams on Bankruptcy*, being Williams and Williams, *The New Law and Practice in Bankruptcy* (1870) 51.

[393] *Peat v Jones & Co* (1881) 8 QBD 147, 149. See also Brett LJ (at 149–150), referring to Malins VC in *Booth v Hutchinson* (1872) LR 15 Eq 30, 35 with respect to the addition of 'mutual dealings' to the set-off section; *Sovereign Life Assurance Co v Dodd* [1892] 2 QB 573, 582; Williams and Williams, *The New Law and Practice in Bankruptcy* (1870) 51.

[394] See para 6.65 above.

[395] (1828) 8 B & C 105, 108 ER 982.

by the creditor and then returned to the bankrupts as indorsers. It was held that the creditor could set off a debt owing to him by the bankrupts against his liability to them on the bill, the important point being that the bankrupts were required to take up the bill again as a result of a prior obligation. Yet at the date of the bankruptcy the bill was held by the third party, and so it is difficult to see how it could be said that a set-off occurred at that date.[396] Consider also the decision of the High Court of Australia in *Hiley v The Peoples Prudential Assurance Co Ltd*.[397] A mortgagee before its liquidation assigned the mortgage to a third party as security for moneys owing. After the liquidation the mortgage was transferred back to the mortgagee. When the mortgagee's liquidator brought proceedings to enforce the mortgage debt, it was held that the mortgagor could set off a cross-demand that he had against the mortgagee. The justification for the set-off was that the mortgage had been assigned by way of security, so that the mortgagee had an equity of redemption, and the mortgagee got back the claim by virtue of this right subsisting at the commencement of the winding up. By itself the equity of redemption was not regarded as sufficient to give rise to a set-off, at least to the extent of the amount of the debt in respect of which the mortgage had been assigned by way of security.[398] If the mortgage had not been transferred back, a set-off would not have occurred to the extent of that amount.[399] But once again, the view that a set-off occurred at the date of the liquidation would not be easy to explain in this context, given that the mortgage at that date was held by a third party.

The ordinary meaning of 'hindsight', in terms of seeing what has happened after the event,[400] accurately describes the process when a contingent debt owing *by* a bankrupt is valued as at the bankruptcy date for the purpose of proof and set-off. Subsequent events may be looked at, including a subsequent occurrence of the contingency, in order to ascertain what was the true value of the contingent debt as at the date of the bankruptcy. That process does not involve deeming an event to have occurred that did not occur. Since *Stein v Blake*, however, the concept of 'hindsight' seems to have taken on broader meaning, so as to assume the characteristics of a fiction.[401] Thus, the House of Lords said in that case that 'due' in the insolvency set-off section means 'treated as having been owing at the bankruptcy

6.95

---

[396] In *Re Anglo-Greek Steam Navigation and Trading Co* (1869) LR 4 Ch App 174 Selwyn LJ followed *Bolland v Nash* as an alternative ground for his decision. See also *Ex parte Banes, re the Royal British Bank* (1857) 28 LTOS 296.

[397] (1938) 60 CLR 468.

[398] Compare *Re Asphaltic Wood Pavement Co. Lee & Chapman's Case* (1885) 30 Ch D 216, explained in *Hiley* (1938) 60 CLR 468, 497–499, *per* Dixon J. See paras 11.27–11.29 below.

[399] See *Re City Life Assurance Co. Stephenson's Case* [1926] 1 Ch 191, 214, explained in *Hiley* (1938) 60 CLR 468, 501–505, *per* Dixon J, and see Rich J at 488.

[400] See *The Oxford English Dictionary* (2nd edn, 1989) vol VII, p 244, and para 6.91 above.

[401] Contrary to the view that has been expressed, that the spirit of the times does not favour the preservation or creation of legal fictions. See Gummow J in *Pyrenees Shire Council v Day* (1998) 192 CLR 330, 387, and again in *Scott v Davis* (2000) 204 CLR 333, 376 para 128.

date with the benefit of the hindsight and, if necessary, estimation prescribed by the bankruptcy law'.[402] The Court of Appeal expressed a similar view in *Re Bank of Credit and Commerce International SA (No 8)*,[403] commenting that 'the hindsight principle enables debts to be treated as owing or not on [the date of bankruptcy] with the benefit of hindsight . . .'. Those statements on their face would extend not only to a contingent debt owing by a bankrupt but also to a contingent debt on the other side of the account, in other words a contingent debt owing *to* a bankrupt, where the contingency occurs after the bankruptcy so as *then* to become due and accordingly susceptible to a set-off.[404] They suggest that the debt nevertheless may be treated as having been due at the earlier bankruptcy date, notwithstanding that the contingency had not then occurred, and notwithstanding the absence of a mechanism for valuing such a debt as at that date for the purpose of the administration of the estate. Further, in order to reconcile cases such as *Bolland v Nash* and *Hiley* (above) with the views expressed in *Stein v Blake*, presumably it would have to be said that the hindsight principle may extend also to deeming a debt to have been owing to a party at the date of the bankruptcy or liquidation, when in truth at that date it was owing to someone else.

BCCI v Habib Bank

6.96 The hindsight principle was applied in a questionable manner in *Bank of Credit and Commerce International (Overseas) Ltd v Habib Bank Ltd*.[405] The liquidator of BCCI had obtained a default judgment against Habib Bank for payment of a number of debts owing to BCCI. Habib Bank sought to set aside the default judgment on a number of grounds, including that BCCI was indebted to it, so that a set-off was available in the liquidation. The liquidator responded that BCCI's debts to Habib Bank had been assumed by other third-party banks after the liquidation, and had been paid by them. Applying the automatic theory, however, that should not have affected the position as between BCCI and Habib Bank. When the debts were assumed by the third-party banks a set-off would already have taken place, on the date of the liquidation. The set-off would have extinguished the cross-demands as at that date, so that to that extent BCCI would no longer have been indebted to Habib Bank. Accordingly nothing would have remained which could have been the subject of a later assumption of liability. Park J nevertheless held that the payments by the third-party banks precluded a set-off, on the

---

[402] [1996] AC 243, 256.
[403] [1996] Ch 245, 269.
[404] See paras 8.27–8.37 below.
[405] [1999] 1 WLR 42, 50–53.
[406] Habib Bank had submitted proofs for the debts said to be owing to it, which the liquidator rejected. Park J said that Habib Bank should have applied to the court for the liquidator's decision to be reversed, and its failure to do so precluded it from asserting the debts by way of a set-off. It is suggested, however, that the failure to take that course of action should not have precluded a set-off. See para 6.113 below.

basis of the hindsight principle.[406] He acknowledged that Lord Hoffmann had referred to the hindsight principle in *Stein v Blake* in the context of contingent debts, where a debt did not exist at the date of the liquidation but arose subsequently, whereas he pointed out that the situation in *BCCI v Habib Bank* was the converse of that, in that the debts owing to Habib Bank had existed at the commencement of the liquidation but did not exist when it became necessary to ascertain the state of the account. Nevertheless, in his Lordship's view the principle must be the same: 'just as the law takes account of the arising of debts in the intervening period, so it must take account of the disappearance of debts in the intervening period'.[407] To illustrate the issue, he referred to an example in which Habib Bank owed 150 units of value to BCCI at the date of the liquidation, and BCCI owed 100 to Habib Bank. In that context, Park J continued:[408]

> It follows that in my example of cross-debts of 150 and 100, if one of those debts is in some way eliminated after the commencement of the liquidation, the automatic set-off, under rule 4.90, though done at the liquidation date, leaves out of account the debt which is eliminated. So if the debt of 100 which BCCI(O) owed to Habib Bank was paid to Habib Bank in full by a third party . . . the set-off is of 150 owed by Habib Bank to BCCI(O) against nil owed by BCCI(O) to Habib Bank.

The difficulty with this analysis is the notion that the third party banks paid **6.97** BCCI's debts to Habib Bank. In truth they did not, because a set-off had already occurred on the date of the liquidation, and a set-off is regarded as equivalent to payment.[409] BCCI's debts therefore had already been extinguished before the third-party banks purported to assume liability, and so it could not be said that they had paid the debts. It is true that in *Re Bank of Credit and Commerce International SA (No 8)*[410] the Court of Appeal canvassed the possibility that, in a three-party situation, discharge by set-off may not be equivalent to discharge by payment. That was in the context of suretyship. It was suggested, but without expressing a concluded view, that, while a payment by the surety to the creditor would discharge the principal debtor, and a set-off under the insolvency set-off section as between the creditor and the surety would discharge the surety, a set-off as between those parties may not discharge the debtor. As a consequence, it was suggested that the creditor may be able to sue the principal debtor, notwithstanding a set-off as between the creditor and the surety, and if the creditor recovered from the principal debtor it could then be said with hindsight that nothing was owing by the

---

[407] [1999] 1 WLR 42, 52.

[408] [1999] 1 WLR 42, 52.

[409] *Ex parte Barnett, re Deveze* (1874) LR 9 Ch App 293, 297; *Inland Revenue Commissioners v John Dow Stuart Ltd* [1950] AC 149, 164; *Re Loteka Pty Ltd* [1990] 1 Qd R 322, 324; *M S Fashions v Bank of Credit and Commerce International* [1993] Ch 425, 439, *per* Hoffmann LJ, 448, CA. The House of Lords in *Re Bank of Credit and Commerce International SA (No 8)* [1998] AC 214, 225 referred in a discussion of set-off to 'payment or deemed payment'. See also *Gye v Davies* (1995) 37 NSWLR 421, 431–432 ('moneys deemed paid by them in consequence of the set-off').

[410] [1996] Ch 245, 268–269 (decision affirmed [1998] AC 214, HL).

surety to the creditor and, also with hindsight, that there was no set-off as between them. That suggestion is criticized later.[411] But leaving aside that criticism, the Court of Appeal nevertheless accepted that a discharge of the principal debtor by a set-off as between the creditor and the principal debtor is not subject to the same principle. The set-off in that circumstance would discharge the surety.[412] In *BCCI v Habib Bank* Habib Bank was a principal debtor and, even if one were to accept the view floated by the Court of Appeal in *BCCI (No 8)*, a set-off as between BCCI and Habib Bank should have been equivalent to a discharge by payment as between those parties. The basis upon which the third-party banks assumed liability is not clear from the report, but it may have been by way of a novation as opposed to the assumption of a suretyship obligation as such.[413] Nevertheless, the set-off should have been an effective discharge as against them also.

6.98 If then BCCI's debts to Habib Bank had been discharged by a set-off, where did that leave the third-party banks? This would depend on the terms of their contracts, but they may have paid under a mistake. They assumed that they were liable to pay Habib Bank whereas the debts in question had ceased to exist. Since the payments by the third-party banks in truth did not discharge the debts which were owing by BCCI, it is difficult to see how the hindsight principle could have any application in the liquidation of BCCI. Park J expressed a concern that, if a set-off were recognized, Habib Bank in effect would have obtained an undue profit. In the example posited, the net position of Habib Bank at the date of the liquidation was minus 50, whereas he said that, if a set-off were allowed, Habib Bank's net position would not have been minus 50 but plus 50; it would have received 100 from the third-party banks but would have owed only 50 to BCCI. But that ignores the possibility that the third-party banks may have been entitled to recover the payments made to Habib Bank as mistaken payments. If that occurred, Habib Bank's net position would have been the same as at the date of the liquidation, ie minus 50. The effect of the judgment was that BCCI, which should have borne the burden of any set-off arising in its liquidation, shifted that burden on to the third-party banks, by denying them the opportunity of recovering the sums that they had paid to Habib Bank where then was no obligation to do so.

(2) Australia

6.99 The difficulties noted above in relation to the automatic theory would also be relevant to Australia. Indeed, in Australia there is an additional problem. The quali-

---

[411] See paras 12.26–12.36 below.

[412] [1996] Ch 245, 268, referring to *Ex parte Hanson* (1806) 12 Ves Jun 346, 33 ER 131.

[413] Reference is made in the judgment ([1999] 1 WLR 42, 50) to Habib Bank itself having assumed liability for the debts of BCCI's Pakistan branch under a statutory scheme and a novation agreement.

fication to the insolvency set-off section[414] is drafted differently to that in England. For example, in the context of company liquidation, section 553C(2) of the Corporations Act 2001 (Cth) provides: 'A person is not entitled under this section to claim the benefit of a set-off if, at the time of giving credit to the company, or at the time of receiving credit from the company, the person had notice of the fact that the company was insolvent.' This suggests that a set-off is something that is claimed, which is inconsistent with the notion of an automatical cancellation. Further, the terms of the qualification seem inapt to deny a set-off in a situation where the creditor had the requisite notice but in the particular case the set-off is sought, not by the creditor, but by the trustee in bankruptcy or liquidator.[415] Once again, the notion that the occurrence of a set-off may depend upon which party is claiming it seems inconsistent with the automatic theory. Nevertheless, as in England, the automatic theory now appears established in Australia.

Prior to *Stein v Blake*, the High Court of Australia had considered the nature of in- **6.100** solvency set-off in *Gye v McIntyre*[416] in the context of a composition[417] under the Bankruptcy Act 1966 (Cth).[418] In doing so it made some observations[419] which support the automatic theory. That was so notwithstanding an earlier decision of the High Court which is difficult to reconcile with that theory.[420] The High Court observed in *Gye v McIntyre*:[421]

---

[414] See the Bankruptcy Act 1966 (Cth), s 86(2), and the Corporations Act 2001 (Cth), s 553C(2).

[415] As in *Re Parker* (1997) 80 FCR 1. See para 6.53 above.

[416] (1991) 171 CLR 609.

[417] In the case of a composition an automatic set-off would occur at the date of the composition. See *Gye v Davies* (1995) 37 NSWLR 421, 428.

[418] It has been said that the word 'creditor' is used in various senses throughout the Bankruptcy Act, and that it takes its colour from the particular context. See *Staples v Milner* (1998) 83 FCR 203, 209, referring to *Pyramid Building Society v Terry* (1997) 189 CLR 176, 192. But certainly where a bankrupt submits a proposal for a composition to his creditors under the Bankruptcy Act, it has been held that a determination by the trustee under s 64ZA as to whether a person is a creditor so as to be entitled to vote is to be made after considering any set-off under s 86. In making that determination it is the trustee's duty to make a judgment about the prospects of a cross-claim. See *Re Dingle; Westpac Banking Corp v Worrell* (1993) 47 FCR 478.

[419] The High Court's observations as to the automatic nature of insolvency set-off have been said to be part of the ratio decidendi. See *G M & A M Pearce and Co Pty Ltd v RGM Australia Pty Ltd* [1998] 4 VR 888, 896. At least in relation to the composition of Mr Perkes this would appear to be correct, since the application to the Federal Court for a declaration in relation to the set-off was made after the trustee issued his certificate that Mr Perkes had carried out the terms of his composition (see the dates set out in the judgment of Gummow and von Doussa JJ in the Federal Court in *McIntyre v Perkes* (1990) 22 FCR 260, 265–266), and there was no procedural step before then which would have brought about a set-off.

[420] *Hiley v The Peoples Prudential Assurance Co Ltd* (1938) 60 CLR 468. See para 6.94 above.

[421] (1991) 171 CLR 609, 622. See also *Lord v Direct Acceptance Corporation Ltd* (1993) 32 NSWLR 362, 372, NSW Court of Appeal; *Citicorp Australia Ltd v Official Trustee* (1996) 71 FCR 550, 567; *G M & A M Pearce and Co Pty Ltd v RGM Australia Pty Ltd* [1998] 4 VR 888 (deed of company arrangement); *Wily v Rothschild Australia Ltd* (1999) 47 NSWLR 555, 565–566. Compare Gummow and von Doussa JJ in the Federal Court in *McIntyre v Perkes* (1990) 22 FCR 260, 270. Compare also *Day v Dent Constructions Pty Ltd v North Australian Properties Pty Ltd*

Section 86[422] is a statutory directive ('shall be set off') which operates as at the time the bankruptcy takes effect. It produces a balance upon the basis of which the bankruptcy administration can proceed. Only that balance can be claimed in the bankruptcy or recovered by the trustee. If its operation is to produce a nil balance, its effect will be that there is nothing at all which can be claimed in the bankruptcy or recovered in proceedings by the trustee. The section is self-executing in the sense that its operation is automatic and not dependent upon 'the option of either party' . . .

6.101 Subsequently Drummond J in *Re Capel, ex p Marac Finance Australia Ltd v Capel*[423] suggested a different interpretation of that passage which constitutes a half-way position between the procedural view and the automatic extinguishment theory later favoured by the House of Lords in *Stein v Blake. Re Capel* concerned an assignment of a claim by a trustee in bankruptcy back to the bankrupt in circumstances where the debtor on the claim had a provable debt against the bankrupt which had not been proved, and where an account otherwise had not been taken in the bankruptcy. Drummond J followed the analysis of the Court of Appeal in *Stein v Blake*,[424] his judgment being delivered after that of the Court of Appeal and before the subsequent appeal to the House of Lords in *Stein v Blake*, and held that the insolvency set-off section did not prevent the assignment. In relation to *Gye v McIntyre*, he expressed the view that the High Court in that case was not saying that the insolvency set-off section operates automatically at the date of the bankruptcy or liquidation to extinguish the cross-demands. Rather, all that the High Court meant was that 'the account, whenever taken, is to be taken by reference to the position obtaining at that date', and that, independently of whether an account has ever been taken, the rights of the parties to the cross-claims 'are to be taken to be the right to recover or to prove for the balance (if any) that would exist if the two claims were set-off against each other at the date of the sequestration order. That is not at all the same as saying that the various claims are extinguished by the operation of the section on the day the sequestration order is made'.[425] However, this does not appear to be what the High Court had in mind, and later cases bear that out.[426] In *Citicorp Australia Ltd v Official Trustee in*

(1982) 150 CLR 85, 109, in which Murphy J appeared to distinguish between the date of the winding up and the time when the account was taken. Similarly some comments by Mason J in that case (at 107) appear to support the procedural view, but it is suggested that little weight should now be attached to those comments in this context given that his Honour, as Chief Justice, headed the Court in *Gye v McIntyre* (n 404 above).

[422] The Bankruptcy Act 1966 (Cth), s 86 is the set-off section applicable to bankruptcies in Australia.

[423] (1994) 48 FCR 195. See also *Re Turner, ex p Mulley* (Federal Court of Australia, Northrop J, 22 June 1995).

[424] [1994] Ch 16. See para 6.82 above.

[425] (1994) 48 FCR 195, 206–207.

[426] In addition to the cases referred to below, see *Lord v Direct Acceptance Corp* (1993) 32 NSWLR 362, 372 (NSW Court of Appeal). In subsequent proceedings in the *Gye v McIntyre* litigation (Federal Court of Australia, 8 October 1992), Beaumont J appeared to accept that the

Bankruptcy[427] the Full Court of the Federal Court[428] said of the decision of the House of Lords in *Stein v Blake* that it applied the reasoning of the High Court in *Gye v McIntyre*, and that the reasoning of the House of Lords should be followed. Similarly the Victorian Court of Appeal in *G M & A M Pearce and Co Pty Ltd v RGM Australia Pty Ltd*,[429] in applying *Gye v McIntyre*, accepted the automatic nature of insolvency set-off in the context of a deed of company arrangement,[430] so that it was immaterial to the question of set-off in that case that the creditor failed to make a claim under the deed before it terminated.[431]

One of the decisions that Drummond J considered in *Re Capel* was *Martin v Lewis*.[432] A debt which was owing to a bankrupt, and which had vested in the trustee in bankruptcy, was assigned back to the bankrupt after he had obtained his discharge.[433] The debtor had a cross-claim against the bankrupt, but a proof of debt had not been lodged in the bankruptcy and nor had an account otherwise been taken in the bankruptcy. The effect of a discharge from bankruptcy is to release the bankrupt from all bankruptcy debts.[434] Notwithstanding that an account had not been taken in the bankruptcy, the Queensland Supreme Court[435] held that the assignee took subject to a set-off in respect of the cross-claim. While the circumstances in issue in *Re Capel* were similar, the cases differed in one respect. Whereas in *Martin v Lewis* the assignment occurred after the bankrupt's discharge from bankruptcy, in *Re Capel* it occurred before discharge, although the question of the efficacy of the assignment did not arise until later. Drummond J doubted the correctness of *Martin v Lewis*. Since the cause of action in that case was assigned after the bankrupt's discharge, he found it difficult to see how the creditor could retain the right to set off the amount owing to him when the bankrupt had

6.102

---

insolvency set-off section operates as an automatic extinction, so that thereafter all that is owing is the balance of the account. See also Powell JA in *Gye v Davies* (1995) 37 NSWLR 421, 428 ('for the purposes of s 86 of the [Bankruptcy] Act, the set-off . . . was to be made as at the dates of their respectively entering into a composition with their creditors . . .').

[427] (1996) 71 FCR 550, 567.

[428] Foster, von Doussa and Sundberg JJ.

[429] [1998] 4 VR 888.

[430] The deed of company arrangement in the *Pearce* case did not exclude the prescribed provisions in Schedule 8A of the Corporations Regulations, including clause 8 which incorporated the insolvency set-off section in s 553C of the Corporations Law (now the Corporations Act 2001 (Cth)), and so the set-off section was incorporated into the deed. See the Corporations Act 2001 (Cth), s 444A(5), and para 6.08 above. See also *Metal Manufacturers Ltd v Hall* (2002) 41 ACSR 466; *Handberg v Smarter Way (Aust) Pty Ltd* (2002) ACLC 856.

[431] Compare the *ex tempore* judgment of Young J in the New South Wales Supreme Court in *Winterton Constructions Pty Ltd v M A Coleman Joinery Co Pty Ltd* (1996) 20 ACSR 671, 674–677, in which it seems to have been assumed that set-off pursuant to the deed was procedural.

[432] Full Court of the Queensland Supreme Court, 7 June 1985.

[433] This was possible because the right of action remained vested in the trustee notwithstanding the discharge. See *Piwinski v Corporate Trustees of the Diocese of Armidale* [1977] 1 NSWLR 266.

[434] See the Insolvency Act 1986, s 281 and, in Australia, the Bankruptcy Act 1966 (Cth), s 153.

[435] Andrews ACJ, Kelly and Shepherdson JJ.

been released from liability.[436] In *Re Capel*, on the other hand, where the assignment occurred before the discharge, Drummond J accepted that the creditor could still assert a set-off against the assignee notwithstanding the later discharge, on the basis that the assignee took subject to the prior equity constituted by the right of set-off otherwise available to the debtor in the bankruptcy.[437] He considered that the essence of the equity to which the assignee took subject was that the account, whenever it was taken, was to be taken by reference to the position obtaining at the date of the bankruptcy, and that this also applied when the account was taken outside the bankruptcy administration in the context of a claim by the assignee.[438] Because the assignment occurred before the discharge, the debt when assigned had the equity 'attached'[439] to it, and in a later accounting reference would have to be made to the position at the time of the bankruptcy when the bankrupt was still liable to the creditor.

6.103 Subsequently Northrop J in *Re Turner, ex p Mulley*[440] expressed approval of Drummond J's analysis in *Re Capel*. Nevertheless, given the later acceptance of the automatic theory of insolvency set-off by both the Full Court of the Federal Court in *Citicorp v Official Trustee* and by the Victorian Court of Appeal in the *Pearce* case,[441] it is unlikely that Drummond J's analysis would now be adopted. *Martin v Lewis* is consistent with the automatic theory, and also with the similar decision in England of Neill J in *Farley v Housing and Commercial Development*[442] in the context of company liquidation, and on the basis of that authority it is likely to be followed.

N. Foreign Currencies

6.104 Consider that one or both of the cross-demands between a bankrupt and a creditor is in a foreign currency.[443]

Proof of debts

6.105 For the purpose of proving a debt in a bankruptcy or a company liquidation, the Insolvency Rules provide that a foreign currency claim is to be converted into sterling at the rate prevailing at the date of the bankruptcy order or, as the case may

---

[436] See the discussion at (1994) 48 FCR 195, 205.
[437] This may have been what French J had in mind in *Re Nguyen* (1992) 35 FCR 320, 327.
[438] See the discussion at (1994) 48 FCR 195, 206–207.
[439] (1994) 48 FCR 195, 203.
[440] Federal Court of Australia, 22 June 1995.
[441] See para 6.101 above. See also the New South Wales Court of Appeal in *Lord v Direct Acceptance Corporation* (1993) 32 NSWLR 362, 372, NSW CA.
[442] (1984) 26 BLR 66.
[443] The following discussion assumes that the obligation in question is a money obligation. See paras 9.11–9.22 below.

be, on the date when the company went into liquidation,[444] as opposed to the date of payment of the dividend. This accords with the rule applied with respect to the valuation of debts for the purpose of proof. Debts or liabilities which do not have a certain value at the commencement of a bankruptcy or a liquidation are valued as at that date. Admittedly later events may be looked at, but only in the sense that they may provide evidence of the true value that the debt in fact had at the relevant date. In the case of a foreign currency claim however there is no need to look at later events. The exchange rate current at the commencement of the bankruptcy or the liquidation provides a clear measure for ascertaining its value as at that date.[445] It is also consistent with the principle accepted by the House of Lords in *Miliangos v George Frank (Textiles) Ltd*,[446] that in an action to enforce a foreign currency debt an English court can give judgment expressed in the foreign currency, with the debt being converted into sterling for the purpose of enforcement of the judgment at the exchange rate applicable on the date that the claimant is given leave to enforce. Since bankruptcy and company liquidation provide a process of collective enforcement, the Court of Appeal in *Re Lines Bros Ltd*[447] considered that it is in accordance with the *Miliangos* case to convert currencies for the purpose of proof by reference to the rate prevailing at the commencement of that process.[448]

Set-off

That sets out the position with respect to proof of debts. In relation to set-off, the **6.106** House of Lords in *Stein v Blake*[449] held that the set-off section in the insolvency legislation takes effect automatically upon the occurrence of the bankruptcy or

---

[444] See the Insolvency Rules 1986, r 4.91 (company liquidation) and r 6.111 (bankruptcy). For the position prior to the Insolvency Rules, see *Re Dynamics Corporation of America* [1976] 1 WLR 757; *Re Lines Bros Ltd* [1983] 1 Ch 1; *Re Amalgamated Investment and Property Co Ltd* [1985] 1 Ch 349, 364. In relation to company liquidation in Australia, see the Corporations Act 2001 (Cth), s 554C. A company goes into liquidation if it passes a resolution for voluntary winding up, or an order for its winding up is made by the court at a time when it has not already gone into liquidation by passing such a resolution. See the Insolvency Act 1986, s 247(2). Compare *Re Pearce* (1933) 6 ABC 126 (conversion at the date when the debt became payable), which was decided before *Miliangos v George Frank (Textiles) Ltd* [1976] AC 443 (discussed below).

[445] *Re Dynamics Corporation of America* [1976] 1 WLR 757, 767–768. See also *Re Lines Bros Ltd* [1983] 1 Ch 1, 19–20.

[446] [1976] AC 443.

[447] [1983] 1 Ch 1 (in particular, see Lawton LJ at 12–13 and Brightman LJ at 20).

[448] In *Miliangos* [1976] AC 443, 498, Lord Wilberforce and Lord Cross of Chelsea suggested that, in the case of a liquidation, conversion should take place at the date when the creditor's claim is admitted by the liquidator. Those statements however were obiter, and the Court of Appeal in *Re Lines Bros* said that the date of the liquidation in fact is more in accordance with the principle actually applied by the House of Lords in *Miliangos*. The approach adopted in *Re Lines Bros* was also accepted in *Re Amalgamated Investment and Property Co Ltd* [1985] 1 Ch 349, 364, and in Australia in *Re Gresham Corp Pty Ltd* (1989) 15 ACLR 461.

[449] [1996] AC 243.

liquidation.[450] The discharge of the cross-demands by way of a set-off does not depend upon the procedural step of taking an account. The conversion of a foreign currency claim on either side of the account therefore should take place by reference to the date of the bankruptcy or liquidation,[451] since according to the automatic theory that date is the date of payment.

Insolvent's foreign currency cross-claim exceeds the creditor's provable debt

6.107   If the bankrupt's or the company's foreign currency cross-claim overtops the creditor's provable debt, the remainder of the cross-claim not extinguished by the set-off may be converted at a different rate. The trustee or the liquidator would sue for payment of the surplus, and once judgment is obtained against the creditor for that amount, conversion should take place in accordance with the *Miliangos* case at the exchange rate applicable when leave to enforce is given.

O. Interest

6.108   When a bankruptcy occurs, and there are cross-demands the subject of a set-off under the insolvency set-off section, interest should stop running, not only on the creditor's claim against the bankrupt, but also on the bankrupt's claim against the creditor. While in *Ex parte Prescot*[452] interest appears to have been allowed on the bankrupt's claim for the period between the bankruptcy and the taking of the account, that could no longer stand following the decision of the House of Lords in *Stein v Blake*,[453] that the set-off takes effect automatically upon the occurrence of the bankruptcy.

P. Set-off as a Void Disposition of Property

6.109   The Insolvency Act 1986, section 127 provides that a disposition of a company's property after the commencement of a court-ordered winding up is void unless the court otherwise orders. In *Barclays Bank Ltd v TOSG Trust Fund Ltd*[454]

---

[450] See paras 6.79–6.103 above.

[451] *Stein v Blake* [1996] AC 243, 252. In Australia, conversion for the purpose of proof takes place by reference to the 'relevant date' (see s 554C of the Corporations Act 2001 (Cth)), which term is defined in s 9 in terms of Part 5.6, Division 1A of the Corporations Act. The 'relevant date' determines generally what debts are provable in a liquidation (see s 553), and there is also authority which suggests that it is the date when a set-off would be regarded as having occurred in accordance with the automatic theory. See the discussion of *Re Parker* (1997) 80 FCR 1, 15 in paras 6.36–6.45 above.

[452] (1753) 1 Atk 230, 26 ER 147.

[453] [1996] AC 243. See paras 6.81–6.82 above.

[454] [1984] BCLC 1, 25–26.

Nourse J said that, where there is a conflict between the then equivalent of section 127[455] and the insolvency set-off section, section 127 must prevail. That view cannot be supported. Section 127 refers to a disposition after the commencement of the winding up, which in a winding up by the court which is not preceded by a resolution for a winding up is the time of the presentation of the petition.[456] But it would always be the case in that circumstance that a set-off would occur later, when the order is made for a winding up.[457] In other words, there would always be a conflict between section 127 and the insolvency set-off section. If the set-off section is to operate effectively in a compulsory winding up, it must prevail over section 127.

Q. Mistake as to Set-off

Payment to the insolvent's estate without asserting a set-off

6.110 It may be that a person possessed of a cross-claim against a bankrupt paid a sum of money to the trustee in bankruptcy in satisfaction of a liability owing to the bankrupt, in the mistaken belief that a set-off was not available.[458] Ordinarily the payment should be recoverable, whether the mistake was one of fact or of law.[459] In the case of bankruptcy the assets of the bankrupt vest in the trustee for division amongst the bankrupt's creditors.[460] Unlike the bankrupt, the trustee is not insolvent, and so the mistaken payment should be recoverable in full from the trustee in an action for money had and received.[461] On the other hand the assets of a company in liquidation ordinarily do not pass to the liquidator,[462] who, it has been said, is principally and really an agent of the company who occupies a position which is fiduciary in some respects and is bound by the statutory duties imposed on him by the insolvency legislation.[463] The money will have vested instead in the

---

[455] Companies Act 1948, s 227.

[456] Insolvency Act 1986, s 129(2).

[457] See para 6.32 above, and paras 6.79–6.103 above in relation to the automatic nature of insolvency set-off.

[458] In relation to the rule in *Cherry v Boultbee* (1839) 4 My & Cr 442, 41 ER 171, see para 14.81 below.

[459] The former principle, that a payment made under a mistake of law is not recoverable, no longer applies. See *Kleinwort Benson Ltd v Lincoln City Council* [1999] 2 AC 349. In Australia, see *David Securities Pty Ltd v Commonwealth Bank of Australia* (1992) 175 CLR 353.

[460] See the Insolvency Act 1986, s 306, and in Australia the Bankruptcy Act 1966 (Cth), s 58.

[461] As in *Bize v Dickason* (1786) 1 TR 285, 99 ER 1097. See also *Edmeads v Newman* (1823) 1 B & C 418, 107 ER 155; *Booth v Hutchinson* (1872) LR 15 Eq 30.

[462] Note however the Insolvency Act 1986, s 145, and in Australia the Corporations Act 2001 (Cth), s 474(2), each of which enables the court, on the application of the liquidator, to direct that the property of the company is to vest in the liquidator.

[463] *Thomas Franklin & Sons Ltd v Cameron* (1935) 36 SR (NSW) 286, 296, NSW SC, *per* Davidson J; *Re Timberland Ltd* (1979) 4 ACLR 259, 285, Vic SC, *per* Marks J. See also *Ayerst v C & K (Constructions) Ltd* [1976] AC 167, 176–177.

insolvent company. In order to recover it in full from the insolvent company the payer's right to it ordinarily should be proprietary in nature. In *Chase Manhattan Bank NA v Israel-British Bank (London) Ltd*[464] Goulding J held that 'a person who pays money to another under a factual mistake retains an equitable property in it and the conscience of that other is subjected to a fiduciary duty to respect his proprietary right'. Subsequently Lord Browne-Wilkinson in *Westdeutsche Landesbank Girozentrale v Islington LBC*[465] doubted the breadth of that proposition. He considered that a trust could only arise after the recipient became aware of the mistake, because it would only be at that time that the recipient's conscience would be affected. If in the circumstances there is a subsisting trust, the mistaken payment should be recoverable *in toto*. In *Re Cushla Ltd*[466] a payment was made to a company in liquidation in circumstances where the payer did not realize that it had a right of set-off. Vinelott J held that the payer was entitled to recover the money and that a set-off should proceed, although the question of a trust was not considered.

6.111 But even if there is no trust, the rule in *Ex parte James*[467] may provide relief. The essence of that rule is that trustees in bankruptcy are officers of the court, and as such may be ordered by the court not to rely on their strict legal rights when to do so would be regarded as dishonourable. It allows recovery of payments made under a mistake of fact or of law,[468] including the law of set-off.[469] A liquidator in a compulsory winding up certainly is an officer of the court,[470] and indeed on two occasions[471] recourse has been had to the rule as a means of ordering the return of a sum of money mistakenly paid to a liquidator in a compulsory winding up in satisfaction of a liability to the company. As a result, a set-off based upon that liability could proceed against an independent indebtedness of the company to the payer. A liquidator in a voluntary winding up however is not an officer of the court, and so he is not amenable to the *Ex parte James* principle.[472]

---

[464] [1981] 1 Ch 105, 119. The *Chase Manhattan* case has been both criticized and applauded. Compare Tettenborn 'Remedies for the Recovery of Money Paid by Mistake' [1980] CLJ 272 with Jones, Comment [1980] CLJ 275.

[465] [1996] AC 669, 714–715. Compare Millett, 'Restitution and Constructive Trusts' (1998) 114 LQR 399, 412–13.

[466] [1979] 3 All ER 415.

[467] *Ex parte James, re Condon* (1874) LR 9 Ch App 609.

[468] *Re Tyler, ex p The Official Receiver* [1907] 1 KB 865; *R v Tower Hamlets LBC* [1988] AC 858, 874–876.

[469] See *Re Paddington Town Hall Centre Ltd* (1979) 41 FLR 239.

[470] See for example *Re Associated Dominions Assurance Society Pty Ltd* (1962) 109 CLR 516.

[471] *Re Cushla Ltd* [1979] 2 All ER 415; *Re Paddington Town Hall Centre Ltd* (1979) 41 FLR 239.

[472] *Re T H Knitwear (Wholesale) Ltd* [1988] 1 All ER 860 (overruling *Re Temple Fire and Accident Assurance Co*, which is noted at (1910) 129 LT Jo 115). See also *Re David A Hamilton and Co Ltd* [1928] NZLR 419. In Australia, compare *Re Autolook Pty Ltd* (1983) 8 ACLR 419, 421, *per* Needham J.

Creditor proves without asserting a set-off

Another possibility is that a creditor, in ignorance of the availability of a set-off, **6.112** lodges a proof in the debtor's bankruptcy in respect of the debt. On its own this should not preclude the creditor from subsequently asserting a set-off. The proof can be amended to reflect the set-off.[473] But what if the creditor, before asserting the set-off, is paid a dividend? It may be said in such a case that the debt has been paid, so that there is nothing 'due' to the creditor within the meaning of the set-off section, and that therefore the creditor has lost his right of set-off. There is some support for that view in the judgment of Knight Bruce VC in *Ex parte Staddon, Re Wise*.[474] In that case the Vice Chancellor, in allowing a set-off, said that he would disregard a proof of debt made by the creditor since the creditor had not received a dividend or obtained any benefit from the proof. However, under the automatic extinction theory of insolvency set-off approved by the House of Lords in *Stein v Blake*,[475] the analysis now would be that a set-off took place automatically at the date of the bankruptcy, in which case the subsequent receipt of a dividend should not affect the position. Consistent with that view, Hoffmann LJ (as he then was) in *MS Fashions v Bank of Credit and Commerce International SA*[476] suggested that the receipt of the dividend would not preclude the creditor from relying on the full claim as a set-off, although credit would have to be given for the dividend received.

Rejection of the creditor's proof by the trustee in bankruptcy or liquidator

Alternatively the creditor may have lodged a proof of debt, but the proof was re- **6.113** jected by the trustee in bankruptcy. Can the creditor then assert a set-off based upon the debt? The issue arose in *Bank of Credit and Commerce International (Overseas) Ltd v Habib Bank Ltd*.[477] Habib Bank had lodged a proof of debt in the liquidation of BCCI. The liquidator rejected the proof, on the ground that the debt had been paid by a third party after the winding up commenced. BCCI's liquidator later sued Habib Bank for payment of a debt owing by Habib Bank to BCCI, and obtained default judgment, whereupon Habib Bank sought to set aside the judgment inter alia on the ground that it had a set-off based on the debt the subject of the rejected proof. Park J held that, because of the rejection of the proof, and Habib Bank's failure to apply to the court for the liquidator's decision to be reversed,[478] Habib Bank was precluded from relying on the debt as a set-off. He said that, if a person who claims to be a creditor has his proof rejected but does

---

[473] *Re Parker* (1997) 80 FCR 1, 9.
[474] (1843) 3 Mont D & De G 256, 12 LJ Bcy 39.
[475] [1996] AC 243. See paras 6.79–6.103 above.
[476] [1993] Ch 425, 435.
[477] [1999] 1 WLR 42.
[478] Pursuant to the Insolvency Rules 1986, r 4.83.

not exercise his right to apply to the court, he could not have a second bite at the cherry by submitting a second proof in respect of the same debt, and equally he should not be permitted to have a second attempt at recovery of the alleged debt by way of a set-off.[479] That conclusion seems doubtful. A set-off would have had the effect that the debt allegedly owing to Habib Bank would have been extinguished automatically to the extent of the set-off at the date of the liquidation.[480] If that was case, it could not thereafter have been the subject of a proof, in which case one may query why Habib Bank should have been prejudiced by its failure to apply to the court to have the liquidator's rejection of the proof reversed. The assertion of a set-off would not have provided a ground for reversing the decision to reject the proof; on the contrary, it was entirely consistent with that rejection.[481] But apart from that, it is difficult to support the decision on the facts. The proof was rejected, not because the liquidator was of the view that the debt had never existed, or that it had been paid prior to the liquidation, but rather because it was paid by a third party after the commencement of the liquidation. However that should not have affected an automatic set-off occurring at the date of the liquidation as between BCCI and Habib Bank. Rather, the question should have been whether the third-party payer was entitled to recover the payment made to Habib Bank on the ground that the payment was made under a mistake.[482]

R. Multiple Claims, and Preferential Debts

6.114 The insolvency legislation accords preferential status to certain classes of debts. In the event of a bankruptcy or a company liquidation, those debts, or at least in some cases a part of them, are paid in priority to other debts of the bankrupt or the company.[483] If the preferred creditor is possessed of a second, separate claim against the bankrupt or the company, or the amount of the claim in question is greater than the amount for which preferential status is accorded, the question may arise whether a set-off should take effect in the first instance against the pre-

---

[479] [1995] 1 WLR 42, 49–50.

[480] See paras 6.79–6.103 above.

[481] Park J found support for that view in *Brandon v McHenry* [1891] 1 QB 538, but the case may be distinguished. A trustee in bankruptcy rejected a proof of debt, and the person lodging the proof did not appeal against the rejection. Subsequently the bankruptcy was annulled, and the person then sought to sue the former bankrupt for payment of the alleged debt. The Court of Appeal held that the action was barred by the rejection of the proof. The decision however was based on the terms of the Bankruptcy Act 1869, s 81, which provided that, where a bankruptcy was annulled, all acts done by the trustee nevertheless remained valid. See now the Insolvency Act 1986, s 282(4), and in Australia the Bankruptcy Act 1966 (Cth), s 154(1). A rejection of a proof was regarded as an act done by the trustee within the meaning of the section. Therefore the rejection remained valid after the annulment, and precluded a subsequent action on the debt. There was no similar provision operating in *BCCI v Habib Bank*.

[482] See the discussion of *BCCI v Habib Bank* in paras 6.96–6.98 above.

[483] See the Insolvency Act 1986, ss 175, 328 and 386.

ferred debt, or the preferred part of the debt, or whether it should operate first against the debt or the part of it which is not preferred, or indeed any other way. The creditor would be better off if the set-off occurred first against the non-preferred debt, because the preferred debt still in existence after the set-off would have priority in the bankruptcy or the liquidation, whereas the creditor could not claim priority if the set-off instead extinguished the debt which otherwise would have been preferred.

An early authority on point is *Ex parte Boyle, re Shepherd*, a decision of Lord Eldon   **6.115**
which appears not to have been reported but which is noted in Cooke's *Bankrupt Laws*.[484] The case concerned some promissory notes drawn by Lord Cork at the request of the bankrupt, the bankrupt having agreed to indemnify Lord Cork in respect of payments made pursuant to them. Lord Cork paid one of the notes before the bankruptcy and two of them afterwards. In addition, Lord Cork was separately indebted to the bankrupt. Under the bankruptcy legislation then in force, Lord Cork could only have proved in the bankruptcy for the payment made before the bankruptcy, but it was considered that his right to an indemnity for the subsequent payments, although not provable, could still be the subject of a set-off.[485] It would have been better for Lord Cork if his liability to the bankrupt could be set off against the claim for an indemnity which was not provable, because he would still have had a right to receive a dividend on the provable claim, and this indeed was the effect of the order made by Lord Eldon.

Lord Eldon's approach favoured the creditor. Buckley J however adopted the op-   **6.116**
posite approach in *Re E J Morel (1934) Ltd*.[486] In his view, the set-off section in the insolvency legislation should be applied on the basis that the debt which would otherwise be preferential in a company liquidation should be the first claim brought into an account. His Lordship said that the result of a set-off is to give a creditor payment in full of his claim to the extent of the set-off, and in that way he is better off than creditors who merely have to rely on their right to prove and receive a dividend. Accordingly, if he obtains payment in full by means of a set-off, it was 'reasonable' that that payment should be treated as being in respect of the debt which would rank first in priority.

Walton J subsequently considered the issue in *Re Unit 2 Windows Ltd*.[487] While   **6.117**
there was no discussion of Lord Eldon's decision in *Ex parte Boyle*, Walton J did consider *Re Morel*, but he was not persuaded by Buckley J's analysis. As his Lordship remarked, 'reasonableness' often depends on the point of view of the person considering it. He proposed a third approach. He said that the maxim that

---

[484] Cooke, *The Bankrupt Laws* (8th edn, 1823) vol 1, 571–2.
[485] Compare paras 7.15–7.17 below.
[486] [1962] 1 Ch 21.
[487] [1985] 1 WLR 1383.

equality is equity should apply, and accordingly he held that the set-off in that case should occur rateably as between the preferential and the non-preferential parts of the indebtedness of the company in liquidation.[488] This has since been followed in Australia,[489] and it would now appear to represent the law.

6.118 The same analysis should apply when a creditor has two or more claims against a company in liquidation, none of which is preferential, and the creditor is separately indebted to the company. The set-off should take effect rateably as between the claims.

6.119 The *Unit 2 Windows* approach would not appear to apply however in relation to preferential debts when a receiver is appointed to a company under a floating charge.[490] Further, it is not relevant when a creditor of a bankrupt or a company in liquidation has two debts owing to him, one secured and the other unsecured. The creditor is entitled to rely on his security in respect of the secured debt and not have it dealt with in the bankruptcy or the liquidation, in which case the debt would not be susceptible to a set-off under the insolvency legislation. If the bankrupt or the company has a cross-demand, it could only be set off against the unsecured debt.[491]

S. Secured Debts

6.120 In *Ex parte Barnett, re Deveze*[492] Lord Selborne LC said of the bankruptcy set-off section that: 'the fact that nothing is said about security or lien one way or the other in the section seems to me only to shew that the existence of security is not to affect its operation'. Similarly, in *Hiley v Peoples Prudential Assurance Co Ltd*[493] Dixon J in the Australian High Court commented that 'secured debts or liabilities

---

[488] See also *Re South Blackpool Hotel Co* (1869) LR 8 Eq 225 in relation to debentures which ranked equally. In Scotland compare *Turner, Petitioner* [1993] BCC 299. Similarly, if a creditor receives a dividend upon a debt partly secured by a guarantee, the dividend should be applied rateably to the whole debt, and the creditor cannot appropriate it to the excess of the debt above the sum guaranteed unless the guarantee provides otherwise. See *Raikes v Todd* (1838) 8 Ad & E 846, 112 ER 1058, and *Rowlatt on Principal and Surety* (5th edn, 1999) 99 para 4–83.

[489] *Central Brakes Service (Newcastle) Pty Ltd v Central Brakes Service (Sydney) Pty Ltd (in liq)* (1989) 7 ACLC 1199, 1202 (although the question was left open on appeal: *Central Brake Service (Sydney) Pty Ltd v Central Brake Service (Newcastle) Pty Ltd* (1992) 27 NSWLR 406, 411).

[490] See paras 17.85–17.87 below.

[491] *Re Norman Holding Co Ltd* [1991] 1 WLR 10. See below.

[492] (1874) LR 9 Ch App 293, 295–296.

[493] (1938) 60 CLR 468, 498. See also *A E Goodwin Ltd v A G Healing Ltd* (1979) 7 ACLR 481, 488. Dixon J referred to *Ex parte Barnett, re Deveze* (1874) LR 9 Ch App 293 and *Ex parte Law, re Kennedy* (1846) De Gex 378 as support for the proposition. *Ex parte Barnett* was a case in which the bankrupt was the secured creditor (see para 6.122 below), while in *Ex parte Law* the petitioner submitted to the jurisdiction of the bankruptcy court by applying to the Commissioner to value the annuity for the purpose of a set-off.

are no less the subject of set-off than unsecured debts as mutual debts, credits or dealings. To the extent that the secured debt is answered by set-off the security is freed . . .'. More recently, Dillon LJ in delivering the judgment of the Court of Appeal in *M S Fashions Ltd v Bank of Credit and Commerce International*[494] said that: 'If there are indeed mutual credits or mutual debts or mutual dealings between a company, or a bankrupt, and a creditor, then the set-off applies, notwithstanding that one or other of the debts or credits may be secured.' The difficulty with these statements is that they draw no distinction between, on the one hand, a secured debt owing by a bankrupt or a company in liquidation, and on the other a secured debt owing to the bankrupt or the company, and indeed they suggest that the same result should follow in either case. In truth they should each attract a different analysis.

Security provided by the insolvent

As those statements indicate, the fact that a creditor of a bankrupt or a company   **6.121** in liquidation has security for the debt owing to him[495] on its own does not preclude the operation of the set-off section.[496] A secured creditor has a choice. The creditor can surrender the security and prove for the whole debt, or value the security and prove for the difference between the amount of the debt and the value, or enforce the security and prove for the balance remaining of the debt. In any of those situations the provable debt should be able to be the subject of a set-off.[497] Consider that the creditor chooses to rely on the security for all or part of the debt and to that extent does not prove in the bankruptcy or the liquidation. For the insolvency set-off section to apply there must be a creditor 'proving or claiming to prove',[498] but in the situation posited, in which the creditor has chosen to rely on the security, he is not 'proving or claiming to prove'. The insolvency set-off section therefore should not apply. Mervyn Davies J accepted an argument to this effect in *Re Norman Holding Co Ltd*,[499] and it is also consistent with Rose LJ's comment

---

[494] [1993] Ch 425, 446.

[495] Including from a third party. See *McKinnon v Armstrong Brothers & Co* (1877) 2 App Cas 531.

[496] This also applies in the case of set-off under the Statutes of Set-off. See *Lechmere v Hawkins* (1798) 2 Esp 626, 170 ER 477.

[497] See the discussion in *Re Norman Holding Co Ltd* [1991] 1 WLR 10. In *Clark v Cort* (1840) Cr & Ph 154, 41 ER 449 a set-off was allowed in equity to the extent of the difference between the value of the bankrupt's indebtedness and the proceeds of realization of a security for that debt.

[498] See the Insolvency Act 1986, s 323(1) and, for company liquidation, the Insolvency Rules, r 4.90(1). In Australia, the Bankruptcy Act 1966 (Cth), s 86 refers to a creditor 'claiming to prove', while in company liquidation the Corporations Act 2001 (Cth), s 553C requires that there should be a person who 'wants to have a debt or claim admitted against the company'.

[499] [1991] 1 WLR 10, 14–15. See also *Brown v Cork* [1985] BCLC 363, 370–371, where the Court of Appeal seemed to accept the respondent's argument to this effect. Compare Powell J in *McColl's Wholesale Pty Ltd v State Bank of NSW* [1984] 3 NSWLR 365, 380, who considered that the requirement that debts be set off means that a secured creditor may *only* enforce his rights under the security to the extent of the balance of the cross-debts.

in delivering the judgment of the Court of Appeal in *Re Bank of Credit and Commerce International SA (No 8)*[500] that: 'Set-off ought not to prejudice the right of a secured creditor to enforce his securities in any order he chooses and at a time of his choice.' The creditor may have both a secured and an unsecured debt owing to him. In that circumstance, Mervyn Davies J held in *Re Norman Holding* that the creditor is entitled to rely on the security in respect of the secured debt and to utilize the unsecured debt in a set-off.[501]

Security held by the insolvent

6.122 Alternatively, it may be that a bankrupt or a company in liquidation is a secured creditor. In that situation, if the bankrupt or the company is separately indebted to the debtor on the secured debt, the debtor would be 'proving or claiming to prove' for the separate debt,[502] in which case there is no reason why the insolvency set-off should not apply. The cases indeed support that view.[503] To the extent of the set-off, the security would be freed.

Payment to the secured creditor

6.123 When a negotiable instrument is lodged as security for an advance, the trustee in bankruptcy of the debtor on the instrument is entitled to recover the instrument after tendering the amount of the advance, and the creditor is not entitled to retain it for a set-off against another debt owing to him by the debtor.[504]

Surplus proceeds, after realizing the security

6.124 After a security is realized the proceeds may be more than sufficient to satisfy the secured moneys. The question whether the creditor may set off his obligation to account for the surplus proceeds against a separate unsecured debt owing to him by the debtor is discussed below.[505]

---

[500] [1996] Ch 245, 256.

[501] This is consistent with the principle that a secured creditor is entitled to apply the security in discharge of whatever secured liability of his debtor he may think fit. See *Re William Hall (Contractors) Ltd* [1967] 1 WLR 948. The debtor in that case was in liquidation, and Plowman J held that the creditor could appropriate the proceeds first in discharge of a non-preferential claim, leaving the creditor free to prove for the whole of the preferential part of the claim.

[502] It is not necessary that a proof be lodged, however. See para 6.04 above.

[503] *Lord Lanesborough v Jones* (1716) 1 P Wms 325, 24 ER 409; *Ex parte Barnett, re Deveze* (1874) LR 9 Ch App 293; *Hiley v Peoples Prudential Assurance Co Ltd* (1938) 60 CLR 468; *Re ILG Travel Ltd* [1995] 2 BCLC 128, 158–160. Compare *Clarke v Fell* (1833) 4 B & Ad 404, 110 ER 507, which is explained in *Ex parte Barnett* at 296.

[504] *Key v Flint* (1817) 8 Taunt 21, 129 ER 289, petition in equity dismissed *Ex parte Flint* (1818) 1 Swans 30, 36 ER 285. See also *Trustee of the Property of Ellis and Co v Dixon-Johnson* [1925] AC 489.

[505] See paras 10.32–10.42 below.

A debt as property the subject of a security

A debt itself may be property the subject of a security. This situation is considered **6.125** later in the context of mutuality.[506]

7

DEBTS, CREDITS AND DEALINGS

A. Mutual Credit, and Dealings

The insolvency set-off section applies when there are mutual credits, mutual debts **7.01** or other mutual dealings. It was not always in this form. The original set-off section in 1705[1] referred only to mutual credit, and in 1732 it was expressed in terms of mutual credit and mutual debts.[2] It was not until 1869 that 'mutual dealings' was added.[3]

Debts and credits

The courts have interpreted 'mutual debts' as referring to debts that were both in **7.02** existence and presently payable before the bankruptcy.[4] It is apparent that 'mutual credits' would include mutual debts, in the sense that, in the case of a debt, credit is given to the debtor for payment. But it is broader than that.

An early authority is *Rose v Hart*.[5] The question in issue was whether a fuller with **7.03** whom cloths had been deposited by a bankrupt prior to the bankruptcy could retain them as a set-off against a debt owing by the bankrupt. Gibbs CJ said that mutual credit meant 'such credits only as must in their nature terminate in debts, as where a debt is due from one party, and credit given by him on the other for a

---

[1] (1705) 4 & 5 Anne, c 17, s 11. See para 6.25 above.
[2] (1732) 5 Geo II, c 30, s 28.
[3] Bankruptcy Act 1869, s 39.
[4] *Ex parte Prescot* (1753) 1 Atk 230, 26 ER 147, and see also *Young v Bank of Bengal* (1836) 1 Moore 150, 164–165, 12 ER 771, 777. Compare the definition of 'debt' in r 13.12 of the Insolvency Rules 1986 in relation to a debt to which a company in liquidation is subject, and for bankruptcy the definition of 'bankruptcy debt' in the Insolvency Act 1986, s 382.
[5] (1818) 8 Taunt 499, 129 ER 477.

sum of money payable at a future day, and which will then become a debt, or where there is a debt on one side, and a delivery of property with directions to turn it into money on the other; in such case the credit given by the delivery of the property must in its nature terminate in a debt . . .'.[6] Since the cloths in that case had not been deposited with authority to turn them into money, there was not mutual credit for the purpose of the set-off section.

7.04 According to the formulation in *Rose v Hart*, mutual credit extends only to credits which must in their nature end in a debt. In later cases, however, this requirement was relaxed,[7] so that it came to be regarded as sufficient if the transaction in question was such that it would naturally or in the ordinary course of business end in a debt,[8] or if it would probably result in a debt,[9] or if a debt was the likely result[10] or a natural outcome.[11] Therefore, where rights are vested in a party[12] before a bankruptcy which would naturally, and which ultimately do, result in a debt, the vesting of the rights is regarded as constituting the giving of credit, so that the resulting debt may be included in a set-off notwithstanding that it may not arise until after the bankruptcy. This relaxation is consistent with the courts' expressed policy of construing the set-off section liberally.[13]

7.05 In 1861 the range of provable debts was expanded, the principal change being the inclusion of a right of proof in respect of damages claims for breach of contract.[14] In addition, the Bankruptcy Act 1869 contained a general right of proof in respect of debts and liabilities to which the bankrupt became subject after the bankruptcy by reason of an obligation incurred before the bankruptcy.[15] This was broader than the situation which had applied under the Bankrupt Law Consolidation Act

---

[6] (1818) 8 Taunt 499, 506, 129 ER 477, 480. See also *Gibson v Bell* (1835) 1 Bing (NC) 743, 754, 131 ER 1303, 1308; *Clarke v Fell* (1833) 4 B & Ad 404, 409, 110 ER 507, 509; *Young v Bank of Bengal* (1836) 1 Moore 150, 168–169, 12 ER 771, 779, PC; *Groom v West* (1838) 8 Ad & E 758, 772–773, 112 ER 1025, 1030.

[7] Compare *Young v Bank of Bengal* (1836) 1 Moore 150, 168–169, 12 ER 771, 779.

[8] *Day & Dent Constructions Pty Ltd v North Australian Properties Pty Ltd* (1982) 150 CLR 85, 95, *per* Gibbs CJ, 103–104, *per* Mason J, referring to *Naoroji v The Chartered Bank of India* (1868) LR 3 CP 444, 451. See also *Palmer v Day & Sons* [1895] 2 QB 618, 621; *Re Mid-Kent Fruit Factory* [1896] 1 Ch 567, 569; *Wreckair Pty Ltd v Emerson* [1992] 1 Qd R 700, 707–708; *Smith's Leading Cases* (12th edn, 1915) vol 2, 281.

[9] *Sovereign Life Assurance Co v Dodd* [1892] 1 QB 405, 411–412.

[10] *Easum v Cato* (1822) 5 B & Ald 861, 867, 106 ER 1406, 1408.

[11] *Re Daintrey* [1900] 1 QB 546, 568 ('the natural outcome of previous transactions'); *Re Parker* (1997) 80 FCR 1, 12.

[12] In *Hiley v Peoples Prudential Assurance Co Ltd* (1938) 60 CLR 468, 487, 499 Rich and Dixon JJ spoke in terms of prior 'rights'. Compare the formulation in *Gye v McIntyre* (1991) 171 CLR 609, 623, 626 in relation to 'dealings'.

[13] *Eberle's Hotels and Restaurant Co Ltd v E Jonas & Brothers* (1887) 18 QBD 459, 465; *Day & Dent Constructions Pty Ltd v North Australian Properties Pty Ltd* (1982) 150 CLR 85, 108; *Gye v McIntyre* (1991) 171 CLR 609, 619; *Re Kolb* (1994) 51 FCR 31, 34; *Re Parker* (1997) 80 FCR 1, 8.

[14] See the Bankruptcy Act 1861, ss 149–154. Damages claims for breach of contract were dealt with in s 153.

[15] Bankruptcy Act 1869, s 31.

1849, by which only certain types of contingent liabilities were provable.[16] A set-off section that referred only to mutual debts and mutual credit would not have been adequate to bring about an expansion in the scope of the insolvency set-off section that corresponded to these changes, since mutual debts and mutual credit encompassed only debts which were in existence and presently payable before the bankruptcy, and debts which came into existence subsequent to the bankruptcy but which were a natural result of a prior transaction. A damages claim is not a debt, and it does not come within those concepts.[17] As Lord Russell of Killowen CJ remarked in relation to the giving of credit,[18] 'the credits must be such as either must terminate in debts or have a natural tendency to terminate in debts, and must not be such as terminate in claims differing in nature from debts'. Moreover, a debt which arose after the bankruptcy pursuant to a prior transaction would not have come within the concept of giving credit if for some reason the debt could not be said to be a natural result of that transaction. It appears that 'mutual dealings' was added to the set-off section in the 1869 Act in order to accommodate these increases in the range of provable debts,[19] a view which is consistent with judicial observations equating the scope of the set-off section in that Act with the ambit of the proof of debt provision.[20] It is also consistent with the observation by Brett LJ in *Peat v Jones & Co*,[21] that 'mutual dealings was added to get rid of any questions which might arise whether a transaction would end in a debt or not'. This statement takes in damages claims for breach of contract, which the courts quickly settled were within the scope of the mutual dealings head of the 1869

---

[16] See the Bankrupt Law Consolidation Act 1849, ss 174–178. For example, s 177 conferred a right of proof in respect of contingents *debts*. While s 178 also conferred a right of proof in respect of contingent *liabilities*, this was confined to traders.

[17] *Rose v Sims* (1830) 1 B & Ad 521, 109 ER 881; *Palmer v Day & Sons* [1895] 2 QB 618, 621. See also *Harrop v Fisher* (1861) 10 CB(NS) 196, 204, 142 ER 426, 429. In *Gibson v Bell* (1835) 1 Bing (NC) 743, 131 ER 1303 and *Groom v West* (1838) 8 Ad & E 758, 112 ER 1025 the claim was framed in damages, and a set-off was allowed. In each case however the transaction was regarded as one which of necessity would end in a debt, and that in truth was the substance of the claim, notwithstanding the form of the pleading. Compare *Makeham v Crow* (1864) 15 CB(NS) 847, 143 ER 1018, in which an unliquidated damages claim arising out of a contract of sale was set off in an action by the vendor's assignees in bankruptcy for the price. However the purchaser presented alternative arguments for a set-off. It was based not only upon the scope of the proof of debt provision in the 1861 Act, but also equitable set-off. The report is silent as to which of these was regarded as the justification for the decision. Certainly, in cases decided after the 1869 Act, set-off of unliquidated damages was justified on the basis of mutual dealings as opposed to mutual credit. In *Booth v Hutchinson* (1872) LR 15 Eq 30, 32 Malins VC said that he probably would have concluded that the damages claim in that case could not have been set off under the old law. He said (at 34) that there was no mutual debt, and there was hardly a mutual credit, but that there was certainly a mutual dealing.

[18] *Palmer v Day & Sons* [1895] 2 QB 618, 621.

[19] In *Turner v Thomas* (1871) LR 6 CP 610, 613–614 Willes J discussed the 'very large extension of the law of set-off' in the 1869 Act by reference to the proof of debt provision.

[20] See eg *In Re Asphaltic Wood Pavement Co. Lee & Chapman's Case* (1885) 30 Ch D 216, 222, *per* Brett MR, 224, *per* Cotton LJ.

[21] (1881) 8 QBD 147, 149.

set-off section.[22] In addition, it would encompass any debt which arises after the bankruptcy as a result of a prior transaction, and without the intervention of any new and independent transaction,[23] irrespective of whether the situation is such as to come within the judicially accepted definition of giving credit. In such a case the debt is still the product of a dealing between the parties, and accordingly it may be included in a set-off on that ground.

7.06 In *Gye v McIntyre*[24] the High Court of Australia suggested, but without deciding the point, that it was 'strongly arguable' that a damages claim for fraudulent misrepresentation may come within the ambit of the expression 'mutual credits'. This issue may be significant in Australia, not simply for the determination whether there are mutual debts, mutual credits or other mutual dealings, but also because the qualification to the set-off section is drafted in terms of having the requisite notice at the time of giving or receiving credit.[25] The suggestion in *Gye v McIntyre* was made in the context of a discussion of a comment by Byles J in *Naoroji v Chartered Bank of India*,[26] that mutual credit encompasses reciprocal demands which must (or would) naturally terminate in a debt. In *Gye v McIntyre* the claim in issue had been liquidated by judgment after the relevant date for determining rights of set-off, and the High Court may have had in mind that a damages claim would naturally terminate in a judgment debt. However, in relation to the question whether credit has been given, as opposed to whether a set-off may be based upon a claim arising out of a prior dealing, the relevant inquiry is whether the claim would naturally end in a debt, as opposed to whether it does end in debt, and the courts have never considered the fact that a damages claim may end in a judgment debt as sufficient to bring it within the concept of giving credit. If that view had prevailed, there would not have been any necessity for the courts after 1869 to have recourse to the concept of mutual dealings in order to allow a damages claim for breach of contract to be set off in a bankruptcy. Therefore, in *Peat v Jones & Co*[27] Cotton LJ said that the damages claim for breach of contract in that case would not have come within the earlier mutual credit clauses, but it did come within the mutual dealing head in the 1869 Act.[28]

---

[22] See, for example, *Booth v Hutchinson* (1872) LR 15 Eq 30; *Peat v Jones & Co* (1881) 8 QBD 147; *Mersey Steel & Iron Co v Naylor, Benzon & Co* (1884) 9 App Cas 434; *Re Asphaltic Wood Pavement Co. Lee & Chapman's Case* (1885) 30 Ch D 216.

[23] See *Hiley v The Peoples Prudential Assurance Co Ltd* (1938) 60 CLR 468, 487, *per* Rich J, 499, *per* Dixon J.

[24] (1991) 171 CLR 609, 625.

[25] See the Bankruptcy Act 1966 (Cth), s 86(2), and for company liquidation the Corporations Act 2001 (Cth), s 553C(2). See also paras 6.50–6.53 above.

[26] (1868) LR 3 CP 444, 451.

[27] (1881) 8 QBD 147, 150.

[28] See also *Booth v Hutchinson* (1872) LR 15 Eq 30, 33, and the reference to 'mutual dealings' in *In Re Asphaltic Wood Pavement Co. Lee & Chapman's Case* (1885) 30 Ch D 216, 224.

Dealings

The High Court in *Gye v McIntyre*[29] noted that the expression 'or *other* mutual   **7.07**
dealings'[30] in the insolvency set-off section gives rise to a linguistic problem, in
that 'credits' and 'debts' ordinarily represent the outcome of dealings rather than
the dealings themselves, whereas dealings do not of themselves, as distinct from
their outcome, represent claims susceptible to a set-off. What the section requires
is that there be debts, credits or claims arising from dealings. In relation to 'dealings', the High Court observed:[31]

> There will . . . be mutual dealings at the date of the sequestration order if there ex-
> isted at that date 'dealings' which involved the bankrupt and the other party and
> which were capable of giving rise to, and subsequently did give rise to, 'mutual'
> claims between them . . .

What constitutes a dealing for the purpose of the insolvency set-off section? The   **7.08**
expression has never been precisely defined, but not every claim can be said to
arise out of a dealing. As Lord Esher MR commented:[32]

> There are, no doubt, matters which give rise to claims, but are not dealings within
> the section. If one man assaults another or injures him through negligence, that
> gives rise to a claim, but is not a dealing; but I am disposed to think that whatever
> comes within the description of an ordinary business transaction would be a dealing
> within the section.

A misappropriation of assets or a conversion of property is not a dealing.[33]

In Australia, the High Court in *Gye v McIntyre*[34] noted that 'dealings' has been   **7.09**
construed as referring to matters having a commercial or business flavour.[35] On
the other hand, their Honours suggested that the term is used in a non-technical
sense in the set-off section, and that it is a term of very wide scope. It embraces far
more than a legally binding contract or 'deal'. They went on to say that,[36]

> Even if it is correct to construe 'dealings' in [the set-off section] as confined to a com-
> mercial or business setting, it covers the communings, the negotiations, verbal and
> by correspondence, and other matters which occur or exist in that setting. Whatever
> may be the outer limits of the word 'dealings' in [the set-off section], it encompasses,
> as a matter of ordinary language, commercial transactions and the negotiations lead-
> ing up to them.

---

[29] (1991) 171 CLR 609, 623.
[30] Emphasis added by the High Court.
[31] (1991) 171 CLR 609, 623.
[32] *Eberle's Hotels and Restaurant Co Ltd v E Jonas & Brothers* (1887) 18 QBD 459, 465, referred
to with evident approval in *Re H E Thorne & Son, Ltd* [1914] 2 Ch 438, 451–452, *per* Astbury J.
[33] *Manson v Smith* [1997] 2 BCLC 161, 164; *Smith v Bridgend County BC* [2002] 1 AC 336, 351
para 35.
[34] (1991) 171 CLR 609, 625.
[35] See also *Re Kolb* (1994) 51 FCR 31, 34.
[36] (1991) 171 CLR 609, 625.

Thus, where a fraudulent misrepresentation was made in the course of negotiations leading up to a contract, but was not a term of the contract itself, the High Court said that the misrepresentation nevertheless was part of a dealing for the purpose of the set-off section. That was so notwithstanding that the resulting contract was not entered into with the person who had made the misrepresentation, but with a company associated with her.

B. The Requirement of a Dealing

7.10   It has been suggested that the set-off section is limited to claims that arise out of contract,[37] a view that Brightman J rejected in *Re D H Curtis (Builders) Ltd.*[38] The purpose of insolvency set-off, he said, is to do substantial justice between a bankrupt and his creditors.[39] On that basis, he concluded that 'one would expect to find that any mutual demands capable of being proved in bankruptcy can be the subject-matter of set-off whether or not arising out of contract'.[40] In the *Curtis* case the Crown had a claim for unpaid taxes against a company in liquidation, and at the same time the Crown was indebted to the company for the repayment of another tax. It was held that the cross-demands could be set off, even though they were statutory rather than contractual in origin. This has been accepted and applied in subsequent cases.[41] It may be thought nevertheless that Brightman J had strained the language of the section. The set-off section stipulates that there should be 'mutual credits, mutual debts or other mutual dealings' between the creditor and the bankrupt or, as the case may be, between a company in liquidation and a creditor. The concept of a 'dealing' may be said to connote a contractual relationship between the parties. Further, the insertion of 'other' before 'mutual dealings' appears to qualify both mutual credits and mutual debts, so that they should also have arisen out of a dealing between the parties to the proposed set-off. There are two difficulties with that analysis, however.

7.11   The first is that 'dealing' would appear to be a broader concept than 'contract', a point emphasized by the High Court of Australia in *Gye v McIntyre*.[42] It would en-

---

[37]   *Palmer v Day & Sons* [1895] 2 QB 618, 621; *Re Mid-Kent Fruit Factory* [1896] 1 Ch 567, 571; *Re Canada Cycle & Motor Agency (Queensland) Ltd* [1931] St R Qd 281; *Re Hurburgh* [1959] Tas SR 25, 46.

[38]   [1978] 1 Ch 162.

[39]   Brightman J referred to *Forster v Wilson* (1843) 12 M & W 191, 203–204, 152 ER 1165, 1171, *Ex parte Cleland, re Davies* (1867) LR 2 Ch App 808, 812–813, and *Re City Life Assurance Co* [1926] Ch 191, 216.

[40]   [1978] 1 Ch 162, 173. See paras 7.15–7.17 below in relation to the suggestion that all provable demands can be the subject of a set-off.

[41]   *Re Cushla* [1979] 3 All ER 415; *Re Unit 2 Windows Ltd* [1985] 1 WLR 1383; *Re Kolb* (1994) 51 FCR 31; *Re Parker* (1997) 80 FCR 1, 10. In Australia, the High Court in *Gye v McIntyre* (1991) 171 CLR 609, 630–634 similarly rejected the view that the claims must have arisen out of contract.

[42]   (1991) 171 CLR 609, 625.

compass claims which arise out of the negotiations which lead up to a commercial transaction, and not just claims which arise out of an ensuing contract. The second is that, in any event, it has never been a necessary requirement for a set-off that the claims should have arisen out of a dealing between the parties.[43] The current form of set-off section first appeared in section 39 of the Bankruptcy Act 1869. Prior to that enactment, the section only encompassed mutual credit and mutual debts. In determining whether the case was one of mutual credit or mutual debts, it was not necessary that the parties should have dealt directly with each other. This is apparent from the decision in 1789 in *Hankey v Smith*,[44] in which it was held that an indebtedness of a bankrupt acceptor upon a bill of exchange could be brought into an account by the holder, even though the bankrupt was unaware that the bill had been indorsed to the holder.[45] The acceptor and the holder had not dealt with each other, and yet a set-off was allowed. As Buller J noted in his judgment, in order to constitute mutual credit it is not necessary that the parties should have intended to trust each other in the transaction in question. If a bill of exchange is sent out into the world, he said that credit is given to the acceptor by every person who takes the bill. A similar result occurred in *Forster v Wilson*[46] in the context of bearer promissory notes, while the same point may be made in relation to the situation in which one of the parties to the proposed set-off gained a right to sue the other only as a result of an assignment to him of the other's indebtedness.[47] When the set-off section was re-cast in 1869 in terms of mutual credits, mutual debts or other mutual dealings, it was not suggested that this had the effect of narrowing the scope of mutual credits and mutual debts, so that henceforth they should be considered as encompassing only debts and credits arising out of dealings between the parties. On the contrary, as Sir George Jessel MR remarked in the context of the 1869 Act,[48] the whole tendency of the history of the insolvency legislation has been to extend the principle upon which the right of set-off is founded.

Because traditionally a dealing has not been considered to be a prerequisite to a **7.12**
set-off, the better view is that the word 'other' before 'mutual dealings' should be

---

[43] *Re Parker* (1997) 80 FCR 1, 10. *Quaere* whether *Manson v Smith* [1997] 2 BCLC 161, 164 was intended to suggest the contrary.

[44] (1789) 3 TR 507n, 100 ER 703.

[45] See also *Collins v Jones* (1830) 10 B & C 777, 109 ER 638; *Ex parte Hastie and Hutchinson, re Alexander and Co* (1850) 14 LTOS 402; *Re Morris and M'Murray* (1874) 5 AJR 157, aff'd at 185 (in which it was specifically argued that there was no dealing between the parties, but a set-off nevertheless was allowed).

[46] (1843) 12 M & W 191, 152 ER 1165.

[47] *Clark v Cort* (1840) Cr & Ph 154, 41 ER 449; *Mathieson's Trustee v Burrup, Mathieson and Co* [1927] 1 Ch 562; *Southern Cross Construction Ltd v Southern Cross Club Ltd* [1973] 1 NZLR 708; *Kon Strukt Pty Ltd v Storage Developments Pty Ltd* (1989) 96 FLR 43. Compare *Re Eros Films Ltd* [1963] 1 Ch 565 and *Law v James* [1972] 2 NSWLR 573, in which the assignment occurred after the company law equivalent of notice of an act of bankruptcy.

[48] *Peat v Jones & Co* (1881) 8 QBD 147, 149.

regarded as otiose. There are admittedly problems with that view. It is difficult to reconcile with Lawrence LJ's comment in *Re Fenton, ex p The Fenton Textile Association Ltd*,[49] that 'the account which has to be taken . . . is an account of what is due from the one party to the other in respect of the mutual dealings'. Further, it is contrary to the opinion of Winn LJ in the Court of Appeal in *Rolls Razor Ltd v Cox*,[50] that the proper construction of the set-off section 'involves placing emphasis primarily upon the concept of mutual dealings and consequentially regarding the debts and credits referred to as such mutual debts and mutual credits as arise from mutual dealings'. Moreover it does not sit well with the stipulation in the set-off section that an account is to be taken of what is due from each party to the other 'in respect of the mutual dealings'. Once again, this suggests that the set-off section only applies to claims which arose out of a dealing. However, in order to give an intelligible meaning to the section in the light of its history, this should be interpreted as referring to an account of sums due in respect of cross-demands each of which constitutes a debt, a credit or the product of a prior dealing.

7.13 If indeed it is not necessary for a set-off that the parties should have dealt with each other, there is no justification for limiting the scope of the section to cross-demands that arose out of contracts. This is not to suggest that it would never be necessary to show a dealing. In the *Curtis* case there were mutual debts, and for that a dealing is not required. Similarly a dealing is not necessary for mutual credit. If, on the other hand, it is sought to base a set-off upon a claim that is neither a presently existing debt at the date of the bankruptcy, nor a debt which is a natural result of a prior transaction so as to constitute the giving of credit within the meaning ascribed to that expression by the courts, the claim should not be capable of being employed in a set-off unless it arose out of a dealing between the parties.[51] This is apparent from the plain words of the set-off section. It is particularly relevant to the reform set out in the 1986 Insolvency legislation, by which damages claims in tort became provable.[52] The issue of set-off against damages claims, including claims in tort, is considered later.[53]

---

[49] [1931] 1 Ch 85, 113.

[50] [1967] 1 QB 552, 574. See also the discussion in *Gye v McIntyre* (1991) 171 CLR 609, 623.

[51] This is consistent with Brightman J's explanation in *Curtis* [1978] Ch 162, 172 of the comment of Lord Russell in *Palmer v Day & Sons* [1895] 2 QB 618, 621 regarding the necessity for the claims to arise out of contract. See also Pincus J in the Federal Court in *McIntyre v Perkes* (1990) 22 FCR 260, 262, referring to the earlier judgment of Hill J in that case at (1989) 89 ALR 460, 470–471.

[52] See the Insolvency Act 1986, s 322, 'bankruptcy debt' being defined in s 382 as including tortious liabilities. For companies, see r 13.12 on the Insolvency Rules. In Australia see the Corporations Act 2001 (Cth), s 553(1) in relation to company liquidation.

[53] See paras 8.42–8.47 below.

C. Different Dealings and Contracts

In *Peat v Jones & Co*[54] Jessel MR said that: 'a contract of sale and purchase is in its   **7.14**
nature mutual, imposing reciprocal obligations on the vendor and purchaser. Any
claim arising out of the mutual dealings could be set off.'[55] Reciprocal obligations
under a contract usually would be mutual,[56] but when it is sought to base a set-off
upon a damages claim for breach of contract the principle of mutuality does not
require that the cross-demand should have arisen out of the same contract.[57]
Further, when the only justification for allowing a claim to be brought into an account is that it arose out of a prior dealing, it should not be necessary that the
cross-claim similarly should have been derived from a dealing between the parties,
notwithstanding the contrary impression that may be gained from the use of the
plural in the expression 'mutual dealings'. For example, one of the demands may
be for damages for breach of contract, and therefore it may be included in a set-off
only because it is derived from a dealing. In addition, the party possessed of the
damages claim may be the acceptor of a bill of exchange, and he may be unaware
that the bill had been endorsed to the party liable for the damages. The acceptor's
liability to the holder in that situation is not derived from a dealing between them.
A set-off nevertheless should be available in respect of the cross-claims, notwithstanding that, while one of the demands is based upon a dealing, the other can
only be brought into account because it is a debt, or alternatively the product of
giving credit. In order for the set-off section to apply, there must be mutual credits, mutual debts or other mutual dealings. Mutuality means that the cross-
demands must be between the same parties and they must be held in the same
capacity or right.[58] The requirements of the set-off section should be satisfied if,
on each side of the account, there is either a presently existing and payable debt at
the date of the bankruptcy, or a debt arising after the bankruptcy in respect of
which credit had been given before the bankruptcy, or a money demand arising
either before or after the bankruptcy as a result of a prior dealing, and if in addition mutuality is present. When it is sought to have recourse to the 'mutual dealings' head, it should not be necessary that both demands should have arisen out of
a dealing. This is consistent with the view that the set-off section should be given
the widest possible scope.[59]

---

[54] (1881) 8 QBD 147.
[55] (1881) 8 QBD 147, 149. See also *Jack v Kipping* (1882) 9 QBD 113, 116.
[56] Unless, for example, the benefit of the contract is held on trust for someone else.
[57] *McIntyre v Perkes* (1990) 22 FCR 260, 263 (Pincus J, referring to *Hiley v The Peoples
Prudential Assurance Co Ltd* (1938) 60 CLR 468), and also 'Set-off in Case of Mutual Dealings'
(1882) 26 Sol Jo 575.
[58] See para 11.01 below.
[59] *Eberle's Hotels and Restaurant Co Ltd v E Jonas & Brothers* (1887) 18 QBD 459, 465; *Day &
Dent Constructions Pty Ltd v North Australian Properties Pty Ltd* (1982) 150 CLR 85, 108; *Gye v
McIntyre* (1991) 171 CLR 609, 619; *Re Kolb* (1994) 15 FCR 31, 34.

D. The Insolvent's Liability

7.15 For the insolvency set-off section to apply there must be mutual credits, mutual debts or other mutual dealings between the bankrupt and 'any creditor of the bankrupt proving or claiming to prove for a bankruptcy debt'. The set-off available pursuant to rule 4.90 of the Insolvency Rules 1986 in the case of a company liquidation is expressed in similar terms. The requirement that there should be a person proving or claiming to prove for a debt in the bankruptcy has as a corollary that the creditor's claim against the bankrupt should be capable of proof. But in addition the courts have often indicated that the converse proposition also applies, that the fact that a claim may be proved means that it should also be capable of being employed in a set-off.[60] This proposition would appear to be based on the notion that insolvency set-off is an aspect of the rules relating to proof of debts.[61] There is, nevertheless, a difficulty with the view that it constitutes a principle of general application, and that is that there is nothing in the set-off section which expressly supports it.[62] The section states that the creditor must be proving or claiming to prove a debt, but it does not say that it is sufficient that the claim is provable. In deciding whether a claim may be employed in a set-off, the primary question should always be whether the cross-demands are such as to come within the language of the section. In other words, there must be mutual credits, mutual debts or other mutual dealings. Indeed, the connection between proof and set-off has not always been emphasized by the courts, particularly in the early years of the bankruptcy legislation. For example, in 1791 it was held in *Smith v Hodson*[63] that an accommodation acceptor paying after the bankruptcy of the drawer could employ his claim for an indemnity in a set-off, even though prior to 1809 an acceptor paying under those circumstances did not have a right of proof.[64]

---

[60] *Graham v Russell* (1816) 5 M & S 498, 501, 105 ER 1133, 1134; *Re Asphaltic Wood Pavement Co. Lee & Chapman's Case* (1885) 30 Ch D 216, 222, 224; *Palmer v Day & Sons* [1895] 2 QB 618, 621; *Re Taylor. Ex parte Norvell* [1910] 1 KB 562, 580; *Paddy v Clutton* [1920] 2 Ch 554, 567; *Ellis and Company's Trustee v Dixon-Johnson* [1924] 1 Ch 342, 357; *Re City Life Assurance Co Ltd. Grandfield's Case* [1926] 1 Ch 191, 210–211, 212; *Re Fenton* [1931] 1 Ch 85, 113; *Hiley v The Peoples Prudential Assurance Co Ltd* (1938) 60 CLR 468, 490; *Kitchen's Trustee v Madders* [1950] 1 Ch 134, 143; *Re Bank of Credit and Commerce International SA (No 8)* [1996] Ch 245, 256, CA. See also *Peat v Jones & Co* (1881) 8 QBD 147, 150; *Sovereign Life Assurance Co v Dodd* [1892] 1 QB 405, 412; *Re D H Curtis (Builders) Ltd* [1978] 1 Ch 162, 173–174; *Re Cushla Ltd* [1979] 3 All ER 415, 420; *Willment Brothers Ltd v North West Thames Regional Health Authority* (1984) 26 BLR 51, 59; *Re Charge Card Services Ltd* [1987] 1 Ch 150, 179, 181, 187.

[61] See *Mersey Steel and Iron Co v Naylor, Benzon & Co* (1884) 9 App Cas 434, 437–438, *per* Earl of Selborne; *Re Bank of Credit and Commerce International SA (No 8)* [1996] Ch 245, 256, CA.

[62] The qualification to the set-off section could preclude a set-off in respect of an otherwise provable debt. See paras 6.49–6.64 above.

[63] (1791) 4 TR 211, 100 ER 979. See also *Ex parte Boyle, re Shepherd* unreported, but noted in Cooke, *The Bankrupt Laws* (8th edn, 1823) vol 1, 571, and *Ex parte Wagstaff* (1806) 13 Ves Jun 65, 33 ER 219.

[64] *Chilton v Whiffin* (1768) 3 Wils KB 13, 95 ER 906; *Young v Hockley* (1772) 3 Wils KB 346, 95 ER 1092; *Snaith v Gale* (1797) 7 TR 364, 101 ER 1023. The statute (1809) 49 Geo III, c 121,

Smith v Hodson concerned the 1732 set-off section, which only applied to mutual   **7.16**
debts and mutual credit. The section did not refer to any connection between set-
off and provable debts, so that on its face there was nothing objectionable in the
decision in *Smith v Hodson*. In 1825 new legislation (6 Geo IV, c 16) came into
force. While the set-off section (section 50) was still confined to mutual credit and
mutual debts, it contained an express statutory recognition of the principle that
all provable debts could be set off.[65] A provision to that effect also appeared in the
set-off section in the bankruptcy legislation of 1849.[66] Neither of those sections,
however, addressed the question of the susceptibility to a set-off of demands that
were not in the nature of provable debts. Sometimes, when the courts held that a
particular claim could not be employed in a set-off pursuant to the 1825 or the
1849 set-off section, the justification was that the demand was not provable, although this was not always the case. There are instances in which the courts instead had regard to the definition of mutual credit adopted in *Rose v Hart* as a
means of rejecting an argument for a set-off. For example, in *Abbott v Hicks*[67] it
was held that a contingent liability of the bankrupt could not be the subject of a
set-off, the court emphasizing that the liability was not provable.[68] That should be
compared to *Rose v Sims*,[69] in which a person indebted to a bankrupt sought to set
off a claim that he had against the bankrupt for damages for breach of contract.
Prior to 1861 damages claims were not provable in a bankruptcy.[70] It was held in
Rose v Sims that the cross-demand could not be employed in a set-off, not because
it was not provable, but on the basis of the principle that mutual credit was confined to transactions that would end in debts, and a damages claim is not a debt.[71]

s 8 introduced a right of proof in favour of a surety who paid after the bankruptcy of the debtor.
Though at common law an accommodation acceptor was not regarded as a surety (see *Fentum v Pocock* (1813) 5 Taunt 192, 128 ER 660, but compare the position in equity, for which see *Coles Myer Finance Ltd v Commissioner of Taxation* (1993) 67 ALJR 463, 466–467, 481–482), it was considered nevertheless that the statute applied to accommodation acceptors. See Cooke, *The Bankrupt Laws* (8th edn, 1823) vol 1, 175, referring to *Ex parte Yonge* (1814) 3 V & B 31, 39–40, 35 ER 391, 394.

[65] The section provided that, 'every Debt or Demand hereby made proveable against the Estate of the Bankrupt, may also be set off in manner aforesaid'.

[66] Bankrupt Law Consolidation Act 1849, s 171.

[67] (1839) 5 Bing (NC) 578, 132 ER 1222.

[68] See in particular the judgments of Coltman and Erskine JJ. Thus, *Abbott v Hicks* was cited in *Smith's Leading Cases* (2nd edn, 1842) vol 2, 182 as authority for the proposition that a demand that was not provable under the fiat could not be set off. While s 56 of the statute (1825) 6 Geo IV, c 16 allowed a right of proof in respect of contingent debts, the contingent liability in *Abbott v Hicks* was not within the ambit of that section.

[69] (1830) 1 B & Ad 521, 109 ER 881.

[70] See the Bankruptcy Act 1861, s 153.

[71] While *Rose v Hart* was not mentioned in the judgments, it was referred to in a note to the re-port, and it is evident that the decision in *Rose v Sims* was based upon that case. Even though a claim may have been framed as a claim for damages, if in truth it was liquidated, so that the amount could be ascertained without the intervention of a jury, it could be proved in a bankruptcy, and similarly it could be the subject of a set-off. See, as to proof, *Utterson v Vernon* (1790) 3 TR 539, 100 ER 721 and, as to set-off, *Gibson v Bell* (1835) 1 Bing (NC) 743, 131 ER 1303 and *Groom v West* (1838) 8 Ad & E 758, 112 ER 1025.

7.17 The stipulation in the 1825 and the 1849 set-off sections, that all provable debts
could be set off, was omitted from the 1869 and the subsequent sections, although
the courts continued to emphasize the principle. The continued emphasis of the
principle however should be considered in the context of the changes to the proof
of debt and the set-off sections that occurred in 1861 and 1869. In 1861, damages
claims for breach of contract became provable. A claim for damages is not a debt
and nor does it constitute the giving of credit.[72] If therefore it was intended that
such claims should be able to be included in a set-off, it would not have been satisfactory to rely on a general statement that all provable debts could be set off if at
the same time the scope of the set-off section was confined to mutual debts and
mutual credit. In the 1869 Act, the reference found in the earlier legislation to
provable debts being able to be set off was omitted from the set-off section, and
the scope of the section instead was expanded to include mutual dealings.
Subsequent judicial statements to the effect that a provable debt can be included
in a set-off may well have been a correct summary of the position that applied after
1869, and that continued to apply in relation to the 1883 and the 1914
Bankruptcy Acts, in light of the scope of the right of proof in those Acts. It should
not however be regarded as a fixed principle that applies regardless of the language
of the set-off section and of any changes to the right of proof. In truth, as Mason
J remarked in the High Court of Australia,[73] the fact that a claim against a bankrupt is provable should only provide indirect assistance in considering whether it
can be set off. The set-off section requires that the claim against the bankrupt
must be capable of proof, but this is expressed as a necessary, rather than a sufficient, condition for a set-off. Thus, in *Bank of Credit and Commerce International
SA v Al-Saud*[74] Neill LJ commented that, while it is true that a debt which is not
eligible for proof is not eligible for set-off, this does not mean that all debts which
are eligible for proof are eligible for set-off. The primary question should always
be whether there are mutual credits, mutual debts or other mutual dealings.[75] In
that regard, the Insolvency Act 1986 further increased the range of provable debts,
by allowing a proof in respect of a damages claim in tort,[76] but without any corresponding change to the set-off section. The position accordingly would appear to
be that, if a claim in tort arose out of a prior dealing between the parties, it should

---

[72] See para 7.05 above.
[73] *Day & Dent Constructions Pty Ltd v North Australian Properties Pty Ltd* (1982) 150 CLR 85,
108.
[74] [1997] 1 BCLC 457, 466.
[75] As Lord Hoffmann remarked in *Stein v Blake* [1996] AC 243, 251, insolvency set-off 'applies
to any claim arising out of mutual credits or other mutual dealings before the bankruptcy for which
a creditor would be entitled to prove as a "bankruptcy debt" '.
[76] See the Insolvency Act 1986, s 322, 'bankruptcy debt' being defined in s 382 as including liabilities in tort. For company liquidation, see r 13.12 of the Insolvency Rules 1986. In Australia, a liability in tort is still not provable in a bankruptcy (see the Bankruptcy Act 1966 (Cth), s 82(2)),
although it may now be proved in a company liquidation. See the Corporations Act 2001 (Cth),
s 553(1).

be able to be included in a set-off. But if the claim in question did not arise out of a dealing, it is difficult to see what basis there is for including it in a set-off, notwithstanding that it is provable, since it is not a debt and nor does it come within the concept of giving credit.[77]

E. The Insolvent's Claim

The bankrupt's claim, and proof in bankruptcy

Consider the claim on the other side of the account, being the bankrupt's or the   **7.18**
company's claim against the creditor. In *Graham v Russell*[78] Lord Ellenborough said that, 'in taking an account between parties, the question, whether any particular item shall be introduced into it, must depend upon the nature and character of the item itself, and not upon the side of the account at which it is to be placed'. The case concerned a statute[79] which allowed an insured under a policy of insurance to prove a claim on the policy in the bankruptcy of the underwriter, even though the loss may not have occurred until after the bankruptcy.[80] *Graham v Russell* differed from the situation contemplated by the statute in that it was the insured rather than the underwriter who was bankrupt, and the underwriter wanted to set off a liability that had accrued on the policy after the insured's bankruptcy against a prior debt of the insured for premiums. Because the bankrupt's claim against the underwriter would have been provable in the underwriter's bankruptcy, and could have been the subject of a set-off, if the underwriter instead had been the bankrupt party, Lord Ellenborough in delivering the judgment of the Exchequer Chamber held that the underwriter could employ his liability on the claim in a set-off when the question arose in the context of the bankruptcy of the insured. The proposition which is the converse of that approach is that, if the bankrupt's claim against the creditor is such that it could not have been proved if the creditor instead had been bankrupt, it similarly should not be capable of being employed in a set-off in the present bankruptcy, irrespective of whether it arises out of a dealing between the parties.

In Australia, the High Court rejected that converse proposition in *Gye v*   **7.19**
McIntyre,[81] as did Gummow and von Doussa JJ in the Federal Court in that case.[82] The High Court reached its conclusion without considering *Graham v Russell*.

---

[77] See paras 8.44–8.47 below.
[78] (1816) 5 M & S 498, 502, 105 ER 1133, 1135.
[79] (1746) 19 Geo II, C 32, s 2.
[80] Prior to 1825 (see s 56 of 6 Geo IV, c 16) contingent debts as a general rule could be neither proved nor set off in a bankruptcy.
[81] (1991) 171 CLR 609, 628–629.
[82] (1990) 22 FCR 260, 273–274. Compare the earlier judgment of Hill J at (1989) 89 ALR 460, 471, 472.

However *Graham v Russell* was considered in the Federal Court, Gummow and von Doussa JJ distinguishing it on the ground that it was concerned only with facilitating, not restricting, the right of set-off. It is true that, in *Graham v Russell*, Lord Ellenborough looked at whether the bankrupt's claim would have been provable if the creditor had been bankrupt as a means of allowing a set-off. It is nevertheless correct to say that the rationale underlying Lord Ellenborough's judgment was that the question whether an item can be included in a set-off should depend upon the nature and character of the item itself, and not upon the side of the account at which it is to be placed.[83] Recourse was had to that notion in *Graham v Russell* in order to allow a set-off. But given that, since 1869, it has been a requirement of the set-off section that the creditor's claim against the bankrupt be provable, the rationale upon which the decision in *Graham v Russell* was based suggests that the bankrupt's claim should also now be in the nature of a provable debt. *Graham v Russell* suggests that it is the nature of the claim that matters, not the side of the account on which it appears. There are other cases which support that view. In *Young v Bank of Bengal*[84] debtors defaulted after the date of their bankruptcy in payment of a secured debt. The creditor realized the security and, after satisfying the secured debt, held a surplus. The creditor then sought to apply the surplus in reduction of a separate unsecured debt of the bankrupts. One of the reasons that the Privy Council gave for holding against a set-off was that the creditor's contingent liability to account for any surplus would not have been a provable debt under the then current legislation if the creditor instead had been made bankrupt before selling the security.[85] In other words, provability was used to restrict the right of set-off in the context of the bankrupt's claim. This was also the approach adopted by Maule J, with whom Cresswell and Williams JJ concurred, in *Bell v Carey*.[86] The bankrupt in that case had a claim in damages against a creditor. Maule J said that the claim could not be the subject of a set-off because, under the bankruptcy legislation in force at the time, 'you could not say that the damages, great or small, would be a demand provable under a fiat'.[87] Reference also may be made to *Booth v Hutchinson*,[88] in which Malins VC, in deciding that a claim for rent which accrued to a landlord after the landlord had executed a deed of assignment could be the subject of a set-off,[89] relied on the definition of 'liabil-

---

[83] (1816) 5 M & S 498, 502, 105 ER 1133, 1135.

[84] (1836) 1 Moore 150, 12 ER 771.

[85] See the discussion at (1836) 1 Moore 150, 166–167, 12 ER 771, 778. This view is also consistent with Brightman J's comment in *Re D H Curtis (Builders) Ltd* [1978] Ch 162, 173, that a natural assumption would be that the set-off section is intended to cover the same subject-matter as the section dealing with proof of debt.

[86] (1849) 8 CB 887, 137 ER 757.

[87] (1849) 8 CB 887, 894, 137 ER 757, 760. See also the comments of Cresswell J during argument at 892, 759.

[88] (1872) LR 15 Eq 30 (esp at 35).

[89] The case concerned a deed of assignment rather than a bankruptcy, but it was considered that it was subject to the same principle as for a bankruptcy.

ity' in section 31 of the Bankruptcy Act 1869 in relation to the right of proof.[90] These cases, which suggest that the availability of a set-off in relation to a bankrupt's claim is limited by the scope of the proof of debt provision, were not considered in *Gye v McIntyre*. More recently, Rose LJ in delivering the judgment of the Court of Appeal[91] in *Re Bank of Credit and Commerce International SA (No 8)*[92] also accepted that view. He said that 'a claim is not capable of set-off unless it is admissible to proof', and that: 'This is true of both sides of the account. The right to set off a particular claim depends on the nature and character of the claim itself and not upon the side of the account on which it is to be placed: *Graham v Russell* (1816) 5 M & S 498, 501.'[93]

On appeal however the House of Lords doubted that proposition,[94] referring to **7.20** *Gye v McIntyre*. The view expressed in *Gye v McIntyre* would seem to be correct. The question is one of construction of the insolvency set-off section, and there is nothing in the section to suggest that the bankrupt's claim against the creditor should be in the nature of a provable debt. The question simply is whether the claim constituted a debt at the date of the bankruptcy, or whether it is a debt which arose later but which was a natural result of a prior transaction so as to come within the concept of giving credit, or whether the claim in any event arose out of a prior dealing.

Gye v McIntyre concerned two debtors who had entered into compositions with **7.21** their creditors, one of whom was liable to the debtors in tort for damages for fraudulent misrepresentation.[95] The misrepresentations arose in the course of negotiations for the purchase of a hotel by the debtors from a company associated with the creditor. The misrepresentations did not arise out of a contract between the debtors and the creditor, the parties to the contract instead being the debtors and the company. They did arise however in the course of the negotiations between the debtors and the creditor leading up to the contract. The High Court said that the concept of 'dealing' in the set-off section includes contractual negotiations. It is not confined to the resulting contract. Accordingly, the claim in this case did arise out of a dealing and could be set off. The claim in question was a claim in tort. Unlike the Insolvency Act in England, the proof of debt provision in the Australian Bankruptcy Act 1966 (Cth) does not extend to tortious demands.[96]

---

[90] The decision nevertheless is unsatisfactory, because the Vice Chancellor failed to consider the question of mutuality which may arise in lease cases as a result of privity of estate. See paras 13.58–13.65 below.

[91] Rose, Saville and Millett LJJ.

[92] [1996] Ch 245.

[93] [1996] Ch 245, 256.

[94] *Re Bank of Credit and Commerce International SA (No 8)* [1998] AC 214, 228.

[95] The Bankruptcy Act 1966 (Cth), s 243 provides that the set-off section (s 86) is to apply to compositions.

[96] See the Bankruptcy Act 1966 (Cth), s 82(2). This is no longer the case however in a company liquidation. See the Corporations Act 2001 (Cth), s 553.

Nevertheless, the High Court said that there was nothing in the language of the set-off section which required that the bankrupt's claim (or, as in that case, the claim of the debtors subject to the compositions) should be in the nature of a provable debt.[97]

The bankrupt's claim must vest in the trustee

7.22   On the other hand, the High Court in *Gye v McIntyre* indicated that the availability of a set-off in relation to the bankrupt's claim is not unqualified. Clearly, in order to come within the set-off section, the bankrupt's claim must be a presently payable debt at the date of the bankruptcy, or the product of giving credit, or it must arise out of a prior dealing between the parties. In addition, however, the High Court suggested, although without expressing a concluded view, that the claim should be such that it would vest in a trustee in bankruptcy,[98] an opinion earlier expressed by Wood.[99] This would exclude, for example, claims for damages for personal injury or wrong done to the bankrupt.[100] The requirement was thought to follow from the stipulation in the set-off section that the balance of the account should be provable in the bankruptcy, or, as the case may be, payable to the trustee in bankruptcy. If the balance is payable to the trustee, the section could only apply if the bankrupt's claim has vested in the trustee. This view would appear to be correct. It should also apply in England, where tortious demands are now provable. The better view is that a damages claim in tort should not be able to be employed in a set-off unless it arose out of a dealing between the parties to the proposed set-off, since the claim does not constitute a debt and nor does it come within the judicially accepted definition of giving credit.[101] Normally, the claims in tort which do not pass to the trustee, for example a damages claim for personal injury, are unlikely to arise out of a dealing. But if in an exceptional case

---

[97]   (1991) 171 CLR 609, 628–629.

[98]   (1991) 171 CLR 609, 626–627. See also *De Mattos v Saunders* (1872) LR 7 CP 570, 582. In *Gye v McIntyre* it was unnecessary for the High Court to express a concluded view on this point since the claim for fraudulent misrepresentation against Mrs McIntyre would, if a sequestration order had been made at the time of the composition, have vested in the trustee in bankruptcy. See (1991) 171 CLR 609, 627.

[99]   Wood, *English and International Set-off* (1989), 315–16.

[100]   See, for example, *Beckham v Drake* (1849) 2 HLC 579, 604, 621, 9 ER 1213, 1222, 1228; *Ex parte Vine, re Wilson* (1878) 8 Ch D 364; *Wilson v United Counties Bank Ltd* [1920] AC 102; *Heath v Tang* [1993] 1 WLR 1421, 1423. When a bankrupt has a cause of action in negligence, which includes a head of damage relating to property and another head of damage relating to personal injury, there is but one cause of action, and since it relates to property it vests in the trustee. On the other hand, the right to recover the damages which are personal, and any damages recovered, are held by the trustee on constructive trust for the bankrupt. See *Ord v Upton* [2000] 1 All ER 193 (esp at 206). Because the constructive trust relates not only to the damages recovered but also to the right to recover them, that part of the claim should not be the subject of a set-off in the bankruptcy. In Australia, the Bankruptcy Act 1966 (Cth), s 116(2)(g) specifically exempts any right of the bankrupt to recover damages or compensation for personal injury or wrong done to the bankrupt from the property which is divisible among the creditors.

[101]   See paras 8.44–8.47 below.

the claim is derived from a dealing, the fact that it does not vest in the trustee should mean that it cannot be set off.

Assignment of a debt

A similar principle applies in the case of an assignment of a debt. If a creditor assigns the debt to a third party, and the creditor later becomes bankrupt, the assigned debt does not vest in the trustee in bankruptcy as part of the insolvent's estate,[102] and the debtor therefore cannot invoke the insolvency set-off section as a defence to an action for payment.[103]   **7.23**

Compositions, in Australia

Gye v McIntyre concerned compositions entered into by two debtors under Part X of the Bankruptcy Act 1966 (Cth), rather than bankruptcy. The claim possessed by each of the debtors had not been included in the composition, but the High Court considered that it would be unjust if a statutory majority of creditors, by excluding a claim of the debtor against a particular creditor from the property vesting in the trustee of the composition, could deprive that creditor of the benefit of a set-off to which he would have been entitled if a bankruptcy had occurred.[104] The important point for a set-off was that the claim would have vested in a trustee in bankruptcy, if the case had involved a bankruptcy. A set-off therefore was allowed.   **7.24**

---

[102] See the Insolvency Act 1986, ss 283(3) and 306.

[103] *De Mattos v Saunders* (1872) LR 7 CP 570; *In Re Asphaltic Wood Pavement Co. Lee & Chapman's Case* (1885) 30 Ch D 216, 225; *Popular Homes Ltd v Circuit Developments Ltd* [1979] 2 NZLR 642, 657. See also *Turner v Thomas* (1871) LR 6 CP 610, 615, and generally paras 11.06 and 17.28 below.

[104] (1991) 171 CLR 609, 627–628.

8

CLAIMS SUSCEPTIBLE TO INSOLVENCY SET-OFF

In the preceding chapter some general observations were made on the meaning of **8.01** mutual credit and mutual dealings. The purpose of this chapter is to consider the application of the insolvency set-off section to various categories of claims.

A. Presently Existing Debts

Presently payable

A debt which is both presently existing and payable at the relevant date for deter- **8.02** mining rights of set-off in a bankruptcy or liquidation[1] may be the subject of a set-off. This includes a debt in equity,[2] other than an equitable debt in the form of an obligation to account for a trust fund.[3]

---

[1] See paras 6.31–6.45 above.
[2] *Ryall v Rowles* (1750) 1 Ves Sen 348, 376, 27 ER 1074, 1090.
[3] See ch 10 below.

Payable at a future date

8.03 Similarly a debt on either side of the account which is in existence at the relevant date, although not payable until a future date, may be the subject of a set-off.[4] In some early cases doubts were expressed as to whether this was strictly a debt for the purpose of the expression 'mutual debts', but in any event it was held to constitute the giving of credit so as to be available as a set-off on that ground.[5]

Unquantified debts

8.04 A set-off is also available in respect of a debt which, although existing, was unquantified at the relevant date,[6] for example where the amount depended upon a valuation by a valuer,[7] or where an arithmetical calculation had to be undertaken,[8] or where an award of costs had been made before the relevant date but it was not taxed until after that date.[9] In *Re the West Australian Lighterage, Stevedoring and Transport Co Ltd*,[10] a shareholder who was indebted to the company became bankrupt. Prior to the bankruptcy the company had gone into voluntary liquidation. Its assets were more than sufficient to pay its liabilities, although the extent of the surplus had not as yet been ascertained. When the liquidator subsequently declared a dividend, the Western Australian Supreme Court held that the company could set off in the bankruptcy the bankrupt's dividend entitlement against the bankrupt's indebtedness to it, the point being that, because the company went into voluntary liquidation before the bankruptcy under circumstances where there would be a surplus, the bankrupt at the date of the bankruptcy had a claim for a share of the surplus which could be the subject of a set-off, notwithstanding that the amount of the claim had not been ascertained at that date.

Discount for early payment

8.05 When a creditor proves in a bankruptcy or a liquidation for a debt the due date for payment of which has not yet occurred, rule 11.13 of the Insolvency Rules pro-

---

[4] See eg *Ex parte Prescot* (1753) 1 Atk 230, 26 ER 147 (debt owing to the bankrupt); *Atkinson v Elliott* (1797) 7 TR 378, 101 ER 1030 (debt owing by the bankrupt); *Rolls Razor Ltd v Cox* [1967] 1 QB 552, 569, 576.

[5] *Ex parte Prescot* (1753) 1 Atk 230, 26 ER 147; *Atkinson v Elliott* (1797) 7 TR 378, 381, 101 ER 1030, 1031. See also *Hankey v Smith* (1789) 3 TR 507n, 100 ER 703; *Re Morris and M'Murray* (1874) 5 AJR 157 (affirmed at 185).

[6] See *Re Daintrey, ex p Mant* [1900] 1 QB 546 (although compare the interpretation put upon that case in *Day and Dent Constructions Pty Ltd v North Australian Properties Pty Ltd* (1982) 150 CLR 85, 92, 94, 103 and in *Re Charge Card Services Ltd* [1987] 1 Ch 150, 182–183, 188), and *Handberg v Smarter Way (Aust) Pty Ltd* (2002) 20 ACLC 856, 868.

[7] *Ex parte Hope, re Hanson* (1858) 3 De G & J 92, 44 ER 1203. See also *Re Rushforth, ex p J R Holmes and Sons* (1906) 95 LT 807.

[8] *Greater Britain Insurance Corp Ltd v C T Bowring & Co (Insurance) Ltd* (1926) 24 Ll L Rep 7, 9.

[9] *Shand v M J Atkinson Ltd* [1966] NZLR 551; *Re Collinson; Smith v Sinnathamby* (1977) 33 FLR 39. Compare *Ex parte Rhodes* (1809) 15 Ves Jun 539, 33 ER 858.

[10] (1903) 5 WAR 132.

vides that, for the purpose of dividend 'and for no other purpose', the amount of the creditor's proof is to be discounted according to a formula to take into account that payment is to be received early. The rule would not appear to apply to the extent that the debt is to be employed in a set-off, because to that extent there is no dividend payable. It should be contrasted with section 554B of the Corporations Act 2001 (Cth) in Australia, which is drafted in terms that the 'amount of a debt that is admissible to proof' is to be reduced by an amount worked out in accordance with the regulations. The reduction is not expressed to occur solely for the purpose of payment of a dividend, but rather for the purpose of calculating the debt that may be proved. Insolvency set-off is regarded as an aspect of the rules relating to the proof of debts,[11] which may suggest that a reduction in a proof would have a corresponding effect on the value of the debt for the purpose of a set-off. The better view however is that the same position obtains as in England. Regulation 5.6.44 of the Corporations Regulations 2001, which sets out the calculation of the discount, provides that the amount payable is to be reduced by 8 per cent per annum calculated from the declaration of the dividend to the time when the debt would have become payable. But there is no dividend declared on a debt to the extent that the debt is extinguished in a set-off, which suggests that the provision does not apply in that context. In any event, section 554B only provides for a reduction in the case of the company's debt to the creditor. If the debt instead is payable *to* the company, there is no basis for reducing the amount of the debt to compensate for early payment by means of a set-off.[12]

Capitalized interest

A presently existing debt payable at a future date should be distinguished from the **8.06** case of a deposit made on terms that interest is to be capitalized so that, upon maturity, the value of the deposit will have increased. If prior to the maturity the depositor becomes bankrupt, and the depositee has a cross-demand against the depositor available by way of set-off, the automatic theory of insolvency set-off[13] dictates that the debt representing the deposit would have been extinguished on the date of the bankruptcy as a result of a set-off occurring on that date. To the extent that the debt has ceased to exist interest should cease to accrue on it. Therefore, for the purpose of the set-off, the amount of the debt should be the initial deposit together with accrued interest as at the bankruptcy date,[14] as opposed

---

[11] *Mersey Steel and Iron Co v Naylor, Benzon & Co* (1884) 9 App Cas 434, 437–438; *Re Bank of Credit and Commerce International SA (No 8)* [1996] Ch 245, 256.

[12] See eg *Ex parte Prescot* (1753) 1 Atk 230, 26 ER 147.

[13] See paras 6.79–6.103 above.

[14] If the deposit-taker rather than the depositor is bankrupt or in liquidation, interest in any event would cease to accrue as from the date of commencement of the bankruptcy or liquidation. See the Insolvency Rules 1986, r 4.93, and for bankruptcy the Insolvency Act 1986, s 322(2).

to the value that the debt would have had if interest had continued to be capitalized until the agreed maturity date.

B. Contingent Debt Owing by the Insolvent

(1) Introduction

8.07 The insolvency set-off section requires that there be a creditor proving or claiming to prove for a debt in the bankruptcy or the liquidation. It is therefore a requirement of a set-off that the claim against the bankrupt or the company be provable. When a person who becomes bankrupt or goes into liquidation has a contingent debt pursuant to a prior contract,[15] the fact of the bankruptcy or the liquidation will sometimes[16] constitute a repudiation of the contract which, if accepted, would give rise to a vested liability in damages.[17] The damages claim could be proved and it could be the subject of a set-off.[18] If however the case is not one involving an accepted repudiation, the insolvency legislation requires the trustee or the liquidator to estimate the value of a contingent debt[19] as at the date of the bankruptcy or the liquidation,[20] and a proof may be lodged for that amount. If the contingency subsequently occurs the full amount of the debt may be proved notwithstanding an earlier estimation, and if a proof has already been lodged based upon the estimation the proof may be adjusted, but not so as to disturb prior dividends.[21] The reason that a subsequent occurrence of the contingency is taken into account is not that the bankruptcy or the liquidation is deemed to have accelerated the contingency, so as to fix the value of the claim on the basis of the contingency having occurred on the date of the bankruptcy or the liquidation. Rather, it is because the fact of the occurrence of the contingency is the best evidence of the true value of the claim as at that date.[22]

---

[15] Note that, in the case of a primary obligation, as opposed to a secondary obligation such as a guarantee, a provision for a demand in writing is not regarded as creating a contingency. See *M S Fashions Ltd v Bank of Credit and Commerce International SA* [1993] Ch 425, 435–436, referring to *Re J Brown's Estate* [1893] 2 Ch 300.

[16] But not always. See para 9.05 below.

[17] *Re Northern Counties of England Fire Insurance Co, Macfarlane's Claim* (1880) 17 Ch D 337, 341; *Baker v Lloyd's Bank Ltd* [1920] 2 KB 322, 326.

[18] See para 8.41 below.

[19] See the Insolvency Act 1986, s 322, and the Insolvency Rules 1986, r 4.86.

[20] *Ellis and Company's Trustee v Dixon-Johnson* [1924] 1 Ch 342, 356–357 (date of the receiving order under the Bankruptcy Act 1914); *Re Dynamics Corporation of America* [1976] 1 WLR 757, 767 (winding up).

[21] *Ellis and Company's Trustee v Dixon-Johnson* [1924] 1 Ch 342, 357, and the Insolvency Rules 1986, r 4.86.

[22] *Ellis and Company's Trustee v Dixon-Johnson* [1924] 1 Ch 342, 356–357; *Re Dynamics Corp of America* [1976] 1 WLR 757, 767–768; *Re Hurren* [1983] 1 WLR 183, 189. See also *Transit Casualty Co v Policyholders Protection Board* [1992] 2 Lloyd's Rep 358, 359, 361.

(2) The Rule Against Double Proof

The meaning of the rule

While contingent debts generally are provable, this is subject to the rule against **8.08**
double proof, which provides that there can only be one dividend in respect of
what in substance is the same debt, even though various claims for a dividend may
be based upon different contracts.[23] The rule can apply in a number of situations,[24] but often finds its expression in the context of guarantees.

A guarantor who has guaranteed the whole of the debt owing to a creditor, and **8.09**
who pays the creditor in accordance with the guarantee, is entitled to be indemnified by the debtor. Prior to payment to the creditor the guarantor's right of indemnity is subject to a contingency. If the debtor is bankrupt, and the guarantor
pays the creditor after the bankruptcy but before the creditor has lodged a proof
in the bankruptcy, the guarantor may prove for his claim for an indemnity
notwithstanding that at the date of the bankruptcy it was still contingent.[25]
Different considerations apply however if the creditor has not been paid in full,
and has either proved in the debtor's bankruptcy or, if he has not proved, he is entitled to do so.[26] The guarantor in those circumstances still has a contingent claim
for an indemnity which prima facie would appear to be provable in the debtor's
bankruptcy, on the basis of a valuation of the claim by the trustee in bankruptcy.
But if the creditor has proved or is entitled to prove in the bankruptcy, and in addition the guarantor were allowed to prove for his contingent claim, the debtor's
estate could be subjected to two proofs in respect of what essentially is the same
debt. The creditor is the party who is out of pocket, and so his right of proof
should be preferred. Therefore, in order to prevent the possibility of a double
proof against the debtor's estate, the guarantor is not permitted to prove for his
contingent claim.[27] The same principle applies if the guarantor makes a payment
to the creditor after the creditor has a lodged a proof, including in the form of a

---

[23] *Re Oriental Commercial Bank* (1871) LR 7 Ch App 99, 103–104. See generally *Barclays Bank
v TOSG Trust Fund Ltd* [1984] 1 AC 626; *WA v Bond Corp Holdings Ltd* (1992) 8 ACSR 352, 364
et seq.

[24] See eg *Deering v Bank of Ireland* (1886) 12 App Cas 20; *The Liverpool (No 2)* [1960] 3 WLR 597.

[25] *Re Fenton* [1931] 1 Ch 85, 118.

[26] See eg *Re Fenton* [1931] 1 Ch 85, in which not all the creditors had proved in the principal
debtor's liquidation and the rule against double proof was held to apply.

[27] *Re Fenton* [1931] 1 Ch 85 (esp at 107, 114, 118–119), not following *Re Herepath and Delmar*
(1890) 7 Morr 129, 190; *Staples v Milner* (1996) 83 FCR 203, 211. It was held in *Re Paine, ex p Read*
[1897] 1 QB 122, and again in *Re Blackpool Motor Car Co Ltd* [1901] 1 Ch 77, that a surety before
payment to the creditor is a 'creditor' of the bankrupt for the purpose of the preference provision.
In *Re Fenton* both Lord Hanworth MR (at 106) and Romer LJ (at 118–120) agreed that those cases
were correctly decided, but they said that the issue determined was separate from the question
whether the surety should be entitled to prove in the bankruptcy. See also *The Liverpool (No 2)*
[1960] 3 WLR 597, 606; *Re Bruce David Realty Pty Ltd* [1969] VR 240, 243; *Re Glen Express Ltd*
(Ch D, Neuberger J, 15 Oct 1999).

dividend in the guarantor's own bankruptcy. Indeed, the principle is still applicable if the creditor, having proved in the debtor's bankruptcy and received a dividend, is paid the full amount which remains outstanding by the guarantor. Because the creditor has proved in the debtor's bankruptcy, the debtor's estate cannot be subjected to a second proof from the guarantor for the same debt.[28] On the other hand, if the guarantor's payment is such that the creditor is paid in full, the guarantor is entitled to be subrogated to the benefit of the creditor's proof in the bankruptcy as regards future dividends to the extent required to indemnify him for his payment to the creditor.[29] It has been suggested that the guarantor is only entitled to be subrogated to the rights of the creditor if the guarantor himself has paid the full amount of the debt,[30] although in Australia the courts have adopted the preferred the view that the right of subrogation arises when the creditor is paid in full, whether or not entirely by the guarantor.[31]

Guarantee limited to a stated amount

8.10 The guarantee may be limited to a stated amount. If that amount is less than the debt owing to the creditor, and the guarantor pays the full amount for which he is liable under the guarantee, the question whether the rule against double proof applies depends upon whether the guarantee is of the whole of the indebtedness, with a limitation of liability to a certain amount, or whether the guarantee is of only part of the debt.[32] In the former case a proof by the guarantor would be in respect of the same debt owing by the debtor to the creditor, so that the rule would apply.[33] Nor would the guarantor be subrogated to a part of the creditor's proof before the creditor has been paid in full.[34] If, however, the guarantee is merely in respect of part of the debt, and the guarantor has paid the creditor that part in accordance with the guarantee before the creditor has proved, the guarantor may prove in the debtor's bankruptcy for an indemnity relation to that part and the

---

[28] *Re Oriental Commercial Bank* (1871) LR 7 Ch App 99; *Re Fenton* [1931] 1 Ch 85, 115.

[29] *Re Whitehouse, Whitehouse v Edwards* (1887) 37 Ch D 683, 694–695; *Re Fenton* [1931] 1 Ch 85, 118; *Westpac Banking Corp v Gollin & Co Ltd* [1988] VR 397, 403; *Western Australia v Bond Corp Holdings Ltd (No 2)* (1992) 37 FCR 150, 163.

[30] See eg *Re Fenton* [1931] 1 Ch 85, 115, *per* Lawrence LJ, *Ex parte Brett, re Howe* (1871) LR 6 Ch App 838, 841, *per* Mellish LJ, and *Ex parte Turquand, re Fothergill* (1876) 3 Ch D 445, 450, *per* James LJ. Compare *Gedye v Matson* (1858) 25 Beav 310, 312, 53 ER 655, 656, *per* Sir John Romilly MR.

[31] *A E Goodwin Ltd v A G Healing Ltd* (1979) 7 ACLR 481; *McColl's Wholesale Pty Ltd v State Bank of NSW* [1984] 3 NSWLR 365, 378; *Raffle v AGC (Advances) Ltd* (1989) ASC 55–933 NSW SC, *per* Young J; *Bayley v Gibsons Ltd* (1993) 1 Tas R 385; *Macedone v Collins* (1996) 7 BPR 15,127, 15,142; *Austin v Royal* (1999) 47 NSWLR 27, 32. See also *Westpac Banking Corp v Gollin & Co Ltd* [1988] VR 397, 402.

[32] See generally the discussion in *Barclay's Bank Ltd v TOSG Trust Fund Ltd* [1984] 1 AC 626, 643–644.

[33] *Re Fenton* [1931] 1 Ch 85, 115.

[34] This is consistent with the discussion in *Re Sass* [1896] 2 QB 12, 15, and see also *Westpac Banking Corp v Gollin & Co Ltd* [1988] VR 397, 405–406.

creditor may prove for the unpaid part.[35] If the creditor has already proved for the whole debt, the guarantor upon payment of the part guaranteed becomes subrogated to the proof to the extent of that part.[36] When a guarantee in truth relates only to a part of a debt, that part as between the creditor and the guarantor is treated as a separate debt.[37]

Guarantee of the whole debt, where there is a part payment

When a guarantee is of the whole indebtedness, the creditor is entitled to prove for the full amount of the debt in the debtor's bankruptcy or liquidation despite having received a payment from a guarantor, if a part of the debt remains unpaid.[38] There is however an exception in the case of bills of exchange. The position of the drawer and a prior indorser of a bill as regards the holder is similar to that of a guarantor, but it is nevertheless accepted that the holder in proving in the bankruptcy of the acceptor must give credit for anything that he received from the drawer or the indorser before the proof.[39] In such a case Wood's view would appear to be correct, that the rule against double proof would not apply so as to prevent a proof by the drawer or the indorser.[40]   **8.11**

Contribution between guarantors

The rule against double proof is also important in the context of rights of contribution between guarantors. When there is more than one guarantor of the same debt, a guarantor who has paid more than his share is entitled to contribution from a co-guarantor.[41] Consider that the co-guarantor has become bankrupt. Prior to payment to the creditor the paying guarantor has a contingent right to contribution from the co-guarantor, but since the creditor has a provable debt in the co-guarantor's bankruptcy the paying guarantor cannot prove for his   **8.12**

---

[35] *Re Sass* [1896] 2 QB 12, 15; *Seabird Corp Ltd v Sherlock* (1990) 2 ACSR 111, 116.

[36] *Re Sass* [1896] 2 QB 12, 15; *Westpac Banking Corp v Gollin & Co Ltd* [1988] VR 397, 405.

[37] See *Re Sass* [1896] 2 QB 12, 15.

[38] *Re Sass* [1896] 2 QB 12, 14–15; *Ulster Bank Ltd v Lambe* [1966] NI 161; *Westpac Banking Corp v Gollin & Co Ltd* [1988] VR 388, 401, 403; *Seabird Corp Ltd v Sherlock* (1990) 2 ACSR 111, 115–116 (guarantee of the whole of the debt but with a limit on the liability); *Farrow Finance Co Ltd v ANZ Executors and Trustee Co Ltd* [1998] 1 VR 50, 76. If the aggregate amount received by the creditor from both sources exceeds the debt, the excess must be held by the creditor in trust for the guarantor. See *Midland Montague Australia Ltd v Harkness* (1994) 35 NSWLR 150, 166.

[39] The acceptor however is not obliged to reduce his proof in respect of anything paid to him after lodging the proof. See generally *Re Houlder* [1929] 1 Ch 205, 212. This principle is confined to negotiable instruments. See *Re Blackburne* (1892) 9 Morr 249, 252, and also the discussion in *Westpac Banking Corp v Gollin & Co Ltd* [1988] VR 388, 407–408. If on the other hand the acceptor is not bankrupt or in liquidation, and the holder is suing the acceptor in an action at law on the bill, the holder need not reduce his claim to the extent of a part payment received from the drawer or a prior indorser, although to the extent of that part payment he sues as trustee for the drawer or the prior indorser, as the case may be. See *Thornton v Maynard* (1875) LR 10 CP 695.

[40] Wood, *English and International Set-off* (1989) 611.

[41] See eg *Craythorne v Swinburne* (1807) 14 Ves Jun 160, 33 ER 482.

contingent claim. Further, if the paying guarantor has paid more than his just share, but the creditor nevertheless has not been paid in full so that the creditor remains entitled to prove in the co-guarantor's bankruptcy, the rule against double proof would still operate to prevent a proof by the paying guarantor. This would also be the case if the paying guarantor pays more than his share after the creditor has lodged a proof in the co-guarantor's bankruptcy. On the other hand, once the creditor has been paid in full, the paying guarantor is entitled to be subrogated to the creditor's proof and to receive the dividends until he has received an amount sufficient to satisfy his claim for contribution.[42]

Set-off

8.13 If the rule against double proof operates to deny a contingent creditor a right of proof, the contingent creditor similarly could not employ his claim in a set-off, since the set-off section stipulates that there should be a creditor proving or claiming to prove for a debt. In *Re Fenton, ex p Fenton Textile Association Ltd*[43] a debtor had gone into liquidation, and a guarantor of the debt had executed a scheme of arrangement. The creditor had lodged a proof in the scheme, but had not been paid anything by either the debtor or the guarantor. The guarantor by reason of the rule against double proof did not have a debt which was provable in the debtor's liquidation, and the Court of Appeal held that the trustee of the guarantor's estate under the scheme similarly was not permitted to employ the guarantor's contingent claim for an indemnity in a set-off in the liquidation.

(3) Set-off Where There is no Double Proof

The principle

8.14 Consider that the rule against double proof does not apply, so that a contingent debt arising out of a prior agreement is provable. A prime example is the case of a guarantor who pays the creditor in full after the debtor's bankruptcy or liquidation but before the creditor has lodged a proof.[44] As a matter of principle the debt should be able to be employed in a set-off, either because the debt is a natural result of a prior transaction so as to come within the concept of giving credit,[45] or alternatively because the debt arose out of a prior dealing between the parties to the proposed set-off. This assumes that the qualification to the set-off section is not a bar to a set-off in respect of contingent debts. According to the qualification,[46] sums due from a bankrupt may not be included in an account if the creditor had

---

[42] *Ex parte Stokes* (1848) De Gex 618; *Re Parker. Morgan v Hill* [1894] 3 Ch 400.

[43] [1931] 1 Ch 85. See also *Western Australia v Bond Corp Holdings Ltd (No 2)* (1992) 37 FCR 150, 163; *Re Glen Express Ltd* (Ch D, Neuberger J, 15 Oct 1999).

[44] *Re Fenton* [1931] 1 Ch 85, 118.

[45] See paras 7.01–7.06 above.

[46] Insolvency Act, s 323(3) and, for companies, the Insolvency Rules, r 4.90(3).

notice at the time they became 'due' that a bankruptcy petition was pending. In the case of a contingent debt the better view is that this refers to the creditor's knowledge at the time that a contract was entered into out of which a debt subsequently arose, as opposed to the time that a liability vested upon the occurrence of the contingency.[47] Assuming that it is possible in principle for a contingent debt owing by a bankrupt or a company in liquidation to be employed in a set-off,[48] the contrary conclusion would mean that the operation of the qualification in most cases would preclude a set-off.

The cases

Apart from the question of the possible application of the qualification, there is **8.15** authority for the view that a debt which is contingent at the relevant date cannot be the subject of a set-off. *Re A Debtor (No 66 of 1955), ex p The Debtor v The Trustee of the Property of Waite (A Bankrupt)*[49] concerned a bankrupt surety. After the bankruptcy the surety's trustee in bankruptcy paid the creditor in full in order to obtain the release of security given by the surety to the creditor. The trustee then sought to recover this amount from the debtor. When the debtor failed to pay, the trustee issued a bankruptcy notice against him. The debtor argued in response that, because of a separate debt owing to him by the surety, he had a right of set-off in the surety's bankruptcy against his indemnity obligation, and that after a set-off the amount for which he was indebted would have been less than the amount required for a bankruptcy notice. The Court of Appeal rejected the argument on the ground that a claim which is merely contingent at the relevant date, and consequently not 'due', cannot be employed in a set-off. In that case the surety, rather than the principal debtor, was the bankrupt party. It was not a case in which a bankrupt had a contingent liability at the relevant date. The bankrupt had a contingent claim, and *Re A Debtor (No 66 of 1955)* is considered later in that context.[50] Nevertheless the Court of Appeal based its decision to deny a set-off on a general proposition, that both demands must be 'due' at the relevant date so that, irrespective of whether the principal debtor or the surety is the bankrupt party, a surety's right to an indemnity will not give rise to a set-off as between those parties if the right was still contingent at the relevant date.[51]

---

[47] See paras 6.54–6.59 above.
[48] See below.
[49] [1956] 1 WLR 1226.
[50] See paras 8.27–8.37 below.
[51] See Lord Evershed MR and Hodson LJ at [1956] 1 WLR 1226, 1230, 1237. In later cases *Re A Debtor (No 66 of 1955)* has been regarded as authority for that proposition. See *Carreras Rothmans Ltd v Freeman Matthews Treasure Ltd* [1985] 1 Ch 207; *Re Hawkins, dec'd* (Walton J, 2 February 1978); *Re Charge Card Services Ltd* [1987] 1 Ch 150, 188–190. See also *Re Bruce David Realty Pty Ltd* [1969] VR 240, 243 (in which Adam J accepted that a surety must have paid the creditor before the principal debtor's bankruptcy in order to have a set-off in the bankruptcy), and *Brown v Cork* [1985] BCLC 363, 368, 376, CA. In Canada see *Re Mitchell, Houghton Ltd* (1970) 14 CBR 301.

8.16   The Court of Appeal distinguished an earlier decision of that court in *Re Daintrey*,[52] on the ground that the *Daintrey* case was not concerned with a contingent debt but rather with a debt which was due at the relevant date but which remained to be quantified.[53] A business had been sold on terms that the price was to be calculated as a proportion of the profits made over a three-year period. The vendor became bankrupt before any profits had been earned. At the end of the three-year period, when the price was calculated in accordance with the agreed formula, it was held that the purchaser could set off his resulting liability against a separate debt owing to him by the vendor. However the debt for the price would appear to have been contingent. No profits had been earned at the date of the bankruptcy, so that the debt was contingent at that date upon profits subsequently being earned.[54] *Re Daintrey* therefore supports the view that a contingent debt may be the subject of a set-off.

8.17   Subsequently, the Court of Appeal in *Brown v Cork*[55] referred to *Re A Debtor (No 66 of 1955)* with approval in the context of a contingent claim possessed by a company in liquidation.[56] Nevertheless, in so far as *Re A Debtor* supports a general proposition that a debt which is contingent at the relevant date cannot be set off, it should not be followed. That would appear to be the position in Australia, following the criticism of the case by the High Court in *Day & Dent Constructions Pty Ltd v North Australian Properties Pty Ltd*.[57] In *Stein v Blake*[58] the House of Lords assumed that a contingent debt can be set off, and the contrary view is also inconsistent with Dixon J's often-quoted statement in the Australian High Court in *Hiley v The People's Prudential Assurance Co Ltd*[59] that: 'It is enough that at the

---

[52] [1900] 1 QB 546. The Court of Appeal in *Re A Debtor (No 66 of 1955)* also relied on dicta in *Re Fenton* [1931] 1 Ch 85, although, as Gibbs CJ commented in *Day and Dent Constructions Pty Ltd v North Australian Properties Pty Ltd* (1982) 150 CLR 85, 94, the dicta in question appear to be ambiguous, if not conflicting. Indeed, Mason J (at 102) said that, according to his reading of the judgments, the surety would have been entitled to a set-off in *Re Fenton* if he had paid the debt.

[53] This view has been expressed on other occasions. See eg *Re National Benefit Assurance Co Ltd* [1924] 2 Ch 339, 343, *per* Eve J; *Carreras Rothmans Ltd v Freeman Matthews Treasure Ltd* [1985] 1 Ch 207, 230, *per* Peter Gibson J.

[54] See Millett J in *Re Charge Card Services Ltd* [1987] 1 Ch 150, 182–183, and the cases to which he refers. As Millett J noted, this was the view of Gibbs CJ and Mason J in the High Court of Australia in *Day and Dent Constructions Pty Ltd v North Australian Properties Pty Ltd* (1982) 150 CLR 85, 92, 94, 103. Compare Lindley MR in the Court of Appeal in *Daintrey* [1900] 1 QB 546, 572.

[55] [1985] BCLC 363, 368, 376.

[56] See para 8.34 below.

[57] (1982) 150 CLR 85. Gibbs CJ (at 94) left open the question whether *Re A Debtor (No 66 of 1955)* was correctly decided, on the ground that the surety, rather than the debtor, was bankrupt, and the payments were made by the trustee to enable him to obtain the bankrupt's property. The better view is that this circumstance would not have justified the result. The discussion in paras 13.32–13.51 below would be relevant to this point.

[58] [1996] 1 AC 243, 252. See also Hoffmann LJ in the Chancery Division in *M S Fashions Ltd v Bank of Credit and Commerce International SA* [1993] Ch 425, 435.

[59] (1938) 60 CLR 468, 496–497.

commencement of the winding up mutual dealings exist which involve rights and obligations whether absolute or contingent of such a nature that afterwards in the events that happen they mature or develop into pecuniary demands capable of set-off.' There are also a number of cases, in addition to *Re Daintrey*, in which English courts have recognized that a contingent debt could be included in a set-off.[60] For example, the holder of a bill of exchange has been permitted to set off his claim against the drawer or an indorser of the bill in the drawer's or the indorser's bankruptcy, even though dishonour by the acceptor only occurred after the bankruptcy.[61] Similarly, it has been held that an accommodation acceptor or indorser of a bill could set off his claim for an indemnity in the drawer's bankruptcy notwithstanding that the bill was paid after the bankruptcy.[62] In *Graham v Russell*,[63] Lord Ellenborough in delivering the judgment of the Exchequer Chamber accepted that an insured could set off the underwriter's liability on a loss which occurred after the underwriter's bankruptcy, despite the contingent nature of the underwriter's liability at the relevant date. It has also been held that the holder of a policy of life insurance who was indebted to the insurance company could set off the value of the policy in the winding up of the company, even though the policy had not matured at the relevant date for determining rights of set-off in the liquidation either by payment of the requisite number of premiums or by death.[64] In *Lee & Chapman's Case*[65] a damages claim for breach of contract against a company, where the breach occurred after the liquidation, was the subject of a set-off.[66]

---

[60] In addition to the cases referred to below, see *Jones v Mossop* (1844) 3 Hare 568, 571, 67 ER 506, 508 (on the assumption that Richard Reed was bankrupt); *Re Taylor, ex p Norvell* [1910] 1 KB 562, 568; *Baker v Lloyd's Bank Ltd* [1920] 2 KB 322; *Hiley v The Peoples Prudential Assurance Co Ltd* (1938) 60 CLR 468, 491, 497; *Re Northside Properties Pty Ltd* [1971] 2 NSWLR 320, 324. In *Willment Brothers Ltd v North West Thames Regional Health Authority* (1984) 26 BLR 51 Ackner and O'Connor LJJ said that, even if the creditor's claim against the company in liquidation was merely contingent at the date of the liquidation, it could still be employed in a set-off, although no mention was made of the earlier decision in the *Waite* case (n 49 above).

[61] *Arbouin v Tritton* (1816) Holt 408, 171 ER 287; *Alsager v Currie* (1844) 12 M & W 751, 152 ER 1402.

[62] *Smith v Hodson* (1791) 4 TR 211, 100 ER 979; *Ex parte Boyle, re Shepherd*, unreported but noted in Cooke, *The Bankrupt Laws* (8th edn, 1823) vol 1, 571; *Ex parte Wagstaff* (1806) 13 Ves Jun 65, 33 ER 219; *Hulme v Muggleston* (1837) 3 M & W 30, 150 ER 1043; *Russell v Bell* (1841) 8 M & W 277, 151 ER 1042; *Bittleston v Timmis* (1845) 1 CB 389, 135 ER 591.

[63] (1816) 5 M & S 498, 105 ER 1133.

[64] *Re City Life Assurance Co Ltd, Grandfield's Case* [1926] 1 Ch 191 (not following *Ex parte Price, re Lankester* (1875) LR 10 Ch App 648 and *Paddy v Clutton* [1920] 2 Ch 554). See also *Sovereign Life Assurance Co v Dodd* [1892] 2 QB 573, in which the insured paid the final premium after the petition and before the winding-up order, although the date of the petition seems to have been regarded as the relevant date. Compare *Re National Benefit Assurance Co Ltd* [1924] 2 Ch 339 (and see also *Hiley v The Peoples Prudential Assurance Co Ltd* (1938) 60 CLR 468, 493), in which the winding up was treated as a repudiation by the company.

[65] *Re Asphaltic Wood Pavement Co. Lee & Chapman's Case* (1885) 30 Ch D 216.

[66] See also para 8.43 below.

Must the debt be exclusively referable to a prior agreement?

8.18 Subsequently Millett J considered the question in *Re Charge Card Services Ltd*.[67] The case concerned a company which operated a charge card scheme. The company assigned its receivables to a factor, the agreement providing that, if the company went into liquidation, the factor could require it to repurchase the debts at face value. One of the issues in dispute was whether, if a notice of repurchase was given after the liquidation, the factor could set off the company's resulting liability to pay the price against a debt owing by the factor to the company. The company's liability to pay the price was contingent at the date of the liquidation, a notice of repurchase not having then been given, and accordingly it was argued that *Re A Debtor (No 66 of 1955)* was authority against a set-off in this situation. Millett J however held that a contingent claim can be employed in a set-off provided that it is exclusively referable to a prior agreement between the parties to the proposed set-off.[68] In the case of a principal debtor's obligation to indemnify the surety, the obligation is not exclusively referable to a contract between the principal debtor and the surety. Rather, it is referable to the contract of guarantee to which the principal often is not a party. On the other hand, since the contingent liability in issue in *Re Charge Card Services* was exclusively referable to a contract between the parties to the proposed set-off, he concluded that *Re A Debtor (No 66 of 1955)* did not constitute authority against a set-off in the case before him.

8.19 The source of Millett J's analysis appears to have been a comment by Lord Evershed MR in *Re A Debtor (No 66 of 1955)*,[69] in which the Master of the Rolls distinguished the case before him from *Re Daintrey*[70] on the ground that in *Re Daintrey* the amount of the indebtedness in question was exclusively referable to an obligation to pay the price incurred prior to the relevant date. However that comment was in the context of Lord Evershed's characterization of *Re Daintrey* as a case in which there was a prior debt which merely remained to be quantified after the relevant date, as opposed to a subsequently arising debt.[71] A quantification of a debt would require that the quantum be exclusively referable to the debt. If on the other hand the question is whether a contingent debt can be included in a set-off, it is unclear why there should be a requirement that it be exclusively referable to a prior agreement between the parties to the proposed set-off. The requirement may have resulted from a perception that only a claim that arises out of mutual

---

[67] [1987] 1 Ch 150.

[68] See the discussion at [1987] 1 Ch 150, 189–190.

[69] [1956] 1 WLR 1226, 1230. Millett J referred to this passage in *Re Charge Card Services* [1987] 1 Ch 150, 188–189.

[70] [1900] 1 QB 546.

[71] See para 8.16 above.

dealings between the parties can be the subject of a set-off.[72] But while 'mutual dealings' constitutes a ground for allowing a set-off, when it is sought to base a set-off upon the concept of giving credit it is not necessary to show that there was a dealing between the parties.[73] For example, an acceptor of a bill of exchange may not have been aware at the time of his bankruptcy that the bill had been endorsed to the holder. While in such a case the bankrupt and the holder had not dealt with each other in relation to the bill, and nor was the indebtedness of the acceptor to the holder 'exclusively referable' to an agreement between them, it was held in *Hankey v Smith*[74] that the holder could employ the claim on the bill in a set-off in the bankruptcy, on the ground that credit nevertheless had been given by the holder. Mutual dealings as a ground for a set-off first appeared in the set-off section in the 1869 Act,[75] but even before then there were instances in which contingent debts were the subject of a set-off,[76] which suggests that it is not necessary to base a set-off in such a case on the mutual dealings head. Indeed, the 1825 and 1849 Bankruptcy Acts each specifically provided that all debts provable against the estate could be set off, and the legislation in each case allowed a right of proof to a person who was a surety at the time of the bankruptcy of the principal debtor, if the surety paid the debt.[77] The contingent debt was allowed to be set off on the ground that credit was given at the date of the debtor's bankruptcy. In other words, there was a prior transaction which would naturally, or in the ordinary course of business, end in a debt.[78] Further, when it is sought to base a set-off of a contingent debt upon the mutual credit head, *Hankey v Smith* demonstrates that it is not necessary that the parties to the transaction of which the debt was the natural result should be the same as the parties to the set-off.

---

[72] On other occasions it has been said that a contingent debt may be set off if it arose out of mutual dealings. See eg *Re Taylor, ex p Norvell* [1910] 1 KB 562, 568, *per* Phillimore J, and Buckley LJ in the Court of Appeal in that case at 580. See also Romer LJ in *Re Fenton* [1931] 1 Ch 85, 117 ('For contingent liabilities are in general debts provable in bankruptcy, and it is well settled that, provided there be mutuality of dealings, claims provable may be set off'). In *Hiley v The Peoples Prudential Assurance Co Ltd* (1938) 60 CLR 468, 496 Dixon J said that it is 'enough' for a set-off that 'at the commencement of the winding up mutual dealings exist which involve rights and obligations whether absolute or contingent of such a nature that afterwards in the events that happen they mature or develop into pecuniary demands capable of set-off'.

[73] See para 7.11 above.

[74] (1789) 3 TR 507n, 100 ER 703.

[75] Bankruptcy Act 1869, s 39.

[76] See eg *Smith v Hodson* (1791) 4 TR 211, 100 ER 979 and *Russell v Bell* (1841) 8 M & W 277, 151 ER 1042 (accommodation acceptor paying after the bankruptcy of the drawer permitted to set off his claim for an indemnity in the drawer's bankruptcy); *Arbouin v Tritton* (1816) Holt 408, 171 ER 287 and *Alsager v Currie* (1844) 12 M & W 751, 152 ER 1402 (holder of a bill of exchange permitted to set off his claim against the drawer or an indorser of the bill in the drawer's or the indorser's bankruptcy, even though dishonour by the acceptor occurred after the bankruptcy). See also *Graham v Russell* (1816) 5 M & S 498, 105 ER 1133. Compare Millett J in *Re Charge Card Services Ltd* [1987] 1 Ch 150, 179.

[77] See (1825) 6 Geo IV, c 16, ss 50 & 52, and the Bankrupt Law Consolidation Act 1849, ss 171 and 173.

[78] See para 7.04 above.

Surety paying after the debtor's bankruptcy

8.20   Consider the case of a surety who pays the creditor after the debtor's bankruptcy. If the rule against double proof does not apply, the surety's claim for an indemnity should be able to be employed in a set-off, on the basis that the debt was a natural result of a prior transaction and therefore it constituted the giving of credit. This was the ground upon which the High Court of Australia upheld the surety's claim for a set-off in *Day and Dent Constructions Pty Ltd v North Australian Properties Pty Ltd*.[79] It should not be necessary to show that the parties to the proposed set-off had dealt with each other, or had intended to trust each other, or, in Millett J's terminology, that the debt in question is exclusively referable to an agreement between them. But even if, contrary to this view, a dealing is required when it is sought to base a set-off upon a debt in respect of which credit had been given, the surety's claim usually would arise out of a dealing between the principal debtor and the surety,[80] the dealing being the giving of the guarantee at the request (express or implied) of the principal debtor.[81] While the surety's claim admittedly may not be *exclusively* referable to that dealing, it is difficult to understand why there should be a requirement of exclusivity. Millett J was bound by the decision of the Court of Appeal in *Re A Debtor*, and in order to justify a set-off in the *Charge Card* case he had to find grounds for distinguishing the earlier case. The better view is that *Re A Debtor (No 66 of 1955)* was wrongly decided.

8.21   *Day and Dent Constructions*[82] does not stand alone in relation to the surety's right of set-off.[83] In *Hiley v The Peoples Prudential Assurance Co Ltd*[84] Starke J indicated that that a surety paying the creditor after the debtor's bankruptcy could employ his claim for an indemnity in a set-off, and this is also consistent with a suggestion by Wigram VC in *Jones v Mossop*[85] that, if the person who in that case was the principal debtor on some promissory notes in respect of which the plaintiff was surety

---

[79] (1982) 150 CLR 85.

[80] Thus Hodson LJ in *Re A Debtor (No 66 of 1955)* [1956] 1 WLR 1226, 1237 agreed that there were mutual dealings in that case. See also *Re Fenton* [1931] 1 Ch 85, 117.

[81] In essence, this was the view expressed by counsel in *Re Charge Card Services* but not adopted by Millett J. See [1987] 1 Ch 150, 189–190. It was held in *Owen v Tate* [1976] 1 QB 402 that, if a surety acted officiously in giving the guarantee, he is not entitled to an indemnity from the principal debtor, in which case he would not have a provable debt which could be set off. *Quaere* whether *Owen v Tate* would be followed. See Birks, *An Introduction to the Law of Restitution* (1989) 311–12, and Goff and Jones, *The Law of Restitution* (5th edn, 1998) 128–9 (where it is suggested that subrogation may apply).

[82] (1982) 150 CLR 85.

[83] In addition to the cases referred to below, see *Re Last, ex p Butterell* (1994) 124 ALR 219. In *Stein v Blake* [1996] 1 AC 243, 256 the House of Lords referred to *Day and Dent Constructions* without suggesting that it was wrongly decided.

[84] (1938) 60 CLR 468, 491. See also Latham CJ (at 483) and Dixon J (at 500–501), referring to *Re The Moseley Green Coal and Coke Co Ltd, Barrett's Case (No 2)* (1865) 4 De G J & S 756, 46 ER 1116, 34 LJ Bcy 41, discussed below.

[85] (1844) 3 Hare 568, 571, 67 ER 506, 508.

had been made bankrupt, the plaintiff subsequently paying the notes would have had a right of set-off. It is also supported by *Re The Moseley Green Coal and Coke Co Ltd Barrett's, Case (No 2)*.[86] *Barrett's Case* was distinguished in *Re A Debtor (No 66 of 1955)* on the ground that the surety's claim against the principal debtor was based on a promissory note given as security to the creditor, but it is difficult to see why this should justify a different result, given that a surety's right to securities held by the creditor is just as much a consequence of the payment to the creditor as is the right to an indemnity.[87] In *Day and Dent Constructions*[88] both Gibbs CJ and Mason J considered that *Barrett's Case* was directly on point.

(4) Subrogation, Where the Creditor had Proved Before the Surety's Payment

The creditor may have proved for the debt in the debtor's bankruptcy before pay- **8.22** ment in full by the surety, in which case the rule against double proof would preclude the guarantor from lodging a second proof. It has been suggested that, where the guarantor is denied the right to lodge a separate proof in the debtor's bankruptcy after payment in full to the creditor, the guarantor similarly could not set off his claim for an indemnity against a liability that he has to the debtor.[89] If that were the law it would be unsatisfactory, but the better view is that a set-off may be available to the guarantor. The set-off section admittedly stipulates that there should be a person proving or claiming to prove for a bankruptcy debt.[90] The guarantor himself does not have a provable debt. That much is clear.[91] Nevertheless, upon payment in full to the creditor the guarantor is entitled to be subrogated to the creditor's proof in the bankruptcy.[92] The court of bankruptcy is a court of equitable jurisdiction,[93] and although the proof is still nominally the creditor's it should be possible to go behind it and proceed on the basis that as a matter of equity the proof has become the proof of the guarantor. As far as equity

---

[86] (1865) 4 De G J & S 756, 46 ER 1116, 12 LT 193, 34 LJ Bcy 41.

[87] Two points should be noted in relation to *Barrett's Case*. The first is that the set-off was against a liability to the company in liquidation for an unpaid call. While it is now accepted that a set-off is not available in such a case (see paras 8.50–8.62 below), the applicable legislation when *Barrett's Case* was decided specifically allowed a set-off to a contributory in respect of any sums due to him from the company on an independent contract or dealing. See the Joint Stock Companies Amendment Act 1858, s 17. The second point is that the set-off section in the bankruptcy legislation had not been incorporated at that time into the joint stock companies legislation, although it was nevertheless accepted that the right of set-off allowed to a contributory should be governed by the same principles. See the comments of Lord Cranworth in subsequent proceedings at (1865) 4 De G J & S 756, 762, 46 ER 1116, 1119.

[88] (1982) 150 CLR 85, 94, 106. As Mason J noted (at 106), the interposition of the surety's sister in *Barrett's Case* was not relevant, since the surety still paid the debt pursuant to the guarantee, albeit indirectly.

[89] Wood, *English and International Set-off* (1989) 303, 608.

[90] See the Insolvency Act, s 323(1).

[91] *Re Whitehouse, Whitehouse v Edwards* (1887) 37 Ch D 683, 694–695.

[92] *Re Whitehouse* (1887) 37 Ch D 683, 694–695; *Re Fenton* [1931] 1 Ch 85, 118; *Westpac Banking Corp v Gollin & Co Ltd* [1988] VR 397, 403.

[93] *Mathieson's Trustee v Burrup, Mathieson & Co* [1927] 1 Ch 562, 569.

is concerned, the position should be the same as if the surety had acquired a right to prove in his own name upon payment to the creditor, so that *Day and Dent Constructions*[94] should apply. The important point is that the guarantor's entitlement to the benefit of the proof is exclusively referable to an obligation incurred before the bankruptcy, and it does not involve any new and independent transaction.[95] That analysis may not apply, however, if the creditor receives payment in full from a number of sureties, so that there is more than one surety subrogated to the proof.[96] The surety's right of subrogation has been described as a class right,[97] in which case there may not be mutuality as between the proof to which the sureties are subrogated and a separate debt owing by one of the sureties to the principal debtor.[98]

Acquisition of an interest after bankruptcy or liquidation

8.23 In the case of a single surety, the fact that the surety only acquires an interest in the proof by way of subrogation after the principal debtor's bankruptcy or liquidation should not preclude a set-off. In New South Wales, *MPS Constructions Pty Ltd v Rural Bank of New South Wales*[99] suggests the contrary. A building contractor had entered into a contract with a local council for the construction of a building. The contract provided for the establishment of a retention fund, by the deposit into a bank account of a percentage of the progress payments due to the contractor. The account was required to be in the joint names of the council and the contractor, and it was to be held by them on trust for the council subject to the discharge by the contractor of its obligations. Before final completion the contractor went into liquidation. The liquidator decided to complete the contract, which would have had the effect of releasing the retention moneys. The bank then asserted that it was entitled to set off the account against a separate debt owing to it by the contractor. One of the reasons given by Helsham CJ in Eq for not allowing the set-off was that at the commencement of the liquidation the account was held on trust for the council, so that there was a lack of mutuality.[100] The contractor's interest in the account at that time was still contingent on completion of construction. But the fact that the contractor was not then the beneficial owner of the debt should not have been sufficient to prevent a set-off. The contractor gave credit to the

---

[94] (1982) 150 CLR 85. See para 8.20 above.

[95] *Hiley v The Peoples Prudential Assurance Co Ltd* (1938) 60 CLR 468, 499, *per* Dixon J, and see also Rich J at 487.

[96] This assumes that it is sufficient for subrogation that the creditor has been paid in full, and that it is not necessary that a surety claiming subrogation should have paid the whole debt himself. See para 8.09 above.

[97] *A E Goodwin Ltd v A G Healing Ltd* (1979) 7 ACLR 481, 489, and see also *Rowlatt on Principal and Surety* (5th edn, 1999) 157.

[98] See paras 12.02–12.07 below.

[99] (1980) 4 ACLR 835.

[100] (1980) 4 ACLR 835, 845.

bank before the liquidation,[101] by entering into a transaction with the bank (along with the council) which would naturally or in the ordinary course of business, and without the interposition of any new and independent transaction,[102] end in a debt owing by the bank in which the contractor alone would be beneficially interested. This should have provided a basis for a set-off. The acquisition of the sole beneficial interest in this situation would not have involved a new and independent transaction, because it was the contemplated end to the transaction which gave rise to the deposit. Further, the fact that the liquidator may have used the company's resources to complete the contract for the benefit of creditors should not have been a sufficient reason for denying a set-off.[103] Nevertheless, in the circumstances the *MPS Constructions* case may have been correctly decided. It involved a contingent claim possessed by a company in liquidation, as opposed to a contingent liability. Unlike a contingent liability, when a contingent claim is in issue the contingency must have occurred before an account can be taken,[104] whereas it appears from the report that the liquidator had not yet obtained the final certificate discharging the council's interest in the account.

Surety's set-off where the creditor had received a dividend

The creditor may have been paid a dividend in the debtor's bankruptcy before the **8.24** guarantor paid the balance of the debt. It has been suggested that a guarantor is only entitled to be subrogated to the rights of the creditor if the guarantor himself has paid the full amount of the debt,[105] but there is much to commend the view, which has been adopted in Australia,[106] that the right of subrogation arises when the creditor is paid in full, whether or not entirely by the guarantor. Assuming that this view is followed, so that the guarantor has a right of subrogation, the fact of the dividend received by the creditor from the debtor's estate means that the guarantor will be subrogated to a debt the face amount of which is greater than the amount that he in fact has paid to the creditor, and in respect of which he has a claim for an indemnity. The guarantor nevertheless should still be entitled to receive future dividends on the full amount of the debt. A similar issue has arisen in

---

[101] See paras 7.02–7.04 above.

[102] *Hiley v The Peoples Prudential Assurance Co, Ltd* (1938) 60 CLR 468, 499, *per* Dixon J, and see also Rich J at 487.

[103] See paras 13.32–13.51 below, and in particular *Re Asphaltic Wood Pavement Co. Lee & Chapman's Case* (1885) 30 Ch D 216.

[104] See paras 8.27–8.37 below.

[105] *Re Fenton* [1931] 1 Ch 85, 115, *per* Lawrence LJ; *Ex parte Brett, re Howe* (1871) LR 6 Ch App 838, 841, *per* Mellish LJ; *Ex parte Turquand, re Fothergill* (1876) 3 Ch D 445, 450, *per* James LJ. Compare *Gedye v Matson* (1858) 25 Beav 310, 312, 53 ER 655, 656, *per* Sir John Romilly MR.

[106] *A E Goodwin Ltd v A G Healing Ltd* (1979) 7 ACLR 481; *McColl's Wholesale Pty Ltd v State Bank of New South Wales* [1984] 3 NSWLR 365, 378; *Raffle v AGC (Advances) Ltd* (1989) ASC 55–933, NSW SC, *per* Young J; *Bayley v Gibsons Ltd* (1993) 1 Tas R 385; *Macedone v Collins* (1996) 7 BPR 15,127, 15,142; *Austin v Royal* (1999) 47 NSWLR 27, 32. See also *Westpac Banking Corporation v Gollin & Co Ltd* [1988] VR 397, 402.

the context of contribution between guarantors. Consider that there are two guarantors of a debt, one of whom has become bankrupt, and the creditor has proved for the full amount of the debt in the bankruptcy. Subsequently the creditor is paid in full, including as a result of a payment from the solvent guarantor which is more than his pro rata share. The solvent guarantor is entitled to be subrogated to the creditor's proof in the co-guarantor's bankruptcy, and to be paid dividends until he has received an amount sufficient to satisfy his claim for contribution.[107] The right of subrogation extends in this case to the full amount of the debt for which the creditor proved, and not just to a part equal to the claim for contribution itself, although the guarantor could not recover by way of dividend more than his contribution entitlement. The same analysis should apply when a guarantor is subrogated to the creditor's proof in the debtor's bankruptcy.

8.25 But how would that concept work if the guarantor wishes to use the creditor's proof to which he is subrogated in a set-off? In the first place, credit should be given in the set-off for any dividend already paid to the creditor.[108] Unless that occurs, the bankrupt debtor's estate will have paid twice in respect of the debt, once in the form of a dividend to the creditor and a second time through a set-off. Further, while the right of subrogation extends to the full amount proved by the creditor, the guarantor would not be entitled to receive by way of dividend more than his actual entitlement. Similarly, if the guarantor wishes to utilize the proof to which he is subrogated in a set-off against a separate debt that he owes to the bankrupt debtor, or to a bankrupt co-guarantor, he should not be entitled to do so for an amount in excess of his entitlement.

(5) Must the Contingency Have Occurred?

8.26 In the case of a debt subject to a contingency, the debt may be proved before the contingency has occurred, based upon an estimate of its value made by the trustee in bankruptcy or the liquidator. Similarly it should not be necessary for a set-off that the contingency should have occurred.[109] The test as to whether credit has been given requires a characterization of the nature of the transaction that was entered into. In other words, is the transaction of the kind that would naturally or in

---

[107] *Ex parte Stokes* (1848) De Gex 618; *Re Parker, Morgan v Hill* [1894] 3 Ch 400.

[108] See in a different context *M S Fashions Ltd v Bank of Credit and Commerce International SA* [1993] Ch 425, 435, ChD, *per* Hoffmann LJ.

[109] Compare Millett J's comment in *Re Charge Card Services Ltd* [1987] 1 Ch 150, 183, that: 'In every case the claim to set off requires that any contingency to which the liability was still subject at the date of the receiving order has since occurred.' On other occasions it has been said that 'it is enough' for a set-off of a contingent debt that it has matured into a pecuniary demand. See *Hiley v The Peoples Prudential Assurance Co Ltd* (1938) 60 CLR 468, 497, *per* Dixon J; *Day and Dent Constructions Pty Ltd v North Australian Properties Pty Ltd* (1982) 150 CLR 85, 95, *per* Gibbs CJ; *Gye v Davies* (1995) 37 NSWLR 421, 428, *per* Powell JA. See also Murphy J in the *Day and Dent* case at 109.

the ordinary course of business end in a debt?[110] There must also be a sum 'due' for a set-off, but an estimate of the contingent debt for the purpose of proof[111] should suffice to satisfy that requirement.[112] The estimated value may be regarded as the sum 'due' from the bankrupt for the purpose of the set-off section.

C. Contingent Debt Owing to the Insolvent

Set-off, when the debt remains contingent

Alternatively, a creditor of an insolvent may be contingently indebted to the in- **8.27** solvent at the date of the insolvent's bankruptcy or liquidation. The insolvency legislation only empowers a trustee in bankruptcy or a liquidator to estimate the value of a contingent debt owing by the insolvent. The power does not extend to a contingent debt on the other side of the account. Therefore, while the debt to the bankrupt or the company remains contingent,[113] the fact that nothing is 'due' in respect of it, whether by way of an estimate of its value or otherwise, should mean that it cannot be brought into account in a set-off.[114]

Set-off, when the contingency has occurred

The inability to include the debt in a set-off only continues while it remains **8.28** contingent. If the contingency occurs after the bankruptcy or the liquidation, there would then be a sum 'due' to the insolvent which should be able to be the subject of a set-off, given that it arose out of a prior obligation.[115] In *Re*

---

[110] See para 7.04 above.

[111] See the Insolvency Act 1986, s 322, and the Insolvency Rules 1986, r 4.86.

[112] *Re Daintrey* [1900] 1 QB 546, 557, *per* Wright J; *M.S. Fashions Ltd v Bank of Credit and Commerce International SA* [1993] Ch 425, 435, ChD, *per* Hoffmann LJ.

[113] Note that, in the case of a primary obligation to pay, as opposed to a secondary obligation such as that of a guarantor, a provision in the contract for a demand in writing upon the debtor is not regarded as creating a contingency. See *M S Fashions Ltd v Bank of Credit and Commerce International SA* [1993] Ch 425, 435–436, referring to *Re J Brown's Estate* [1893] 2 Ch 300.

[114] *Re Daintrey* [1900] 1 QB 546, 557, 565, 573; *M S Fashions Ltd v Bank of Credit and Commerce International SA* [1993] 1 Ch 425, 435, *per* Hoffmann LJ. See also *Re Bank of Credit and Commerce International SA (No 8)* [1998] AC 214, 224 (the depositor's liability to the bank in liquidation remained contingent after the liquidation because a demand had not been made), and *MPS Constructions Pty Ltd v Bank of New South Wales* (1980) 4 ACLR 835 (see para 8.23 above). Compare *Re Taylor, ex p Norvell* [1910] 1 KB 562, 568, *per* Phillimore J, aspects of which seem contrary to this view.

[115] In addition to the cases discussed below, see *Wreckair Pty Ltd v Emerson* [1992] 1 Qd R 700; *Re Taylor, ex p Norvell* [1910] 1 KB 562, 568, *per* Phillimore J; *M S Fashions Ltd v Bank of Credit and Commerce International SA* [1993] Ch 425, 435, ChD, *per* Hoffmann LJ; *Stein v Blake* [1996] 1 AC 243, 252–253. See also the cases concerned with a temporary suspension of mutuality in paras 6.65–6.67 above. In *Ex parte Hope, re Hanson* (1858) 3 De G & J 92, 44 ER 1203 the bankrupts' claim for improvements appears to have been contingent at the date of the bankruptcy on the lease being determined. When this subsequently occurred, a set-off was allowed in respect of the

Daintrey,[116] a business was sold on terms that the price was to be calculated as a proportion of the profits earned over a three-year period. The vendor became bankrupt before the expiration of the period and before any profits had been made. At the end of the three-year period, when the price was calculated in accordance with the agreed formula, the Court of Appeal held that the purchaser could set off his liability for the price against a separate debt owing to him by the vendor. *Re Daintrey* is sometimes characterized as a case in which there was a presently existing debt at the relevant date for determining rights of set-off which only remained to be quantified,[117] but in truth it is an example of a contingent debt.[118] No profits had been earned as at the relevant date, so that any debt to the bankrupt was contingent upon profits subsequently being earned.

8.29 There are other examples. In *Palmer v Day & Sons*[119] a person before his bankruptcy had delivered some pictures to auctioneers for the purpose of sale. The sale occurred after the bankruptcy, and it was held that the auctioneers could employ their liability to account for the proceeds of sale in a set-off. *Palmer v Day & Sons* is an example of a set-off based upon the principle enunciated by Gibbs CJ in *Rose v Hart*.[120] According to that principle, where property has been deposited with a person with directions or authority to turn it into money, the depository may set off the obligation to account for the proceeds against a separate debt owing to him by the depositor. In a number of cases this has been held to apply even though the proceeds were received after the depositor's bankruptcy.[121] While these *Rose v Hart* cases may be criticized on the ground that the proceeds of sale may have been impressed with a trust, in which case prima facie they should not have been susceptible to a set-off,[122] they nevertheless were instances in which a set-off occurred against a sum that first became due to a bankrupt after the bankruptcy as a result of a prior dealing.

---

claim. Similarly, in *Thornton v Maynard* (1872) LR 10 CP 695 the bankrupt drawer's estate first obtained the claim against the acceptor after the bankruptcy when the dividend was paid to the plaintiff indorsee. However this arose out of the prior obligation incurred as drawer, and a set-off was allowed. See also *Re Inglis, ex p The Trustee* (1932) 5 ABC 255. A contract for the sale of wheat was on terms that the purchaser could elect to pay cash or deliver wheat of equal quality. The wheat was delivered before the vendor's bankruptcy, but it was not until later that the purchaser elected to pay cash. It was held that the resulting debt could be the subject of a set-off. Compare *MPS Constructions Pty Ltd v Rural Bank of NSW* (1980) 4 ACLR 835, for which see para 8.23 above.

[116] [1900] 1 QB 546.

[117] *Re National Benefit Assurance Co Ltd* [1924] 2 Ch 339, 343; *Re A Debtor (No 66 of 1955)* [1956] 1 WLR 1226, 1230, 1238; *Carreras Rothmans Ltd v Freeman Matthews Treasure Ltd* [1985] 1 Ch 207, 230.

[118] *Re Taylor, ex p Norvell* [1910] 1 KB 562, 580–581; *Re Fenton* [1931] 1 Ch 85, 113; *Re Charge Card Services Ltd* [1987] 1 Ch 150, 182–183; *Day and Dent Constructions Pty Ltd v North Australian Properties Pty Ltd* (1982) 150 CLR 85, 92, 94, 103.

[119] [1895] 2 QB 618.

[120] (1818) 8 Taunt 499, 506, 129 ER 477, 480. See paras 10.11–10.31 below.

[121] In addition to *Palmer v Day & Sons*, see *French v Fenn* (1783) 3 Dougl 257, 99 ER 642; *Olive v Smith* (1813) 5 Taunt 56, 128 ER 607; *Astley v Gurney* (1869) LR 4 CP 714.

[122] See paras 10.15–10.17 below.

Graham v Russell[123] provides an early illustration of a set-off in this situation. It   **8.30**
concerned the statute (1746) 19 Geo II, c 32, s 2, which allowed an insured to
prove a claim on a policy in the underwriter's bankruptcy when the loss occurred
after the bankruptcy.[124] Since the insured's claim could have been proved, Lord
Ellenborough said that it could have grounded a set-off, and if the insured's claim
on the policy could have been set off if the underwriter had been bankrupt, he
concluded that the underwriter similarly should be able to set off his liability on
the policy when the insured instead was bankrupt, even though the loss occurred
after the insured's bankruptcy.[125] Another example is *Lee & Chapman's Case*.[126] A
contractor under a construction contract went into liquidation. The liquidator
subsequently completed the work, whereupon the price became payable to the
company. The Court of Appeal held that the debt for the price could be the subject of a set-off. Further, Dixon J seems to have had in mind both sides of the account when he said in *Hiley v The Peoples Prudential Assurance Co Ltd*[127] that: 'It
is enough that at the commencement of the winding up mutual dealings exist
which involve rights and obligations whether absolute or contingent of such a nature that afterwards in the events that happen they mature or develop into pecuniary demands capable of set-off.'

In Victoria, Hayne J held that a claim for post liquidation licence fees, which   **8.31**
existed only as a contingent claim at the date of the payee's liquidation, could be
included in a set-off in the liquidation.[128] Similarly in *Booth v Hutchinson*[129]
Malins VC accepted that rent accruing to a bankrupt landlord[130] after the bankruptcy could be the subject of a set-off. The judgment is unsatisfactory because
the Vice Chancellor failed to consider issues of mutuality which arise in lease cases
as a result of privity of estate.[131] It nevertheless indicates an acceptance of the view
that a debt arising in favour of a bankrupt after the bankruptcy but pursuant to a
prior contract can be included in an account in a bankruptcy.

The set-off section admittedly provides that an account is to be taken of what is   **8.32**
due from each party 'to the other', and in the case of a bankruptcy a debt arising

---

[123] (1816) 5 M & S 498, 105 ER 1133

[124] *Graham v Russell* was decided before 1825, when the bankruptcy legislation was amended to
allow contingent debts to be set off. The set-off section in the 1825 Act (6 Geo IV, c 16, s 50) stipulated that 'every debt or demand hereby made provable against the estate of the bankrupt, may also
be set-off in the manner aforesaid against such estate', and the 1825 bankruptcy legislation was the
first to provide for proof in respect of contingent debts. See s 56.

[125] The court declined to follow *Glennie v Edmunds* (1813) 4 Taunt 775, 128 ER 536. Compare
also *Ex parte Blagden* (1815) 19 Ves Jun 465, 34 ER 589.

[126] *Re Asphaltic Wood Pavement Co. Lee & Chapman's Case* (1885) 30 Ch D 216.

[127] (1938) 60 CLR 468, 497.

[128] *Old Style Confections Pty Ltd v Microbyte Investments Pty Ltd* [1995] 2 VR 457.

[129] (1872) LR 15 Eq 30, 35.

[130] In fact, the landlord had executed a deed of assignment of his estate upon trust for his creditors, but the deed provided that all questions should be decided according to bankruptcy law.

[131] See paras 13.58–13.65 below.

after the bankruptcy pursuant to a prior contract is a debt due to the trustee rather than to the bankrupt, given that the property of the bankrupt is vested in the trustee.[132] Therefore, at no time could it be said that there is, or has been, a sum due to the bankrupt himself. But that should not preclude a set-off. When a debt arises in this manner as a result of a prior contract between the bankrupt and a creditor, 'to the other' should be interpreted as including 'to the trustee', on the basis that the trustee takes subject to the prior equity resulting from mutual credits, mutual debts or other mutual dealings. The whole thrust of the set-off section is to look at the position prior to the bankruptcy, and if there have been prior mutual credits or mutual dealings one would expect that a set-off ordinarily would follow. *Re Daintrey, Booth v Hutchinson* and *Palmer v Day & Sons* all suggest this view. In any event, there should not be the same difficulty in that regard in the case of a company liquidation, since the assets of the company after its liquidation ordinarily do not vest in the liquidator,[133] and so any debt arising in favour of the company after the liquidation would still be a debt due to the company. While the House of Lords has held that the company in this period is divested of the beneficial title to its assets,[134] which includes debts owing to the company, it is still not possible to identify another person to whom it can be said that the debt is owing.[135] In Australia on the other hand there is authority for the view that liquidation does not deprive the company of the beneficial title to its assets.[136] If that view is followed, the point under discussion would be even less likely to be regarded as an issue there.

8.33 The allowance of a set-off in this situation admittedly is inconsistent with *Re A Debtor (No 66 of 1955).*[137] The Court of Appeal held in that case that a bankrupt surety's claim for an indemnity from the principal debtor could not be the subject of a set-off, since the payment to the creditor only occurred after the bankruptcy, and therefore at that date there was nothing due for the purpose of the set-off section. In other words, it was regarded as essential that an amount be due at the date of the bankruptcy, even though the resulting debt had its source in a prior obligation. *Re A Debtor* is difficult to reconcile with earlier authority,[138] and it should not be followed.[139]

---

[132] Insolvency Act 1986, s 306.

[133] *Re Oriental Inland Steam Co* (1874) LR 9 Ch App 557, 560. Note however that the Insolvency Act 1986, s 145 empowers the court on the application of a liquidator to direct that all or part of the company's property shall vest in the liquidator.

[134] *Ayerst v C & K Construction Ltd* [1976] AC 167.

[135] *Ayerst v C & K Construction Ltd* [1976] AC 167, 178–179.

[136] *Franklin's Selfserve Pty Ltd v Federal Commissioner of Taxation* (1970) 125 CLR 52.

[137] [1956] 1 WLR 1226.

[138] See above.

[139] See also para 8.20 above. In *Day and Dent Constructions* (1982) 150 CLR 85, 94 Gibbs CJ left open the question whether *Re A Debtor (No 66 of 1955)* was correct, on the ground that the payment was due to the trustee to enable him to obtain the bankrupt's property. Mason J on the other hand (at 106) said that it was anomalous and should not be followed.

Nevertheless, the Court of Appeal later accepted the authority of *Re A Debtor* in **8.34**
Brown v Cork.[140] The judgment of the Court was delivered by Oliver LJ, who referred to *Re A Debtor* as supporting a proposition that, where a guarantor in liquidation was entitled to claim contribution from a co-guarantor as a result of a payment made to the creditor after the liquidation,[141] the claim could not be the subject of a set-off in the liquidation against a separate debt owing by the paying guarantor to the co-guarantor.[142] In the circumstances in issue in *Brown v Cork*, that proposition is doubtful. The source of the claim for contribution was a joint and several cross-guarantee executed by the members of a group of companies in favour of a bank, by which each company guaranteed to the bank the payment of the liabilities to the bank of the other companies. The cross-guarantee constituted a prior dealing between the parties to the proposed set-off for the purpose of the insolvency set-off section. The fact that the claim for contribution was contingent at the date of the paying guarantor's liquidation therefore should not have been a ground for objection. After *Brown v Cork*, the House of Lords in *Stein v Blake*[142a] indeed accepted that set-off in bankruptcy can extend to debts on both sides of the account which were contingent at the bankruptcy date.

Likelihood of the contingency occurring

It has been suggested[143] that the question whether a contingent debt owing to an **8.35**
insolvent can be the subject of a set-off if the contingency subsequently occurs may depend upon whether it could be said at the insolvency date that the claim was likely to mature into an actual liquidated debt during the course of the insolvency proceedings. That view appears to be based upon the commonly-accepted definition of mutual credit.[144] However, since the expansion of the set-off section in 1869[145] to include mutual dealings, it should be sufficient if the debt arose out of a prior dealing between the parties to the proposed set-off without the intervention of any new and independent transaction.[146] It should not be necessary in such a case to show likelihood.[147]

---

[140]   [1985] BCLC 363, *per* Oliver, Parker and Balcombe LJJ. In addition to *Brown v Cork*, see in Australia *A E Goodwin Ltd v A G Healing Ltd* (1979) 7 ACLR 481 and *Westmex Operations Pty Ltd v Westmex Ltd* (1994) 12 ACLC 106, 110 (guarantee provided to the NCSC pursuant to a Class Order in order to obtain exemption from filing individual company accounts).

[141]   The creditor was paid in full, so that there was no question of a double proof. See paras 8.08–8.13 above.

[142]   [1985] BCLC 363, 368, 376.

[142a]   [1996] 1 AC 243, 252.

[143]   Wood, *English and International Set-off* (1989) 592.

[144]   See para 7.04 above.

[145]   Bankruptcy Act 1869, s 39.

[146]   See *Hiley v The Peoples Prudential Assurance Co Ltd* (1938) 60 CLR 468, 487, *per* Rich J, 499, *per* Dixon J.

[147]   See para 7.05 above.

Proof in the contingent creditor's insolvency before the contingency occurs

8.36   Consider that, before the contingency occurred, the person contingently liable
had proved in the bankruptcy or liquidation of the contingent creditor in respect
of a debt separately owing to him, and had received a dividend. If after the occurrence of the contingency the bankrupt's trustee or the company's liquidator sues
him for payment of the resulting debt, the better view was expressed by Hoffmann
LJ in the Chancery Division in *M S Fashions Ltd v Bank of Credit and Commerce
International SA*,[148] that the person may still rely on his provable debt in a set-off,
notwithstanding that he had been paid a dividend, but he must give credit for the
dividend in the set-off.

Contract for the sale of property or for the performance of work

8.37   When a trustee in bankruptcy or a liquidator completes a prior contract for the
sale of property or for the performance of work so as to earn the price, the purchaser's resulting debt would have been contingent at the relevant date for determining set-offs. It has been suggested that a lack of mutuality may be an objection
to employing the debt in a set-off. The question of the availability of a set-off in
such cases is considered later.[149]

D. Insolvent Corporate Group

8.38   It is common for the members of a group of companies to provide guarantees supported by fixed and floating charges to a major creditor, usually a bank, in order to
secure the indebtedness of one or more group members to the creditor. In addition, the group members may be indebted to each other on trading accounts or
inter-company loans. In the event of the collapse of the group and the liquidation
of the companies the creditor would realize its securities. If the creditor is not paid
in full, the rule against double proof would operate to deny rights of contribution
to group members that have paid more than their share of the debt as against underpaying members. Similarly, rights of subrogation would not be available.[150]
Alternatively, the creditor may be paid in full and may hold a surplus from the securities. The question then will arise as to how the surplus is to be dealt with. In
particular, the issue may be complicated where some of the members whose assets
were used to pay a greater proportion of the debt, and who therefore would be entitled to contribution from underpaying members, are indebted on inter-company accounts to the underpaying members.

---

[148] [1993] Ch 425, 435.
[149] See paras 13.32–13.51 below.
[150] See paras 8.08–8.13 above.

The circumstances of each case would require consideration, but the problem is **8.39** illustrated by *Brown v Cork*.[151] The members of a group of companies executed a joint and several cross-guarantee, whereby each guaranteed to a bank the liability of each of the other companies to the bank. In addition, the cross-guarantee was supported by fixed and floating charges granted by each company which covered the whole of the company's assets. The group got into difficulties, and the bank appointed a receiver pursuant to the securities. The receiver realized the companies' assets secured to the bank, and after paying the bank he held a surplus. One of the companies had gone into liquidation before the bank was paid, and the other companies went into liquidation after payment to the bank. The question arose as to how the surplus was to be applied. The Court of Appeal held that the surplus should be distributed amongst the companies in proportions, on the basis that each company (so far as the money realized from its charge permitted) would have discharged its own indebtedness to the bank, and also an equal share of the deficiency attributable to the indebtedness to the bank of those companies which were unable to discharge their own indebtedness in full.[152] Oliver LJ in delivering the judgment of the Court rejected an alternative proposal, that a separate account should be prepared for each company showing the amounts due to and from it by way of contribution to or from its co-sureties, and in making the calculation there should be set off against contribution liabilities any sums due from one company to another on their inter-company trading accounts.

The issue with which the Court of Appeal was concerned was whether a set-off **8.40** was available. Two reasons appear in the judgment as to why it was not. The company that went into liquidation before payment in full to the bank had paid more than its share. Oliver LJ said[153] in relation to that company that there was no set-off because the liability of the underpaying companies for contribution under the cross-guarantee arose after the liquidation, and a set-off in that circumstance was precluded by the earlier decision of the Court of Appeal in *Re A Debtor*.[154] This aspect of the case was criticized earlier.[155] It is suggested that the fact that the debt arose after the liquidation should not have precluded a set-off in circumstances where it arose out of a prior dealing between the parties in the form of the cross-guarantee. Oliver LJ however noted another, more general, argument put forward

---

[151] [1985] BCLC 363, *per* Oliver, Parker and Balcombe LJJ. In Australia, see also *A E Goodwin Ltd v A G Healing Ltd* (1979) 7 ACLR 481, and *Westmex Operations Pty Ltd v Westmex Ltd* (1994) 12 ACLC 106, 110 (guarantee provided by a group of companies to the National Companies and Securities Commission pursuant to a class order in order to obtain exemption from filing individual company accounts).

[152] See Lightman and Moss, *The Law of Receivers and Administrators of Companies* (3rd edn, 2000) 315.

[153] [1985] BCLC 363, 368.

[154] [1956] 1 WLR 1226.

[155] See para 8.34 above.

by the respondent, which Oliver LJ seemed to accept.[156] Each of the companies which had paid more than its share had a right of contribution from the others, and for the purpose of obtaining contribution it was entitled to be subrogated to the securities provided to the bank by the other companies. The subrogation entitlement extended also to the surplus in the receiver's hands.[157] To that extent the indebtedness of each of the companies to the other for contribution was a secured indebtedness. Because of the security there was no question of an overpaying surety having to prove in the liquidation of an underpaying surety, in which case a set-off under the insolvency set-off section would not have occurred in the liquidation. The overpaying surety was entitled to rely on its security and to call on the receiver to hand over the moneys in his hands to the extent of the charge. Further, Oliver LJ rejected an argument that the proviso to section 5 of the Mercantile Law Amendment Act 1856, to the effect that a surety is entitled to recover from a co-surety no more than the 'just proportion' to which the co-surety is liable, itself required a set-off in respect of other debts as between the parties.

8.41 The difficulty with the second argument is that it only considered the effect of the liquidation of an underpaying surety. In that liquidation, an overpaying surety was a secured creditor. As such it was entitled to elect not to prove but to rely on its security, in which case the better view is that, in that liquidation, the insolvency set-off section indeed did not apply.[158] But the overpaying sureties themselves were in liquidation, so that the question of set-off in the liquidation of an overpaying surety also had to be considered. Unlike the case of a secured creditor of a company in liquidation, when a company in liquidation itself holds security for a debt there is no question of an election. If the debtor on the secured debt is also owed a debt by the company in liquidation, an automatic set-off[159] may occur in that liquidation in relation to the debts, in which case, to the extent of the set-off, the security would be released.[160] Furthermore, for the reason given above it should not have mattered, in the case of one of the overpaying sureties, that it went into liquidation before the debt arose. It is suggested, therefore, that there should have been a set-off in *Brown v Cork*.[161]

---

[156] See [1985] BCLC 363, 369–371.

[157] See also *Bayley v Gibsons Ltd* (1993) 1 Tas R 385, 387–388, 390.

[158] See para 6.121 above.

[159] See paras 6.79–6.103 above.

[160] See para 6.122 above.

[161] In *A E Goodwin Ltd v A G Healing Ltd* (1979) 7 ACLR 481, 491 Powell J similarly concluded that an overpaying surety's claim for contribution from an underpaying surety could not be the subject of a set-off in respect of an inter-company debt, in circumstances where it appears that both companies were in liquidation. Powell J justified that conclusion on a different ground, that subrogation was a class right which enured to the benefit of all the sureties, and therefore there was a lack of mutuality for the purpose of a set-off. However, while the view that subrogation operated as a class right would have been relevant to the question of subrogation to the creditor's securities, it should not have impacted on the personal liability of an underpaying surety to pay contribution to an overpaying surety, for the purpose of a set-off in the overpaying surety's liquidation. Thus, in

E. Damages Claims

(1) Breach of Contract

Prior to 1869 the set-off section in the insolvency legislation was confined to mutual **8.42**
credit and mutual debts. The concept of giving credit itself related to debts, in that
it encompassed a debt arising out of a transaction entered into before the relevant
date for determining rights of set-off where it could be said that the transaction was
of the type that would naturally, or in the ordinary course of business, end in a
debt.[162] Accordingly, a claim for damages for breach of contract was regarded as not
being within the ambit of the set-off section.[163] Nor would the amendment of the
bankruptcy legislation in 1861, by which damages claims for breach of contract became provable,[164] have been sufficient to remedy that situation. After the amendment the point nevertheless remained that, as long as the set-off section was cast only
in terms of mutual debts and mutual credits, it did not contemplate a set-off in relation to a damages claim.[165] In 1869 however the set-off section was expanded to include mutual dealings.[166] This, in conjunction with the 1861 amendment to the
proof of debt provision, had the effect of allowing a damages claim for breach of a
contract entered into before the bankruptcy to be included in a set-off, since in such
a case the claim arose out of a prior dealing between the parties to the set-off.[167]

In *Carreras Rothmans Ltd v Freeman Matthews Treasure Ltd*[168] Peter Gibson J held **8.43**
that a claim for damages for breach of a prior contract could only be employed in

---

Brown v Cork [1985] BCLC 363, 369 the Court of Appeal seems to have accepted that the claims
for contribution in that case could have been the subject of a set-off, were it not for the points that
it made (see above) to the effect that the indebtedness for contribution was a secured indebtedness
and, in relation to one of the companies, that the debt arose after its liquidation.

[162] See paras 7.04–7.06 above.

[163] *Rose v Sims* (1830) 1 B & Ad 521, 109 ER 881.

[164] Bankruptcy Act 1861, s 153.

[165] Compare *Makeham v Crow* (1864) 15 CB(NS) 847, 143 ER 1018, in which an unliquidated
damages claim arising out of a contract of sale was set off in an action by the vendor's assignees in
bankruptcy for payment of the price. However, the purchaser presented alternative arguments for a
set-off. A set-off was claimed, not only under the bankruptcy legislation based upon the scope of the
proof of debt provision in the 1861 Act, but also on equitable set-off. The report is silent as to which
of these was regarded as the justification for the decision. Certainly, in cases decided after the
Bankruptcy Act 1869, which introduced 'mutual dealings' into the set-off section, set-off of unliquidated damages claims was justified on that ground. Thus, in *Booth v Hutchinson* (1872) LR 15 Eq
30, 32 Malins VC said that he would probably have concluded that the damages claim in that case
could not have been set off under the old law. He said (at 34) that there was no mutual debt, and
there was hardly a mutual credit, but that there was certainly a mutual dealing.

[166] Bankruptcy Act 1869, s 39.

[167] See eg *Booth v Hutchinson* (1872) LR 15 Eq 30; *Peat v Jones & Co* (1881) 8 QBD 147; *Mersey
Steel & Iron Co v Naylor, Benzon & Co* (1884) 9 App Cas 434; *Re Asphaltic Wood Pavement Co. Lee
& Chapman's Case* (1885) 30 Ch D 216; *Palmer v Day & Sons* [1895] 2 QB 618, 621. See also *Baker
v Lloyd's Bank Ltd* [1920] 2 KB 322, in which Roche J treated the declaration of insolvency as a repudiation, although there is no indication as to whether the repudiation in fact was accepted.

[168] [1985] 1 Ch 207.

a set-off if the breach occurred on or before the relevant date for determining rights of set-off. This proposition was said to be supported by *Re A Debtor (No 66 of 1955)*,[169] but the better view is that that case was wrongly decided.[170] The *Carreras Rothmans* case is contrary to *Re Asphaltic Wood Pavement Co. Lee & Chapman's Case*,[171] in which a set-off was allowed notwithstanding that the breach occurred after the winding up of the company,[172] as well as the decision of Roche J in *Telsen Electric Co Ltd v J J Eastick & Sons*[173] in relation to the alternative finding that the breach occurred when the liquidator refused to accept the return of the goods. This aspect of the *Carreras Rothmans* case should not be regarded as good law, which indeed was the view of Millett J in *Re Charge Card Services Ltd*.[174]

(2) Tort

The necessity for a dealing

8.44   It used to be the case that a claim in tort which remained unliquidated at the date of the bankruptcy or liquidation was not provable,[175] and similarly it could not be employed in a set-off.[176] The position changed in 1986, when the Insolvency Act introduced a right of proof in respect of an unliquidated claim in tort,[177] and this has since been adopted in Australia in the context of company liquidation.[178] But this should not have the consequence that a tortious claim which is still unliquidated at the relevant date for determining rights of set-off[179] can always be employed in a set-off.[180] In order for the set-off section to apply there must be mutual

---

[169] [1956] 1 WLR 1226.

[170] See paras 8.20 and 8.33 above.

[171] (1885) 30 Ch D 216.

[172] See Millett J's explanation of *Lee & Chapman's Case* in *Re Charge Card Services Ltd* [1987] 1 Ch 150, 180–181.

[173] [1936] 3 All ER 266.

[174] [1987] 1 Ch 150, 178, 190.

[175] See the former Bankruptcy Act 1914, s 30(1). Compare *Re Berkeley Securities (Property) Ltd* [1980] 1 WLR 1589 in relation to a claim in tort that had been liquidated by judgment after winding up but before the claimant lodged a proof in the winding up, although the development in that case was short-lived. See *Re Islington Metal and Plating Works Ltd* [1984] 1 WLR 14, and *Re Autolook Pty Ltd* (1983) 2 ACLC 30.

[176] *Aliter* if judgment had been obtained and the claim liquidated before the relevant date. See *Re D H Curtis (Builders) Ltd* [1978] 1 Ch 162, 172, and, with respect to proof, *Page v Commonwealth Life Assurance Society Ltd* (1935) 36 SR (NSW) 85, 90, *Re Berkeley Securities (Property) Ltd* [1980] 1 WLR 1589, 1606, and *Re Autolook Pty Ltd* (1983) 2 ACLC 30. An award of costs made in the tort action, being a mere addition or appurtenance to the damages, followed the same rule. See *Re Newman, ex p Brooke* (1876) 3 Ch D 494, 497.

[177] See s 322, 'bankruptcy debt' being defined in s. 382 as including tortious liabilities. For company liquidation, see the Insolvency Rules 1986, r 13.12.

[178] See the Corporations Act 2001 (Cth), s 553(1). The old position still applies in bankruptcy, however. See the Bankruptcy Act 1966 (Cth), s 82(2).

[179] See paras 6.31–6.45 above.

[180] Compare the position in New Zealand in relation to bankruptcy. Claims in tort are provable if capable of estimation (see the Insolvency Act 1967, ss 87, 98 and 99), and according to s 93 it suffices for a set-off that a person entitled to prove in respect of any debt or demand is indebted or

debts, mutual credits or other mutual dealings. A damages claim is not a debt, unless it has been liquidated by judgment prior to the relevant date.[181] Similarly the
concept of giving credit is confined to a transaction which would naturally end in
a debt,[182] as opposed to a damages claims.[183] Not only is a damages claim in tort
not a debt, nor the subject of giving credit, but in many cases it would not result
from a dealing between the parties, in which case it would not come within the
language of the set-off section. As Lord Esher MR once remarked:[184] 'There are,
no doubt, matters which give rise to claims, but are not dealings within the section. If one man assaults another or injures him through negligence, that gives rise
to a claim, but is not a dealing . . .'. Thus, it was held in New South Wales that a
wrongful taking of property giving rise to a liability for damages in conversion was
not a dealing for the purpose of the set-off section.[185]

This is not to suggest that a tortious claim can never arise out of a dealing. One sit- **8.45**
uation that was recognized before the 1986 Insolvency legislation is the case of a
claim for damages for misrepresentation inducing a contract. The claim, although
based upon tort, was considered to be provable[186] on the ground that it is in the
nature of a claim under the contract.[187] Similarly it could be employed in a set-off,
the justification being that it arose out of a dealing between the parties.[188] Further,

---

liable to the bankrupt in respect of any debt or demand. Compare the Companies Act 1993 (NZ),
s 310, which sets out the right of set-off in company liquidation.

[181] This is implicit in Brightman J's comment in *Re D H Curtis (Builders) Ltd* [1978] 1 Ch 162,
172.

[182] *Palmer v Day & Sons* [1895] 2 QB 618, 621, and see paras 7.04–7.06 above.

[183] *Rose v Sims* (1830) 1 B & Ad 521, 109 ER 881. In Australia the High Court in *Gye v McIntyre*
(1991) 171 CLR 609, 625 suggested, although without determining the question, that a damages
claim for fraudulent misrepresentation could constitute the giving of 'credit' for the purpose of the
expression 'mutual credits'. That view is doubtful, however. See paras 7.05 and 7.06 above.

[184] *Eberle's Hotels and Restaurant Co Ltd v E Jonas & Brothers* (1887) 18 QBD 459, 465.

[185] *Re Leeholme Stud Pty Ltd* [1965] NSWR 1649.

[186] See *Jack v Kipping* (1882) 9 QBD 113, 117, and also the discussion in *Gye v McIntyre* (1991)
171 CLR 609, 631. Compare *Re Giles, ex p Stone* (1889) 61 LT 82, in which the damages for misrepresentation were sought from someone who was not a party to the contract.

[187] See *Jack v Kipping* (1882) 9 QBD 113, 117; *Palmer v Day & Sons* [1895] 2 QB 618, 622;
Tilley v Bowman Ltd [1910] 1 KB 745, 753.

[188] *Jack v Kipping* (1882) 9 QBD 113; *Re Mid-Kent Fruit Factory* [1896] 1 Ch 567, 571–572;
Tilley v Bowman Ltd [1910] 1 KB 745. Compare *Kitchen's Trustee v Madders* [1950] 1 Ch 134, in
which there was an undertaking not to prove the damages claim in the bankruptcy. The allowance
of a set-off in *Jack v Kipping* has been said to give rise to difficulty. See *Tilley v Bowman Ltd* at 752,
and note also *Provident Finance Corp Pty Ltd v Hammond* [1978] VR 312, 318. It is not easy to reconcile with the principle which has been applied in the case of an assignment of a debt, that an assignee does not take subject to a cross-claim for damages for fraud inducing the contract out of
which the assigned debt arose, on the ground that the damages claim is not a claim arising under the
contract itself. See *Stoddart v Union Trust Ltd* [1912] 1 KB 181. *Quaere* whether *Stoddart v Union
Trust* was correctly decided. See para 17.26 below. In Australia, it has been questioned whether the
claim for fraudulent misrepresentation inducing a contract in *Jack v Kipping* in fact was provable,
and therefore whether the insolvency set-off section indeed applied to it. Rather, it has been suggested that the case should be treated as illustrating the availability of equitable set-off. See *Re NIAA
Corp Ltd (in liq)* (NSW Supreme Court, McLelland CJ in Eq, 2 December 1994), referred to in

in *Shirlaw v Lewis*[189] Hodgson J in the New South Wales Supreme Court considered that, if there had been a liability in conversion in that case, in the circumstances in issue it would have arisen out of a prior dealing between the parties, and he contemplated the possibility that it could have been included in a set-off. But unless a claim in tort arose out of a dealing between the parties to the proposed set-off, it would not be within the ambit of the set-off section. It should not suffice that the claim is provable. While it is true to say that set-off is an aspect of the rules relating to proof of debts,[190] this notion should not import an absolute principle that all provable debts are capable of being set off.[191] Rather, the principle is as Lord Hoffmann expressed it in *Stein v Blake*,[192] that: 'Bankruptcy set-off . . . applies to any claim arising out of mutual credits or other mutual dealings before the bankruptcy for which a creditor would be entitled to prove.'

Bankrupt's claim must vest in the trustee

8.46 The Insolvency Act, section 323 provides that only the balance of the account taken under the section is provable in the bankruptcy or, as the case may be, is to be paid to the trustee in bankruptcy. As a corollary, the High Court of Australia in *Gye v McIntyre*[193] said that the bankrupt's claim against the creditor must be such that it would vest in a trustee in bankruptcy.[194] This would exclude claims for damages for personal injury or wrong done to the bankrupt.[195] Normally claims of this nature are unlikely to arise out of a dealing between the parties, so that in any event they should not be able to be employed in a set-off. But even if in an exceptional case the claim is derived from a dealing, the fact that it does not vest in the trustee should mean that it cannot be set off.

Aliferis v Kyriacou (2000) 1 VR 447, 463 para 48, *per* Charles JA. On the other hand, the High Court of Australia in *Gye v McIntyre* (1991) 171 CLR 609, 630–631 regarded *Jack v Kipping* as an authority on insolvency set-off.

[189] (1993) 10 ACSR 288, 295–296.

[190] *Mersey Steel and Iron Co v Naylor, Benzon & Co* (1884) 9 App Cas 434, 437–438; *Re Bank of Credit and Commerce International SA (No 8)* [1996] Ch 245, 256.

[191] See paras 7.15–7.17 above.

[192] [1996] 1 AC 243, 251 (emphasis added).

[193] (1991) 171 CLR 609, 626–627.

[194] Wood earlier had expressed this view in *English and International Set-off* (1989) 315–16.

[195] See, for example, *Beckham v Drake* (1849) 2 HLC 579, 604, 621, 9 ER 1213, 1222, 1228; *Ex parte Vine, re Wilson* (1878) 8 Ch D 364; *Wilson v United Counties Bank Ltd* [1920] AC 102; *Heath v Tang* [1993] 1 WLR 1421, 1423. When a bankrupt has a cause of action in negligence, which includes a head of damage relating to property and another head of damage relating to personal injury, there is but one cause of action, and since it relates to property it vests in the trustee. On the other hand, the right to recover the damages which are personal, and any damages recovered, are held by the trustee on constructive trust for the bankrupt. See *Ord v Upton* [2000] 1 All ER 193 (esp at 206). Because the constructive trust relates not only to the damages recovered but also to the right to recover them, that part of the claim should not be the subject of a set-off in the bankruptcy. In Australia, the Bankruptcy Act 1966 (Cth), s 116(2)(g) specifically exempts any right of the bankrupt to recover damages or compensation for personal injury or wrong done to the bankrupt from the property which is divisible among the creditors.

Australia

In Australia, damages claims in tort are now provable in company liquidation,[196] **8.47**
but they are still not provable in bankruptcy.[197] This should have the consequence
in Australia that a damages claim in tort against a bankrupt cannot be included in
a set-off.[198] On the other hand, while the set-off section requires that the claim
against the bankrupt be provable, the High Court in *Gye v McIntyre*[199] said that
there is no such principle that the bankrupt's claim against the creditor must be in
the nature of a provable debt.[200] Therefore, an unliquidated damages claim in tort
available to a bankrupt against a creditor should be able to be included in a set-off
if it arose out of a dealing between the parties, even though it would not have been
provable in the creditor's bankruptcy if the creditor instead had been the bankrupt
party.

F. Breach of Trust

The introduction in 1861 of a right of proof in respect of claims for unliquidated **8.48**
damages only applied to damages arising by reason of a contract or promise.[201]
This was extended in the Bankruptcy Act 1883, section 37 to damages for breach
of trust. However, the liability of a trustee who disposed of trust property in
breach of trust traditionally has been regarded in equity as being in the nature of
an obligation to restore the property or to pay compensation, and as creating an
equitable debt, as opposed to being for unliquidated damages.[202] Therefore, even
before the amendment to the proof of debt section in 1883, the equitable debt
could be proved in a bankruptcy.[203]

When a beneficiary is bankrupt, there is an issue as to whether the trustee should **8.49**
be permitted to profit from his own breach of trust by employing his liability for
breach of trust in a set-off in the bankruptcy.[204] Consider however that the trustee
is the bankrupt party, and it is the beneficiary who is asserting a set-off. The beneficiary's claim against the trustee for wrongfully disposing of trust property is in

---

[196] Corporations Act 2001 (Cth), s 553(1).
[197] Bankruptcy Act 1966 (Cth), s 82(2).
[198] See paras 7.15–7.17 above.
[199] (1991) 170 CLR 609.
[200] See para 7.19 above.
[201] Bankruptcy Act 1861, s 153.
[202] *Ex parte Adamson, re Collie* (1878) 8 Ch D 807, 819; *Wickstead v Browne* (1992) 30 NSWLR
1, 14–15. See also *Target Holdings Ltd v Redferns* [1996] AC 421, 434. Compare *Space Investments
Ltd v CIBC* [1986] 1 WLR 1072, 1074.
[203] *Ex parte Westcott, re White* (1874) LR 9 Ch App 626; *Emma Silver Mining Co v Grant* (1880)
17 Ch D 122. See also Williams, *The Law and Practice in Bankruptcy* (2nd edn, 1876) 161.
[204] See para 8.72 below.

the nature of an equitable debt. When a set-off is based upon mutual debts or mutual credits, it is not necessary to show that the debt in question had its origin in a dealing between the parties to the proposed set-off.[205] Accordingly, where the trustee's liability is in the nature of an equitable debt, and that debt arose before the bankruptcy, it should not be necessary to show a prior dealing between the parties in order that the claim may come within the ambit of the set-off section, although usually in these cases there would be a dealing for the purpose of the set-off section arising from the circumstances giving rise to the trust. If on the other hand the breach of trust occurred after the bankruptcy, albeit where the trust was subsisting before then, it seems doubtful that a claim for a set-off could be based on the concept of giving credit, since it could hardly be said that a trust would naturally, or in the ordinary course of business, end in an equitable debt as a result of a breach.[206] Rather, it would be necessary to show a prior dealing between the trustee and the beneficiary.

G. Calls on Shares

Introduction

8.50 Section 17 of the Joint Stock Companies Amendment Act 1858 provided that, in fixing the amount payable by a contributory in the event of the winding up of a joint stock company, a set-off could occur between the amount of the call made upon him and any sum due to him on an independent contract or dealing with the company. It applied not only to companies in which contributories had unlimited liability, but also to companies where the liability was limited pursuant to the Joint Stock Companies Act 1856.[207] In the Companies Act 1862, however, the right to a set-off was restricted. Section 101 was drafted in terms similar to the current Insolvency Act 1986, section 149, in that it only provided for a set-off against a call where the company was an unlimited company and, in addition, the call had been made before the winding up.[208] In *Grissell's Case*[209] it was held in the context of the 1862 Act, and it has since become an established principle, that when a lim-

---

[205] See paras 7.10–7.12 above.

[206] See para 7.04 above.

[207] See eg *Garnet and Mosely Gold Mining Co of America Ltd v Sutton* (1862) 3 B & S 321, 122 ER 121. This would explain Dixon J's query in *Hiley v The Peoples Prudential Assurance Co Ltd* (1938) 60 CLR 468, 500 in relation to *Re The Moseley Green Coal and Coke Co Ltd. Barrett's Case (No 2)* (1865) 4 De G J & S 756, 46 ER 1116 (the application of s 17 of the 1858 Act in that case is more readily apparent from the reports in 12 LT 193 and 34 LJ Bcy 41).

[208] However any money due to the contributory as a member of the company in respect of any dividend or profit is excluded from the set-off. See the Insolvency Act 1986, 149(2)(a).

[209] *Re Overend, Gurney, and Co. Grissell's Case* (1866) LR 1 Ch App 528. The subsequent introduction of the rules of bankruptcy into the law of company liquidation has not affected the principle enunciated in *Grissell's Case*. See *Re General Works Co. Gill's Case* (1879) 12 Ch D 755; *Re North Queensland Brick and Pottery Co Ltd. MacBrair's Case* [1902] St R Qd 286.

ited liability company is being wound up, a shareholder who is also a creditor of the company may not set off the company's debt to him against his liability for unpaid calls.[210] Nor may he set off the dividend payable on the debt against the call. Indeed, given that there is no right of set-off, the rule in *Cherry v Boultbee*[211] dictates that the call, being an obligation to contribute to the fund represented by the company's assets, must be paid in full before the shareholder is entitled to participate in the fund by receiving a dividend along with the other creditors on the debt owing to him.[212] Despite early authority to the contrary,[213] it is now settled that the rule extends to voluntary liquidations.[214] Moreover, it makes no difference that the call may have been made before the winding up,[215] or that the call is being enforced in a common law action brought by the liquidator in the name of the company rather than in a proceeding in the winding up,[216] or that the company's unpaid capital has been charged or assigned to a third party.[217] Further, an agreement for a set-off between the company and the shareholder will not be effective to exclude the rule if the set-off has not been effected pursuant to the agreement

---

[210] Compare *Re The London and Scottish Bank; Logan's Case* (1870) 21 LT 742. A counterclaim similarly will not succeed. See *Government Security Investment Co v Dempsey* (1880) 50 LJQB 199.

[211] (1839) 4 My & Cr 442, 41 ER 171. See ch 14 below.

[212] *Re Overend, Gurney, and Co. Grissell's Case* (1866) LR 1 Ch App 528, 536; *Re China Steamship Co, ex p MacKenzie* (1869) LR 7 Eq 240, 244; *Ramsay v Jacobs* (1987) 12 ACLR 595, 597. Note also the effect of the Insolvency Act 1986, s 74(2)(f), that a sum due to a member of a company, payable to that member in his character of a member (by way of dividends, profits or otherwise), is not deemed to be a debt of the company payable to that member in competition with other creditors, but any such sum may be taken into account for the purpose of the final adjustment of the rights of the contributories among themselves. In Australia, see the Corporations Act 2001 (Cth), s 563A, and also s 553A, which provides that a debt owed by a company to a person in the person's capacity as a member of the company is not admissible to proof unless the person has paid all amounts that he is liable to pay as a member of the company.

[213] *Brighton Arcade Co Ltd v Dowling* (1868) LR 3 CP 175. See also *Groom v Rathbone* (1879) 41 LT 591.

[214] *Re International Life Assurance Society. Gibbs and West's Case* (1870) LR 10 Eq 312, 330; *Re Paraguassu Steam Tramroad Co. Black & Co's Case* (1872) LR 8 Ch App 254, 262–263; *Re Whitehouse & Co* (1878) 9 Ch D 595; *Hoby and Co Ltd v Birch* (1890) 62 LT 404; *Re Pyle Works* (1890) 44 Ch D 534, 585–586; *Ramsay v Jacobs* (1987) 12 ACLR 595.

[215] *Re Breech-Loading Armoury Co. Calisher's Case* (1868) LR 5 Eq 214; *Re Stranton Iron and Steel Co, Barnett's Case* (1875) LR 19 Eq 449; *Re Whitehouse and Co* (1878) 9 Ch D 595; *Re Auriferous Properties Ltd* [1898] 1 Ch 691, 696; *Re Hiram Maxim Lamp Co* [1903] 1 Ch 70; *Re John Dillon Ltd (In Liq), ex parte Jefferies* [1960] WAR 30.

[216] *Re Whitehouse & Co* (1878) 9 Ch D 595, 604–605; *Alliance Film Corp Ltd v Knoles* (1927) 43 TLR 678. For the form of proceeding in a winding up to enforce payment of a call, see *Palmer's Company Law* (looseleaf, 1993) vol 3, para 15.404.

[217] See *Re International Life Assurance Society. Gibbs and West's Case* (1870) LR 10 Eq 312, 327 (in which the calls had been charged); *Bank of Australasia v Zohrab* (1891) 10 NZLR 310; *Re John Dillon, ex p Jefferies* [1960] WAR 30. See also *Re Matheson Bros & Co Ltd, ex p Matheson* (1884) NZLR 3 SC 323, 324 in the context of an assignment of calls by a liquidator after the commencement of the winding up. While an assignee of calls takes free from any debt owing by the company to the contributory, the contributory may bring into account an indebtedness of the assignee himself. See *Re Matheson* at 324.

before the liquidation,[218] even though the shareholder may have been induced to take the shares on the faith of the agreement.[219] If a set-off against a call has taken place before the company's liquidation, it nevertheless may be avoided by the liquidator if the circumstances were such as to give rise to a voidable preference.[220]

Rationale

8.51 Sir George Jessel sought to explain the denial of a set-off on the basis of lack of mutuality.[221] He said that, once a winding up commences, a liability to contribute unpaid capital no longer takes the form of a debt owing to the company, but rather it constitutes a liability to contribute to the assets of the company enforceable by the liquidator, and there is a lack of mutuality between that liability and an indebtedness of the company.[222] This theory has been criticized however on the ground that a call in a winding up does in fact give rise to a debt due to the company.[223] The fact that the call may be made by the liquidator does not mean that it is a liability owed to the liquidator.[224] Nor should the fact that the machinery for making a call in a compulsory winding up is the exercise by the liquidator as an officer of the court of the court's power[225] have the consequence that it is not a debt due to the company. In that regard, the liability to contribute unpaid capital differs from the obligation to repay a preference, against which there similarly cannot be a set-off.[226] In the case of unpaid capital, the shareholder had a liability to contribute the capital before the winding up, albeit that the liability was contingent upon a call being made.[227] A preferential payment on the other hand is voidable only by order of the court on the application of the liquidator.[228] Indeed,

---

[218] *Re Law Car and General Insurance Corp* [1912] 1 Ch 405; *Harding and Co Ltd v Hamilton* [1929] NZLR 338. Compare *Re Blakely Ordnance Co; Blakely's Case* (1867) 17 LT 307. *Contra* if the set-off is effected before liquidation. See eg *Re Harmony and Montague Tin and Copper Mining Co. Spargo's Case* (1873) LR 8 Ch App 407; *Re Jones, Lloyd & Co Ltd* (1889) 41 Ch D 159 (which is explained in *Harding v Hamilton*); *Re The Switchback Railway and Outdoor Amusement Co Ltd, ex p Mount* (1890) 16 VLR 339, 341; *Re New Zealand Pine Co Ltd, ex p The Official Liquidator: Guthrie's Case* (1898) 17 NZLR 257; *Randall v The Liquidator of the Santa Claus Gold Mining Co Ltd* (1906) 8 WALR 36. See also *Ramsay v Jacobs* (1987) 12 ACLR 595, 597–598 (payment in advance).

[219] *Re Paraguassu Steam Tramroad Co. Black & Co's Case* (1872) LR 8 Ch App 254.

[220] *Re Land Development Association. Kent's Case* (1888) 39 Ch D 259; *Re Washington Diamond Mining Co* [1893] 3 Ch 95; *Re Atlas Engineering Co (Davy's Case)* (1889) 10 LR (NSW) Eq 179, 6 WN (NSW) 64; *Mitchell v Booth* [1928] SASR 367.

[221] *Re Whitehouse & Co* (1878) 9 Ch D 595.

[222] See also *Ex parte Branwhite* (1879) 40 LT 652; *Monkwearmouth Flour Mill Co Ltd v Lightfoot* (1897) 13 TLR 327; *Re GEB, A Debtor* [1903] 2 KB 340, 346, 352.

[223] See Cotton and Lindley LJJ in *Re Pyle Works* (1890) 44 Ch D 534, 575, 585–586. See also *Re A Debtor (No 41 of 1951)* [1952] 1 Ch 192 in the context of a voluntary winding up.

[224] Compare Wood, *English and International Set-off* (1989) 729.

[225] See the Insolvency Rules 1986, r 4.202.

[226] See paras 13.07–13.16 below.

[227] Compare *Palmer's Company Law* (looseleaf, 1998) vol 1, para 6.202 in relation to public companies.

[228] Insolvency Act 1986, s 239. In Australia, see the Corporations Act 2001 (Cth), s 588FF(1) in the context of company liquidation.

the lack of mutuality theory is difficult to reconcile with *Re China Steamship Co,
ex p MacKenzie*.[229] *Ex parte MacKenzie* concerned a shareholder who, after the
commencement of the company's liquidation, assigned to a third party a debt
owing to him by the company. It was held that the assignee took subject to a right
in the company[230] to set off a call subsequently made on the assignor's shares
against the debt. An assignee takes subject to equities, including rights of set-off,
available to the debtor against the assignor.[231] But if lack of mutuality were the reason that a shareholder after the commencement of the winding up is denied a set-
off against a call, there should not have been an equity available to the company
against the shareholder/assignor in *Ex parte MacKenzie* to which the assignee was
subject. An alternative explanation is that the insolvency legislation itself forbids
a set-off. The legislation, when taken as a whole, contemplates that the proceeds
of a call are to be used with the other assets of the company in the pari passu payment of the company's debts, and it would be contrary to that principle to allow a
set-off against the call.[232] But perhaps the simplest explanation is that the change
to the legislation which occurred in 1862, by which the right of set-off that was
formerly available to a contributory against a call was confined to unlimited companies where the call had been made before the winding up,[233] gave rise to an
implication that in the case of a limited company Parliament intended that the
call should be paid without set-off,[234] and this principle has since become
entrenched.

Set-off asserted by the company rather than the contributory

While *Grissell's Case* operates to prevent the creditor from asserting a set-off, *Ex   **8.52**
parte MacKenzie*[235] shows that there is no such objection when the set-off is asserted by the company. In the *MacKenzie* case a shareholder after the commencement of the company's liquidation assigned to a third party a debt owing to him
by the company, and Lord Romilly MR held that the assignee took subject to a
right in the company to set off a subsequent call against the debt. The set-off
in issue would have been based upon the Statutes of Set-off, given that, at the time,
the bankruptcy set-off section had not been incorporated into the law of company

---

[229] (1869) LR 7 Eq 240.
[230] See below.
[231] See ch 17 below.
[232] *Re Overend, Gurney and Co. Grissell's Case* (1866) LR 1 Ch App 528, 535–536; *Re Paraguassu
Steam Tramroad Co. Black & Co's Case* (1872) LR 8 Ch App 254, 262, 265; *Re Auriferous Properties
Ltd* [1898] 1 Ch 691, 696; *Re Patrick Corporation Ltd and the Companies Act* (1980) ACLC 40–643
at p 34,272.
[233] See para 8.50 above.
[234] See *Re Breech-Loading Armoury Co. Calisher's Case* (1868) LR 5 Eq 214, 217, although compare *Re Stranton Iron and Steel Co. Barnett's Case* (1875) LR 19 Eq 449, 452.
[235] *Re China Steamship Co, ex p MacKenzie* (1869) LR 7 Eq 240.

liquidation.[236] But could a liquidator now assert against an assignee the wider right of set-off available under the insolvency legislation? A potential difficulty is the view that has gained general acceptance by the courts, that the insolvency set-off section is self-executing and operates automatically on the occurrence of a liquidation.[237] It would hardly be consistent with that analysis to hold that the section can be invoked by one party but not the other. Nevertheless, the question may be academic. When a debt is assigned after the commencement of a liquidation, any proof in respect of it should be lodged in the name of the assignor as the creditor at the relevant date for determining the provable debts.[238] The assignee is not considered to be in any better position than the assignor.[239] The liquidator in *Ex parte MacKenzie* undoubtedly would have been entitled to invoke *Grissell's Case* against the assignor, and similarly he should have been entitled to assert the same equity against the assignee. In fact it was the liquidator in *MacKenzie* who sought the set-off, while it was the assignee who relied on *Grissell's Case* in an attempt to prevent a set-off occurring. It seems to have been assumed that, in the absence of a set-off, the assignee would have been entitled to receive a dividend on the assigned debt, and the liquidator would have had to look to the assignor for payment of the call. A set-off therefore was perceived to be a means by which the company in effect could obtain payment to the extent that its liability on the assigned debt was thereby extinguished. Yet it would have been more valuable for the liquidator to assert *Grissell's Case* against the assignee, since the liquidator should have been entitled to decline to pay anything to the assignee by way of dividend until the call had been satisfied in full.[240] This course of action, for some reason that is not apparent, was not adopted.

Assignment

8.53 In the case of an assignment of a debt, the assignee does not take subject to a set-off in respect of a debt owing by the assignor to the debtor that only came into existence after the debtor received notice of the assignment, even if the assignor's indebtedness was the result of a contract entered into before notice.[241] The assignee does take subject however to a debt that arose before notice, whether or not the debt was presently payable at that date.[242] The order of events in *Ex parte MacKenzie* was (1) commencement of the winding up, (2) assignment, and notice

---

[236] The incorporation first occurred with the enactment of the Supreme Court of Judicature Act 1875, s 10. See para 6.07 above. The set-off in *MacKenzie* occurred in the context of a claim to prove in the liquidation, but the Statutes of Set-off strictly should not have applied in that context. See para 17.31 below.

[237] See paras 6.79–6.103 above.

[238] *Ex parte Dickenson, re Gibson* (1832) 2 Deac & Ch 520.

[239] *Re Wickham* (1917) 34 TLR 158. See also *Ex parte Deey* (1796) 2 Cox 423, 30 ER 196.

[240] *Re Overend, Gurney and Co. Grissell's Case* (1866) LR 1 Ch App 528, 536.

[241] *Watson v Mid Wales Railway Co* (1867) LR 2 CP 593. See para 17.12 below.

[242] *Re Pinto Leite and Nephews, ex p Visconde des Olivaes* [1929] 1 Ch 221. See para 17.11 below.

of assignment given to the company, and (3) call made in the winding up. Normally a shareholder before a call would be regarded as having only a contingent liability to contribute unpaid capital.[243] But this must be considered in the context of section 80 of the Insolvency Act 1986,[244] which stipulates that the liability of a contributory in a winding up creates a debt accruing due from him at the time when his liability commenced but payable when the call is made. Even though the call in *Ex parte MacKenzie* was made after notice of the assignment, the effect of the then equivalent of s 80[245] was that the liability to contribute was deemed to have had reference back so as to give rise to an existing debt (payable *in futuro*) before notice.[246] Sir John Romilly said that the debt had reference back to the time when the winding-up began.[247] It was on that ground that Stirling J in *Christie v Taunton, Delmard, Lane and Co*[248] held that, when the assignment of the company's debt instead had taken place before the winding up, the assignee did not take subject to a right in the company to set off the assignor's liability for calls made after the winding up. The debt for calls in that case was not considered to have had reference back to the time before notice of the assignment. There is an alternative interpretation of section 80, however, and that is that the debt is deemed to have been created when the contributory first took out the shares.[249] If that view were applied, it would be difficult to see why, as a matter of principle, the existence or otherwise of a right in the company to set off the calls against the assignee's claim on the assigned debt should depend on whether the assignment took place before or after the commencement of the winding up. But whatever the position is in that regard, if both the call and the assignment took place before the winding up, and notice of the assignment was not given until after the call, the assignee will take subject to the company's pre-existing right of set-off.[250]

---

[243] Compare *Palmer's Company Law* (looseleaf, 1998) vol 1, para 6.202 with respect to public companies.

[244] In Australia, see the Corporations Act 2001 (Cth), s 527.

[245] Companies Act 1862, s 75.

[246] For another instance in which a reversion back of a title resulted in a set-off, see *Bailey v Johnson* (1872) LR 7 Ex 263 in the context of an annulment of a bankruptcy. See para 11.05 below.

[247] See also Pennington, *Company Law* (7th edn, 1995) 610–11.

[248] [1893] 2 Ch 175, following a dictum of Lord Romilly in *Re China Steamship Co, ex p MacKenzie* (1869) LR 7 Eq 240, 244. See also *Re The McKay Harvesting Machinery Co* (1894) 20 VLR 153; *Re Matheson Bros & Co* (1884) NZLR 3 SC 323, 325.

[249] See *Buckley on the Companies Acts* (14th edn, 1981) vol 1, 507 (in relation to the Companies Act 1948, s 214), referring to *Ex parte Canwell, re Vaughan* (1864) 4 De G J & S 539, 46 ER 1028, *Williams v Harding* (1866) LR 1 HL 9, and *Re West of England Bank, ex p Hatcher* (1879) 12 Ch D 284. In *Re Northern Assam Tea Co, ex p Universal Life Assurance Co* (1870) LR 10 Eq 458, 463 Lord Romilly agreed with counsel's argument to that effect.

[250] *Christie v Taunton, Delmard, Lane and Co* [1993] 2 Ch 175. Notwithstanding the winding up, when there is a prior assignment set-off under the Statutes of Set-off is in issue. See para 17.31 below.

Solvent company

8.54 The prohibition against setting off a call against a debt only applies in a winding up. When a company is a going concern, a set-off may take effect under the Statutes of Set-off.[251] It may be that a set-off is pleaded as a defence to an action brought by a company for payment of a call while the company is a going concern, but before judgment the company commences to be wound up. Since a set-off under the Statutes does not take place until a judgment for a set-off is given, the demands will not have been extinguished at the commencement of the winding up, and so the ordinary rule that a set-off may not proceed in a liquidation will apply.[252]

Bankrupt contributory

8.55 *Grissell's Case* does not apply when the contributory is bankrupt. In *Re Duckworth*[253] the Court of Appeal held that, when the liquidator of a company lodges a proof in the bankruptcy of a contributory in respect of a call, the contributory's trustee may bring into account a debt owing by the company to the contributory.[254] This was considered to be a consequence of the power conferred upon the liquidator by the Companies Act 1862 to prove in the bankruptcy of a contributory for any 'balance' against his estate.[255] The current English provision similarly is drafted in terms of a liquidator proving for a 'balance',[256] although this is no longer the case in Australia.[257] There is however a second justification for the set-off, and that is that, while the insolvency legislation prima facie may purport to prohibit a set-off in the company's liquidation, it does not have the effect of overriding the statutory right of set-off otherwise available in the bankruptcy under the bankruptcy legislation.[258] This explains why a set-off may proceed when the question arises in the context of a proof lodged by the bankrupt's trustee

---

[251] *Re Stranton Iron and Steel Co. Barnett's Case* (1875) LR 19 Eq 449, 451. See also *Re White Star Line Ltd* [1938] 1 Ch 458, 470, *per* Clauson J.

[252] *Re Hiram Maxim Lamp Co* [1903] 1 Ch 70; *Re A Shadler Ltd. McPhillamy's Case* (1904) 4 SR (NSW) 619 (verdict by consent for a set-off obtained after the liquidation held to be ineffective); *Re John Dillon Ltd; ex p Jefferies* [1960] WAR 30.

[253] (1867) LR 2 Ch App 578. See also *Ex parte Cooper, re A Trust Deed* (1867) 15 LT 637. In Australia see *Re Patrick Corp Ltd and the Companies Act* (1980) ACLC 40–643. The estimated amount claimable from a bankrupt in respect of future calls by a solvent company may be brought into an account in the bankruptcy. See *Re Anderson* [1924] NZLR 1163.

[254] However, because the set-off only arises after the contributory has become bankrupt, a petition presented by the liquidator of a company for the bankruptcy of a contributory based upon the non-payment of calls may not be impugned because of a set-off that will become available in the bankruptcy on the basis of a debt owing by the company to the contributory. See *Re John Sloss, ex p Robison Bros, Campbell & Sloss Ltd* (1893) 19 VLR 710; *Re GEB, A Debtor* [1903] 2 KB 340.

[255] Companies Act 1862, s 95. Compare the explanation offered by Romer LJ in *Re GEB, A Debtor* [1903] 2 KB 340, 352.

[256] See the Insolvency Act 1986, s 167, and also s 165 with respect to voluntary liquidations, in each case referring to Sch 4, Pt III.

[257] See the Corporations Act 2001 (Cth), s 477(2)(e).

[258] See *Re Duckworth* (1867) LR 2 Ch App 578, 580–582.

in the winding up,[259] as opposed to the case of a liquidator proving for the 'balance' in the contributory's bankruptcy. Nevertheless, it should still be necessary to show that a set-off is available in the bankruptcy according to the principles generally applicable to bankruptcy set-off. On that basis, it is difficult to understand the decision of Giffard LJ in *Re Universal Banking Corporation, ex p Strang*.[260] A shareholder assigned a debt owing to him by the company to a third party after an order was made to wind up the company. Subsequently the shareholder executed a deed of composition, which incorporated the principles of bankruptcy. It was held that the shareholder's liability for a call made in the winding up could be set off against the assigned debt. However the assignment occurred before the composition, so that at the date of the composition the position was that the company's debt was owing to the assignee while the shareholder was the party liable for the call. There was therefore no mutuality at that date, which should have prevented a set-off under the bankruptcy set-off section.[261] Nor would a set-off have been available in the company's liquidation on the basis of *Ex parte MacKenzie*,[262] since the company (through the liquidator) was not the party asserting a set-off. *Ex parte Strang* should be compared to *Re Matheson Bros & Co*,[263] a decision of Williams J in the New Zealand Supreme Court. In *Re Matheson* the benefit of a call made by a liquidator, as opposed to a debt owing by the company to the contributory, was assigned before the contributory's bankruptcy, and Williams J held, correctly, it is submitted, that lack of mutuality prevented a set-off in the bankruptcy against the company's debt. Nor could it be said in a case such as *Re Matheson* that an assignee of calls takes subject to a prior right of set-off available to the contributory in the liquidation, since the effect of *Grissell's Case* is that there would not have been any such right. But if the assignee of the call himself happens to be indebted to the contributory, a set-off should be available in the contributory's bankruptcy against the assigned call, since the assignee would be claiming payment of the call personally, and there would not be any reason in such a case for applying *Grissell's Case*.[264]

The ambit of the set-off where the contributory is bankrupt is sometimes framed in terms of a contributory who becomes bankrupt after the commencement of the winding up.[265] It is not clear that the availability of the set-off would be so limited, however, particularly if the debt resulting from a call has relation back to the date of the acquisition of the shares rather than the date of the winding up.[266] In any

8.56

---

[259] *Re Anglo-Greek Steam Navigation and Trading Co. Carralli & Haggard's Claim* (1869) LR 4 Ch App 174; *Re The Oxford and Canterbury Hall Co Ltd, ex p Morton* (1869) 38 LJ Ch 390.
[260] (1870) LR 5 Ch App 492.
[261] See eg *De Mattos v Saunders* (1872) LR 7 CP 570.
[262] *Re China Steamship Co, ex p MacKenzie* (1869) LR 7 Eq 240. See para 8.52 above.
[263] (1884) NZLR 3 SC 323.
[264] *Re Matheson Bros & Co* (1884) NZLR 3 SC 323, 324.
[265] See McPherson, *The Law of Company Liquidation* (4th edn, 1999) 423.
[266] See para 8.53 above.

event, it is apparent from *Re Duckworth* that it is not an objection to a set-off that the call is made after the commencement of the bankruptcy.

Contributory is a company in liquidation

8.57 In *Re Auriferous Properties Ltd*[267] Wright J held that a set-off is not available when the contributory is a company that has gone into liquidation, as opposed to a bankrupt.[268] Rather *Grissell's Case* applied, so that the contributory company had to pay the call in full before receiving a dividend on the debt.[269] It seems difficult to justify this distinction between an incorporated contributory and a contributory who is a natural person, since the statutory right of set-off conferred by the insolvency legislation in a contributory's insolvency is equally applicable to both cases.

Costs and expenses of the winding up

8.58 The preceding discussion concerned the right to set off a debt incurred by the company before its liquidation. The costs and expenses of the winding up, including debts or liabilities incurred by the company or the liquidator in the course of carrying on the company's business after the commencement of the winding up, stand on a different footing. These debts have priority in the liquidation, and are payable in full.[270] Alternatively the creditor may employ the debt in a set-off, including against a liability to pay a call on shares.[271]

Unlimited companies

8.59 The Insolvency Act 1986, section 149[272] empowers the court, at any time after the making of a winding-up order, to make an order on a contributory to pay any moneys due from him to the company, exclusive of any sum payable by him by virtue of a call made in pursuance of the Insolvency Act.[273] The only sum which could be payable by virtue of a call made in pursuance of the Act is a call made in the winding up,[274] so that the effect is to exclude those calls. It does not, however, exclude a call made by the directors before the winding up which remains un-

---

[267] [1898] 1 Ch 691.

[268] Wright J in *Re Auriferous Properties* expressed doubt as to the correctness of *Re Duckworth* (see para 8.55 above), but he said that it had stood for too long to be interfered with. It was held in *Re West Hartlepool Iron Co Ltd, Gunn's Case* (1878) 38 LT 139 that the exception in *Re Duckworth* does not apply when the estate of a deceased peron is being administered in bankruptcy, although compare *Re Bailey, deceased: Duchess Mill Ltd v Bailey* (1932) 76 Sol Jo 560.

[269] *Re Auriferous Properties Ltd (No 2)* [1898] 2 Ch 428.

[270] See eg *Re International Marine Hydropathic Co* (1884) 28 Ch D 470.

[271] *Re London and Colonial Co, ex p Clark* (1869) LR 7 Eq 550. Compare *Re General Exchange Bank* (1867) LR 4 Eq 138 with respect to the costs of the petition, although the set-off in that case was sought by the liquidator rather than the contributory.

[272] In Australia, see the Corporations Act 2001 (Cth), s 483(2).

[273] Section 149 also excludes a call made pursuant to the Companies Act 1985, although that exclusion would now have little practical significance.

[274] See the Insolvency Act 1986, s 150, and also the Insolvency Rules, r 4.202. For voluntary liquidation, see s 165(4).

paid.[275] Section 149(2) goes on to provide that, if the company is an unlimited company, the court in making the order may allow[276] the contributory to set off any sum due to him on an independent dealing or contract with the company.[277] Thus, the effect of section 149 is to allow to a contributory in an unlimited company a set-off in respect of a prior unpaid call made by the directors.

There is competing authority as to whether *Grissell's Case* extends to unlimited companies so as to prevent a set-off against a call made *after* the winding up. Malins VC in *Gibbs and West's Case*,[278] following a dictum of Lord Chelmsford in *Grissell's Case*,[279] held in favour of a set-off, although the judgment is not satisfactory because the Vice Chancellor assumed, mistakenly, that the then equivalent of section 149[280] in fact extended to this situation. Fry J on the other hand held that a set-off was not available in *Ex parte Branwhite*.[281] The relevant question is whether Parliament, by specifically allowing a set-off in relation to calls made before the winding up of an unlimited company, evinced an intention that calls made after the winding up could not be the subject of a set-off. On that basis, Fry J's conclusion in *Ex parte Branwhite* is to be preferred.   **8.60**

All creditors have been paid in full

The Insolvency Act 1986, section 149(3)[282] provides that, when all the creditors   **8.61**
of a company, whether it is limited or unlimited, have been paid in full, any money due on any account whatever to a contributory may be allowed to him by way of set-off against any subsequent call. Lord Romilly once said[283] that it is difficult to put an intelligible construction upon this provision because, if all the creditors have been paid in full, prima facie there would not appear to be any scope for a set-off. It has been suggested,[284] however, that it may refer to a sum due to a member in his character of member by way of dividend or profit, on the ground that this is not considered to be a debt of the company.[285]

---

[275] *Re Whitehouse & Co* (1878) 9 Ch D 595, 601.

[276] The court has a discretion in the matter. See *Re Norwich Equitable Fire Assurance Co; Brasnett's Case* (1885) 53 LT 569, in which the shareholder's claim against the company required further investigation.

[277] This does not include any money due to the contributory as a member of the company in respect of any dividend or profit.

[278] *Re International Life Assurance Society. Gibbs and West's Case* (1870) LR 10 Eq 312.

[279] (1866) LR 1 Ch App 528, 536. *Grissell's Case* itself was concerned with a call made after the winding up. See also *Re Paraguassu Steam Tramroad Co. Black & Co's Case* (1872) LR 8 Ch App 254, 265.

[280] See the Companies Act 1862, s 101.

[281] *Ex parte Branwhite, re The West of England and South Wales District Bank* (1879) 40 LT 652.

[282] In Australia, see the Corporations Act 2001 (Cth), s 483(2).

[283] *Re Breech-Loading Armoury Co. Calisher's Case* (1868) LR 5 Eq 214, 217.

[284] *Buckley on the Companies Act* (14th edn, 1981) vol 1, 628, cited with approval in *Re Compania de Electricidad de la Provincia de Buenos Aires Ltd* [1980] 1 Ch 146, 172.

[285] See the Insolvency Act 1986, s 74(2)(f). In Australia, see the Corporations Act 2001 (Cth), s 563A, which postpones debts due to a person in his capacity as a member of a company, whether

Debt for equity swap

8.62   In Australia the courts have held that a debt for equity swap entered into between an insolvent company not in liquidation and creditors of the company, by which the creditors are issued with fully paid shares on terms that the allotment is paid for by setting off debts equal to the nominal value of the shares, does not amount to an issue of shares at a discount, provided that the debts were genuinely created in the course of the company's business and are immediately payable.[286] In such circumstances it is not to the point that the company otherwise had insufficient assets to pay its debts in full, since the value of the debts the subject of the set-off is still considered to be the face value of the legally and immediately enforceable obligations that they represent.

H. Basing a Claim for a Set-off Upon a Wrongful Act

8.63   It is sometimes suggested that a person may not rely on his own wrongful act in order to found a set-off,[287] although this would appear to be expressed too broadly. A principle to that effect has been applied in the case of misfeasance claims against directors and promoters of companies, and it may extend to a claim for breach of trust in dealing with another's property and to some cases involving dishonesty or fraud. But beyond those circumstances it is doubtful if there is any such principle.

(1) Misfeasance Claims Against Directors and Promoters

8.64   If in the course of a winding up it appears that any person who has taken part in the formation, promotion, or management of the company, or any liquidator or officer of the company, has misapplied or become accountable for any of the company's money or other property, or if he has been guilty of any misfeasance or breach of fiduciary duty in relation to the company, then the Insolvency Act 1986, section 212[288] provides a summary procedure by which the official receiver, or the liquidator or any creditor or contributory, may apply to the court for an order compelling the person to repay or account for the money or other property. In *Ex*

---

by way of dividends, profits or otehwise, to other debts of the company, and also s 553A, which restricts the right of proof where the member is liable to the company in his capacity as member.

[286]   *Pro-Image Studios v Commonwealth Bank of Australia* (1991) 4 ACSR 586; *Re Keith Bray Pty Ltd* (1991) 23 NSWLR 430. The courts in each case declined to follow *Re Jarass Pty Ltd* (1988) 13 ACLR 728.

[287]   See eg Shelford, *The Law of Bankruptcy and Insolvency* (3rd edn, 1862) 522; Doria, *The Law and Practice in Bankruptcy* (1874) 685; Williams and Muir Hunter, *The Law and Practice in Bankruptcy* (19th edn, 1979) 197.

[288]   In Australia, see the Corporations Act 2001 (Cth), s 598.

parte Pelly[289] the Court of Appeal held, and it has since been confirmed,[290] that a person liable in misfeasance proceedings to repay money may not bring into account a cross-demand that he has against the company. This result has been supported on a number of grounds.

Brett LJ in *Ex parte Pelly*[291] said that a right of set-off arises only when there is an **8.65** action at law, whereas a provision such as section 212 provides a summary remedy without an action. This is not a satisfactory explanation for the rule however because, while an action at law is a prerequisite to a set-off under the Statutes of Set-off,[292] it is not necessary for set-off under the insolvency legislation.

More recently, Millett LJ in an ex tempore judgment in *Manson v Smith*[293] sought **8.66** to explain the denial of a set-off on two grounds. In the first place, he said that mis-appropriation of a company's money or assets by a director is not a dealing between him and the company.[294] The difficulty with that as an explanation is that the in-solvency set-off section does not require that the claims should have arisen out of dealings between the parties. A set-off can be based on a prior debt which is not the result of a dealing.[295] A company director is in a fiduciary relationship with the company, and the liability of a director who has misapplied company funds is sim-ilar to that of a trustee who has misapplied trust funds.[296] The trustee's obligation in such a case is to restore the trust estate or to pay compensation, which is regarded as giving rise to an equitable debt as opposed to a liability in damages.[297] A director, while a fiduciary, admittedly is not a trustee in the strict sense of the words,[298] but breach of the fiduciary duty attracts the same remedy of equitable compensa-tion.[299] Where there is an equitable debt in the form of an obligation to pay equi-table compensation, ordinarily it should not be necessary to show a dealing.[300]

---

[289] *Re Anglo-French Co-operative Society, ex p Pelly* (1882) 21 Ch D 492.

[290] *Re Exchange Banking Co. Flitcroft's Case* (1882) 21 Ch D 519; *Re Carriage Co-operative Supply Association* (1884) 27 Ch D 322; *Re Leeds and Hanley Theatres of Varieties Ltd* [1904] 2 Ch 45. Compare *Re Toowoomba Welding Works Pty Ltd (No 2)* [1969] Qd R 337.

[291] (1882) 21 Ch D 492, 507.

[292] Indeed, both Sir George Jessel MR and Brett LJ in *Ex parte Pelly* (1882) 21 Ch D 492, 502, 507 seem to have assumed that the Statutes of Set-off provided the only form of set-off that could have applied.

[293] [1997] 2 BCLC 161.

[294] [1997] 2 BCLC 161, 164.

[295] See para 7.07 above.

[296] It was regarded as such in *Ex parte Pelly* (1882) 21 Ch D 492, 495, 496, *per* Hall VC, 500–501, *per* Jessel MR, 504, *per* Brett LJ.

[297] See para 8.48 above.

[298] *Jacobs' Law of Trusts in Australia* (6th edn, 1997) 9–10; *Permanent Building Society v Wheeler* (1992) 10 WAR 109, 142–143. Compare *Belmont Finance Corp v Williams Furniture Ltd (No 2)* [1980] 1 All ER 393, 405.

[299] *Nocton v Lord Ashburton* [1914] AC 932, 946, 956–958; *Tavistock Pty Ltd v Saulsman* (1990) 3 ACSR 502, 510. See generally Gummow, 'Compensation for Breach of Fiduciary Duty', in Youdan (ed), *Equity, Fiduciaries and Trusts* (1989) ch 2.

[300] See para 8.49 above.

8.67 Millett LJ went on to suggest a second justification for the rule, that a set-off under the insolvency section cannot exist if one of the two debts came into being only in the course of liquidation, and in a misfeasance proceeding a debt only comes into being as a result of a judgment, which occurs after the liquidation.[301] However it is difficult to reconcile this explanation with the view that the misfeasance section is purely procedural. In other words, as Lord Evershed MR expressed it, the section 'does not create any new cause of action; it only provides a method of litigating particular claims; and, in providing a method, it is not exclusive'.[302] The Master of the Rolls went on to explain that the acts which are covered by the section are acts which are wrongful according to the established rules of law or equity.[303] The section therefore does not bring a debt into being by way of a judgment in a proceeding under the section. Rather, it provides a summary method of enforcing a pre-existing claim. This claim often would exist before the winding up.

8.68 It has also been suggested that a set-off is denied on the ground of lack of mutuality, since the summons is brought in the name of the liquidator, or another authorized person, rather than in the name of the company.[304] Lack of mutuality may indeed explain the denial of a set-off in some cases, for example where the claim being enforced in misfeasance proceedings is in respect of a disposition of the company's property after the commencement of its winding up[305] or for the recovery of a preference.[306] Set-off in relation to these situations is considered later.[307] In other circumstances, however, the fact that the claim is brought in the name of the liquidator does not provide a satisfactory explanation for the principle because, while the liquidator may take out the summons, section 212 is only procedural, in the sense that it provides a summary procedure for enforcing a liability that the director (or other such person) has to the company.[308] The liability

---

[301] The passages in the judgment of Hall VC to which Millett LJ referred (at [1997] 2 BCLC 161, 164) may have resulted from confusion between the right of set-off under the Statutes of Set-off and set-off under the insolvency legislation. Indeed, in the Court of Appeal in *Ex parte Pelly* both Sir George Jessel MR and Brett LJ seem to have assumed that set-off under the Statutes was in issue. See n 292 above.

[302] *Re B Johnson & Co (Builders) Ltd* [1955] 1 Ch 634, 647. See also *Cavendish Bentinck v Fenn* (1887) 12 App Cas 652, 669; *Re Asiatic Electric Co Pty Ltd* [1970] 2 NSWR 612, 613; *Re Oasis Merchandising Services Ltd* [1998] Ch 170, 181; *Halsbury's Laws of England* (4th edn, 1996) vol 7(3), 1694 para 2451. There may however be cases where the right enforced in a misfeasance proceeding is created only by the winding up. See *Halsbury, loc cit*, and *Couve v J Pierre Couve Ltd* (1933) 49 CLR 486, 494–496 (disposition of the company's property after the commencement of winding up); *Re Washington Diamond Mining Co* [1893] 3 Ch 95 (esp at 115) (preference). See also para 8.68 below.

[303] *Re B Johnson & Co* [1955] 1 Ch 634, 648.

[304] *Re Buena Vista Pty Ltd* [1971] 1 NSWLR 72, 74.

[305] See eg *Couve v J Pierre Couve Ltd* (1933) 49 CLR 486.

[306] As apparently occurred in *Re Washington Diamond Mining Co* [1893] 3 Ch 95.

[307] See paras 13.07–13.19 below.

[308] See above.

is enforced on behalf of the company, and the proceeds become part of the company's assets.[309] It differs from a claim for repayment of a preference, in relation to which lack of mutuality is properly regarded as a ground for denying a set-off.[310] In the event of misfeasance, where for example the claim is against a director or a person involved in the promotion, formation or management of the company, the company itself will have had a claim against the person before the liquidation, whereas the same cannot be said in relation to a preference.[311]

In cases where lack of mutuality is not an issue, the denial of a set-off is better explained on policy considerations. Thus, it has been said that, if an innocent contributory liable to pay a call on shares is denied a set-off, then a director or other officer of the company who has misapplied company money certainly should not have the benefit of a set-off. [312] Further, as Millett LJ pointed out in *Manson v Smith*,[313] the contrary view would lead to an anomaly. A director who was owed a debt by the company, and who was able to persuade his fellow directors to pay the debt in view of the company's impending liquidation, would be faced with the prospect of having the payment avoided as a preference in the liquidation. He could hardly be in a better position by misappropriating the money from the company, and then in subsequent misfeasance proceedings claiming an entitlement to set off his liability to repay the money against the debt owing to him. **8.69**

The policy consideration which operates to deny a set-off is that the liability to repay is a liability of a delinquent in breach of a duty in the nature of a breach of trust,[314] and it should not be treated in the delinquent's favour as a debt due from him to the company so as to entitle him to a set-off.[315] Admittedly it is difficult to reconcile this explanation with the view of Vaughan Williams J in *Re Bassett, ex p Lewis*,[316] that a set-off could occur if the liability is enforced in an action brought against the delinquent instead of the liquidator proceeding by way of summons under a provision such as the Insolvency Act 1986, section 212. It is on the other hand consistent with Maugham J's judgment in *Re Etic Ltd*.[317] After noting that the misfeasance section applies only to cases where there has been a misapplication or retention of moneys or property of the company or a positive misfeasance or **8.70**

---

[309] *Re Bassett, ex p Lewis* (1895) 2 Mans 177, 181.

[310] See para 13.08 below.

[311] As to the distinction between a misfeasance claim and a preference claim, see *Re Asiatic Electric Co Pty Ltd* [1970] 2 NSWR 612, 613; *Re Fresjac Pty Ltd* (1995) 65 SASR 334, 342; *Re Oasis Merchandising Services Ltd* [1998] Ch 170, 181.

[312] See Jessel MR and Cotton LJ in *Ex parte Pelly* (1882) 21 Ch D 492, 503, 509–510.

[313] [1997] 2 BCLC 161, 165.

[314] *Cavendish Bentinck v Fenn* (1887) 12 App Cas 652, 669, *per* Lord Macnaghten; *Re Etic Ltd* [1928] 1 Ch 861, *per* Maugham J; *Couve v J Pierre Couve Ltd* (1933) 49 CLR 486, 495.

[315] See Hall VC in the earlier judgment to which he referred at first instance in *Ex parte Pelly* (1882) 21 Ch D 492, 498.

[316] (1895) 2 Mans 177, 181.

[317] [1928] 1 Ch 861.

breach of trust,[318] including a breach of trust by way of negligence, Maugham J commented that: 'the fact that under [the misfeasance section] there is no right of set-off is itself an indication that the Courts have considered that the jurisdiction under [the section] is a special one *and is confined to claims by the company against the officer in which it would not be right for the officer of the company to be entitled to set up a right of set-off*'.[319] This suggests, contrary to Vaughan Williams J's opinion in *Re Bassett*, that a set-off similarly would be unavailable if the claim is enforced by way of action rather than under section 212,[320] which is the preferred view. Indeed, the contrary view is difficult to reconcile with the automatic nature of insolvency set-off, which has now been accepted by the courts.[321] If the claims are such that, apart from the suggested policy consideration, they would give rise to a set-off under the insolvency set-off section, the set-off would take effect automatically at the date of the liquidation, regardless of the form of proceeding later taken to enforce a perceived claim against a delinquent director or other such person. There is no justification, therefore, for a different result depending on the form of proceeding used.

8.71 If a director's or a promoter's liability for misfeasance is unable to be employed in a set-off, the right of the director or the promoter to receive a dividend on a debt owing to him should be subject to the rule in *Cherry v Boultbee*.[322] *Cherry v Boultbee* is considered later.[323]

(2) Fraud, and Breach of Trust in Dealing With Another's Property

8.72 If one accepts that policy consideration is a justification for denying a set-off in misfeasance proceedings, there is no reason why it should not apply generally to cases involving breach of trust in dealing with another's property. Consider that a trustee ('T') holds property on trust for a beneficiary ('B'), and that T in breach of trust disposes of the property. In such a case, T is obliged to restore the property or pay compensation, this obligation being regarded as an equitable debt.[324] If T becomes bankrupt the equitable debt would be provable in the bankruptcy,[325] and in addition it should be capable of being employed in a set-off.[326] If on the other hand B is the bankrupt party, it is suggested that T should not be entitled to a set-

---

[318] [1928] 1 Ch 861, 873, referred to in *Re B Johnson & Co (Builders) Ltd* [1955] 1 Ch 634, 649.

[319] [1928] 1 Ch 861, 873 (emphasis added).

[320] See also the statement of the principle in *Re Bailey Cobalt Mines Ltd* (1919) 44 OLR 1.

[321] See para 6.79 *ff* above.

[322] (1839) 4 My & Cr 442, 41 ER 171.

[323] See ch 14 below.

[324] *Ex parte Adamson, re Collie* (1878) 8 Ch D 807, 819; *Webb v Stenton* (1883) 11 QBD 518, 530; *Wickstead v Browne* (1992) 30 NSWLR 1, 14–15; *Goodwin v Duggan* (1996) 41 NSWLR 158, 166. See also *Target Holdings Ltd v Redferns* [1996] AC 421, 434. Compare *Space Investments Ltd v CIBC* [1986] 1 WLR 1072, 1074.

[325] Insolvency Act 1986, ss 322 and 382.

[326] See para 8.48 above.

off in the bankruptcy based upon his own breach of trust,[327] given that, if he had retained the trust property, he would have had to account to B's estate without the benefit of a set-off.[328] The contrary view would mean that the trustee would profit from the breach of trust.

Some cases, apart from misfeasance claims, which involve dishonesty or fraud **8.73** may attract similar considerations, particularly where the conduct was designed to gain an advantage in another's insolvency, but there is little authority on point.[329] Fraud did not preclude a set-off in *Ex parte Minton, re Green*.[330] An insolvent entered into a composition with her creditors by which each was to receive a rateable dividend, although she agreed with one creditor to pay him in full so as to induce him to sign the composition deed. The payment had been extorted by the creditor, and constituted a fraud upon the other creditors. It was held[331] that the payment was recoverable by the insolvent, and that this claim had passed to her assignees in bankruptcy, but that it could be set off against a separate debt owing to the creditor. However, the case should be considered in the context that the primary question was the liability of the creditor to repay the money, and further that it was the commissioners in the bankruptcy, as opposed to the creditor, who said that the liability should be set off against the separate debt.

(3) Deliberate Breach of Contract in Order to Obtain a Set-off

It is doubtful whether the principle that a person cannot rely on his own wrong- **8.74** ful act in order to obtain a set-off would extend further than breach of trust, or misfeasance in the nature of breach of trust, or possibly some cases involving fraud or dishonesty. It has been suggested that a set-off also might not arise in favour of a creditor of a bankrupt if the creditor has purposely broken his contract in order to obtain a set-off.[332] In considering that suggestion, however, it should be borne in mind that failure to pay any debt on time constitutes a breach of contract.[333] Set-off constitutes a form of security in the event of the bankruptcy of a party to

---

[327] This would be the case if the trustee were ordered to restore or pay compensation to the trust estate, rather than to pay compensation to the beneficiary directly. See para 10.02 below.

[328] See paras 10.03–10.06 below.

[329] Some comments in *Re Pollitt, ex p Minor* [1893] 1 QB 175, 179–180 and *Atkinson v Learmouth* (1905) 11 ALR 191, 195 suggest support for this proposition. The decisions in those cases however may be explained on the ground that the funds in question were held subject to a trust so as to preclude a set-off. See paras 10.43–10.54 below. On the other hand, a claim by an insolvent for fraudulent misrepresentation inducing a contract may be the subject of a set-off. See *Gye v McIntrye* (1991) 171 CLR 609.

[330] (1834) 3 Deac & Ch 688.

[331] By Erskine CJ, Sir J Cross and Sir G Rose.

[332] *Turner v Thomas* (1871) LR 6 CP 610, 614. See also *Re Pollitt, ex p Minor* [1893] 1 QB 175, 179–180 (decision affirmed [1893] 1 QB 455); *Atkinson v Learmouth* (1905) 11 ALR 191, 195; *Re H E Thorne & Son Ltd* [1914] 2 Ch 438, 450. *Williams and Muir Hunter on Bankruptcy* (19th edn, 1979) 197.

[333] See Maugham J at first instance in *Re City Equitable Fire Insurance Co Ltd* [1930] 2 Ch 293, 302.

mutual dealings,[334] and a party to a transaction may breach the contract by refusing to pay a debt when the bankruptcy of the creditor is imminent, relying instead on the security that his indebtedness will constitute for the creditor's own indebtedness to him. A creditor who is aware of his debtor's impending insolvency, and who consequently withholds payment of his own debt to the debtor as a form of security, would not be denied a set-off, and it is difficult to see why a simple breach of contract in any other form should be treated differently. For example, when a creditor who had purchased goods from an insolvent debtor prior to the latter's bankruptcy immediately refused to pay the price, offering instead to treat that debt as satisfaction for the debtor's indebtedness to him, he was still allowed a set-off in the debtor's subsequent bankruptcy, even though the set-off was based upon his own deliberate breach in not tendering payment.[335] There is also *Bolland v Nash*,[336] in which it was the creditor claiming the benefit of a set-off who had dishonoured his own acceptance and thereby caused the bill to be returned to the bankrupts as indorsers. In other words, the mutuality necessary for the set-off was revived as a result of the creditor's breach of his own engagement as acceptor to pay the bill according to the tenor of his acceptance.[337] In *Willment Brothers Ltd v North West Thames Regional Health Authority*[338] an employer under a building contract stopped payment on a cheque that had been forwarded to the contractor in payment of a debt so as to obtain a right of set-off in the contractor's liquidation, the liquidation having commenced after the cheque was sent to the contractor. The Court of Appeal allowed the set-off.

Breach of contract in not establishing a trust

8.75   A contract may stipulate that a sum of money equal in amount to the indebtedness of one of the parties to the other is to be set aside in a separate fund and held on trust. If a trust is established, the trustee would be denied a set-off in the beneficiary's bankruptcy in relation to his obligation to account for the trust fund.[339] It may be however that, in breach of contract, the person failed to establish the trust, in which case the question may arise whether a set-off should be allowed in respect of the resulting damages liability. In some cases the maxim that equity deems as

---

[334]   See para 6.12 above.

[335]   *Southwood v Taylor* (1818) 1 B & Ald 471, 106 ER 173, and see also *Holmes v Tutton* (1855) 5 El & Bl 65, 119 ER 405.

[336]   (1828) 8 B & C 105, 108 ER 982.

[337]   See the Bills of Exchange Act 1882, s 54(1).

[338]   (1984) 26 BLR 51.

[339]   See paras 10.03–10.06 below.

done that which ought to be done may apply, so that equity would deem a notional trust to have been created against which there may not be a set-off.[340] In other cases however the bankruptcy of the party having recourse to the maxim may make it difficult for him to obtain an order for specific performance, and the application of the maxim depends upon the availability of such an order.[341] One possible objection to a set-off is that the person claiming the benefit of the set-off himself is in breach of contract, in not setting aside a separate fund to which the trust may attach. The contrary argument is that this is no worse than a creditor neglecting to pay, or indeed choosing not to pay, a debt owing by him to his debtor on another transaction on the due date, and if a set-off may arise in the one case then similarly it should be available in the other. A second possible objection is that, by stipulating for a trust, the parties impliedly had agreed to exclude a set-off, although under the current state of the law that argument would not be tenable[342] since the House of Lords has held that the parties to mutual dealings cannot contract out of the operation of the mutual credit provision.[343] If neither of these objections would be valid individually, they should not be valid cumulatively, and so, unless equity would deem a notional trust fund to have been set up, it is suggested that a set-off would be available.[344]

---

[340] *Re Arthur Sanders Ltd* (1981) 17 BLR 125. Compare *Re ILG Travel Ltd* [1995] 2 BCLC 128, 162, in which ILG acquiesced in the agent's failure to pay the money into a separate account, and also *GPT Realisations Ltd v Panatown Ltd* (1992) 61 BLR 88 (application for mandatory interlocutory injunction to set up a separate trust account refused).

[341] *Re Anstis* (1886) 31 Ch D 596, 605–606; *Re Plumptre* [1910] 1 Ch 609, 619. Similarly, the insolvency of the party against whom it is sought to apply the maxim may prevent its application. See *Mac-Jordan Construction Ltd v Brookmount Erostin Ltd* [1992] BCLC 350. Compare *Re Arthur Sanders Ltd* (1981) 17 BLR 125. The Greater London Council had failed to pay retention money relating to work performed by a contractor (now in liquidation) and various sub-contractors into a separate trust account, despite a contractual obligation to do so. Nourse J said that, in the case of a solvent employer such as the GLC, equity would deem as done that which ought to have been done and would find a notional trust. While the availability of an order for specific performance was not considered, it appears that the remaining work under the contract in fact had been completed by another contractor.

[342] See *Re ILG Travel Ltd* [1995] 2 BCLC 128, 160–161.

[343] *National Westminster Bank Ltd v Halesowen Presswork and Assemblies Ltd* [1972] AC 785. See para 6.71 above.

[344] See *Mac-Jordan Construction Ltd v Brookmount Erostin Ltd* [1992] BCLC 350, 359.

9

COMMENSURABLE DEMANDS

A. The Requirement of Commensurability

For the insolvency set-off section to apply the demands must be commensurable, **9.01** in other words the claim on each side of the account must be a money demand.[1] Set-off under the Statutes of Set-off and equitable set-off are subject to the same requirement.[2] A claim which is not monetary in nature is not susceptible to a set-off even if its value is measurable with precision in money terms.[3] Thus, a set-off has been denied in the context of a claim for the return of specific property in circumstances where the court nevertheless accepted that the property in question had a particular value.[4] In the case of insolvency set-off there are two reasons for the principle. The first, which has been emphasized in the cases, is the perceived difficulty in producing a balance on the account when one of the demands is not a money claim. As Lord Russell of Killowen CJ once remarked: 'There could not

---

[1] *Eberle's Hotels and Restaurant Co Ltd v E Jonas & Brothers* (1887) 18 QBD 459; *Palmer v Day & Sons* [1895] 2 QB 618, 622; *Re Taylor, ex p Norvell* [1910] 1 KB 562, 567; *Hiley v The Peoples' Prudential Assurance Co, Ltd* (1938) 60 CLR 468, 490, 497; *Gye v McIntyre* (1991) 171 CLR 609, 623; *Lloyds Bank NZA Ltd v National Safety Council* [1993] 2 VR 506, 510; *Re Parker* (1997) 80 FCR 1, 10. See also *Rose v Hart* (1818) 8 Taunt 499, 129 ER 477; *Ex parte Roy, re Sillence* (1877) 7 Ch D 70; *Re Winter, ex p Bolland* (1878) 8 Ch D 225; *Peacock v Anderson* (1878) 4 NZ Jur (NS) SC 67; *Lord (Trustee of) v Great Eastern Railway Co* [1908] 2 KB 54 (reversed on other grounds [1909] AC 109); *Ellis and Co's Trustee v Dixon-Johnson* [1925] AC 489; *Re Leeholme Stud Pty Ltd (in liq)* [1965] NSWR 1649; *Smith v Bridgend County BC* [2002] 1 AC 336, 351 para 36.

[2] For the Statutes of Set-off, see *Tony Lee Motors Ltd v M S MacDonald & Son (1974) Ltd* [1981] 2 NZLR 281, 288 and *Grant v NZMC Ltd* [1989] 1 NZLR 8, 11. For equitable set-off, see *Tony Lee Motors* at 211, and para 3.02 above.

[3] Compare Balcombe LJ in the Court of Appeal in *Stein v Blake* [1994] Ch 16, 22 ('measurable in money terms').

[4] See eg *Eberle's Hotels and Restaurant Co Ltd v E Jonas & Brothers* (1887) 18 QBD 459; *Ellis and Co's Trustee v Dixon-Johnson* [1925] AC 489 (shares readily available on the stock exchange).

be an 'account' as between goods and money, and no balance could be struck.'[5]
The second is that the requirement of money demands is inherent in the stipulation in the set-off section that 'the *sums* due from one party shall be set off against the *sums* due from the other'. In so far as the Statutes of Set-off are concerned, the requirement of money demands follows from the very basis of the Statutes, that there must be mutual debts.

Rolls Razor v Cox criticized

9.02 There is one case in which a set-off was allowed in respect of a claim to recover property. In *Rolls Razor Ltd v Cox*[6] a salesman employed by a company had been entrusted with goods for the purpose of sale. The company subsequently went into liquidation. When the liquidator of the company brought an action for the return of the goods, the Court of Appeal held that the salesman could retain them as a set-off against the company's indebtedness to him for retained commissions. For the purpose of the set-off the goods were valued at the price at which the salesman had been authorized to sell them. It has been suggested that the right enforced in the *Rolls Razor* case may be explicable as some sort of lien rather than a set-off,[7] but the question of a lien was specifically argued before and rejected by the Court of Appeal. It is clear from the judgments that the right in question was regarded as a set-off. The better view is that the *Rolls Razor* case was wrongly decided. In *Smith v Bridgend County BC*[8] Lord Hoffmann said that, in the absence of a lien or other security, a defendant could not retain an asset belonging to a plaintiff by way of set-off against a money claim. This comment was made in the context of equitable set-off, but the judgment suggests that it was thought to apply also to insolvency set-off.[9]

9.03 Lord Denning MR in the leading judgment in the *Rolls Razor* case relied on a comment by Gibbs CJ in 1818 in *Rose v Hart*,[10] to the effect that credit may be given for the purpose of the set-off section where there is a delivery of property with a direction to turn it into money. The Chief Justice however went on to speak in terms of setting off the 'debt' resulting from the direction to turn the property into money, and while it is true that on another occasion he said that credit is created when goods are deposited for the purpose of sale and not just when the goods are sold,[11] the set-off itself nonetheless related to the 'debt' arising from the receipt

---

[5] *Palmer v Day & Sons* [1895] 2 QB 618, 622. See also *Eberle's Hotels v Jonas* (1887) 18 QBD 457, 465, 467, 468, 469.
[6] [1967] 1 QB 552.
[7] Wood, *English and International Set-off* (1989) 564.
[8] [2002] 1 AC 336, 351 para 36.
[9] See [2002] 1 AC 336, 351 para 35. See also *Tony Lee Motors Ltd v M S MacDonald & Son (1974) Ltd* [1981] 2 NZLR 281 in the context of the Statutes of Set-off.
[10] (1818) 8 Taunt 499, 506, 129 ER 477, 480.
[11] *Graham v Russell* (1816) 3 Price 227, 231, 146 ER 244, 246.

of the money as a result of carrying out the directions. *Rose v Hart* is considered in greater detail later.[12] The point is there made that Gibbs CJ was concerned to limit the perception that the earlier decision of Lord Hardwicke in *Ex parte Deeze*[13] stood as authority for the proposition that there could be a set-off against goods. Lord Hardwicke himself later remarked in *Ex parte Ockenden*[14] that in *Ex parte Deeze* there had been evidence of a custom of the trade by which packers could retain goods, not only as security for the price of their work upon the goods, but also for the separate debts of the owner. In subsequent cases, however, *Ex parte Deeze* had been referred to as an authority on set-off,[15] and Gibbs CJ in his judgment in *Rose v Hart* was attempting to rationalize the decisions in those cases with the stipulation in the set-off section in the bankruptcy legislation of 1732[16] that 'one debt may be set against another'. In the cases in question the direction to turn the property into money had been carried out, so that in each case there was in fact a debt in existence when the account was to be taken. On the other hand, the debts were not in existence at the relevant date for determining rights of set-off, a problem that Gibbs CJ overcame in *Rose v Hart* by ascribing a wider meaning to mutual credits than to mutual debts. Therefore, a debt which arose after the relevant date could be brought into an account, provided that it was based upon a credit given before that date. Nevertheless, he still required a 'debt' at the taking of the account, so that 'one debt may be set against another' in accordance with the 1732 Act. A proper statement of the rule is that, when goods are deposited for sale, credit is given for any proceeds of sale that *in fact* are received. This is reflected in the marginal note to Moore's report of *Rose v Hart*,[17] that: 'In order to constitute a mutual credit, within 5 Geo 2, c 30, s 28, it must be confined to *pecuniary* demands on such credits only as in their nature will terminate in a debt.'

B. Repudiation, and Specific Performance

Consider that A has entered into a contract for the purchase of goods from B, B **9.04** being a creditor of A on another transaction, but prior to delivery the purchaser (A) goes into liquidation.

---

12 See paras 10.11–10.31 below.
13 (1748) 1 Atk 228, 26 ER 146.
14 (1754) 1 Atk 235, 237, 26 ER 151, 152.
15 See eg *French v Fenn* (1783) 3 Dougl 257, 99 ER 642; *Smith v Hodson* (1791) 4 TR 211, 100 ER 979. Compare *Olive v Smith* (1813) 5 Taunt 56, 128 ER 607.
16 (1732) 5 Geo II, c 30, s 28.
17 (1818) 2 Moore CP 547 (emphasis added).

Insolvency as a repudiation

9.05 Insolvency of itself generally does not terminate outstanding contracts to which the insolvent is a party.[18] Nor does it necessarily constitute a repudiation of the contracts so as to entitle the other contracting party to elect to treat the contract as terminated.[19] A repudiation may occur if insolvency is coupled with other circumstances. For example, insolvency may have the effect of putting it beyond the insolvent's power to perform his obligations under a contract.[20] Thus, an order that an insurance company be wound up because of insolvency has been said to constitute a repudiation by the company of its contracts of insurance, on the basis that the deficiency in the company's funds makes it impossible to pay claims in full.[21] Similarly, if a bank has discounted bills of exchange for a customer prior to the customer's insolvency, the customer has already obtained the benefit of the contract and only has an obligation to reimburse the bank, which he could not do in view of his insolvency.[22] Repudiation may also occur if the conduct of the insolvent or his trustee in bankruptcy shows that the contract has been abandoned.[23] In that regard the courts have indicated that, if one contracting party notifies the other that he is insolvent, that may be treated as a notice of repudiation if he does not also inform the other that he still intends to complete the contract.[24]

---

[18] See eg *Re Sneezum* (1876) 3 Ch D 463, 473; *Shipton Anderson & Co (1927) Ltd v Micks, Lambert & Co* [1936] 2 All ER 1032, 1037; *Official Receiver v Henn* (1981) 40 ALR 569, 572; *Re Palmdale Insurance Ltd* [1982] VR 921, 929.

[19] The ensuing discussion should be distinguished from the situation in which a contract in its terms is such that it is to remain in operation only so long as one of the parties continues in business, so that cessation of business consequent upon insolvency terminates the contract without giving rise to a liability for damages for breach of contract. See for example *Rhodes v Forwood* (1876) 1 App Cas 256 and *Re Arawa Dairy Co Ltd* [1938] NZLR 411, although compare *Reigate v Union Manufacturing Co (Ramsbottom) Ltd* [1918] 1 KB 592.

[20] See for example the comments of Cotton LJ in *Re Asphaltic Wood Pavement Co. Lee & Chapman's Case* (1885) 30 Ch D 216, 223–224 in relation to the obligation of the company in liquidation to maintain the street for a period of fifteen years. See also *Ogdens Ltd v Nelson* [1905] AC 109, in which the company had sold its business prior to going into voluntary liquidation.

[21] *Re National Benefit Assurance Co Ltd* [1924] 2 Ch 339, 343; *Re The Federal Building Assurance Co Ltd* (1934) 34 SR (NSW) 499, 506; *Hiley v The Peoples Prudential Assurance Co Ltd* (1938) 60 CLR 468, 493; *Re Palmdale Insurance Ltd* [1982] VR 921, 929. See also *Re Northern Counties of England Fire Insurance Co, Macfarlane's Claim* (1880) 17 Ch D 337, 341, but compare the comments of Lord Cairns in the *Albert Arbitration* (reported as a footnote to *Re English Assurance Co, Holdich's Case* (1872) LR 14 Eq 72). *Quaere* whether English courts would now reach the same conclusion in relation to insurance companies carrying on long-term business in view of the liquidator's statutory obligation to carry on the insurer's business so far as it consists of those contracts, with a view to its being transferred as a going concern to a person who may lawfully carry out those contracts. See the Financial Services and Markets Act 2000, s 376 and *MacGillivray on Insurance Law* (9th edn, 1997) 182 paras 7-68 and 7-69.

[22] *Baker v Lloyd's Bank Ltd* [1920] 2 KB 322, 326.

[23] As in *Morgan v Bain* (1874) LR 10 CP 15. See also *Lawrence v Knowles* (1839) 5 Bing (NC) 399, 132 ER 1152; *Re Tru-Grain Co Ltd* [1921] VLR 653.

[24] *Morgan v Bain* (1874) LR 10 CP 15, 25–26. Compare *Mess v Duffus and Co* (1901) 6 Com Cas 165, in which the notice was held not to constitute notice of intention not to perform the contract.

Generally though, in the absence of any such circumstances, the courts have shown a marked reluctance to conclude that insolvency of itself constitutes a repudiation of contracts that could return a profit for the insolvent's estate.[25] An example is the case of a contract for the sale of goods. The mere fact that the purchaser becomes insolvent before delivery of the goods is not considered to be a sufficient reason to entitle the vendor to treat the contract as rescinded.[26] In view of his precarious position the vendor is entitled to insist that the whole of the price be tendered to him before delivery, even if the sale was otherwise expressed to be on credit terms.[27] But the insolvency itself, without some additional circumstance, is not regarded as a repudiation of the contract. This is based upon a sound policy consideration, that the insolvent's beneficial contracts should be preserved for the benefit of the creditors.[28] If the contract can be performed at a profit, it would make good sense for the purchaser's trustee in bankruptcy to use the funds of the estate to pay the price and complete the contract.

Specific performance

If in a contract for the sale of goods the purchaser's trustee wishes to proceed with the contract and tenders the price, the vendor could not accept payment and refuse to deliver the goods as a set-off against a separate debt owing to him, since the contractual obligation to deliver is not a money obligation. The vendor nevertheless may adopt a different approach. He may decide that he would be better off if he repudiated the contract, on the premise that he would thereby incur a monetary damages liability to the purchaser which could be set off against the debt owing to him, and at the same time he would be able to retain the goods for sale elsewhere. In that regard it should not be an objection to a set-off that the damages liability would be incurred to the purchaser after the commencement of the bankruptcy, since the liability would have arisen out of a prior dealing between the parties.[29] Nor should it be an objection that the set-off would be based upon

9.06

---

[25] In addition to the cases cited in the next footnote, see *Brooke v Hewitt* (1796) 3 Ves Jun 253, 30 ER 997; *Re Tru-Grain Co Ltd* [1921] VLR 653, 656; *Lindley on Companies* (6th edn, 1902) vol 2, 1014; *Gore-Browne on Companies* (44th edn, looseleaf) para 34.3. See also *Jennings Trustee v King* [1952] 1 Ch 899; *Shipton, Anderson & Co (1927) Ltd v Micks, Lambert & Co* [1936] 2 All ER 1032, 1037.

[26] *Tolhurst v Associated Portland Cement Manufacturers (1900) Ltd* [1902] 2 KB 660 (esp at 671, referring to *Ex parte Chalmers, re Edwards* (1873) LR 8 Ch App 289 and *Morgan v Bain* (1874) LR 10 CP 15). Similarly, the insolvency of a vendor is not a sufficient reason to entitle the purchaser to put an end to the contract. See *Mess v Duffus and Co* (1901) 6 Com Cas 165.

[27] *Ex parte Chalmers, re Edwards* (1873) LR 8 Ch App 289. See also *Gunn v Bolckow, Vaughan & Co* (1875) LR 10 Ch App 491, 501; *Re Phoenix Bessemer Steel Co* (1876) 4 Ch D 108, 112, 114; *Re Sneezum* (1876) 3 Ch D 463, 473–474; *Grice v Richardson* (1877) 3 App Cas 319. This principle has been codified in the sale of goods legislation. See the Sale of Goods Act 1979, s 41(1)(c).

[28] *Ex parte Chalmers, re Edwards* (1873) LR 8 Ch App 289, 294.

[29] See para 8.43 above.

the vendor's own conduct in deliberately breaching the contract for the express purpose of obtaining a set-off.[30] Ultimately, however, the vendor's prospect of success may depend upon whether the purchaser's trustee is able to obtain an order for specific performance of the contract. If specific performance is available, the vendor could be compelled to perform the obligation under the contract to deliver the goods and, since this obligation is not a money obligation, it could not be the subject of a set-off.

9.07   If the article the subject of the sale is unique, the court, subject to other discretionary considerations, ordinarily would decree specific performance. On the other hand, if the contract concerns goods readily available in the market at an ascertainable market price, the courts incline against specific relief. It has been suggested that in such a case specific performance is not available under any circumstances.[31] However that view seems contrary to principle, and it is of doubtful validity.[32] Specific performance is denied, not on an absolute jurisdictional basis, but rather because in the vast majority of cases damages are an adequate remedy,[33] this being the original foundation of the decree of specific performance.[34] As a corollary, if in a particular case damages at law would not be an adequate remedy, the court in principle should have a discretion to grant specific relief.[35] There is nevertheless a difficulty in relation to contracts for the sale of unascertained goods. The Sale of Goods Act 1979, section 52 expressly provides for specific performance of a contract to sell specific or ascertained goods, and Atkin LJ in *Re Wait*[36] said of the corresponding provision in earlier legislation[37] that it set out the full extent of equitable remedies in the context of contracts for the sale of goods, so that specific performance is not available where the goods are unascertained. Comments by Lord Brandon of Oakbrook in delivering the judgment of the House of Lords in *Leigh and Sillavan Ltd v Aliakmon Shipping Co Ltd*[38] suggest that he would have agreed with the view expressed by Atkin LJ in re-

---

[30] See para 8.74 above.

[31] *Price v Strange* [1978] 1 Ch 337, 369, *per* Buckley LJ.

[32] It is questioned in Jones and Goodhart, *Specific Performance* (2nd edn, 1996) 278. See also the more cautious approach of Goff LJ in *Price v Strange* [1978] 1 Ch 337, 359.

[33] *Adderley v Dixon* (1824) 1 Sim & St 607, 610, 57 ER 239, 240; *Falcke v Gray* (1859) 4 Drewry 651, 657–658, 62 ER 250, 252; *Re Clarke* (1887) 36 Ch D 348, 352; *Thomas Borthwick & Sons (Australasia) Ltd v South Otago Freezing Co Ltd* [1978] 1 NZLR 538, 548, PC ('A contract for the sale of goods obtainable on the market will not *normally* be specifically enforced' (emphasis added)); Spry, *Equitable Remedies* (6th edn, 2001) 55 n 18, 65–67.

[34] *Harnet v Yeilding* (1805) 2 Sch & Lef 549, 553, *per* Lord Redesdale.

[35] See in this regard *Sky Petroleum Ltd v VIP Petroleum Ltd* [1974] 1 WLR 576 (esp at 578–579).

[36] [1927] 1 Ch 606, 630.

[37] Sale of Goods Act 1893, s 52.

[38] [1986] 1 AC 785, 812.

lation to specific performance.[39] On the other hand, Lord Atkin's view has been criticized by commentators.[40]

Recent amendments to the Sale of Goods Act 1979[41] have ameliorated to some ex- **9.08**
tent the position in relation to unascertained goods. The definition of 'specific goods' in section 61 has been amended so as to include within the meaning of that term an undivided share, specified as a fraction or percentage, of goods identified and agreed on at the time a contract of sale was made. This has the effect that, where a specified fraction or percentage of an identified and agreed bulk is sold, the agreement may be specifically enforced pursuant to section 52.[42] The amendment does not apply however when the agreement relates to a sale of a specified quantity to be taken from an identified bulk, as opposed to a fraction or a percentage, although as a result of another amendment to the Act[43] the buyer in such a case, once he pays the price, becomes the owner of an undivided share in the bulk.[44] If on the other hand there is no identified bulk, the reforms have no application.

The adequacy of damages

In determining whether damages are an adequate remedy, it is not simply a mat- **9.09**
ter of considering whether the amount of the loss can be adequately quantified and expressed in a judgment. This is apparent from the decision of the House of Lords in *Beswick v Beswick*.[45] The defendant had breached a contract with the plaintiff to make periodic payments to a third party. A judgment for nominal damages arguably would have constituted an accurate reflection of the plaintiff's own loss, but it would not have been adequate to meet the justice of the case. Accordingly, specific performance was granted. The question is whether a judgment for damages would put the claimant in a situation as beneficial to him as if the agreement were specifically enforced,[46] or, in other words, whether damages would provide a 'complete remedy'.[47] Thus, the courts have indicated that it is

---

[39] See also *Re Goldcorp Exchange Ltd* [1995] 1 AC 74, 90–91 in relation to the question of equitable title. In New South Wales, compare *Electrical Enterprises Retail Pty Ltd v Rodgers* (1989) 15 NSWLR 473, 492–493, although the legislation in issue differed from that in England. *Re Wait* has been followed in Victoria. See *King v Greig* [1931] VLR 413, 438–439.

[40] Treitel, 'Specific Performance in the Sale of Goods' [1966] JBL 211, 222–4; Jones and Goodhart, *Specific Performance* (2nd edn, 1996) 147–50. See also Spry, *Equitable Remedies* (6th edn, 2001) 54–5; Pollock, 'Re Wait' (1927) 43 LQR 293; Pettit, *Equity and the Law of Trusts* (9th edn, 2001) 633 n 19.

[41] See the Sale of Goods (Amendment) Act 1995.

[42] See *Benjamin's Sale of Goods* (5th edn, 1997) 967 para 17-090.

[43] See s 20A, introduced by the Sale of Goods (Amendment) Act 1995.

[44] *Benjamin's Sale of Goods* (5th edn, 1997), 967 para 17-090

[45] [1968] AC 58.

[46] *Harnett v Yeilding* (1805) 2 Sch & Lef 549, 556; Spry, *Equitable Remedies* (6th edn, 2001) 59–60.

[47] *Adderley v Dixon* (1824) 1 Sim & St 607, 610, 57 ER 239, 240, *per* Sir John Leach.

appropriate to consider whether the defendant for any reason is unlikely to satisfy a judgment for damages.[48] In that regard, if the reason that the defendant is unlikely to satisfy the judgment is insolvency, and he has other creditors, the court may refuse to grant relief on the basis that specific performance would have the effect of preferring the claimant over the general body of creditors, if in fact there is no other reason apart from inadequacy of damages for granting relief.[49] In the absence of that countervailing circumstance, however, the actual amount that the claimant is likely to receive in his hands as a result of a judgment for damages, in comparison to what his position would be if specific performance were granted, is a relevant factor.

9.10 In the situation posited,[50] an award of damages would not constitute an adequate remedy to the insolvent purchaser's estate, even where the goods are readily available in the market at an ascertainable price. If the vendor were to perform his obligation and deliver the goods, the estate would have the full benefit of the contract, and at the same time would only have to pay a dividend on the separate debt owing to the vendor. If, however, the purchaser is remitted to a claim for damages against the vendor after the vendor's repudiation, the vendor's liability for damages ordinarily should be capable of set-off against the debt, given that it is not an objection to a set-off that the vendor may have deliberately breached a contract in order to obtain a set-off. The allowance of a set-off where none otherwise would be available may have a considerable effect on the funds available for distribution to the purchaser's creditors, and on that basis an award of damages would not put the purchaser and his creditors in a situation as beneficial as if the contract in question were specifically performed. As a matter of principle there is much to be said for the view that specific performance should be available in this situation, subject to other relevant discretionary considerations.

C. Foreign Exchange Contracts[51]

Introduction

9.11 The requirement of commensurability has come into prominence in recent years in the context of foreign exchange contracts.

---

[48] *Hodgson v Duce* (1856) 2 Jur NS 1014; *Evans Marshall & Co Ltd v Bertola SA* [1973] 1 WLR 349, 380–381; *The Oakworth* [1975] 1 Lloyd's Rep 581, 583. See also Horack, 'Insolvency and Specific Performance' (1918) 31 Harvard Law Review 702; Spry, *Equitable Remedies* (6th edn, 2001) 68.

[49] *Re Wait* [1927] 1 Ch 606. See also *Hewett v Court* (1983) 149 CLR 639, 658; Spry, *Equitable Remedies* (6th edn, 2001) 55 n 20, 68–9.

[50] See para 9.06 above.

[51] The following discussion is adapted from Derham, 'Set-off and Netting of Foreign Exchange Contracts in the Liquidation of a Counterparty' [1991] JBL 463.

For the sake of simplicity, consider the following situation. A bank has entered **9.12** into two foreign exchange contracts with a customer or with another bank (referred to as the 'counterparty').[52] In the first contract entered into on, say, 1 September, the bank has agreed to provide an amount expressed in currency 1 to the counterparty in consideration of the counterparty's agreement to provide an amount expressed in currency 2. Performance of the contract is to take place on 31 December. Pursuant to a second contract, entered into on 1 October, the counterparty has agreed to provide an amount expressed in currency 3 to the bank in consideration of the bank's agreement to provide an amount expressed in currency 4. This contract is also to be performed on 31 December. However, on 15 November the counterparty goes into liquidation.

In the event of the liquidation of a counterparty, the liquidator could be expected **9.13** to disclaim any foreign exchange contract which, because of movements in exchange rates, is considered to be unprofitable,[53] and keep on foot any contract which is profitable to the counterparty. If a contract is disclaimed, a person who sustains consequential loss or damage is deemed by the Insolvency Act[54] to be a creditor of the company to the extent of the loss, and accordingly may prove for the loss in the liquidation. If the liquidator of a counterparty were to disclaim one contract as unprofitable but elect to perform another profitable contract, the bank would wish to set off its obligation arising under the continuing contract against its damages claim against the counterparty in liquidation arising as a result of the disclaimer. The question of where the bank would stand in the event of a liquidation of the counterparty is of paramount concern to banks. It affects dealing limits that banks can set for their counterparties. In addition, where the bank requires cash cover (for example, a margin deposit) as 'security' in the event of default by the counterparty, it may affect the amount of cover or margin deposit required. It also may be important for capital adequacy purposes, that is, in the determination of the amount of capital that the bank is required by the relevant central bank to have to cover its risk assets.

The nature of foreign money obligation

In considering the question, a critical issue is the nature of the foreign money **9.14** obligation under a foreign exchange contract.

The traditional view, as expressed by Dr Mann,[55] is that foreign money may func- **9.15** tion either as money or as a commodity, depending on the circumstances. He said

---

[52] Often there will be a large number of contracts with a particular counterparty involving different currencies and performance dates.

[53] Pursuant to the Insolvency Act 1986, s 178. In Australia, see the Corporations Act 2001 (Cth), s 568.

[54] Insolvency Act 1986, s 178(6).

[55] Mann, *The Legal Aspect of Money* (5th edn, 1992) 191 *et seq.*

that foreign money should be regarded as money where it serves monetary functions, for example in the case of a foreign currency debt.[56] However, in the particular situation in which foreign money is dealt in and quoted on the foreign exchange market, he considered that it is the object of commercial intercourse and therefore is a commodity.[57] In other words, it is similar to a contract to deliver so many tons of wheat. Nussbaum[58] and Rabel[59] expressed similar views. Nussbaum justified the conclusion by reference to the distinction between acting as a measure and being measured, between *mensura* and *mensuratum*. Money in a general sense is a standard or measure of the value of goods and services.[60] As a corollary, it is correct to say that the value of goods and services is measured by reference to money. Indeed, money has been described as the common denominator of value.[61] But while money is a measure, it is an abstract unit of measurement (in England, the pound sterling) which cannot be precisely defined.[62] Money as such is not measured by anything else. Money is *mensura*, not *mensuratum*.[63] Yet, when foreign money is sold or exchanged it is being measured. It is measured by its fluctuating exchange value against the fixed unit of account in which domestic money is denominated, the rate of exchange of a foreign currency being the price of that currency in terms of a country's own currency.[64] According to Nussbaum,[65]

---

[56] See particularly the comments of Lord Radcliffe in *Re United Railways of Havana and Regla Warehouses Ltd* [1961] AC 1007, 1059–1060.

[57] See Mann (n 55 above) 191. This view is not affected by the decision of the House of Lords in *Miliangos v George Frank (Textiles) Ltd* [1976] AC 443. See Derham "Set-off and Netting of Foreign Exchange Contracts in the Liquidation of a Counterparty" [1991] JBL 463, 475–477.

[58] See Nussbaum, *Money in the Law National and International* (1950) 340–4 for a discussion of foreign money in the context of a foreign currency debt, and at 24 (and see also at 319) in relation to foreign money functioning as a commodity when it is purchased or exchanged on the foreign exchange market.

[59] Rabel, *The Conflict of Laws* (2nd edn, 1964) vol 3, 26.

[60] Nussbaum (n 58 above) 14, referred to in Mann (n 55 above) 49.

[61] Nussbaum (n 58 above) 11.

[62] Mann (n 55 above) 49, 86. As Nussbaum (n 58 above) 14 put it in relation to the United States dollar, 'the dollar concept existing at any given time is as little susceptible of definition as, say, the concept of "blue".'

[63] Nussbaum (n 58 above) 28, and see also the discussion in Mann (n 55 above) 43–9. Under the Bretton Woods Agreement, the 'par value' of the currency of each member was expressed in terms of gold, in the sense that the par value determined the price for the purchase and sale of gold. See Mann (n 55 above) 33–6. It is therefore correct to say that the par value constituted a measure. See Mann (n 55 above) 46. That system effectively had ceased to apply by 1973. See *Lively Ltd v City of Munich* [1976] 1 WLR 1004, 1010–1013.

[64] See Mann (n 55 above) 61.

[65] Nussbaum said (n 58 above) 24 that: 'in special situations pieces of money are dealt with as commodities. This happens mainly in the market of foreign exchanges. Ever since there has been a theory of money, it has been recognized that money may have a 'second use',—namely, to be purchased or exchanged. In the language of Thomas Aquinas, money, if sold or exchanged, is 'measured, not a measure;' '*mensuratum*,' not '*mensura*'. Its intrinsic or exchange value as distinct from the extrinsic or nominal (face) value is controlling in the situation. The latter value is a matter of the law; the former is the result of economic conditions. While the intrinsic value is subject to fluctuations, the extrinsic one is invariable.'

when foreign money is measured in that manner it has the character of a commodity.[66]

There is support for the view that foreign money in the context of a foreign **9.16** exchange contract is a commodity.[67] It is consistent with references to foreign exchange contracts in a number of cases in terms of a sale and purchase,[68] although, if the obligation on both sides of the contract is a foreign money obligation, the contract would be more appropriately described as one of exchange, similar to a barter. In *Drexel Burnham Lambert International NV v El Nasr*[69] Staughton J described Swiss francs the subject of forward contracts of sale and purchase as a commodity, and in New South Wales Lee J referred to the opinions of Mann and Nussbaum with evident approval when he held that a foreign exchange contract that made provision for physical delivery was a commodity agreement for the purposes of the Futures Industries Code formerly applicable in that jurisdiction.[70] While 'commodity' admittedly had a particular definition in the Code,[71] his Honour said that: 'it is a natural use of the word to apply it to foreign currency in circumstances in which it is dealt with in commercial transactions of the kind under consideration'.[72] On another occasion Lord Radcliffe in the House of

---

[66] That should not be the case, however, in relation to the periodic payment obligations that arise under a currency and interest rate swap. See Derham, 'Set-off and Netting of Foreign Exchange Contracts in the Liquidation of a Counterparty' [1991] JBL 463, 468–9.

The concept of acting as a measure of the value of goods and services is a general function of money, and Nussbaum's thesis would not require that, if in a particular situation 'money' is not being used specifically for that purpose, it is not money. This would be the case, for example, when money is transferred by way of gift. But where foreign money is being measured, Nussbaum considered that in that circumstance it is not functioning as money. Further, the notion that foreign money when sold or exchanged is measured against domestic money should be distinguished from the situation in which parties have agreed that what is admittedly a foreign currency debt should be converted into domestic money at a specified exchange rate for certain purposes, for example because payment is to be made in domestic money, or in order to ascertain whether security 'top up' is required. The measurement as against domestic money is applied to the debt, which itself is not money. See Mann, *The Legal Aspect of Money* (5th edn, 1992) 5 in relation to bank accounts.

[67] The following authorities are in addition to cases which have dealt with money in a bag, or specific coins. See for example *Taylor v Plumer* (1815) 3 M & S 562, 105 ER 721; *Moss v Hancock* [1899] 2 QB 111.

[68] *Re British American Continental Bank Ltd. Goldzieher and Penso's Claim* [1922] 2 Ch 575, 586, *per* Warrington LJ ('The subjects of these contracts for sale and purchase were sums of foreign currency'); *Bank of India v Patel* [1982] 1 Lloyd's Rep 506, 508, 509, and on appeal [1983] 2 Lloyd's Rep 298, 299, 302; *Isaac Naylor & Sons Ltd v New Zealand Co-operative Wool Marketing Association Ltd* [1981] 1 NZLR 361, 366.

[69] [1986] 1 Lloyd's Rep 356.

[70] *Shoreline Currencies (Aust) Pty Ltd v Corporate Affairs Commission (NSW)* (1986) 10 ACLR 847. See also *Carragreen Currency Corporation Pty Ltd v Corporate Affairs Commission (NSW)* (1986) 11 ACLR 298; *Corporate Affairs Commission (NSW) v Lombard Nash International Pty Ltd* (1986) 11 ACLR 566, 569 ('there is a bet made on the relative price of a commodity, such as *currency*, gold or platinum' (emphasis added)).

[71] 'Commodity' was defined in s 4 of the Futures Industries Code as 'a thing that is capable of delivery pursuant to an agreement for its delivery; or . . . an instrument creating or evidencing a thing in action.' See now the definition in the Corporations Act 2001 (Cth), s 9.

[72] (1986) 10 ACLR 847, 855 (emphasis added).

Lords[73] recognized that there is a distinction between, on the one hand, a contract to pay foreign money abroad in satisfaction of a debt and, on the other, 'a contract to deliver foreign currency in this country or abroad or a true exchange contract', which he defined as a contract to exchange the currency of one country for the currency of another. He specifically rejected the view that foreign currency debts payable abroad give rise to an obligation to deliver a commodity as opposed to an obligation to pay money. On the other hand he seems to have regarded foreign exchange contracts as contracts for the delivery of a commodity. More recently, Austin J recognized the distinction in the New South Wales Supreme Court:[74]

> Where the foreign currency functions as money, an English or Australian court is likely to regard the legal character of the obligation as being inherently identical with an obligation to pay a sum of domestic money. But if the foreign money is the object of commercial intercourse, as in a typical foreign exchange contract and certain currency futures contracts, it is likely to be treated as a commodity. This approach comes closest to reconciling the case law, while producing sensible commercial results.

Set-off consequences of the characterization of the obligation

9.17 If the foreign money obligation in a foreign exchange contract is not a money obligation, the set-off consequences may differ depending on which of the parties has that obligation. The situation posited is that a contract has been disclaimed by the counterparty's liquidator because it is considered to be unprofitable. As a result the bank has a damages claim against the counterparty which may be proved in the liquidation. The liquidator however has not disclaimed a second contract, because this contract is considered to be profitable from the counterparty's point of view. In view of the counterparty's insolvency, the bank would not be obliged to perform its obligation under the second contract until the counterparty has first performed its own obligation, despite any term of the contract that may suggest otherwise.[75] If the liquidator accordingly makes available the requisite amount of the currency in question, the bank would wish to set off its resulting obligation to perform its side of the contract against the damages claim that it has against the counterparty arising from the disclaimer of the first contract.

9.18 Consider first that the counterparty has the foreign money obligation, while the bank's obligation is to pay a sum expressed in sterling. The bank in this circumstance ordinarily should be entitled to a set-off in the counterparty's liquidation, since it has a money obligation that arose out of a contract entered into before the liquidation. This should be so notwithstanding the decision of Watkin Williams J in *Ince Hall Rolling Mills Co Ltd v The Douglas Forge Co.*[76] In that case the

---

[73] *Re United Railways of Havana and Regla Warehouses Ltd* [1961] AC 1007, 1059–1060.
[74] *Daewoo Australia Pty Ltd v Suncorp-Metway Ltd* (2000) 48 NSWLR 692, 702 para 33.
[75] See *Ex parte Chalmers, re Edwards* (1873) LR 8 Ch App 289, and para 9.05 above.
[76] (1882) 8 QBD 179.

liquidator of a supplier delivered goods to a purchaser pursuant to a contract that had been entered into before the liquidation, and it was held that the purchaser was not entitled to a set-off in respect of its resulting liability for the price. The better view however is that the *Ince Hall* case was wrongly decided,[77] and that a bank with a sterling liability on a foreign exchange contract which becomes due and payable after the counterparty's liquidation should be able to employ that liability in a set-off in the liquidation.

Alternatively, the bank may have the foreign money obligation. In such a case, if **9.19** the obligation is not a money obligation,[78] the requirement of commensurability would mean that it could not be employed in a set-off in the counterparty's liquidation. There would not be a sum 'due' for the purpose of the insolvency set-off section. Nor would the fact that the obligation nevertheless has a readily ascertainable value affect that conclusion. In cases concerned with a claim for the return of specific property, there have been instances in which the courts accepted that the property had a particular value, but it was nevertheless held that the value could not form the basis of a set-off.[79]

The possibility that there may not be a set-off in a liquidation in relation to for- **9.20** eign exchange transactions has caused consternation to participants in the foreign exchange markets, and various arguments have been put forward as to why that conclusion may not follow.[80]

A recent view—*Camdex v Bank of Zambia*

In England this may no longer be an issue, however. In *Camdex International Ltd* **9.21** *v Bank of Zambia*[81] the Court of Appeal rejected the view that the foreign money obligation under a foreign exchange contract is not a money obligation. Simon Brown LJ commented:[82]

> When indeed one asks for what purpose it is sought to categorise foreign exchange transactions variously as commodity or as money transactions one is lost for an answer. What in other words is the point of the distinction . . . Of course if one is concerned with rare coins or the manufacture of bank notes or something of that

---

[77] See paras 13.32–13.51 below.

[78] Whether or not it is an obligation to deliver a commodity. See Derham, 'Set-off and Netting of Foreign Exchange Contracts in the Liquidation of a Counterparty' [1991] JBL 463, 470–5.

[79] See, for example, *Eberle's Hotels and Restaurant Co Ltd v E Jonas & Brothers* (1887) 18 QBD 459; *Ellis and Co's Trustee v Dixon-Johnson* [1925] AC 489 (shares readily available on the stock exchange).

[80] See generally Derham, 'Set-off and Netting of Foreign Exchange Contracts in the Liquidation of a Counterparty' [1991] JBL 463, and Wood, *English and International Set-off* (1989) 339–42. See also Wood, 'Netting Agreements in Organised and Private Markets' in Kingsford-Smith (ed), *Current Developments in Banking and Finance* (1989) 1; Wood and Terray, 'Foreign Exchange Netting in France and England' International Financial Law Review, October 1989, 18.

[81] [1997] 6 Bank LR 43.

[82] [1997] 6 Bank LR 43, 51–52.

kind, money may indeed be a commodity rather than a medium of exchange. But where, as is the usual case, the obligation in question is simply the payment of a stipulated sum in a stipulated currency, then, whether that obligation arises from a loan, or any other contract or set of circumstances, it is an obligation properly described as one of debt.

Similarly Phillips LJ said:[83]

> In my judgment, where a contract expressly provides for the payment of a sum in a foreign currency, the obligation is a money obligation and breach of it gives rise primarily to a claim in debt, whether the obligation is by way of repayment of money loaned, payment for goods or services or payment for other currencies.
>
> So far as the last type of contract is concerned, I recognise that an exchange transaction is *sui generis*, but its true nature is the incurring of mutual money obligations, not the barter of commodities.

The analysis in the *Camdex* case has been criticized,[84] but if it is followed it would provide greater certainty to participants in foreign exchange markets.

9.22 But even if the *Camdex* case is not followed, a properly drafted netting agreement may provide protection to a bank against the liquidation of a counterparty. Netting agreements are considered later.[85]

---

[83] [1997] 6 Bank LR 43, 57.
[84] Brindle and Cox (eds), *Law of Bank Payments* (2nd edn, 1999) 29–33.
[85] See paras 16.28–16.42 below.

10

TRUST FUNDS

A. Introduction

The subject of discussion in this chapter is the question whether, and if so under **10.01** what circumstances, the obligation of a person who holds a fund impressed with a trust to account for the trust fund may be the subject of a set-off against a debt owing to him in his personal capacity. It should be distinguished from the situation in which a beneficiary of a trust is obliged to contribute to the trust fund. That situation is not one of set-off, but rather of the application of a principle known as the rule in *Cherry v Boultbee*,[1] which is considered later.[2]

Dissipation of the trust fund

It is assumed in the following discussion that the trustee has retained the trust **10.02** fund or its traceable proceeds. If a trustee in breach of trust has dissipated the trust assets, the court may order the trustee to restore the trust estate, either by restoring assets that have been lost or by paying sufficient compensation to the trust estate to put it back to what it would have been had the breach not been committed.[3] The better view is that the trustee could not set off against that obligation a separate debt owing to him in his personal capacity by a beneficiary. The obligation to restore the trust estate and the claim against the beneficiary personally would not be mutual.[4] Alternatively, the court may order the trustee to pay

---

[1] (1839) 4 My & Cr 442, 41 ER 171.
[2] See ch 14 below.
[3] See the discussion in *Target Holdings Ltd v Redferns* [1996] AC 421, 434. See also *Maguire v Makaronis* (1997) 188 CLR 449, 469–470.
[4] Compare *Baillie v Edwards* (1848) 2 HLC 74, 9 ER 1020. See para 6.19 above.

compensation directly to a beneficiary. An order in that form ordinarily is appropriate in the case of a beneficiary who is absolutely entitled to the trust fund.[5] The obligation to pay compensation for breach of trust is an equitable debt,[6] and as such it may constitute a debt for the purpose of a statutory set-off. In the circumstances however a set-off may be unjust.[7] In particular, if the beneficiary is insolvent, it is suggested that the trustee should not be permitted a set-off based upon his own breach of trust, in circumstances where the trustee otherwise would have had to account for the trust fund to the beneficiary and would have been confined to a dividend on his separate claim against the beneficiary,[8] since in comparison to that result a set-off would mean that the trustee would profit from the breach.[9] If in that circumstance the court were to order the trustee to restore the trust fund, the order should preclude a set-off,[10] although an order in that form ordinarily is not made in the case of a bare trust, as opposed to a traditional trust in which there is no one beneficiary who is absolutely entitled to the trust property.[11]

B. Insolvency Set-off

10.03 If T holds a sum on trust for B, and B becomes bankrupt, T must account for the trust fund to B's trustee in bankruptcy without a set-off in respect of an independent debt owing by B to T in T's personal capacity.[12] Thus, a sum held on trust by a solicitor for a bankrupt client cannot be the subject of a set-off in bankruptcy,[13] and similarly an insurance broker is not entited to a set-off in respect of subroga-

---

[5] *Target Holdings Ltd v Redferns* [1996] AC 421, 434–435. Lord Browne-Wilkinson emphasized however (at 435) that he would not rule out in this circumstance the possibility of an order to reconstitute the trust fund.

[6] *Ex parte Adamson, re Collie* (1878) 8 Ch D 807, 819; *Webb v Stenton* (1883) 11 QBD 518, 530; *Wickstead v Browne* (1992) 30 NSWLR 1, 14–15; *Goodwin v Duggan* (1996) 41 NSWLR 158, 166. See also para 8.72 above. Compare *Space Investments Ltd v CIBC* [1986] 1 WLR 1072, 1074.

[7] See *Reed v Oury* [2002] EWHC 369 (Ch) at para 62, but compare *Taylor v Taylor* (1875) LR 20 Eq 155, which is considered in para 10.09 below.

[8] See para 10.03 below.

[9] See para 8.72 above.

[10] See above

[11] *Target Holdings Ltd v Redferns* [1996] AC 421, 434–436.

[12] In addition to the cases referred to below, see the special purpose payment cases referred to in paras 10.43–10.54 below. See also *Re The United Ports and General Insurance Co, ex p The Etna Insurance Co* (1877) 46 LJ Ch 403, 406; *Elgood v Harris* [1896] 2 QB 491, 494; *Re McMahon and Canada Permanent Trust Co* (1979) 108 DLR (3d) 71; *Lloyds Bank NZA Ltd v National Safety Council of Australia* [1993] 2 VR 506. In *Hamilton v Commonwealth Bank of Australia* (1992) 9 ACSR 90, 108 Hodgson J queried whether the principle applies in Australia in relation to moneys held by a creditor as fiduciary for the debtor, following *Gye v McIntyre* (1991) 171 CLR 609. It is suggested that the principle is not affected by that case.

[13] *Wright v Watson* (1883) Cab & El 171, and see also *Stumore v Campbell & Co* [1892] 1 QB 314 (Statutes of Set-off). Compare *Shand v M J Atkinson Ltd* [1966] NZLR 551, which was concerned with the construction of the Law Practitioners Act 1955 (NZ).

tion moneys held on trust for a bankrupt underwriter.[14] In an early case,[15] a creditor of a bankrupt was indebted to one of the assignees in bankruptcy in the assignee's private capacity. When the creditor himself later became bankrupt, the fact of the assignee's trusteeship was held to preclude a set-off in relation to the dividend payable to the creditor and the creditor's own indebtedness to the assignee. The denial of a set-off in these cases may be explained on the ground of lack of mutuality[16] in that, while T has a personal claim against the bankrupt, the bankrupt has a claim *in specie* against a trust fund. It is true that a trustee is referred to as an equitable debtor,[17] and the interest of a beneficiary has been described as a right *in personam* against the trustee.[18] The prevailing view, however, is that a beneficiary has a proprietary interest in the trust assets,[19] and it is that proprietary interest which destroys mutuality for the purpose of a set-off.

In considering the principle, two points should be noted. The first is that it applies **10.04** when the question of set-off arises in relation to an obligation to account for a trust fund to which the beneficiary of the trust is absolutely entitled. If on the other hand a creditor has an interest by way of security in a fund in the hands of the debtor,[20] a set-off in some circumstances may occur against the secured debt.[21] To the extent of the set-off the secured debt would be paid, and to that extent the fund would be released from the security.[22] The second point is that the obligation to account for a trust fund, while not susceptible to a set-off under the insolvency set-off section, may be the subject of contractual deductions agreed between the parties in relation to other sums payable under the agreement,[23] or indeed arising

---

[14] See *Elgood v Harris* [1896] 2 QB 491, although in that case the trust moneys in any event were received after the bankruptcy.

[15] *Ex parte White* (1742) 1 Atk 90, 26 ER 59, and see also *Ex parte Bailey, re Howarth* (1840) 1 Mont D & De G 263. Compare *Ex parte Nockold* (1734), unreported but noted in Cooke, *The Bankrupt Laws* (8th edn, 1823) vol 1, 509, which has not been followed. See *Re Henley, Thurgood & Co* (1863) 11 WR 1021, 1022.

[16] *National Westminster Bank Ltd v Halesowen Presswork and Assemblies Ltd* [1972] AC 785, 821; *Lloyds Bank NZA Ltd v National Safety Council of Australia* [1993] 2 VR 506, 515. Mutuality is not always necessary for equitable set-off, however. See para 4.48 above. Therefore, depending on the circumstances, the fact of a trust may not be fatal to that form of set-off. Similarly a trustee may have a lien on the trust fund for his expenses. See *Obaray v Gateway (London) Ltd* [2001] L & TR at para 53. In *Baillie v Edwards* (1848) 2 HLC 74, 9 ER 1020, 20 Baillie was not personally liable but rather there was a right of indemnity from his estate, and the circumstances were held to give rise to an equitable set-off. See para 6.19 above.

[17] *Webb v Stenton* (1883) 11 QBD 518, 526. See also para 10.02 above.

[18] Most notably, by Professor Maitland. See Maitland, *Equity* (2nd edn (rev by Brunyate), 1936) 106 *et seq.*

[19] *Archer-Shee v Garland* [1931] AC 212; Pettit, *Equity and the Law of Trusts* (9th edn, 2001) 78–81; Meagher, Gummow and Lehane, *Equity Doctrines and Remedies* (3rd edn, 1992) 96–8.

[20] A trust and a charge are distinct institutions. See *Associated Alloys Pty Ltd v ACN 001 452 106 Pty Ltd* (2000) 202 CLR 588, 595–596 paras 5 and 6.

[21] See para 6.120 *ff* above.

[22] *Re ILG Travel Ltd* [1995] 2 BCLC 128, 158–160. See para 6.122 above.

[23] *Re ILG Travel Ltd* [1995] 2 BCLC 128, 157–158; *Obaray v Gateway (London) Ltd* [2001] L & TR 20. See also *Re Tout and Finch Ltd* [1954] 1 WLR 178, 186.

on other accounts.[24] The deductions allowed by the contract operate to limit the amount to which the beneficiary is entitled under the trust.[25]

Express stipulation for a trust

10.05 In *Re ILG Travel Ltd*,[26] Jonathan Parker J suggested that a stipulation in a contract between T and B, that T is to hold a sum on trust for B, would not preclude a set-off in B's liquidation against a debt owing by B to T under the contract, the reason being that, if insolvency set-off is mandatory and cannot be contracted out of,[27] the parties could not avoid that result by simply using the word 'trust'. If however a trust has been established,[28] prima facie the principle which precludes a set-off against a trust fund should apply. There is a lack of mutuality, and it should not matter for that analysis whether the trust in issue is an express trust or a trust arising by operation of law. Nor should it matter for mutuality whether the demands have their source in the same contract or different contracts.[29] It is not simply a case of the parties purporting to contract out of the operation of the insolvency set-off section where the section otherwise would apply. Rather, the requirements of the section are not satisfied.

An exception

10.06 There is an apparent exception to the general principle which precludes a set-off against an obligation to account for a trust fund in the situation in which property has been deposited with another with directions or authority to turn it into money. This is considered below in the context of a discussion of *Rose v Hart*.[30]

C. Statutes of Set-off

10.07 Set-off under the Statutes of Set-off is subject to the same principle. If T is a trustee of a fund for B, and he is sued by B for payment, T may not deduct a debt owing

---

[24] See *Re McMahon and Canada Permanent Trust Co* (1979) 108 DLR (3d) 71, 77–78; *Lloyds Bank NZA Ltd v National Safety Council of Australia* [1993] 2 VR 506, 510, 513, 514.

[25] It has been suggested that the agreement should be construed as creating a charge on the fund, so that the trustee is not a bare trustee but one whose trust obligation applies only to the balance remaining after deducting the amount due to him. See Goode, *Principles of Corporate Insolvency Law* (2nd edn, 1997) 191, and *Obaray v Gateway (London) Ltd* [2001] L & TR 20. Compare that view with the analysis in *Associated Alloys Pty Ltd v ACN 001 452 106 Pty Ltd* (2000) 202 CLR 588.

[26] [1995] 2 BCLC 128, 160–161.

[27] See para 6.71 *ff* above.

[28] See [1995] 2 BCLC 128, 156–157. An entitlement to mix money with one's own is usually regarded as being inconsistent with a trust. See para 10.46 below.

[29] Compare [1995] 2 BCLC 128, 161. See paras 11.01–11.02 above.

[30] (1818) 8 Taunt 499, 129 ER 477. See paras 10.11–10.31 below.

to him in his personal capacity by B.[31] Ordinarily equity will act by analogy with the right of set-off available at law under the Statutes of Set-off if the demands are equitably, but not legally, mutual.[32] As in the case of insolvency set-off, however, when the claim is for payment of a trust fund there is a lack of mutuality.[33] On the one hand the trustee has a personal claim against the beneficiary, and on the other the beneficiary has a claim *in specie* against the trust fund.

Lack of mutuality should be regarded as the proper basis for the early decision in **10.08** *Whitaker v Rush.*[34] A testator bequeathed £400 to a legatee, who assigned the legacy to the plaintiff. When the plaintiff brought this bill seeking payment of the legacy, the executor asserted that the legatee was indebted to him on a partnership account and for money lent, and that he was not obliged to pay to the plaintiff more than what was due on the balance of accounts. Sir Thomas Clark said that there was no case where a debt in one right had been set off against a debt in another right, and he disallowed a set-off. This seems correct. While the legatee was liable to the executor in the executor's personal capacity, the executor was not personally liable for the legacy, which was payable out of the fund constituted by the proceeds of the testator's estate.

Whitaker v Rush should be contrasted with *Taylor v Taylor,*[35] which concerned an **10.09** intestacy.[36] The deceased had left two sons, the plaintiff and the defendant. Letters of administration were granted to the defendant in 1856. In 1860 he submitted an account to the plaintiff, and in accordance with the terms of the account he paid the plaintiff a sum of money. In 1871 the plaintiff filed this bill, alleging that he had recently discovered that he was entitled to more than had been paid to him under the intestacy. Sir George Jessel agreed with him on this point, and held that the defendant as administrator was liable to pay the difference. He also held however that the defendant could set off a debt owing to him in his personal capacity by the plaintiff. The Master of the Rolls said that it was 'clear, on every principle of equity, on every principle of common sense and common justice, and on every principle derived by analogy from the Statute of Set-off, or otherwise, that the

---

[31] *Talbot v Frere* (1878) 9 Ch D 568, 573; *Stumore v Campbell & Co* [1892] 1 QB 314, 316; *Zemco Ltd v Jerrom-Pugh* [1993] BCC 275 (following *Guinness plc v Saunders* [1988] 1 WLR 863). See also *Re Jeffrey's Policy* (1872) 20 WR 857 (proceeds of life policy deposited as security). Malins VC did not consider the possibility of a trust when he held in *Thomas v Howell* (1874) LR 18 Eq 198 that an agent could set off a sum remaining in his hands on account of rent collected for his principal against the principal's liability for unpaid commission. Compare *Smit Tek International Zeesleepen BV v Selco Salvage Ltd* [1988] 2 Lloyd's Rep 398, 408 in the context of a set-off asserted by the beneficiary of a trust, as opposed to the trustee.

[32] See para 3.06 above.

[33] *National Westminster Bank Ltd v Halesowen Presswork and Assemblies Ltd* [1972] AC 785, 821.

[34] (1761) Amb 407, 27 ER 272. See also *Medlicot v Bowes* (1749) 1 Ves Sen 207, 27 ER 985; *Freeman v Lomas* (1851) 9 Hare 109, 68 ER 435.

[35] (1875) LR 20 Eq 155.

[36] An administrator of an intestate's estate, once he has completed the administration, holds as trustee for the beneficiaries on the intestacy. See *Re Cockburn's Will Trusts* [1957] 1 Ch 438, 439.

Defendant . . . is entitled to the set-off claimed, and I intend to allow it'.[37] *Whitaker v Rush* was cited in argument, but Sir George Jessel did not mention it in his judgment. While the cases were similar, they differed in the following respect. In *Whitaker v Rush* the claim of the legatee related to a subsisting fund. In *Taylor v Taylor* on the other hand it seems clear that there was no longer a fund in existence into which the proceeds of the testator's estate could traced. The plaintiff only had a personal claim against the defendant for payment of the sum to which he was entitled.[38] Consequently, as Sir George Jessel described the defendant's successful argument, this was a case in which the defendant was saying to the plaintiff: 'You have come into equity for a personal equitable debt due from me to you. I ask to set off a personal legal debt due from you to me.'[39] In fact, *Taylor v Taylor* has been cited as authority for a different proposition. While it is agreed that a debt owing to an executor in his own right cannot be set off against a legacy, it has been suggested, on the authority of the *Taylor* case, that a debt due from one of the next of kin to an administrator may be set off against the next of kin's share in the estate.[40] However Sir George Jessel did not draw any such distinction between an executor and an administrator, and it would be difficult to justify. The case is better explained on the basis suggested above.

10.10 *Taylor v Taylor* was followed in *Re Jones, Christmas v Jones*.[41] A son had been appointed administrator in his mother's intestacy. In addition, he was executor of his father's will. Two people, who were also next of kin of the intestate, brought an action for revocation of the probate of the will. They were unsuccessful, and were ordered to pay the executor's costs. When they demanded payment of their shares of the intestate's estate the administrator paid the proceeds of the estate into court, and said that he was entitled to bring into account the next of kins' indebtedness for costs. Kekewich J held that *Taylor v Taylor* was an authority in favour of a set-off, and that accordingly it should be allowed. This would have been a correct conclusion if the *Taylor* case indeed supports a general proposition that an administrator is in a different position to an executor with respect to set-offs. The contrary view is that the distinguishing feature in the *Taylor* case was the absence of a specific fund in respect of which a claim could have been made. There was merely a personal liability in the administrator. In *Re Jones*, on the other hand, there was still a specific fund, which had been paid into court. The better view is that there was no mutuality for the purpose of a set-off between the next of kins' liability to the administrator for costs and their right to participate in the fund.

---

[37] (1875) LR 20 Eq 155, 160.
[38] Thus, the amount which a defaulting trustee is bound to pay to make good a breach of trust is regarded as an equitable debt. See para 10.02 above.
[39] (1875) LR 20 Eq 155, 160.
[40] *Withers on Reversions* (2nd edn, 1933) 260. See also *Halsbury's Laws of England* (4th edn, 1999) vol 42, 267 para 460 (compare para 458 in relation to executors).
[41] [1897] 2 Ch 190.

D. The Delivery of Property—*Rose v Hart*

(1) The General Principle

Set-off only applies when the claims the subject of the proposed set-off are com- **10.11**
mensurable, in other words when they are such that they would result in money
demands.[42] This was established authoritatively by Gibbs CJ in *Rose v Hart*,[43]
when he held that a fuller with whom cloths had been deposited by a person who
later became bankrupt could not retain the cloths as a set-off against the bankrupt's indebtedness to him. On the other hand, the Chief Justice recognized that
there may be a set-off where goods were deposited with a direction to turn them
into money.

> Something more is certainly meant here by mutual credits than the words mutual
> debts import; and yet, upon the final settlement, it is enacted merely that one debt
> shall be set against another. We think this shews that the legislature meant such
> credits only as must in their nature terminate in debts, as where a debt is due from
> one party, and credit given by him on the other for a sum of money payable at a fu-
> ture day, and which will then become a debt, or where there is a debt on one side,
> and a delivery of property with directions to turn it into money on the other; in such
> case the credit given by the delivery of the property must in its nature terminate in a
> debt, the balance will be taken on the two debts, and the words of the statute will in
> all respects be complied with: but where there is a mere deposit of property, without
> any authority to turn it into money, no debt can ever arise out of it, and, therefore,
> it is not a credit within the meaning of the statute.[44]

It has been argued[45] that the allowance of a set-off when there is a direction to turn **10.12**
property into money owes its existence to the omission of a relevant fact from the
report of Lord Hardwicke's judgment in *Ex parte Deeze*.[46] In the *Deeze* case a
packer was allowed to retain six bales of cloth sent to him for packing and pressing as against the assignee in bankruptcy of the owner, not only for the cost of his
work upon the cloth, but also for the owner's debt to him on a loan. In the course
of his judgment Lord Hardwicke made a number of references to the law of mutual credit, although later in *Ex parte Ockenden*[47] he said that there had been evidence in *Ex parte Deeze* that it was usual for packers to lend money to clothiers,
and for a packer to retain cloths as security, not only for the work done upon them,
but also for any loans made. The case, then, was not one of set-off at all, but it

---

[42] See ch 9 above.
[43] (1818) 8 Taunt 499, 129 ER 477.
[44] (1818) 8 Taunt 499, 506, 129 ER 477, 480.
[45] Bishop, 'Set-off in the Administration of Insolvent and Bankrupt Estates' (1901) 1 Columbia
Law Review 377. See also *Young v Bank of Bengal* (1836) 1 Moore 150, 169–171, 12 ER 771,
779–780.
[46] (1748) 1 Atk 228, 26 ER 146.
[47] (1754) 1 Atk 235, 237, 26 ER 151, 152.

rather concerned a lien arising from the custom of the trade.[48] Despite this, *Ex parte Deeze* was still treated in subsequent cases as an authority on set-off.[49] Gibbs CJ in *Rose v Hart* said that he 'could not persuade [himself] to break in upon a class of cases so long established',[50] and his statement of the law represented an attempt to reconcile the cases decided after *Ex parte Deeze* with the stipulation in the set-off section in the bankruptcy legislation of 1732[51] that 'one debt may be set against another'. One such case was *French v Fenn.*[52] The bankrupt and the defendant together had purchased a string of pearls, the agreement between them being that the defendant would sell the pearls and that they would then share in any resulting profit. The pearls were sold after the bankruptcy, and it was held that the defendant could set off the bankrupt's share of the profit against the bankrupt's debt to the defendant for the bankrupt's share of the purchase money, which had been advanced by the defendant. There were also the cases of *Parker v Carter*[53] and *Olive v Smith*,[54] in each of which an insurance broker had been entrusted with a policy of insurance with authority to collect the insurance money in the event of a loss. It was held that the broker could set off insurance money received after the insured's bankruptcy against the insured's general indebtedness to him.[55] This included debts which were not a part of the insurance account, and consequently were not within the insurance broker's general lien.

10.13 Since *Rose v Hart* the principle has been applied in a number of other situations, for example where goods or their documents of title[56] were delivered to a person for the purpose of sale,[57] and where bills of exchange were deposited with a bank to collect and remit the proceeds.[58]

---

[48] This omission from the report of *Ex parte Deeze* inspired Lord Mansfield's condemnation of Atkyn's reports as 'extremely inaccurate'. See *Olive v Smith* (1813) 5 Taunt 56, 64, 128 ER 607, 610. An extract from Lord Hardwicke's notes on *Ex parte Deeze* is set out in a note to *Young v Bank of Bengal* (1836) 1 Moore 150, 170, 12 ER 771, 779. Lord Henley inclined to the view that Lord Hardwicke in fact had changed his mind in *Ex parte Ockenden* as regards his earlier decision in *Ex parte Deeze*, and that Lord Hardwicke took hold of the circumstance of there being evidence of a usage in *Ex parte Deeze* in order to reconcile his two decisions. See Henley, *A Digest of the Bankrupt Law* (3rd edn, 1832) 190.

[49] See eg *French v Fenn* (1783) 3 Dougl 257, 99 ER 642; *Smith v Hodson* (1791) 4 TR 211, 100 ER 979. Compare *Olive v Smith* (1813) 5 Taunt 56, 128 ER 609.

[50] (1818) 8 Taunt 499, 505, 129 ER 477, 480. See also Lord Mansfield in *Olive v Smith* (1813) 5 Taunt 56, 67, 128 ER 607, 611.

[51] (1732) 5 Geo II, c 30, s 28.

[52] (1783) 3 Dougl 257, 99 ER 642.

[53] (1788), unreported but noted in Cooke, *The Bankrupt Laws* (8th edn, 1823) vol 1, 578.

[54] (1813) 5 Taunt 56, 128 ER 607.

[55] See also *Chalmers v Page* (1820) 3 B & Ald 697, 106 ER 816.

[56] *M'Gillivray v Simson* (1826) 2 Car & P 320, 172 ER 145, affirmed 5 LJOSKB 53 (bills of lading).

[57] *Palmer v Day & Sons* [1895] 2 QB 618 (sale by an auctioneer); *Hunter v Official Assignee of Bispham* (1898) 17 NZLR 175 (sale by an auctioneer); *Re Lindsay* (1890) 9 NZLR 192; *Re Rose, ex p Hasluck & Garrard* (1894) 1 Mans 218; *Re Clements* (1931) 7 ABC 255; *Rolls Razor Ltd v Cox*

Gibbs CJ said in *Rose v Hart* that, for mutual credit, the transaction in question **10.14** must be such that it 'must' end in a debt, and it was on that ground that the Privy Council in *Young v Bank of Bengal*[59] later criticized the decision in *Olive v Smith*. Since *Rose v Hart* however the courts have expanded the concept of giving credit, so that it is now regarded as sufficient if the transaction would naturally or in the ordinary course of business end in a debt. It is not necessary that the transaction be such that it must of necessity have that result.[60] Moreover, since the *Young* case the scope of the set-off section has been enlarged to include claims arising out of mutual dealings. The decision in *Olive v Smith* may be objectionable on the ground that the insurance proceeds may have been impressed with a trust, depending on whether it was intended that they be kept separate from the broker's own funds or whether they should form an item in the account between the parties, but this is a difficulty with the *Rose v Hart* cases generally.[61] Apart from that possible objection, and notwithstanding a recent suggestion to the contrary,[62] *Olive v Smith* would appear to be alive and well.

Set-off against a trust fund

In some cases the allowance of a set-off in the circumstances contemplated by *Rose* **10.15** *v Hart* may produce an anomaly. Often when property is deposited with a person with directions to turn it into money the depository's status is that of a fiduciary, and any money received in respect of the property is impressed with a trust. Accordingly, the allowance of a set-off may conflict with the general principle that a trustee must account for the trust fund without a set-off in respect of an independent debt due to him in his personal capacity.[63] In the *Rose v Hart* cases, on the other hand, the depository's authority to turn the property into money and to receive the proceeds has been regarded as a sufficient source of credit to found a set-off in the depositor's bankruptcy, and the courts in reaching that conclusion have not considered the possibility of a trust.[64]

[1967] 1 QB 552 (company salesman). See also *Holmes v Kidd* (1858) 3 H & N 891, 157 ER 729, in which it was agreed that the proceeds of sale of property were to be applied in reduction of the debt, and *New Zealand and Australian Land Co v Watson* (1881) 7 QBD 374, in which the court rejected the view that the proceeds in that case were impressed with a trust in favour of the owner.

58 *Naoroji v The Chartered Bank of India* (1868) LR 3 CP 444.
59 (1836) 1 Moore 150, 12 ER 771. See also Parke B during argument in *Alsager v Currie* (1844) 12 M & W 751, 754–755, 152 ER 1402, 1403, commenting on *Young v Bank of Bengal.*
60 See para 7.04 above.
61 See below.
62 It is suggested in Wood, *English and International Set-off* (1989), 563 that *Olive v Smith* was probably overruled by *Rose v Hart*, although Gibbs CJ in *Rose v Hart* seems to have regarded *Olive v Smith* as consistent with his formulation of the principle.
63 See para 10.03 above.
64 In addition to the cases referred to below, compare *Naoroji v The Chartered Bank of India* (1868) LR 3 CP 444 with *Re Brown, ex parte Plitt* (1889) 6 Morr 81 in the context of a bill deposited with a bank to collect and remit the proceeds.

10.16   It is not universally accepted that the *Rose v Hart* set-off is anomalous. Professor Goode has suggested that the cases in question constitute instances in which the proceeds are not in fact impressed with a trust.[65] His argument is that the depository in these cases extends credit to the depositor in reliance on his prospective receipt of the proceeds of the property, for which the depositor gives credit to him. Accordingly the true basis of *Rose v Hart* is said to be that the depository has implied authority, by virtue of their mutual dealings, to regard himself as a debtor for a sum equal to the proceeds, and not as a trustee of the proceeds themselves. This would not explain all the cases, however. It is, of course, correct to say that, while a depository is often a trustee in respect of the proceeds of property deposited with him with directions to turn it into money, this is not always the case. For example, if there is an on-going business relationship between the depositor and the depository such that the depository is regularly entrusted with property to be turned into money, the courts may conclude that it was intended that the nature of the relationship in respect of the proceeds should be one of debt rather than trust.[66] The question essentially is whether it was intended that the depository should keep the proceeds separate from his own money.[67] But in the case of the *Rose v Hart* set-off the turning of property into money has not always been the subject of an on-going business arrangement between the parties. Further, in the absence of a relationship of that nature, the argument that the basis of *Rose v Hart* is that the depository extends credit in reliance on his prospective receipt of the proceeds would not apply when the depositor's indebtedness to the depository arose before, rather than after, the deposit. In such a case it could hardly be said that there was reliance by the depository in extending credit.[68]

10.17   Consider *Palmer v Day & Sons*.[69] In September 1894 one Langton gave instructions to the defendant auctioneers to sell some furniture, and also to sell his house. The furniture auction took place on 15 and 19 October. The house was put up for auction on 8 November, but no sale was effected. A sum of approximately £31 was due to the auctioneers in respect of their charges for the auctions, of which approximately £24 related to the unsuccessful attempt to sell the house. Between the

---

[65] Goode, *Principles of Corporate Insolvency Law* (2nd edn, 1997), 190–191.

[66] Finn, *Fiduciary Obligations* (1977), 105. See eg the retention of title cases, *Hendy Lennox (Industrial Engines) Ltd v Grahame Puttick Ltd* [1984] 1 WLR 485 and *Re Andrabell Ltd* [1984] 3 All ER 407, referred to in Goode, *Principles of Corporate Insolvency Law* (2nd edn, 1997) 191.

[67] *Re Nanwa Gold Mines Ld* [1955] 1 WLR 1080; *Re Bond Worth Ltd* [1980] 1 Ch 228, 160–161; *Westdeutsche Landesbank Girozentrale v Islington LBC* [1996] AC 669, 712; *Royal Trust Bank v National Westminster Bank plc* [1996] 2 BCLC 682, 701; *Triffit Nurseries v Salads Etcetera Ltd* [2000] 1 BCLC 761, 764; Millett, 'Restitution and Constructive Trusts' (1998) 114 LQR 399, 407. Compare *Stephens Travel Service International Pty Ltd v Qantas Airways Ltd* (1988) 13 NSWLR 331, 349, referred to in *Re ILG Travel Ltd* [1995] 2 BCLC 128.

[68] The relationships of debt and trust are not mutually exclusive. See *Barclays Bank Ltd v Quistclose Investments Ltd* [1970] AC 567.

[69] [1895] 2 QB 618. See also *Webb v Smith* (1885) 30 Ch D 192 (Statutes of Set-off) and *Hunter v Official Assignee of Bispham* (1898) 17 NZLR 175.

date of the furniture auction and the attempted auction of the house, some pictures which had been passed in at the furniture auction were sent to the auctioneers for the purpose of sale. This sale took place after the attempt to sell the house, and also after Langton became bankrupt. Lord Russell of Killowen CJ and Charles J held that the auctioneers could set off against the bankrupt's indebtedness to them for £31 in respect of the unpaid charges their obligation to account for the proceeds of sale of the pictures.[70] However, the instructions to sell the house were given before the pictures were sent to the auctioneers for sale, in which case it seems difficult to say that the auctioneers gave credit to Langton for their charges in respect of the auction of the house in reliance on their prospective receipt of the proceeds of sale of the pictures. There was no discussion in the judgment as to whether the proceeds were impressed with a trust, which is curious given that the Court of Appeal only some eight years earlier had held that auctioneers receive proceeds of sale in a fiduciary capacity for their customers.[71] This suggests that the existence or otherwise of a trust was not considered to be relevant to the question of set-off. Nor is there anything in the judgment to suggest that this was a case in which there was an on-going business relationship such that it may have been intended that the relationship should only be one of debt.

Proceeds received before the bankruptcy

In *Rose v Hart* the proceeds obtained from turning property into money were re- **10.18**
ceived after bankruptcy,[72] but the same result should follow when the receipt of
the proceeds occurred before then. Furthermore, set-off under the Statutes of Set-
off is probably subject to the same principle.[73]

(2) The Circumstances in Which the Set-off Applies

The *Rose v Hart* set-off applies in the following circumstances. **10.19**

Authority to turn the property into money

A person holding chattels without authority to turn them into money, and who is **10.20**
sued by the owner's trustee in bankruptcy for their return, cannot bring the value
of the chattels into account as a set-off against the bankrupt's indebtedness to him.

---

[70] It was held that there were separate contracts for the sale of the house and the furniture (including the pictures), so that the auctioneers' lien on the proceeds did not extend to their charges in respect of both sales.

[71] *Crowther v Elgood* (1887) 34 Ch D 691.

[72] See eg *French v Fenn* (1783) 3 Dougl 257, 99 ER 642; *Olive v Smith* (1813) 5 Taunt 56, 128 ER 607; *Naoroji v The Chartered Bank of India* (1868) LR 3 CP 444 (it appears more clearly from the report in 37 LJCP 221 that the proceeds in respect of most of the bills were received after the date of the deed of inspectorship); *Astley v Gurney* (1869) LR 4 CP 714; *Palmer v Day & Sons* [1895] 2 QB 618.

[73] In *Webb v Smith* (1885) 30 Ch D 192 the Court of Appeal assumed that the auctioneer had a right of set-off under the Statutes of Set-off in respect of proceeds of sale in his hands.

The claims are not commensurable.[74] This has been held to be the case when the chattels are in that person's possession wrongfully,[75] or merely for use,[76] or for the performance of work upon them,[77] or, having been lodged as a security, the secured debt has been paid.[78] It would also apply when a company had granted a charge over chattels to a creditor, but the charge is void as against a liquidator under the Companies Act 1985, section 395 for non-registration.[79]

The remedies under the Torts (Interference With Goods) Act

10.21 The Torts (Interference With Goods) Act 1977, section 2 abolished detinue, which is the action formerly used to obtain the return of goods wrongfully detained. Section 3 instead provides that, in proceedings against a person who is in possession or control of the goods of another for wrongful interference with the goods, the relief can take the form of:

(a) an order for delivery of the goods, and for payment of any consequential damages, or
(b) an order for delivery of the goods, but giving the defendant the alternative of paying damages by reference to the value of the goods, together in either alternative with payment of any consequential damages, or
(c) damages.

Relief under (a) is at the discretion of the court, and the claimant may choose between the others.

10.22 The better view is that the Act has not changed the position in relation to set-off. If a claimant claims the return of the goods under (b), it should not make any difference for the purpose of set-off that the defendant may choose to pay damages. This is consistent with the position formerly applicable in an action in detinue.[80] The form of judgment in a detinue action was for delivery of the chattel or payment of its assessed value together with damages for detention. The defendant in effect had an option, although the Common Law Procedure Act 1854, section 78 gave the court the power to order delivery up of the chattel, without giving the defendant the option of paying its assessed value. In *Eberle's Hotels and Restaurant Co*

---

[74] See ch 9 above.

[75] *Lord (Trustee of) v Great Eastern Railway Co* [1908] 2 KB 54; *Re Leeholme Stud Pty Ltd* [1965] NSWR 1649. See also *Peacock v Anderson* (1878) 4 NZ Jur (NS) SC 67.

[76] *Ex parte Roy, re Sillence* (1877) 7 Ch D 70; *Re Winter, ex parte Bolland* (1878) 8 Ch D 225; *Rolls Razor Ltd v Cox* [1967] 1 QB 552.

[77] *Rose v Hart* (1818) 8 Taunt 499, 129 ER 477.

[78] *Eberle's Hotels and Restaurant Co Ltd v E Jonas & Brothers* (1887) 18 QBD 459. See also *Key v Flint* (1817) 8 Taunt 21, 129 ER 289, petition in equity dismissed *Ex parte Flint* (1818) 1 Swans 30, 36 ER 285.

[79] See *Smith v Bridgend County BC* [2002] 1 AC 336 in relation to equitable set-off, but it should also apply to insolvency set-off. See in particular at 351 paras 35 and 36.

[80] See generally the discussion in *General and Finance Facilities Ltd v Cooks Cars (Romford) Ltd* [1963] 1 WLR 644, 650.

Ltd v E Jonas & Brothers[81] the plaintiff company had deposited some cigars with the defendants as security for a debt. The company was ordered to be wound up, and the debt secured by the cigars having been subsequently paid the liquidator brought an action in detinue for their return. The defendants claimed that they were entitled to have the value of the cigars assessed and then set off against another unsecured debt owing to them by the plaintiff. The Court of Appeal however held that the plaintiff was entitled to the return of the cigars without being subjected to a set-off. An interesting aspect of the case is a comment by counsel during argument, and the responses of Fry LJ and Lord Esher MR. Counsel suggested that, if the judge in a detinue action declined to order delivery of the chattels, so that the defendant instead could pay their assessed value, the claim would be a money claim which could be set off. Fry LJ responded that the application or otherwise of the insolvency set-off section depended on the state of things at the time of the winding up, and at that time there was a right to delivery of the cigars on payment of the secured debt. That was not a right that was susceptible to a set-off.[82] Similary Lord Esher asked,[83] 'Can the applicability of [the set-off section] depend on what the judge may do at the trial? Must it not depend on the nature of the respective rights of the parties antecedently to the action?' This suggests that, even if specific restitution had not been ordered, a set-off would have been denied. Similarly, under the regime set out in the Torts (Interference With Goods) Act, if the claimant seeks an order for the delivery of the goods in accordance with section 3(2)(a), the availability of a set-off under the insolvency legislation should not depend upon whether the defendant subsequently elects to pay damages. Nor would equity provide relief by way of an equitable set-off in this situation.[84] That conclusion in relation to insolvency set-off is also suggested by cases in which property that initially was in issue was sold with the consent of the parties after the owner's bankruptcy. The courts emphasized that the right at the date of the bankruptcy was to the return of the property, and the fact that the dispute subsequently became one over the proceeds of sale did not let in a set-off.[85]

Destruction of the goods

Similarly, if the goods deposited with another party are destroyed after the depositor's bankruptcy, so that at the date of the bankruptcy the bankrupt's estate was entitled to the return of the goods, the fact that the only remedy later available to the trustee is to claim damages should not let in a set-off. However, what if the goods were destroyed before the bankruptcy, so that at the date of the bankruptcy **10.23**

---

[81] (1887) 18 QBD 459.

[82] (1887) 18 QBD 459, 463. See also Fry LJ at 469 and 470.

[83] (1887) 18 QBD 459, 464.

[84] This is suggested by *Smith v Bridgend County BC* [2002] 1 AC 336, esp at 351 para 36.

[85] *Re Winter, ex p Bolland* (1878) 8 Ch D 225; *Lord (Trustee of) v Great Eastern Railway Co* [1908] 2 KB 54 (reversed on other grounds [1909] AC 109). See also *Ex parte Ockenden* (1754) 1 Atk 235, 26 ER 151.

specific restitution was not possible, and the trustee accordingly is only in a position to claim damages under section 3(2)(c) of the Act?[86] A set-off may be available,[87] but it will depend on the circumstances. A set-off can only proceed where there are mutual debts, mutual credits or other mutual dealings. A damages claim is not a debt. Nor does it come within the concept of giving credit.[88] Moreover, a damages claim for wrongful interference with goods or chattels often will not arise out of a dealing between the parties. In *Re Winter, ex p Bolland*[89] Bacon VC said that a mere authority to possess or use particular chattels unaccompanied by a power to sell is not a dealing, although Lord Esher MR adopted a less dogmatic approach in the *Eberle's Hotels* case.[90] In his view, whatever comes within an ordinary business transaction would be a dealing for the purpose of the set-off section,[91] and he suggested that the deposit of the cigars in that case to secure a debt would have constituted a dealing. On the other hand, it would be difficult to categorize a wrongful taking of property as a dealing for the purpose of the set-off section.[92]

Money claims

10.24 The essence of a *Rose v Hart* set-off is that property was deposited with a person with authority to turn it into money, under circumstances not amounting to a preference.[93] The authority must have been acted upon, so that the claim against the depository is for a sum of money which can be set off against the depositor's own indebtedness to produce a balance on the account. In *Rolls Razor Ltd v Cox*[94] a set-off admittedly was allowed notwithstanding that the authority had not been acted upon, but the better view is that the case was wrongly decided.[95]

Unrevoked authority

10.25 An effective revocation of the authority to turn the property into money should prevent a set-off.[96] According to the Court of Appeal in *Rolls Razor v Cox*,[97] how-

---

[86] Cozens Hardy MR left the question open in *Lord (Trustee of) v Great Eastern Railway Co* [1908] 2 KB 54, 78.

[87] Compare *Peacock v Anderson* (1878) 4 NZ Jur (NS) SC 67, 70, although the comment by Richmond J was made in the context that a set-off was not available generally against an unliquidated claim. That would not be relevant to the current insolvency set-off section. See paras 8.42–8.47 above.

[88] *Palmer v Day & Sons* [1895] 2 QB 618, 621. See paras 7.05 and 7.06 above.

[89] (1878) 8 Ch D 225, 228.

[90] (1887) 18 QBD 459, 465.

[91] See para 7.07 above.

[92] *Re Leeholme Stud Pty Ltd* [1965] NSWR 1649, 1650.

[93] *Castendyck and Focke v Official Assignee of S A McLellan* (1887) 6 NZLR 67, 75.

[94] [1967] 1 QB 552.

[95] See para 9.02 above.

[96] *Palmer v Day & Sons* [1895] 2 QB 618, 623.

[97] [1967] 1 QB 552.

ever, a revocation before the bankruptcy or liquidation of the depositor will not always be effective. In that case the authority of the company's salesman to sell the company's goods was revoked after the board of directors publicly announced that the company was insolvent, which occurred before the resolution to wind up the company. The Court of Appeal nevertheless allowed the salesman to set off the value of the goods still in his possession, Lord Denning commenting that 'this right [of set-off] could not be taken away by the insolvent person at the last moment revoking the power of sale'.[98] The courts should reconsider this decision. The state of the company's solvency before the relevant date may go to the question whether there was notice of a pending petition or of the summoning of a meeting of creditors for the purpose of the qualification to the mutual credit provision in rule 4.90(3) of the Insolvency Rules.[99] However, that date merely defines a point beyond which a set-off may not be acquired, as opposed to a point beyond which the parties may no longer act so as to deprive the other of a set-off. There is no justification in the language of the set-off section for the view that a company may not act before the commencement of the liquidation in the interests of the general body of creditors in order to prevent the depletion of the estate through a set-off. Indeed, Lord Denning's view would appear to conflict with an opinion earlier expressed by Pollock MR in *Re City Life Assurance Co Ltd, Stephenson's Case*[100] in relation to the Bankruptcy Act 1914, s 31, which was in similar terms to the current set-off section.

> It is suggested that there was an equity between the policy holder and the company that the policy holder should be able to invoke the principle of s 31 if and when he required to do so, and that the company are not entitled to say that there is no mutuality, because under the dealings between the policy holders and the company the principles of s 31 ought to have remained available to the policy holder. That argument does not, to my mind, carry weight. There is no equity that the rights which govern the parties, if and when s 31 applies, should be always available. Sect 31 appears to me to be applicable if and when there is a bankruptcy or winding up of a company, but until that time has come, the law which governs the rights of the parties is not in force and cannot be held to be an inchoate right which the policy holder had as against the company at the time when the winding up of the company had not been commenced or, indeed, thought of.

Pollock MR referred to the time before the winding up had been thought of, but his thesis was that there is no equity at any time before the winding up that the possibility of a set-off should be always available. Lord Denning noted that the set-off section sanctions the taking of an account where 'there have been mutual

10.26

---

[98] [1967] 1 QB 552, 571. The point was not considered by the other member of the majority, Danckwerts LJ, but since he upheld the salesman's right to a set-off he presumably agreed with Lord Denning. Winn LJ in his dissenting judgment said that the revocation of the authority was effective to stop a set-off.

[99] For bankruptcy, see the Insolvency Act 1986, s 323(3). See para 6.49 *ff* above.

[100] [1926] 1 Ch 191, 217.

credits'. He said that the use of the past tense indicated that 'when the mutual dealings *have been* such as to give rise to mutual credits, there is a right of set-off'.[101] If that were a correct interpretation, however, it is difficult to see why it would be that only a 'last moment' revocation would be ineffective. Moreover, if an insolvent debtor may not act at the last moment to take away the possibility of a set-off by revoking a power of sale, the question would arise whether an insolvent debtor could adopt other courses of action which similarly would have the effect of destroying the possibility of a set-off in a future bankruptcy or liquidation, for example an assignment by the debtor to a third party of the benefit of his cross-claim against his creditor.[102] But there is no reason why the debtor should be restricted in that regard. The better view is that the set-off section requires not only that there should 'have been' mutual credits at some stage before the bankruptcy or liquidation, but that those mutual credits should still be subsisting at that date. It introduces uncertainty into the law to say that a debtor facing bankruptcy or a winding up may not revoke an authority 'at the last moment'.[103] In *Rolls Razor Ltd v Cox* there was a public declaration of insolvency, but in many cases it would be difficult to say when a debtor became aware that bankruptcy or a winding up was unavoidable.

Bankruptcy and liquidation as a revocation of authority

10.27 In applying *Rose v Hart* it appears not to make any difference that the proceeds in question may have been received after the depositor's bankruptcy or liquidation,[104] provided that the deposit of the property occurred before then under circumstances not giving rise to a preference,[105] and provided also that the authority had not been revoked.[106] As Dr Oditah has queried,[107] however, it is not clear why the fact of bankruptcy itself in some cases would not operate as a revocation of an otherwise revocable authority in accordance with normal principles. In *Elliott v Turquand*[108] the Privy Council said that:

---

[101] [1967] 1 QB 552, 571.

[102] Compare *Re City Life Assurance Co Ltd. Stephenson's Case* [1926] 1 Ch 191, 214.

[103] In *Rolls Razor Ltd v Cox* this meant about a month before the extraordinary resolution to wind up the company.

[104] See eg *French v Fenn* (1783) 3 Dougl 257, 99 ER 642; *Olive v Smith* (1813) 5 Taunt 56, 128 ER 607; *Naoroji v The Chartered Bank of India* (1868) LR 3 CP 444 (it appears more clearly from the report at 37 LJCP 221 that the proceeds in respect of most of the bills were received after the date of the deed of inspectorship); *Astley v Gurney* (1869) LR 4 CP 714; *Palmer v Day & Sons* [1895] 2 QB 618.

[105] *Castendyck and Focke v Official Assignee of S A McLellan* (1887) 6 NZLR 67, 75.

[106] See *Naoroji v The Chartered Bank of India* (1868) LR 3 CP 444, 452 (in the context of a deed of inspectorship under the Bankruptcy Act 1861 which, when registered, had an effect equivalent to an adjudiction in bankruptcy), and *Palmer v Day & Sons* [1895] 2 QB 618, 623. Compare *Rolls Razor Ltd v Cox* [1967] 1 QB 552 (above).

[107] Oditah, 'Assets and the Treatment of Claims in Insolvency' (1992) 108 LQR 459, 467 n 55, and also Oditah, *Legal Aspects of Receivables Financing* (1991) 248 n 72.

[108] (1881) 7 App Cas 79, 88.

Authorities given in the course of mutual dealings, and necessary to the continuance of those dealings, are, by implication, excepted from the rule that authorities are revoked by . . . bankruptcy. They continue and remain unrevoked by virtue of the provision which protects such dealings, in the same way as powers necessary to give effect to protected sales continue and remain unrevoked by . . . bankruptcy. If this were not so, in some cases of mutual credits the protection professed to be given would be illusory.

The notion that an authority to sell was necessary for the continuance of the parties' mutual dealings, so as to prevent its revocation by bankruptcy, would not always explain the *Rose v Hart* cases. Consider for example *Palmer v Day & Sons*,[109] to which reference was made earlier.[110] There is nothing in the report to suggest that there was an on-going business relationship such that the deposit was necessary for the continuance of mutual dealings, or that the auctioneer gave credit to the depositor on the strength of the prospective receipt of the proceeds of sale. In that case, the trustee in bankruptcy upon his appointment wrote to the auctioneer requesting him to proceed with the sale of the goods previously deposited with him by the bankrupt. The auctioneer did so, and when he received the proceeds he was allowed to utilize them in a set-off under *Rose v Hart* against a separate debt owing to him by the bankrupt. One would have thought that this was a case in which the auctioneer's original authority to sell was revoked, but that he was then authorized by the trustee to sell as the *trustee's* agent, the goods in question having vested in the trustee upon his appointment. On that analysis, a set-off should have been denied because of lack of mutuality.

Unless an authority to sell is coupled with an interest,[111] the authority in any event **10.28** should be revoked when the depositor is a company which is the subject of a court-ordered winding up. In such a case the Insolvency Act 1986, section 127 provides that a disposition of the company's property made after the commencement of the winding up is void unless the court otherwise orders.[112] It would be difficult to assert in the face of that provision that an agent of the depositor, such as an auctioneer,[113] would have continuing authority to sell the company's property.[114]

---

[109] [1895] 2 QB 618.

[110] See para 10.17 above.

[111] See below.

[112] Compare s 284 in relation to bankruptcy, which avoids a disposition in the period beginning with the presentation of the petition and ending with the vesting of the estate in the trustee, at which time the bankrupt would no longer have title to his estate so as to be able to dispose of it in any event.

[113] If the agent is a receiver appointed under a debenture, s 127 would not affect the authority to sell.

[114] Compare *Rolls Razor v Cox*, which concerned a voluntary liquidation so that the equivalent of s 127 in force at the time was not applicable.

Demand for the return of the goods by the depositor's trustee in bankruptcy

10.29 In *Palmer v Day & Sons* the trustee requested the auctioneer to proceed with the sale. However, given that the property deposited with the auctioneer had vested in the trustee upon his appointment, why could not the trustee have demanded its return as the legal owner? He could not have done so if the authority to sell was coupled with an interest, and the comments of the Privy Council in *Elliott v Turquand* (above) may be said to support the view that an authority given in the course of mutual dealings is of that nature. But is that the case? If the authority to sell is coupled with an interest, it could not be revoked by the depositor himself before bankruptcy, but the mere fact that authority is given in the course of mutual dealings would not suffice to preclude the depositor from revoking it.[115] There would have to be other circumstances arising from the mutual dealings which establish an interest. *Rolls Razor v Cox* admittedly suggests that a liquidator cannot demand the return of the company's property handed over for sale so as to defeat a set-off. There are difficulties with the reasoning in the case however, and it is suggested that it should be reconsidered.[116] In any event, it should not be extended to bankruptcy, given that the property of the bankrupt is vested in the trustee. The trustee's reason for demanding its return may not be based solely on a desire to avoid a set-off. He may regard the method or timing of the sale as not being the most beneficial as far as the estate as a whole is concerned, particularly if the debtor before his bankruptcy delivered goods for sale on a 'fire sale' basis in order to obtain funds to overcome what he thought was a temporary liquidity problem but which culminated in bankruptcy. There may indeed be only a small debt owing to the depository, and in such a case it hardly seems satisfactory that the trustee should be locked into a sale by the depository solely in order to secure that debt.

Deposit of the means of completing the transaction

10.30 The essence of a *Rose v Hart* set-off is not merely the conferral of authority to receive the proceeds obtained from turning property into money, but rather that authority given under circumstances not amounting to a preference,[117] coupled with

---

[115] In *Palmer v Day & Sons* [1895] 2 QB 618, 623 Lord Russell of Killowen assumed that the authority to sell could have been revoked. While he also commented that no action could have been taken by the depositor when the receiving order was made to recover the goods, that was in the context of an argument that the depositor himself could not have maintained an action in detinue for the return of the goods, in which action a set-off admittedly would not have been available, unless he had taken steps to alter the terms on which the goods had been left with the auctioneer. Lord Russell agreed with that view. Since the depositor had not altered the terms, he could not have sued in detinue at the date of the receiving order. See also *Naoroji v Chartered Bank of India* (1868) LR 3 CP 444, 452, *per* Montague Smith J.

[116] See above, and also paras 9.02 and 10.25 above.

[117] *Castendyck and Focke v Official Assignee of S A McLellan* (1887) 6 NZLR 67, 75.

a deposit of whatever may be necessary for the depository to complete the transaction and receive the money. For example, in the case of a chattel for sale, usually this would mean a deposit of the chattel itself. Gibbs CJ in *Rose v Hart* was concerned with cases in which there had been a deposit of property before the relevant date, but the proceeds obtained from turning the property into money were not received by the depository until after that date. The deposit of the property was regarded as the basis of the credit in these cases, presumably because it was thought to confer upon the depository the means by which he could proceed with the transaction himself despite the bankruptcy. He could hand over that property to the third party and receive the money in return. Possession of the means of completing the transaction however would not always require an actual deposit of the property concerned. For example, in the case of goods, it would be sufficient if bills of lading are handed over[118] or, as in *Easum v Cato*,[119] if the conduct of the parties is such that it is 'as if' the goods had been put into the person's hands.[120] Moreover, physical delivery is not feasible when the transaction concerns the sale of immoveable property such as land. In such a case, a *Rose v Hart* set-off would require a deposit of the documentation necessary for the sale. In *Elliott v Turquand*[121] an agent had been authorized to receive the proceeds of sale of land. The Privy Council said that if the agent had been entrusted with the deed of conveyance for the purpose of receiving the purchase money, 'the case would be very like some of the instances referred to in *Rose v Hart*'.[122]

In *Elliott v Turquand* there was insufficient evidence of a deed of conveyance having been handed over to the agent for the purpose of receiving the proceeds of sale. Nevertheless, the agent had actually received the proceeds under an unrevoked authority before the principal's bankruptcy, and he was allowed to bring them into an account. An agent is often, but not always, a trustee of moneys received in the course of his agency.[123] While the existence or otherwise of a trust was not canvassed by the Privy Council, it did comment[124] that the agent was authorized to   **10.31**

---

[118] *M'Gillivray v Simson* (1826) 2 Car & P 320, 172 ER 145, affirmed 5 LJOSKB 53.

[119] (1822) 5 B & Ald 861, 106 ER 1406.

[120] Prior to their bankruptcy, the bankrupts in *Easum v Cato*, being desirous of making a shipment of goods to Rio de Janeiro for sale, but not in their own names, represented to the merchants through whom the consignment was to be made that the goods belonged to the defendant. When the defendant received the proceeds of sale after the bankruptcy, it was held that he could set off his obligation to account for them to the bankrupts against a separate debt owing by him to the bankrupts, Abbott CJ commenting that 'this case is to be considered as if the bankrupts had actually put the goods into the hands of the defendant . . .'. See (1822) 5 B & Ald 861, 866, 106 ER 1406, 1408.

[121] (1881) 7 App Cas 79.

[122] (1881) 7 App Cas 79, 87. See also *Castendyck and Focke v Official Assignee of S A McLellan* (1887) 6 NZLR 67, 74. In *Castendyck* the agent was authorized merely to find a purchaser, and not to receive the purchase money, and so he was not allowed to set off the money when it came into his hands.

[123] Compare *Palette Shoes Pty Ltd v Krohn* (1937) 58 CLR 1, 30, *per* Dixon J, with *Henry v Hammond* [1913] 2 KB 515.

[124] (1881) 7 App Cas 79, 85, 87.

receive the purchase money and to credit it to the mutual account existing between them, which suggests that there was not a trust. Accordingly, even though the case strictly did not come within the principle discussed in *Rose v Hart*, that did not matter. Because there was no question of a trust there was nothing objectionable in a set-off.

E. Surplus Proceeds After Realizing a Security

10.32 Consider that a bankrupt or a company in liquidation prior to the insolvency gave security for a debt, and after default in payment of the debt the creditor turned the property constituting the security into money, either through the exercise of a power of sale or, if the security consists of an insurance policy or a negotiable instrument or a debt owing by a third party, by collecting the proceeds. If a surplus remains after the secured debt has been satisfied, the creditor may wish to set off the obligation to account for the surplus against a separate unsecured debt owing to him by the bankrupt or the company.

Mortgagee's right of retainer, and tacking

10.33 Before considering the issue two lines of authority should be distinguished. The first was developed by Sir John Romilly who, instead of relying on the law of set-off, attempted to develop a mortgagee's right of retainer. In both *Spalding v Thompson*[125] and *Re Haselfoot's Estate, Chauntler's Claim*[126] a policy of life assurance had been mortgaged to secure a debt, and when the testator died and the insurance moneys were received, he held that the mortgagee could retain the surplus against a separate unsecured debt of the testator. In *Re Haselfoot's Estate*[127] he said that the right was not one of set-off, but rather it was a right in the mortgagee to retain a part of the testator's estate in his possession in satisfaction of the testator's debt. Subsequently Malins VC applied this right of retainer in a case where there was a surplus remaining after a sale by a mortgagee.[128] In later cases, however, it has been criticized and disregarded,[129] and it would appear that it no longer applies. The second line of authority relates to tacking. When a mortgagor died, equity in a number of cases allowed the mortgagee to tack an unsecured debt onto the mortgage as against the successors in title to the equity of redemption, in so far as the mortgaged property was an asset available for payment of the unsecured debt. However, this was only allowed as a means of preventing circuity of action, and it

---

[125] (1858) 26 Beav 637, 53 ER 1044.

[126] (1872) LR 13 Eq 327.

[127] (1872) LR 13 Eq 327, 331.

[128] *Re General Provident Assurance Co, ex p National Bank* (1872) LR 14 Eq 507. Compare *Pile v Pile* (1872) 23 WR 440, where the sale of the mortgaged property took place under a court order and the proceeds of sale did not come into the mortgagee's hands.

[129] See *Talbot v Frere* (1878) 9 Ch D 568 and *Re Gregson. Christison v Bolam* (1887) 36 Ch D 223.

could not be used to obtain priority over other creditors when the mortgagor's estate was insolvent.[130] In any event, the right appears to have been abolished in relation to mortgages of land as a result of the general abolition of tacking (save in respect of further advances) by the Law of Property Act 1925, section 94.[131]

Set-off

With respect to set-off, the fundamental point should be that a mortgagee is a **10.34** trustee for the mortgagor, or as the case may be a subsequent encumbrancer,[132] in respect of any surplus remaining after exercising a power of sale and paying the secured debt.[133] This is not a recent development. Dr Waters[134] has suggested that it would have been obvious to judicial minds at least since *Cholmondeley v Clinton*[135] in 1820. Therefore the obligation to account for the surplus should not be susceptible to a set-off.[136] *Talbot v Frere*[137] supports that view. Sir George Jessel MR said in that case, in the context of a deceased mortgagor's insolvent estate, that: 'the mortgagee cannot plead set-off. He is a trustee of the money for the estate, and his claim is only a simple contract debt against that estate.'[138] It was also on that ground that the Victorian Supreme Court in *Lloyds Bank NZA Ltd v National Safety Council of Australia*[139] declined to allow a set-off against a surplus obtained from the exercise of a power of sale after the liquidation of the mortgagor. Nor would there appear to be any reason for encouraging a set-off. A secured creditor should not be entitled to use the security to obtain priority over other creditors in relation to a debt that otherwise was unsecured.[140] Apart from the *Talbot* and *Lloyd's Bank* cases, however, the authorities are in an unsatisfactory state.

---

[130] See eg *Irby v Irby* (1855) 22 Beav 217, 52 ER 1091; *Pile v Pile* (1875) 23 WR 440; *Talbot v Frere* (1878) 9 Ch D 568, 572–573. See generally *Fisher and Lightwood's Law of Mortgage* (11th edn, 2002), 718–19 para 24.82

[131] In Australia, see eg the Property Law Act 1958 (Vic), s 94 and the Conveyancing and Law of Property Act 1884 (Tas), s 38, neither of which is expressed to apply to mortgages of Torrens title land (see s 86 of the Victorian Act and s 91 of the Tasmanian Act), and in Queensland the Property Law Act 1974, s 82 (which does extend to Torrens land: see s 5(1)(b)).

[132] *Tanner v Heard* (1857) 23 Beav 555, 53 ER 219.

[133] *Matthison v Clarke* (1854) 3 Drewry 3, 4, 61 ER 801; *Charles v Jones* (1887) 35 Ch D 544; *Lloyds Bank NZA Ltd v National Safety Council of Australia* [1993] 2 VR 506, 510–511, 514; *Sheahan v Carrier Air Conditioning Pty Ltd* (1997) 189 CLR 407, 429–430. See also the Law of Property Act 1925, s 105.

[134] Waters, *The Constructive Trust* (1964) 207.

[135] (1820) 2 Jac & W 1, 37 ER 527.

[136] This is in the absence of a prior agreement by the mortgagor that the mortgagee may apply the surplus in satisfaction of another debt. See *Lloyds Bank NZA Ltd v National Safety Council of Australia* [1993] 2 VR 506, 508, 510, 513, 514.

[137] (1878) 9 Ch D 568.

[138] (1878) 9 Ch D 568, 573.

[139] [1993] 2 VR 506. See also *Re Parker* (1997) 80 FCR 1, 18.

[140] *Lloyds Bank NZA Ltd v National Safety Council* [1993] 2 VR 506, 522, referring to *Re Pearce* [1909] 2 Ch 492, 499–500, *per* Buckley LJ and *Eberle's Hotels and Restaurant Co Ltd v E Jonas & Brothers* (1887) 18 QBD 459, 470, *per* Fry LJ.

Deceased's Insolvent Estate

10.35 In *Talbot v Frere*[141] a testator had mortgaged policies of life assurance to a creditor. The testator died insolvent, and the creditor received the policy moneys which were more than sufficient to pay the mortgage debt. Sir George Jessel held that the creditor could not keep the surplus in payment of another unsecured debt. The creditor was a trustee for the estate,[142] and his obligation to account for the trust fund was not susceptible to a set-off.[143] The same issue arose on similar facts in *Re Gregson. Christison v Bolam*.[144] A set-off was also denied, but on a different ground. North J said that the debt was owing by the testator, whereas the testator himself never had a right to the surplus which first became payable after his death to the use of the executor. Accordingly, there was a lack of mutuality.[145] If on the other hand surplus proceeds of security had been received in the testator's lifetime, he suggested that there might have been a set-off.[146] It is difficult however to reconcile that view with *Talbot v Frere*. If there is a trust it should prevent a set-off whether the proceeds are received before or after death.[147]

10.36 Those cases concerned a deceased's insolvent estate. More commonly the issue will arise in the context of a bankruptcy or a liquidation of the mortgagor.

Proceeds received before the debtor's insolvency

10.37 If the security is realized and the proceeds are received before the debtor's bankruptcy, there is support for the view that a surplus can be set off.[148] *Young v Bank of Bengal*[149] concerned a security over some promissory notes. While the security was not realized until after the bankruptcy, and a set-off accordingly was denied for the reason explained below, Lord Brougham nevertheless accepted, on the authority of *Atkinson v Elliott*,[150] that a set-off would have been available if the bank

---

[141] (1878) 9 Ch D 568.

[142] In *Roxburghe v Cox* (1881) 17 Ch D 520, 525 James LJ said of *Talbot v Frere* that: 'That was a case of trustee and *cestui que trust*.'

[143] The set-off in issue in *Talbot v Frere* was pursuant to the Statutes of Set-off, since the deceased had died before the bankruptcy set-off section had been made applicable to deceaseds' insolvent estates by the Supreme Court of Judicature Act 1875, s 10. See paras 13.121–13.125 below.

[144] (1887) 36 Ch D 223.

[145] See also *Re Gedney. Smith v Grummitt* [1908] 1 Ch 804.

[146] (1887) 36 Ch D 223, 227.

[147] In *Re Gregson* (1887) 36 Ch D 223, 230 North J doubted whether the mortgagees in that case could 'strictly speaking' be said to be trustees. Nevertheless his judgment suggests that he contemplated that there was a form of trust, commenting that the balance in the hands of the mortgagees was money received 'to the use of the executor'. He may have had in mind what has been termed a quasi-trust (see *Foley v Hill* (1848) 2 HLC 28, 35–36, 9 ER 1002, 1005), or in modern parlance a constructive trust. See Finn, *Fiduciary Obligations* (1977) 89.

[148] See also *Samuel, Samuel & Co v West Hartlepool Steam Navigation Co* (1907) 12 Com Cas 203 (Statutes of Set-off).

[149] (1836) 1 Moore 150, 12 ER 771.

[150] (1797) 7 TR 378, 101 ER 1030.

had realized the security and received the surplus prior to the bankruptcy, 'for then they would have been debtors in that amount to Palmer and Co, and the case would have been one of mutual debts'.[151]

In *Astley v Gurney*[152] a set-off was allowed where the proceeds of the security were   **10.38**
received before bankruptcy, although the circumstances were unusual. As security for two debts, the debtor deposited bills of lading for shipments of cotton and coffee, and also some bills of exchange. Prior to his bankruptcy, and prior to the due date for payment, the debtor agreed that the creditor should sell the cotton and the coffee. The cotton was sold before the bankruptcy, but the sale of the coffee was not effected until later. The proceeds of sale of the cotton, together with an amount received on one of the bills of exchanged that matured before the bankruptcy, were sufficient to pay both debts, leaving a surplus. It was held that this surplus could be set off against a separate unsecured debt. The justification for allowing a set-off was the debtor's assent to a sale before the debt was due and before bankruptcy, which was taken to include also authority to receive the proceeds.[153] Cleasby B in the Exchequer Chamber said that this authority altered the position of the parties so that, as soon as it was given, credit was given to the creditor for the proceeds of sale.[154] He distinguished it from a deposit of property as security, because in that case the deposit is not made for the purpose of being converted into money, but rather with the intention of its being returned.[155] This is not a satisfactory explanation, however. All that occurred as a result of the sale was that one form of security (cotton) was replaced with another, in the form of the proceeds of the sale. The question still should have been how the proceeds were to be treated. In Victoria, Marks J suggested that the authority given to the creditor in *Astley v Gurney* to receive the proceeds of sale was interpreted as authority to apply the proceeds in satisfaction of other debts.[156] While this is not stated expressly in the judgments, it seems the best explanation for the decision.

In neither *Young v Bank of Bengal* nor *Astley v Gurney* was the question of a trust   **10.39**
canvassed, but it was considered in *Re H E Thorne & Son Ltd*.[157] A company had mortgaged some machinery, the mortgage agreement containing a covenant by the mortgagor to insure. The machinery was destroyed by fire, and the insurance

---

[151] (1836) 1 Moore 150, 168, 12 ER 771, 778.

[152] (1869) LR 4 CP 714.

[153] See Bovill CJ in the Common Pleas (1869) LR 4 CP 714, 719–720, and Cleasby B on appeal in the Exchequer Chamber at 722–723.

[154] (1869) LR 4 CP 714, 722. The appeal to the Exchequer Chamber was only in respect of the coffee sold after the bankruptcy (see below), but Cleasby B's comments were expressed generally, in relation to both the cotton and the coffee. Indeed, he said (at 723) that it did not matter whether the sale occurred before or after bankruptcy.

[155] (1869) LR 4 CP 714, 721–722.

[156] *Lloyds Bank NZA v National Safety Council* [1993] 2 VR 506, 512.

[157] [1914] 2 Ch 438.

money was paid to the mortgagee. Some two weeks later the company went into liquidation. It was held that the mortgagee could set off the surplus over and above the mortgage debt against a separate unsecured debt of the mortgagor.[158] It was argued that the surplus was held on trust and that therefore it was not susceptible to a set-off, but Astbury J was not persuaded. Instead, he based his decision upon a statement by Lord Esher in *Eberle's Hotels v Jonas*,[159] that 'wherever in the result the dealings on each side would end in a money claim, [the set-off section] would be applicable'. He said that the liquidator's argument that there may not be a set-off 'where a creditor holds the balance of a realized security in trust for his debtor so that the creditor is not entitled to deal with it in his account . . . would form a serious limitation on the general rule in *Eberle's Hotels Co v Jonas*'.[160] However this view would seem to allow any trust fund arising from a dealing to be employed in a set-off, a conclusion that would hardly be accepted.[161]

Proceeds received after the debtor's insolvency

10.40   Alternatively, the security may be enforced and the proceeds received *after* the debtor's bankruptcy or liquidation. In *Young v Bank of Bengal*[162] a debtor pledged promissory notes as security for a debt, but became bankrupt prior to default in payment. When default subsequently occurred the bank exercised its security rights and sold the notes. The Privy Council held that a surplus remaining after satisfying the secured debt had to be accounted for without a set-off against a sep-

---

[158] The insurance money received under a policy taken out pursuant to a covenant to insure would have taken the place of the property destroyed, and would have been held as security until it was applied in payment of the mortgage debt. See *Edmonds v The Hamilton Provident and Loan Society* (1891) 18 OAR 347.

[159] (1887) 18 QBD 459, 465. Astbury J found further support for his conclusion in another statement in Lord Esher's judgment in *Eberle's Hotels* (at 466) that: 'These cigars were deposited to secure a debt with power to sell them at once, even before default in payment of the monthly instalments. If the defendants had sold them before the debt was paid, I am disposed to think that the plaintiffs' claim for an account of their proceeds would then have been a mere money claim.' However this comment should be understood in the context of a letter written by the plaintiffs to the defendants authorizing them to dispose of the cigars and to 'put the proceeds to their credit'. See at 459–460. In other words, it was contemplated that, if the cigars were sold, the proceeds were not to be kept separate but rather were to be credited to the general account between them.

[160] [1914] 2 Ch 438, 453. In *Lloyds Bank NZA v National Safety Council* [1993] 2 VR 506, 512 Marks J distinguished *Re Thorne* on the ground that a credit in fact had been raised at the time of the liquidation, the surplus moneys having been credited to the account of the company before its liquidation. He also suggested that authority to credit proceeds against existing debts was open to implication in the *Thorne* case. It appears that there had been correspondence between the parties in *Re Thorne* prior to the liquidation in which the company's indebtedness was shown after deducting the insurance proceeds. See [1914] 2 Ch 438, 440. However, neither of the matters to which Marks J referred formed part of Astbury J's reasons in the *Thorne* case.

[161] In particular, Astbury J's analysis fails to account for the denial of a set-off in the special-purpose payment cases. These were distinguished, unsatisfactorily, by Astbury J on the ground that the exercise of a right of set-off would have amounted to a breach of a specific contract. See the discussion of these cases in paras 10.43–10.54 below.

[162] (1836) 1 Moore 150.

arate unsecured debt. The denial of a set-off has been explained on the ground that the security was deposited only for a particular or special purpose,[163] although this is not the reason that was given. Indeed, it is difficult to reconcile that explanation with Lord Brougham's view that a set-off would have been available if the security had been enforced before the bankruptcy.[164] A set-off in fact was denied because it was thought that credit had not been given[165] within the meaning ascribed to that expression by Gibbs CJ in *Rose v Hart*. The Privy Council adopted a strict interpretation of *Rose v Hart*, and said that it was necessary to show that the transaction was such that it *must* end in a debt.[166] This could not be said with certainty in the *Young* case, because default had not occurred at the date of the bankruptcy. Therefore there was no authority to sell at that time, and indeed the security could have been redeemed by the assignees in bankruptcy.

The question of set-off in this context also arose in *Astley v Gurney*,[167] to which reference was made earlier.[168] Briefly, a debtor provided as security bills of lading for shipments of cotton and coffee, and also some bills of exchange. Most of the bills of exchange were collected after the bankruptcy, and the Common Pleas held, on the authority of *Young v Bank of Bengal*, that the surplus proceeds arising in relation to them could not be set off against a separate unsecured debt. It was never intended that the proceeds of the bills of exchange should be applied to anything but the debt for which they were given as security. Credit therefore was not given for the surplus.[169] The position was different, however, in relation to the coffee, which was also sold after the bankruptcy. This was the subject of an appeal to the Exchequer Chamber,[170] which held that those surplus proceeds could be set off against a separate unsecured debt. The set-off in this instance was justified on the same ground referred to earlier in relation to the cotton,[171] that the debtor had authorized a sale before the debt had matured and before the bankruptcy, which

10.41

---

[163] *Alsager v Currie* (1844) 12 M & W 751, 757–758, 152 ER 1402, 1404; *Naoroji v Chartered Bank of India* (1868) LR 3 CP 444, 448, *per* Byles J (*arguendo*); *Re Daintrey* [1900] 1 QB 546, 559. See also *M S Fashions Ltd v Bank of Credit and Commerce International SA* [1993] Ch 425, 451, and *Key v Flint* (1817) 8 Taunt 21, 23, 129 ER 289, 289–290.

[164] (1836) 1 Moore 150, 168, 12 ER 771, 778, and see para 10.37 above.

[165] Because the security was enforced and the proceeds were obtained *after* the bankruptcy, there was not a 'debt' in existence at the date of the bankruptcy. If therefore a set-off was to proceed, it was necessary to find that credit was given. See paras 7.02–7.04 above.

[166] See the discussion at (1836) 1 Moore 150, 168–169, 12 ER 771, 779. In later cases it was said to be sufficient if the transaction would naturally or in the ordinary course of business end in a debt. See eg *Naoroji v Chartered Bank of India* (1868) LR 3 CP 444, 451, 452, and para 7.04 above. In the *Naoroji* case, Byles J (at 452) described *Young v Bank of Bengal* as 'a very doubtful authority'.

[167] (1869) LR 4 CP 714.

[168] See para 10.38 above.

[169] (1869) LR 4 CP 714, 720.

[170] (1869) LR 4 CP 714. The report suggests that the Exchequer Chamber reversed the decision of the Common Pleas, whereas this is not obvious from a reading of the judgments. The discrepancy is explained in a footnote to another report of the case at 38 LJCP 357, 359.

[171] See para 10.38 above.

included authority to receive the proceeds. That authority constituted the giving of credit for the proceeds of sale when they were received.[172]

Criticism of the cases

10.42   The rationale in those cases for denying a set-off when the security was realized after the bankruptcy, in the absence of prior instructions to sell, was that credit had not been given at the date of the bankruptcy. The difficulty with relying on that explanation now is that the set-off section has been expanded to include claims arising out of mutual dealings.[173] Accordingly, if the question of a trust is left aside, the ostensible reason given in the cases for denying a set-off would no longer apply.[174] The 'debt' in respect of the surplus would be the product of a prior dealing between the parties, and therefore it would be part of their mutual dealings. It would no longer be to the point that it may have been uncertain whether the security would be sold because, as Brett LJ remarked in *Peat v Jones & Co*,[175] mutual dealings was added to the set-off section in order to get rid of questions which might arise as to whether a transaction would end in a debt or not. Therefore, if the courts were to ignore the trust impressed upon the surplus proceeds, it should not matter whether the security was realized before or after bankruptcy. The better approach is to recognize that surplus proceeds from the realization of a security are usually impressed with a trust. Unless in a particular case it is intended that the surplus be credited to an account between the parties, so that there is no trust, a creditor therefore should not be entitled to obtain priority over other creditors in relation to another unsecured debt owing to him by setting off the surplus against that debt.[176] This is the position in Victoria.[177] According to this view, it should not matter when the security was realized.[178]

---

[172]   Oditah, *Legal Aspects of Receivables Financing* (1991) 249–50 sought to explain the set-off on the ground that the security over the coffee had been released, but this does not solve the problem. It was merely agreed that the creditor could sell the coffee and receive the proceeds. One may assume that it was intended that the proceeds would then form the security.

[173]   See ch 7 above.

[174]   See Derham, 'Some Aspects of Mutual Credit and Mutual Dealings' (1992) 108 LQR 99, 109, a point also made by Phillips J in the Victorian Supreme Court in *Lloyds Bank NZA v National Safety Council* [1993] 2 VR 506, 520–522.

[175]   (1881) 8 QBD 147, 149.

[176]   Compare *Baker v Lloyd's Bank Ltd* [1920] 2 KB 322, although Roche J seems to have accepted (at 328) that the security in that case was not intended to be confined to the specific advance in respect of which it was given.

[177]   *Lloyd's Bank NZA Ltd v National Safety Council* [1993] 2 VR 506.

[178]   Indeed, an issue for consideration in relation to the surplus produced from the exercise of a power of sale governed by the Law of Property Act 1925 is whether the allowance of a set-off is consistent with s 105, which provides that any surplus received by a mortgagee, after paying prior claims, 'shall be paid to the person entitled to the mortgaged property'. In Australia see eg the Property Law Act 1958 (Vic), s 105. A similar provision is to be found in the Consumer Credit Act 1974, s 121(3) in relation to pawnbrokers.

F. Special-Purpose Payments

Failure of the purpose

If a person ('the depositor') has paid a sum of money to another ('the depository')   **10.43**
to be applied for a special purpose which has failed, or which has not been carried
into effect, the depositor is entitled to recover the money undiminished by a set-
off. This applies when the defence of set-off as between solvent parties under the
Statutes of Set-off is in issue,[179] and also, if the depositor has become bankrupt or
is a company which has gone into liquidation, when it is sought to base a defence
on the insolvency set-off section. In *Re Pollitt, ex p Minor*[180] a client was indebted
to his solicitor, who refused to act further unless the client deposited a sum of
money to cover future costs. The client accordingly placed money in the solicitor's
hands for that purpose. Subsequently the client became bankrupt, after which the
solicitor continued to act on his behalf. The Court of Appeal held that the solicitor was only entitled to his costs for the work performed before notice of the act of
bankruptcy, when his authority to act was revoked. Therefore the purpose for
which the money had been lodged with him had failed, and he was obliged to return the residue to the bankrupt's trustee without deducting the bankrupt's prior
debt to him. The leading judgment in the Court of Appeal was delivered by Lord
Esher MR, who commented:[181] 'If the money was given to the solicitor for a specific purpose, then, as between him and the bankrupt, there could not be a set-off.'

Residue remaining after the purpose is carried out

Alternatively, the purpose may have been carried out but there is a residue re-   **10.44**
maining in the hands of the depository. In *Re Mid-Kent Fruit Factory*[182] a company
gave two cheques to its solicitors for the purpose of discharging the claims of its
creditors, the solicitors being instructed to settle for less if possible. The solicitors
managed to settle for less in some cases, although the company was not informed
of this. When the company went into liquidation the solicitors sought to set off
the balance remaining against the company's liability for costs. Vaughan Williams
J considered that, when money is deposited for a special purpose, and after the
purpose is fulfilled a balance remains with the depository, the depository cannot
set off the balance in the depositor's bankruptcy unless the depository can show
that he retained it with the consent of the depositor.[183] In the case before him the

---

[179] *Stumore v Campbell & Co* [1892] 1 QB 314.
[180] [1893] 1 QB 455, affirming [1893] 1 QB 175.
[181] [1893] 1 QB 455, 458.
[182] [1896] 1 Ch 567. See also *Re City Equitable Fire Insurance Co Ltd* [1930] 2 Ch 293, 313–314.
[183] Compare *Buchanan v Findlay* (1829) 9 B & C 738, 749, 109 ER 274, 278, in which the depository would have been entitled under the agreement to retain the surplus if the proceeds of the
bills entrusted with him had been applied as directed.

company was not aware of the surplus, and so it could not be said that the company had consented to the solicitors retaining it. A set-off therefore was not available.[184]

Collection of the proceeds of a negotiable instrument

10.45 A similar principle may apply when a negotiable instrument is deposited with a person to collect the proceeds and apply them in a particular way. If the person instead retains the proceeds, and does not apply them as directed, the trustee in bankruptcy of the depositor may recover the proceeds undiminished by a set-off.[185]

The justification for denying a set-off

10.46 In some of these special-purpose payment cases the courts, when denying the depository a set-off, have emphasized the proprietary nature of the depositor's claim. Sometimes the deposit has been said to give rise to a trust,[186] and in other cases a bailment.[187] There is however authority which suggests that the rule is based upon a broader concept, and that the depository may be denied a set-off in the depositor's bankruptcy even though the relationship between the parties is only one of debt. In *Re City Equitable Fire Insurance Co Ltd*[188] a reinsurer under a treaty of reinsurance had agreed to accept a share of all fire insurance policies accepted or renewed by the insurer, and in order to secure the due performance of the reinsurer's obligations under the treaty the insurer was entitled to retain (as a 'deposit') 40 per cent of all premiums credited to the reinsurer in the first year. The reinsurer went into liquidation, and after all its obligations to the insurer under the treaty had been satisfied the insurer still retained a substantial fund. It was held that the deposit constituted money left in the hands of the insurer for a special purpose, and that the balance remaining after the purpose was satisfied had to be returned to the liquidator without a set-off against other debts owing by the reinsurer to the insurer. Counsel for the insurer argued that the deposit was not a trust fund but rather it was a loan with a conditional right to payment, and on that basis it should be able to employed in a set-off. It is an essential feature of a trust that it should be intended that the moneys in question be kept separate,[189] but it appears that the

---

[184] The depository has the onus of showing the depositor's consent.

[185] *Buchanan v Findlay* (1829) 9 B & C 738, 109 ER 274; *Atkinson v Learmouth* (1905) 11 ALR 191. See also *Alder v Keighley* (1846) 15 M & W 117, 153 ER 785 (though this case was decided by reference to the form of action employed).

[186] See *Wright v Watson* (1883) Cab & El 171, and also *Stumore v Campbell & Co* [1892] 1 QB 314.

[187] See *Re Mid-Kent Fruit Factory* [1896] 1 Ch 567, 572, and also *Buchanan v Findlay* (1829) 9 B & C 738, 749, 109 ER 274, 278 (bills of exchange deposited for a specific purpose).

[188] [1930] 2 Ch 293.

[189] See *Re Nanwa Gold Mines Ltd* [1955] 1 WLR 1080; *Re Bond Worth Ltd* [1980] 1 Ch 228, 260–261; *Westdeutsche Landesbank Girozentrale v Islington LBC* [1996] AC 669, 712; *Royal Trust*

insurer was not obliged to keep the deposit separate from its own funds. Further, the insurer was required to pay interest to the reinsurer on the deposit,[190] a factor which is usually considered to be a powerful indication of a debt rather than a trust relationship.[191] However, the existence or otherwise of a trust was not treated as critical to the decision. At first instance Maugham J commented:[192] 'It does not seem to me to matter much whether it is or is not regarded as a trust fund. It is, to my mind, moneys "deposited for a specific purpose" . . .'. On appeal, the Court of Appeal failed to mention the presence or absence of a trust. Lord Hanworth MR, with whom Lawrence and Romer LJJ agreed, was content to find that the accumulated fund was intended to be held for a specific purpose, as security for the due performance of the reinsurer's obligations under the treaty, and that therefore it should be set aside from any account between the parties.

Winn LJ in the Court of Appeal in *Halesowen Presswork and Assemblies Ltd v Westminster Bank Ltd*[193] suggested that the parties to mutual dealings may 'separate out' a particular debt, so that it is not to be regarded as mutual for the purpose of the insolvency set-off section. However Lord Kilbrandon on appeal doubted that proposition.[194] and it is inconsistent with the accepted view that the insolvency set-off section cannot be contracted out of.[195] Mutuality in truth is concerned with the status of the parties and their relationship with each other, not with the circumstances under which a debt arose.[196] Alternatively, Willes J once suggested[197] that 'some difficulty might arise' in allowing a defendant a set-off if he has 'purposely broken his contract in order to create the claim', and Astbury J had **10.47**

Bank v National Westminster Bank plc [1996] 2 BCLC 682, 701; *Triffit Nurseries v Salads Etcetera Ltd* [2000] 1 BCLC 761, 764; Finn, *Fiduciary Obligations* (1977) 103–4. Compare *Stephens Travel Service International Pty Ltd v Qantas Airways Ltd* (1988) 13 NSWLR 331, 349, referred to in *Re ILG Travel Ltd* [1995] 2 BCLC 128, 148–152, 156.

[190] Since the interest was to be paid to the reinsurer, and not retained by the insurer as part of the retention fund, it was held that it could be set off.

[191] *Pott v Clegg* (1847) 16 M & W 321, 327, 153 ER 1212, 1214, *per* Parke B, (*arguendo*); *Foley v Hill* (1848) 2 HLC 28, 36, 9 ER 1002, 1005; *Re Broad, ex p Neck* (1884) 13 QBD 740; Finn, *Fiduciary Obligations* (1977) 108. An agreement to pay interest is not conclusive evidence of a debt. For example, if the person receiving the money has agreed to invest it for the payer, and to pay the interest that is actually received, a trust is created. See Scott, *The Law of Trusts* (4th edn, 1987) vol 1, 135–6 para 12.2, and *Re Exchange Travel (Holdings) Ltd (No 3)* [1996] BCLC 524, 534. However, in cases like the *City Equitable Fire* case, where the agreement is to pay interest at a defined rate whether or not the money is invested, that circumstance almost certainly indicates that the payee is to have the use of the money, and that the transaction gives rise to a debt and not a trust. See Scott, *The Law of Trusts, loc cit.*

[192] [1930] 2 Ch 293, 303.

[193] [1971] 1 QB 1, 43–44, referring to his earlier judgment in *Rolls Razor Ltd v Cox* [1967] 1 QB 552, 575.

[194] *National Westminster Bank Ltd v Halesowen Presswork and Assemblies Ltd* [1972] AC 785, 821.

[195] See paras 6.71–6.72 above.

[196] See para 11.01 below.

[197] *Turner v Thomas* (1871) LR 6 CP 610, 614.

recourse to a similar notion in *Re H E Thorne & Son Ltd*[198] in order to explain the special-purpose payment cases. He said that a depository is denied a set-off in these cases 'if it involves a breach of the contract under which he obtained the money'.[199] Other judgments support that view. In *Re Pollitt*[200] Vaughan Williams J said that: 'The attempt to use the money deposited as security for another purpose than that for which it was deposited is an attempt to do wrong.' In an Australian case, *Atkinson v Learmouth*,[201] a debtor had handed a promissory note to the creditor with instructions to collect the proceeds and to pay them (less a discount) into the debtor's bank account. The creditor duly collected the proceeds, but instead of applying them as directed he retained them in satisfaction of the debtor's debt to him. While there are statements in the joint judgment of Hodges and Holroyd JJ which suggest that the claim brought by the debtor's assignee in bankruptcy for payment of the proceeds was regarded as proprietary in nature,[202] they commented in disallowing a set-off that:[203] 'we should expect that the law would not allow a man by dishonestly breaking his contract, and keeping another man's money, to gain any advantage'. The problem with this as an explanation is that there is no such general principle which precludes a person from basing a set-off upon his own breach of contract, even where the contract is purposely broken in order to bring about that result.[204] For example, failure to pay a debt on time constitutes a breach of contract,[205] but a creditor who is aware of the debtor's insolvency and who consequently withholds payment of his own debt to the debtor is not for that reason denied a set-off. It is difficult to see why a simple breach of contract in any other form should be treated differently. But even if there were a general principle to the effect that a set-off may not arise when a contract has been breached for the very purpose of gaining a set-off, it would not be relevant to special-purpose payment cases in which the purpose has failed for some other reason, or when the purpose has been carried out leaving a surplus.

10.48   Nor is the breach of contract theory supported by the old common law cases which established that, when either money or a negotiable instrument was lodged with a depository to be applied by him to a specific purpose, and the depository instead wilfully retained the money, or the instrument or its proceeds, in purported satisfaction of the depositor's indebtedness to him, there could not be

---

[198] [1914] 2 Ch 438.
[199] [1914] 2 Ch 438, 450.
[200] [1893] 1 QB 175, 179 (decision affirmed [1893] 1 QB 455).
[201] (1905) 11 ALR 191.
[202] Hodges and Holroyd JJ emphasized (at (1905) 11 ALR 191, 194–195) that the debtor was the owner of the note and the proceeds. They also said (at 196) that the difference between their approach and that of the dissentient, Hood J, was the statement by Hood J that the dealing in the note was intended to terminate in a debt.
[203] (1905) 11 ALR 191, 195.
[204] See para 8.74 above.
[205] *Re City Equitable Fire Insurance Co Ltd* [1930] 2 Ch 293, 302, *per* Maugham J.

a set-off if the depositor brought a special action for breach of duty, although a set-off was allowed if the depositor waived the breach and sued instead for money had and received.[206] These cases are explicable on the basis of the form of action employed. Actions for damages for breach of duty are unliquidated in nature, and before 1861[207] claims of that nature could not be proved in a bankruptcy, and consequently could not be set off.[208] While it was generally considered in these cases that a set-off was available in an action for money had and received,[209] they were decided at common law where the presence of absence of a trust arising out of the stated purpose ordinarily would not have been considered.[210]

The only justification for denying a set-off to a depository against the obligation **10.49** to account for the remains of a fund received for a special purpose is that the money was held subject to a trust. If the money was not intended to be kept separate from the depository's own funds before the purpose was carried out, there would not be a trust,[211] in which case a set-off in principle should be available to the depository in the depositor's bankruptcy. This was the view of the Court of Appeal in the context of set-off between solvent parties,[212] and it should apply equally to insolvency set-off. The *City Equitable Fire* case therefore should only be regarded as correctly decided if, notwithstanding the obligation to pay interest, there was a trust so that the insurer would have been obliged to pay the retention moneys into a separate account. Given that there does not appear to have been an obligation to keep the deposit separate, a set-off should have been available.

---

[206] See generally *Colson v Welsh* (1795) 1 Esp 378, 170 ER 391; *Atkinson v Elliott* (1797) 7 TR 378, 101 ER 1030; *Thorpe v Thorpe* (1832) 3 B & Ad 580, 110 ER 211; *Hill v Smith* (1844) 12 M & W 618, 152 ER 1346; *Alder v Keighley* (1846) 15 M & W 117, 153 ER 785; *Bell v Carey* (1849) 8 CB 887, 137 ER 757. Compare *Buchanan v Findlay* (1829) 9 B & C 738, 109 ER 274, in which a set-off was disallowed in an action for money had and received in relation to the proceeds of bills, although in that case the bankrupts prior to their bankruptcy had demanded the return of the bills, so that the defendants had no right to receive the proceeds.

[207] Compare the Bankruptcy Act 1861, s 153.

[208] *Rose v Sims* (1830) 1 B & Ad 521, 109 ER 881. Compare *Gibson v Bell* (1835) 1 Bing (NC) 743, 131 ER 1303 and *Groom v West* (1838) 8 Ad & E 758, 112 ER 1025. It was held in these cases that, when a purchaser of goods who had agreed to pay the price by accepting a bill of exchange in fact failed to do so, and the vendor's assignees in bankruptcy brought a special action of assumpsit against him for breach of contract, the purchaser could set off in that action an independent indebtedness of the bankrupt vendor to him (but compare *Hutchinson v Reid* (1813) 3 Camp 329, 170 ER 1400 in the context of the Statutes of Set-off). This was justified on the ground that the claim in reality was for the price of the goods themselves, so that effectively it was liquidated in nature. Indeed, Lord Denman CJ in *Groom v West* distinguished the liquidated nature of the demand before him from the case of a claim for unliquidated damages for breach of duty in not applying a special purpose payment in the required manner.

[209] See eg *Colson v Welsh* (1795) 1 Esp 378, 380, 170 ER 391, 391–392; *Atkinson v Elliott* (1797) 7 TR 378, 101 ER 1030; *Hill v Smith* (1844) 12 M & W 618, 631, 152 ER 1346, 1351 (in relation to the Statutes of Set-off). Compare *Buchanan v Findlay* (1829) 9 B & C 738, 109 ER 274, explained in *Thorpe v Thorpe* (1832) 3 B & Ad 580, 583–584, 110 ER 211, 212.

[210] Compare para 2.81 above in relation to set-off of judgments.

[211] See para 10.46 above.

[212] *Anglo Corporation Ltd v Peacock AG* [1997] EWCA Civ 992.

Subsequently Lord Kilbrandon and Lord Simon of Glaisdale referred to the *City Equitable Fire* case without criticism in *National Westminster Bank Ltd v Halesowen Presswork and Assemblies Ltd*,[213] but their respective explanations for the special-purpose payment cases each seem to countenance a form of trust fund. Lord Kilbrandon said that the funds in these cases were 'impressed with quasi-trust purposes',[214] a concept that has also been used to explain the status of property held under a fiduciary obligation that is similar to a trust, but which is not a trust in the strict technical sense of the word.[215] Indeed, Lord Kilbrandon referred in his judgment to the 'fund' held by way of guarantee against the non-performance of the obligations in the *City Equitable Fire* case, which suggests that he assumed that there was a trust in that case. The use of the expression 'quasi-trust' was criticized by Lord Simon of Glaisdale as giving 'uncertain guidance in the law'. He preferred to say that: 'money is paid for a special (or specific) purpose so as to exclude mutuality of dealing within [the set-off section] if the money is paid in such circumstances that it would be a misappropriation to use it for any other purpose than that for which it is paid'.[216] It is not clear what he meant by 'misappropriation', but it suggests that the parties should have intended that there be a separate fund which is not to be misappropriated, and such a fund may be characterized as a trust fund.

Bank accounts, and other debt relationships

10.50 In *National Westminster v Halesowen* a company's current account with its bank was overdrawn. It was agreed between the company and the bank that the account should be frozen, and that a new account should be opened through which the company's current business henceforth should pass. It was held that this new account was not precluded from being set off in the company's liquidation against the overdrawn account by virtue of being a special-purpose account. This view seems correct. The account had credited to it the company's own money. It was a normal bank account giving rise to a debtor/creditor relationship. There are other cases to a similar effect. In *Pedder v The Mayor, Aldermen, and Burgesses of Preston*[217] the Corporation of Preston had an account with a bank for the Corporation's general municipal functions. In addition the Corporation had been constituted the Local Board of Health under the Public Health Act 1848, and for this a separate account was opened with the same bank. The bank entered into an arrangement with its creditors under the Bankrupt Law Consolidation Act 1849,

---

[213] [1972] AC 785.

[214] [1972] AC 785, 821.

[215] *Foley v Hill* (1848) 2 HLC 28, 35–36, 9 ER 1002, 1005. In modern parlance this is called a constructive trust. See Finn, *Fiduciary Obligations* (1977) 89.

[216] [1972] AC 785, 808. See also *Re Arthur Sanders Ltd* (1981) 17 BLR 125, 133, and the comments of Vaughan Williams J in the Divisional Court in *Re Pollitt* [1893] 1 QB 175, 179.

[217] (1862) 12 CB(NS) 535, 142 ER 1251.

at which time the general account was overdrawn and the Local Board of Health account was in credit. Section 87 of the 1848 Act provided that the money received by the Local Board of Health 'shall be applied . . . in defraying such of the Expenses incurred or to be incurred by the said Local Board in carrying this Act into execution', but it was nevertheless held that the Corporation could set the credit balance on that account against its indebtedness on the other. A second case is *Ex parte Pearce, re Langmead*.[218] Commissioners had been appointed for the purposes of improving the harbour of Teignmouth and the navigation of the river Teign. The Commissioners opened two accounts with a bank, headed respectively 'No 1 Harbour Account' and 'No 2 River Account'. The Harbour Account was in credit and the River Account in debit. It was held in the bankruptcy of the bank that the two accounts could be set off, notwithstanding that an Act of Parliament provided that the sums standing to the credit of the Harbour Account were to be used in improving Teignmouth Harbour. In the *Pedder* and *Pearce* cases the debtor on the special purpose account was bankrupt, whereas in the *Halesowen* case the creditor on the account was the insolvent party, but the principle should be the same. In *M S Fashions Ltd v Bank of Credit and Commerce International SA*[219] the Court of Appeal[220] held that an account into which money had been deposited as security for a third party's debt to the bank was not exempt from set-off on the basis of the special-purpose payment cases.[221]

A different result occurred in New South Wales in *National Mutual Royal Bank v Ginges*.[222] The *Ginges* case concerned an account opened by a company in similar circumstances to the account in the *Halesowen* case. Brownie J accepted that its purpose was to provide creditors participating in a moratorium with a 'fund' to which they could look for payment, and held that it could not be set off in the company's liquidation. But unless the creditors had an equitable interest in the account,[223] which was not discussed,[224] the purpose for which the account was **10.51**

---

[218] (1841) 2 Mont D & De G 142.
[219] [1993] Ch 425, 448–451.
[220] Dillon, Nolan and Steyn LJJ.
[221] See also *Bank of Credit and Commerce Hong Kong Ltd (in liq) v Mahadumrongkul* (8 May 1997), in which the Privy Council (on appeal from the Court of Appeal of Hong Kong) rejected the view that a deposit made by a director of a company with a bank as security for the company's debt to the bank was held on trust.
[222] Supreme Court of New South Wales, 15 March 1991.
[223] See paras 11.04–11.07 below.
[224] The judgment records that the bank paid the money into court pursuant to Part IV of the Trustee Act 1925 (NSW), and that Waddell CJ in Eq in earlier proceedings (30 April 1990) had ordered that the money be paid to the liquidator. However the reason for the order does not appear in Brownie J's judgment in the *Ginges* case, in particular whether the question of set-off was raised before Waddell CJ in Eq. Nor was the question of a trust discussed in these proceedings. The bank was suing the defendants as guarantors of the company's overdrawn account, and the guarantors argued unsuccessfully by way of defence that the overdrawn account should have been set off in the company's liquidation against the account in credit.

opened should not have prevented a set-off. As between the bank and the customer the account simply gave rise to a debt.[225]

10.52 When the relationship is one of debt, for example where money is paid into a bank account to be applied to a particular purpose which has not been carried out, other factors nevertheless may affect the availability of a set-off. In the first place, there may have been an agreement (express or implied) that the debt is not to be set off, although this would not be effective to exclude a set-off once bankruptcy or liquidation occurs[226] Secondly, if the money was paid to the bank under circumstances where it was specifically appropriated to meet a liability owing by the depositor to a third party, the circumstances may be such as to give rise to an equitable assignment or, if the bank has communicated its assent to the arrangement to the third party, possibly it may constitute an attornment so as to entitle the third party to sue on the basis of money had and received,[227] although attornment where there is no fund remains a matter of controversy.[228] In either case this would destroy mutuality for the purpose of set-off against the depositor.

The principle rephrased

10.53 If the existence of a trust is recognized as the reason for denying a set-off in the special-purpose payment cases, the statements of law found in *Re Pollitt* and *Re Mid-Kent* should be rephrased. The principle is better stated in terms that, if a payment is made for a special purpose, and either the purpose fails or, it if has been carried out, a residue remains, the depository may not set off the obligation to return the money if the depositor has retained a beneficial interest in the money so that it is subject to a trust in his favour.[229] In the *Mid-Kent Fruit Factory* case[230] Vaughan Williams J said that, if there is a residue remaining after the purpose has been carried out, the depository may not bring it into an account unless he can show that it remained in his hands with the depositor's consent. While the depositor's consent to the money remaining with the depository may militate against a trust, it is not conclusive. The question is the terms upon which the money was to be retained, in particular whether the depositor could

---

[225] Nevertheless Clarke JA referred to *National Mutual v Ginges* without adverse comment in *Central Brake Service (Sydney) Ltd v Central Brake Service (Newcastle) Ltd* (1992) 27 NSWLR 406, 412. Compare also Helsham CJ in Eq's comments in *MPS Constructions Pty Ltd v Rural Bank of New South Wales* (1980) 4 ACLR 835, 845 in relation to the bank account set up in that case for the payment of retention money pursuant to a building contract.

[226] See paras 6.71–6.72 above.

[227] *W P Greenhalgh and Sons v Union Bank of Manchester* [1924] 2 KB 153.

[228] See the criticism of *Shamia v Joory* [1958] 2 QB 448 in Goff and Jones, *The Law of Restitution* (5th edn, 1998) 691–2.

[229] See *Barclays Bank Ltd v Quistclose Investments Ltd* [1970] AC 567, 581–582, as explained by Lord Millett in *Twinsectra Ltd v Yardley* [2002] 2 AC 164, 186 para 77 *et seq.*

[230] [1896] 1 Ch 567. See para 10.44 above.

mix it with his own funds or whether he was required to keep it separate for the benefit of the depositor.[231]

The distinction between a debt and a trust is important not only for set-off, but **10.54** also in the determination of the depositor's rights as against the depository where the depository became bankrupt before the money was applied to the purpose. If the fund was deposited subject to a trust, and the purpose has failed, the depositor as the beneficial owner of the money can recover it in full from the bankrupt's estate.[232] If however the relationship between the parties is simply one of debtor and creditor, as was the case in *Re Barned's Banking Co Ltd. Massey's case* where a bank was provided with funds to cover the acceptance of a bill of exchange,[233] the depositor is confined to a proof in the depository's bankruptcy.

---

[231] See para 10.46 above.

[232] Insolvency Act 1986, s 283(3). See eg *Ex parte Dumas* (1754) 2 Ves Sen 582, 28 ER 372; *Re Rogers, ex p Holland and Hannen* (1891) 8 Morr 243; *Barclays Bank Ltd v Quistclose Investments Ltd* [1970] AC 567. See also *Tooke v Hollingworth* (1793) 5 TR 215, 101 ER 121, affirmed (1795) 2 H Bl 501, 126 ER 670 for the position at common law.

[233] (1870) 39 LJ Ch 635. See also *Pott v Clegg* (1847) 16 M & W 321, 153 ER 1212. Compare *Farley v Turner* (1857) 26 LJ Ch 710, where the bank had specifically appropriated the money to the purpose before its bankruptcy.

11

MUTUALITY—INTRODUCTION

A. The Meaning of Mutuality

For both the insolvency set-off section and the Statutes of Set-off there must be **11.01** mutuality.[1] Mutuality does not require that the claims should arise at the same time,[2] nor that there should be any connection between them.[3] It is irrelevant, moreover, that the claims may be of a different nature. As the High Court of Australia expressed it in *Gye v McIntyre*,[4] 'the word "mutual" conveys the notion of reciprocity rather than that of correspondence'. Thus, an obligation arising out of an instrument under seal may be set off against a simple contract debt,[5] and a secured debt may be set off against an unsecured debt.[6] Mutuality in fact refers to two characteristics, that the demands must be between the same parties, and that

---

[1] Compare paras 4.48–4.54 above in relation to equitable set-off. Lack of mutuality is also a defence to proceedings for specific performance, but it is there used in a different sense, that as a matter of discretion the court will not compel a defendant to perform his obligations specifically if it cannot at the same time ensure that any unperformed obligations of the claimant will be specifically performed, unless damages would be an adequate remedy for any default by the claimant. See *Price v Strange* [1978] 1 Ch 337, 367–368, *per* Buckley LJ.

[2] *Halsbury's Laws of England* (4th edn, 1999) vol 42, para 421 n 2. See also the reference in *Day and Dent Constructions Pty Ltd v North Australian Properties Pty Ltd* (1981) 34 ALR 595, 600, Federal Court of Australia, to the submission to that effect in relation to the Statutes of Set-off, which was not disputed.

[3] *Naoroji v Chartered Bank of India* (1868) LR 3 CP 444, 452; *Re Daintrey* [1900] 1 QB 546.

[4] (1991) 171 CLR 609, 623.

[5] See eg *Ex parte Law, re Kennedy* (1864) De Gex 378.

[6] See paras 6.120–6.125 above in relation to insolvency set-off.

they must be held in the same capacity, or right, or interest.[7] It is concerned with the status of the parties and their relationship to each other. It is not concerned with the nature of the claims themselves. The nature of the claims is dealt with instead by the requirement of 'debts', or, in insolvency set-off, of 'debts', 'credits' or claims arising out of prior 'dealings'.[8] The requirement of same parties means that A's right to sue B may not be set off against A's indebtedness to C, or that a joint demand may not be set off against a separate demand.[9] In the case of insolvency set-off, the requirement that the demands be held in the same capacity or right or interest means that each of the parties, who is liable to the other, must be the beneficial owner of the cross-claim against that other.[10] In other words, 'there must be identity between the persons beneficially interested in the claim and the person against whom the cross-claim existed'.[11] The principle differs slightly for the Statutes of Set-off. In that context mutuality strictly is determined by reference to legal titles, although equity may confer or deny a set-off depending on whether there is mutuality in equity.[12] In the case of a company, a change in control of the company between the dates that the cross-demands were contracted does not affect mutuality, if in truth the same legal entity was the contracting party in both cases.[13]

11.02 The form of the arrangements by which the cross-demands came into existence does not affect mutuality. It is not correct to say, as Lord Denning suggested in the Court of Appeal in *Halesowen Presswork and Assemblies Ltd v Westminster Bank Ltd*,[14] that the nature of the arrangements entered into may be 'so special as to deprive them of mutuality', an approach that Lord Cross of Chelsea on appeal in the House of Lords[15] criticized as being too narrow in the light of the decided cases.[16] In *Rolls Razor Ltd v Cox*[17] Winn LJ advanced the theory that mutuality essentially is concerned with the intentions of the parties.[18] Subsequently however Jonathan

---

[7] *Ince Hall Rolling Mills Co Ltd v The Douglas Forge Co* (1882) 8 QBD 179, 183 ('between the same parties and in the same interest'); *Shand v M J Atkinson Ltd* [1966] NZLR 551, 570 ('by and against a person in the same right'); *Peel v Fitzgerald* [1982] Qd R 544, 547 ('between the same parties and in the same right').

[8] See ch 7 above.

[9] See ch 12 below.

[10] See paras 11.04–11.07 below.

[11] *West Street Properties Pty Ltd v Jamison* [1974] 2 NSWLR 435, 441, *per* Jeffrey J.

[12] See paras 11.08–11.10 below.

[13] *Central Brake Service (Sydney) Pty Ltd v Central Brake Service (Newcastle) Pty Ltd* (1992) 27 NSWLR 406 (official management).

[14] [1971] 1 QB 1, 36.

[15] *National Westminster Bank Ltd v Halesowen Presswork and Assemblies Ltd* [1972] AC 785, 812.

[16] Compare Viscount Dilhorne, who said (at [1972] AC 785, 806) that the arrangements before him were not of this special character, without offering an opinion in relation to Lord Denning's view.

[17] [1967] 1 QB 552, 574.

[18] See also the reference to intention in *Gore-Browne on Companies* (44th edn, looseleaf) §34.9, p 34.046.

Parker J in *Re ILG Travel Ltd*[19] rejected the proposition that the subjective intentions of the parties can be decisive of the question whether dealings between them are mutual dealings, and indeed in insolvency set-off the notion that intention is relevant to mutuality is contrary to the proposition that the insolvency set-off section cannot be contracted out of.[20] Later Winn LJ commented that the set-off section in the insolvency legislation 'applies only to cross-claims arising *directly* from dealings between a person who has become a bankrupt and another person all of which are properly called "mutual" '.[21] In essence, this appears to be no more than a restatement of the argument that was rejected in 1798 in *Hankey v Smith*,[22] that for mutual credit the parties should have meant to trust each other in the transaction in question. It was held in that case that an indebtedness of a bankrupt acceptor upon a bill of exchange could be brought into an account by the holder, even though the bankrupt was unaware that the bill had been indorsed to the holder. A similar result has occurred in the context of the Statutes of Set-off.[23] The notion of 'direct' dealings, or of the element of trust, fails to explain the undoubted right of set-off in cases like *Hankey v Smith*, or indeed in any case in which one of the parties to the proposed set-off gained a right to sue the other only as a result of an assignment to him of the other's indebtedness.[24] Rather, those cases support the view that for mutuality one should look only to the identity of the persons entitled to the benefit and subject to the burden of the cross-demands.

The necessity for mutuality

It has been said that mutuality must always be present,[25] but the rule is better **11.03** stated that cross-demands which are not mutual may not be set off 'except under special circumstances'.[26] Reference is made in the following discussion

---

[19] [1995] 2 BCLC 128, 160.

[20] See para 6.71 above.

[21] *Halesowen Presswork and Assemblies Ltd v Westminster Bank Ltd* [1971] 1 QB 1, 43, CA (emphasis added).

[22] (1789) 3 TR 507n, 100 ER 703. There have nevertheless been other occasions when mutuality has been defined in terms of mutual trust. See Story, *Commentaries on Equity Jurisprudence* (14th edn, 1918) vol 3, 471 (and the cases referred to in note 4), and *Knox v Cockburn* (1862) 1 QSCR 80. See also *Koster v Eason* (1813) 2 M & S 112, 118, 105 ER 324, 326–327, where Lord Ellenborough spoke in terms of 'consent'.

[23] See eg *Cornforth v Rivett* (1814) 2 M & S 510, 105 ER 471.

[24] See eg *Clark v Cort* (1840) Cr & Ph 154, 41 ER 449; *Mathieson's Trustee v Burrup, Mathieson and Co* [1927] 1 Ch 562; *Southern Cross Construction Ltd v Southern Cross Club Ltd* [1973] 1 NZLR 708; *Kon Strukt Pty Ltd v Storage Developments Pty Ltd* (1989) 96 FLR 43. See also, with respect to the Statutes of Set-off, *Bennett v White* [1910] 2 KB 643.

[25] *Re Mid-Kent Fruit Factory* [1896] 1 Ch 567, 571. See also *Knox v Cockburn* (1862) 1 QSCR 80, 83; *Re City Life Assurance Co Ltd* [1926] 1 Ch 191, 216; *Day and Dent Constructions Pty Ltd v North Australian Properties Pty Ltd* (1981) 34 ALR 595, 601, Federal Court of Australia.

[26] *Freeman v Lomas* (1851) 9 Hare 109, 113–114, 68 ER 435, 437, *per* Sir George Turner. See also *West Street Properties Pty Ltd v Jamison* [1974] 2 NSWLR 435, 441.

to a number of situations in which the courts have allowed a set-off despite the absence of strict mutuality.

B. Equitable Interests—Insolvency Set-off

11.04 A fundamental principle of insolvency set-off is that mutuality is determined by reference to the equitable interests of the parties rather than their bare legal rights.[27] Therefore the beneficial owner of a debt may set off the debt against a liability that he has to the debtor.[28] Thus, where an equitable assignee of a debt is being sued by the debtor's trustee in bankruptcy in respect of a separate liability that he owes to the debtor, he may bring the assigned debt into an account.[29] Conversely, a set-off will be denied if one of the parties to the proposed set-off holds the claim as a bare trustee for someone else,[30] or if he has assigned it in favour of a third party,[31] although in such a case there is the possibility of a set-off between the debtor on the assigned debt and the true beneficial owner.[32] The emphasis on equitable rights is a consequence of the influence of equity in matters of bankruptcy. The Chancellor more or less assumed control over bankruptcy in the nineteenth century, and ever since the creation of a separate Court of Bankruptcy in 1831[33] and its subsequent amalgamation with the Supreme Court of Judicature in

---

[27] *Re Hett, Maylor and Co* (1894) 10 TLR 412; *Hiley v Peoples Prudential Assurance Co Ltd* (1938) 60 CLR 468, 488, 497; *Gye v McIntyre* (1991) 171 CLR 609, 623. As Byles J remarked during argument in *Watkins v Clark* (1862) 12 CB (NS) 277, 282, 142 ER 1149, 1152, 'The bankrupt law deals with beneficial interests only.'

[28] *Crosse v Smith* (1813) 1 M & S 545, 105 ER 204; *Bailey v Johnson* (1872) LR 7 Ex 263; *Ex parte Morier, re Willis, Percival & Co* (1879) 12 Ch D 491, 496, 500, 502; *Hiley v Peoples Prudential Assurance Co Ltd* (1938) 60 CLR 468, 497. See also *Cochrane v Green* (1860) 9 CB (NS) 448, 142 ER 176. The observations of Sir George Jessel MR in *Middleton v Pollock, ex p Nugee* (1875) LR 20 Eq 29, 36–37 (and see also *Welton v Harnett* (1886) 7 NSWR 74) on the necessity for some 'special jurisdiction' should not be regarded as correct.

[29] *Mathieson's Trustee v Burrup, Mathieson and Co* [1927] 1 Ch 562.

[30] For example, when a creditor of a bankrupt on a negotiable instrument holds the instrument as trustee for a third party, the creditor may not employ it in a set-off. See *Fair v M'Iver* (1812) 16 East 130, 104 ER 1038; *Belcher v Lloyd* (1833) 10 Bing 310, 131 ER 924; *Lackington v Combes* (1839) 6 Bing (NC) 71, 133 ER 28; *Forster v Wilson* (1843) 14 M & W 191, 152 ER 1165; *London, Bombay, and Mediterranean Bank v Narraway* (1872) LR 15 Eq 93; *Tapper v Matheson* (1884) NZLR 3 SC 312. Why did the fact that Rawilla Pty Ltd was a trustee of a discretionary trust not preclude a set-off in *Re Last, ex p Butterell* (1994) 124 ALR 219? See para 17.93, n 499 below.

[31] *Boyd v Mangles* (1874) 16 M & W 337, 153 ER 1218; *Re Asphaltic Wood Pavement Co. Lee & Chapman's Case* (1885) 30 Ch D 216; *Re W Guthrie and Allied Companies* (1901) 4 GLR 155 (NZSC). See also *De Mattos v Saunders* (1872) LR 7 CP 570; *Re City Life Assurance Co Ltd. Stephenson's Case* [1926] 1 Ch 191, 214 (as explained by Dixon J in *Hiley v Peoples Prudential Assurance Co Ltd* (1938) 60 CLR 468, 501–505); *Re Patrick Corp Ltd and the Companies Act* (1980) ACLC 40–643; *Thomas v National Australia Bank Ltd* [2000] 2 Qd R 448, 455.

[32] See eg *Thornton v Maynard* (1875) LR 10 CP 695, discussed below.

[33] See (1831) 1 & 2 Will IV, c 56. The Bankruptcy Act 1869 replaced the Court of Bankruptcy with the London Bankruptcy Court.

1883,[34] the court administering bankruptcy has been a court of both common law and equity.[35] As Clauson J aptly remarked:[36]

> The Bankruptcy Act . . . is an Act regulating the proceedings of a Court which has always been a Court of equity, proceeding on equitable principles, recognizing equitable debts, subject of course to such infirmities as are sometimes present, but drawing no distinction between equitable and legal rights for purposes of administering the estate of the bankrupt.

When a debt is held on trust, the notion that the debt may be set off against a cross-claim owing by the beneficiary to the debtor assumes that the debt is held on trust only for that beneficiary. If the debt was contracted on behalf of a number of beneficiaries, a set-off may be denied on the ground that a jointly-owned claim may not be set off against a debt owing by one only of the joint claimants.[37]

Beneficial title acquired after the relevant date

For a set-off to proceed under the insolvency legislation, the beneficial title ordinarily should have been acquired before the relevant date for determining rights of set-off,[38] so that, for example, a set-off may not be based upon an assignment or other acquisition of title that took place after that date.[39] There may be a set-off however if a beneficial title, although not acquired until after the relevant date, nevertheless reverts back to a time before then. This may occur when a bankruptcy is annulled. In *Bailey v Johnson*[40] the defendant had been adjudicated a bankrupt, so that his property vested in his trustee in bankruptcy on trust for his creditors. The trustee realized the estate, and paid the proceeds into a bank account. The bank was also a creditor of the defendant. Subsequently the bank itself was adjudicated bankrupt, and after that the defendant's bankruptcy was annulled. The bank's trustee in bankruptcy sued the defendant for payment of the debt owing to the bank, whereupon the defendant sought to set off the proceeds of his estate paid into the bank. The annulment took place after the bank's bankruptcy, at which time the defendant's estate was held on trust for his general body of creditors. On the other hand, the bankruptcy legislation provides a mechanism

11.05

---

[34] The Supreme Court of Judicature Act 1873, ss 3 and 16 originally contemplated the consolidation of the London Bankruptcy Court with the newly created Supreme Court of Judicature, but the proposal was abandoned with the enactment of s 9 of the Supreme Court of Judicature Act 1875, and was not carried into effect until the enactment of the Bankruptcy Act 1883, s 93.

[35] The Lord Chancellor in 1921, pursuant to the power conferred upon him by the Bankruptcy Act 1914, s 97, assigned the jurisdiction in bankruptcy to the Chancery Division of the High Court. See the Order of the Lord Chancellor, 15 August 1921, No 1741 (L 21).

[36] *Mathieson's Trustee v Burrup, Mathieson and Co* [1927] 1 Ch 562, 569.

[37] See paras 12.02–12.07 below.

[38] See paras 6.31–6.48 above. Compare the criticism of *MPS Constructions Pty Ltd v Rural Bank of New South Wales* (1980) 4 ACLR 835 in para 8.23 above.

[39] *Middleton v Pollock, ex p Nugee* (1875) LR 20 Eq 29.

[40] (1872) LR 7 Ex 263.

by which, upon an annulment, the property of the debtor may 'revert' to him.[41] This was held to operate retrospectively, so that the money should be considered as having been the defendant's when it was paid into the bank. A set-off therefore was allowed.

Insolvent assignor or trustee

11.06 When a claimant is suing only as an assignor or as a trustee, the debtor in some circumstances is permitted to set off a debt owing to him by the assignor or the trustee, notwithstanding that a third person is beneficially interested in the action. The circumstances in which this may occur are considered later.[42] If the assignor or the trustee is bankrupt or is a company in liquidation, the debtor's right of set-off in such a case is not derived from the insolvency legislation,[43] but rather it is based upon the notion that the beneficial owner should take subject to the legal right of set-off available to the debtor against the assignor under the Statutes of Set-off, or alternatively subject to an equitable set-off when the demands are sufficiently closely connected. This has the consequence that, unless the circumstances are such as to give rise to an equitable set-off, both demands must be liquidated, and also be due and payable, at the date of the action.[44] Since the bankrupt is not entitled to the benefit of the claim, it would not have passed to his trustee in bankruptcy as property of the bankrupt, in which case the insolvency set-off section cannot be invoked against the person who is beneficially interested. For example, in *De Mattos v Saunders*[45] the plaintiff was an insured under a policy of marine insurance, and was suing the underwriter for an indemnity for a total loss on behalf of a third party who had made advances on the shipping documents. A claim under a policy of indemnity insurance is regarded as a claim for unliquidated damages, and accordingly it cannot be set off under the Statutes of Set-off.[46] Therefore there was no right of set-off under the Statutes to which the third party in *De Mattos v Saunders* could be made to take subject. The plaintiff had executed a deed of inspectorship under the Bankruptcy Act 1861, which incorporated the principles of bankruptcy,[47] but it was held that the mutual credit section applicable in bankruptcy did not assist the underwriter. The plaintiff's

---

[41] See the Insolvency Act 1986, s 282(4), and in Australia, the Bankruptcy Act 1966 (Cth), s 154(1).

[42] See ch 17 below.

[43] *De Mattos v Saunders* (1872) LR 7 CP 570; *Re Asphaltic Wood Pavement Co. Lee & Chapman's Case* (1885) 30 Ch D 216, 225; *Popular Homes Ltd v Circuit Developments Ltd* [1979] 2 NZLR 642, 657. See also *Turner v Thomas* (1871) LR 6 CP 610, 615; *Hoverd Industries Ltd v Supercool Refrigeration and Air Conditioning (1991) Ltd* [1995] 3 NZLR 577. See also para 17.28 below.

[44] Note that the position in relation to the Statutes of Set-off differs in some Australian states. See paras 2.55–2.67 above.

[45] (1875) LR 7 CP 570.

[46] See para 2.26 above.

[47] See the Bankruptcy Act 1861, s 197.

claim was not available for the benefit of his creditors under the deed, and therefore the section did not apply.

Insolvent beneficial owner

Alternatively, it may be that the beneficial owner of a claim, as opposed to the legal   **11.07**
owner, is bankrupt. In that circumstance, the debtor may assert a set-off under the
insolvency set-off section in respect of the bankrupt's liability to him when the
legal owner is suing on behalf of the bankrupt. In *Thornton v Maynard* [48] the plaintiff as holder of several bills of exchange was suing the acceptor, although he had
already been paid a dividend on the bills in the bankruptcy of the drawer. When
the acceptor of a bill is bankrupt, the holder in proving in the bankruptcy must
give credit for anything that he received from the drawer or an indorser before
lodging the proof, [49] but this principle does not apply if the acceptor is solvent. In
such a case the holder may sue the acceptor for the full amount of the bill, but to
the extent of anything received from the drawer he sues as trustee for him. It was
held in *Thornton v Maynard* that, because the holder to the extent of the dividend
received from the drawer's estate was suing as trustee, the acceptor was entitled to
that extent to a set-off under the bankruptcy legislation in respect of a debt owing
to him by the drawer. [50]

C. Statutes of Set-off

It is sometimes assumed that mutuality for the purpose of determining the avail-   **11.08**
ability of a set-off under the Statutes of Set-off similarly is determined by reference
to the equitable title to the cross-demands, [51] but, as Meagher, Gummow and
Lehane in Australia have explained, [52] that statement is not accurate. The Statutes
permit a set-off in an action if there is mutuality by reference to the legal title to
the debts. If there is not mutuality at law but there is in equity, equity nevertheless
may act by analogy with the legal right of set-off available pursuant to the Statutes
and recognize a set-off. [53] Alternatively, if there is mutuality at law by reference to

---

[48] (1872) LR 10 CP 695.

[49] *Re Blackburne* (1892) 9 Morr 249, 252; *Re Houlder* [1929] 1 Ch 205, 212.

[50] The claim accruing to the bankrupt estate was still contingent at the date of the bankruptcy,
but this is not sufficient to prevent a set-off. See paras 8.27–8.37 above.

[51] See eg Russell LJ (with whom Sellers LJ agreed) in *Robbie & Co Ltd v Witney Warehouse Co Ltd*
[1963] 1 WLR 1324, 1339. See also in Canada *Coba Industries Ltd v Millie's Holdings (Canada) Ltd*
[1985] 6 WWR 14, 28–29; *Telford v Holt* (1987) 41 DLR (4th) 385, 394.

[52] Meagher, Gummow and Lehane, *Equity Doctrines and Remedies* (3rd edn, 1992) 720–1. See
also *Hoverd Industries Ltd v Supercool Refrigeration and Air Conditioning (1991) Ltd* [1995] 3 NZLR
577, 587.

[53] *Freeman v Lomas* (1851) 9 Hare 109, 116, 68 ER 435, 438; *Cavendish v Geaves* (1857) 24 Beav
163, 53 ER 319; *Cochrane v Green* (1860) 9 CB (NS) 448, 142 ER 176; *Agra and Masterman's Bank
Ltd v Leighton* (1866) LR 2 Ex 56, 65; *Union Bank of Australia v Waterston* (1894) 12 NZLR 672;

the legal titles but one of the debts has been assigned in equity or is held on trust for another party, a court of equity may regard it as unconscionable for a set-off at law to occur, and accordingly would not permit the set-off.[54] But apart from these instances of equitable intervention, the Statutes themselves applied to cross-debts at law between the parties to a common law action.[55] Consider the case of an equitable assignment of a debt. The general rule is that an equitable assignee takes subject to a right of set-off accruing to the debtor against the assignor before the debtor received notice of the assignment.[56] The determinative date is the date of notice, not the date of the assignment.[57] When a cross-debt accrues to the debtor against the assignor after notice, the reason that a set-off is denied to the debtor as against the assignee is not simply that mutuality in equity is absent. There is still mutuality at law as between the debtor and the assignor, and therefore there is a right of set-off at law. The question is whether it is unconscionable for the debtor to rely on the right of set-off otherwise available at law when the equitable title to one of the debts is in someone else.[58] The answer to that question depends on when the cross-debt was acquired. If it was acquired after notice of the assignment, equity regards it as unconscionable for the debtor to rely on the set-off available at law, and equity accordingly will not permit him to do so.[59]

11.09 The correctness of this analysis is apparent if one looks instead at the position that obtains when the debtor acquired the liquidated cross-claim against the assignor after the equitable assignment but before the debtor had notice of the assignment. In such a case it is recognized that the third party assignee takes subject to the debtor's right of set-off, a result that is hardly consistent with mutuality being determined solely by reference to equitable interests. The giving of notice is not nec-

---

Barclays Bank Ltd v Aschaffenburger Zellstoffwerke AG [1967] 1 Lloyd's Rep 387. Indeed, it appears that the common law courts in some early cases took notice of a trust for the purpose of recognizing a set-off. Two such cases, *Bottomley v Brooke* and *Rudge v Birch*, both unreported, were mentioned by counsel during argument in *Winch v Keeley* (1787) 1 TR 619, 621–622, 99 ER 1284, 1285–1286. Compare however *Tucker v Tucker* (1833) 4 B & Ad 745, 110 ER 636. In *Bennett v White* [1910] 2 KB 643 the defendant was an assignee under a statutory assignment, and so there was mutuality at law.

[54] *Re Whitehouse & Co* (1878) 9 Ch D 595, 597; *Re Paraguassu Steam Tramroad Co. Black & Co's Case* (1872) LR 8 Ch App 254, 261; *Mercer v Graves* (1872) LR 7 QB 499, 504, *per* Blackburn J.

[55] *Chitty's Blackstone* (1826) vol 3, 305 n 37; *Popular Homes Ltd v Circuit Developments Ltd* [1979] 2 NZLR 642, 655. See also *Isberg v Bowden* (1853) 8 Ex 852, 155 ER 1599, as explained by Keating J in *Watkins v Clark* (1862) 12 CB(NS) 277, 281–282, 142 ER 1149, 1151 ('the statutes of set-off are confined to legal debts between the parties').

[56] See para 17.03 below.

[57] See eg *Moore v Jervis* (1845) 2 Coll 60, 63 ER 637 and *Brice v Bannister* (1878) 3 QBD 569, 578, and para 17.16 below.

[58] See *Wilson v Gabriel* (1863) 4 B & S 243, 247–248, 122 ER 450, 452, *per* Blackburn J, referred to in *Christie v Taunton, Delmard, Lane and Co* [1893] 2 Ch 175, 182. As Bramwell B expressed it in *Higgs v The Northern Assam Tea Co. Ltd* (1869) LR 4 Ex 387, 394, the question is, 'taking the set-off to be available at law, would equity restrain the defendants from relying on it?' See also *Watson v Mid Wales Railway Co* (1867) LR 2 CP 593, 600, *per* Montague Smith J.

[59] *Hoverd Industries Ltd v Supercool Refrigeration and Air Conditioning* [1995] 3 NZLR 577, 587.

essary to complete the title of an equitable assignee.[60] Notice is desirable in order to ensure that the assignee has priority over other assignees in accordance with the rule in *Dearle v Hall*,[61] and in order to oblige the debtor to tender payment to the assignee rather than the assignor.[62] Notice is not necessary however for the equitable title to pass to the assignee, which occurs at the date of the assignment. Therefore, in the period between the assignment and notice of the assignment, when the cross-debt was incurred, there was not mutuality in equity between the assigned debt and the cross-debt. In equity the assigned debt was owing to the assignee, while the cross-debt was incurred by the assignor. Accordingly, when the question of set-off later arises, it can be seen that there is not, and never has been, mutuality in equity. Why, then, is a set-off allowed? The reason is that the debtor has a right of set-off at law under the Statutes of Set-off, since the position at law is that the assigned debt is still owing to the assignor and accordingly there is mutuality at law. Moreover, it is not unconscionable for the debtor to rely on the legal right to a set-off, since the cross-debt was incurred before he had notice of the equitable assignment. While there are statements in judgments of Sir George Jessel MR[63] and Lord Selborne LC[64] which seem to suggest that equity never permits a set-off under the Statutes where cross-demands are mutual at law but not in equity, the allowance of a set-off when the cross-debt is incurred after the assignment but before notice shows that the rule is not inflexible, and that the principle is one of unconscionability.[65] As Jeffrey J remarked in the New South Wales Supreme Court in *West Street Properties Pty Ltd v Jamison*,[66] 'Lack of mutuality in equity can be a reason for denying a right to set-off at law, . . . but that is not to say that its presence is invariably necessary before allowing any right of set-off at all.' This analysis admittedly does not sit comfortably with the view that has been expressed in recent times, that the principles, as well as the courts, of common law and equity have now been fused.[67] That view is much criticized, however,[68] and it

---

[60] *Gorringe v Irwell India Rubber and Gutta Percha Works* (1886) 34 Ch D 128; *Ward v Duncombe* [1893] AC 369, 392; *Re City Life Assurance Co Ltd. Stephenson's Case* [1926] 1 Ch 191, 219–220; *Re Trytel* [1952] 2 TLR 32, 34; *Thomas v National Australia Bank Ltd* [2000] 2 Qd R 448.

[61] (1828) 3 Russ 1, 38 ER 475.

[62] *Brice v Bannister* (1878) 3 QBD 569; *Re Trytel* [1952] 2 TLR 32, 34; *Halsbury's Laws of England* (4th edn (Reissue), 1991) vol 6, 47 para 70.

[63] *Re Whitehouse & Co* (1878) 9 Ch D 595, 597.

[64] *Re Paraguassu Steam Tramroad Co. Black & Co's Case* (1872) LR 8 Ch App 254, 261.

[65] This is also evident from the decision of the Court of Appeal in *Rother Iron Works Ltd v Canterbury Precision Engineers Ltd* [1974] 1 QB 1 in relation to receivership. See para 17.78 below.

[66] [1974] 2 NSWLR 435, 441–442.

[67] *United Scientific Holdings Ltd v Burnley Borough Council* [1978] AC 904. See also *Bank of Credit and Commerce International SA v Ali* [2002] 1 AC 251, 263 para 17, *per* Lord Bingham ('More than a century and a quarter have passed since the fusion of law and equity . . .'); Burrows, 'We Do This at Common Law But That in Equity' (2002) 22 OJLS 1, 4.

[68] Baker, 'The Future of Equity' (1977) 93 LQR 529; Meagher, Gummow and Lehane, *Equity Doctrines and Remedies* (3rd edn, 1992) 67–8; Martin, 'Fusion, Fallacy and Confusion; A Comparative Study' [1994] The Conveyancer 13. See also *MCC Proceeds Inc v Lehman Bros*

does not provide a satisfactory framework for explaining the allowance of a set-off when a cross-debt arises after the assignment but before notice.

11.10 When liquidated cross-demands are mutual having regard to equitable rights, it is not necessary for the defendant show some additional 'equity' to support an equitable set-off, since equity in such a case may act by analogy with the legal right under the Statutes. Observations to the contrary[69] are difficult to support.

D. Ascertained Beneficial Interests

11.11 It has been said that, in order to achieve mutuality where a debt is held on trust for a beneficiary, the beneficial ownership must be clear and ascertained without inquiry.[70] This requires an explanation. The early cases referred to as authority for the proposition[71] concerned either a residuary legatee under a will or a person entitled under an intestacy, where the administration of the estate had not been completed. Prior to completion of the administration, a residuary legatee or a person entitled in an intestacy does not have a beneficial interest in the estate. All that the legatee or the person so entitled has is an equitable chose in action, in the form of a right to require the due administration of the estate. That was confirmed by the Privy Council in *Commissioner of Stamp Duties (Queensland) v Livingston*[72] in relation to a residuary legatee, and the principle is equally applicable in the case of an intestacy.[73] The early set-off cases which have been cited as requiring a clear and ascertained beneficial ownership[74] in fact are authorities for a different proposition, that the court will not take an account of the assets of the estate, and of the debts and charges that still have to be satisfied out of it, so as to allow a present set-off to the extent of the interest that it is anticipated that the legatee or the person entitled in an intestacy will have in the future. This should apply in relation to both insolvency set-off and set-off between solvent parties.

International (Europe) [1998] 4 All ER 675, 690–691 (equitable title not sufficient to found a common law claim in conversion). Sir Peter Millett writing extra-judicially ('Equity—The Road Ahead' (1995) 9 Tolley's Trust Law International 35, 37) commented that the fusion theory is now widely discredited. In *Bank of Boston Connecticut v European Grain and Shipping Ltd* [1989] 1 AC 1056, 1109 the House of Lords remarked that the Judicature Acts, 'while making important changes in procedure, did not alter and were not intended to alter the rights of the parties'.

[69] *Middleton v Pollock, ex p Nugee* (1875) LR 20 Eq 29, 36–37; *Welton v Harnett* (1886) 7 NSWR 74.

[70] Wood, *English and International Set-off* (1989) 779–80, 1081–2.

[71] *Bishop v Church* (1748) 3 Atk 691, 26 ER 1197; *Ex parte Morier, re Willis, Percival & Co* (1879) 12 Ch D 491; *Phillips v Howell* [1901] 2 Ch 773.

[72] [1965] AC 694. See also *Ex parte Morier* (1879) 12 Ch D 491, 496, *per* James LJ, and para 13.116 below. Similarly, the object of a discretionary trust does not have a legal or a beneficial interest in the trust property. See *Gartside v IRC* [1968] AC 553; *Chief Commissioner of Stamp Duties v ISPT Pty Ltd* (1998) 45 NSWLR 639, 655.

[73] *Re Leigh's Will Trusts* [1970] 1 Ch 277, 281–282.

[74] See above.

Proof of a presently existing beneficial interest

Alternatively, it may be that the facts alleged, if proved, would disclose a presently **11.12** existing beneficial interest in a debt, but the facts are in dispute. The question of the availability of a set-off in that circumstance has arisen in the context of nominee bank accounts. In both *Bhogal v Punjab National Bank*[75] and *Uttamchandami v Central Bank of India*[76] a bank alleged that an account in the name of A in truth was held for the benefit of B. When A sued the bank for payment of the credit balance on the account, and applied for summary judgment, the bank argued that it was entitled to leave to defend on the basis of a set-off arising out of an indebtedness of B on another account. The set-off alleged was an equitable set-off, based upon equity acting by analogy with the Statutes of Set-off.[77] Usually the defendant in an application for summary judgment will be granted leave to defend if he can show an arguable case, but it was held in the *Bhogal* and *Uttamchandami* cases that the bank was not entitled to unconditional leave to defend in the absence of clear and indisputable evidence[78] that the account was merely a nominee account.[79]

Two comments may be made in relation to that proposition. **11.13**

The first is that both Dillon and Bingham LJJ in respective judgments in the **11.14** *Bhogal* case relied on the earlier decision of the Court of Appeal in *Ex parte Morier*,[80] but that case was concerned with a different issue.

In *Ex parte Morier*, a brother and sister were executors of their deceased father's **11.15** will, and accordingly opened an account in their joint names with a bank. The son, who was the residuary legatee under the will, kept another account of his own with the bank. The bank filed a liquidation petition, at which time there was a balance standing to the credit of the joint account, whereas the son's separate account was overdrawn. The son sought to set off the balance due from him to the bankers on his own account against the sum due from the bankers on the executors' joint account, on the ground that he was the residuary legatee and the sum standing to the credit of the joint account belonged in equity to himself alone. The son's argument to that effect failed before the Court of Appeal. A number of debts remained to be paid out of the estate, and the Court was not prepared to take an account in relation to the testator's estate in order to ascertain the son's entitlement as residuary legatee. In a short judgment Brett LJ said that:[81]

---

[75] [1988] 2 All ER 296.

[76] Unreported, but noted in (1989) 139 New Law Journal 222.

[77] See para 3.06 above.

[78] See Dillon LJ in *Bhogal v Punjab National Bank* [1988] 2 All ER 286, 301, and Lloyd LJ in *Uttamchandami v Central Bank of India* (1989) 139 New Law Journal 222, 223.

[79] As in *Re Hett, Maylor and Co* (1894) 10 TLR 412.

[80] (1879) 12 Ch D 491, CA.

[81] (1879) 12 Ch D 491, 502.

> My view is this, that, the account standing in the names of the brother and sister, the case could not have been brought within the rules of equitable set-off or mutual credit, unless the brother was so much the person solely beneficially interested that a Court of Equity, without any terms or any further inquiry, would have obliged the sister to transfer the account into her brother's name alone.

Both that comment, however, and the decision in *Ex parte Morier* should be considered in the context that the *Morier* case was concerned with the position of a residuary legatee prior to completion of the administration of the estate. Since there were a number of debts which remained outstanding, it was clear that there was not at the date of the liquidation a presently existing beneficial interest, and the Court of Appeal held that it would not take an account of the assets of the estate and the debts and liabilities payable out of the estate in order to ascertain what the beneficial interest ultimately would be. Thus James LJ, in a judgment with which Brett LJ agreed,[82] commented:

> It is said A and B were executors, and A was also the residuary legatee, and therefore entitled to the whole of the fund. *But the fund had never been liquidated so as to become a trust fund.*[83]

And later:

> I think the Court has never yet taken accounts in order to see how much of a fund standing in the name of two persons in a bank would *ultimately*, upon the balance of the accounts, turn out to be the property of one of them, so as to enable that balance to be a set-off against a sum due by that one to the bank.[84]

That situation should be compared to the *Bhogal* and *Uttamchandami* cases, in which the facts alleged, if proved, would have established a presently existing interest, and the question was whether the court should investigate those facts. The issue, then, was entirely different, and so *Ex parte Morier* did not require the decisions in the later cases.

11.16 The second comment is that considerable emphasis was also placed in the *Bhogal* case on the responsibilities of banks to honour their obligations promptly. Both Dillon and Bingham LJJ quoted with approval a passage from the judgment of Scott J at first instance who, in rejecting the bank's defence, said that:[85] 'The commercial banking commitment that a bank enters into with a person who deposits money with it is just as needful of immediate performance as are a bank's obligations under a letter of credit or bank guarantee.' Bingham LJ also referred[86] to another comment by Scott J, to the effect that he was not satisfied that banks should be treated like other debtors in relation to summary judgment. In addition,

---

[82] (1879) 12 Ch D 491, 500.
[83] (1879) 12 Ch D 491, 496 (emphasis added).
[84] (1879) 12 Ch D 491, 499–500 (emphasis added).
[85] [1988] 2 All ER 296, 299–300, 306.
[86] [1988] 2 All ER 296, 306.

Dillon LJ emphasized a bank's duty to honour a customer's cheque drawn in accordance with the mandate, provided that the customer has sufficient funds in the account to cover it.[87] Thus, banks were perceived as occupying a special position in relation to their obligations as debtors.

Mixed account

In the *Bhogal* case, the bank argued that accounts in the name of Mr Basna and Mr **11.17** Bhogal were each nominee accounts beneficially owned by a Mr Sanger. It asserted that Mr Sanger was either the sole and absolute beneficial owner of the moneys in the account or he had a substantial beneficial interest in them. Because of that interest the bank argued, in applications for summary judgment against it for payment of the credit balances on the accounts, that it was entitled to leave to defend because of another overdrawn account upon which Mr Sanger was liable to it. The Court of Appeal rejected the bank's contention, because there was not clear and indisputable evidence that the accounts were nominee accounts. But apart from that, Dillon LJ also suggested that, for a set-off to occur in relation to a nominee account, the totality of the money in the account must belong to the principal of the nominee, whereas in the case of the Basna account it appeared that at least some of the money in the account belonged to Mr Basna. Therefore, even if the bank were able to show that the Basna account was a mixed account, fed in part by moneys belonging to Mr Sanger and in part by moneys which belonged to the nominee, there could be no equitable set-off in view of Mr Basna's own entitlement.[88] Similarly Bingham LJ said that he was willing to accept that a bank could challenge its customer's title to money in the customer's account on its own behalf only when its claim is against a sole beneficiary.[89] When the account is a mixed account, Dillon LJ seems to have regarded the situation as analogous to a joint claim possessed by a partnership,[90] the courts having accepted that a joint claim generally cannot be set off against a debt owing separately by one of the partners.[91] The analogy is not complete, however, because a partnership contracts on a joint basis, which is not the position when the moneys of a number of persons are deposited in an account held by one of them.

Subsequently, a differently constituted Court of Appeal considered the question **11.18** of set-off in the context of a mixed nominee account in *Bank of Credit and Commerce International SA (in liq) v Al-Saud*.[92] The defendant, Prince Fahd bin Salman bin Abdul Aziz Al-Saud, had given a guarantee to the plaintiff bank in

---

[87] See [1988] 2 All ER 296, 300, 301.
[88] [1988] 2 All ER 296, 301.
[89] [1988] 2 All ER 296, 307.
[90] See Dillon LJ's reference (at [1988] 2 All ER 296, 301) to *Addis v Knight* (1817) 2 Mer 117, 35 ER 885, which concerned a joint liability of a partnership.
[91] See paras 12.02–12.07 below.
[92] [1997] 1 BCLC 457, *per* Neill, Simon Brown and Waite LJJ.

respect of a loan made by the bank to a company. The company defaulted, whereupon the bank, which was now in liquidation, sued the Prince on the guarantee and applied for summary judgment. The Prince responded that he was entitled to leave to defend because of a set-off available against the claim, based on three accounts with the plaintiff which were in credit. The accounts were in the name of a third party, one Mr Ghazzawi, but both the Prince and Mr Ghazzawi said that the moneys paid into the accounts belonged to the Prince. It appeared however that there had been some intermingling of Mr Ghazzawi's own money in the accounts, and also that Mr Ghazzawi was entitled to defray some expenses from the accounts, so that an inquiry would have been necessary in order to ascertain the precise state of the accounts between the Prince and Mr Ghazzawi. Neill LJ in delivering the judgment of the Court of Appeal accepted, on the authority of the *Morier* case, that, unless the Prince's beneficial interest in the three accounts could be established by clear evidence and without the necessity for the taking of an account, there would be a lack of mutuality. On the facts of *BCCI v Al-Saud*, where it was accepted that some inquiry would have been necessary, the Court of Appeal held that there was no arguable defence of set-off. If on the other hand the extent of the Prince's interest in the account had been clear and ascertained, the judgment suggests that a set-off would have been available to that extent.[93] Thus, Neill LJ commented that:[94] 'It is true that Mr Ghazzawi has asserted in his affidavits that the money in the accounts belongs in the main to the Prince, but it seems to be a sensible rule that a beneficial interest has to be established by clear evidence and without the necessity for the taking of an account.' And further on:[95] 'In my judgment counsel for BCCI was correct in his submission that unless the Prince's entitlement to the moneys in the three Park Lane accounts can be shown to be clear and ascertained there is a lack of mutuality or reciprocity between himself and BCCI.' The suggestion, that a set-off may be available against a person interested in a mixed account where that person's interest is clear and ascertained, should be contrasted with the strict view expressed in the *Bhogal* case, that there should be a sole beneficiary to whom the totality of the money in the account belongs.

11.19 Two points may be made in relation to these respective views.

11.20 The first is that the opinions in the *Bhogal* case were justified by reference to passages in the judgments of James and Brett LJJ in *Ex parte Morier*. Bingham LJ in

---

[93] In Northern Ireland, Carswell LJ (with whose judgment Hutton LCJ agreed) left open the question whether a set-off was available to a bank in relation to an account, where the bank could show with sufficient clarity that the person against whom the set-off was sought to be exercised was entitled to a part only of the account, albeit a specific and ascertainable part. He nevertheless said that at least an arguable case for a set-off could have been put forward. See *Abbey National plc v McCann* [1997] Northern Ireland Judgments Bulletin 158, 172–173. Compare Capper, 'Deceit, Banker's Set-off and Mareva Undertakings—The Abbey's Bad Habits' [1999] LMCLQ 21, 24–5.

[94] [1997] 1 BCLC 457, 465.

[95] [1997] 1 BCLC 457, 466.

the *Bhogal* case[96] said that the requirement of a 'sole beneficiary' reflected Brett LJ's short judgment in the *Morier* case,[97] while Dillon LJ[98] regarded his view in relation to a mixed account as following from a comment by James LJ in *Ex parte Morier*, to the effect that it is not sufficient that the result of taking an account would merely show an ultimate balance belonging to the principal of an alleged nominee account holder.[99] However the passages from *Ex parte Morier* should be considered in the context of the circumstances in issue in that case,[100] in particular that the administration of the deceased's estate had not been completed. Therefore a trust had not yet arisen in favour of the residuary legatee in relation to the executorship account which the residuary legatee was seeking to set off against his overdrawn personal account. Hence Brett LJ's comment in the *Morier* case, that the amount standing to the credit of the account could not be set off 'unless the [residuary legatee] was so much the person solely beneficially interested that a Court of Equity, without any terms or any further inquiry, would have obliged the [co-executor] to transfer the account into the [residuary legatee's] name alone'. In the circumstances of the case, a trust would not have arisen until the completion of the administration, at which time the residuary legatee would have become solely beneficially interested in the account. But until the completion of the administration, it could not be said that the residuary legatee had a beneficial interest. The statements in the *Morier* case did not comprehend the situation in which two or more persons have clear and ascertained *present* beneficial interests in a bank account in the name of a nominee.

Secondly, the broader view suggested by *BCCI v Al-Saud* is consistent with cases concerning debts other than bank accounts, where the courts have recognized that a set-off may occur in relation to a beneficial interest in a debt that is not the sole beneficial interest.[101] For example, in *Manley & Sons Ltd v Berkett*[102] an auctioneer was suing for the price of goods sold to the defendant. The auctioneer had a first claim on the proceeds for his charges and expenses, but to the extent of the proceeds that the auctioneer would have had to hand over to the vendor, and in which the vendor accordingly was beneficially interested, the purchaser was allowed a

11.21

---

[96] [1988] 2 All ER 296, 307.
[97] See para 11.15 above.
[98] [1988] 2 All ER 296, 301.
[99] See (1879) 12 Ch D 491, 496. Dillon LJ paraphrased James LJ's comments in terms that, 'it is not enough if the taking of an account would merely show an ultimate balance, *and not the totality of the money in an account*, to belong to the principal of an alleged nominee account holder'. The italicized words however do not appear in the passage in James LJ's judgment to which Dillon LJ referred.
[100] See para 11.15 above.
[101] It was suggested in the *Bhogal* and *Uttamchandami* cases that banks should be treated differently to other debtors (see para 11.16 above), but if the interest of a person in a bank account is clear and ascertained, albeit not extending to the totality of the moneys in the account, that factor should not be relevant.
[102] [1912] 2 KB 329.

set-off against a debt owing to him by the vendor. There was in that case an agreement for a set-off between the vendor and the purchaser, but Bankes J nevertheless characterized the set-off set up by the purchaser as an equitable set-off. There are also examples in the context of insolvency set-off. Thus, when a debt due to a creditor is assigned by the creditor to a third party as security for a debt owing by the creditor to the third party, but the debt owing to the third party is for a smaller amount than the assigned debt, so that there is a residue from the assigned debt to be paid over to the creditor/assignor, and the creditor has gone into liquidation, a cross-demand by the debtor against the creditor in some circumstances may be set off against the residue to which the creditor would be entitled.[103] *Thornton v Maynard*[104] provides another illustration. The holder of some bills of exchange was suing the acceptor for payment. It appeared however that the holder had already been paid a dividend in the drawer's bankruptcy in respect of the bills, and to the extent of the dividend he was suing as trustee for the drawer. It was held that the acceptor to that extent was entitled to set off a debt owing to him by the drawer. While the drawer was bankrupt, so that the set-off is explicable as arising under the bankruptcy legislation,[105] Lord Coleridge CJ in delivering the judgment of the Common Pleas[106] nevertheless referred to it as a set-off in equity.

Insolvency set-off

11.22 The form of set-off in issue in *BCCI v Al-Saud* differed from that in the *Bhogal* case. *Bhogal v Punjab National Bank* concerned equitable set-off arising by analogy with the Statutes of Set-off, whereas in the *Al-Saud* case insolvency set-off was in issue. Insolvency set-off raises different considerations.

11.23 In the *Morier* case, the residuary legatee seeking a set-off did not have a present beneficial interest in the executors' account. Where however the substance of the allegation relates to an alleged present beneficial interest, the extension of a perceived requirement of clear and indisputable evidence of the interest to insolvency set-off is not without difficulty. In the case of insolvency set-off, the set-off section provides that an account 'shall be taken' of what is due from each party to the other in respect of their mutual dealings.[107] The statutory injunction to take an account seems contrary to the view that a set-off should be denied unless the beneficial interest is clear and ascertained. Furthermore, the court in the *Bhogal* case emphasized a bank's responsibilities to honour its obligations to its customers

---

[103] *Hiley v Peoples Prudential Assurance Co Ltd* (1938) 60 CLR 468, 497–498, *per* Dixon J, referring to *Re Asphaltic Wood Pavement Co. Lee & Chapman's Case* (1885) 30 Ch D 216. See paras 11.27–11.31 below.

[104] (1875) LR 10 CP 695.

[105] See the Bankruptcy Act 1869, s 39.

[106] Lord Coleridge CJ, Brett and Archibald JJ.

[107] See the Insolvency Rules, r 4.90 for company liquidation, and for bankruptcy the Insolvency Act 1986, s 323.

promptly,[108] which would not be relevant if the bank or the customer is in liquidation given that the banker/customer relationship would have terminated.[109] The notion of the bank's responsibilities particularly would not have any application if the bank is in liquidation, since the customer in any event would be confined to a proof in the liquidation. Moreover, there may be a question of set-off as between the bank and the alleged nominee. Consider that a bank is in liquidation, and an account in credit in the name of A is alleged to be held wholly or partly for the benefit of B. If a set-off is not permitted as between the bank and B in relation to the account unless the interest of B in the account is clear and ascertained, what is the position if A also happens to be indebted to the bank? If there is not clear and indisputable evidence that B has an interest in the account, it may equally be the case that it is not clear and indisputable that A is the beneficial owner of the account, in which case would A also be denied a set-off? Alternatively, if the principle only operates to deny B a set-off, could A then have a set-off for an amount greater than his true beneficial interest in the account? These questions suggest that the court should in fact ascertain the interests of A and B and permit or deny set-offs accordingly.

11.24 The *Al-Saud* case nevertheless is authority for the view that the principle applied in the *Bhogal* and *Uttamchandani* cases extends also to insolvency set-off. That view should be reconsidered.

E. Security Over a Debt

(1) Introduction

11.25 A debt owing to a creditor may be the subject of a security given by the creditor to a third party.[110] A security over a debt may take a number of forms, and it is appropriate to consider the results that may follow in relation to each of them.

(2) Assignment by Way of Mortgage

11.26 In the first place, a debt may be assigned by way of mortgage. In so far as set-offs between the debtor and the mortgagor/creditor are concerned, the relevant principles essentially are as follows. The assignment has the result that prima facie there is not mutuality in equity,[111] and this is so whether or not default has occurred under the mortgage. Prima facie therefore the insolvency set-off section would not apply. On the other hand the mortgagee, being an assignee, is subject

---

[108] See para 11.16 above.

[109] See *Halesowen Presswork and Assemblies Ltd v Westminster Bank Ltd* [1971] 1 QB 1, 23, 24 (Roskill J) in relation to the winding up of the customer.

[110] See also paras 6.120–6.125 above.

[111] Compare the discussion below of the situation in which the assigned debt is greater than the secured debt.

to the same principle applicable generally to assignments, that an assignee takes subject to an equitable set-off available to the debtor against the assignor, or to a set-off that accrued to the debtor under the Statutes of Set-off before the debtor had notice of the assignment.[112]

Assigned debt exceeds the secured debt

11.27   What if the debt assigned by way of security exceeds the debt owing by the mortgagor to the mortgagee for which it is security, and the assigned debt is being enforced? In Australia, Dixon J in *Hiley v The Peoples Prudential Assurance Co Ltd*[113] said, in the context of a debt owing by a company in liquidation which had been assigned by the creditor by way of security to a third party:

> In the third place, it is settled that if a creditor of a liquidating company, that is, the person entitled to a legal chose in action, has before the winding up assigned it equitably to a third party by way of charge as security for a debt owing by him to the third party but of smaller amount so that there is a residue to be paid over to the assignor, the liquidating company may set off against the residue a cross-demand upon the assignor.

It is difficult to accept this proposition as a general statement of principle. There is an apparent lack of mutuality for the purpose of the insolvency set-off section, since the mortgagee has security over the whole of the debt assigned to him, and there is no part in which the mortgagor alone is beneficially interested. The question is whether this is an instance in which a set-off nevertheless is appropriate. Prima facie it is not. The security in this case is a debt owing to the mortgagor. If the debtor is insolvent the true value of the security would not be the face value of that debt. It would be less, depending on the dividend payable by the debtor. Accordingly, where a mortgagee has a debt of £x owing to him by the mortgagor which is secured by a mortgage over a debt of £y owing to the mortgagor by a debtor in liquidation, it would hardly be fair to allow a set-off as between the mortgagor and the debtor to the extent of £$(y-x)$, since this would deplete the security. Dixon J's proposition assumes that, if £x is still owing by the debtor after the set-off, the mortgagee's position is protected, but the mortgagee would not be protected if the debtor is insolvent.

11.28   It would nevertheless be appropriate to recognize a set-off in the circumstances contemplated by Dixon J if two conditions are satisfied. The first, which is suggested by Wood,[114] is that the security should be presently enforceable and it should be in the process of being enforced, so that the mortgagee's position after taking into account the set-off is presently ascertainable. Unless this limitation is

---

[112]   See paras 17.10–17.12 (Statutes of Set-off) and paras 17.22–17.27 (equitable set-off).
[113]   (1938) 60 CLR 468, 497. See also Rich J at 489 (referring to *Re Asphaltic Wood Pavement Co. Lee & Chapman's Case* (1885) 30 Ch D 216).
[114]   Wood, *English and International Set-off* (1989) 782.

imposed, the mortgagee may find when the security is later enforced that it has been depleted by a set-off as between the mortgagor and the debtor. The second condition is that the debtor on the assigned debt should be solvent so that, after setting off an amount equal to £(y − x), the remaining £x owing by the debtor in fact is worth £x. There is nothing objectionable in recognizing a set-off as between a debtor and a creditor when the debt is assigned by way of security and the creditor/mortgagor is insolvent, but there is when the debtor is the insolvent party. Indeed, in the case to which Dixon J referred as authority for his proposition, the creditor rather than the debtor was insolvent. *Lee & Chapman's Case*[115] concerned a charge granted by a company over a debt owing to it by the Commissioners of Sewers. The company later went into liquidation. There was no suggestion that the Commissioners were insolvent, and accordingly there was nothing unfair in the Court of Appeal's decision to allow the Commissioners to set off their debt to the extent of the amount over and above the secured debt owing by the company. While the question of mutuality was not considered in *Lee & Chapman's Case*, when a creditor grants security over the debt to a third party and the creditor also happens to be liable to the debtor, the creditor should be regarded as having a sufficient interest in the surplus over and above the secured debt for the purpose of the requirement of mutuality if the security is being enforced and the debtor is solvent, so that the secured creditor's position is both presently ascertainable and sufficiently protected.

Auctioneer's lien

A similar principle has been recognized in the context of an auctioneer's lien.[116] An **11.29** auctioneer has a lien on the proceeds of sale for his charges and expenses. If a purchaser of goods at auction removes the goods before payment in full the auctioneer may sue for the price, but the purchaser is permitted to set off in that action a debt owing to him by the vendor to the extent that the proceeds would be handed over to the vendor.[117] While the auctioneer would have had a prior interest in the whole of the claim in order to satisfy the lien, mutuality should be satisfied if the purchaser is solvent and the auctioneer's lien accordingly is protected.

---

[115] *Re Asphaltic Wood Pavement Co. Lee & Chapman's Case* (1885) 30 Ch D 216. See also *Union Bank of Australia v Waterston* (1894) 12 NZLR 672 (agreement for set-off between the mortgagor and the debtor).

[116] See para 13.93 below.

[117] *Manley & Sons Ltd v Berkett* [1912] 2 KB 329 (in which there was an agreement for a set-off between the purchaser and the vendor, although Bankes LJ (at 333–334) nevertheless approached the question on the basis that an equitable set-off was in issue). See also *Holmes v Tutton* (1855) 5 El & Bl 65, 82, 119 ER 405, 412.

Set-off between the mortgagee and the debtor

11.30   What about the position as between the mortgagee and the debtor? Wood[118] has
suggested that, if the mortgagor is not in default, the assigned debt cannot be set
off against a debt that the mortgagee owes to the debtor, on the ground that the
mortgagor's interest in the assigned debt in the form of the equity of redemption
otherwise will have been used to pay the debt owing by the mortgagee. It would
mean that the mortgagee will have foreclosed before default by the mortgagor.
This seems correct. The fact that the mortgagor still has the equity of redemption
means that he still has a proprietary interest in the assigned debt which would destroy mutuality as between the mortgagee and the debtor. As Wood has also
pointed out,[119] however, the cases suggest that the result would be different if the
mortgagee is enforcing the debt after default. Thus, where an insurance broker
took out a policy of marine insurance in his own name, so that he could sue upon
it, and the broker had a general lien on the policy for the balance of the insured's
account with him exceeding the claim on the policy, the broker, upon being sued
by the underwriter's assignees in bankruptcy for unpaid premiums for which he
was personally liable, was allowed to set off the underwriter's liability on the policy arising out of a loss.[120] Moreover, where an agent selling the goods of his principal was entitled by virtue of a lien on the goods to receive payment of the price,
it was held that an agreement between the purchaser and the agent's assignees in
bankruptcy by which the price was set off against a debt owing by the agent to the
third party was binding on the principal.[121]

Secured creditor has other security

11.31   A creditor may have assigned the debt by way of security to a third party, but the
third party has other security from the creditor which is sufficient to satisfy the secured debt. Can the debtor in that circumstance set off the assigned debt against
a liability of the creditor in the creditor's bankruptcy or liquidation? The issue
arose in *Ex parte Staddon, re Wise*.[122] The petitioner had borrowed £500 from the
bankrupts, who were country bankers, and gave them a promissory note for that
amount. The bankrupts in turn had deposited the promissory note, together with

---

[118] Wood, *English and International Set-off* (1989) 780, 916.

[119] Wood, *English and International Set-off* (1989) 919–21. In addition to the cases referred to
below, see *Moore v Jervis* (1845) 2 Coll 60, 63 ER 637 in which Knight Bruce VC said (at 71) that
the bank had an equitable interest in the promissory note deposited with it as security sufficient to
support a set-off against the maker of the note.

[120] *Parker v Beasley* (1814) 2 M & S 423, 105 ER 438 (in which the brokers had a lien by virtue
of their accepting bills of exchange on the credit of the goods insured); *Davies v Wilkinson* (1828) 4
Bing 573, 130 ER 889.

[121] *Hudson v Granger* (1821) 5 B & Ald 27, 106 ER 1103, and see also *Warner v M'Kay* (1836)
1 M & W 591, 150 ER 571.

[122] (1843) 12 LJ Bcy 39, 3 Mont D & De G 256.

other securities, with London bankers for the purpose of securing a debt due from them to the London bankers. After the bankruptcy the London bankers called upon the petitioner to pay the amount of the promissory note, which he did. The securities held by the London bankers were more than sufficient to satisfy the debt due to them, and the surplus securities were returned to the assignees in bankruptcy. Before the bankruptcy the petitioner had taken up some notes of the bankrupts in the course of business, and he presented a petition to the Court of Bankruptcy against the assignees praying that they might be ordered to pay him the sum that he had paid to the London bankers. Sir James Knight Bruce VC declared in his order that the petitioner, as against the estate of the bankrupts, was entitled to set off the amount of the bankrupts' notes that he had taken up against the amount due on his own promissory note, and that he was entitled to a lien for the amount that he had paid on the funds and securities which the assignees had received from the London bankers after the debt to the London bankers was paid. The Vice Chancellor emphasized that the petitioner was ignorant that the bankrupts had parted with his promissory note, and that the petitioner had regulated his dealings on that footing by taking up the bankrupts' own notes in the ordinary course of business. However the case should not be confined to that circumstance, but should also apply where a debtor had acquired a claim against the creditor before the creditor provided the debt as security. Thus, Sir James Knight Bruce commented that, since the securities held by the London bankers were more than sufficient to satisfy the debt to them, in a sense the property in the petitioner's promissory note had never left the bankrupts' hands, and the bankrupts therefore retained such an interest in it that the insolvency set-off section would have applied. While he said that he did not put the case mainly or exclusively on that ground, it nevertheless suggests a general application for the decision. In *Ex parte Staddon* the debtor paid the secured creditor, but where there is other security a similar result should follow if the instrument upon which the debtor is liable is returned to the creditor/mortgagor,[123] either because the secured creditor had recourse to the other security or because the creditor's trustee in bankruptcy or liquidator redeemed the security by payment.[124] On the other hand, the order in the *Staddon* case referred to a set-off 'as against the estate of the bankrupts'.[125] A set-off should not apply as against the secured creditor before the

---

[123] When in a case such as *Staddon* a debtor's instrument is returned to the creditor's trustee in bankruptcy or liquidator, it may be a case in which there was a temporary suspension of mutuality, so as in any event to permit a set-off on that ground. See paras 6.65–6.67 above.

[124] In the *Staddon* case the assignees in bankruptcy paid the balance of the secured debt after the payment by the petitioner and the remaining securities were returned to them. The remaining securities were realized, and the report states (at (1843) 3 Mont D & De G 256, 259) that they produced a 'much larger sum' than the amount paid by the petitioner and the balance paid by the assignees. See also para 11.36 below in relation to redemption of a security.

[125] The terms of the order are set out at (1843) 12 LJ Bcy 39, 40.

secured creditor has been paid.[126] If a set-off were available before payment, on the ground that the secured creditor had other security sufficient to pay the secured debt, the secured creditor would be exposed to the risk of a reduction in the value of the remaining security.

(3) Floating Security[127]

11.32 A company instead may grant a floating security over its assets, including over debts owing to it. Before crystallization, the existence of the floating security has no effect upon rights of set-off accruing to the debtor against the company. The debtor will not be deprived of a set-off by reason of the fact that, at the time that either of the cross-debts was incurred, he had notice of the security.[128] The position changes, however, once crystallization occurs. Upon crystallization, the security attaches to the company's assets, and it is commonly said that any debts owing to the company and coming within the ambit of the security are assigned in equity to the secured creditor.[129] In Australia, the proposition that crystalliza-tion results in an equitable assignment of the company's assets the subject of the security has been described as 'too imprecise',[130] and indeed crystallization of a floating security is often expressed to result in a fixed equitable charge over the as-sets[131] as distinct from an assignment by way of mortgage. But it has also been said in Australia that the appellation 'equitable assignment' is sufficient for some pur-poses,[132] and the cases suggest that crystallization of a floating security which is in the form of a charge is to be equated with an equitable assignment for the purpose of determining rights of set-off.[133] The principles discussed above in the context of mortgages accordingly are relevant, on the basis that an equitable assignment occurs at the date of crystallization.

---

[126] See also para 11.28 above.

[127] See also paras 17.73–17.87 below.

[128] *Biggerstaff v Rowatt's Wharf Ltd* [1896] 2 Ch 93.

[129] *Biggerstaff v Rowatt's Wharf Ltd* [1896] 2 Ch 93; *N W Robbie & Co Ltd v Witney Warehouse Co Ltd* [1963] 1 WLR 1324 (referred to with evident approval in *Security Trust Co v Sovereign Bank of Canada* [1976] AC 503, 518); *National Mutual Life Nominees Ltd v National Capital Development Commission* (1975) 37 FLR 404, 407–410; *Rendell v Doors and Doors Ltd* [1975] 2 NZLR 191; *Business Computers Ltd v Anglo-African Leasing Ltd* [1977] 1 WLR 578, 582; *Hoverd Industries Ltd v Supercool Refrigeration and Air Conditioning (1991) Ltd* [1995] 3 NZLR 577, 587; *Roadshow Entertainment Pty Ltd v (ACN 053 006 269) Pty Ltd* (1997) 42 NSWLR 462, 482; *Re Parker* (1997) 80 FCR 1, 17. See generally *Ferrier v Bottomer* (1972) 126 CLR 597, 607; *George Barker (Transport) Ltd v Eynon* [1974] 1 WLR 462, 467; *Moodemere Pty Ltd v Waters* [1988] VR 215, 228; *Re ELS Ltd* [1995] Ch 11; *Wily v Commonwealth* (1996) 66 FCR 206, 220–221.

[130] *Sheahan v Carrier Air Conditioning Pty Ltd* (1997) 189 CLR 407, 422–423, *per* Brennan CJ. See also *Re Parker* (1997) 80 FCR 1, 17–18; *G & M Aldridge Pty Ltd v Walsh* [1999] 3 VR 601, 610–611 para 26 (decision affirmed (2001) 203 CLR 662, HC).

[131] See below.

[132] *G & M Aldridge Pty Ltd v Walsh* [1999] 3 VR 601, 610 para 26.

[133] See eg *N W Robbie & Co Ltd v Witney Warehouse Co Ltd* [1963] 1 WLR 1324; *Business Computers Ltd v Anglo-African Leasing Ltd* [1977] 1 WLR 578, 580, 582; *Hoverd Industries Ltd v Supercool Refrigeration and Air Conditioning (1991) Ltd* [1995] 3 NZLR 577, 587; *Roadshow Entertainment Pty Ltd v (ACN 053 006 269) Pty Ltd* (1997) 42 NSWLR 462, 482.

If after crystallization the company goes into liquidation, a debt otherwise owing   **11.33**
to the company at the date of the liquidation will have become the subject of a
fixed security in favour of the secured creditor as a result of the crystallization,
whether by way of an assignment or a fixed equitable charge. The debtor accordingly could not rely on the insolvency set-off section in the company's liquidation,[134] except, in the circumstances referred to above,[135] to the extent that the debt
in question exceeds the amount secured. The question whether the insolvency set-
off section would apply if the security is redeemed by the company after its liquidation is considered below.[136]

(4) Fixed Equitable Charge

A third possibility is a fixed equitable charge on a debt taking effect as a mere en-   **11.34**
cumbrance, as opposed to an assignment. This form of charge creates in equity a
specific charge on the proceeds of the debt as soon as they are received.[137]
However, while an equitable charge also confers a form of proprietary interest in
the debt the subject of the charge,[138] in the sense that the chargor no longer has an
unfettered title to deal with it, and upon default the chargee is entitled to realize
the debt through the appointment of a receiver or by disposing of it without the
chargor's consent so as to confer upon the transferee an unencumbered title,[139] an
equitable charge does not purport to transfer the beneficial ownership title in the
debt to the chargee.[140] For this reason it has been suggested that the fact that a debt
is the subject of a fixed charge does not affect mutuality as between the debtor and
the creditor/chargor, so that the chargee should take subject to any right of set-off
as between those parties whether arising before or after the debtor has notice of the
charge.[141] The better view, however, is that an equitable charge has the same effect

---

[134] *Re Parker* (1997) 80 FCR 1, 16–18. This appears from cases such as *Handley Page Ltd v
Commissioners of Customs and Excise and Rockwell Machine Tool Co Ltd* [1970] 2 Lloyd's Rep 459;
Rendell v Doors and Doors Ltd [1975] 2 NZLR 191; *Hoverd Industries Ltd v Supercool Refrigeration
and Air Conditioning (1991) Ltd* [1995] 3 NZLR 577, 585 *et seq*. See also para 11.04 above, and
para 17.84 below.
[135] See para 11.28 above.
[136] See para 11.36 below.
[137] *Siebe Gorman & Co Ltd v Barclays Bank Ltd* [1979] 2 Lloyd's Rep 142, 159.
[138] *Re Bank of Credit and Commerce International SA (No 8)* [1998] AC 214, 226.
[139] If the instrument creating the charge has not included an express power of sale or a right to
appoint a receiver, the chargee may apply to the court for an order for either remedy.
[140] *Re Bank of Credit and Commerce International SA (No 8)* [1998] AC 214, 226; *Re Cosslett
(Contractors) Ltd* [1998] Ch 495, 508; *Tancred v Delagoa Bay and East Africa Railway Co* (1889) 23
QBD 239, 242; *Morris v Woodings* (1997) 25 ACSR 636, 640–641; Gough, *Company Charges* (2nd
edn, 1996) 18–19.
[141] Goode, 'Centre Point' [1984] JBL 172, and see also Grantham, 'The Impact of Security on
Set-off' [1989] JBL 377, 386–8. Compare Professor Goode's later discussion in *Legal Problems of
Credit and Security* (2nd edn, 1988) 117.

upon mutuality as a mortgage.[142] The important point is that an equitable charge, while it does not involve a full transfer of the beneficial ownership, nevertheless confers an immediate proprietary interest in the debt,[143] so that it is not merely a security over the proceeds.[144] If the chargor becomes bankrupt the charged debt would not vest in his trustee in bankruptcy for the benefit of creditors generally, in which case it should not be the subject of a set-off under the insolvency set-off section as between the chargor and the debtor.[145] For example, in *Lee & Chapman's Case*[146] the security in issue was described as a charge,[147] and it was held that the charged debt was not available for a set-off as between the debtor and the creditor/chargor in the latter's liquidation to the extent of the amount of the debt that was required to discharge the security. Similarly, when the debtor on the charged debt is bankrupt, any proof in the bankruptcy would be lodged for the benefit of the chargee, not the chargor, so that it should not be the subject of a set-off in respect of a debt owing by the chargor to the debtor.

Statutes of Set-off

11.35 In so far as set-off under the Statutes of Set-off is concerned, the availability of a set-off as against a debt the subject of an equitable charge similarly should be subject to the same principles as for a mortgage. In other words, the equitable chargee should only take subject to a right of set-off that accrued to the debtor against the

---

[142] In *Hoverd Industries Ltd v Supercool Refrigeration and Air Conditioning (1991) Ltd* [1995] 3 NZLR 577, 587 the New Zealand Court of Appeal in considering mutuality equated a fixed charge with an equitable assignment. See also *Roadshow Entertainment Pty Ltd v (ACN 053 006 269) Pty Ltd* (1997) 42 NSWLR 462, 482, and the cases dealing with crystallization of a floating charge, for which see para 11.32 above.

[143] This immediate and attached security interest should be distinguished from the interest which the holder of a floating security has prior to crystallization. While this is a present security (*Smith v Bridgend County BC* [2002] 1 AC 336, 357 paras 61 and 62; Gough, *Company Charges* (2nd edn, 1996) 97; *Wily v St George Partnership Banking Ltd* (1999) 84 FCR 423, 425–427, 430–434). It is, as Professor Goode has explained (*Legal Problems of Credit and Security* (2nd edn, 1988) 49), a security over a fund of assets without attaching to any particular asset. See also *Evans v Rival Granite Quarries Ltd* [1910] 2 KB 979, 999; *Moodemere Pty Ltd v Waters* [1988] VR 215, 228. It has also been said that the interest created by a floating charge, although existing, is dormant until crystallization. See *Smith v Bridgend* at 357 para 61, *per* Lord Scott. These analyses may provide a solution to the problem to which Mr Grantham adverted in his article, 'The Impact of a Security Interest on Set-off' [1989] JBL 377, 386–7.

[144] Compare an assignment of the proceeds of a debt, for which see para 17.53 below.

[145] *De Mattos v Saunders* (1872) LR 7 CP 570, 582; *Re Asphaltic Wood Pavement Co. Lee & Chapman's Case* (1885) 30 Ch D 216, 225; *Popular Homes Ltd v Circuit Developments Ltd* [1979] 2 NZLR 642, 657. See also *Turner v Thomas* (1871) LR 6 CP 610, 615, and paras 17.28 and 17.84 below.

[146] *Re Asphaltic Wood Pavement Co. Lee & Chapman's Case* (1885) 30 Ch D 216.

[147] See the statement of facts, and also the judgment of Bacon VC at first instance, at (1881) 26 Ch D 624, 627–628, 634, and on appeal Brett MR (1885) 30 Ch D 216, 220–222, although compare Cotton LJ at 224–226.

chargor before he had notice of the charge.[148] When the cross-debt arose after notice there admittedly is still mutuality at law, so that the Statutes prima facie apply. On the other hand, it would be unconscionable for the debtor to base a defence on a cross-debt that accrued to him after he was aware that someone else had a proprietary interest in the debt,[149] and the debtor should not be permitted to rely on any such defence in an action to enforce the debt.[150] This is consistent with the floating charge cases.[151] While it was generally said in those cases that crystallization of the security brought about an equitable assignment of the debt in favour of the debenture-holder, in many of them the debenture in fact provided for a charge upon crystallization as opposed to a mortgage,[152] and in that respect they support the view that a charge has an effect similar to an assignment as far as rights of set-off are concerned. Thus, Jeffrey J in the New South Wales Supreme Court in *West Street Properties Pty Ltd v Jamison*[153] referred, in the context of a crystallized floating charge, to the principle 'which prevents a cross-action for a legal debt from being maintained against a plaintiff suing on behalf of an equitable chargee where the substantial consequence of doing so would be to allow the defendant, as no more than an unsecured creditor of the plaintiff, to defeat the equitable chargee's security'. It has been assumed in New Zealand that the same principle applies in the case of an equitable charge as for a mortgage.[154]

(5) Redemption of the Security

11.36 When a debt is the subject of a security, and the security is redeemed, the full beneficial title to the debt reverts to the security provider, and rights of set-off should be determined accordingly. Therefore, in a subsequent liquidation of the security provider, the debt should be able to be set off pursuant to the insolvency set-off section against a cross-debt owing by the security provider to the debtor. However, what if the security is redeemed after the security provider's liquidation? If the security provider held the debt before the debt became the subject of a fixed security, it should not matter that redemption occurs after liquidation. It would

---

[148] See para 11.26 above. Compare *Rother Iron Works Ltd v Canterbury Precision Engineers Ltd* [1974] 1 QB 1 (see para 17.78 below) in the context of a receiver who carried on the company's business.

[149] *Hoverd Industries Ltd v Supercool Refrigeration and Air Conditioning (1991) Ltd* [1995] 3 NZLR 577, 587, referring to Meagher, Gummow and Lehane, *Equity Doctrines and Remedies* (3rd edn, 1992) 720–1 para 2867. The analysis of James LJ in *Roxburghe v Cox* (1881) 17 Ch D 520, 526 would appear to apply equally to an equitable charge.

[150] See para 11.08 above.

[151] See para 11.32 above and paras 17.73–17.87 below.

[152] See eg *N W Robbie & Co Ltd v Witney Warehouse Co Ltd* [1963] 1 WLR 1324 in which the security took the form of a charge (see the terms of the security at 1326), and the discussion in *Biggerstaff v Rowatt's Wharf, Ltd* [1896] 2 Ch 93 (the terms of the security being set out at 94). See also *National Mutual Life Nominees Ltd v National Capital Development Commission* (1975) 37 FLR 404, 408–410 (criticized in Sykes and Walker, *The Law of Securities* (5th edn, 1993) 960).

[153] [1974] 2 NSWLR 435, 441.

[154] *Dalgety and Co Ltd v National Mortgage and Agency Co Ltd* (1910) 13 GLR 379.

simply be a case of a suspension of mutuality,[155] and *Hiley v The Peoples Prudential Assurance Co Ltd*[156] supports the availability of a set-off in that circumstance. Consider however that the security is a floating security over all the assets of a company, and the debt the subject of the security was incurred to the security provider after the floating security crystallized.[157] If, as is usually the case, the security extends to future assets, the debt when it came into existence would have been the subject of an immediate equitable assignment to the secured creditor.[158] The situation in that circumstance would differ from that in the *Hiley* case, in which there was merely a suspension of mutuality. The company in the *Hiley* case was owed the debt, it assigned it by way of mortgage, and it redeemed the security after its liquidation. In the situation posited, on the other hand, the security provider prior to the liquidation was never owed the debt free of the security.[159] The secured creditor from the beginning was beneficially interested in the dealing which gave rise to the debt the subject of the security, and so there would not appear to have been strict mutuality in equity prior to the liquidation. On that basis, it would not be a case of a suspension of mutuality. A set-off nevertheless may still be available. If the secured creditor had sufficient other security to satisfy the secured debt, it is suggested that the company providing the security would have retained a sufficient interest in the redeemed debt so as to permit a set-off.[160] In a case in which the security was over all the company's assets, and the security was redeemed so that the full beneficial interest in the debt reverted to the company, ordinarily it would follow that the secured creditor had sufficient other security.

---

[155] See paras 6.65–6.67 above.

[156] (1938) 60 CLR 468.

[157] Chilwell J's dictum in *Rendell v Doors and Doors Ltd* [1975] 2 NZLR 191, 202–203 (which is criticized in Wood, *English and International Set-off* (1989) 922) should be considered in this context.

[158] *N W Robbie & Co Ltd v Witney Warehouse Co Ltd* [1963] 1 WLR 1324.

[159] The comments of Deane J in *Federal Commissioner of Taxation v Everett* (1978) 21 ALR 625, 644, referring to *Re Lind* [1915] 2 Ch 345, 360 in relation to an assignment of future property are relevant here.

[160] See paras 11.27–11.31 above.

12

MUTUALITY—SAME PARTIES

A. Introduction

In the absence of an agency or a trust relationship which brings about mutuality **12.01** in equity, or alternatively, before bankruptcy or liquidation, of a set-off agreement between the parties,[1] A's right to sue B may not be set off against A's indebtedness to C.[2] This applies where B and C are related companies,[3] and also where C is a director of company B[4] or is the beneficial owner of company B.[5]

B. Joint Claims and Liabilities

(1) The General Principle

The requirement of same parties often arises in the context of joint debts and **12.02** demands. Joint debtors may employ the debt in a set-off against a cross-demand

---

[1] See ch 16 below in relation to set-off agreements.

[2] See eg *North and South Wales Bank Ltd v Macbeth* [1908] AC 137, 141, HL.

[3] *Bank of Credit and Commerce International (Overseas) Ltd v Habib Bank Ltd* [1999] 1 WLR 42; *Meridien BIAO Bank GmbH v Bank of New York* [1997] 1 Lloyd's Rep 437. See also *First National Bank of Chicago v West of England Shipowners Mutual Protection and Indemntiy Asociation (The Evelpidis Era)* [1981] 1 Lloyd's Rep 54. *Aliter* if the corporate veil can be lifted so that C's asset, in the form of the claim against A, can be considered as an asset of B. Compare *Meridien BIAO Bank v Bank of New York* at 446. It makes no difference that B and C are in liquidation and their liquidators have entered into a pooling arrangement. See *BCCI v Habib Bank* at 48–49.

[4] *Re Barker, ex p Michell* (1958) 18 ABC 195.

[5] *Re Bank of Credit and Commerce International SA (No 8)* [1998] AC 214. See also *Hamilton Ice Arena Ltd v Perry Developments Ltd* [2002] 1 NZLR 309 (equitable set-off).

possessed by them jointly against the creditor,[6] but a set-off generally will not arise as between, on the one hand, a joint debt or a joint demand, and on the other a separate demand or a separate debt of one of the joint parties.[7] Thus, in the case of a partnership,[7a] a joint debt of the partnership generally cannot be set off against a debt owed separately to one of the partners,[8] and a separate debt of one of the partners cannot be set off against an obligation owing to the firm.[9] Further, an agreement between a partner and his separate creditor, by which the partner's liability is to be set off against a debt owing by the creditor to the partnership, may be impugned in equity by the other partners to the extent of their interest in the debt to the partnership if the creditor had notice that it was a partnership asset.[10] Even if all the partners separately are indebted to a creditor of the firm, the separate debts give rise to separate claims, and they may not be set off against a liability of the creditor to the partnership.[11] Conversely, in *Ex parte Christie*[12] the partners were jointly indebted to a creditor, who was indebted to each of the partners separately, and a set-off was denied in the creditor's bankruptcy.

The parties may act to bring about a set-off

12.03   The parties nevertheless may act to bring about a set-off. Thus, a partnership may agree with a debtor to the firm that the firm is to be responsible for debts owing separately by its members to the debtor, and that those separate debts are to be set

---

⁶   See eg *Stackwood v Dunn* (1842) 3 QB 822, 114 ER 723; *Forster v Wilson* (1843) 12 M & W 191, 152 ER 1165.
⁷   In addition to the cases referred to below, see *Arnold v Bainbrigge* (1853) 9 Ex 153, 156 ER 66; *Jones v Fleeming* (1827) 7 B & C 217, 108 ER 704.
⁷ᵃ   Note that it is now possible to have a limited liability partnership which, unlike a normal partnership, is a separate legal entity from its members. See the Limited Liability Partnerships Act 2000. Mutuality therefore should be determined on the same basis as for a company.
⁸   *M'Gillivray v Simson* (1826) 2 Car & P 320, 172 ER 145, affirmed 5 LJOSKB 53; *Tyso v Pettit* (1879) 40 LT 132. See also *Addis v Knight* (1817) 2 Mer 117, 35 ER 885; *Vale of Clwydd Coal Co v Garsed* (1885) 2 WN (NSW) 14 (joint debt); *Re Pennington and Owen Ltd* [1925] 1 Ch 825. Compare *James v Kynnier* (1799) 5 Ves Jun 108, 31 ER 496, in which the sum paid by the partner to the partnership creditor was treated as a payment of the partnership debt, as opposed to giving rise to a separate debt owing by the creditor to the partner.
⁹   *Ex parte Riley* (1731) W Kel 24, 25 ER 476; *Ex parte Twogood* (1805) 11 Ves Jun 517, 32 ER 1189; *Ex parte Soames, re Pestell* (1833) 3 Deac & Ch 320; *France v White* (1839) 6 Bing (NC) 33, 133 ER 13; *Baker v Gent* (1892) 9 TLR 159. See also *Middleton v Pollock, ex p Nugee* (1875) LR 20 Eq 29; *Bowyear v Pawson* (1881) 6 QBD 540; *McEwan v Crombie* (1883) 25 Ch D 175; *Tapper v Matheson* (1884) NZLR 3 SC 312; *Loughnan v O'Sullivan* [1922] 1 IR 103 (affirmed [1922] 1 IR 160) (joint judgment for costs in favour of A and B against C could not be set off in C's bankruptcy against B's separate debt to C). In *Ex parte Ross, re Fisher* (1817) Buck 125, a firm consisting of two partners was dissolved, although the business was continued by one of the former partners. It was held that a debt due to the former partners could not be set off against a liability incurred by the remaining partner after the dissolution.
¹⁰   See *Piercy v Fynney* (1871) LR 12 Eq 69, but compare Lord Esher MR in *Harper v Marten* (1895) 11 TLR 368.
¹¹   *Tyso v Pettit* (1879) 40 LT 132.
¹²   (1804) 10 Ves Jun 105, 32 ER 783.

off against the debt owing to the firm.[13] Similarly, the conduct of the parties may be such as to indicate an agreement that a claim possessed by a partner against a third party is to be amalgamated with a debt owing by himself and his partners to that party.[14] In these cases, however, the agreement will not be effective in a bankruptcy when it involves an asset of the bankrupt unless the set-off has occurred prior to the bankruptcy.[15] Alternatively, if a member is a separate creditor, his right to sue may be assigned to the firm, which may then set it off against a joint indebtedness.[16] A more common situation arises when a partner retires. A retiring partner remains liable for debts incurred by the firm before his retirement. But if a creditor has agreed to a novation, so that the firm constituted by the remaining partners is to be treated as the debtor and the old firm which included the retired partner is discharged, the debt may be set off against a debt subsequently incurred by the creditor to the new firm.[17] Without a novation the partnership in debt would be differently constituted from the partnership in credit, and mutuality would be lacking.[18]

Severance of a joint claim

In the case of joint creditors, they may agree that the debt should be severed.[19] If **12.04** the debtor is a party to the agreement it may take effect by way of novation, by which the joint claim is extinguished and is replaced by a separate claim in favour of each creditor for his proportion. Each creditor would then be able to employ his separate claim in a set-off against a debt that he owes to the debtor. Alternatively, if the debtor is not a party, an agreement amongst the creditors to sever the joint claim may take effect by way of an equitable assignment of part of the debt to each creditor.[20] The creditors would then hold the debt jointly as trustees for themselves as tenants in common of distinct portions of the debt,[21] and questions of set-off would be determined by reference to the same principles

---

[13] *Kinnerley v Hossack* (1809) 2 Taunt 170, 127 ER 1042. There must be evidence of an agreement for payment by means of a set-off. A mere understanding by one party is not sufficient. See *Ex parte Soames, re Pestell* (1833) 3 Deac & Ch 320, 324, and also *Tyso v Pettit* (1879) 40 LT 132.

[14] *Ell v Harper* (1886) NZLR 4 SC 307.

[15] *British Eagle International Air Lines Ltd v Compagnie Nationale Air France* [1975] 1 WLR 758. See paras 16.18–16.20 below.

[16] Compare *Watts v Christie* (1849) 11 Beav 546, 50 ER 928, where the assignment took place in circumstances such that a set-off would have constituted a fraudulent preference. See para 6.61 above.

[17] *Burgess v Morton* (1894) 10 TLR 339, reversed on other grounds [1896] AC 136.

[18] As in *Re Jane, ex p The Trustee* (1914) 110 LT 556.

[19] Compare *Bowyear v Pawson* (1881) 6 QBD 540, in which a creditor entered into an agreement by which he assigned the claim to himself and another person in equal shares as tenants in common. Watkin Williams and Mathew JJ held that this was not sufficient to sever the debt so as to entitle the other person to set off his interest in it against a separate debt that he owed to the debtor.

[20] Since it is not possible to have a legal assignment of part of a debt, the assignment in this situation must of necessity be an equitable assignment. See *McIntyre v Guy* (1994) 51 FCR 472, 479.

[21] *McIntyre v Gye* (1994) 51 FCR 472, 479.

applicable generally to equitable assignments of debts.[22] Thus, each creditor in re-spect of his portion would take subject to a set-off available to the debtor against the joint creditors before the debtor received notice of the assignment. If the debtor raises the defence against only one of the creditors suing as an equitable assignee, that creditor should be entitled to contribution from the other creditors.

(2) Insolvency Set-off and Partnerships

12.05   In order for the insolvency set-off section to apply in relation to partnership lia-bilities,[22a] the partnership must be in the process of being wound up under the Insolvent Partnerships Order 1994, either as an unregistered company[23] or in cir-cumstances where a joint bankruptcy petition has been presented by all members of the insolvent partnership.[24] If an action is brought to recover a debt owing to a partnership, the insolvency set-off section will not apply in relation to a cross-claim against the partnership merely because one of the partners has become bankrupt.[25]

(3) Equitable Interests

12.06   Since mutuality in insolvency set-off is determined by reference to the equitable interests of the parties,[26] a set-off may proceed despite the fact that at law one claim may be joint and the other separate if in equity the same parties are inter-ested in the cross-demands. Therefore, a debt owing to a number of creditors (Cl and C2) jointly may be set off against the separate indebtedness of one of the cred-itors (Cl), if Cl and C2 are merely trustees of the debt for Cl so that he is the only person beneficially interested in it.[27] Conversely, a set-off may be denied where there is mutuality at law but not in equity.[28]

12.07   In relation to the Statutes of Set-off,[29] a defence of set-off may arise at law if there is mutuality by reference to the legal title to cross-debts, and equity acting by ana-

---

[22]   See *Adamopoulos v Olympic Airways SA* (1991) 25 NSWLR 75, 87, and ch 17 below.
[22a]   In the case of a limited liability partnership, see para 6.05 above.
[23]   See the Insolvent Partnerships Order 1994, arts 7, 8, 9 and 10 (SI 1994/2421), together with Part V (in particular s 221(1)) of the Insolvency Act 1986 and art 18 of the Insolvent Partnerships Order.
[24]   See the Insolvent Partnerships Order 1994, art 11 and Sch 7. In Australia, see the Bankruptcy Act 1966 (Cth), ss 45, 46 and 56A. In Australia a partnership of more than five members may be wound up under the Corporations Act 2001 as a Part 5.7 body, in which case the set-off section (s 553C) applies. See s 583.
[25]   *Staniforth v Fellowes* (1814) 1 Marsh 184; *New Quebrada Co Ltd v Carr* (1869) LR 4 CP 651; *London, Bombay and Mediterranean Bank v Narraway* (1872) LR 15 Eq 93.
[26]   See para 11.04 above.
[27]   Compare *Re Imperial Mercantile Credit Association, ex p Smith and Ford* (1867) 15 WR 1069, in which the beneficial entitlement of one of the trustees only related to the interest payable on the debt. Compare also *Ex parte Morier, re Willis, Percival & Co* (1879) 12 Ch D 491, in which the es-tate had not been fully administered by the executors, and so a trust as yet had not been imposed in favour of the executor who was the residuary legatee. See para 13.117 below.
[28]   *Tapper v Matheson* (1884) NZLR 3 SC 312.
[29]   See paras 11.08–11.10 above.

logy with the Statutes similarly may recognize a set-off if there is mutuality in equity. Conversely, if a creditor holds a debt on trust for or if the creditor has assigned it in equity to a third party, equity may regard it as unconscionable for a set-off at law to occur as between the debtor and the creditor, and accordingly not permit a set-off. Thus, the same result often (but not always[30]) follows in relation to the Statutes as if mutuality were determined by reference to equitable titles.

(4) Exceptions

The courts have been reluctant to depart from the principle that a joint demand and a separate demand may not be brought into an account. There are nevertheless a number of instances in which a set-off has been allowed, despite an apparent absence of mutuality. Some of these in truth are not exceptions to the principle of mutuality, in that, properly regarded, they do not constitute instances in which a set-off was allowed under the insolvency set-off section where there was not mutuality. Rather, they are examples of equitable set-off, for which mutuality is not a strict requirement.[31]

12.08

A surety made jointly liable

In *Ex parte Hanson*,[32] one of two joint debtors on a bond given as security for a debt had joined in the bond only as a surety. Lord Eldon held that the principal debtor was entitled in equity to employ the joint debt in a set-off against a separate claim that he had against the bankrupt creditor. A set-off was allowed because, 'the joint debt was nothing more than a security for the separate debt; and upon equitable considerations a creditor, who has a joint security for a separate debt, cannot resort to that security without allowing what he has received on the separate account'.[33] A similar notion was applied in *Hamp v Jones*.[34] A judgment had been obtained at law against both Hamp and his bailiff for damages for wrongful distress. In addition, Hamp had a separate claim against the judgment creditor. The creditor was insolvent, but not apparently bankrupt. Because the demands were not mutual they could not be set off at law. Hamp however had agreed to indemnify the bailiff on the judgment, and so Sir Lancelot Shadwell VC held that Hamp could set off the judgment against his separate claim, the Vice Chancellor commenting that:[35] 'If, as the bill states, Mr Hamp has agreed to indemnify his bailiff, that, it seems to me, is a reason for the interference of the Court.' In this

12.09

---

[30] See para 11.09 above.
[31] See paras 4.48–4.54 above, and *Bank of New Zealand v Harry M Miller & Co Ltd* (1992) 26 NSWLR 48, 55.
[32] (1811) 18 Ves Jun 232, 34 ER 305, affirming (1806) 12 Ves Jun 346, 33 ER 131. See also *Ex parte Hippins, re Sikes* (1826) 2 Gl & J 93, 4 LJOS Ch 195; *Clarkson v Smith & Goldberg* [1926] 1 DLR 509, 511.
[33] (1811) 18 Ves Jun 232, 233–234, 34 ER 305, *per* Lord Eldon.
[34] (1840) 9 LJ Ch 258.
[35] (1840) 9 LJ Ch 258.

case, a private agreement for an indemnity provided the basis for a set-off. If on the other hand an agreement for an indemnity in truth is nothing more than a device to obtain an advantage over other creditors by means of a set-off, it is unlikely that an equitable set-off would be permitted.

Judgments

12.10 The common law courts, in the exercise of what has been described as a form of equitable jurisdiction for the purpose of preventing absurdity or injustice,[36] will permit a set-off of judgments in appropriate cases.[37] In exercising this jurisdiction the courts have been prepared to allow a set-off where A has a judgment against B and C, and B has a separate judgment against A.[38] In those cases however there was no question of bankruptcy. If there is a bankruptcy, a set-off of judgments will not be permitted in circumstances extending beyond the insolvency set-off section.[39]

Fraud

12.11 Equity will permit Dl, one of two joint debtors Dl and D2, to set off the joint debt in the creditor's bankruptcy against the creditor's separate debt to D1, if the creditor's debt arose as a result of the creditor's fraud and the creditor concealed the fraud until after the joint debt was incurred. This proposition is based on two decisions of Lord Eldon. In *Vuillamy v Noble*[40] a customer (Dl) had deposited some stock with a bank as security for a loan. The customer paid off the loan, but neglected to request a retransfer of the security. In the meantime he had become a joint debtor with D2 to the bank in a separate transaction. After the bank's bankruptcy, Dl discovered that the bank had sold the stock, so that instead of being the owner of stock he was merely a creditor of the bank for its value.[41] Lord Eldon held that Dl could set off the bank's indebtedness to him in his separate capacity against the joint debt of himself and D2 to the bank.[42] In doing so he referred to his

---

[36] *Edwards v Hope* (1885) 14 QBD 922, 926.

[37] See paras 2.78–2.86 above.

[38] *Roberts v Biggs* Barnes 146, 94 ER 848; *Mitchell v Oldfield* (1791) 4 TR 123, 100 ER 929; *Dennie v Elliott* (1795) 2 H Bl 587, 126 ER 719. See para 2.83 above.

[39] *Doe v Darnton* (1802) 3 East 149, 102 ER 554.

[40] (1817) 3 Mer 593, 36 ER 228.

[41] When a secured debt is paid but the security is not returned, the security is held on trust for the former debtor. See *Pearce v Morris* (1869) LR 5 Ch App 227, 230; *Holme v Fieldsend* [1911] WN 111. If the property constituting the security is sold by the trustee, the beneficial owner may trace it to the proceeds of sale, and if the proceeds have been mixed with part of the trustee's own funds, the beneficial owner has a charge on the whole of the blended fund, the onus being on the trustee to prove which part of it is his own. See *Re Hallett's Estate. Knatchbull v Hallett* (1880) 13 Ch D 696; *Re Tilley's Will Trusts, Burgin v Croad* [1967] 1 Ch 1179. Ordinarily, then, someone in the position of the customer in *Vuillamy* (n 40 above) would have effective real rights for the recovery of the sum owing to him, and a set-off would only be required if the proceeds cannot be traced, or, having been traced, if the fund with which it is mixed is insufficient to satisfy the charge.

[42] Compare the interpretation of *Vuillamy* (n 40 above) put forward by Sir George Jessel MR in *Middleton v Pollock, ex p Knight and Raymond* (1875) LR 20 Eq 515, 521–523, that the stock

earlier decision in *Ex parte Stephens*.[43] The separate debt of the bankrupt creditors in that case to one of their two joint and several debtors (Dl) similarly had arisen as a result of the creditors' own fraud, in retaining Dl's money for their own use rather than using it to purchase annuities as instructed. Lord Eldon enjoined the creditors' assignees in bankruptcy from suing the other joint and several debtor (D2) for payment of the debt, and ordered that Dl should be allowed to set off the joint and several debt of herself and D2 against her separate claim arising as a result of the creditors' fraud.

Ex parte Stephens is generally regarded as having turned on the element of fraud,[44] and indeed Lord Eldon later doubted whether the decision would have been right but for the fraud.[45] It would not be crucial in a similar case today, however.[46] Since the liability was several as well as joint, the view now would be that the several liability of D1 and D1's cross-claim constitute mutual debts or claims arising out of mutual dealings which are capable of set-off under the insolvency set-off section.[47] The case nevertheless is still relevant as an illustration of the circumstances in which a set-off may be available against a joint debt.[48] **12.12**

In discussing *Ex parte Stephens* in *Vuillamy v Noble*,[49] Lord Eldon emphasized that, when D1 in *Ex parte Stephens* incurred the liability to the bankers, she was unaware that they had her money in their hands for which they were accountable.[50] If D1 in a similar case was aware of the fraud at the time of entering into a joint debt, so that D1 was cognizant of the position, it would not generally be appropriate to give D1 a preference over other creditors by means of a set-off. **12.13**

---

was retained by the bank under an agreement that it should constitute security for the joint debt. Therefore it was said that the case was not concerned with set-off at all, because equity would have applied the proceeds of sale in reduction of the joint debt for which it was security, so that only the balance would have been payable. However, Lord Eldon (at (1817) 3 Mer 593, 612–613, 36 ER 228, 236) queried what evidence there was of an agreement that the stock was to be held as security for the joint loan, and in his judgment he treated the issue as one of set-off.

[43] (1805) 11 Ves Jun 24, 32 ER 996. See also the discussion of *Ex parte Stephens* in para 12.27 *ff* below.

[44] *Ex parte Hanson* (1806) 12 Ves Jun 346, 348–349, 33 ER 131, 132; *Ex parte Blagden* (1815) 19 Ves Jun 465, 467, 34 ER 589, 590; *Jones v Mossop* (1844) 3 Hare 568, 573, 67 ER 506, 509; *Ex parte Staddon, re Wise* (1843) 12 LJ Bcy 39, 40; *Middleton v Pollock, ex p Knight and Raymond* (1875) LR 20 Eq 515, 519–520; *McIntyre v Perkes* (1990) 22 FCR 260, 271; *Lord v Direct Acceptance Corp Ltd* (1993) 32 NSWLR 362, 369–370; *Re Bank of Credit and Commerce International SA* [1996] Ch 245, 267–268. See also *Strong v Foster* (1855) 17 CB 201, 217, 139 ER 1047, 1053.

[45] *Ex parte Blagden* (1815) 19 Ves Jun 465, 467, 34 ER 589, 590.

[46] See Hoffmann LJ in *M S Fashions Ltd v Bank of Credit and Commerce International SA* [1993] Ch 425, 438.

[47] See para 12.21 below.

[48] In *Vuillamy* (1817) 3 Mer 593, 621, 36 ER 228, 239 Lord Eldon regarded it as relevant in that context.

[49] (1817) 3 Mer 593, 621, 36 ER 228, 239.

[50] See also *Re Bank of Credit and Commerce International SA (No 8)* [1996] Ch 245, 266, CA.

12.14 The situation is different if the fraudulent conduct of a bankrupt has resulted in a debt owing to two creditors (Cl and C2) jointly, one of whom (Cl) is a separate debtor of the bankrupt. A joint owner of property may not apply the property to his own exclusive use. The joint property in this case consists of the claim arising from fraud, and if Cl would not have had the right to apply it to his own exclusive use before the bankruptcy he should not be entitled to do so after the bankruptcy. C1 therefore should not be entitled to set off the joint claim against his separate indebtedness. *Middleton v Pollock, ex p Knight and Raymond*[51] illustrates the point. The joint creditors in that case admittedly were trustees for third parties, and it was emphasized that payment could not properly have been tendered to one of the trustees alone. But even if there were no trust, the result should have been the same. Moreover, the fact of the trust should have sufficed to preclude a set-off irrespective of the joint legal ownership. Mutuality in bankruptcy is determined by reference to the equitable interests of the parties, and fraud would not justify joint creditors applying the debt owing to them as trustees in satisfaction of the indebtedness of one of them, when the equitable ownership of the joint creditors' claim is in someone else.

Dormant partner

12.15 In *Stracey, Ross, et al v Deey*[52] a partnership carried on trade as grocers. Only one partner was active in the business, however, the other partners being dormant. A debtor of the business had also dealt separately with the active partner, who in the course of those dealings became indebted to the debtor. When the partnership sued the debtor on the grocery account, Lord Kenyon allowed the debtor to set off the active partner's separate debt to him. The *Stracey* case appears as a note to the report of the decision in *George v Clagett*,[53] the seminal authority on the right of a person dealing with someone acting as an agent for an undisclosed principal to set off the agent's indebtedness to him against his liability to the principal on that dealing.[54] But while the position of a dormant partner has been said to be analogous to that of an undisclosed principal,[55] the analogy has been criticized on the ground that the dormant partner's right to sue, and his liability to be sued, do not arise because he is an undisclosed principal intervening on his agent's contracts, but rather because the dormant partner is a party to the contracts.[56] Accepting that

---

[51] (1875) LR 20 Eq 515.

[52] (1789) 7 TR 361n, 101 ER 1021, 2 Esp 469n, 170 ER 422.

[53] (1797) 7 TR 359, 101 ER 1019.

[54] See paras 13.71–13.91 below.

[55] *Beckham v Drake* (1841) 9 M & W 79, 85, 152 ER 35, 37, *per* Parke B, and see also *Watteau v Fenwick* [1893] 1 QB 346, 349.

[56] See Pollock (1893) 9 LQR 111; Montrose, 'Liability of Principal for Acts Exceeding Actual and Apparent Authority' (1939) 17 Canadian Bar Review 693, 703–4. See also *Bowstead and Reynolds on Agency* (17th edn, 2001) 349 Stoljar, *The Law of Agency* (1961) 57. Compare *Construction Engineering (Aust) Pty Ltd v Hexyl Pty Ltd* (1985) 155 CLR 541.

distinction, the *Stracey* case nevertheless should still be followed.[57] If a partnership acts in such a way as to conceal the interest of a dormant partner in the business, and consequently it gives the impression that it consists only of the active partners, it should not be allowed to deny a third party a set-off that would have arisen if the partnership had in fact been so constituted. However the availability of a set-off may be subject to the same limitation which applies to undisclosed principals, that it is confined to the case of mutual debts under the Statutes of Set-off or, in an appropriate case, to equitable set-off, as opposed to the wider right of set-off conferred by the insolvency legislation.[58]

The converse situation instead may apply. A partnership may conduct business **12.16** under the name of A and B, although B is an employee and not a partner. A third party who deals with the firm in ignorance of the true situation would contract with A and B jointly, but A and B nevertheless would enter into the contract as agent for A as an undisclosed principal. If A intervenes on the contract and sues the third party, the third party may set off in that action a debt owing to him by A.[59]

The set-off in a case such as *Stracey* is based upon the third party's belief that the **12.17** active partner was the only principal in the business. In that regard, the circumstances must not have been such as to put the third party on inquiry as to whether there was a dormant partner. In *Baker v Gent*[60] a partnership consisted of two partners, Lachmann and Phillips, but the interest of Phillips in the business was concealed. The business traded under the name of Lachmann and Co. This was held to constitute notice to the defendant that someone else may have been involved in the firm, and accordingly he was not allowed to set off his indebtedness to the firm against Lachmann's separate debt to him. On the other hand, a name such as Lachmann and Co should not put a person dealing with the firm upon inquiry as to the existence of a dormant partner if there were two or more active partners involved in the business.

The generally accepted explanation for the set-off in the undisclosed principal **12.18** cases is that it is based upon representation and estoppel. In the same way, whether or not the partnership cases are thought to involve an undisclosed principal, the set-off in those cases is said to arise from 'some default in the other partners, or some assent on their part'.[61] It is not sufficient that a person dealt with one member of a partnership in the erroneous belief that that member was the only

---

[57] See for example *Muggeridge's v Smith and* Co (1884) 1 TLR 166.
[58] *Turner v Thomas* (1871) LR 6 CP 610, and see para 13.74 below.
[59] *Spurr v Cass* (1870) LR 5 QB 656.
[60] (1892) 9 TLR 159.
[61] *Gordon v Ellis* (1846) 2 CB 821, 828–829, 135 ER 1167, 1170, *per* Tindal CJ *(arguendo)*.

principal in the business.[62] In *Harper v Marten*[63] two partners, Forster and Peake, traded under the name of Forster, Peake, and Co. The defendant dealt only with Peake, and assumed that Peake was trading on his own account. The defendant entered into an agreement with Peake by which her indebtedness resulting from those dealings should be set off against a claim that she had against Peake alone. The Court of Appeal upheld the agreement despite the express reference to Forster in the partnership name. Two points should be noted, however. The first is that the defendant had inquired of Peake as to from whom she was ordering the goods, and he replied himself. The second is the court's finding that Forster had placed the most implicit confidence in Peake and had allowed him to have the whole control and management of the business, and moreover Forster had refrained from making any demand on the defendant for payment of her account when he might reasonably have been expected to do so. Therefore, as Lord Esher MR remarked, while Forster had not authorized Peake to tell a lie, he had enabled Peake to do so and had allowed it to look like the truth.

Common partners in two partnerships

12.19 Another Lord Kenyon judgment has provided a further possible exception. In *Puller v Roe*[64] a partnership consisting of four partners, A, B, C, and D (known as A & Co), held a promissory note made by the defendants. C and D were also partners in another firm. A & Co were indebted to this other partnership, and so the note was indorsed by A & Co to C and D. Subsequently A, B, C, and D all became bankrupt. The assignees in bankruptcy of the second partnership of C and D sued the defendants on the note, whereupon Lord Kenyon held that the defendants could set off some debts owing to them by A & Co, his Lordship commenting that partners 'cannot as between themselves raise a distinct account, though they might indorse to a third person. The affairs of the company are in presumption of law known to all the partners, and all are equally liable.'[65] Nevertheless, while the decision appears to represent a commonsense result, unless C and D in truth held the note as trustees for A & Co it is not easy to explain the set-off. The holder in due course of a negotiable instrument takes free of equities, including rights of set-off.[66] In order to be a holder in due course a person inter alia must have taken the instrument in good faith and for value, and at the time that it was indorsed to him he must not have had notice of any defect in the title of the person who negotiated it.[67] Mere knowledge of a possible right of set-off between prior parties does not

---

[62] *Gordon v Ellis* (1846) 2 CB 821, 135 ER 1167. Compare *Harper v Marten* (1895) 11 TLR 368 (Lord Esher MR).

[63] (1895) 11 TLR 368.

[64] (1793) Peake 260, 170 ER 149.

[65] (1793) Peake 260, 263, 170 ER 149, 150.

[66] Bills of Exchange Act 1882, s 38.

[67] Bills of Exchange Act 1882, s 29.

affect the negotiability of an instrument,[68] and therefore the partners' presumed knowledge of the state of the account between A & Co and the defendants should not have impugned their good faith. Nor indeed is it regarded as fraud for an indorser and an indorsee to agree to the negotiation of the instrument in order to defeat a right of set-off otherwise available against the indorser.[69] *Puller v Roe* possibly may be explained on the basis of the old common law rule that one partnership could not sue another if one or more of the partners were common to both firms, since those partners in effect would be both plaintiffs and defendants in the one suit.[70] Consequently the discharge of A & Co's debt to C and D in *Puller v Roe* may not have been perceived as value given for taking the note.[71] The fact of common partners however should no longer be an objection to an action between two firms.[72] Moreover, the debt may be the subject of an account in equity between the partners,[73] in which case its discharge should be sufficient value. Thus, an antecedent debt which has been rendered unenforceable by statute may afford sufficient consideration for a negotiable instrument.[74]

Setting off a joint creditor's interest in the debt

There is early Chancery support for the view that when C1, one of a number of **12.20** partners C1 and C2, is bankrupt, and a debtor to C1 and C2 has a separate claim against the bankrupt, the debtor may set off the bankrupt's *interest* in his indebtedness to the bankrupt and C2 jointly against the bankrupt's separate debt to him,[75] provided that the extent of the bankrupt's interest in the joint claim is not disputed, and provided also that the partnership assets are otherwise sufficient to satisfy the partnership debts.[76] In *Lord Lanesborough v Jones*[77] Lord Cowper suggested (obiter) that a debtor to C1 and C2 who has a separate claim against C1 may bring into an account, in C1's bankruptcy, C1's interest in the debtor's indebtedness to them, 'if there be a surplus beyond what will pay the partnership

---

[68] *Oulds v Harrison* (1854) 10 Ex 572, 576, 156 ER 566, 568, *per* Parke B (*arguendo*).

[69] See *Oulds v Harrison* (1854) 10 Ex 572, 156 ER 566 in relation to the more unlikely case of an overdue bill (see para 17.57 below), and also *Metropolitan Bank v Snure* (1860) 10 UC (CP) 24.

[70] See *Bosanquet v Wray* (1815) 6 Taunt 597, 128 ER 1167 and *Mainwaring v Newman* (1800) 2 Bos & Pul 120, 126 ER 1190.

[71] Normally an antecedent debt or liability may constitute valuable consideration for a bill of exchange or promissory note. See the Bills of Exchange Act 1882, s 27(1)(b).

[72] See *Lindley and Banks on Partnership* (18th edn, 2002) 430 para 14.13.

[73] See eg *Meyer and Company v Faber (No 2)* [1923] 2 Ch 421, 439.

[74] *Sharpe v Ellis* (1971) 20 FLR 199, 208.

[75] See, and compare, *McEwan v Crombie* (1883) 25 Ch D 175, in which the claim was not truly joint.

[76] The second proviso would be required to protect the creditors of the partnership in the event of its bankruptcy, because the debts owing to the partnership would be joint property distributable in the first instance amongst the joint creditors. See the Insolvent Partnerships Order 1994, Sch 4, Pt II (s 175A) and Sch 7 (s 328A). In Australia this restriction would apply whether or not the joint creditors are partners. See the Bankruptcy Act 1966 (Cth), s 110.

[77] (1716) 1 P Wms 325, 326–327, 24 ER 409, 410.

debts', while the principle was applied in *Ex parte Quintin*,[78] where Lord Loughborough emphasized that the solvent partner (C2) had paid all the partnership debts, and had also agreed that he was only interested to the extent of a quarter in the debts due to the partnership.[79] However Lord Eldon effectively overruled the *Quintin* case in *Ex parte Twogood*,[80] the Lord Chancellor expressing concern that the administration of the bankruptcy would be delayed unduly until the state of the partnership accounts could be ascertained.[81] Nevertheless, despite Lord Eldon's condemnation of the *Quintin* case, the possibility of a set-off has been kept alive in Victoria by *Re John Sloss, ex p Robison Brothers, Campbell & Sloss Ltd*,[82] in which the Supreme Court seemed to accept that the *Quintin* case was still good law. In fact a set-off was denied in *Re Sloss* because of lack of evidence as to the extent of the entitlement of the bankrupt partner in the debt owing to the partnership. On the other hand, Madden CJ cited the *Quintin* case with evident approval, and although he made no mention of *Ex parte Twogood* in his judgment, that case had been brought to the attention of the court during argument. Perhaps the courts may be inclined to apply the *Quintin* case when the partnership accounts are relatively simple, or when the assets of the partnership are patently sufficient to satisfy the partnership debts, so that the administration of the bankruptcy would not be unduly delayed. However, it would hardly be satisfactory that the question whether a debtor to a partnership is entitled to a set-off should depend on the state of the partnership accounts, and the better view is that a set-off is not available in this situation, in accordance with Lord Eldon's judgment in *Ex parte Twogood*.

C. Several Persons Separately Liable

Joint and several debt

12.21 In the case of a joint and several debt,[83] each of the debtors is severally as well as jointly liable.[84] The creditor in such a case may sue all the debtors in the one

---

[78] (1796) 3 Ves Jun 248, 30 ER 994.

[79] Lord Loughborough referred to *Ex parte Edwards* (1745) 1 Atk 100, 26 ER 66, in which Lord Hardwicke ordered that an action against a debtor to a partnership should be stayed pending the taking of an account as to how much was owing to the partnership, and how much was owing to the debtor by one of the partners. However the report is silent as to whether a set-off eventually was allowed.

[80] (1805) 11 Ves Jun 517, 32 ER 1189. See also *Addis v Knight* (1817) 2 Mer 117, 122, 35 ER 885, 887.

[81] Lord Eldon also remarked that the effect of a set-off would be to prefer the particular creditor over the general body of the bankrupt partner's separate creditors, but every set-off in insolvency has that effect.

[82] (1893) 19 VLR 710.

[83] This includes the case of a breach of trust where there is more than one trustee. The liability of trustees for breach of trust is joint and several, and gives rise to an equitable debt. See *Goodwin v Duggan* (1996) 41 NSWLR 158.

[84] See generally Glanville Williams, *Joint Obligations* (1949) 34–5.

action, or he may proceed against one or more of them separately.[85] The indebtedness of a truly joint and several debtor, and a debt owing by the creditor to that debtor, constitute mutual debts, and may be set off.[86] The occurrence of the set-off would bring about a *pro tanto* reduction in the joint and several debt, and would release the other debtors as well.[87] In that regard, when debtors are jointly and severally liable, and either the creditor or one of the debtors is bankrupt, a set-off under the insolvency set-off section, according to the view that has prevailed as to the operation of the section,[88] would occur automatically at the date of the bankruptcy. If the creditor is the bankrupt party, and two or more of the debtors have cross-claims eligible for a set-off, a set-off should take effect on a pro rata basis.[89] Insolvency set-off should be compared to set-off under the Statutes of Set-off, which is not automatic but rather it operates as a procedural defence to an action at law.[90] The creditor could sue whichever of the debtors he chooses. In such a case the joint and several debtor being sued could not bring into account an indebtedness of the creditor to one of the other joint and several debtors. The debts would not be mutual. A right of contribution between the debtors does not justify a set-off in that circumstance.[91] If on the other hand joint and several debtors are sued together, judgment for a set-off in favour of one of the debtors to that extent would discharge the debt, and therefore the judgment against the other debtors should also be reduced accordingly.[92]

Guarantees and bills of exchanges

Apart from joint and several debts, there are other situations in which a number **12.22** of persons may be sued separately in respect of what in substance is the same debt. This may arise, for example, when a guarantee is given in respect of another person's debt, or in the case of a bill of exchange on which the drawer or an indorser is liable as well as the acceptor. Further, while in some cases of joint and several liability none of the parties may be principally liable *inter se*, in others one party

---

[85] Glanville Williams, *Joint Obligations* (1949) 59–62.

[86] *Fletcher v Dyche* (1787) 2 TR 32, 100 ER 18; *Owen v Wilkinson* (1858) 5 CB(NS) 526, 141 ER 213; *Re Last, ex p Butterell* (1994) 124 ALR 219; *Re Kolb* (1994) 51 FCR 31; *Re Bank of Credit and Commerce International SA (No 8)* [1998] AC 214, 224–225. See also *Paulson v Murray* (1922) 68 DLR 643 (set-off of judgments), and *Ferrum Inc v Three Dees Management Ltd* (1992) 7 OR (3d) 660, 669.

[87] *Owen v Wilkinson* (1858) 5 CB(NS) 526, 527, 141 ER 213 (Willes J, referring to *Pothier on Obligations*, by Evans, vol 2 at p 68); *Goodwin v Duggan* (1996) 41 NSWLR 158, 167; *Re Bank of Credit and Commerce International SA (No 8)* [1998] AC 214, 224–225; *Handberg v Smarter Way (Aust) Pty Ltd* (2002) 20 ACLC 858 (judgment for costs).

[88] See para 6.79 *ff* above.

[89] This would be consistent with the approach adopted when there are two debts owing to a creditor, one of which has priority in the debtor's bankruptcy or liquidation. See para 6.114 *ff* above.

[90] See paras 2.33–2.48 above.

[91] *Bowyear v Pawson* (1881) 6 QBD 540; *Lord v Direct Acceptance Corp Ltd* (1993) 32 NSWLR 362, 371–372; *Goodwin v Duggan* (1996) 41 NSWLR 158, 166, 167–168.

[92] *Goodwin v Duggan* (1996) 41 NSWLR 158.

may be the principal debtor, with the liability of the other joint and several debtors intended to be secondary. The contract in that circumstance effectively is one of suretyship. Similarly, in the case of a bill of exchange the acceptor has the principal liability and the liability of the drawer and the indorsers is secondary, unless it is an accommodation acceptance in which case, as between the drawer and the acceptor, equity regards the drawer as the person principally liable.[93] In those situations, one of the parties may have a separate claim against the creditor, and the creditor may have become bankrupt or is a company in liquidation. In a number of early cases the question arose as to whether the creditor's trustee (or assignees) in bankruptcy could avoid a set-off by proceeding against one party rather than another for payment, or alternatively whether there was an obligation to facilitate a set-off by proceeding against a particular party. The cases established the following propositions.

(1) If one of the debtors was principally liable *inter se*, so that ultimately he was to pay the debt, he could insist that the creditor's trustee proceed against him so that he could have the benefit of a set-off.[94] Thus, in *Ex parte Hippins, re Sikes*[95] Lord Eldon held that the drawer of an accommodation bill, as the person principally liable in equity, could demand that the bill be delivered up in part discharge of a debt owing to him by the bankrupt holders.

(2) A trustee in bankruptcy holding a bill of exchange that had been dishonoured by the acceptor could not be compelled to have recourse to the drawer or an indorser of the bill who was also a creditor of the bankrupt, and who therefore would have had a set-off against his liability on the bill, but instead could insist on suing the acceptor as the party principally liable. Commissioner Holroyd adopted that view in *Ex parte Banes, re The Royal British Bank*,[96] following an earlier decision by Lord Eldon to the same effect in *Ex parte Burton, Franco and Corea, re Kensington*.[97] Conversely, a bankrupt acceptor's trustee could not require the holder to have recourse to an indorser so as to avoid a set-off.[98] *Ex parte Banes* and *Ex parte Burton* should still apply in a situation in which a bankrupt has a contingent claim against one of a number of debtors.

---

[93] The common law on the other hand considered that the accommodation acceptor was principally liable. See *Coles Myer Finance Ltd v Commissioner of Taxation* (1993) 67 ALJR 463, 466–467, 481–484.

[94] *Ex parte Hanson* (1811) 18 Ves Jun 232, 34 ER 305; *Ex parte Hippins, re Sikes* (1826) 2 Gl & J 93, 4 LJOS Ch 195; *Ex parte Banes, re The Royal British Bank* (1857) 28 LTOS 296, 297.

[95] (1826) 2 Gl & J 193, 4 LJOS Ch 195.

[96] (1857) 28 LTOS 296.

[97] (1812) 1 Rose 320. In *Ex parte Hippins, re Sikes* (1826) 2 Gl & J 93, 96 Lord Eldon said that, after examining the secretary's book, it appeared that the bill in *Ex parte Burton* was not an accommodation acceptance.

[98] *McKinnon v Armstrong Brothers & Co* (1877) 2 App Cas 531. See also *Crosse v Smith* (1813) 1 M & S 545, 105 ER 204, in which it was held that a bankrupt drawer could not compel the holder to proceed against the acceptor, and thereby avoid a set-off in his bankruptcy.

The claim, while it remains contingent, cannot be the subject of a set-off,[99] and those cases support the view that the trustee in bankruptcy is not obliged to facilitate a set-off against that debtor by taking steps to cause the liability to vest, for example by making a demand. That situation should be distinguished from *M S Fashions Ltd v Bank of Credit and Commerce International SA*,[100] in which the claim of the bank in liquidation against the guarantor in the circumstances was held not to be contingent.[101]

Surety expressed to be liable as a principal

The House of Lords has held that the insolvency set-off section takes effect auto-   **12.23** matically upon the occurrence of a bankruptcy or a liquidation.[102] On that basis, it should not generally be relevant to ask whether a trustee in bankruptcy or a liquidator can avoid a set-off by proceeding against one party rather than another, or whether he is obliged to facilitate a set-off by having recourse to a debtor who has a cross-claim. Rather, the question is whether a set-off has or has not occurred. The point is illustrated by *M S Fashions Ltd v Bank of Credit and Commerce International SA*.[103] The case concerned a bank which had gone into liquidation. Prior to the liquidation it had provided loans to various companies, in each case secured by a cash deposit made by a director as surety. The deposit was charged in favour of the bank as security for the company's debt, and the charge in each case provided that the director was liable as a principal debtor. In one case the charge also included a personal guarantee of the debt. In another case there was no express guarantee, but the stipulation that the director was to be liable as a principal debtor was interpreted as creating a personal liability in the director not exceeding the amount of the deposit.[104] In each case the liquidator adopted the stance that he was entitled to proceed against the company for repayment of the advance, and to confine the surety to a dividend in the liquidation in respect of the deposit. The Court of Appeal however held that a set-off occurred automatically in the liquidation as between the bank's debt to the surety on the deposit and the surety's liability to the bank, and that this operated also to extinguish the principal debt owed by the company.[105]

In one of the cases considered in the *M S Fashions* case, the surety's liability was ex-   **12.24** pressed to be payable on demand. The liquidator argued that, because a demand had not been made upon the surety, the bank's claim against the surety was still

---

[99] See para 8.27 above.
[100] [1993] Ch 425.
[101] See below.
[102] *Stein v Blake* [1996] AC 243; *Re Bank of Credit and Commerce International SA (No 8)* [1998] Ch 214, 223. See paras 6.79–6.103 above.
[103] [1993] Ch 425. See also *Handberg v Smart Way (Aust) Pty Ltd* (2002) 20 ACLC 856, 866.
[104] See Hoffmann LJ at first instance [1993] Ch 425, 431.
[105] [1993] Ch 425, 448. See also Hoffmann LJ at first instance at 439.

contingent. Under the insolvency set-off section a contingent liability of a bankrupt or a company in liquidation may be the subject of a set-off,[106] but there cannot be a set-off in relation to a contingent claim possessed by the bankrupt or the company if the contingency has not occurred.[107] Therefore, if indeed the claim of the bank in liquidation had been contingent, the liquidator's argument would have been correct.[108] The Court of Appeal however referred to earlier authority to the effect that, where a surety contracted on the basis of being liable as a principal debtor, he could be sued on his engagement without a demand having been made, notwithstanding that the agreement may have provided for a demand.[109] This had the consequence that the surety's liability to the bank in liquidation was not contingent, and it was held that it could be the subject of an automatic set-off.

12.25   It is doubtful whether indeed there should have been a set-off in the *M S Fashions* case. It was not simply a case of a surety having a cross-claim against a creditor in liquidation. Rather, the cross-claim took the form of a deposit which was charged in favour of the creditor, and the charge should have had the effect of destroying mutuality for the purpose of a set-off.[110] This aspect of the case is considered later.[111]

The *BCCI (No 8)* case—choice of remedy?

12.26   The issue of set-off in the liquidation of a creditor, in circumstances where there is a surety for the debt and the surety has a cross-claim against the creditor available by way of set-off in the liquidation, was the subject of further analysis by the Court of Appeal[112] in *Re Bank of Credit and Commerce International SA (No 8)*.[113] In delivering the judgment of the Court, Rose LJ acknowledged the self-evident proposition that the creditor's liquidator could not both set off against the surety and recover from the principal debtor.[114] On the other hand, he canvassed the

---

[106] See paras 8.14–8.21 above

[107] See para 8.27 above.

[108] Compare Calnan, 'The Insolvent Bank and Security Over Deposits' (1996) 11 Journal of International Banking and Financial Law 185, 188–9. It is suggested that Calnan's reference to *Stein v Blake* [1996] AC 243 does not assist the argument in favour of a set-off, since it begs the question as to whether the requirements of the insolvency set-off section have been satisfied, in particular that there must be a sum 'due' on each side of the account.

[109] [1993] Ch 425, 447–448, referring to *Rowe v Young* (1820) 2 Bligh 391, 465–466, 4 ER 374. See also Hoffmann LJ at first instance in *M S Fashions Ltd v Bank of Credit and Commerce International SA* [1993] Ch 425, 436, referring to *Esso Petroleum Co Ltd v Alstonbridge Properties Ltd* [1975] 1 WLR 1474, 1483. In Australia, compare *Re Taylor, ex p Century 21 Real Estate Corporation* (1995) 130 ALR 723.

[110] In *Re Bank of Credit and Commerce International SA (No 8)* [1998] AC 214, 225 the House of Lords left open the question whether the existence of the charge would have affected mutuality, while the Court of Appeal [1996] Ch 245, 273 suggested that the *M S Fashions* case may require reconsideration (although not specifically on this ground).

[111] See paras 16.68–16.70 below.

[112] Rose, Saville and Millett LJJ.

[113] [1996] Ch 245, 268–269. The decision was affirmed by the House of Lords: see [1998] AC 214.

[114] [1996] Ch 245, 269.

possibility that the liquidator may have a choice as to which remedy to pursue, notwithstanding the automatic nature of insolvency set-off.[115]

The impetus for that view was a perceived need to reconcile *Ex parte Stephens*[116] **12.27** with the automatic theory of insolvency set-off that has now been accepted by the courts. In *Ex parte Stephens*, Miss Stephens and her brother had given a joint and several promissory note to bankers in respect of a loan to the brother of £1,000, Miss Stephens signing as surety. In addition, Miss Stephens had a cross-claim against the bankers, arising from their failure to comply with her instructions to invest the proceeds obtained from realizing certain securities in the purchase of other securities, and their concealment of that fact. The bankers subsequently became bankrupt. Their assignees in bankruptcy brought an action on the promissory note against the brother alone, thereby attempting to avoid the set-off that was available to Miss Stephens. Miss Stephens and her brother then brought this proceeding in equity to prevent that occurring. Lord Eldon held that Miss Stephens was entitled to set off the bank's liability to her against her liability on the joint and several note. He ordered that the assignees be restrained from suing either Miss Stephens or her brother on the note, and that the note be delivered up to her.

It has been said that *Ex parte Stephens* turned on the bankers' fraud, in failing to **12.28** carry out Miss Stephens' instructions and concealing their failure from her,[117] and indeed Lord Eldon later commented that, but for the fraud, he doubted much whether the decision would have been right.[118] The case, as Rose LJ noted in the *BCCI (No 8)* case,[119] proceeded on the basis that a joint and several debtor could set off a debt owed to him by the creditor, but that, in the absence of a special circumstance such as fraud, the creditor could avoid the set-off by proceeding against another joint and several debtor. But on the basis of the automatic theory of insolvency set-off, the presence or absence of fraud should not have mattered.[120] There were mutual debts as between Miss Stephens and the bankers which would have given rise to a set-off between them at the date of the bankruptcy, thereby resulting in payment of the joint and several note. In order to attempt to reconcile

---

[115] The argument was noted, but not commented upon, by the House of Lords on appeal. See [1998] AC 214, 225.

[116] (1805) 11 Ves Jun 24, 32 ER 996. See para 12.11 above.

[117] *Ex parte Hanson* (1806) 12 Ves Jun 346, 348–349, 33 ER 131, 132; *Ex parte Blagden* (1815) 19 Ves Jun 465, 467, 34 ER 589, 590; *Jones v Mossop* (1844) 3 Hare 568, 573, 67 ER 506, 509; *Ex parte Staddon, re Wise* (1843) 12 LJ Bcy 39, 40; *Middleton v Pollock, ex p Knight and Raymond* (1875) LR 20 Eq 515, 519–520; *McIntyre v Perkes* (1990) 22 FCR 260, 271; *Lord v Direct Acceptance Corporation Ltd* (1993) 32 NSWLR 362, 369–370; *Re Bank of Credit and Commerce International SA (No 8)* [1996] Ch 245, 267–268. See also *Strong v Foster* (1855) 17 CB 201, 217, 139 ER 1047, 1053.

[118] *Ex parte Blagden* (1815) 19 Ves Jun 465, 467, 34 ER 589, 590.

[119] [1996] Ch 245, 268.

[120] See Hoffmann LJ (as he then was) in *M S Fashions v Bank of Credit and Commerce International* [1993] Ch 425, 438.

Ex parte Stephens with the automatic theory, Rose LJ sought to draw a distinction between, on the one hand, a discharge of the surety as against the creditor which is based upon a set-off as between those parties, and on the other a discharge which arises as a result of payment by the surety to the creditor.[121] He accepted that discharge of the principal debtor, whether by payment by the principal debtor or by way of set-off as between the principal debtor and the creditor, necessarily discharges the surety.[122] Further, discharge of the surety as a result of actual payment by the surety would also discharge the principal debtor. On the other hand, he suggested that the principal debtor is not discharged when the surety is discharged by way of set-off. In *Ex parte Stephens*, Miss Stephens had joined in the promissory note as surety for her brother, and on Rose LJ's analysis a discharge of Miss Stephens as surety by way of a set-off as between her and the bankers was not sufficient to discharge the brother as principal debtor. Only *actual* payment by Miss Stephens would have had that effect. As a consequence of that analysis, Rose LJ postulated that the creditor has a choice of which remedy to pursue. The creditor can rely on the set-off against the surety. Alternatively, Rose LJ suggested that, in the absence of fraud by the creditor, the surety's set-off would not prevent the creditor from suing the principal debtor, since the principal debtor has not been discharged by the set-off. If the creditor sued the principal debtor, Rose LJ said that the recovery from the principal debtor would be treated as notionally taking place at the date of the bankruptcy. It could then be said, with hindsight, that nothing in fact was due from the surety at the date of the bankruptcy. Therefore, there would not have been a set-off as against the surety, so that the surety would be entitled to prove in respect of the debt owing to him.[123]

12.29 The Court of Appeal's comments on this point were obiter, since it was held that the depositors in the *BCCI (No 8)* case had not assumed a personal obligation to the bank to pay the principal debt, and so there was no personal covenant against which the deposits could be set off.[124] But apart from that, there are difficulties

---

[121] See the discussion at [1996] Ch 245, 268–269.

[122] [1996] Ch 245, 268, referring to *Ex parte Hanson* (1806) 12 Ves Jun 346, 33 ER 131 (affirmed (1811) 18 Ves Jun 232, 34 ER 305). In Australia, see also counsel's submission to which Sheller JA referred without adverse comment in *Lord v Direct Acceptance Corporation Ltd* (1993) 32 NSWLR 362, 368–369, and generally *McDonald v Dennys Lascelles Ltd* (1933) 48 CLR 457, 479–480. Compare *Bank of Credit and Commerce International (Overseas) Ltd v Habib Bank Ltd* [1999] 1 WLR 42 (assumption of a debtor's liability by way of novation after the debtor's liquidation), for which see para 6.96 *ff* above.

[123] Rose LJ said: 'The only question is whether the principal debtor is discharged by the set-off simultaneously available to the surety or whether the creditor can recover from the principal debtor and, having recovered, submit to a proof from the surety without any discount on the basis that, with hindsight, it has appeared that nothing was due from the surety at the date of bankruptcy. The mischief against which bankruptcy set-off is directed would indicate that the correct approach is in the latter sense.' [1996] Ch 245, 269.

[124] See para 12.38 below.

with the analysis, and the better view is that discharge of the surety by way of set-off also discharges the principal debtor.

12.30 In the first place, the *M S Fashions* case supports the contrary view. The surety in the *M S Fashions* case had assumed the liability of a principal debtor, and it stands as authority for the proposition that the creditor's trustee in bankruptcy in that circumstance cannot sue the 'true' principal debtor to the extent that the debt has been extinguished by the surety's set-off. Alternatively, the surety may not have contracted as a principal debtor. In that circumstance, the surety's liability usually would be conditional upon a demand being made.[125] Until the creditor has made a demand, the claim against the surety is still subject to a contingency and cannot be included in a set-off in the creditor's insolvency.[126] If on the other hand the creditor makes a demand on the surety, a set-off, according to the automatic theory of insolvency set-off, would be deemed to have occurred at the date of the liquidation. The creditor would have chosen to pursue a remedy against the surety by way of set-off, and the decision in the *M S Fashions* case would apply so as to prevent a further action against the principal debtor to the extent of the set-off.

12.31 Further, the suggested distinction between discharge by set-off and discharge by payment is contrary to the generally accepted view that set-off is equivalent to payment.[127] Dillon LJ assumed the correctness of that proposition in the Court of Appeal in the *M S Fashions* case, wherein he equated a set-off as between a surety and the creditor with a payment by the surety, which he regarded in turn as operating in reduction of the principal debt. Speaking of the effect of a set-off under the insolvency set-off section, he said that:[128]

> The statutory set-off . . . operates to reduce or extinguish the liability of the guarantor and necessarily therefore operates as in effect a payment by him to be set against the liability of the principal debtor. A creditor cannot sue the principal debtor for an amount of the debt which the creditor has already received from a guarantor.

This reflects a similar view expressed by Hoffmann LJ at first instance.[129]

---

[125] *M S Fashions Ltd v Bank of Credit and Commerce International SA* [1993] Ch 425, 436, *per* Hoffmann LJ, 447, CA.

[126] See para 8.27 above.

[127] *Ex parte Barnett, re Deveze* (1874) LR 9 Ch App 293, 297; *Inland Revenue Commissioners v John Dow Stuart Ltd* [1950] AC 149, 164 *per* Lord Porter ('Set-off is payment . . .'); *Re Loteka Pty Ltd* [1990] 1 Qd R 322, 324; *M S Fashions Ltd v Bank of Credit and Commerce International SA* [1993] Ch 425, 439, *per* Hoffmann LJ, 448, CA. The House of Lords in *Re Bank of Credit and Commerce International SA (No 8)* [1998] AC 214, 225 referred in the context of r 4.90 of the Insolvency Rules (the insolvency set-off provision in company liquidation) to 'payment or deemed payment'. See also *Gye v Davies* (1995) 37 NSWLR 421, 431–432 ('moneys deemed paid by them in consequence of the set-off').

[128] [1993] Ch 425, 448.

[129] [1993] Ch 425, 439 ('the set-off is equivalent to payment').

Ex parte Stephens explained

12.32 The point that should be borne in mind when considering cases such as *Ex parte Stephens* is that it is only in recent times that the automatic theory of insolvency set-off has gained acceptance by the courts.[130] It was not current when *Ex parte Stephens* was decided. This is apparent from the form of pleading used in the nineteenth century when a defendant in an action brought against him by assignees in bankruptcy sought to rely on a set-off. The defendant in such a case would not deny that he was indebted on the basis of a set-off that had already occurred at the date of the bankruptcy. Rather, the defence was pleaded by way of an allegation that the bankrupt 'was, *and still is*, indebted to the defendant'.[131] The pleading assumed that the cross-demands still retained their separate identities after the bankruptcy, when the action was brought. Further, when Sir George Jessel MR in 1881[132] sought to explain why the insolvency set-off section could be relied on as a defence to an action at law brought by a trustee in bankruptcy for payment of a debt owing to the bankrupt, as opposed to the set-off being given effect in the Bankruptcy Court, he did not do so, as one would have expected if it was thought to be the case, by reference to a notion that the cross-demands had already been discharged by a set-off that had occurred automatically at the bankruptcy date, so that to that extent that was no debt remaining which could be the subject of a common law action. On the contrary, he said that the bankruptcy legislation contemplated the set-off being allowed in the Bankruptcy Court, and that if a debtor were sued instead in a common law court the debtor could apply to the Court of Bankruptcy for an injunction to restrain the assignees in bankruptcy from suing. He said that the common law courts, having regard to 'the equity of the statute',[133] then went a step further and allowed the debtor to plead the set-off in the common law court itself, without the necessity of applying for an injunction.[134] That explanation is hardly consistent with the set-off being thought of as operating by way of an automatic discharge at the bankruptcy date. If the set-off were thought

---

[130] See also para 6.84 above.

[131] See eg *Hulme v Muggleston* (1837) 3 M & W 30, 31, 150 ER 1043, 1044; *Russell v Bell* (1841) 8 M & W 277, 278, 151 ER 1042, 1043; *Bittleston v Timmis* (1845) 1 CB 389, 391, 135 ER 591, 592. See also *West v Baker* (1875) 1 Ex D 44, 45. In *Gibson v Bell* (1835) 1 Bing NC 743, 131 ER 1303 the defendant pleaded (at 746, 1305) that 'the said sum of money still remained unpaid and unsatisfied to the Defendant'. In Bullen & Leake, *Precedents of Pleading* (2nd edn, 1863) 580, the plea was expressed in terms that a debt owing by the bankrupt 'at the commencement of this suit was and still is due to the defendant'. Later editions set out the pleading in similar terms. See para 6.84 n above.

[132] *Peat v Jones & Co* (1881) 8 QBD 147, 149.

[133] For a discussion of the concept of the equity of a statute, see *Nelson v Nelson* (1995) 184 CLR 538, 552–554.

[134] See also Sir George Jessel's later discussion in *Mersey Steel and Iron Co v Naylor, Benzon & Co* (1882) 9 QBD 648, 664.

of as operating automatically at that date, it would not have been necessary to have recourse to a concept such as the equity of the statute.

Consistent with that view, Lord Eldon's judgment in *Ex parte Stephens* itself sug- **12.33** gests that he did not regard a set-off as having already occurred between Miss Stephens and the bankers under the bankruptcy legislation. In the course of his judgment he referred to 'the balance, for which she would have been creditor, *if* the assignees had sued her, or arranged the account upon the principle of mutual debt and credit'.[135] This suggests that, until an account was taken, either by the court in an action by the assignees against Miss Stephens, or as a result of the as-signees themselves arranging the account on the basis of mutual credit, the cross-demands between her and the bankers were regarded as retaining their separate identities.

Once it is appreciated that, when *Ex parte Stephens* was decided, it was not the pre- **12.34** vailing view that set-off under the bankruptcy legislation occurred automatically at the date of the bankruptcy, the importance of the element of fraud in the case becomes apparent. The promissory note was joint and several. The bankers' as-signees in bankruptcy accordingly could have sued either Miss Stephens or her brother or both. They chose to sue the brother alone. When the action was com-menced the note had not been discharged, either by payment or by way of set-off. Miss Stephens had a *right* of set-off, which would have provided her with a de-fence, but she was not being sued. A set-off had not taken place pursuant to that right, so that it had not operated to discharge either Miss Stephens or her brother. Further, the brother was not possessed of a cross-claim against the bankers, so that he did not have a defence to the action. Hence the importance of fraud. It pro-vided the justification for equity to intervene in the assignees' action against the principal debtor, by restraining the action and ensuring that Miss Stephens ob-tained the benefit of her set-off.

Ex parte Stephens therefore is explicable on the basis that a set-off was not regarded **12.35** as having taken place in the bankruptcy at the time when Miss Stephens presented her petition in equity, and the effect of Lord Eldon's order was allow a set-off in eq-uity in her favour by way of a common injunction restraining an action on the promissory note.[136] It will be recalled that an injunction restraining common law

---

[135] (1805) 11 Ves Jun 24, 27, 32 ER 996, 997 (emphasis added).

[136] In *Re BCCI (No 8)* [1996] Ch 245, 269 Rose LJ offered a different interpretation of the order in *Ex parte Stephens*. He said that Lord Eldon's order was not that Miss Stephens was discharged by set-off (which, he said, was never in dispute), but rather that 'the assignees [in bankruptcy] held £1,000 of her money on trust to discharge the note'. On that basis, the discharge of the principal debtor in *Ex parte Stephens* could be regarded as occurring by way of a payment, rather than by way of a set-off available to Miss Stephens as surety. Two comments may be made in relation to this. The first is the point already made, that it is not correct to say that it was 'never in dispute' that Miss Stephens herself was 'discharged by set-off'. She had a right of set-off, but it was not thought that she had been discharged by it. Secondly, it is true that Lord Eldon commented in his judgment (at

proceedings was the method by which courts of equity gave effect to equitable set-offs before the Judicature Acts.[137] Thus, Sir William Grant in *Addis v Knight*[138] referred to *Ex parte Stephens* as having established that, 'under certain circumstances, there may be a set-off in Equity when there can be none at Law'.

12.36 In the Court of Appeal's judgment in the *BCCI (No 8)* case,[139] Miss Stephen is variously described as having had a 'right of set-off' and as having been 'discharged' by set-off. These expressions appear to have been used inter-changeably. In truth, while Miss Stephens had a 'right of' set-off, Lord Eldon did not regard her as having been 'discharged' by set-off. Because *Ex parte Stephens* proceeded on the assumption that a creditor on a joint and several debt normally could avoid a set-off available to one debtor by proceeding against another debtor, the Court of Appeal in the *BCCI (No 8)* case opined that this could only be on the basis that, in a three-party situation, discharge by set-off is not to be equated with discharge by payment.[140] That in turn formed the basis of the proposition that a creditor, faced with an automatic set-off available to a surety, could still sue the principal debtor. In fact, *Ex parte Stephens* provides no support for that proposition. It does not stand as authority for the view that a discharge by way of set-off as between a creditor and a surety does not discharge the debtor, because on the view of the operation of the insolvency set-off section then current, the surety had not been discharged by way of set-off. It was Lord Eldon's order which was regarded as bringing about a set-off, in the manner in which that was done by courts of equity at the time, by way of an injunction restraining common law proceedings and an order for delivery up of the promissory note.

Set-off between the creditor and the principal debtor as a discharge of the surety

12.37 The Court of Appeal in the *BCCI (No 8)* case nevertheless accepted that a set-off of debts between the creditor and the principal debtor under the insolvency set-off section would discharge the surety.[141] It should be compared in that regard to

---

(1805) 11 Ves Jun 24, 28, 32 ER 996, 998) that Miss Stephens, 'has a clear right to say, they shall hold £1000 of her money in discharge of the note; and shall deliver up the note'. But, as Sir George Jessel MR's discussion of *Ex parte Stephens* in *Middleton v Pollock, ex p Knight and Raymond* (1875) LR 20 Eq 515, 520–521 makes plain, that referred simply to a right of set-off, which indeed is reflected in the order that was made. The order, as summarized in the final paragraph of the report of *Stephens* (at 28), was not that £1,000 be held on trust to discharge the debt, but rather that Miss Stephens 'be at liberty to set off the amount of the promissory note against the demand she has upon the bankrupts', with consequential orders that the promissory note be delivered up to her and the assignees be restrained from suing either her or her brother. See also the discussion of the *Stephens* case in *Lord v Direct Acceptance Corporation Ltd* (1993) 32 NSWLR 362, 369–370.

   [137] See para 3.01 above.
   [138] (1817) 2 Mer 117, 121, 35 ER 885, 887.
   [139] [1996] Ch 245, 266–269.
   [140] [1996] Ch 245, 268.
   [141] [1996] Ch 245, 268. See para 12.28 above.

Bank of Credit and Commerce International (Overseas) Ltd v Habib Bank Ltd.[142] In that case a third party assumed liability for the debts of a debtor after the debtor's liquidation, apparently by way of a novation, and Park J accepted that payments made by the third party to a creditor precluded a set-off as between the debtor and the creditor at the date of the liquidation. That aspect of the case was considered, and criticized, earlier.[143]

D. Separate Depositor Does not Assume a Personal Obligation

In the *M S Fashions* case,[144] the person who provided the bank with a deposit as se- **12.38**
curity for the company's liability on the loan had also assumed a personal liability for the loan. The assumption of a personal liability was crucial to the decision to recognize a set-off as between the depositor and the bank in the bank's liquidation, because it provided the means of bringing about mutuality. Where, however, a depositor has not assumed a personal liability, but merely provided the deposit by way of collateral security for a loan to a company, there is no mutuality between, on the one hand, the bank's indebtedness to the depositor in relation to the deposit, and on the other the bank's claim against the company.[145] In that circumstance, the House of Lords in *Re Bank of Credit and Commerce International SA (No 8)*[146] confirmed that the deposit and the loan will not be the subject of a set-off under the insolvency set-off section in the event of the bank's liquidation.[147] The liquidator can proceed against the company for repayment of the loan, and confine the depositor to a proof in the liquidation in respect of the deposit.[148]

The *BCCI (No 8)* case should also be contrasted with *Clarkson v Smith and* **12.39**
Goldberg,[149] a decision of the Appellate Division of the Ontario Supreme Court. In that case a bank provided an overdraft to a partnership, taking as security a

---

[142] [1999] 1 WLR 42.

[143] See paras 6.96–6.98 above.

[144] [1993] Ch 425. See para 12.23 above.

[145] The charge on the deposit in favour of the bank is an additional reason for finding a lack of mutuality. See paras 16.68–16.70 below. In *Re Bank of Credit and Commerce International SA (No 8)* [1998] AC 214, 225 the House of Lords left open the question whether the existence of the charge has that effect.

[146] [1998] AC 214.

[147] See also *Lord v Direct Acceptance Corporation Ltd* (1993) 32 NSWLR 362; *Tam Wing Chuen v Bank of Credit and Commerce Hong Kong Ltd* [1996] 2 BCLC 69 (PC). Nor is this a ground for an equitable set-off. See paras 4.51–4.54 above.

[148] If the customer had also provided a separate security to the bank in the form of a mortgage, the doctrine of marshalling would not apply so as to compel the bank to have recourse first to the deposit. See *Re Bank of Credit and Commerce International SA (No 8)* [1996] Ch 245, 271–272, CA, [1998] AC 214, 230–231, HL.

[149] [1926] 1 DLR 509.

charge over a separate deposit by one of the partners. The bank went into liquidation, and the liquidator sought to recover the debt from the partnership without allowing a set-off in respect of the deposit charged as security. The Appellate Division rejected the liquidator's approach and allowed an equitable set-off. In addition to his liability as a partner the depositor had assumed a separate personal liability,[150] but that was not the basis of the set-off. It was based upon the partnership debt.[151] The partners were jointly liable, and a judgment against the partnership could be levied against the firm's assets or the separate assets of the partners. Since the partner who provided the security could be required to pay the whole debt out of his personal assets, or to contribute to payment through his interest in the firm assets, it was regarded as manifestly unjust that he should be refused the use of his deposit to pay the debt. In the *BCCI (No 8)* case, on the other hand, the depositor had no liability, other than as security provider, to contribute to the payment of the principal debt, so that the reasoning is not applicable to that case.

12.40 The denial of a set-off in the *BCCI (No 8)* case, when compared to the allowance of a set-off in the *M S Fashions* case, has been described as anomalous and paradoxical, because it means that a bank's position is better in its own liquidation when it had not obtained a personal guarantee from the depositor than when it had.[152] In truth, there is no paradox. When a surety provides a security deposit to a bank, the bank may also require a personal covenant from the depositor in order to give it an additional avenue for obtaining repayment of the debt in the event that the borrower defaults. But if there is a set-off the bank obtains repayment in full. The purpose of taking the security therefore is achieved. It would be commercially unrealistic to suggest that a lender in structuring security arrangements is concerned additionally with the position that may apply in its own liquidation. In any event, there should not have been a set-off under the insolvency set-off section in the *M S Fashions* case, because the charge over the deposit in favour of the bank should have prevented mutuality arising in relation to the depositor's personal liability to the bank and the deposit. This aspect of the *M S Fashions* case is considered later.[153]

Obligation to set off

12.41 The Court of Appeal in the *BCCI (No 8)* case[154] noted that the terms of the deposit in that case merely authorized the bank to set off the deposit against the loan to

---

[150] The partner drew a cheque on his account and gave it to the bank as security.

[151] The point was made in the judgment that a right of set-off ordinarily does not exist between a debt due by a firm and an amount due to a separate partner, but even apart from that principle the charge over the separate partner's deposit would have destroyed mutuality. See para 16.68–16.70 below.

[152] See *Re Bank of Credit and Commerce International SA (No 8)* [1996] Ch 245, 253, 273, CA, [1998] AC 214, 224–225, HL; *Tam Wing Chuen v Bank of Credit and Commerce Hong Kong Ltd* [1996] 2 BCLC 69, 71–72; Richard Millett, 'Pleasing Paradoxes' (1996) 112 LQR 524.

[153] See paras 16.68–16.70 below.

[154] [1996] Ch 245, 273.

the company. The bank was not obliged to do so. But what if the terms had been such as to require a set-off, and a set-off had not occurred at the date of the bank's liquidation? That was the situation in *Bank of Credit and Commerce Hong Kong Ltd (in liq) v Mahadumrongkul*,[155] a decision of the Privy Council on appeal from the Court of Appeal of Hong Kong. As in the *BCCI (No 8)* case, a shareholder had placed a deposit with a bank to secure a loan to the company, apparently without having assumed a personal liability as a guarantor. In a letter to the depositor, the bank said that, upon default by the borrower, 'we shall . . . automatically apply any monies standing to the credit of the [Deposit] Account' in settlement of the principal, interest and margin owing in respect of the loan. Subsequently the bank went into liquidation, and after that the borrower defaulted. The point in issue was the date upon which the deposit was required to be applied in reduction of the loan pursuant to the agreement. The question whether a set-off in fact occurred on that date was not specifically addressed, but it seems to have been assumed that a set-off would then have occurred.[156] At least in England,[157] however, an agreement in those terms would not result in a set-off after the liquidation if a set-off was not available in any event under the insolvency set-off section,[158] and in this case there was a lack of mutuality as between the bank's indebtedness to the depositor and its claim against the borrower. As the Court of Appeal remarked in the *BCCI (No 8)* case[159] in relation to the deposit in that case:

> The appellants were indebted to the bank. Their controlling shareholders deposited moneys with the bank. If the case had stopped there, there could have been no question of set-off in the bank's insolvency. The bank could not have set off the debts which it owed to the depositors against the debts which their companies owed to the bank. The requirement of mutuality would have been absent. *Even if all parties agreed that the bank should set off the amounts in question*, it could not have done so after the bankruptcy. In the absence of the necessary mutuality, the set-off would have contravened the statutory scheme of distribution in insolvency. Once insolvency supervenes, rule 4.90 of the Insolvency Rules 1986 requires set-off in the situations in which it is applicable and public policy forbids it where it is not.

---

[155] [1997] UKPC 20 (Lord Goff of Chieveley, Lord Slynn of Hadley, Lord Lloyd of Berwick, Lord Nicholls of Birkenhead and Lord Hoffmann).

[156] The borrower was ordered to be wound up on 2 March 1992. The depositor and the borrower (a company of which the depositor was a director) asserted that the agreement required that a set-off be effected against outstanding principal 20 days after 28 June 1991, whereas the liquidator said that the relevant date under the agreement was 16 July 1992. The significance of the date of the set-off was that the continued accrual of interest on the loan until the later date, together with the cessation of the bank's liability to pay interest on the deposit as from the commencement of the winding up, would have meant that the money owing to the bank exceeded the amount owing on the deposit. The Privy Council held that the later date was correct, referring to it as 'the effective date for the set-off', which suggests that a set-off was regarded as having occurred on that date in accordance with the agreement.

[157] And also in Australia.

[158] *British Eagle International Air Lines Ltd v Compagnie Nationale Air France* [1975] 1 WLR 758. See paras 16.18–16.20 below.

[159] [1996] Ch 245, 272 (emphasis added).

This should apply whether the agreement is couched in terms that a set-off is to occur automatically in the event of a default, or whether an act by the bank is required in order to effect the set-off.

E. Deceased Insolvent Partner

12.42   The Partnership Act 1890, section 9 provides that the estate of a deceased partner is severally as well as jointly liable for the debts of the firm, although this is expressed to be subject to the prior payment of his separate debts. In keeping with that priority, a debtor to a deceased partner cannot set off a debt owing to the debtor by the partnership,[160] at least if the deceased's estate has insufficient assets to pay the deceased's separate debts.[161] If it were otherwise, an asset of the deceased partner would be used to pay the firm's debts before his separate debts had been paid.

12.43   Where two or more partners jointly own the beneficial interest in a claim, and all except one die, the common law courts applied the principle that the claim passed to the survivor, so that there was mutuality for the purpose of a set-off between the original joint claim and a separate debt owing by the survivor.[162] In equity, however, the claim must be brought into account in determining the entitlement of the deceased partners' estates in relation to the partnership.[163] The better view is that this entitlement of the deceaseds' estates destroys mutuality in equity for the purpose of a set-off.[164]

---

[160] *Addis v Knight* (1817) 2 Mer 117, 35 ER 885.

[161] *Lindley and Banks on Partnership* (18th edn, 2002) 451 para 14–79.

[162] *Slipper v Stidstone* (1794) 5 TR 493, 101 ER 277, and see also *French v Andrade* (1796) 6 TR 582, 101 ER 715.

[163] See eg *McClean v Kennard* (1874) LR 9 Ch App 336, and generally *Lindley on the Law of Partnership* (15th edn, 1984) 521 (where the explanation of the historical position is more clearly set out than in *Lindley and Banks on Partnership* (18th edn, 2002) 515 para 18–66). See also the Insolvency Act 1986, s 421A).

[164] See *Lindley and Banks on Partnership* (18th edn, 2002) 451 para 14–79. Compare Wood, *English and International Set-off* (1989) 1034–5. *Aliter* if the debt owing is a partnership debt as opposed to a separate debt of the survivor. See *Lindley and Banks, loc cit.*

13

MUTUALITY—SAME RIGHT

A. Introduction

In the case of insolvency set-off, the requirement that the demands be held in the **13.01** same right means that each of the parties, who is liable to the other, should be the beneficial owner of a cross-demand against the other.[1] It should be compared to the Statutes of Set-off, which contemplate mutuality by reference to the legal title to the debts. Equity on the other hand may allow a set-off by analogy with the Statutes if there is mutuality in equity but not at law, or alternatively it may refuse

---

[1] See para 11.01 above.

to allow a set-off if there is mutuality at law but not in equity, so that the same result usually would follow in the case of the Statutes as if mutuality were determined by reference to equitable interests.[2]

Different personal capacities

13.02   As long as the demands in that sense are mutual, the dealings are not considered to be in a different right merely because each may relate to a different personal status or capacity possessed by one of the parties.[3] For example, in an action brought by a trustee against a beneficiary of the trust for an indemnity as to costs and expenses incurred in connection with the trust, the Queensland Supreme Court held that the beneficiary could set off an indebtedness of the trustee in his personal capacity.[4] On another occasion an executor was the sole person interested in the estate of the testator, and all claims against the estate had been satisfied. When the executor brought an action to recover a debt owing to the estate, the debtor was allowed to set off a personal indebtedness of the executor to him in a matter unrelated to the estate.[5] While neither of these cases concerned a bankruptcy or a company liquidation, they should apply equally to insolvency set-off. A further illustration is to be found in the cases which support the proposition that a local authority which has vested in it a number of statutory functions may set off a credit balance arising on a bank account which relates to one function against its indebtedness on an account relating to another. In *Pedder v The Mayor, Aldermen, and Burgesses of Preston*,[6] the Corporation of Preston had an account with a bank for the corporation's general municipal functions. In addition the Corporation had been constituted the Local Board of Health under the Public Health Act 1848, and for this a separate account was opened with the same bank. The bank entered into an arrangement with its creditors under the Bankrupt Law Consolidation Act 1849, at which time the general account was overdrawn and the Local Board of Health account was in credit. Though section 87 of the 1848 Act provided that the money received by the Local Board of Health 'shall be applied . . . in defraying such of the Expenses incurred or to be incurred by the said Local Board in carrying this Act into execution', it was held that the Corporation could set the credit balance on that account against its indebtedness on the other.

---

[2] See paras 11.08–11.10 above.
[3] See *Gye v McIntyre* (1991) 171 CLR 609, 625–626.
[4] *Peel v Fitzgerald* [1982] Qd R 544.
[5] *Williams v MacDonald* [1915] VLR 229. See also, and compare, *Knowles v Maitland* (1825) 4 B & C 173, 107 ER 1024, in which the cross-demands both related to the capacity of colonel of the regiment.
[6] (1862) 12 CB (NS) 535, 142 ER 1251. See also *Ex parte Pearce, re Langmead* (1841) 2 Mont D & De G 142.

Trustees in bankruptcy

A right accruing to, or a liability incurred by, a trustee in bankruptcy in his own **13.03** right may not be the subject of a set-off in the bankruptcy.[7] Nor can the trustee set off the dividend payable to a creditor against the creditor's indebtedness to the trustee in his private capacity.[8]

A liability incurred by the trustee in his own right is a liability which gives rise to **13.04** a direct claim against the trustee personally, as opposed to a provable debt. A right accruing to the trustee in his own right includes a right founded upon the trustee's title as trustee of the estate, as opposed to the title of the bankrupt. An example of the latter is a right arising in favour of the estate after the bankruptcy which is not derived from an obligation incurred by or a transaction entered into with the debtor before the bankruptcy. Thus, there may be an award of costs made in favour of the trustee in an action brought to recover a debt owing to the bankrupt's estate. The defendant's obligation to pay the costs only arises after the bankruptcy as a result of his failure to pay the debt to the trustee upon demand, and so it may not be brought in as a set-off against a liability of the bankrupt.[9] Another illustration is *Ex parte Young, re Day & Sons*.[10] The trustee in bankruptcy of a firm opened an account with a bank, and paid into it a sum of money received on behalf of the estate. Subsequently the bank filed a liquidation petition. It was held that the firm's trustee could not set off the bank's debt to him for the money deposited against an independent indebtedness of the bankrupt firm to the bank for which a proof had been lodged.[11] On the other hand, while the decision was correct in relation to set-off, it is suggested that the trustee should have been able to invoke an independent principle known as the rule in *Cherry v Boultbee*,[12] and on that basis refuse to pay a dividend to the bank until the bank had accounted for the money received.[13] *Cherry v Boultbee* is considered later.[14]

---

[7] *Re A Debtor, ex p The Peak Hill Goldfield Ltd* [1909] 1 KB 430, 437.

[8] *Ex parte White* (1742) 1 Atk 90, 26 ER 59; *Ex parte Bailey, re Howarth* (1840) 1 Mont D & De G 263; *Ex parte Saunders, re Innes* (1842) 2 Mont D & De G 529, 530–531. The reason for this is that the demands are due in different rights. See *Ex parte Alexander, re Elder* (1832) 1 Deac & Ch 513, 524, *per* Erskine CJ. A second reason is that the creditor is a *cestui que trust* of the trustee, and so is entitled to receive the dividend undiminished by a set-off. See *Re Henley, Thurgood & Co* (1863) 11 WR 102l, 1022, and ch 10 above.

[9] *West v Pryce* (1825) 2 Bing 455, 130 ER 382.

[10] (1879) 41 LT 40.

[11] Similarly, it has been held that a sum of money received by a creditor of a bankrupt on behalf of the estate may not be brought into an account. See *Groom v Mealey* (1835) 2 Bing (NC) 138, 132 ER 54; *Elgood v Harris* [1896] 2 QB 491. Compare *Bailey v Johnson* (1872) LR 7 Ex 263, in which the bankruptcy under which the trustee paid the money into the bank was annulled after the bank's bankruptcy. See para 11.05 above.

[12] (1839) 4 My & Cr 442, 41 ER 171.

[13] As in *Ex parte Bebb* (1812) 19 Ves Jun 222, 34 ER 501 and *Ex parte Graham* (1814) 3 V & B 130, 35 ER 428. See para 14.33 below.

[14] See ch 14 below.

The effect of company liquidation

13.05 In so far as companies are concerned, a liquidation does not affect the corporate personality of the company.[15] Nor generally does it result in a *cessio bonorum* in favour of the liquidator. In contrast to bankruptcy,[16] the legal title to the company's assets remains with the company.[17] A liquidator 'is principally and really an agent for the company but occupies a position which is fiduciary in some respects and is bound by the statutory duties imposed upon him by the [Insolvency] Act'.[18] However the making of a winding-up order in a compulsory liquidation, or the passing of a resolution for a voluntary liqudation, should have the same effect upon mutuality as far as the company's claims accruing after the winding up are concerned as the appointment of a trustee has in a bankruptcy. In *Ayerst v C & K (Construction) Ltd*[19] the House of Lords confirmed that, while a winding-up order in a compulsory liquidation does not divest the company of the legal title to its assets, it does deprive it of the beneficial title.[20] This is a consequence of the vesting of the custody and control of the company's property in the liquidator to be applied by him in discharge of the company's liabilities and, in the case of a surplus, to be distributed amongst the members. Admittedly, uncertainty as to the property divisible amongst the creditors, as well as uncertainty as to the creditors entitled to share in the realization of the property, means that a creditor who is entitled to share in the proceeds is not invested with the beneficial title to any part of the company's property while it is still being administered by the liquidator.[21] Nevertheless, the House of Lords concluded that it could still be said that the company itself is not possessed of the beneficial title. If a company does not have

---

[15] See the Insolvency Act 1986, s 87(2) in relation to a voluntary winding up. This is also the case in a compulsory liquidation. See *Reigate v Union Manufacturing Co (Ramsbottom) Ltd* [1918] 1 KB 592, 606.

[16] A trustee in bankruptcy upon his appointment has vested in him the property belonging to the bankrupt at the commencement of the bankruptcy. See the Insolvency Act 1986, ss 283(1) and 306. This includes things in action. See s 436.

[17] *Re A Debtor* [1927] 1 Ch 410, 420; *John Mackintosh and Sons Ltd v Baker's Bargain Stores (Seaford) Ltd* [1965] 1 WLR 1182; *Re Northside Properties Pty Ltd* [1971] 2 NSWLR 320, 326; *National Westminster Bank Ltd v Halesowen Presswork and Assemblies Ltd* [1972] AC 785, 796. When a company is being wound up by the court, there is provision for the liquidator to apply to the court for an order vesting the company's property in him. See the Insolvency Act 1986, s 145. The effect of such an order is to vest the company's property in the liquidator in his official, as opposed to his personal, capacity. See *Graham v Edge* (1888) 20 QBD 683. It appears that the section is rarely invoked. See *Buckley on the Companies Act* (14th edn, 1981) vol 1, 597–8.

[18] *Thomas Franklin & Sons Ltd v Cameron* (1935) 36 SR (NSW) 286, 296, *per* Davidson J, referred to with approval in *Re Timberland Ltd* (1979) 4 ACLR 259, 285, *per* Marks J. See also *Re Windsor Steam Coal Co (1901) Ltd* [1928] 1 Ch 609. A liquidator is entitled to examine a proof lodged in the winding up in the light of any possible right of set-off. See *Re National Wholemeal Bread and Biscuit Co* [1892] 2 Ch 457.

[19] [1976] AC 167. See also *Mitchell v Carter* [1997] 1 BCLC 673, 686, *per* Millett LJ.

[20] This also applies to a voluntary winding up. See [1976] AC 167, 176.

[21] [1976] AC 167, 178–179.

the beneficial title to its assets after the commencement of its liquidation, for the purpose of mutuality in equity the effect, as far as claims accruing subsequently to the company are concerned, accordingly should be the same as in the case of the appointment of a trustee in bankruptcy. That proposition brings into question *Monkwearmouth Flour Mill Co v Lightfoot*.[22] The defendant was appointed after the commencement of the plaintiff company's liquidation to collect outstanding debts due to the company. When he was sued for the money he had received he was allowed to set off the company's prior indebtedness to him. At no stage however could it be said that the company itself was the beneficial owner of any right against him. Nor was his liability the result of a dealing entered into with the company before the commencement of its liquidation.[23] A set-off therefore should have been denied on the ground of lack of mutuality.[24]

There is Australian authority which is inconsistent with the *Ayerst* case. Some five   **13.06** years prior to that case, Menzies J in *Franklin's Selfserve Pty Ltd v Federal Commissioner of Taxation*[25] held that the fact that a company was being wound up did not mean that it could no longer be regarded as the beneficial holder of shares in a subsidiary company for the purpose of the income tax legislation. But even if that view were to prevail and be applied generally,[26] the *Monkwearmouth* case would still be difficult to explain, since the company's claim accrued after the relevant date for determining rights of set-off,[27] without it being related to a prior transaction.

B. Transactions Impugned by a Trustee or Liquidator

(1) Preferences

Bankruptcy

If, within the period of six months[28] prior to the presentation of a petition against   **13.07** a debtor, the debtor did anything or suffered anything to be done which had the effect of putting a particular creditor into a better position in the debtor's bankruptcy than the creditor would otherwise have been, the court on the application

---

[22] (1897) 13 TLR 327.
[23] See paras 7.07–7.09 above.
[24] See in this regard *Sankey Brook Coal Co Ltd v Marsh* (1871) LR 6 Ex 185.
[25] (1970) 125 CLR 52. See also *Mineral & Chemical Traders Pty Ltd v Tymczyszyn Pty Ltd* (1994) 15 ACSR 398, 417.
[26] In *FCT v St Hubert's Island Pty Ltd* (1978) 138 CLR 210, 233, 249–250 the High Court of Australia declined to resolve the conflict between the *Ayerst* and *Franklin's Selfserve* cases, although in *CPH Property Pty Ltd v Commissioner of Taxation* (1998) 88 FCR 21, 50–51 Hill J said that as 'presently advised' he would prefer the latter. See also Meagher, Gummow and Lehane, *Equity: Doctrines and Remedies* (3rd edn, 1992) 109–10.
[27] See paras 6.46–6.48 above.
[28] Or two years for a person associated with the bankrupt. See the Insolvency Act 1986, s 341(1).

of the trustee may make such order as it thinks fit for restoring the position to what it would have been if the debtor had not given the preference.[29] A creditor who is liable to return a preferential payment is not entitled to set off against that liability the debt for which the payment was intended to be satisfaction,[30] or indeed any other liability of the bankrupt to him.[31] The trustee's right to the return of the preference accrues in his own right as trustee, and is not derived from an obligation incurred by the creditor to the bankrupt. The creditor's liability and the creditor's claim against the bankrupt accordingly are not mutual.[32] In any event, public policy would dictate that a transaction which Parliament has said should be avoided as a preference should not be able to ground a set-off, because otherwise the efficacy of the preference provision would be severely limited.[33] In Australia, the courts have also had regard to the qualification to the set-off section[34] as a reason for denying a set-off.[35] The creditor's notice of the debtor's insolvency, which under the Australian Bankruptcy Act would operate to deny to the creditor the defence of purchaser, payee or encumbrancer in good faith in a preference action,[36] usually would also preclude a set-off.

---

[29]   See the Insolvency Act 1986, s 340. In Australia see the Bankruptcy Act 1966 (Cth), s 122.

[30]   *Courtney v King* (1870) 1 VR (L) 70; *Re A Debtor* [1927] 1 Ch 410; *Re Grezzana, Painter v Charles Whiting and Chambers Ltd* (1932) 4 ABC 203: *Re Smith, ex p The Trustee; J Bird Pty Ltd and Tully (Respondents)* (1933) 6 ABC 49. See also *Calzaturificio Zenith Pty Ltd v NSW Leather and Trading Co Pty Ltd* [1970] VR 605. Compare *Morris v Flower* (1863) 2 SCR (NSW) 196.

[31]   *Wood v Smith* (1838) 4 M & W 522, 527, 150 ER 1536; *Hamilton v Commonwealth Bank of Australia* (1992) 9 ACSR 90, 107; *Re Armour* (1956) 18 ABC 69, 74–76. See also *Re K B Docker* (1938) 10 ABC 198, 238–239 (in relation to the alternative ground). A similar principle applied when a voluntary settlement was avoided by a trustee in bankruptcy, in circumstances where money the subject of the settlement was not paid in satisfaction of a debt owing by the bankrupt. The recipient was required to return the settlement without a set-off in respect of a debt owing to him or her. See *Lister v Hooson* [1908] 1 KB 174; *Re Hermann, ex p The Official Assignee* (1916) 16 SR (NSW) 264.

[32]   See *Courtney v King* (1870) 1 VR (L) 70, 73; *Lister v Hooson* [1908] 1 KB 174 (voluntary settlement); *Re Armour* (1956) 18 ABC 69, 75–76. A similar analysis formerly applied under the doctrine of relation back, when the trustee's title related back to encompass a sum of money paid by the bankrupt to a creditor before the sequestration order. See *Re Pollitt* [1893] 1 QB 455, and also *Tamplin v Diggins* (1809) 2 Camp 312, 170 ER 1167; *Thomason v Frere* (1809) 10 East 418, 103 ER 834; *Kinder v Butterworth* (1826) 6 B & C 42, 108 ER 369. Mutuality was lacking only when the obligation of the creditor to account for a sum of money was based *solely* upon relation back, as opposed to an indebtedness that the creditor had incurred to the bankrupt himself. Compare *Elliott v Turquand* (1881) 7 App Cas 79; *Re Jackson, ex p The Official Assignee* (1888) 6 NZLR 417. The doctrine of relation back no longer applies in England under the Insolvency Act 1986.

[33]   See *Re Grezzana* (1932) 4 ABC 203, 206. This is particularly so when the argument for a set-off is based upon the original debt for which the preferential payment was intended to be satisfaction. See *Courtney v King* (1870) 1 VR (L) 70, 73; *Re A Debtor* [1927] 1 Ch 410, 415–416, 419–420; *Re Grezzana* (above).

[34]   See paras 6.49–6.64 above.

[35]   *Re Hardman* (1932) 4 ABC 207; *Re Smith* (1933) 6 ABC 49; *Re Pitts and Lehman Ltd* (1940) 40 SR (NSW) 614; *Re K B Docker* (1938) 10 ABC 198, 238–239. See also *Russell Wilkins & Sons Ltd v The Outridge Printing Co Ltd* [1906] St R Qd 172.

[36]   Bankruptcy Act 1966 (Cth), s 122(4)(c).

Company liquidation

The same principle applies in the liquidation of an insolvent company,[37] so that a **13.08** creditor of the company is not entitled to a set-off against an obligation to repay a preference.[38] It has been said that it is more likely that the denial of a set-off in the case of a company liquidation is attributable to considerations of policy rather than of strict logic,[39] but the fact that the creditor's obligation only arises after the liquidation, and therefore after the relevant date for determining rights of set-off, should be a sufficient justification for denying a set-off.[40] There is also a lack of mutuality. While the proceeds of a preference action form part of the fund of assets that is available for payment of the claims of unsecured creditors,[41] in England neither the right to recover a preference nor the proceeds of the action is regarded as the property of the company.[42] Rather, it is a statutory right given to the liquidator for the purpose of the winding up[43] and for the benefit of the general body of creditors.[44] Thus, a right to recover a preferential payment is not caught by a debenture granted by the company over its present and future assets.[45] Since the right is not the property of the company, there is not mutuality in equity as between it and a debt owing by the company to the creditor.[46]

---

[37] See the Insolvency Act 1986, ss 239 & 240. In Australia see the Corporations Act 2001 (Cth), s 588FA.

[38] *Re A Debtor* [1927] 1 Ch 410; *Calzaturificio Zenith Pty Ltd v NSW Leather and Trading Co Pty Ltd* [1970] VR 605; *Re Exchange Travel (Holdings) Ltd* [1997] 2 BCLC 579, 594. The absence of a *cessio bonorum* in a company liquidation makes no difference. See *Re A Debtor* at 420, *per* Clauson J.

[39] McPherson, *The Law of Company Liquidation* (4th edn, 1999) 565.

[40] See *Re A Debtor* [1927] 1 Ch 410, *per* Astbury J.

[41] *Re Starkey* [1994] 1 Qd R 142, 154.

[42] *Re M C Bacon Ltd* [1991] Ch 127, 136–137; *Re Oasis Merchandising Services Ltd* [1998] Ch 170, 181–183 (and the cases there referred to); *Lewis v Commissioner of Inland Revenue* [2001] 3 All ER 499 (see in particular at paras 36–37); Gough, *Company Charges* (2nd edn, 1996) 122. Compare para 13.15 below in relation to Australia.

[43] *Re Fresjac Pty Ltd* (1995) 65 SASR 334, 347.

[44] *Willmott v London Celluloid Co* (1886) 34 Ch D 147, 150; *Re Yagerphone Ltd* [1935] 1 Ch 392, 396; *Re M C Bacon Ltd* [1991] Ch 127, 137; *Sheahan v Carrier Air Conditioning Pty Ltd* (1997) 189 CLR 407, 428. Similarly, in the context of a voluntary settlement in bankruptcy, Fletcher Moulton LJ in *Lister v Hooson* [1908] 1 KB 174, 179 explained the denial of a set-off against the obligation to account to the trustee on the ground that the proceeds are 'considered to be due to the estate for the purposes of the bankruptcy, ie, for paying the creditors of the estate'.

[45] *Re Yagerphone Ltd* [1935] 1 Ch 392; *N A Kratzmann Pty Ltd v Tucker (No 2)* (1968) 123 CLR 295, 299–301; *N W Robbie & Co Ltd v Witney Warehouse Co Ltd* [1963] 1 WLR 1324, 1338; *Re Fresjac Pty Ltd* (1995) 65 SASR 334, 346–347; *Re Oasis Merchandising Services Ltd* [1998] Ch 170, 181–182; *Sheahan v Carrier Air Conditioning Pty Ltd* (1997) 189 CLR 407, 428; *Hamilton v National Australia Bank Ltd* (1996) 66 FCR 12, 37; *Re Exchange Travel (Holdings) Ltd* [1997] 2 BCLC 579, 596.

[46] See para 11.04 above. Similarly an equitable set-off ordinarily should not be available. See *Re Buchanan Enterprises Pty Ltd* (1982) 7 ACLR 407.

Administration order in relation to a company

13.09 The preference section also applies when an administration order is made in relation to a company,[47] in which case the same principle should apply. A set-off[48] should not be available against a claim by the administrator to recover a preference, either because of lack of mutuality or as a matter of implication from the insolvency legislation.

No preference if a set-off would have been available

13.10 If A and B are indebted to each other, and A makes a payment to B in satisfaction of his indebtedness in circumstances where B similarly discharges his indebtedness to A, or if A and B merely agree that the cross-demands should be set one against the other and cancelled,[49] then A's payment, or the agreement for a set-off, will not be construed as a preference in his subsequent bankruptcy if the cross-demands were such that in any event they would have given rise to a set-off. The fact that the debts would have been set off in the bankruptcy means that the arrangements have not worked to the detriment of the other creditors of the bankrupt. 'You cannot prefer a man . . . by merely putting him in the very position in which he would be if a bankruptcy followed.'[50] That was not the case however in *Re Washington Diamond Mining Co.*[51] A director of a company was owed directors' fees. At the same time he held shares in the company which were not fully paid up, so that he had a potential liability to contribute the amount unpaid on the shares. The company went into liquidation. Before the liquidation, but dur-

---

[47] See the Insolvency Act 1986, s 239(1), referring to s 238(1).

[48] The insolvency set-off section does not apply to a company which is subject to an administration order. See para 6.08 above.

[49] It should not be necessary for a preferential 'payment' that money changed hands. See Lindley LJ in *Re Washington Diamond Mining Co* [1893] 3 Ch 95, 109–110.

[50] *Re Washington Diamond Mining Co* [1893] 3 Ch 95, 104, *per* Vaughan Williams J. See also *Hamilton v Commonwealth Bank of Australia* (1992) 9 ACSR 90, 106–108; *Wily v Rothschild Australia Ltd* (1999) 47 NSWLR 555, 566; *Wily v St George Partnership Banking Ltd* (1999) 84 FCR 423, 435–436 (mutual payments) *Minister for Transport v Francis* (2000) 35 ACSR 584, 594. Compare *Wily v Bartercard Ltd* (2000) 34 ACSR 186 (esp at 197), in which there would not have been a set-off if the transaction were set aside. The decision in the *Bartercard* case was affirmed on appeal. See (2001) 39 ACSR 94. Compare also *Re B P Fowler Ltd* [1938] 1 Ch 113, in which Crossman J held that the payments constituted a preference notwithstanding that he left open (at 120) whether there would have been a set-off in the liquidation. In that respect the judgment is unsatisfactory. In considering whether the qualification to the set-off section (see paras 6.49–6.64 above) would have precluded a set-off, the question of notice is to be determined by reference to the circumstances at the time of the incurring of the obligations, as opposed to the time of effecting a set-off pursuant to the agreement, because the question of a preference is to be determined on the assumption that the agreement is set aside. See *Minister for Transport v Francis* (above).

[51] [1893] 3 Ch 95. See also *Re Land Development Association. Kent's Case* (1888) 39 Ch D 259; *Re Atlas Engineering Co (Davy's Case)* (1889) 10 LR (NSW) Eq 179, 6 WN (NSW) 64; *Mitchell v Booth* [1928] SASR 367. Compare *Re Masons' Hall Tavern Co. Habershon's Case* (1868) LR 5 Eq 286.

ing the preference period, the director gave a cheque to the company for the amount remaining unpaid on his shares, and received at the same time a cheque from the company for a like amount on account of his fees.[52] Lindley LJ in the Court of Appeal characterized the arrangement as an attempt by the director to pay up his shares in full without really parting with any money,[53] and said that the exchange of cheques was simply a mode for setting off the amount due for fees against the amount due on the shares.[54] If the debts could have been set off in any event in the liquidation, the arrangement would not have been a preference. But while there may be a set-off in an action at law by a solvent company to enforce a call on shares, a call for unpaid capital is not such a claim that may give rise to a set-off in a liquidation.[55] The Court of Appeal therefore held that the arrangement constituted a preference, with the result that the director was required to contribute the full amount of the unpaid capital to the company and to lodge a proof in the liquidation in respect of his claim for fees. When an agreement for a set-off is set aside as a preference, it has the effect of putting the parties in the same position as if the demands had not been set against each other.[56]

Other arrangements constituting preferences

A preference also may take the form of an arrangement between a creditor and a **13.11** debtor by which the creditor is to become indebted to the debtor, so that a possible set-off situation may arise. In such cases the preference provision will override any right to a set-off.[57] For example, there may be a preference where a debtor sells goods or other property on credit to a creditor, the preference arising from the possibility of the creditor setting off the purchase price against the bankrupt's indebtedness to him.[58] An alternative to the credit sale is a delivery of goods to the creditor with authority to sell and to receive the proceeds,[59] or merely an authority to receive the proceeds of a sale conducted by someone else.[60] In such a case

---

[52] The company's account was in credit only for a trifling amount. The cheque given to the company was deposited first, and it was only after the amount of the cheque was received by the company's bankers that the cheque given to the director was cashed.

[53] [1893] 3 Ch 95, 109.

[54] [1893] 3 Ch 95, 110.

[55] See 8.50–8.62 above.

[56] See the Insolvency Act 1986, ss 239(3) and 340(2), and the discussion in *Hamilton v Commonwealth Bank of Australia* (1992) 9 ACSR 90, 107. See also in Australia the Bankruptcy Act 1966 (Cth), s 122(5).

[57] *Re Clements* (1931) 7 ABC 255, 268–269.

[58] *Sempill v Vindin* (1868) 7 SCR (NSW) 361. Compare *Smith v Hodson* (1791) 4 TR 211 and *Donaldson v Couche* (1867) 4 WW & A'B (L) 41, in which the assignees in bankruptcy affirmed the sale by suing for the price.

[59] The provision of property by a debtor to a creditor for sale and to retain the proceeds, or a credit given in an account, may be characterized as a 'payment made' by the debtor. See *Findlay v Trevor* (1993) 11 ACLC 483, 490, 499.

[60] There would not be a set-off in any event if the proceeds are received subject to a trust. See ch 10 above.

the creditor may be ordered to return the proceeds of sale undiminished by a set-off.[61]

Desire to produce a preference

13.12 The preference provision in the English Insolvency legislation stipulates that the debtor should have been 'influenced' by a 'desire to produce' a situation in which the creditor may be preferred.[62] There should have been some desire to confer a preference, so that an arrangement involving a sale of goods on credit or a delivery of property for sale will only be held to constitute a preference, with the consequent denial of a set-off against the purchase price or the obligation to pay the proceeds of sale, if the debtor was influenced by a desire that the creditor should set off the purchase price or the proceeds of sale against his indebtedness.[63] It should be compared to the position in Australia, where the preference provision merely looks to the *effect* of the transaction. A transfer of property[64] in favour of a creditor is void as against the debtor's trustee in bankruptcy if it had the effect of giving the creditor a preference.[65] The intention of the debtor to prefer is irrelevant.[66] On the other hand, in a case in which a debtor deposited goods with his creditor for the purpose of sale by the creditor, it was said that any retainer of the proceeds of sale by the creditor would not be a 'payment' for the purpose of the preference section unless the debtor had authorized the creditor, either expressly or impliedly, to satisfy the debt from the proceeds.[67]

---

[61] *Castendyck and Focke v The Official Assignee of S A McLellan* (1887) 6 NZLR 67; *Re Hardy* (1901) 19 NZLR 845; *Re Clements* (1931) 7 ABC 255; *Re Wade (deceased)* (1943) 13 ABC 116. See also *Re Grezzana* (1932) 4 ABC 203. Compare *Re Smith* (1933) 6 ABC 49 and *Re McConnell* (1911) 18 ALR 90, [1912] VLR 102, in which the creditor acted in good faith, for valuable consideration, and in the ordinary course of business, and therefore was protected. Compare also *Simson v Guthrie* (1873) 4 AJR 182; *Re Lindsay* (1890) 9 NZLR 192.

[62] See the Insolvency Act 1986, s 340(4), and for company liquidation s 239(5).

[63] See also in New Zealand *Re Reimer* (1896) 15 NZLR 198 and *Hunter v The Official Assignee of Bispham* (1898) 17 NZLR 175.

[64] This includes a payment of money. See the Bankruptcy Act 1966 (Cth), s 122(8)(a).

[65] See the Bankruptcy Act 1966 (Cth), s 122, and for company liquidation the Corporations Act 2001 (Cth), ss 588FA(1) and 588FC.

[66] *S Richards and Co Ltd v Lloyd* (1933) 49 CLR 49.

[67] *Re Clements* (1931) 7 ABC 255, 270. Therefore Paine J held in *Re Clements* that the creditor in that case was not precluded from setting off the obligation to account for the proceeds against the debt. In *Hamilton v Commonwealth Bank of Australia* (1992) 9 ACSR 90, 108 Hodgson J criticized the availability of a set-off in *Re Clements* in that circumstance. He said that it was difficult to see why, as a matter of justice, a creditor should be better off where it received the proceeds of sale not as a payment, but merely because it was given authority by the debtor to sell the goods and receive the proceeds as agent. That criticism is well-founded. Hodgson J suggested that Paine J should have found that the money was received by the agent as a fiduciary for the debtor, and accordingly it should have been accounted for to the trustee. The difficulty with that suggestion is that a set-off in relation to sale proceeds is based upon *Rose v Hart* (1818) 8 Taunt 499, 129 ER 477, which seems to apply regardless of whether the proceeds are impressed with a trust. See paras 10.15–10.17 above.

Acting inconsistently with a right to avoid a transaction

Formerly, the preference provision in the the bankruptcy legislation entitled the   **13.13**
trustee in bankruptcy himself to avoid the payment or transfer of property.[68] It was
not necessary for the trustee to apply for an order from the court. When there had
been a transfer of property, the denial of a set-off was premised on the assumption
that the trustee did not adopt a course of action that was inconsistent with his
statutory right to avoid the transfer and to seek either a return of the property or
damages for its conversion. In *Smith v Hodson*[69] the preference took the form of a
sale of goods on credit to a creditor, thereby leaving open the possibility of the
creditor obtaining an advantage over the other creditors by means of a set-off
against his indebtedness for the purchase price. The bankrupt's assignees in bankruptcy had a choice. They could either have avoided the contract of sale as a preference and sued for the recovery of the property, or they could have affirmed the
transaction and sued for the purchase price. Since they adopted the latter course
they let in a set-off.[70] The current preference provision in the Insolvency Act
1986[71] does not empower the trustee himself to avoid a preference. He must apply
to the court for an order to that effect. But if in a *Smith v Hodson* situation the
trustee fails to seek an order and instead sues for the price, a set-off ordinarily
should be available to the creditor.[72]

Right of proof

Where a payment is avoided as a preference, the Insolvency Act[73] provides that the   **13.14**
court may make such order as it thinks fit with respect to the rights of the recipient of the avoided payment to prove for the debt which was discharged by it. In
Australia, the High Court has held that the recipient may not prove until the preference has been repaid in full.[74]

---

[68] See eg the Bankruptcy Act 1914, s 44(1). This is still the case in Australia in relation to bankruptcy (see the Bankruptcy Act 1966 (Cth), s 122), but not in company liquidation. See the
Corporations Act 2001 (Cth), s 588FF.

[69] (1791) 4 TR 211, 100 ER 979. See also *Holmes v Tutton* (1855) 5 El & Bl 65, 119 ER 405.

[70] See also *Donaldson v Couche* (1867) 4 W W & A'B (L) 41.

[71] See s 340 for bankruptcy, and s 239 for company liquidation.

[72] In England the qualification to the set-off section only applies in relation to sums becoming
due *from* the bankrupt. In Australia, on the other hand, the qualification is drafted in terms of both
giving and receiving credit, and so it may apply so as to prevent a set-off in this situation. See para
6.53 above.

[73] See s 241(1)(g) for company liquidation, and s 342(1)(g) for bankruptcy. In Australia, see the
Corporations Act 2001 (Cth), s 588FF(1)(g) in the context of company liquidation.

[74] *N A Kratzmann Pty Ltd v Tucker (No 2)* (1968) 123 CLR 295. See also the Corporations Act
2001 (Cth), s 588 FI.

(2) Preferences in Australia

13.15 In Australia, the view as to the nature and effect of the right to take action in respect of a preference differs in some respects from that in England. Thus, English courts have said that the proceeds of a preference when recovered by a liquidator are impressed with a trust in the liquidator's hands for those creditors amongst whom the liquidator has to distribute the assets.[75] In Australia on the other hand the notion of a trust, in the full sense of the word, has been doubted.[76] Further, for the purpose of a liquidator's power to sell all or part of the company's property pursuant to section 477(2)(c) of the Corporations Act 2001 (Cth), it has been held that the proceeds of a successful claim to recover a preference constitute property of the company,[77] whereas the prevailing view in England is that the right is not the property of the company.[78] In adopting that view in Australia, particular significance has been attached to sectiion 588FF(1) of the Corporations Act, which provides that the court may order the recipient of a preference to pay the amount in question 'to the company'.[79] None of these matters however should affect the principle that a set-off is not available against an obligation to repay a preference.[80] There is still a lack of mutuality.[81]

13.16 An application to set aside a preference is made by the liquidator, not the company,[82] and it is made for the benefit of unsecured creditors and for the purpose of

---

[75] *Re Yagerphone Ltd* [1935] Ch 392, 396; *Re M C Bacon Ltd* [1991] Ch 127, 137.

[76] *Re Starkey* [1994] 1 Qd R 142, 154; *Re Fresjac Pty Ltd* (1995) 65 SASR 334, 348.

[77] *Re Tosich Construction Pty Ltd* (1997) 73 FCR 219; *Elfic Ltd v Macks* (2001) 181 ALR 1. See also *Re Addstone Pty Ltd* (1998) 83 FCR 583, 588. There is however authority to the contrary. Prior to the amendment of the Corporations Law in 1992 which introduced s 588FF (see below), it was said that neither the right to recover a preference nor the proceeds recovered formed part of the property of the company. In relation to the claim itself, see *Bibra Lake Holdings Pty Ltd v Firmadoor Australia Pty Ltd* (1992) 7 WAR 1, 7; *Re Fresjac Pty Ltd* (1995) 65 SASR 334, 346–347. In relation to the proceeds when recovered, see *Bibra Lake v Firmadoor* above at 5, 6–7 (referring to *Horn v York Paper Co Ltd* (1991) 23 NSWLR 622, 623); *Re Starkey* [1994] 1 Qd R 142, 154.

[78] See para 13.08 above.

[79] *Re Tosich Construction Pty Ltd* (1997) 73 FCR 219, 235; *Elfic Ltd v Macks* (2001) 181 ALR 1, 18 para 98, 42 para 205.

[80] *Re A Debtor* [1927] 1 Ch 410; *Calzaturificio Zenith Pty Ltd v NSW Leather and Trading Co Pty Ltd* [1970] VR 605; *Re Exchange Travel (Holdings) Ltd* [1997] 2 BCLC 579, 594. Indeed, prior to the introduction of s 588FF it was said that the appropriate order in the case of a preference was that payment be made to the company, as opposed to the liquidator. See *Octavo Investments Pty Ltd v Knight* (1979) 144 CLR 360, 372; *Bibra Lake Holdings Pty Ltd v Firmadoor Australia Pty Ltd* (1992) 7 WAR 1, 6–7; *Re Fresjac Pty Ltd* (1995) 65 SASR 334, 343. Therefore, the inclusion of the stipulation in s 588FF that payment is to be made 'to the company' simply reflects the pre-existing view as to the appropriate order.

[81] See also Bennetts, 'Voidable Transactions: Consequences of Removing Avoidance Powers from the Liquidator and Vesting Them in the Court' (1994) 2 Insolvency Law Journal 136, 137–9.

[82] See the Corporations Act 2001 (Cth), s 588FF ('on the application of a company's liquidator'), and also *Olsen v Nodcad Pty Ltd* (1999) 32 ACSR 118, 120. Before the introduction of s 588FF the liquidator was regarded as the proper plaintiff in the action. See *Bibra Lake Holdings Pty Ltd v Firmadoor Australia Pty Ltd* (1992) 7 WAR 1; *Re Fresjac Pty Ltd* (1995) 65 SASR 334, 343.

the winding up.[83] Courts in Australia, like those in England,[84] have accepted that a charge granted by a company over its present and future assets does not catch a right to recover a preference or the proceeds of recovery of a preference.[85] Similarly neither a right to set aside a preference in a liquidation nor the proceeds of recovery could be assigned by the company prior to its liquidation as future property.[86] Those propositions should not be affected by the stipulation in section 588FF that payment is to be made 'to the company'.[87] The reason why a security granted by a company does not attach to the proceeds of a preference claim is that the right to apply for relief in relation to a preference is given for the benefit of the general body of creditors and for the purpose of the winding up.[88] This is still the case under section 588FF, notwithstanding the stipulation as to payment.[89] If the company cannot charge the right to make an application to the court in relation to a preference because the right is one given for the benefit of unsecured creditors, and if the company similarly cannot assign it prior to liquidation, it is evident that, while the stipulation as to payment in section 588FF may result in the company having the legal title to the recovery, it is not the beneficial owner of the claim.[90] If it is not

---

[83] *Sheahan v Carrier Air Conditioning Pty Ltd* (1997) 189 CLR 407, 428; *Re Fresjac Pty Ltd* (1995) 65 SASR 334, 347; *Willmott v London Celluloid Co* (1886) 34 Ch D 147, 150; *Re M C Bacon Ltd* [1991] Ch 127, 137.

[84] See para 13.08 above.

[85] *N A Kratzmann Pty Ltd v Tucker (No 2)* (1968) 123 CLR 295, 299–301; *Re Fresjac Pty Ltd* (1995) 65 SASR 334, 346–347; *Sheahan v Carrier Air Conditioning Pty Ltd* (1997) 189 CLR 407, 428; *Hamilton v National Australia Bank Ltd* (1996) 66 FCR 12, 37.

[86] *UTSA Pty Ltd v Ultra Tune Australia Pty Ltd* [1997] 1 VR 667, 698.

[87] This was assumed in *Hamilton v National Australia Bank Ltd* (1996) 66 FCR 12, 37, *per* Lehane J. Compare *Jonsson, Milner & Riaps Pty Ltd v Tim Ferrier Pty Ltd* [2001] QSC 9 at para 16, and Bennetts, 'Voidable Transactions: Consequences of Removing Avoidance Powers from the Liquidator and Vesting Them in the Court' (1994) 2 Insolvency Law Journal 136, 139–40. Bennetts has referred to some comments by Knox J in *Re Produce Marketing Ltd (No 2)* [1989] BCLC 520 in the context of a claim for wrongful trading under the English Insolvency Act 1986 as supporting the contrary view. However those comments no longer reflect the position in England. In *Re Oasis Merchandising Services Ltd* 1998] Ch 170, 181 the Court of Appeal accepted that a right of action by a liquidator for wrongful trading, and the fruits of such an action, are not property of the company and are not caught by a debenture. See also *Re M C Bacon Ltd* [1991] Ch 127, 138 and *Lewis v Commissioner of Inland Revenue* [2001] 3 All ER 499 (preference).

[88] In *Sheahan v Carrier Air Conditioning Pty Ltd* (1997) 189 CLR 407, 428 Dawson, Gaudron and Gummow JJ said that: 'The right to have such preferential dealings set aside, statutory in nature, is given for the benefit of the general body of creditors. Hence, the security would not attach to the proceeds of the judgments the appellant recovered at first instance in the present litigation.'

[89] In *Re Fresjac Pty Ltd* (1995) 65 SASR 334, 343 Doyle CJ noted, in relation to the position prior to the introduction of s 588FF into the Corporations Law in 1992, that the appropriate order in the case of a preference was for the payment of any sum recovered to be made to the company, and commented that this 'suggests that the fact that money is received by the company is not sufficient of itself to enable a charge to attach to the money, because it is clear that in the case of the recovery of a preferential payment such recovery is for the benefit of the general creditors and not for the benefit of a secured creditor'.

[90] See also para 13.26 below. Thus, when it was said prior to the enactment of s 588FF in 1992 that the appropriate order in a preference action was for payment to the company rather than the liquidator, this was explained on the ground that the *legal* title to the assets of a company being

the beneficial owner, there would not be mutuality in equity in relation to the obligation to repay a preference and a debt owing to the creditor by the company for the purpose of a set-off under the insolvency set-off section.[90a]

(3) Other Impugned Transactions

13.17 There are other provisions in the Insolvency Act 1986 which enable a trustee in bankruptcy or a liquidator to take action in relation to certain transactions, for example in relation to transactions at an undervalue,[91] transactions defrauding creditors,[92] and in situations in which there has been fraudulent trading[93] or wrongful trading.[94] Moreover, a disposition of a company's property made after the commencement of a court-ordered winding up is void without the consent of the court.[95] An obligation to make or return a payment under those provisions should be subject to the same rule which obtains in the case of a preference, that it cannot be the subject of a set-off. A similar comment may be made in respect of the obligation to account for the proceeds of execution completed after the bankruptcy or liquidation of the debtor.[96]

13.18 The view that a set-off is not available is a reflection of the distinction which English courts have drawn in the context of company liquidation, between assets which are the property of the company at the commencement of the liquidation, including rights of action which arose and might have been pursued by the com-

---

wound up remained with the company. See *Bibra Lake Holdings Pty Ltd v Firmadoor Australia Pty Ltd* (1992) 7 WAR 1, 7; *Amatek Ltd v Botman* (1995) 127 FLR 160, 172.

[90a] See para 11.04 above.

[91] Insolvency Act 1986, s 238, and for bankruptcy s 339. Section 238 also applies when an administration order is made in relation to a company. As in the case of a preference, a set-off should not be available in response to an application by an administrator for an order in relation to a transaction at an undervalue. See para 13.09 above.

[92] Insolvency Act 1986, s 423.

[93] Insolvency Act 1986, s 213.

[94] Insolvency Act 1986, s 214.

[95] Insolvency Act 1986, s 127. See also s 284 with respect to individuals, which applies to dispositions in the period beginning with the presentation of the petition and ending with the vesting of the bankrupt's estate in the trustee.

[96] See the Insolvency Act 1986, ss 183 and 346. Compare the exceptional case of *Ex parte Elliott, re Jermyn* (1838) 3 Deac 343. The petitioner had paid a sum of money in order to prevent a distress being levied on the bankrupt's goods. The petitioner sold some of the goods, and was sued by the bankrupt's assignees for the proceeds. It had been held in a previous action ((1837) 2 Deac 179) that the sum paid on behalf of the bankrupt to prevent the distress was not a provable debt, but the court in the present case said that the assignees could not recover the proceeds without giving credit for the sums paid by the petitioner. However this was not justified on the basis of the principles of set-off. Rather, the action to recover the proceeds was characterized as an action for money had and received. The action for money had and received, although founded in the common law, is of an equitable nature. See *Roxborough v Rothmans of Pall Mall Australia Ltd* (2001) 76 ALJR 203, 223 [96]–[99], *per* Gummow J, 244 [202]–[203], *per* Callinan J. It only entitles the claimant to recover what in conscience he is entitled to. In particular, he must give credit for any benefits that he has received. See *Westdeutsche Landesbank Girozentrale v Islington LBC* [1994] 4 All ER 890, 940–941.

pany itself prior to the liquidation, and assets which only arise after the liquidation and which are recoverable only by the liquidator through the exercise of rights conferred on him alone by statute.[97] A claim by the liquidator within the latter category is not regarded as constituting property of the company, and accordingly it would not be caught by a charge granted by the company over its present and future assets.[98] Thus, in England a claim to recover a fraudulent preference is not considered to be property of the company,[99] and nor is a claim for fraudulent or wrongful trading,[100] or a right to assert that a disposition of the company's property after the commencement of its winding up is void.[101] Therefore it has been held in England that the right to recover a void disposition cannot be assigned by the liquidator pursuant to a power to sell any of the company's property.[102] Similarly in South Australia[103] Doyle CJ (with whom Matheson J agreed) concluded that the right to recover property the subject of a void disposition is not property of the company,[104] and therefore it is not a right to which a charge granted by the company would attach.[105] As in the case of a preference,[106] there would not in these situations be mutuality in equity for the purpose of the insolvency set-off section in relation to the right in question and a separate debt owing by the company.[107]

In Australia, *Shirlaw v Lewis*[108] suggests that in some circumstances there may be **13.19** a set-off in relation to a void disposition. Two companies entered into a contract

---

[97] *Re Oasis Merchandising Services Ltd* [1998] Ch 170, 181–183, CA; *Re Ayala Holdings Ltd (No 2)* [1996] 1 BCLC 467, 480–481, 483.

[98] *Re Oasis Merchandising Services Ltd* [1998] Ch 170, 181–182.

[99] See para 13.08 above. The contrary view has been expressed in Australia. See para 13.15 above.

[100] *Re Oasis Merchandising Services Ltd* [1998] Ch 170, 181; *Re M C Bacon Ltd* [1991] Ch 127, 138 (referring to the Insolvency Act 1986, s 214). In Australia, compare the Corporations Act 2001 (Cth), s 588W, which is considered below. On the other hand, a claim against directors for misfeasance is property of the company which can be charged, since the right of action in such a case arises and was available to the company before the winding up. See *Re Oasis Merchandising Services Ltd* [1998] Ch 170, 181; *Re Fresjac Pty Ltd* (1995) 65 SASR 334, 342 (referring to *Re Asiatic Electric Co Pty Ltd* [1970] 2 NSWLR 612).

[101] Insolvency Act 1986, s 127.

[102] *Re Ayala Holdings Ltd* [1996] 1 BCLC 467.

[103] *Re Fresjac Pty Ltd* (1995) 65 SASR 334.

[104] Compare *Elfic Ltd v Macks* (2001) 181 ALR 1 in relation to a preference. See para 13.15 above.

[105] (1995) 65 SASR 334, 345. Similarly, Doyle CJ said that the *proceeds* of the exercise of the right do not fall to be treated as property of the company caught by a pre-existing charge. On the other hand the Chief Justice accepted that, when the property disposed of is specific property the subject of a charge, as opposed to money, that property, if recovered, would again become subject to the charge.

[106] See para 13.08 above.

[107] Similarly equitable set-off ordinarily would not be available. See *Re Buchanan Enterprises Pty Ltd* (1982) 7 ACLR 407. Compare *Thomas v Hatzipetros* (1997) 24 ACSR 286 which concerned a different question, whether a disposition of property should be validated on the ground that the company was no worse off by the disposition because the bank as the disponee in any event would have claimed a set-off.

[108] (1993) 10 ACSR 288.

for the sale of a business. The purchaser went into possession prior to completion, but the contract provided that if the purchaser defaulted the vendor was entitled to terminate the purchaser's licence to conduct the business and to resume possession, whereupon the vendor would purchase all of the purchaser's goods and saleable stock in trade used in the business. The purchaser repudiated the contract, so as to give rise to a liability in damages to the vendor. The vendor accepted the repudiation, thereby terminating the contract, and Hodgson J in the New South Wales Supreme Court accepted that a sale of the goods and stock in trade was intended to take effect in that circumstance. A winding up of the purchaser commenced, after which the vendor retook possession. It then proceeded on the basis that it was the purchaser of the stock pursuant to the contract and on-sold it. The liquidator of the purchaser asserted that the sale of the stock to the vendor after the commencement of the winding up was a void disposition, and sought damages for conversion from the vendor because of the on-sale. Hodgson J held that, whether the claim against the vendor was characterized as being in the nature of a claim for unjust enrichment or a claim in conversion,[109] the vendor was entitled to set off its damages claim arising from the repudiation, since the taking of the stock arose out of the pre-liquidation dealings of the parties. It is difficult to support that view. The purpose of the statutory power to avoid a disposition of property is to enable the recovery of the property with a view to a rateable distribution among the general creditors,[110] and if a particular creditor who is a recipient of the property could set off the debt owing to him against a liability in damages for converting the property, the purpose of the section would be defeated. If the power to avoid the disposition is exercisable for the benefit of creditors generally, so should the right to sue in conversion. The company itself therefore should not be the beneficial owner of the claim in conversion so as to satisfy the requirement of mutuality in equity in relation to that claim and the debt owing by the company to the creditor.[111] In view of the set-off Hodgson J said that it was unnecessary to consider an alternative argument, that the disposition should be validated by the court,[112] but that would have been a preferable basis for a decision in favour of the vendor.

---

[109] Hodgson J in fact doubted (at (1993) 10 ACSR 288, 295) that a retrospective avoidance of a disposition can retrospectively make a disposal of goods a wrongful act of conversion, but compare *Sydlow Pty Ltd v Melwren Pty Ltd* (1994) 13 ACSR 144, 147.

[110] *Re Fresjac Pty Ltd* (1995) 65 SASR 334, 343, 344–345.

[111] In relation to a claim in conversion, Doyle CJ in *Re Fresjac Pty Ltd* (1995) 65 SASR 334, 347 referred to *Re Quality Camera Co Pty Ltd* [1965] NSWR 1330 as illustrating the proposition that money recovered as a preference is not caught by a charge over the company's assets, even when the money is the value of specific goods which themselves were caught by the charge. The Chief Justice considered (see in particular at 349) that the same conclusion applied in the case of a void disposition.

[112] Pursuant to the Corporations Law, s 468. See now the Corporations Act 2001 (Cth), s 468.

(4) Wrongful Trading in Australia

Another decision in Australia that would benefit from reconsideration is that of **13.20**
Mansfield J in *Re Parker*.[113] It concerned sections 588V and 588W of the
Corporations Law,[114] which imposed liability on a holding company for insolvent
trading by a subsidiary. In essence, section 588V provides that a holding company
contravenes the section if its subsidiary incurred debts when it was insolvent and,
having regard to the nature and extent of the holding company's control over the
subsidiary's affairs, it is reasonable to expect that the holding company would have
been aware that there were reasonable grounds for suspecting the subsidiary's insolvency. If the subsidiary goes into liquidation, and the holding company has
contravened section 588V, the liquidator pursuant to section 588W may recover
from the holding company, 'as a debt due to the company', the amount of any loss
or damage suffered by unsecured creditors because of the subsidiary's insolvency.

In *Re Parker*, the liquidator of a subsidiary alleged that the holding company was **13.21**
liable under section 588W. In addition, the subsidiary was indebted to the holding company, and the liquidator said that the subsidiary's debt should be set off
pursuant to section 553C of the Corporations Law against the holding company's
liability under section 588W. The impetus for this was that the holding company
was in receivership, and its assets (including any dividend payable to the holding
company) were expected to be absorbed in satisfying the charge to the secured
creditor. Therefore, in the absence of a set-off, the holding company would have
received a dividend in the liquidation in respect of the debt owing to it and at the
same time there would not have been any assets available to satisfy the holding
company's liability under section 588W.[115] Mansfield J accepted the liquidator's
argument, and held that a section 588W claim could be the subject of a set-off.[116]

---

[113] (1997) 80 FCR 1.

[114] Now, the Corporations Act 2001 (Cth).

[115] Normally, if a floating charge granted by a company crystallizes before the company's liquidation, a debt owing to the company and coming within the ambit of the charge would become the
subject of a fixed security in favour of the secured creditor, so that there would not be mutuality in
equity at the date of the liquidation as between the charged debt and a debt owing by the company
to the debtor. See para 11.33 above. In *Re Parker*, however, an administrator had been appointed to
the subsidiary prior to crystallization of the charge, and Mansfield J accepted that s 513B of the
Corporations Law had the effect that the date of the administration was the relevant date for determining rights of set-off. See paras 6.35–6.45 above, where that view is criticized. Since the administrator was appointed before crystallization, Parker J accepted that there was mutuality in equity at
the relevant date for the purpose of a set-off under the insolvency set-off section. Furthermore, the
fact that the charge crystallized before the winding up would have had the consequence that the
liquidator could not have invoked the rule in *Cherry v Boultbee* (1839) 4 My & Cr 442, 41 ER 171.
See paras 14.19–14.22 below.

[116] One of the conditions for liability under ss 588V & 588W is that, at the time when the subsidiary incurred the debts, it was reasonable to expect that the holding company would have been
aware that there were reasonable grounds for suspecting that the subsidiary was insolvent. Often,
that notice would bring into effect the qualification to the insolvency set-off section, in s 553C(2),
so as to preclude a set-off in the subsidiary's liquidation. See paras 6.49–6.53 above. Section

13.22   The question of the availability of a set-off involved the determination of two issues. The first was whether the holding company's liability under section 588W
constituted a debt or a credit or a claim arising out of a dealing for the purpose of
the insolvency set-off section, and the second was whether there was mutuality.

13.23   In relation to the first issue, a claim pursuant to section 599W does not exist prior
to the liquidation. On the contrary, liquidation is a pre-condition to it. Mansfield
J was also prepared to accept in *Re Parker* that the claim may not arise from a prior
dealing between the holding company and the subsidiary, or at least he declined
to decide the case on that basis.[117] On the other hand, he pointed out that the
events which constituted the contravention occurred before the commencement
of the subsidiary's liquidation. Mansfield J said that the claim under section
588W was the 'natural outcome' of those events, which justified the application
of the set-off section[118] He derived support for that view from an earlier comment
by Bigham J in *Re Daintrey*,[119] which was quoted by Rich J in *Hiley v Peoples
Prudential Assurance Co Ltd*,[120] and to which the High Court referred with approval in *Gye v McIntyre*.[121] Bigham J said of the appellants in *Re Daintrey* that they
'are not seeking to alter the rights of the parties by reference to subsequent transactions, but are seeking to ascertain them by reference to the natural outcome of
previous transactions . . .'.[122] In the *Hiley* case, however, both Rich and Dixon JJ
also emphasized that the company's right to the debt which it was sought to include in a set-off in that case[123] arose out of subsisting *rights* in the company when
the winding up began,[124] and Rich J in particular emphasized the importance generally of prior rights when it is sought to include a claim arising after the liquidation in a set-off:

553C(2) on the other hand is drafted in terms of the person claiming the benefit of the set-off having the requisite notice. Moreover, it is clear from the context that it contemplates the creditor of the
company and not the company itself. Since in *Re Parker* the liquidator, as opposed to the holding
company, was claiming the set-off, the qualification on its face did not apply. The point may be
made however that it seems inconsistent with the mandatory and automatic nature of insolvency
set-off that the question whether a set-off occurs should depend on which party is claiming it. See
para 6.53 above.

[117] (1997) 80 FCR 1, 10–11.
[118] (1997) 80 FCR 1, 12.
[119] [1900] 1 QB 546.
[120] (1938) 60 CLR 468, 487.
[121] (1991) 171 CLR 609, 630.
[122] [1900] 1 QB 546, 568.
[123] An insurance company prior to its liquidation had assigned a debt owing to it to a third party
by way of security, and after the winding up began the debt was transferred back to the company.
Since the debt had come back to the company, the High Court held that the debtor could employ it
in a set-off in the liquidation, notwithstanding that at the date of the liquidation it was held by the
third party. The important point was that the company had an equity of redemption, and the debt was
got back by virtue of rights subsisting at the commencement of the winding up. See para 6.65 above.
[124] (1938) 60 CLR 468, 489, *per* Rich J, 499, *per* Dixon J. Similarly in *Re Daintrey* [1900] 1 QB
546, to which Rich J referred in *Hiley* (see above), there were subsisting rights at the date of the bankruptcy arising out of the contract for the sale of the business.

> But this . . . does not mean that at the time when the winding up commences there must exist claims which then and there can be made the subject of account and set-off . . . Rights must be vested in the creditor and in the company which, without any new transaction, grow in the natural course of events into money claims capable of forming items in an account or capable of settlement by set-off.

In *Re Parker*, on the other hand, the subsidiary had no rights against its holding company prior to the liquidation. Section 588V describes certain events which must have occurred before the liquidation in order to support a claim in the liquidation under section 588W. Those events themselves however do not confer any rights on the subsidiary prior to its liquidation. They are simply pre-conditions to the statutory right coming into being. For a set-off to occur, there must have been mutual debts, mutual credits or mutual dealings. The section 588W claim arose after the liquidation, and therefore the set-off could not have been based upon mutual debts in existence at the date of the liquidation.[125] Moreover, Mansfield J proceeded on the basis that the section 588W claim did not arise out of a prior dealing. The justification for the set-off therefore must have been that the subsidiary gave credit to the holding company prior to the liquidation. But if the subsidiary had no 'rights' against the holding company prior to the liquidation, whether arising from a prior transaction or otherwise, it is difficult to see how it could be said that the subsidiary ever gave credit to the holding company before the liquidation.[126] It is true, as Mansfield J noted, that it is not necessary for a set-off that the claims should have arisen out of prior dealings.[127] In the cases to which he referred,[128] however, a creditor had acquired the bankrupt's debt before the bankruptcy, as a result of a third party having negotiated to the creditor an instrument upon which the bankrupt was liable. That did not involve a dealing between the bankrupt and the creditor, but there was nevertheless an existing debt owing to the creditor on the instrument at the date of the bankruptcy, and the creditor gave credit in relation to that debt before the bankruptcy. The credit therefore was founded upon the prior rights that the creditor had pursuant to the instrument negotiated to it. In *Re Parker* on the other hand there were no prior rights which could be said to have constituted the giving of credit in relation to the subsequent section 588W claim.

13.24 In any event there was a lack of mutuality. Mansfield J did not consider that mutuality presented a problem. He noted that section 588W is expressed in terms that the subsidiary's liquidator may recover from the holding company 'as a debt due to the company'. He regarded this as sufficient to establish mutuality as

---

[125] See para 7.02 above.
[126] See para 7.04 above.
[127] (1997) 80 FCR 1, 10–11. See paras 7.10–7.13 above.
[128] *Hankey v Smith* (1789) 3 TR 507n, 100 ER 703 and *Forster v Wilson* (1843) 12 M & W 191, 152 ER 1165.

between the subsidiary's section 588W claim and the holding company's claim against the subsidiary.[129] The section should not have that effect, however.

13.25   The stipulation that a claim under section 588W is recoverable 'as a debt due to the company' may result in the subsidiary having the legal title to the claim. In insolvency set-off, however, mutuality is determined by reference to equitable interests,[130] and it seems difficult to say that the subsidiary itself is the beneficial owner of any claim that may accrue to it under section 588W. For example, the subsidiary prior to its liquidation could not charge any subsequently accruing claim under section 588W. In the first place, that proposition arises by implication from section 588Y, which states that an amount paid to a company under section 588W is not available to pay a secured debt of the company unless all the company's unsecured debts have been paid in full. Further, the Explanatory Memorandum circulated with the Corporate Law Reform Bill 1992, which introduced sections 588V and 588W, made it clear that the purpose of the section is to benefit unsecured creditors,[131] in which case the comment of the High Court in *Sheahan v Carrier Air Conditioning Pty Ltd*[132] in the context of a right to have a preference set aside should be equally applicable to s 588W: 'The right to have such preferential dealings set aside, statutory in nature, is given for the benefit of the general body of creditors. *Hence*, the security would not attach to the proceeds of the judgments . . .'.[133] Similarly, because of the interest of unsecured creditors, the subsidiary prior to its liquidation could hardly assign for its own benefit a potential claim under section 588W as future property.[134] These factors suggest that the company is not the beneficial owner of the claim.[135] If the company is not the beneficial owner, there would not be mutuality for the purpose of a set-off as between the claim and a debt owing by the company. It is true that in *Re Parker* the allowance of a set-off benefited the unsecured creditors, since it removed the holding company as a proving creditor in circumstances where the cross-claim against the holding company pursuant to section 588W would not have yielded anything. But that is not the point. If a set-off is available to one party it should be equally available to the other, and in other cases it would be contrary to the interests of unsecured creditors if the holding company were permitted to set off its liability under section 588W against a separate debt owing to it by the subsidiary.

---

[129] (1997) 80 FCR 1, 11.

[130] See paras 11.04–11.07 above.

[131] The Explanatory Memorandum stated (in para 1128) that the liquidator 'may take proceedings against the holding company to recover, for the benefit of unsecured creditors, loss or damage suffered by unsecured creditors as a result of the holding company's contravention of 588V'.

[132] (1997) 189 CLR 407.

[133] (1997) 189 CLR 407, 428 (emphasis added).

[134] In *UTSA Pty Ltd v Ultra Tune Australia Pty Ltd* [1997] 1 VR 667, 698 Hansen J at first instance accepted that a claim under the Corporations Law, s 588FF is not assignable by the company.

[135] See also para 13.16 above in relation to preferences.

There is admittedly authority for the view that a claim under section 588W is **13.26** property of the company for the purpose of a liquidator's power to sell pursuant to section 477(2)(c) of the Corporations Act 2001 (Cth).[136] But while the claim may be property of the company for the purpose of enabling the liquidator to deal with it as a saleable asset pursuant to section 477(2)(c), that proposition does not require the conclusion that the company itself is the beneficial owner. The company would hold the claim for the benefit of unsecured creditors. There may not be a trust in the full sense of the word,[137] but that does not matter. The important point for mutuality is that the company itself is not the beneficial owner. An analogy may be drawn with the position of an executor of a deceased's estate prior to completion of the administration.[138] Before the completion of the administration a legatee does not have a beneficial interest in the assets the subject of the bequest,[139] and nor does the executor. The testator's property comes to the executor in full ownership, in the sense that he has the whole right of property, to the extent that there are property rights. Nevertheless he holds it for the purpose of carrying out the functions and duties of administration, not for his own benefit. The executor therefore is not the beneficial owner of the estate.[140]

(5) Assignment of Book Debts

The Insolvency Act, section 344 provides that an assignment of book debts by a **13.27** person engaged in any business is void as against the person's trustee in bankruptcy as regards book debts which were not paid before the presentation of the petition, unless the assignment has been registered under the Bills of Sale Act 1878. Where an assignment is void the purchaser may be liable to account to the vendor's trustee for the proceeds of debts received. In Victoria there is authority to the effect that the purchaser may set off a cross-claim against his liability to account for proceeds under the insolvency set-off section,[141] but the case should be understood in the context of the legislation in issue. The Book Debts Act 1896 (Vic) provided that an assignment of book debts had no validity at law or in

---

[136] *Re Movitor Pty Ltd* (1996) 64 FCR 380, 392. The question in the *Movitor* case was whether the fruits of an action under s 588W were property of the company for the purpose of the Corporations Law, s 477(2)(c). Drummond J also said however (at 392) that the 'debt' can properly be regarded as property of the company which the liquidator is empowered to sell. In England, the Court of Appeal in *Re Oasis Merchandising Services Pty Ltd* [1998] Ch 170, 184–185 distinguished *Re Movitor* on the basis of the different language in the Australian wrongful trading provision. See also *Re William Felton Co Pty Ltd* (1998) 28 ACSR 228, 235–236; *Re Addstone Pty Ltd* (1998) 83 FCR 583, 592.

[137] See *Re Starkey* [1994] 1 Qd R 142, 154, *per* McPherson JA and *Re Fresjac Pty Ltd* (1995) 65 SASR 334, 348, *per* Doyle CJ in relation to preferences.

[138] See *Re Starkey* [1994] 1 Qd R 142, 154 in relation to preferences, and para 13.116 below.

[139] *Official Receiver in Bankruptcy v Schultz* (1990) 170 CLR 306, 312, 314.

[140] *Commissioner of Stamp Duties (Queensland) v Livingston* [1965] AC 694, 707–708; *Ayerst v C & K (Construction) Ltd* [1976] AC 167, 177–178.

[141] *Savage v Thompson* (1903) 29 VLR 436.

equity until it was registered. The Victorian legislation should be compared to the English Insolvency Act, which provides that the assignment is void *as against the trustee*.[142] The only obligation to account for the proceeds is to a trustee in bankruptcy. In such a case a question of mutuality would arise which was not in issue in Victoria.

(6) Set-off, After the Avoidance of an Assignment of a Debt

13.28 A bankrupt prior to the bankruptcy may have assigned to X a debt owing to the bankrupt by Y. If the assignment is subsequently avoided, for example as a transaction at an undervalue or a transaction defrauding creditors, so that the debt reverts to the bankrupt, there is then the possibility of the debt forming the basis of a set-off as between the bankrupt and Y.[143] The issue of mutuality, when the effect of avoiding a transaction is that a payment must be made to the trustee, would not arise.

C. Performance of Contracts After Insolvency

(1) Disclaimer

13.29 The fact that one of the parties to a contract has become bankrupt or has gone into liquidation may constitute a repudiation of the contract, but insolvency is not always a repudiation.[144] If a contract is not repudiated, any rights arising under it in favour of the insolvent will become an asset of the estate available for distribution amongst creditors. If the insolvent's side of the contract still requires performance, the trustee or the liquidator may choose to disclaim it as an unprofitable contract.[145] Alternatively, the contract may be regarded as profitable and therefore it may not be disclaimed. In that circumstance, the question may arise whether rights and liabilities arising pursuant to the contract as a result of later performance or non-performance may be the subject of a set-off.

---

[142] After the assignment is avoided any proceeds received by the purchaser may be subject to a constructive trust, and therefore not be susceptible to a set-off in any event on that ground. See ch 10 above.

[143] *Re Last, ex p Butterell* (1994) 124 ALR 219. Why did the fact that Rawilla Pty Ltd was a trustee of a discretionary trust not have the consequence that there was not mutuality in equity? See para 17.93 below.

[144] See eg *Brooke v Hewitt* (1796) 3 Ves Jun 253, 30 ER 997; *Jennings' Trustee v King* [1952] 1 Ch 899; *Official Receiver v Henn* (1981) 40 ALR 569. See also paras 9.04–9.05 above.

[145] See the Insolvency Act 1986, s 315, and, for company liquidation, s 178. In Australia see the Bankruptcy Act 1966 (Cth), s 133, and for companies the Corporations Act 2001 (Cth), ss 568–568F.

Bankruptcy

Consider first the case of a bankruptcy. A trustee in bankruptcy ordinarily is not **13.30**
liable personally for a breach of the bankrupt's contracts occurring after the bankruptcy, including as a result of a disclaimer. Rather, the other contracting party is
remitted to a proof in the bankruptcy for his damages claim,[146] and since the claim
arises out of a prior dealing with the bankrupt he should also be able to use it in a
set-off.[147] Often, though, when a contract imposing onerous obligations on a
bankrupt is in issue,[148] the other contracting party will serve a notice on the bankrupt's trustee requiring him to decide within twenty-eight days whether or not he
is going to disclaim the contract, and if he does not disclaim the Insolvency Act
states that the trustee is deemed to have adopted the contract.[149] Two interpret-
ations of this provision have been suggested.[150] The first is that the trustee is
deemed to have adopted the contract in his personal capacity, so that he becomes
personally liable for any subsequent breach of the contract, subject only to a possible right of indemnity from the estate.[151] Since the burden of a contract, as distinct from the benefit, cannot be assigned, this interpretation contemplates a form
of novation of the contract, by which the trustee in his personal capacity replaces
the bankrupt as the party responsible for carrying out the contract. The second is
also based on a novation, but in this case the trustee representing the estate and the
creditors generally is substituted for the trustee as representing the bankrupt.[152]
On this interpretation, it has been suggested[153] that the other contracting party
would be a first priority creditor entitled to be paid ahead of the other creditors.
Either interpretation, however, should mean that the other contracting party
could not bring a prior debt that he owes to the bankrupt into an account.
Mutuality would be lacking in relation to the debt and his claim against either the
trustee representing the estate or the trustee in his personal capacity. Usually this
would not be significant, because the right of the other contracting party to proceed against the trustee personally, or to have a direct claim against the estate,
would obviate the necessity for a set-off. Indeed, if the value of the claim of the
other contracting party is greater than his indebtedness to the bankrupt, both

---

[146] *Re Sneezum, ex p Davis* (1876) 3 Ch D 463. See also *Stead Hazel and Co v Cooper* [1933] 1 KB
840 for companies. In the event of a disclaimer, the Insolvency Act 1986, ss 178(6) and 315(5) confer a right of proof for loss suffered as a result of the disclaimer.

[147] See paras 8.42–8.43 above.

[148] For a discussion of onerous contracts, see Melville, 'Disclaimer of Contracts in Bankruptcy'
(1952) 15 MLR 28.

[149] Insolvency Act 1986, s 316(2). In Australia see the Bankruptcy Act 1966 (Cth), s 133(6).

[150] Melville, 'Disclaimer of Contracts in Bankruptcy' (1952) 15 MLR 28, 33–4.

[151] Robson, *Law of Bankruptcy* (7th edn, 1894) 473–4. In the case of a lease, if a trustee does not
disclaim he becomes personally liable for rent. The basis of the liability is privity of estate. See eg *Ex
parte Dressler, re Solomon* (1878) 9 Ch D 252, and paras 13.58–13.62 below.

[152] Williams and Muir Hunter, *The Law and Practice in Bankruptcy* (19th edn, 1979) 394–5.

[153] Melville, 'Disclaimer of Contracts in Bankruptcy' (1952) 15 MLR 28, 34.

these alternatives would be preferable to a set-off, because set-off only enables a creditor to obtain the full value of his claim to the extent of his indebtedness. On the other hand, the other contracting party may suffer from the loss of a set-off if the section is interpreted as imposing personal liability on the trustee and the trustee himself is insolvent.

Company liquidation

13.31 Disclaimer has a similar operation in company liquidation. If the liquidator disclaims a contract the resulting damages claim should be able to be the subject of a set-off, since it arises out of a prior dealing with the company.[154] Liquidation differs from bankruptcy, however, in that the company's property does not vest in the liquidator as the person administering the estate.[155] Consistent with that distinction, if a notice is served upon a liquidator requiring him to decide whether or not he is going to disclaim a contract, and he fails to disclaim within the twenty-eight day period, the Insolvency Act 1986 does not provide that the liquidator himself is deemed to have adopted the contract.[156] Any subsequent breach of contract would be a liability of the company, and in accordance with normal principles it should be able to be the subject of a set-off.

(2) Contract by Insolvent to Sell Property or Perform Work

13.32 A person may have contracted to sell property or to perform work, but have become bankrupt or gone into liquidation before the contract has been performed.[157] If the contract subsequently is performed, so that the price becomes payable, the other contracting party liable to pay the price may wish to set off against that liability a separate debt owing to him by the bankrupt or the company.

Beneficial ownership had vested in the purchaser before the vendor's insolvency

13.33 If the contract is for the sale of real property, and the beneficial ownership of the property had vested in the purchaser prior to the vendor's bankruptcy or liquidation, the purchaser ordinarily is entitled to specific performance of the contract, subject to the usual requirement of being able to show that he is ready and willing to perform his own essential obligations under the contract. If the vendor happens to be separately indebted to the purchaser, and the debt is otherwise capable of

---

[154] See paras 8.42–8.43 above.

[155] See para 13.05 above.

[156] Compare in Australia the Corporations Act 2001 (Cth), s 568(8) which provides that, if the liquidator does not disclaim within the appointed time, 'he or she' shall be deemed to have adopted it.

[157] Compare *Shirlaw v Lewis* (1993) 10 ACSR 288, in which the sale occurred after the winding-up summons was filed but before the winding-up order.

being included in a set-off under the insolvency set-off section, the Court of Appeal in *Re Taylor, ex p Norvell*[158] held that specific performance may be decreed on terms that the purchaser pay the balance (if any) in favour of the vendor.

Beneficial title had not passed before the vendor's insolvency

Consider however that the contract is for the sale of property the beneficial own- **13.34**
ership of which had not vested in the purchaser prior to the vendor's insolvency.
This may occur, for example, in the case of a contract for the sale of a quantity of
unascertained goods for delivery at a future date. Often in such a case the price is
not payable until delivery occurs. If in the interim the vendor has become bankrupt or has gone into liquidation, the trustee in bankruptcy or the liquidator may
disclaim the contract if it is unprofitable.[159] Alternatively, if the contract is profitable, the trustee or the liquidator may decide to complete it for the benefit of the
unsecured creditors and deliver the goods in question. There should not be any
difficulty if the goods are delivered and accepted on a 'cash on delivery' basis. If
however delivery takes place without immediate payment, the purchaser may assert that he is entitled to a set-off against the debt for the price. The same issue may
arise in the context of a prior contract for the performance of work. If the trustee
or the liquidator decides to complete the contract because it is profitable and performs the work, the question may arise whether the resulting payment obligation
may be the subject of a set-off.

Prima facie a set-off should be possible. A debt which arises in favour of a bank- **13.35**
rupt or a company in liquidation after the bankruptcy or the liquidation but pursuant to a prior contract is capable of being employed in a set-off.[160] Since the debt
for the price is a natural result of the prior transaction it should be a case of giving
credit for the purpose of the set-off section, although in any event the debt should
be available as a set-off on the ground that it is a money demand arising out of a
prior dealing between the parties to the proposed set-off.[161] Further, the requirement of mutuality should be satisfied. For mutuality, the cross-demands must be
between the same parties and they must be held in the same right and interest[162]
The fact that a debt for the price first arises after the bankruptcy or liquidation
does not affect mutuality, notwithstanding that the debt from the time that it accrued would have been vested in the trustee or, in the case of a company liquidation in which there is no *cessio bonorum*, notwithstanding that the company itself
would never have had a beneficial interest in the accrued debt.[163] The critical point

---

[158] [1910] 2 KB 562.
[159] See the Insolvency Act 1986, s 315 and, for company liquidation, s 178.
[160] See paras 8.27–8.37 above.
[161] See ch 7 above.
[162] See para 11.01 above.
[163] See paras 13.05–13.06 above. In Australia compare *Franklin's Selfserve Pty Ltd v Federal
Commissioner of Taxation* (1970) 125 CLR 52, in which Menzies J held that liquidation does not

is that the debt arose out of a prior contract between the parties to the proposed set-off, and mutuality therefore should be satisfied as at the relevant date for determining rights of set-off in relation to the debt and a cross-claim between the parties.[164] As Dixon J expressed the principle in the High Court of Australia in *Hiley v The Peoples Prudential Assurance Co Ltd*:[165]

> It is enough that at the commencement of the winding up mutual dealings exist which involve rights and obligations of such a nature that afterwards in the events that happen they mature or develop into pecuniary demands capable of set-off. If the end contemplated by the transaction is a claim sounding in money so that, in the phrase employed in the cases, it is commensurable with the cross-demand, no more is required than that at the commencement of the winding up liabilities shall have been contracted by the company and the other party respectively from which cross money claims accrue during the course of the winding up . . .

However the decision of Watkin Williams J in *Ince Hall Rolling Mills Co Ltd v The Douglas Forge Co*[166] is authority against the availability of a set-off.

The *Ince Hall* case

13.36 The *Ince Hall* case concerned a contract for the sale of a quantity of unascertained goods, where the contract was entered into before the liquidation of the supplier. After the liquidation the liquidator was authorized by the court to carry on the business for the purpose of winding up the company, whereupon the liquidator determined to complete the contract and to deliver the goods contracted for. Payment did not take place upon delivery, and when the liquidator subsequently sued for the price the purchaser sought to set off a separate debt owing to it. Watkin Williams J held that the debt for the price could not be the subject of a set-off. He said that there was a lack of mutuality, the reason being that, when a company completes a transaction after the commencement of its liquidation, albeit pursuant to a prior contract, it does so in a new interest and a new capacity:[167]

> Every transaction entered into by the company from [the commencement of liquidation] is void unless sanctioned by the Court; no contracts can be executed nor can the business of the company be carried on in a single particular except for the purposes of winding-up and for the benefit of the creditors, and, although the company continues in existence and under the same name, and may, if allowed by the Court, continue to carry on its business and enter into or complete transactions, it does so

---

deprive a company of the beneficial title to its assets. On that basis, lack of mutuality is even less likely to be an objection in Australia.

[164] This is implicit in the cases referred to in paras 8.28–8.37 above.

[165] (1938) 60 CLR 468, 497. This has since been accepted as a correct statement of the law. See *Re Charge Card Services Ltd* [1987] 1 Ch 150, 178, *per* Millett J; *Gye v McIntyre* (1991) 171 CLR 609, 624; *Old Style Confections Pty Ltd v Microbyte Investments Pty Ltd* [1995] 2 VR 457, 463, 464, *per* Hayne J.

[166] (1882) 8 QBD 179.

[167] (1882) 8 QBD 179, 184.

in a new interest and a new capacity, and solely for the purpose of winding-up its affairs in the interest of its creditors and shareholders . . . The practical effect of the defendants' contention would be that the company by a transaction which is void, unless sanctioned and ratified by the Court, would be paying one creditor in full out of the assets of the insolvent company in preference to the other creditors; such a result may well make one pause before giving effect to such a contention.

Criticism of the *Ince Hall* case

The decision in the *Ince Hall* case has been referred to in later cases, generally with- **13.37** out criticism.[168] Nevertheless, if goods are supplied to a purchaser pursuant to a contract entered into before the supplier's liquidation, the purchaser may ask why the fact that delivery takes place after liquidation rather than before should affect his position, particularly given that he may have been induced to enter into the transaction on the basis of a perception that mutual debts could be set off. A debt for the price arises upon delivery, and the question whether delivery will occur is in the hands of the supplier's liquidator, not the purchaser. If the liquidator instead had disclaimed the contract, the resulting damages claim against the company would have been a provable debt in the liquidation,[169] and similarly it would have been able to be the subject of a set-off.[170]

Philip Wood[171] has sought to explain the *Ince Hall* case on the basis of a suggested **13.38** general principle, that if an insolvency representative 'earns' a payment under a

---

[168] *Ince Hall Rolling Mills v The Douglas Forge Co* was referred to with evident approval by the Western Australian Supreme Court in *Re The West Australian Lighterage, Stevedoring and Transport Co Ltd* (1903) 5 WAR 132, 138. Further, the New South Wales Court of Appeal in *Central Brake Service (Sydney) Ltd v Central Brake Service (Newcastle) Ltd* (1992) 27 NSWLR 406, 409 noted the decision without adverse comment. In *Re Taylor, ex p Norvell* [1910] 1 KB 562, 575 (and see also at 576) Fletcher Moulton J in his dissenting judgment said (without referring to the *Ince Hall* case) that 'it cannot be doubted' that a trustee in bankruptcy electing to perform a prior contract to sell goods would be entitled to be paid the price in cash and not by a set-off. See also Gibbs CJ's discussion in *Day and Dent Constructions Pty Ltd v North Australian Properties Pty Ltd* (1982) 150 CLR 85, 94 of the Court of Appeal's decision in *Re A Debtor (No 66 of 1955)* [1956] 1 WLR 1226. In *Re A Debtor* a surety's trustee in bankruptcy paid the creditor under the guarantee in order to obtain the release of security given to the creditor, and it was held that the surety's resulting claim for an indemnity from the debtor could not be the subject of a set-off. The ostensible reason for the decision was that at the date of the bankruptcy the surety merely had a contingent right to an indemnity, the creditor not having been paid at that date, and it was not considered to be possible to base a set-off upon a claim that was merely contingent, and consequently not due, at that date. While Gibbs CJ criticized that ground for the decision, he nevertheless suggested (although without deciding) that, since 'the payments were made by the trustee to enable him to obtain the bankrupt's property', that 'may justify a conclusion that there were no mutual dealings between the trustee and the debtor'. On the other hand, Hayne J in *Old Style Confections Pty Ltd v Microbyte Investments Pty Ltd* [1995] 2 VR 457, 462–463, 464 left open the question whether the *Ince Hall* case was correctly decided.

[169] See the Insolvency Act 1986, s 178(6). The equivalent provision for bankruptcy is s 315(5).

[170] See para 13.31 above. In the converse case of a company which failed to purchase goods after its liquidation notwithstanding a prior agreement to do so, it was held that the resulting damages claim against the company could be set off. See *Telsen Electric Co Ltd v J J Eastick & Sons* [1936] 3 All ER 266.

[171] Wood, *English and International Set-off* (1989) 326, 329.

contract by the use of the insolvent's assets, for example by delivering property or performing work or continuing a lease of the insolvent's property, the price or the rent which is then earned is non-mutual with a separate debt of the insolvent, and so it is not available for a set-off. The reason for this is said to be that the assets of the estate available for distribution generally in effect would be used to pay one creditor in full. The insolvent would be divested of the assets used to perform the contract, and the estate would also lose the entitlement to the price or the rent as a result of the set-off. Apart from the *Ince Hall* case, however, it is difficult to find support in set-off cases for any such general principle.

13.39 In the first place, the lease cases to which Wood has referred[172] were concerned with bankruptcies, and in that context the denial of a set-off in respect of post-insolvency rent where the landlord has become bankrupt is explicable by the concept of privity of estate.[173]

13.40 Secondly, aspects of the decision of the High Court of Australia in *Hiley v The Peoples Prudential Assurance Co Ltd*[174] militate against the suggested principle. The *Hiley* case concerned a policy-holder in a life insurance company who had borrowed money from the company secured by a mortgage over some property. The company then transferred the mortgage, including the policy-holder's debt, to an assignee by way of security. After the company went into liquidation the liquidator redeemed the mortgage, whereupon it was held that the policy-holder could employ the debt in a set-off in the liquidation. The redemption of the security occurred as a result of a compromise of rights involving the life company and the assignee, although the tenor of the judgments, particularly that of Dixon J,[175] suggests that the same result would have followed if the redemption had occurred as a result of a payment of money by the liquidator. In either case the liquidator would have used assets of the company which otherwise would have been available for distribution generally, in the form of either the compromised rights or the company's funds, in order to redeem the policy-holder's debt to the company, and yet that circumstance was not regarded as fatal to a set-off. It is true that in the *Hiley* case the recipient of the company's property was not the person claiming the set-off, but looked at from the perspective of a liquidator, who used the company's property to obtain the right, that factor should not be significant.

13.41 Thirdly, *Re Asphaltic Wood Pavement Co. Lee & Chapman's Case*[176] suggests that there is no such principle in relation to contracts for the performance of

---

[172] Wood, *English and International Set-off* (1989) 342–3.
[173] See para 13.58 below.
[174] (1938) 60 CLR 468.
[175] See eg Dixon J's discussion at (1938) 60 CLR 468, 505 of *Re City Life Assurance Co Ltd. Stephenson's Case* [1926] 1 Ch 191.
[176] (1885) 30 Ch D 216, referred to with evident approval in *Hiley v The Peoples Prudential Assurance Co Ltd* (1938) 60 CLR 468, 497–498, *per* Dixon J.

work.[177] A company had contracted with the Commissioners of Sewers to pave a street for a stated price. In addition the contract provided that, if within two years following completion the Commissioners by notice in writing to the company should so require, the company had to keep the road in repair for a period of fifteen years, for which the company was to be paid at a fixed annual rate. The company went into liquidation before the completion of the work. The liquidator was empowered by the court to complete the contract, and for that purpose to expend all necessary moneys for wages, materials and incidental expenses, which he duly did.[178] On the other hand, given the liquidation, the company was not in a position to fulfil its obligation to repair for the fifteen-year period, the Commissioners having served the requisite notice. Prior to the liquidation the company had granted a charge to a third party which encompassed part of the moneys payable under the contract, but the Court of Appeal[179] held that the residue of the contract sum owing by the Commissioners could be set off against the Commissioners' claim for damages for anticipatory breach of contract arising from failure to keep the road in repair for fifteen years. This was so notwithstanding that the Commissioners' debt to the company for the price only arose after the liquidation when the work was completed. The company's money would have been used after the liquidation to complete the contract for the benefit of the company's creditors, in buying materials, paying wages etc, and in that sense *Lee & Chapman's Case* is similar to the *Ince Hall* case. Yet a set-off was allowed. The *Ince Hall* case was mentioned in argument before the Court of Appeal, but Brett LJ responded that the decision in that case had no bearing upon the case before him.[180] It is not clear what he meant by that. It is true that in *Lee & Chapman's Case* a great part of the work had been completed before the liquidation, whereas in the *Ince Hall* case performance by the company occurred entirely after the liquidation. However, to the extent that the company's funds were expended after the liquidation, and the expenditure of those funds was necessary in order for the

---

[177] Compare Wood, *English and International Set-off* (1989) 336. As Wood noted, *Alloway v Steere* (1882) 10 QBD 22 was concerned with a lease, for which special considerations apply. See para 13.59 below.

[178] The contract was entered into on 22 September 1882. On 9 December 1882 the company presented a petition for a winding-up order, and by orders made on 12 and 16 December 1882 the provisional official liquidator appointed to the company was empowered to complete the contract. On 13 January 1883 the company was ordered to be wound up, and on 29 January the official liquidator, having completed the work, forwarded an account to the Commissioners. On 8 March 1883 the Commissioners' engineer certified that the work was complete. On 25 May 1883 the Commissioners served the company with a formal notice that they required the company to repair and maintain the street for the further period for fifteen years.

[179] Brett MR, Cotton and Lindley LJJ

[180] (1885) 30 Ch D 216, 219.

company's creditors to obtain the benefit of the contract,[181] the cases would appear to be similar.[182]

13.42 In *Lee & Chapman's Case* the Commissioners' claim was based upon a breach by the company of an obligation that arose out of the same contract as the Commissioners' liability to pay the contract sum, and for that reason Wood has suggested that the set-off enforced in *Lee and Chapman's Case* is an example of an equitable (or a transaction) set-off, as opposed to a set-off under the bankruptcy legislation.[183] Equitable set-off was not mentioned in any of the judgments, however. The only right of set-off that was discussed was the right arising under the mutual credit provision in the bankruptcy legislation,[184] and it is clear that this was the form of set-off that was considered to be in issue. In other words, it must have been accepted that there was mutuality for the purpose of the bankruptcy set-off section, even though the contract was completed after the liquidation for the benefit of creditors.

13.43 Given that *Lee & Chapman's Case* in truth was concerned with insolvency set-off, is there a satisfactory basis for distinguishing it from the *Ince Hall* case? The cases differed in relation to the destination of the company's property. While they are similar, in that in each a claim accrued to a company after the commencement of its liquidation as a result of the use by the liquidator of the company's assets or funds, in the *Ince Hall* case the person liable on the claim was the direct recipient of property of the company that otherwise would have been available for distribution generally, whereas in *Lee & Chapman's Case* the company's funds would have been remitted to third parties (suppliers of materials, employees receiving wages etc). This point was addressed above in relation to *Hiley v The Peoples Prudential Assurance Co Ltd*,[185] but the distinction should be of even less significance for *Lee & Chapman's Case* where, as in the *Ince Hall* case, the party claiming the set-off benefited directly from the performance of the contract. In both those cases, the person asserting a set-off against the debt to the company arising from performance of the contract received full consideration for the debt, in the *Ince Hall* case as a result of the delivery of the goods the subject of the contract of sale, and in *Lee & Chapman's Case* by reason of the street being paved. This circumstance is not a reason for denying a set-off, however. It has never been a principle of insolvency

---

[181] See Bacon VC at first instance (1884) 26 Ch D 624, 634.

[182] Indeed, the analysis of Watkin Williams J in the *Ince Hall* case on the question of mutuality is at odds with the tenor of Cotton LJ's judgment in *Lee & Chapman's Case* (1885) 30 Ch D 216, 224 (and see also Brett MR at 220), although the context admittedly was different. In *Old Style Confections Pty Ltd v Microbyte Investments Pty Ltd* [1995] 2 VR 457, 462 Hayne J commented that the *Ince Hall* case 'may well be said' to be inconsistent with *Lee & Chapman's Case*, but without deciding the point.

[183] Wood, *English and International Set-off* (1989) 331, 337.

[184] See in particular (1885) 30 Ch D 216, 222, *per* Brett MR, 224, *per* Cotton LJ, referring to the Bankruptcy Act 1869, s 39.

[185] See para 13.40 above.

set-off that a person indebted to a bankrupt or a company in liquidation should be precluded from employing the debt in a set-off merely because that person in any event had received full consideration from the bankrupt or the company. This is apparent from cases in which goods were delivered by a vendor to a purchaser on credit terms before the vendor became bankrupt, and the price was not payable until after the bankruptcy. It was held in these cases that the purchaser was entitled to a set-off against the price even though he already had the goods.[186] Indeed, in a loan the borrower receives full consideration, in the form of the money the subject of the loan, and he is not precluded by that fact from subsequently asserting the debt in a set-off.

The *Ince Hall* case concerned a contract for the sale of goods. There would be a **13.44** stronger case in bankruptcy than in company liquidation for arguing that performance by the trustee of a prior contract for the sale of goods should not result in a set-off, given that the bankrupt's assets vest in the trustee. The trustee accordingly uses his own property to perform the contract. This would not assist with the *Ince Hall* case itself, since a company liquidation was in issue, and a liquidation does not result in a *cessio bonorum* in favour of the liquidator.[187] But even in a bankruptcy, the fact that the property had vested in the trustee should not affect the position. Performance still takes place pursuant to a contract made with the bankrupt before the bankruptcy.[188] It should not matter whether the trustee uses his own property, or indeed anyone else's, in order to perform the contract. The debt still arises out of the bankrupt's contract, which constitutes a dealing for the purpose of the insolvency set-off section. If on the other hand goods were delivered pursuant to a new contract made with the trustee after the bankruptcy, a set-off would not be available.[189]

Receivership

The *Ince Hall* case also produces a different result to that which obtains in a re- **13.45** ceivership, as a consequence of the decision of the Court of Appeal in *Rother Iron Works Ltd v Canterbury Precision Engineers Ltd.*[190] Apart from the fact that *Ince Hall v The Douglas Forge Co* concerned a liquidation and *Rother Iron Works v Canterbury Precision Engineers* a receivership, the similarity between the cases is striking. In both cases a company had contracted to sell goods to a person who was

---

[186] *Smith v Hodson* (1791) 4 TR 211, 100 ER 979; *Groom v West* (1838) 8 Ad & E 758, 112 ER 1025 (in which it was specifically argued, unsuccessfully, that a set-off should be denied because the purchaser already had the goods); *Gibson v Bell* (1835) 1 Bing (NC) 743, 131 ER 1303; *Russell v Bell* (1841) 8 M & W 277, 151 ER 1042.

[187] See para 13.05 above.

[188] Compare Lindley LJ's explanation of the *Ince Hall* case in *Mersey Steel and Iron Co v Naylor, Benzon & Co* (1882) 9 QBD 648, 669, CA. See below.

[189] Compare *Re Henley, Thurgood & Co* (1883) 11 WR 1021.

[190] [1974] 1 QB 1. See para 17.78 below.

a creditor on another transaction. The purchaser became indebted for the price when the goods were delivered, which in each case occurred after the relevant event (liquidation in the *Ince Hall* case, and receivership in the *Rother Iron Works* case). Yet, while a set-off was denied in *Ince Hall v The Douglas Forge Co*, the purchaser in *Rother Iron Works v Canterbury Precision Engineers* was permitted to set off the debt for the price against a prior cross-debt owing by the company. Russell LJ in *Rother Iron Works v Canterbury Precision Engineers* referred to the *Ince Hall* case, but distinguished it on the ground that the liquidation of a company produces a vital change in the status of the company and does not operate only as an equitable assignment by way of charge. It undoubtedly is true that liquidation and receivership are different, and it is also true that different set-off rules apply in each case,[191] but there is nevertheless some similarity between them. When the floating charge crystallized in the *Rother Iron Works* case, the goods which were later sold became subject to a fixed charge in favour of the secured creditor, and were set aside to satisfy the debt owing to the creditor. Similarly a winding up under English law divests the company of the beneficial title to its assets, which are collected and applied in the first instance for the benefit of creditors in discharge of the company's debts.[192] In both cases, then, the company was not the full beneficial owner of the goods delivered, and in that respect they are similar. There are indeed indications that Russell LJ was not comfortable with the decision in the *Ince Hall* case. In response to the argument that the allowance of a set-off in the *Rother Iron Works* case would produce an illogical distinction between liquidation and receivership, his Lordship remarked that he was 'not satisfied that the *Ince Hall* case does necessarily show such an illogical distinction',[193] which is not a particularly confident assertion as to the differences between the two cases. Moreover, as an alternative basis for distinguishing the earlier case, he referred to a statement by Lindley LJ in *Mersey Steel and Iron Co v Naylor, Benzon & Co*[194] to the effect that *Ince Hall* was a case where the liquidator, after the winding up had commenced, entered into a new contract. In fact this is not a proper interpretation of the *Ince Hall* case, because Watkin Williams J in that case proceeded on the basis that the goods were supplied after the liquidation in execution of a contract entered into by the company before then.[195]

---

[191] As Templeman J noted in *Business Computers Ltd v Anglo-African Leasing Ltd* [1977] 1 WLR 578, 585. The insolvency set-off section applies in a liquidation, whereas in receivership rights of set-off are governed by the Statutes of Set-off and the principles of equitable set-off.

[192] *Ayerst v C & K (Construction) Ltd* [1976] AC 167. Compare Australia, where the position is uncertain. See para 13.06 above.

[193] [1974] 1 QB 1, 5 (emphasis added).

[194] (1882) 9 QBD 648, 669.

[195] See the question framed by Watkin Williams J in the opening paragraph of his judgment at (1882) 8 QBD 179.

Assignment of future business receipts

There is a line of cases which, it has been suggested,[196] is consistent with the deci-   **13.46**
sion in the *Ince Hall* case. The cases established the principle that an assignment
by a trader of the future receipts of his business is, as regards receipts which accrue
after the commencement of his bankruptcy, inoperative as against the title of the
trustee in bankruptcy.[197] The basis of the principle, as explained by Lord Esher
MR in *Re Davis & Co, ex p Rawlings*,[198] is that the payments 'would only arise in
case the business of the bankrupts should be carried on, and in case, by reason of
its being carried on, payments should be made to the person who was carrying it
on. If the business was being carried on by the trustee the payments would never
become due to the bankrupts, they would become due to the trustee'. Since
payments arising from the carrying on of the business after bankruptcy do not become due to the bankrupt, they cannot be assigned by him before the bankruptcy
so as to defeat the trustee's title. The earnings received as a result of the trustee
operating the business after the bankruptcy are regarded as the earnings of the
trustee, not the bankrupt.[199]

The trustee's title to receipts is readily apparent when the trustee in carrying on the   **13.47**
business enters into new contracts,[200] and it is clear that sums payable under those
contracts could not be set off in the bankruptcy against debts owing by the bankrupt. But what if the trustee simply performs a contract made with the bankrupt
himself prior to the bankruptcy? The courts have accepted that the principle still
applies in that circumstance.[201] The contract receipts are regarded as having been
earned by the trustee in carrying out the contract. However set-off raises different
issues.[202] The receipts still arise out of the bankrupt's contract, and an action to

---

[196] See Wood, *English and International Set-off* (1989) 326, 334–6.

[197] *Ex parte Nichols, re Jones* (1883) 22 Ch D 782; *Wilmot v Alton* [1897] 1 QB 17; *Re Irvine*
[1919] NZLR 351; *Re Collins* [1925] Ch 556. Compare *Drew & Co v Josolyne* (1887) 18 QBD 590,
Official Assignee of Palmer v Sharpe [1921] NZLR 460 and *Re Tout and Finch Ltd* [1954] 1 WLR
178, in which the debt assigned represented retention moneys already earned but not yet payable at
the date of the bankruptcy or liquidation. Similarly, in *Re Davis & Co, ex p Rawlings* (1888) 22 QBD
193 and *Ex parte Moss, re Toward* (1884) 14 QBD 310 the debt assigned was in existence at the date
of the bankruptcy although not payable until a future date, and so the title of the assignee took
precedence over that of the trustee in bankruptcy.

[198] (1888) 22 QBD 193, 198. See also *Ex parte Nicholls, re Jones* (1883) 22 Ch D 782, 785–786,
per Jessel MR; *Re Green* [1979] 1 WLR 1211, 1220–1221.

[199] *Re Green* [1979] 1 WLR 1211, 1223–1224; *Official Assignee of Palmer v Sharpe* [1921] NZLR
460, 462.

[200] See eg *Ex parte Moss, re Toward* (1884) 14 QBD D 310, 316–317.

[201] *Wilmot v Alton* [1897] 1 QB 17; *Re Collins* [1925] 1 Ch 556. The principle does not apply,
however, where the bankrupt had wholly executed his part of the contract before the bankruptcy, so
that nothing by way of further performance was required of him. See *Wilmot v Alton* at 22–23, *per*
Rigby LJ; *Re Trytel* [1952] 2 TLR 32.

[202] A security granted by a company over its present and future assets does not catch a right to recover a preferential payment, a proposition that was referred to earlier as indicating a lack of mutuality in equity in relation to the right of recovery and a debt owing by the company to the preferred

enforce payment would be based on that contract. This is critical for insolvency set-off, which is not concerned with the identity of the person to whom the money is to be paid but rather with cross-demands originating from mutual credits, mutual debts or other mutual dealings.[203] A debt which accrues after a bankruptcy, but which relates to a prior contract with the bankrupt, arises out of a prior dealing with the bankrupt, and prior mutual dealings give rise to an 'equity' pursuant to the insolvency set-off section to which the bankrupts' trustee takes subject. As Dixon J expressed the principle in the Australian High Court in *Hiley v Peoples Prudential Assurance Co*:[204] 'If the end contemplated by the transaction is a claim sounding in money . . . *no more is required* than that at the commencement of the winding up liabilities shall have been contracted by the company and the other party respectively from which cross money claims accrue during the course of the winding up.'

13.48 The view that the cases concerning assignments of business receipts do not impact upon rights of set-off is also suggested by *Lee & Chapman's Case*.[205] In that case a set-off was allowed in the liquidation of a company in respect of a claim that accrued after the commencement of the liquidation but pursuant to a prior contract, as a result of the liquidator carrying on the company's business. Lindley LJ was one of the judges in the Court of Appeal in that case. Two years earlier he was also one of the judges in the Court of Appeal in *Ex parte Nichols*[206] who accepted the principle precluding an assignment of future receipts after bankruptcy, and yet

---

creditor. See paras 13.08 and 13.16 above. That situation differs, however, from the principle applicable in the case of business receipts after bankruptcy. In the case of a preference, the statutory right to recover is given for the benefit of the general body of creditors, and not for the benefit of the company itself. See *Re M C Bacon Ltd* [1991] Ch 127, 137, *per* Millett J. On the other hand, when a bankrupt prior to the bankruptcy entered into a contract which produces business receipts after bankruptcy, the bankrupt would have entered into it for his own benefit. Further, a right to recover a preference in its nature is such that it cannot be charged. Business receipts on the other hand are capable of being charged; it is only in the situation in which the trader becomes bankrupt that the charge is ineffective as against the title of the trustee in bankruptcy.

[203] See also the cases in which a claim in favour of a bankrupt's estate which was contingent at the date of the bankruptcy but which subsequently vested was held to give rise to a set-off. See paras 8.28–8.37 above.

[204] (1938) 60 CLR 468, 497 (emphasis added), referred to with approval in *Re Charge Card Services Ltd* [1987] 1 Ch 150, 178, *per* Millett J and *Gye v McIntyre* (1991) 171 CLR 609, 624. In *Old Style Confections Pty Ltd v Microbyte Investments Pty Ltd* [1995] 2 VR 457, 463 Hayne J said that, 'the mere fact that performance of the contract made before liquidation may not take place until after liquidation does not determine whether the debt due under that contract may be set-off against other dealings with the company'.

[205] *Re Asphaltic Wood Pavement Co. Lee & Chapman's Case* (1885) 30 Ch D 216, referred to with evident approval in *Hiley v The Peoples Prudential Assurance Co Ltd* (1938) 60 CLR 468, 497–498, *per* Dixon J. See also *Clarke v Fell* (1833) 4 B & Ad 404, 110 ER 507, in which the bankrupt completed the repairs to the carriage after the bankruptcy, and the tenor of the judgments suggests that a set-off would have been allowed to the owner of the carriage against the cost of the repairs but for the agreement to pay in ready money.

[206] *Ex parte Nichols, re Jones* (1883) 22 Ch D 782.

he apparently did not regard that case as deserving mention when, along with Brett MR and Cotton LJ, he upheld the claim for a set-off in *Lee & Chapman's Case*. Further, when the Court of Appeal in *Wilmot v Alton*[207] subsequently followed *Ex parte Nichols*, Brett MR, who by then was Lord Esher MR, did not consider it necessary to explain his earlier judgment in *Lee & Chapman's Case*. This suggests that the principle was not regarded as relevant to set-off.

A possible explanation for *Lee & Chapman's Case* is that the assignment principle **13.49** does not apply in the case of a company liquidation,[208] although it has been assumed otherwise.[209] In *Re Green*[210] Walton J explained the principle on the ground that, in a bankruptcy, the business and its profit-making apparatus vest in the trustee,[211] so that when profits from carrying on the business arise they are profits of a business vested in the trustee. In a company liquidation, on the other hand, the assets of the company ordinarily do not vest in the liquidator.[212] But distinguishing *Lee & Chapman's Case* on that basis would not assist in explaining *Ince Hall v The Douglas Forge Co*, since that case was also concerned with a company liquidation.

In any event, set-off and the principle which impacts upon an assignment of busi- **13.50** ness receipts after bankruptcy attract different considerations. In the latter case, when a person in the course of his business enters into a contract which requires him to perform obligations in the future, and the person becomes bankrupt before the obligations have been performed, the trustee in bankruptcy, if he regards it as being for the benefit of the estate, may carry on the business and perform the contract. But the trustee is not obliged to do so. He could instead decide not to have anything to do with the contract, in which case nothing would be payable under it, including to an assignee of business receipts. If on the other hand the trustee elects to go on with the contract, he would do so for the benefit of the estate, and any moneys when they become due would belong to the estate.[213] The assignee once again would not receive anything, so that the assignee is put in the same position in the event that the contract is performed that he would have been

---

[207] [1897] 1 QB 17.

[208] *Lee & Chapman's Case* itself lends support to that view. Ninety per cent of the earnings under the contract in that case had been charged to a third party, so that the set-off only related to the ten per cent to which the company itself remained entitled. Not only was the set-off upheld, but the charge was also regarded as effective notwithstanding that the contract was completed after liquidation.

[209] See Wynn-Parry J in *Re Tout and Finch Ltd* [1954] 1 WLR 178, 186–89 (although in the circumstances the assignment principle was held not to apply because the retention moneys had been earned before the liquidation, notwithstanding that they were not payable until later), and also Goode *Principles of Corporate Insolvency Law* (2nd edn, 1997) 133–4.

[210] [1979] 1 WLR 1211, 1220–1221, 1224.

[211] Thus Walton J held in *Re Green* that the principle does not apply to an assignment of the future personal earnings of the bankrupt.

[212] See para 13.05 above.

[213] *Wilmot v Alton* [1897] 1 QB 17, 20–21, *per* Lord Esher MR, 23, *per* Rigby LJ.

in if the trustee had decided not to perform the contract. This would not be the consequence in relation to set-off, however, if the rule were that the other contracting party is denied a set-off in relation to sums payable to the trustee through performance of the contract. This is because, if the trustee had elected not to perform, the other contracting party in that circumstance would have had a provable claim in the bankruptcy for any damage suffered consequent upon the bankrupt's breach of contract, and that claim could have been employed in a set-off.[214] There is another point. If a trustee elects to carry on the business after the bankruptcy for the benefit of the estate, but business receipts after the bankruptcy went to a prior assignee, the estate would not benefit from the performance. A set-off on the other hand would not have that result. If a set-off were allowed it would not be a case of the estate obtaining no benefit from the contract. The contract sum would still enure to the benefit of he estate, although not by way of a cash payment. Rather, payment would be effected by a set-off against a debt which otherwise would have been provable in competition with the other creditors.[215]

The relevance of the time that property passed

13.51   In the case of a contract for the sale of land or goods where the seller has become insolvent prior to completion, Philip Wood has suggested that the availability of set-off depends upon whether the beneficial ownership of the property in question passed prior to the insolvency date. [216] A set-off may be available if the beneficial ownership has passed, and conversely it is said that a set-off is denied if it has not passed. As authority for the latter proposition, reference is made to the *Ince Hall* case. However set-off is not concerned with property rights as such, but rather with money claims arising from the giving of credit or from prior dealings between the parties. The time of passing of the beneficial interest should only be incidentally relevant, in the sense that it can affect the parties' remedies. If the beneficial ownership has already passed, the vendor's trustee or liquidator could not disclaim the contract.[217] Furthermore, the court ordinarily would order specific performance of the contract on the application of the purchaser, on terms that he pay the balance of the price after deducting a debt owing to him by the insolvent vendor.[218] If on the other hand the beneficial ownership has not passed, the contract may be able to be disclaimed as an unprofitable contract,[219] in which case it

---

[214]   See para 13.30 above.

[215]   See the comments of Hayne J (in a different context) in *Old Style Confections Pty Ltd v Microbyte Investments Pty Ltd* [1995] 2 VR 457, 466.

[216]   Compare Wood, *English and International Set-off* (1989) 327–36.

[217]   *Re Bastable, ex p The Trustee* [1901] 2 KB 518.

[218]   *Re Taylor, ex p Norvell* [1910] 1 KB 562. See para 13.33 above.

[219]   *Quaere* whether, in the determination of whether a contract is unprofitable, a trustee in bankruptcy or liquidator may take into account the effect of any set-off that may be available to the other party, or whether regard may be had only to whether the contract itself is a bad bargain. In *Old Style Confections Pty Ltd v Microbyte Investments Pty Ltd* [1995] 2 VR 457, 466 Hayne J considered that

could not be specifically enforced.[220] The purchaser would then be left to his remedy in damages, which in turn should be able to be the subject of a set-off.[221] But if in a case such as *Ince Hall v The Douglas Forge Co* the contract is performed, the availability of a set-off should not be confined to the situation in which the beneficial ownership of the property in question passed to the purchaser prior to the vendor's bankruptcy or liquidation.

(3) Contract to Sell Property to or to Perform Work for an Insolvent

The converse of the situation considered above is that the purchaser (as opposed **13.52** to the seller) of property to be delivered or of work to be performed becomes bankrupt or goes into liquidation before completion of the contract. Once again, if the contract is disclaimed a resulting damages claim would be provable,[222] and it should also be capable of being employed in a set-off.[223] Consider however that the contract remains on foot. In the first place, questions of set-off are unlikely to arise in this situation because, in the case of a contract to sell goods, if the purchaser has become insolvent the vendor is entitled to insist that the price be tendered to him before delivery, even if the sale was otherwise expressed to be on credit terms.[224] A similar principle would appear to apply to contracts for the performance of work.[225] But if in a particular case the goods are delivered without payment having first been received, or the work is performed without the price having first been secured, for reasons similar to those given above in criticizing the decision in the *Ince Hall* case[226] the resulting debt should be able to be employed in a set-off,[227] given that it resulted from a prior contract and it would be provable in the bankruptcy or the liquidation.

(4) Options

The preceding discussion concerned the situation in which there is an uncondi- **13.53** tional contract for the sale of goods or for the performance of work, and bankruptcy or liquidation intervenes before the contract has been performed. Alternatively, a creditor may have an option to purchase the debtor's property, and upon exercise of the option the creditor may wish to set off the resulting debt for

---

the availability of a set-off against contract payments is not a relevant consideration. Note that in Australia a liquidator or trustee can disclaim any contract, though if it is not an unprofitable contract the leave of the court is required. See the Bankruptcy Act 1966 (Cth), ss 133(1A) and 133(5A), and the Corporations Act 2001 (Cth), ss 568(1)(f) and 568(1A).

[220] See Jones and Goodhart, *Specific Performance* (2nd edn, 1996) 221.
[221] See paras 13.30–13.31 above.
[222] See the Insolvency Act 1986, ss 178(6) & 315(5).
[223] See paras 13.30–13.31 above.
[224] *Ex parte Chalmers* (1873) LR 8 Ch App 289; Sale of Goods Act 1979, s 41(1)(c).
[225] *Re Sneezum, ex p Davies* (1876) 3 Ch D 463, 473–474.
[226] (1882) 8 QBD 179. See paras 13.35–13.51 above.
[227] Compare Wood, *English and International Set-off* (1989) 308–9.

the price against the debt owing to him by the debtor. If the option is exercised before the debtor becomes bankrupt or goes into liquidation there should not be any difficulty. The debt for the price should be capable of giving rise to a set-off against the debt due to the creditor.[228] Consider however that the option is not exercised until after the debtor's bankruptcy or liquidation. For the reasons given above in the context of the discussion of the *Ince Hall* case,[229] the fact that the property sold pursuant to the option otherwise would have been available for distribution amongst creditors should not affect the question of mutuality. Nor should the creditor be denied a set-off simply because he will have received full consideration for the debt for the price, in the form of the property the subject of the option.[230] There is nevertheless authority for the proposition that the creditor on exercising the option must pay the price without a set-off against the separate debt owing by the debtor.

13.54 In *Re Kidsgrove Steel, Iron, and Coal Co*[231] the owner of a colliery and iron works leased them to a company, the lease giving the owner the option, after the end or determination of the lease, of purchasing at a valuation all plant and fixtures that might be erected by the company as lessee. The company went into liquidation, after which the lease was determined. The owner thereupon exercised the option to purchase the plant and fixtures erected on the premises. Chitty J held that the resulting debt for the price could not be the subject of a set-off, since the contract to purchase was not in existence at the date of the liquidation. He said that the contract only arose subsequently, when the option was exercised. Recently the New Zealand Court of Appeal in *Paganini v The Official Assignee*[232] also held against a set-off in similar circumstances, although without referring to *Re Kidsgrove*. The Court of Appeal justified its decision on a number of grounds, but the principal ground was that, since the option was not exercised until after the liquidation of the debtor/vendor, there was not at the date of the liquidation a debt owing to the debtor for the price and nor had the parties at that date engaged in mutual dealings.[233]

---

[228] See eg *Shirlaw v Lewis* (1993) 10 ACSR 288, in which the purchase of goods and stock in trade pursuant to the prior agreement occurred after the winding-up summons was filed but before the winding-up order, when the vendor of the business re-took possession, and Hodgson J accepted that it could be the subject of a set-off.

[229] (1882) 8 QBD 179. See paras 13.35–13.51 above.

[230] See para 13.43 above.

[231] (1894) 38 Sol Jo 252.

[232] CA308/98, Gault, Thomas and Keith JJ, 22 March 1999, affirming *Paganini v Official Assignee* (1999) 8 NZCLC 261, 811. See also *Re Proudfoot* [1961] NZLR 268, 282, referred to in the Court of Appeal in *Paginini* at para 12. To the extent that reliance was placed in *Proudfoot* (at 282) and *Paginini* (para 12) on *Re A Debtor (No 66 of 1955)* [1956] 1 WLR 1226, that case is of doubtful authority. See para 8.15 *ff* above. For a discussion of the *Paginini* case, see Taylor, 'The Year in Review—New Zealand Insolvency Law in 1999' [1999] Insolvency Law Journal 212.

[233] See para 13 of the judgment. In addition, Keith J in delivering the judgment of the Court of Appeal referred (at paras 13–17) to the requirement of mutuality. The essence of the argument was

The New Zealand Court of Appeal treated the exercise of the option as the rele-   **13.55**
vant dealing, which occurred after the liquidation. An alternative view is that the
dealing was the entry before the liquidation into the contract containing the option. The creditor in exercising the option was simply pursuing rights conferred
by the earlier contract, and the exercise of the option itself did not involve a new
and independent transaction. In Australia, Dixon J employed similar language in
allowing a set-off in *Hiley v Peoples Prudential Assurance Co Ltd.*[234] In the *Paganini*
case the exercise of the option seems to have been regarded as a separate transaction or dealing, notwithstanding that it had its source in an earlier contract. That
view also seems to have informed Chitty J's reason for refusing a set-off in *Re
Kidsgrove*, that the contract to purchase arose after the date of the liquidation. An
option is sometimes described as an irrevocable offer,[235] and on that basis the exercise of the option could be characterized as a new contract. But that view is not
universally accepted. There is a competing view, that an option is a conditional
contract,[236] and on that analysis the contract would be formed before the debtor's
bankruptcy or liquidation. Indeed the grant of an option itself is regarded as giving rise to an interest in the property the subject of the option,[237] which militates
against the view that the subsequent exercise of the option constitutes a new or
independent transaction or dealing.

It may be sought to justify the decisions in the *Kidsgrove* and *Paganini* cases on the   **13.56**
basis of a perceived policy consideration, that it should not be open to a creditor
who holds an option over the debtor's property to improve his position at the expense of the other creditors, by choosing to exercise the option after the debtor's

---

that that the debt for the price arose after the liquidation, when the company no longer had the beneficial interest in its property. But if the relevant dealing were characterized as the entry into the
agreement which gave rise to the option as opposed to the exercise of the option (see below), there
would have been mutuality since the dealing was entered into before the liquidation. The Court of
Appeal also considered that policy considerations supported its conclusion. See below. At first instance ((1999) 8 NZCLC 261, 811) Robertson J relied on the decision of Richmond J in *Felt and
Textiles of New Zealand Ltd v R Hubrich Ltd* [1968] NZLR 716. *Felt and Textiles* however was concerned with set-off under the Statutes of Set-off in the context of a receivership, as opposed to set-
off in company liquidation. See para 17.81 below. The Statutes of Set-off were confined to mutual
debts. They did not extend to debts arising out of mutual dealings, and in the case of an option the
relevant dealing may be characterized as the entry into the option itself.

[234] (1938) 60 CLR 468, 499. See also Rich J at 487. In *M S Fashions Ltd v Bank of Credit and
Commerce International SA* [1993] Ch 425, 446 Dillon LJ (with whom Nolan and Steyn LJJ agreed)
referred to the *Hiley* case with evident approval.

[235] *Helby v Mathews* [1895] AC 471, 477, *per* Lord Herschell LC, 479–480, *per* Lord Watson.

[236] *Griffith v Pelton* [1958] 1 Ch 205, 225; *Laybutt v Amoco Australia Pty Ltd* (1974) 132 CLR
57, 75–76. In *Spiro v Glencrown Properties Ltd* [1991] Ch 537, 544 Hoffmann J (as he then was) rejected the view that an option strictly speaking is either an offer or a conditional contract, and suggested instead that it is a relationship *sui generis*.

[237] *London v South Western Railway Co v Gomm* (1881) 30 Ch D 562, 581, *per* Sir George Jessel
MR; *Spiro v Glencrown Properties Ltd* [1991] Ch 537, 543. In Australia see *Laybutt v Amoco
Australia Pty Ltd* (1974) 132 CLR 57, 75–76, and generally Farrands, *The Law of Options* (1992) 26
et seq.

bankruptcy or liquidation and then setting off the debt for the price against a debt in respect of which the creditor otherwise would only have received a dividend. The creditor has the choice whether to purchase the property the subject of the option, and that choice available to the option-holder distinguishes this situation from the *Ince Hall* case, which is criticized above.[238] In that case, it was the vendor's liquidator, rather than the purchaser, who decided to complete the contract. In truth, however, when one considers this perceived policy consideration, it does not provide a compelling reason for denying a set-off. In the first place, if the sale pursuant to the option would be unprofitable for the vendor, the vendor's trustee in bankruptcy or liquidator could disclaim the contract. More importantly, there is no general principle which precludes a creditor from acting in order to bring about a situation in which a set-off would be available in the debtor's bankruptcy or liquidation, save to the extent that the qualification to the set-off section may apply.[239] Consider in that regard *Re The Moseley Green Coal and Coke Co Ltd, Barrett's Case.*[240] A debt the subject of a guarantee was secured by a promissory note given by the debtor to the creditor. After the debtor had been ordered to be wound up the surety's sister paid the creditor, and the promissory note was indorsed and delivered to her. Subsequently the sister agreed to hand over the promissory note to the surety in exchange for his own promissory note. Lord Westbury held that the surety could bring the claim on the promissory note into an account with a debt that he owed to the debtor, since his acquisition of the promissory note related to the prior obligation that he had assumed as surety. It appears however that the sister was not pressing the surety for payment, and that the arrangement was entered into with the sister at the suggestion of the surety's own legal advisers for the specific purpose of obtaining a set-off for the surety.[241] Consider also *Re Inglis, ex p The Trustee,*[242] a decision of Paine J in the South Australian Insolvency Court. A debtor delivered wheat to the creditor for storage on terms that the creditor had the option of either purchasing the wheat at market price or delivering to the debtor or to his order wheat of the same quality. The debtor became bankrupt after delivering the wheat but before an election was made. Paine J accepted that the creditor could choose to purchase the wheat at market price and thereby obtain a set-off against the resulting debt.

13.57   *Lee & Chapman's Case*[243] is also relevant. The contract in that case provided that the Commissioners of Sewers could give a notice to the company requiring it to keep the road in repair for a period of fifteen years at a stated price. The notice was

---

[238] See paras 13.36–13.51 above.
[239] See paras 6.49–6.64 above.
[240] (1865) 4 De G J & S 756, 46 ER 1116, 34 LJ Bcy 41.
[241] See the statement of the facts at (1865) 34 LJ Bcy 41, 42.
[242] (1932) 5 ABC 255.
[243] *Re Asphaltic Wood Pavement Co. Lee & Chapman's Case* (1885) 30 Ch D 216. See para 13.41 above.

given after the company's liquidation, and it was the company's resulting liability for damages to the Commissioners for anticipatory breach of contract in relation to that obligation that was the subject of the set-off. The set-off was allowed notwithstanding that it was the result of the exercise of an option after liquidation. The circumstances admittedly differed from those in the *Kidsgrove* and *Paganini* cases. In *Lee & Chapman's Case* the party exercising the option was a debtor of the company, and it was the claim against the company resulting from the exercise of the option (for damages, for failure to carry out the repair obligation) that was set off against the debt owing to the company. In the *Kidsgrove* and *Paganini* cases on the other hand the option-holder was a creditor. The creditor incurred a liability for the price as a result of exercising the option, and sought to set off that liability against a debt that otherwise would only have yielded a dividend. *Lee & Chapman's Case* nevertheless suggests that it is not fatal to a set-off that it is based upon the exercise of an option by the party asserting a set-off after the bankruptcy or liquidation of the other party.

D. Leases

(1) Bankruptcy

Bankruptcy does not result in a vesting of the bankrupt's contracts in his trustee, **13.58** but rather a vesting of the bankrupt's rights under the contracts. The contract is still the contract of the bankrupt. Any action by the bankrupt's trustee to obtain a benefit which has accrued under the contract prior to the bankruptcy would be an action on the original contract. Similarly, if the trustee decides to carry on the contract after the bankruptcy for the benefit of the estate, then, apart from the possible statutory novation which may be brought about by serving a notice under the Insolvency Act 1986, section 316,[244] any rights subsequently obtained or obligations subsequently incurred would still relate to the bankrupt's contract, and any action by or against the estate would be based upon the privity that the bankrupt himself has in the contract. Mutuality therefore should still be present in relation to the claim and a cross-debt arising pursuant to a prior independent dealing between the bankrupt and the other contracting party.[245] A different analysis applies however when the relationship between the bankrupt and the other party was that of landlord and tenant. Any rights possessed or liabilities incurred by the bankrupt pursuant to a lease of real property prior to the bankruptcy ordinarily would be capable of giving rise to a set-off.[246] On the other hand, the bankrupt's interest in the lease vests in the trustee in bankruptcy immediately

---

[244] See para 13.30 above.
[245] See para 11.01 above.
[246] See eg *Ex parte Hope, re Hanson* (1858) 3 De G & J 92, 44 ER 1203, in which a set-off was allowed against rent overdue before the tenants' bankruptcy.

upon the trustee's appointment taking effect,[247] and the trustee himself becomes the landlord or the tenant, as the case may be. The trustee may disclaim the interest under the Insolvency Act, section 315 as onerous property, in which case the trustee is relieved from personal liability for breach of the terms of the lease as from the commencement of his trusteeship.[248] If on the other hand the trustee fails to disclaim, any rights or liabilities subsequently obtained or incurred by the trustee under covenants annexed to the land[249] accrue in his own right as trustee, *as the landlord or tenant*. This includes, in the case of the landlord, the right to payment of rent. Privity of estate, as opposed to privity of contract, enables the trustee and the other party to enforce *inter se* their rights under the covenants.[250]

Mutuality

13.59 When the property of a bankrupt vests in his trustee, so that in the case of a lease the trustee himself becomes the landlord or the tenant, as the case may be, there is a lack of mutuality between any right accruing to, or any liability incurred by, the trustee in his own right as trustee under a covenant annexed to the land, and an independent cross-demand between the bankrupt and the other party to the claim on the covenant.[251] This is consistent with the principle that, unlike an assignee of a chose in action who sues under the assignor's privity of contract, an assignee of an estate or interest in land who sues does not take subject to personal defences that the defendant would have had against the assignor.[252] For example, in *Alloway v Steere*[253] a debtor was the tenant of a farm. There was a local custom by which the person who was the tenant of farmland was entitled at the expiration of the tenancy to an allowance for any tillages and cultivation. During the currency of

---

[247] Insolvency Act 1986, s 306.

[248] See the Insolvency Act 1986, s 315(3), and in Australia the Bankruptcy Act 1966 (Cth), s 133(2).

[249] See the Landlord and Tenant (Covenants) Act 1995, s 3.

[250] The covenants which are binding on and which accrue to the benefit of an assignee of the lease or the reversion formerly were limited to those which 'touch and concern' the land, but (subject to s 3(6)) that limitation no longer applies in relation to new tenancies under the Landlord and Tenant (Covenants) Act 1995. See s 3, and the definitions of 'landlord covenant' and 'tenant covenant' in s 28.

[251] While the trustee in bankruptcy of a tenant from the time of his appointment is liable personally on the basis of privity of estate for the payment of rent and the performance of other covenants annexed to the land, he usually would be entitled to an indemnity from the estate. See *Lowrey v Barker & Sons* (1880) 5 Ex D 170, 173, 175, and *Titterton v Cooper* (1882) 9 QBD 473, 492, but compare *Re Page Brothers, ex p Mackay* (1884) 14 QBD 401.

[252] *David v Sabin* [1893] 1 Ch 523.

[253] (1882) 10 QBD 22. See also *Ex parte Sir W Hart Dyke, re Morrish* (1882) 22 Ch D 410; *Titterton v Cooper* (1882) 9 QBD 473. Compare *Re Wilson, ex p Lord Hastings* (1893) 10 Morr 219, in which Vaughan Williams J found a custom in the county of Norfolk by which the landlord could deduct any arrears of rent, including arrears owing by the bankrupt as a previous tenant, from an allowance payable to the bankrupt's trustee for fixtures, growing crops etc left in the hands of the landlord. Apparently there is a similar custom in a number of other counties. See Williams and Muir Hunter, *The Law and Practice in Bankruptcy* (19th edn, 1979) 198 n 98.

the tenancy the debtor instituted proceedings under the Bankruptcy Act 1869 for liquidation of his affairs by arrangement or composition with his creditors, with the result that the tenancy vested in his trustee. When the trustee subsequently claimed the allowance, the landlord was not allowed to set off arrears of rent owing by the debtor from the period before the liquidation proceedings.[254] As Manisty J remarked:[255]

> The relative rights and liabilities of the landlord and the trustee appear clearly from the case of *Titterton v Cooper* ((1882) 9 QBD 473), where the whole question was fully considered. and the conclusion arrived at by the Court of Appeal was that a trustee in bankruptcy, not disclaiming, was in the position of an ordinary assignee of the lease, and as such liable for the rent, and for the performance of the covenants during the time the lease was vested in him. No one could suggest that an ordinary assignee could be made liable for breaches of covenant, or of the contract of tenancy, which occurred before the assignment to him, and the breach of contract in respect of which the landlord claims a set-off in the present case is such a breach.

Bankrupt landlord

13.60 Similarly, when the landlord in *Kitchen's Trustee v Madders*[256] became bankrupt, the tenants were not allowed to set off a damages claim against the landlord for which they had obtained judgment against their obligation to pay rent to the landlord's trustee in bankruptcy relating to the period after the trustee's appointment.[257]

13.61 The principle applied in *Kitchen's Trustee v Madders* is that the landlord's trustee is in the same position with regard to the tenant as any other assignee of the property from the landlord, and in that capacity himself becomes the landlord.[258] This principle was not applied three years later in *Bradley-Hole v Cusen*,[259] but, while the case has enjoyed the support of text-writers,[260] the decision is questionable. The rent paid by the tenant of a dwelling-house to the landlord before the landlord's bankruptcy was greater than the rent lawfully recoverable by the landlord

---

[254] Compare *Ex parte Hope, re Hanson* (1858) 3 De G & J 92, 44 ER 1203, in which the assignees in bankruptcy elected not to continue the tenancy.

[255] (1882) 10 QBD 22, 29.

[256] [1950] 1 Ch 134.

[257] See also *Graham v Allsopp* (1848) 3 Ex D 186, 154 ER 809 (in relation to the quarter's rent due after Christmas). Compare *Booth v Hutchinson* (1872) LR 15 Eq 30 in which Sir Richard Malins VC permitted a set-off in respect of rent accruing due after the date of the landlord's deed of assignment, although the question of mutuality appears not to have been considered.

[258] See the discussion of *Kitchen's Trustee* in *Old Syle Confections Pty Ltd v Microbyte Investments Pty Ltd* [1995] 2 VR 457, 463.

[259] [1953] 1 QB 300.

[260] See Megarry, *The Rent Acts* (10th edn, 1967) vol 1, 346; *Woodfall's Law of Landlord and Tenant* (looseleaf edn, 1994) vol 3, para 23.004; Hill and Redman's *Law of Landlord and Tenant* (17th edn, 1982) vol 1, 988; *Halsbury's Laws of England* (4th edn (reissue), 1994) vol 27(1), 722 para 752 n 4. The decision was also referred to without adverse comment in *Mulvey v Secretary of State for Social Security* [1997] UKHL 10.

under the Rent Restriction Acts. The legislation conferred upon the tenant the right to recover the overpayment from the landlord who received it, or to deduct it from rent payable by him to the landlord.[261] The issue was whether the deduction could be made from rent payable to the landlord's trustee for the period after the bankruptcy. Jenkins LJ delivered the judgment of the Court of Appeal. He was prepared to assume, although without finally deciding the point, that the deduction could not have been made from rent payable to an ordinary assignee of the landlord. He referred however to *Bendall v McWhirter*,[262] in which Somervell and Romer LJJ held that a deserted wife had a personal licence to remain in occupation of the matrimonial home owned by the husband, and also that the husband's trustee in bankruptcy was no more entitled to revoke this licence than was the husband himself.[263] Jenkins LJ concluded from that decision that a trustee in bankruptcy must be something other than an ordinary assignee, because an ordinary assignee of the husband's property would not have taken subject to the husband's personal obligations. By analogy, he thought that a landlord's trustee should take subject to the tenant's right of deduction in the case before him. Subsequently the House of Lords in *National Provincial Bank Ltd v Ainsworth*[264] overruled *Bendall v McWhirter*, and in doing so rejected the notion that *Bendall v McWhirter* could be supported on the ground that a trustee in bankruptcy is in any special position,[265] or that a distinction could be drawn between trustees in bankruptcy on the one hand and purchasers and mortgagees on the other.[266] As Lord Upjohn remarked, 'a trustee in bankruptcy succeeds only to the property of the bankrupt in its then plight and condition and is not concerned with personal rights that do not affect that property'.[267] That effectively rejects the reasoning employed by Jenkins LJ, and so the decision in *Bradley-Hole v Cusen* could only be correct if the deduction could have been made against an ordinary assignee of the landlord. While Lord Wilberforce in the *Ainsworth* case was prepared to accept that the *Cusen* case was correctly decided,[268] Jenkins LJ in that case would seem to have been correct in his assumption that an ordinary assignee would not have been so bound, which brings into question the basis for making the deduction from rent payable to the trustee. The definition of 'landlord' in the Rent Restriction Acts,[269] as including any person deriving title under the original land-

---

[261] The relevant provision was the Increase of Rent and Mortgage Interest (Restrictions) Act 1920, s 14(1), which was in similar terms to the Rent Act 1977, ss 57(1) and (2).

[262] [1952] 2 QB 466.

[263] Lord Denning went further, and said that the deserted wife had an equity which was binding not only on the husband's trustee but also on third parties generally.

[264] [1965] AC 1175.

[265] See Lord Hodson at 1226.

[266] See Lord Wilberforce at 1256.

[267] [1965] AC 1175, 1240.

[268] [1965] AC 1175, 1258.

[269] See now the Rent Act 1977, s 152.

lord, is expressed not to apply when the context requires otherwise. The stipulation in the legislation that the tenant may recover the overpayment from the
landlord who received it[270] would seem to indicate that 'landlord' indeed is used
in a narrower sense in this context,[271] because a person who derived his title from
the landlord who received the money himself would not be the landlord who
received it.

It has been suggested that *Bradley-Hole v Cusen* in truth is an example of an equit- **13.62**
able set-off, and that on that basis it was correctly decided.[272] There are two difficulties with that view, however. The first is that equitable set-off was not
mentioned in the judgment. The second is that the demands in any event do not
appear to have been sufficiently closely connected to give rise to an equitable set-
off.[273] Given that a trustee in bankruptcy is in the same position as any other assignee of the reversion, a claim for rent by an assignee in relation to a period after
the assignment would not be impeached, for the purpose of an equitable set-off,[274]
by the tenant's claim for an overpayment to the original landlord. Moreover,
applying the formulation approved by the House of Lords in *Bank of Boston
Connecticut v European Grain and Shipping Ltd,*[275] the cross-claim could not be
said to have arisen out of the same transaction as the trustee's claim for rent due to
him in his capacity as assignee of the reversion.

(2) Company Liquidation

In a company liquidation, the company's interest in a leasehold property does not **13.63**
vest in the liquidator.[276] If the lease is not disclaimed or otherwise terminated, the
company itself remains as the landlord or the tenant, as the case may be, and the
concept of privity of estate applicable to trustees in bankruptcy does not apply.[277]
Therefore, when the company is the tenant, the landlord cannot proceed against
the liquidator personally for payment of rent. The landlord may be entitled to be
paid in full for rent which has accrued after liquidation as an expense incurred in
the winding up, if the liquidator has retained possession for the convenience of the

---

[270] Recovery could also be had from the landlord's personal representative. A personal representative ordinarily means an executor or an administrator (see *Re Best's Settlement Trusts* (1874) LR 18
Eq 686, 691), as opposed to a trustee in bankruptcy.

[271] See *Murray v Webb* (1925) 59 Ir LT 41.

[272] Wood, *English and International Set-off* (1989) 343. Wood uses 'transaction set-off' as a
generic term encompassing both equitable set-off and common law abatement.

[273] See *Reeves v Pope* [1914] 2 KB 284, which is considered in paras 17.60–17.66 below. Wood's
suggestion (*English and International Set-off* (1989) 343) that *Booth v Hutchinson* (1872) LR 15 Eq
30 similarly may be explained on the basis of equitable set-off is open to the same objection.

[274] See ch 4 above.

[275] [1989] 1 AC 1056. See para 4.15 above.

[276] See para 13.05 above.

[277] *Old Style Confections Pty Ltd v Microbyte Investments Pty Ltd* [1995] 2 VR 457, 463.

winding up.[278] But if that is not the case, the landlord's only remedy is to prove in the liquidation.

Extent of the right of proof for rent

13.64 The Insolvency Rules 1986, rule 4.92[279] provides that, in the case of rent and other payments of a periodic nature, the creditor may prove for any amounts due and unpaid up to the date when the company went into liquidation and, where at that date any payment was accruing due, the creditor may prove for so much as would have fallen due at that date, if accruing from day to day.[280] This does not mean that a landlord cannot prove for rent which accrues after the liquidation.[281] The rule is permissive in its operation, not prohibitory. It was originally introduced into the bankruptcy legislation in order to give a landlord a right of proof that he did not otherwise have.[282] A provision to this effect first appeared in the Bankruptcy Act 1861.[283] Prior to that Act, a landlord could only prove in the tenant's bankruptcy for rent which had accrued due at the time of the filing of the petition for adjudication. He could not prove for a proportionate part of a payment that had as yet not accrued due. It was in order to remedy that situation that section 150 of the 1861 Act was introduced, so as to allow a right of proof for a proportionate part of rent and other periodic payments up to the date of adjudication.[284] It is now accepted that, if a lease is not disclaimed or otherwise terminated, the landlord may prove for rent which relates to the period after the bankruptcy or liquidation,[285] but there is an element of uncertainty as to the extent of the right.[286] The preferred approach is that the provisions in the Insolvency Act dealing with estimating the value of contingent and future claims also apply to a periodic obligation to pay rent, so that an estimate should be made for the purpose of proof of the landlord's loss as a result of the tenant's liquidation and subsequent dissolution.[287] There is

---

[278] *Re ABC Coupler & Engineering Co Ltd (No 3)* [1970] 1 WLR 702; *Re Downer Enterprises Ltd* [1974] 1 WLR 1460; *Re H H Realisations Ltd* (1975) 31 P & C R 249.

[279] The equivalent provision in bankruptcy is set out in the Insolvency Rules 1986, r 6.112.

[280] In Australia, see the Corporations Regulations, reg 5.6.43(1). For bankruptcy, see the Bankruptcy Act 1966 (Cth), s 96.

[281] Compare Wood, *English and International Set-off* (1989) 309, 310–11.

[282] See Cotton LJ in *Ex parte Dressler, re Solomon* (1878) 9 Ch D 252, 259 in relation to the Bankruptcy Act 1869, s 35.

[283] Bankruptcy Act 1861, s 150.

[284] Robson, *A Treatise on the Law of Bankruptcy* (3rd edn, 1876) 260.

[285] In addition to the cases referred to below, see *Re ABC Coupler and Engineering Co Ltd (No 3)* [1970] 1 WLR 702; *Re H H Realisations Ltd* (1975) 31 P & C R 249. While these cases, and a number of the cases referred to below, were concerned with company liquidation, they should also be relevant to bankruptcy.

[286] See *Brash Holdings Ltd v Katile Pty Ltd* [1996] 1 VR 24, 35–36.

[287] *Re Lucania Temperance Billboard Halls (London) Ltd* [1966] 1 Ch 98, 106; *James Smith & Sons (Norwood) Ltd v Goodman* [1936] 1 Ch 216; *Lam Soon Australia Pty Ltd v Molit (No 55) Pty Ltd* (1996) 70 FCR 34, 43–44 (and see also at first instance (1996) 63 FCR 391, 398–401); McPherson, *The Law of Company Liquidation* (4th edn, 1999) 547–8.

an alternative view that, while the landlord is entitled to claim for the whole of the rent to the end of the term, he can only prove for rent which in fact has become due and payable.[288] But whatever the extent of the right of proof, a set-off should be available to the landlord in relation to the provable debt and a separate debt owing to the tenant.

Landlord in liquidation

In the situation in which a landlord is a company that has gone into liquidation, **13.65** and privity of estate accordingly is not relevant, it has been suggested that rent payable after the insolvency is not normally available for set-off against a pre-insolvency debt owed by the landlord to the tenant, the reason being that the rent is 'earned' by the landlord's estate and, since it is payable for the benefit of the general body of creditors, there is a lack of mutuality in relation to it and a pre-insolvency debt incurred by the insolvent to the lessee.[289] The better view is that there is no general principle that precludes a set-off when a debt is earned by the use after insolvency but pursuant to a prior contract of property otherwise available for distribution generally.[290] If privity of estate does not apply, it is difficult to see why rent accruing to a company in liquidation should not be available for a set-off if it arises out of a prior lease.[291] In the language of Rich J in the High Court of Australia in *Hiley v The Peoples Prudential Assurance Co Ltd*,[292] it is a case where rights are vested in the tenant and in the company which, without any new transaction, grow in the natural course of events into money claims capable of forming items in an account. Dixon J commented in similar terms in that case.[293] In the case of a lease, rent becomes payable without the intervention of a new transaction.

E. Periodic Payment Obligations After Insolvency

A common form of periodic payment obligation is the payment of rent pursuant **13.66** to a lease of land. Set-off in that context was considered above. In the case of other

---

[288] *Metropolis Estates Co Ltd v Wilde* [1940] 2 KB 536, 541–542, referring to *Re New Oriental Bank Corporation (No 2)* [1895] 1 Ch 753; *Re Oak Pitts Colliery Co* (1882) 21 Ch D 322, 329; Williams and Muir Hunter, *The Law and Practice in Bankruptcy* (19th edn, 1979) 154; Hill and Redman's *Law of Landlord and Tenant* (17th edn, 1982) vol 1, 595; *Buckley on the Companies Act* (14th edn, 1981) vol 1, 717–18; *Palmer's Company Law* (1997, looseleaf) vol 3, para 15.432.

[289] Wood, *English and International Set-off* (1989) 342.

[290] See paras 13.38–13.51 above.

[291] This assumes that a debt which arises in favour of a company after its liquidation but pursuant to a prior contract is capable as a matter of principle of being employed in a set-off. See paras 8.27–8.37 above. In *Old Style Confections Pty Ltd v Microbyte Investments Pty Ltd* [1995] 2 VR 457 Hayne J held that a periodic licence fee payable to a company after its liquidation could be the subject of a set-off. See below.

[292] (1938) 60 CLR 468, 487.

[293] (1938) 60 CLR 468, 499.

periodic payment obligations arising after bankruptcy or liquidation, the applicable principles should be the same as those discussed for rent in the case of a company liquidation, where privity of estate does not apply. Thus, it has been held in Victoria that a periodic licence fee accruing to a company after its liquidation may be the subject of a set-off.[294] The same result should follow in the case of hire payable under a contract for the hire of goods which, unlike a lease of land, is not subject to privity of estate.[295]

F. Agency

(1) Introduction

13.67 In an agency situation mutuality generally is determined by the principal/third-party relationship, as opposed to that of the agent and the third party. For example, when a bill of exchange is indorsed to an agent for the purpose of collection, the acceptor may bring his indebtedness on the bill into an account with a claim possessed by him against the indorser.[296] Conversely, a person holding a bill as agent for another generally could not employ the bill in a set-off against a debt of his own to the acceptor. A similar rule applies when an agent entering into a contract with a third party discloses that he is acting on behalf of a principal.[297] The principal is the contracting party, and lack of mutuality would operate to deny the third party the right to set off a debt owing to him by the agent against his liability on the contract to the principal.[298] This may also be the case in many commercial transactions where the agent discloses that he is acting on behalf of a principal but without disclosing the principal's identity. The third party in that circumstance may be regarded as having agreed to treat as a party to the contract anyone on whose behalf the agent may have been authorized to contract,[299] and in an action by the principal the third party could not set off a liability of the agent to him.[300]

---

[294] *Old Style Confections Pty Ltd v Microbyte Investments Pty Ltd* [1995] 2 VR 457.

[295] Compare Wood, *English and International Set-off* (1989) 309, 342.

[296] See *Re Anglo-Greek Steam Navigation and Trading Co. Caralli and Haggard's Claim* (1869) LR 4 Ch App 174. The agent for collection in that case admittedly had indorsed the bill back to the inspectors of the indorser appointed under the indorser's deed of inspectorship. Nevertheless, Giffard LJ said that it was immaterial whether the bills had been got back. See also *Barclays Bank Ltd v Aschaffenburger Zellstoffwerke AG* [1967] 1 Lloyd's Rep. 387.

[297] Compare the case of an undisclosed principal. See paras 13.71–13.91 below.

[298] *Richardson v Stormont, Todd & Co Ltd* [1900] 1 QB 701. See also *Moore v Clementson* (1809) 2 Camp 22, 170 ER 1068.

[299] See *Teheran-Europe Co Ltd v S T Belton (Tractors) Ltd* [1968] 2 QB 545, 555, *per* Diplock LJ. See also *N & J Vlassopulos Ltd v Ney Shipping Ltd (The Santa Carina)* [1977] 1 Lloyd's Rep. 478, 481, 484; *Marsh & McLennan Pty Ltd v Stanyers Transport Pty Ltd* [1994] 2 VR 232; Goodhart and Hamson, 'Undisclosed Principals in Contract' (1932) 4 CLJ 320, 339. Compare *Bowstead and Reynolds on Agency* (17th edn, 2001) 469–70.

[300] *Hornby v Lacy* (1817) 6 M & S 166, 105 ER 1205. For set-off as between the agent and the third party, see paras 13.99–13.101 below.

(2) Set-off Agreement Between the Agent and the Third Party[301]

An agent may be authorized to receive payment of a sum of money from a third **13.68**
party on behalf of the principal. The mere existence of authority to that effect
would not justify an attempt by the third party to obtain payment of a debt owing
to him by the agent by way of a set-off against the debt to the principal.[302] Nor
ordinarily would it authorize the agent to enter into an agreement for a set-off
against his own debt to the third party.[303] Furthermore, an alleged custom to that
effect would be unreasonable,[304] so that it would not bind the principal unless he
knew of the custom and had agreed to be bound by it.[305]

There are, nevertheless, some situations in which a set-off agreement between the **13.69**
agent and the third party involving the principal's claim would be valid. If the
principal is indebted to the agent, and has authorized the agent to pay himself out
of the proceeds of the third party's debt to the principal, the agent may receive
payment by means of a set-off against a debt that he owes to the third party.[306]
Further, an agent selling the goods of his principal may be entitled by virtue of a
lien to receive payment of the price. In such a case an agreement between the purchaser and the agent[307] to set off the price against a debt owing by the agent to the
purchaser will be binding upon the principal to the extent of the principal's
indebtedness to the agent secured by the lien.[308] In addition, where the principal
is undisclosed, an agreement for a set-off between the agent and the third party
entered into before the third party had notice that the person with whom he
was dealing was merely an agent should be binding on the principal,[309] although a

---

[301] See ch 16 below in relation to set-off agreements.
[302] *Bartlett v Pentland* (1830) 10 B & C 760, 109 ER 632; *Pearson v Scott* (1878) 9 Ch D 198;
Stolos Compania SA v Ajax Insurance Co Ltd (The Admiral C) [1981] 1 Lloyd's Rep 9.
[303] *Jell v Pratt* (1817) 2 Stark 67, 171 ER 575; *Young v White* (1844) 7 Beav 506, 49 ER 1162;
Wrout v Dawes (1858) 25 Beav 369, 53 ER 678; *Coupe v Collier* (1890) 62 LT 927. See also *Trading
and General Investment Corp v Gault Armstrong & Kemble Ltd (The Okeanis)* [1986] 1 Lloyd's Rep
195, 199.
[304] See *Pearson v Scott* (1878) 9 Ch D 198; *Crossley v Magniac* [1893] 1 Ch 594; *Blackburn v
Mason* (1893) 68 LT 510; *Anderson v Sutherland* (1897) 13 TLR 163. See also *Cooke & Sons v
Eshelby* (1887) 12 App Cas 271, 280 with respect to the alleged custom.
[305] *Blackburn v Mason* (1893) 68 LT 510. There is a custom at Lloyd's by which a broker may set
off the amount of a loss against his debt for premiums due to the underwriter. This method of payment will bind the insured if it can be shown that the broker was authorized to settle losses in accordance with the custom. See *Stewart v Aberdein* (1838) 4 M & W 211, 150 ER 1406, and *Stolos
Compania SA v Ajax Insurance Co Ltd (The Admiral C)* [1981] 1 Lloyd's Rep. 9, 10, and generally
Arnould's Law of Marine Insurance and Average (16th edn, 1981) vol 1, 124–7 paras 188–90.
[306] *Barker v Greenwood* (1837) 2 Y & C Ex 414, 160 ER 458. See also *Pariente v Lubbock* (1856)
8 De G M & G 5, 44 ER 290.
[307] Or his trustee in bankruptcy, as in *Hudson v Granger* (1821) 5 B & Ald 27, 106 ER 1103.
[308] *Hudson v Granger* (1821) 5 B & Ald 27, 106 ER 1103. See also *Warner v M'Kay* (1836) 1 M
& W 591, 150 ER 571, and paras 13.99–13.101 below.
[309] See also *Bowstead and Reynolds on Agency* (17th edn, 2001) 368–9.

set-off may be available to the third party at common law in that circumstance even apart from the agreement.[310]

13.70   Consider that the principal has authorized the agent to employ the third party's liability to the principal in a set-off against the agent's personal debt to the third party. If a set-off is effected before any of them becomes bankrupt or goes into liquidation, there would not ordinarily be a problem.[311] Where however the principal becomes bankrupt before a set-off has occurred, a subsequent set-off would not be valid unless the source of the agent's authority is a security over the principal's claim so that to that extent it is not an asset available for distribution amongst the principal's creditors. Apart from that exception, authority conferred by the principal in favour of the agent would not bind the principal's trustee in bankruptcy in whom the claim is vested as part of the principal's estate. This should also be the case when the third party has become bankrupt. The use of the third party's asset in the form of the claim against the agent, in order to satisfy the third party's liability to the principal in circumstances where the insolvency set-off section does not apply, would be contrary to the requirement of a pari passu distribution of the bankrupt's estate, and the agreement accordingly would not be binding as against the trustee.[312] Consider however that the agent is the party who has become bankrupt. If the occurrence of the bankruptcy terminated the authority, a set-off could not occur. But if the authority is not terminated, the bankruptcy should not affect the position.[313] A set-off should only be objectionable if it involves the use of an asset otherwise available for distribution amongst the insolvent's creditors. This is not the case in relation to the agent, since the set-off is against the agent's liability. This admittedly is contrary to the view expressed by the Court of Appeal in *Re Bank of Credit and Commerce International SA*,[314] that 'if A owes B £x and B owes C £y and any of them becomes insolvent the two debts cannot be set off even if there is an express agreement by the three of them that B may set them off; such an agreement is contrary to the scheme of distribution on insolvency and cannot prevail over the rules which require pari passu distribution . . .'. However to the extent that this statement includes the situation in which A is the insolvent party, it is difficult to see what the objection is.[315]

---

[310] See below.

[311] This is subject to the set-off not being impugned in a subsequent insolvency on the ground that it is a transaction at an undervalue or a transaction defrauding creditors. See the Insolvency Act 1986, ss. 238, 339 and 423.

[312] See the discussion of *British Eagle International AirLines Ltd v Compagnie Nationale Air France* [1975] 1 WLR 758 in paras 16.18–16.20 below.

[313] Compare Wood, *English and International Set-off* (1989) 1001–2, 1010.

[314] [1996] Ch 245, 257 (emphasis added). See also on appeal in the House of Lords [1998] AC 214, 223.

[315] See para 16.20 below.

(3) Undisclosed Principals

A person may contract in his own name but as agent for an undisclosed princi- **13.71**
pal.[316] The status of an undisclosed principal is anomalous in English law. A principal whose existence is unknown to a third party could hardly be said to be a party
to a contract with the third party. The agent is the contracting party, and therefore
the agent may sue and be sued on the contract. But in addition the principal may
sue and be sued if there is nothing in the contract which is inconsistent with someone other than the agent being the 'principal'.[317] This right to sue and the liability
to be sued is not based upon privity of contract, because the principal is not a contracting party. Rather, the undisclosed principal is treated as having a right to
intervene on the agent's contract.[318] This intervention was described by Sir
Frederick Pollock as being 'inconsistent with the elementary doctrines of the law
of contract'.[319] Various writers over the years have made a number of attempts to
provide a theoretical justification for it,[320] but none has been entirely successful. It
is probably best to regard the doctrine as an anomaly introduced by the common
law for reasons of mercantile convenience.[321]

If the undisclosed principal, when discovered, is sued on the contract by the third **13.72**
party, the principal could not set off a claim that he has against the agent.[322] Nor
could the principal bring into account a claim that the agent has against the third
party, although a set-off may be available in accordance with normal principles if
the third party is liable to the principal.[323] Alternatively, it may be that the principal is the party who takes action by intervening on the contract and enforcing
it against the third party.[324] In such a case there is the possibility of a set-off in

---

[316] For a discussion of the situations in which the undisclosed principal doctrine applies, see
Reynolds, 'Practical Problems of the Undisclosed Principal Doctrine' (1983) 36 Current Legal
Problems 119.

[317] *Dunlop Pneumatic Tyre Co Ltd v Selfridge and Co Ltd* [1915] AC 847, 864; *Siu Yin Kwan v
Eastern Insurance Co Ltd* [1994] 2 AC 199, 207–209. See generally Powell, *The Law of Agency*
(1952) 130–1 and *Bowstead and Reynolds on Agency* (17th edn, 2001) 352.

[318] *Welsh Development Agency v Export Finance Co Ltd* [1992] BCLC 148, 173, 182. See generally Goodhart and Hamson (1932) 4 CLJ 320, 345 *et seq*, criticizing McCardie J in *Said v Butt* [
1920] 3 KB 497, 500. Compare however Glanville Williams, 'Mistake as to Party in the Law of
Contract' (1945) 23 Canadian Bar Review 380, 404.

[319] (1887) 3 LQR 358, 359. See also *Siu Yin Kwan v Eastern Insurance Co Ltd* [1994] 2 AC 199,
207.

[320] See the discussion in Stoljar, *The Law of Agency* (1961) 228–33. See also *Bowstead and
Reynolds on Agency* (17th edn, 2001) 342–4; Fridman, *The Law of Agency* (7th edn, 1996) 257.

[321] Fridman, *The Law of Agency* (7th edn, 1996) 258; *Siu Yin Kwan v Eastern Insurance Co Ltd*
[1994] 2 AC 199, 207. See also *Bowstead and Reynolds on Agency* (17th edn, 2001) 343.

[322] *Waring v Favenck* (1807) 1 Camp 85, 170 ER 886; *Kymer v Suwercropp* (1807) 1 Camp 109,
170 ER 894.

[323] See eg *Spurr v Cass* (1870) LR 5 QB 656.

[324] If the agent has a direct pecuniary interest in enforcing the contract, in the form of a 'lien' over
the proceeds for his charges and expenses, or for the balance of his general account with the principal, payment by the third party to the principal when the third party has notice of the lien would not

relation to a cross-demand available to the third party against the principal. In addition, however, the third party may bring into account a debt owing to him by the agent that arose before the third party had notice that the person with whom he was dealing in fact was acting as an agent. The leading case is *George v Clagett*.[325] A factor sold goods for his principal in his own name without disclosing that he was an agent. When the principal sued the third party for the price,[326] the third party was allowed to set off the agent's separate debt to him. The set-off is not limited to cases involving a sale of goods, but is of general application. Bowen LJ in *Montagu v Forwood*[327] described its scope in the following terms:

> If A employs B as his agent to make any contract for him, or to receive money for him, and B makes a contract with C, or employs C as his agent, if B is a person who would be reasonably supposed to be acting as a principal, and is not known or suspected by C to be acting as an agent for any one, A cannot make a demand against C without the latter being entitled to stand in the same position as if B had in fact been a principal. If A has allowed his agent B to appear in the character of a principal he must take the consequences.[328]

The plaintiff in that case had employed an agent to collect a general average loss from Lloyd's underwriters. The agent in turn employed Lloyd's brokers as sub-agents. The policy had been effected in the name of the agent,[329] and the sub-agents thought that the loss was payable to the agent on his own account. When the sub-agents were sued by the plaintiff as an undisclosed principal for the money received from the underwriters, they were allowed to set off the agent's debt to them.[330]

13.73 As a preliminary point, it is assumed in the following discussion that the third party would have a right of set-off against the agent in accordance with normal principles. This would not be the case if the third party, instead of being a debtor,

---

be a defence to a later action brought against him by the agent. See *Robinson v Rutter* (1855) 4 El & Bl 954, 119 ER 355. In relation to an insurance broker's lien, see *Arnould's Law of Marine Insurance and Average* (16th edn, 1981) vol 1, 134 para 200. If the third party is uncertain as to whether he should pay the principal, he should interplead. See Powell, *The Law of Agency* (1952) 223 note 2.

[325] (1797) 7 TR 539, 101 ER 1019.

[326] The question of a set-off, in the proper sense of that word, usually would only arise when the principal sues for the price. It should be distinguished from the situation in which the principal disputes the title of the purchaser to goods bought through the principal's agent on the ground that the agent exceeded his authority in selling in a particular manner, for example by setting off the price against a debt owing by the agent to the purchaser. See for example *Lloyds and Scottish Finance Ltd v Williamson* [1965] 1 WLR 404; *Tingey and Co Ltd v John Chambers and Co Ltd* [1967] NZLR 785.

[327] [1893] 2 QB 350.

[328] [1893] 2 QB 350, 355–356.

[329] This only appears from the report of the case at 69 LT 371.

[330] For other sub-agency cases involving a sale of goods, see *New Zealand and Australian Land Co v Watson* (1881) 7 QBD 374 and *Knight v Matson & Co* (1902) 22 NZLR 293, although compare *Kaltenbach, Fischer & Co v Lewis & Peat* (1885) 10 App Cas 617, 626–627. See also *Bowstead and Reynolds on Agency* (17th edn, 2001) 140–6 in relation to the principal and sub-agent relationship.

is holding a fund on trust, the obligation to account for which is not susceptible to a set-off.[331]

Insolvency set-off

The set-off to which the principal takes subject is not that conferred by the mu- **13.74** tual credit provision in the insolvency legislation in the event of the bankruptcy or liquidation of the agent, but rather it is confined to defences of set-off available between solvent parties, in other words set-off under the Statutes of Set-off and equitable set-off. In *Turner v Thomas*[332] an agent for an undisclosed principal contracted to sell goods to a third party. The agent was separately indebted to the third party, and later became bankrupt, whereupon the third party refused to proceed with the contract. He was then sued by the principal for damages for breach of contract. While the third party's damages liability could have been set off in the agent's bankruptcy if the agent had contracted as principal, it could not have formed the basis of a defence to an action at law under the Statutes of Set-off, since the Statutes required mutual debts. Accordingly it was held that the agent's debt could not be set off in accordance with *George v Clagett* against the damages liability in the principal's action. One reason given for the limitation on the third party's right of set-off was that the possibility of the agent's bankruptcy would not have been contemplated by the third party when deciding whether or not to deal with the agent, although that generalization may not always hold true.[333] A second, more substantial reason given for the limitation was that the insolvency set-off section is only intended for the settlement of accounts between the bankrupt and a person dealing with him, rather than between that person and some other party such as an undisclosed principal who stands outside the bankruptcy. The principal, by intervening on the contract and suing in his own name, takes the claim outside the operation of the insolvency legislation, in which case the insolvency set-off section should not be relevant.[334]

Equitable set-off

The doctrine of the undisclosed principal is a common law doctrine, and *George* **13.75** *v Clagett* was decided at common law. Consistent with its origin, the right of set-off that the courts have enforced in these cases is the defence available in the common law courts under the Statutes of Set-off. In an appropriate case, however, there is no reason why the third party could not assert equitable defences of set-off

---

[331] See ch 10 above.

[332] (1871) LR 6 CP 610. See also *Thornton v Maynard* (1875) LR 10 CP 695, 700; *Montagu v Forwood* [1893] 2 QB 350, 354, *per* Lord Esher MR (and see also Bowen LJ in the report of the case at 69 LT 371, 373).

[333] See eg *Cooke & Sons v Eshelby* (1887) 12 App Cas 271, 280.

[334] Similarly the insolvency set-off section cannot be invoked against an assignee of a debt when the assignor has become bankrupt. See para 17.28 below.

against the undisclosed principal. Similarly, when the third party is suing on the contract, and there is a cross-claim against the third party arising out of the contract which is sufficiently closely connected to give rise to an equitable set-off, the third party's title to sue would be impeached, whether the action is against the principal or the agent

Due and payable

13.76   Set-off under the Statutes of Set-off requires that both debts be due and payable.[335] It is clear from *George v Clagett*, however, that it is not necessary that both debts should have been payable when the third party received notice of the principal. The purchase in that case took place before the date of notice, but the price was not payable until a later date, while the indebtedness of the agent was based upon a bill of exchange accepted by the agent but not payable until four days after notice. On the other hand, the debts should have arisen before notice.[336] In *Kaltenbach, Fischer & Co v Lewis and Peat*[337] merchants employed an agent to sell goods, and the agent in turn employed a firm of brokers as sub-agents. The brokers sold the goods to a purchaser who was allowed six-months' credit for the price. Before the period had elapsed, and while the brokers were still in possession of the goods, the merchants gave notice of their interest in the transaction to the brokers, and claimed the return of the goods or their net proceeds. The agent had pledged the goods to the brokers to secure a debt, and it was accepted that the brokers' interest was protected by the Factors Act, so that they were entitled to a lien for that amount and to deduct it from the proceeds of sale. But the brokers asserted that they were also entitled to set off the balance of the proceeds against other amounts due to them by the agent, and they accordingly credited the balance to the agent's account. The House of Lords held that they were not entitled to do so. Lord Bramwell dealt with the case on the basis that it involved a claim for property.[338] The brokers still retained the goods when notice was given to them, and the merchants as principals had a right to possession at that time, subject to the lien. The principals' claim accordingly was proprietary in nature, and therefore it was not susceptible to a set-off. Lord Watson proceeded on a different analysis,[339] emphasizing instead that there was no debt owing by the brokers when they received notice of the true ownership. A debt did not arise until later, when

---

[335]   See para 2.29 above.

[336]   The requirement of existing debts at the time of notice also applies to a debtor's right to set off a debt owing to him by the assignor in an action brought against him by an assignee of his indebtedness. See para 17.12 below.

[337]   (1885) 10 App Cas 617, discussed in Goodhart and Hamson 'Undisclosed Principals in Contract' (1934) 4 CLJ 320, 333–4.

[338]   (1885) 10 App Cas 617, 635–637.

[339]   (1885) 10 App Cas. 617, 626–628.

the price was received from the purchaser, and his Lordship said that the brokers could not avail themselves of a set-off arising in that manner after notice.[340]

Belief that the agent was a principal

The set-off only arises if the third party believed that the agent was the principal **13.77** when the third party became indebted under the transaction,[341] or if the cross-debt owing by the agent to the third party arose after the entry into the transaction on behalf of the undisclosed principal,[342] if the third party still held the belief at that time.[343] Both debts therefore must have been incurred before notice. Knowledge of the agency sufficient to preclude a set-off need not point to the agent as being the agent of the claimant. It suffices if it points to him as being an agent, whether for the claimant or for anyone else.[344] Furthermore it is not necessary that the third party personally should know of the agency. It would suffice if his own agent is aware of it in circumstances where that knowledge would be imputed to the third party.[345] The principle in relation to set-off should be contrasted with the situation in which an insurance broker with a general lien on the policy for the balance of the insured's account discovers that the nominal insured is only an agent. In such a case the broker is still allowed to exercise a lien over any money received by him from the insurer after notice of the agency, provided that he held the policy before notice and provided also that the lien can only be exercised in respect of the amount due to him at the date of notice.[346]

Duty of inquiry

If the circumstances are such as to put the third party on inquiry as to the status of **13.78** the agent, and he fails to make an inquiry, he may be denied a set-off.[347] In effect

---

[340] If the brokers had received the price before they had notice of the undisclosed principals, Lord Watson said that it was possible that they might have been entitled to set it off against the agent's balance, but that in the circumstances it was not necessary to offer an opinion on the point. See (1885) 10 App Cas 617, 627. Lord Fitzgerald (at 640–641) appears to have proceeded on the same basis as Lord Watson, although his judgment is not clear on this point.

[341] *Carr v Hinchliff* (1825) 4 B & C 547, 107 ER 1164; *Fish v Kempton* (1849) 7 CB 687, 137 ER 272. See also *Kaltenbach, Fischer & Co v Lewis and Peat* (1885) 10 App Cas 617, discussed above.

[342] See *Moore v Clementson* (1809) 2 Camp. 22, 170 ER 1068, as explained by Parke B in *Warner v M'Kay* (1836) 1 M & W 591, 596, 150 ER 571, 573.

[343] See for example *Borries v Imperial Ottoman Bank* (1873) LR 9 CP 38; *Salter v Purchell* (1841) 1 QB 209, 213–214, 113 ER 1110, 1111, *per* Parke B (*arguendo*).

[344] *Semenza v Brinsley* (1865) 18 CB (NS) 467, 144 ER 526; *Maspons y Hermano v Mildred, Goyeneche & Co* (1882) 9 QBD 530, affirmed (1883) 8 App Cas 874. See also *Walshe v Provan* (1853) 8 Ex 843, 155 ER 1595; *Busby v MacLurcan and Lane Ltd* (1930) 48 WN (NSW) 2, 5.

[345] *Dresser v Norwood* (1864) 17 CB (NS) 466, 144 ER 188.

[346] *Mann v Forrester* (1814) 4 Camp 60, 171 ER 20; *Near East Relief v King, Chasseur and Co Ltd* [1930] 2 KB 40, 46. See generally *Arnould's Law of Marine Insurance and Average* (16th edn, 1981) vol 1, 132 para 197.

[347] *Baring v Corrie* (1818) 2 B & Ald 137, 144, 106 ER 317, 320; *Pratt v Willey* (1826) 2 Car & P 350, 172 ER 158. See also *Pearson v Scott* (1879) 9 Ch D 198, 202; *Cooke & Sons v Eshelby* (1887)

this is the same as saying that the third party's belief should be reasonable,[348] or that there should be 'nothing to lead the person who deals with him to suppose, *and* he does not in fact know, that he is acting as an agent'.[349] It has been said that 'the only question to be decided is whether the defendant really dealt with the agent in the honest belief that he was dealing with a principal'.[350] Nevertheless, the cases suggest that an honest belief will not be sufficient if the third party failed to make an inquiry when one was called for. This duty of inquiry has a common law origin, and it is therefore independent of the equitable doctrine of constructive notice.

13.79   The question whether a third party was put on inquiry will depend upon the facts of each case. In particular, the circumstances in which the agent contracted may be such as to indicate that he must have been acting only as an agent. In *Maanns v Henderson*[351] an English subject in time of war, although acting for a neutral foreigner, opened a policy of insurance in his own name with a broker, and informed the broker that the property was neutral. This was held to be a sufficient indication to the broker that the English subject was acting as an agent and not on his own account. In some cases documents accompanying a sale may indicate that the sale is being made on behalf of another person. In one case the principal was named as the seller on a ticket accompanying the goods being sold by the agent in the agent's own name, and accordingly it was held that the third party ought to have inquired into the nature of the situation of the agent.[352] That case should be compared to *Cooper v Strauss & Co.*[353] A sale note contained the words 'Sold for and on account of', but without the name of a principal having been inserted. Kennedy J said that those words appeared in the sale note because factors sometimes sold on their own account, but more generally for a principal. While a set-off was disallowed because the agent in fact had informed the third party that he was selling on behalf of the real owners, the contents of the sale note evidently were not considered to be sufficient to achieve that result. The sale note also mentioned the name and address of the real principal. This information however was only included as a description of the goods being sold, and Kennedy J did not consider that it would convey to a purchaser that the contract of sale was being made

---

12 App Cas 271, 277–278; *Montagu v Forwood* [1893] 2 QB 350, 356. For an analogous case concerning a dormant partner, see *Baker v Gent* (1892) 9 TLR 159 (see para 12.17 above).

[348]   *Cooke & Sons v Eshelby* (1887) 12 App Cas 271, 278; Montagu *v Forwood* [1893] 2 QB 350, 355.

[349]   *Montagu v Forwood* [1893] 2 QB 350, 355, *per* Lord Esher MR (emphasis added).

[350]   *Knight v Matson & Co* (1902) 22 NZLR 293, 309, *per* Williams J. See also *Fish v Kempton* (1848) 7 CB 687, 691–692, 693, 137 ER 272, 274, 275.

[351]   (1802) 1 East 335, 102 ER 130.

[352]   *Pratt v Willey* (1826) 2 Car & P 350, 172 ER 158. Compare *Greer v Downs Supply Co* [1927] 2 KB 28, in which the third party raised the matter with the agent.

[353]   (1898) 14 TLR 233.

on behalf of that person as owner. Similarly, in *Knight v Matson & Co*[354] a cattle-dealer sold cattle with the brand of the real owner upon them. However a cattle-dealer buying cattle would not obliterate or change the existing brands, and so the presence of a brand upon cattle being sold by a dealer was not considered to be sufficient to put the third party on inquiry as to their true ownership.

In the case of a sale of goods, where the sale concerns goods presently owned and existing,[355] the third party could not deny that he was put on inquiry if the agent at the time of the sale did not have actual possession of the goods or of their *indicia* of title.[356] Indeed, it has been said that in order to make a valid defence under *George v Clagett* the plea should show that the contract was made by a person whom the principal had entrusted with possession.[357] In *Wynen v Brown*[358] the goods had been entered in the name of the brokers at the Custom House, they had been warehoused in the brokers' name, and the order to the wharfinger for their delivery had also been in the brokers' name. Those circumstances were regarded as sufficient to give rise to a set-off, even though the brokers did not have the bills of lading or other *indicia* of title and even though the goods had been wharfed in the principal's name. The case is inadequately reported, but it may be queried whether on the facts as disclosed the third party should have questioned the brokers or the wharfinger as to the ownership of the goods.

13.80

It may be that the third party is aware that the person with whom he is contracting sometimes deals as an agent for other persons. The cases in point are noticeable for their lack of consistency. Lord Ellenborough in *Moore v Clementson*[359] thought that a mere general knowledge possessed by the third party that the other contracting party was a factor by itself would not deprive him of a set-off. It appears from the headnote to *Wynen v Brown*[360] that the person selling was known to be a broker, but a set-off was allowed without any indication of an inquiry having been made.[361] Similarly, in *Dresser v Norwood*[362] the Common Pleas allowed the third party a set-off even though he himself had employed the other party as a selling agent on two occasions. The jury's finding that the third party believed that he was dealing directly with the owner was considered to be sufficient for a

13.81

---

[354] (1902) 22 NZLR 293.

[355] Compare for example *Cooke & Sons v Eshelby* (1887) 12 App Cas 271.

[356] See *Baring v Corrie* (1818) 2 B & Ald 137, 106 ER 317. In cases such as *Montagu v Forwood* [1893] 2 QB 350, in which an agent is employed to collect a sum of money from a third party, the agent should have possession of any requisite documents.

[357] *Semenza v Brinsley* (1865) 18 CB (NS) 467, 477, 144 ER 526, 530. See also *Borries v The Imperial Ottoman Bank* (1873) LR 9 CP 38.

[358] (1826) 4 LJOSKB 203.

[359] (1809) 2 Camp 22, 170 ER 1068.

[360] (1826) 4 LJOSKB 203.

[361] See also *Garrett v Bird* (1872) 11 SCR (NSW) 97, which was concerned with the agent's standing to sue.

[362] (1863) 14 CB (NS) 574, 143 ER 570.

set-off.[363] On the other hand, in *Baring v Corrie*[364] the third party knew that the persons with whom they were dealing acted both as brokers and merchants, and Abbott CJ said that the third party should have inquired. In *Pearson v Scott*[365] a solicitor had been instructed to sell some stock. He in turn employed a stockbroker. When the sale was completed the stockbroker forwarded the proceeds to the solicitor, less a deduction to cover an indebtedness of the solicitor to him on a separate transaction. While the solicitor was known as a person who speculated in stock on his own account, Fry J held that, since the stockbroker knew that the person who employed him was a solicitor, he should have realized that he was dealing with a person who may have been acting upon the instructions of a client, and therefore he should have made some inquiry. Since the stockbroker had not initiated an inquiry he could not be heard to say that he dealt with the solicitor in any other character than as agent for the principals now suing for the proceeds, and so his act of crediting part of the proceeds to the solicitor's account with him was held not to discharge him from liability to the principals. In *Knight v Matson & Co*[366] the agent was a dealer in cattle, but the third party had been informed in a prior transaction that the dealer on that occasion was acting as an agent. While one of the members of the majority, Williams J, said that the only question was whether the third party really dealt with the agent in the honest belief that they were dealing with a principal,[367] Edwards J decided the case on the basis that the third party had not been put on inquiry.[368] The dealer was in the business of selling cattle on his own account, and knowledge of a single isolated occasion on which he had acted as an agent was not regarded as sufficient to deny the third party a set-off on the ground of failure to inquire as to the ownership of the cattle. Stout CJ dissented. He said that the third party should have known from the previous transaction that the dealer might have been acting as an agent, and he considered that the third party's failure to inquire into the dealer's status in the second dealing should deprive them of a set-off.[369]

13.82   The imposition of a duty of inquiry when the third party is aware that the other contracting party has dealt in the past as an agent only becomes important when the third party asserts that he believed that the other party on this occasion was

---

[363] Subsequently the Exchequer Chamber reversed the decision, but on the ground that the third party himself had acted through an agent who was aware of the identity of the real owner. This knowledge was imputed to the third party. There is nothing in the report however to indicate that the third party's own awareness that the other contracting party was in the habit of selling as a factor was thought to prevent a set-off. See *Dresser v Norwood* (1864) 17 CB (NS) 466, 144 ER 188.

[364] (1818) 2 B & Ald 137, 106 ER 317.

[365] (1878) 9 Ch D 198.

[366] (1902) 22 NZLR 293.

[367] (1902) 22 NZLR 293, 309, 311.

[368] (1902) 22 NZLR 293, 315–317.

[369] See also *Cooke & Sons v Eshelby* (1887) 12 App Cas 271; *London Joint Stock Bank v Simmons* [1892] AC 201, 229–230.

dealing as a principal, but in the circumstances that belief was unreasonable. The cases suggest that this may give rise to a duty to inquire, but its imposition, and the reasonableness of the belief, would depend upon the facts of each case. Lord Ellenborough's opinion in *Moore v Clementson*, that a mere general knowledge that the other party is a factor will not result in the loss of a set-off, is almost certainly too wide. When the third party is aware that the nature of the business of the person with whom he is dealing is such that he often acts as an agent for others,[370] it is unlikely that his expressed belief that the person was acting as a principal in the particular transaction in issue would be reasonable in the absence of an inquiry. On the other hand, the belief generally would be reasonable in a case like *Knight v Matson & Co*, or *Dresser v Norwood*, where the agent as a matter of business usually deals on his own account, although he is known to have dealt occasionally in the past as an agent for others.

Basis of the set-off

In the absence of a proper theoretical justification for the intervention of an undis-   **13.83**
closed principal on his agent's contract,[371] it is difficult to explain the basis for the third party's right of set-off against the principal. There have been statements suggesting that the set-off may be based upon a notion that an undisclosed principal takes subject to equities or defences available to the third party against the agent before notice.[372] In other words, an undisclosed principal should be treated in the same way as an assignee of a chose in action.[373] Goodhart and Hamson[374] sought to explain the doctrine of the undisclosed principal as being a primitive form of assignment, although there are differences between the concepts.[375] An assignment results from an act of the parties, whereas the rights and liabilities of an undisclosed principal arise as a matter of law. Moreover, an assignment usually occurs after the relationship between the assignor and the debtor has come into existence, whereas the interest of the undisclosed principal in his agent's contract arises contemporaneously with the entry into that contract. Further, a contract

---

[370] As in *Cooke & Sons v Eshelby* (1887) 12 App Cas 271.

[371] See para 13.71 above.

[372] See *Isberg v Bowden* (1853) 8 Ex 852, 859, 155 ER 1599, 1602; *Dresser v Norwood* (1863) 14 CB (NS) 574, 588–589, 143 ER 570, 576; *Turner v Thomas* (1871) LR 6 CP 610, 613; *Montgomerie v United Kingdom Mutual Steamship Association, Ltd* [1891] 1 QB 370, 372. See also the early judgments in *Rabone v Williams* (1785) 7 TR 360n, 101 ER 1020 and *Stracey, Ross et al v Deey* (1789) 7 TR 361n, 101 ER 1021. The Privy Council in *Browning v Provincial Insurance Co of Canada* (1873) LR 5 PC 263, 272 said that 'an undisclosed principal may sue and be sued upon mercantile contracts made by his agent in his own name, subject to any defences or equities which without notice may exist against the agent'.

[373] See ch 17 below.

[374] Goodhart and Hamson, 'Undisclosed Principals in Contract' (1932) 4 CLJ 320.

[375] See Glanville Williams, 'Mistake as to Party in the Law of Contract' (1945) 23 Canadian Bar Review 380, 408; Powell, *The Law of Agency* (1952) 138–9; Stoljar, *The Law of Agency* (1961), 232; *Siu Yin Kwan v Eastern Insurance Co Ltd* [1994] 2 AC 199, 210.

which provides that it is not assignable cannot be assigned, but such a provision does not preclude intervention by an undisclosed principal.[376] In any event, before the enactment of the Judicature Acts a chose in action was not assignable at common law,[377] and so an analogy between assignments and the common law treatment of the undisclosed principal would not have a strong historical foundation. Perhaps reflecting those difficulties with the assignment theory, the generally accepted explanation for the set-off is not that it is based upon a notion of taking subject to equities, but rather upon estoppel.

13.84   The leading case is *Cooke & Sons v Eshelby*.[378] Brokers sold goods to Cooke & Sons in their own name, but acting on behalf of a principal. The principal gave notice that the sale was made on his behalf, and sued the purchasers for the price. The purchasers were asked in interrogatories as to whether they did not believe that the brokers in the transaction were acting on behalf of principals, and they replied that they 'had no belief on the subject', and that they dealt with the brokers 'not knowing whether they were acting as brokers on behalf of principals, or on their own account as the principals'. The House of Lords held that, because the purchasers had not been led to believe that the brokers were acting as principals rather than agents, they were not entitled to set off a debt due to them from the brokers.[379] The set-off was regarded as being based upon an estoppel,[380] and before the principal could be estopped from denying the set-off there had to be a representation and reliance upon that representation. As Lord Watson remarked,[381]

> These decisions appear to me to establish conclusively that, in order to sustain the defence pleaded by the appellants, it is not enough to shew that the agent sold in his own name. It must be shewn that he sold the goods as his own, or, in other words, that the circumstances attending the sale were calculated to induce, and did induce, in the mind of the purchaser a reasonable belief that the agent was selling on his own account and not for an undisclosed principal; and it must also be shewn that the agent was enabled to appear as the real contracting party by the conduct, or by the authority, express or implied, of the principal. The rule thus explained is intelligible and just: and I agree . . . that it rests upon the doctrine of estoppel.

---

[376]   *Siu Yin Kwan v Eastern Insurance Co Ltd* [1994] 2 AC 199, 210. In relation to a prohibition on assignment, see *Linden Gardens Trust Ltd v Lenesta Sludge Disposals Ltd* [1994] 1 AC 85.

[377]   See *Lampet's Case* (1612) 10 Co Rep 46b, 48a, 77 ER 994, 997.

[378]   (1887) 12 App Cas 271.

[379]   Compare Reynolds, who has argued that this may have been a case of an unnamed, as opposed to an undisclosed, principal. See Reynolds, 'Practical Problems of the Undisclosed Principal Doctrine' (1983) 36 Current Legal Problems 119, 133.

[380]   See also *Montagu v Forwood* [1893] 2 QB 350, 355, *per* Bowen LJ; *Cooper v Strauss and Co* (1898) 14 TLR 233; *Farquharson Brothers & Co v King* (1901) 70 LJKB 985, 987, *per* Vaughan Williams LJ (*arguendo*); *Tingey and Co Ltd v John Chambers and Co Ltd* [1967] NZLR 785. In *Fish v Kempton* (1849) 7 CB 687, 691, 137 ER 272, 274 Wilde CJ explained the set-off in terms savouring of estoppel, and see also the judgments in *Baring v Corrie* (1818) 2 B & Ald 137, 106 ER 317.

[381]   (1887) 12 App Cas 271, 278.

Similarly Lord Halsbury, while not actually mentioning estoppel, nevertheless explained the undisclosed principal cases in terms embodying the elements of that doctrine.[382] The answer to the interrogatory indicated that the element of reliance was absent.

The requirement of showing reliance upon a representation is inconsistent with **13.85** the view that the set-off is based simply on a notion of taking subject to equities. Nevertheless it provides a sound approach to the issue.[383] There is no justification for shifting the burden of the liability for the agent's indebtedness onto the undisclosed principal unless the third party had been led to believe, erroneously, that when he was dealing with the agent he was in fact dealing directly with a principal. A third party in a case such as *Cooke v Eshelby*, who had no belief as to whether the person with whom he was dealing was a principal, may be taken to have assumed the risk that there may have been an undisclosed principal who could intervene, in which case the possibility of a set-off against the agent is unlikely to have been a factor influencing his decision to deal with the agent.[384] Having said that, estoppel does not explain the allowance of a set-off in all the undisclosed principal cases, irrespective of whether the estoppel is thought to be based upon conduct of the principal as constituting a representation, or whether the representation is thought to be made by the agent which then becomes binding upon the principal.[385]

Consider first the possibility of the principal's own conduct as constituting a rep- **13.86** resentation, in the context of a sale of goods. A representation sufficient to induce the belief that the agent is contracting as principal should indicate that the agent is the owner of the goods in question. In other words, the representation should be sufficient to satisfy the doctrine of apparent ownership.[386] This doctrine, as

---

[382] 'The ground upon which all these cases have been decided is that the agent has been permitted by the principal to hold himself out as the principal, and that the person dealing with the agent has believed that the agent was the principal, and has acted on that belief.' (1887) 12 App Cas 271, 275. Compare Lord Fitzgerald, who said (at 282–283) that he had 'some hesitation' in accepting the view that the set-off rests upon estoppel. However, as noted in Spencer Bower and Turner, *The Law Relating to Estoppel by Representation* (3rd edn, 1977) 25, he then proceeded to state the proposition in terms of his own choosing which differed in no substantial respect from those in which estoppel by representation are usually expressed.

[383] Compare Pollock (1887) 3 LQR 358, 359, who doubted the wisdom of extending the anomalous rights of an undisclosed principal.

[384] Compare the evidence to the contrary referred to by Lord Fitzgerald in *Cooke v Eshelby* (1887) 12 App Cas 271, 280, based upon an alleged custom in the Liverpool Cotton Market which was not proved, that the third party may set off the broker's indebtedness to him against any obligation to pay the price to an undisclosed principal, even when aware of the possibility of the existence of such a principal.

[385] I acknowledge my debt in the following discussion to *Bowstead and Reynolds on Agency* (17th edn, 2001) 367–71.

[386] While the doctrine of apparent ownership is also said to be based upon an estoppel (see eg *Mercantile Credit Co Ltd v Hamblin* [1965] 2 QB 242, 271), the fact that it confers a real title, as opposed to operating merely between the parties themselves, has been said to militate against an

Bowstead and Reynolds on Agency[387] explains, is concerned with the validity of a disposition of property, and with overcoming the *nemo dat* principle, whereas in the set-off cases the validity of the disposition is conceded. However, unless the agent has been held out as the owner of the goods, and as such able to transfer a good title in his own right, it can hardly be said that anything done by the undisclosed principal has constituted a representation that the agent is selling as a principal. The difficulty, as *Bowstead and Reynolds* also points out in criticizing the estoppel theory,[388] is that, while the third party evidently may found a set-off upon the mere fact of the agent having had possession of the goods for sale, or of their *indicia* of title,[389] possession is not sufficient to create a situation of apparent ownership.[390] Something further is required, for example that the real owner has allowed the goods to stand in another's name,[391] or that the real owner has given another person an acknowledgement in writing that the other person has bought and paid for the goods,[392] or that the real owner has signed a document offering to buy the goods from the other person.[393] It seems then that the set-off in these cases may be based upon conduct that would not be sufficient to constitute a representation by the undisclosed principal that the agent is owner of the goods being sold.

13.87 There is another way of approaching the estoppel theory, and that is that the agent himself, by contracting in his own name, represents that he is the principal in the transaction, and if the undisclosed principal has authorized this he becomes bound by the representation.[394] This approach avoids the difficulty that the principal's conduct may not have been sufficient to constitute a representation that the agent was contracting as a principal in his own right. However, even if it is accepted that the agent makes such a representation by contracting in his own name,[395] it still fails to explain the right of set-off in cases in which the agent had

---

estoppel, or at least against the traditional view that an estoppel does not establish a title. Compare *Bowstead and Reynolds on Agency* (17th edn, 2001) 386, 389 with Spencer Bower and Turner, *The Law Relating to Estoppel by Representation* (3rd edn, 1977) 17–18.

[387] *Bowstead and Reynolds on Agency* (17th edn, 2001) 369.

[388] *Bowstead and Reynolds on Agency* (17th edn, 2001) 369–70 (and see also at 386–7, 390).

[389] See *Semenza v Brinsley* (1865) 18 CB (NS) 467, 477, 144 ER 526, 530, and also *Borries v The Imperial Ottoman Bank* (1873) LR 9 CP 38.

[390] *Rimmer v Webster* [1902] 2 Ch 163, 169; *Motor Credits (Hire Finance) Ltd v Pacific Motor Auctions Pty Ltd* (1963) 109 CLR 87, 99. Compare *Lloyds and Scottish Finance Ltd v Williamson* [1965] 1 WLR 404, criticized, and possibly explained, in *Bowstead and Reynolds on Agency* (17th edn, 2001) 390 n 54, and see also Fridman, *The Law of Agency* (7th edn, 1996) 279–80.

[391] See eg *Henderson & Co v Williams* [1895] 1 QB 521 (goods warehoused in another's name).

[392] *Rimmer v Webster* [1902] 2 Ch 163.

[393] *Eastern Distributors Ltd v Goldring* [1957] 2 QB 600.

[394] See Spencer Bower and Turner, *The Law Relating to Estoppel by Representation* (3rd edn, 1977) 122. In *Borries v The Imperial Ottoman Bank* (1873) LR 9 CP 38, 47 Brett J referred to the agents as representing themselves to be the real owners.

[395] Compare Goodhart and Hamson's view ((1932) 4 CLJ 320, 344), that 'normally a person contracting in his own name does not, by that mere fact, make any representation that he is not

been instructed to reveal the fact of his agency, or at least had not been authorized to use his own name when contracting.[396] There have been statements which assume that the set-off only applies when the principal has authorized the agent to contract as though he were the principal.[397] Indeed, in *Baring v Corrie*[398] a third party who bought goods from a broker selling in his own name was denied a set-off against the undisclosed principal, inter alia because a broker's authority was confined to selling in the name of his principal.[399] Nevertheless, it was held by the Court of Appeal in *Ex parte Dixon, re Henley*,[400] and again by the New Zealand Court of Appeal in *Knight v Matson & Co*,[401] that an express direction to the agent to reveal the fact of his agency will not deprive the third party of a set-off if the agent ignores the direction and contracts in his own name without disclosing that he is an agent.[402] It may be thought unfair that the principal should be subjected to a set-off that would not have arisen if the agent had acted in accordance with his instructions. Equally, though, it is unfair that a private communication from the principal to the agent should have the effect of depriving the third party of a set-off when the possibility of a set-off may have been an inducement for the third party to contract with the agent. If the principal chooses to deal through an agent, he should be expected to take the risk that the agent may exceed his authority and act as though he himself is the principal.[403]

Before discussing these cases in the context of the agent's authority to make the **13.88** representation, it should be noted that *Knight v Matson* may be explained on another ground. Edwards J found that a situation of apparent ownership had been created. The agent in that case was a dealer in cattle in his own right. It has been suggested that a deposit of goods with a person who in the normal course of his

---

contracting as trustee for, or for the benefit of, another'. As support for that proposition, Goodhart and Hamson referred to two cases, *Nash v Dix* (1898) 78 LT 445 and *Dyster v Randall and Sons* [1926] Ch 932, although these may have been concerned with the materiality of the representation (as defined in Spencer Bower and Turner, *The Law of Actionable Misrepresentation* (3rd edn, 1974) 144), as opposed to whether there had been any representation.

[396] The mere fact that the agent was authorized not to reveal the name of the principal does not mean that he was authorized to contract as though he was the principal. See *Cooke v Eshelby* (1887) 12 App Cas 271, 281–282, *per* Lord Fitzgerald.

[397] For example, Lord Halsbury LC in *Cooke v Eshelby* (1887) 12 App Cas 271, 275 spoke of the 'permission of the real principal to the agent to assume his character'. In *Dresser v Norwood* (1863) 14 CB (NS) 574, 143 ER 570, the authority given to the agent to sell in his own name was emphasized. See also *Fish v Kempton* (1849) 7 CB 687, 691, 137 ER 272, 274, *per* Wilde CJ *(arguendo); Semenza v Brinsley* (1865) 18 CB (NS) 467, 477, 144 ER 526, 530.

[398] (1818) 2 B & Ald 137, 106 ER 317.

[399] For the distinction formerly drawn between brokers and factors, see *Bowstead and Reynolds on Agency* (17th edn, 2001) 30–1.

[400] (1876) 4 Ch D 133, explaining *Semenza v Brinsley* (1865) 18 CB (NS) 467, 144 ER 526.

[401] (1902) 22 NZLR 293.

[402] The agent's failure to reveal his agency would not affect his authority to sell. This is clear from the *Dixon* and *Matson* cases, and see also *Stevens v Biller* (1883) 25 Ch D 31.

[403] See Powell, *The Law of Agency* (1952) 148–9, where this point is made without reference to either *Ex parte Dixon* or *Knight v Matson*.

business is known to sell goods of that type on his own account may be sufficient to satisfy the doctrine of apparent ownership.[404] Therefore, the conduct of the undisclosed principal in entrusting his cattle for sale with a person who bought and sold cattle in his own right in the normal course of his business may have constituted a representation to those dealing with that person that he in fact was the owner of the cattle. Since an estoppel may be explained on the basis of the principal's own representation, the agent's disregard for the instructions given to him as to the disclosure of the agency would lose its significance. That explanation however would not appear to be available in relation to *Ex parte Dixon*.[405] The agent was an iron and metal merchant. In the transaction in question he sold a particular type of pig-iron to the third person on behalf of an undisclosed principal. While it may be accepted that an iron and metal merchant would buy and sell pig iron in his own right in the normal course of his business, this was not emphasized either in the statement of facts set out in the report or in the judgments, which suggests that the case did not turn on it. Rather, the Court of Appeal in allowing a set-off had recourse to the scope of the authority usually possessed by a factor.

13.89   If the agent has been instructed to reveal the fact of his agency, it is difficult to see how it could be said that the principal has authorized the agent to represent that he is the principal. Clearly the agent does not possess actual authority. Moreover, an argument based upon apparent authority would not be open to the third party seeking a set-off. Apparent authority arises when a person by words or conduct represents or permits it to be represented that another has authority to act on his behalf.[406] However, the essence of the set-off in these cases is that the third person believed that the person with whom he was dealing was contracting as a principal in his own right. He could hardly argue that the other party was held out as having authority to contract in his own name though on behalf of the real principal, and at the same time assert that he believed that he was dealing with the principal in the transaction. As Scrutton LJ once remarked,[407] 'you cannot rely on the apparent authority of an agent who did not profess in dealing with you to act as agent'. While this may seem clear, the Court of Appeal in *Ex parte Dixon*[408] nevertheless based its decision to allow a set-off upon the notion that the agent could be taken as having had authority to sell in his own name. Thus Brett JA said:[409]

---

[404] See *Bowstead and Reynolds on Agency* (17th edn, 2001) 390, referring to *Motor Credits (Hire Finance) Ltd v Pacific Motor Auctions Pty Ltd* (1963) 109 CLR 87, 99.

[405] Edwards J in *Matson* (1902) 22 NZLR 293, 315, however, seemed to regard *Ex parte Dixon* as a case of apparent ownership.

[406] *Bowstead and Reynolds on Agency* (17th edn, 2001) 307.

[407] *Underwood Ltd v Bank of Liverpool and Martins* [1924] 1 KB 775, 792.

[408] (1876) 4 Ch D 133.

[409] (1876) 4 Ch D 133, 137, referred to with approval by Williams J in the *Matson* case (1902) 22 NZLR 293, 308–309.

Now, the rule of law is, that the extent of an agent's authority as between himself and third parties is to be measured by the extent of his usual employment. That being so, the very fact of entrusting your goods to a man as a factor, with the right to sell them, is *prima facie* authority from you to him to sell in his own name.

Similarly, James LJ in deciding in favour of the set-off said that:[410] 'As regards third parties, the powers of an agent are measured by the apparent scope of his authority, and cannot be limited by any private communication with him.'

There was no mention in *Ex parte Dixon* of the apparent inconsistency of basing **13.90** the third party's right of set-off upon the authority usually possessed by a factor, when the set-off is only allowable if the third party did not know that the person with whom he was dealing was a factor.[411] This aspect of the decision in *Ex parte Dixon* is reminiscent of the later case of *Watteau v Fenwick*,[412] in which it was held that the owner of a business was liable on contracts entered into by an agent who was the manager of the business but who appeared to be the principal, even though the agent had been instructed not to enter into that type of transaction. Wills J said that: 'the principal is liable for all the acts of the agent which are within the authority usually confided to an agent of that character, notwithstanding limitations, as between the principal and the agent, put upon that authority'.[413] This case has often been criticized on the same ground as that mentioned above, that the agent had neither actual nor apparent authority, and therefore the principal should not have been liable on the contract.[414] But even apart from that criticism, *Watteau v Fenwick* does not support the approach adopted in *Ex parte Dixon*. In *Watteau v Fenwick* the third party did not know that the other contracting party was only an agent. Nevertheless, the decision in that case is still consistent with the result that would have followed if the third party had been informed of that fact, ie the principal would have been liable on the contract. This is not so in relation to *Ex parte Dixon*, however. If the third party had been aware that he was dealing with a factor, he would have been denied the relief that was granted by the Court of Appeal, ie a right to set off the agent's indebtedness to him against his liability to the principal. In other words, the form of authority which the court found in

---

[410] (1876) 4 Ch D 133, 136.

[411] Brett JA in *Ex parte Dixon* seemed to contemplate the situation in which the agent is a factor in the traditional sense of the word, so that his 'usual employment' is to sell the goods of others in his own name. However Williams J in *Knight v Matson* (1902) 22 NZLR 293, 308–309, in applying Brett JA's statement, evidently considered that the analysis should not be limited to that type of agent.

[412] [1893] 1 QB 346.

[413] [1893] 1 QB 346, 348–349.

[414] See *Bowstead and Reynolds on Agency* (17th edn, 2001) 92–4, 349–51and Fridman, *The Law of Agency* (7th edn, 1996) 72–6. Bingham J doubted the authority of *Watteau v Fenwick* in *Rhodian River Shipping Co SA v Halla Maritime Corporation (The Rhodian River)* [1984] 1 Lloyd's Rep 373, and the British Columbia Court of Appeal declined to follow it in *Sign-O-Lite Plastics Ltd v Metropolitan Life Insurance Co* (1990) 73 DLR (4th) 541. See also *McLaughlin v Gentles* (1919) 51 DLR 383 and *International Paper Co v Spicer* (1906) 4 CLR 739, 763.

Ex parte Dixon was an even more tenuous basis for the decision in that case than the authority found in *Watteau v Fenwick*.

13.91 Unless possibly *Ex parte Dixon* is treated as a case in which the goods had been delivered to an agent who was accustomed to deal in goods of that type on his own account in the normal course of his business, so as to come within the doctrine of apparent ownership, it is difficult to explain the allowance of a set-off on the basis of an estoppel. The notion that the agent dealt in goods of that type on his own account was not emphasized in the judgments, and it seems that the decision did not turn on it. The case may be regarded as wrongly decided on the ground that the representation made by the agent was not authorized by, and consequently was not binding upon, the undisclosed principal. That would not be a welcome result, however, because a private communication between the principal and the agent should not have the effect of denying the third party a set-off that he otherwise may have expected to have, particularly when it was the principal himself who chose to deal through an agent. Alternatively, the courts may come to recognize that the estoppel theory put forward by the House of Lords in *Cooke v Eshelby*,[415] which was decided only eleven years after *Ex parte Dixon*[416] without any mention being made of that case, is not a satisfactory explanation for the *George v Clagett* set-off,[417] and that, as the principal's very right of intervention on his agent's contract is an anomaly without a proper juristic explanation,[418] so is the third party's right of set-off.

(4) Set-off Between the Principal and the Third Party

13.92 When a contract is effected through an agent, the parties to the contract usually are the principal and the third party.[419] The agent is not a party, and accordingly he may not enforce the contract in an action brought in his own name.[420] This is not an invariable rule, however, because there are a number of situations in which the agent contracts personally, and in which he may sue.[421] This is the case when the agent contracts for an undisclosed principal. It may also apply, depending on

---

[415] (1887) 12 App Cas 271.

[416] (1876) 4 Ch D 133.

[417] The statement of the principle in terms of estoppel is criticized in Powell, *The Law of Agency* (1952) 147–8, and also in *Bowstead and Reynolds on Agency* (17th edn, 2001) 369–70.

[418] See para 13.71 above.

[419] Compare the case of an undisclosed principal, who is not a party to the agent's contract. See para 13.71 above.

[420] See eg *Storaker v Southouse & Long Ltd* (1920) 20 SR (NSW) 190. The fact that the agent may be on a del credere commission does not affect this conclusion. See *Bramwell v Spiller* (1870) 21 LT 672. Nor would it make any difference if the agent paid the contract sum to the principal under the terms of the commission. See *Jordeson and Co and Simon Kahn v London Hardwood Co* (1913) 19 Com Cas 161; *Coghlan v McKay* (1902) 8 ALR 155. See also *Flatau, Dick & Co v Keeping* (1931) 39 Li L Rep 232 (advances made by the agent to his principal on the goods).

[421] See generally *Bowstead and Reynolds on Agency* (17th edn, 2001) 464 *et seq*.

the circumstances, in the case of an agent for an unnamed principal,[422] that is, when the agent discloses that he is acting as an agent but without disclosing the principal's identity, and when a person enters into a contract in his own name but he is expressed to do so 'and/or as agent', so that he may or may not be contracting as a principal.[423] Similarly a factor,[424] an auctioneer of goods,[425] and an agent who effects insurance in his own name on behalf of another with that other's authority[426] may each sue. If indeed the agent rather than the principal sues, the question whether the third party may set off in that action a debt owing to him by the principal prima facie should depend on whether it can be said that the agent in bringing the action does so as trustee for the principal, because otherwise the demands would not be mutual in equity.[427] In fact, it is not easy to find a trust in all cases.

Auctioneer's lien

Consider the case of a sale of goods by auction. The purchaser may have removed **13.93** the goods without immediate payment and subsequently been sued by the auctioneer for the price, the auctioneer's entitlement to sue arising either by virtue of a special property that he has in the goods, or alternatively from a contract implied by law between him and the purchaser whereby the purchaser has agreed to pay the price to the auctioneer.[428] The purchaser may set off in that action a debt owing to him by the vendor/principal, provided that the auctioneer is adequately

---

[422] In *Teheran-Europe Co Ltd v S T Belton (Tractors) Ltd* [1968] 2 QB 545, 558 Diplock LJ contemplated the situation in which both the principal and the agent may be entitled to sue on the contract. See generally *Bowstead and Reynolds on Agency* (17th edn, 2001) 469–71.

[423] See *Lee v Bullen* (1858) 27 LJQB 161. See also *Greater Britain Insurance Corp. Ltd v C T Bowring & Co (Insurance) Ltd* (1925) 22 Ll L Rep 538, in which Greer J allowed brokers a set-off in respect of policies effected by them 'and/or as agents'. For the terms of the policy, see (1925) 23 Ll L Rep 285. Greer LJ's reliance on *Koster v Eason* (1813) 2 M & S 112, 105 ER 324 and *Parker v Beasley* (1814) 2 M & S 423, 105 ER 438 suggests that he considered that the brokers could have sued in their own name. His decision subsequently was affirmed by the Court of Appeal ((1926) 24 Ll L Rep 7), but on the alternative ground that the agreement between the parties modified their relationship.

[424] *Drinkwater v Goodwin* (1775) 1 Cowp 251, 98 ER 1070.

[425] See *Williams v Millington* (1788) 1 H Bl 81, 126 ER 49; *Chelmsford Auctions Ltd v Poole* [1973] 1 QB 542. This is not the case, however, in relation to an auctioneer of land. See *Cherry v Anderson* (1876) Ir R 10 CL 204.

[426] *Provincial Insurance Co of Canada v Leduc* (1874) LR 6 PC 224, 244, and see generally *Arnould's Law of Marine Insurance and Average* (16th edn, 1981) vol 2, 1132 para 1354.

[427] Compare *Atkyns and Batten v Amber* (1796) 2 Esp 493, 170 ER 431 in which a set-off was denied, although the broker in that case had made advances to the principal on the goods sold so that he would have been suing on his own account. *Quaere* whether the agent in the *Atkyns* case should have been allowed to sue in his own name. See *Bramwell v Spiller* (1870) 21 LT 672. The sale note in *Atkyns and Batten v Amber* said that the goods were sold by the agent 'on account of' the principal, so that the agent himself would not appear to have been a party to the contract. See for example *Jordeson & Co and Simon Kahn v London Hardwood Co* (1931) 19 Com Cas 161 ('as agents for'); *Flatau, Dick & Co v Keeping* (1931) 39 Ll L Rep 232 ('sold for account of our principals').

[428] *Chelmsford Auctions Ltd v Poole* [1973] 1 QB 542, 549, 550, referring to *Benton v Campbell, Parker and Co* [1925] 2 KB 410, 416.

protected in respect of his lien[429] for his expenses and charges in auctioning the goods,[430] and for any other right of deduction previously agreed to by the vendor in respect of other debts owing to him by the vendor.[431] The use of the word 'lien' to describe the auctioneer's rights in respect of the proceeds of sale is criticized in *Bowstead and Reynolds on Agency*[432] on the same basis that the term 'banker's lien' has been said to be inappropriate to describe a banker's right to treat accounts as combined.[433] In other words, it is difficult to see how a lien can be exercised over money, which normally would become the property of the holder subject to an obligation to account for it. It is suggested in *Bowstead* that the auctioneer's lien over the proceeds may refer to a number of rights. Thus, it may be explained as a right of set-off when the auctioneer is sued by the principal, or it may refer to the auctioneer's right to sue the purchaser for the price and then retain the proceeds, or it may refer to the rule that the purchaser, to the extent of the lien, may not set off against the auctioneer a claim that he has against the vendor. But in considering the auctioneer's position, it should also be appreciated that it differs from that of a banker, since the auctioneer holds the proceeds of sale subject to a trust.[434] When the price is received there is therefore a fund which is to be kept separate, and from which the amount secured by the lien can be retained. A bank on the other hand is a debtor, not a trustee.[435] However the essence of the view in Bowstead would appear to be correct, that an auctioneer's lien should be regarded as a package or rights, including the right to sue the purchaser for the price and to retain from the trust fund representing the proceeds an amount sufficient to satisfy his entitlement.

13.94   In *Benton v Campbell, Parker and Co*,[436] Salter J suggested that a set-off in respect of a debt owing by the vendor is not available in the auctioneer's action before the debt secured by the lien has been paid, but the better view is that it is sufficient if allowance is given for the auctioneer's entitlement in the set-off, by only permit-

---

[429]   An auctioneer only has a particular lien over goods for his charges and expenses in respect of those particular goods. See *Webb v Smith* (1885) 30 Ch D 192. The auctioneer's position should be compared to that of a factor, who has a general lien for the balance of his account with the principal. See *Kruger v Wilcox* (1755) Amb 252, 27 ER 168; *Baring v Corrie* (1818) 2 B & Ald 137, 148, 106 ER 317, 321.

[430]   *Jarvis v Chapple* (1815) 2 Chit 387; *Holmes v Tutton* (1855) 5 El & Bl 65, 82, 119 ER 405, 412; *Manley & Sons Ltd v Berkett* [1912] 2 KB 329. See also *Bulgin v McCabe* (1859) unreported but mentioned at 1 QSCR 83–84; *Grice v Kenrick* (1870) LR 5 QB 340, 345; *Benton v Campbell, Parker & Co Ltd* [1925] 2 KB 410, 416; *Chelmsford Auctions Ltd v Poole* [1973] 1 QB 542, 549. Compare *Coppin v Craig* (1816) 7 Taunt 243, 129 ER 97, in which the auctioneer had sold the goods of one person under another's name.

[431]   *Manley & Sons Ltd v Berkett* [1912] 2 KB 329.

[432]   *Bowstead and Reynolds on Agency* (17th edn, 2001) 284. See also *Re Clune* (1988) 14 ACLR 261, 267. Compare Dal Pont, *Law of Agency* (2001) 463–4.

[433]   See para 15.03 below.

[434]   *Crowther v Elgood* (1887) 34 Ch D 691; *Re Cotton (deceased), ex p Cooke* (1913) 108 LT 310.

[435]   *Foley v Hill* (1848) 2 HLC 28, 9 ER 1002.

[436]   [1925] 2 KB 410, 416. See also *Holmes v Tutton* (1855) 5 El & Bl 65, 82, 119 ER 405, 412.

ting the purchaser to set off the price less an amount equal to the sum necessary to protect the auctioneer's entitlement.[437] This right of set-off available to the purchaser in the auctioneer's action has been described as a right in equity by way of equitable defence.[438]

Insolvency set-off

Consider the position in relation to insolvency set-off. When the vendor is bankrupt or is a company in liquidation there is a conceptual difficulty in allowing a set-off as between the purchaser and the vendor before the auctioneer's charges and expenses have been met, and that is that the demands in such a case strictly would not be mutual. Once the auctioneer has received the sale proceeds a trust may arise in favour of the principal after the auctioneer has made the necessary deduction in order to obtain reimbursement.[439] However, the insolvency legislation is cast in terms of mutual debts, credits, and dealings, and mutuality is determined by reference to the equitable title to the demands,[440] as opposed to the eventual equitable title to the proceeds of the demands. The difficulty is that, until the auctioneer's lien has been satisfied, it can hardly be said that the auctioneer holds the right to sue solely as trustee for the principal, since the auctioneer at that stage will have the prior right to look to anything that may be recovered in order that he may satisfy his lien. The auctioneer may be a trustee, first for himself, and, after that, for the principal. Nevertheless, the auctioneer would be the first beneficiary, and his beneficial interest would extend to the whole claim as the source from which his lien is to be satisfied. While the principal may be said to have a beneficial interest in the remainder, that interest would be subject to the interest of the auctioneer, and strictly it should not be sufficient to render the claim mutual with an indebtedness of his own to the purchaser. However, at least if the purchaser is solvent, this objection is unlikely to prevail. An analogous situation occurred in *Lee & Chapman's Case*.[441] A debt owing to a company was charged to a third party. The company went into liquidation, and it was held that the debtor was entitled to a set-off in the liquidation against the part of the debt over and above the amount required to satisfy the secured debt owing to the third party as chargee. On the other hand, a set-off ordinarily should not be available as between the vendor and the purchaser if the purchaser is insolvent, unless the auctioneer's prior interest is

13.95

---

[437] *Manley & Sons Ltd v Berkett* [1912] 2 KB 329. A set-off should be denied, however, if the auctioneer previously had tendered the sale price to the vendor, so that he is suing entirely on his own account, as in *Chelmsford Auctions Ltd v Poole* [1973] 1 QB 542.

[438] *Manley & Sons Ltd v Berkett* [1912] 2 KB 329, 333. See also *Holmes v Tutton* (1855) 5 El & Bl 65, 82, 119 ER 405, 412. In *Chelmsford Auctions Ltd v Poole* [1973] 1 QB 542, 549 Lord Denning referred to the set-off as an 'equity'.

[439] *Re Cotton (deceased), ex p Cooke* (1913) 108 LT 310.

[440] See paras 11.04–11.07 above.

[441] *Re Asphaltic Wood Pavement Co. Lee & Chapman's Case* (1885) 30 Ch D 216.

otherwise secured.[442] If the purchaser is insolvent, a set-off would reduce the debt over which the auctioneer has a 'lien' without any certainty that the proceeds eventually received in respect of the remainder of the debt would be sufficient to satisfy the lien.

Set-off agreement

13.96 The effectiveness as against the auctioneer of an agreement for a set-off between the vendor and the purchaser should be determined by reference to similar principles. The agreement will not provide a defence to an action by the auctioneer unless his charges and expenses have been paid,[443] or at least, if the purchaser is solvent, the set-off may be reduced so as to leave an amount sufficient to cover them.[444] In *Grice v Kenrick*[445] the auctioneer's lien had been satisfied, and although he was aware of a set-off agreement between the vendor and the purchaser, the auctioneer himself paid the price to the vendor and proceeded to sue the purchaser. The set-off agreement was held to constitute a defence to the auctioneer's action, although the court suggested that the auctioneer would have succeeded if he had been deceived by the purchaser, or if there had been anything accompanying the receipt of the goods from which a promise on the defendant's part to pay the auctioneer could have been inferred.

Undisclosed principal

13.97 A similar analysis should apply when an agent who contracted on behalf of an undisclosed principal is suing the third party,[446] and the third party, having discovered the identity of the principal, wishes to set off in that action a debt owing to him by the principal. While the agent ordinarily would hold any proceeds received under the contract on trust for the principal,[447] the Privy Council in *Allen v F O'Hearn and Co*[448] considered that, *as regards the third party*, the agent is not a trustee for the undisclosed principal.[449] Prima facie that should have the consequence that, as between the agent and the third party in the agent's action, there is a lack of mutuality in relation to the cross-demands. There was a similar lack of

---

[442] See paras 11.28 and 11.29 above.

[443] *Grice v Kenrick* (1870) LR 5 QB 340.

[444] *Manley & Sons Ltd v Berkett* [1912] 2 KB 329.

[445] (1870) LR 5 QB 340.

[446] The agent as the contracting party is entitled to sue on the contract. See *Garrett v Bird* (1872) 11 SCR (NSW) 97. See also *Sims v Bond* (1833) 5 B & Ad 389, 393, 110 ER 834, 835–836, and generally *Bowstead and Reynolds on Agency* (17th edn, 2001) 467.

[447] *Pople v Evans* [1969] 2 Ch 255, 261, and see also *Allen v F O'Hearn and Co* [1937] AC 213, 218.

[448] [1937] AC 213, 218.

[449] See also *Pople v Evans* [1969] 2 Ch 255. Compare Ames, 'Undisclosed Principal—His Rights and Liabilities' (1909) 18 Yale Law Journal 443, 446, 448, and Higgins, 'The Equity of the Undisclosed Principal' (1965) 28 MLR 167. Compare also Wood, *English and International Set-off* (1989) 980–1.

mutuality however in the auctioneer cases, and they suggest that this objection is unlikely to prevent a set-off given that the principal is the party who will benefit from the claim. If the principal intervened and himself sued the third party there would be mutuality, and the existence or otherwise of a right of set-off should not depend on whether the principal or the agent sues. Furthermore, if either the principal or the third party is bankrupt or in liquidation, a set-off may occur between them in any event under the insolvency set-off section without the necessity for an action.[450]

Unnamed principal

Alternatively, the agent may have informed the third party that he was acting on behalf of a principal, but without naming the principal. In other words, the case may concern a disclosed principal who nevertheless is unnamed. Sometimes the agent in these cases will contract personally and therefore will be liable on the contract, this liability being in addition to that of the principal,[451] in which case the agent also may be entitled to bring proceedings.[452] Once again, the third party generally should be entitled to set off a cross-demand that he has against the principal. However, whether the principal is undisclosed or merely unnamed, the availability of a set-off should be subject to the same principle applicable to auctioneers, that a set-off should not be available if it would prejudice a prior interest that the agent has in the action.   **13.98**

(5) Set-off Between the Agent and the Third Party, Where the Agent Can Enforce the Contract[453]

When an agent is entitled to enforce a contract made on behalf of the principal,[454] and the agent is independently indebted to the third party, a set-off should be permissible as between them to the extent that the agent has a prior interest in the action, for example as a result of an auctioneer's lien for his charges and expenses. This is implicit in *Hudson v Granger*.[455] An agent who sold the goods of his principal was entitled by virtue of a lien on the goods to receive the price. It was held that an agreement between the purchaser and the agent's assignees in bankruptcy,   **13.99**

---

[450] *Stein v Blake* [1996] AC 243. See para 6.79 *ff* above.

[451] *Bowstead and Reynolds on Agency* (17th edn, 2001) 469–70. Compare *N & J Vlassopulos Ltd v Ney Shipping Ltd (The Santa Carina)* [1977] 1 Lloyd's Rep 478.

[452] As in *Short v Spackman* (1831) 2 B & Ad 962, 109 ER 1400. See Fridman, *The Law of Agency* (7th edn, 1996) 249–50, though compare Stoljar, *The Law of Agency* (1961) 250–1. In *Teheran-Europe Co Ltd v S T Belton (Tractors) Ltd* [1968] 2 QB 545, 558 Diplock LJ contemplated the situation in which both the principal and the agent may be entitled to sue, and may be liable to be sued, on the contract.

[453] See also paras 13.68–13.70 above.

[454] See para 13.92 above.

[455] (1821) 5 B & Ald 27, 106 ER 1103. See also *Warner v M'Kay* (1836) 1 M & W 591, 150 ER 571.

by which the price was set off against a debt owing by the agent to the third party, was binding on the principal. On the other hand, to the extent that the principal is the party interested in the claim, a debt owing to the agent personally should not be able to be set off.[456]

Insurance brokers in marine insurance

13.100 The question of a set-off as between an agent and a third party has arisen in the context of marine insurance. As a result of a mercantile custom, which since has received statutory recognition,[457] a broker who effects a policy of marine insurance on behalf of an insured is directly responsible as a principal to the underwriter for the premium.[458] In a number of cases in which a broker was being sued by an underwriter's trustee (or, formerly, assignees) in bankruptcy for premiums, the broker sought to set off the underwriter's liability to the insured for losses on policies effected through the broker.[459] The prima facie rule is that, unless the broker effected the policy on his own account,[460] the underwriter's liability to the insured and the broker's indebtedness to the underwriter are not mutual, so that a set-off against the broker's debt is not permitted.[461] That would also apply in a case where the underwriter is being sued by the insured in respect of a loss.[462] Nor would an agreement for a set-off between the broker and the underwriter bind the insured.[463] Consider however that the policy is taken out in the broker's name,[464] so that he may sue upon it,[465] and moreover that the broker has an interest in the claim on the policy as a result of a lien for an amount owing to him by the in-

---

[456] Compare the contrary view expressed at common law by Denman CJ in *Gibson v Winter* (1833) 5 B & Ad 96, 102, 110 ER 728, 730.

[457] Marine Insurance Act 1906, s 53(1). In Australia see the Marine Insurance Act 1909 (Cth), s 59(1).

[458] See generally *Arnould's Law of Marine Insurance and Average* (16th edn, 1981) vol 1, 112–13. Apparently this is not so in non-marine insurance, although an agent authorized to receive payment on behalf of an insurer will be liable to account for premiums actually received. See *Re Palmdale Insurance Ltd* [1982] VR 921.

[459] The cases are collected and discussed in *Arnould on the Law of Marine Insurance and Average* (12th edn, 1939) vol 1, 163 *et seq.* In Australia, note the Insurance (Agents and Brokers) Act 1984 (Cth), s 37, which provides that moneys paid to a person (not being a registered insurance broker) as agent of an insurer are subject to a trust in favour of the insurer and are not capable of being made subject to a set-off.

[460] See *Koster v Eason* (1813) 2 M & S 112, 105 ER 324, although this is unlikely to be the case in modern business. See *Arnould's Law of Marine Insurance and Average* (16th edn, 1981) vol 1, 118 n 62.

[461] See eg *Wilson v Creighton* (1782) 3 Dougl 132, 99 ER 576; *Bell v Auldjo* (1784) 4 Dougl 48, 99 ER 761.

[462] *Stolos Compania SA v Ajax Insurance Co Ltd (The Admiral C)* [1981] 1 Lloyd's Rep 9.

[463] *Jell v Pratt* (1817) 2 Stark 67, 171 ER 575.

[464] The name inserted in the policy is 'frequently—perhaps usually—that of the brokers acting on behalf of others'. *The Yasin* [1979] 2 Lloyd's Rep 45, 53, *per* Lloyd J.

[465] See *Provincial Insurance Co of Canada v Leduc* (1874) LR 6 PC 224, 244, and generally *Arnould's Law of Marine Insurance and Average* (16th edn 1981) vol 2, 1132, para 1354.

sured.[466] In those circumstances, if the broker is sued by the underwriter's trustee in bankruptcy for unpaid premiums the courts have held that the broker may set off the insured's claim on the policy.[467] In the cases in question the amount owing to the broker secured by the lien exceeded the claim on the policy. If on the other hand the lien is for an amount less than the loss, a set-off should only be permitted to the extent of the lien. The contrary conclusion would mean that the insured's asset would be used to pay the broker's liability.[468] Moreover, a claim on a policy of marine insurance is regarded as being unliquidated in nature,[469] even after the loss has been adjusted,[470] so that a set-off would not appear to be available under the Statutes of Set-off if both the broker and the underwriter are solvent.[471]

Non-marine insurance

In non-marine insurance a broker effecting a policy of insurance on behalf of a **13.101** client ordinarily would not do so in his own name. Therefore, the preceding discussion of the broker's right to set off losses when the name inserted in the policy is that of the broker would not be relevant. On the other hand, an attempt was made in New South Wales to introduce a right of set-off between the insurer and the broker based upon custom or usage. In *Re Colin Williams (Insurance) Pty Ltd*[472] an insurance company and an insurance broker had adopted a practice by which the company would debit the broker in its accounts with the amount of the premium,[473] and credit the broker with the appropriate commission. If a policy

---

[466] For a discussion of an insurance broker's lien, see *Arnould's Law of Marine Insurance and Average* (16th edn, 1981) vol 1, 129–34. Presumably this would encompass the common practice by which the broker, on receiving credit for a claim from the underwriter, pays the insured forthwith. See Arnould, *op cit* vol 1, 111, 116 n 56.

[467] *Parker v Beasley* (1814) 2 M & S 423, 105 ER 438 (in which the brokers had a lien by virtue of their accepting bills on the credit of the goods insured); *Davies v Wilkinson* (1828) 4 Bing 573, 130 ER 889.

[468] See Lord Ellenborough in *Koster v Eason* (1813) 2 M & S 112, 119–120, 105 ER 324, 327.

[469] *Luckie v Bushby* (1853) 13 CB 864, 138 ER 1443; *Pellas v Neptune Marine Insurance Co* (1879) 5 CPD 34; *William Pickersgill & Sons Ltd v London and Provincial Marine and General Insurance Co Ltd* [1912] 3 KB 614, 622; *Jabbour v Custodian of Israeli Absentee Property* [1954] 1 WLR 139, 145; *Chandris v Argo Insurance Co Ltd* [1963] 2 Lloyd's Rep 65, 73–74; *Edmunds v Lloyd Italico* [1986] 1 WLR 492, 493; *Accident Compensation Commission v C E Heath Underwriting & Insurance (Aust) Pty Ltd* [1990] VR 224, 231; *Penrith City Council v Government Insurance Office* (1991) 24 NSWLR 564, 568; *I M Properties plc v Cape & Dalgleish* [1999] QB 297, 304.

[470] *Luckie v Bushby* (1853) 13 CB 864, 138 ER 1443; *Jabbour v Custodian of Israeli Absentee Property* [1954] 1 WLR 139, 143.

[471] See para 2.26 above.

[472] [1975] 1 NSWLR 130. See also *Re Palmdale Insurance Ltd* [1982] VR 921.

[473] In non-marine insurance a broker ordinarily is not principally liable for the premium, although an agent of the insurer authorized to receive premiums on behalf of the insurer will be liable to account for premiums actually received. See *Re Palmdale Insurance Ltd* [1982] VR 921. Compare the custom at Lloyd's, which renders the broker principally liable. See *MacGillivray on Insurance Law* (9th edn, 1997) 962 para 35-12, and also *Grover and Grover Ltd v Mathews* (1910) 15 Com Cas 249, 260 (Lloyd's fire policy). There does not appear to be any authority establishing the existence of a similar custom in non-marine insurance in Australia. See *Norwich Fire Insurance Society Ltd v*

was cancelled so that a proportion of the premium was returnable, the insurance company would credit the broker's account with the rebate of premium, and debit that account with a rateable proportion of the commission.[474] Both the insurer and the broker went into liquidation. The insurer cancelled all its policies, and as a result became liable for returns of premium. The insurer's liquidator proposed to credit the broker with the returns, and debit it with the rebate of commission together with the sums owing by the broker for premiums. The broker's liquidator, on the other hand, said that the return premiums were payable to the policyholders, and so could not be set off against the sums owing by the broker. Evidence was given of a practice in the insurance industry by which an insurance broker is credited with any return premium on a policy arranged through the broker and subsequently cancelled. Helsham J pointed out however that the policies all had provisions to the effect that, if the policy were cancelled, the unearned premium would be refunded *to the insured*. His Honour said that any alleged usage would be unreasonable if it was inconsistent with the terms of the contract between the insurer and the insured. In any event, even apart from the wording of the policies, he said that a usage by which an underwriter credits a broker's account with return premiums would be unreasonable, and consequently would not be binding upon the insured, unless the insured had knowledge of the practice when he entered into the contract.[475]

(6) Set-off Against an Agent With a Lien, Where the Agent Cannot Sue

13.102 We have seen that, where an insurance broker has taken out a policy of insurance on behalf of an insured but in his own name, so that the broker can sue upon it, and the broker is indebted to the underwriter, the courts have permitted the broker to employ an accrued claim on the policy in a set-off in the underwriter's bankruptcy against the debt to the extent that the broker has a lien on the policy.[476] In

---

Brennans (Horsham) Pty Ltd [1981] VR 981, 989, and also, in England, *Wilson v Avec Audio-Visual Equipment Ltd* [1974] 1 Lloyd's Rep 81. *Quaere* whether, in the absence of an agreement between the parties, the broker in *Re Colin Williams (Insurance) Pty Ltd* (n 472 above) in fact would have been liable to the insurance company for premiums. See *Norwich Winterthur Insurance (Australia) Ltd v Con-Stan Industries of Australia Pty Ltd* [1983] 1 NSWLR 461, 474 (result affirmed (1986) 160 CLR 226).

[474] Helsham J accepted that there was a usage by which an insurer, upon cancelling a policy in respect of which a broker's commission had been paid, could claim a proportionate part of the commission. He further held that this usage was not unreasonable. See also *Re Palmdale Insurance Ltd* [1982] VR 921.

[475] Helsham J referred to similar cases in marine insurance in which it was held that a usage at Lloyd's, by which an underwriter could settle a loss by setting it off against a broker's liability for premiums, would not bind the insured, unless the insured had knowledge of the existence of the usage, or in any event the broker from the course of dealing between himself and the insured had authority to settle losses in accordance with it. See *Sweeting v Pearce* (1859) 7 CB (NS) 449, 141 ER 890, (1861) 9 CB (NS) 534, 142 ER 210, and generally *Arnould's Law of Marine Insurance and Average* (16th edn, 1981) vol 1, 125–27.

[476] See para 13.100 above.

the cases in question however it was crucial to the set-off that the policy was in the broker's own name. As Lord Ellenborough remarked,[477] the underwriter in such a case 'had consented that [the brokers] should be at liberty to stand in the character and situation of principals, that in case of loss they should be entitled to act in all respects as his creditors, and that they should be considered as giving him credit upon the policy at their own risk, and on their account'. If on the other hand the policy was not in the broker's name he was not entitled to a set-off, notwithstanding that he had a lien. The important point as far as mutuality for a set-off is concerned is that a broker's lien is not equitable in origin, but rather it has its source in the common law. Furthermore, apart from the intervention of statute in the form of the Judicature Acts, the common law courts never contemplated an assignment of a debt, so that any suggestion that the lien operates as a form of assignment would hardly be accurate.[478] Rather, the common law gave effect to the lien by allowing the broker to retain the policy in his possession, and to apply any proceeds of a claim that the broker in fact received in reduction of the debt owing to him.[479] Nor, given its common law origin and nature, would the lien confer an equitable interest in the insured's claim,[480] notwithstanding that equitable remedies, for example an injunction, would be available in an appropriate case in aid of the common law right. Consistent with that view, it was held that, where the broker could not sue, there was a lack of mutuality between the insured's claim against the underwriter on the policy and the underwriter's demand against the broker for premiums, and consequently no set-off.[481]

(7) Del Credere Commissions

There are a number of old set-off cases concerning agents who contracted on the **13.103** basis of a del credere commission, in other words where the agent undertook to indemnify his employer against loss arising from the failure of persons with whom he contracted to carry out their contracts.[482] In *Grove v Dubois*[483] an insurance

---

[477] *Koster v Eason* (1813) 2 M & S 112, 118, 105 ER 324, 326–327.

[478] Compare Wood, *English and International Set-off* (1989) 919.

[479] See eg *Mann v Forrester* (1814) 4 Camp 60, 171 ER 20; *Eide UK Ltd v Lowndes Lambert Group Ltd* [1999] QB 199, 208–211.

[480] Compare Wood, *English and International Set-off* (1989) 1004–5. The comments of the Privy Council in *Allen v F O'Hearn* [1937] AC 213, 218, in relation to whether an agent for an undisclosed principal is a trustee of the claim, should be considered in this context. See para 13.97 above.

[481] See *Koster v Eason* (1813) 2 M & S 112, 105 ER 324; *Xenos v Wickham* (1863) 14 CB (NS) 435, 465–466, 143 ER 515, 528; *Wilson v Creighton* (1782) 3 Dougl 132, 99 ER 576. See also *Cumming v Forester* (1813) 1 M & S 494, 105 ER 185 (set-off between solvent parties). Nor did it matter whether or not the broker acted on a del credere commission. See *Peele v Northcote* (1817) 7 Taunt 478, 129 ER 192. Compare Wood, *English and International Set-off* (1989) 918–19, 1006–7.

[482] *Halsbury's Laws of England* (4th edn (reissue), 1990) vol 1(2), 11 para 13. See generally Chorley, 'Del Credere' (1929) 45 LQR 221, (1930) 46 LQR 11.

[483] (1786) 1 TR 112, 99 ER 1002. See also *Bize v Dickason* (1786) 1 TR 285, 99 ER 1097; *Wienholt v Roberts* (1811) 2 Camp 586, 170 ER 1260.

broker on a del credere commission took out policies in his own name on behalf of foreign correspondents. When he was sued by an underwriter's assignees in bankruptcy for unpaid premiums, it was held that he could set off claims that had accrued on the policies. The Court of King's Bench in allowing a set-off laid considerable emphasis on the fact of the commission, and indeed Lord Mansfield in his judgment said that the 'whole turns on the nature of a commission del credere'.[484] The view seems to have been that, if the broker had made himself liable to the principal for the loss, the broker in turn must have given credit to, or trusted, the underwriter for the amount of the loss.[485] That basis for the decision has been criticized, however, particularly by Lord Ellenborough, on the ground that a contract between the insured and the broker for a del credere commission ought not vary the rights between the broker and the underwriter, who is a stranger to it, and empower the broker to set up a claim against the underwriter that is derived from the contract.[486] Nevertheless, despite that criticism, the case has not been overruled. Rather it has been suggested that the dealing in *Grove v Dobois* was with the broker as a principal,[487] the broker having insured for foreign correspondents who were unknown to the underwriter. In truth this is not the basis on which the judgments in *Grove v Dubois* proceeded.[488] A more fundamental question was in issue, whether a del credere agent assumed a primary or a secondary obligation.[489] Lord Mansfield in *Grove v Dubois*[490] said that it was primary. Lord Ellenborough on the other hand considered that it took effect as a guarantee,[491] and therefore was secondary. This is the view that has prevailed. A del credere commission is regarded as an agreement to indemnify the principal if the

---

[484] (1786) 1 TR 112, 115, 99 ER 1002, 1004.

[485] See the discussion in the note to the report of *Baker v Langhorn* (1816) 4 Camp 396, 399, 171 ER 126, 127. In *Lee v Bullen* (1858) 27 LJQB 161 the del credere commission was said to give the broker an 'interest' in the contract of insurance. See also *Tapper v Matheson* (1884) NZLR 3 SC 312, 314.

[486] *Cumming v Forester* (1813) 1 M & S 494, 499, 105 ER 185, 186; *Koster v Eason* (1813) 2 M & S 112, 119, 105 ER 324, 327; *Hornby v Lacy* (1817) 6 M & S 166, 171, 105 ER 1205, 1207, *per* Lord Ellenborough (although compare Lord Ellenborough's earlier judgment in *Wienholt v Roberts* (1811) 2 Camp 586, 170 ER 1260). See also *Baker v Langhorn* (1816) 6 Taunt 519, 521, 128 ER 1136, 1137, *per* Gibbs CJ; *Peele v Northcote* (1817) 7 Taunt 478, 480, 485, 129 ER 192, 193, 195, *per* Gibbs CJ; *Hornby v Lacy* at 172, 1207, *per* Abbott CJ. *Quaere* whether this is a satisfactory ground for criticism. For example, an assignment by A to B of a debt owing by C may provide B with a defence to an action brought against him by C on another transaction.

[487] *Cumming v Forester* (1813) 1 M & S 494, 499, 105 ER 185, 187, *per* Lord Ellenborough. In *Parker v Smith* (1812) 16 East 382, 385–386, 104 ER 1133, 1135 Lord Ellenborough said that *Grove v Dubois* was determined on the ground that there were 'dealings virtually had with the assured themselves'. See also *Arnould on the Law of Marine Insurance and Average,* (12th edn, 1939) vol 1, 164–5.

[488] Chorley, 'Del Credere' (1929) 45 LQR 221, 227.

[489] Chorley, 'Del Credere' (1929) 45 LQR 221, 229–30.

[490] (1786) 1 TR 112, 115, 99 ER 1002, 1004.

[491] *Morris v Cleasby* (1816) 4 M & S 566, 574, 105 ER 943, 947; *Hornby v Lacy* (1817) 6 M & S 166, 171, 105 ER 1205, 1207.

third party fails to pay through insolvency, or something that makes it impossible to recover as in the case of insolvency.[492]

Given this characterization of a del credere agency, if the agent has paid the prin- **13.104**
cipal in accordance with the commission, and the case is one in which the agent in any event can sue the third party in his own name, for example because he acted for an undisclosed principal or an unnamed principal,[493] the position is simple. There is mutuality both at law and in equity between the agent and the third party.[494] Since the agent after payment under the del credere commission holds the claim for his own benefit and not for the benefit of the principal, there is no other beneficial interest which can affect mutuality. Where the third party has become bankrupt or has gone into liquidation, so that the insolvency set-off section governs the question, the availability of a set-off would depend on the principles discussed earlier in relation to contingent debts and guarantees.[495] Thus, the agent would not be entitled to a set-off if payment has not been made under the commission.[496] The principal in such a case would still have a right of proof in the insolvency, and the rule against double proof would prevent a set-off as between the agent and the third party.[497]

Consider that the case is one in which the agent does not have standing to sue, and **13.105**
the third party is insolvent. Usually the del credere commission would not have been given at the request of the third party, in which case *Owen v Tate*[498] suggests that after payment the agent as a surety would not have a claim for reimbursement from the third party which could be set off. That view is consistent with some of the early common law cases in which *Grove v Dubois* was criticized and a set-off was denied.[499] However *Owen v Tate* has not been favourably received by

---

[492] *Thomas Gabriel & Sons v Churchill & Sim* [1914] 3 KB 1272, affirming [1914] 1 KB 449.

[493] See *Teheran-Europe Co Ltd v S T Belton (Tractors) Ltd* [1968] 2 QB 545, 558 in relation to an agent for an unnamed principal.

[494] See *Koster v Eason* (1813) 2 M & S 112, 105 ER 324, in which Lord Ellenborough emphasized (at 118, 326–327) the title to sue. This is the proper explanation of *Lee v Bullen* (1858) 27 LJQB 161, in which the brokers contracted in their own names 'and/or as agents'. Wightman J emphasized that the brokers might have sued and recovered in their own names, but compare Compton J at 162.

[495] See paras 8.07–8.26 (contingent debt owing by the insolvent) and paras 8.27–8.37 (contingent debt owing to the insolvent) above. In particular, a guarantor who pays the creditor after the creditor has proved in the debtor's bankruptcy or liquidation should be subrogated to the creditor's proof, and because of that beneficial interest in the proof the guarantor should be entitled to a set-off. See paras 8.22–8.25 above. Accordingly, it should not be fatal to a set-off that the agent paid under the del credere commission after the principal had lodged a proof in the third party's bankruptcy or liquidation. Compare however Wood, *English and International Set-off* (1989) 1007.

[496] *Koster v Eason* (1813) 2 M & S 112, 119–120, 105 ER 324, 327.

[497] See paras 8.08–8.13 above.

[498] [1976] 1 QB 402.

[499] See eg *Cumming v Forrester* (1813) 1 M & S 494, 105 ER 185; *Morris v Cleasby* (1816) 4 M & S 566, 105 ER 943; *Peele v Northcote* (1817) 7 Taunt 478, 129 ER 192.

commentators,[500] and it may not be followed. Moreover, it may not have the effect of precluding a remedy to the del credere agent by way of subrogation to the principal's rights against the third party, either on the basis of the equitable right[501] or pursuant to the statutory right conferred on a surety by s 5 of the Mercantile Law Amendment Act 1856.[502] Even if it is the case, on the authority of *Owen v Tate*, that the agent has no direct right of reimbursement from the third party, but subrogation is available, the interest obtained in the principal's action consequent upon the right of subrogation may provide a sufficient basis for a set-off.[503] Nor should it make any difference that the interest is acquired after the third party's bankruptcy by payment to the principal, since it still arises out of a prior obligation in the form of the del credere agency.[504] The basis of the set-off is the giving of credit, in that the del credere commission would naturally or in the ordinary course of business end in a debt[505] owing by the third party to the agent as a result of the right of subrogation. When it is sought to base a set-off upon the concept of giving credit, it is not necessary to show that the debt arose out of a dealing between the parties to the proposed set-off.[506] If the del credere commission would naturally result in money becoming payable by the third party to the agent, credit is given by the agent to the third party whether or not the third party is aware of it.

(8) Set-off Between the Agent and the Third Party, Where the Agent is Personally Liable as Agent

13.106 An agent contracting for a principal may undertake a personal liability to the third party,[507] which should be capable of being set off against a personal claim that he has against the third party.[508] On the other hand, the agent should not be entitled to bring into an account a liability of the third party to the principal. While the principal may be obliged to indemnify the agent, this would be of no concern to the third party, and it should not be sufficient to bring about mutuality between the agent's personal liability to the third party and a claim possessed by the prin-

---

[500] Goff and Jones, *The Law of Restitution* (5th edn, 1998) 128–9; Birks, *An Introduction to the Law of Restitution* (1989) 311–12; Burrows, *The Law of Restitution* (1993) 213–16.

[501] Goff and Jones, *The Law of Restitution* (5th edn, 1998) 128–9; Beatson, *The Use and Abuse of Unjust Enrichment* (1991) 199. Compare Mitchell, *The Law of Subrogation* (1994) 166–7.

[502] O'Donovan and Phillips, *The Modern Contract of Guarantee* (3rd edn, 1996) 660–1; Burrows, *The Law of Restitution* (1993) 215.

[503] See para 8.22 above.

[504] See para 8.23 above, criticizing *MPS Constructions Pty Ltd v Rural Bank of New South Wales* (1980) 4 ACLR 835.

[505] See para 7.04 above.

[506] See para 7.11 above. Compare *Re Charge Card Services Ltd* [1987] 1 Ch 150, 189–190, *per* Millett J, for which see paras 8.18–8.20 above.

[507] See generally *Bowstead and Reynolds on Agency* (17th edn, 2001) 461 *et seq.*

[508] See *Kent v Munroe* (1904) 8 OLR 723 in relation to McDiarmid.

cipal against the third party.[509] This is subject to two exceptions, however. The first applies when the agent in truth had contracted only as a surety, rather than as a principal debtor in his own right. If the third party proceeds against the agent/surety, the agent may be able to defend the action on the basis of a set-off that would have been available to the principal debtor.[510] The second may arise when the cross-demands are sufficiently closely connected to give rise to an equitable set-off, since mutuality is not a strict requirement of equitable set-off.[511]

(9) Set-off Between the Principal and the Agent

If the agent incurs a liability to the third party for which he is entitled to be reimbursed by the principal, there may be a set-off as between the principal and the agent in respect of the agent's right of reimbursement and a separate indebtedness of the agent to the principal.[512]   **13.107**

An agent may be obliged to account to the principal for sums received in the course of the agency. The question whether the agent is entitled to a set-off may depend on whether the sums in question are impressed with a trust.[513]   **13.108**

G. The Crown

Prior to the enactment of the Crown Proceedings Act 1947, it was not possible for the defendant in an action at law brought against him by the Crown to set off a cross-demand that he had against the Crown. A subject could only make good a claim against the Crown by means of a petition of right, and he could not avoid that procedure by refusing to pay a debt of his own to the Crown and then asserting his claim as a set-off.[514] The inability to rely on a set-off against the Crown was remedied by section 13 of the Crown Proceedings Act,[515] which provided that all civil proceedings by or against the Crown were to be instituted and proceeded with in accordance with the rules of court and not otherwise. RSC O 77 r 6[516]   **13.109**

---

[509] See *Nelson v Roberts* (1893) 69 LT 352, and Angas Parsons J in *Rex v Ray, ex p Chapman* [1936] SASR 241, 249 (liability of personal representative for costs). See also *Kent v Munroe* (1904) 8 OLR 723.

[510] See paras 18.07–18.35 below.

[511] See paras 4.48–4.54 above.

[512] *Cropper v Cook* (1868) LR 3 CP 194.

[513] See ch 10 above.

[514] *Attorney-General v Guy Motors, Ltd* [1928] 2 KB 78. Compare *Hettihewage Siman Appu v The Queen's Advocate* (1884) 9 App Cas 571, in which there was a right to sue the Crown under the laws of Ceylon. In *Re Ind, Coope & Co Ltd* [1911] 2 Ch 223, 235–236 Warrington J left open the question whether a set-off could have been exercised against the Crown. The Crown on the other hand could plead a set-off in answer to a petition of right. See *De Lancey v The Queen* (1871) LR 6 Ex 286, 288, *per* Kelly CB, referring to (1860) 23 & 24 Vict, c 34, s 7.

[515] For the County Court, see s 15.

[516] See the Crown Proceedings Act 1947, s 35(2)(g). RSC O 77 r 6 continues to apply under the new Civil Procedure Rules 1998. See r 50.1, and Sch 1.

however contains a number of restrictions on the availability of set-off and counterclaim in proceedings by and against the Crown. Briefly, a person may not plead a set-off or make any counterclaim in proceedings by the Crown if they are for the recovery of, or the proposed set-off or counterclaim arises out of a right or claim to repayment in respect of, any taxes, duties, or penalties. Furthermore, a counterclaim may not be made nor a set-off pleaded by the Crown in proceedings against the Crown, or by any person in proceedings by the Crown, without the permission of the court:

(a) if the Crown is sued or sues in the name of a Government department and the subject-matter of the counter-claim or set-off does not relate to that department, or

(b) if the Crown is sued or sues in the name of the Attorney-General.

13.110 The Civil Procedure Rules do not apply to insolvency proceedings under the Insolvency Act 1986. On the other hand, rule 7.51 of the Insolvency Rules 1986 provides that, except so far as they are inconsistent with the Insolvency Rules, the Rules of the Supreme Court apply to insolvency proceedings in the High Court. In relation to insolvency set-off, the House of Lords has held that it takes effect automatically upon the occurrence of a bankruptcy or a liquidation.[517] It does not depend on a proceeding, and therefore O 77 r 6 in relation to proceedings by or against the Crown can have no application to insolvency set-off. In the context of the Bankruptcy Act 1914, it was accepted that a set-off could occur in relation to obligations to pay tax to and rights to tax refunds from revenue authorities,[518] and that should still be the case.

Government departments

13.111 The Crown includes government departments that are headed by a Minister.[519] The fact that legislation may provide that a department is entitled to enforce rights acquired in the exercise of its functions and is liable in respect of liabilities 'as if it were acting as a principal' does not mean that the rights or liabilities are not those of the Crown so as to destroy mutuality. A provision to that effect may be purely procedural, in the sense that the department is capable of suing and being sued as a principal, but in the eyes of the law it is still an agent of the Crown.[520]

13.112 Debts arising from dealings with the one government department would be mutual for the purpose of a set-off. An analogous case is *Knowles v Maitland*,[521] in

---

[517] *Stein v Blake* [1996] AC 243. See paras 6.79–6.103 above.

[518] *Re D H Curtis (Builders) Ltd* [1978] 1 Ch 162; *Re Cushla Ltd* [1979] 3 All ER 415; *Re Unit 2 Windows Ltd* [1985] 1 WLR 1383.

[519] Hogg and Monahan, *Liability of the Crown* (3rd edn, 2000) 11.

[520] *Cullen v Nottingham Health Authority* [1986] BCC 99,368.

[521] (1825) 4 B & C 173, 107 ER 1024, as explained by Lord Tenterden CJ in *Earl of Dalhousie v Chapman* (1829) 7 LJOSKB 233.

which the colonel of a regiment was both debtor and creditor in that capacity, and a set-off was allowed. On the other hand, a person may be liable to one government department and have a claim against another. Because of the theory that the Crown is one and indivisible the demands should be mutual, although, where the debtor is neither bankrupt nor a company in liquidation, a set-off would be subject to RSC O 77 r 6.

Criticism of Crown set-off

The Cork Committee,[522] following similar comments by the Blagden Committee in 1957,[523] considered that this right of set-off available to the Crown conferred upon it an unwarranted preference in the bankruptcy of a subject. Accordingly it recommended that government departments should be treated as separate entities for the purpose of set-off, and moreover that there should not be any right of set-off between contractual and statutory obligations. On the other hand it also recommended that set-off in relation to one statutory obligation and another, and in relation to one contractual obligation and another, in each case relating to the same government department, should be allowed in accordance with the principle of mutuality. While those recommendations were not included in the Insolvency Act 1986, there is much to commend them, although it is debatable whether the Crown indeed should be allowed to set off one statutory obligation against another when the one government department is involved. Statutory rights and obligations arise independently of any desire by the parties to deal with each other. If the possibility of a right of set-off could not have acted as a stimulus for either of the parties to enter into a dealing, there is no real justification for allowing either of them preferential treatment by means of a set-off in the event of the insolvency of the other.[524]

13.113

Public corporations

It may be that a public corporation, as opposed to a department of state, is liable to a bankrupt or a company in liquidation, or that a public corporation has a claim against the bankrupt or the company. The question then may arise whether there is mutuality in relation to that demand and a cross-demand that relates to a department of state, or another public corporation. In Australia it has been held that the fact that a public corporation is a party to one of the demands does not destroy mutuality as long as the corporation may be considered to be an agent of the Crown, a concept that is determined by the measure of control that the Crown, through its Ministers, has over the body in question.[525] This should also apply in

13.114

---

[522] *Cork Committee Report*, 306–7, 309.
[523] *Blagden Committee Report*, 29.
[524] See paras 6.11 and 6.12 above.
[525] Hogg and Monahan, *Liability of the Crown* (3rd edn, 2000) 333–4.

England. An illustration is *Re Duncan and Wakefield's Assignment*, a decision of the Western Australian Supreme Court.[526] Debtors who had executed a deed of assignment were owed money by the Minister of Lands, but were also indebted to the State Saw Mills. Dwyer J noted that the State Saw Mills:[527]

> is a trading concern created to carry on a profit making business, it is administered by one of the State Ministers as part of his normal ministerial duties, the property it holds belongs to the State and has always so belonged, its funds are provided from time to time out of the consolidated revenue, and its profits go into consolidated revenue, there is no special beneficiary or group of beneficiaries to be advantaged, the benefit from its operations is for the State as a whole and not for any particular class or restricted number of persons, and any loss must be borne similarly.

His Honour concluded that the corporation was an agent of the Crown, and accordingly it was allowed to bring into an account the Minister's liability to the debtor. In *Re Mathrick*[528] two public corporations were involved. The Board of Land and Works owed a sum of money to a bankrupt, while the Forests Commission was a creditor of the bankrupt. Lukin J held that both bodies were agents of the Crown. In each case the corporation was financed out of consolidated revenue, and all moneys were received on account of consolidated revenue. Moreover, each was subject to a large amount of ministerial control. Because they were both agents of the Crown, a set-off could proceed.[529] If on the other hand a public corporation is independent of the government, with independent powers and discretions, it does not represent the Crown,[530] and mutuality would be lacking where a cross-demand relates to another public corporation or the Crown.

The federal system in Australia

13.115 In a federal system such as Australia's, a person may be a debtor to the Crown in right of one state and a creditor of the Crown in right of another state, or of the Commonwealth, and vice versa. The aphorism that 'the Crown is one and indivisible'[531] suggests that the demands are mutual and may be set off. However, as Latham CJ once observed, when this aphorism is 'stated as a legal principle, it tends to dissolve into verbally impressive mysticism'.[532] In truth, the Crown in right of each state and of the Commonwealth represents a separate government and a separate legal person. The better view is that the demands are not mutual,

---

[526] (1932) 34 WALR 138.

[527] (1932) 34 WALR 138, 139.

[528] (1941) 12 ABC 212.

[529] Lukin J overruled an earlier decision of his own in *Re McCann and Edwards' Deed of Arrangement* (1932) 4 ABC 145, in which a set-off had been denied in similar circumstances.

[530] *Skinner v Commissioner for Railways* (1937) 37 SR (NSW) 261, 270; *Grain Elevators Board (Victoria) v Dunmunkle Corp* (1946) 73 CLR 70, 76.

[531] See eg *Amalgamated Society of Engineers v Adelaide Steamship Co Ltd* (1920) 28 CLR 129, 152.

[532] *Minister for Works for Western Australia v Gulson* (1944) 69 CLR 338, 350.

and that a set-off should not be allowed.[533] Nor, one imagines, would a government of one state be happy that its claim against a person could be used to satisfy the liability of another state.

H. Set-off in Relation to a Deceased's Estate

(1) Executors and Administrators

An executor or administrator of a deceased's estate still in the course of adminis- **13.116**
tration strictly is not a trustee of the deceased's property, which includes any debts owing to the estate. A trust requires that there should be specific subjects identifiable as the trust fund, and while the estate is still being administered it is impossible to identify, in the case of residuary legatees and persons entitled upon an intestacy, the person in whom the beneficial ownership of any particular asset forming part of the estate is vested.[534] An executor has a number of fiduciary obligations with respect to the assets that come into his hands in right of his office, but the residuary legatees do not have a beneficial property interest in those assets before the completion of the administration.[535] Rather, their only right consists of a chose in action to have the estate properly administered. Those principles were accepted by the Privy Council in *Commissioner of Stamp Duties (Queensland) v Livingston*.[536] Viscount Radcliffe in delivering the judgment also said of an executor that the testator's property comes to him 'in full ownership, without distinction between legal and equitable interests. The whole property was his'.[537] This does not mean that an executor is the beneficial owner of the assets. The executor has the 'full ownership', but in the sense that he has vested in him 'the whole right of property'[538] to the extent that there are property rights in those assets. As Lord

---

[533] See *Vass v Commonwealth* (2000) 96 FCR 272, 288–289, although that was not simply a case of different governments.

[534] *Ayerst v C & K (Construction) Ltd* [1976] AC 167, 178, referring to *Commissioner of Stamp Duties (Queensland) v Livingston* [1965] AC 694, 707–708, PC. This applies equally in the case of a specific bequest. See *Official Receiver in Bankruptcy v Schultz* (1990) 170 CLR 306, 312.

[535] 'What equity did not do was to recognise or create for residuary legatees a beneficial interest in the assets in the executor's hands during the course of administration. Conceivably, this could have been done, in the sense that the assets, whatever they might be from time to time, could have been treated as a present, though fluctuating, trust fund held for the benefit of all those interested in the estate according to the measure of their respective interests. But it never was done. It would have been a clumsy and unsatisfactory device from a practical point of view; and, indeed, it would have been in plain conflict with the basic conception of equity that to impose the fetters of a trust upon property, with the resulting creation of equitable interests in that property, there had to be specific subjects identifiable as the trust fund.' *Commissioner of Stamp Duties (Queensland) v Livingston* [1965] AC 694. 707–708, *per* Viscount Radcliffe, PC.

[536] [1965] AC 694. See also *Official Receiver in Bankruptcy v Schultz* (1990) 170 CLR 306, 312–314 (although the Australian High Court (at 314) left open the question whether the estate is held on trust for the beneficiaries *as a class*, so as to confer a proprietary interest on all beneficiaries).

[537] [1965] AC 694, 707.

[538] [1965] AC 694, 712.

Diplock later remarked: 'No one would suggest that an executor, who was not also a legatee, was beneficial owner as well as legal owner of any of the property which was in the full ownership of the deceased before his death.'[539] It would seem then that, during the administration of the estate, neither the executor nor a residuary legatee is regarded as the beneficial owner of a debt which constitutes an asset of the estate. This concept also applies in the case of an intestacy, so that neither the administrator nor any person entitled on the intestacy is the beneficial owner of an asset which forms part of the unadministered estate.[540] An unadministered estate is similar in that regard to a valid non-charitable purpose trust, for example a trust for a monument. There is no beneficiary who it can be said is the beneficial owner of the trust fund, but that does not mean that the trustee is the beneficial owner. Given these principles, consider the case of a debtor to an estate who is being sued by an executor or an administrator. In the first place, the debtor could not set off a claim that he has against the executor or administrator in that person's personal capacity. Nor, if the estate has not been administered, could the debtor bring the debt into an account in a bankruptcy with a debt owing to him by a residuary legatee personally, or, as the case may be, by a person entitled to a share of the intestate's estate.[541] Mutuality in equity would be lacking.

13.117 Once an executor or an administrator has completed the administration of the estate he becomes a trustee holding for the beneficiaries under the terms of the will or on an intestacy.[542] If in that circumstance the executor himself is the sole person beneficially interested in the estate, a debt owing by the executor may be set off against a debt due to the estate.[543] Until the administration has been completed, however, a court of equity generally will not inquire whether the estate has sufficient assets to satisfy the testator's debts and testamentary expenses, and the expenses of the administration, in order to facilitate a set-off either by or against the residuary legatee or person entitled on an intestacy.[544] As Sir George Jessel MR once remarked, 'for the mere purpose of set-off the Court will not take the

---

[539] *Ayerst v C & K (Construction) Ltd* [1976] AC 167, 178. Even when a person is solely entitled to the full beneficial ownership of property, both at law and in equity, it is not correct to say that the person enjoys an 'equitable interest' in the property. Rather, the legal title carries with it all rights. Therefore, if the person disposes of the property in circumstances which give rise to a trust in his favour, it is not correct to say that the person 'retains' the equitable interest. See *Westdeutsche Landesbank Girozentrale v Islington LBC* [1996] AC 669, 706, 714.

[540] *Re Leigh's Will Trusts* [1970] 1 Ch 277, 281–282. Similarly a beneficiary in a discretionary trust has no proprietary interest in the trust assets. See *Gartside v IRC* [1968] AC 553; *Chief Commissioner of Stamp Duties v ISPT Pty Ltd* (1997) 45 NSWLR 639, 655.

[541] See *Bishop v Church* (1748) 3 Atk 691, 26 ER 1197; *Phillips v Howell* [1901] 2 Ch 773.

[542] *Re Cockburn's Will Trusts* [1957] 1 Ch 438, 439.

[543] *Williams v MacDonald* [1915] VLR 229. For a discussion of the question whether an executor is required to make an assent in his own favour in this situation, see *Williams, Mortimer and Sunnucks on Executors, Administrators and Probate* (18th edn, 2000) 1073. Assuming that the administration of the estate had been completed, *quaere* why a set-off was not allowed in *Harvey v Wood* (1821) 5 Madd 459, 56 ER 971.

[544] *Bishop v Church* (1748) 3 Atk 691, 26 ER 1197.

account'.[545] In *Ex parte Morier, re Willis, Percival & Co*[546] a brother and sister were executors of their deceased father's will, and accordingly opened an executorship account with a bank in their joint names. The son, who was the sole residuary legatee, also kept a separate account with the bank in his personal capacity. The bank stopped payment and entered into an arrangement with its creditors for its liquidation,[547] at which time the executorship account was in credit and the son's personal account in debit. Securities had been set aside to answer the specific legacies bequeathed by the will, and the testator's debts and funeral and testamentary expenses had all been paid. At the date of the arrangement however the executors were still jointly liable for some rates and taxes, and in addition a solicitor's bill of costs had not been paid. The administration therefore had not been completed at that date, with the result that a trust had not arisen in favour of the son as the residuary legatee so as to enable him to employ the bank's debt in a set-off. Nor was the Court of Appeal prepared to take an account of the testator's estate in order to ascertain whether there would be a surplus accruing to the residuary legatee.

Two cases in which a set-off was permitted

There are nevertheless two cases in which a debt constituting an asset of a deceased's estate was allowed to be brought in as a set-off against a separate indebtedness of the residuary legatee before the completion of the administration, although neither decision is free of difficulty. **13.118**

The first case, *Jones v Mossop*,[548] concerned an assent in an intestacy. An assent is a **13.119** method by which a personal representative indicates that he does not require certain property for the discharge of the liabilities of the estate, and that therefore it may pass to the legatee.[549] After the assent, the beneficial interest in the property concerned vests in the legatee. He may bring an action to recover it, including against the personal representative.[550] The facts of *Jones v Mossop* are complicated, but may be summarized as follows. Jones was indebted on a bond to John Reed. John Reed died intestate, leaving Richard Reed his only child and next of kin, and as such entitled to a clear residue of his personal estate. Richard Reed obtained a grant of administration of his father's estate. Before he could undertake the administration however he became insolvent, and he later died. Mossop was appointed assignee in his insolvency. After the death of Richard Reed, Mossop obtained letters of administration *de bonis non* of John Reed, and commenced an

---

[545] *Middleton v Pollock, ex p Nugee* (1875) LR 20 Eq 29, 34.
[546] (1879) 12 Ch D 491.
[547] See the Bankruptcy Act 1869, s 125.
[548] (1844) 3 Hare 568, 67 ER 506.
[549] Williams, *The Law Relating to Assents* (1947) 1.
[550] *Williams, Mortimer and Sunnucks on Executors, Administrators and Probate* (18th edn, 2000) 1077.

action against Jones on the bond. Jones was a creditor of Richard Reed, and accordingly he sought to have his claim set off against his debt to John Reed's estate, the residue of which after payment of John Reed's debts would vest in Richard Reed. A number of the debts of John Reed still remained unpaid, but Wigram VC nevertheless allowed a set-off because of some admissions made by Mossop as administrator. Mossop said that he believed that the personal estate exclusive of the bond was more than sufficient to pay John Reed's debts, that the money due upon the bond was part of the net residue of the estate, and that it had become legally and equitably the absolute property of Richard Reed. The Vice Chancellor said that the case 'is the same in principle as where an assent has been given to a legacy whereby the property has passed to the legatee, being himself an executor, in which case the legacy is separated from the estate of the testator, and becomes the property of the legatee'.[551] But notwithstanding the admissions, the decision is still open to question on the basis of the view that has been expressed, that an administrator, as opposed to an executor, cannot assent in respect of pure personalty which passes on an intestacy,[552] and a debt owing to the deceased is personalty.

13.120   The second case is *Bailey v Finch*.[553] The defendant was the sole executor of a testatrix's will, and was also the residuary legatee. An executorship account opened by him with a banking firm showed a credit balance of £500 when the firm was adjudged bankrupt. At the date of the bankruptcy the defendant had not provided specifically for two bequests, but there were in the hands of the defendant, besides the credit balance with the firm, other personal assets of the testatrix which would have been more than sufficient to provide for the bequests. The defendant also had his own personal account with the firm, which was overdrawn to the extent of £300. It was held in this action brought against him on the overdrawn account by the trustee of the bankrupts' estate that he could set off the credit balance on the executorship account, even though the administration had not been completed at the time of the bankruptcy, and even though there had not been a prior assent in respect of any part of the residuary estate. The set-off was based upon the court's finding that there was a right of set-off existing at law.[554] The defendant was the sole creditor on the executorship account. Therefore at law there was mutuality between that claim and his personal debt to the bank. The executorship account had not been set aside to answer any other specific bequest. Therefore there was no other person who could be identified as having the equitable title to

---

[551] (1844) 3 Hare 568, 576, 67 ER 506, 510.

[552] See *Williams, Mortimer and Sunnucks on Executors, Administrators and Probate* (18th edn, 2000) 1072. Compare *Parry and Clark on the Law of Succession* (10th edn, 1996) 480.

[553] (1871) LR 7 QB 34.

[554] See Cockburn CJ at (1871) LR 7 QB 34, 40, and Blackburn J at 43–44 (and also during argument at 36). See also the explanation of *Bailey v Finch* in *Ex parte Morier, re Willis, Percival & Co* (1879) 7 Ch D 491, 498–499, *per* James LJ, 501–502, *per* Cotton LJ.

it. Moreover, the rest of the estate was more than sufficient to satisfy the specific bequests, and so it was considered that there was no reason in equity for disallowing this set-off permitted at law. The fact of mutuality at law was the ground upon which James and Cotton LJJ later distinguished *Bailey v Finch* in *Ex parte Morier*.[555] In the *Morier* case, the executorship account was in the joint names of the two executors. Therefore, in contrast to *Bailey v Finch*, there was a lack of mutuality at law between the executors' joint demand against the bank and the bank's separate claim against the executor who was the residuary legatee, so that a set-off would not have been available at law. Nevertheless, the analysis in *Bailey v Finch* is not without difficulty, and indeed Cotton LJ in *Ex parte Morier*[556] appears to have been uncomfortable with the decision. The firm had been made bankrupt, in which case the set-off section in the insolvency legislation alone should have determined the availability of a set-off.[557] Mutuality under the insolvency set-off section is determined by reference to the equitable interests of the parties, rather than their dry legal rights.[558] While an estate is still in the course of administration it is impossible to identify, at least in the case of residuary legatees, the person in whom the beneficial ownership in any particular property forming part of the estate is vested.[559] Since the administration had not been completed at the time of the bankruptcy in *Bailey v Finch*, and nor had there been an assent, it was not possible to say at that date that the defendant himself was the beneficial owner of the executorship account.[560] On that basis, a set-off should not have been allowed. In other words, the distinction is between a set-off at law, which may take effect when the demands are mutual at law unless there is another person whom it can be said has an equitable title to either of the demands sufficient to prevent a set-off, or there is some other reason in equity as to why a set-off should not proceed,[561] and a set-off in insolvency, in which it must be shown that the parties themselves to the proposed set-off have the equitable titles to the demands.

(2) Set-off Between a Third Party and a Deceased's Estate

If a creditor of a deceased sues the estate for payment, the executor or administrator of the estate cannot set off a debt owing to him in his personal capacity by the   **13.121**

---

[555] (1879) 12 Ch D 491. See para 13.117 above.

[556] (1879) 12 Ch D 491, 501–502.

[557] See paras 6.13–6.15 above.

[558] See paras 11.04–11.07 above.

[559] *Ayerst v C & K (Construction) Ltd* [1976] AC 167, 178. This applies also in the case of a specific bequest. See *Official Receiver in Bankruptcy v Schultz* (1990) 170 CLR 306, 312.

[560] See Blackburn J (1871) LR 7 QB 34, 45 ('this money, which at the time of the bankruptcy was legally in the defendant, and not also equitably only because some other persons had a small claim on it'), although compare Cockburn CJ at 40 and Mellor J at 46.

[561] See paras 11.08–11.10 above.

creditor.[562] Alternatively, the creditor may be indebted separately to the estate as a result of a liability incurred to the deceased, in which case the creditor may wish to set the debts against each other, particularly if the estate is insolvent.

Equitable set-off, and the Statutes of Set-off

13.122 Consider first the question of set-off when the estate is not being administered in bankruptcy. In such a case, if the demands are sufficiently closely connected there is no reason why an equitable set-off should not be available.[563] Further, the Statutes of Set-off may apply. The first Statute, (1729) 2 Geo II, c 22, s 13, provided that 'where there are mutual debts between the plaintiff and defendant, or if either party sue or be sued as executor or administrator, where there are mutual debts between the testator or intestate and either party, one debt may be set against the other'. This has been interpreted as requiring that the debts the subject of a set-off originally should have existed between two living persons.[564] In other words, there must have been cross-debts between the testator (or the intestate) and the creditor before the death.[565] *Wilkinson v Cawood*[566] is not inconsistent with that view. A sub-lessee paid rent to the wife of his deceased landlord after the death, and she in turn paid ground rent to the superior landlord. When she was sued by the deceased's executor in respect of the rent that she had received, it was held that she could set up the payments she had made for ground rent that had accrued due before (but not after) the death, even though those payments did not give rise to a debt owing to her by the deceased before the death. *Wilkinson v Cawood* should be compared to *Shipman v Thompson*.[567] A testator had appointed

---

[562] *Medlicot v Bowes* (1749) 1 Ves Sen 207, 208, 27 ER 985, 986. Similarly, in an action by an executor or administrator for money had and received after the death to the use of the executor or the administrator, the defendant cannot set off a debt owing to him by the deceased. See *Schofield v Corbett* (1836) 11 QB 779, 116 ER 666.

[563] See ch 4 above.

[564] *Rees v Watts* (1855) 11 Ex 410, 414, 156 ER 891, 893.

[565] *Lambarde v Older* (1853) 17 Beav 542, 51 ER 1144; *Rees v Watts* (1855) 11 Ex 410, 156 ER 891 (in which the early cases are discussed); *Allison v Smith* (1869) 10 B & S 747, 148 RR 589; *Newell v The National Provincial Bank of England* (1876) 1 CPD 496; *Hallett v Hallett* (1879) 13 Ch D 232; *Re Gregson. Christison v Bolam* (1887) 36 Ch D 223; *Re Wickham's Will. Grant v Union Trustee Co of Australia Ltd* (1898) 9 QLJ 102 (though note the discussion of *Re Wickham's Will* in para 14.35 below in the context of the rule in *Cherry v Boultbee* (1839) 4 My & Cr 442, 41 ER 171). See also *Beckwith v Bullen* (1858) 8 El & Bl 683, 120 ER 254 (deceased underwriter's liability on policy still unliquidated at the date of death), and *Mardall v Thellusson* (1856) 6 El & Bl 976, 119 ER 1127. Compare *Parker v Jackson* [1936] 2 All ER 281, which is criticized in paras 2.42–2.47 above, and also *Blakesley v Smallwood* (1846) 8 QB 538, 115 ER 978, which is discussed in *Rees v Watts* (1855) 11 Ex 410, 415–416, 156 ER 891, 893–894. The relevant date is the date of death, as opposed to the date of notice of death, although compare Wood, *English and International Set-off* (1989) 1104 in relation to the debt owing by the deceased. In *Rogerson v Ladbroke* (1822) 1 Bing 93, 130 ER 39 the banker's right of combination was in issue, as opposed to set-off under the Statutes of Set-off. See ch 15 below.

[566] (1797) 3 Anst 905, 145 ER 1077.

[567] (1738) Willes 103, 125 ER 1078.

an agent to collect rent. After the testator's death the agent received payments of rent that were due and payable before the death, and it was held that he had to account for them to the estate without set-off in respect of a debt owing to him by the testator. *Shipman v Thompson* accords with the traditional interpretation of the Statutes. The agent was not indebted to the testator before the death, so that the Statutes did not apply. The rent was not received by the agent to the use of the testator, but rather to the use of the executor. There is no inconsistency however between *Wilkinson v Cawood* and *Shipman v Thompson*, because the former case in truth did not concern set-off under the Statutes of Set-off. Rather, the payments of ground rent to the superior landlord were treated as a discharge *pro tanto* of the rent due to the intermediate landlord,[568] so that there was no longer an obligation to account for it.

It is not clear from the cases whether the debts should not only have been in **13.123** existence but also have been due and payable before death, although the Statutes of Set-off point to the latter as being the correct principle. The Statutes allowed a set-off between two living persons in the case of mutual debts, and 'debts' has been interpreted in that context as referring to debts which are not only in existence but also due and payable.[569] In the case of an action by or against an executor or administrator the Statutes similarly provided that there could be a set-off if there were mutual debts between the testator and the other party to the proposed set-off. Ordinary rules of statutory interpretation suggest that 'debts' should be given the same meaning in this context, in which case it would refer to debts due and payable between those parties. This has been held to be the case in Canada,[570] while North J, in discussing the availability of a set-off where one of the parties had died in *Re Gregson*,[571] framed the relevant question in terms of a debt *payable* to the testator in his lifetime.[572] It is not clear, however, that the courts will adopt that position.[573] The tendency of the courts in recent times has been to enlarge the circumstances in which set-off is available, which suggests that they would be sympathetic to the broader interpretation.

---

[568] See also *Sapsford v Fletcher* (1792) 4 TR 511, 100 ER 1147, to which MacDonald CB referred in *Wilkinson v Cawood*.

[569] See para 2.29 above.

[570] *Trusts & Guar Co v Royal Bank* [1931] 2 DLR 601. Compare *Ontario Bank v Routhier* (1900) 32 OR 67 and *Royal Trust Co v Molsons Bank* (1912) 8 DLR 478, in which it was accepted that the bank could have applied the testator's deposit against the promissory notes maturing after the death, although these cases appear to have been concerned with a banker's right of combination of accounts (see ch 15 below) rather than set-off under the Statutes.

[571] (1887) 36 Ch D 223, 226–227.

[572] See also *Newell v The National Provincial Bank of England* (1876) 1 CPD 496, although the promissory note in that case was given as surety.

[573] While there is a presumption that a word appearing in different parts of the same section in an Act of Parliament has the same meaning, this is not an invariable rule. See eg *Doe d Angell v Angell* (1846) 9 QB 328, 355, 115 ER 1299, 1309; *Re Smith. Green v Smith* (1883) 24 Ch D 672, 678; *Clyne v Deputy Commissioner of Taxation* (1982) 150 CLR 1, 10, 15.

Bankruptcy

13.124   In 1875 the rules of bankruptcy, including the insolvency set-off section, were incorporated for the first time into the administration of a deceased's estate when it
is insolvent.[574] Prior to 1875 rights of set-off were only available under the Statutes
of Set-off, and accordingly were subject to the limitation inherent in the Statutes,
that both debts had to be owing, and possibly also be due and payable,[575] between
the parties before the deceased's death. However, since the administration of
insolvent estates has been brought within the ambit of the insolvency legislation,[576] that restriction would no longer apply. Rather, the demands which may be
brought into an account are regulated by the terms of the insolvency set-off section, so that it is sufficient if the credits or dealings in question were mutual in
their origin.[577] Thus claims which are contingent at the relevant date, or which
only become due and payable after that date, may be included in a set-off, in accordance with principles applicable generally to insolvency set-off.

13.125   If a debtor by or against whom a bankruptcy petition has been presented dies, the
proceedings in the matter are continued as if he were still alive, unless the court orders otherwise.[578] If on the other hand the deceased died before presentation of the
petition, the Administration of Insolvent Estates of Deceased Persons Order 1986
now stipulates that the equivalent of the commencement of the bankruptcy,
which is the relevant date for determining rights of set-off under the Insolvency
Act, is the date of the insolvency administration order, this being an order for the
administration in bankruptcy of the insolvent estate of a deceased debtor.[579] This
should not mean however that the date of the order is the relevant date for determining rights of set-off.[580] In so far as the claim against the deceased is concerned,

---

[574]   See the Supreme Court of Judicature Act 1875, s 10.

[575]   See above.

[576]   See now the Administration of Insolvent Estates of Deceased Persons Order 1986 (SI
1986/1999), made pursuant to the Insolvency Act 1986, s 421. For Australia, see the Bankruptcy
Act 1966 (Cth), Pt XI, and also the various state laws regarding the administration of insolvent estates, eg the Administration and Probate Act 1958 (Vic), s 39(1).

[577]   *Watkins v Lindsay and Co* (1898) 67 LJQB 362, 364.

[578]   See the Administration of Insolvent Estates of Deceased Persons Order 1986 (SI 1986/1999),
Art 5. In Australia, see the Bankruptcy Act 1966 (Cth), ss 63 and 245.

[579]   See the Administration of Insolvent Estates of Deceased Persons Order 1986, Sch 1, Pt 1.

[580]   Compare the position in Australia. The date of the sequestration order is the relevant date for
the purpose of the set-off section (see para 6.34 above), and the Bankruptcy Act 1966 (Cth),
s 248(3)(a) provides that 'a reference to a sequestration order shall be read as a reference to an order
for administration of an estate' under Part XI. An order that the estate of a deceased person should
be administered under the bankruptcy legislation is not made on the basis of an act of bankruptcy.
It is not altogether clear, then, how the qualification to the set-off section in s 86(2) of the
Bankruptcy Act dealing with notice of an act of bankruptcy would operate under the Australian legislation when a debt owing by the deceased is acquired after the date of death but before the order.
If in fact the creditor had notice of an act of bankruptcy committed by the deceased within the six-
month period before the date of the order, there is no reason why the proviso should not apply in
the normal way. This is consistent with s 247A (relation back under Part XI). In other cases, where

the Order also provides that, in the definition of 'bankruptcy debt' in the Insolvency Act 1986, the date of death of the deceased is to be substituted for the commencement of the bankruptcy,[581] so that the provability of a claim is to be determined by reference to that date. Since the set-off section requires that there be a creditor proving or claiming to prove for a bankruptcy debt, in practice the date of death should be the relevant date for the claim against the estate.[582] In substance this should also be the position in relation to the cross-demand possessed by the estate. If a creditor becomes indebted to the deceased's estate after the date of death but before the order, and the debt does not arise out of a prior dealing that the creditor had with the deceased himself, there would be a lack of mutuality between that debt and the debt owing by the deceased to the creditor, so that a set-off would not be available on that ground. In *Re Gedney. Smith v Grummitt*[583] a person purchased some simple contract debts and a mortgage owing by the deceased, the purchase taking place after the death but before an order for the administration of the estate in bankruptcy. He realized the mortgage and, having applied the proceeds in satisfaction of the mortgage debt, he held a surplus which he claimed to set off against the other debts due to him. Even apart from the question whether a set-off should have been denied because the surplus was impressed with a trust,[584] Warrington J held that the surplus never belonged to the testator and accordingly there was never a debt due to him. Nor did it arise out of a dealing with the testator. There was no basis, therefore, for a set-off.[585] On the same principle, the proceeds of a deceased's estate deposited with a bank may not be brought into an account with an indebtedness of the deceased himself to the bank,[586] and an order for costs made against a creditor of the estate in favour of the executor for successfully defending an action by the creditor against the estate cannot be set off against the debt owing to the creditor.[587] Similarly, if an executor

---

a person acquires a debt owing by the deceased between the date of death and the date of the order, the courts may apply the qualification on the basis that the person should not be entitled to employ the debt in a set-off if at the time of acquisition he was aware that the estate was insolvent. See eg *Law v James* [1972] 2 NSWLR 573 and *Wily v Rothschild Australia Ltd* (1997) 47 NSWLR 555, 566 in relation to companies. This is not an issue in England, where the qualification to the set-off section is now drafted in terms of notice of the petition rather than notice of an act of bankruptcy. See para 6.49 above.

[581] See the Administration of Insolvent Estates of Deceased Persons Order 1986, Sch I, Pt II, para 31.

[582] Under the Bankruptcy Act 1914, the date of death seems to have been the relevant date. See *Re Bailey, deceased: Duchess Mill Ltd v Bailey* (1932) 76 Sol Jo 560.

[583] [1908] 1 Ch 804.

[584] See paras 10.32–10.42 above.

[585] See also *Re Gregson. Christison v Bolam* (1887) 36 Ch D 223.

[586] *National Bank of Australasia v Swan* (1872) 3 VR (L) 168. In the *Swan* case the deceased's debt arose pursuant to a guarantee, although default by the principal debtor did not occur until after the death. Stawell CJ (at 171) rejected an argument that, because the debt arose after the death, it was the administrator's, and not the intestate's, debt.

[587] *Re Dickinson. Marquis of Bute v Walker, ex p Hoyle, Shipley and Hoyle* [1888] WN 94.

or administrator sells an asset of the estate to a person who is a creditor of the deceased, the creditor cannot set off the price against the debt owing to him, in the absence of an agreement to that effect.[588]

Debts incurred by the personal representative

13.126 It may be that a personal representative has carried on the deceased's business, and in doing so has incurred some debts. A personal representative who carries on the business renders himself personally liable for all debts which he contracts in so doing, although if he was authorized to carry on the business he is entitled as against the beneficiaries to be indemnified out of that part of the testator's estate which he was authorized to employ in the business.[589] *Nelson v Roberts*[590] is authority for the proposition that this personal liability of the personal representative to a creditor and a debt owing by the creditor to the estate are not mutual.[591]

Charge on the estate for costs and expenses

13.127 A personal representative is entitled to an indemnity for his costs and expenses incurred in performing his duties. If the assets are insufficient to pay the creditors of the deceased, these costs are a first charge on the estate. Nevertheless, a charge on the estate is not a personal claim, and it generally could not be the subject of a set-off.[592]

(3) Set-off by a Beneficiary of the Estate

13.128 If a beneficiary of the estate is also indebted to it, so that he has a right to participate as well as an obligation to contribute to the fund constituting the estate, the rule in *Cherry v Boultbee*[593] may apply, with the consequence that his obligation to contribute may be appropriated as satisfaction of his right to participate as beneficiary.[594]

13.129 An executor or administrator may be personally liable to a beneficiary if he fails to apply the estate in accordance with his duties. There is authority which suggests that the executor or administrator can set off against that liability a debt owing to him in his personal capacity by the beneficiary,[595] though this may depend on the circumstances.[596]

---

[588] *Lambarde v Older* (1853) 17 Beav 542, 51 ER 1144.

[589] *Labouchere v Tupper* (1857) 11 Moore 198, 14 ER 670.

[590] (1893) 69 LT 352. See also *Staniar v Evans* (1886) 34 Ch D 470, 476–477; *Rex v Ray, ex p Chapman* [1936] SASR 241, 249.

[591] *Quaere* whether *Nelson v Roberts* should be followed. See paras 17.92–17.94 below.

[592] *Monypenny v Bristow* (1832) 2 Russ & M 117, 39 ER 339. Compare para 3.04 above.

[593] (1839) 4 My & Cr 442, 41 ER 171.

[594] See ch 14 below.

[595] See *Taylor v Taylor* (1875) LR 20 Eq 155, which is explained in paras 10.09–10.10 above.

[596] See para 10.02 above.

14

THE RULE IN *CHERRY v BOULTBEE*

A. Introduction

The notion which underlies the equitable principle in *Cherry v Boultbee*[1] is that, **14.01** 'where a person entitled to participate in a fund is also bound to make a contribution in aid of that fund, he cannot be allowed so to participate unless and until he has fulfilled his duty to contribute'.[2] It is an illustration of a more fundamental principle of equity, that he who seeks equity must do equity.[3] Many of the cases concerned with *Cherry v Boultbee* have involved a debtor of a deceased person who is also entitled to a pecuniary legacy under the deceased's will. Unless a contrary intention is manifested in the will,[4] the executor may decline to hand over

---

[1] (1839) 4 My & Cr 442, 41 ER 171.

[2] *Re Peruvian Railway Construction Co Ltd* [1915] 2 Ch 144, 150, *per* Sargant J (affirmed [1915] 2 Ch 442). See also *Re Akerman* [1891] 3 Ch 212, 219; *Re Fenton (No 2)* [1932] 1 Ch 178, 186; *Re Davies Chemists Ltd* [1993] BCLC 544, 546.

[3] *Courtenay v Williams* (1844) 3 Hare 539, 553–554, 67 ER 494, 500; *Stephenson Nominees Pty Ltd v Official Receiver* (1987) 16 FCR 536, 558.

[4] *Harvey v Palmer* (1851) 4 De G & Sm 425, 64 ER 897. See also *Re Eiser's Will Trusts* [1937] 1 All ER 244. Compare *Re Kowloon Container Warehouse Co Ltd* [1981] HKLR 210, in which it was held that a provision in a company's articles, to the effect that the company should have a lien upon the shares of a member for his debts owing to the company, did not purport to exclude *Cherry v Boultbee*.

anything in satisfaction of the legacy to the extent of the debt. The executor will be particularly keen to exercise this right if the debtor is insolvent or if for some other reason the debtor is unlikely to satisfy the liability.

14.02 The principle was applied by the courts a long time before 1839, when *Cherry v Boultbee*[5] was decided.[6] However, it was not until Lord Cottenham's judgment in that case that it was expressly distinguished from the right of set-off.[7] The Lord Chancellor commented:[8]

> It must be observed that the term 'set-off' is very inaccurately used in cases of this kind. In its proper use, it is applicable only to mutual demands, debts and credits. The right of an executor of a creditor to retain a sufficient part of a legacy given by the creditor to the debtor, to pay a debt due from him to the creditor's estate, is rather a right to pay out of the fund in hand, than a right of set-off.

Since then the courts have emphasized that *Cherry v Boultbee* has a wider application than set-off, and that it rests upon quite different principles.[9] Thus, *Cherry v Boultbee* applies in relation to a right to participate in a trust fund, whereas the general rule with respect to set-off is that a set-off may not be based upon an obligation to account for a sum held on trust.[10]

The nature of the principle

14.03 Lord Cottenham described the operation of the principle as a right in the executor to 'retain' a part of a legacy as payment of the debt, but the courts on a number of occasions have rejected retainer as a description of the right.[11] As Kekewich J once remarked,[12] 'Nothing is in truth retained by the representative of the estate; nothing is in strict language set off'. There has still nevertheless been a tendency to refer

---

[5] (1839) 4 My & Cr 442, 41 ER 171.

[6] The earliest reported example appears to be *Jeffs v Wood* (1732) 2 P Wms 128, 24 ER 668.

[7] Compare eg Lord Cottenham's earlier judgment in *Houlditch v Wallace* (1838) 5 Cl & Fin 629, 666, 7 ER 543, 557. In subsequent cases the right occasionally has still been referred to as a set-off. See eg *Freeman v Lomas* (1851) 9 Hare 109, 68 ER 435, *per* Sir George Turner.

[8] (1839) 4 My & Cr 442, 447, 41 ER 171, 173.

[9] *Re Rhodesia Goldfields Ltd, Partridge v Rhodesia Goldfields Ltd* [1910] 1 Ch 239, 246–247; *Re Smelting Corp, Seaver v The Company* [1915] 1 Ch 472, 476; *Re National Live Stock Insurance Co Ltd* [1917] 1 Ch 628, 632; *Re Melton* [1918] 1 Ch 37, 58–59; *Re Fenton (No 2), ex p Fenton Textile Association Ltd* [1932] 1 Ch 178, 188; *Selangor United Rubber Estates Ltd v Cradock (No 4)* [1969] 1 WLR 1773, 1778; *Re Davies Chemists Ltd* [1993] BCLC 544, 548.

[10] See ch 10 above.

[11] *Re Akerman* [1891] 3 Ch 212, 219; *Smith v Smith* (1861) 3 Giff 263, 271, 66 ER 408, 411; *Re Melton. Milk v Towers* [1918] 1 Ch 37, 59 (but compare Warrington LJ at 55); *In the Will of Bickerdike, deceased, Bickerdike v Hill* [1918] VLR 191, 196. See also *Re Rhodesia Goldfields Ltd, Partridge v Rhodesia Goldfields Ltd* [1910] 1 Ch 239, 245–246; *Re National Live Stock Insurance Co Ltd* [1917] 1 Ch 628, 631–632.

[12] *Re Akerman* [1891] 3 Ch 212, 219.

to the principle in terms of retainer,[13] and indeed in a later case Sargant J criticized the rejection of that epithet by Kekewich J.[14] Kekewich J would appear to have been correct, however. The more popular explanation, which can be traced back to the judgment of Sir Joseph Jekyll in 1723 in *Jeffs v Wood*,[15] is that the principle in effect provides a method of payment. The person administering the fund[16] may assert that the debtor already has an asset of the fund in his own hands, in the form of the debt, which should be appropriated as *pro tanto* payment of his right to participate.[17] The administrator in truth does not 'retain' anything as payment of the debt.[18] Rather, he directs the debtor to satisfy his entitlement to a share of the fund from a particular source. The principle is better described as a right to appropriate a particular asset as payment, as opposed to a right of set-off or a right of retainer.

B. Executor's Right of Retainer

Cherry v Boultbee should be distinguished from the executor's right of retainer. The **14.04**
common law developed the principle that an executor or an administrator of a deceased's estate could retain from the estate an amount sufficient to cover any debts owing to him by the deceased[19] in priority to the costs of the administration,[20] and

---

[13] See eg *Corr v Corr* (1879) 3 LR Ir 435, 446, 448; *Re Taylor, Taylor v Wade* [1894] 1 Ch 671; *Re Watson, Turner v Watson* [1896] 1 Ch 925; *Jackson v Yeats* [1912] 1 IR 267; *Re Lennard. Lennard's Trustee v Lennard* [1934] 1 Ch 235, 241; *Stephenson Nominees Pty Ltd v Official Receiver* (1987) 16 FCR 536, 558. Compare Sargant J in *Re Peruvian Railway Construction Co Ltd* [1915] 2 Ch 144, 151 ('right of retainer or quasi-retainer').

[14] *Re Savage. Cull v Howard* [1918] 2 Ch 146.

[15] (1732) 2 P Wms 128, 130, 24 ER 668.

[16] Henceforth the term 'administrator' is used generally to describe a person charged with the responsibility of collecting assets into a fund, and distributing the fund amongst a group of persons.

[17] See eg *Campbell v Graham* (1831) 1 Russ & M 453, 39 ER 175; *Courtnay v Williams* (1846) 15 LJ Ch 204, 208; *Re Akerman, Akerman v Akerman* [1891] 3 Ch 212, 219–220; *Re Goy & Co Ltd. Farmer v Goy & Co Ltd* [1900] 2 Ch 149, 153; *Re Mayne, ex p The Official Receiver* [1907] 2 KB 899, 901; *Turner v Turner* [1911] 1 Ch 716, 719; *Re Pennington and Owen Ltd* [1925] 1 Ch 825, 830, 832–833; *Picken v Lord Balfour of Burleigh* [1945] 1 Ch 90, 104. See also *Dingle v Coppen* [1899] 1 Ch 726, 740 and *Re Melton* [1918] 1 Ch 37, 54, 59, and the second formulation of the principle applicable to defaulting trustees referred to in para 14.70 below. Compare *Dodson v Sandhurst and Northern District Trustees Executors and Agency Co Ltd* [1955] VLR 100, 104.

[18] Compare *Re Hurburgh. National Executors and Trustees Co of Tasmania Ltd v Hurburgh* [1959] Tas SR 25, 40–42, where Crawford J suggested that *Cherry v Boultbee* confers a right *in rem*. However, the two reasons adduced to support that contention may be explained on other grounds. The first reason, regarding the effect of a bankruptcy or an assignment, may be explained by reference to the principle that a trustee in bankruptcy or an assignee takes subject to equities. See paras 14.52–14.56 below. The second reason regarding the effect of proving for the debt in the bankruptcy may be explained on the basis of a waiver of the right conferred by *Cherry v Boultbee*. See paras 14.49–14.51 below.

[19] If the debts were owing by the deceased himself, they would be unconnected with the administration of his estate. This should be distinguished from a trustee's right to an indemnity from the capital and income of the trust for costs properly incurred by him in the administration of the trust. See *Stott v Milne* (1884) 25 Ch D 710.

[20] *Re Wester Wemyss, Tilley v Wester Wemyss* [1940] Ch 1.

also in priority to the claims of creditors of an equal or lower degree.[21] This right was not a right of set-off, in the sense that the word is used to describe the process by which cross-demands are brought into an account so as to produce a balance, but rather it was a right to retain assets in payment of a debt. Thus, while it is a prerequisite to the common law defence of set-off under the Statutes of Set-off that the debt sought to be set off must be enforceable by action, an executor could exercise a right of retainer in respect of a debt which, although existing, was unenforceable as a result of a time bar.[22] The executor's right of retainer is also distinct from *Cherry v Boultbee*, which is not properly described as a right of retainer. They had different origins. The executor's right of retainer was developed by the common law courts,[23] while *Cherry v Boultbee* is an equitable doctrine.

14.05 The executor's right of retainer has now been abolished in England, although a personal representative who pays himself from the estate is not required to account for the sum so paid if he acted in good faith and at the time had no reason to believe that the deceased's estate was insolvent.[24] It has also been abolished in Western Australia,[25] New South Wales,[26] South Australia,[27] Victoria,[28] Queensland[29] and New Zealand,[30] in each case (apart from Queensland) without a similar saving provision. While it has attracted a considerable amount of case law, in view of the limited application that it now has[31] it is not proposed to discuss it further.[32]

C. The Scope of the Rule

14.06 *Cherry v Boultbee* has been described as a principle of wide utility and broad equity, and not dependent upon refined or technical considerations.[33] It is not

---

[21] *Attorney-General v Jackson* [1932] AC 365.

[22] *Hill v Walker* (1858) 4 K & J 166, 70 ER 69.

[23] *Attorney-General v Jackson* [1932] AC 365, 370. Since this right of retainer was developed by the common law, originally it could only be exercised against the legal, and not the equitable, assets of the estate, and moreover the executor's right was not prejudiced if he was a trustee of the debt for a third party. See however the Administration of Estates Act 1925, s 34(2), discussed in *Re Rudd. Royal Exchange Assurance v Ballantine* [1942] 1 Ch 421. See also in Tasmania the Administration and Probate Act 1935, s 34(2).

[24] Administration of Estates Act 1971, s 10.

[25] Administration Act 1903, s 10(2).

[26] Wills, Probate and Administration Act 1898, s 82(2), which amendment was introduced by Act No 14 of 1906, s 4.

[27] Administration and Probate Act 1919, s 62.

[28] Administration and Probate Act 1958, s 36(3).

[29] Succession Act 1981, s 58(1).

[30] Administration Act 1969, s 40.

[31] It still applies in Tasmania.

[32] For a discussion of the executor's right of retainer, see Meagher, Gummow and Lehane, *Equity: Doctrines and Remedies* (3rd edn, 1992) 825–8.

[33] *Stephenson Nominees Pty Ltd v Official Receiver* (1987) 16 FCR 536, 558, *per* Gummow J, referring to *Re Jewell's Settlement* [1919] 2 Ch 161, 174, 177.

confined to cases in which a legatee who was indebted to the testator is the beneficiary of a 'bounty' from the testator in the form of a legacy,[34] but applies generally whenever a person who is entitled to a share of a fund is also liable to
contribute to the fund. Thus, it may be invoked by an administrator of an intestate's estate against a next of kin,[35] and it may apply to a person with a derivative
title to a legacy, being a person who obtained a right to the legacy under the will or
as a result of the intestacy of another originally entitled to it.[36] It can also apply
when the beneficiary of a trust is indebted to the trust,[37] including in one instance
where resulting trusts impressed upon matrimonial property in proportion to the
expenditure incurred by the husband and wife respectively were being dissolved.[38]

Bankruptcy and company liquidation

Cherry v Boultbee may be relevant when a trustee in bankruptcy or a liquidator[39] is **14.07**
administering the fund represented by the estate available for distribution.[40]
Normally it is not in the interests of the general body of creditors that a claim
against the estate should be set off against a liability of the estate, because this
reduces the dividend payable generally. Consider, however, that a creditor of a
company in liquidation is also liable to the company,[41] but that the liability for
some reason cannot be employed by the creditor in a set-off. The creditor is entitled to receive a dividend in the liquidation, but is also required to make a contribution to the extent of the liability. The liquidator may assert that the creditor

---

[34] Compare *Dingle v Coppen* [1899] 1 Ch 726, 739, 740. For an application of the principle in
the case of a *power* to pay moneys to a person indebted to the testator, see *Re Bleechmore. Public
Trustee v Bleechmore* [1922] SASR 399.

[35] *Re Cordwell's Estate. White v Cordwell* (1875) LR 20 Eq 644.

[36] *Dodson v Sandhurst and Northern District Trustees Executors and Agency Co Ltd* [1955] VLR
100; *Re Milnes; Milnes v Sherwin* (1885) 53 LT 534. See also with respect to defaulting trustees (see
paras 14.67–14.78 below) *Re Dacre. Whitaker v Dacre* [1916] 1 Ch 344.

[37] See eg *Priddy v Rose* (1817) 3 Mer 86, 36 ER 33; *Re Akerman* [1891] 3 Ch 212.

[38] *Cowcher v Cowcher* [1972] 1 WLR 425.

[39] In *Fused Electrics Pty Ltd v Donald* [1995] 2 Qd R 7, 8–9 Williams J doubted whether *Cherry
v Boultbee* is applicable in the case of a company liquidation, on the ground that it may not be correct to categorize the assets of a company in liquidation as a fund. The authorities suggest otherwise,
however. See the cases referred to below in the context of liability for misfeasance or for unpaid calls,
and also *Re Davies Chemists Ltd* [1993] BCLC 544. Liquidation gives rise to an entitlement in creditors to share in the proceeds of realization of the company's property (see *Ayerst v C & K
(Construction) Ltd* [1976] AC 167, 178–179), which is a sufficient basis for applying the equitable
principle. See also *Re Saltergate Insurance Co Ltd (No 2)* [1984] 3 NSWLR 389 (proceeds of a reinsurance treaty received by the liquidator of an insurance company constituting a separate fund in the
winding up).

[40] In addition to the cases referred to below, see *Rowe v Anderson* (1831) 4 Sim 267, 58 ER 100.

[41] In Australia, when the creditor is a member of the company, and the debt is owed by the company to the creditor in the creditor's capacity as a member, whether by way of dividends, profits or
otherwise, the Corporations Act 2001 (Cth), s 553A provides that the debt is not admissible to
proof against the company unless the creditor has paid all amounts that the creditor is liable to pay
as a member of the company. See also the Corporations Act 2001 (Cth), s 563A, and in England the
Insolvency Act 1986, s 74(2)(f).

should satisfy the right to receive the dividend from the obligation to contribute. For example, *Cherry v Boultbee* may entitle the liquidator of a company to refuse to pay a dividend to a creditor who is liable for damages for misfeasance,[42] or who is liable for unpaid calls,[43] neither of which may be employed in a set-off in a winding up.[44] Similarly, *Cherry v Boultbee* may be invoked to prevent a shareholder of a company which is in liquidation, but which has a surplus available for distribution amongst the shareholders, from receiving a rateable proportion of the surplus without satisfying a debt that he owes to the company.[45] It may be that a creditor of a bankrupt has become indebted to the bankrupt's trustee for costs in litigation conducted on behalf of the estate. While lack of mutuality would prevent a set-off,[46] the liability for costs is still a contribution required to be made in aid of the fund,[47] and so the dividend payable to the creditor may be deemed to be paid to the extent of the costs.[48]

Equitable principle

14.08 On the other hand, *Cherry v Boultbee*, being an equitable principle, will not apply where it is contrary to statute or contrary to the agreement of the parties, or where the circumstances otherwise show that it would not be in accordance with good conscience that it should apply.[49] In a case in Queensland, a person who was liable to a company which had gone into liquidation was awarded costs in proceedings brought against him by the liquidator on behalf of the company, and the entitlement to the costs was accorded priority by the applicable companies legislation on the basis that they were costs, charges and expenses of the winding up. Because of the statutory priority, the liquidator was not permitted to invoke *Cherry v Boultbee.*[50]

---

[42] *Re Leeds and Hanley Theatres of Varieties Ltd* [1904] 2 Ch 45. See also *Re Cobalt Mines Ltd* (1918) 44 OLR 1, 7–8; *Re Jewell's Settlement, Watts v Public Trustee* [1919] 2 Ch 161, 175–176; *Re VGM Holdings Ltd* [1942] 1 Ch 235; *Selangor United Rubber Estates Ltd v Cradock (No 4)* [1969] 1 WLR 1773.

[43] *Re Auriferous Properties Ltd (No 2)* [1898] 2 Ch 428; *Re National Live Stock Insurance Co Ltd* [1917] 1 Ch 628; *Re Hattons Confectionery Co Ltd* [1936] NZLR 802; *Re White Star Line Ltd* [1938] 1 Ch 458.

[44] See paras 8.64–8.71 (misfeasance) and 8.50–8.62 (unpaid calls) above.

[45] *Re Peruvian Railway Construction Co Ltd* [1915] 2 Ch 144, 151; *Re Kowloon Container Warehouse Co Ltd* [1981] HKLR 210.

[46] *West v Pryce* (1825) 2 Bing 455, 130 ER 382.

[47] See para 14.32 below.

[48] *Re Mayne, ex p The Official Receiver* [1907] 2 KB 899; *Re Davies Chemists Ltd* [1993] BCLC 544 (company liquidation).

[49] *Perpetual Trustees (WA) Ltd v Equus Corp Pty Ltd* (NSWSC, Young J, 5 March 1998, at p 7). In *Perpetual Trustees*, the fact that the rights of the beneficiaries of a trust to receive moneys pursuant to the trust were set out in great detail in the trust deed was not regarded as negativing the operation of *Cherry v Boultbee*.

[50] *Fused Electrics Pty Ltd v Donald* [1995] 2 Qd R 7. See also *Process Engineering Pty Ltd v Derby Meat Processing Co Ltd* [1977] WAR 145. *Re Bank of Hindustan, China and Japan, ex p Smith* (1867) LR 3 Ch App 125, to which Williams J referred in the *Fused Electrics* case, may be distinguished on the ground that the solicitor's lien would have prevented the application of *Cherry v Boultbee*.

Fund

The essence of *Cherry v Boultbee* is that there is a right to participate in, and an **14.09** obligation to contribute to, a fund.[51] The concept of a 'fund' is flexible;[52] it includes a trust fund,[53] an estate administered under a will or in an intestacy, and the pool of assets of a bankrupt or a company in liquidation which is administered in accordance with the relevant statutory scheme.[54] It does not include, however, a company's assets while the company is still a going concern.[55] On the other hand, it is not necessary that the fund should consist of anything of value other than the obligation in respect of which the principle is sought to be invoked.[56]

Other circumstances

While the principle in *Cherry v Boultbee* is concerned with a right to participate in **14.10** and an obligation to contribute to a fund, the equitable principle which underlies it nevertheless may be relevant in other circumstances. For example, if A is claiming a constructive trust remedy against B, and A himself in breach of a fiduciary duty to B has misapplied B's funds, it may be made a condition of equitable relief that A must first do equity by accounting for the misapplied funds.[57]

D. Who May Invoke the Rule?

The principle considered in *Cherry v Boultbee* operates in favour of the fund, and **14.11** generally it can only be invoked by the person administering the fund.[58] Accordingly, a person obliged to contribute to a fund who also has a right to participate which for some reason is unenforceable could not insist that the obligation to

---

[51] See eg *Re Peruvian Railway Construction Co Ltd* [1915] 2 Ch 144, 150; *Re Melton* [1918] 1 Ch 37, 55, *per* Warrington LJ.

[52] *Perpetual Trustees (WA) Ltd v Equus Corp Pty Ltd* (NSWSC, Young J, 5 March 1998, at p 9).

[53] In *Perpetual Trustees (WA) Ltd v Equus Corp Pty Ltd* (NSWSC, Young J, 5 March 1998) this was held to include a pool of fees received by a trustee, where the trustee was obliged simply to distribute them (less authorized deductions) within thirty days.

[54] In relation to company liquidation, see *Hiley v The Peoples Prudential Assurance Co Ltd* (1938) 60 CLR 468, 496.

[55] *Re Peruvian Railway Construction Co Ltd* [1915] 2 Ch 144, 151; *Selangor United Rubber Estates Ltd v Cradock (No 4)* [1969] 1 WLR 1773, 1779.

[56] As may have been the case in *Re VGM Holdings Ltd* [1942] 1 Ch 235. See also *Ex parte Turpin, re Brown* (1832) Mont 443, for which see para 14.50 below.

[57] *Stephenson Nominees Pty Ltd v Official Receiver* (1987) 16 FCR 536, 538, *per* Gummow J. This may be what Young J in the New South Wales Supreme Court had in mind when he suggested in *Perpetual Trustees (WA) Ltd v Equus Corp Pty Ltd* (5 March 1998) that a fund may not be a prerequisite for the application of *Cherry v Boultbee*.

[58] Thus, Gibson J in *Re Hurburgh* [1959] Tas SR 25, 37 said of the principle in *Cherry v Boultbee* that it 'does not operate to quantify the share to be paid to a legatee until the executors (or trustees) choose to assert it'.

contribute be satisfied by his unenforceable right.[59] There is nevertheless an exception in the situation in which the administrator of the fund is the person against whom the principle may be invoked. For example, a trustee who is also a beneficiary of the trust may have acted in breach of trust. In that circumstance the other beneficiaries may apply for an order that the principle should apply in respect of the trustee's entitlement, if their own entitlements would be affected.[60]

What if the administrator of the fund does not invoke *Cherry v Boultbee*?

14.12   What if the administrator of the fund does not invoke *Cherry v Boultbee* against a contributor, so as to appropriate a right to participate in satisfaction of the obligation to contribute? Can the contributor be compelled to contribute, and then be required to wait for a distribution from the fund in respect of the right to participate? The emphasis in the equitable principle considered in *Cherry v Boultbee* is on circumscribing the ability of a person to claim a distribution from a fund in circumstances where it would be unconscionable to do so, as opposed to laying down an inflexible rule regarding satisfaction of an obligation to contribute, and it has been said that a person should not be ordered to pay that part of a liability which would come back to him on a distribution.[61] However in *Staniar v Evans*[62] North J said that an order for payment of the full amount of the liability to contribute is the usual order, and that an order for payment only of the balance after deducting the entitlement to participate may be made as a matter of favour only. He said that, in order to obtain an order for payment of the balance, the contributor should be 'perfectly able, and ready, and willing' to pay the contribution.[63] If the contributor cannot show his ability and readiness and willingness to pay, for example because of insolvency, the order instead should be in terms that the full amount of the contribution must be paid before the right to participate can be exercised. *Staniar v Evans* concerned a defaulting trustee who was entitled to costs out of the estate,[64] but North J indicated that the principle is equally applicable where the right to participate consists of a right to a share of the trust estate.[65] Special considerations apply to cases involving defaulting trustees, and the principle is considered later in that context,[66] but the courts nevertheless have adopted

---

[59]   Compare paras 14.15–14.18 below in relation to an unenforceable obligation to contribute.
[60]   See eg *Fox v Buckley* (1876) 3 Ch D 508.
[61]   *Re VGM Holdings Ltd* [1942] 1 Ch 235; *Selangor United Rubber Estates Ltd v Cradock (No 4)* [1969] 1 WLR 1773. See also *RWG Management Ltd v Commissioner for Corporate Affairs* [1985] VR 385, 397–398 (defaulting trustee); *Cumming v Sands* [2001] NSWSC 706.
[62]   (1886) 34 Ch D 470.
[63]   (1886) 34 Ch D 470, 473–474.
[64]   See also *Lewis v Trask* (1882) 21 Ch D 862; *Re Gloag's Estate* (1892) 11 NZLR 90.
[65]   (1886) 34 Ch D 470, 473.
[66]   See paras 14.74–14.78 below.

a similar approach to that suggested by North J in other cases not concerned with defaulting trustees.[67]

In *Staniar v Evans* the obligation to contribute exceeded the right to participate. **14.13** North J's order benefited the trust estate, because in a bankruptcy of the default-ing trustee the trust estate could have proved and received a dividend on the whole debt, as opposed to proving and receiving a dividend only in relation to the bal-ance. On the other hand, Lord Eldon's judgment in *Ex parte Graham*[68] suggests that, if the person obliged to contribute pays an amount such that the remaining obligation to contribute equals the obligor's entitlement to participate, the debt may then be regarded as paid. The fund in *Ex parte Graham* arose in the bank-ruptcy of a firm. The firm's assignees in bankruptcy deposited £28,079 19s 10d with bankers, Kensington and Co, who themselves became bankrupt. Prior to their bankruptcy Kensington and Co had lodged a proof in the firm's bankruptcy for a debt due to them, in the amount of £8,247 18s. The assignees in bankruptcy of the firm initially lodged a proof in Kensington and Co's bankruptcy for the amount of the deposit less a dividend of £1,649 11s 7d that had been declared in the firm's bankruptcy in favour of Kensington and Co. Subsequently, however, the assignees brought this petition praying that they might in addition be permitted to prove in Kensington and Co's bankruptcy for the amount by which they had re-duced their proof, and that the assignees in bankruptcy of Kensington and Co might be restrained from receiving a dividend in the firm's bankruptcy until the amount deposited with Kensington and Co had been repaid.[69] Lord Eldon said in his judgment that:

> until that Sum of £28,079, 19s 10d has been paid *minus* all the Dividends, to which Kensington and Co would have a Claim under their Proof, they are not entitled to those Dividends: but, whenever so much of that Sum of £28,079, 19s 10d is paid as leaves no more with Kensington and Co than the Amount of their Dividend upon the £8247, 18s then that Sum of £28,079, 19s 10d is paid.[70]

Lord Eldon made an order in accordance with the prayer in the petition, but with liberty to the assignees of Kensington and Co to apply whenever they shall have furnished to the firm's estate the sum of £28,079, 19s 10d minus the amount of

---

[67] *Ex parte Bebb* (1812) 19 Ves Jun 222, 34 ER 501; *Ex parte Graham* (1814) 3 V & B 130, 35 ER 428; *Ex parte Bignold, re Charles* (1817) 2 Madd 470, 56 ER 408; *Re Auriferous Properties Ltd (No 2)* [1898] 2 Ch 428 (obligation to contribute unpaid capital); *Re White Star Line Ltd* [1938] 1 Ch 458 (obligation to contribute unpaid capital); *N A Kratzmann Pty Ltd v Tucker (No 2)* (1968) 123 CLR 295 (obligation to repay a preference). See also *Ex parte Turpin, re Brown* (1832) Mont 443 (see para 14.50 below); *Ex parte Young, re Prior* (1835) 4 Deac & Ch 645; *Ex parte Crofts, re Last and Casey* (1837) 2 Deac 102; *Ex parte King, re Severn* (1835) 1 Deac 143; *Re Walter, ex p Walter's Assignees* (1859) 32 LTOS 396; *Ex parte Gonne, re March* (1837) 6 LJ Bcy 57.

[68] (1814) 3 V & B 130, 35 ER 428.

[69] When a fund consists of a bankrupt's estate, a creditor's right to participate for the purpose of *Cherry v Boultbee* is the dividend payable on the debt. See para 14.80 below.

[70] (1814) 3 V & B 130, 132, 35 ER 428, 429.

the dividends to which Kensington and Co would be entitled upon their proof. This approach is consistent with the view that a person should not be required to pay when the payment would come back to him in a distribution.[71]

14.14   If the person the subject of the order is a trustee of a trust, and the right to participate takes the form of an indemnity from the fund for his expenses, an order for payment of the balance may be made in the circumstances contemplated in *Staniar v Evans* notwithstanding that the fund may be insufficient to make all the required distributions out of the trust. This is because the trustee in any event has a first charge on the trust fund for his expenses incurred in the administration of the trust.[72] In other circumstances, however, the court should consider whether there are any prior ranking claims on the trust fund which may require that payment of all or part of the obligation to contribute to the fund should be made, and also the effect that an order for payment of the balance may have on the entitlements of other parties. This may be the case, for example, when the person the subject of the order is the beneficiary of a trust, and the trustee has a first charge on the trust estate for expenses incurred. If the beneficiary has an obligation to contribute, an order that he need only tender the balance after deducting the entitlement to participate in the trust would prejudice the trustee if it would mean that the fund in hand would be insufficient to reimburse the trustee for his expenses. If a fund is insolvent, the person obliged to contribute would only receive a dividend in respect of the right to participate,[73] and so an order for payment of the balance should only be made if the dividend is presently ascertainable.[74] When a person liable to contribute to a fund is entitled to a percentage of the fund, as opposed to a fixed entitlement, and it is otherwise appropriate that an order be made for payment of the balance, the court in making the order should ascertain the person's share by first taking into account any expenses that will have to be met from the fund, for example costs incurred in litigation in order to establish the liability, which costs are over and above those included in an order for costs made by the court. Once the fund actually available for distribution has been ascertained in this way, the court in its discretion may order that only the excess of the obligation to contribute over the right to participate in the fund is required to be paid.[75]

---

[71]   See above.

[72]   *Stott v Milne* (1884) 25 Ch D 710.

[73]   See para 14.80 below.

[74]   Compare *Ex parte Graham* (1814) 3 V & B 130, 35 ER 428 above, and *Cumming v Sands* [2001] NSWSC 706 at para 9.

[75]   *Selangor United Rubber Estates Ltd v Cradock (No 4)* [1969] 1 WLR 1773.

E. Enforceable Rights and Obligations

Unenforceable obligation to contribute

The distinction between a right of set-off and a right under the principle in *Cherry* **14.15**
v Boultbee may be illustrated by the different treatment accorded by each to the
usual form of statute of limitation, which takes away the creditor's right to enforce
the debt owing to him but does not affect the existence of the debt. It is a prerequisite to a set-off under the Statutes of Set-off that the debts the subject of the
set-off be enforceable by action,[76] but the fact that the liability to contribute to a
fund is time-barred, and consequently unenforceable, generally does not preclude
the right to invoke *Cherry v Boultbee*.[77] The administrator of the fund does not set
up the liability as a form of cross-action. Rather he says that, although the claim
against the contributor is unenforceable, it is still an existing asset of the estate.
Since the person claiming a share of the fund holds an asset constituting a part of
the fund, he should pay himself *pro tanto* out of that asset. A right under *Cherry v
Boultbee* is similar in that regard to the right of a lienee at law to withhold possession even when the debt upon which the lien is based is existing but unenforceable
as a result of a time bar.[78] There is one case in which it was held that *Cherry v
Boultbee* could not be invoked in respect of an unenforceable obligation to contribute. In *Dingle v Coppen*[79] a person indebted to a testatrix obtained judgment
against the estate for damages for waste committed by the testatrix during her lifetime. When the testatrix died the limitation period for the debt owing to her had
expired. Byrne J held that the executors could not apply *Cherry v Boultbee* so as to
oblige the debtor to satisfy his claim for damages by appropriating the estate's asset
represented by his unenforceable indebtedness. In *Dingle v Coppen* there were two
cross-demands, each of which in its nature was such that, when it arose, it could
have been made the subject of an action at law between the debtor and the testatrix personally. Because of the expiration of the limitation period, however, the
testatrix at the time of her death could not have enforced the debt owing to her.
Nor could she have employed it as a defence to an action brought against her in

---

[76] See paras 2.49–2.51 above.

[77] *Courtnay v Williams* (1846) 15 LJ Ch 204; *Smith v Smith* (1861) 3 Giff 263, 66 ER 408; *Coates
v Coates* (1864) 33 Beav 249, 55 ER 363; *Gee v Liddell (No 2)* (1866) 35 Beav 629, 55 ER 1041; *Re
Cordwell's Estate, White v Cordwell* (1875) LR 20 Eq 644; *Re Knapman. Knapman v Wreford* (1881)
18 Ch D 300, 304; *Re Milnes; Milnes v Sherwin* (1885) 53 LT 534; *Re Akerman* [1891] 3 Ch 212;
Re Langham; Otway v Langham (1896) 74 LT 611; *Re Allison* (1900) 1 Tas LR 169. See also *Rose v
Gould* (1852) 15 Beav 189, 51 ER 509; *Poole v Poole* (1871) LR 7 Ch App 17. If a debt is time-
barred, an action cannot be brought in respect of it, and so damages in the form of interest cannot
be awarded at a trial. Consequently interest cannot be deducted under *Cherry v Boultbee*. See *In the
Will of Bickerdike, deceased, Bickerdike v Hill* [1918] VLR 191, 197.

[78] *Spears v Hartly* (1800) 3 esp 81, 170 er 545; *Higgins v Scott* (1831) 2 B & AD 413, 109 ER
1196.

[79] [1899] 1 Ch 726.

respect of the waste.[80] In those circumstances Byrne J considered that the fact of her death should not make any difference, and that the estate should not be able to achieve the same effect as a set-off by means of *Cherry v Boultbee*. He distinguished the case from the situation in which a person is given a bounty in the form of a legacy under a will. In that situation there is nothing inequitable in applying *Cherry v Boultbee* on the basis that a time-barred obligation to contribute should be taken into account.

Statute of Frauds

14.16 *Cherry v Boultbee* similarly should be available as a general rule when the obligation to contribute to the fund is unenforceable for any other reason,[81] for example because of failure to comply with the requirements of the Statute of Frauds. The Court of Appeal in *Re Rownson, Field v White*[82] admittedly held that, while an executor or an administrator may exercise a right of retainer in satisfaction of a debt owing to him by the deceased that has become unenforceable because of a time bar, he is not entitled to a similar right of retainer when the debt is unenforceable because of failure to comply with the Statute of Frauds. However, the principle in *Cherry v Boultbee* is separate and distinct from an executor's right of retainer,[83] and indeed there is a sound reason for distinguishing the two in this respect. The Court of Appeal in *Rownson* regarded the right of a personal representative to pay any creditor of the deceased, including himself, in respect of a debt that has become time-barred, as an exception to his general duty not to waste an estate that is not his own. The Court was not prepared to extend that exception to the case of a debt owing to the personal representative that is unenforceable instead under the Statute of Frauds. That consideration does not apply, however, when *Cherry v Boultbee* is in issue. Rather, the personal representative acts in the interests of the estate by directing a person, who otherwise would deplete the estate by withdrawing his own entitlement, to obtain payment from an asset of the estate in his own hands that otherwise would have no value because of its unenforceability.

The obligation to contribute must not have ceased to exist

14.17 In order to invoke *Cherry v Boultbee*, the right to share in the fund must be due and payable.[84] By this it is meant that, until the right to participate has become payable, the administrator may not appropriate an obligation to contribute as

---

[80] This was apart from the question whether the nature of the demands was such that a set-off would have been available in any event.

[81] See also *Herskope v Perpetual Trustees (WA) Ltd* (2002) 41 ACSR 707 (covenant not to sue).

[82] (1885) 29 Ch D 358.

[83] See para 14.04 above.

[84] See *Campbell v Graham* (1831) 1 Russ & M 453, 465, 39 ER 175, 179 (affirmed *Campbell v Sandford* (1834) 8 Bligh NS 622, 5 ER 1073).

satisfaction of the right to participate.[85] For example, the principle may not be invoked in respect of a legacy while that legacy is still only a right in reversion[86] or, in the case of a residuary legacy, until the residue is ascertained.[87] A corollary of this principle is that the liability to contribute to the fund should not have ceased to exist, as opposed to being unenforceable, at the time that the share of the fund becomes payable,[88] unless in a particular case the terms governing the fund provide otherwise.[89] Thus, *Cherry v Boultbee* will not apply if the debt is one for which the person claiming the share has been released as a result of a discharge from bankruptcy,[90] or pursuant to a composition or deed of arrangement,[91] or if the debt has been extinguished by moratorium legislation.[92]

Consider that a debtor to a deceased testator has become bankrupt while his right **14.18** to a legacy under the will is still only a right in reversion.[93] If the executor chooses to prove for the debt in the bankruptcy, he waives his right to invoke *Cherry v*

---

[85] Thus interest still accumulates on the debt until the share becomes payable. See *Re Akerman* [1891] 3 Ch 212; *Re Watson* [1896] 1 Ch 925.

[86] See *Re Batchelor, Sloper v Oliver* (1873) LR 16 Eq 481, 483–484 (referred to with evident approval in *Re Watson* [1896] 1 Ch 925, 932); *Re Baird (Decd), Hall v Macky* [1935] NZLR 847, 852. See also *Re Hurburgh* [1959] Tas SR 25, 43–46, *per* Crawford J, criticizing *Richards v Richards* (1821) 9 Price 219, 147 ER 72, and seeking to explain *Burridge v Row* (1842) 1 Y & C CC 183, 62 ER 846, affirmed (1844) 13 LJ Ch 173, on the basis of set-off. Certainly Lord Lyndhurst in *Burridge* based his decision on both set-off and the principle in *Cherry v Boultbee*. However, the insolvency legislation only allows the trustee to estimate the value of a liability of the bankrupt, so that a dividend in respect of it may be paid immediately. See the Insolvency Act 1986, s 322(3). There is no corresponding power to put a present value on a sum payable to the bankrupt in the future and to demand payment of that sum immediately. Consequently it should not be possible for a set-off to proceed while the right of the bankrupt is still only a right in reversion.

[87] See *Re Hurburgh* [1959] Tas SR 25, 32–33.

[88] In addition to the cases cited below, see *Re Palmer. Palmer v Clarke* (1894) 13 R 233 (with respect to the disclaimed contract); *Re Wheeler. Hankinson v Hayter* [1904] 2 Ch 66; *In the Will of Bickerdike, deceased, Bickerdike v Hill* [1918] VLR 191; *Woodcock v Eames* (1925) 69 Sol Jo 444. Compare *Re Pink. Pink v Pink* [1912] 1 Ch 498. *Quaere* whether there should be an existing debt at that date, or whether it is sufficient that the liability is contingent although almost certainly bound to vest. See para 14.31 below.

[89] See *Re Ainsworth. Millington v Ainsworth* [1922] 1 Ch 22, in which a direction in a will, that a debt due to the testator from his son should be deducted from the moiety of the residuary estate bequeathed to the son, was held not to be affected by the son's discharge from bankruptcy.

[90] *Re Akerman* [1891] 3 Ch 212, 217; *Re Watson* [1896] 1 Ch 925, 933; *Re Baird* [1935] NZLR 847. Compare *Re Hope, De Cetto v Hope* [1900] WN 76, which is explained on other grounds in *Re Hurburgh* [1959] Tas SR 25, 48. *Re Melton* [1918] 1 Ch 37 is cited as authority to the contrary in *Withers on Reversions* (2nd edn, 1933) 246, although it appears from the statement of the facts in *Re Melton* (at 38) that the bankrupt in that case had never obtained his discharge. *Quaere* why the fact of the debtor's discharge from bankruptcy in *Re Palmer* (1894) 13 R 233 did not take away the executor's right to invoke *Cherry v Boultbee* in relation to the £700.

[91] See *Re Sewell. White v Sewell* [1909] 1 Ch 806, and the cases cited therein, and also *Re Hurburgh* [1959] Tas SR 25. Compare *Re Powell. Powell v Powell* (1904) 20 TLR 374. However, *Cherry v Boultbee* may be invoked in respect of any sum payable as a dividend under the composition or scheme. See *Re Orpen. Beswick v Orpen* (1880) 16 Ch D 202.

[92] *Parkes Property and Stock Co Ltd v Perpetual Trustee Co Ltd* (1936) 36 SR (NSW) 457.

[93] See *Re Hurburgh* [1959] Tas SR 25, 50–51.

Boultbee.[94] If on the other hand he decides to wait until the debtor's legacy falls into possession and then to rely on *Cherry v Boultbee* as a means of obtaining the full value of the debt, he runs the risk that the debtor may be discharged from bankruptcy while the right to the legacy is still only in reversion. If that were to happen, the fact that the debtor has been released from liability on the debt as a result of the discharge[95] would mean that the principle could not be invoked against him, and so the testator's estate will have lost the chance of receiving anything in respect of the debt. However the provision in the Insolvency Act, by which a bankrupt may be discharged automatically after either two or three years from the date of the bankruptcy,[96] offers some guidance to an executor faced with the choice of which approach to adopt in this situation.

F. Mutuality

14.19 In order for the principle in *Cherry v Boultbee* to apply, there must at one time have been a person who was both entitled to participate in, and also liable to contribute to, a fund. The administrator of the fund may not invoke the principle in respect of a debt due to some other person, rather than to the fund,[97] and similarly it is not sufficient that the person entitled to participate is indebted to a third party who is under an obligation to contribute.[98]

Bankruptcy

14.20 The requirement of a person being at the one time entitled to participate in and obliged to contribute to the fund may come into issue in the event of the bankruptcy of the person entitled to participate. This was the case in *Cherry v Boultbee.*[99] A legatee under a will was indebted to the testatrix. After incurring the debt, but before the testatrix died, the legatee became bankrupt. The bankruptcy did not affect the liability on the debt, which remained the liability of the legatee. On the other hand, since the legatee had become bankrupt during the lifetime of

---

[94] See para 14.49 below.

[95] See the Insolvency Act 1986, s 281.

[96] Insolvency Act 1986, s 279. Compare the former Bankruptcy Act 1914, s 26. In Australia, see the Bankruptcy Act 1966 (Cth), s 149.

[97] See *Re Watson* [1896] 1 Ch 925, 937, and also *Stammers v Elliott* (1868) LR 3 Ch App 195, 199 (with respect to the £150).

[98] See *Avison v Holmes* (1861) 1 J & H 530, 70 ER 855, and also *Smee v Baines* (1861) 29 Beav 661, 54 ER 784.

[99] (1839) 4 My & Cr 442, 41 ER 171, not following *Ex parte Man* (1829) Mont & M 210. See also *Bell v Bell* (1849) 17 Sim 127, 60 ER 1077; *Re Hodgson, deceased, Hodgson v Fox* (1878) 9 Ch D 673; *Re Orpen. Beswick v Orpen* (1880) 16 Ch D 202; *Re Peruvian Railway Construction Co Ltd* [1915] 2 Ch 144; *Re Reiter, ex p Hislop* (1932) 5 ABC 98. Sir George Turner in *Freeman v Lomas* (1851) 9 Hare 109, 115–116, 68 ER 435, 438 had reservations about the decision in *Cherry v Boultbee.*

the testatrix, and had not obtained a discharge from bankruptcy,[100] the legatee himself never had a right to the legacy.[101] Rather, the right to it was vested at all times in his assignee in bankruptcy on behalf of the estate. Consequently 'there never was a time at which the same person was entitled to receive the legacy and liable to pay the entire debt; the right, therefore, of retaining a sufficient sum out of the legacy to pay the debt can never have been vested in anyone'.[102] If on the other hand the legatee's bankruptcy had occurred after the death, the executors would have been permitted to invoke the principle. The legatee himself at one time would have been entitled to share in the fund. Moreover, since the bankrupt's assignees in bankruptcy could claim no better title than the bankrupt himself, the principle could have been invoked against them also.[103]

While it was held in *Cherry v Boultbee* that the executors could not apply the principle in respect of the full amount of the debt owing to the fund, Lord Cottenham nevertheless accepted that it could be invoked in respect of the dividend payable in the bankruptcy.[104] In other words, the executors could insist that the legacy should be considered as paid to the extent of the dividend payable on the debt. The one party, in the form of the assignee in bankruptcy, was entitled to participate in the fund, by receiving the legacy on behalf of the insolvent estate, and was also obliged to contribute to the fund, by paying a dividend out of the insolvent estate.[105] **14.21**

The relevant date

The relevant date in these insolvent debtor cases is the date of the event which precipitates the setting up of the fund. Thus, where the fund consists of a deceased's estate, the precipitating event is the death. In a bankruptcy or a company liquidation, it is the commencement of the bankruptcy or the liquidation. The principle may be invoked by the administrator of the fund as long as the person liable to contribute to the fund was also possessed of a right to participate at some time **14.22**

---

[100] If the legatee had obtained a discharge from bankruptcy the terms of the will were such that he would have obtained an absolute right to the legacy, but he died before obtaining the discharge. See Lord Langdale at first instance (1838) 2 Keen 319, 325, 48 ER 651, 654.

[101] Compare the case of a company liquidation, in which the assets remain vested in the company. See *Re Kowloon Container Warehouse Co Ltd* [1981] HKLR 210, 226.

[102] (1839) 4 My & Cr 442, 448, 41 ER 171, 173, *per* Lord Cottenham.

[103] *Jeffs v Wood* (1723) 2 P Wms 128, 24 ER 668; *Bousfield v Lawford* (1863) 1 De G J & S 459, 46 ER 182; *Ranking v Barnard* (1820) 5 Madd 32, 56 ER 806; *Richards v Richards* (1821) 9 Price 219, 147 ER 72.

[104] (1839) 4 My & Cr 442, 448, 41 ER 171, 173.

[105] See also in this regard *Re Orpen* (1880) 16 Ch D 202; *Re Peruvian Railway Construction Co Ltd* [1915] 2 Ch 144; *Re Fenton (No 2), ex p Fenton Textile Association Ltd* [1932] 1 Ch 178, 187. Compare *Re Hodgson* (1878) 9 Ch D 673, in which a dividend had not been declared in the bankruptcy. *Quaere* whether a foreign bankruptcy of the debtor to the fund may be recognized for the purpose of *Cherry v Boultbee*. See the discussion in *Re Kowloon Container Warehouse Co Ltd* [1981] HKLR 210 with respect to a foreign liquidation.

after the precipitating event. For example, when a company in liquidation had a surplus available for distribution amongst its shareholders, and one of the shareholders, who was indebted to the company, died insolvent, Sargant J considered that the liquidator could only have invoked the principle if the death had occurred after the commencement of the liquidation. He said that, when the liquidation commenced, 'the rights in respect of the shares may be considered to have been converted into a right or expectation of receiving a rateable proportion of the surplus moneys remaining after satisfying the liabilities of the company'.[106] The precipitating event, as Sargant J also remarked, is the '*earliest* possible moment at which any right of retainer or set-off or the like could arise'.[107] It means that the principle in *Cherry v Boultbee* may not be invoked if the debtor to the fund did not have a right to share in it personally some time after the precipitating event.[108] In the case in issue, the shareholder had died before the liquidation. At the date of the liquidation the deceased shareholder was still the person indebted to the company, but the shares, and the right to participate in the surplus, had vested in the executor. The liquidator therefore was not entitled to apply the principle in relation to the debt owing to the company. On the other hand, consistent with *Cherry v Boultbee*, Sargant J recognized that the principle could be invoked in respect of the dividends payable by the executors out of the deceased's insolvent estate to the company.

14.23   While the same person at some time at least must have been entitled to share in the fund and also liable to contribute to it, it is not necessary that the right and the liability should each have been presently payable, or indeed vested, at that time. For example, if a legatee becomes bankrupt after the testator's death, the executors may invoke the principle when the legacy becomes due and payable even if the legatee only had an interest in reversion at the time of his bankruptcy,[109] or if the right to participate otherwise was payable *in futuro* when the bankruptcy occurred. Similarly it is sufficient if the liability to contribute was merely contingent at the date of the bankruptcy, for example when the testator had guaranteed the legatee's debts and the executors were not called upon to make a payment under the guarantee until after the legatee's bankruptcy.[110] As long as there has been in

---

[106]   *Re Peruvian Railway Construction Co Ltd* [1915] 2 Ch 144, 151 (affirmed [1915] 2 Ch 442).

[107]   [1915] 2 Ch 144, 151 (emphasis added).

[108]   The principle may be invoked when the obligation to contribute only arises after the precipitating event. See eg the cases referred to in paras 14.32–14.35 below in relation to the proposition that the contribution need only be in aid of the fund. See also *Re Palmer; Palmer v Clarke* (1894) 13 R 233, in which an option to purchase the testator's property was exercised after the testator's death.

[109]   See *Re Watson. Turner v Watson* [1896] 1 Ch 925; *Re Lennard. Lennard's Trustee v Lennard* [1934] 1 Ch 235. See also *Re Melton. Milk v Towers* [1918] 1 Ch 37; *Re Hurburgh* [1959] Tas SR 25, 40, *per* Crawford J ('the legatee is entitled in possession or in reversion or even contingently to a general legacy or a share of residue').

[110]   *Willes v Greenhill (No 1)* (1860) 29 Beav 376, 54 ER 673; *Re Whitehouse, Whitehouse v Edwards* (1887) 37 Ch D 683; *Re Watson. Turner v Watson* [1896] 1 Ch 925; *Re Melton* [1918] 1 Ch 37.

this sense a situation in which the one person had both a right to participate and an obligation to contribute before the bankruptcy, an equity to invoke the principle arises in favour of the administrator of the fund to which the trustee in bankruptcy of the person entitled to participate takes subject.[111] A judgment creditor is in the same position in that regard as a trustee in bankruptcy, and accordingly takes subject to the equity in the form of the right to invoke the principle.[112]

Mutuality is concerned with the relationship to the fund

Mutuality for the purpose of *Cherry v Boultbee* is concerned with the relationship **14.24** between the fund and the person indebted to the fund.[113] Generally it should be determined by reference to principles similar to those applicable to set-off. They differ in one respect, however. Set-off applies where A is indebted to B and B is indebted to A, whereas in the case of *Cherry v Boultbee* it is not necessary that the debt should have been incurred to the person in respect of whose estate the fund was set up. It is sufficient if the debt is incurred to the administrator of the fund, as long as the proceeds of the debt will be in aid of the fund.[114] In other respects, similar principles apply. *Cherry v Boultbee* can be invoked when the person liable to contribute is the same as the person entitled to participate,[115] having regard to equitable rights. For example, if A holds his right to participate in the fund merely as a trustee, the administrator of the fund could not appropriate it as payment of a debt owing by A personally.[116] On the other hand, the administrator may appropriate as payment a debt owing by a person who is the beneficial owner of the right to participate.[117] Conversely, *Cherry v Boultbee* will not apply if the testator was only a trustee of a legatee's indebtedness,[118] or if the debt is owing to the administrator of the fund in his personal capacity, even though the administrator may be entitled to the residue of the fund and consequently would be benefited by the deduction.[119] In *Re Binns*[120] a will stipulated that the residuary estate was to be held on trust for the children of the deceased, but if any child died the children of that child were to take his share. It was held that a grandchild claiming under the

---

[111] The obligation to contribute nevertheless must still be in existence when the right to participate becomes due and payable. See para 14.17 above.

[112] *Kilworth v Mountcashell* (1864) 15 Ir Ch Rep 565, 581.

[113] The principle 'is applied only where there is a direct and specific mutuality between the mass and the particular debtor'. See *Re Pennington and Owen Ltd* [1925] 1 Ch 825, 830, *per* Pollock MR.

[114] See paras 14.32–14.35 below.

[115] *Reeve v Richer* (1847) 1 De G & Sm 624, 63 ER 1224; *Re Bruce. Lawford v Bruce* [1908] 2 Ch 682.

[116] If, however, the trust is created after the precipitating event, the person acquiring the beneficial title would take subject to equities. See paras 14.52–14.56 below.

[117] *Re Kent County Gas Light and Coke Co Ltd* [1913] 1 Ch 92, 97; *Re Kowloon Container Warehouse Co Ltd* [1981] HKLR 210.

[118] *Richardson v Richardson* (1867) LR 3 Eq 686, 695.

[119] *Freeman v Lomas* (1851) 9 Hare 109, 68 ER 435.

[120] [1929] 1 Ch 677.

will after the death of his parent, who in turn was a child of the testator, was not liable to have his interest reduced to the extent of a debt owing by his deceased parent to the testator. While *Cherry v Boultbee* would have applied if the deceased parent himself had claimed under the will, the child of that deceased parent was entitled in his own right.

Same fund

14.25 Similarly, the obligation to contribute and the right to participate ordinarily should relate to the same fund.[121] In *Re Towndrow, Gratton v Machen*[122] a person appointed executor under a will was also entitled to a legacy, for which an assent had been given by the executors. In addition he was appointed trustee of the residuary personal estate, although he himself had no beneficial interest in that estate. While acting in his capacity of trustee he misappropriated a part of the residue. Because of the assent, the specific legacy was held on a trust which was separate and distinct from the trusts upon which the rest of the estate were held.[123] Therefore Parker J held that the trustee was not required to make good his default to the residuary estate before he (or the person to whom he had mortgaged his right to the legacy) could claim the legacy. Parker J correctly applied the principle in *Cherry v Boultbee* on the assumption that the legacy was the subject of a valid assent,[124] but it has been doubted whether the case nevertheless was correctly decided. Younger J in *Re Jewell's Settlement Re Watts v Public Trustee*[125] said that *Towndrow* might have been decided differently if *Morris v Livie*[126] had been cited to the court. *Morris v Livie* is considered later in the context of defaulting trustees.[127] Knight Bruce VC in that case put forward the view that, when a trustee appointed under a will is also named as a legatee, the legacy is presumed to be consideration for his performing the duties of trustee. *Cherry v Boultbee* specifically contemplates the existence of a right to participate, but dictates that a particular asset may be appropriated as payment of that right. The effect of *Morris v Livie* on the other hand is that the trustee is deprived of a right to participate while he is in default. In *Re Towndrow* there was an assent. But an executor can only assent to a

---

[121] In addition to the cases cited below, see *Price v Loaden* (1856) 21 Beav 508, 52 ER 955 and *Re Saltergate Insurance Co Ltd (No 3)* [1984] 3 NSWLR 389, 393–594.

[122] [1911] 1 Ch 662.

[123] As soon as executors assent to a bequest it ceases to be a part of the testator's assets. See *Dix v Burford* (1854) 19 Beav 409, 412, 52 ER 408, 410, and also para 13.119 above.

[124] See also *Ballard v Marsden* (1880) 14 Ch D 374 and *Re Milnes; Milnes v Sherwin* (1885) 53 LT 534, 535. Compare *Cole v Muddle* (1852) 10 Hare 186, 68 ER 892, the correctness of which is doubted in *Withers on Reversions* (2nd edn, 1933) 241 note a, on the ground that one of several executors should be able to assent to a legacy in which he is interested. Compare also *Hastie v Hastie* (1876) 24 WR 242, in which there was a strong case of fraud.

[125] [1919] 2 Ch 161.

[126] (1842) 1 Y & C CC 380, 62 ER 934.

[127] See para 14.68 below.

legacy in favour of the legatee to whom it is given, and not in favour of a stranger.[128] Similarly, while it is has been said that an assent is irrevocable,[129] it may be that an assent made in favour of a trustee would not be binding if in truth the result of the trustee's conduct was that he was not entitled to the legacy while he remained in default. The assent should be binding however as against a purchaser of the legacy for value and in good faith from the defaulting trustee on the faith of the assent.[130]

Settlement involving two or more funds

An apparent exception to the requirement of a single fund exists in the case of a set- **14.26**
tlement. Two or more funds may be settled under the one settlement but on different trusts. Nevertheless, the courts 'consider everything that is brought or expressed to be brought into settlement by anybody from any source as one aggregate trust fund'.[131] Consequently the trustees may invoke *Cherry v Boultbee* against a person seeking to participate in the settlement if he is also obliged to contribute to it,[132] even though the 'right' and the 'obligation' may relate to different funds encompassed by the settlement.[133] Similarly, separate trusts, or bequests, under the one will may be treated as constituting the one fund, unless the executors have already set apart a particular legacy so that the estate is no longer in bulk.[134]

---

[128] *Re West, West v Roberts* [1909] 2 Ch 180, 186.

[129] See eg Williams, *The Law Relating to Assents* (1947) 98, although compare *Williams, Mortimer, and Sunnucks on Executors, Administrators and Probate* (18th edn, 2000) 1078.

[130] *Williams, Mortimer and Sunnucks on Executors, Administrators and Probate* (18th edn, 2000) 1077. See also *Edgar v Plomley* [1900] AC 431, which concerned a fund in court in an administration suit ordered to be carried to a separate account in the name of a trustee whom it was later discovered was in default.

[131] *Codrington v Lindsay* (1873) LR 8 Ch App 578, 592, *per* James L.J. See generally *Withers on Reversions* (2nd edn, 1933) 241.

[132] See for example *Priddy v Rose* (1817) 3 Mer 86, 36 ER 33; *Kilworth v Mountcashell* (1861) 12 Ir Ch Rep 43 (subsequent proceedings (1864) 15 Ir Ch Rep 565); *Corr v Corr* (1879) 3 LR Ir 435; *Ballard v Marsden* (1880) 14 Ch D 374, 377; *Re Weston. Davies v Tagart* [1900] 2 Ch 164. The liability to contribute need not arise out of the terms of the settlement, but may arise subsequently as a result of a misappropriation. See eg *Woodyatt v Gresley* (1836) 8 Sim 180, 59 ER 72. Moreover it makes no difference that the settlement may be voluntary, provided that it has been so completed as to be enforceable by the court. See *Re Weston*. Compare *Hallett v Hallett* (1879) 13 Ch D 232, in which the fund for which the action was brought was expressly excluded from the settlement.

[133] See *Burridge v Row* (1844) 13 LJ Ch 173 (affirming 1 Y & C CC 183, 62 ER 846); *Re Jewell's Settlement. Watts v Public Trustee* [1919] 2 Ch 161. The courts seem to incline in favour of finding that there is a single settlement. See eg *Woodyatt v Gresley* (1836) 8 Sim 180, 59 ER 72.

[134] *In the Estate of Tolley, deceased* (1972) 5 SASR 466, and see also *MacPhillamy v Fox* (1932) 32 SR (NSW) 427. Harvey CJ in Eq in *MacPhillamy v Fox* criticized *Re Towndrow* [1911] 1 Ch 662 (see above), although the criticism would appear to be misplaced, except possibly to the extent that the case concerned a defaulting trustee. *Re Towndrow* is not inconsistent with the Chief Justice's contention that the whole of the funds held by a trustee under a will constitute one fund for the purpose of adjustment, because an assent has the effect of setting apart the particular fund in question from the fund in bulk. In *MacPhillamy v Fox* there had not been an assent in respect of the bequest in issue.

Joint and separate rights and obligations

14.27 The prohibition against setting off joint demands and separate demands[135] also applies to *Cherry v Boultbee*.[136] Thus, an executor may not appropriate as payment of a legacy a debt owing to the fund by a number of joint debtors of whom the legatee is one.[137] Similarly in Ireland a legatee was indebted to a firm in which the testator was a partner, and it was held that the executor could not appropriate the joint claim as payment of the legacy.[138] There was on the other hand a curious decision by Stuart VC in *Smith v Smith*.[139] A residuary legatee under a will was a partner in a firm that was indebted to the testator. The firm became bankrupt. Stuart VC held that the executors could appropriate the joint debt of the firm as payment of the legacy due to the partner in his separate capacity. Cozens-Hardy MR in *Turner v Turner*[140] offered a possible explanation for the decision, but without finally deciding whether the case was correctly decided. He said that in *Smith v Smith* the assignees in bankruptcy were seeking payment of the legacy in their capacity of assignees of the separate estate of the partner, rather than as assignees of the joint estate of the firm, and moreover he said that the legatee's separate estate was liable to the testator's estate for the debt. Since the testator's executors in *Smith v Smith* could have proved for the debt against the separate estate of the legatee, which estate was vested in the assignees, the executors could appropriate the debt as payment of the legacy owing to the partner.[141] That explanation is doubtful. Formerly, when a partnership became bankrupt, the principle was that the joint estate was applicable in the first instance in payment of the joint debts and the separate estate of each partner was applicable in the first instance in payment of his separate debts. If there was a surplus of the separate estates it was dealt with as part of the joint estate, and if there was a surplus of the joint estate it was dealt with as part of the respective separate estates in proportion to the interest of each partner in the joint estate.[142] Thus, the separate estate of each partner was only liable to be applied in payment of a partnership debt to the extent of any surplus remaining after the partner's separate creditors had been paid in full. The

---

[135] See paras 12.02–12.07 above.

[136] See eg *Re Pennington and Owen Ltd* [1925] 1 Ch 825. Note also *McEwan v Crombie* (1883) 25 Ch D 175, which appears to have been a case involving *Cherry v Boultbee* rather than set-off.

[137] *Turner v Turner* [1911] 1 Ch 716.

[138] *Jackson v Yeats* [1912] 1 IR 267.

[139] (1861) 3 Giff 263, 66 ER 408.

[140] [1911] 1 Ch 716.

[141] Cozens-Hardy MR in *Turner v Turner* [1911] 1 Ch 716, 721 said with regard to *Smith v Smith* that the case 'is consistent with the principle in *Cherry v Boultbee* because the testatrix's executors could have proved against the separate estate of William Smith, whose separate estate was vested in the assignees, and that brings us practically to the same position as though there had never been a firm and the debt had originally been due from the legatee'.

[142] See eg art 10 of the Insolvent Partnerships Order 1986 (SI 1986/2142). In Australia see the Bankruptcy Act 1966 (Cth), s 110.

principle has been modified under the Insolvent Partnerships Order 1994, so that, to the extent of any deficiency in the joint estate, a claim may now be made against the separate estates pari passu with other separate creditors.[143] Nevertheless, it is still the case that the separate estate of each partner is only liable to be applied in payment of partnership debts to the extent that those debts are not capable of being satisfied from the partnership assets. The order in *Smith v Smith* had the effect of allowing a separate asset of a partner to be used to satisfy a partnership debt before the joint estate had been taken into account, which could have disadvantaged the separate creditors of that partner. This potential disadvantage to separate creditors is still relevant under the new distribution rules.

Cherry v Boultbee may apply on the other hand when the liability to contribute is **14.28** joint and several rather than joint.[144] If there are joint and several debtors to a fund, and the administrator of the fund appropriates the debt as *pro tanto* payment of the right of one of the debtors to participate, all the debtors are discharged to the extent of the right to participate, although the debtor whose right was appropriated should be entitled to contribution from the other debtors.[145]

G. The Obligation to Contribute

Damages liability

Cherry v Boultbee is not confined to cases in which the obligation to contribute to **14.29** the fund is for a liquidated sum enforceable either as a debt or by means of an order for specific performance,[146] but encompasses also a liability sounding in damages,[147] for example a liability for breach of contract for failure to keep up a policy of life insurance settled on trust,[148] or a liability for damages for misfeasance.[149]

Obligation to contribute which is contingent or not presently payable

There is authority for the view that the administrator of a fund may not invoke **14.30** *Cherry v Boultbee* when the liability of the person seeking to share in the fund is

---

[143] See Sch 4, Pt II (s 175A) and Sch 7 (s 328A) of the Insolvent Partnerships Order 1994 (SI 1994/2421).

[144] *Selangor United Rubber Estates Ltd v Cradock (No 4)* [1969] 1 WLR 1773.

[145] This seems to have been recognized in *Selangor United Rubber Estates Ltd v Cradock (No 4)* [1969] 1 WLR 1773, 1776.

[146] For specific performance, see *Re Palmer, Palmer v Clarke* (1894) 13 R 233, 236.

[147] *Stephenson Nominees Pty Ltd v Official Receiver* (1987) 16 FCR 536, 558.

[148] *Re Jewell's Settlement, Watts v Public Trustee* [1919] 2 Ch 161, distinguishing *Re Smelting Corporation, Seaver v The Company* [1915] 1 Ch 472.

[149] See the discussion of *Re Milan Tramways Co, ex p Theys* (1884) 25 Ch D 587 in *Re Jewell's Settlement* [1919] 2 Ch 161, 174–176. See also *Re Leeds and Hanley Theatres of Varieties Ltd* [1904] 2 Ch 45.

not payable until a future date. Thus, when a residuary legatee was indebted to the testator on a debt payable by instalments, the executors were not permitted to invoke the principle in respect of instalments payable in the future.[150] This result was justified on the ground that, if the debt could be appropriated as payment of the right to participate before the debt was presently payable, the contract under which the debt arose will have been altered.[151] On the other hand, in *Re Rhodesia Goldfields Ltd*[152] neither the existence nor the amount of a liability had been established or ascertained, but if there was a liability it would have been presently payable. Swinfen Eady J held that, pending the ascertainment and establishment of the amount (if any) due to the fund, the share of the fund for which payment was sought should be retained and carried to a separate account.

14.31 The view that *Cherry v Boultbee* may not be invoked when the liability to contribute, although presently existing, is payable *in futuro*, brings into question some judicial statements which suggest that the principle may apply when the obligation to contribute is merely contingent. In other words, the liability is not only not presently payable, but it is not even presently existing. Thus, when a testator was a surety for one of his legatees, Warrington LJ said that at 'the death of the testator' the executors 'had a right to be indemnified against any claim which they *might ultimately have to satisfy* as the result of the guarantee; and to retain in their hands so much of [the legatee's] share as was sufficient to provide for that indemnity'.[153] The statements to that effect were made in the context of a bankrupt principal debtor, and they should be confined to that context. In such a case the surety's estate almost certainly would be called upon to honour the obligation under the contract of suretyship, and consequently a liability in the principal debtor to indemnify the estate would almost certainly arise. In other situations, however, if it is not possible to invoke *Cherry v Boultbee* in respect of a present debt payable *in futuro*, the principle certainly should not apply when the liability is merely contingent.[154] For example, there is authority for the view that executors

---

[150] *Re Abrahams, Abrahams v Abrahams* [1908] 2 Ch 69. See also *Re Rees, Rees v Rees* (1889) 60 LT 260; *Jeffryes v Agra and Masterman's Bank* (1866) LR 2 Eq 674, 680; *Re Watson* [1896] 1 Ch 925, 933–934; *Re Rhodesia Goldfields Ltd* [1910] 1 Ch 239, 242, *per* Swinfen Eady J (*arguendo*).

[151] *Re Abrahams* [1908] 2 Ch 69, 72.

[152] [1910] 1 Ch 239.

[153] *Re Melton, Milk v Towers* [1918] 1 Ch 37, 54–55 (emphasis added). See also Swinfen Eady LJ at 51–52, approving of a dictum by North J to this effect in *Re Binns, Lee v Binns* [1896] 2 Ch 584, 587–588.

[154] In *Re Mitchell, Freelove v Mitchell* [1913] 1 Ch 201, 206 Parker J said that, when the principal debt is due and payable, but the surety has not paid anything under the guarantee, the 'surety's right is confined to a right to come into equity in order to get an indemnity against his liability to the creditor'. The surety's right in such a case, however, is not that he should be paid a sum of money by the debtor as an indemnity for his liability as a guarantor, but rather that he should be entitled to an order from a court of equity compelling the debtor to relieve him from liability by paying off the debt to the creditor. This right to *quia timet* relief should not entitle the administrator of the surety's estate to appropriate the debtor's right to a share of the fund as an indemnity for the surety's liability as a guarantor.

cannot invoke *Cherry v Boultbee* against a legatee who is a guarantor for a third party and whose liability has not yet vested.[155]

The obligation to contribute need only be 'in aid of' the fund

It is not necessary that the contribution should directly form a part of the fund in **14.32** question. Rather, it is sufficient if it is 'in aid of' the fund.[156] For example, *Cherry v Boultbee* may be invoked when the liability to contribute is based upon an award of costs made in favour of the administrator of the fund as a result of litigation conducted on behalf of the fund.[157] The administrator ordinarily would have a right of indemnity from the fund in respect of his costs. If he has already exercised the right, anything paid to him under the award of costs would be paid by him into the fund. If on the other hand he has not been indemnified from the fund, the costs paid to him will still be in aid of the fund because they will relieve the fund of the burden of indemnifying him.[158] When the fund is constituted by an estate being administered in bankruptcy, lack of mutuality would operate to deny the debtor for costs the right to set off the costs against the bankrupt's debt to him.[159] The bankrupt's trustee on the other hand could invoke *Cherry v Boultbee* in relation to the debtor's right to receive a dividend on the debt owing by the bankrupt.[160]

The notion that it is sufficient that the obligation to contribute is in aid of the **14.33** fund explains two early decisions of Lord Eldon. In each of *Ex parte Bebb*[161] and *Ex parte Graham*[162] a banking firm was appointed to act as bankers for the estate of a customer being administered in bankruptcy, the bank being a creditor of the customer. The customer's assignees in bankruptcy paid the proceeds of the estate into the bank, which subsequently itself became bankrupt. It was held that the

---

[155] See *Smee v Baines* (1861) 29 Beav 661, 54 ER 784, as explained in *Withers on Reversions* (2nd edn, 1933) 255.

[156] See Sargant J's formulation of the principle in *Re Peruvian Railway Construction Co Ltd* [1915] 2 Ch 144, 150. This may explain *Irby v Irby (No 3)* (1858) 25 Beav 632, 53 ER 778.

[157] *Re Knapman* (1881) 18 Ch D 300 (but note the explanation of the case in *Re Pain. Gustavson v Haviland* [1919] 1 Ch 38); *Re Mayne, ex p The Official Receiver* [1907] 2 KB 899; *Dodson v Sandhurst and Northern District Trustees Executors and Agency Co Ltd* [1955] VLR 100. *Cherry v Boultbee* may also apply in the converse situation, in which a person who is liable to contribute to a trust fund has obtained an order for payment of costs out of the trust fund. See *Re Harrald; Wilde v Walford* (1884) 51 LT 441.

[158] *Dodson v Sandhurst and Northern District Trustees Executors and Agency Co Ltd* [1955] VLR 100, 102–103.

[159] *West v Pryce* (1825) 2 Bing 455, 130 ER 382.

[160] *Re Mayne* [1907] 2 KB 899. Compare *Ex parte Whitehead, Re Kirk* (1821) 1 Gl & J 39, in which the debtor for costs had assigned his estate, including his claim against the bankrupt, to trustees for the benefit of his creditors before the liability for costs arose. Therefore, at no time was the right to participate and the liability to contribute vested in the same person. See the discussion of mutuality in paras 14.19–14.28 above.

[161] (1812) 19 Ves Jun 222, 34 ER 501.

[162] (1814) 3 V & B 130, 35 ER 428.

bankers' estate was not entitled to receive a dividend in the customer's bankruptcy until the whole of the sum received as bankers under the commission had been repaid. This sum was owing to the customer's assignees in bankruptcy, who had deposited the proceeds in the bank, rather than to the customer. However, the bank's liability still represented a contribution required to be made in aid of the customer's estate.[163] Subsequently Sir Thomas Plumer in *Ex parte Bignold, re Charles*[164] considered that the same result should follow in the case of an assignee of a bankrupt who was a creditor of the bankrupt, and who himself became bankrupt while holding proceeds of the estate in his capacity as assignee. Once again, the assignee was not indebted to the bankrupt personally, but rather to the other assignees in bankruptcy. Nevertheless his required contribution was still in aid of the bankrupt's estate.[165] Consistent with those cases, it should not be an objection to the operation of *Cherry v Boultbee* that a legatee's liability arises as a result of a dealing with the executor of a testator's estate, as opposed to the testator, as long as the fruit of the liability will be in aid of the estate rather than accruing to the executor personally.[166]

14.34 The principle that the obligation to contribute need only be in aid of the fund brings into question the decision in *Re Henley, Thurgood & Co.*[167] Henley & Co ('Henleys') were trade creditors of Fairhead & Son ('Fairheads'), who executed an inspectorship deed under the Bankruptcy Act 1861. The inspectors of the deed continued to trade with Henleys, and as a result a balance became due to the inspectors in respect of those dealings. Henleys themselves later became bankrupt, whereupon the inspectors asserted that they could 'retain or set off' the dividend payable to Henleys' assignee in bankruptcy against the debt owing to the inspectors as a result of their own dealings with Henleys. Clearly there could not be a set-off. There was a lack of mutuality.[168] Moreover the creditors under the deed, including

---

[163] See also *Fuller v Knight* (1843) 6 Beav 205, 49 ER 804 in the context of a loan of trust moneys. Compare *Re Wickham's Will, Grant v Union Trustee Co of Australia Ltd* (1898) 9 QLJ 102, which is considered in para 14.35 below, and *Ex parte Young; Re Day & Sons* (1879) 41 LT 40, for which see para 13.04 above.

[164] (1817) 2 Madd 470, 56 ER 408.

[165] Compare *Ex parte Alexander, re Elder* (1832) 1 Deac & Ch 513, in which a creditor of the bankrupt had been employed to liquidate the bankrupt's estate and effects. The creditor then retained from the proceeds a sum more than sufficient to cover his reasonable commission and expenses. It was held that the official assignee could not direct the creditor to look to the excess still in his hands as payment of his right to receive a dividend on the debt owing to him by the bankrupt. The case however turned on the extent of the duties of the official assignee, and it should not be regarded as authority for the view that *Cherry v Boultbee* could not have been invoked in this situation.

[166] A comment by Sir John Romilly in *Smee v Baines* (1861) 29 Beav 661, 663, 54 ER 784, 785, suggesting that there should have been a transaction with the testator himself, should be considered in the context of the facts in issue in that case.

[167] (1863) 11 WR 1021.

[168] The dealing was with the inspectors themselves rather than Fairheads, while Henleys were creditors of Fairheads.

Henleys, were *cestuis que trust* of the inspectors for the dividend, and an obligation to account for a share of a trust fund is not susceptible to a set-off.[169] But Commissioner Holroyd also concluded that 'retainer' (a term evidently intended to refer to *Cherry v Boultbee*) did not apply, with the consequence that the inspectors could not appropriate Henleys' liability to them on the dealings transacted after the deed as satisfaction of Henleys' right to receive a dividend on Fairheads' debt incurred before the deed. It is suggested that the case was wrongly decided on this point. While Henleys became indebted to the inspectors rather than to Fairheads, the debt was due to the inspectors in their capacity as such. The proceeds would have swelled the fund available for distribution amongst Fairheads' creditors, and accordingly the liability was in aid of the fund. *Cherry v Boultbee* admittedly could not have been invoked by Henleys' assignee in bankruptcy. In so far as the assignee was concerned, the right to participate in Henleys' estate was vested from the commencement of the bankruptcy in Fairheads' inspectors, while Fairheads themselves were the party indebted to Henleys. It was not then a case of the one person being entitled to participate in and also liable to contribute.[170] But Fairheads' inspectors had a different perspective. The Henleys' bankruptcy occurred after the inspectorship deed and after the dealings between Henleys and the inspectors. From the perspective of the inspectors, Henleys prior to their bankruptcy had a right to participate and were also liable to make a contribution in aid of Fairheads' fund, which should have given rise to an equity to invoke *Cherry v Boultbee* to which the assignee in bankruptcy of Henleys should have taken subject.[171]

There are also doubts as to the correctness of the decision of the Queensland **14.35** Supreme Court in *Re Wickham's Will, Grant v Union Trustee Co of Australia Ltd.*[172] The widow of a testator borrowed a sum of money from the plaintiffs as trustees of her husband's estate. Subsequently she purchased a share of one of the residuary legatees under the will. Griffith CJ, with whom Chubb J concurred, held that the trustees could not set off the loan against the share of the residuary estate when that share became payable. As far as set-off was concerned, the decision undoubtedly was correct. The demands were not mutual for the purpose of a set-off.[173] However there was no consideration given in the judgment to *Cherry v Boultbee.*[174] In that regard, if assignees in bankruptcy could invoke the principle

---

[169] See ch 10 above.

[170] See the discussion of mutuality in paras 14.19–14.28 above.

[171] See para 14.20 above.

[172] (1898) 9 QLJ 102.

[173] The widow's debt did not arise out of a dealing with the husband himself.

[174] Griffith CJ based his decision as to set-off upon *Hallett v Hallett* (1879) 13 Ch D 232, although Fry J in that case considered both set-off and *Cherry v Boultbee*. Fry J similarly held that lack of mutuality prevented a set-off, but he denied the operation of *Cherry v Boultbee* on a different ground, that the sum claimed from the trustees was never intended to be a part of the settlement. Therefore, while there was an obligation to contribute to the fund, the sum claimed was not based upon a right to participate in the fund.

against a bank with whom they had deposited the proceeds of the estate,[175] it should also be relevant when trust funds are invested in a loan to a person who acquires a right to participate.[176] The concepts of mutuality in set-off and under *Cherry v Boultbee* differ in this respect. For set-off one looks only to the persons possessed of the legal and equitable titles to the demands. In the case of *Cherry v Boultbee*, on the other hand, mutuality is concerned with the relationship between the fund and the person entitled to participate in the fund. Mutuality is preserved as long as the person is under an obligation to make a payment which will go to swell, or will be in aid of, the fund.

There must be an obligation

14.36 *Cherry v Boultbee* may not be invoked if the liability to contribute was extinguished before the right to participate became due and payable.[177] Similarly it does not apply when there never has been a liability to contribute.[178] This was held to

---

[175] See *Ex parte Bebb* (1812) 19 Ves Jun 222, 34 ER 501 and *Ex parte Graham* (1814) 3 V & B 130, 35 ER 428, referred to in para 14.33 above. Compare *Ex parte Young; Re Day & Sons* (1879) 41 LT 40, for which see para 13.04 above.

[176] In fact, the widow in *Re Wickham's Will* had mortgaged the share of the residuary estate to a bank. The share took the form of a reversionary interest in a trust fund which was subject to her own life interest. The widow had died, and so the bank was claiming payment of this share. Before the mortgage the one person, the widow, had both an obligation to contribute to, and a right to participate in, the fund. Moreover, it is not a valid objection to a claim to invoke *Cherry v Boultbee* against an assignee of the right to participate that the right was only a right in reversion when the administrator received notice of the assignment. See *Willes v Greenhill (No 1)* (1860) 29 Beav 376, 54 ER 673, and generally para 14.57 below. Griffith CJ considered that, even if a right of 'set-off' otherwise had been available to the trustees as against the administrators of the widow's estate, the bank would not have taken subject to it. It is suggested however that that would not have been the result under *Cherry v Boultbee*. In support of his view that the bank in any event would not have taken subject to a set-off, Griffith CJ referred to *Watson v Mid Wales Railway Co* (1867) LR 2 CP 593, in which it was held that a set-off could not be based upon a debt arising after notice though as a result of a contract entered into before notice. The *Watson* case is distinguishable from *Re Wickham's Will*, however. *Watson v Mid Wales Railway Co* concerned a debt which did not exist before notice, whereas the reversionary interest in the fund in the *Wickham* case was a present interest, although one which was not payable until a future day. Similarly, a set-off may be based upon a debt which is in existence before notice, but which is not payable until after notice. See *Re Pinto Leite and Nephews, ex p Visconde des Olivaes* [1929] 1 Ch 221, and para 17.11 below.

[177] See para 14.17 above.

[178] See *Re Morley, Morley v Saunders* (1869) LR 8 Eq 594. The requirement of a subsisting liability brings into question some comments by Lord Greene MR, with whom Finlay and Morton LJJ concurred, in *Picken v Lord Balfour of Burleigh* [1945] 1 Ch 90. A compulsory superannuation scheme provided that every employee should contribute a percentage of his salary to the fund. Upon retirement the employee became entitled to benefit payments based upon a percentage of his average salary during the period of his membership. The managers of the scheme calculated contributions on the basis of the bare rate of pay applicable to the grade of the particular employee, without taking into account certain bonuses that were also paid. It was held that these bonuses in fact constituted a part of the salary of each member, and that accordingly the benefits payable should have been calculated on the basis of an average salary which included those sums. It was also held, however, that the members could not claim this increased benefit without bringing into account the deficit in past contributions. The case itself may be explained on the basis of the second reason advanced by Lord Greene (at 102), that 'the right to a pension is conditional on the contributions

be the case when a sum of money was paid by mistake out of a fund to a person who incidentally was also entitled to participate in the fund, and that sum was not recoverable because the mistake was a mistake of law rather than of fact.[179] The House of Lords has now accepted that the principle by which sums paid under a mistake of law are not recoverable no longer forms part of English law.[180] But even before that development, the courts recognized an exception in the case of a trustee who, acting under an honest mistake of law, made a payment to a beneficiary in excess of the beneficiary's entitlement. The trustee in such a case could deduct the overpayment from future trust payments to the beneficiary.[181] This was also held to apply when a trustee in bankruptcy overpaid a creditor in the first dividend.[182] Neville J stated the principle in terms that 'the Court in a proper case—of course there may be cases in which it would be most inequitable to do it—will adjust the rights between the *cestui que trust* and the trustee who has overpaid through an honest and, so to speak, permissible mistake of construction, or of fact'.[183] This was not strictly an application of the *Cherry v Boultbee* principle, but was a principle *sui generis*. It applied even though there was no right of recovery from the beneficiary personally in respect of the overpayment,[184] so that it was not based upon the notion underlying *Cherry v Boultbee*, of a person being both entitled to participate in and also liable to contribute to a fund. Given however that moneys paid under a mistake may now be recovered notwithstanding that the mistake was one of law, the trustee's right would now be regarded as coming within the ambit of *Cherry v Boultbee*.

---

having been paid'. However, the Master of the Rolls (at 100) also justified the result by reference to the 'very well-known principle of equity' that a member 'ought not to be allowed to take money from the fund without himself contributing to it what he ought to have contributed in the past'. His Lordship apparently was of the view that this principle applied even where the only method of contribution was by way of deduction from salary, so that if the deduction was not made there was no obligation to pay sums that should have been, but in fact were not, deducted. The better view is that *Cherry v Boultbee* does not apply in this situation. Lord Greene expressed the principle in terms of 'what he ought to have contributed in the past'. A better expression of the principle in *Cherry v Boultbee* is that a member ought not to be allowed to take money from the fund without himself having contributed to it any sum which he is obliged to contribute.

[179]   *Re Hatch. Hatch v Hatch* [1919] 1 Ch 351.

[180]   *Kleinwort Benson Ltd v Lincoln City Council* [1999] 2 AC 349. In Australia, see *David Securities Pty Ltd v Commonwealth Bank of Australia* (1992) 175 CLR 353.

[181]   *Re Ainsworth. Finch v Smith* [1915] 2 Ch 96; *Re Reading. Edmands v Reading* [1916] WN 262; *Re Musgrave, Machell v Parry* [1916] 2 Ch 417; *Re Wooldridge. Wooldridge v Coe* [1920] WN 78; *IVS Enterprises v Chelsea Cloisters Management* (CA, 27 January 1994), discussed in Mathews, 'Restitution 0, Trusts 0 (After Extra Time)—A Case of Set-off' [1994] Restitution Law Review 44.

[182]   *Re Searle, Hoare and Co* [1924] 2 Ch 325.

[183]   *Re Musgrave* [1916] 2 Ch 417, 425.

[184]   *Hilliard v Fulford* (1876) 4 Ch D 389. In relation to an overpaid creditor in a bankruptcy, see *Re Searle, Hoare and Co* [1924] 2 Ch 325, 328.

Interest

14.37   When the obligation to contribute is an interest-bearing debt, it has been held
that *Cherry v Boultbee* should be applied first as against accrued interest, and then
as against the principal sum.[185]

H. The Right to Participate

14.38   *Cherry v Boultbee* only applies when the right to participate in the fund is for a sum
of money. It may not be invoked when a debtor to a testator's estate is entitled to
a specific bequest of freeholds or leaseholds, or of chattels, because in such a case
the right to participate cannot be measured against a monetary obligation to contribute.[186] It makes no difference that the bequest may be in respect of property
that could easily be converted into money,[187] although, if the testator directs that
his real and/or personal property is to be sold and the proceeds divided, *Cherry v
Boultbee* may be invoked in relation to a right to participate in the proceeds.[188] It
is no objection that the debtor is a specific legatee if the legacy is pecuniary in nature.[189]

14.39   There is, nevertheless, a situation in which a failure to satisfy an obligation will affect a non-monetary entitlement to participate in a fund. When there is an obligation arising under the terms of a settlement to contribute to the trusts of the
settlement, and this has not been done, the person obliged will not be permitted
to claim any property to which he would otherwise have been entitled pursuant to
the settlement.[190] In contrast to *Cherry v Boultbee*,[191] this may be described as a
right of retainer.

14.40   It may be that the right of a person indebted to a fund to participate in the fund is
periodic in nature. If so, the administrator may appropriate a part of the debt as

---

[185] *Campbell v Graham* (1831) 1 Russ & M 453, 39 ER 175, affirmed *Campbell v Sandford*
(1834) 8 Bligh NS 622, 5 ER 1073.
[186] *Re Akerman* [1891] 3 Ch 212. See also *Re Taylor. Taylor v Wade* [1894] 1 Ch 671, 674;
Dodson v Sandhurst and Northern District Trustees Executors and Agency Co Ltd [1955] VLR 100,
104.
[187] *Re Savage. Cull v Howard* [1918] 2 Ch 146.
[188] See eg *Re Akerman* [1891] 3 Ch 212; *Re Melton* [1918] 1 Ch 37. Compare *Re Milnes; Milnes
v Sherwin* (1885) 53 LT 534, which concerned the old rule in *Ackroyd v Smithson* (1780) 1 Bro CC
503, 28 ER 1262 that, when a legacy of a share of the proceeds of sale of real estate has failed, for example because the person named as legatee died before the testator, the share should be treated as
real property rather than personalty.
[189] *Re Taylor* [1894] 1 Ch 671; *Re Baird* [1935] NZLR 847. Earlier observations to the contrary
by Kekewich J in *Re Akerman* [1891] 3 Ch 212 have not been followed.
[190] *Re Weston. Davies v Tagart* [1900] 2 Ch 164.
[191] See para 14.03 above.

payment of each right to participate as it accrues due, until such time as the asset of the estate represented by the debt has been exhausted.[192]

I. Discretionary Relief

Since *Cherry v Boultbee* is an equitable remedy, the conduct of the party claiming **14.41** the benefit of the principle is relevant to the question whether he should be permitted to do so. In *Houlditch v Wallace*[193] a beneficiary of a trust was entitled to an annuity under the trust. Over a period of some twelve years, before the beneficiary assigned the annuity to the plaintiff, the beneficiary had appropriated income of the trust to his own use in excess of the amount to which he was entitled under the annuity. The other beneficiaries were aware of this, but took no steps to remedy their loss.[194] Lord Cottenham held that the other beneficiaries could not arrest future payments of the annuity as satisfaction of the sums owing by the assignor for the period before the assignment, inter alia because of their laches in not enforcing their equity immediately.

In *Re Pain. Gustavson v Haviland*[195] the usual principle by which an assignee of an **14.42** interest in a trust fund takes free of equities arising after notice of the assignment[196] was held not to apply. The assignees in that case had stood by and allowed the assignor to commence proceedings against the trustee. The assignor lost, and was the subject of an order for costs. This was an equity against the assignor which arose after notice of the assignment, but Younger J held that it could be asserted against the assignees. They had allowed the action to proceed when they might have stopped it, knowing that they would have benefited if it had been successful.

J. Suretyship, and the Rule Against Double Proof

The rule against double proof provides that an insolvent's estate ought not to pay **14.43** twice in respect of what is substantially the same debt.[197] Consider, for example,

---

[192] See *Priddy v Rose* (1817) 3 Mer 86, 36 ER 33; *Skinner v Sweet* (1818) 3 Madd 244, 56 ER 499; *Ex parte Turpin, re Brown* (1832) Mont 443; *Smith v Smith* (1835) 1 Y & C Ex 338, 160 ER 137; *Kilworth v Mountcashell* (1864) 15 Ir Ch Rep 565; *Re Jewell's Settlement. Watts v Public Trustee* [1919] 2 Ch 161; *Dodson v Sandhurst and Northern District Trustees Executors and Agency Co Ltd* [1955] VLR 100. Compare the order made by Lord Thurlow in *Ex parte Mitford* (1784) 1 Bro CC 398, 28 ER 1202 (the terms of which are set out in *Priddy v Rose* at 105–106, 40).

[193] (1838) 5 Cl & Fin 629, 7 ER 543.

[194] An injunction had been obtained to restrain the beneficiary from receiving the income of the trust, but the order was not acted upon.

[195] [1918] 1 Ch 38.

[196] See paras 14.52–14.66 below.

[197] See paras 8.08–8.13 above.

that a principal debtor is bankrupt, and that the creditor has proved and received a dividend on the debt. The creditor then proceeds against a surety for the balance of the debt owing to him. The surety in such a case cannot prove in the bankruptcy for an indemnity for the sum paid by him to the creditor. In substance, the debtor's liability to the surety for an indemnity is in respect of the same debt as that owing to the creditor, and because a dividend had already been paid to the creditor the debtor's estate is not liable to pay a second dividend to the surety.[198] Moreover, since the surety cannot prove for an indemnity, he cannot employ his claim in a set-off.[199] On the other hand, the status of *Cherry v Boultbee* in relation to double proof is not free from doubt.

14.44   Luxmoore J adopted a strict view in *Re Fenton (No 2), ex p Fenton Textile Association Ltd.*[200] Fenton, who had guaranteed advances by some banks to the Association, executed two deeds of arrangement in favour of his creditors. Subsequently the Association was ordered to be wound up. After the winding-up order the banks proved against Fenton's estate for the full amount of the guarantees, and received a dividend. Fenton was also a debtor of the Association, to which a dividend accordingly was also payable. Luxmoore J held that the rule against double proof precluded the operation of *Cherry v Boultbee* in relation to the fund being administered under the deeds of arrangement, and that consequently the trustee of the two deeds could not insist that the liquidator's claim for a dividend on the debt owing by Fenton to the Association be satisfied out of the Association's liability to indemnify Fenton's estate for the sum paid under the guarantee.[201] The rule against double proof was said to apply because the banks had only received a dividend from Fenton's estate, and so they were still entitled to prove against the assets of the Association for the full value of the debt.[202]

14.45   There was no mention in *Re Fenton* of the earlier Court of Appeal decision in *Re Melton. Milk v Towers.*[203] A testator bequeathed a one-fourth reversionary share in

---

[198]   *Re Oriental Commercial Bank, Ex p European Bank* (1871) LR 7 Ch App 99. See also *Re Moss, ex p Hallett* [1905] 2 KB 307.

[199]   *Re Fenton* [1931] 1 Ch 85.

[200]   [1932] 1 Ch 178.

[201]   Luxmoore J said that, because the Association had gone into liquidation before the surety's estate had paid anything to the creditor, *Cherry v Boultbee* was authority for the proposition that the principle in any event could only have been invoked in respect of a sum equal to the appropriate *dividend* payable in the liquidation on the obligation to indemnify the surety's estate. *Cherry v Boultbee* was a case in which the right to participate arose after the bankruptcy of the legatee. See para 14.20 above. *Re Fenton* is distinguishable, because there was a contingent obligation to contribute before the Association's liquidation. Indeed, Luxmoore J's dictum is inconsistent with the cases in which the principle was applied in respect of the full amount of a liability that vested after, but was contingent before, the debtor's bankruptcy. See *Re Melton* [1918] 1 Ch 37; *Willes v Greenhill (No 1)* (1860) 29 Beav 376, 54 ER 673; *Re Whitehouse* (1887) 37 Ch D 683; *Re Watson* [1896] 1 Ch 925. After the execution of the deeds, the Association had a right to participate and also a contingent obligation to contribute.

[202]   See *Re Sass, ex p National Provincial Bank of England Ltd* [1896] 2 QB 12.

[203]   [1918] 1 Ch 37. See also the further discussion of *Re Melton* in paras 14.60–14.62 below.

a residuary fund to a legatee. The legatee was indebted to a creditor, and the testa-tor was a surety for the debt up to a limited specified amount. The surety died, and the debtor later became bankrupt. The creditor proved in the debtor's bankruptcy and received a dividend. The creditor then proceeded against the surety's estate under the contract of suretyship for the sum for which the surety had agreed to be liable, and received payment in full of that amount from the estate. When the bankrupt debtor's right to a share of the residuary estate later became payable, the Court of Appeal[204] unanimously held[205] that the executors of the surety could in-voke the principle in *Cherry v Boultbee* in respect of their right to an indemnity for the sum paid to the creditor. Warrington LJ proceeded on the basis that *Cherry v Boultbee* operates as a right of retainer, and for that reason his judgment is not en-tirely satisfactory. In his view, *Cherry v Boultbee* conferred upon the surety's ex-ecutors the right to retain the debtor's entitlement, and to use it to satisfy the claim for an indemnity under the guarantee. This was an equity that came into existence at the date of the death, which was prior to the bankruptcy. The amount necessary to make good the claim accordingly never formed part of the debtor's estate, with the result that the rule against double proof did not apply.[206] That analysis should be compared to the approach of Scrutton LJ, which conformed with the preferred view of *Cherry v Boultbee*.[207] As Scrutton LJ remarked: 'how in any way does it in-fringe the rule against double proof that, when the bankrupt claims his share, the representatives of the surety should say, "Certainly, but you must ascertain your share in the proper way"? '[208] The principal debtor in *Re Melton* was entitled to a percentage of the residuary estate. The value of the residue was the sum actually held by the executors in their hands, plus the indemnity obligation owing to the fund. There was no infringement of the rule against double proof, because it was not a question of the debtor's estate being called upon to pay twice in respect of the same debt. Rather, the surety's executors were acknowledging their obligation to pay the debtor's share, but in paying that share they were exercising their right to take into account that the debtor already held an asset forming a part of the fund. Swinfen Eady LJ expressed his conclusion in similar terms.[209]

The *Fenton* and *Melton* cases differed in that, in *Re Melton*, the creditor had al-ready received a dividend from the principal debtor's estate, whereas in *Re Fenton* the rule against double proof was said to be relevant because the creditor was still possessed of a right to prove in the principal debtor's bankruptcy for the full value of the debt. There is nothing of substance in that distinction, however. Wood has **14.46**

---

204 Swinfen Eady, Warrington and Scrutton L.JJ
205 Overruling *Re Binns, Lee v Binns* [1896] 2 Ch 584.
206 See Warrington L.J's judgment at [1918] 1 Ch 37, 55–56.
207 See para 14.03 above.
208 [1918] 1 Ch 37, 61.
209 See the last sentence of his judgment at [1918] 1 Ch 37, 54.

sought to explain the different results on another ground.[210] In *Re Melton* it appears that the creditor had been fully paid,[211] whereas this was not the case in *Re Fenton*. Because the creditor had been fully paid, the surety's estate would have been subrogated to the creditor's proof in the debtor's bankruptcy,[212] and Wood has suggested that the debtor's legacy could have been 'retained' in respect of this proof, up to the amount of the proof less any dividends paid to the creditor, as opposed to being in respect of the surety's own right to an indemnity. However, this is not the basis upon which the Court of Appeal decided the case. The reasoning of the Court proceeded along the lines that the rule against double proof was irrelevant to *Cherry v Boultbee* given the nature of the right that arises under it, rather than that the rule against double proof did not apply to prevent the operation of *Cherry v Boultbee* because the surety's estate had the benefit of the creditor's proof by way of subrogation. It was not crucial that the creditor was fully paid. The judgments in the *Fenton* and *Melton* cases in fact are difficult to reconcile. The reasoning of Scrutton LJ in *Re Melton* should be preferred over that of Luxmoore J in *Re Fenton*.

14.47 Subsequently Clauson J followed *Re Melton* in *Re Lennard. Lennard's Trustee v Lennard*,[213] without mentioning *Re Fenton*. The facts in *Re Lennard* were similar to those in *Re Melton*, but the case illustrates the further proposition that the surety's executors cannot discharge the surety's obligation as guarantor in a more liberal manner than is strictly necessary, and expect to be able to charge the overpayment as against the principal debtor's trustee in bankruptcy. The guarantee was in respect of an annuity. The creditor valued the annuity, and proved in the debtor's bankruptcy for that value. The surety's executors however ignored the fact of the proof altogether. They made a number of payments to the creditor, and then purchased another annuity for her. Clauson J held that the executors could exercise their rights under *Cherry v Boultbee* against the principal debtor's right to share in the residue, but only to the extent of the difference between the value placed on the annuity in the bankruptcy and the dividend paid on that value, as opposed to the amount that they paid in instalments and in purchasing a new annuity. Because the creditor had elected to value the annuity and to prove in the bankruptcy, the surety's executors were entitled to pay the creditor the amount of the valuation and to take over the proof. This would have discharged the surety's estate from further liability under the contract of suretyship. In so far as they had spent a larger sum than was strictly necessary, they could not employ *Cherry v Boultbee* in respect of the surplus.

---

[210] Wood, *English and International Set-off* (1989) 440–1.
[211] Compare however Warrington LJ at [1918] 1 Ch 37, 55.
[212] See para 8.09 above.
[213] [1934] 1 Ch 235.

It may be that the sum brought into account by the representatives of the surety's **14.48**
estate under *Cherry v Boultbee*, together with any dividend paid to the creditor, is
greater than the principal debt itself. In such a case Scrutton LJ in *Re Melton*[214]
said that: 'If in the end it turns out that the debtor has paid more than 20*s* in the
pound he will get this overpayment back from either the principal creditors or the
representatives of the surety. If in the end it turns out that the creditors have got
more than 20*s* in the pound the surplus will be returned to the surety or the
debtor, whichever ought to have it.'

K. Waiver, and Proof of Debt

Cherry v Boultbee cannot be invoked if the person entitled to participate in the **14.49**
fund has been released from the liability to contribute as a result of an order of discharge from bankruptcy.[215] In addition, the administrator of the fund is denied recourse to the principle if he has proved the debt in the debtor's bankruptcy and
received a dividend,[216] or, if the fund is entitled to be subrogated to someone else's
proof,[217] if the administrator has elected to rely on that proof.[218] The leading case
is *Stammers v Elliott*.[219] In the course of his judgment in that case Lord Chelmsford
said: 'If he [the executor], therefore, proves a debt under a bankruptcy . . . the debt
must be held to be satisfied.'[220] However, the notion that proof constitutes satisfaction, or payment, of the debt[221] requires an explanation. The Court of
Appeal[222] in *Re West Coast Gold Fields Ltd. Rowe's Trustee's Claim*[223] commented,
'No doubt it is true that proof deprives the creditor of any other remedy against
the debtor or his estate, and in that sense proof is payment'.[224] Similarly, Lord
Westbury once remarked that: 'Proof against a bankrupt's estate is payment in this
sense, that the party making proof could not afterwards have a personal remedy
against the bankrupt.'[225] Proof does not constitute payment in an absolute sense

---

[214] [1918] 1 Ch 37, 61.
[215] See eg *Re Akerman* [1891] 3 Ch 212, 217, and para 14.17 above.
[216] *Stammers v Elliott* (1868) LR 3 Ch App 195; *Re Watson* [1896] 1 Ch 925, 933; *Armstrong v Armstrong* (1871) LR 12 Eq 614. See also *Re Kent County Gas Light and Coke Co Ltd* [1913] 1 Ch 92. The administrator should be able to withdraw the proof before a dividend has been received and rely instead on *Cherry v Boultbee*. See *Re Dicken, ex p Dicken* (1817) Buck 115, as explained in *Re Sewell* [1909] 1 Ch 806, 809.
[217] For example, when the testator guaranteed a beneficiary's debts and the testator's estate has paid the creditor under the guarantee.
[218] *Re Whitehouse* (1887) 37 Ch D 683.
[219] (1868) LR 3 Ch App 195.
[220] (1868) LR 3 Ch App 195, 200.
[221] See eg *Ex parte Hornby, re Tarleton* (1817) Buck 351, 354 ('proof is equivalent to payment').
[222] Vaughan Williams, Stirling and Cozens-Hardy LJJ.
[223] [1906] 1 Ch 1.
[224] [1906] 1 Ch 1, 8, referred to with evident approval in *Re Hurburgh* [1959] Tas SR 25, 41–42.
[225] *Ewart v Latta* (1865) 4 Macq 983, 990.

so that, as in the *West Coast Gold Fields* case, the mere fact that a company in voluntary liquidation has received a dividend in a shareholder's bankruptcy for a call in relation to partly paid shares does not mean that the shares are considered to be fully paid for the purpose of a distribution of the surplus assets of the company.[226] Rather, these observations may be interpreted to mean that the creditor, by proving, abandons or waives any other remedy that he has against the debtor.[227]

14.50   The conduct of the administrator in proving in the bankruptcy could only be said to constitute an abandonment of the right to invoke *Cherry v Boultbee* if the debt could have been satisfied by means of the principle had the administrator decided not to prove. It may be said that this would not have been the case if the sole asset of the estate was the debt owing by the bankrupt, because until the debt was paid there would not have been a fund in respect of which *Cherry v Boultbee* could have been invoked. This provides a possible explanation for the decisions in cases such as *Ex parte Turpin, re Brown*.[228] The *Turpin* case concerned a husband who, upon his marriage, gave a bond for £3,000 to trustees to be settled upon trust for himself for life, with the remainder to the wife and children. The husband became bankrupt without ever having paid anything under the bond, and so the trustees proved in the bankruptcy and obtained a dividend on the debt. It was held that the husband's assignees in bankruptcy were not entitled to the income received by the trustees on the proceeds of the dividend during the husband's life, but rather the trustees could retain and accumulate the income until the full debt of £3,000 had been realized.[229] There is nothing in the judgments in these cases however to indicate that they were based upon the ground suggested above, and indeed later cases seem to support the view that the same result would have ensued if the trustees in any event had been possessed of a fund at the time that they lodged a proof in respect of the debt.[230] There was no mention of this line of cases in

---

[226]   The court appeared to accept ([1906] 1 Ch 1, 8, and see also Buckley J at first instance [1905] 1 Ch 597, 602) that the holders of the other shares which were fully paid were alone entitled to share in the surplus assets until the amount paid on their shares was reduced to that which in fact had been paid on the bankrupt's shares.

[227]   Crawford J in *Re Hurburgh* [1959] Tas SR 25 41–42 noted that a secured creditor who proves his debt loses the benefit of his security, and so he concluded that *Cherry v Boultbee* similarly must take effect as a right in security. However the principle may be explained instead on the basis of an abandonment or a waiver of a personal right against the debtor available to the fund.

[228]   (1832) Mont 443.

[229]   See also *Ex parte Young, re Prior* (1835) 4 Deac & Ch 645 (explaining *Ex parte Shute, re Shute* (1833) 3 Deac & Ch 1); *Ex parte Crofts, re Last & Casey* (1837) 2 Deac 102 (in which the debtor was jointly and severally, and not just jointly, liable); *Re Walter, ex p Walter's Assignees* (1859) 32 LTOS 396. In addition see *Ex parte King. Re Severn* (1835) 1 Deac 143, although it is not clear whether the fund in that case consisted of anything other than the dividends.

[230]   See *Ex parte Smith, re Manning* (1836) 1 Deac 385, and note also *Ex parte Gonne, re March* (1837) 6 LJ Bcy 57. In *Fuller v Knight* (1843) 6 Beav 205, 49 ER 804 a trustee acted in breach of trust in lending part of the trust fund to the tenant for life. The tenant for life subsequently executed a creditor's deed, to which the trustee was a party, which provided for his assets, including his interest under the settlement, to be applied in payment of certain debts. It was held that the trustee

Stammers v Elliott,[231] but they may be distinguished on the following ground.[232] In *Stammers v Elliott,* and the cases following it, the obligation to contribute took the form of a debt that arose independently of the terms of the trust governing the fund. In the *Turpin* line of cases, on the other hand, the obligation to contribute to the settlement was undertaken as part of the terms of the settlement itself, so that both the liability to contribute and the right to participate were a part of the same transaction. Equity in this latter situation is more rigorous in ensuring that the estate of the bankrupt does not derive any benefit from the trust until the bankrupt's liability has been satisfied in full.[233] In other words, 'the Court, on looking at the settlement, and finding that the bankrupt had not fulfilled the covenants of the settlement, says, No, if you come here for equity, you must do equity first; and the Court will retain the dividend until the deficiency has been supplied'.[234]

There is a further exception to the principle that proof constitutes a waiver of the right to invoke *Cherry v Boultbee*. In two early nineteenth-century cases,[235] the bank in which the proceeds of a bankrupt customer's estate had been deposited itself became bankrupt. The bank was also a creditor of the bankrupt customer. It was held in each case that the bank was not entitled to receive a dividend on the debt owing to it until its liability to the estate on the deposit had been paid *in toto*. This was not affected by a proof lodged in the bank's bankruptcy. The bank remained liable to contribute the residue of its indebtedness, after paying a dividend to the customer's estate, before it could exercise its own right to participate in the bankruptcy in respect of the debt owing to it.[235a] This same principle has been held to apply in the case of an assignee in bankruptcy who was also a creditor of the bankrupt, and who himself became bankrupt after having received proceeds of the estate.[236]   **14.51**

---

nevertheless should not be prevented from applying the income otherwise available to the life tenant to make good the breach of trust. The agreement embodied in the creditor's deed could not be brought forward in order to prevent the trustee from acting to remedy his breach of trust.

[231]   (1868) LR 3 Ch App 195.

[232]   The distinction that Lord Chelmsford in *Stammers v Elliott* (1868) LR 3 Ch App 195, 200 drew between an executor and a trustee seems doubtful. See *Re Sewell* [1909] 1 Ch 806, 809, *per* Parker J.

[233]   *Cherry v Boultbee* should no longer be available however once the bankrupt is discharged from bankruptcy, so that he is released from his debt. See *Re Sewell* [1909] 1 Ch 806, 808 (defaulting trustee's debt released by composition), and para 14.17 above.

[234]   *Ex parte Gonne* (1837) 6 LJ Bcy 57, 59, *per* Erskine CJ *(arguendo)*.

[235]   *Ex parte Bebb* (1812) 19 Ves Jun 222, 34 ER 501; *Ex parte Graham* (1814) 3 V & B 130, 35 ER 428.

[235a]   See however the order in *Ex parte Graham* (1814) 3 V & B 130, 35 ER 428, discussed in para 14.13 above.

[236]   *Ex parte Bignold, re Charles* (1817) 2 Madd 470, 56 ER 408.

L. Assignments

(1) The General Principle

14.52   The leading authority on the effect of an assignment upon rights under *Cherry v Boultbee* is *Stephens v Venables (No 1)*.[237] Executors and trustees granted a lease of part of the testator's property to a residuary legatee. Subsequently the legatee charged his legacy to the plaintiff, and notice of the charge was given to the trustees. When the plaintiff as chargee claimed the legatee's interest after completion of the administration, a question arose as to whether the trustees could invoke the principle in *Cherry v Boultbee* against the plaintiff in respect of arrears of rent owing by the legatee to the estate. Consistent with the principle applicable to set-off,[238] Sir John Romilly MR held that the plaintiff took subject to equities, including rights under the principle in *Cherry v Boultbee*, which were in existence at the date that the trustee received notice of the assignment (or charge).[239]

> When a trustee or executor receives notice that a legatee has charged his legacy in favor of a stranger, the trustee is bound to withhold all further payments to that legatee, unless made with the consent of the mortgagee of the legacy. All rights of set-off and adjustment of equities between the legatee and the executor already existing at the date of the notice have priority over the charge, and may properly be deducted from the amount coming to the mortgagee; but the trustees can create no new charge or right of set off after that time. A debt due to the trustees before the notice of charge received by him may be set off against the share of the legatee, but no debt which accrued due subsequently to that period can be allowed to work any deduction from the share charged to the mortgagee.[240]

The trustees therefore could invoke the principle in respect of arrears of rent as at the date they were given notice of the charge, but not in respect of subsequently accruing rent.[241]

Exceptions

14.53   The general principle is that an assignee takes free of equities arising after notice, but there are exceptions[242] in the case of defaulting trustees and executors, and

---

[237] (1862) 30 Beav 625, 54 ER 1032.

[238] The Master of the Rolls referred to rights of 'set-off' in his judgment, although in truth rights under *Cherry v Boultbee* were in issue. The obligation to contribute should not have ceased to exist when the right to participate becomes due and payable. See eg *Re Baird* [1935] NZLR 847, and para 14.17 above.

[239] While the case concerned a charge, which does not involve an assignment, the same principle applies as for an assignment, in the sense that the chargee takes subject to equities. See paras 11.34–11.35 above.

[240] (1862) 30 Beav 625, 627, 54 ER 1032, 1033.

[241] See the further discussion of *Stephen v Venables* in para 14.58 below.

[242] See also paras 17.22–17.27 below in relation to equitable set-off.

also, in some circumstances, where a beneficiary becomes liable to the estate for costs. These exceptions are considered later.[243]

A competing principle

Sir John Romilly spoke in terms of a trustee. In *Stephens v Venables*, however, the **14.54** administration of the estate had not been completed at the date of the assignment of the interest in the residuary estate.[244] The assignment therefore did not involve an existing equitable interest under a trust. All that the residuary legatee was entitled to was 'a chose in action, capable of being invoked for any purpose connected with the proper administration of his estate'.[245] In other words, the subject of the assignment in equity was a presently existing chose in action against the executor, together with the right to receive the fruits of that chose in action when they matured.[246] Consider a case in which the subject of an assignment instead is an existing equitable interest under a trust. There is a competing equitable principle, that an assignee of an equitable interest takes subject to prior equities,[247] although the court will not interfere with the assignee's title if he is a purchaser of the equitable interest for valuable consideration without notice of the prior equity.[248] This differs from the principle applied in *Stephens v Venables*, and also in the case of set-off, in two respects. It allows an exception of purchaser for value without notice, and in addition the dividing line is the date of the assignment as opposed to the date of notice of the assignment. While it is usually stated in terms of an equitable estate or interest in land, as opposed to a trust fund, there would appear to be a sound reason for distinguishing between an assignment of a personal chose in action and an assignment of a beneficial interest in a trust. The rule that an equitable assignee of a chose in action takes subject to equities in existence at the date of notice is based upon the notion that the assignee steps into the shoes of the assignor.[249] The subject of the assignment is the personal rights possessed by

---

[243] For defaulting executors and trustees, see paras 14.67–14.71 below, and for costs see paras 14.42 above and 14.63 below.

[244] This appears more clearly from the report of subsequent proceedings in *Stephens v Venables (No 2)* (1862) 31 Beav 124, 54 ER 1084.

[245] *Commissioner of Stamp Duties (Queensland)* v *Livingston* [1965] AC 694, 717, PC. See para 13.116 above.

[246] *Re Leigh's Will Trusts* [1970] 1 Ch 277, 282.

[247] For this competing equitable principle, the prior equity should be 'ancillary to or dependent upon' an equitable title. An equity that is purely personal between the original parties will not suffice. See *National Provincial Bank Ltd v Ainsworth* [1965] AC 1175, 1238, *per* Lord Upjohn. This should encompass *Cherry v Boultbee*. The administrator of the fund says that the person claiming an interest in the fund already has an asset of the fund in his own hands, and therefore to that extent his right to participate is satisfied.

[248] *Westminster Bank Ltd v Lee* [1956] 1 Ch 7; *Phillips v Phillips* (1861) 4 De G F & J 208, 218, 45 ER 1164, 1167. Note that a disposition of an equitable interest or trust subsisting at the time of the disposition must be in writing. See the Law of Property Act 1925, s 53(1)(c). In Australia, see eg the Property Law Act 1958 (Vic), s 53(1)(c).

[249] Tudsbery, *Equitable Assignments* (1912) 87.

the assignor against the other party (usually, a debtor), together with the fruits of those rights. Therefore the general rule is that the assignee is bound by all equities and defences available against the assignor whose personal rights he is enforcing.[250] As an exception, however, equity will not allow the debtor to diminish the rights of the assignee by relying on events occurring after he has become aware of the assignment.[251] For that reason the date of notice to the debtor is the important date. On the other hand, the subject of an assignment of an equitable interest in a trust fund is not just the assignor's personal rights, but also a share of a specific fund. A proprietary interest in the fund is assigned. The assignee can rely upon his own equitable title, as opposed to that of the assignor. Moreover, the assignee of an equitable interest in a trust becomes the beneficiary as soon as the assignment takes place. Notice may be important for the question whether the trustee discharges his obligation by tendering payment to the assignor. It is not necessary however in order to perfect the title of the assignee.[252] Therefore, as from the time of the assignment, the assignee's interest in the trust is based upon his own title, and not that of the assignor, and so anything that occurs after the assignment between the trustee and the assignor should not affect his title.

14.55 There is some support for the view that the purchaser for value principle applies in the case of a right to participate in a trust fund.[253] For example, *Lewin on Trusts* states that, if a beneficiary joins in a breach of trust, all the benefit that would have accrued to him from the trust fund may be stopped by the beneficiaries as against him, and also against those claiming under him, except so far as the defence of

---

[250] Compare the case of a statutory assignment under the Law of Property Act 1925, s 136(1). If the requirements of the section are satisfied, the legal right to the debt is transferred. See *Read v Brown* (1888) 22 QBD 128, 132. The date of notice is still the dividing line, however. While the assignee takes subject to equities, notice is essential for the validity of the statutory assignment.

[251] *Roxburghe v Cox* (1881) 17 Ch D 520, 526. See para 17.03 below.

[252] *Ward v Duncombe* [1893] AC 369, 392. See also *Gorringe v Irwell India Rubber and Gutta Percha Works* (1886) 34 Ch D 128; *Re City Life Assurance Co Ltd. Stephenson's Case* [1926] 1 Ch 191, 219–220; *Re Trytel* [1952] 2 TLR 32, 34; *Thomas v National Australia Bank Ltd* [2000] 2 Qd R 448.

[253] In addition to the following, see *Houlditch v Wallace* (1838) 5 Cl & Fin 629, 7 ER 543 and *Cloutte v Story* [1911] 1 Ch 18, 24. In *Houlditch v Wallace* an estate was conveyed by its owner to trustees upon trust to pay to himself an annual sum, and to pay the surplus rent to his creditors in satisfaction of his debts. Subsequently he assigned a part of his right to the annuity by way of security. Both before and after the assignment the owner appropriated income of the estate in excess of the annual sum payable to himself. In relation to sums misappropriated after the assignment, the assignee took free from any equity that the owner's creditors, as the other trust beneficiaries, otherwise would have had to make a deduction from the annual payments. See (1838) 5 Cl & Fin 629, 665, 7 ER 543, 557. In relation to misappropriations before the assignment, Lord Cottenham held that the creditors were precluded by their laches from asserting their equity against the assignee. See para 14.40 above. Apart from that, the question whether there could have been a deduction from future payments under the annuity was thought to depend upon whether the assignee had notice of the equity. However the annuity was payable out of the estate, and counsel for the assignee argued (though without the point being addressed specifically by Lord Cottenham, and compare counsel for the creditors at 660, 555) that it created an interest charged upon the land. See at 652–653, 552. If that were the case, the subject of the assignment itself would have been an interest in the land.

purchase for value may be applicable.[254] The proposition is also consistent with a comment by Sir John Romilly MR in *Irby v Irby (No 3)*,[255] a case decided some four years before *Stephens v Venables*. Herbert de Crespigny was a beneficiary under his father's marriage settlement. He was also in default in his capacity of executor of his father's will, which gave rise to a right in the trustees to impound his entitlement under the settlement. The Master of the Rolls said[256] that 'this equity would be good against all persons who had taken an assignment of a charge upon Herbert de Crespigny's share, after having had notice of the claim of the trustees upon him'. The case concerned an equitable interest in a trust, and prior notice would only have been important if the defence of purchaser of an equitable interest for value without notice was relevant.

The weight of opinion however favours the view that the principle applied in the case of an assignment of a personal chose in action is also relevant when a chose in equity, in the form of an equitable interest in a trust fund, is assigned.[257] In accepting this view, the courts and text-writers have not considered the difference between an assignment of a personal chose in action and an assignment of an equitable proprietary interest in a fund.   **14.56**

(2) Presently Existing Rights and Obligations

Not presently payable at the date of notice

It is not necessary that the right to participate and the obligation to contribute should be presently payable at the date of notice, if indeed they are existing at that   **14.57**

---

[254] *Lewin on Trusts* (17th edn, 2000) 1239. In *Kilworth v Mountcashel* (1864) 15 Ir Ch Rep 565, 578, 580 Sir Thomas Smith MR adopted a similar statement in an earlier edition of *Lewin*, although he held (at 581) that a judgment creditor is not a purchaser, and therefore is not entitled to the benefit of the exception of purchaser for value.

[255] (1858) 25 Beav 632, 53 ER 778.

[256] (1858) 25 Beav 632, 638, 53 ER 778, 780.

[257] See *Phipps v Lovegrove* (1873) LR 16 Eq 80, 88; *Cumming v Austin* (1902) 28 VLR 347, affirmed (1903) 28 VLR 622; *Re Pain. Gustavson v Haviland* [1919] 1 Ch 38 (esp at 46); *Southern British National Trust Ltd v Pither* (1937) 57 CLR 89, 105, *per* Rich J; *White and Tudor's Leading Cases in Equity* (9th edn, 1928) vol 1, 136 (referred to with evident approval by Latham CJ in *Pither's* case at 102); *Halsbury's Laws of England* (4th edn (reissue), 1991) vol 6, 41 para 61, 44 para 66; *Withers on Reversions* (2nd edn, 1933) 239 (although neither of the cases cited in *Withers* concerned an equitable interest in a trust, or indeed commented upon an assignment of such an interest). See also *Cockell v Taylor* (1852) 15 Beav 103, 118, 51 ER 475, 481. In Underhill and Hayton, *Law Relating to Trusts and Trustees* (15th edn, 1995) 913 the principle that a bona fide purchaser of the interest of a trustee/beneficiary in default takes subject to a deduction to make good the default, even when the purchaser is without notice, is explained by the notion that 'the equitable interest in question was a chose in action, and purchasers of choses in action take subject to all equities'. In fact, the defaulting trustee cases have been explained on either of two grounds, neither of which is based on the principle that a purchaser of a chose in action takes subject to all equities. See paras 14.67–14.71 below. The second of those grounds, regarding a payment in advance, would also explain *Dibbs v Goren* (1849) 11 Beav 483, 50 ER 904. See *Livesey v Livesey* (1827) 3 Russ 287, 296, 38 ER 583, 587.

date. The administrator of the fund cannot appropriate an obligation to contribute as payment of a right to participate until the right has become due and payable. However he will not be denied the right to invoke *Cherry v Boultbee* against an assignee of the right to participate merely because the right was still only a right in reversion when the administrator received notice of the assignment,[258] or if it was otherwise still contingent.[259]

Contingent obligation to contribute

14.58 An assignee of a debt does not take subject to a set-off in respect of a cross-debt owing by the assignor to the debtor when the cross-debt arose after notice, albeit that it was the result of a contract entered into before notice.[260] This notion is criticized in the discussion of assignments in relation to set-off[261] on the ground that the existence or otherwise of a right of set-off should depend on when the debtor and the assignor entered into a binding contract, as opposed to when a debt arose pursuant to the contract. That criticism is equally relevant to the principle in *Cherry v Boultbee*, but *Stephens v Venables (No 1)*[262] is authority for the proposition that the restriction nevertheless also applies in that context. The case concerned a legatee who was granted a lease of part of the testator's property by the executors and trustees of the will for a period of twenty-one years. Subsequently he charged his right to the legacy, and notice of the charge was given to the trustees. When the legacy became payable, Sir John Romilly MR held that the trustees could invoke the principle in respect of the rent due from the legatee up to the date of notice, but that the chargees in enforcing their security took free from the legatee's indebtedness for rent arising after notice.[263] It made no difference that the liability for rent was based upon an obligation incurred under a lease entered into before notice. Sir John Romilly, in holding that only debts arising before notice could be taken into account, said:[264] 'Were it otherwise, the charge made by the legatee, whether residuary or pecuniary, would be worth nothing, the trustees might, after the receipt of notice of the charge, embark in a speculation with the legatee, and if, in the course of it, a balance accrued due to the trustee from the legatee, he

---

[258] See *Willes v Greenhill (No 1)* (1860) 29 Beav 376, 54 ER 673; *Re Batchelor. Sloper v Oliver* (1873) LR 16 Eq 481, 484. Compare *Re Wickham's Will. Grant v Union Trustee Co of Australia Ltd* (1898) 9 QLJ 102 (see para 14.35 above), in which the judgment proceeded on the basis of set-off rather than *Cherry v Boultbee*. In the case of *Cherry v Boultbee*, the right to participate must be payable before there can be an appropriation. See para 14.17 above.

[259] See *Re Batchelor* (1873) LR 16 Eq 481, 483–484, and also *Re Hurburgh* [1959] Tas SR 25, 31, 40.

[260] *Watson v Mid Wales Railway Co* (1867) LR 2 CP 593, and see also *Business Computers Ltd v Anglo-African Leasing Ltd* [1977] 1 WLR 578.

[261] See para 17.12 below.

[262] (1862) 30 Beav 625, 54 ER 1032. See also *Re Pain, Gustavson v Pain* [1919] 1 Ch 38, 47–48.

[263] See also *Hill v Hicken* [1897] 2 Ch 579.

[264] (1862) 30 Beav 625, 627–628, 54 ER 1032, 1033–1034.

might set it off against the legacy and leave the mortgagee with nothing.' This would not be a valid objection, however, if the debt, although arising after notice, is based upon a contract entered into before notice.

Furthermore, *Stephens v Venables* seems difficult to reconcile with other cases **14.59** which support the proposition that an assignee of a legacy takes subject to the principle in *Cherry v Boultbee* in circumstances where the legatee becomes obliged after the testator's death to indemnify the estate for a sum paid on the legatee's behalf under a guarantee given by the testator in relation to the legatee's debts, even though the trustees tendered payment to the creditor after they had notice of the assignment. In other words, the liability of the legatee/assignor to indemnify the estate was only contingent at the date of notice, and the essence of a contingent liability is that there is no actual liability until the occurrence of the event upon which the contingency depends, in this case payment by the surety's estate to the creditor. Curiously, the first of the cases is a decision of Sir John Romilly MR himself. In *Willes v Greenhill (No 1)*,[265] the testator was a surety on two promissory notes for a legatee to whom the testator had bequeathed a reversionary share in his residuary estate. The testator's death occurred before the notes became payable. Subsequently the trustees of the estate paid the creditor on the notes, but prior to the payment the legatee had assigned his legacy by way of mortgage to one of the trustees. This particular trustee, as assignee, obviously had notice of the assignment, and Sir John Romilly held that the notice that he had also constituted notice to the other trustees. Apparently it was not considered to be an objection to the trustees' right to invoke *Cherry v Boultbee* when the legacy became payable, that the legatee's liability to indemnify the estate for the sum paid on his behalf was only contingent at the date of the assignment, and therefore at the date of notice. Admittedly the question in *Willes v Greenhill* arose in the context of a priorities dispute between two mortgages, the legatee subsequently also having mortgaged the legacy to the trustees generally in order to secure the moneys to be paid on his behalf on the two notes. In the case of successive assignments, priority depends on which of the assignees first gives notice to the debtor. The Master of the Rolls, in following *Browne v Savage*,[266] said that it was in the interest of the single trustee taking the first mortgage to disclose the mortgage to his fellow trustees in order to obtain priority over any subsequent assignments, and so it could be assumed that in fact he had done this. Therefore, it was held that his mortgage had priority over the subsequent mortgage to the trustees generally. But the same reasoning should also have been relevant to the priorities dispute between the mortgage to the single trustee and the right of the trustees generally to invoke *Cherry v Boultbee*. In other words, it could be assumed that the trustees had notice of the assignment

---

[265] (1860) 29 Beav 376, 54 ER 673.
[266] (1859) 4 Drewry 635, 62 ER 244.

when they paid the creditor, and yet they were not precluded by that notice from invoking *Cherry v Boultbee* against the assignee notwithstanding that the legatee's obligation to contribute was still contingent at the date of notice. *Willes v Greenhill* is consistent in that regard with the principle applied in the case of a bankrupt legatee/principal debtor. The fact that the testator's estate pays the creditor after the bankruptcy, but under a contract of suretyship entered into by the testator before the bankruptcy, will not deprive the executors of the right to invoke the principle against the bankrupt's trustee in bankruptcy.[267] Similarly, it does not seem to be an objection to the operation of *Cherry v Boultbee* that an assignment may have taken place when the right to participate was still only contingent.[268]

14.60   Consider also *Re Melton*,[269] which was referred to earlier in the context of suretyship and the rule against double proof.[270] Some additional facts should be noted. The principal debtor in *Re Melton* had mortgaged his interest in the legacy to the creditor after the testator's death, but before his own bankruptcy. Notice of the mortgage was given to the surety's executors before they paid the creditor. The creditor had valued the security, and only proved in the debtor's bankruptcy for the balance of the debt. The creditor therefore retained the benefit of the security. After payment by the executors under the suretyship agreement, the creditor assigned the security to the appellant in order to obtain payment of the sum still outstanding on the principal debt.[271] The appellant, as assignee from the creditor, had no better title than the creditor itself had. It was held that the rule against double proof did not deprive the surety's executors of the right to invoke *Cherry v Boultbee* in respect of the sum paid on behalf of the principal debtor. But the principal debtor was only contingently liable to indemnify the estate at the date of notice to the executors, payment to the creditor not yet having taken place, and it is implicit in the decision that the fact that the obligation to contribute to the estate was only contingent at that date was not considered to be an objection to the operation of the principle.

14.61   Wood[272] has sought to explain *Willes v Greenhill* and *Re Melton* on the ground that in both cases the beneficiary who assigned the interest was also an executor. In the context of assignments, special rules indeed apply to trustees and executors who are entitled to participate in the estate but who have defaulted in the performance of their duties as such.[273] An assignee of the trustee's or the executor's interest takes

---

[267]   *Re Watson* [1896] 1 Ch 925; *Re Lennard* [1934] 1 Ch 235. See para 14.23 above.

[268]   See *Re Batchelor* (1873) LR 16 Eq 481, 483–484, and also *Re Hurburgh* [1959] Tas SR 25, 31, 40.

[269]   [1918] 1 Ch 37.

[270]   See para 14.45 above.

[271]   See Warrington LJ at [1918] 1 Ch 37, 55.

[272]   Wood, *English and International Set-off* (1989) 449–50.

[273]   See paras 14.67–14.78 below.

subject to a deduction for an amount required to remedy the default even where the default occurred after notice of the assignment. The basis of the principle is default in the performance of a fiduciary obligation, and an assignee from an executor or a trustee takes the risk of a subsequent breach of fiduciary duty.[274] In neither *Willes v Greenhill* nor *Re Melton* however was there any question of a default of that nature, and so the fact that the beneficiary assigning the interest also happened to be an executor should not have been relevant.

It is difficult to see why *Cherry v Boultbee* should have been available in cases such **14.62** as *Willes v Greenhill* and *Re Melton*, in which the debtor's liability to the fund arose after notice of the assignment but as a result of a contract of suretyship entered into before notice, but that it should not have been available in a case such as *Stephens v Venables*, where the indebtedness for rent came into existence after notice but as a result of a lease entered into before notice. *Stephens v Venables* is consistent with the principle applied in the law of set-off,[275] while in the suretyship cases the fact that a liability only vested after the notice was not emphasized. The principle enunciated in *Stephens v Venables* is generally regarded as representing the current state of the law.[276] Nevertheless, it constitutes an unwarranted restriction on the operation of *Cherry v Boultbee*, as well as on the right of set-off, and there is much to commend the view that the approach evidenced by the suretyship cases should be applied generally whenever a debt arises after notice although as a result of a contract entered into before notice.

(3) Costs in Pending Proceedings

If a beneficiary of a trust commences a suit against a trustee and, while the pro- **14.63** ceedings are still pending, the beneficial interest is assigned, the assignee will take subject to an order for costs ultimately made against the beneficiary if the suit fails.[277] Where, however, the suit was commenced after the trustee was notified of the assignment, the assignee ordinarily will take free of a costs order made against the assignor, except to the extent of the trustee's usual right of indemnity out of the *entire* trust fund for all costs and expenses properly incurred by him in relation to the trust.[278] On the other hand, the assignee may lose his priority if he stands by and allows costs to be incurred that he could have prevented.[279]

---

[274] *Cock v Aitken* (1912) 15 CLR 373, 384, *per* Isaacs J.

[275] Indeed, Sir John Romilly seemed to treat the case as one of set-off, although in truth rights under *Cherry v Boultbee* were in issue.

[276] See eg *Re Milan Tramways Co, ex p Theys* (1884) 25 Ch D 587 (esp Fry LJ at 594).

[277] See *Re Pain, Gustavson v Haviland* [1919] 1 Ch 38, 48–49, explaining *Re Knapman, Knapman v Wreford* (1881) 18 Ch D 300. See also *Re Mayne, ex p The Official Receiver* [1907] 2 KB 899, and *Re Jones, Christmas v Jones* [1897] 2 Ch 190 (esp at 203–204).

[278] *Re Pain. Gustavson v Haviland* [1919] 1 Ch 38, 49, and see also Isaacs J in the High Court of Australia in *Cock v Aitken* (1912) 15 CLR 373, 383–384.

[279] *Re Pain. Gustavson v Haviland* [1919] 1 Ch 38.

(4) Assignee Has Obligation to Contribute

14.64 The assignee of a right to participate takes subject not only to equities available against the assignor, but also to equities available against himself. If the assignee is liable to contribute to the fund, his obligation may be appropriated as payment of the right to participate when the right becomes due and payable.[280] *Cherry v Boultbee* is an equitable principle, and it may be applied by a court of equity as against the person with the equitable title to the right to participate, whoever that person may be.

(5) Agreement not to Assert Equities Against Assignees

14.65 While an assignee of a chose in action generally takes subject to equities available to the debtor against the assignor, a debtor may contract with the creditor on terms that the debtor will not raise against an assignee any rights which he may possess against the creditor. For example, debentures issued by a company may provide that the principal and interest secured by the debentures will be paid without regard to any equities between the company and the original or any intermediate holder thereof. This clause will be effective in the winding up of the company when there is a fund available for payment of the debentures, so that a registered transferee who is a bona fide purchaser for value will be entitled to receive the sum payable in the winding up in respect of the debentures without any deduction under *Cherry v Boultbee*.[281] On the other hand, a transferee who is not a bona fide purchaser for value cannot rely on the clause.[282] In that regard, a trustee under a creditors' deed executed by a debtor was held not to be a purchaser of debentures assigned by the debtor to the trustee pursuant to the deed, the trustee having become the registered holder. Therefore, the trustee took subject to equities available to the company against the debtor notwithstanding that the debentures provided that they were to be paid without regard to equities between the company and the original holder.[283] Similarly, neither a trustee in bankruptcy nor a judgment creditor is considered to be a purchaser.[284]

---

[280] *Burridge v Row* (1844) 13 LJ Ch 173. See also *Re Milan Tramways Co, ex p Theys* (1884) 25 Ch D 587, 592–593, *per* Cotton LJ. Compare *Campbell v Graham* (1831) 1 Russ & M 453, 39 ER 175 (and on appeal *Campbell v Sandford* (1834) 8 Bligh NS 622, 5 ER 1073), in which the assignee of the legacies was not personally liable on the bonds.

[281] *Re Goy & Co Ltd. Farmer v Goy & Co Ltd* [1900] 2 Ch 149 (esp at 153, where Stirling J emphasized that the transfer was for value and in good faith, as to which see also *Re Blakely Ordnance Co* (1867) LR 3 Ch App 154, 159). *Aliter* if the debentures do not contain a clause to that effect. See *Re Rhodesia Goldfields Ltd* [1910] 1 Ch 239.

[282] *Re Brown & Gregory Ltd, Shepheard v Brown & Gregory Ltd* [1904] 1 Ch 627, affirmed [1904] 2 Ch 448.

[283] *Re Brown & Gregory Ltd* [1904] 1 Ch 627, affirmed [1904] 2 Ch 448.

[284] *Kilworth v Mountcashell* (1864) 15 Ir Ch Rep 565, 581; *Re Marquis of Anglesey* [1903] 2 Ch 727, 732.

(6) Successive Assignments

Consider that A, who has a right to participate in a fund, assigns the right to B, who   **14.66**
in turn assigns it to C. Subject to the principles discussed above, the administrator
of the fund may invoke *Cherry v Boultbee* in respect of an obligation that A has to
contribute to the fund. However the question may arise whether *Cherry v Boultbee*
may be invoked when B instead has the obligation to contribute. The issue of successive assignments is considered later.[285]

M. Defaulting Trustees and Executors

'It has always been a rule of the Court of Chancery that, if a trustee misappropri-   **14.67**
ates trust money, and has an equitable interest under the trust deed, the Court will
not allow him to receive any part of the trust fund in which he is equitably interested under the trust until he has made good his default as trustee.'[286] A possible
explanation for this principle is *Cherry v Boultbee*. It could be said that the defaulting trustee or executor[287] is directed to satisfy his beneficial entitlement from
the trust assets in his own hands in the form of his liability to compensate the trust
for the breach. In fact, two slightly different formulations have been adopted. The
principle is often called a right to impound, or stop, the beneficial interest of the
defaulting trustee,[288] although in truth this is not an accurate description of either
of the formulations. Moreover, both formulations have been said to give a wider
remedy in the case of an assignment than that otherwise available against an assignee under *Cherry v Boultbee*. An assignee only takes subject to equities in existence before notice. Yet the courts have said that there is no such limitation in the
case of a defaulting trustee, so that the assignee of the trustee's beneficial interest
under the trust will take subject to a possible deduction to the extent required to
remedy the breach irrespective of whether the assignment occurred before or after
default. This applies also to a trustee's liability to pay costs to the estate because
of the trustee's misconduct.[289] An important limitation, however, is that this

---

[285] See paras 17.47–17.50 below.
[286] *Re Brown, Dixon v Brown* (1886) 32 Ch D 597, 600, *per* Kay J. In addition to the cases cited
below, see *Skinner v Sweet* (1818) 3 Madd 244, 56 ER 499; *Woodyatt v Gresley* (1836) 8 Sim 180,
59 ER 72; *Staniar v Evans* (1886) 34 Ch D 470. Compare *Hallett v Hallett* (1879) 13 Ch D 232, in
which the trustee's beneficial interest related to a trust which was separate and distinct from the settlement in respect of which he was in default.
[287] This same principle applies to a defaulting executor. See *Sims v Doughty* (1800) 5 Ves Jun
243, 31 ER 567; *Re Dacre* [1916] 1 Ch 344.
[288] See eg *Courtenay v Williams* (1844) 3 Hare 539, 554, 67 ER 494, 500; *Fox v Buckley* (1876)
3 Ch D 508, 509, *per* Little VC, at first instance.
[289] An assignee of a trustee's right to participate will take subject to a deduction in respect of costs
payable by the trustee even if the assignment took place before the liability arose. See *Hopkins v
Gowan* (1828) 1 Mol 561, 562 (IR), and *Re Pain, Gustavson v Haviland* [1919] 1 Ch 38, 47. This

extended principle in relation to assignments is only relevant when the assignor was a trustee or an executor at the time of the assignment. If the assignor subsequently becomes a trustee or an executor, and then defaults, it does not apply.[290] Moreover, it only applies when the obligation to contribute arises out of a default in the performance of a fiduciary obligation.[291] An obligation to contribute which is derived from another source will not suffice.[292]

The first formulation

14.68 The first formulation is set out in *Morris v Livie*.[293] A person appointed trustee under a will committed a breach of trust after he had assigned a right that he had in reversion as a residuary legatee to participate in the trust. When the assignee later sought payment of the legacy, it was held that he took subject to the trustee's obligation to reimburse the trust for the breach. Knight Bruce VC said that the right to participate was given subject to a condition that the trustee would properly perform the duties of trustee. If the trustee acted in breach of trust, the right to participate could not be exercised until the breach had been remedied.

> It may, I conceive, be properly said that [the trustee's] legacy was given under a condition raised and implied by law, that undertaking he should duly fulfil the duties and obligations imposed on him by the instrument giving it. This he could not do without performing the trust as to the stock legacy, which, before his own legacy became due, he had, by his own misconduct, disabled himself from performing. The condition, if existing, accompanied his legacy until its discharge, and applied to it as much after as before its assignment.[294]

Cherry v Boultbee specifically contemplates the existence of a right to participate, but allows the administrator of the fund to appropriate a particular asset as payment of the right. Under *Morris v Livie*, on the other hand, the trustee's breach

---

is not the case however for a beneficiary who is not also an executor or a trustee, and who is liable for costs incurred after notice of an assignment of his interest. The assignee does not take subject to a deduction, except to the extent of the trustee 's usual right to indemnity out of the *entire* trust fund for all costs and expenses properly incurred by him in relation to the trust. See *Re Pain*, explaining *Re Knapman, Knapman v Wreford* (1881) 18 Ch D 300. See also *Cock v Aitken* (1912) 15 CLR 373, 383–384, *per* Isaacs J. On the other hand, it was held in *Re Pain* that the assignee may lose his priority if he stands by and allows the assignor to incur costs that he could have prevented. See also para 14.63 above.

[290] *Re Pain, Gustavson v Haviland* [1919] 1 Ch 38, 47; *White and Tudor's Leading Cases in Equity* (9th edn, 1928) vol 1, 139, citing *Irby v Irby (No 3)* (1858) 25 Beav 632, 53 ER 778. Compare *Cumming v Austin* (1903) 28 VLR 622, 629.

[291] See *Cock v Aitken* (1912) 15 CLR 373, 384, *per* Isaacs J.

[292] Compare the discussion of *Willes v Greenhill (No 1)* (1860) 29 Beav 376, 54 ER 673 and *Re Melton* [1918] 1 Ch 37 in para 14.61 above.

[293] (1842) 1 Y & C CC 380, 62 ER 934. See also *Wilkins v Sibley* (1863) 4 Giff 442, 445–446, 66 ER 780, 781–782; *Cock v Aitken* (1912) 15 CLR 373, 384; *Re Pain. Gustavson v Haviland* [1919] 1 Ch 38, 46–47.

[294] (1842) 1 Y & C C CC 380, 388–389, 62 ER 934, 938.

impugns his very entitlement to participate in the trust to the extent of the breach. Strictly, this is not a case of the trustee's interest being impounded. Rather, it is said that, in the event of a breach, the trustee does not have an interest. Since an assignee can only claim what the trustee himself could claim, the assignee should also take subject to the obligation to remedy the breach, regardless of when the breach may have occurred.

Morris v Livie is not confined to the case of a trustee who is also a residuary lega-   **14.69**
tee.[295] It has been cited as authority for the general proposition that 'every person taking an assignment from a cestui que trust of a portion of the testator's estate, at all events takes it subject to the liability to make good all breaches of trust on the part of the assignor if he fill the fiduciary position of a trustee, even though the breaches of trust be subsequent to the assignment'.[296] Nevertheless, *Morris v Livie* should not be relevant if it is clear that the bequest was intended to be independent of the office of trustee,[297] because it could not be said in such a case that the bequest was conditional upon the trustee properly performing his duties. On that basis, it is difficult to explain the decision in *Re Hervey, Short v Parratt*[298] by reference to *Morris v Livie*. The case concerned an intestacy. The administratrix was one of the next of kin of the intestate, and as such was entitled, after payment of the debts, to one moiety of the residue. She committed a breach of trust,[299] and so she herself could take nothing out of the personal estate until the amount which she was liable to replace had been made good. Prior to the default she had settled all her property, which included after-acquired property,[300] but it was held, on the authority of *Morris v Livie*, that the trustees of the settlement were subject to the same equity, even though the default occurred after the assignment. In an intestacy, however, nothing is 'given' by the intestate as such, and nor is the administrator appointed

---

[295] Compare *Withers on Reversions* (2nd edn, 1933) 242. For example, the trustee in *Barnett v Sheffield* (1852) 1 De G M & G 371, 42 ER 595 was entitled to a specific legacy in the form of an annuity, but because of a misappropriation of trust funds it was held that he could not demand that anything be paid to him under the annuity. Knight Bruce VC (at 382, 599) described the annuity as 'a guarantee for a full account on his part as to all the transactions in which he as a trustee should be engaged in respect of the trust'.

[296] *Re Knapman* (1881) 18 Ch D 300, 307, *per* Hall VC. It is not necessary that the defaulting trustee should be the only trustee of the trust. See *Barnett v Sheffield* (1852) 1 De G M & G 371, 42 ER 595.

[297] See Little VC at first instance in *Fox v Buckley* (1876) 3 Ch D 508, 509. Compare *Barnett v Sheffield* (1852) 1 De G M & G 371, 42 ER 595, in which the court rejected the argument that the will in that case specifically contemplated that the legacy should be paid despite any misappropriation. For a discussion of when a legacy may be said to be attached to the office of executor, see *Williams on Wills* (7th edn, 1995) vol 1, 268–9.

[298] (1889) 61 LT 429.

[299] An administrator of an intestate's estate becomes a trustee as soon as the administration is completed. See *Re Cockburn's Will Trusts* [1957] 1 Ch 438, 439.

[300] The assignment of the beneficial interest would have become effective as soon as the trust was created and a beneficial interest was acquired. See *Palette Shoes Pty Ltd v Krohn* (1937) 58 CLR 1, 27.

by the intestate. It is difficult then to see the basis for suggesting that the administrator's right to participate in the estate was given subject to a condition of properly performing the office, in accordance with *Morris v Livie.*

The second formulation

14.70 The second formulation of the principle in these defaulting trustee or executor cases is similar to, but is nonetheless distinct from, *Cherry v Boultbee.* Instead of saying that the trustee's obligation to contribute should be appropriated as payment of the right to participate when the right becomes due and payable, it is said that the trustee is deemed to have paid himself in advance, or in anticipation, from the money in his hands constituted by the misappropriated funds.[301] Strictly, this is not a case of impounding the trust fund; rather, the trustee is treated as if he has already had what he could claim.[302] It is not important for this formulation that there should be any connection between the beneficial entitlement and the proper performance by the trustee of his duties. In this respect it is wider than *Morris v Livie.*[303] For example, it applies even if the trustee acquired a beneficial interest only derivatively.[304] It has been said that it still applies when the breach of trust is committed after the assignment.[305] If indeed that were correct, it would justify a deduction in a case such as *Hervey,*[306] in which there was no connection between the office of administratrix and the right to share in the estate. It is questionable, however, whether the terms of this second formulation are apt to allow a deduction in respect of a breach occurring after the assignment or, at any rate, if there are other trustees of the trust, after they received notice of the assignment. The point is that, if a trustee has notice of an assignment of an equitable interest under the trust, he could not discharge his obligation by paying the assignor. He must tender payment to the assignee.[307] This should also apply when the assignor is the trustee. Payment to himself after notice would not discharge the trust obligation to the assignee, and so it is difficult to see how a notion of a payment in advance to a defaulting trustee could bind the assignee if default occurred after notice of the assignment. There must of course be a valid notice. In that regard, if there are

---

[301] *Irby v Irby (No 3)* (1858) 25 Beav 632, 638, 53 ER 778, 780; *Re Carew* [1896] 1 Ch 527, 535; *Edgar v Plomley* [1900] AC 431, 443; *Re Towndrow* [1911] 1 Ch 662, 668; *Re Dacre* [1916] 1 Ch 344; *RWG Management Ltd v Commissioner for Corporate Affairs* [1985] VR 385, 398.

[302] *Jacubs v Rylance* (1874) LR 17 Eq 341, 342.

[303] On the other hand, *Morris v Livie* would still apply when the trustee personally has not derived any advantage from the breach, but *quaere* whether this second formulation would be relevant in that case. See *Re Pain, Gustavson v Haviland* [1919] 1 Ch 38, 46–47.

[304] *Jacubs* v *Rylance* (1874) LR 17 Eq 341; *Doering v Doering* (1889) 42 Ch D 203; *Cumming v Austin* (1903) 28 VLR 622; *Re Dacre* [1916] 1 Ch 344. See also *Brandon v Brandon* (1859) 3 De G & J 524, 44 ER 1371 with respect to the purchased shares.

[305] *Doering v Doering* (1889) 42 Ch D 203, 207; *Cumming v Austin* (1903) 28 VLR 622; *Re Dacre* [1916] Ch 344, 347.

[306] (1889) 61 LT 429.

[307] *Brice v Bannister* (1878) 3 QBD 569.

a number of trustees an assignee need give notice to only one of them, although when the assignor himself is a trustee the notice that the assignor/trustee obviously has is not considered to be sufficient for that purpose.[308] The assignee should protect his interest by giving notice to another trustee. Alternatively, the assignor may be a sole trustee. In the context of a priorities dispute under *Dearle v Hall*[309] between successive assignees, it has been said that notice to, or the knowledge possessed by, a sole assignor/trustee is not effective to alter priorities.[310] This should not apply, however, when a question of payment is in issue. Notice is not necessary in order to perfect the title of the assignee. He becomes the trust beneficiary as from the date of the assignment.[311] A sole assignor/trustee could hardly discharge the trust obligation to the assignee by paying a complete stranger whom the trustee knows is not the beneficiary, and equally he should not be able to discharge that obligation by paying himself when he knows that he ceased to be the beneficiary as from the time of the assignment.

Consequences of the formulations

It would seem, then, that neither *Morris v Livie* nor the second theory of a payment in advance offers a satisfactory explanation as to why an assignee of a defaulting trustee's beneficial interest should take subject to a deduction to make good the breach if, as in *Re Hervey*, the trustee's entitlement was not dependent upon the proper performance of the office of trustee, and moreover if the breach occurred after the trustees received notice of the assignment, or, in the case of a sole trustee, after the assignment itself. **14.71**

One consequence of both formulations is that, unlike under *Cherry v Boultbee*, it should not make any difference that the liability to contribute ceased to exist before the right to participate became due and payable, for example because of a discharge from bankruptcy, or as a result of a composition or scheme of arrangement.[312] The discharge should not be relevant, because the breach would mean that the right to participate has already been impugned (under *Morris v Livie*), or it has already been satisfied by a notional payment in advance to the defaulting trustee.[313] Similarly, in the case of *Morris v Livie*, the fact of proving the debt and receiving a dividend in the bankruptcy should not constitute a waiver of the right **14.72**

---

[308] *Browne v Savage* (1859) 4 Drewry 635, 62 ER 244; *Cumming v Austin* (1902) 28 VLR 347, affirmed (1903) 28 VLR 622. Compare the case of an assignment *to* a trustee. See para 14.59 above.

[309] (1828) 3 Russ. 1, 38 ER 475.

[310] *Re Dallas* [1904] 2 Ch 385, and compare *Ipswich Permanent Money Club Ltd v Arthy* [1920] 2 Ch 257.

[311] *Ward v Duncombe* [1893] AC 369, 392. See also *Gorringe v Irwell India Rubber and Gutta Percha Works* (1886) 34 Ch D 128; *Re City Life Assurance Co Ltd. Stephenson's Case* [1926] 1 Ch 191, 219–220; *Re Trytel* [1952] 2 TLR 32, 34; *Thomas v National Australia Bank Ltd* [2000] 2 Qd R 448.

[312] Compare para 14.17 above in relation to *Cherry v Boultbee*.

[313] Compare the comments of Parker J in *Re Sewell. White v Sewell* [1909] 1 Ch 806, 808–809.

to invoke the principle either before or after discharge,[314] since the trustee's right should still be impugned until such time as the default is remedied *in toto*. While *Re Sewell*[315] is authority to the contrary, the point may be made that Parker J did not analyse the case in terms of the defaulting trustee formulations.

Non-monetary bequest

14.73 *Cherry v Boultbee* is confined to the situation in which a right to participate is for a sum of money. It is not available against a legatee entitled to a specific bequest of freeholds or leaseholds, or of chattels.[316] This restriction should not apply, however, in the case of a defaulting executor or trustee under the *Morris v Livie* formulation. It is doubtful whether the second formulation could be invoked in this situation. If an executor or a trustee entitled to a specific bequest of that nature misappropriates funds of the estate, it would not be appropriate to characterize the misapplied funds as a 'payment' of the bequest in advance, because a person to whom specific property has been bequeathed could not claim instead a sum of money. With respect to *Morris v Livie*, on the other hand, if the bequest was conditional upon the executor or trustee properly performing the duties ancillary to the office, failure to perform those duties should impugn the right to the bequest.[317] Admittedly there have been cases in which a trustee appointed under a will was given a life interest in realty, and it was held that the interest was not liable to be appropriated to make good deficiencies in the trust caused by his own breach.[318] But that was because a devise of realty formerly took place outside the will, so that it was not bound by the trust.[319] Moreover, since the devise took place outside the will, it could not be said that it was connected with the office of trustee, so as to support an argument that it was subject to a condition that the devisee would properly perform the duties of executor and trustee.[320] However real estate now devolves on the personal representative,[321] and so the old rule should no longer apply.

Bankrupt defaulting trustee

14.74 The preceding discussion concerned the situation in which the defaulting trustee, or an assignee, seeks payment of the trustee's beneficial entitlement under the

---

[314] Compare para 14.49 above in relation to *Cherry v Boultbee*.
[315] [1909] 1 Ch 806.
[316] See para 14.38 above.
[317] *Palmer v The Permanent Trustee Co* (1915) 16 SR (NSW) 162.
[318] *Egbert v Butter* (1856) 21 Beav 560, 52 ER 976; *Fox v Buckley* (1876) 3 Ch D 508. See also *Re Milnes; Milnes v Sherwin* (1885) 53 LT 534, 535.
[319] See *Re Brown. Dixon v Brown* (1886) 32 Ch D 597, 600.
[320] See Little VC at first instance in *Fox v Buckley* (1876) 3 Ch D 508, 509.
[321] Administration of Estates Act 1925, s 1(1), and see generally *Williams, Mortimer and Sunnucks on Executors, Administrators and Probate* (18th edn, 2000) 479, 1037 n 32.

trust. Consider the converse situation, in which the defaulting trustee is bankrupt and other trustees of the trust wish to prove in the bankruptcy in respect of the breach. For what amount, if any, can they prove? In considering this question, a distinction can be drawn between the two defaulting trustee formulations.

Under the second formulation, the defaulting trustee is deemed to have paid **14.75** himself in advance, or in anticipation, from the misappropriated funds. Since payment is deemed to have occurred, this would seem to require the striking of a balance between what was due from the defaulting trustee by way of compensation and what was due to the defaulting trustee, so that the claim against the defaulting trustee should be limited to the balance. In Victoria, comments by Brooking J in *RWG Management Ltd v Commissioner for Corporate Affairs*[322] support this approach in the context of a defaulting trustee with a right of indemnity from the estate. However it is contrary to views expressed by North J in *Staniar v Evans*.[323] *Staniar v Evans* concerned a defaulting trustee who was entitled to costs out of the estate. North J said that the usual order in such a case is that the trustee cannot receive any costs until the default has been made good. He said that an order may be made for payment of the balance only, but that an order in that form is made as a matter of favour only in circumstances where the trustee in any event is perfectly able and ready and willing to pay what he owes. If the trustee is not able and ready and willing to pay, the order should be for payment of the full amount necessary to make good the default. On this view, if the trustee is bankrupt and therefore is unable to pay what he owes, the proof should be for the full amount. *Staniar v Evans* concerned a claim for costs out of the trust estate, but North J indicated that the principle is also relevant when the trustee is entitled to a share of the trust estate.[324] A similar approach has been adopted in other situations.[325] It would seem to be particularly apt in the case of the first formulation. If a bequest is given to a trustee of an estate under an implied condition that he should fulfil the duties and obligations imposed on him by the instrument, the trustee, having defaulted, would not be entitled to the bequest until the breach is remedied. It could therefore be said that the other trustees should be entitled to prove for the full amount of the breach, and that the bankrupt's estate should not be entitled to participate in the trust until the default has been remedied *in toto*.[326]

In fact the courts have not always proceeded on the *Staniar v Evans* approach **14.76** when the first formulation would apply, at least when the bankrupt otherwise

---

[322] [1985] VR 385, 397–398.

[323] (1886) 34 Ch D 470. See also *Lewis v Trask* (1882) 21 Ch D 862, and para 14.12 above.

[324] (1886) 34 Ch D 470, 473.

[325] See para 14.83 below.

[326] The proof in the bankruptcy should not constitute a waiver of the right to invoke *Morris v Livie*, or indeed *Cherry v Boultbee*, since the right to participate and the obligation to contribute both arise out of the trust itself. See *Ex parte Turpin* (1832) Mont 443, and para 14.50 above.

would have had a present right to a definite part of the trust fund at the date of bankruptcy.[327] Rather, the right of proof in the bankruptcy has been limited to the difference between the defaulting trustee's liability and the trustee's beneficial interest in the trust estate, which includes the trust asset represented by his own liability. This has the consequence that the other beneficiaries of the trust effectively are deprived of the benefit of *Morris v Livie*. It has been justified on the basis of set-off. In *Ex parte Turner, re Crosthwaite*[328] a trustee appointed under a will was one of two residuary legatees. He misapplied trust funds, and became bankrupt. The other residuary legatee was also appointed a trustee. He sought to prove in the bankruptcy for the full amount of the default, and to retain the dividends and not pay anything to the defaulting trustee until the default was made good. Lord Cranworth and Knight Bruce LJ rejected that approach, and held that set-off applied. Lord Cranworth commented that, 'being one of the residuary legatees, he or his estate is entitled, on the doctrine of mutual credit, to set off against the sum due from him his share of whatever is due to him'.[329] He analysed the position as follows. He said that, if before the bankruptcy, the defaulting trustee had tendered the value of the residue of his liability after setting off his own beneficial interest in the trust, the question between the parties would have been settled. Therefore the trustees should be remitted to a proof for the difference remaining after the set-off. The decision in *Ex parte Turner* was followed in *Re Chapman. Ex parte Parker*,[330] Mathew J commenting: 'We should be flying in the face of [the insolvency set-off section[331]] if we did not ascertain what the exact liability of the bankrupt was, and that exact liability can only be ascertained by giving the bankrupt credit for his share.'[332]

14.77 With respect, it is not easy to see how the insolvency set-off section can be said to apply. In the first place, the defaulting trustee's right to participate in the trust is a claim *in specie* for a share of a trust fund, and so it should not be within the ambit of the set-off section.[333] Secondly, the essence of a set-off is the existence of cross-demands between the parties. The bankrupt defaulting trustee in the *Turner* case was allowed a deduction in respect of his interest in the total trust estate, which included the trust asset represented by his own liability. Yet it could hardly be said that the bankrupt had a cross-demand against the other trustees in respect of his 'interest' in his own unsatisfied liability. Thirdly, according to *Morris v Livie*, the defaulting trustee's entitlement is conditional upon the breach being remedied.

---

[327] Compare *Re Gloag's Estate* (1892) 11 NZLR 90 (esp at 94), discussed below.

[328] (1852) 2 De G M & G 927, 42 ER 1134.

[329] (1852) 2 De G M & G 927, 932, 42 ER 1134, 1136. Knight Bruce LJ adopted a similar analysis.

[330] (1887) 4 Morr 109.

[331] The relevant provision was the Bankruptcy Act 1883, s 38.

[332] (1887) 4 Morr 109, 112.

[333] See paras 10.03–10.06 above.

Until that occurs, the bankrupt's entitlement, and any demand in relation to it, would be contingent. Unlike a contingent liability of a bankrupt, a contingent claim possessed by a bankrupt cannot be the subject of a set-off until the contingency has occurred and an amount accordingly has become due to the bankrupt.[334] In the situation under discussion, the contingency would not occur until the default has been remedied. In truth, it is not easy to see how the doctrine of mutual credit can be said to be relevant to a case such as *Turner.*

Ex parte Turner was not applied in a case in New Zealand. In *Re Gloag's Estate*[335] a **14.78** trustee was entitled to a life interest in the whole of the trust fund and, having misapplied the fund, she became bankrupt. Williams J held[336] that the representative of the trust estate in the interest in reversion of the other beneficiaries was entitled to prove for the whole of the misapplied fund, and that the bankrupt's estate could not participate in the income obtained from the dividend payable on the proof until the original fund had been replaced *in toto.* His Honour distinguished the *Turner* case on the ground that the defaulting trustee in that case had a present right to a definite share of the trust fund. The trustee before the bankruptcy could have discharged his obligation to the other beneficiary by paying him a certain sum after deducting his immediate share. This was not the case in the *Gloag* case, however. The defaulting trustee could not have discharged herself by paying to the other beneficiaries the present value of their reversionary interests after her life interest. She could only discharge herself by replacing the corpus, and there was nothing which could be set against that obligation.[337]

N. The Method of Application of *Cherry v Boultbee*

Cherry v Boultbee entitles the administrator of the fund to assert that a debtor to **14.79** the fund should appropriate a particular asset of the fund, in the form of his own indebtedness, as *pro tanto* payment of his right to participate. The application of this principle is straightforward when the right to participate is for a fixed sum. [338] If on the other hand the debtor is entitled to a certain percentage of the fund, the administrator in invoking the principle calculates the debtor's share on the basis that the fund has been increased by the debtor's own debt, and the debtor becomes

---

[334] See paras 8.27–8.37 above.

[335] (1892) 11 NZLR 90.

[336] Following *Ex parte King, Re Severn* (1835) 1 Deac 143.

[337] See also *Ex parte Stone, re Welch* (1873) LR 8 Ch App 914 (no set-off in respect of debtor/trustee's reversionary interest).

[338] If there are a number of fixed sum legacies, but there is a deficiency in the fund, an abatement may be necessary in order to calculate the amount of the right to participate in respect of which *Cherry v Boultbee* can operate. See *Re King, King v King* (1914) 31 WN (NSW) 55. Compare *Re Richardson, ex p Thompson v Hutton* (1902) 86 LT 25, although it is not clear from the report how the amount due on abatement was calculated.

entitled to the requisite percentage of this total estate, which includes the debt. The administrator then directs the debtor to appropriate the debt as *pro tanto* payment of his share, and so the net sum (if any) payable to him is the difference between the share calculated in this manner and his indebtedness to the fund.[339]

14.80 In the case of a fund represented by the assets of a company in liquidation or a bankrupt's estate,[340] a creditor's right to participate is confined to the dividend payable on the debt owing to him.[341] *Cherry v Boultbee* is applied in the following manner. The dividend rate payable by the fund should be calculated by dividing the total assets of the fund, including the creditor's liability to the company or the bankrupt, by the total provable liabilities of the fund, which include the debt owing to the creditor.[342] The dividend payable to the creditor is the product of this dividend rate and his claim against the company or the bankrupt. The creditor's own liability to the company or the bankrupt is then appropriated as *pro tanto* payment of this sum, and the net amount (if any) payable to the creditor is the remainder of the dividend after subtracting the value of the creditor's liability.[343]

14.81 It may be that a bankrupt is liable to contribute to a fund, and his trustee is seeking to enforce a right vested in the bankrupt to participate in the fund. The administrator of the fund may bring into account the full value of the bankrupt's liability, despite the fact of the bankruptcy, since the bankrupt's trustee is not considered to be in any better position than the bankrupt himself.[344] Thus *Cherry v Boultree* in this situation operates substantively, in the sense that it allows the administrator to treat the debt owing to the fund as payment of a right to participate to the extent of the full value of the debt, even though the fund otherwise would only have received a dividend. In effect the same result is achieved as for a set-off in the bankruptcy. If the administrator of the fund mistakenly pays the bankrupt's trustee without invoking *Cherry v Boultbee*, the rule in *Ex parte James*[345] may provide relief.[346]

---

[339] *Willes v Greenhill (No 1)* (1860) 29 Beav 376, 383, 54 ER 673, 675–676; *Re Melton* [1918] 1 Ch 37, 46, 54, 59.

[340] See para 14.07 above.

[341] See eg *Ex parte Graham* (1814) 3 V & B 130, 35 ER 428; *Re Mayne, ex p The Official Receiver* [1907] 2 KB 899. *Cherry v Boultbee* would only be important in the context of a bankruptcy or a company liquidation if for some reason a set-off is not available to the creditor.

[342] Obviously there can never be a dividend rate greater than one.

[343] In some cases the estate in fact may be able to pay a full dividend when the creditor's obligation to contribute is taken into account in this manner. If in such a case the creditor's liability exceeds the dividend notionally payable to him, the difference will represent a subsisting liability still owing by the creditor.

[344] *Corr v Corr* (1879) 3 LR Ir 435; *Re Weston. Davies v Tagart* [1900] 2 Ch 164. See also *Ex parte Metcalfe* (1805) 11 Ves Jun 404, 408, 32 ER 1143, 1144–1145; *Re Brown. Dixon v Brown* (1886) 32 Ch D 597; *Re Kowloon Container Warehouse Co Ltd* [1981] HKLR 210.

[345] (1874) LR 9 Ch App 609. See para 6.111 above.

[346] See *Re Brown* (1886) 32 Ch D 597, and note also *Ex parte Bignold, re Charles* (1817) 2 Madd 470, 56 ER 408.

While these principles generally are straightforward, the problem becomes more **14.82** complex when there are two prima facie insolvent estates, each of which has a claim against the other, and the situation is such that the cross-demands may not be employed in a set-off. For example, it may be that a company in liquidation is liable in the liquidation of another company to pay a call on shares,[347] or is liable for misfeasance,[348] and the first company is also a creditor of the second on a separate transaction. The liquidator of the second company may assert that the first company should not be allowed to participate in the liquidation by receiving a dividend on the debt owing to it until the first company has made its required contribution in the form of a call,[349] or has satisfied its misfeasance liability, and the liquidator of the first company may adopt a similar stance. The problem is that neither company in fact may have sufficient assets to satisfy its liability *in toto*. That was the case in *Re Leeds and Hanley Theatres Of Varieties Ltd.*[350] Two companies, the Finance Company (F) and the Theatres Company (T), were in liquidation. F was a creditor of T for £5,100 on debentures issued by T, while T had a claim against F for £4,323 as a result of a judgment obtained against F for damages for misfeasance. Because of the nature of the latter claim, the two demands could not be set off.[351] Moreover, neither company had sufficient assets in hand with which to pay its own liability in full. F had no assets other than the dividend payable by T on the debentures, but had other creditors to the extent of £5,490. T had other assets totalling in value £8,277, and other liabilities of £4,685. Buckley J adopted the following procedure for settling the rights of the parties:[352]

> The proper administration in my judgment, therefore, is this. Notionally treat the Finance Company as having paid the £4,323 to the Theatres Company; take the aggregate notional sum thus arrived at and treat it as applied in payment of a dividend upon all the debts of the Theatres Company—that is to say, upon the £5,100 due to the Finance Company and the £4,685 due to other people. That will attribute to the Finance Company a certain sum. If that sum be greater than the £4,323 that they owe, they will get the difference. If it be less, or equal, they will receive nothing. If the dividend thus arrived at on the £4,685 cannot be satisfied in full (because the notional sum, of course, is not really paid), then the £4,685 would take the whole of the assets of the Theatres Company, although it be less than the notional dividend calculated upon the footing that the Finance Company have paid that which they have not paid.

---

[347] See paras 8.50–8.62 above.

[348] See paras 8.64–8.71 above.

[349] See *Re Auriferous Properties Ltd (No 2)* [1898] 2 Ch 428; *Re National Live Stock Insurance Co Ltd* [1917] 1 Ch 628; *Re White Star Line Ltd* [1938] 1 Ch 458.

[350] [1904] 2 Ch 45.

[351] *Ex parte Pelly* (1882) 21 Ch D 492. See paras 8.64–8.71 above.

[352] [1904] 2 Ch 45, 51–52.

In essence this is an application in favour of T of the method suggested above for calculating the net sum payable when a creditor of a bankrupt or a company in liquidation is also liable to make a contribution.[353] A notional payment of £4,323 by F to T would have produced an aggregate fund in T of £12,600. Its total liabilities were only £9,785 (being £5,100 plus £4,685), and so T could pay a full dividend of 100p in the £. Therefore F was entitled to receive £5,100 from T, but since F was indebted to T for £4,323 the net sum payable was reduced to £777.

14.83 Buckley J only notionally treated F as having paid its debt. Consequently, only T obtained the benefit of the operation of *Cherry v Boultbee*. A greater sum would have been payable by T if instead F had been treated as the recipient of the notional payment.[354] Buckley J's decision to give T the benefit of the principle in *Cherry v Boultbee* may have been prompted by the fact that the summons was taken out in the winding up of T, and so he was only called upon to consider the position as between T and its creditors.[355] It also may be justified however on another ground, that a party such as F which is liable for misfeasance not only may not employ the liability in a set-off against a cross-demand, but in addition it should be required to satisfy the liability *in toto* before a right to receive a dividend on the cross-demand accrues. The courts have applied a similar principle where a

---

[353] See para 14.80 above. Buckley J's approach has been approved in other cases. See *Re National Live Stock Insurance Co Ltd* [1917] 1 Ch 628; *Re Hattons Confectionery Co Ltd* [1936] NZLR 802; *Re Mitchell, Houghton Ltd* (1970) 14 CBR 301. Compare *West Mercia Safetywear Ltd v Dodd* [1988] BCLC 250. It has also been criticized, however. See Luckett and Dean, 'Cross Debts: Notional Calculations in Liquidations' (1983) 11 Australian Business Law Review 69. They noted that, as a result of the order, F received £777 from T for distribution amongst its other creditors, who each would have received a resulting dividend of 2s 10d in the pound, whereas T as a creditor of F in effect received payment in full for its own claim against F. Accordingly, they proposed an alternative procedure which would have the effect of treating all the creditors of each company in an equal manner. See also Dean, Luckett and Houghton, 'Notional Calculations in Liquidations Revisited' (1993) 11 Companies and Securities Law Journal 204. However, a feature of *Cherry v Boultbee* in the situation in which the debtor/creditor of the fund is insolvent is that it has the effect of enabling the fund to obtain the full value of the debt owing to it to the extent of the right to participate. See para 14.81 above. This is a consequence of the right of the administrator of the fund to direct the debtor to satisfy his right to participate from his own obligation to contribute.

[354] The dividend rate payable by F, on the assumption that T has notionally paid its debt, would have been obtained by dividing its total assets, including T's debt, by its total liabilities, which would have equalled £5,100 + 0/(£5,490 + £4,323). This produces a dividend rate of 0.5197. Thus the value of T's right of participation would have been the product of 0.5197 and £4,323, or £2,246.74. Under *Cherry v Boultbee*, F's liquidator would have been entitled to direct T to appropriate a part of its own liability to contribute (being £5,100) in part satisfaction of this right to participate, after which T would still have had a residual liability to F of £2,853.26. The dividend rate payable by T on this debt, being its total assets divided by its liabilities (the assets of T would no longer include F's liability for £4,323), would have been £8,277/(£4,685 + £2,853.26). Since this is greater than one, T could have paid a full dividend to its creditors, so that F would have received the full value of the residue of T's debt for £2,853.26. The end result is that, while the judgment of Buckley J obliged T to pay to F £777, T would have been required to pay the greater sum of £2,853.26 if the notional payment had been deemed to have been made by T rather than F.

[355] See Buckley J at [1904] 2 Ch 45, 51. *Quaere* what would have happened on this view if a summons had also been taken out in the winding up of F.

company in liquidation was liable in the liquidation of another company to pay a call on shares,[356] and where a company in liquidation was obliged to return a payment invalidated as a preference in the liquidation of the payer, so that the first-mentioned company had to repay the preference in full before it could receive a dividend on the original debt for which the payment was intended to constitute satisfaction.[357] There have also been cases in which a banker, or an assignee in bankruptcy, who received proceeds from the realization of a bankrupt's estate, and who also happened to be a creditor of the bankrupt, himself became bankrupt. The banker's, or the assignee's, estate was held not to be entitled to receive a dividend on the bankrupt's indebtedness until the proceeds had been repaid.[358] A person liable for misfeasance is unlikely to be treated more leniently than, for example, an innocent contributory liable to pay a call on shares,[359] and so it is understandable that F, the party liable for misfeasance, should have been chosen as the party to make a notional payment, rather than T.

The calculation of the notional dividend rate in the *Leeds and Hanley* case was **14.84** premised on the assumption that T had a valuable asset to the full extent of F's liability. This was a valid assumption in *Re Leeds and Hanley*, since the dividend payable by T to F was greater than F's liability to T, and therefore all of the asset represented by F's liability was employed in order to reduce the sum otherwise payable to F. It would not have been the case however if F's liability had been greater than the dividend notionally payable in T's liquidation. F would have had a residual liability remaining after the application of *Cherry v Boultbee*, and if F was insolvent it would only have been able to pay a fractional dividend on this residue. This means that F in effect would have received credit for a higher dividend rate in the *Cherry v Boultbee* calculation than that payable to T's other creditors, who would have been paid a dividend calculated on the basis of the true resulting asset value of the company. However, the effect on the dividend rate in a case such as this often would be marginal.

---

[356] *Re Auriferous Properties Ltd (No 2)* [1898] 2 Ch 428; *Re White Star Line Ltd* [1938] 1 Ch 458.

[357] *N A Kratzmann Pty Ltd v Tucker (No 2)* (1968) 123 CLR 295. In Australia, see also the Corporations Act 2001 (Cth), s 588 FI.

[358] *Ex parte Bebb* (1812) 19 Ves Jun 222, 34 ER 501; *Ex parte Graham* (1814) 3 V & B 130, 35 ER 428; *Ex parte Bignold, re Charles* (1817) 2 Madd 470, 56 ER 408. See however the order in *Ex parte Graham*, discussed in para 14.13 above.

[359] See *Ex parte Pelly* (1882) 21 Ch D 492, 503, 509–510.

15

COMBINATION OF BANK ACCOUNTS

A. Introduction

When a customer has more than one account with a bank, one of which is in **15.01** credit and another in debit, it is said that the bank in some circumstances may combine, or consolidate, the accounts and proceed on the basis that there is only one debt for the balance. The accounts need not be at the same branch.[1] Nor is it necessary that the account in credit should have resulted from a deposit by the customer himself. A combination may arise in relation to an account that originally was opened by a third party, but which became vested in the customer.[2]

Combination is particularly important if the bank is suspicious of the customer's **15.02** solvency, because it provides the bank with a means by which it can obtain the

---

[1] *Garnett v M'Kewan* (1872) LR 8 Ex 10, and see para 15.31 below.
[2] See Bacon VC in *Roxburghe v Cox* (1881) 17 Ch D 520, who (incorrectly) characterized the right in question as a lien. See below. While James and Lush LJJ on appeal in the Court of Appeal decided the case instead by reference to the principles of set-off under the Statutes of Set-off, Baggallay LJ (at 527–8) said that he did not dissent from Bacon VC's conclusion.

benefit of the account in credit, by setting it against the account in debit, before the customer has dissipated the credit balance. For example, if combination applies, a bank may refuse to honour a cheque drawn by a customer on an account in credit if the customer has a debit balance on another account, unless the overall credit balance on the two accounts taken together is sufficient to satisfy the cheque, or the balance in any event is within an agreed overdraft limit.[3] In this sense it has been said that combination may be used as a sword as well as a shield.[4]

B. The Nature of the Right of Combination

The principle

15.03 A bank has a lien on all securities deposited with it as banker unless there is an express contract, or circumstances showing an implied contract, inconsistent with a lien.[5] On occasions it has been assumed that combination of accounts is merely an aspect of the banker's lien,[6] though the courts have been critical of the use of the term 'lien' in this context.[7] The lien to which a bank is entitled is a common law possessory lien. This form of lien merely confers upon a creditor the right to retain possession of tangible property held by the creditor until such time as the debtor pays the debt. Once the creditor loses possession, the lien is lost. Thus a cheque or other negotiable security deposited with a bank for collection may be the subject of a lien while it remains in the possession of the bank. But when the cheque is cleared the bank loses possession, with the result that the lien comes to an end. Since the relationship of banker and customer is one of debt rather than trust[8] the proceeds of the cheque received by the bank become the property of the bank,

---

[3] *Garnett v M'Kewan* (1872) LR 8 Ex 10.

[4] *Barclays Bank Ltd v Okenarhe* [1966] 2 Lloyd's Rep 87, 97. See also *National Bank of New Zealand v Heslop* (1882) NZLR 1 CA 47; *Royal Trust Co v Molsons Bank* (1912) 8 DLR 478, 480.

[5] *Brandao v Barnett* (1846) 3 CB 519, 531, 136 ER 207, 212–213.

[6] See eg *Misa v Currie* (1876) 1 App Cas 554, 569, *per* Lord Hatherley ('all monies paid into a bank are subject to a lien'); *Bower v Foreign and Colonial Gas Co* (1874) 22 WR 740; *Roxburghe v Cox* (1881) 17 Ch D 520; *T and H Greenwood Teale v William Williams Brown and Co* (1894) 11 TLR 56; *Baker v Lloyd's Bank, Ltd* [1920] 2 KB 322, 327; *Greenhalgh and Sons v Union Bank of Manchester* [1924] 2 KB 153, 164; *Halesowen Presswork and Assemblies Ltd v Westminster Bank Ltd* [1971] 1 QB 1, 19 (Roskill J, at first instance). Ungoed-Thomas J in *Re Keever* [1967] 1 Ch 182 referred to a lien, but that was in the context of the bank's lien on the cheque (and its proceeds) which was security for the balance on the customer's account (see at 190), as opposed to combination of the accounts in order to ascertain the balance secured.

[7] *Re Morris, deceased. Coneys v Morris* [1922] 1 IR 136; *Halesowen Presswork and Assemblies Ltd v Westminster Bank Ltd* [1971] 1 QB 1, 33–34, *per* Lord Denning MR, 46, *per* Buckley LJ, which view was endorsed on appeal by Viscount Dilhorne ([1972] AC 785, 802) and by Lord Cross of Chelsea (at 810). See also *Royal Trust Co v Molsons Bank* (1912) 8 DLR 478, 480–481; *Broad v Commissioner of Stamp Duties* [1980] 2 NSWLR 40; *MPS Constructions Pty Ltd v Rural Bank of New South Wales* (1980) 4 ACLR 835, 840–841; *Duke Finance Ltd v Commonwealth Bank of Australia* (1990) 22 NSWLR 236, 251.

[8] *Foley v Hill* (1848) 2 HLC 28.

rather than of the customer, and it can hardly be correct to say that the bank has a lien on its own property. The bank, when it receives the proceeds and credits the customer's account in credit, becomes a debtor to the customer. A debt is not tangible property, and so the use of the word 'lien' to describe the bank's rights in relation to the account is inappropriate.[9] Lord Denning in the Court of Appeal in *Halesowen Presswork and Assemblies Ltd v Westminster Bank Ltd*[10] said that, 'we should discard the use of the word "lien" in this context and speak simply of a banker's "right to combine accounts": or a right to "set off" one account against the other'.[11] The term "ser-off" however similarly does not convey the true nature of combination of accounts. It suggests that there are independent debts in existence which the bank may set off by the exercise of a right so as to produce a single debt for the balance, but this is not the traditional basis of combination. Rather, the explanation found in the cases is that, unless a particular account is separated out by agreement (express or implied) or it is separate as a matter of law, the debt owing by either party to the other at any particular time can only be ascertained by looking at the balance of all the accounts together. In other words, it is not so much a right to set off independent debts as a recognition that the debt owing is the balance of all the accounts. Expressed more concisely, combination is an accounting situation rather than a set-off situation.[12] On that basis, a specific act of combination should not be required.[13] The accounting does not bring about the single debt, but rather it is undertaken in order to ascertain what the debt is. When combination is referred to as a set-off, that expression is not inapt if it is meant to convey a set-off of debits against credits[14] in order to calculate the debt, but it is inaccurate if it is intended to mean a set-off of independent obligations. The principle has its justification in the notion that, no matter how many accounts belonging to a customer a bank may have entered in its books, there is still only one banker/customer relationship.[15] As Kelly CB expressed it, in a case where a customer had a credit balance at one branch which was almost exactly equalled by a debit balance at another

---

[9] *Halesowen Presswork and Assemblies Ltd v Westminster Bank* Ltd [1971] 1 QB 1, 46, *per* Buckley LJ. See also on appeal in the House of Lords [1972] AC 785, 802, *per* Viscount Dilhorne, 810, *per* Lord Cross of Chelsea.

[10] [1971] 1 QB 1.

[11] [1971] 1 QB 1, 34.

[12] *Halesowen Presswork and Assemblies Ltd v Westminster Bank Ltd* [1971] 1 QB 1, 46, *per* Buckley LJ; *Re Charge Card Services Ltd* [1987] 1 Ch 150, 173–174, *per* Millett J.

[13] Even on the view that combination operates as a set-off of independent accounts (see below) a physical combination of the accounts in the bank's books may not be necessary, if the right is otherwise properly asserted. See Roskill J at first instance in *Halesowen Presswork and Assemblies Ltd v Westminster Bank Ltd* [1971] 1 QB 1, 19, and also *Direct Acceptance Corporation Ltd v Bank of New South Wales* (1968) 88 WN (Pt. 1) (NSW) 498, 502.

[14] See *Matthews v Geraghty* (1986) 43 SASR 576, 580.

[15] See *Halesowen Presswork and Assemblies Ltd v Westminster Bank Ltd* [1971] 1 QB 1, 46, *per* Buckley LJ, and *Welsh Development Agency v Export Finance Co Ltd* [1992] BCLC 148, 167, *per* Dillon LJ.

branch,[16] 'The defendant's bank, therefore, had scarcely a shilling of his money, and I cannot see why they were bound to honour his cheque at Leighton Buzzard just because there was a balance at that branch in his favour.'

15.04 While this analysis has its supporters,[17] it also has its critics.[18] In Wood's opinion the right in question, which he calls current account set-off, is indeed a set-off, in the sense that it requires an act by the bank to set what are otherwise distinct reciprocal claims against one another.[19] Wood regards the various judicial statements which suggest that there is only one amount owing as being no more than an expression of the fact that, in the absence of an agreement to the contrary, the bank at any time may set off accounts without notice to the customer and accordingly treat divided accounts as a single blended account.[20] However, this does not appear to be what the judges had in mind. But the rejection of that view does not mean that nothing follows from the fact that separate accounts are recorded in the bank's books. It is unlikely that the courts in saying that a number of accounts form one entire account intended to refer to the operation of the accounts themselves. Rather, they appear to have had in mind the question whether, and to what extent, a debt is owing at any particular time by the bank or the customer to the other. Accordingly, for certain purposes the accounts should indeed be treated as separate, for example for the calculation and payment of interest, and for questions relating to the order and appropriation of payments in accordance with *Clayton's Case*.[21] In truth, as Byrne J remarked at first instance in *Mutton v Peat*,[22] in response to an argument that as between banker and customer all accounts form but one account, this 'is true for certain purposes'. On the other hand, unless there is an express or implied agreement to the contrary which would preclude a combination in any event, the courts have recognized that a bank is entitled to give effect to the principle of combination in its books by moving debits or credits from one account to another.[23] When that occurs the accounts cease to be

---

[16]   *Garnett v M'Kewan* (1872) LR 8 Ex 10, 12.

[17]   Shea, 'Statutory Set-off' (1986) 3 Journal of International Banking Law 152, 154; Penn, Shea and Arora, *The Law Relating to Domestic Banking* (1987) 143–4; McCracken, *The Banker's Remedy of Set-off* (2nd edn, 1998) ch 1; Cranston, *Principles of Banking Law* (1997) 176.

[18]   See Wood, *English and International Set-off* (1989) 92–4; Salter, 'Remedies For Banks: An Outline of English Law' in Blair (ed), *Banks and Remedies* (2nd edn, 1999) 49–52; Cresswell *et al,* *Encyclopedia of Banking Law* (looseleaf) C640.1; Goode, *Principles of Corporate Insolvency Law* (2nd edn, 1997) 176. Ellinger, Lomnicka and Hooley, *Modern Banking Law* (3rd edn, 2002), 201, 203–4 also suggests this view. Compare also *Paget's Law of Banking* (11th edn, 1996) 530–1, 535–6, which is equivocal.

[19]   Wood, *English and International Set-off* (1989) 92, 94.

[20]   Wood, *English and International Set-off* (1989) 92.

[21]   (1816) 1 Mer 572, 35 ER 781.

[22]   [1899] 2 Ch 556, 560.

[23]   In the *Halesowen* case, see Roskill J at first instance [1971] 1 QB 1, 20–21, Lord Denning MR in the Court of Appeal at 35 and Lord Kilbrandon in the House of Lords [1972] AC 785, 819, each criticizing a dictum by Swift J to the contrary in *Greenhalgh and Sons v Union Bank of Manchester* [1924] 2 KB 153, 164. See also *Garnett v M'Kewan* (1872) LR 8 Ex 10 (esp Kelly CB at 13); *Re*

separate for those purposes as well. But as Canadian courts have emphasized, the book-keeping entry itself does not constitute a payment of the account in debit, since there was in any event only one debt.[24]

The cases

The first case suggesting that combination in truth is an accounting situation is *Ex* **15.05** *parte Pearce, re Langmead.*[25] Commissioners appointed under an Act of Parliament had two accounts with a bank, designated respectively the river account and the harbour account. The river account was overdrawn, but the harbour account had a credit balance exceeding the debit balance on the river account. The bank became bankrupt, whereupon the assignees in bankruptcy commenced proceedings at law against the customer for payment of the debit balance on the river account. Sir John Cross granted an injunction restraining the action, commenting that: 'There was only one account of banker and customer between the bank and the commissioners.'[26] The assignees therefore had no just cause to bring the action. It is true that he referred later in his judgment to set-off, and to the 'debts' on each of the accounts, although these expressions may not have been used in their technical sense. Nor could his reference to a single account be explained as a recognition of the concept that the bank at any time could have combined without notice, because the bank, or, at least, its assignees in bankruptcy, was the party attempting to treat the accounts as separate.

Bailey v Finch[27] also concerned the bankruptcy of a bank. The defendant as ex- **15.06** ecutor under a will had an executorship account with the bank. In addition he had three accounts in his personal capacity with the bank, two of which were overdrawn and the third of which was in credit. On the three accounts there was an overall balance against him. The question was whether the defendant could set off the executorship account against the overall debit balance on the three accounts, and the case was discussed earlier in that context.[28] For present purposes the interesting point is the characterization by Blackburn J of the position in relation to the three accounts. He said that:[29]

Sutcliffe & Sons Ltd, ex p Royal Bank [1933] 1 DLR 562 (esp at 569); *Re T C Marines Ltd* (1973) 34 DLR (3d) 489; *Re Plasky* (1981) 39 CBR 186, 194; *Deep v Bank of Montreal* (1991) 47 OAC 319. In *Clark v Ulster Bank Ltd* [1950] NILR 132, 143 Black LJ referred to this as crystallizing the position.

[24] *Re Sutcliffe & Sons Ltd, ex p Royal Bank* [1933] 1 DLR 562 (esp at 569); *Ross v Royal Bank of Canada* (1965) 52 DLR (2d) 578; *Re Plasky* (1981) 39 CBR 186; *Re T C Marines Ltd* (1973) 34 DLR (3d) 489. For the same reason, the book-keeping entry does not constitute a seizure of assets. See *Deep v Bank of Montreal* (1991) 47 OAC 319.

[25] (1841) 2 Mont D & De G 142.

[26] (1841) 2 Mont D & De G 142, 145.

[27] (1871) LR 7 QB 34.

[28] See para 13.120 above.

[29] (1871) LR 7 QB 34, 40.

> [W]hat we have to look to is, what were the facts at the time of the bankruptcy; and the rights of the parties must be regulated by what those facts were. It appears that at that time Mr Finch, the defendant, had an account with the bank, or rather several accounts, which for convenience he had called by different names; it matters not what they were, he had for convenience three accounts. There is no doubt whatever, as between him and the bank, those three accounts all formed in reality one account; and that a debt was owing by him to the bank upon those three accounts, being the balance of the whole three taken together. That would have been independent of any question of set-off and mutual credit.

Blackburn J was speaking of the position at the time of the bankruptcy. At that time he considered that there was one debt for the balance of the three accounts, and this was independent of any question of set-off under the bankruptcy legislation. Moreover, there is nothing in the report to suggest that there had been an act of combination at that time. On the contrary, the comments of Blackburn J suggest otherwise. Nor, one imagines, would the trustee in bankruptcy have regarded it as being in the interests of the estate to effect a combination, if indeed an act of combination was thought to be necessary in order to produce a single debt, since the bank rather than the customer was insolvent.

15.07 Subsequently James LJ considered *Bailey v Finch* in *Ex parte Morier, re Willis, Percival & Co*,[30] his Lordship commenting in relation to that case:[31]

> There all the judges start with this . . . , that really *in point of law* there was but one account, and there was no debt except upon taking the two accounts together. The mere fact of the two accounts being put upon different pages of the ledger could have no more effect than if an account had gone over from one page of the bank's ledger to another, or than if a man, as a mere matter of account, had kept different accounts, such as a farm account, a colliery account, or a house account, merely for his own convenience for ascertaining how moneys came in and how they had been applied.

James LJ described the notion, that there was no debt except upon taking the two accounts together, as the position 'in point of law'. It was not intended to be a description of the position that applied as a matter of substance, based on a notion that the bank could have set off the accounts at any time without notice to produce a single account. Nor was James LJ's opinion on the point recently formed. Some seven years earlier, in *Re European Bank. Agra Bank Claim*,[32] he said, in a judgment with which Mellish LJ agreed, that: 'It was only for convenience that the loan account was kept separately . . . . In truth, as between banker and customer, whatever number of accounts are kept in the books, the whole is really but one account . . .'.

---

[30] (1879) 12 Ch D 491.
[31] (1879) 12 Ch D 491, 498–499 (emphasis added).
[32] (1872) LR 8 Ch App 41, 44, referred to with approval in *Re Keever* [1967] 1 Ch 182, 190.

In *Ex parte Douglas*[33] Luxmoore J adopted James LJ's statement in *Ex parte* **15.08**
Morier, although not in the context of banker and customer. A partnership had
lent some money to a second partnership, the amount of the loan being carried to
a loan account. James Douglas was a member of both firms, and when he died a
general trading account between them showed a credit balance in favour of the
second partnership. Luxmoore J referred to James LJ's judgment as support for the
proposition that:[34] 'In law there was in fact at James Douglas's death but one account between the two firms, and taking the two accounts together, there was no
debt.' Once again, that was regarded as the position *in law*. At the date of the
death, when there had not been any purported act of combination, there was nevertheless only one debt for the balance.

Consider *Mutton v Peat*.[35] Stockbrokers had two accounts with a bank, a current **15.09**
account with a credit balance of £1,362 10s and a loan account upon which they
owed £7,500. In addition, the brokers had deposited some bonds by way of security for their indebtedness to the bank. When the brokers ceased trading the bank
made a point of carrying the credit balance on the current account to a separate
liquidation account, rather than applying it in reduction of the loan account, and
it was argued that the security applied only to the loan account without taking
into account the credit account.[36] In this case the bank had gone out of its way to
avoid setting off the accounts, but Lindley MR in the leading judgment did not
regard the bank's action as significant. He said[37] that the amount of the indebtedness secured by the bonds was:

> the amount, taking the deposit account[38] and current account together (you cannot
> separate them), which is due to the bankers on the two accounts. With that amount
> his bonds must stand charged. I do not care how the bankers may have manipulated
> their books or how many accounts they may have kept. When you come to ascertain
> what is the amount due from [the brokers] to the bankers the question admits of
> only one solution—it is the balance due on the loan account after deducting the
> 1362*l*10s.

---

[33] [1930] 1 Ch 342.
[34] [1930] 1 Ch 342, 349.
[35] [1900] 2 Ch 79.
[36] The bank had sold the bonds. However, unknown to the bank, the bonds were not the property of the stockbrokers but belonged to clients. Similarly, once again unknown to the bank, some of
the money paid into the current account was clients' money. The plaintiff was a client whose bonds
had been deposited as security. He sought a declaration that the balance remaining in the hands of
the bank represented the net proceeds of sale of the bonds, and that he was entitled to have paid to
him so much of those moneys as represented the purchase moneys received for his bonds. The money
remaining would only have included money belonging to him if the bonds were provided as security
for the general indebtedness of the brokers to the bank, and not merely the indebtedness on the loan
account. The defendants on the other hand included a client whose money had been paid into the
current account. He argued, unsuccessfully, that the security related only to the loan account, so that
the current account, into which his money could be traced, remained untouched.
[37] [1900] 2 Ch 79, 85.
[38] This should refer to the loan account.

The amount due represented the debt on the basis of combination of accounts.[39] In *Halesowen Presswork and Assemblies Ltd v Westminster Bank Ltd*[40] Lord Denning sought to explain *Mutton v Peat* on the ground that a customer has the right to call upon the bank to combine accounts, while on another occasion Mocatta J referred to it as a case in which the bank was obliged to combine.[41] In truth the case was not decided on those grounds. Rather, Sir Nathaniel Lindsay proceeded on the basis that an act of combination was not necessary, since there was in any event only one debt for the balance. Consistent with that view, Rigby LJ considered that the correct analysis was that the bank was bound to allow the credit balance in account in determining the indebtedness, rather than that they ought to have appropriated it in reduction of the loan.[42]

15.10 The next case is *Garnett v M'Kewan*.[43] A customer had an account in credit at one branch of a bank and another account in debit at another branch. The bank transferred the debit balance in reduction of the credit balance, and refused to honour cheques drawn on that account. The Court of Exchequer held that the bank was entitled to do so. There was in this case an act of combination, but the later explanation of the decision by the Privy Council in *Prince v Oriental Bank Corp*[44] suggests that it did not turn on that point. Sir Montague Smith, in delivering the judgment of the Privy Council,[45] said of *Garnett v M'Kewan* that:[46]

> [T]he Court held that money of the Plaintiff lodged at one branch, and being still there to the credit of his account, was to be treated as part of the customer's entire account with the bank, and that the whole account was to be looked at to see on which side as between him and the bank the balance stood.

Consistent with that observation, Bramwell B in *Garnett v M'Kewan*[47] said that 'the customer has no claim, for he is indebted to the bank on his whole account in such an amount as to reduce his assets to almost nothing'. Martin B referred to the account in credit as an 'apparent balance'. He said that[48] 'the mere existence of an

---

[39] See the discussion of *Mutton v Peat* in *Halesowen Presswork and Assemblies Ltd v Westminster Bank Ltd* [1971] 1 QB 1, 22, *per* Roskill J, at first instance, 34, *per* Lord Denning MR, 42, *per* Winn LJ, 46, *per* Buckley LJ.

[40] [1971] 1 QB 1, 34.

[41] *Barclays Bank Ltd v Okenarhe* [1966] 2 Lloyd's Rep 87, 95–96. See also Ellinger, Lomnicka and Hooley, *Modern Banking Law* (3rd edn, 2002) 219.

[42] Rigby LJ commented: 'I think we are bound to say that the bankers ought to have appropriated the 1362*l* 10*s* in reduction of the 7500*l* loan, or perhaps it would be more correct to say that they were bound to allow the 1362*l* 10*s* in account whether they appropriated it or not, and even if they endeavoured not to appropriate it. The security was given for the indebtedness of [the stockbrokers] to the bankers and for nothing else, and that indebtedness was the 7500*l* minus the 1362*l* 10*s*, and that only.' See [1900] 2 Ch 79, 86.

[43] (1872) LR 8 Ex 10.

[44] (1878) 3 App Cas 325.

[45] Sir James Colville, Sir Barnes Peacock, Sir Montague Smith and Sir Robert Collier.

[46] (1878) 3 App Cas 325, 333.

[47] (1872) LR 8 Ex 10, 15.

[48] (1872) LR 8 Ex 10, 13–14.

apparent balance, if there is no real balance, is not enough to render the bank liable to pay a cheque at the branch where the apparent balance is'. Similarly Pigott B referred to the bank 'taking into account the state of the plaintiff's balance as a whole . . .'.[49] According to Kelly CB,[50] 'The question substantially raised by the pleadings is whether any money of the plaintiff's was in the hands of the London and County Bank', which captures the essence of the principle underlying combination.

More recently, the view that combination is a matter of account rather than a set-   **15.11** off of debts was emphasized by Buckley LJ in the Court of Appeal in the *Halesowen* case:[51]

> Where the relationship of the banker and customer is a single relationship . . . albeit embodied in a number of accounts, the situation is not, in my judgment, a situation of lien at all. A lien postulates property of the debtor in the possession or under the control of the creditor. Nor is it a set-off situation, which postulates mutual but independent obligations between the two parties. It is an accounting situation, in which the existence and amount of one party's liability to the other can only be ascertained by discovering the ultimate balance of their mutual dealings.

Millett J referred to that passage with evident approval in *Re Charge Card Services Ltd*,[52] as did Otton J in *Re K (Restraint Order)*.[53] In the latter case, Otton J said[54] that combination 'is a means of establishing the indebtedness of the customer to the bank and the bank to the customer'. He went on to observe that the bank, in exercising the right, 'is merely carrying out an accounting procedure so as to ascertain the existence and amount of one party's liability to the other. This can only be ascertained by discovering the ultimate balance of their mutual dealing'.[55]

A similar position has been adopted in other jurisdictions. In Scotland, Lord   **15.12** Dunedin in *James Kirkwood & Sons v Clydesdale Bank*,[56] in a judgment with which Lord Kinnear, Lord M'Laren and Lord Pearson concurred, observed that, 'the state of affairs between a banker and his customer as at any given time must be taken to be the state of affairs upon all the accounts',[57] and that 'upon a true accounting between the parties concerned there were no funds in the hands of the

---

[49] (1872) LR 8 Ex 10, 14.
[50] (1872) LR 8 Ex 10, 12.
[51] [1971] 1 QB 1, 46. See also his earlier comments in *Re E J Morel (1934) Ltd* [1962] 1 Ch 21, 32.
[52] [1987] 1 Ch 150, 173–174.
[53] [1990] 2 QB 298, 303. While Otton J referred (at 305) to the account in credit itself as a chose in action, that was in the context of a discussion of the bank's rights arising under a letter of set-off as opposed to common law combination.
[54] [1990] 2 QB 298, 304.
[55] The bank in this case had a letter of set-off empowering it to set off the accounts, but the comments related to the position apart from the letter. See [1990] 2 QB 298, 304–305.
[56] [1908] SC 20.
[57] [1908] SC 20, 24.

Clydesdale Bank belonging to this gentleman'.[58] In Ireland Sir Andrew Porter MR posed the question: 'Now what is the meaning of a No 2 account? It no doubt often means that the account refers to another subject-matter or department of business for mere convenience, but is not otherwise legally separate from the No 1 account of the customer . . . .'[59] In Northern Ireland, Black CJ adopted a similar view in *Clark v Ulster Bank Ltd*,[60] commenting:[61] 'The balance at credit of No 2 account was merely one of the elements to be taken into account in conjunction with the balance at debit of No 1 Account in computing the indebtedness between Mr Clark and the bank.'

15.13   This is also the position in Canada. Indeed, Middleton JA in the Ontario Court of Appeal in *Re Sutcliffe & Sons Ltd, ex p Royal Bank*[62] could not have expressed the principle in clearer terms when he said, in the context of a loan account with a debit balance in excess of the credit balance on a current account, that[63] 'the fact that there were two accounts kept by the bank is utterly immaterial. There was in law but one account to be ascertained by bringing all items into consideration. The bank is not and never was, in this case, a debtor in any sense. It was and is a creditor.' Canadian courts have adopted this approach on other occasions.[64]

15.14   It has also been recognized in Australia,[65] with McPherson JA in the Queensland Court of Appeal in *Re Bank of Queensland Ltd*[66] referring to the principle described by Buckley LJ in the *Halesowen* case (above) as the 'single indebtedness' principle. Observations in the New South Wales Court of Appeal in *Cinema Plus Ltd v Australia and New Zealand Banking Group Ltd*[67] also support that view. Sheller JA in that case said that: 'Strictly the consolidation or combination may be regarded as a matter of account rather than set off. The balance of all such

---

[58] [1908] SC 20, 25.

[59] *Re Johnson & Co Ltd* [1902] 1 IR 439, 442. Sir Andrew Porter continued: 'and in such cases the balance on the one account can be set off against the other'. Having made the point that the accounts are not legally separate, it is suggested that he meant by that comment an accounting exercise in order to ascertain the balance, as opposed to a set-off of independent debts.

[60] [1950] NILR 132, 142–143.

[61] [1950] NILR 132, 143

[62] [1933] 1 DLR 562.

[63] [1933] 1 DLR 562, 569.

[64] *Ross v Royal Bank of Canada* (1965) 52 DLR (2d) 578; *Re T C Marines Ltd* (1973) 34 DLR (3d) 489. See also *Deep v Bank of Montreal* (1991) 47 OAC 319. Compare *Royal Trust Co v Molsons Bank* (1912) 8 DLR 478, in which it was assumed that an act of combination was required.

[65] In addition to the following, see Hood J in *Mercantile Bank of Australia Ltd v Weigall* (1895) 16 ALT 192, 193 ('As a matter of fact the two accounts were really one, though kept separate in the bank books'); *Re Tonkin* (1938) 6 ABC 197, 210; *Re Deague* (1951) 15 ABC 197, 202; *Matthews v Geraghty* (1986) 43 SASR 576, 580, *per* King CJ ('The allocation of moneys which the customer has advanced to the bank between various accounts is, in the absence of special contract, a mere matter of mutual convenience'). In New Zealand, see *Horton v Bank of New Zealand* (1889) 7 NZLR 582, 591 (although in that case the several accounts admittedly were opened at the instance of the bank for convenience of bookkeeping).

[66] [1997] 2 Qd R 129, 137–138.

[67] (2000) 49 NSWLR 513.

accounts represents the debt . . .'.[68] Similarly Giles JA commented in relation to combination that, 'It is necessary that there be "really but one account" . . .'.[69]

Cases supporting the contrary view

There are nevertheless statements to be found in the cases that support the contrary **15.15** view.[70] In New Zealand Conolly J suggested that, until the accounts were amalgamated, they had to be considered as separate,[71] and Hawkins J in *York City and County Banking Co v Bainbridge*[72] seemed to be of the same opinion. Reference also may be made to *Barclays Bank Ltd v Okenarhe*,[73] in which Mocatta J in an unreserved judgment aassumed that an act of combination was required.[74] Further, the courts and text-writers have been accustomed to refer to combination as a right of set-off,[75]

---

[68] (2000) 49 NSWLR 513, 543 para 116, referring to *Re Charge Card Services Ltd* [1987] 1 Ch 150, 173–174 (where Millett J quoted with evident approval Buckley LJ in *Halesowen Presswork and Assemblies Ltd v Westminster Bank Ltd* [1971] 1 QB 1, 46 (see para 15.11 above)). Earlier in his judgment (at [113]) Sheller JA commented that a banker 'has a prima facie right in law to combine the accounts of a customer and set off debits against credits', which is consistent with an accounting exercise in order to ascertain the balance of the account as between banker and customer, as opposed to a set-off of independent debts.

[69] (2000) 49 NSWLR 513, 549 para 142, referring to *Re European Bank* (1872) LR 8 Ch App 41, 44 (see above).

[70] In addition to the cases referred to below, see *Barclays Bank Ltd v TOSG Trust Fund Ltd* [1984] BCLC 1, 23, in which Nourse J referred to 'the process of debits and credits which were necessary to combine the accounts', although one of the four accounts in that case related to a separate company, and so it could only have been combined with the other three as a result of the letter of set-off which contemplated an act of combination. Similarly in *Royal Bank of Scotland plc v Wallace International Ltd* [2000] EWCA Civ 16 the set-off involved accounts of a number of companies, and it appears (see paras 8 and 48) that a contractual right was in issue. In New South Wales, Hodgson J in *Hamilton v Commonwealth Bank of Australia* (1992) 9 ACSR 90, 106–107 assumed that an act of combination was required, although that view also seems to have been a consequence of an agreement between the parties. In particular, the loan was not repayable until 15 January 1989, and Hodgson J (at 107) referred to the 'understanding' between the customer (Skinnys) and the bank which would have enabled the bank to dishonour cheques prior to that date.

[71] *National Bank of New Zealand v Grace* (1890) 8 NZLR 706. Compare the comments of Richmond J in *Horton v Bank of New Zealand* (1889) 7 NZLR 582, 591, which accord with orthodoxy. The decision in the *Grace* case in any event may be explained on another ground. The question was whether interest had to be calculated on the net position, but the single debt theory does not require that result before the bank has given effect to the combination in its books by an appropriate entry. See para 15.18 below.

[72] (1880) 43 LT 732, 734.

[73] [1966] 2 Lloyd's Rep 87.

[74] See Mocatta J's discussion of events at [1966] 2 Lloyd's Rep 87, 90.

[75] See eg *Ex parte Kingston, re Gross* (1871) LR 6 Ch App 632; *Garnett v M'Kewan* (1872) LR 8 Ex 10, 12, 13, *per* Kelly CB, 14, *per* Pigott B; *Bank of New South Wales v Goulburn Valley Butter Co Pty Ltd* [1902] AC 543, 550, PC; *Re Morris, deceased, Coneys v Morris* [1922] 1 IR 136; *Re Shaw; ex p Andrew v Australia and New Zealand Banking Group Ltd* (1977) 31 FLR 118, 122; *Oceanica Castelana Armadora SA v Mineralimportexport* [1983] 1 WLR 1294; Pennington, Hudson and Mann, *Commercial Banking Law* (1978) 29; Goode, *Legal Problems of Credit and Security* (2nd edn, 1988) 147; Holden, *The Law and Practice of Banking* (5th edn, 1991) vol 1, 71; Wood, *English and International Set-off* (1989) 93; Ellinger, Lomnicka and Hooley, *Modern Banking Law* (3rd edn, 2002) 203–4; *Paget's Law of Banking* (11th edn, 1996) 529 *et seq*.

or a right in a bank to consolidate or combine accounts.[76] This includes Roskill J at first instance[77] and Lord Denning MR and Winn LJ in the Court of Appeal in the *Halesowen* case,[78] while in the House of Lords in that case Viscount Dilhorne, Lord Cross of Chelsea and Lord Kilbrandon each used language suggestive of a right or a power in the bank to consolidate or combine.[79] Expressions such as these may suggest that, in the absence of an exercise of the right or power, the accounts represent separate debts. It is true that Winn LJ in the *Halesowen* case doubted that a number of accounts could be said to give rise to a single account.[80] But apart from that, when it was said in the *Halesowen* case that a bank has a right to combine or consolidate accounts, there was no criticism of the explanation put forward by Buckley LJ in the Court of Appeal, and in the cases which pre-dated *Halesowen Presswork and Assemblies v Westminster Bank*, that the principle is based on the view that the debt at any particular time is the balance of all the accounts. In truth, the nature of the principle of combination was not considered by the House of Lords. In so far as the cases may refer to a right or a power to set off or consolidate or combine, a number of points may be made. In the first place, they may in some instances have contemplated an accounting exercise, in other words a process of setting off debits against credits[81] as an accounting procedure for the purpose of calculating the amount owing, as opposed to a set-off of independent debts, together with the right to take action consequent upon the state of that account, for example the dishonouring of a cheque. Secondly, the bank may give effect to the principle of combination in its books,[82] and while that in itself does not involve a payment of one account by the use of another, because there was in any event one debt, it does have significance for some purposes, in particular for the calculation of interest and the application of *Clayton's Case*. In that sense, the entry made in the bank's books may be said to constitute the exercise of a 'right'. Thirdly, *Halesowen* was a case in which there was an agreement that the accounts should be kept separate, although the bank could put an end to the agreement in the event of a material change of circumstances. If there were materially changed circumstances, the question of termination of the agree-

---

[76] See eg *Re E J Morel (1934) Ltd* [1962] 1 Ch 21, 30; *Barclays Bank Ltd v Okenarhe* [1966] 2 Lloyd's Rep 87, 95; *Direct Acceptance Corp Ltd v Bank of New South Wales* (1968) 88 WN (Pt 1) (NSW) 498, 504; *Matthews v Geraghty* (1986) 43 SASR 576, 580; *Welsh Development Agency v Export Finance Co Ltd* [1992] BCLC 148, 167. In *Inglis v Commonwealth Trading Bank of Australia* (1973) 47 ALJR 234, 234–235 Mason J referred to a right to consolidate accounts, but that was following termination of an agreement to keep the accounts separate. See paras 15.27–15.29 below.

[77] [1971] 1 QB 1, 19. Roskill J regarded combination as a manifestation of or a right analogous to the banker's right of lien. See however para 15.03 above.

[78] [1971] 1 QB 1, 34, 35, *per* Lord Denning, 38, *per* Winn LJ.

[79] [1972] AC 785, 807, *per* Viscount Dilhorne, 810, *per* Lord Cross of Chelsea, 819–820, *per* Lord Kilbrandon.

[80] [1971] 1 QB 1, 40.

[81] See the language used in *Matthews v Geraghty* (1986) 43 SASR 576, 580 and *Cinema Plus Ltd v Australia and New Zealand Banking Group Ltd* (2000) 49 NSWLR 513, 543 para 113, *per* Sheller JA.

[82] See para 15.04 above.

ment, and of a consequential combination or consolidation of the accounts, would have involved the exercise of a right or power by the bank.[83] While some of the comments in the House of Lords in the *Halesowen* case in relation to combination were expressed generally,[84] they nevertheless should be considered with these points in mind.[85]

C. Criticisms

This analysis of combination has been said to be inconsistent with many of the features of bank accounts,[86] although in truth any difficulty is more apparent than real. In particular, some of the criticisms assume that statements by judges to the effect that all the accounts constitute a single account were intended to refer to the operation of the accounts, and not just to the ascertainment of the debt at any particular time. The important point is that the accounts are not treated as one for all purposes. While the existence and the amount of the debt owing by the bank or the customer to the other can only be ascertained by looking at the balance of all the accounts together, for some purposes the accounts retain their separate identities until the bank effects a physical combination in its books.[87]   **15.16**

As a preliminary point, one effect of the view that there is at any particular time a single debt would be that an account could not be sued for separately if there is a second account which reduces or cancels the balance on the first,[88] unless it has been separated out by agreement. This is unlikely to have any practical significance, however. Neither the bank nor the customer is likely to suffer an action against it in such a case. Whether the defence is based upon the notion that there is only one debt or upon a set-off, the result would be the same. A similar comment may be made in respect of the argument that an account may be assigned or garnished.[89] The assignee or the creditor would take subject to equities,[90] including rights of set-off, so that the theory that combination operates as a set-off would produce the same result in any event as the view that it is simply an accounting exercise.   **15.17**

---

[83] See also para 15.28 below.
[84] See Lord Cross of Chelsea and Lord Kilbrandon [1972] AC 785, 810, 819–820.
[85] In relation to the third point, see in particular Viscount Dilhorne at [1972] AC 785, 807.
[86] Wood, *English and International Set-off* (1989) 93; Salter, 'Remedies For Banks: An Outline of English Law' in Blair (ed), *Banks and Remedies* (2nd edn, 1999) 52.
[87] See para 15.04 above.
[88] Compare Wood, *English and International Set-off* (1989) 93.
[89] *ibid.*
[90] See paras 17.02–17.72 below (assignments) and paras 17.104–17.112 below (garnishee orders).

Interest

15.18 Before accounts are combined in the bank's books,[91] interest ordinarily is calculated on the balance of each account, without reference to the balance on any other account. This method of calculating interest however is not inconsistent with the suggested explanation of combination.[92] The parties can agree that interest is to be calculated on whatever basis they choose, and the bank and its customer ordinarily would contract on the basis that, while an account retains its separate identity in the bank's books,[93] interest is to be calculated by reference to the balance on that account.[94]

Clayton's Case, **and the order of combination**

15.19 Nor is the notion that combination is a matter of accounting rather than of set-off inconsistent with the application of *Clayton's Case*[95] to each of the accounts. The accounting simply goes to the question whether, and to what extent, there is a debt owing at any particular time by one party to the other in their banking relationship. This does not impact upon how debits and credits are treated within an account. If a customer pays an amount to the credit of one of a number of current accounts, *Clayton's Case* operates so as to appropriate the payment to the earliest drawing on that account, as opposed to the earliest drawing on the accounts taken together.[96] Any other result would be contrary to the presumed intention of the parties, which is the basis of *Clayton's Case*.[97] The parties nevertheless may have expressed an intention that *Clayton's Case* is not to be applied in that manner, or there may be special circumstances from which such an intention may be implied, in which case appropriation of payments will be dealt with in accordance with

---

[91] See para 15.04 above.

[92] Compare *Pott v Clegg* (1847) 16 M & W 321, 327, 153 ER 1212, 1214, *per* Parke B (*arguendo*).

[93] Compare *Royal Trust Co v Molsons Bank* (1912) 8 DLR 478. Assuming that the promissory notes came to the bank as part of the banker/customer relationship (see paras 15.39–15.45 below), *Royal Trust Co v Molson* would have been correctly decided if (as Falconbridge CJKB postulated, at 480) the bank were regarded as having applied the deposit against the indebtedness on the notes.

[94] See *Barclays Bank Ltd v Okenarhe* [1966] 2 Lloyd's Rep 87, 98. Compare *National Bank of New Zealand v Grace* (1890) 8 NZLR 706 (esp at 712), in which Conolly J, in holding that interest is payable on an overdrawn account without reference to a credit balance on another account, assumed that, until the accounts were closed and the balance sued for, the accounts had to be considered as separate accounts for all purposes.

[95] (1816) 1 Mer 572, 35 ER 781.

[96] *Horton v Bank of New Zealand* (1889) 7 NZLR 582, 593–594 (Richmond J having accepted (at 591) that the accounts in law were combined); *Re Yeovil Glove Co Ltd* [1963] 1 Ch 528, 543 (affirmed [1965] 1 Ch 148); *Re James R Rutherford & Sons Ltd* [1964] 1 WLR 1211, 1216–1217. See also the formulation of the principle by the Earl of Selborne in *Re Sherry* (1884) 25 Ch D 692, 702. Compare *Mutton v Peat* [1899] 2 Ch 556 (reversed [1900] 2 Ch 79).

[97] See *Re Hallett's Estate* (1880) 13 Ch D 696, 738–739.

their intention.[98] An illustration is *Re E J Morel (1934) Ltd.*[99] In the *Morel* case, drawings from a No 3 account were regarded as having come from a credit balance on a No 2 account. The circumstances were exceptional, however. A drawing could not be made from the No 3 account unless the No 2 account had a credit balance sufficient to cover it, so that they were interdependent and, in substance, were the one account.[100]

The question of how accounts are to be appropriated in relation to combination **15.20** may arise in some circumstances.[101] Consider that two accounts, a No 1 account and a No 2 account, are in debit, while a third No 3 account has a credit balance. At any particular time the customer's or the bank's debt to the other can be ascertained only by looking at the balance of all three accounts, and the ascertainment of the balance does not depend upon the order in which the accounts are set against each other. However the bank is entitled to give effect to the principle of combination in its books by moving assets and liabilities from one account to another, unless there is an express or an implied agreement to the contrary,[102] and it is at that point that the question of the order of the combination may arise. In the example, does the credit balance on the No 3 account reduce first the No 1 account or the No 2 account? While the bank's book entry itself would not constitute a payment, since there was in any event only one debt for the balance,[103] it could affect issues such as the calculation of interest and the application of *Clayton's Case* in relation to future debits and credits. In *Re E J Morel (1934) Ltd*[104] Buckley J (as he then was) said that the bank can combine the accounts in whatever way it chooses, a view that was also accepted by Nourse J at first instance in *Barclays Bank Ltd v TOSG Trust Fund Ltd.*[105] That view is consistent with the rules applicable to appropriation of payments. If a debtor makes a payment to a creditor, he can appropriate it as he pleases. If the debtor does not make an appropriation, however, and *Clayton's Case* is not applicable, the right of appropriation devolves upon the creditor.[106] On a similar principle, if the customer has not chosen to apply the No 3 credit account in a particular way, for example by withdrawing funds from that account and crediting them to either the No 1 or the No 2 account, or by otherwise requesting the bank to make the appropriate book

---

[98] *Re Hallett's Estate* (1880) 13 Ch D 696, 738–739.

[99] [1962] 1 Ch 21. See para 15.56 below.

[100] Compare the arrangement adopted in *Re James R Rutherford & Sons Ltd* [1964] 1 WLR 1211.

[101] See eg the discussion of time bars in paras 15.34–15.38 below.

[102] See para 15.04 above.

[103] *Re Sutcliffe & Sons Ltd, ex p Royal Bank* [1933] 1 DLR 562 (esp at 569); *Ross v Royal Bank of Canada* (1965) 52 DLR (2d) 578; *Re T C Marines Ltd* (1973) 34 DLR (3d) 489; *Re Plasky* (1981) 39 WWR 186.

[104] [1962] 1 Ch 21, 31–32.

[105] [1984] BCLC 1, 22.

[106] *Cory Bros & Co Ltd v The Owners of the Turkish Steamship 'Mecca' (The Mecca)* [1897] AC 286.

entries, the question of how the No 3 account should be dealt with should devolve upon the bank, given that *Clayton's Case* does not apply as between accounts.

15.21 It is true that Walton J in *Re Unit 2 Windows Ltd*[107] held that, when there is a claim going one way and two cross-claims going the other, or, as in that case, one cross-claim which is partly preferential and partly non-preferential in the liquidation of the debtor, the set-off should occur rateably as between the cross-claims. *Unit 2 Windows* however was decided on the basis of the interpretation of the set-off section in the insolvency legislation. When common law principles of combination are in issue, as opposed to a question of statutory interpretation, the position at common law regarding appropriation of payments would appear to provide the appropriate analogy. Nor would the principles ever conflict. If as a matter of the law of combination there is only one debt for the balance, the insolvency set-off section would not apply. The set-off section requires mutual but independent obligations, whereas under the principle of combination there is only one obligation.[108]

Guarantees and securities

15.22 A guarantee may be given in respect of a customer's indebtedness. If the customer has two accounts with the bank, one in debit and the other in credit, it would be to the advantage of the guarantor if the two accounts were combined so as to produce a single debt for the balance. The guarantor's liability in such a case would be reduced.[109] Alternatively, a customer may have provided security to a bank for his indebtedness to the bank, and the customer has one account with a debit balance and another in credit. The question whether the debt secured is the balance of the two accounts taken together,[110] or whether regard is to be had only to the account in debit,[111] would depend principally on the terms of the security, but it could also depend on whether the accounts are combined. In relation to these issues, a number of general comments may be made. In the first place, it may be relevant to consider whether the circumstances surrounding the provision of the guarantee or the security in relation to a particular account evidence an agreement that that

---

[107] [1985] 1 WLR 1383. See para 6.117 above.

[108] See Buckley LJ in *Halesowen Presswork and Assemblies Ltd v Westminster Bank Ltd* [1971] 1 QB 1, 46.

[109] See eg *Re Tonkin* (1933) 6 ABC 197, 210–211. Compare *York City and County Banking Co v Bainbridge* (1880) 43 LT 732, in which a surety's liability in respect of a loan made to a customer was not reduced by a credit balance on the customer's current account, since the accounts were separate. In that regard, there is usually an implied agreement that a loan account and a current account are to be kept separate. See para 15.52 below.

[110] As in *Re European Bank. Agra Bank Claim* (1872) LR 8 Ch App 41 and *Mutton v Peat* [1900] 2 Ch 79. See also *Horton v Bank of New Zealand* (1889) 7 NZLR 582; *Re Sherry* (1884) 25 Ch D 693, 706; *National Bank of Nigeria Ltd v Awolesi* [1964] 1 WLR 1311, 1316–1317.

[111] See *Royal Bank of Canada v Bank of Montreal* [1976] 4 WWR 721, although it is unclear whether the current account in fact had a credit balance.

account is to be separated from other accounts.[112] Alternatively, notwithstanding the principle of combination, there is no reason why a guarantee or a security in its terms could not be confined to a particular account, treating it for the purpose of the guarantee or the security as if it were a separate debt.[113] On the other hand, where the accounts would otherwise be regarded as separate, the terms of the guarantee or the security should be examined to see whether, as a matter of construction of the contract, it is in any event only intended to benefit the bank to the extent of any net balance on all the accounts.[114] Further, if accounts are separate, and a guarantee is given in respect of the customer's indebtedness on one of the accounts, the customer as the principal debtor would have a defence of set-off under the Statutes of Set-off to the extent of the credit balance on the second account if he was sued for payment of the debit balance on the first account. The guarantor in that situation might also be able to rely on the principal debtor's defence in an action on the guarantee,[115] although the question whether a guarantor is entitled to rely on the principal debtor's defence under the Statutes remains uncertain.[116] It also may be the case that a guarantee in its terms contemplates a single unbroken account, so that, if the bank permits the principal debtor to open a second account into which credit funds are deposited, the guarantor may be prejudiced so as to discharge him from the guarantee.[117]

The question of combination in the context of a guarantee arose in *Bradford Old* **15.23** *Bank Ltd v Sutcliffe*.[118] A bank provided a fixed loan and a current account with an overdraft limit to a company, supported by a guarantee from the directors. One of the directors subsequently became insane. This had the consequence that the guarantee ceased to be continuing in relation to that guarantor, so that it only extended to debts in existence at that date. The company nevertheless continued to operate the current account for a number of years, when a demand was made on the guarantee. The current account was overdrawn, but in accordance with *Clayton's Case*[119] payments into the current account during the intervening period

---

[112] This may apply in particular where an account in credit is charged back to the bank. See para 16.74 below. The giving of separate securities to a bank in relation to two or more accounts may indicate that the accounts are to be treated as separate. See *Lloyds Bank NZA Ltd v National Safety Council* [1993] 2 VR 506, 523.

[113] In *Re Bank of Queensland Ltd* [1997] 2 Qd R 129, 137 McPherson JA said that, 'the principle [of combination] applies in relation to cases in which the bank holds securities for one only of two accounts'.

[114] See the discussion of *Mutton v Peat* [1900] 2 Ch 79 in para 15.09 above.

[115] Compare *York City and County Banking Co v Bainbridge* (1880) 43 LT 732.

[116] See paras 18.26–18.28 below.

[117] *National Bank of Nigeria Ltd v Awolesi* [1964] 1 WLR 1311. If the guarantee on its proper construction permits the opening of a second account, so as to cover all such accounts, the Privy Council in the *Awolesi* case considered that the guarantor may still be discharged if the accounts are allowed to be operated so as to increase the burden on him, for example in the calculation of interest.

[118] [1918] 2 KB 833.

[119] (1816) 1 Mer 572, 35 ER 781.

had had the effect of satisfying the debt on that account as it stood when the guarantee ceased to be continuing. The director therefore was no longer liable under the guarantee in relation to the current account. In so far as the loan account was concerned, the Court of Appeal held that there was an implied agreement that it was to be kept separate from the current account.[120] The amount owing on the loan account therefore was not satisfied by subsequent payments into the current account, and the guarantor remained liable for the debt on that account. A curious aspect of the case is that it seems to have been assumed that, if the accounts had not been separate, *Clayton's Case* would have operated on the basis that payments into the current account would have reduced the loan account, but it is suggested that that would not have been the case. *Clayton's Case* ordinarily should be confined in its operation to an individual account notwithstanding the principle of combination.[121]

15.24 A similar situation occurred in *Re Sherry*.[122] A bank provided an overdraft to a customer secured by a guarantee. The guarantor died, whereupon the guarantee was determined as to future advances. The bank accordingly closed the account, and opened a new account to which subsequent payments in were credited and drawings debited. When the guarantee was later enforced, it was held that *Clayton's Case* did not apply so as to appropriate the payments credited to the second account in reduction of the guaranteed debt on the first account. Nor was it a term of the guarantee that payments received from the debtor should be regarded as appropriated in that manner. *Re Sherry* is not inconsistent with the notion that combination is a matter of account.[123] The fact that *Clayton's Case* was applied only in relation to the second account does not show any inconsistency.[124] Further, the second account had a debit balance so that, even assuming that the case was one in which there was a single debt between banker and customer represented by the balance of both accounts, there was no account in credit which could have had the effect of reducing the guaranteed debt.[125]

---

[120] See para 15.52 below.

[121] See para 15.19 above. The current account was overdrawn, but if the current account had had a credit balance when the proceeding commenced which exceeded the loan, and if the current account and the loan account had not been separate so as to preclude combination, the principle of combination would have dictated that the company would not have been indebted to the bank, and the bank therefore could not have sued the director on the guarantee.

[122] (1884) 25 Ch D 692. See also *Kirby v Duke of Marlborough* (1813) 2 M & S 18, 105 ER 289; *Williams v Rawlinson* (1825) 3 Bing 71, 130 ER 440.

[123] Compare Wood, *English and International Set-off* (1989) 93 (referring to para 10–223).

[124] See para 15.19 above.

[125] Compare *Hollond v Teed* (1848) 7 Hare 50, 68 ER 20 (explained in *Re Sherry* (1884) 25 Ch D 692, 704–705). In that case there was a balance standing to the credit of an account at the date the guarantee determined. However, at that date the outstanding bills of exchange the subject of the guarantee had not matured, and the amount standing to the credit of the account was withdrawn before maturity. Accordingly, it could not have been a case of combination.

A bank has a lien on cheques and other securities deposited with it,[126] which **15.25** should include a right to set off the proceeds against the customer's debt to the bank.[127] The lien is applicable in respect of the balance on all accounts between the bank and the customer, including a loan account.[128]

Notice of combination

It has been suggested that the question may still be open as to whether a bank may **15.26** be required to give notice before exercising its combination rights, and that any such requirement would be inconsistent with the view that at any particular time there is only one debt.[129] The answer is that there is no requirement of notice for combination as such, and nor is the bank obliged to give notice of its intention to rely upon the principle.[130] Accordingly, there is no inconsistency.

There may, however, be a requirement of notice where there is an agreement be- **15.27** tween the parties to keep the accounts separate, and the bank wishes to terminate the agreement. For example, when a customer has both a current account in credit and a loan account, the courts usually imply an agreement that the accounts are to be kept separate,[131] because otherwise the customer could not safely draw cheques on the current account. Consistent with the view that reasonable notice is required to close a current account in credit,[132] it may be that the agreement can be terminated if reasonable notice is given.[133] The question of reasonableness would depend upon the circumstances of the case,[134] but in any event provision would have to be made for outstanding cheques.[135]

A similar issue was the subject of discussion in the House of Lords in the **15.28** *Halesowen* case.[136] The bank in that case had agreed that it would not require

---

[126] *Re Keever* [1967] 1 Ch 182, 189.

[127] See para 15.115 below.

[128] *Re Keever* [1967] 1 Ch 182, 190, citing *Re European Bank* (1872) LR 9 Ch App 41.

[129] Salter, 'Remedies For Banks: An Outline of English Law' in Blair (ed), *Banks and Remedies* (2nd edn, 1999) 52.

[130] *Garnett v M'Kewan* (1872) LR 8 Ex 10; *Irwin v Bank of* Montreal (1876) 38 UCQB 375, 393; *Wallinder v Imperial Bank of Canada* [1925] 4 DLR 390, 392; *Deep v Bank of Montreal* (1991) 47 OAC 319. See also *Re Shaw* (1977) 31 FLR 118, 122 in relation to a contractual right to set off accounts.

[131] *Bradford Old Bank Ltd v Sutcliffe* [1918] 2 KB 833. See para 15.52 below.

[132] *Joachimson v Swiss Bank Corp* [1921] 3 KB 110, 127; *Tai Hing Cotton Mill Ltd v Liu Chong Hing Bank Ltd* [1986] 1 AC 80, 105. Compare *Paget's Law of Banking* (11th edn, 1996) 167 with respect to an overdraft.

[133] See *Buckingham and Co v London and Midland Bank* (1895) 12 TLR 70, 72, and also *Cumming v Shand* (1860) 5 H & N 95, 157 ER 1114. Compare *Inglis v Commonwealth Trading Bank of Australia* (1973) 47 ALJR 234, in which the current account was overdrawn so that the bank was not obliged to honour further cheques. Mason J accordingly held that the bank could consolidate the accounts without notice, following breach of the agreement by the customer to maintain the working (current) account in credit. Compare also Roskill J at first instance in the *Halesowen* case. See para 15.52 below.

[134] *Prosperity Ltd v Lloyds Bank Ltd* (1923) 39 TLR 372, 373.

[135] *Joachimson v Swiss Bank Corp* [1921] 3 KB 110, 125.

[136] [1972] AC 785.

repayment of a frozen current account for a period of four months unless there was a material change in circumstances. This gave rise to an implied term that, during the period, the bank would not combine or consolidate the account with another current account in credit. Viscount Dilhorne left open the question whether the bank would have been required to give notice of termination in the event of a material change in circumstances,[137] but Lord Cross of Chelsea inclined to the better view, that notice was required, albeit notice having immediate effect as opposed to reasonable notice.[138] A requirement of reasonable notice would have enabled the customer to defeat the object with which it was given, by immediately withdrawing the funds standing to the credit of the current account. On the other hand, Lord Cross considered that the bank would still have been required to honour cheques drawn before notice up to the limit of the credit balance on the account. The bank's right to terminate the arrangement upon the occurrence of a material change of circumstances carried with it a consequential power to combine the accounts.[139] This would have differed from the ordinary case of combination which does not depend upon termination of an agreement to keep accounts separate, because combination ordinarily operates on the basis that the accounts are combined in a single debt without the exercise of a right or a power.[140]

15.29 In a case where an agreement to keep accounts separate is terminated, combination may not require a book entry by the bank. An assertion that the accounts are combined may suffice.[141]

The bank's, rather than the customer's, right, and different branches

15.30 It is sometimes suggested that the right to combine accounts is a right possessed by the bank only, and not the customer,[142] but that in some circumstances the bank may be obliged to combine.[143] The case generally cited in support of the second of these propositions is *Mutton v Peat*,[144] though this is not an accurate description of the ground upon which the case was decided. In truth, the presence

---

[137] [1972] AC 785, 807.

[138] [1972] AC 785, 810, referring to Buckley LJ in the Court of Appeal [1971] 1 QB 1, 47.

[139] See also *Inglis v Commonwealth Trading Bank of Australia* (1973) 47 ALJR 234.

[140] See para 15.03 above.

[141] See Roskill J at first instance in *Halesowen Presswork and Assemblies Ltd v Westminster Bank Ltd* [1971] 1 QB 1, 19, and also *Direct Acceptance Corp Ltd v Bank of New South Wales* (1968) 88 WN (Pt 1) (NSW) 498, 502. This also accords with the bank's contention in *Neste Oy v Lloyds Bank plc* [1983] 2 Lloyd's Rep 658, 662–663.

[142] *Barclays Bank Ltd v Okenarhe* [1966] 2 Lloyd's Rep 87, 95; Herzberg, 'Bankers' Rights of Combination' (1982) 10 Australian Business Law Review 79, 82, 83.

[143] *Barclays Bank Ltd v Okenarhe* [1966] 2 Lloyd's Rep 87, 95–96; *Halesowen Presswork and Assemblies Ltd v Westminster Bank Ltd* [1971] 1 QB 1, 34; *Paget's Law of Banking* (11th edn, 1996) 532; Ellinger, Lomnicka and Hooley, *Modern Banking Law* (3rd edn, 2002), 219.

[144] [1900] 2 Ch 79.

or absence of an act of combination was regarded as irrelevant, because it was considered that there was in any event only one debt for the balance.[145]

In so far as the view that only the bank may combine is concerned, it is based on **15.31** what has been described as the 'apparent anomaly'[146] that arises in relation to accounts at different branches of the same bank. A bank may look upon various accounts as combined notwithstanding that they are kept at separate branches. Thus a bank may refuse to honour a cheque drawn by a customer on one branch at which he has an account in credit if there is a countervailing account in debit at another branch, such that the overall credit balance is insufficient to cover the cheque.[147] On the other hand, when a customer has two current accounts at separate branches, he may only draw upon either account to the extent of the balance on the account at the branch where the account is kept. If he draws on either account for an amount in excess of the credit balance on that account, or in excess of an agreed overdraft limit, he is not entitled to have the cheque honoured on the ground that the combined balance on both accounts is more than sufficient to cover it.[148] While this has been said to be inconsistent with the notion that combination is a matter of account rather than set-off,[149] it may be explained on the basis that the bank only promises to repay any part of the amount due on an account against the customer's written order if the order is addressed to the bank at the branch at which the account is kept.[150] It is not necessary to say that combination is a right only of the bank. If there is only one debt for the balance *vis-à-vis* the bank, there should also be only one debt *vis-à-vis* the customer,[151] although the customer's right to have his cheques honoured is subject to the terms of the contract with the bank.

It may be that, instead of having two accounts in credit at different branches, both **15.32** accounts are at the same branch. A cheque may be drawn on the first account for an amount which is in excess of the credit balance on that account, although it

---

[145] See the discussion of *Mutton v Peat* in para 15.09 above.

[146] *Barclays Bank Ltd v Okenarhe* [1966] 2 Lloyd's Rep 87, 95.

[147] *Garnett v M'Kewan* (1872) LR 8 Ex 10, approved of by the Privy Council in *Prince v Oriental Bank Corp* (1878) 3 App Cas 325. See also *Irwin v Bank of Montreal* (1876) 38 UCQB 375, 393; *Wallinder v Imperial Bank of Canada* [1925] 4 DLR 390, 392; *Barclays Bank Ltd v Okenarhe* [1966] 2 Lloyd's Rep 87; *National Bank of New Zealand v Heslop* (1882) NZLR 1 CA 47.

[148] *Garnett v M'Kewan* (1872) LR 8 Ex 10, 12, *per* Kelly CB ('if the plaintiff had had a balance in his favour at both places he could of course have drawn at either to the extent of the balance there'), 14–15, *per* Bramwell B; *Barclays Bank Ltd v Okenarhe* [1966] 2 Lloyd's Rep 87, 95. See also *National Bank of New Zealand v Grace* (1890) 8 NZLR 706, 710.

[149] Salter, 'Remedies For Banks: An Outline of English Law' in Blair (ed), *Banks and Remedies* (2nd edn, 1999) 52.

[150] See *Joachimson v Swiss Bank Corp* [1921] 3 KB 110, 127; *Prince v Oriental Bank Corp* (1878) 3 App Cas 325, 332; *Woodland v Fear* (1857) 7 El & Bl 519, 119 ER 1339.

[151] In *Re Bank of Queensland Ltd* [1997] 2 Qd R 129, 137 McPherson JA said that, 'where a customer has two accounts with a bank, either the bank or the customer is entitled to treat those two accounts . . . as one'.

would be covered if both accounts were taken together. The question arises whether the bank is obliged to honour the cheque by transferring part of the balance on the second account to the first account. Ellinger, Lomnicka and Hooley considered the issue in the situation in which the second account is a savings account.[152] In their opinion, the maintenance of different types of accounts manifests an intention that they are to be kept separate, and accordingly the bank could dishonour the cheque. Their conclusion would appear to be correct. If a cheque cannot be drawn on a savings account, it would be contrary to the parties' agreement to that effect if the bank were required to transfer a part of the balance on a savings account to a current account in order to honour a cheque. They went on to suggest that in practice the bank would permit the customer to overdraw the current account and leave the savings account intact as a form of security. This differs from a transfer of part of the savings account to the current account, however, because the customer would be debited with interest on the overdrawn account at a rate which exceeds the interest that would be earned on the savings account if it were left intact.

15.33 The question is more difficult where the second account is another current account rather than a savings account. If there is an express or implied agreement between the bank and the customer that the accounts are to be kept separate, that would be the end of the matter. The bank could not utilize part of the credit balance on the second account to pay a cheque drawn on the first account. In the absence of an agreement to that effect, however, the argument that the bank should honour the cheque is not without merit. The accounts in such a case would be regarded as combined, in the sense that they produce a single debt for the balance. That should be so from the perspective of both the bank and the customer. They are regarded as the one account, and it may be said that it was only for convenience that they were entered in the bank's books under different names.[153] In the situation in which a customer has two or more accounts at different branches, it is said that the bank is not required to honour a cheque drawn on one account for an amount greater than the balance on that account, notwithstanding that the account at the second branch has sufficient funds to cover the shortfall, because each branch of a bank could not be expected to know the state of the customer's account at every other branch.[154] This would hardly apply however when both current accounts are with the same branch, if indeed it is still

---

[152] Ellinger, Lomnicka and Hooley, *Modern Banking Law* (3rd edn, 2002) 218–219.

[153] *Bailey v Finch* (1871) LR 7 QB 34, 40; *Ex parte Morier, re Willis, Percival & Co* (1879) 12 Ch D 491, 498–499; *Re Johnson & Co Ltd* [1902] 1 IR 439, 442; *Clark v Ulster Bank Ltd* [1950] NILR 132, 142. See also *Re European Bank. Agra Bank Claim* (1872) LR 8 Ch App 41, 44; *Garnett v M'Kewan* (1872) LR 8 Ex 10, 12.

[154] *Barclays Bank Ltd v Okenarhe* [1966] 2 Lloyd's Rep 87, 95. See also *National Bank of New Zealand v Grace* (1890) 8 NZLR 706, 710; *Joachimson v Swiss Bank Corp* [1921] 3 KB 110, 129–130; *Prince v Oriental Bank Corp* (1878) 3 App Cas 325, 332–333.

appropriate in modern times in the context of separate branches. Moreover, when Atkin LJ in *Joachimson v Swiss Bank Corp*[155] discussed the terms implied in the banker/customer contract, he referred to the bank's obligation to honour the customer's written orders addressed to the bank at the branch where the account is kept. The emphasis was on the branch, as opposed to a particular account. Nevertheless, the question of the bank's obligation when there is more than one account was not an issue in the *Joachimson* case, and indeed Bankes LJ in that case warned against placing too much reliance upon the language used in a judgment when the judge had not the precise point before him.[156] The better view is that the bank is not obliged to honour the cheque, notwithstanding that the accounts may be combined to form a single debt. The opening of separate accounts is likely to be regarded as giving rise to an implied term in the banker/customer contract that the bank is only obliged to honour a cheque drawn on a particular account to the extent of the credit balance on that account.

Time bars

It has also been suggested that a debit balance may become statute-barred as a re- **15.34** sult of the expiration of a limitation period and hence ineligible for a set-off, and that this is inconsistent with the notion that only one amount is owing on all the accounts.[157] The proposed analysis of combination indeed suggests that an account that otherwise would have been time-barred if it had existed in isolation may be included in a combination. If at the same time there is a second account in credit, the first account to the extent of the credit balance will have been paid. This may not always be the case, however. If, for example, the second account only came into existence after the expiration of the limitation period for the first account, there may well be an implied agreement that it is to be kept separate. The circumstances of each case would require consideration.

Two comments may be made in respect of the criticism of the view that an account **15.35** that otherwise would be time-barred may be included in a combination.

The first is that there is nothing in the cases which is inconsistent with that result. **15.36** The two cases which have been cited as authority to the contrary in fact were not concerned with combination. In *Pott v Clegg*[158] the assignees in bankruptcy of a bankrupt banker sued the executor of William Turner for the balance owing on an account. The executor pleaded set-off based upon an account that had been opened in the joint names of Turner and one Mawdesley, the limitation period for

---

[155] [1921] 3 KB 110, 127.
[156] *Joachimson v Swiss Bank Corp* [1921] 3 KB 110, 120.
[157] Wood, *English and International Set-off* (1989) 93, and see also Salter, 'Remedies For Banks: An Outline of English Law' in Blair (ed), *Banks and Remedies* (2nd edn, 1999) 52.
[158] (1847) 16 M & W 321, 153 ER 1212.

which had elapsed. Mawdesley had died, and the account accordingly had vested in Turner, although it still remained in the bank's books in the joint names. It was held that Turner's executor could not employ the time-barred account in a set-off. The case turned on the availability of a set-off under the Statutes of Set-off, for which it is accepted that the debt sought to be set off must be enforceable by action.[159] It was not a case of combination, because the basis of that principle is a single relationship of banker and customer,[160] whereas in *Pott v Clegg* separate banker/customer relationships were in issue. A similar comment may be made in respect of *Re Morris. Coneys v Morris.*[161] A customer with a deposit account was liable as a surety on a promissory note given to the bank. After the limitation period for a claim on the note had expired the bank purported to set off the amount of the note against the deposit. It was held that the bank was not entitled to do this, given that an action could not have been brought on the note. Once again, however, this was not a case of combination, since the customer's liability on the note as a surety did not arise out of the banker/customer relationship.

15.37 The second comment is that, even if combination of accounts were properly characterized as a set-off rather than an accounting situation,[162] the fact that one of the accounts is time-barred should still not preclude an exercise of the right. In other words, the position should be the same whichever way combination is characterized. This conclusion should apply notwithstanding comments by Sir John Ross LC in the Irish High Court of Appeal in *Re Morris* which suggest that an account in respect of which the limitation period has expired could not be the subject of combination.[163] A statute of limitation commonly takes away the remedy of enforcing a debt in an action at law but leaves the debt itself intact. Assume that combination indeed operates by way of set-off. The set-off would be effected by the bank without recourse to the courts, in which case the expiration of a limitation period should not affect the right. There are indeed a number of situations in which the courts have recognized that a creditor may exercise rights and remedies in relation to a time-barred debt in circumstances where recourse to the courts is not required. For example, the common law has recognized that a possessory lien may be exercised in respect of a statute-barred debt,[164] and one would have thought that the same principle should apply in relation to a common law right to

---

[159] See para 2.49 above.
[160] See Buckley LJ in the Court of Appeal in *Halesowen Presswork and Assemblies Ltd v Westminster Bank Ltd* [1971] 1 QB 1, 46, and para 15.03 above.
[161] [1922] 1 IR 136, affirming [1922] 1 IR 88.
[162] Compare para 15.03 above.
[163] [1922] 1 IR 136, 137. Compare O'Connor MR, whose judgment consisted primarily of a rejection of the argument that the bank had a 'lien' on the deposit account. In relation to set-off, his only discussion was in the context of pleading set-off as a defence to an action at law, presumably pursuant to the Statutes of Set-off, for which an enforceable debt is required.
[164] *Spears v Hartly* (1800) 3 Esp 81, 170 ER 545; *Higgins v Scott* (1831) 2 B & Ad 413, 109 ER 1196.

combine accounts which, like a lien, takes effect extra-judicially. Consistent with that view, Mocatta J commented in *Barclays Bank Ltd v Okenarhe*[165] that a bank should not be in any worse position with respect to money deposited with it than it would be with respect to securities over which it had a lien. A similar stance has been adopted in equity in relation to both the substantive defence of equitable set-off[166] and the principle in *Cherry v Boultbee*.[167] Another illustration is the right that an executor formerly enjoyed to retain a sufficient amount from the estate in order to pay a debt owing to him by the deceased in priority to other creditors.[168] While it has now been abolished in England,[169] it was nevertheless held that the expiration of the limitation period for the debt did not affect the executor's right.[170] Further, reference may be made to the case of a debtor who makes a payment to the creditor without directing that it be paid in reduction of a particular debt. The right of appropriation in such a case devolves upon the creditor, and he may apply the payment to a time-barred debt rather than to another debt that is still enforceable.[171] It is true that, in the case of set-off under the Statutes of Set-off, the common law courts have required that the cross-debt sought to be set off must be enforceable by action,[172] and that may well be what Sir John Ross had in mind in *Re Morris*. This form of set-off however is a procedural defence to an action at law, which requires a court order to bring about a set-off.[173] It differs in that respect from combination of accounts.

How would combination work in practice in relation to an account that otherwise **15.38** would be time-barred? Consider that there are two accounts, account No 1 which is in credit, and account No 2 which has a debit balance and in respect of which the limitation period has expired. In such a case the customer could only sue for the balance of the two accounts if the credit balance on account No 1 exceeds the debit balance on account No 2. If on the other hand the debit balance on account No 2 exceeds the debit balance on account No 1, the bank's claim for the ultimate balance would be unenforceable. It may be that there are two accounts with debit balances, account No 2 which is time-barred and account No 3 which is not. In such a case the principle should be that, in the absence of an appropriation by the customer, the bank could treat the credit balance on account No 1 as reducing first the debit balance on account No 2.[174] To the extent that any part of the balance on account No 2 is not reduced in that manner, an action in respect of it, being an

---

[165] [1966] 2 Lloyd's Rep 87, 97.
[166] See para 4.39 above.
[167] (1839) 4 My & Cr 442, 41 ER 171. See para 14.15 above.
[168] See para 14.04 above.
[169] Administration of Estates Act 1971, s 10.
[170] *Hill v Walker* (1858) 4 K & J 166, 70 ER 69.
[171] *Mills v Fowkes* (1839) 5 Bing (NC) 455, 132 ER 1174.
[172] See para 2.49 above.
[173] See paras 2.33–2.48 above.
[174] See para 15.20 above.

action founded upon simple contract, would be precluded by the Limitation Act 1980, section 5.

D. Banker and Customer Relationship

15.39 Combination only extends to obligations owing to a bank in its capacity as banker.[175] A debt due to it as a result of carrying on another business will not suffice.[176] Moreover, the obligations should relate to the same bank, a requirement that probably would not be satisfied where a bank uses separate corporate structures for its trading and savings bank functions.[177]

Banking business

15.40 Combination is a common law concept, and it should apply in the case of institutions that are regarded at common law as carrying on the business of banking.[178] In Australia, Isaacs J in *State Savings Bank of Victoria v Permewan Wright & Co Ltd*[179] described the essential characteristics of the business of banking as: 'the collection of money by receiving deposits upon loan, repayable when and as expressly or impliedly agreed upon, and the utilization of the money so collected by lending it again in such sums as are required. These are the essential functions of a bank as an instrument of society.' In other words, the business of banking essentially is the borrowing and lending of money. Isaacs J went on to say that the methods by which the functions of a bank are effected, as by current account, deposit account at call, fixed deposit account, orders, cheques, secured loans, discounting bills, letters of credit, telegraphic transfers and other modes, are merely auxiliary circumstances, any of which may or may not exist in any particular case. In particular, he said that banks are not bound by law to open current accounts, but may confine themselves to deposit accounts. Subsequently the English Court of Appeal in *United Dominions Trust Ltd v Kirkwood*[180] rejected Isaacs J's approach as not reflecting modern practice,[181] the court emphasizing instead the importance that

---

[175] See Roskill J in *Halesowen Presswork and Assemblies Ltd v Westminster Bank Ltd* [1971] 1 QB 1, 20 ('whenever a customer is indebted to a banker as a banker'), and the discussion in *Barclays Bank Ltd v Okenarhe* [1966] 2 Lloyd's Rep 87, 98–99 in relation to whether the loan was made in the ordinary course of banking business.

[176] See Pigott and Bramwell BB in their judgments in *Garnett v M'Kewan* (1872) LR 8 Ex 10, 14. Bramwell B gave as an example the business of brewer.

[177] Herzberg, 'Bankers' Rights of Combination' (1982) 10 Australian Business Law Review 79, 86.

[178] See also *Paget's Law of Banking* (11th edn, 1996) 103.

[179] (1913) 19 CLR 457, 470–471. See also *Melbourne Corp v Commonwealth* (1947) 74 CLR 31, 54, 63, *per* Latham CJ, 64–65, *per* Rich J; *Mason v Savings Bank of South Australia* [1925] SASR 198, 204; *PP Consultants Pty Ltd v Finance Sector Union of Australia* (2000) 201 CLR 648, 655–656 para 17.

[180] [1966] 2 QB 431. See also *Re Roe's Legal Charge* [1982] 2 Lloyd's Rep 370, CA.

[181] [1966] 2 QB 431, 445–446, *per* Lord Denning, 464, *per* Diplock LJ.

cheques now play as a means of paying and receiving money.[182] Consistent with that view, Harman and Diplock LJJ regarded it as an essential characteristic of banking business that the bank conducts current accounts,[183] while Lord Denning described the keeping of current accounts as a characteristic 'usually' found in banks.[184]

This does not mean that banking business, and combination of accounts,[185] is confined to current accounts. The conduct of current accounts may be regarded in England as an essential characteristic of modern banking business, in that an institution is not properly regarded as a bank unless it provides current accounts, but the business of banking encompasses more than that. A banker conducts the business of banking with customers,[186] and the main criterion for determining whether a person is a customer of a bank is whether that person has an account with the bank through which transactions are passed.[187] It does not have to be a current account. It has been said that a deposit account will suffice,[188] and indeed Paget suggests that a continued practice of getting bills discounted by a bank would probably be enough to establish a person as a customer.[189] **15.41**

Lease finance facilities

It is now common for banks to provide lease finance facilities to customers. Typically this involves the bank acquiring items of equipment and leasing them to **15.42**

---

[182] [1966] 2 QB 431, 446, *per* Lord Denning, 459 , *per* Harman LJ, 465, *per* Diplock J.

[183] [1966] 2 QB 431, 457–458, 459, *per* Harman LJ, 465, *per* Diplock LJ.

[184] [1966] 2 QB 431, 447. Lord Denning (at 453–454) said that there are other characteristics which go to make a banker, including stability, soundness and probity, and the reputation of the firm amongst ordinary commercial men. Diplock LJ (at 473–475) also thought that regard could be had to reputation (although for a reason different from that which commended itself to Lord Denning), though compare Harman LJ at 460–461.

[185] See paras 15.46–15.48 below. Compare Ireland, where it has been said that combination is confined to current accounts. See *Bank of Ireland v Martin* [1937] IR 189, 202–203; Earley, 'Set-off Rights Available to Banks in Ireland' [1997] 4 Journal of International Banking Law 153, 154.

[186] In *Melbourne Corp v Commonwealth* (1947) 74 CLR 31, 51 Latham CJ said that: 'A banker conducts a business of banking with customers. The customer of a banker does his banking business with the banker. That which the banker does as a banker is the business of banking, and that which the customer does as a customer of the banker is also the business of banking.'

[187] *Paget's Law of Banking* (11th edn, 1996), 106, and see also Ellinger, Lomnicka and Hooley, *Modern Banking Law* (3rd edn, 2002) 90–2.

[188] *Great Western Railway Co v London and County Banking Co Ltd* [1901] AC 414, 420–421; *Hart v Sangster* [1957] 1 Ch 329, 336, 337; *Warren v Colonial Catering Co Ltd* [1975] 1 NZLR 273, 276; *Paget's Law of Banking* (11th edn, 1996) 108; Ellinger, Lomnicka and Hooley, *Modern Banking Law* (3rd edn, 2002) 90; Weaver and Craigie, *The Law Relating to Banker and Customer in Australia* (looseleaf) vol 1, [5.30]; *Halsbury's Laws of England* (4th edn, 1989) vol 3(1), 181 para 214.

[189] *Paget's Law of Banking* (11th edn, 1996) 108. See also Weaver and Craigie, *The Law Relating to Banker and Customer in Australia* (looseleaf) vol 1, [5.20]. In *Great Western Railway Co v London and County Banking Co Ltd* [1901] AC 414, 422–423 Lord Brampton left open the question whether the keeping of an ordinary bank account is essential to constitute a person a customer of a bank.

the customer. The question arises whether the customer's payment obligations pursuant to the lease, including as a result of early termination, may be the subject of combination with a credit balance on another account. The issue came before the New South Wales Court of Appeal in *Cinema Plus Ltd v ANZ Banking Group Ltd*.[190] A customer defaulted under a lease facility, and the bank argued that the amount payable by the customer consequent upon the default could be combined with a credit balance on the customer's current account. Both Sheller and Giles JJA considered that combination did not apply. Sheller JA thought that the situation was governed by the principle that a loan account cannot be combined with a current account in credit,[191] while Giles JA said that, for combination to apply, there must be 'really but one account', and the current account and the lease finance facility served different functions which were inimical to their combination.[192] It is suggested that the same conclusion could have been reached by reference to a more fundamental principle, that combination only applies to amounts owing to a bank as banker. While it has been said that the meaning of 'banking business' can change from time to time,[193] when a bank leases equipment to a customer one would have thought that payments under the lease are due to it in its capacity as the owner and lessor of the equipment, as opposed to the capacity of banker. Thus, in *United Dominions Trust Ltd v Kirkwood*[194] Lord Denning said of a facility whereby a finance house acquired goods and let them to a customer on hire purchase terms that it was not banking.

Guarantor of another customer's debt

15.43 Combination should not apply when a person who has a deposit account with a bank gives a guarantee to the bank in respect of a second customer's indebtedness.[195] The guarantee in that circumstance would not be given in the capacity of a customer, but rather to assist the bank in its relationship with the second customer. If the bank wishes to be able to utilize the deposit in order to secure the liability under the guarantee, it should obtain an express contractual right of set-off from the guarantor.[196]

---

[190] (2000) 49 NSWLR 513.
[191] (2000) 49 NSWLR 513, 543 paras 113 and 114. See para 15.52 below.
[192] (2000) 49 NSWLR 513, 549 para 142.
[193] Ellinger, Lomnicka and Hooley, *Modern Banking Law* (3rd edn, 2002) 60, referring inter alia to *Woods v Martins Bank Ltd* [1959] 1 QB 55, 70. See also *United Dominions Trust Ltd v Kirkwood* [1966] 2 QB 431, 464.
[194] [1966] 2 QB 431, 449.
[195] *Bank of Ireland v Martin* [1937] IR 189, although in any event it was said in that case (at 202–203) that combination is confined to current accounts. See however para 15.46 below.
[196] See ch 16 below in relation to set-off agreements.

Joint account

When two or more persons have a joint account with a bank, and one of those persons has another account in his own right, separate banker/customer relationships would be in issue so as to preclude a combination.[197] **15.44**

Different names

Alternatively, the same person may open two or more accounts for his own benefit though under different names. While in this situation there is the same bank and the same customer, it is doubtful whether it can be said that there is the one relationship. In *Barclays Bank Ltd v Okenarhe*[198] Mocatta J in an unreserved judgment allowed combination of accounts in this situation, but the circumstances were exceptional and the case may be confined to its facts. **15.45**

E. The Scope of Combination

Combination is not confined to current accounts

Combination may apply in the case of two current accounts.[199] Indeed, it has been said in Ireland that combination is confined to that context,[200] while in *Re E J Morel (1934) Ltd*[201] Buckley J suggested that combination does not apply **15.46**

---

[197] *Watts v Christie* (1849) 11 Beav 546, 50 ER 928, and see also *Ex parte Morier, re Willis, Percival & Co* (1879) 12 Ch D 491 (in which the joint executors in any event were not beneficial owners of the account). Compare Ellinger, Lomnicka and Hooley, *Modern Banking Law* (3rd edn, 2002) 212–13 (referring to *Hill v Bank of Hochelaga* [1921] 3 WWR 430). *Quaere* whether a joint and several liability owing to a bank would give rise to a combination under general law. In *York City and County Banking Co v Bainbridge* (1880) 43 LT 732, 734 Hawkins J contemplated that possibility, but he assumed that the right in question took the form of a right in the bank to set one account against another, as opposed to a notion that the accounts in any event are combined. The better view is that combination does not apply in this situation. If a number of the joint and several debtors are customers of the bank, it could hardly be said that the liability is combined at one and the same time with all the customers' individual accounts in credit. In the absence of an agreement for a set-off, the bank should be confined to a set-off, either as a procedural defence to an action at law under the Statutes of Set-off or pursuant to the insolvency legislation. Combination may apply, however, in relation to joint accounts in the same names. See *Houben v Bank of Nova Scotia* (1970) 3 NBR (2d) 366, 374.

[198] [1966] 2 Lloyd's Rep 87.

[199] *Garnett v M'Kewan* (1872) LR 8 Ex 10; *Re E J Morel (1934) Ltd* [1962] 1 Ch 21, 30, 31–32; *Clark v Ulster Bank Ltd* [1950] NILR 132.

[200] *Bank of Ireland v Martin* [1937] IR 189, 202–203; Earley, 'Set-off Rights Available to Banks in Ireland' [1997] 4 Journal of International Banking Law 153, 154. In *National Westminster Bank Ltd v Halesowen Presswork and Assemblies Ltd* [1972] AC 785, 819 Lord Kilbrandon referred to the case of two current accounts, but that would seem to have been in the context of providing an example, as opposed to a definition, of combination.

[201] [1962] 1 Ch 21, 31–32.

where accounts are of a different character, for example when a customer has a current account and another account which is not a current account.[202] Combination should not be so limited, however, in principle it would appear to extend to accounts of a different character, including non-current accounts, unless there is an agreement, express or implied, to keep them separate.[203] Thus, when Roskill J (as he then was) at first instance in the *Halesowen* case[204] characterized combination as a manifestation of or a right analogous to the exercise of the banker's right of lien,[205] he said of the lien, and inferentially of combination, that it is 'a right which is of general application and not in principle (apart from special agreement whether express or implied) limited to current or other similar accounts'. For example, there is authority for the view that an overdrawn current account and a deposit account may be regarded as combined,[206] at least when the deposit account is at call. If the deposit is withdrawable after a specified period of notice by the customer, Roskill J in the *Halesowen* case[207] considered that the deposit would be treated as separate until the expiration of the requisite period after the customer has given notice, whereupon combination may apply. Similarly the Ontario Court of Appeal in *Deep v Bank of Montreal*[208] accepted that a bank was entitled to apply the proceeds of a maturing term deposit against an overdrawn current account.

---

[202] Compare Buckley LJ's later, and more general, discussion in *Halesowen Presswork and Assemblies Ltd v Westminster Bank Ltd* [1971] 1 QB 1, 46, in particular his reference to *Re European Bank* (1872) LR 8 Ch App 41 and *Mutton v Peat* [1900] 2 Ch 79 as examples of combination. Those cases each concerned a current account and a loan account, as opposed to accounts of the same character. In *Oceanica Castelana Armadora SA v Mineralimportexport* [1983] 1 WLR 1294 Lloyd J held that a Mareva injunction granted in relation to a defendant's assets, which included a deposit with a bank, should be varied so as to allow the bank to exercise any right of 'set-off' that it may have in respect of facilities afforded by the bank to the defendant prior to the injunction. See para 15.76 below. In particular, Lloyd J referred to a right of 'set-off' against the deposit in respect of interest accruing to the bank on term loans provided to the defendant, and also in respect of payments made by the bank on letters of credit opened at the request of the defendant. The judgment however was premised on the assumption that the bank had such a right of 'set-off'. The nature of the right in that case was not explored. In particular, it is not clear if Lloyd J considered that the common law principle of combination applied, or whether it was based on set-off clauses in the facility documentation.

[203] See paras 15.50–15.62 below.

[204] [1971] 1 QB 1, 19.

[205] See however para 15.03 above.

[206] *Re K (Restraint Order)* [1990] 2 QB 298. The bank in that case had a letter of set-off, but Otton J (at 304) considered the position in relation to combination apart from the letter. See also *Wallinder v Imperial Bank of Canada* [1925] 4 DLR 390, 392; *Houben v Bank of Nova Scotia* (1970) 3 NBR (2d) 366, 374; *O'Hearn v Bank of Nova Scotia* [1970] SCR 341 (savings account and loan account). In Ireland, compare *Bank of Ireland v Martin* [1937] IR 189, 203–204.

[207] [1971] 1 QB 1, 21–22. In Australia, see also Weaver and Craigie, *The Law Relating to Banker and Customer in Australia* (looseleaf) vol 1, [7.1000], referring to *Marosvary v Bank of NSW* (WA District Court, Gunning DCJ, 23 May 1979).

[208] (1991) 47 OAC 319.

There have also been instances in which combination has been recognized in rela- **15.47**
tion to a loan account and a current account in credit.[209] More recent cases suggest
that combination ordinarily would not apply in that situation,[210] but the reason
given is not that combination is confined to current accounts, or accounts of the
same character, but rather that, in the circumstances, the courts usually imply an
agreement that the accounts are to be kept separate. It is the implied agreement
which results in their separation, as opposed to a view that the different nature of
the accounts precludes combination.[211] Moreover, there is authority which suggests that combination may apply to a loan account and a deposit account upon
which the customer may not draw cheques, if the accounts are presently payable
upon demand. [212]

Bills of exchange and promissory notes

The broader view of combination is also reflected in some cases in which a bank **15.48**
held a bill of exchange or a promissory note upon which its customer was liable,
and the courts recognized that the bank could appropriate the customer's account
in credit towards satisfaction of the bill or the note.[213] It is not made clear in the reports of some of the cases whether the bank obtained the bill or the note as a result
of discounting it for the customer, or whether the bank obtained it from a third

---

[209] *Re European Bank* (1872) LR 8 Ch App 41; *Mutton v Peat* [1900] 2 Ch 79; *Re Tonkin* (1933)
6 ABC 197 (esp at 210–211). See also *Hamilton v Commonwealth Bank of Australia* (1992) 9 ACSR
90, 106. In Canada, see *Re Sutcliffe & Sons Ltd* [1933] 1 DLR 562 and *Ross v Royal Bank of Canada*
(1965) 52 DLR (2d) 578 (esp at 587–590).

[210] See para 15.52 below.

[211] Thus, Lord Denning MR and Buckley LJ in the Court of Appeal in *Halesowen Presswork and
Assemblies Ltd v Westminster Bank Ltd* [1971] 1 QB 1, 34, 46 accepted the earlier cases as examples
of combination.

[212] *Barclays Bank Ltd v Okenarhe* [1966] 2 Lloyd's Rep 87 (the sum paid to the customer being
treated as a loan).

[213] *National Bank of New Zealand v Heslop* (1882) NZLR 1 CA 47 (in which the customer's
claim against the bank was for damages, for failure to honour a cheque, so that it could not have
been a case of set-off of mutual debts under the Statutes of Set-off); *Royal Trust Co v Molsons Bank*
(1912) 8 DLR 478; *Re T C Marines Ltd* (1973) 34 DLR (3d) 489. See also *Ontario Bank v
Routhier* (1900) 32 OR 67, *Coulls v English, Scottish and Australian Chartered Bank* (1872) 6
SALR 44 (in which the proceeds of the bill of exchange discounted by the bank for the customer
were appropriated by the bank to the customer's earlier overdue bill held by the bank) and *Baker
v Lloyd's Bank Ltd* [1920] 2 KB 322, 327 (the bank's right against the credit balance on the current account being described as a 'lien'). In *Pollard v Ogden* (1853) 2 El & Bl 459 it is not clear if
the bank, having paid the bill as indorser, was entitled to debit its customer's account, or whether
a defence of set-off under the Statutes of Set-off was in issue. Compare *Rogerson v Ladbroke* (1822)
1 Bing 93, in which the bank received notice of the customer's death before the promissory note
matured. It is also necessary to distinguish cases such as *Rogerson v Ladbroke* (in relation to the bill
of exchange) and *Roy v Canadian Bank of Commerce* (1917) 38 DLR 742, in which the bill was
made payable at the bank. If a customer of a bank accepts a bill and makes it payable at the bank,
that fact constitutes authority to the bank to apply the customer's funds in paying the bill. See
Kymer v Laurie (1849) 18 LJQB 218.

party.[214] The discounting of bills of exchange has been described as a method by which the functions of a bank are effected,[215] so that it may take place as part of the banker and customer relationship. If on the other hand a bank obtains a bill or a note upon which the customer is liable as a result of a dealing with a third party, it would be difficult to say that the customer's obligation to the bank arises out of the banker/customer relationship,[216] when the negotiation of the bill or the note to the bank took place outside that relationship. In that circumstance combination should not apply.[217]

Presently matured obligations

15.49   A combination only arises when the accounts are otherwise presently payable,[218] which in this context includes presently payable on demand.[219] Thus a combination may not be based upon an obligation to the bank that will only mature at a future date, or an obligation that is merely contingent,[220] unless there is an agreement to the contrary.[221]

---

[214] See *Royal Trust Co v Molsons Bank* (1912) 8 DLR 478, *Ontario Bank v Routhier* (1900) 32 OR 67 and *Coulls v English, Scottish and Australian Chartered Bank* (1872) 6 SALR 44. In *National Bank of New Zealand v Heslop* (1882) NZLR 1 CA 47 the report states that the bank discounted the bill, but it is not clear for whom. The bill was accepted by the customer, but it was drawn by third parties (Stratford and Coupe) and it was made payable at another bank.

[215] *Commissioners of the State Savings Bank of Victoria v Permewan Wright & Co Ltd* (1913) 19 CLR 457, 471, *per* Isaacs J, but compare Lord Denning in *United Dominions Trust Ltd v Kirkwood* [1966] 2 QB 431, 448–449.

[216] See paras 15.39–15.45 above.

[217] In *Flanagan v National Bank Ltd* [1939] IR 352 a customer was liable to a bank on promissory notes otherwise than as a result of the bank having discounted them for her, and it was held that the bank could not appropriate the customer's deposit in satisfaction of the notes.

[218] *Matthews v Geraghty* (1986) 43 SASR 576, 580. Compare *Agra and Masterman's Bank v Hoffman* (1864) 34 LJ Ch 285, which concerned equitable set-off. In the *Hoffman* case, bankers refused to honour cheques drawn by a customer on an account in credit because of an unmatured liability of the customer on some bills of exchange. The customer accordingly brought an action against the bank for damages and for payment of the balance of the account. After the action was commenced several of the bills, to a larger amount than the balance, were dishonoured, whereupon the bankers filed a bill in equity for an account and for an injunction to restrain the action at law. Stuart VC granted the injunction, on the ground that the customer's legal right was impeached in equity. However it is difficult to see what connection there was between the demands which would have been sufficient to give rise to an equitable set-off on that ground. See paras 4.02–4.28 above.

[219] As in the case of a bank's liability to its customer on a current account in credit. Compare *Joachimson v Swiss Bank Corp* [1921] 3 KB 110.

[220] *Rogerson v Ladbroke* (1822) 1 Bing 93, 130 ER 39; *Bower v Foreign and Colonial Gas Co* (1874) 22 WR 740. See also *Jeffryes v Agra and Masterman's Bank* (1866) LR 2 Eq 674, 680, *per* Sir William Page Wood VC ('you cannot retain a sum of money which is actually due against a sum of money which is only becoming due at a future time'), *Ontario Bank v Routhier* (1900) 32 OR 67, 68, and *Paget's Law of Banking* (11th edn, 1996) 525–6 (criticizing Abbott CJ in *Bolland v Bygrave* (1825) 1 Ry & M 271, 171 ER 1017 with respect to a banker's lien on securities, although Abbott CJ's judgment was cited with evident approval by Ungoed-Thomas J in *Re Keever* [1967] 1 Ch 182, 189–190). Compare *Baker v Lloyd's Bank Ltd* [1920] 2 KB 322, in which the declaration of insolvency was held to constitute a repudiation of the obligation to pay the bills of exchange at maturity.

[221] See paras 15.66–15.70 below.

F. Express and Implied Agreements to Keep Accounts Separate

It is not necessary to show an agreement between the bank and the customer that **15.50** the accounts should be combined. If combination would otherwise apply, the principle is that two or more accounts kept by a customer with a bank give rise to a single debt unless there is an agreement, express or implied, to keep them separate.[222] This is a conclusion of law[223] which follows from the circumstance that there is a single banker/customer relationship.[224]

The mere act of opening two or more accounts does not constitute an agreement **15.51** to keep them separate.[225] On the other hand, there may be an agreement to separate out an account after the accounts have been established. For example, a customer may have a number of accounts with a bank which otherwise would be regarded as combined, but the parties may agree to strike a balance on one or more of the accounts on the basis of an account stated,[226] so that the balance on that account may be sued for separately. In *Cumming v Shand*[227] the course of dealing between the bank and the customer was held to give rise to an implied agreement that a current account would not be debited with the sums paid on the customer's behalf by the bank, and the bank was required to give reasonable notice of its intention to discontinue the arrangement. If a customer gives a cheque to his bank with instructions to cash it and pay him the proceeds, as opposed to crediting the proceeds to an account, the better view is that the instructions would preclude a combination in relation to the proceeds,[228] although there is authority in Australia which suggests the contrary.[229]

---

[222] See Roskill J at first instance in *Halesowen Presswork and Assemblies Ltd v Westminster Bank Ltd* [1971] 1 QB 1, 20–21 (who incorrectly characterized the right as an aspect of the banker's lien: see para 15.03 above), and Lord Denning in the Court of Appeal in the *Halesowen* case (at 35), each criticizing the dictum of Swift J in *W P Greenhalgh and Sons v Union Bank of Manchester* [1924] 2 KB 153, 164 suggesting that the customer's assent to a combination is required. See also Lord Kilbrandon in the House of Lords in *National Westminster Bank Ltd v Halesowen Presswork and Assemblies Ltd* [1972] AC 785, 819 (in relation to two current accounts) and *Re Bank of Queensland Ltd* [1997] 2 Qd R 129, 137–138.

[223] In *Ex parte Morier* (1879) 12 Ch D 491, 498 James LJ said that, 'in point of law there was but one account'. Compare Dr McCracken, *The Banker's Remedy of Set-off* (2nd edn, 1998) 27–30, who has sought to explain combination on the basis of an implied term.

[224] See para 15.03 above.

[225] *Halesowen Presswork and Assemblies Ltd v Westminster Bank Ltd* [1971] 1 QB 1, 35, *per* Lord Denning MR.

[226] *Siqueira v Noronha* [1934] AC 332, 337, and see also *Opal Maritime Agencies Pty Ltd v 'Skulptor Konenkov'* (2000) 98 FCR 519, 568.

[227] (1860) 5 H & N 95, 157 ER 1114.

[228] *Rouxel v Royal Bank of Canada* [1918] 2 WWR 791.

[229] *Coulls v English, Scottish and Australian Chartered Bank* (1872) 6 SALR 44.

Current account and a loan account

15.52 A customer may have a loan from a bank and at the same time have a current account in credit. While there are cases which suggest that the accounts may be regarded as combined,[230] the generally accepted view is that there is an implied agreement that they should be kept separate.[231] The reason, as Scrutton LJ explained, is that: 'No customer could otherwise have any security in drawing a cheque on his current account if he had a loan account greater than his credit balance on current account.'[232] In New South Wales, on the other hand Giles JA justified the conclusion in terms that the loan account and the current account are not kept separate simply for convenience, but rather to serve different functions inimical to their consolidation.[233] The view that there is no combination is subject to an agreement to the contrary.[234] As Lord Cross of Chelsea remarked in the House of Lords in the *Halesowen* case,[235] a loan account and a current account are regarded as separate 'unless the bank makes it clear to the customer that it is retaining the right at any moment to apply the credit balance on the current account in reduction of the debt on the loan account'. Roskill J at first instance in the *Halesowen* case[236] postulated that, if a customer has a loan account on (say) seven

---

[230] *Re European Bank* (1872) LR 8 Ch App 41; *Mutton v Peat* [1900] 2 Ch 79; *Re Tonkin* (1933) 6 ABC 197, 210–211. See also *Hamilton v Commonwealth Bank of Australia* (1992) 9 ACSR 90, 106. In Canada, see *Re Sutcliffe & Sons Ltd* [1933] 1 DLR 562 and *Ross v Royal Bank of Canada* (1965) 52 DLR (2d) 578 (esp at 587–590).

[231] *Buckingham & Co v London and Midland Bank* (1895) 12 TLR 70 (action for damages for failing to honour the customer's cheques); *Bradford Old Bank Ltd v Sutcliffe* [1918] 2 KB 833 (in which the Court of Appeal held that sums paid into a current account, in the period after a guarantee relating both to that account and a loan account had ceased to be a continuing guarantee, could not be considered as constituting satisfaction of the indebtedness on the loan account, with the result that the surety remained liable for the sum outstanding on the loan account); *Re E J Morel* (*1934*) *Ltd* [1962] 1 Ch 21, 30–31; *Halesowen Presswork and Assemblies Ltd v Westminster Bank Ltd* [1971] 1 QB 1, 20, 22 CA, *per* Roskill J (at first instance), 34, *per* Lord Denning MR, and, on appeal in the House of Lords ([1972] AC 785), *per* Lord Cross of Chelsea at 809 and Lord Kilbrandon at 819; *Bhogal v Punjab National Bank* [1988] 2 All ER 296, 300; *Cinema Plus Ltd v Australia and New Zealand Banking Group Ltd* (2000) 49 NSWLR 513, 543, 549. See also *York City and County Banking Co v Bainbridge* (1880) 43 LT 732; *Re Deague* (1951) 15 ABC 197, 202; *Barclays Bank Ltd v Okenarhe* [1966] 2 Lloyd's Rep 87, 96. Compare *Matthews v Geraghty* (1986) 43 SASR 576, in which the bank had an express contractual right of set-off.

[232] *Bradford Old Bank Ltd v Sutcliffe* [1918] 2 KB 833, 847. See also Pickford LJ at 839.

[233] *Cinema Plus Ltd v Australia and New Zealand Banking Group Ltd* (2000) 49 NSWLR 513, 549 para 142.

[234] 'The critical question must always be, "What was the contract?" and not whether a particular account or accounts bear one title rather than another.' *Halesowen Presswork and Assemblies Ltd v Westminster Bank Ltd* [1971] 1 QB 1, 21, *per* Roskill J (at first instance). Thus Roskill J (at 22) distinguished *Re European Bank* (1872) LR 8 Ch App 41 and *Mutton v Peat* [1900] 2 Ch 79 on the ground that it was not part of the arrangements between the parties in those particular cases that the accounts should be kept separate.

[235] *National Westminster Bank Ltd v Halesowen Presswork and Assemblies Ltd* [1972] AC 785. 809. See also Roskill J at first instance [1971] 1 QB 1, 22.

[236] [1971] 1 QB 1, 21.

days call, and a current account in credit, it would be a term of the contract between the parties that the accounts may be 'set off' if the call is made and payment is not tendered within the requisite period. As a general proposition this is doubtful. Unless the terms of an agreement between the parties to keep accounts separate are such that the agreement is determinable by notice having immediate effect,[237] the better view is that any such implied term would require the bank to give reasonable notice of termination. This would be consistent with the view that reasonable notice is required to close a current account in credit.[238]

Current account and other accounts

The justification for implying a term that a current account in credit is to be kept **15.53** separate from a loan account should be equally relevant in relation to other debts owing to the bank, for example where the customer is indebted to the bank on a bill discount facility,[239] or where the customer has defaulted under a lease facility provided by the bank and is indebted for a termination amount.[240]

Deposit account upon which cheques cannot be drawn

That justification would not be relevant however to a loan account and a deposit **15.54** account upon which the customer may not draw cheques, and there is authority which suggests that those accounts may be combined, at least when the deposit and the loan are both presently payable on demand.[241]

Termination of the banker/customer relationship—the customer's liquidation

Roskill J at first instance in the *Halesowen* case considered that the implied agree- **15.55** ment to keep separate a loan account and a current account in credit only subsists while the banker/customer relationship remains in existence.[242] The relationship

---

[237] See para 15.28 above.

[238] See paras 15.27–15.28 above.

[239] See para 15.48 above.

[240] *Cinema Plus Ltd v Australia and New Zealand Banking Group Ltd* (2000) 49 NSWLR 513, 549 para 142, *per* Giles JA, and see also Sheller JA at 543 paras 113 and 114 (the 'loan facilities' included the lease finance facility: see at 529 para 72). In any event, it is suggested that amounts due to a bank under a lease may be precluded from combination on the more fundamental ground that they are not due to the bank in its capacity as banker. See para 15.42 above.

[241] This would seem to be the effect of Mocatta J's decision in *Barclays Bank Ltd v Okenarhe* [1966] 2 Lloyd's Rep 87, in which the sum paid to the customer was treated as a loan. Compare *Rogerson v Ladbroke* (1822) 1 Bing 93, 130 ER 39, in which the bank had notice of the customer's death before the loan secured by the promissory note matured. See para 15.114 below.

[242] [1971] 1 QB 1, 23–24, following *Re Keever* [1967] 1 Ch 182. See also *Thomas v Howell* (1874) LR 18 Eq 198, 202–203 (death of customer). The *Halesowen* case involved an express agreement between the bank and the customer to keep the accounts separate, but Roskill J's opinion evidently was also intended to encompass the implied agreement arising in the case of a loan account and a current account. See also Lord Kilbrandon in the House of Lords [1972] AC 785, 819. Compare *Re Johnson & Co Ltd* [1902] 1 IR 439, in which the agreement was entered into specifically in contemplation of a winding up.

terminates upon the death or insanity of the customer or upon his bankruptcy or its liquidation,[243] but not upon the appointment of a receiver.[244] When termination occurs, Roskill J accepted that the bank becomes entitled to combine the accounts.[245] He suggested that the judgment of Buckley J in *Re E J Morel (1934) Ltd*[246] constitutes authority to the contrary, but he said that on this point Buckley J should be regarded as wrong.[247] Two points may be made in relation to the general proposition, and Roskill J's criticism of Buckley J's judgment in *Re E J Morel*. The first is that both the *Morel* and *Halesowen* cases concerned a company in liquidation. If a banker/customer relationship is terminated as a result of the bankruptcy or liquidation of the customer, the question should not arise as to whether the accounts may be combined after the termination of the implied agreement to keep them separate. This is because of the prevailing view as to the operation of the insolvency set-off section, that it takes effect automatically upon the occurrence of the bankruptcy or liquidation.[248] There would not be any scope for combination after the set-off has occurred.[249] The second point is that in any event there is nothing in Buckley J's judgment which is inconsistent with the general proposition accepted by Roskill J.

15.56 *Re E J Morel* concerned the Companies Act 1948, s 319(4) which, subject to certain limitations, conferred a right of priority in the liquidation of a company in favour of a person who had advanced money for the payment of wages to an employee of the company.[250] A company's current account was substantially overdrawn. This account (the No 1 account) was frozen, and a No 2 account, being a

---

[243] *Halesowen v National Westminster Bank Ltd* [1971] 1 QB 1, 24, *per* Roskill J. A demand by a bank upon a customer for repayment does not terminate the banker and customer relationship. See *National Bank of Greece v Pinios Shipping Co No 1* [1990] 1 AC 637, 684.

[244] *Direct Acceptance Corp Ltd v Bank of New South Wales* (1968) 88 WN (Pt 1) (NSW) 498, 504 (in which there was an express agreement not to set off).

[245] *Quaere* whether combination in this circumstance would require an act, or at least an assertion, of combination, given that the banker/customer relationship has terminated. See also paras 15.28 and 15.29 above.

[246] [1962] 1 Ch 21.

[247] Conversely, Roskill J said (at [1991] 1 QB 1, 23) that it could not be contended that the accounts remain separate after bankruptcy or liquidation without also contending that *Re Keever* [1967] 1 Ch 182 was wrongly decided. That conclusion does not necessarily follow, however. In the *Keever* case, a customer had three accounts with a bank, one in credit and two in debit (being a 'private' account and a loan account). The bank received a cheque from the customer for collection. It collected the cheque the next day, and on that day the customer also became bankrupt. Ungoed-Thomas J held that the bank had a lien on the cheque for the amounts owing, and that it was entitled to set off the proceeds against the debit balances. However that does not require a conclusion about combination of the accounts. The case is explicable on the ground that the indebtedness on the private and the loan accounts, whether combined or separate, was secured by the lien, and that upon receipt of the proceeds the bank was entitled to apply them against the amounts owing, as an incident of the security conferred by the lien. See para 15.115 below.

[248] See para 6.79 *ff* above.

[249] The contrary seems to have been assumed in the House of Lords in *Halesowen* [1972] AC 785, 807, *per* Viscount Dilhorne, 811–812, *per* Lord Cross of Chelsea, 820, *per* Lord Kilbrandon.

[250] See now the Insolvency Act 1986, ss 175 and 386, referring to Sch 6 (in particular category 5).

normal business current account, and a No 3 account, called a wages account, were opened. The company was allowed to draw on the No 3 account in order to pay the wages of its employees. However it was a term of the arrangement that the No 2 account had to have at all times a credit balance in excess of the debit on the No 3 wages account. Buckley J held that the credit balance on the No 2 account should be treated as reducing the debit on the wages account, rather than the debit on the No 1 account. Therefore the bank had a reduced claim to priority for sums advanced for the payment of wages, and it was left with a right of proof on the No 1 account for which no priority was accorded. In order for the bank to have succeeded in its claim to priority, it had to be shown that the bank had actually made advances for the purpose of paying wages. Buckley J said that, because of the agreement to freeze the No 1 account so as no longer to be capable of being operated in the ordinary way as a current account, it had assumed the character of a loan account.[251] Therefore the arrangement usually implied in the case of a loan account and a current account in credit was applicable, that the No 1 frozen account and the No 2 current account should be regarded as separate and distinct,[252] which in turn meant that payments credited to the No 2 account could not be regarded as having operated to reduce the prior debit balance on the No 1 account.[253] In so far as the No 3 wages account was concerned, the parties had agreed that any debit balance on that account was always to be covered by a credit balance on the No 2 account, which led Buckley J to conclude that these two accounts were not separate, but were interdependent. In substance, they constituted the one account. The bank itself therefore had not made any advances for the payment of wages, except to the extent that at the final date the debit on the wages account was less than the credit on the No 2 account. Rather, the wages had been paid from the customer's own 'money' in the No 2 account. Buckley J was not concerned with the question whether a combination could occur after termination of the banker/customer relationship as a result of the liquidation. Indeed, this should not be an issue in any event if the insolvency set-off section takes effect automatically upon the occurrence of the liquidation.[254] The essence of his analysis simply was that the bank had not made an advance on each occasion when resort was had to the wages account for the purpose of paying wages. The source of the payment instead was the company's own 'money' in the No 2 account. The

---

[251] Similarly, the assertion by counsel in the *Halesowen* case [1971] 1 QB 1, 9, that once the overdrawn No 1 account in that case was frozen it became for all practical purposes a loan account, was not disputed. See eg in the House of Lords [1972] AC 785, 809, *per* Lord Cross of Chelsea, 819, *per* Lord Kilbrandon.

[252] See also *Re Deague* (1951) 15 ABC 197, 202. Riley J's dictum in *Re Shaw* (1977) 31 FLR 118, 122, that independently of the letter of set-off the bank had a right to combine the working current account in credit with the frozen overdrawn current account, should be regarded as doubtful.

[253] Compare the arrangement adopted in *Re James R Rutherford & Sons Ltd, Lloyd's Bank Ltd v Winter* [1964] 1 WLR 1211.

[254] See para 15.55 above.

point upon which the judgment proceeded was how the accounts operated prior to the liquidation, as opposed to how they were to be dealt with after the liquidation.

15.57 Buckley J then went on to consider the position that would have applied if he was wrong in the view that he had taken in relation to the No 2 account and the wages account, in other words if all three accounts were separate so that the debit balance on the wages account indeed represented sums advanced by the bank for the purpose of paying wages. In that circumstance he said that the insolvency set-off section would have operated on the basis that the claim which otherwise would be preferred in the winding up should be the first claim to be brought into account with the creditor's own liability to the company. This would have had the effect that the debit balance on the wages accounts would have been paid by a set-off against the credit balance on the No 2 account, and so the same result would have been achieved. This aspect of Buckley J's judgment is probably no longer good law following *Re Unit 2 Windows Ltd*.[255] In that case Walton J advocated a different approach to the question of set-off where a creditor of a company in liquidation has both a preferred and a non-preferred claim. He had recourse to the maxim that equality is equity, and accordingly considered that a set-off should occur rateably as between the claims.[256] On that analysis, *Re E J Morel* is a case in which the operation of the principle of combination prior to the liquidation produced a different result to that which would have obtained after the liquidation under the insolvency set-off section on the assumption that the accounts were separate.

Freezing an overdrawn current account and opening a new account

15.58 An arrangement similar to that in the *Morel* case is sometimes adopted when a bank is concerned as to the solvency of a customer with a substantially overdrawn current account. The overdrawn account is frozen, and a new current account is opened through which the customer's current business henceforth is to pass. This second current account is required to remain in credit, the intention being that the customer's indebtedness on the frozen account should be reduced progressively by occasional payments into it from the credit balance on the operating current account. As Buckley J noted in the *Morel* case, the act of freezing an overdrawn current account converts it into a loan account so that, even apart from any express agreement between the parties that the bank should not have a right of set-off,[257] the courts would usually find an implied agreement to the effect that the accounts should not be combined during the subsistence of the banker/customer relationship. The presumption that the accounts are intended to be separate will not be

---

[255] [1985] 1 WLR 1383.
[256] See paras 6.114–6.119 above.
[257] As in *Direct Acceptance Corporation Ltd v Bank of New South Wales* (1968) 88 WN (Pt 1) (NSW) 498.

rebutted by the agreement that the debit on the frozen account should be reduced progressively, as long as the intention is that any transfers from one account to the other should be made on the instructions of the customer rather than on the initiative of the bank alone, albeit at the insistence of the bank.[258] Nor would the presumption be rebutted by an agreement that interest due on the frozen overdraft may be debited to the new account.[259] It may be, however, that, prior to this arrangement, the customer had given a letter of set-off to the bank authorizing the bank at any time without notice to apply a credit balance on any of the customer's accounts as payment of any account in debit. In the absence of a later agreement negativing the operation of the letter, this may have the effect that the usual implied term precluding combination in such cases would not arise.[260]

Agreement to exclude set-offs

The parties may wish to exclude a set-off in the event of the customer's bankruptcy **15.59** or liquidation. For example, a company in financial difficulty may have proposed a moratorium with its creditors, or it may intend to realize its assets as a means of paying its debts. In order to prevent a situation arising in which its bank alone is benefited by any payments deposited with it, the parties may agree that the company's overdrawn account should be frozen and that a new account should be opened which is to remain in credit, and moreover that the bank should not be entitled to set off the credit balance on this new account against the debit balance on the frozen account. The House of Lords in *National Westminster Bank Ltd v Halesowen Presswork and Assemblies Ltd*[261] struck down this form of arrangement in the event of the bankruptcy or liquidation of the customer, by holding that the operation of the set-off section in the insolvency legislation cannot be excluded by agreement between the parties.[262] As a result, it is necessary for the customer in this situation to open a working account with a different bank if it is intended that the first bank is not to be preferred by means of a set-off at the expense of the other creditors in the event of bankruptcy or winding-up proceedings. The Cork Committee described this as 'an unnecessary and undesirable complication',[263] and recommended that a creditor should be permitted to agree in advance with a debtor to waive the operation of the insolvency set-off section, particularly given that the creditor is the party who otherwise would be benefited by a set-off. This is a salutary proposal, and it is a matter for regret that in England a provision giving effect to it was not included in the Insolvency Act 1986.

---

[258] *Re E J Morel (1934) Ltd* [1962] 1 Ch 21, 26.
[259] This is apparent from the *Halesowen* case [1972] AC 785.
[260] See eg *Re Shaw* (1977) 31 FLR 118, and para 15.67 below.
[261] [1972] AC 785.
[262] See paras 6.71–6.72 above.
[263] *Cork Committee Report* 306.

Bank's conduct precluding combination

15.60 Roskill J at first instance in the *Halesowen* case[264] said that a bank by its actions may preclude itself from asserting a combination. This observation requires further explanation. If the general principle is that accounts are combined in a single debt unless there is an agreement to the contrary, the bank's actions should not preclude a combination unless those actions have the effect of giving rise to an agreement with the customer that henceforth the accounts should be regarded as separate, or the bank is otherwise estopped from asserting that there is an agreement in those terms. For example, the fact that a bank debits and credits interest to each account separately is not sufficient to preclude the bank from asserting that the accounts are combined.[265] Nor should separate bank statements have that effect. Separate statements merely reflect the undoubted fact that a bank has a number of accounts entered in its books, and, as Lindley MR noted in *Mutton v Peat*,[266] no matter how many accounts a bank may have entered in its books the amount due to the bank is the balance of all of them.

Deposit for a specific purpose

15.61 If money is deposited with a bank for a specific purpose known to the bank, for example, in order to provide funds to meet a particular cheque or bill of exchange, the courts may imply an agreement that the money should not be combined with an overdrawn account.[267]

Consequences of an agreement to keep accounts separate

15.62 Usually an express or an implied agreement that accounts are separate would simply mean that each account should be considered as giving rise to a separate debt. It would deprive the bank of the right to act unilaterally based upon an assumption that there is only one debt arising out of the banker/customer relationship.

---

[264] [1971] 1 QB 1, 19.

[265] See para 15.18 above. Mocatta J, in expressing this view in *Barclays Bank Ltd v Okenarhe* [1966] 2 Lloyd's Rep 87, 98, postulated that, in certain circumstances, the crediting of interest on an account might be evidence that the parties had reached agreement that the accounts should be kept separate. He conceded however that 'the circumstances would probably have to be somewhat exceptional since . . . the general practice is that interest is either credited or debited after calculation by reference to one account and not to all the accounts between a customer and his bank'.

[266] [1900] 2 Ch 79, 85.

[267] *Garnett v M'Kewan* (1872) LR 8 Ex 10, 13 (citing *Hill v Smith* (1844) 12 M & W 618); *MPS Constructions Pty Ltd v Rural Bank of New South Wales* (1980) 4 ACLR 835, 841–842 (account opened for retention money under a building contract). See also *W P Greenhalgh and Sons v Union Bank of Manchester* [1924] 2 KB 153. Compare *Oceanica Castelana Armadora SA v Mineralimportexport* [1983] 1 WLR 1294, in which the customer had deposited money for the purpose of securing a guarantee intended to be given by the bank to a third party, though that purpose failed. In some cases there may also be a trust, as in *Barclays Bank Ltd v Quistclose Investments Ltd* [1970] AC 567. See para 15.83 below.

The bank could not, for example, dishonour a cheque on the basis of the customer's entire position with the bank. Depending on the terms of the agreement, however, it may not have the additional effect of negating a right of set-off under the Statutes of Set-off as a defence to an action at law by the customer for payment of the balance on an account in credit,[268] or indeed under the insolvency set-off section in the event that the recommendation of the Cork Committee that contracting out should be permitted is ever adopted.[269] The agreement would bring about the very situation necessary for a set-off, ie mutual and independent cross-demands. In relation to the Statutes of Set-off, the defence is only available in the case of mutual debts.[270] The customer's action therefore would have to be for payment of a debt, in the form of the balance standing to the credit of an account. The bank would not have a defence under the Statutes if the customer is suing instead for damages, for example for failure to honour a cheque.

G. Combination and Nominee Accounts

An account may be opened in the name of A who, unknown to the bank, is merely **15.63** a nominee for B. If B also happens to be a customer in his own right, and with a separate account of his own, the bank, when it discovers the nomineeship, may wish to assert that a credit balance on one of the accounts is combined with a debit balance on the other. Notwithstanding some comments in the Court of Appeal in *Bhogal v Punjab National Bank*[271] that suggest that combination may occur where the beneficial interest of B is clear and indisputable, and that the bank in that circumstance may dishonour cheques drawn on the nominee account,[272] the better view is that combination is not available in this situation. When an account is opened and, unknown to the bank at the time, it is a nominee account, the

---

[268] *Bank of Ireland v Martin* [1937] IR 189, 205; *Flanagan v National Bank Ltd* [1939] IR 352. See also *Hill v Smith* (1844) 12 M & W 618, 631, 152 ER 1346, 1351 (money deposited with a bank for a specific purpose).

[269] See para 15.59 above. See also eg *Ex parte Pearce, re Langmead* (1841) 2 Mont D & De G 142, and *Pedder v The Mayor, Aldermen, and Burgesses of Preston* (1862) 12 CB (NS) 535, 142 ER 1251, with respect to special-purpose local government accounts. The denial of a set-off in cases such as *Hill v Smith* (1844) 12 M & W 618, 631, 152 ER 1346, 1351 and *Bell v Carey* (1849) 8 CB 887, 137 ER 757, when the customer's assignees in bankruptcy sued for damages rather than for money had and received, may be explained on the ground that, before the Bankruptcy Act 1861, a damages claim could neither be proved in the bankruptcy nor set off. See para 10.48 above.

[270] See paras 2.14–2.28 above.

[271] [1988] 2 All ER 296, 301, *per* Dillon LJ.

[272] *Barclays Bank Ltd v Okenarhe* [1966] 2 Lloyds Rep 87 (see para 15.45 above) would also support this view. In *Uttamchandami v Central Bank of India*, unreported but noted in (1989) 139 New Law Journal 222, it is not clear if Lloyd LJ's remarks (at 223) concerning a case in which the account is indisputably a nominee account were intended to refer to the availability of equitable set-off as a defence to an action for payment of the balance on that account, or to combination giving the bank a right to dishonour cheques.

nominee would be the customer, not the person for whom the account is held. The banker/customer relationship is one of contract, and the nominee ordinarily would be the contracting party.[273] The same banker/customer relationship therefore would not be in issue in relation to the accounts for the purpose of a combination. There may, however, be instances in which the person for whom the nominee has opened the account is disclosed to the bank,[274] so that that person is regarded by all parties as the customer. Depending on the circumstances, combination may be appropriate in relation to that account and another account possessed by the customer.

15.64   Consider that a cheque payable to B is deposited into A's account for the purpose of collection on behalf of B, and B happens to be separately indebted to the bank. In *Abbey National plc v McCann*,[275] Carswell LJ in the Northern Ireland Court of Appeal suggested that, when a cheque deposited in those circumstances was collected and the proceeds credited to A's account, there was an arguable case that the part of A's account representing B's beneficial entitlement to the proceeds could be combined with B's debt.[276] Ordinarily that should not be the case, however. The debt is owing to the bank by B, but the deposit is into A's account. The deposit does not occur in the course of B's banking relationship with the bank, but rather through the medium of A's relationship. Separate banker/customer relationships therefore are in issue, so that there should not be a combination.

15.65   If combination does not apply, a set-off nevertheless may be available as a defence to an action at law for payment of the credit balance on one of the accounts. This is the form of set-off that was in issue in *Bhogal v Punjab National Bank*, and it is based upon the Statutes of Set-off.[277] The Statutes are confined to mutual debts. Moreover, unlike combination, set-off under the Statutes only provides a procedural defence to an action, in the sense that the demands are not set against each other until there is judgment for a set-off.[278] For example, the defence would not entitle the bank to dishonour a cheque, and it would not avail the bank in an action against it for damages for failing to honour the cheque. Furthermore, when

---

[273] When an agent contracts on behalf of an undisclosed principal, the agent is the contracting party. See para 13.71 above.

[274] As occurred in *Re Hett, Maylor & Co* (1894) 10 TLR 412.

[275] [1997] Northern Ireland Judgments Bulletin 158, 172–173.

[276] Carswell LJ (at [1997] NIJB 158, 172) referred to this as 'equitable set-off', which he said was 'basically the right to combine accounts'. See also Hutton LCJ at 180. Compare Nicholson LJ, who said (at 183) that there was no right of 'equitable set-off'.

[277] The set-off in issue in *Bhogal v Punjab National Bank* was an equitable set-off based upon equity acting by analogy with the Statutes. See para 11.12 above. While 'combination' appears in the headnote to the report of the *Bhogal* case, it does not appear in the judgments, and in that respect the headnote is misleading. At first instance in the *Bhogal* case Scott J said that: 'This is not a case . . . in which the bank is seeking to exercise its common law right as a banker of combining accounts.' See [1988] 2 All ER 296, 305.

[278] See para 2.33 above.

A commences proceedings against a bank for payment of a credit balance on an account, and the bank asserts that the account is a nominee account and that the true owner, B, is separately indebted to the bank, the bank will not be granted leave to defend unless there is clear and indisputable evidence of the nomineeship.[279]

H. Agreements Permitting Combination

A customer may agree with his bank that the bank may set off or consolidate or combine all or any of his accounts at any time without notice.[280] An agreement in those terms contemplates an act of combination by the bank.[281] In considering the effect of the agreement, however, two situations should be distinguished.

15.66

In the first place, it may be that two accounts are in issue which prima facie come within the ambit of the law of combination, being accounts arising pursuant to the one banker/customer relationship, but that in the circumstances the courts usually would imply an agreement that the accounts are to be kept separate, for example so that the customer can deal safely with third parties in the knowledge that he has an account in credit against which he can draw cheques. It is for that reason that the courts usually find an implied agreement that a loan account should be kept separate from a current account in credit.[282] Yet, in a case such as this, one would have thought that an agreement empowering the bank to combine the accounts at any time without notice[283] would abrogate the very reason for implying a term to keep them separate.[284] Therefore, even though the agreement may seem to contemplate some form of act of combination by the bank, it may be that the fact that the customer has authorized the bank to effect a set-off at any time without notice would mean that the accounts in any event are combined in a single debt. Alternatively, it may be that the agreement contemplates that a credit balance on an account may be applied in satisfaction of a liability in circumstances in

15.67

---

[279] See paras 11.11–11.23 above.

[280] In *Voyer v Canadian Imperial Bank of Commerce* [1986] 1 WWR 174 a bank improperly exercised a contractual right of set-off against a deposit account, and the customer sued in conversion in respect of the sum removed from the account. Conversion is not an appropriate form of action in this circumstance, however, since conversion relates to interference with the right to possession of a chattel (see *MCC Proceeds Inc v Lehman Bros International (Europe)* [1998] 4 All ER 675, 685–686), and a bank account is not a chattel. The appropriate remedy is a declaration that the account was improperly debited. See *Clerk and Lindsell on Torts* (18th edn, 2000) 744 n 52.

[281] Depending on the terms of the agreement, this may not require a book entry. It may suffice if the bank asserts that the accounts are combined. See para 15.67 below.

[282] See para 15.52 above.

[283] As in *Matthews v Geraghty* (1986) 43 SASR 576. See also the letters of set-off in *Re Shaw* (1977) 31 FLR 118, 120 and *Re K (Restraint Order)* [1990] 2 QB 298, 299–300.

[284] This may explain Riley J's comments in *Re Shaw* (1977) 31 FLR 118, 122, given that a closed overdraft account is regarded as a loan account and therefore it cannot be the subject of a combination with another current account in credit. See para 15.56 above.

which a combination would not otherwise be recognized, not because of an implied agreement in order to safeguard a credit account against which cheques may be drawn, but because there are separate banker/customer relationships. Thus, the letter may allow the bank to appropriate a customer's separate credit balance as satisfaction of a joint liability,[285] or it may entitle the bank to consolidate the accounts of the various companies in a group. An appropriation of the credit balance could only arise as a result of an act by the bank which is authorized by the set-off agreement. If an act of combination is required, it may not necessitate an actual book entry.[286] An assertion that the accounts have been consolidated or combined may suffice.[287]

Contingent obligation

15.68 Whether a right of set-off conferred by a set-off agreement extends to an amount which is not presently due and payable depends on the construction of the agreement.[288] In that regard, a bank is sometimes empowered to set off an account in credit against a liability which is contingent. Professor Goode has suggested that an agreement in those terms may be interpreted in either of two ways.[289] The more likely construction is that the bank is entitled to suspend payment of the account in credit until such time as the liability may vest, followed, if it does vest, by a set-off. Alternatively, there may be cases where the effect of the agreement is that the bank's liability on the account in credit is immediately cancelled to the extent of the maximum contingent liability, with an obligation to re-credit the customer if and to the extent that the contingent liability does not become an actual liability.

Account subject to an assignment or a trust

15.69 An agreement authorizing a bank to set off accounts will not be effective in relation to an account where moneys credited to the account were the subject of a prior assignment or trust in favour of a third party, and the bank had notice of the assignment or trust.[290] If the bank did not have notice, it will obtain priority if it was a bona fide purchaser for value.[291]

---

[285] See para 15.44 above.

[286] There may be an express provision to that effect in the agreement. See eg the letter of set-off in *Re Shaw* (1977) 31 FLR 118 (the material terms of the letter are set out at 120).

[287] See Roskill J at first instance in *Halesowen Presswork and Assemblies Ltd v National Westminster Bank Ltd* [1971] 1 QB 1, 19, and also *Direct Acceptance Corporation Ltd v Bank of New South Wales* (1968) 88 WN (Pt 1) (NSW) 498, 502.

[288] Compare *Matthews v Geraghty* (1986) 43 SASR 576, 580.

[289] Goode, *Legal Problems of Credit and Security* (2nd edn, 1988) 173.

[290] *Re Marwalt Ltd* [1992] BCC 32.

[291] *Neste Oy v Lloyds Bank plc* [1983] 2 Lloyd's Rep 658, 666; *Re Marwalt Ltd* [1992] BCC 32, 38. See paras 15.85–15.104 below.

Customer's liquidation

An exercise of a contractual right of combination or set-off in relation to a cus- **15.70**
tomer's credit account after the commencement of the customer's liquidation, in
circumstances where the insolvency set-off section does not apply, would be
struck down as contrary to the pari passu principle.[292]

I. Different Currencies

An issue that is yet to be determined is whether combination applies to accounts **15.71**
in different currencies.[293]

A discussion of the issue must begin with the fundamental point, that combin- **15.72**
ation is an accounting situation in which the existence and amount of one party's
liability to the other can only be ascertained by looking at the ultimate balance of
all the accounts. The concept is dynamic in nature. At any particular point in time
there is as a matter of law only one debt for the balance.[294] Therefore, for combination to apply to a foreign currency account, there should be a defined mechanism for converting the account into sterling such that at any point in time both
parties could calculate the combined position. Further, since the basis of combination is the banker/customer relationship, the exchange rate should be the rate
that the bank would make available to the customer for the account in question.
In this sense it would differ from a currency conversion effected for the purpose of
proof of debts in a bankruptcy or a liquidation, or for the purpose of enforcing a
foreign currency judgment obtained in accordance with the decision of the House
of Lords in *Miliangos v George (Frank) Textiles Ltd.*[295] In those situations, a general
objectively ascertainable market rate would suffice.[296] This would not be appropriate, however, in the case of combination, which should look to the rate that
would be offered by that bank to that customer.

What rate, then, would be applied for conversion if the parties have not expressly **15.73**
agreed a conversion mechanism? It could be said that there is an implied term in
the contract between the bank and its customer that conversion would occur at
the bank's rate for the relevant currency applicable at the time, for example the rate
quoted by the bank on its web site. There are problems with that view, however.

---

[292] See para 16.18 below.
[293] See generally Horrigan, 'Combining Bank Accounts in Different Currencies—A Conceptual
Analysis' (1991) 65 Australian Law Journal 14.
[294] See para 15.03 above.
[295] [1976] AC 443.
[296] For example, the Practice Direction published after the decision in *Miliangos v George (Frank)
Textiles Ltd* [1976] AC 443 referred to the rate current in London at the close of business on the day
in question. See [1976] 1 WLR 83.

In the first place, it is difficult to see why the customer should be taken to have agreed to accept that rate, given that it may be lower than that offered by other financial institutions. Secondly, the quoted rate may be expressed to be applicable only to transactions up to a stated amount. Thirdly, the bank's rate appearing on the screen may only be used as a guide by the bank when it is asked to quote a rate in a particular case. Rates move during the day, and the rate that is quoted to a customer may vary from the screen rate, depending on the bank's perception of where the market is going. Therefore, at any point in time a customer with a large foreign currency account may not be in a position to know with certainty what its combined position is. It could be said that the customer can request the bank at any time to advise the appropriate rate for conversion so that it may know the position at that time, but that would not be a convenient solution. Moreover it may not be feasible outside banking hours. While the bank may continue to trade in foreign currencies overnight, this may be limited to only some currencies, and the customer therefore may not be in a position to obtain advice in relation to a particular currency after hours.

15.74 In *Garnett v M'Kewan*[297] Bramwell B justified the bank's right to dishonour a cheque drawn on an account where there was another account in debit on the ground that, 'to limit [the customer's] drawing to the amount of his total actual balance is no hardship on him, for he always knows, or can know if he likes, the state of his account as a whole'. As a corollary, where the customer at any point in time cannot know the state of the accounts on a combined basis with certainty, it is suggested that combination should not apply.[298] In any event, the bank's applicable rate to an extent would be within the bank's discretion, which would hardly be a satisfactory basis for combination from the customer's point of view, particularly where large amounts of money are in issue. Having said that, there is authority in Canada to the effect that combination may apply in relation to foreign currency accounts. In *Deep v Bank of Montreal*[299] the Ontario Court of Appeal held that a bank was entitled to apply a maturing Deutschmark term deposit against a Canadian dollar overdraft. The court simply assumed however that combination applies to foreign currency accounts. Further, there was no discussion of the conversion mechanism.

15.75 Alternatively, the bank may have an express contractual right to combine accounts, including foreign currency accounts. Unlike for the common law prin-

---

[297] (1872) LR 8 Ex 10, 15.

[298] Other writers however have expressed the contrary view. See Wood, *English and International Set-off* (1989) 97; McCracken, *The Banker's Remedy of Set-off* (2nd edn, 1998) 32; Goode, *Legal Problems of Credit and Security* (2nd edn, 1988) 171; Ellinger, Lomnika and Hooley, *Modern Banking Law* (3rd edn, 2002) 209. Compare *Paget's Law of Banking* (11th edn, 1996) 537.

[299] (1991) 47 OAC 319.

ciple of combination, an act of combination would be required in this situation.[300] In such a case the agreement should specify the mechanism for converting foreign currency accounts into sterling for the purpose of a combination.

J. Mareva Injunctions and Restraint Orders

In *Oceanica Castelana Armadora SA v Mineralimportexport*,[301] the plaintiff in a suit   **15.76** against a foreign defendant had obtained a Mareva injunction restraining the defendant from removing or disposing of its assets situated within the jurisdiction up to a stated maximum amount. Barclays Bank held funds deposited with it by the defendant. However, the bank had also made substantial loans to the defendant, and so it applied to the court for an order to vary the injunction in order that it might exercise its right of 'set-off'. Lloyd J granted the variation on the grounds that a Mareva injunction was not intended to interfere with the ordinary rights and remedies of a third party. He accepted that the funds held by the bank prima facie were covered by the wording of the injunction before him, and that therefore it was necessary that the bank should come to court for a variation.[302] His Lordship said that this was unsatisfactory, and suggested that henceforth all Mareva injunctions intended to be served on banks should contain a suitable proviso exempting the bank's right of 'set-off' from the operation of the injunction.[303] If however the case is truly one of combination, it is not at all clear that a bank should be required to apply to the court for a variation in the absence of a specific proviso protecting its rights. In such a case a right to set off independent cross-demands is not in issue. Rather, the bank is entitled to say that there is only one debt owing by or to the customer for the balance of all the accounts arising in the course of the banker/customer relationship, unless a particular item has been separated out by agreement. Therefore a particular account in credit with the bank should not be regarded as a separate asset of the customer coming within the ambit of a Mareva injunction, if there are other accounts in debit which must be brought into account in order to ascertain the debt owing by the bank or the customer to the other. Thus, Canadian courts have recognized that, when a bank makes an entry in its books giving effect to the principle of combination, the entry itself does not constitute payment of an account in debit, since there was in any

---

[300] See paras 15.66–15.67 above. Depending on the terms of the agreement, an assertion that the accounts are combined, without a book entry to that effect, may suffice. See para 15.29 above.

[301] [1983] 1 WLR 1294.

[302] See also *Project Development Co Ltd SA v KMK Securities Ltd* [1982] 1 WLR 1470.

[303] Lloyd J expressed approval of a clause suggested by counsel: 'Provided that nothing in this injunction shall prevent [the bank] from exercising any rights of set-off it may have in respect of facilities afforded by [the bank] to the defendants prior to the date of this injunction'.

event only one debt for the balance.[304] Consistent with that approach, Otton J in *Re K (Restraint Order)*[305] held that a bank's assertion of a right of combination in relation to a deposit account and an overdraft account was not in conflict with the terms of a restraint order under section 8 of the Drug Trafficking Offences Act 1986, which restrained all dealings with the accounts. As his Lordship noted,[306] combination in truth is merely an accounting procedure in order to ascertain the existence and amount of one party's liability to the other.

15.77 Alternatively, the 'set-off' asserted by the bank may not be in respect of accounts that are combined in that sense, but rather it may be based upon a contractual right of set-off in respect of separate debts. In that circumstance, the bank would require the protection contemplated by Lloyd J.

15.78 When an account in credit has been frozen as a result of a Mareva injunction, Lloyd J considered that the bank's right of 'set-off' should be protected in relation to all liabilities of the customer arising in connection with facilities granted to the customer before the bank received notification of the injunction. Thus, he considered that the bank should be permitted to debit the account in respect of any liability which it may incur on confirmed letters of credit opened at the request of the customer before notice.[307] Further, he said that any right of set-off possessed by the bank may be exercised in respect of interest accruing due both before and after notification, provided that the facility in question was granted to the customer before notification.[308]

K. Preferences

15.79 Given the true nature of the principle of combination, that in the absence of an express or implied agreement to the contrary an account in credit and another account with a debit balance are combined in a single debt, it should follow that the mere fact that the bank may make an entry in its books giving effect to the combination by itself should not constitute a preference, since there was in any event only one debt.[309]

---

[304] *Re Sutcliffe & Sons Ltd, ex p Royal Bank* [1933] 1 DLR 562 (esp at 569); *Ross v Royal Bank of Canada* (1965) 52 DLR (2d) 578; *Re T C Marines Ltd* (1973) 34 DLR (3d) 489; *Re Plasky* (1981) 39 CBR 186. For the same reason, the book-keeping entry does not constitute a seizure of assets. See *Deep v Bank of Montreal* (1991) 47 OAC 319.

[305] [1990] 2 QB 298.

[306] [1990] 2 QB 298, 304.

[307] See *Oceanica Castelana* [1983] 1 WLR 1294, 1301.

[308] [1983] 1 WLR 1294, 1301.

[309] This has been held to be the case in Canada. See *Re Sutcliffe & Sons Ltd, ex p Royal Bank* [1933] 1 DLR 562 (esp at 569); *Ross v Royal Bank of Canada* (1965) 52 DLR (2d) 578; *Re T C Marines Ltd* (1973) 34 DLR (3d) 489; *Re Plasky* (1981) 39 CBR 186. See also *Salter and Arnold Ltd v Dominion Bank* [1926] SCR 621, which nevertheless proceeded upon a different analysis. In Australia, Riley J in *Re Shaw* (1977) 31 FLR 118, 123 inclined to the view that a payment for the purpose of the

Rather, the question whether the preference section[310] applies should be ascertained by an examination of the circumstances surrounding the deposits made by the customer with the bank.[311]

It may be, however, that a customer has two accounts which, it has been expressly **15.80** or impliedly agreed, are to be regarded as separate, but the bank is empowered by a letter of set-off to combine them.[312] The question whether the bank's action in doing so constitutes a preference is considered later in the context of a discussion of set-off agreements.[313]

L. Trust Accounts

(1) Introduction

A customer may be a trustee in respect of an account in credit opened in his name. **15.81** This by itself would not preclude the application of the principle that all the accounts kept by a customer with a bank are combined in a single debt.[314] If however the bank has knowledge of the trust, the principle of combination would not apply.[315] Nor may the bank rely on a set-off agreement entered into with the

---

preference section occurred when the cheque was deposited with the bank and presented for payment (13 September), or alternatively when the funds represented by the cheque were made available to the bank, as opposed to when the bank debited the account with a sum sufficient to cover the overdrawn account. See also *Matthews v Geraghty* (1986) 43 SASR 576; *Re Tonkin* (1933) 6 ABC 197, 210–211. In *Re Shaw, quaere* why the date of payment was not simply the date of deposit of the cheque (12 September).

[310] See the Insolvency Act 1986, s 340, and, for companies, s 239.

[311] As in *Hamilton v Commonwealth Bank of Australia* (1992) 9 ACSR 90 (following (at 109–110) *Matthews v Geraghty* (1986) 43 SASR 576), although in the circumstances of that case Hodgson J accepted (at 106) that the accounts at the date of the payment were separate.

[312] This assumes that the giving of the letter of set-off does not have as a consequence that there is no implied agreement to keep the accounts separate. See para 15.67 above.

[313] See paras 16.04–16.17 below.

[314] See *Union Bank of Australia, Ltd v Murray-Aynsley* [1898] AC 693; *Bank of New South Wales v Goulburn Valley Butter Co Pty Ltd* [1902] AC 543, 550; *Clark v Ulster Bank Ltd* [1950] NILR 132. Compare *Garnett v M'Kewan* (1872) LR 8 Ex 10, 14, *per* Pigott B, 14–15, *per* Bramwell B.

[315] *Bank of New South Wales v Goulburn Valley Butter Co Pty Ltd* [1902] AC 543, 550. See also *Re Branston & Gothard Ltd* [1999] Lloyd's Rep Bank 251; *Bodenham v Hoskyns* (1852) 2 De G M & G 903, 905, 42 ER 1125, 1126; *Houben v Bank of Nova Scotia* (1970) 3 NBR (2d) 366, 381; *Law Society of Upper Canada v Toronto Dominion Bank* (1995) 36 CBR (3d) 220. In the latter case a bank employed a solicitor to act for it in relation to a loan, and credited the solicitor's trust account with the amount of the proposed loan. The trust account, although in credit, had a shortfall as a result of defalcations by the solicitor, and when the bank was informed of the shortfall it purported to debit the account with the amount that it had credited to it. It sought to justify the debit on the ground that it was entitled to revoke the trust and then to set off the solicitor's resulting debt to it against the part of the trust account constituted by its funds credited to the account. Farley J in the Ontario General Division held that the bank was not entitled to do so. He said that, when a trust account has a shortfall, it is held on trust on a pro rata basis for all persons whose moneys are in the account, and there was no separate part of it to which the bank alone was entitled, and which could be the subject of a set-off.

customer in that circumstance,[316] unless the beneficiaries of the trust had consented to it or the circumstances otherwise are such as to give rise to an estoppel.[317] If the customer becomes bankrupt or goes into liquidation, the fact of the trust would mean that there would be a lack of mutuality in equity,[318] which in turn would have the consequence that the bank could not set off the accounts under the insolvency set-off section. For that reason it may be crucial that, despite the trust, combination should apply.

15.82 The principle that an account in a customer's name which is known to be a trust account cannot be combined with another account held by the customer in his personal capacity potentially could be explained on either of two grounds. If the customer when he opened the trust account made it clear that it was subject to a trust, for example by specifically labelling it as a trust account, the circumstances could be regarded as giving rise to an implied agreement that it is to be kept separate. In fact, that approach is not reflected in the cases.[319] Rather, the principle that combination does not apply has been based simply on the notion that the bank cannot use moneys which in equity are the property of a third party in order to satisfy the customer's personal debt. If on the other hand the bank did not know of the trust, it should be able to obtain the benefit of the trust account in a combination where the defence of bona fide purchaser for value is available.[320]

(2) The Requirement of a Trust

15.83 The money deposited by the customer must have been impressed with a trust in his hands. An important decision in that regard is *Barclays Bank Ltd v Quistclose Investments Ltd*,[321] in which the House of Lords held that a trust may arise when a sum of money is advanced by A to B for a specific purpose, for example, in order to pay B's creditors, or, as in the *Quistclose* case itself, in order that B may pay a dividend. The fact that the money is advanced by way of loan does not preclude the court from finding that it is subject to a trust. As Lord Wilberforce remarked in delivering the judgment of the Law Lords,[322] 'There is surely no difficulty in recognising the co-existence in one transaction of legal and equitable rights and

---

[316] *Pannell v Hurley* (1845) 2 Coll 241, 245, 63 ER 716, 718; *Neste Oy v Lloyds Bank plc* [1983] 2 Lloyd's Rep 658; *Royal Bank of Scotland plc v Wallace International Ltd* [2000] EWCA Civ 16 (see paras 8 and 48).

[317] Compare *Royal Bank of Scotland plc v Wallace International Ltd* [2000] EWCA Civ 16.

[318] See paras 11.04–11.07 above.

[319] See paras 15.105–15.108 below.

[320] See *Re Marwalt Ltd* [1992] BCC 32, 38; *Neste Oy v Lloyds Bank plc* [1983] 2 Lloyd's Rep 658, 666.

[321] [1970] AC 567.

[322] Lord Reid, Lord Morris of Borth-y-Gest, Lord Guest, Lord Pearce and Lord Wilberforce.

remedies.'[323] Lord Wilberforce analysed the position in terms of a primary and a secondary trust. He said that there is a primary trust in favour of the persons intended to benefit from the payment, and A has an equitable right to see that the money in fact is applied to this designated purpose. If the purpose is carried out, B becomes a debtor to A. If however the purpose fails, it becomes necessary to see whether the parties intended that a secondary trust should arise in favour of A. In the instant case the purpose had failed,[324] and in the circumstances Lord Wilberforce said that it was clear that the parties had intended that there should be a secondary trust. Moreover, the bank with which B had deposited the money had been informed that the money had been raised by means of a loan advanced for the sole purpose of enabling B to satisfy its liability to pay the dividend. That was sufficient to give the bank notice that the money was impressed with a trust, notwithstanding that it may not have been aware of the identity of the lender[325] or of the detailed terms of the trust.[326] Because of the notice, the bank could not set off the account into which the trust money had been paid against B's overdraft. The nature of the trust in the *Quistclose* case has been much debated. In *Twinsectra Ltd v Yardley*[327] Lord Millett rejected the suggestion that there are successive trusts. He favoured the view that the lender remains the beneficial owner of the money, but with a mandate given to the transferee to apply it for the stated purpose.[328] But whatever its nature, the possibility of a trust in these circumstances is now widely accepted.

The justification for the trust in the *Quistclose* case was the presumed intention of the parties. It should be contrasted with the constructive trust found in *Neste Oy v Lloyds Bank plc*,[329] which was based upon a perception of what fairness and good conscience required. In the *Neste Oy* case, a principal made a number of payments **15.84**

---

[323] [1970] AC 567, 581. Note also the comments of Dixon J in *Palette Shoes Pty Ltd v Krohn* (1937) 58 CLR 1, 30. The money may be advanced in accordance with an antecedent contractual obligation, rather than by way of loan. In *Carreras Rothmans Ltd v Freeman Mathews Treasure Ltd* [1985] 1 Ch 207, Peter Gibson J applied *Barclays Bank Ltd v Quistclose Investments Ltd* in a case in which the money was paid by A into a specially labelled bank account to be used by B solely for the purpose of paying C, when B was liable as a principal to C but with a right of reimbursement from A.

[324] Why had the purpose failed as a result of the resolution to wind up the company? See Goodhart and Jones, 'The Infiltration of Equitable Doctrine into English Commercial Law' (1980) 43 MLR 489, 494, referring to the statement of facts by Harman LJ in the Court of Appeal [1968] 1 Ch 540, 549–551, and *Twinsectra Ltd v Yardley* [2002] 2 AC 164, 191–192 at para 98, *per* Lord Millett.

[325] See Lord Wilberforce in the House of Lords [1970] AC 567, 582.

[326] See Sachs LJ in the Court of Appeal in *Barclays Bank Ltd v Quistclose Investments Ltd* [1968] 1 Ch 540, 567.

[327] [2002] UKHL 2 AC 164, 186 at para 77 *et seq*.

[328] See also Lord Hoffmann at [2002] 2 AC 164, 168–169 at para 13, whose opinion, though confined to the circumstances in issue, was consistent with Lord Millett's analysis. Lord Hutton at para 25 agreed with Lord Hoffmann and Lord Millett that there was a trust, and Lord Slynn of Hadley at para 2 agreed with Lord Hoffmann's reasons.

[329] [1983] 2 Lloyd's Rep 658.

to its agent, by way of credit to a bank account, for the purpose of meeting expenses. One such payment was received after the directors of the agent's holding company had determined that the group and its members should cease trading and that the group's bank should be requested to appoint a receiver.[330] Bingham J held that this gave rise to a trust, notwithstanding that payments received from the principal in the normal course were not intended to be kept separate from the agent's own funds, but were paid by the principal directly into the agent's general banking account, so that it was apparent that the parties had contracted on a debtor/creditor basis.[331] In the case of the payment credited to the agent after the resolution to cease trading, the trust was justified on the ground that no honest person receiving money from another in that circumstance, when there was bound to be a total failure of consideration, could in good conscience retain it. Further, Bingham J accepted that the bank in all probability was aware of the decision to cease trading before it credited the money to the agent's account.[332] Therefore it had prior notice of the circumstances giving rise to the constructive trust, and so it was obliged to refund the money to the principal notwithstanding that the account was the subject of a contractual right of set-off in favour of the bank. In some respects *Neste Oy v Lloyds Bank plc* is similar to *Sinclair v Brougham*,[333] in which depositors with a building society were allowed to follow their money by reason of the fact that the purpose for which they had handed the money to the directors was incapable at law of fulfilment.[334] The cases are distinguishable, however. The 'purpose' in *Sinclair v Brougham* was that the money should be deposited with the building society on the basis of a banker/customer relationship, and that it should be recoverable at a later date as a debt. That purpose failed because repayment was ultra vires. The depositors lacked the personal remedy against the building society for which they had bargained, and so the court found a proprietary remedy. On the other hand, the principal in the *Neste Oy* case still had the personal right of a creditor against the agent which had been the basis of their relationship. The justice of finding a constructive trust is by no means clear when the principal provided the money as an unsecured creditor and still retained the rights of a creditor.[335] The principal took the risk of the agent's insolvency, and the imposition of a constructive trust in such a case would seem to

---

[330] The sequence of events is set out at [1983] 2 Lloyd's Rep 658, 662.

[331] [1983] 2 Lloyd's Rep 658, 664–665.

[332] See [1983] 2 Lloyd's Rep 658, 667.

[333] [1914] AC 398.

[334] See *Re Diplock. Diplock v Wintle* [1948] 1 Ch 465, 540–541.

[335] See Goff and Jones, *The Law of Restitution* (5th edn, 1999) 705. Compare *Re Kayford Ltd* [1975] 1 WLR 279, in which the company had set up a separate trust account for its customers' moneys. Note the criticism of the decision in *Re Kayford* by Goodhart and Jones, 'The Infiltration of Equitable Doctrine into English Commercial Law' (1980) 43 MLR 489, 494–97, but see *Re Branston & Gothard Ltd* [1999] Lloyd's Rep Bank 251, 258–259.

confer an unjustified priority in the event of the agent's liquidation.[336] *Sinclair v Brougham* has now been overruled by the House of Lords,[337] and it is suggested that *Neste Oy v Lloyds Bank plc* similarly should be reconsidered.[338]

(3) The Defence of Bona Fide Purchaser for Value

The bank in these cases asserts that it is entitled to look upon the credit balance on the trust account as combined with the trustee's personal account in debit. The beneficiaries on the other hand say that the moneys deposited with the bank were subject to a trust in their favour, that those moneys can be traced into the bank's debt to the customer on the account in credit, that the account accordingly is held on trust for them, and that the fact of the trust therefore precludes combination in relation to the account. The bank may then respond by way of defence that it was a bona fide purchaser for value without notice of the moneys deposited with it,[339] so that it is not affected by the trust in relation to either those moneys or the account into which they can be traced. On that basis, the bank says that it should not be precluded by the trust from looking upon the accounts as combined.[340] **15.85**

The defence of bona fide purchaser raises the issues of the bank's knowledge and whether it gave value. **15.86**

Knowledge of the trust

Sometimes the account will be headed in such plain terms that the bank cannot fail but to know that it is a trust account, for example when a county treasurer opened accounts headed 'Superannuation Fund' and 'Police Account'.[341] If on the other hand there is nothing on the face of the account to show that it stood on any different footing from other accounts kept by the customer, or if there is nothing to indicate that the moneys deposited by the customer were impressed with a trust, the Privy Council in *Union Bank of Australia Ltd v Murray-Aynsley*[342] said that it is incumbent upon the *cestuis que trust* 'to prove that the moneys for which they now sue were, in the knowledge of the bank, trust funds'. In that regard a **15.87**

---

[336] The resolution in the *Neste Oy* case was merely to cease trading. There is no mention in the report of a subsequent liquidation, although the resolution was based upon the directors' perception that the group and its companies could not meet credit as it fell due.

[337] *Westdeutsche Landesbank Girozentrale v Islington LBC* [1996] AC 669.

[338] In *Kingscraft Insurance Co Ltd v H S Weavers (Underwriting) Agencies Ltd* [1993] 1 Lloyd's Rep 187, 195 Harman J nevertheless referred to *Neste Oy v Lloyds Bank plc* with approval.

[339] As to the onus of proof, see *Polly Peck International plc v Nadir (No 2)* [1992] 4 All ER 769, 781.

[340] See *Neste Oy v Lloyds Bank Plc* [1983] 2 Lloyd's Rep 658, 666, and also *Re Marwalt Ltd* [1992] BCC 32, 38.

[341] *Ex parte Kingston, re Gross* (1871) LR 6 Ch App 632. See also *Greenwell v National Provincial Bank* (1883) 1 Cab & El 56; *Re Branston & Gothard Ltd* [1999] Lloyd's Rep Bank 251 ('client money requirement' account).

[342] [1898] AC 693, 697.

bank would have knowledge if it wilfully shut its eyes to the obvious, since this is regarded as actual knowledge.[343] Moreover, it suffices if the bank has knowledge of the circumstances giving rise to a trust.[344] It is not necessary that the bank should appreciate the legal consequences of those circumstances.

The difference between knowledge and notice

15.88 When a prior equitable interest in property is asserted against a transferee of the legal title to the property, the question whether the transferee takes free of the prior equitable interest traditionally is expressed in terms whether the transferee is a bona fide purchaser of the legal interest for value without notice. Notice includes the equitable doctrine of constructive notice.[345] But consistent with the statement of the principle in *Union Bank v Murray-Aynsley*, when money is paid into a bank, 'knowledge' rather than 'notice' has been said to be the appropriate concept.[346] These expressions are not synonymous.[347] Knowledge is a narrower concept. As Vinelott J remarked in *Eagle Trust plc v SBC Securities Ltd*:[348]

> However, 'notice' is often used in a sense or in contexts where the facts do not support the inference of knowledge. A man may have actual notice of a fact and yet not know it. He may have been supplied in the course of a conveyancing transaction with a document and so have actual notice of its content, but he may not in fact have read it; or he may have read it some time ago and have forgotten its content . . . . So also by statute a man may be deemed to have actual notice of a fact which is clearly not within his knowledge.

In particular, the doctrine of constructive notice was developed in the field of property transactions in which a full and complete investigation of title is called for, and there is time to investigate title.[349] An investigation of that nature is inappropriate in the case of a commercial transaction involving the payment of money in the ordinary course of business,[350] and the courts have shown a marked reluc-

---

[343] *English and Scottish Mercantile Investment Co v Brunton* [1892] 2 QB 700, 707–708; *John T Ellis Ltd v Walter T Hinds* [1947] 1 KB 475, 483; *Macquarie Bank Ltd v Sixty-Fourth Throne Pty Ltd* [1998] 3 VR 133, 163.

[344] *Barclays Bank Ltd v Quistclose Investments Ltd* [1970] AC 567, 582.

[345] Constructive notice is a wholly equitable doctrine. See *English and Scottish Mercantile Investment Co v Brunton* [1892] 2 QB 700, 708.

[346] *Polly Peck International plc v Nadir (No 2)* [1992] 4 All ER 769, 781–782, *per* Scott LJ.

[347] *Cresta Holdings Ltd v Karlin* [1959] 3 All ER 656, 657, *per* Hodson LJ; *Carl Zeiss Stiftung v Herbert Smith & Co (No 2)* [1969] 2 Ch 276, 296; *Re Montagu's Settlement Trusts* [1987] 1 Ch 264, 271, 285, *per* Megarry VC; *Eagle Trust plc v SBC Securities Ltd* [1992] 4 All ER 488, 497–498, *per* Vinelott J; *Polly Peck International plc v Nadir (No 2)* [1992] 4 All ER 769, 781, *per* Scott LJ. In *Montagu's Settlement Trusts* Megarry VC said (at 285) that a person is not to be taken to have knowledge of a fact that he once knew but has genuinely forgotten, and that it is doubtful whether there is a general doctrine of 'imputed knowledge' that corresponds with 'imputed notice'.

[348] [1992] 4 All ER 488, 497–498.

[349] See Vinelott J in *Eagle Trust plc v SBC Securities Ltd* [1992] 4 All ER 488, 507, referring to *Manchester Trust v Furness* [1895] 2 QB 539, 545. See also *Cowan de Groot Properties Ltd v Eagle Trust plc* [1992] 4 All ER 700, 759–760.

[350] *Eagle Trust plc v SBC Securities Ltd* [1992] 4 All ER 488, 507–508.

tance to extend the doctrine to those circumstances.[351] On the other hand, where it is not the custom or practice to investigate title, and there is no recognized procedure for doing so, it has been said that an analogous concept may apply in a situation in which an honest and reasonable man would have made inquiry.[352] It has also been said, however, that in an ordinary commercial context it would be difficult to establish that the circumstances were such as to put a party to the transaction on inquiry.[353]

Trust moneys paid directly into an overdrawn account

The issue of a trust in relation to combination of accounts arises in the situation in which trust moneys are paid into an account in credit, so that they can be traced into that account, and the beneficiaries of the trust assert that their consequent interest in the account precludes a combination in respect of it. A similar issue may arise in another context. Instead of being paid into a separate account, the trust moneys may be paid in breach of trust directly into the trustee's overdrawn private account, and the bank in an action against it for repayment of the trust moneys asserts that they are not repayable because they were used to reduce or discharge the debit balance on the trustee's account.[354] In principle, this should produce the same result. If combination is merely an accounting exercise in order to ascertain what the debt is at any particular time,[355] it should not make any difference whether trust funds are deposited in an account in credit where there is another overdrawn account, or whether they are credited directly to the trustee's personal overdrawn account in reduction of the debt on that account. It is relevant therefore to consider

15.89

---

[351] *Greer v Downs Supply Co* [1927] 2 KB 28; *The Njegos* [1936] P 90, 103; *Northside Development Pty Ltd v Registrar-General* (1987) 11 ACLR 513, 523; *Polly Peck International plc v Nadir (No 2)* [1992] 4 All ER 769, 782.

[352] See Millett J in *El Ajou v Dollar Land Holdings plc* [1993] 3 All ER 717, 739 and in *Macmillan Inc v Bishopsgate Investment Trust plc* [1995] 1 WLR 978, 1000, and also his extra-judicial discussion in 'Equity—The Road Ahead' (1995) 9 Tolley's Trust Law International 35, 40. See also *Neste Oy v Lloyds Bank plc* [1983] 2 Lloyd's Rep 658, 667, and Scott LJ's reference to 'constructive knowledge' in the context of an equitable proprietary tracing claim against a bank in *Polly Peck International plc v Nadir (No 2)* [1992] 4 All ER 769, 776, 781–782.

[353] Millett, 'Equity's Place in the Law of Commerce' (1998) 114 LQR 214, referring to *Sanders Bros v Maclean & Co* (1883) 11 QBD 327, 343 and *Barclays Bank plc v Quincecare Ltd* [1992] 4 All ER 363, 377, *per* Steyn J ('trust, not distrust, is also the basis of a bank's dealings with its customers'). In particular, Millett J warned in *Macmillan Inc v Bishopsgate Investment Trust plc (No 3)* [1995] 1 WLR 978, 1014 that bank officers are not detectives. See also *Lloyds Bank Ltd v Chartered Bank of India, Australia and China* [1929] 1 KB 40, 73, and *Lipkin Gorman v Karpnale Ltd* [1987] 1 WLR 987, 1006. Further, if an inquiry is made and an answer is received which the inquirer may reasonably believe to be true, he is entitled to act on it. See *Selangor United Rubber Estates Ltd v Cradock (No 3)* [1968] 1 WLR 1555, 1607, and also *Baden v Société Générale pour Favoriser le Developpement du Commerce et de l'Industrie en France SA* [1992] 4 All ER 161, 246.

[354] See eg *Thomson v Clydesdale Bank, Ltd* [1893] AC 282; *British America Elevator Co Ltd v Bank of British North America* [1919] AC 658; *Westpac Banking Corp v Savin* [1985] 2 NZLR 41. See also *Bodenham v Hoskyns* (1852) 2 De G M & G 903, 42 ER 1125.

[355] See para 15.03 above.

under what circumstances a bank would be liable when trust moneys are paid in breach of trust directly into the trustee's overdrawn account.

15.90   If trust moneys are paid to a person in breach of trust, and the recipient retains the money, or the trust money can be traced into other property held by the recipient, the beneficiaries may have a proprietary remedy.[356] This would not be the case however if the payment is made to the credit of an overdrawn bank account. When money is deposited with a bank, the money itself becomes part of the bank's general pool of assets, and ordinarily it would not be traceable into any particular asset belonging to the bank.[357] The beneficiaries therefore would have to seek a personal remedy against the bank on the basis of a constructive trust, either because the bank knowingly received trust property transferred to it in breach of trust or because it was an accessory to a breach of trust.[358] In the case of accessory liability, the test for liability is dishonesty,[359] which often would be difficult to prove, and so the beneficiaries may look instead to the question whether the bank is liable personally as having received and dealt with trust property.[360]

The bank as 'recipient'

15.91   The bank will not be regarded as a recipient of the trust moneys deposited with it unless it received them for its own use and benefit, and for that to have occurred the moneys should have brought about a reduction or discharge in the trustee's debt.[361] In that regard, the mere continuation of a running account in overdraft would not suffice to render the bank liable as a recipient.[362] The bank in that circumstance would be acting simply as the customer's agent, and not as the recipient of the money for its own use and benefit.

---

[356]   See generally *Boscawen v Bajwa* [1996] 1 WLR 328, 334–335.

[357]   *Space Investments Ltd v Canadian Imperial Bank of Commerce* [1986] 1 WLR 1072, 1074. Compare the equitable charge or lien on the bank's assets recognized by the Privy Council in *Space Investments* and also *Re Goldcorp Exchange Ltd* [1995] 1 AC 74, 109–110, as explained in *Stephenson Nominees Pty Ltd v Official Receiver* (1987) 16 FCR 536, 556, *per* Gummow J and *Bishopsgate Investment Management Ltd v Homan* [1995] Ch 211, 221–222, *per* Leggatt LJ.

[358]   *Barnes v Addy* (1874) LR 9 Ch App 244, 251–252.

[359]   *Royal Brunei Airlines v Tan* [1995] 2 AC 378; *Twinsectra Ltd v Yardley* [2002] 2 AC 164.

[360]   As in *Westpac Banking Corp v Savin* [1985] 2 NZLR 41 (see in particular at 52–53, 60, 69–70).

[361]   *Agip (Africa) Ltd v Jackson* [1990] 1 Ch 265, 292; *Nimmo v Westpac Banking Corp* [1993] 3 NZLR 218, 224–226 (criticizing the distinction drawn in *Polly Peck International plc v Nadir (No 2)* [1992] 4 All ER 769, 777 between the sterling transfers and the currency exchanges); *Stephens Travel Service International Pty Ltd v Qantas Airways Ltd* (1988) 13 NSWLR 331, 361–366; *Cigna Life Insurance New Zealand Ltd v Westpac Securities Ltd* [1996] 1 NZLR 80, 86–87 (also criticizing the distinction drawn in the *Polly Peck* case); *Sansom v Westpac Banking Corp* (1996) Aust Torts Reports 81–383 at pp 63,325–63,326; Millett, 'Tracing the Proceeds of Fraud' (1991) 107 LQR 71, 82–3. Compare Bryan, 'The Liability of Banks to Make Restitution for Wrongful Payments' (1998) 26 Australian Business Law Review 93, 106–109.

[362]   Millett, 'Tracing the Proceeds of Fraud' (1991) 107 LQR 71, 83 n 46; *Stephens Travel Service International Pty Ltd v Qantas Airways Ltd* (1989) 13 NSWLR 331, 361–366.

The degree of knowledge required

Assuming that the bank is a recipient in that sense, the question is what degree of **15.92** knowledge of the trust is required of the bank in order to make it personally liable as a recipient of the trust money paid to it. In *Thomson v Clydesdale Bank Ltd*[363] a broker was instructed to sell shares and to pay the proceeds into a bank account in the principal's name, but instead he paid the proceeds into his own overdrawn account. The House of Lords held that the bank was not obliged to repay the money to the principal. Lord Watson emphasized that it was not enough to show that the bank had acted negligently. Rather, he said that it had to be shown that the bank knew that the money did not belong to the broker and that the broker had no authority from the true owner to pay it into his bank account.[364] Lord Herschell in his judgment said that 'under ordinary circumstances' a bank that takes money in discharge of a debt is not bound to inquire into the manner in which the person paying the debt acquired the money.[365] On the other hand, he indicated that the bank would not have succeeded if it had 'reason to believe' that the money was trust money, but in the circumstances he concluded that there was no such reason to believe.[366] Similarly Lord Shand rejected the argument that the circumstances were such as to put the bank on inquiry.[367]

In an often-quoted classification, Peter Gibson J in *Baden v Société Générale pour* **15.93** *Favoriser le Developpement du Commerce et de l'Industrie en France SA*[368] accepted that knowledge can comprise any one of five different mental states. The use of these categories has been criticized on the ground that they do not have clear and precise boundaries, but may merge imperceptibly into one another.[369] Nevertheless they have formed the basis of discussion of knowledge in many of the recent cases on knowing receipt, and it has been said that assistance may still be gained by reference to them.[370] The categories are:

---

[363] [1893] AC 282.

[364] [1893] AC 282, 290.

[365] [1893] AC 282, 287. Compare *Bank of New South Wales v Goulburn Valley Butter Co Pty Ltd* [1902] AC 543, 550.

[366] [1893] AC 282, 287–288.

[367] [1893] AC 282, 293.

[368] [1992] 4 All ER 161, 235.

[369] See eg *Polly Peck International plc v Nadir (No 2)* [1992] 4 All ER 769, 777; *Koorootang Nominees Pty Ltd v Australia and New Zealand Banking Group Ltd* [1998] 3 VR 16, 105. In *Royal Brunei Airlines v Tan* [1995] 2 AC 378, 392 the Privy Council suggested, in the context of accessory liability, that the *Baden* scale of knowledge is best forgotten. See also *Twinsectra Ltd v Yardley* [2002] 2 AC 164, 195 at para 113, *per* Lord Millett.

[370] See eg *Bank of Credit and Commerce International (Overseas) Ltd v Akindele* [1999] BCC 669, 677, *per* Carnwath J (at first instance); *Koorootang Nominees Pty Ltd v Australia and New Zealand Banking Group Ltd* [1998] 3 VR 16, 85; *Macquarie Bank Ltd v Sixty-Fourth Throne Pty Ltd* [1998] 3 VR 133, 164; *Equiticorp Industries Group Ltd v The Crown* [1996] 3 NZLR 586, 604. See also *Bank of Credit and Commerce International (Overseas) Ltd v Akindele* [2001] Ch 437, 454–455, CA.

(1) actual knowledge;

(2) wilfully shutting one's eyes to the obvious;

(3) wilfully and recklessly failing to make such inquiries as an honest and reasonable man would make;

(4) knowledge of circumstances which would indicate the facts to an honest and reasonable man;

(5) knowledge of circumstances which would put an honest and reasonable man on inquiry.

15.94   In *Re Montagu's Settlement Trusts*[371] Megarry VC said that want of probity is essential for the imposition of personal liability as a constructive trustee on the knowing receipt ground, and that accordingly it is necessary to establish knowledge in categories (1), (2) and (3). This view has substantial support.[372] It was favoured by Alliott J at first instance in *Lipkin Gorman v Karpnale Ltd,*[373] by Steyn J in *Barclays Bank plc v Quincecare,*[374] and by Arden J in *Eagle Trust plc v SBC Securities Ltd (No 2).*[375] In *Dubai Aluminium Co Ltd v Salaam,*[376] Rix J commented that the test in knowing receipt cases is likely to be the same as that for knowing assistance, in other words based on dishonesty, and similarly Potter LJ in delivering the judgment of the Court of Appeal in *Twinsectra Ltd v Yardley*[377] seemed to regard honesty as the test for both knowing receipt and knowing assistance. Aikens J in *Bank of America v Arnell*[378] also shared that view. There are other opinions however that favour a more expansive approach.[379] Lord Millett on appeal in the House of Lords in the *Twinsectra* case[380] said that there is no basis for requiring dishonesty in this context, and that constructive notice of a breach of trust is sufficient. Similarly in *Houghton v Fayers*[381] Nourse LJ, with whose judgment

---

[371]   [1987] 1 Ch 264, 285.

[372]   In addition to the cases referred to below, see *Cowan de Groot Properties Ltd v Eagle Trust plc* [1992] 4 All ER 700, 758–760 (in relation to a bona fide purchaser for value); *Hillsdown Holdings plc v Pensions Ombudsman* [1997] 1 All ER 862, 902–903. See also *Eagle Trust plc v SBC Securities Ltd* [1992] 4 All ER 488, 509 in relation to commercial transactions (in other contexts, compare at 506–507).

[373]   [1987] 1 WLR 987, 1005.

[374]   [1992] 4 All ER 363, 375.

[375]   [1996] 1 BCLC 121, 152. Arden J emphasized, however, that her view was confined to cases where the receipt occurs in the discharge of a lawful debt, or at least where the case arises out of a transaction which does not itself constitute a breach of trust.

[376]   [1999] 1 Lloyd's Rep 415, 453.

[377]   [1999] Lloyd's Rep Bank 438 (in particular at 462–465 paras 101–108, and see also the extract from the first instance judgment of Carnwath J at 449 para 46).

[378]   [1999] Lloyd's Rep Bank 399, 406–407 para 15.

[379]   In *Polly Peck International plc v Nadir (No 2)* [1992] 4 All ER 769, 777 Scott LJ expressed doubt as to the sufficiency of the fifth category, but left the question open. On the other hand, he accepted (at 781–782) that constructive knowledge would suffice. See also Millett J in *El Ajou v Dollar Land Holdings plc* [1993] 3 All ER 717, 739, and, writing extrajudicially, in 'Tracing the Proceeds of Fraud' (1991) 107 LQR 71, 80–2.

[380]   *Twinsectra Ltd v Yardley* [2002] 2 AC 164, 194 at para 105.

[381]   [2000] 1 BCLC 511, 516.

Ferris J agreed, said that it is unnecessary for a finding of dishonesty to be made in a knowing receipt case. He said that it is enough for the claimant to establish that the recipient knew or ought to have known that money had been paid to him in breach of fiduciary duty. Subsequently Nourse LJ adopted a different approach in giving the judgment of the Court of Appeal in *Bank of Credit and Commerce International (Overseas) Ltd v Akindele*.[382] He reiterated his view that dishonesty is not a necessary ingredient in knowing receipt liability, and he also said that he had grave doubts as to the utility of the *Baden* categorization in this context. Rather than expressing the question in terms whether the recipient knew or ought to have known of the breach of trust, as in *Houghton v Fayers*, he suggested that there should be a single test of knowledge. He said that all that is necessary is that the recipient's state of knowledge should be such as to make it unconscionable for him to retain the benefit of the receipt. In New Zealand, on the other hand, it has been said that all five categories of knowledge are relevant to the knowing receipt head of constructive trust,[383] while in Australia it has been suggested that the first four categories may result in liability but not the fifth.[384] Alternatively, consistent with the view that has been expressed that the liability of a recipient of trust property is restitution-based,[385] there is support for the proposition that the liability should be strict but subject to defences of bona fide purchase and change of position.[386]

The law in relation to liability as a knowing recipient of trust property awaits a definitive treatment by the House of Lords. But however the issue ultimately may be determined, there is much to be said for the view that an analogous approach should be adopted when combination against a trust account is in issue, despite the difference in the way that the case is presented when combination rather than payment in reduction of an overdraft is in issue.[387] In the case of combination the **15.95**

---

[382] [2001] Ch 437.

[383] *Westpac Banking Corp v Savin* [1985] 2 NZLR 41, 52–53; *Equiticorp Industries Group Ltd v Hawkins* [1991] 3 NZLR 700, 728; *Powell v Thompson* [1991] 1 NZLR 597, 608–609. Compare *Equiticorp Industries Group Ltd v The Crown* [1996] 3 NZLR 586, 604–605 (summary), [1998] 2 NZLR 481, 636–638.

[384] *Koorootang Nominees Pty Ltd v Australia and New Zealand Banking Group Ltd* [1998] 3 VR 16, 85, 105; *Hancock Family Memorial Foundation Ltd v Porteous* (1999) 32 ACSR 124, 142 [79]. See also *Macquarie Bank Ltd v Sixty-Fourth Throne Pty Ltd* [1998] 3 VR 133, 165.

[385] *Royal Brunei Airlines v Tan* [1995] 2 AC 378, 386; *Twinsectra Ltd v Yardley* [2002] 2 AC 164, 194 at para 105, *per* Lord Millett.

[386] *Koorootang Nominees Pty Ltd v Australia and New Zealand Banking Group Ltd* [1998] 3 VR 16, 99–105; *Twinsectra Ltd v Yardley* [2002] 2 AC 164, 194 at para 105, *per* Lord Millett; Lord Nicholls, 'Knowing Receipt: The Need for a New Landmark', in Cornish (ed), *Restitution Past, Present and Future* (1998) 231. This view was criticized in *Bank of Credit and Commerce International (Overseas) Ltd v Akindele* [2001] Ch 437, 455–456, CA. In Victoria, Tadgell JA noted the point in *Macquarie Bank Ltd v Sixty-Fourth Throne Pty Ltd* [1998] 3 VR 133, 156 without offering an opinion.

[387] Indeed, this would follow if the courts were to accept that the liability of a recipient of trust property is restitution-based, and therefore liability prima facie is strict (see above), because the question then would be whether the bank could establish a defence of bona fide purchase, which is also the defence that the bank would assert in the case of combination.

beneficiaries assert their beneficial interest in the account as a reason for denying that the bank can regard the account as combined with another account of the trustee/customer, whereas when trust money is paid directly into an overdrawn account the issue arises instead in the context of an attempt to render the bank personally liable as a constructive trustee as a consequence of having received trust property. The analogy is suggested given the nature of combination of accounts,[388] and notwithstanding that the courts have emphasized the difference between the doctrines of purchaser without notice and constructive trust. [389]

15.96 One thing that is clear, however, is that a mere request by a customer that the money be put into a separate account by itself is not sufficient to constitute knowledge.[390] Nor generally is it sufficient that the bank is aware that the customer occupies a position in which he often receives money on behalf of others, for example as a solicitor or stockbroker. Thus, in *T and H Greenwood Teale v William Williams Brown and Co*[391] a solicitor paid clients' money into an 'office account', while in *Clark v Ulster Bank Ltd*[392] the money was paid by a solicitor into a 'No 2 Account'. In each case it was held that the bank did not have sufficient knowledge of the fiduciary nature of the account to prevent combination.[393] In that regard, the Solicitors' Act 1974, section 85(b) prohibits a bank from having recourse against money standing to the credit of an account kept by a solicitor with the bank in pursuance of the rules applicable to solicitors' client accounts, other than in respect of a liability in connection with the account itself. This would preclude set-off against or combination with an overdrawn account of the solicitor. Prima facie it would not prevent combination in relation to an account into which clients' moneys have been paid if the account is not kept in pursuance of the rules, although in accordance with the principles discussed above the combination may be impugned if the bank in any event is aware that the account is a trust account.[394]

The relevant time for knowledge

15.97 The question arises whether it is necessary to show that the bank had the requisite knowledge (or notice) of the trust when it received the trust money and credited it to the customer's account, or whether knowledge at a later date would suffice. On the one hand, in *Grigg v Cocks*[395] the bank became aware of the circumstances

---

[388] See para 15.89 above.
[389] *Re Montagu's Settlement* [1987] 1 Ch 264, 272–273, 278, *per* Sir Robert Megarry VC; *Linter Group Ltd v Goldberg* (1992) 7 ACSR 580, 636; *Bank of Credit and Commerce International (Overseas) Ltd v Akindele* [2001] Ch 437, 452, CA.
[390] *Barclays Bank Ltd v Quistclose Investments Ltd* [1970] AC 567, 582.
[391] (1894) 11 TLR 56.
[392] [1950] NILR 132.
[393] See also *Thomson v Clydesdale Bank, Ltd* [1893] AC 282 (stockbroker).
[394] See *Clark v Ulster Bank Ltd* [1950] NILR 132, 141.
[395] (1831) 4 Sim 438, 58 ER 163.

giving rise to the trust affecting the bill of exchange after the proceeds of the bill were received and credited to the customer's account but before the bank made a book entry combining the account with another. Sir Lancelot Shadwell held that the bank was entitled to consider itself as debtor for the balance of the accounts, notwithstanding the notice.[396] In Northern Ireland Black CJ adopted a similar approach in *Clark v Ulster Bank Ltd*.[397] On the other hand, the Privy Council in *Union Bank of Australia Ltd v Murray-Aynsley*[398] seems to have considered that notice of a trust conveyed to the bank after it received the money could still be relevant.[399] Further, in *Barclays Bank Ltd v Quistclose Investments Ltd*[400] Lord Reid left open the question whether subsequent notice could have affected the bank's position,[401] although the case seems to have proceeded on the basis that set-off under the insolvency set-off section was in issue as opposed to combination of accounts.[402]

When a customer has a number of accounts with a bank, and the requirements of combination are satisfied, the principle of combination dictates that the accounts constitute a single debt unless there is an agreement (express or implied) that they should be kept separate.[403] On that basis, notice of a trust received after money has been credited to an account should not affect the position in relation to combination.[404] The credit will already have been subsumed into the debt constituted by the overall balance on all the accounts. Similarly, a later entry by the bank reflecting the combination in its books should not be characterized a dealing with trust property so as to give rise to liability as a constructive trustee. There was in any event only one debt for the balance, in which case the book entry itself would not **15.98**

---

[396] See in particular (1831) 4 Sim 438, 453–454, 58 ER 163, 169.

[397] [1950] NILR 132, 142–143.

[398] [1898] AC 693.

[399] Lord Watson, in delivering the advice of the Privy Council, commented that 'there is nothing to prove or even to suggest that any notice was subsequently conveyed to the bank of the trust character of the funds which the respondents are claiming in this action'. [1898] AC 693, 698. See also *Taylor v Forbes* (1830) 7 Bligh NS 417, 5 ER 828, which is difficult to follow given that separate banker/customer relationships appear to have been in issue.

[400] [1970] AC 567, 578.

[401] Compare Russell LJ in the Court of Appeal [1968] 1 Ch 540, 556, 561, who approached the problem in terms whether the bank in that case had notice when it received the money and credited it to an account, and also Lord Wilberforce in the House of Lords [1970] AC 567, 582.

[402] See para 15.101 below.

[403] See para 15.03 above.

[404] The contrary was assumed in *Houben v Bank of Nova Scotia* (1970) 3 NBR (2d) 366, 381, St John County Court, New Brunswick. Compare the situation in which the accounts are separate, and the bank effects a set-off pursuant to a set-off agreement. See para 15.103 below. Compare also the case of a constructive trust arising as a result of the transfer of trust property to a person in breach of trust, where the person received the property initially unaware of the trust but subsequently acquired knowledge of it. See Millett, 'Tracing the Proceeds of Fraud' (1991) 107 LQR 71, 80, and *Agip (Africa) Ltd v Jackson* [1990] 1 Ch 265, 290, 291.

have constituted an appropriation by the bank of the trust account in reduction of a debt owing to the bank on another account.[405]

Value

15.99 In order to obtain the benefit of the bona fide purchaser principle in relation to a trust account, so as to be able to rely on combination in relation to that account and the trustee's overdrawn personal account,[406] the bank must have given value.

15.100 When money is paid into an account in credit in circumstances where combination is not in issue, the bank is not regarded as having given value merely because of the promise to repay a like amount.[407] On the other hand, when a bank receives money in reduction or discharge of a debt, the fact of the reduction or discharge does constitute value,[408] and that should also apply in a case of combination. The position should be the same whether the customer has one overdrawn account to which trust moneys are credited, or whether the customer has a number of accounts the balance of which at any particular time represents a debt owing to the bank.[409] Because there is only one debt in any event, payment into an account in credit, where there is a second account which is overdrawn to a greater extent than the credit balance on the first account, should have the same effect at law as a payment to the credit of the overdrawn account itself, in that it brings about a reduction in the customer's debt to the bank.

15.101 The question of value was considered in *Neste Oy v Lloyd's Bank plc*.[410] The case was referred to earlier[411] in the context of a payment made by a principal which

---

[405] *Re Sutcliffe & Sons Ltd, ex p Royal Bank* [1933] 1 DLR 562.

[406] See *Re Marwalt Ltd* [1992] BCC 32, 38 and *Neste Oy v Lloyds Bank plc* [1983] 2 Lloyd's Rep 658, 666.

[407] *Lipkin Gorman v Karpnale Ltd* [1991] 2 AC 548, 562, 576–577. See also Lord Wilberforce in *Barclays Bank Ltd v Quistclose Investments Ltd* [1970] AC 567, 582 (discussed below), although compare Harman LJ in the Court of Appeal in *Quistclose* [1968] 1 Ch 540, 555.

[408] *Taylor v Blakelock* (1886) 32 Ch D 560 (esp at 570); *Thomson v Clydesdale Bank Ltd* [1893] AC 282, 289–290, 291–292; *P T Garuda Indonesia Ltd v Grellman* (1992) 35 FCR 515, 530–532 (an antecedent debt constitutes valuable consideration for a payment in discharge of that debt); *Kyra Nominees Pty Ltd v National Australia Bank Ltd* (1986) 4 ACLC 400, 407; Millett, 'Tracing the Proceeds of Fraud' (1991) 107 LQR 71, 82; Goode, *Legal Problems of Credit and Security* (2nd edn, 1986) 120. See also *Thorndike v Hunt* (1859) 3 De G & J 563, 570, 44 ER 1386, 1388–9. *Re Leslie Engineers Co Ltd* [1976] 1 WLR 292, 299; *Barclays Bank Ltd v W J Simms Son & Cooke (Southern) Ltd* [1980] 1 QB 677, 695; *Australia and New Zealand Banking Group Ltd v Westpac Banking Corp* (1988) 164 CLR 662, 673 (although compare at 677–678); *David Securities Pty Ltd v Commonwealth Bank of Australia* (1992) 175 CLR 353, 405–406. Where a customer pays money into an account in credit, in circumstances where there is a second account which is overdrawn, the customer may not intend to reduce or discharge the debt to the bank, but he should nevertheless be bound by the consequences that follow at law from his act.

[409] See para 15.89 above.

[410] [1983] 2 Lloyd's Rep 658.

[411] See para 15.84 above.

was credited to its agent's account after the bank was aware of a decision that the group of companies of which the agent was a member was to cease trading. In addition, there were five other payments credited to the agent's account prior to the decision, which Bingham J held could be applied by the bank against other accounts in debit. The primary reason for the decision was that the payments were not received subject to a trust, but if he was wrong on that point he accepted that the bank in any event was a bona fide purchaser for value without notice. He said that the bank gave value when the payments were credited to the account.[412] He went on to comment that the bank certainly gave value when it continued lending in the belief that the overall debt was reduced by the sum of the payments. But even where a bank does not continue lending, if a payment into an account brings about a permanent reduction in the customer's debt value is given. It is true that in *Barclays Bank Ltd v Quistclose Investments Ltd*[413] Lord Wilberforce said that the bank in that case had not in any real sense given value when it received the money or thereafter changed its position.[414] In that case, however, the bank had agreed that the money paid into the account was only to be used for the purpose of funding the payment of a dividend, which would have precluded a combination in respect of it.[415] The question instead concerned set-off under the insolvency set-off section, the customer having gone into liquidation.[416] It was not therefore a case in which it could be said that the deposit itself operated to reduce the customer's debt to the bank so as to constitute the giving of value on that ground.

A deposit may result in a net credit to the customer, as opposed to operating in reduction or discharge of the customer's debt. If in such a case the bank subsequently acquires notice of the trust, it may be liable as a constructive trustee if it nevertheless assists the trustee in dealing with the money in a manner which is inconsistent with the trust.[417]   **15.102**

---

[412] His Lordship said ([1983] 2 Lloyd's Rep 658, 667) that: 'It appears to me that the bank gave value when these first five payments were credited to PSL's account, certainly when the bank continued lending in the belief that the group's overall debt was reduced by the sum of the payments . . .'. The case however concerned a set-off effected pursuant to a set-off agreement. See para 15.103 below.

[413] [1970] AC 567. See para 15.83 above.

[414] [1970] AC 567, 582. See also Russell LJ in the Court of Appeal [1968] 1 Ch 540, 563, although compare the view of Harman LJ (at 555) that: 'The bank stands . . . in the position of an assignee for value, the consideration being the promise to repay.'

[415] See Russell LJ in the Court of Appeal [1968] 1 Ch 540, 563.

[416] In the Court of Appeal, Harman LJ [1968] 1 Ch 540, 551 noted that the bank informed the board of the customer that it was exercising its 'statutory' right to combine accounts. See also the reference by Russell LJ (at 563) to the decision in *Rolls Razor Ltd v Cox* [1967] 1 QB 552, which concerned the question whether the operation of the insolvency set-off section could be excluded by agreement between the parties, and the reference by Sachs LJ (at 567) to the Bankruptcy Act 1914, s 31, which was the set-off section then applicable to company liquidations under the Companies Act 1948, s 317.

[417] See eg *Selangor United Rubber Estates Ltd v Cradock (No 3)* [1968] 1 WLR 1555 and *Karak Rubber Co Ltd v Burden (No 2)* [1972] 1 WLR 602. The test for liability as an accessory is dishonesty. See *Twinsectra Ltd v Yardley* [2002] 2 AC 164.

(4) Set-off Agreement

15.103   A customer may have a number of accounts with a bank that are separate from each other, and which accordingly are not subject to the principle of combination, but the bank has a set-off agreement entitling it to combine the accounts and set them off.[418] If one of the accounts is a trust account in credit, and the trustee has a second account with a greater debit balance, the payment of money into the trust account by itself should not constitute the giving of value, since, if the accounts are separate, the payment in would not result in a reduction in or discharge of the debt to the bank. Questions of knowledge of the trust and of the giving of value generally should be determined instead as at the date that the bank purports to effect a set-off in accordance with the agreement. The discharge or reduction of the customer's debt to the bank as a result of the bank's exercise of the contractual right of set-off would constitute the giving of value, and the question then would be whether the bank had knowledge of the trust at that time.[419]

15.104   It may not always be the case, however, that the date of the set-off is the relevant date. If the deposit was required as a condition to the grant of a loan or other facility, the making of the loan itself may constitute value, and the question of knowledge of the trust similarly should be determined as at that time. Alternatively, the provision of the loan in that circumstance may justify a defence to the bank of innocent change of position.[420]

(5) Labelling an Account as a Trust Account, Where the Customer is not a Trustee

15.105   An account kept by a customer with a bank may be labelled as a trust account, but despite the label it is not a trust account but rather it contains the customer's own money. In that circumstance, one would have thought that the fact of the label shows an intention that the account is to be kept separate from the customer's other accounts, and that an agreement to that effect therefore should be implied so as to preclude combination, notwithstanding that the customer himself is beneficially interested in the credit balance. That approach is not reflected in the cases, however, and there is authority for the proposition that combination may occur in relation to the account.

15.106   *Bailey v Finch*[421] concerned an account opened by a customer in his capacity as executor of an estate, and labelled as such. In the course of his judgment, Blackburn J contemplated the possibility that the account could have been combined with another account held by the customer in his personal capacity,[422] in

---

[418]   See paras 15.66–15.70 above.
[419]   See *Neste Oy v Lloyds Bank plc* [1983] 2 Lloyd's Rep 658, 667, and also *Re Marwalt Ltd* [1992] BCC 32, 38, 43.
[420]   See generally *Boscawen v Bajwa* [1996] 1 WLR 328, 334.
[421]   (1871) LR 7 QB 34.
[422]   See (1871) LR 7 QB 34, 41–42, 43.

circumstances where the customer was also the residuary legatee and there were other assets in the estate which were sufficient to satisfy the specific bequests and charges upon the estate. The remarks were obiter, however, and the position was not the subject of detailed consideration. The case itself concerned insolvency set-off, the bankers in that case having become bankrupt, and moreover, as an alternative to combination prior to the bankruptcy, Blackburn J suggested that the Statutes of Set-off may have provided a defence to the customer to an action at law by the bank to obtain payment of the customer's personal account in debit.[423] Set-off under the Statutes is premised on the assumption that there are independent debts, which is the consequence when there is an implied agreement that the accounts are to be kept separate, and it applies in circumstances where there is mutuality at common law and there is no reason in equity as to why a set-off at law should not proceed.[424] An implied agreement to keep accounts separate, while it would preclude combination, ordinarily should not affect a set-off under the Statutes.[425]

Two other cases are relevant, one Canadian and the other from New Zealand. In **15.107** *Bank of Montreal v R & R Entertainment Ltd*[426] an account was labelled as a trust account, although the customer in truth was not a trustee. The judgment is not altogether clear, but the New Brunswick Court of Appeal appears to have accepted the view adopted by the trial judge, that the bank was entitled to apply the account against a second overdrawn account possessed by the customer personally, so as to justify the bank's initial act in dishonouring cheques drawn on the 'trust' account.[427] The circumstances were peculiar, however.[428] It appears that both the

---

[423] See paras 2.04–2.54 above.

[424] See the discussion of *Bailey v Finch* in para 13.120 above. Blackburn J in *Bailey v Finch* referred (at (1871) LR 7 QB 34, 42) to *Ex parte Kingston* (1871) LR 6 Ch App 632, in which a set-off seems to have been allowed to the bank in relation to the part of the 'Police Account' which represented the customer's own money. However the set-off may be explained as having occurred under the insolvency set-off section, the customer having become bankrupt, for which different considerations apply. See para 15.108 below. The customer in *Ex parte Kingston* had indicated to the bank that the account was to be kept separate (see at 634), which ordinarily would preclude combination. Nevertheless the county court judge in the *Kingston* case, to whose judgment Blackburn J referred in *Bailey v Finch* at 42, evidently regarded the case as involving a bankers 'lien' on the account. See the judgment set out in a footnote in *Ex parte Kingston* at 635–637.

[425] See para 15.62 above.

[426] (1984) 13 DLR (4th) 726.

[427] The facts of the case were unusual. Because of the debit on the customer's account the bank dishonoured some cheques drawn on the trust account, whereupon the payee of the cheques threatened to sue the bank on the ground that the account was held on trust for it. The bank settled the claim, and sought in this action to recover from the customer and some guarantors. The Court of Appeal held that the account was not a trust account, and that therefore the bank was entitled to dishonour the cheques. Furthermore, the bank had withdrawn the credit balance from the trust account and credited it to another account in order to secure the customer's debt. Therefore, when the bank settled the action it did so with its own money. Its claim against the customer and the guarantors accordingly failed.

[428] See (1984) 13 DLR (4th) 726, 734.

bank and the customer had transferred funds from one account to the other from time to time, and had treated the trust account as an extension of the customer's general account. The trust account was overdrawn almost every month from the time it was established, and funds were transferred from one account to the other when either of the accounts was overdrawn. The question whether the labelling of the account gave rise to an implied term that it was to be regarded as separate was not considered, but it is apparent that the parties' own conduct was inconsistent with that conclusion. Furthermore, notwithstanding the general nature of the discussion,[429] the right of set-off which the trial judge accepted and to which the Court of Appeal referred may have rested in contract rather than on the common law doctrine.[430]

15.108 The second case is *McMillan v Bank of New Zealand*,[431] a decision of the New Zealand Supreme Court.[432] A debtor executed a deed of assignment for the benefit of his creditors whereby he was to be permitted to carry on business, but paying one half of the gross takings for distribution among his creditors. Of his own accord he opened an account with his bank in his own name for that purpose but with the words 'trust account' added. The creditors refused to assent to the deed, whereupon the bank transferred an amount standing to the credit of the account in reduction of another account possessed by the customer in debit. The bank's action in doing so was upheld, since the account was not subject to a trust. Once again, however, there was no consideration given to the possibility that the accounts may have been separate as a result of an implied agreement arising out of the labelling of the account as a trust account, so as to preclude the principle of combination. If that view had been adopted in the *McMillan* case, the result may have been the same in any event. The customer had become bankrupt, and a set-off may have been available under the insolvency set-off section so as to bring about the same practical result as a combination. The insolvency set-off section was not considered in the judgment, but in that form of set-off one would look beyond the mere labelling of the account in order to ascertain the true beneficial interests, and if there is mutuality in equity a set-off ordinarily should proceed.[433]

(6) Account Containing Both Trust and Personal Moneys

15.109 An account in credit may have had deposited into it both trust moneys and the customer's personal moneys. In such a case Wood's view[434] would appear to be correct, that, consistent with the principle applicable to tracing trust moneys into an

---

[429] See (1984) 13 DLR (4th) 726, 732.
[430] See the terms of the 'Authority to Charge Accounts' set out at (1984) 13 DLR (4th) 726, 734.
[431] (1882) NZLR 1 SC 332.
[432] Prendergast CJ and Richmond J.
[433] See para 11.04 above.
[434] Wood, *English and International Set-off* (1989) 1067.

account,[435] a combination would reduce first the part of the account in which the customer is personally interested. If another account in debit kept by the customer is more than sufficient to extinguish that amount on the basis of combination, the question whether combination will then apply in relation to the trust moneys should be determined by reference to the principles discussed above.

If on the other hand the account is specifically labelled as a trust account, there is **15.110** much to be said for the view that the label may give rise to an implied agreement that it is to be kept separate so as to preclude combination.[436] This approach, however, is yet to be reflected in the cases, which instead suggest that combination may apply to the extent that the customer is personally interested in the credit balance on the trust account.[437] But even if the accounts are not combined, if the customer sues the bank for payment of the balance on the account a set-off should be available to the bank in any event under the Statutes of Set-off to the extent of the customer's personal interest,[438] or alternatively the insolvency set-off section may apply to that extent if the customer is bankrupt or is in liquidation.[439]

(7) Overdrawn Trust Account

The preceding discussion concerned a trust account in credit. If on the other hand **15.111** a trust account is overdrawn for some reason, the customer would be personally liable.[440]

If an account is labelled as a trust account, it was suggested earlier that this should **15.112** give rise to an implied agreement that it is to be treated as separate from the customer's private accounts,[441] and an agreement in those terms should continue to be relevant when the trust account is overdrawn. In other words, it should still be a separate account.[442] In that circumstance combination should not apply, in which case the bank should be confined to a procedural defence of set-off in an action at law under the Statutes of Set-off, or alternatively insolvency set-off. In

---

[435] *Re Hallett's Estate* (1880) 13 Ch D 696.
[436] See para 15.105 above.
[437] See paras 15.105–15.108 above.
[438] See para 15.106 above.
[439] See para 15.108 above.
[440] *Daniels v Imperial Bank of Canada* (1914) 19 DLR 166, 169; *Bailey v Finch* (1871) LR 7 QB 34, 41 (in relation to an overdrawn executorship account). See also, and compare, *Coutts and Co v The Irish Exhibition in London* (1891) 7 TLR 313.
[441] See para 15.105 above.
[442] There is some support for this view in the discussion of Walsh J in the Alberta Supreme Court in *Daniels v Imperial Bank of Canada* (1914) 19 DLR 166, 168–169. The judgment is not entirely clear, but it seems to have been concluded that the defendant was entitled to succeed on the basis of a defence of set-off (see below), as opposed to combination of accounts. On the other hand, the New Brunswick Court of Appeal in *Bank of Montreal v R & R Entertainment Ltd* (1984) 13 DLR (4th) 726, 733 referred to *Daniels v Imperial Bank of Canada* in the context of a 'bank's right of set-off', by which it was apparently meant combination.

the case of the Statutes, the accounts would not be set against each other until such time as judgment for a set-off is given,[443] which would have the consequence that the bank would be liable for damages if, prior to judgment, it failed to honour a cheque drawn by the customer on his private account in credit because of the presence of a debit balance on the trust account. However the proposition that an implied term arises from the labelling of the account as yet is unsupported by authority,[444] and the question of combination in relation to an overdrawn trust account therefore remains uncertain.

M. Assignments[445]

15.113 An assignment of an account in credit is governed by principles similar to those applicable in the trust cases, so that the assignee takes subject to a combination arising before the bank had notice (or knowledge) of the assignment.[446] Prior to notice there is still the one banker/customer relationship in relation to the accounts. Where one of the accounts is payable on demand, an assignee may be subject to a combination notwithstanding the absence of a demand before the bank had notice of the assignment.[447]

N. Deceased Customer

15.114 A deceased customer in whose name there is a credit balance on an account may also have a loan which matures after the date of death. Since a combination does not arise in relation to an account that is neither presently payable nor presently payable on demand,[448] the accounts at the date of death would not have been combined in a single debt. When the loan matures, the liability will still be the liability of the deceased customer, but from the moment of death the right to receive the credit balance will have been vested in his executor.[449] Nevertheless, consistent with the principle applicable to assignments, it was held in *Rogerson v Ladbroke*[450]

---

[443] See paras 2.33–2.48 above.

[444] See paras 15.105–15.108 above.

[445] See also para 15.17 above.

[446] *Roxburghe v Cox* (1881) 17 Ch D 520; *Jeffryes v Agra and Masterman's Bank* (1866) LR 2 Eq 674, 680. Compare *Re Jane, ex p The Trustee* (1914) 110 LT 556, in which the accounts would have been separate, being a current account in credit and a loan account, and *Re Marwalt Ltd* [1992] BCC 32, in which the bank had notice of the assignment.

[447] See para 15.49 above.

[448] See para 15.49 above.

[449] *Williams, Mortimer and Sunnucks on Executors, Administrators and Probate* (18th edn, 2000) 467.

[450] (1822) 1 Bing 93, 130 ER 39.

that the estate will take subject to a combination if the loan matured before the bank had notice of the death.[451]

O. Banker's Lien Over a Negotiable Instrument

A bank has a lien on all bills of exchange and cheques coming into its possession **15.115** as banker for the general balance of moneys due from the customer.[452] The lien is not merely over the paper on which the order to pay is written, but is over the chose in action which the order creates.[453] This should also include a power to collect the proceeds upon maturity.[454] When the bank collects the proceeds, however, the lien will come to an end. The bank will no longer have possession of the instrument, and the proceeds themselves ordinarily would not be tangible property which can be the subject of a possessory lien.[455] Nevertheless the bank's security rights derived from the lien should entitle it to apply the proceeds in reduction of the debt secured by the lien,[456] unless there is an agreement to the contrary. A contrary agreement would arise, for example, where the bank had specifically agreed to account to the customer for the proceeds.[457]

---

[451] In the absence of information as regards the date of death, *quaere* whether *Thomas v Howell* (1874) LR 18 Eq 198 was correctly decided. The case was distinguished, on other grounds, in *Halse v Rumford* (1878) 47 LJ Ch 559. In *Royal Trust Co v Molsons Bank* (1912) 8 DLR 478 the customer died before the promissory notes became due, although it is not clear when the bank received notice of the death. A similar comment may be made in respect of *Ontario Bank v Routhier* (1900) 32 OR 67.

[452] *National Australia Bank Ltd v KDS Construction Services Pty Ltd* (1987) 163 CLR 668, 678, referring to *Brandao v Barnett* (1846) 12 Cl & Fin 787, 809, 8 ER 1622, 1631. The lien is a common law lien. It is doubtful if it would apply when a trustee deposits a cheque for collection and the beneficiary rather than the trustee is indebted to the bank. See *Abbey National plc v McCann* [1997] Northern Ireland Judgments Bulletin 158, 171–172, 183.

[453] *Sutters v Briggs* [1922] 1 AC 1, 20; *Re Keever* [1967] 1 Ch 182, 189; *National Australia Bank Ltd v KDS Construction Services Pty Ltd* (1987) 163 CLR 668, 679.

[454] *Duke Finance Ltd v Commonwealth Bank of Australia* (1990) 22 NSWLR 236, 249.

[455] *Halesowen Presswork and Assemblies Ltd v Westminster Bank Ltd* [1971] 1 QB 1, 46, *per* Buckley LJ. See also on appeal in the House of Lords [1972] AC 785, 802, *per* Viscount Dilhorne, 810, *per* Lord Cross of Chelsea, and para 15.03 above.

[456] *Duke Finance Ltd v Commonwealth Bank of Australia* (1990) 22 NSWLR 236; *Re Keever* [1967] 1 Ch 182. See also *National Australia Bank Ltd v KDS Construction Services Pty Ltd* (1987) 163 CLR 668, 678–679. Compare *Abbey National plc v McCann* [1997] Northern Ireland Judgments Bulletin 158, 172–173. Similarly an insurance broker who has a lien over a policy is entitled to apply the proceeds collected under the policy in satisfaction of the debt secured by the lien. See *Eide UK Ltd v Lowndes Lambert Group Ltd* [1999] QB 199, 208–211.

[457] *Rouxel v Royal Bank of Canada* [1918] 2 WWR 791.

16

SET-OFF AGREEMENTS

A. Introduction

Parties dealing with each other may enter into an agreement for the satisfaction of **16.01** their cross-demands by bringing them into an account, on the basis that a set-off is to occur either immediately or at a later date at the option of one of the parties. Generally this is not objectionable.[1] It merely constitutes an agreed method of payment.[2] The agreement may not be effective, however, where trust moneys are

---

[1] Unless a contractual deduction or set-off is precluded by statute. See eg *VHE Construction plc v RBSTB Trust Co Ltd* [2000] BLR 187, 192 in relation to the Housing Grants, Construction and Registration Act 1996 where a notice of intention to withhold payment has not been given.

[2] See eg *Jeffs v Wood* (1723) 2 P Wms 128, 129, 24 ER 668, 669; *Kinnerley v Hossack* (1809) 2 Taunt 170, 127 ER 1042; *Cheetham v Crook* (1825) M'Cle & Yo 307, 148 ER 429; *Re Kelly* (1932) 4 ABC 258, 267; *Federal Commissioner of Taxation v Steeves Agnew and Co (Vic) Pty Ltd* (1951) 82 CLR 408, 420; *First National Bank of Chicago v West of England Shipowners Mutual Protection and Indemnity Association (The Evelpidis Era)* [1981] 1 Lloyd's Rep 54, 63; *Matthews v Geraghty* (1986) 43 SASR 576, 582; *Pro-Image Studios v Commonwealth Bank of Australia* (1991) 4 ACSR 586, 588–589; *Re Keith Bray Pty Ltd* (1991) 5 ACSR 450, 451; *Opal Maritime Agencies Pty Ltd v 'Skulptor Konenkov'* (2000) 98 FCR 519, 562, 568. A set-off agreement may extend to debts owing to affiliates. See *Sinochem International Oil (London) Co Ltd v Mobil Sales and Supply Corp* [2000] 1 All ER (Comm) 474, and also *Latreefers Inc v Tangent Shipping Co Ltd* [2000] 1 BCLC 805 (multi-party). A contractual set-off can be express, it may arise by custom, or it may be inferred from conduct. See *Commercial Factors Ltd v Maxwell Printing Ltd* [1994] 1 NZLR 724, 737–739 (cheque swapping arrangement held to constitute a contractual set-off). In Australia the courts have upheld a contractual set-off in the

in issue.[3] If a customer has deposited trust moneys into an account with a bank, and the bank, acting pursuant to a set-off agreement, purports to set off the account against a second overdrawn account held by the customer in his personal capacity, the bank may be liable to account to the person beneficially entitled to the trust moneys unless it can rely on defences of purchaser for value without notice or change of position.[4]

Contingent debts

16.02 A set-off agreement may extend to contingent debts of a debtor. Professor Goode has suggested that an agreement in those terms may operate in either of two ways.[5] In the first place, it may be intended that the creditor is to have the right to suspend payment of his own debt to the debtor until the debtor's contingent liability matures, with an ensuing right of set-off, or until it is clear that the contingency will not occur. Alternatively, the creditor may have an immediate right to set off the maximum potential liability of the debtor, upon terms of re-crediting the debtor with the appropriate amount if the actual liability proves to be less or if the contingency fails to occur. Professor Goode considered that in most cases the former construction is likely to prevail. This may not be the case, however, if the deposit is already subject to a contractual restriction on withdrawals, in other words the deposit is flawed.[6] In that circumstance, a right to suspend payment upon the occurrence of the contingency would not add anything to the existing arrangement, in which case the second construction may reflect more accurately the parties' intention.

B. Bankruptcy and Company Liquidation

16.03 In the event of a bankruptcy or a liquidation of a company, the validity of a set-off effected pursuant to an agreement to which the bankrupt or the company is a party is subject to two limitations. The first relates to preferences and other impugned transactions under the insolvency legislation, and the second concerns the *pari passu* principle which governs distributions in bankruptcy and company liquidation.

---

context of a debt for equity swap. See para 8.62 above. If a set-off agreement is terminated, the agreement nevertheless may continue to operate in respect if items covered by the agreement prior to the termination. See *Opal Maritime Agencies v 'Skulptor Konenkov'* at 563 (though compare *Opal Maritime Agencies Pty Ltd v Baltic Shipping Co* (1998) 158 ALR 416, 422).

 [3] See eg *P C Harrington Contractors Ltd v Co Partnership Developments Ltd* (1998) 88 BLR 44 (retention fund held on trust).
 [4] See paras 15.85 and 15.103 above.
 [5] Goode, *Legal Problems of Credit and Security* (2nd edn, 1988) 173.
 [6] See para 16.92 below.

(1) Preferences and Other Impugned Transactions

The first limitation is that a set-off of debts effected pursuant to a contract may be **16.04** impugned[7] if it is a transaction at an undervalue,[8] or a transaction defrauding creditors,[9] or if it is a disposition of the company's property after the commencement of its winding up,[10] or if it constitutes a voidable preference.[11] This is subject to qualification, however. In the first place, if the subject of the set-off is two bank accounts which in any event would be regarded as combined in a single debt pursuant to the principle of combination of accounts,[12] a book-keeping entry by the bank setting off the debit and credit balances against each other should not constitute a preference, since there was in any event a single debt for the balance.[13] Secondly, a contractual set-off effected prior to the bankruptcy or liquidation of one of the parties will not be struck down as a preference if the cross-demands would have been set off in any event under the insolvency set-off section.[14] When

---

[7] In Australia, an additional issue in a bankruptcy is the relation back of the trustee's title, in the case of a creditor's petition to the time of the act of bankruptcy. See the Bankruptcy Act 1966 (Cth), ss 115 and 116. This applies to debts owing to the bankrupt, which constitute property of the bankrupt. See the definition of 'property' in s 5. On the other hand, the trustee takes subject to equities to which the bankrupt was subject (see *Mitford v Mitford* (1803) 9 Ves Jun 87, 99–100, 32 ER 534, 439), and a set-off agreement may constitute an equity. See paras 17.38–17.46 below.

[8] Insolvency Act 1986, s 238 and, for bankruptcy, s 339.

[9] Insolvency Act 1986, s 423.

[10] Insolvency Act 1986, s 127. In Australia, there is a suggestion in *Couve v J Pierre Couve Ltd* (1933) 49 CLR 486, 494 that the exercise of a contractual right of set-off may constitute a void disposition (although the avoidance of the disposition of the goods the subject of the sale in that case meant that there was no debt for the price, and therefore no set-off against that debt), and see also *Barclays Bank Ltd v TOSG Trust Fund Ltd* [1984] BCLC 1, 25–26; Goode, *Principles of Corporate Insolvency Law* (2nd edn, 1997) 424–5. On the other hand, Otton J in *Re K (Restraint Order)* [1990] 2 QB 298, 305 considered that the exercise of a contractual right of set-off was not a 'disposing of' assets for the purpose of the Drug Trafficking Offences Act 1986. Compare also *Re Loteka Pty Ltd* [1990] 1 Qd R 322, 324.

[11] Insolvency Act 1986, s 340 and, for company liquidation, s 239. See generally *Re Washington Diamond Mining Co* [1893] 3 Ch 95; *Re Land Development Association. Kent's Case* (1888) 39 Ch D 259; *Re Atlas Engineering Co (Davy's Case)* (1889) 10 LR (NSW) Eq 179, 6 WN (NSW) 64; *Mitchell v Booth* [1928] SASR 367.

[12] See ch 15.

[13] See para 15.79 above.

[14] *Re Washington Diamond Mining Co* [1893] 3 Ch 95, 104, 111. See also *Hamilton v Commonwealth Bank of Australia* (1992) 9 ACSR 90, 106–108; *Wily v Rothschild Australia Ltd* (1999) 47 NSWLR 555, 566; *Wily v St George Partnership Banking Ltd* (1999) 84 FCR 423, 435–436 (mutual payments); *Minister of Transport v Francis* (2000) 35 ACSR 584, 594. Compare *Wily v Bartercard Ltd* (2000) 34 ACSR 186 (decision affirmed ((2001) 39 ACSR 94), in which there would not have been a set-off had the transaction been set aside. In *Wily v Rothschild*, a bank had provided a 'gold loan' to a company, which obliged the company to repay to the bank an equivalent amount of gold. In addition, the bank held funds on deposit for the company. On the day that the directors of the company resolved to wind up the company, the bank used the funds on deposit to purchase gold and apply it in reduction of the gold loan. Windeyer J held that this was not a preference, since a set-off would have been available in any event, and the payment therefore did not have the effect of preferring the bank over other creditors. A difficulty with that view is that at the date of the payment the demands were not commensurable, in that the bank was liable as a

a payment is avoided as a preference, the parties so far as possible are put in the same position as if the payment had not been made.[15] In the same way, if a contractual set-off were set aside, the debts would revive,[16] and they potentially would be available for set-off pursuant to the insolvency legislation. If the insolvency set-off section would have applied in any event, the contractual set-off would not be a preference. As Vaughan Williams J once remarked, 'You cannot prefer a man, it seems to me, by merely putting him in the very position in which he would be if a bankruptcy followed.'[17] Furthermore, in considering whether the qualification to the set-off section[18] would have precluded a set-off, on the basis that the creditor had notice that a bankruptcy petition was pending, or in the case of company liquidation that the creditor had notice that a meeting of creditors had been summoned under section 98 of the Insolvency Act or that a petition for the winding up of the company was pending,[19] the question of notice is to be determined by reference to the circumstances at the time of the incurring of the obligations, as opposed to the time that the contractual set-off is effected. This is because the question whether there has been a preference, in other words whether there would have been a set-off in any event, is to be tested on the assumption that the contractual set-off is set aside.[20]

16.05 If the form of set-off agreement between two parties, A and B, is such that it entitles A to act unilaterally and in his discretion to bring about a set-off, and A effects a set-off within the preference period applicable in B's bankruptcy or liquidation,

---

debtor on the account while the company's obligation was to deliver gold. Therefore the circumstances at that date were not such as to give rise to a set-off in a liquidation. See ch 9. The decision nevertheless would appear to be correct. If the bank had not purchased the gold and applied it in reduction of the gold loan, either of two things would have happened. Either the liquidator himself would have performed the contract by delivering gold, or the company would have defaulted, thereby giving rise to a liability in damages to the bank which could have been set off in the liquidation against the debt on the deposit. See para 8.43 above. In either case the bank would have been protected, so that the bank's action did not put it in a better position than it otherwise would have been in the liquidation.

[15] Insolvency Act 1986, ss 239(3) and 340(2); *Hamilton v Commonwealth Bank of Australia* (1992) 9 ACSR 90, 107. In Australia, see also the Bankruptcy Act 1966 (Cth), s 122(5).

[16] See eg the order in *Wily v Bartercard Ltd* (2000) 34 ACSR 186, 197–198, in which the circumstances were not otherwise such as to give rise to a set-off under the insolvency set-off section. The decision subsequently was affirmed by the NSW Court of Appeal. See *Bartercard Ltd v Wily* (2001) 39 ACSR 94.

[17] *Re Washington Diamond Mining Co* [1893] 3 Ch 95, 104. Thus, Professor Goode has made the point that payment by a company into an overdrawn account with its bank would not be a preference in the company's subsequent liquidation, if the payment does not exceed the amount of a credit balance on another account held by the company which otherwise would have been available as a set-off against the first account, because the effect of the payment is to reduce the set-off so that the position of other creditors is unaffected. See Goode, *Principles of Corporate Insolvency Law* (2nd edn, 1997) 402.

[18] See paras 6.49–6.64 above.

[19] See the Insolvency Act 1986, s 323(3) and, for company liquidation, the Insolvency Rules 1986, r 4.90(3).

[20] *Minister of Transport v Francis* (2000) 35 ACSR 584, 594.

A's act in doing so on its own should not constitute a preference under the English insolvency legislation.[21] For the preference section to apply, an individual or a company must do something or suffer something to be done which has the effect of putting the creditor in a better position, in the event of the individual's bankruptcy or the company's liquidation, than the creditor would have been in if the thing had not been done, and the individual or the company must have been influenced by a desire to produce that result.[22] If a debtor authorizes the creditor to sell the debtor's property and to apply the proceeds in reduction of the debt, the creditor in doing so may be acting as the debtor's agent.[23] But when a creditor is empowered by a prior agreement to act unilaterally to set off their mutual debts, the creditor usually would be acting on its own behalf and not as an agent.[24] Nothing would be done by the debtor,[25] and nor could it be said that the debtor is suffering anything to be done if the debtor has no means of preventing the occurrence of a set-off.[26] The act of effecting a set-off therefore should not be a preference, and the question whether there has been a preference should be determined instead by reference to the circumstances surrounding the incurring of the debts the subject of the set-off, or the entry into the set-off agreement.[27] It is at that point that the question of a desire to produce a preference should be determined. This may also be relevant where the cross-demands were such that the insolvency set-off section would have applied in any event. While in that situation the act of setting off the cross-demands on its own would not be a preference,[28] the

---

[21] See also Wood, *English and International Set-off* (1989) 373–4, and Goode, *Principles of Corporate Insolvency Law* (2nd edn, 1997) 402. Compare the position in Australia. See paras 16.07–16.17 below. The preference provision in Australia differs from that in England in that the question of a desire to produce a preference is not relevant. See para 13.12 above.

[22] Insolvency Act 1986, s 340(3)(b) and (4), and for company liquidation s 239(4)(b) and (5).

[23] See *Re Kelly* (1932) 4 ABC 258, 262–267, and also *Re Hamling* (1957) 18 ABC 121, 127. *Aliter* if the agreement operates as an equitable assignment of the proceeds. Compare *Re Kelly* at 262–267.

[24] In *Cinema Plus Ltd v Australia and New Zealand Banking Group Ltd* (2000) 49 NSWLR 513 the New South Wales Court of Appeal held that a bank which exercised a contractual power to consolidate accounts was not acting 'on behalf of' the customer, for the purpose of the Corporations Law, s 437D. See para 16.08 below.

[25] Compare the situation in which a debtor is required by a prior agreement to do something, for example to execute a charge in favour of a creditor upon request. The execution of a charge may constitute a preference. See *Re Eric Holmes (Property) Ltd* [1965] 1 Ch 1052.

[26] In *British Eagle International Air Lines Ltd v Compagnie Nationale Air France* [1975] 1 WLR 758 (see para 16.19 below), the clearing house arrangement was considered not to involve a fraudulent preference, because it could not be said to have been made with a view of giving a preference within the terms of the Bankruptcy Act 1914, s 44. See Lord Morris of Borth-y-Gest at 762, and also the Court of Appeal [1974] 1 Lloyd's Rep 429, 431. It was not suggested (compare the reference to counsel's argument in the House of Lords at 779) that the striking of a balance itself pursuant to the arrangement was a preference.

[27] Compare *Re Deague* (1951) 15 ABC 197, although in that case the customer himself transferred funds from one account to another. See also the discussion of *Re Deague* in *Hamilton v Commonwealth Bank of Australia* (1992) 9 ACSR 90, 106

[28] See para 16.04 above.

circumstances giving rise to the cross-demands, for example the making of a deposit with a bank, could be impugned as preferential.[29]

16.06 When a company owes a debt to A, and as a result of a prior arrangement the company is entitled, without A's consent, to set off the debt against a separate debt owing by B to the company, the company's act in effecting a set-off in accordance with the arrangement would not be a preference to A in the company's liquidation. In *Katz v McNally*[30] two directors of a company, GM and RM, had loan accounts with the company. GM's account had a credit balance in his favour of £135,001 but that of RM was in debit to the extent of £61,607. An administration order was made against the company, and subsequently it went into liquidation. Within the preference period the company paid £73,394 to GM, representing the sum of £135,001 due to him less the amount of £61,607 owing by RM to the company, which amount was set off against RM's debt. One of the questions for determination was whether the preferential payment to GM was limited to the amount actually paid to him (£73,393), or whether it included also the sum of £61,607 the subject of the set-off. This was thought to depend on whether the company had a right to set off RM's debt to it against its debt to GM. The Court of Appeal accepted that, if the company was entitled to effect a set-off without GM's consent, the effect of such a set-off could not be treated as a preferential payment to GM. If on the other hand a set-off could not have been effected without GM's consent, the payment would fall to be treated as an application of £135,001 to or at the direction of GM. The evidence indicated that the company had a right of set-off and that it did no need the consent of GM. The preference to GM accordingly was limited to the amount actually paid to him.

Preferences in Australia—bankruptcy

16.07 In Australia, the preference section in bankruptcy[31] applies where there was a 'transfer of property by a person who is insolvent ("the debtor")' within the preference period in the debtor's bankruptcy. A transfer of property is defined as including a payment of money.[32] The word 'transfer' has been described as one of the widest terms that can be used.[33] 'Payment' similarly has been said to be a very wide term, such that it may include a mere transfer of figures in an account without any money passing.[34] The exercise of a contractual right of set-off therefore should

---

[29] See *Hamilton v Commonwealth Bank of Australia* (1992) 9 ACSR 90, 106–110.
[30] [1999] BCC 291, affirming *Re Exchange Travel (Holdings) Ltd (No 3)* [1996] 2 BCLC 524 (Rattee J).
[31] Bankruptcy Act 1966 (Cth), s 122.
[32] Bankruptcy Act 1966 (Cth), s 122(8).
[33] *Gathercole v Smith* (1881) 17 Ch D 1, 7, 9; *Re Hardman* (1932) 4 ABC 207, 210.
[34] *Re Hardman* (1932) 4 ABC 207, 210; *Findlay v Trevor* (1993) 11 ACLC 483, 499; *Driver v Federal Commissioner of Taxation* (1999) 42 ATR 510, 513 (decision affirmed [2000] NSWCA 247).

constitute a transfer of property for the purpose of the preference section.[35] In order to constitute a voidable preference, however, the payment must have been made *by the debtor*. This raises a similar issue to that considered in relation to contractual set-offs in England.[36] If a creditor is empowered by a prior agreement to act unilaterally to set off mutual money obligations as between it and the debtor, is the creditor's act in effecting a set-off, in circumstances where the cross-demands otherwise would not have been set off in the bankruptcy,[37] properly characterized as a payment 'by' the debtor so as to be voidable as a preference?

Cinema Plus Ltd v Australia and New Zealand Banking Group Ltd[38] suggests that **16.08** the creditor's act in effecting the set-off does not constitute a payment 'by' the debtor. One of the issues in the case concerned the meaning of section 437D(1) of the Corporations Law,[39] which operated to avoid a transaction or dealing entered into by a person 'on behalf of' a company under administration which affected the property of the company. The New South Wales Court of Appeal held that a bank which exercised a contractual right to consolidate, or set off, the accounts of a company was not acting 'on behalf of' the company for the purpose of section 437D(1). The clause in issue provided that the bank at any time could 'consolidate . . . any of your accounts . . . towards payment of money which is then, or will become, due and payable by you to us . . .'. Spigelman CJ said that the reference in the clause to 'payment' was not a reference to an act of the company, or an act on behalf of the company.[40] Sheller JA, with whose reasons Giles JA agreed, referred to an earlier discussion by Dixon J of the expression 'on behalf of'. In the context there under consideration, Dixon J said that it meant 'for the purposes of, as an instrument of, or for the benefit and in the interest of . . .'.[41] Sheller JA considered that, even giving the expression 'on behalf of' in section 437D(1) that meaning, the bank was not so acting when it consolidated the accounts.[42] The clause empowered the bank to act independently and in no sense on behalf of the company. The bank acted on its own behalf. The *Cinema Plus* case concerned a company under administration, but the same reasoning should apply when the bank's customer is an individual. When a bank sets off an individual's accounts

---

[35] Similarly, the provision of property by a debtor to a creditor for sale and to retain the proceeds may be characterized as a 'payment made' by the debtor for the purpose of the preference section. See *Findlay v Trevor* (1993) 11 ACLC 483, 499; *Re Wade* (1943) 13 ABC 116; *Re McConnell* (1911) 18 ALR 90, [1912] VLR 102.

[36] See para 16.05 above.

[37] See para 16.04 above. For example, the creditor may have given or received credit after the creditor had notice of an act of bankruptcy, which would preclude a set-off in the subsequent bankruptcy. See the Bankruptcy Act 1966 (Cth), s 86(2), and paras 6.49–6.64 above.

[38] (2000) 49 NSWLR 513.

[39] Now, the Corporations Act 2001 (Cth).

[40] (2000) 49 NSWLR 513, 525 para 56.

[41] *R v Portus, ex p Federated Clerks Union of Australia* (1949) 79 CLR 428, 438.

[42] (2000) 49 NSWLR 513, 544 para 118.

pursuant to a prior contractual right, the act of effecting payment in that manner would not be an act of the individual through the bank as its instrument, and nor would it be an act on behalf of the individual in the other senses referred to by Dixon J. It should not then be a payment 'by' the individual for the purpose of the preference section in the individual's subsequent bankruptcy.

16.09   The judgments of King CJ and Bollen J in the South Australian Supreme Court in *Matthews v Geraghty*[43] are also consistent with that view. The case concerned section 453(5) of the Companies (South Australia) Code, which applied in the situation in which a disposition of property made by a company within six months before the commencement of its winding up conferred a preference upon a creditor of the company, with the consequent effect of discharging an officer of the company from a liability as guarantor.[44] In those circumstances, the liquidator could recover from the officer an amount equal to the value of the property. In *Matthews v Geraghty* a bank had made a loan to a company which was guaranteed by the directors. In addition, the company had executed a set-off agreement which entitled the bank to set off debit and credit balances. Some two weeks before the company went into liquidation the company deposited a sum of money to the credit of a current account, and four days later the bank acting pursuant to the agreement set off the resulting credit balance against the loan. The set-off had the effect of discharging both the company from its liability on the loan and the directors from their liability to the bank as guarantors. It was argued that the section did not apply because, while the deposit with the bank was a disposition of property, the deposit itself did not confer a preference, which occurred as a result of the subsequent act of the bank manager in setting off the accounts. However King CJ said that it was a natural and reasonably foreseeable consequence of the deposit that the bank would apply the resulting credit balance in satisfaction of the loan. The deposit put it in the power of the bank to apply the money in that manner. In his opinion, therefore, the disposition of property consisting of the deposit conferred a preference on the bank as a creditor, and it also had the effect of discharging the guarantors from their liability under the guarantee. The section accordingly applied.[45] Bollen J adopted a similar analysis. Both King CJ and Bollen J regarded the deposit as the relevant disposition of property made 'by' the

---

[43] (1986) 43 SASR 576.

[44] See now the Corporations Act 2001 (Cth), s 588FH. In England the preference section itself may apply to the guarantor, by virtue of the Insolvency Act 1986, s 239(4)(a) and, for company liquidation, s 340(3)(a). See also *West Mercia Safetyware Ltd v Dodd* [1988] BCLC 250, in which it was held to be a breach of duty by a director to cause a transfer of the company's funds when the company was known to be insolvent for the purpose of relieving the director of personal liability under a guarantee.

[45] See also the discussion of *Matthews v Geraghty* in *Hamilton v Commonwealth Bank of Australia* (1992) 9 ACSR 90, 109–110.

company, not the bank's act in setting off the credit balance against the debit balance pursuant to the prior set-off agreement.[46]

The third member of the Supreme Court, Cox J, similarly held that there was a **16.10** disposition of property for the purpose of the section, but he described the transaction differently. In a short judgment, he said that, since the transfer from the current account to the loan account was authorized by the terms of the arrangement between the bank and the company, the 'whole transaction', in other words the deposit together with the set-off, was a relevant disposition of property by the company within the meaning of the section.[47] The set-off on its own, however, was still not regarded as a disposition of property made by the company.

In *Matthews v Geraghty* the subject of the set-off was a debt arising from a deposit. **16.11** King CJ and Bollen J viewed the deposit as the relevant disposition of property by the company, while Cox J regarded the subsequent contractual set-off as part of the same transaction as the deposit. Those analyses would not be available if the debt the subject of the set-off is not the result of a disposition of property, for example in the case of a contract to perform work. There is other authority however which suggests that a creditor's act in effecting a set-off pursuant to a prior set-off agreement by itself could constitute a preference for the purpose of the bankruptcy legislation.

In *Driver v Federal Commissioner of Taxation*[48] a company was assessed to pay **16.12** amounts to the Commissioner of Taxation as income tax in respect of two tax returns. In each case the company lodged a request for an amended assessment, which resulted in a credit to the company. Pursuant to a power conferred by the income tax legislation, the Commissioner of Taxation applied the credits in reduction of the company's outstanding tax liabilities. The company went into liquidation, and the liquidator asserted that the application of the credits to the unpaid tax constituted a preference. Windeyer J rejected the argument. His decision turned on the language of the preference provisions set out in the Corporations Law for company liquidation,[49] the effect of which is considered

---

[46] See also Madden CJ's comment in *Re McConnell* [1912] VLR 102, 109, (1911) 18 ALR 90, 94, that the words of the preference section 'connote an active operation by the insolvent himself . . .'. A'Beckett J, with whom Hood J concurred, differed from Madden CJ, holding (at [1912] VLR 102, 112) that the appropriation by the agent of the insolvent's money in discharge of the insolvent's debt in that case was a 'payment made' by the insolvent. However, that view was premised on his Honour's assumption (at 111) that the creditor could not have sold the debtor's goods without the debtor's assent. Madden CJ, on the other hand, considered that the authority to sell was an authority coupled with an interest and therefore it was irrevocable by the debtor.

[47] Hodgson J adopted Cox J's analysis as an alternative basis for his decision in *Hamilton v Commonwealth Bank of Australia* (1992) 9 ACSR 90, 109–110. See also *Re Emanuel (No 14) Pty Ltd; Macks v Blacklaw & Shadforth Pty Ltd* (1997) 147 ALR 281 in relation to company liquidation. See para 16.15 below.

[48] (1999) 42 ATR 510, affirmed [2000] NSWCA 247.

[49] Corporations Law, ss 588FA–588FF. See now the Corporations Act 2001 (Cth).

below.[50] If, however, the question had arisen under the earlier Companies (New South Wales) Code, he said that the Commissioner's unilateral act in applying the credit to the outstanding tax liability would have been a preference. The preference section in the Code[51] applied in circumstances where there was: 'A settlement, a conveyance or transfer of property, a charge on property, a payment made, or an obligation incurred, by a company . . .'. This was similar in effect to the current bankruptcy provision. Windeyer J said that the application of the credit in reduction of the outstanding tax would have been characterized as a 'payment' for the purpose of that section, and that it would have constituted a preference under the Code.[52]

16.13   Windeyer J's discussion of the earlier legislation was obiter. Furthermore, while he referred to the meaning of 'payment', accepting that this may include a mere transfer of figures in an account without any money passing, the further requirement that the payment had to be made 'by' the company was not explored. Nevertheless, in a subsequent appeal to the New South Wales Court of Appeal, Sheller JA expressed agreement with Windeyer J's judgment, including, it would seem, his Honour's assessment of what the position would have been under the earlier legislation.[53] If indeed the Commissioner's unilateral application of the credits in reduction of the tax liability pursuant to a power in the income tax legislation constituted a payment 'by' the company, *a fortiori* that would be the case where a creditor's unilateral act in effecting a set-off occurred pursuant to a power conferred by a prior set-off agreement with the debtor. The preferred view, which is consistent with *Cinema Plus Ltd v Australia and New Zealand Banking Group Ltd*, is that the set-off constitutes a payment, but it is not a payment 'by' the debtor. The creditor, acting on his own behalf and not on behalf of the debtor, pays himself from a designated asset of the debtor.[54] On its own, therefore, this should not be a preference. On the other hand, the circumstances surrounding the

---

[50] See paras 16.14–16.17 below.

[51] Section 451(1).

[52] Windeyer J found support for this view in comments by Tipping J in the New Zealand Supreme Court in *Re Peter Austin Ltd* [1990] 2 NZLR 245, 248 in relation to the equivalent New Zealand provision.

[53] *Driver v Commissioner of Taxation* [2000] NSWCA 247 at paras 19 and 20.

[54] In *Sheahan v Carrier Air Conditioning Pty Ltd* (1997) 189 CLR 407, 437 Dawson, Gaudron and Gummow JJ noted (referring to *Re Stevens* (1929) 1 ABC 90, 93) that there may be a payment made by a debtor within the meaning of the preference section in the bankruptcy legislation where the debtor directs a third party who holds funds at the direction of the debtor, or is otherwise obliged to the debtor, to account to the debtor, not by payment to the debtor, but to a creditor of the debtor. But the High Court went on to comment that the third party in that circumstance is to be treated as acting 'on behalf of' the debtor, whereas on the basis of *Cinema Plus Ltd v Australia and New Zealand Banking Group Ltd* (n 38 above) that explanation would not be available in the case of a set-off effected pursuant to a prior set-off agreement.

incurring of the debts the subject of the set-off,[55] or the entry into the set-off agreement itself, could give rise to a preference.

Preferences in Australia—company liquidation

In Australia, a new scheme governing preferences and other voidable transactions in company liquidation was introduced into the Corporations Law in 1992, and subsequently it was re-enacted as part of the Corporations Act 2001 (Cth). An analysis of the question whether the exercise by a creditor of a contractual right of set-off prior to the debtor's liquidation may be a preference, in circumstances where the cross-demands otherwise would not have been set off in the liquidation,[56] involves a number of steps.   **16.14**

Section 588FA provides that a transaction may be an unfair preference in a company's liquidation if the company and the creditor are parties to it, and it results in the creditor receiving more from the company in respect of an unsecured debt than the creditor would receive if the transaction were set aside. The first step, then, is to identify the 'transaction'. Because of the requirement that the company be a party to the transaction, Windeyer J held in *Driver v Federal Commissioner of Taxation*[57] that the Commissioner of Taxation's action in applying a company's tax credits in reduction of its tax liabilities was not a preference in the company's liquidation, a view that was affirmed on appeal by the New South Wales Court of Appeal.[58] The exercise of a contractual set-off differs from the circumstances in issue in the *Driver* case in that the set-off occurs as a result of a power conferred by the debtor on the creditor. However the debtor usually is still not a party to the ultimate act of effecting a set-off, and so ordinarily the act of effecting the set-off should not be a transaction for the purpose of s 588FA.[59] In some cases the analysis in *Re Emanuel (No 14) Pty Ltd; Macks v Blacklaw & Shadforth Pty Ltd*[60] may qualify that proposition. In *Re Emanuel*, the Federal Court[61] accepted that there may be a transaction to which a debtor (A) is a party notwithstanding that it is made up of a composite of dealings in not all of which A participates. That view   **16.15**

---

[55] Including as a result of a deposit of money, as in *Matthews v Geraghty* (1986) 43 SASR 576. See above.

[56] See para 16.04 above.

[57] (1999) 42 ATR 510. See para 16.12 above.

[58] [2000] NSWCA 247. See also *Macquarie Health Corp Ltd v Commissioner of Taxation* (1999) 96 FCR 238, 269–271 in relation to a notice given by the Commissioner under the Income Tax Assessment Act 1936 (Cth), s 218 (see now s 260–5 in Schedule 1 of the Tax Administration Act 1953 (Cth)).

[59] Compare Cox J in *Matthews v Geraghty* (1986) 43 SASR 576, 581–582 in relation to the expression 'a disposition of property is made by a company', where a company made a deposit with a bank which the bank set off against an overdrawn account. However King CJ and Bollen J adopted a different analysis. See paras 16.9 and 16.10 above.

[60] (1997) 147 ALR 281.

[61] O'Loughlin, Branson and Finn JJ.

was expressed in the context of an agreement between A and B that, as part of a settlement of the claims between them, B would make a payment to C who was A's creditor. The court rejected an argument that, since the payment was made by B and not A, A was not a party to the transaction constituting the payment, and therefore the payment was not a preference in A's liquidation. The transaction consisted of a composite of dealings, and it did not matter that A did not participate in the final act of payment to C. In discussing the point, however, the court emphasized that its observations were confined to a course of dealing initiated by a debtor for the purpose, and having the effect, of extinguishing a debt. It referred to the situation in which the debtor 'procures the intended outcome'.[62] In the case of a set-off agreement, however, commonly it would not be the debtor's intention at the time of entering into the agreement that the creditor would exercise the right. Rather, the contractual set-off would be intended to provide a form of security as part of an ongoing commercial arrangement between the parties.

16.16   In any event, the entry into the set-off agreement, or the incurring of an obligation the subject of the set-off, itself could be a transaction for the purpose of section 588FA, given that the company was a party to those acts. Ordinarily, then, section 588FA should direct attention initially to those matters as the foundation of a preference argument. Once a transaction is characterized as an unfair preference for the purpose of section 588FA, section 588FC provides that it may be an insolvent transaction, and therefore it potentially may be avoided by a liquidator, if it was entered into when the company was insolvent, or if an act was done for the purpose of giving effect to the transaction when the company was insolvent. But what if the obligations the subject of the contractual set-off were incurred, and the set-off agreement was entered into, before the company's insolvency, though the set-off was effected after insolvency? It suffices for section 588FC that an act is done for the purpose of giving effect to the transaction, but the section does not stipulate who must perform the act. It is not limited in that regard to the company. If the transaction is characterized as the entry into the set-off agreement, the creditor's act in setting off the demands pursuant to the agreement may be characterized as an act done for the purpose of giving effect to the transaction. If the set-off was effected within the preference period[63] and while the company was insolvent, the set-off may be voidable.[64]

---

[62]   (1997) 147 ALR 281, 288. See also *V R Dye & Co v Peninsula Hotels Pty Ltd* [1999] 3 VR 201, 215 and *Re Imobridge Pty Ltd (No 2)* [2000] 2 Qd R 280, 295.

[63]   Corporations Act 2001 (Cth), s 588FE.

[64]   In order to constitute a preference, the transaction must 'result' in the creditor receiving more from the company in respect of an unsecured debt than the creditor would receive if the transaction were set aside. When a creditor unilaterally effects a set-off pursuant to a prior set-off agreement, and a set-off would not otherwise have been available in the liquidation (see para 16.04 above), it is the creditor's own action, rather than the earlier transaction to which the company was a party, which is the immediate cause of the creditor receiving more than it would have received in the liquidation. The connection nevertheless should be established, because the set-off is the natural and reasonably

The creditor nevertheless will be protected if it can satisfy the requirements of sec- **16.17**
tion 588FG(2). An examination of that issue once again directs attention to the
transaction (entry into the set-off agreement or the incurring of the obligations),
as opposed to the act done for the purpose of giving effect to it. Section 588FG(2)
protects a creditor if a number of conditions are satisfied. In summary, these are:
(a) that the creditor became a party to the transaction in good faith, (b) that, at the
time when the creditor became a party, it had no reasonable grounds for suspecting that the company was insolvent at that time or would become insolvent as a
result of an act done for the purpose of giving effect to the transaction, and moreover a reasonable person in the creditor's circumstances would have had no such
grounds for so suspecting, and (c) that the creditor provided valuable consideration under the transaction or changed its position in reliance on the transaction.
If those requirements are satisfied, the transaction would not be impugned as a
preference.

(2) Set-off Agreement Taking Effect Contrary to the Pari Passu Principle

There is a second limitation on the validity of a set-off effected pursuant to an **16.18**
agreement to which a bankrupt or a company in liquidation is a party. Unless the
agreement is effective to create a charge,[65] the statutory requirement of a pari passu
distribution of the estate amongst the general body of creditors[66] has the consequence that a contractual set-off which involves a claim in favour the bankrupt or
the company[67] will not be effective to the extent that the demands had not been
set against each other, and a balance struck, before the commencement of the
bankruptcy or the liquidation. Rather, a set-off will only occur to the extent that
it is available within the terms of the insolvency set-off section.[68] As Rose LJ remarked in delivering the judgment of the Court of Appeal in *Re Bank of Credit and
Commerce International SA (No 8)*:[69] 'Once insolvency supervenes, rule 4.90 of

---

foreseeable consequence of the transaction. See *Matthews v Geraghty* (1986) 43 SASR 576 (which is
referred to in *Hamilton v Commonwealth Bank of Australia* (1992) 9 ACSR 90, 109–110), and para
16.09 above.

[65] See paras 16.78–16.91 below.

[66] See the Insolvency Act 1986, s 107 (which also applies to compulsory liquidation: see *Webb v
Whiffin* (1872) LR 5 HL 711, 735 and *Attorney-General v McMillan & Lockwood Ltd* [1991]
1 NZLR 53), and r 4.181 of the Insolvency Rules. For bankruptcy, see the Insolvency Act 1986,
s 328(3).

[67] Compare the discussion below of a set-off agreement where the set-off concerns only a *liability* of the bankrupt or the company.

[68] *Re Charge Card Services Ltd* [1987] Ch 150, 177; *Re Bank of Credit and Commerce
International SA (No 8)* [1996] Ch 245, 257, 272–273; *Sinochem International Oil (London) Co Ltd
v Mobil Sales and Supply Corp* [2000] 1 All ER (Comm) 474, 480. Compare *Sturdy v Arnaud* (1790)
3 TR 599, 100 ER 754, and *Hanford v Moseley*, unreported but referred to in *Jones v Mossop* (1844)
3 Hare 568, 572–574, 67 ER 506, 508–509. Compare also *Dobson v Lockhart* (1793) 5 TR 133,
101 ER 77, in which the agreement in question was interpreted as making the debt to the bankrupt
conditional.

[69] [1996] Ch 245, 272.

the Insolvency Rules 1986 requires set-off in the situations in which it is applicable and public policy forbids it where it is not.' Thus, where a surety places a deposit with a creditor charged as security for the principal debtor's liability, and the creditor becomes bankrupt or goes into liquidation, lack of mutuality would prevent a set-off under the insolvency set-off section in relation to the deposit and the principal debt,[70] and a prior agreement that the deposit is to be set off against the debt in the event of default in payment would not be effective in the bankruptcy or the liquidation.[71]

16.19   The leading authority on this second limitation is *British Eagle International Air Lines Ltd v Compagnie Nationale Air France*.[72] The International Air Transport Association had established a clearing house system for the monthly settlement of debits and credits arising when members performed services for one another. A balance would be struck between the total sum owing to a particular member in respect of services supplied by it *for* all other members, and the total owing by that member in respect of services supplied *by* all other members. The clearance took effect within five days after the thirtieth day of each calendar month in relation to the month prior to that calendar month. Members with an overall debit balance would pay into the clearing house the amount of the debit, while the clearing house would pay to members with an overall credit balance the sums due to them. British Eagle went into liquidation. The House of Lords said that any clearance that had taken place before the commencement of the liquidation was binding on the liquidator,[73] since there was no question of a preference. The majority[74] held

---

[70]   *Re Bank of Credit and Commerce International SA (No 8)* [1998] AC 214. See para 12.38 above.

[71]   *Re BCCI (No 8)* [1996] Ch 245, 272, CA.

[72]   [19751 1 WLR 758. See also *Re NIAA Corp Ltd* (1993) 33 NSWLR 344, 359.

[73]   As Lord Romilly M.R. remarked in *Re Smith Knight & Co, ex p Ashbury* (1868) LR 5 Eq 223, 226, 'The Act of Parliament unquestionably says, that everbody shall be paid *pari passu*, but that means everybody after the winding-up has commenced. It does not mean that the Court will look into past transactions, and equalise all creditors by making good to those who have not received anything a sum of money equal to that which other creditors have received.' See also *Carreras Rothmans Ltd v Freeman Mathews Treasure Ltd* [1985] 1 Ch 207, in which the money in the account was not an asset of the company at the date of the liquidation.

[74]   Lord Cross of Chelsea, Lord Diplock, and Lord Edmund-Davies concurring. The dissentients, Lord Morris of Borth-y-Gest and Lord Simon of Glaisdale, said that, as a result of the clearing house rules, money was not payable by one member to another, but rather the clearing house itself was the creditor. Therefore the property of the company in liquidation did not include the right to receive money from the other members. The majority on the other hand (see Lord Cross of Chelsea at 778) noted that the framers of the regulations had described the rights of the members *inter se* as debts, and concluded that, notwithstanding that one member could not have brought legal proceedings against another member, each member performing services for another obtained a species of chose in action against that other member which could be enforced against it separately in the liquidation. Compare the Talisman system operated by the London Stock Exchange, which provides that, after clearance, selling member firms have no rights against buying member firms but instead have rights only against the Stock Exchange, and conversely that the Stock Exchange has the right to seek payment of the balance due from any member firm. See Abrams, 'Talisman: A Legal Analysis' (1980) 1 The Company Lawyer 17, and Goode, *Legal Problems of Credit and Security* (2nd edn, 1988) 175–6.

however that the clearing house system could not operate after the commence-ment of the liquidation in respect of debits and credits not actually cleared at that date, because this would be contrary to the statutory injunction that the property of a company is to be applied in its winding up in satisfaction of its liabilities *pari passu*. It made no difference that the parties may have had good business reasons for entering into the arrangement, or that the arrangement was not designed spe-cifically in order to evade the insolvency legislation.[75] Therefore, the liquidator was entitled to recover the uncleared credits owing to the company, while mem-bers with uncleared debits on the company's accounts were each remitted to a proof in respect of them. On the other hand, each member could set off the uncleared sums owing to it individually by the company against its individual indebtedness to the company.

In the context of a set-off agreement, the objection in the *British Eagle* case should **16.20** only be relevant when the agreement provides for a set-off against a claim possessed by a bankrupt or a company in liquidation in circumstances where the insolvency set-off section does not apply. There is no reason why a set-off agree-ment which involves utilizing a liability of the bankrupt or the company should be impugned. For example, A, B and C may agree that A's liability to B may be set off against B's liability to C, and A goes into liquidation before the set-off has occurred. Since A's liability, as opposed to property distributable amongst credi-tors, is in issue, the liquidation should not affect the agreement.[76] The agreement would have the effect that B would no longer be a proving creditor to the extent of the set-off, with a consequent increase in the dividend payable to other credi-tors. Nevertheless, comments made in *Re Bank of Credit and Commerce International SA (No 8)*[77] have cast doubt on that view. In the Court of Appeal, Rose LJ in delivering the Court's judgment said that, 'if A owes B £x and B owes C £y *and any of them becomes insolvent* the two debts cannot be set off even if there is an express agreement by the three of them that B may set them off; such an agreement is contrary to the scheme of distribution on insolvency and cannot pre-vail over the rules which require pari passu distribution . . . .'[78] But why the agree-ment should be regarded as contrary to public policy when A is the insolvent party

---

[75] Compare *Ex parte Mackay* (1873) LR 8 Ch App 643 with respect to the agreement as to the royalties in a bankruptcy. Lord Cross of Chelsea rejected the argument that the parties to the clear-ing house arrangement in the *British Eagle* case (n 72 above) had intended to give one another charges on some of each other's future book debts. Compare *Ex parte Mackay* with respect to the right to half of the royalties.

[76] See also para 13.70 above. Mance LJ's comments in *Sinochem International Oil (London) Co Ltd v Mobil Sales and Supply Corp* [2000] 1 All ER (Comm) 474, 480 with respect to the liquidation of the affiliate may support this view, although it is not clear if his Lordship was referring to a set-off of a debt owing by the insolvent affiliate against a debt owing to Sinochem London or another affil-iate.

[77] [1996] Ch 245, *per* Rose, Saville and Millett LJJ.

[78] [1996] Ch 245, 257 (emphasis added).

is difficult to understand. The decision in that case went on appeal to the House of Lords. In a speech with which the other Law Lords agreed, Lord Hoffmann commented:[79]

> In English law, it [ie insolvency set-off] is strictly limited to mutual claims existing at the bankruptcy date. There can be no set-off of claims by third parties, even with their consent. To do so would be to allow parties by agreement to subvert the fundamental principle of pari passu distribution of the insolvent company's assets . . .

Once again, to the extent that this may encompass an agreement which provides that a third party's (B's) claim against the company is to be set off against B's liability to C, as opposed to the company's asset in the form of a claim being utilized by way of a set-off against a third party's liability, it is difficult to understand why it should be objectionable. The agreement in this situation would not subvert the *pari passu* principle.

C. An Administrator's Indemnity and Lien in Australia

16.21 In Australia, an administrator appointed to a company pursuant to Part 5.3A of the Corporations Act 2001 (Cth) is personally liable for certain debts incurred in the performance or exercise of his or her functions or powers.[80] On the other hand, the administrator is entitled to be indemnified out of the company's property for debts for which the administrator is liable and also for remuneration.[81] The right of indemnity is expressed to have priority over the company's unsecured debts,[82] and is secured by a lien over the company's property.[83] If the property in question consists of a debt owing to the company, and the debtor has a contractual right to set off the debt against a separate debt owing by the company to the debtor, the question may arise whether the administrator's lien on the company's property has priority over the contractual right of set-off.

16.22 In *Cinema Plus Ltd v Australia and New Zealand Banking Group Ltd*[84] a company had a current account with a bank with a substantial credit balance when administrators were appointed to it, and it was also indebted to the bank on a terminated lease facility. The lease documentation entitled the bank to set off the debt against the credit balance, but before it purported to do so the administrators incurred debts in the course of the administration for which they were personally liable. The account represented property of the company in the form of a debt owing to

---

[79] [1998] AC 214, 223.
[80] Corporations Act 2001 (Cth), s 443A.
[81] Corporations Act 2001 (Cth), s 443D.
[82] Corporations Act 2001 (Cth), s 443E.
[83] Corporations Act 2001 (Cth), s 443F.
[84] (2000) 49 NSWLR 513.

it, but if the bank could then set off the account against the company's liability on the terminated facility, the account would have disappeared and the administrators would not have been able to look to it in order to indemnify themselves. The administrators had a lien on the company's property to secure their right of indemnity, and ordinarily a person taking an assignment of or a security over a debt should take subject to a prior contractual right of set-off.[85] The New South Wales Court of Appeal[86] however held that the administrator's lien had priority over the contractual right of set-off, and was not disturbed by it. Spigelman CJ[87] justified that conclusion by reference to the object of Part 5.3A of the Corporations Act,[88] as set out in section 435A. The stated object is to provide for the business, property and affairs of an insolvent company to be administered in a way that maximizes the chances of the company continuing in existence or, if that is not possible, that results in a better return for the company's creditors and members than would result from an immediate winding up of the company. The Chief Justice said that it would best serve the achievement of that object if the reference to 'the company's property' in section 443D were understood as referring to the company's property as it existed at the time when the debts were incurred and the right to remuneration accrued. He thought that persons would be reluctant to accept appointment as administrators if they could not determine in advance whether the statutory indemnity would cover their exposure. If the value of the indemnity could be reduced by subsequent conduct of creditors which retrospectively exposed an administrator to liability or loss of remuneration, the statutory scheme would not operate effectively.

The Court of Appeal rejected an argument that the set-off agreement in issue created a charge.[89] If it had operated as a charge, the bank would have been precluded from enforcing it during the administration without the administrators' consent or the leave of the court.[90] Since the agreement was not a charge the bank was an unsecured creditor, and a result in its favour would have run counter to the stipulation in the Corporations Act that an administrator's right of indemnity has priority over all the company's unsecured debts.[91] The decision therefore would appear to be correct. **16.23**

---

[85] See paras 17.38–17.46 below.
[86] Spigelman CJ, Sheller and Giles JJA.
[87] (2000) 49 NSWLR 513, 527–528 paras 59–69. Sheller and Giles JJA (at 545–546, 549) agreed with Spigelman CJ on this point.
[88] The legislation at the time was the Corporations Law, which subsequently was replaced by the Corporations Act 2001 (Cth), although the relevant provisions are the same.
[89] (2000) 49 NSWLR 513, 523 para 47, *per* Spigelman CJ, 543–544 para 116, *per* Sheller JA and 550 para 145, *per* Giles JA.
[90] Corporations Act 2001 (Cth), s 440B.
[91] Corporations Act 2001 (Cth), s 443E(1).

16.24 On the other hand, the Court of Appeal emphasized that the bank's contractual right of set-off was only impaired to the extent that, at the date of the set-off, the account was subject to the lien. Apart from that, the bank's contractual right was not affected by the administration.[92] This had the consequence that the administrator's priority was limited to remuneration and debts incurred between the date of the appointment and the date of set-off. An administrator's lien attaches to the company's property when the right of indemnity arises, and after the company's account in credit has been consolidated with a debt owing by the company there is no longer any property existing to which a lien can attach for the purpose of *subsequently* incurred debts and *subsequent* remuneration.

D. Partnerships

16.25 One of a number of partners indebted in his personal capacity to a creditor, who in turn is indebted to the partnership, may authorize the creditor to set off his separate debt against the debt owing to the partnership. Before the Judicature Acts the fact of the agreement for a set-off provided a defence to an action at law by the partnership for the recovery of the debt owing to the partnership.[93] In equity however the agreement may be impugned if the creditor had knowledge of the interest of the partnership in his indebtedness.[94]

E. Investment Exchanges and Clearing Houses

16.26 The Companies Act 1989, Part VII introduced provisions designed to overcome the effects of *British Eagle International Airlines Ltd v Compagnie Nationale Air France*.[95] Their scope is limited, however. They relate to the rules of certain investment exchanges and clearing houses recognized under the Financial Services Act 1986. The effect of the legislation is that the 'default rules' of the exchange or clearing house, and other rules of the exchange or clearing house relating to the settlement of market contracts, are not to be invalid on the ground of inconsistency with the insolvency laws relating to the distribution of the assets of a person in bankruptcy or winding up.[96] 'Default rules' are rules which provide for the taking of action in the event of a person appearing to be unable, or likely to be unable,

---

[92] (2000) 49 NSWLR 513, 528 para 69, *per* Spigelman CJ, 545–546 paras 124–128, *per* Sheller JA.

[93] *Gordon v Ellis* (1844) 7 Man & G 607, 135 ER 244.

[94] *Piercy v Fynney* (1871) LR 12 Eq 69.

[95] [1975] 1 WLR 758. See para 16.19 above. For a detailed discussion, see *Gore-Browne on Companies* (44th edn, looseleaf) vol 2, ch 34A.

[96] See in particular the Companies Act 1989, ss 155, 158–165.

to meet his obligations in respect of a market contract.[97] They include provision for the rights and liabilities under unsettled market contracts to which the defaulter is a party to be discharged, and for there to be paid by one party to the other such sum of money (if any) as may be determined in accordance with the rules. They also provide for set-off in relation to sums payable in respect of different contracts.[98] The net sum payable in accordance with the default rules by a bankrupt defaulter, or a defaulter in liquidation, is then provable in the bankruptcy or the liquidation, and may be taken into account for the purpose of a set-off in accordance with the principles otherwise applicable under the insolvency set-off section, in the same way as a debt due before the bankruptcy or the liquidation.[99] The application of the Act has since been extended by regulation to include 'money market contracts'.[100] A money market contract is defined as a contract in relation to which a 'listed person' provides settlement arrangements, and which is a contract for the acquisition or disposal either of currency of the United Kingdom or elsewhere or of rights under a contract the value of which is determined by reference to the value of the ecu. A 'listed person' is a person included in a list maintained by the Financial Services Authority. The effect of the regulations is that the default rules of the listed person are not to be invalid by reason of inconsistency with insolvency laws relating to the distribution of assets, in accordance with Part VII of the Companies Act 1989.

Australia

A similar development has occurred in Australia, with the enactment of the Payment Systems and Netting Act 1998 (Cth). The Act gives effect to the rules of stock and futures exchanges and clearing houses approved by the Minister,[101] which relate to the termination of obligations and the calculation and netting of termination values, including in the 'external administration' of a participant (which includes bankruptcy and liquidation).[102] The Act also applies to 'approved netting arrangements',[103] which include payment systems. To qualify, the system

16.27

---

[97] Companies Act 1989, s 188.
[98] Companies Act 1989, sch 21.
[99] See the Companies Act 1989, s 163(2). This is subject to an exception in s 163(4), where a creditor at the time that he entered into a contract had notice that a bankruptcy petition was pending or (in the case of a company) that a meeting of creditors had been summoned under s 98 of the Insolvency Act 1986 or that a winding-up petition was pending. In those circumstances, the value of any profit to him as a result of a sum arising from the contract being taken into account is recoverable from him by the liquidator or trustee in bankruptcy. The exception does not apply, however, in relation to a sum arising from a contract effected under the default rules themselves. See s 163(5).
[100] Financial Markets and Insolvency (Money Market) Regulations 1995 (SI 1995/2049), amended by the Financial Markets and Insolvency (Ecu Contracts) Regulations 1998 (SI 1998/27).
[101] These are referred to in the Act as 'netting markets'.
[102] Payment Systems and Netting Act 1998 (Cth), Pt 5.
[103] Payment Systems and Netting Act 1998 (Cth), Pt 3.

must provide for netting to occur at least once on each business day and be approved by the Reserve Bank.[104] In relation to approved netting arrangements, however, the efficacy of the netting is subject to a qualification. If a party to an approved netting arrangement goes into external administration, and an obligation owed by that party to another party has been netted under the arrangement, in circumstances where a direct payment by that party to the other would have been voidable in the external administration if it had been made to settle the obligation on the day on which the netting occurred, the liquidator (or the equivalent in other forms of external administration) may recover from the other party an amount equal to the amount of the obligation.[105] Thus, the effect of voidable preferences, and other such insolvency principles allowing for claw-back of payments, is preserved.

F. Netting of Foreign Exchange Contracts

16.28 In relation to contracts for the acquisition or disposal of currencies which are not 'money market contracts' governed by Part VII of the Companies Act 1989,[106] questions of set-off in insolvency are determined by reference to the insolvency set-off section and other principles of general application.

16.29 Consider that a bank and a counterparty have entered into large number of foreign exchange contracts involving various currencies and settlement dates. Prior to the decision of the Court of Appeal in *Camdex International Ltd v Bank of Zambia*,[107] there was a body of opinion of considerable standing to the effect that the foreign money obligation under a foreign exchange contract is not a money obligation.[108] That view in turn resulted in doubt as to whether, in the event of the liquidation of the counterparty, the various obligations under foreign exchange contracts between the counterparty and the bank could be set off.[109] In an attempt to avoid that potential difficulty, participants in foreign exchange and other similar markets have had recourse to close-out netting agreements. In the *Camdex* case, the Court of Appeal expressed the view that the foreign money obligation under an exchange contract is properly characterized as a money obligation,[110] which has added greater certainty to the question of set-off in those markets. The case has been criticized, however,[111] and since then the traditional view, that in a

---

[104] Payment Systems and Netting Act 1998 (Cth), s 12.
[105] Payment Systems and Netting Act 1998 (Cth), s 10(4).
[106] See para 16.26 above.
[107] [1997] 6 Bank LR 43. See para 9.21 above.
[108] See paras 9.15–9.16 above.
[109] See paras 9.17–9.20 above, and also Derham, 'Set-off and Netting of Foreign Exchange Contracts in the Liquidation of a Counterparty' [1991] JBL 463.
[110] [1997] 6 Bank LR 43, 51–52, *per* Simon Brown LJ, 55–57, *per* Phillips LJ.
[111] Brindle and Cox (eds), *Law of Bank Payments* (2nd edn, 1999) 29–33.

foreign exchange contract the foreign money is the object of commercial intercourse and as such it should be treated as a commodity, has been reiterated in Australia.[112] But even apart from the *Camdex* case, in other words even if one were to accept that a foreign money obligation under a foreign exchange contract is not a money obligation, there are cogent arguments that a close-out netting contract would be effective to provide a set-off.

The essence of close-out netting[113] is that, upon the occurrence of a liquidation, **16.30** the foreign exchange contracts are 'closed', and are replaced by an obligation to pay the net money value of the contracts based upon the market exchange rates prevailing at the time. Because the obligation is simply to pay a net money amount, any perceived difficulty in relation to whether a foreign money obligation under a foreign exchange contract may be the subject of a set-off in a liquidation would not arise. There would be no danger of the solvent party being confined to a dividend in the liquidation of the counterparty in respect of contracts disclaimed by the liquidator, and at the same time having to perform contracts which are unprofitable from the solvent party's perspective. However a question which has generated considerable debate in recent years is whether a close-out netting agreement could be struck down as an attempt to evade the operation of the insolvency law, if a set-off otherwise would not have been available in the liquidation under the insolvency set-off section.[114]

The question of what constitutes an evasion of the insolvency law has been ex- **16.31** pressed in various terms. However these are not exclusive of each other and to a considerable extent they overlap.

According to one approach, a comparison is made between what the creditor **16.32** would have received if the other party had not become bankrupt, and what the agreement between them states that he should receive in the event of a bankruptcy. There is an evasion of the insolvency law if something is to accrue to the creditor upon the occurrence of the bankruptcy of the debtor which would put him in a better position than if the debtor had not become bankrupt. For example, James LJ, in striking down a contract as constituting a fraud in the bankruptcy law, said that,[115]

> In my opinion, looking at the whole scope and object of this Deed, at the whole intention of the parties, and taking a common-sense view of the thing, it is impossible not to see that it was intended to make a different distribution of the property of the mortgagors according as they should or should not become bankrupt.

---

[112] *Daewoo Australia Pty Ltd v Suncorp-Metway Ltd* (2000) 48 NSWLR 692, 702 para 33, *per* Austin J.

[113] Alternative forms of netting are payment netting and netting by novation, although neither is entirely satisfactory. See generally Derham, 'Set-off and Netting of Foreign Exchange Contracts in the Liquidation of a Counterparty—Part 2: Netting' [1991] JBL 536, 536–9.

[114] See para 16.29 above.

[115] *Ex parte Williams, re Thompson* (1877) 7 Ch D 138, 143.

Similarly, Tomlin J observed in a later case[116] that: 'He cannot make a bargain with the mortgagor which secures to him, the mortgagee, a greater advantage if the mortgagor becomes bankrupt than he would get if he does not.' The principle is illustrated by *Ex parte Mackay*,[117] in which the Court of Appeal struck down a provision in a contract to the effect that, upon the bankruptcy of the debtor, a part of his property should become subject to a charge in favour of the creditor.[118] This formulation would not describe close-out netting. Netting by close-out does not attempt to confer a greater advantage on either party in the liquidation of the other in comparison with what would have been the case in the absence of a liquidation. Before liquidation each of the parties had obligations to the other pursuant to the foreign exchange contracts. After the liquidation the netting agreement provides for a change in the nature of the obligations, but not in their notional net value. The netting is intended to preserve the value of the contracts to the parties, assuming that no liquidation had occurred.

16.33   There is another line of cases dealing with deprivation of property upon insolvency. Subject to some exceptions, such as the case of an asset which is inherently determinable or where there is a superior or a reversionary interest,[119] a person cannot agree to determine his interest in property in the event of his bankruptcy. For example, if a husband brought property into a marriage settlement, a trust of the income of the property in favour of the husband until his bankruptcy was said to be bad.[120] The principle was also applied in the context of a building contract which provided that, if the builder became bankrupt or insolvent, any of his materials and chattels situated on the premises were to be forfeited to the owner. The provision for forfeiture was an attempt to qualify the interest of the builder in his property upon the occurrence of his bankruptcy, and so was void.[121] However there is nothing objectionable in qualifying contractual rights by a provision for termination of the contract upon liquidation,[122] and so these cases are not directly applicable to netting.

---

[116] *Re Johns* [1928] 1 Ch 737, 748.

[117] (1873) LR 8 Ch App 643.

[118] Similarly, a vendor selling on credit terms cannot contract on the basis that, if the purchaser becomes bankrupt, the price should be doubled. See *Ex parte Mackay* (1873) LR 8 Ch App 643, 647.

[119] See *Money Markets International Stockbrokers Ltd v London Stock Exchange Ltd* [2002] 1 WLR 1150, 1160–1161 para 37, 1174 paras 89 and 90.

[120] See *Mackintosh v Pogose* [1895] 1 Ch 505, 511–512.

[121] *Ex parte Jay, re Harrison* (1880) 14 Ch D 19. See also *Rouch v Great Western Railway Co* (1841) 1 QB 51, 64–65, 113 ER 1049; *Ex parte Barter, re Walker* (1884) 26 Ch D 510 (shipbuilding contract). Compare *Ex parte Newitt, re Garrud* (1881) 16 Ch D 522 in which the default was not based upon bankruptcy, though see the discussion of that case in *Money Markets International Stockbrokers Ltd v London Stock Exchange Ltd* [2002] 1 WLR 1150, 1178 para 104 *et seq, per* Neuberger J.

[122] See para 16.37 below.

The issue may be looked at from another perspective. Instead of making a com- **16.34**
parison between the positions of the parties before and after liquidation, regard
may be had to the position in a liquidation, and a comparison is drawn between
what the result would have been for the creditor in the liquidation in the absence
of the provision in question, and what it is intended to be in the light of that provision. There does not appear to be any case in which a contract was struck down
on this basis in circumstances in which one of the other formulations referred to
above would not also have applied, but it is suggested by a number of judicial
statements. In *Ex parte Mackay*[123] James LJ observed that, 'a man is not allowed,
by stipulation with a creditor, to provide for a different distribution of his effects
in the event of bankruptcy from that which the law provides'. In *Ex parte Jackson*[124]
Cotton LJ described as a fraud on the bankruptcy law a clause that he said was 'an
attempt to alter and disturb the legal distribution of the mortgagor's property in
bankruptcy'. Further, when Lord Cross in the *British Eagle* case[125] distinguished
the decision of the Court of Appeal in *Ex parte Mackay*, by which the Court of
Appeal struck down a provision in a contract to the effect that a charge should
arise upon the bankruptcy of the debtor, he said that the charge 'had been created
deliberately in order to provide for a different distribution of the insolvent's property on his bankruptcy from that prescribed by the law'.

These statements would not impugn a contract which had effect before the **16.35**
liquidation and which was not a sham, as for example a valid security. Nor would
they apply to a floating security which is expressed to crystallize upon liquidation.[126] In the first place, a floating security is a present security even before crystallization.[127] But even apart from that, it is of the essence of a floating security that
it crystallizes upon liquidation even in the absence of an express provision to that
effect, given that the company then ceases to carry on business other than for the
purpose of its winding up.[128] Therefore, the stipulation for crystallization upon
liquidation itself does not result in preferential treatment for the chargee. On the
other hand, the statements could be said to have application in a situation in
which a contract provides for a change in the nature of the parties' rights and

---

[123] (1873) LR 8 Ch App 643, 647. This statement was referred to with evident approval by
Tomlin J in *Re Johns* [1928] Ch 737, 745, and by Lord Morris and Lord Cross in *British Eagle
International Air Lines Ltd v Compagnie Nationale Air France* [1975] 1 WLR 758, 770, 779.

[124] (1880) 14 Ch D. 725, 741.

[125] *British Eagle International Airlines Ltd v Compagnie Nationale Air France* [1975] 1 WLR 758,
780.

[126] Compare Coleman, 'Netting A Red Herring' (1994) 9 Journal of International Banking and
Financial Law 391, 399.

[127] *Evans v Rival Granite Quarries, Ltd* [1910] 2 KB 979, 999; *Smith v Bridgend County BC*
[2002] 1 AC 336, 357 paras 61 and 62.

[128] *Re Crompton & Co Ltd* [1914] 1 Ch 954, 961–965, and see generally Goode, *Legal Problems
of Credit and Security* (2nd edn, 1988) 61.

obligations upon the occurrence of a liquidation,[129] where that change is intended[130] to have the effect of altering the distribution in a liquidation in comparison to what it otherwise would have been so as to result in preferential treatment as against the general creditors.[131] Close-out netting should be considered in that context. Doubts have been expressed in the past as to whether a foreign currency obligation pursuant to a foreign exchange contract is a money obligation, and therefore whether it could be the subject of a set-off in a liquidation. As a result of the netting agreement, however, there is a change in the nature of the obligations upon the occurrence of a liquidation, so that the various obligations (including the foreign currency obligations) are replaced by a single obligation to pay a net sterling amount. This change in the nature of the obligations upon the occurrence of a liquidation has raised the question whether close-out netting is contrary to public policy. In *Camdex International Ltd v Bank of Zambia* the Court of Appeal rejected the view that the foreign money obligation under a foreign exchange contract is not a money obligation, but even apart from that development the better view is that close out netting is not contrary to public policy.[132]

16.36 Two preliminary points should be emphasized in relation to the possible application of the public policy ground to netting.

16.37 The first is that the termination of the obligations on its own would not be objectionable. There is nothing wrong with a contract providing for termination upon liquidation. The termination does not operate to deprive the company's creditors of the benefit of an asset that otherwise would have been available to them in the liquidation, but rather it defines the scope of the rights flowing from the

---

[129] See *Re Johnson* [1904] 1 KB 134, 136–137. Compare *Money Markets International Stockbrokers Ltd v London Stock Exchange Ltd* [2002] 1 WLR 1150, 1178 para 104 *et seq.*

[130] See *Re Stockton Iron Furnace Co* (1879) 10 Ch D 335, 356. See also *Ex parte Williams* (1877) 7 Ch D 138, 143; *Re Johns* [1928] 1 Ch 737, 748; *Re Apex Supply Co Ltd* [1942] 1 Ch 108, 114; *Bombay Official Assignee v Shroff* (1932) 48 TLR 443, 446. Compare *Money Markets International Stockbrokers Ltd v London Stock Exchange Ltd* [2002] 1 WLR 1150, 1177–1178 paras 101–103, 1182 para 118.

[131] Coleman, 'Netting A Red Herring' (1994) 9 Journal of International Banking and Financial Law 391, 399 has suggested that the statements in question do not support any such proposition, on the ground that they beg the question as to what the insolvent's property is. However, 'property' and 'effects' would appear to have been used in the sense of the estate available for distribution generally, as opposed to a particular item of property. This is apparent from the Cotton LJ's reference in *Ex parte Jackson* to *altering* the distribution of the bankrupt's property in bankruptcy. Where a contract purports to take property out of the estate (as, for example, in the case of the charge which was expressed to arise upon liquidation in *Ex parte Mackay* (1873) LR 8 Ch App 643), the effect of the contract, if valid, would be that the property in question would not be distributed in the bankruptcy at all, as opposed to being the subject of a different distribution.

[132] The principle in question would only apply if as a result of the relevant event the estate available for distribution amongst the general body of creditors is lessened. Compare the stock exchange close out rules considered in *Ex parte Grant, re Plumbly* (1880) 13 Ch D 667, discussed in Derham, 'Set-off and Netting' [1991] JBL 536, 545–6.

contract.[133] Nor is there anything objectionable *per se* in a clause in a standard loan agreement which accelerates a payment obligation in the event of liquidation, since the clause merely crystallizes the position between the parties without changing the nature of the obligation. If there is an objection in the case of close-out netting, it would be in the replacement of the obligations upon liquidation, some of which (in the situation posited)[134] may not be money obligations and therefore not susceptible to a set-off under the insolvency set-off section, with a net money obligation.

The second point is that it would be misleading to analyse the situation in terms of a single transaction. The totality of the arrangement would have to be looked at. When there is only one transaction, and that transaction is closed out in the liquidation of one of the parties so as to result in an obligation on one of them to pay the net market value to the other, depending on which way the market has moved, it cannot be said that the insolvent's overall position has been affected. The general body of creditors still obtain the benefit of the contract to the extent of its then current market value, and so closure does not change the distribution in the liquidation.[135] This is because there is no question of set-off within the confines of a single transaction. Were it not for the close-out provision, the position would be that the liquidator would either disclaim or affirm the contract. If he disclaimed, the contract would be terminated, and the solvent party would prove for its loss. If on the other hand the liquidator elected to keep the contract on foot, because it was considered profitable from the insolvent party's perspective, the liquidator would have to perform it,[136] in which case set-off within the contract would not be an issue. A close-out would deprive the liquidator of the opportunity to elect to affirm or disclaim, depending on the state of the market, but apart from that closure in relation to a single contract results in the insolvent's estate obtaining the benefit of the contract in the form of a valuation made by reference to market rates prevailing at the time. That situation should be distinguished from close-out netting of foreign exchange contracts in circumstances where there is a large number of separate contracts between the parties.[136a] In the absence of close-out in that circumstance, each contract would either be affirmed or disclaimed by the liquidator. The solvent party would be confined to a dividend for its losses as a result of the disclaimer of contracts unprofitable to the insolvent defaulter, and therefore profitable to the solvent party. However, in relation to contracts which

16.38

---

[133] The contract is 'inherently limited'. See *Money Markets International Stockbrokers Ltd v London Stock Exchange Ltd* [2002] 1 WLR 1150, 1160–1161 para 37, 1174 para 89, *per* Neuberger J.

[134] See para 16.29 above.

[135] See the discussion of *Shipton, Anderson & Co (1927), Ltd v Micks, Lambert & Co* [1936] 2 All ER 1032 in Derham, 'Set-off and Netting' [1991] JBL 536, 549–50.

[136] See para 9.17 above.

[136a] See the discussion in paras 9.11–9.22 above.

the liquidator has elected to perform, if it is assumed, notwithstanding the views expressed in the *Camdex* case, that a foreign money obligation under a foreign exchange contract is not a money obligation,[137] the solvent party may not be entitled to a set-off in relation to its foreign money obligations under those contracts.[138] In those circumstances, close-out netting would have a substantive effect upon the position of the general body of creditors, by changing the nature of the obligations and thereby letting in a set-off where none otherwise would have been available. If the close-out provisions were considered in the context of each individual foreign exchange contract in isolation, they would not be objectionable.[139] If however the relationship is considered in its entirety, so that it is apparent that closure of the contracts pursuant to the close-out provisions would have the effect of changing the distribution in a liquidation, the question would then arise as to whether the form of netting under consideration is contrary to public policy.

16.39   A mitigating factor is that the bank's position could be protected by alternative mechanisms, in which case close-out netting itself should not be objectionable. For example, it could be made a term of each foreign exchange contract, amounting to a condition,[140] that the counterparty must not go into liquidation.[141] The parties to a contract are entitled to stipulate that any term is of a fundamental character going to the root of the contract, although in some circumstances clear language may be required.[142] If liquidation then occurs, the bank would be entitled under normal common law principles to terminate its future obligations under each contract and to claim damages.[143] When a contract is terminated pursuant to an express power contained in the contract, the party exercising the power ordinarily is confined to damages for any breaches that have occurred up to the date of termination, but (in the absence of a repudiation)[144] not thereafter.[145] When termination occurs as a result of a breach of condition, however, the measure of damages relates to the loss of the whole transaction. It includes compensation for loss of the opportunity to receive performance of the other party's

---

[137]   See para 16.29 above.

[138]   See paras 9.17–9.20 above.

[139]   This seems clear from *Shipton, Anderson & Co (1927) Ltd v Micks, Lambert & Co* [1936] 2 All ER 1032.

[140]   As distinguished from a warranty. A condition in this sense should also be distinguished from the condition precedent to the performance of obligations which appears in the International Swaps and Derivatives Association Master Agreement. See para 16.42 below.

[141]   A similar condition would apply to the bank.

[142]   *Schuler AG v Wickman Machine Tools Sales Ltd* [1974] AC 235, 251; *Bunge Corp v Tradax Export SA* [1981] 1 WLR 711, 715–716; *Lombard North Central plc v Butterworth* [1987] 1 QB 527, 535–536, 546.

[143]   *Wickman Machine Tool Sales Ltd v L Schuler AG* [1972] 1 WLR 840, 851; *Lombard North Central plc v Butterworth* [1987] 1 QB 527, 535.

[144]   Liquidation without more would not constitute a repudiation of foreign exchange contracts. See para 9.05 above, and Derham, 'Set-off and Netting' [1991] JBL 463, 481–4.

[145]   *Lombard North Central plc v Butterworth* [1987] 1 QB 527, 546.

outstanding obligations.[146] In the case of foreign exchange contracts which are wholly executory, this should equate to the cost of obtaining replacement contracts in the market, which would be similar to the close-out amount payable under a netting agreement. Indeed, if each contract is separate,[147] a breach of condition would produce a better result for the bank than netting, because the bank would have a claim for damages in respect of each contract in its favour, and could terminate contracts which were unprofitable from its perspective without having to credit the counterparty in liquidation with the market value of those contracts. The counterparty as the defaulter would not be entitled to damages from the bank. While close out netting provisions are not usually drafted in terms of breach of a condition, the fact that the parties by their contract have agreed that a result should follow which is similar to, or indeed less advantageous for the bank than, that which would apply in such a case, suggests that netting itself is not contrary to public policy.

Further, there are other protections that may be built into netting agreements **16.40** with the aim of bringing about a situation in which the result obtained as a result of netting is similar to that which would follow in any event in the absence of the basic netting provisions.

A master netting agreement may provide that all the foreign currency and sterling **16.41** obligations of the parties that arise out of their foreign exchange transactions constitute a single contract. In other words, this is not a case in which a master agreement sets out terms that apply to each foreign exchange transaction, each of which is regarded as a separate contract. Rather, there is only one contract for the performance of all obligations that arise pursuant to outstanding foreign exchange transactions between the parties. The purpose of the provision is to prevent a liquidator being able to 'cherry pick', in other words, being able to disclaim some transactions but not others. The right of disclaimer applies to a 'contract'.[148] The liquidator cannot enforce one part of the contract and disclaim another part. Therefore, if all the foreign exchange transactions constitute a single contract, the counterparty's liquidator could not 'cherry pick'. He could not disclaim some of the transactions and affirm others. The single contract could analysed in either of two ways. In the first place, it could be said that entry into a new foreign exchange transaction takes effect as an amendment to a prior contract which governed their earlier transactions, so that the obligations of the parties under the contract henceforth consist of their obligations pursuant to their prior outstanding transactions

---

[146] *Lombard North Central plc v Butterworth* [1987] 1 QB 527 (esp at 535). Note however the criticism of *Lombard* in *Chitty on Contracts* (28th edn, 1999) vol 1, 1333–4, para 27-116.

[147] Compare the 'one contract' approach in relation to netting, referred to below.

[148] See the Insolvency Act 1986, s 178(3)(b), and in Australia the Corporations Act 2001 (Cth), s 568(1)(f).

together with the obligations arising under the new transaction.[149] Alternatively, when a new foreign exchange transaction is entered into, a new contract could be formed which includes also the rights and obligations under earlier transactions, so that those rights and obligations henceforth become rights and obligations under the new contract.

16.42 The 'single contract' approach is artificial, and it has its critics. An alternative solution, which is widely favoured by practitioners, is a condition precedent along the lines set out in the International Swaps and Derivatives Association Master Agreement, by which the obligations of each party under foreign exchange transactions the subject of the agreement are expressed to be subject to a condition precedent, that no event of default, including liquidation of the counterparty, has occurred. If the counterparty goes into liquidation after it has performed its side of a particular transaction, it may be debated whether the bank in that circumstance could rely on the clause as a justification for not performing its own obligation pursuant to the transaction.[150] But in relation to transactions which are wholly executory, it is difficult to see, in the absence of a waiver by the bank, what basis the liquidator would have for arguing that the counterparty after the liquidation still has valuable enforceable rights against the bank. An agreement for close out netting in such a case could hardly be described as an attempt to evade the operation of the insolvency law.[151]

G. Netting in Australia

16.43 In view of doubts that had been expressed in some quarters as to the efficacy of netting in the event of the liquidation of a counterparty, the Parliament of Australia enacted legislation in 1998 which gave effect to the principle of close-out netting.[152]

---

[149] This should not entail changing the accounting procedures and records of the parties, since each transaction still remains distinct, although it does not constitute a separate contract in its own right. For that reason, it does not suffer from the same drawback as netting by novation. See Derham, 'Set-off and Netting' [1991] JBL 536, 537–9.

[150] See *A-G v McMillan & Lockwood Ltd* [1991] 1 NZLR 53, CA, and note also the discussion in *British Eagle International Air Lines Ltd v Compagnie Nationale Air France* [1975] 1 WLR 758, 778.

[151] This condition precedent would also provide a solution to the problem posed in Australia by the Banking Act 1959 (Cth), s 13A(3), in relation to the situation in which the counterparty is another bank. Section 13A(3) provides that, in the event that an authorized deposit-taking institution becomes unable to meet its obligations or suspends payment, its assets in Australia are to be available to meet its deposit liabilities in Australia in priority to all other liabilities. This should not affect netting where the condition precedent applies, since in such a case foreign exchange contracts which are still wholly executory would not be valuable assets. In any event, see now the Payment Systems and Netting Act 1998 (Cth), discussed below.

[152] Legislation has also been enacted in New Zealand. See the Companies Amendment Act 1999, s 15, and the Insolvency Amendment Act 1999.

Part 4 of the Payment Systems and Netting Act 1998 (Cth), which deals with **16.44** close-out netting, resulted from a report prepared by a sub-committee of the Companies and Securities Advisory Committee.[153] The sub-committee included in its report a form of draft legislation which confined close-out netting to certain types of financial contracts, principally consisting of products such as swaps, foreign exchange contracts, and various forms of options and derivatives. The Act is not so confined, however. It allows netting in respect of a 'close-out netting contract', which is defined broadly in section 5. Subject to a number of exclusions, a close-out netting contract essentially is a contract under which, upon the happening of a particular event, (a) particular obligations of the parties terminate or may be terminated, (b) termination values of the obligations are calculated or may be calculated, and (c) the termination values are netted or may be netted so that only a net cash amount is payable. In addition, a contract may be declared by regulation to be a close-out netting contract.

Close-out netting contracts need not relate to a particular subject, but may **16.45** encompass obligations of any nature. Thus, a simple contract debt, for example in relation to a bank account, potentially could be the subject of a close-out netting contract. The obligations, it would seem, need not be prospective, but could include obligations already incurred at the date of the close-out netting contract. Further, the legislation is not in its terms confined to bilateral netting, but would allow netting in relation to three or more parties.[154]

Subject to a close-out netting contract having a sufficient nexus with Australia,[155] **16.46** it is provided in section 14(1)(c) that 'obligations may be terminated, termination values may be calculated and a net amount become payable in accordance with the contract'. Further, section 14(1)(d) stipulates that an assignment of rights by a counterparty, or the creation of a security interest over those rights, where it occurs in contravention of a prohibition in the close-out netting contract, will not defeat the netting. The efficacy of netting is further reinforced by section 14(1)(e), which stipulates that, 'for the purposes of any law', the assets of a party to a close-out netting contract are taken to include any net obligation owed to the party under the contract, and are taken not to include obligations terminated under the

---

[153] Netting Sub-Committee of the Companies and Securities Advisory Committee, *Netting in Financial Markets Transactions—Final Report* (June 1997).

[154] See para 16.57 below.

[155] This is satisfied if Australian law governs the close-out netting contract and the contract is entered into in circumstances that are within Commonwealth constitutional reach. See s 14(1). Commonwealth constitutional reach is defined in s 5 in terms of various matters which are recognized heads of Commonwealth power under the Australian Constitution. In addition, if a person who is a party to a close-out netting contract goes into 'external administration' (which is defined in s 5 in terms that would include matters such as company liquidation, receivership and bankruptcy), there is a sufficient nexus for the Act if Australian law governs the external administration. See s 14(2).

contract. This would apply, for example, where a third party seeks to execute a judgment obtained against a party to a close-out netting contract by attaching a debt owing to that party which is subject to the contract. Termination and netting under the contract would defeat the execution creditor.

16.47 Section 14(2) governs the situation in which a counterparty goes into external administration, which is defined in section 5 as including events such as company liquidation, receivership, administration, bankruptcy and a deed of arrangement under Part X of the Bankruptcy Act 1966 (Cth). In any of those circumstances, section 14(2)(c), like section 14(1)(c), provides that obligations may be terminated, termination values may be calculated and a net amount become payable in accordance with the contract. Obligations that have been terminated are to be disregarded in the external administration, and the net obligation is to be provable in the external administration or is to be payable to the external administrator, as the case may be. Section 14(2)(g) goes on to provide that the termination of obligations, the netting of obligations and any payment made to discharge a net obligation are not to be void or voidable in the external administration. This negates the effect of the decision in the *British Eagle* case.[156]

16.48 Netting in the event of liquidation (or other external administration) is subject to two limitations. In the first place, section 14(3) provides that a person may not rely on a close-out netting contract in relation to a right or obligation 'if the person acquired the right or obligation from another person with notice that that other person was at that time unable to pay their debts as and when they became due and payable'. Close-out netting is also restricted by section 14(5). This applies in relation to an obligation owed by a party to a close-out netting contract to another person, in circumstances where the party goes into external administration and the obligation is, or has been, terminated under the contract. If the other person did not act in good faith in entering into the transaction that created the terminated obligation, or the other person had reasonable grounds to suspect insolvency when the transaction that created the terminated obligation was entered into, or the other person neither provided valuable consideration nor changed its position in reliance on the transaction, section 14 will not apply to the obligation. It cannot be netted in the liquidation (or other form of external administration), and similarly the protection provided by section 14 will not apply where netting occurred prior to the external administration.[157]

---

[156] *British Eagle International Air Lines Ltd v Compagnie Nationale Air France* [1975] 1 WLR 758. See para 16.19 above.

[157] This appears from s 14(5)(b), which refers to an obligation which 'has been' terminated under the contract. Apart from subsection (5), netting prior to an external administration is protected by s 14(2) in a subsequent liquidation (or other external administration). Thus, s 14(2) is expressed to apply (in (a)) where a party is, or 'has been', a party to a close-out netting contract, while, according to (d), obligations that are 'or have been' terminated under the contract are to be disregarded in the external administration (subject however to subsection (5)).

A number of points may be made in relation to the legislation.   **16.49**

Section 14(1)(d), dealing with assignments and security interests, and section   **16.50**
14(1)(e), which provides that the assets of a party to a close-out netting contract
are taken, for the purposes of any law, to include the net obligation owed to the
party under the contract, have not been specifically extended to section 14(2) in
relation to external administrations. This may be because section 14(1) is intended to apply in all cases, but if that is the explanation it is not clear what purpose section 14(2)(c) serves, given section 14(1)(c). Alternatively, section
14(1)(d) may not have been extended to section 14(2) because it was thought that
the principles set out in section 14(2) would take effect in accordance with their
terms, and on that basis they would override any assignment or other interest asserted by a third party. In its application to section 14(1), however, paragraph (d)
only subordinates the interest of the assignee or the encumbrancee where the
assignment or the encumbrance is entered into in contravention of a prohibition
in the close-out netting contract. This would not be the case, for example, if the
assignment or the encumbrance occurred before the close-out netting contract.
On the other hand, if in the case of section 14(2) it is sought to rely on the general
language of the subsection in order to defeat the interest of an assignee or the
holder of an encumbrance, the qualification in section 14(1)(d) would not appear
to apply.

Section 14(2) gives supremacy to a close-out netting contract in the event of an ex- **16.51**
ternal administration. The obligations may be terminated, termination values
may be calculated and a net amount become payable in accordance with the
contract, and obligations that have been terminated under the contract are to be
disregarded in the external administration. The definition of external administration includes receivership.[158] On its face, section 14(2) would seem to apply even
where the security pursuant to which the receiver was appointed pre-dated the
netting agreement. For example, a debt to the knowledge of the debtor may be
charged in favour of a third party, and subsequently the chargor/creditor and the
debtor may enter into a close-out netting contract in respect of their obligations,
including the charged debt. In that circumstance, it seems unjust that, if the mortgagee later were to appoint a receiver and the receiver attempts to collect the debt,
the close-out netting contract should prevail. Nevertheless, this would seem to be
the effect of section 14(2). At general law the earlier charge, of which the debtor
was aware, would have priority over a set-off agreement in this situation,[159] and it

---

[158] The definition of 'external administration' in s 5 includes (in (a)) the case of a body corporate
that is an externally administered body corporate within the meaning of the Corporations Act, and
in s 9 of the Corporations Act 'externally-administered body corporate' is defined as including a
body corporate in respect of property of which a receiver, or a receiver and manager, has been appointed (whether or not by the court).

[159] See para 17.46 below.

is difficult to see why close-out netting under the Payment Systems and Netting Act should produce a different result.

16.52 Section 14(3) also presents difficulties. It applies in an external administration. It provides that a person may not rely on the application of section 14(2) to a right or obligation if the person 'acquired the right or obligation' from 'another person' with notice that that other person at the time was unable to pay their debts as and when they became due and payable. The expression 'another person' also appears in section 14(5) (see below), and its use in that context suggests that it includes a counterparty to a close-out netting contract. Subsection (3) seems intended to introduce into the netting legislation a concept similar to the qualification to the insolvency set-off section.[160] The Corporations Act 2001 (Cth), section 553C(2) provides, as a qualification to the right of set-off conferred by section 553C(1) in the case of company liquidation, that a person dealing with a company is not entitled to a set-off in the company's liquidation if at the time of giving or receiving credit from the company the person had notice of the fact that the company was insolvent. In bankruptcy, the corresponding provision[161] is expressed in terms of notice of an available act of bankruptcy. There is however an important distinction between, on the one hand, section 14(3), and on the other section 553C(2) and section 86(2). The latter are drafted in terms of notice of insolvency, or of notice of an available act of bankruptcy, at the time of giving or receiving credit. Those provisions would apply, for example, to the case of a deposit made by an insolvent customer to the credit of an account with a bank, in circumstances where the customer is separately indebted to the bank. The deposit to the credit of the account would result in a debt owing by the bank to the customer, and would constitute the giving of credit by the customer to the bank. Therefore, if the bank had notice of the customer's insolvency at the time of the deposit, it could not employ the debt in a set-off in the customer's subsequent liquidation. Section 14(3), on the other hand, is not well expressed in that regard. It is drafted in terms of acquiring a right or an obligation from another person, as opposed to giving or receiving credit. When a customer makes a deposit with a bank, the bank receives credit from the customer, but it is a misnomer to say that the bank acquires an obligation from the customer. It certainly acquires the funds the subject of the deposit, and moreover it is correct to say that it *incurs* an obligation to the customer as a result of accepting the deposit. But the obligation itself is not acquired from the customer. It is simply a consequence of the deposit.

16.53 Furthermore, section 14(3) on its face would not preclude netting in circumstances where one party with notice of the other's insolvency buys up at a discount debts owing by the other to third parties. Consider that two companies, A and B,

---

[160] See paras 6.49–6.64 above.
[161] Bankruptcy Act 1966 (Cth), s 86(2).

have entered into a close-out netting contract which applies to their respective obligations to each other, and B to the knowledge of A is insolvent. In addition, B is indebted to various third parties. In the hands of the third parties the debts would be of diminished value, given B's insolvency. Therefore, A may buy them from the third parties at a discount, on the assumption that A could obtain their full value in B's liquidation by netting them off against A's own indebtedness to B. Under the insolvency set-off section, the qualification to the section would preclude a set-off in that circumstance. When A purchased the debts, B would have become indebted to A, and A correspondingly would have given credit at that time to B. Because the giving of credit occurred at a time when A had notice of B's insolvency, section 553C(2) would deny a set-off in B's liquidation in respect of the debts.[162] The insolvency, of which there must be notice in order to preclude a set-off, is that of the other party to the set-off, in the example, B. Section 14(3), on the other hand, is drafted in terms of notice of the insolvency of the person from whom the right or obligation was acquired. In the example, A has acquired the rights against B from the third parties, and so section 14(3) prima facie directs attention to notice of the insolvency of the third parties, rather than of B. If section 14(3) is intended to preclude netting in the liquidation of a counterparty to a close-out netting contract in respect of an obligation of the counterparty which was purchased at a discount from a third party with notice of insolvency, it has referred to the wrong party. The notice should relate to the insolvency of the counterparty. The insolvency of the third party from whom the obligation was acquired should not be of any consequence. Alternatively, if section 14(3) is not intended to cover that situation, it should.

According to section 14(4), subsections (1) and (2), which give effect to close-out **16.54** netting contracts both before and during external administration, are to have effect despite any other law, including the 'specified provisions'. These are defined in section 5 as including Division 2 of Part 5.7B of the Corporations Law, and sections 120, 121 and 122 of the Bankruptcy Act 1966 (Cth). Division 2 of Part 5.7B deals with such matters as unfair preferences and uncommercial transactions,[163] and sections 120, 121 and 122 of the Bankruptcy Act deal with similar matters (undervalued transactions, transfers to defeat creditors and preferences) in the context of bankruptcy. Those provisions therefore do not impugn netting under the Payment Systems and Netting Act.

On the other hand, section 14(5) may apply to exclude netting.[164] The exclusion **16.55** is limited, however. It only precludes netting in relation to an obligation owed *by*

---

[162] If B is an individual, and has become bankrupt, a set-off would be denied in the bankruptcy if at the time of the purchase A had notice of an available act of bankruptcy committed by B. See the Bankruptcy Act 1966 (Cth), s 86(2).

[163] Corporations Act 2001 (Cth), ss 588FA and 588FB.

[164] See para 16.48 above.

the party in external administration. It does not extend to an obligation owed *to* that party. Thus, for example, it would not preclude netting in relation to a deposit made by an insolvent customer with a bank, in circumstances where the bank was aware of the insolvency, and the deposit was made in order to advance the bank's position in a subsequent liquidation of the customer, by enabling it to set it off against a debt owing by the bank to the customer or to another insolvent party to the close-out netting contract. The deposit gives rise to an obligation owed to, as opposed to an obligation owed by, the customer, and prima facie section 14(5) would not be relevant. Section 14(3), on the other hand, may apply. Subsection (3), it will be recalled, precludes a person from relying on the protection provided by subsection (2) where it acquired a right or obligation from another person with notice that that other person was unable to pay their debts as and when they became due and payable. The point is made above however that section 14(3) is not well expressed. When a deposit is made with a bank, the bank incurs an obligation to the customer, but it seems a misnomer to say that the obligation has been acquired from the customer.

Close-out netting, where a set-off would not otherwise have been available

16.56   A close-out netting contract could provide a means of bringing about a set-off in the liquidation of a company against an obligation that otherwise is not susceptible to a set-off. For example, a liability for unpaid share capital may not be the subject of a set-off in the company's liquidation against a separate debt owing by the shareholder to the company.[165] The share capital instead must be paid in full before the shareholder is entitled to a dividend in the liquidation.[166] Further, an agreement for a set-off between the company and the shareholder would not be effective to avoid the rule if the set-off has not been effected pursuant to the agreement before the liquidation.[167] This has been explained on a number of grounds,[168] including that the insolvency legislation contemplates that the proceeds of a call for payment of unpaid share capital are to be used with the other assets of the company in the *pari passu* payment of the company's debts, and it would be contrary to that principle to allow a set-off against the call.[169] Similarly, a liability for misfeasance cannot be the subject of a set-off in a liquidation.[170]

---

[165]   See paras 8.50–8.62 above.

[166]   *Re Overend, Gurney and Co. Grissell's Case* (1866) LR 1 Ch App 528, 536; *Re China Steamship Co, ex p MacKenzie* (1869) LR 7 Eq 240, 244; *Ramsay v Jacobs* (1987) 12 ACLR 595, 597.

[167]   *Re Law Car and General Insurance Corp* [1912] 1 Ch 405; *Harding and Co Ltd v Hamilton* [1929] NZLR 338. Compare *Re Blakely Ordnance Co; Blakely's Case* (1867) 17 LT 307. See also *Ramsay v Jacobs* (1987) 12 ACLR 595, 597–598.

[168]   See para 8.51 above.

[169]   *Re Overend, Gurney and Co. Grissell's Case* (1866) LR 1 Ch App 528, 535–536; *Re Paraguassu Steam Tramroad Co. Black & Co's Case* (1872) LR 8 Ch App 254, 262, 265; *Re Auriferous Properties Ltd* [1898] 1 Ch 691, 696.

[170]   See paras 8.64–8.71 above.

However a close-out netting contract could provide a means of circumventing these principles. This assumes nevertheless that there is a valid netting contract. Depending on the circumstances, the entry into the netting contract could constitute a breach of duty by the directors to the company, so as to enable the company to avoid the contract.

Multilateral netting

The Act does not confine close-out netting to bilateral arrangements, but in its terms would extend also to multilateral close-out netting, in other words where there are three or more parties to the contract.[171] For example, if A is indebted to B, but A has a claim against C, B and C being related, and A becomes insolvent, a lack of mutuality would prevent a set-off in A's liquidation,[172] even if there was an express agreement for a set-off between the parties.[173] However the parties could now achieve that result by the use of a close-out netting agreement in accordance with the Act.

16.57

In that situation A's creditors would obtain some benefit from the agreement, in that netting would result in the reduction or discharge of a provable debt in A's liquidation in the form of A's debt to B. Consider however that B is the party in liquidation. Netting in that circumstance would result in B's creditors losing the benefit of an asset otherwise available in the liquidation (the claim against A), without their obtaining any compensating benefit. Furthermore, the netting agreement would not be registrable, so that persons dealing with B may not be aware that an asset appearing in its books may not be available to satisfy B's debts in the event of a liquidation. Multilateral netting can also occur under Part 3 of the Act, dealing with payment systems,[174] as well as under Part 5, relating to the rules of stock and futures exchanges and clearing houses,[175] but the scope of those Parts is confined. Part 3 only applies to an 'approved netting arrangement', being an arrangement approved by the Reserve Bank, and in granting approval the Reserve Bank must be satisfied that systemic disruption to the financial system otherwise could result if a participant went into external administration.[176] Similarly, for Part

16.58

---

[171] The definition of close-out netting contract in s 5 excludes from its scope an 'approved netting arrangement'. That term is defined in terms of a netting arrangement approved under s 12, which applies to multilateral netting arrangements. See s 11. But in order to be an approved netting arrangement, the arrangement must provide for netting to occur at least once on each business day. See s 12(1)(b). That is not ordinarily the case in close-out netting. Therefore, the exclusion of an approved netting arrangement from the definition of close-out netting contract would not preclude a multilateral contract from coming within the definition in circumstances where netting is not to occur at least once on each business day.

[172] For an analogous case, see *Re Bank of Credit and Commerce International SA (No 8)* [1998] AC 214.

[173] *Re Bank of Credit and Commerce International SA (No 8)* [1996] Ch 245, 257, CA.

[174] See in particular the Payment Systems and Netting Act 1998, s 11.

[175] See the definitions of 'market netting contract' and 'netting market' in s 5.

[176] Payment Systems and Netting Act 1998, s 12(1)(a).

5, the exchange or clearing house must be approved by the Minister, or declared by regulation to be within the Act.[177] No such limitations however apply to close-out netting contracts, which are purely private arrangements between the parties to them. On the other hand, Parts 3 and 5 do not contain restrictions similar to those in sections 14(3) and (5) (above) in relation to external administration, so that section 14 to that extent is more confined. Moreover, while in the above example B's creditors are deprived of the benefit of B's asset in the liquidation, that would have been the case in any event if B had given a guarantee to A in respect of C's debt. B's claim against A on the debt, and B's liability to A on the guarantee, would have been mutual and could have been set off in B's liquidation without recourse to the Payment Systems and Netting Act.[178] The Act achieves the same result, but without requiring the use of a guarantee for the purpose of bringing about mutuality.

H. Taking a Charge Over One's Own Debt

The conceptual impossibility argument

16.59 Is it possible for a debtor to take a charge or other security over its own indebtedness?[179] Until the House of Lords settled the question recently in *Re Bank of Credit and Commerce International SA (No 8)*,[180] that deceptively simple question gave rise to much debate. Typically the issue may arise when a bank provides financial accommodation to a customer, for example by way of a bank guarantee or a letter of credit facility, and as security for the customer's liability to indemnify the bank in the event that the bank has to pay under the guarantee or the letter of credit the customer deposits cash with the bank. The deposit gives rise to a debt owing by the bank to the customer, which the customer purports to charge or mortgage in favour of the bank. The question is whether a charge (or mortgage) in fact has been created. The effectiveness of the security has been recognized in Canada,[181]

---

[177] See the definition of 'netting market' in the Payment Systems and Netting Act 1998, s 5.
[178] See paras 8.07–8.26 above.
[179] In some jurisdictions legislation has been enacted to specifically recognize the validity of a charge in this situation. In Bermuda, see the Charge and Security (Special Provisions) Act 1990; in Singapore, s 9A of the Civil Law Act (c 43); in the Cayman Islands, the Property (Miscellaneous Provisions) Law 1994; and in Hong Kong, the Law Amendment and Reform (Consolidation) Ordinance, s 15A.
[180] [1998] AC 214.
[181] *Clarkson v Smith and Goldberg* [1926] 1 DLR 509 (Ontario Supreme Court, Appellate Division). Wood, *English and International Set-off* (1989) 200 also refers to *Re Century Steel and Boiler Ltd* (1981) 94 APR 490, 36 NBR (2d) 490 as an example of the recognition of a charge-back. It is not clear, however, whether the New Brunswick Court of Appeal in that case regarded the landlord as a trustee of the security deposit, in which case the charge would have been over the proceeds of the deposit, including any bank account into which the proceeds could be traced, or whether the landlord was entitled to mix the proceeds with its own funds and therefore was simply a debtor, in which case the question would have involved a charge-back.

but in England[182] and in Australia[183] there developed a body of opinion of considerable standing to the effect that a charge-back is conceptually impossible. According to this view, a 'charge-back' is not without legal effect. It is regarded as operating as a contractual right of set-off which, not being a charge, would not require registration. It does not, however, confer a proprietary interest in the debt, in the form of a charge properly so-called.

If a charge-back were conceptually impossible, and the customer (in the example) **16.60** went into liquidation, the bank's rights would rest on the insolvency set-off section as opposed to the security. In some circumstances, however, those rights could produce different results. The distinction could be important, for example, in relation to the accruing of interest, or for currency conversions where one or both of the debts is in a foreign currency. In the case of an automatic set-off under the insolvency set-off section at the date of the liquidation,[184] both those matters would be determined as at that date,[185] whereas pursuant to a charge that survives liquidation interest would continue to accrue until the debt is paid, and the foreign currency conversion usually would also occur at that date in accordance with express or implied terms in the contract.[186] The distinction could also be important when a company has a contingent debt at the time of its liquidation which is not capable of acceleration. In the case of a set-off, the liquidator would value the contingent debt,[187] and that value, which may be less than its maximum potential amount, would be the subject of an automatic set-off. In the case of a charge, on the other hand, the creditor could retain the security until the contingency occurs, and apply it at that time against the debt which ultimately arises.[188] Richard

---

[182] The conceptual impossibility argument found favour with Millett J (as he then was) in *Re Charge Card Services Ltd* [1987] 1 Ch 150, and subsequently with the Court of Appeal (which included Millett LJ) in *Re BCCI (No 8)* [1996] Ch 245. Professor Goode has been a distinguished supporter of this view. See *Legal Problems of Credit and Security* (2nd edn, 1988) 124–31, and also 'Charges Over Book Debts: A Missed Opportunity' (1994) 110 LQR 592, 606.

[183] *Broad v Commissioner of Stamp Duties* [1980] 2 NSWLR 40; *Griffiths v Commonwealth Bank of Australia* (1994) 123 ALR 111, 120; *First For Finance Pty Ltd v Westpac Banking Corp* (Vic SC, Hansen J, 7 May 1998, esp at 23); *Wily v Rothschild Australia Ltd* (1999) 47 NSWLR 555. See also *Estate Planning Associates (Australia) Pty Ltd v Commissioner of Stamp Duties* (1985) 2 NSWLR 495, in which it was held that *Broad's* case applied in the case of a policy of insurance issued by an insurance company which was deposited back with the company by way of security. In *Jackson v Esanda Finance Corp Ltd* (1992) 59 SASR 416 the principle was applied in the context of a purported charge over a debenture stock certificate. Compare *Cinema Plus Ltd v Australia and New Zealand Banking Group Ltd* (2000) 49 NSWLR 513, 517–521, discussed below.

[184] See para 6.79 *ff* above.

[185] For interest, see para 6.108 above, and for foreign currency debts para 6.106 above.

[186] Compare the Insolvency Rules 1986, r 4.93 in relation to interest on a debt proved in the liquidation. See also Calnan, 'The Insolvent Bank and Security Over Deposits' (1996) 11 Journal of International Banking and Financial Law 185, 187 in relation to debts in different currencies.

[187] Pursuant to the Insolvency Rules 1986, r 4.86, and for bankruptcy see the Insolvency Act 1986, s 322.

[188] See Calnan, 'Security Over Deposits Again: *BCCI (No 8)* in the House of Lords' (1998) 13 Journal of International Banking and Financial Law 125, 127.

Calnan has given another example,[189] relating to the situation in which a guarantor has placed a deposit with a bank charged to secure the guarantee liability to the bank, both the guarantor and the principal debtor have gone into liquidation, and the deposit charged to the bank is less than the principal debt. Consider for example that the principal debt is £100 but the security deposit is only £60. If an automatic set-off occurred in the guarantor's liquidation, the debt would be reduced to £40 and the bank's proof in the principal debtor's liquidation would be limited to that amount. If on the other hand the charge were effective in the liquidation, the bank could delay in enforcing the charge, and could prove for the full £100 in the principal debtor's liquidation.

16.61 The argument against the validity of the security is sometimes said to be stronger in the case of a mortgage than for a charge. A mortgage is a form of security that takes effect by way of assignment. An argument commonly presented is that, if a creditor were to assign the debt to the debtor, the debtor would become his own creditor. The interests would merge, so that there would no longer be a debt and consequently no security. Any document purporting to bring about an assignment could only take effect as a release of the debt or a covenant not to sue.[190] The tenor of Lord Hoffmann's brief reference to merger in *Re BCCI (No 8)*[191] in the context of an equitable charge,[192] where he emphasized that in the case of a charge the depositor retains title, suggests that he may have regarded the question as open in relation to a mortgage.[193] However it is not universally accepted that there would be a merger in the case of a mortgage,[194] because it is said that the equity of redemption that the debtor retains would prevent a merger. In that regard, courts of equity, having regard to the intention of the parties, may treat an interest which merged at law as still subsisting in equity.[195] Thus, while the appointment of a debtor as executor has the effect at common law of extinguishing the debt, on the

---

[189] Calnan, 'The Insolvent Bank and Security Over Deposits' (1996) 11 Journal of International Banking and Financial Law 185, 189.

[190] *Broad v Commissioner of Stamp Duties* [1980] 2 NSWLR 40, 46; *Re Charge Card Services Ltd* [1987] 1 Ch 150, 175. See also *Street v Retravision (NSW) Pty Ltd* (1995) 56 FCR 588, 596; *Re Bank of Credit and Commerce International SA (No 8)* [1996] Ch 245, 261–262 (CA). For the general proposition that a person cannot covenant with himself, or at the same time be both landlord and tenant, see *Rye v Rye* [1962] AC 496, 512, 513–514.

[191] [1998] AC 214, 227.

[192] See below.

[193] See also Segal, 'Conceptual Implausibility in the Court of Appeal' [1996] 8 Journal of International Banking Law 307, 308.

[194] In *Clarkson v Smith and Goldberg* [1926] 1 DLR 509, 510 the Appellate Division of the Ontario Supreme Court commented that, by an hypothecation agreement, a bank's indebtedness on a deposit was 'in effect assigned to the bank', and treated it as a valid security. See also the discussion in *Banco Santander SA v Bayfern Ltd* [2000] 1 All ER (Comm) 776 in relation to an assignment of a joint and several debt to one of the joint and several debtors.

[195] *Capital and Counties Bank Ltd v Rhodes* [1903] 1 Ch 631, 652; *Cinema Plus Ltd v Australia and New Zealand Banking Group Ltd* (2000) 49 NSWLR 513, 520–521 paras 23–30; Meagher, Gummow and Lehane, *Equity Doctrines and Remedies* (3rd edn, 1992) 857, 859.

ground that at law the executor cannot sue himself, this is not so in equity, which fastens upon the executor an equivalent obligation to account to those interested in the estate for the amount of the debt.[196] Further, there is authority which supports the proposition that in equity a debtor can be a trustee of his own indebtedness[197] (although it is criticized in *Scott on Trusts*[198]). But whatever the position in relation to a mortgage, Lord Hoffmann considered that merger is not a problem when an equitable charge is in issue.[199] A charge does not involve an assignment of the subject-matter of the security. Rather, it arises when certain property is specifically made responsible for the discharge of an obligation, without any transfer of title or possession to the obligee.[200] It takes effect as an hypothecation rather than an alienation.[201] It is true that the primary remedies of an equitable chargee are the right to apply to the court for an order for sale or for the appointment of a receiver,[202] whereas a receiver would hardly be apt in the case of a charge-back, and nor would a sale be contemplated. The only remedy that the parties would have had in mind is that the bank itself, without recourse to the courts, would set one demand against another. This should not be an objection, however. There is no reason why the parties to a security contract cannot provide for their own remedies in the event of default,[203] the classic example being the appointment of a receiver out of court. It should not make any difference that the remedy contemplated may be in substitution for the traditional remedies available to an

---

[196] *Commissioner of Stamp Duties (NSW) v Bone* (1976) 135 CLR 223, 227–228, [1977] AC 511, 518 (PC); *Commissioner of Taxation v Orica Ltd* (1998) 194 CLR 500, 544, *per* Gummow J; *Cinema Plus Ltd v ANZ Banking Group Ltd* (2000) 49 NSWLR 513, 520–521 paras 28 and 29, *per* Spigelman CJ.

[197] *Paterson v Murphy* (1853) 22 LJ Ch 882 (the point appears more clearly in that report than in the report of the case at 11 Hare 88, 68 ER 1198); Oditah, 'Financing Trade Credit: Welsh Development Agency v Exfinco' [1992] JBL 541, 557. *Moore v Darton* (1851) 4 De G & Sm 517, 64 ER 938, to which Dr Oditah has also referred, may be explained on the ground that the trust was of the money advanced rather than the debt.

[198] Scott, *The Law of Trusts* (4th edn, 1987) vol 1 at 187 and 197, vol 1A at 494.

[199] [1998] AC 214, 227.

[200] *Re Bank of Credit and Commerce International SA (No 8)* [1998] AC 214, 226; *Re Cosslett (Contractors) Ltd* [1998] Ch 495, 508; *Tancred v Delagoa Bay and East Africa Railway Co* (1889) 23 QBD 239, 242; *Morris v Woodings* (1997) 25 ACSR 636, 640–641; Waldock, *The Law of Mortgages* (2nd edn, 1950) 9–10; Gough, *Company Charges* (2nd edn, 1996) 18; *Fisher and Lightwood's Law of Mortgage* (11th edn, 2002) 25. However the distinction between a charge and an assignment has not always been recognized. See eg *Roadshow Entertainment Pty Ltd v (ACN 053 006 269) Pty Ltd* (1997) 42 NSWLR 462, 482 ('fixed charge which operated as a completed equitable assignment') and *Hoverd Industries Ltd v Supercool Refrigeration and Air Conditioning (1991) Ltd* [1995] 3 NZLR 577, 587 ('A fixed charge would operate as an equitable assignment . . .').

[201] In effect a shadow is cast over the property set aside as security for the debt until the debt is paid. See Sykes and Walker, *The Law of Securities* (5th edn, 1993) 18, referring to *Salmond on Jurisprudence* (12th edn, 1966) 430.

[202] Megarry and Wade, *The Law of Real Property* (6th edn, 2000) 1215, referring to *Tennant v Trenchard* (1869) LR 4 Ch App 537 and *Re Owen* [1894] 3 Ch 220.

[203] As Wigram VC remarked in *Sampson v Pattison* (1842) 1 Hare 533, 535, 66 ER 1143, 'The only question is, what are the terms of the contract?'

equitable chargee, as opposed to being in addition to them. For the same reason, the fact that the debtor cannot enforce the debt by suing himself is not an impediment.[204] It is not necessary for the debtor to do so.

16.62   In *National Westminster Bank Ltd v Halesowen Presswork and Assemblies Ltd*[205] a number of the judges in both the Court of Appeal and the House of Lords commented that a bank cannot have a lien on its own indebtedness,[206] and the statements to that effect have been referred to as supporting a like principle in the case of an equitable charge.[207] These statements however should be considered in the context in which they were made. The courts in the *Halesowen* cases were concerned to distinguish a bank's right to combine accounts[208] from the lien that a bank has on its customer's securities as a security for any indebtedness of the customer arising out of the banker/customer relationship. The lien is a common law possessory lien, which presupposes the existence of tangible property which may be retained and held in possession until the debt in question is paid. A credit balance on a bank account is not tangible property capable of being held in this manner. It is a debt. It was said therefore that the use of the word 'lien' in the context of combination of accounts is inappropriate. The statements in question are not authority for the proposition that it is not possible for a debtor to have a charge over its own indebtedness because, in contrast to the case of a common law possessory lien, intangible property may be the subject of an equitable charge.[209]

16.63   An argument of greater refinement has been proposed,[210] based on the distinction between property and obligation. The argument is that, while as between a cred-

---

[204]   Compare *Re Charge Card Services Ltd* [1987] 1 Ch 150, 176.

[205]   [1972] AC 785, HL, reversing [1971] 1 QB 1, CA.

[206]   See Lord Denning MR and Buckley LJ in the Court of Appeal [1971] 1 QB 1, 34, 46, and Viscount Dilhorne and Lord Cross of Chelsea in the House of Lords [1972] AC 785, 802, 810. See also *MPS Constructions Pty Ltd v Rural Bank of New South Wales* (1980) 4 ACLR 835. In that case a customer had executed a 'lien' in favour of a bank over all moneys deposited by it with the bank. Helsham CJ in Eq, in following the *Halesowen* case, held that this did not encompass moneys standing to the customer's credit in a bank account in his name. However the question of the effect of a charge, as opposed to a lien, was not considered.

[207]   *Broad v Commissioner of Stamp Duties* [1980] 2 NSWLR 40, 46–47; *Re Bank of Credit and Commerce International SA (No 8)* [1996] Ch 245, 259–260, CA.

[208]   See ch 15 above.

[209]   See the discussion of the *Halesowen* case in *Re Bank of Credit and Commerce International SA (No 8)* [1998] AC 214, 226.

[210]   It has been suggested that the question whether an equitable charge may arise depends upon the availability of specific performance, and that accordingly a relevant issue in considering the validity of charge-backs is whether specific performance would be ordered. See Everett, 'Security Over Bank Deposits' (1988) 16 Australian Business Law Review 351, 364, and McCracken, *The Banker's Remedy of Set-off* (2nd edn, 1998) 191–6, 198–201, 264. The better view however is that an equitable charge of present property (as distinct from a promise for valuable consideration to charge future acquired assets) does not depend on specific performance. See *Hewett v Court* (1983) 149 CLR 639 (esp Deane J at 665–667) in relation to an equitable lien, which is a form of equitable charge (see 663). Indeed, it is difficult to see what the substance of the order against the chargor would be (although compare McCracken, *op cit* 201).

itor and a third party the debt is an asset, as between the debtor and the creditor it is not an asset but an obligation. In other words, the creditor does not own the debt, rather the debt is owed to it.[211] However, while it is true to say that the creditor is owed the debt, the creditor as against the debtor also has rights which are a species of property and which should be just as capable of being the subject of a security in favour of the debtor as a third party.[212]

There is on the other hand authority which supports the validity of a charge-back,[213] and consistent with that authority the House of Lords in *Re BCCI (No 8)*[214] rejected the conceptual impossibility argument. While a determination of the point was not necessary for a decision in *BCCI (No 8)*, Lord Hoffmann, with whose judgment the other Law Lords agreed, considered that it should be dealt with given that it had been fully argued.[215]   **16.64**

Lord Hoffmann approached the issue by reference to basic principles, rather than by undertaking a comprehensive analysis of the authorities.[216] He said that a debt is a chose in action, which the law has always recognized as property. A charge over a chose in action can validly be granted to a third party. He then asked, in what respects would the fact that the beneficiary of the charge is the debtor himself be inconsistent with the transaction having one or more of the features of a charge?   **16.65**

---

[211] *Re BCCI (No 8)* [1996] Ch 245, 259, CA; Millett (1991) 107 LQR 680; Goode, *Legal Problems of Credit and Security* (2nd edn, 1988) 125 (and see also, by Professor Goode, 'Security: A Pragmatic Conceptualist's Response' (1989) 15 Monash University Law Review 361, 368, 'Charges Over Book Debts: A Missed Opportunity' (1994) 110 LQR 592, 606 and 'Charge-Backs and Legal Fictions' (1998) 114 LQR 178, 179).

[212] Lindley LJ's comment in *Lister v Stubbs* (1890) 45 Ch D 1, 15, that the employer's claim in that case confounded ownership with obligation, does not assist the argument. An employee received money by way of secret commission which he invested in the purchase of land, and the employer sought to trace the money into the investment. The action failed on the ground that the relation between them was only that of debtor and creditor, rather than trustee and *cestui que trust*. While the employee had an obligation to the employer on a debtor/creditor basis, neither the money itself nor the property into which it could be traced was owned by the employer.

[213] *Ex parte Caldicott, re Hart* (1884) 25 Ch D 716; *Ex parte Mackay* (1873) LR 8 Ch App 643, 42 LJ Bcy 68 (esp at 69); *Swiss Bank Corp v Lloyds Bank Ltd* [1982] AC 584, 614; *Welsh Development Agency v Export Finance Co Ltd* [1992] BCLC 148, 166–167 (and see also Browne-Wilkinson VC in the Chancery Division [1990] BCC 393, 408). These cases were discussed in greater detail in the second edition of this book, at 554–5. See also Oditah, 'Financing Trade Credit: Welsh Development Agency v Exfinco' [1992] JBL 541, 557. A number of other cases are referred to in Wood, *English and International Set-off* (1989) 199–205, although some of them may be explained on other grounds. For example, in *Webb v Smith* (1885) 30 Ch D 192, which is often cited as authority in support of charge-backs, the proceeds of sale would have been impressed with a trust, and the auctioneer's 'lien' would have attached to the trust fund. The auctioneer had paid the proceeds into a bank account, which the auctioneer would have held on trust, first to discharge his lien and then to pay to the vendor or to his order. It was not a simple case of a debt owing at common law by the auctioneer to the vendor. See the discussion of *Webb v Smith* in the Court of Appeal in *Re BCCI (No 8)* [1996] Ch 245, 261.

[214] [1998] AC 214.

[215] [1998] AC 214, 225.

[216] See in particular the discussion at [1998] AC 214, 226–227.

The method by which the property is realized would differ, in that, instead of the beneficiary of the charge having to claim payment from the debtor, the realization would take the form of a book entry, by setting off one debt against the other. But in no other respect would the transaction have any consequence different from that which would attach to a charge given to a third party. It would still be a proprietary interest which, subject to questions of registration and a possible defence of purchaser for value without notice, would be binding upon an assignee, and upon a liquidator or a trustee in bankruptcy. Similarly, the chargor would retain an equity of redemption. In those circumstances, Lord Hoffmann said that he could not see why it could not properly be said that the debtor has a proprietary interest by way of charge over the debt.[217] He also noted that documents purporting to create such charges had been used by banks for many years,[218] and was of the view the law should attempt to uphold a practice adopted by the commercial community, provided that there was no threat to the consistency of the law or an objection on grounds of public policy.[219] This reflects a sentiment earlier expressed by Hammond J in New Zealand, that 'good commercial law should follow good commercial practice (and not vice versa)'.[220]

16.66 Notwithstanding that the view expressed by the House of Lords on the validity of charge-backs strictly was obiter, it was nevertheless a considered opinion after full argument, and it would appear to have settled the law in England.[221] In Australia, on the other hand, decisions of the House of Lords are not binding. They are persuasive, but only, it has been said, to the degree of persuasiveness of their reasoning.[222] In New South Wales, Windeyer J in *Wily v Rothschild Australia Ltd*[223] declined to follow *BCCI (No 8)* on this point. He preferred instead earlier Australian authority, including a decision of the Full Court of the South Australian Supreme Court,[224] in which it had been accepted that a charge-back is conceptually impossible,[225] commenting that he would leave it to an appeal court to determine that those cases should not be followed.[226] He noted that the views

---

[217] [1998] AC 214, 227.

[218] [1998] AC 214, 225–226, 227.

[219] [1998] AC 214, 228.

[220] *Commercial Factors Ltd v Maxwell Printing Ltd* [1994] 1 NZLR 724, 727.

[221] The judgment on this point has been both applauded and criticized. Compare the views of Richard Calnan, 'Fashioning the Law to Suit the Practicalities of Life' (1998) 114 LQR 174, and Professor Roy Goode, 'Charge-Backs and Legal Fictions' (1998) 114 LQR 178.

[222] *Cook v Cook* (1986) 162 CLR 376, 390.

[223] (1999) 47 NSWLR 555.

[224] *Jackson v Esanda Finance Corp Ltd* (1992) 59 SASR 416.

[225] In addition to *Jackson v Esanda Finance Corp Ltd* (1992) 59 SASR 416, see *Broad v Commissioner of Stamp Duties* [1980] 2 NSWLR 40; *Estate Planning Associates (Australia) Pty Ltd v Commissioner of Stamp Duties* (1985) 2 NSWLR 495; *Griffiths v Commonwealth Bank of Australia* (1994) 123 ALR 111, 120; *First For Finance Pty Ltd v Westpac Banking Corp* (Vic SC, Hansen J, 7 May 1998, esp at p 23).

[226] (1999) 47 NSWLR 555, 564.

expressed in *BCCI (No 8)* were not essential for the decision, and said that they seemed partly to have been brought about through a desire to make the law accord with the desires of commerce rather than through totally convincing reasoning.[227] Windeyer J adhered to that view at first instance in *Cinema Plus Ltd v Australia and New Zealand Banking Group Ltd*,[228] but Spigelman CJ later rejected it on appeal in that case.[229] The Chief Justice had recourse to the equitable maxim that 'equity looks to the intent rather then to the form',[230] and said that:[231] 'In my opinion, there is no reason why, in an appropriate case, equity could not find that the intention of the parties to create a charge between a debtor and creditor, over-rides what would be regarded, at common law, as a "conceptual impossibility".'

This reasoning is difficult to follow. It appears to concede that at 'common law' a **16.67** charge over one's own debt is conceptually impossible, but postulates that equity would have regard to the intention of the parties in order to override that result. But a charge is a creature of equity. There is no such thing as a legal charge, except as provided by statute.[232] It is not then a question of the common law maintaining that it is conceptually impossible to have a charge over one's own debt. If on the other hand his Honour used the expression 'common law' as including the doctrines of equity,[233] and in contradistinction to statutory law, his Honour's comment would raise further questions. In particular, why would equity, on the one hand, regard something as conceptually impossible, and on the other suggest that that result could be avoided by looking to the intent rather than the form? If equity were to regard its own institution of a charge as conceptually impossible in a particular situation, that would be the end of the matter. The answer, as the House of Lords has determined, is that in fact there is no conceptual impossibility in the notion of a debtor taking a charge over its own debt.

Charge-backs and mutuality

A charge-back could secure not only a debt owing by the chargor, but also a third **16.68** party's indebtedness. This could arise, for example, where a deposit held by a bank is charged by the depositor to secure financial accommodation provided to a

---

[227] See also McCormack, 'Charge-Backs and Commercial Certainty in the House of Lords' [1998] Company Financial and Insolvency Law Review 111.

[228] (2000) 34 ACSR 621, 627.

[229] *Cinema Plus Ltd v Australia and New Zealand Banking Group Ltd* (2000) 49 NSWLR 513, 517–521. The other members of the Court of Appeal, Sheller and Giles JJA, did not consider the conceptual impossibility argument, determining the charge issue instead on the basis that the clause in question was not apt to create a charge. See Sheller JA at 543–544 and Giles JA at 549.

[230] (2000) 49 NSWLR 513, 520 para 24, referring to Meagher, Gummow and Lehane, *Equity Doctrines and Remedies* (3rd edn, 1992) 88–93 paras 331–8.

[231] (2000) 49 NSWLR 513, 521 para 30.

[232] Goode, *Legal Problems of Credit and Security* (2nd edn, 1988) 14.

[233] As Spigelman CJ contemplated. See (2000) 49 NSWLR 513, 521 para 32, 522 para 39.

related entity.[234] But in the situation in which there are only two parties, so that the debt secured by the charge-back is owing by the depositor, it has been suggested that, as a result of the analysis of the insolvency set-off section accepted in *Stein v Blake*,[235] the charge, even if it were otherwise valid, would not continue after the depositor's liquidation. In *Stein v Blake* the House of Lords held that a set-off takes effect automatically upon the occurrence of a bankruptcy or a liquidation, so as to bring about a cancellation of the cross-demands on that date to the extent of the set-off.[236] It has been argued that the cross-demands therefore would no longer exist, and that a charge over one claim to secure payment of the other accordingly would not survive the winding-up order.[237]

16.69 The principal source of support for the view that the charge would not survive liquidation is *M S Fashions Ltd v Bank of Credit and Commerce International SA*.[238] A bank advanced money to a company, taking as security a deposit from a director which was charged to the bank. In addition, the director assumed a personal liability for the company's debt. Subsequently the bank went into liquidation. It was held that the director's personal liability to the bank and the bank's debt to the director on the deposit were demands arising out of mutual dealings within the ambit of the set-off section, and accordingly were the subject of an automatic set-off upon the occurrence of the liquidation. As a result, the bank could not choose to sue the company for payment and confine the director to a proof in the liquidation in respect of the deposit. Counsel for the liquidator argued that, because of the charge, there was no set-off, but that argument received little sympathy from Hoffmann LJ in the Chancery Division. He said that, even if one ignored the question whether a charge-back is conceptually possible, the charge was over a debt owing by the bank to secure a debt owed to the bank. In that circumstance, '[t]he account to be taken by rule 4.90 must require an unwinding of that arrangement so that the deposit is set off against the debt it was intended to secure'.[239] On appeal the Court of Appeal similarly held that the fact of the charge over the deposit did not prevent a set-off.[240] While the issue was discussed in that forum primarily from a different perspective, as to whether the deposit was a special-purpose payment and therefore not available for a set-off on that ground,[241] the tenor of the judgment, and the result, suggests that the Court of Appeal agreed

---

[234] As in *Re Bank of Credit and Commerce International SA (No 8)* [1998] AC 214.

[235] [1996] AC 243.

[236] See para 6.79 *ff* above.

[237] For a discussion of the issue, see Berg, 'Charges Over Book Debts: A Reply' [1995] JBL 433, 465–7, and 'House of Lords Clarifies Liquidation Netting', International Financial Law Review, August 1995, 20, 21.

[238] [1993] Ch 425. See also the discussion of the *M S Fashions* case in paras 12.23–12.25 above.

[239] [1993] Ch 425, 438.

[240] See the discussion at [1993] Ch 425, 448–451.

[241] See paras 10.43–10.54 above.

with Hoffmann LJ's analysis. That view is also consistent with earlier decisions of the Court of Appeal in *Sovereign Life Assurance Co v Dodd*[242] and *Re City Life Assurance Co Ltd. Grandfield's Case.*[243] In those cases a loan made by an insurance company to an insured was set off in the company's liquidation against the insured's claim on a policy issued by the company, which policy had been mortgaged back to the company as security for the loan.[244] Nevertheless, the effect of the mortgage-back on mutuality was not considered, other than by Bowen and Kay LJJ in *Sovereign Life v Dodd*[245] (see below), who referred to it only briefly. This lack of critical analysis diminishes the weight to be attached to those cases as authorities on this point.

It is difficult to support the proposition that, in the event of a charge-back, a set-off under the insolvency set-off section will occur as between the charged debt and the debt owing by the chargor to the chargee for which it is security,[246] and it is suggested that the *M S Fashions* case is wrong on this point. The essence of Hoffmann LJ's analysis, that the account to be taken under the insolvency set-off section requires an unwinding of the arrangement, begs the question as to whether the requirements of the set-off section in fact have been satisfied so as to justify an account under it. As counsel argued before the Court of Appeal in the *M S Fashions* case,[247] the charge in that case had the consequence that there was no mutuality for the purpose of a set-off. The bank had a claim against the director, and it also had a beneficial interest in the deposit as a result of the charge. Because of the charge the director himself did not have had an unimpeded beneficial interest in the deposit, which should have been sufficient to prevent mutuality arising.[248] A set-off under the insolvency set-off section therefore should not have occurred in *M S Fashions v BCCI.* Under a charge-back the chargee is a secured

16.70

---

[242] [1892] 2 QB 573.

[243] [1926] Ch 191, 199, not following *Ex parte Price, re Lankester* (1875) LR 10 Ch App 648 and *Paddy v Clutton* [1920] 2 Ch 554.

[244] See also *Re National Benefit Assurance Co Ltd* [1924] 2 Ch 339. In *Hiley v The Peoples Prudential Assurance Co Ltd* (1938) 60 CLR 468 an insured executed a 'memorandum of deposit' as collateral security of a loan from the insurance company (a mortgage of land also having been obtained), and deposited the policy with the insurer. The insurer expressly repudiated the policy, and the insured was allowed to set off his cross-claim for damages resulting from the repudiation against the loan. The terms of the 'memorandum of deposit' are not set out in the report, and the nature and ambit of the collateral security are unclear, in particular as to whether it would have extended to a damages claim for repudiation of the policy.

[245] [1892] 2 QB 573, 582, 584–585.

[246] In *Ex parte Mackay* (1872) LR 8 Ch App 643, in which the right to retain the royalties was treated as a charge on a debt, it is apparent that the companies' debt to Jeavons for the royalties and their rights against Jeavons in respect of the loan were not regarded as having been set off under the insolvency set-off section. It is not clear from the report however whether the debt for the royalties was joint or several for the purpose of determining mutuality, and accordingly whether the insolvency set-off section applied.

[247] [1993] Ch 425, 440–441. See also Wood, *English and International Set-off* (1989) 195.

[248] See para 11.34 above.

creditor, and the chargee's position should be governed by the rules relating to the security,[249] including as to the timing of enforcement. It should not be a question of insolvency set-off. Subsequently Lord Hoffmann again referred to the issue in the House of Lords in *Re Bank of Credit and Commerce International SA (No 8)*.[250] He said that the argument that the charge destroyed mutuality 'was somewhat cursorily rejected in the *M S Fashions* case', although without expressing a concluded view on the subject.[251] It nevertheless suggests a willingness to reconsider the opinion that he expressed in the *M S Fashions* case.[252]

16.71 Consider once again the case of a bank which provides a facility to a customer secured by a charge over a deposit provided by the customer. Subsequently the bank goes into liquidation. If, as suggested, the insolvency set-off section does not apply because of lack of mutuality, prima facie the liquidator could sue the customer for payment of the debt, and after it has been paid confine the customer to a proof in the liquidation in relation to the deposit. That seems an unjust result. When a customer provides a deposit as security for the customer's own debt, the intention usually would be that the deposit itself would provide the source of the payment to the bank. It is unlikely that the parties contemplated that the customer would have to find the sum in question twice—once to fund the deposit and a second time to pay the debt. In that circumstance, Richard Calnan has suggested that it would be unconscionable for the bank to insist on recovering the customer's liability in full without taking account of the deposit, and that therefore an equitable

---

[249] *Ex parte Caldicott, re Hart* (1884) 25 Ch D 716, 722.

[250] [1998] AC 214, 225.

[251] Mokel, 'Resolving the *M S Fashions* "Paradox"' [1999] Company Financial and Insolvency Law Review 106, 107–8 has supported Hoffmann LJ's initial stance in the *M S Fashions* case, inter alia on the ground that the charge over the deposit did not reduce its value, but simply affected the depositor's ability to apply it for any purpose other than to pay off the secured debt. That may be accepted, but the charge also had the effect of impeding the depositor's beneficial interest in the deposit. It is that which affects mutuality, not the value of the deposit in the liquidation.

[252] Richard Calnan has queried whether that aspect of the *M S Fashions* case is consistent with *Ex parte Caldicott, re Hart* (1884) 25 Ch D 716. See Calnan, 'The Insolvent Bank and Security Over Deposits' (1996) 11 Journal of International Banking and Financial Law 185, 189. In *Ex parte Caldicott*, a partner in a firm mortgaged his separate property to the firm's bankers in order to secure the firm's indebtedness. In addition, he gave a personal covenant to the bank that the firm would pay the balance due on the firm's current account. Subsequently the partner entered into an agreement to sell the mortgaged property. The bank concurred in the sale on condition that the proceeds be placed on deposit with it, and that they should stand charged with the payment of the firm's debt. The firm later became bankrupt. The Court of Appeal regarded the deposit as a security held by the bank, but since it was not a security on an asset belonging to the firm it was held that it was not necessary that it be deducted from the proof lodged by the bank against the joint estate. As Calnan has pointed out, this assumes that the deposit was not set off in the partner's bankruptcy against his liability on the separate undertaking. In other words, it assumes that there was no mutuality. If a set-off had occurred in the partner's bankruptcy, the firm's debt to that extent would have been paid, in which case the bank's proof in the firm's bankruptcy would have had to be reduced. The only query in relation to that analysis is that the report of the *Caldicott* case simply states that the deposit was charged with payment of the firm's debt. It is not specifically mentioned that it was security also for the partner's separate liability on his undertaking.

set-off may be available.[253] There is a lack of mutuality, but equity does not in all cases regard mutuality as a strict requirement for an equitable set-off.[254] Calnan's argument is contrary to the view that is sometimes expressed, that equitable set-off is not available in bankruptcy or company liquidation in circumstances that are outside the operation of the insolvency set-off section,[255] but it is suggested that that view is doubtful, both as a matter of principle and as a matter of precedent.[256] There are other difficulties with Calnan's view, however. While the parties may indeed have assumed that the deposit would be applied in satisfaction of the debt, the agreement usually would be drafted in terms of giving the bank a discretion to effect a set-off, in which case the notion that equity may require a set-off prima facie would be contrary to the terms of their agreement.[257] The point is that insolvency does not give rise to an equity sufficient to support an equitable set-off.[258] Therefore, if equitable set-off were available, it should be available irrespective of the bank's insolvency. But if that were the case, the contractual stipulation for a discretion would be illusory. Further, the notion that equity would require a set-off is at variance with the view that a secured creditor is not obliged to resort to the security, but can claim repayment from the debtor personally and leave the security alone.[259]

But notwithstanding those difficulties, there is much to commend Calnan's view. **16.72** Moreover, it is supported by comments by Bowen and Kay LJJ in the Court of Appeal in *Sovereign Life Assurance Co v Dodd*.[260] An insurance company provided a loan to an insured customer, the company taking as security a mortgage of a life policy issued by the company to the insured. The company went into liquidation, and it was held that the loan to the insured could be set off against the insured's claim against the company on the policy. Kay LJ considered an argument that there was no debt owing to the insured on the policy because of the mortgage.[261] He dealt with it shortly:[262]

---

[253] Calnan, 'The Insolvent Bank and Security Over Deposits' (1996) 11 Journal of International Banking and Financial Law, 185, 187–8.

[254] See paras 4.48–4.54 above.

[255] *Brown v Cork* [1985] BCLC 363, 376, CA; *Day and Dent Constructions Pty Ltd v North Australian Properties Pty Ltd* (1981) 34 ALR 595, 599, 601, 636–637, Federal Court. See also *Re BCCI (No 8)* [1996] Ch 245, 269–270, CA, although the discussion in that case was confined to two cases (*Ex parte Stephens* (1805) 11 Ves Jun 24, 32 ER 996 and *Jones v Mossop* (1844) 3 Hare 568, 67 ER 506) which were said to support a wider right of set-off in equity than under the insolvency set-off section. See para 6.20 above.

[256] See paras 6.16–6.20 above.

[257] A similar point was made in *Lord v Direct Acceptance Corp Ltd* (1993) 32 NSWLR 362, 369. See para 4.51 above.

[258] *Rawson v Samuel* (1841) Cr & Ph 161, 175, 41 ER 451, 457. See para 4.03 above.

[259] *Re BCCI (No 8)* [1998] AC 214, 222, HL.

[260] [1892] 2 QB 573. The analysis in *Clarkson v Smith and Goldberg* [1926] 1 DLR 509 also supports Calnan's view. See para 12.39 above.

[261] [1892] 2 QB 573, 584. See also counsel's argument at first instance [1892] 1 QB 405, 408.

[262] [1892] 2 QB 573, 585.

There was a clear debt due upon these policies when the present action was brought; and I think we may discard the argument founded upon the fact that there had been an assignment of the policies to the company, for there will be a set-off in equity in cases where, but for some such circumstance as this assignment, there would have been a legal set-off. The company were liable to the defendant for the amount of the policies, subject of course to their charge upon the policies for the advances, and I think that in this action the defendant probably had a set-off against the company wholly independent of the section.

Kay LJ went on to say that there were in any event mutual dealings for the purpose of the insolvency set-off section.[263] This would not appear to have been the case, because the mortgage would have destroyed mutuality. But whatever the position in that regard, he was of the view that a set-off 'probably' was available in equity and that this was independent of the insolvency set-off section. Nor was Kay LJ alone in that regard, Bowen LJ similarly commenting:[264] 'As far as I can see, this is a good set-off at law; but if it were not a good legal set-off by reason of the existence of an assignment of the policies to the secretary of the company, it would, at all events, be a good set-off in equity.' Those remarks support Calnan's view, that a set-off may be available in equity in the case of a charge-back, notwithstanding that the insolvency set-off section does not apply because of lack of mutuality.

16.73   On the other hand, an equitable set-off should not be available when the deposit is made by a third party, such as director of the customer.[265] The effect of allowing an equitable set-off to the customer would be to require the bank to look to the deposit provided by the third party as a security, as opposed to seeking payment from the customer as principal debtor. That would make the surety primarily liable to discharge the debt. As the New South Wales Court of Appeal remarked in *Lord v Direct Acceptance Corporation Ltd*,[266] there is no equity in that result.[267]

Charge-back and combination of accounts

16.74   When a customer has a number of accounts with a bank, the principle of combination may apply so that, unless a particular account has been separated out by agreement or it is separate as a matter of law, the balance of all the accounts represents the debt at any particular time.[268] If however a customer sets up a security deposit at the request of a bank and charges it to the bank, the security interest that the bank has in the account should have the effect of preventing a combination in respect of it, so that the bank's position instead should be governed by the security.

---

263   [1892] 2 QB 573, 586.
264   [1892] 2 QB 573, 582.
265   This was the view also of Calnan, 'The Insolvent Bank and Security Over Deposits' (1996) 11 Journal of International Banking and Financial Law 185, 189.
266   (1993) 32 NSWLR 362, 369. See paras 4.51–4.52 above.
267   See also *Re BCCI (No 8)* [1996] Ch 245, 256, CA in relation to insolvency set-off.
268   See ch 15 above.

Indeed, combination would not be applicable in any event where, as is often the case, the liability secured by the charge is contingent, for example where the deposit secures a contingent liability to the bank on a letter of credit provided by the bank, or a contingent liability under a guarantee of a related company's indebtedness.[269]

Registration

Consider that a deposit with a bank has been charged in its favour by way of a **16.75** charge-back. The question arises whether the agreement would require registration under sections 395 and 396 of the Companies Act 1985 in the event that the party granting the right is a company.[270] If registration is required, failure to register the charge would render it void as against a liquidator or administrator of the company.[271]

Only certain categories of company charges are registrable, one possibility being **16.76** that the agreement constitutes a charge on the company's book debts. The term 'book debts' is not defined in the English legislation,[272] but in its generally accepted sense it refers to debts connected with and growing out of a person's trade or business which would ordinarily be entered in that person's books.[273] Opinions differ as to whether this would include a bank account.[274] The better view is that a bank account is not a book debt, since it does not arise out of the company's trade or business but is merely the consequence of the deposit of surplus funds.[275]

---

[269] See para 15.49 above.

[270] The mere possibility of a set-off under either the Statutes of Set-off or the insolvency set-off section is not registrable. One reason for this is that the possibility does not confer any form of security interest. See *Re John Ewing, A Bankrupt* (1906) 8 GLR 612; *Official Assignee of Reeves and Williams v Dorrington* [1918] NZLR 702, 706. In any event, the creditor's right arises by operation of law, as opposed to being created by the company itself.

[271] Companies Act 1985, s 395(1). Note the new Part IV of the Companies Act 1989 (ss 92–107) in relation to registration of charges, which has not yet been implemented. See *Gore-Browne on Companies* (44th edn, looseleaf) vol 1, §18.33 (supplement 38, July 2001).

[272] Compare Australia, where a charge on a book debt is defined in the Corporations Act 2001 (Cth), s 262(4) in terms of a charge on a debt due 'on account of or in connection with a profession, trade or business carried on by the company, whether entered in a book or not . . .'.

[273] *Shipley v Marshall* (1863) 14 CB (NS) 566, 143 ER 567; *Independent Automatic Sales Ltd v Knowles and Foster* [1962] 1 WLR 974. See also *Waters v Widdows* [1984] VR 503, 519–520.

[274] See generally McCracken, *The Banker's Remedy of Set-off* (2nd edn, 1998), 208–211, and McCormack, 'Charge-Backs and Commercial Certainty in the House of Lords' [1998] Company Financial and Insolvency Law Review 111, 117–19.

[275] In addition to the cases referred to below, see Goode, *Legal Problems of Credit and Security* (2nd edn, 1988) 114–15; Ellinger, Lomnicka and Hooley, *Modern Banking Law* (3rd edn, 2002) 786; *Re Stevens* [1888] WN 110, 116; *Watson v Parapara Coal Co Ltd* (1915) 17 GLR 791; *Perrins v State Bank of Victoria* [1991] 1 VR 749, 754–755; *Re Old Inns of NSW Pty Ltd; Millar v Leach* (1994) 13 ACSR 141, 143. See also *Cox v Smail* [1912] VLR 274, 285; *Re Grimsley* (1938) 10 ABC 88. For the contrary view, see Calnan, 'Security Over Deposits Again: BCCI (No 8) in the House of Lords' (1998) 13 Journal of International Banking and Financial Law 125, 128. In any event, money deposited by an investment company with a bank by way of investment may give rise to a book debt. See Goode, *op cit* 114–15, and Ellinger, Lomnicka and Hooley, *op cit* 786 n 33.

Consistent with that view, in *Re Brightlife Ltd*[276] Hoffmann J held that the expression 'all book debts and other debts' in a debenture did not encompass an amount standing to the credit of a bank account. Some two years later, however, he commented in *Re Permanent Houses (Holdings) Ltd*[277] that *Re Brightlife Ltd* was concerned with the construction of a particular debenture, and that he did not express an opinion in that case as to whether a credit balance is a book debt for the purpose of registration of charges under the Companies Act. More recently, Lord Hoffmann again referred to the issue in delivering the judgment of the House of Lords in *Re BCCI (No 8)*.[278] While emphasizing that he was not expressing a view on the point, he nevertheless referred to the judgment of Hutton LCJ (as he then was) in *Northern Bank Ltd v Ross*,[279] which suggested that an obligation to register is unlikely to arise in the case of bank deposits, in terms suggesting that he also inclined to that view.

16.77 But even if the more confined notion of a book debt is adopted, a charge-back may be registrable on another ground. If the company has the right to operate the account without restriction until such time as the bank effects a set-off, a charge over the account would resemble a floating charge, in which case the agreement may be registrable on that ground. Alternatively, a customer may be required to maintain a minimum credit balance, for example in order to cover a liability that the bank may incur on a guarantee or a letter of credit given on behalf of the customer, and the bank has the right to apply the specified balance in satisfaction of any liability that may arise. The restriction on the company's right to operate and manage the account would be inconsistent with a floating security. It may instead give rise to a fixed equitable charge on part of a debt, in which case, unless it is said that the account is a book debt, it would not be registrable.

I. A Set-off Agreement as a Charge

16.78 Acceptance of the view that a debtor can have a security over his own indebtedness leads to the question whether a set-off agreement itself is a charge.[280] This is not

---

[276] [1987] 1 Ch 200.
[277] [1988] BCLC 563, 566–567.
[278] [1998] AC 214, 227.
[279] [1991] BCLC 504, [1990] BCC 883.
[280] A 'flawed asset', in other words a debt with a restriction on the right of repayment until, for example, the creditor has discharged a debt that he in turn owes to the debtor, is not a charge. See *Re Bank of Credit and Commerce International SA (No 8)* [1998] AC 214, 227, HL. This contractual restriction should be effective in the bankruptcy or liquidation of the creditor. See *Re BCCI (No 8)* [1996] Ch 245, 262–263, CA; [1998] AC 214, 225, 227, HL. Moreover, if a flawed asset is used in conjunction with a charge-back, and the charge-back were registrable (compare the discussion above), a failure to register, while it may render the security void as against a liquidator, should not affect the contractual restriction on the right to repayment. See the analogous case of *Re Cosslett (Contractors) Ltd* [1998] Ch 495, 511.

intended to refer to a situation in which it is agreed that a set-off is to occur immediately or as a matter of course, since this is merely a method of payment.[281] Nor would it apply to a provision in a contract to the effect that the amount payable is the contract price less allowable deductions in respect of expenditure. Rather, the issue may arise when one party (referred to in the following discussion as the debtor) is given a power to set off debts in circumstances where the essence of the arrangement is to provide a form of security to the debtor. For example, it is common for banks to be given a power by contract to set off a customer's credit account against any debt owing by the customer, or a related company, to the bank as a result of the provision of financial accommodation. The question is whether the contractual right of set-off results in the creation of a charge over the credit account in favour of the bank as the debtor on that account. A contractual right of set-off would go beyond the right of set-off conferred by the Statutes of Set-off. The Statutes provide a procedural defence which requires an order of the court for its enforcement.[282] A set-off agreement on the other hand allows the debtor itself to effect a set-off and thereby obtain payment.

If the customer has gone into liquidation, and the circumstances in any event are **16.79** such as to give rise to a set-off under the insolvency set-off section, it would be often of no consequence whether or not the set-off agreement has resulted in a charge in favour of the bank, because the same result would follow in any event. There may be other cases however where the question would assume importance.[283] If a charge has been created it would survive the insolvency of the person entitled to the credit account, and the bank could rely on it[284] notwithstanding that a set-off is not available under the insolvency set-off section. This may be particularly important where, for example, the credit balance is held by one company in a group and banking accommodation is provided to another, because in such a case a lack of mutuality would prevent the operation of the set-off section. The issue whether a set-off agreement is a charge could also arise in the context of a negative pledge which prohibits the granting of security, as well as in jurisdictions in which stamp duty is imposed on charges and other loan securities. Further, when an administration order has been made against a company, section 11(3)(c) of the Insolvency Act prohibits any 'security'[285] being enforced against the property of the company during the period that the order is in force, except with the consent of the administrator or the leave of the court,[286] and the question whether

---

[281] This would include, for example, the clearing arrangement in *British Eagle International Air Lines Ltd v Compagnie Nationale Air France* [1975] 1 WLR 758.

[282] See paras 2.33–2.48 above.

[283] See also para 16.60 above.

[284] Subject to the question of registration. See paras 16.75–16.77 above.

[285] This is defined in the Insolvency Act, s 248(b) as, 'any mortgage, charge, lien or other security'.

[286] See also s 10(1)(b) with respect to the period between the presentation of the petition for an administration order and the making or the dismissal of the order, and para 12(1)(g) of Schedule A1 in relation to a moratorium under s 1A of the Act.

this would prevent a bank exercising rights under a set-off agreement may depend on whether the agreement gives rise to a charge.[287] Similarly, if a company voluntary arrangement is proposed under Part I of the Insolvency Act, the arrangement must not affect the rights of a secured creditor without the concurrence of the creditor concerned,[288] and in that circumstance the question whether a set-off agreement is a charge may be crucial.

16.80 There is not a great deal of authority on point. On the one hand, one may find support for the view that a set-off agreement may give rise to a charge in the judgment of Harman J in *Re Tudor Glass Holdings Ltd, Franik Ltd and Thermal Aluminium Ltd.*[289] An officer of the BA group of companies referred in a letter to a director of the Tudor Glass group to the practice of 'contra accounting'. Harman J was prepared to accept that it was intended to provide security to the BA group in the event of a persistent delay in payment by the members of the Tudor Glass group, by allowing for a set-off of debts as between the two groups of companies. He doubted that the letter was effective to achieve that result, but if it had been he said that it would have constituted a floating charge, in which case it would have been void as against the receiver of the Tudor Glass group for want of registration under the companies legislation. Nevertheless the *Tudor Glass* case goes against the current of opinion, because the predominant view is that a set-off agreement is not a charge.[290] This includes some comments by Lord Hoffmann in delivering

---

[287] The term 'security' in s 11(3)(c) admittedly has been interpreted broadly as including the exercise by a landlord of a right of re-entry for non-payment of rent. See *Exchange Travel Agency Ltd v Triton Property Trust plc* [1991] BCLC 396; *Re Olympia and York Canary Wharf Ltd* [1993] BCLC 453, 455, 456. On that basis, a 'security' possibly could also include a set-off agreement, whether or not it is a charge. However, Neuberger J in *Re Lomax Leisure Ltd* [2000] Ch 502 declined to accept the view expressed in those cases in relation to the right of re-entry (although see now the Insolvency Act 1986, s 11(3)(ba), and also Sch A1, para 12(1)(f) in relation to a moratorium under s 1A of the Act, and ss 252(2)(aa) and 254(1)(a) in relation to an interim order under Pt VIII). In Australia the corresponding restriction, in s 440B of the Corporations Act 2001 (Cth), is expressed to relate to enforcement of a 'charge', and the New South Wales Court of Appeal in *Cinema Plus Ltd v ANZ Banking Group Ltd* (2000) 49 NSWLR 513 held that the set-off agreement in issue in that case was not a charge for the purpose of s 440B. Compare *Timbertown Community Enterprises Ltd v Holiday Coast Line Credit Union Ltd* (1997) 15 ACLC 1679, in which the issue was raised but not determined.

[288] Insolvency Act 1986, s 4(3). In Australia, when it is proposed that a company execute a deed of company arrangement, or the company has executed such a deed, the court may order a secured creditor not to realize the security. See the Corporations Act 2001 (Cth), s 444F(2). However, an order cannot be made under s 444F(2) if the creditor has security over all or substantially all of the company's assets. See s 441A. Schedule 8A, cl 7(d) of the Corporations Regulations, which prescribes provisions to be incorporated into each deed of company arrangement, provides that a creditor may not exercise any right of set-off to which the creditor would not have been entitled had the company been wound up. However, cl 7(d) is expressed to be subject to s 444D, which (subject to the exceptions mentioned therein) preserves the position of secured creditors.

[289] (1984) 1 BCC 98,982.

[290] See *Electro Magnetic (S) Ltd v Development Bank of Singapore Ltd* [1994] 1 SLR 734; *Griffiths v Commonwealth Bank of Australia* (1994) 123 ALR 111, 120; *Broad v Commissioner of Stamp Duties* [1980] 2 NSWLR 40, 48; *Bank of New Zealand v Harry M Miller & Co Ltd* (1992) 26 NSWLR 48, 54; *Commercial Factors Ltd v Maxwell Printing Ltd* [1994] 1 NZLR 724, 738; *Cinema*

the judgment of the House of Lords in *Re Bank of Credit and Commerce International SA (No 8)*,[291] in which a contractual right of set-off appears to have been contrasted with a proprietary interest. The comments were made in passing, however, and the issue was not analysed. What then is the basis of the view that a set-off agreement is not a charge? Statements to the effect that it confers a purely personal right[292] do not advance the argument, because they beg the question as to why the right is to be regarded as purely personal rather than proprietary.

The essence of an equitable charge is that specific property is appropriated to the **16.81** discharge of a debt or other obligation, without there being a change of ownership either at law or in equity.[293] A commonly-cited definition is that of Atkin LJ in *National Provincial and Union Bank of England v Charnley*:[294]

> It is not necessary to give a formal definition of a charge, but I think there can be no doubt that where in a transaction for value both parties evince an intention that property, existing or future, shall be made available as security for the payment of a debt, and that the creditor shall have a present right to have it made available, there is a charge, even though the present legal right which is contemplated can only be enforced at some future date, and though the creditor gets no legal right of property, either absolute or special, or any legal right to possession . . . .

No particular form of words is necessary in order to give rise to an equitable charge,[295] although there must be an intention to create a security.[296] The intention

---

Plus Ltd v ANZ Banking Group Ltd (2000) 49 NSWLR 513, 549–550, *per* Giles JA. Academic writers generally also favour that view. See Cresswell, Blair, Hill, Hooley, Phillips and Wood, *Encyclopedia of Banking Law* vol 1, E2476; Goode, *Legal Problems of Credit and Security* (2nd edn, 1988) 173; Goode, *Commercial Law* (2nd edn, 1995) 657; Wood, *English and International Set-off* (1989) 148–50, 193–4; Hapgood, 'Set-off Under the Laws of England,' in Neate (ed) *Using Set-off as a Security* (1990) 32, 37. On the other hand, prior to *Re BCCI (No 8)* [1998] AC 214, in which the House of Lords affirmed the conceptual validity of a charge-back, some writers had expressed the view that, if the conceptual problem could be overcome, a set-off agreement could give rise to a charge. See Pollard, 'Credit Balances as Security—II' [1988] JBL 219, 220; Everett, 'Multi-Party Set-off Agreements' [1993] Journal of Banking and Finance Law and Practice 180, 183–4 (in relation to a multi-party set-off agreement). See also Blair, 'Charges Over Cash Deposits', International Financial Law Review, November 1983, 14; Yeowart, 'House of Lords Upholds Charge-Backs over Deposits', International Financial Law Review, January 1998, 7, 9.

291 [1998] AC 214, 227.
292 See eg Goode, *Legal Problems of Credit and Security* (2nd edn, 1988) 173.
293 *Carreras Rothmans Ltd v Freeman Matthews Treasure Ltd* [1985] 1 Ch 207, 227; *Re Bond Worth Ltd* [1980] 1 Ch 228, 248; *Re Charge Card Services Ltd* [1987] 1 Ch 150, 176; *Re Cosslett (Contractors) Ltd* [1998] Ch 495, 508; Megarry and Wade, *The Law of Real Property* (6th edn, 2000) 1183. See also *Bristol Airport plc v Powdrill* [1990] 1 Ch 744, 760. Compare *Palmer v Carey* [1926] AC 703, which is explained in *Re Gillott's Settlement* [1934] Ch 97, 109–110 and *Swiss Bank Corp v Lloyds Bank* [1979] 1 Ch 548, 568.
294 [1924] 1 KB 431, 449–450.
295 *National Provincial and Union Bank of England v Charnley* [1924] 1 KB 431, 440, *per* Bankes LJ; *Gorringe v Irwell India Rubber and Gutta Percha Works* (1886) 34 Ch D 128, 134; Megarry and Wade, *The Law of Real Property* (6th edn, 2000) 1183.
296 *Re State Fire Insurance Co* (1863) 1 De G J & S 634, 641, 46 ER 251, 254; *National Provincial and Union Bank of England v Charnley* [1924] 1 KB 431, 449–450; *Swiss Bank Corp v Lloyds Bank Ltd* [1982] AC 584, 595; Megarry and Wade, *The Law of Real Property* (6th edn, 2000) 1183.

is not wholly subjective. As Buckley LJ observed in the Court of Appeal in *Swiss Bank Corp v Lloyds Bank Ltd*,[297] an intention to create a security may be expressed or it may be inferred. An inference to that effect may be drawn from the construction of the agreement in the light of admissible evidence as to the surrounding circumstances, and if an agreement on its proper construction has the effect of creating a charge, it does not matter that the parties themselves did not realize that that was a consequence.[298] Buckley LJ remarked:[299]

> But notwithstanding that the matter depends upon the intention of the parties, if upon the true construction of the relevant documents in the light of any admissible evidence as to surrounding circumstances the parties have entered into a transaction the legal effect of which is to give rise to an equitable charge in favour of one of them over property of the other, the fact that they may not have realised this consequence will not mean that there is no charge. They must be presumed to intend the consequence of their acts.

Brandon and Brightman LJJ agreed with Buckley LJ's judgment, and Browne-Wilkinson J commented to a similar effect at first instance.[300]

16.82   At first blush those principles seem apt to encompass some set-off agreements, for example where a bank as a condition to the grant of a facility requires that a deposit be made with it which the depositor is not permitted to access until all indebtedness under the facility has been paid, and the parties agree that the bank may appropriate the deposit in discharge of the debt in the event of default in payment. The essence of the arrangement is that the depositor's property, in the form of the account in credit, is to function as a security. Indeed, in the case of a charge-back in which express words of charge are used, a contractual set-off is the very remedy that would be contemplated,[301] and the House of Lords has now confirmed that a charge-back can be effective to create a proprietary interest in the indebtedness of the party asserting the right.[302] Why then should an express contractual stipulation for a set-off be regarded as inconsistent with a charge?

16.83   According to Philip Wood, it is a characteristic of set-offs generally that they operate by way of the debtor using his asset to pay his liability. In other words, in a set-off the debtor sets off the cross-claim owed to him to pay the creditor's claim, as opposed to applying the creditor's claim to pay the cross-claim.[303] That view forms

---

[297] [1982] AC 584, 595.

[298] See also *Smith v Bridgend County BC* [2002] 1 AC 336, 352 para 42, 355 para 53.

[299] [1982] AC 584, 595–596.

[300] [1979] 1 Ch 548, 569.

[301] Thus, when the Court of Appeal in *BCCI (No 8)* [1996] Ch 245 held that a charge-back is conceptually impossible, it said (at 262) that the agreement would take effect as a contractual set-off, even if this were not expressly spelt out. Millett J expressed a similar view in *Re Charge Card Services Ltd* [1987] 1 Ch 150, 177.

[302] *Re Bank of Credit and Commerce International (SA) (No 8)* [1998] AC 214.

[303] Wood, *English and International Set-off* (1989) 5.

the basis of a distinction that he has sought to draw between contractual set-off and a charge. In the case of a charge, the debtor applies the creditor's asset over which the debtor has a charge to pay the creditor's liability to him, whereas in the case of a contractual set-off the essence of the agreement is that the debtor may apply his own asset to pay his liability.[304] On that analysis, when a bank has a contractual right of set-off against a customer's account in credit, the agreement does not operate by way of giving the bank a right to use the customer's asset in the form of the account in credit in order to satisfy the customer's debt to the bank. Rather, the bank satisfies its liability to the customer on the credit account by appropriating its own asset in the form of the debt owing to it.

The problem with that view is that the various forms of set-off operate differently, **16.84** and it is difficult to extract from them a general proposition that, in the case of a set-off, a debtor uses his asset to pay his liability. Primarily this is because, in most forms of set-off, the setting of the demands against each other is not effected by the parties themselves. Thus, in the case of set-off in bankruptcy and company liquidation, the courts have now accepted that the set-off occurs automatically at the date of the bankruptcy or the liquidation.[305] In that circumstance, it is not profitable to consider which of the demands is set against the other. They are simply brought together, by force of statute, into an account. In relation to set-off under the Statutes of Set-off, the issue of set-off will arise when a debtor being sued for payment pleads as a defence a debt that the creditor owes to him, and in that sense it can be said that it involves the debtor using his own asset. Nevertheless, it is the judgment of the court which brings about the set-off,[306] not the act of the debtor, and the debts are merged in the judgment.[307] In the case of equitable set-off, the essence of the set-off is that a debtor has a cross-claim against the creditor which renders it unjust for the creditor to treat the debtor as having defaulted in payment. But once again, a right to an equitable set-off does not entitle the debtor to extinguish the debts. For that, a judgment of the court is still required.[308]

Contractual set-off differs fundamentally from those forms of set-off, in that the **16.85** party possessed of the right himself may act to bring about the set-off. In a situation in which a set-off is asserted as a defence, the defendant of necessity is confined to using, or asserting, his own asset in order to plead circumstances that would justify the court in giving judgment for a set-off. There is no such inherent restriction, however, when a debtor is in the position of being able to effect a

---

[304] Wood, *English and International Set-off* (1989) 148–50, 193–4. See also Hapgood, 'Set-off Under the Laws of England' in Neate (ed) *Using Set-off as a Security* (1990) 32, 37.

[305] See paras 6.79–6.103 above.

[306] See paras 2.33–2.48 above.

[307] *Stein v Blake* [1996] AC 243, 251.

[308] See paras 4.31 and 4.32 above.

set-off himself by way of a power to do so in a contract. In that context, one can sensibly ask whether it is a case of the debtor paying his own liability by the application of his asset, or whether instead the essence of the agreement is that the contract allows the debtor to use the creditor's asset (the claim against the debtor) to discharge the creditor's liability to the debtor. If the former is the correct analysis the agreement would not be a charge, whereas in the latter situation the agreement would have the flavour of a charge. The determination of the issue is not assisted by reference to other forms of set-off, because contractual set-off is *sui generis*. The answer must depend on the construction of the particular agreement, but certainly agreements are drafted in the latter form, and they are commonly described as conferring rights of set-off.[309] The term 'set-off' is not inapt in that context. As Rose LJ remarked in giving the judgment of the Court of Appeal in *Re BCCI (No 8)*,[310] 'a debtor's right to appropriate a debt which he owes to his creditor and apply it in reduction or discharge of a debt which is owed to himself whether by the creditor or a third party is in our opinion accurately described as a right of set-off.'

16.86 The relevant question is the intention (whether expressed or inferred) of the parties in the context of the agreement in issue, but often the view that the debtor pays his own liability with his own asset would not reflect the reality of the case. Consider the following scenario. A bank has provided a facility to a customer; as a form of security the bank is given the option of effecting a set-off against a deposit in the customer's (or a related company's) name; the 'trigger' for doing so is the customer's default; the customer (or the related company) has not sought repayment of the deposit; and the bank required the deposit and the set-off as security in the event of the customer's insolvency, in which case the bank's asset would be worth only a fraction of its face value. In the absence of clear language, it would be difficult to support the view that the substance of the transaction is that the bank in effecting a set-off pays its debt by the application of its own asset, which because of the customer's insolvency in truth is of diminished value, rather than that the debt owing by the customer in default is satisfied by the application of the customer's asset. *Kent's Case*[311] shows that the courts indeed are prepared to look at the substance of the matter. Mr Kent held partly paid shares in a company. He took an assignment of a debt owing by the company, and wrote to the directors requesting them to transfer from the amount due in respect of the debt a sum sufficient to pay up his shares in full. The directors then passed a resolution that 'the debt assigned by Mr Eichholz to Mr Kent as aforesaid should be applied in paying up in full the shares mentioned in Mr Kent's letter of this date'. Shortly afterwards

---

[309] See eg the agreements in *Matthews v Geraghty* (1986) 43 SASR 576, 580–581, 582 ('letter of set-off'), *Lord v Direct Acceptance Corp Ltd* (1993) 32 NSWLR 362, 364–365 ('Memorandum of Deposit and Set-off'), *Griffiths v Commonwealth Bank of Australia* (1994) 123 ALR 111, 115–116, 121, and *Marathon Electrical Manufacturing Corp v Mashreqbank PSC* [1997] 2 BCLC 460, 468.

[310] [1996] Ch 245, 262.

[311] *Re Land Development Association, Kent's Case* (1888) 39 Ch D 259.

an order was made to wind up the company, whereupon it was held that the transaction was void as a preference.[312] But for that result to have followed, it must have been regarded as a payment or a transfer of property by the company as a debtor in favour of Kent as a creditor,[313] notwithstanding that Kent's letter and the directors' resolution were cast in terms that Kent's asset should be used to pay his liability. Plainly, given the company's insolvency, that was not the substance of the transaction. There was a similar case in New South Wales. In *Re Atlas Engineering Co (Davy's Case)*[314] a shareholder requested the company to apply a debt due to him from the company in settlement of the amount unpaid on his shares, and he was given a receipt acknowledging that the company had received the sum. As in *Kent's Case*, this was held to be a preference in the company's liquidation, Owen J regarding it as a payment by the company, notwithstanding that the request and the receipt suggested that the shareholder was using his asset to pay his liability.[315]

In New South Wales, Giles JA in *Cinema Plus Ltd v ANZ Banking Group Ltd*[316]   **16.87** offered a different explanation as to why a set-off agreement is not a charge. The case concerned an agreement which entitled a bank at any time to 'combine, consolidate, merge or apply any credit balance in any of [the customer's] accounts' towards payment of any moneys owing by the customer to the bank. The question was whether this was a charge for the purpose of s 440B of the Corporations Law in Australia, which rendered a charge given by a company unenforceable while the company was under administration.[317] His Honour said that a charge, being pro-

---

[312] See also *Re Washington Diamond Mining Co* [1893] 3 Ch 95.

[313] See the Bankruptcy Act 1883, s 48, being the preference section in issue, which was made applicable to company liquidations by the Companies Act 1862, s 164.

[314] (1889) 10 LR (NSW) Eq 179, 6 WN (NSW) 64.

[315] The question could also arise in relation to an allegation that a company's property has been disposed of after the commencement of its winding up, contrary to the Insolvency Act 1986, s. 127. Consider that a company's claim against a debtor is the subject of a contractual right of set-off in favour of the debtor, and a set-off is not available under the insolvency set-off section. After the commencement of the company's liquidation the debtor purports to effect a set-off. If the liquidator asserts that the set-off constituted a void disposition, it is unlikely that the court would be attracted to an argument that the company's property in truth was not disposed of, but rather it was a repayment of the debt owing to the company by an application of the debtor's asset. In *Barclays Bank Ltd v TOSG Trust Fund Ltd* [1984] BCLC 1, 24–26 Nourse J contemplated that a set-off taking effect after the commencement of a winding up could constitute a void disposition, and there is also a suggestion to that effect in *Couve v J Pierre Couve Ltd* (1933) 49 CLR 486, 494 (however the avoidance of the disposition of the goods the subject of the sale in that case meant that there was no debt for the price, and therefore no set-off against that debt). See also Goode, *Principles of Corporate Insolvency Law* (2nd edn, 1997) 424–5. On the other hand, Otton J in *Re K (Restraint Order)* [1990] 2 QB 298, 305 considered that the exercise of a contractual right of set-off was not a 'disposing of' assets for the purpose of the Drug Trafficking Offences Act 1986. Compare also *Re Loteka Pty Ltd* [1990] 1 Qd R 322, 324. Nourse J's comment in the *TOSG* case (at 25–26) that, in the event of a conflict between the insolvency set-off section and the void disposition section, the latter prevails, cannot be supported. See para 6.109 above.

[316] (2000) 49 NSWLR 513, 549–550 paras 144 and 145.

[317] There is an exception in the case of a charge over the whole or substantially the whole of the company's property. See the Corporations Act 2001 (Cth), s 441A.

prietary in nature, must in its nature be assignable. In the case of the agreement in issue, he said that it could only be given effect by the bank by a book entry. Because it could only be given effect in that manner, he said that the agreement was of no use to anyone other than the bank, and effectively it was not assignable. On that basis he concluded that it was a personal right, and did not confer a proprietary interest.

16.88 Giles JA's analysis reflects one of the criteria which Lord Wilberforce in *National Provincial Bank Ltd v Ainsworth*[318] said must be satisfied before a right or interest can be admitted into the category of property, that it must be capable in its nature of assumption by third parties.[319] Indeed, Millett LJ had recourse to this criterion in *Re Cosslett (Contractors) Ltd*[320] as a test for determining whether the circumstances in issue gave rise to an equitable charge. The case concerned a right possessed by an employer under a building contract to retain possession of the contractor's equipment and to use it to complete the works. One of the reasons that Millett LJ gave for holding that this was not an equitable charge was that it did not create a 'transmissible interest'. In Australia, however, the courts have rejected the proposition that an interest must in its nature be assignable in order to be characterized as proprietary. Kitto J emphasized this point in *National Trustees Executors and Agency Co of Australasia Ltd v Federal Commissioner of Taxation*:[321]

> It may be said categorically that alienability is not an indispensible attribute of a right of property according to the general sense which the word 'property' bears in the law. Rights may be incapable of assignment, either because assignment is considered incompatible with their nature, as was the case originally with debts (subject to an exception in favour of the King) or because a statute so provides or considerations of public policy so require, as is the case with some salaries and pensions; yet they are all within the conception of 'property' as the word is normally understood: *Ex parte Huggins, In re Huggins* (1882) 21 Ch D 85, at p 91; *Hollinshead v Hazleton* [1916] 1 AC 428, at p 447.

In *Federal Commissioner of Taxation v Orica Ltd*[322] the High Court of Australia referred to those observations with evident approval. On another occasion Mason J commented that, while it is generally correct to say that proprietary rights are capable in their nature of assumption by third parties, assignability is not in all circumstances an essential characteristic of a right of property.[323] The same point has

---

[318] [1965] AC 1175.

[319] Lord Wilberforce said: 'Before a right or an interest can be admitted into the category of property, or of a right affecting property, it must be definable, identifiable by third parties, capable in its nature of assumption by third parties, and have some degree of permanence or stability.' See [1965] AC 1175, 1247–1248. Similarly, Plowman J in *Re Button's Lease* [1964] 1 Ch 263, 272 said that: 'It is inherent in the nature of a piece of property that the owner of it should be able to dispose of it.'

[320] [1998] Ch 495, 508.

[321] (1954) 91 CLR 540, 583. See also Dixon J at 558.

[322] (1998) 194 CLR 500, 537, *per* Gaudron, McHugh, Kirby and Hayne JJ, 542–543, *per* Gummow J.

[323] *R v Toohey, ex p Meneling Station Pty Ltd* (1982) 158 CLR 327, 342–343.

been made on other occasions,[324] including by English text-writers.[325] On this view, it should not be fatal to the argument that a set-off agreement may be a charge that effectively it may not be assignable.

But even apart from the question whether assignability is necessary for a propri- **16.89** etary interest, the objection raised by Giles JA would not be relevant to all set-off agreements. The set-off agreement in issue in the *Cinema Plus* case referred to a right to 'combine, consolidate, merge or apply' a credit balance. In the case of a right to 'combine', 'consolidate' or 'merge' accounts, it is, as Giles JA pointed out, difficult to see how it could be given effect other than by way of a book entry by the bank holding the deposit. However a set-off agreement may be drafted instead in terms of the bank being entitled to 'appropriate' or 'apply' a customer's account in credit in reduction or discharge of the customer's debt.[326] In that regard, the Court of Appeal in *BCCI (No 8)*[327] accepted that a right in a debtor to appropri- ate a debt which he owes to his creditor and apply it in reduction of a debt which is owed to himself is accurately described as a right of set-off. A right to appropri- ate or apply differs from a right to 'combine', 'consolidate' or 'merge' accounts, in that those latter rights each contemplate the bringing together of two debts to pro- duce a balance, as opposed to a dealing in relation to one of the debts by applying or appropriating that debt in satisfaction or reduction of the other. Further, in contrast to a consolidation or a combination or a merger, a right to appropriate or apply a credit balance could be given effect other than by way of book entry by the bank holding the deposit, in which case it should be capable of assumption by a third party. Thus, the debt representing the credit balance could be appropriated by way of a sale, a court-ordered sale and the appointment by the court of a

---

[324] *Dorman v Rodgers* (1982) 148 CLR 365, 374; *Australian Capital Television Pty Ltd v The Commonwealth* (1992) 177 CLR 106, 165–166; *Georgiadis v Australian and Overseas Telecommunications Corp* (1994) 179 CLR 297, 311–312; *Wily v St George Partnership Banking Ltd* (1998) 84 FCR 423, 432; Meagher, Gummow and Lehane, *Equity Doctrines and Remedies* (3rd edn, 1992) 104 para 403. Jackson (in *Principles of Property Law* (1967) 42) said that the ability to deal with an interest is not a criterion which should be adopted to decide the existence of a proprietary interest, but rather it should be treated as a prima facie right following from the classification of an interest as proprietary. See also in Canada *Delgamuuk v British Columbia* (1997) 153 DLR (4th) 193, 241, *per* Lamer CJC, with whom Cory, McLachlin and Major JJ concurred.

[325] Gray and Gray, *Elements of Land Law* (3rd edn, 2001) 109–10; Pettit, *Equity and the Law of Trusts* (9th edn, 2001) 19.

[326] See, eg, the agreements in *Matthews v Geraghty* (1986) 43 SASR 576 ('appropriate and trans- fer the whole or any part of any credit balance . . . to payment in whole or in part of any debit balance'), *Lord v Direct Acceptance Corp Ltd* (1993) 32 NSWLR 362 ('redeem and/or appropriate the Deposit . . . in total or partial satisfaction of the Debt'), *Griffiths v Commonwealth Bank of Australia* (1994) 123 ALR 111 ('prepay and apply the whole or any part of the deposit . . . in or towards payment of the moneys owing'), and *Marathon Electrical Manufacturing Corp v Mashreqbank PSC* [1997] 2 BCLC 460, 468 ('set off transfer or apply all or any of the monies stand- ing to the credit of any current account or deposit account').

[327] [1996] Ch 245, 262. See para 16.85 above.

receiver being the primary remedies of an equitable chargee.[328] Alternatively, consistent with the principle that security on an asset extends also to its products and proceeds,[329] a right to appropriate or apply a credit balance towards payment should also include a right to appropriate or apply the proceeds of the credit balance.[330] In other words, the credit balance could be repaid, and the proceeds used to pay the security holder. As Millett LJ remarked in *Royal Trust Bank v National Westminster Bank plc*:[331] 'I do not see how it can be possible to separate a debt or other receivable from the proceeds of its realisation.' An agreement in those terms therefore would not suffer from the difficulty suggested by Giles JA in the *Cinema Plus* case. Indeed, a charge is often defined in terms of an 'appropriation' of specific property to the discharge of a debt,[332] and it would be surprising if an agreement expressed in terms of an appropriation of a deposit were to be characterized differently to an agreement which referred instead to a charge.

16.90 Consider then the case of a specific deposit made by a customer as a result of a bank's requirement for 'cash cover' for a facility provided either to the customer or to a third party, the deposit being on terms that it cannot be withdrawn until all amounts actually or contingently owing under the facility have been paid, and in the event of a default the bank is given the right to appropriate or apply the deposit in reduction of amounts owing to it under the facility. Since it is not necessary to use any particular form of words in order to create a charge,[333] once the objection to a debtor taking a charge over its own debt is removed there is force in the argument that the agreement results in the creation of a security interest.[334] This should be so notwithstanding the contrary view expressed by Lee J in Australia in

---

[328] Megarry and Wade, *The Law of Real Property* (6th edn, 2000) 1215; Sykes and Walker, *The Law of Securities* (5th edn, 1993) 198.

[329] Goode, *Commercial Law* (2nd edn, 1995) 642, 667 (and also *Legal Problems of Credit and Security* (2nd edn, 1988) 117); Oditah, *Legal Aspects of Receivables Financing* (1991) 25; *Re Cosslett (Contractors) Ltd* [1998] Ch 495, 508.

[330] Sometimes the clause itself makes this clear. In *Lord v Direct Acceptance Corp Ltd* (1993) 32 NSWLR 362 the clause was in terms of '*redeem* and/or appropriate' the deposit (emphasis added), while in *Griffiths v Commonwealth Bank of Australia* (1994) 123 ALR 111 it referred to the right to '*prepay* and apply' the deposit (emphasis added).

[331] [1996] 2 BCLC 682, 704.

[332] *Carreras Rothmans Ltd v Freeman Matthews Treasure Ltd* [1985] 1 Ch 207, 227; *Re Bond Worth Ltd* [1980] 1 Ch 228, 248; *Re Cosslett (Contractors) Ltd* [1998] Ch 495, 508.

[333] *National Provincial and Union Bank of England v Charnley* [1924] 1 KB 431, 440, *per* Bankes LJ; *Gorringe v Irwell India Rubber and Gutta Percha Works* (1886) 34 Ch D 128, 134.

[334] This conclusion is consistent with the reasoning of Spigelman CJ in *Cinema Plus Ltd v ANZ Banking Group Ltd* (2000) 49 NSWLR 513, 523 para 46. Compare Sheller JA at 543 paras 113–116. He said (at 543 para 116) that the set-off agreement in that case was not a charge because it was 'no greater and no different in nature from the right enjoyed [by the bank] at law to combine current accounts'. That was not the case, however. Combination is entirely different from contractual set-off. Combination proceeds on the basis that the balance of all the accounts represents the debt. See para 15.03 above. A contractual set-off on the other hand assumes that the accounts are separate debts which the bank may set off in order to produce a single debt. The set-off can only operate in a situation in which the accounts are not combined.

Griffiths v Commonwealth Bank of Australia,[335] which concerned an agreement in similar terms to those posited.[336] The agreement would appear to come squarely within Cotton LJ's definition of a charge over a debt in *Gorringe v Irwell India Rubber and Gutta Percha Works:*[337]

> When there is a contract for value between the owner of a chose in action and another person which shews that such person is to have the benefit of the chose in action, that constitutes a good charge on the chose in action. The form of words is immaterial so long as they shew an intention that he is to have such benefit.

That scenario should be contrasted with a standard clause in a bank loan agree- **16.91** ment to the effect that the bank can appropriate any account in credit that the customer may have with the bank in discharge of the loan, but without a deposit specifically being required for the purpose of security, and without there being an obligation to maintain such an account and without imposing restrictions on withdrawals. Ordinarily the clause should not result in the creation of a charge in favour of the bank, because it is not a case of specific property being appropriated to the discharge of a debt, and it does not manifest an intention to create a present right over property of the customer.[338] Nor should it constitute a floating charge. It has been said to be a characteristic of a floating charge that it is a charge on fluctuating assets,[339] but that hardly seems an apt description of a situation in which there may not be and may not ever be an account in credit. The agreement suggests an intention to provide the bank with a simple means of effecting payment to the extent of any cash that may be at hand, but without appropriating an account as security. Indeed, any charge which the agreement might be thought to create would be so precarious that, in the absence of clear language, no such intention ought to be imputed.[340] On that basis, the decision of the Singapore Court of Appeal in *Electro Magnetic (S) Ltd v Development Bank of Singapore Ltd,*[341] that an agreement in those terms was not a charge, would appear to be correct. It

---

[335] (1994) 123 ALR 111, 120.

[336] The agreement in *Griffiths v Commonwealth Bank of Australia* provided that, so long as any moneys remained owing or payable to the bank, the bank was under no obligation to repay the deposit, and 'the bank may without prior notice to me/us prepay and apply the whole or any part of the deposit and interest accrued thereon in or towards payment of the moneys owing or any part thereof'.

[337] (1886) 34 Ch D 128, 134.

[338] See Spigelman CJ in *Cinema Plus Ltd v ANZ Banking Group Ltd* (2000) 49 NSWLR 513, 522 para 42, 523 para 46, referring (at 522 paras 41 and 42) to *National Provincial and Union Bank of England v Charnley* [1924] 1 KB 431, 449–450, Atkin LJ.

[339] *Agnew v Commissioner of Inland Revenue* [2001] 2 AC 710, 721 para 19; *Re Cosslett (Contractors) Ltd* [1998] Ch 495, 510; *Smith v Bridgend County BC* [2002] 1 AC 336, 352 para 41. However, while this is a characteristic usually found in floating charges, it should not be a necessary requirement. Professor Goode has suggested that a floating charge can be made to cover any description of property, including land. See Goode, *Commercial Law* (2nd edn, 1995) 734.

[340] As in *Swiss Bank Corp v Lloyds Bank Ltd* [1982] AC 584, 614.

[341] [1994] 1 SLR 734.

is distinguishable from *Re Tudor Glass Holdings*,[342] because in that case the essence of the arrangement was that there would be cross-demands, the purpose of the arrangement being to provide protection to the BA group of companies for an increase in the indebtedness of the Tudor Glass group.[343]

J. Flawed Asset

16.92 Consider that a bank wishes to provide financial accommodation to a customer secured by a cash deposit provided either by the customer or a third party. As an alternative to a charge-back or a set-off agreement, or as additional protection, the deposit may be on terms constituting it a 'flawed asset'. In other words, repayment of the deposit is expressed to be conditional, or contingent, upon the customer satisfying its obligations to the bank under the facility. Until the obligations are satisfied, the deposit is not repayable.[344] The condition on repayment of the deposit is not a charge,[345] and therefore it is not registrable. Nevertheless it should still be effective in the bankruptcy or liquidation of the depositor.[346] After insolvency it remains a flawed asset subject to the same contractual restriction on repayment as before. That was the view of the Court of Appeal in *Re Bank of Credit and Commerce International SA (No 8)*,[347] and observations on appeal in the House of Lords suggest that their Lordships were of the same opinion.[348] Moreover, if a flawed asset is used in conjunction with a charge-back and, contrary to the view expressed earlier in relation to bank deposits,[349] the charge-back were registrable, failure to register, while it would render the charge void as against a liquidator, should not affect the contractual restriction on the right to repayment.[350]

16.93 If the deposit is made by a third party, and the depositor is not personally liable for the debt,[351] lack of mutuality would prevent a set-off in the depositor's or the

---

[342] (1984) 1 BCC 98,982. See para 16.80 above.

[343] See the discussion at (1984) 1 BCC 98,982, 98,984.

[344] A security deposit may be made on terms that it will mature and become payable if it is to be appropriated by the bank in discharge of a debt owing to the bank, and otherwise it is not repayable until the debt has been repaid in full. See eg *Lord v Direct Acceptance Corp Ltd* (1993) 32 NSWLR 362, 365–366.

[345] This seems to have been assumed in *Re Bank of Credit and Commerce International SA (No 8)* [1998] AC 214, 227. See also *Hoverd Industries Ltd v Supercool Refrigeration and Air Conditioning (1991) Ltd* [1995] 3 NZLR 577, 588.

[346] Compare *Hoverd Industries Ltd v Supercool Refrigeration and Air Conditioning (1991) Ltd* [1995] 3 NZLR 577, 584, 587, in which the New Zealand Court of Appeal accepted that the condition linking the payment obligation with redemption of the preference shares was not intended to apply in a winding up, since it was not possible in a winding up to redeem the shares.

[347] [1996] Ch 245, 262–263.

[348] [1998] AC 214, 227.

[349] See paras 16.75–16.77 above.

[350] See the analogous situation considered in *Re Cosslett (Contractors) Ltd* [1998] Ch 495, 511.

[351] As in *Re BCCI (No 8)* [1998] AC 214.

customer's bankruptcy or liquidation against the customer's debt to the bank. Because of the contractual restriction on withdrawal the bank would not have to repay the deposit, and to that extent it would be protected,[352] but the debts nevertheless would retain their separate identities and would not be set off. Alternatively, the deposit may be made by the customer itself. In that circumstance, if the customer goes into liquidation, the Court of Appeal in *Re BCCI (No 8)*[353] assumed that the deposit may be set off against the customer's debt to the bank under the insolvency set-off section. That assumption is doubtful, however. If the customer is in liquidation, its claim against the bank on the deposit would be contingent upon satisfaction of its debt to the bank. But unlike a contingent liability of a company in liquidation, a contingent claim possessed by the company cannot be set off in its liquidation until the contingency occurs.[354] Therefore, as long as the customer remains indebted to the bank, a set-off should not be available in the customer's liquidation against the deposit. Once again, however, the condition on repayment should have the consequence that the bank would not have to repay the deposit, and to that extent it would remain protected.

---

[352] Compare Calnan, 'The Insolvent Bank and Security Over Deposits' (1996) 11 Journal of International Banking and Financial Law 185, 190, and 'Security Over Deposits Again: BCCI (No 8) in the House of Lords' (1998) 13 Journal of International Banking and Financial Law 125, 127.

[353] [1996] Ch 245, 262–263.

[354] See para 8.27 above.

17

ASSIGNEES, AND OTHER INTERESTED THIRD PARTIES

A. Introduction

Consider that A is indebted to B, and that a third party, C, has an interest in the **17.01** debt. This may arise, for example because C is an assignee, or the holder of a security interest, or the beneficiary of a trust, or an undisclosed principal, or a person with subrogation rights, or a judgment creditor levying execution on B's asset in the form of the debt. If A has a cross-claim against B that otherwise would be eligible for a set-off against the debt, A would be concerned to know whether the set-off is still available notwithstanding the interest of C. Alternatively, if A has a cross-claim against C, the question may arise whether the cross-claim can be set off against A's debt to B, given C's interest in the debt. Some general principles were considered earlier in the context of a discussion of mutuality.[1] The purpose of this chapter is to consider the availability of a set-off in cases involving assignments, crystallized floating securities, trusts, execution creditors and subrogation rights. Undisclosed principals[2] were considered earlier, as were assignments in the context of the principle in *Cherry v Boultbee*[3] and combination of bank accounts.[4] In addition, the Contracts (Rights of Third Parties) Act 1999 in some circumstances permits a person who is not a party to a contract to enforce a term in the contract which purports to confer a benefit on him, and the chapter concludes with a brief discussion of set-off in that situation.

B. Assignments

(1) Introduction

17.02 When a debt is assigned, a set-off may occur as between the assignee's beneficial interest in the assigned debt and a cross-claim that the debtor has against the assignee.[5] In addition, however, there is a general equitable principle[6] that an assignee in some circumstances takes subject to equities, which include rights of set-off, that are available to the debtor as against the assignor.[7]

Equitable assignment

17.03 Consider the case of an equitable assignment.[8] Commonly the question of set-off will arise in the situation in which the assignor is indebted to the debtor on a cross-debt that is independent of the assigned debt. When the assignee sues for payment

---

[1] See ch 11 above.

[2] See paras 13.71–13.91 above.

[3] See paras 14.52–14.66 above.

[4] See para 15.113 above.

[5] See paras 3.06, 11.04 and 11.08 above. See eg *Moore v Jervis* (1845) 2 Coll 60, 63 ER 637; *Horrobin v Australia and New Zealand Banking Group Ltd* (1996) 40 NSWLR 89, 93. Compare *Society of Lloyd's v Leighs* [1997] 6 Re LR 289.

[6] Compare the pre-Judicature Acts, common law case of *Watkins v Clark* (1862) 12 CB (NS) 277, 142 ER 1149.

[7] Save possibly in the case of an equitable set-off, for which strict mutuality is not in all cases necessary (see paras 4.48–4.54 above), the debtor could not set off a debt owing by a person other than the assignor. See *First National Bank of Chicago v West of England Shipowners Mutual Protection and Indemnity Association (The Evelpidis Era)* [1981] 1 Lloyd's Rep 54.

[8] See para 17.04 below in relation to an assignment which complies with the Law of Property Act 1925, s 136(1).

of the assigned debt, the debtor asserts that the debts should be set off under the Statutes of Set-off,[9] notwithstanding the assignment. The basic principle is that, if the cross-debt arose after the debtor had notice of the assignment, the debtor cannot set it off against the assignee, but that a set-off is available if the cross-debt arose before the debtor had notice.[10] In *N W Robbie & Co Ltd v Witney Warehouse Co Ltd*[11] the Court of Appeal sought to explain the denial of a set-off in relation to a post-notice cross-debt on the ground that the demands are not equitably mutual. The assigned debt is owned beneficially by the assignee, whereas the cross-debt constitutes a claim against the assignor. This is not a convincing explanation, however. It fails to explain why a set-off is allowed to the debtor when the cross-debt arose after the assignment but before the debtor had notice of the assignment, because in the period between assignment and notice mutuality determined by reference to beneficial titles similarly would be lacking.[12] The preferred analysis[13] is that at common law mutuality for the purpose of the Statutes of Set-off is determined by reference to legal titles, so that if cross-debts are legally mutual there is a prima facie right to a set-off under the Statutes. The question then becomes whether equity regards it as unconscionable for the debtor to rely on this right of set-off otherwise available at law when the equitable title to one of the debts is in someone else.[14] This reflects the position that applied before the Judicature Acts. An assignment of a debt was not then generally recognized by the common law courts, in the sense that the assignee could not enforce the debt in a common law action brought in his own name.[15] He was required to sue in the name of the assignor. If the assignor refused to allow his name to be used, he could be compelled to do so by a court of equity. As far as the common law was concerned, however, the resulting action to enforce the debt was still the assignor's action, and unless equity intervened defences available to the debtor against the assignor, including pursuant to the Statutes of Set-off, could be asserted in that action. Equity would not enjoin the debtor at the request of the assignee from raising defences that arose before the debtor had notice of the assignment.[16] However,

---

[9] See paras 2.04–2.54 above.

[10] See paras 17.10–17.12 below.

[11] [1963] 1 WLR 1324, 1339, *per* Russell LJ, with whose reasons Sellers LJ (at 1331) agreed. See also *Coba Industries Ltd v Millie's Holdings (Canada) Ltd* [1985] 6 WWR 14, 28–29; *Telford v Holt* (1987) 41 DLR (4th) 385, 394.

[12] See para 11.09 above.

[13] See paras 11.08–11.10 above.

[14] Meagher, Gummow and Lehane, *Equity Doctrines and Remedies* (3rd edn, 1992) 720–1. See also Blackburn J in *Wilson v Gabriel* (1863) 4 B & S 243, 247–248, 122 ER 450, 452, referred to in *Christie v Taunton, Delmard, Lane and Co* [1893] 2 Ch 175, 182, and *Hoverd Industries Ltd v Supercool Refrigeration and Air Conditioning (1991) Ltd* [1995] 3 NZLR 577, 587.

[15] The major reasons put forward for the non-assignability of choses in action at law are discussed in Marshall, *The Assignment of Choses in Action* (1950), 34 *et seq.*

[16] This has been explained on the ground that equity will not intervene when the equities are equal. *Wilson v Gabriel* (1863) 4 B & S 243, 248, 122 ER 450, 452.

it was considered unconscionable for the debtor to diminish the rights of the assignee by relying on defences that accrued after he had notice of the assignment,[17] and so in that situation the assignee could obtain an injunction to restrain the debtor from relying on the defence.[18] The Judicature Acts brought about a fusion of the courts of law and equity,[19] but the courts nevertheless have continued to apply the principle that an assignee is bound by equities arising before notice. Moreover, notwithstanding the fusion, and notwithstanding the modern view as to enforcement, that an equitable assignee may sue in his own name subject to a requirement (which can be dispensed with only in exceptional circumstances)[20] of joining the assignor as a party to the action,[21] the explanation should still be the same.

Statutory assignment

17.04 The Judicature Acts[22] also introduced a statutory form of assignment, the successor of which is set out in section 136(1) of the Law of Property Act 1925.[23] In order to come within this provision the assignment must be in writing, it must be absolute and not by way of charge only, and express notice in writing must be given to the debtor. When the section is complied with the assignee obtains the legal title to the debt, and he may sue in his own name without joining the assignor. However, the principle that an assignee takes subject to equities has been

---

[17] This notion underlies the explanation in *Roxburghe v Cox* (1881) 17 Ch D 520, 526, *per* James LJ. See also Meagher, Gummow and Lehane, *Equity Doctrines and Remedies* (3rd edn, 1992) 720–1; *Long Leys Co Pty Ltd v Silkdale Pty Ltd* (1991) 5 BPR 11,512, 11,519 (NSW CA).

[18] As Bramwell B expressed it, the question was: 'taking the set-off to be available at law, would equity restrain the defendants from relying on it?' See *Higgs v Northern Assam Tea Co Ltd* (1869) LR 4 Ex 387, 394.

[19] It was suggested in *United Scientific Holdings Ltd v Burnley Borough Council* [1978] AC 904 that the Judicature Acts also brought about a fusion of the principles of law and equity. This view has been attacked as heretical. See Baker, 'The Future of Equity' (1977) 93 LQR 529; Meagher, Gummow, and Lehane, *Equity: Doctrines and Remedies* (3rd edn, 1992) 67–8; Martin, 'Fusion, Fallacy and Confusion; A Comparative Study' [1994] The Conveyancer 13. See also *MCC Proceeds Inc v Lehman Bros International (Europe)* [1998] 4 All ER 675, 690–691 (equitable title not sufficient to found a common law claim in conversion) and Sir Peter Millett, 'Equity—The Road Ahead' (1995) 9 Tolley's Trust Law International 35, 37. In *Bank of Boston Connecticut v European Grain and Shipping Ltd* [1989] 1 AC 1056, 1109 the House of Lords said that the Judicature Acts, 'while making changes to procedure, did not alter the rights of the parties'. Compare *Bank of Credit and Commerce International SA v Ali* [2002] 1 AC 251, 263 para 17, *per* Lord Bingham ('More than a century and a quarter have passed since the fusion of law and equity . . .'), and Burrows, 'We Do This at Common Law But That in Equity' (2002) 22 OJLS 1, 4.

[20] Compare *Commercial Factors Ltd v Maxwell Printing Ltd* [1994] 1 NZLR 724; *Thomas v National Australia Bank Ltd* [2000] 2 Qd R 448, 458, 460.

[21] *Three Rivers District Council v Bank of England* [1996] QB 292, 313, 315, *per* Peter Gibson LJ. In Australia, see also *Long Leys Co Pty Ltd v Silkdale Pty Ltd* (1991) 5 BPR 11,512, 11,517; *McIntyre v Gye* (1994) 51 FCR 472, 480; *Brookfield v Davey Products Pty Ltd* (1996) 14 ACLC 303, 305; *Chapman v Luminis Pty Ltd* (1998) 86 FCR 513, 519.

[22] Supreme Court of Judicature Act 1873, s 25(6).

[23] In Australia, see eg the Property Law Act 1958 (Vic), s 134.

expressly preserved,[24] so that the debtor can rely on a right of set-off against the assignee that would have prevailed against an equitable assignee before the Judicature Acts.[25] This includes a set-off at common law under the Statutes of Set-off.[26] On the other hand, because the assignor is not a party to the action, the debtor cannot counterclaim in the action for the excess of the assignor's indebtedness to him over and above the amount of the assigned debt.[27]

Cross-demand must be available as a set-off against the assignor

An assignee takes subject to a cross-demand available to the debtor against the assignor only if the cross-demand would have been available as a set-off as between the assignor and the debtor in circumstances where neither party is bankrupt or is a company in liquidation.[28] It has been suggested in Australia that in some cases a cross-demand that would not have given rise to a set-off in an action by the assignor nevertheless may be asserted against the assignee.[29] This is contrary to the view expressed by the House of Lords in *Bank of Boston Connecticut v European Grain and Shipping Ltd*,[30] and it should not be regarded as correct.   **17.05**

The origin of that suggestion in Australia is a statement by Lord Hobhouse in delivering the advice of the Privy Council in *Government of Newfoundland v Newfoundland Railway Co*[31] in the context of a claim by an assignee for payment of sums due under a construction contract: 'Unliquidated damages may now be set off as between the original parties, and also as against an assignee if flowing out of and inseparably connected with the dealings and transactions which also give rise to the subject of the assignment.' That statement in turn was adopted by Lord Brandon of Oakbrook in the House of Lords in the *Bank of Boston* case as setting out the applicable test for an equitable set-off as between the original parties, to   **17.06**

---

[24] See *Pfeiffer GmbH v Arbuthnot Factors Ltd* [1988] 1 WLR 150, 162.

[25] *Lawrence v Hayes* [1927] 2 KB 111, 120–121; *Roadshow Entertainment Pty Ltd v (ACN 053 006 269) Pty Ltd* (1997) 42 NSWLR 462, 482.

[26] *Glencore Grain Ltd v Agros Trading Co* [1999] 2 Lloyd's Rep 410, 420.

[27] *Young v Kitchin* (1878) 3 Ex D 127; *Mitchell v Purnell Motors Pty Ltd* [1961] NSWR 165, 168.

[28] See paras 17.28 and 17.31 below.

[29] *McDonnell & East Ltd v McGregor* (1936) 56 CLR 50, 60, *per* Dixon J. See also *Re K L Tractors Ltd* [1954] VLR 505, 508; *Bayview Quarries Pty Ltd v Castley Developments Pty Ltd* [1963] VR 445, 449; *Edward Ward & Co v McDougall* [1972] VR 433, 438–439; *Provident Finance Corp Pty Ltd v Hammond* [1978] VR 312, 320; *James v Commonwealth Bank of Australia* (1992) 37 FCR 445, 461–462; *Re Partnership Pacific Securities Ltd* [1994] 1 Qd R 410, 423–424; *Walker v Department of Social Security* (1995) 56 FCR 354, 363–364, 367; *Roadshow Entertainment Pty Ltd v (ACN 053 006 269) Pty Ltd* (1997) 42 NSWLR 462, 482; Spry, 'Equitable Set-offs' (1969) 43 Australian Law Journal 265, 269–70 (although the treatment in Spry, *Equitable Remedies* (6th edn, 2001) 178 is more equivocal); Meagher, Gummow and Lehane, *Equity: Doctrines and Remedies* (3rd edn, 1992) 821–23. In *Clyne v Deputy Commissioner of Taxation* (1981) 150 CLR 1, 20, Mason J said that the word 'equities' in the context of the expression 'an assignment is subject to equities' comprehends 'set-off and counterclaims,' but the point was not discussed in any detail.

[30] [1989] 1 AC 1056, 1105–1106, 1109–1111.

[31] (1888) 13 App Cas 199, 213.

which an assignee also takes subject.[32] Traditionally an equitable set-off was said to be available where the connection between the claimant's claim and the defendant's cross-claim was such that the claimant's title to sue was impeached.[33] Lord Brandon said that the concept of impeachment is not a familiar one today, and formulated the test instead by reference to whether the defendant's cross-claim could be characterized as 'flowing out of and inseparably connected with the dealings and transactions which also give rise to' the claimant's claim.[34] This was said to be merely a different version of the impeachment test,[35] but in truth it is broader. Thus, it is difficult to see how the formulation adopted in the *Bank of Boston* case could ever operate to deny an equitable set-off when the same transaction is the source of both demands, whereas in the context of the traditional impeachment test it has been said that it is not sufficient for an equitable set-off that the cross-demands arose out of the one transaction.[36] In Australia the courts have tended to be more rigorous than those in England in emphasizing impeachment of title as the basis of equitable set-off,[37] and in order to distinguish the statement in the *Government of Newfoundland* case, which formed the foundation of the test approved in *Bank of Boston Connecticut v European Grain and Shipping Ltd*, it has been suggested that the *Government of Newfoundland* case in truth was not concerned with determining the availability of an equitable set-off as between the debtor and the assignor in that case, but rather with the question whether an assignee of a contract could recover moneys owing under it without being met by a counterclaim for breach by the assignor of the same contract.[38] By confining the case to assignments, it has been said in Australia that *Government of Newfoundland v Newfoundland Railway Co* does not provide a good juridical root for any changed doctrine of equitable set-off.[39] The *Government of Newfoundland* case concerned Newfoundland legislation similar to section 25(6) of the Supreme Court of Judicature Act 1873 (UK),[40] which provided that an assignee took 'sub-

---

[32] [1989] 1 AC 1056, 1106, 1110–1111. The Appellate Division of the Alberta Supreme Court in *Kaps Transport Ltd v McGregor Telephone and Power Construction Co Ltd* (1970) 73 WWR 549, 552 similarly treated this as a test for set-off between original parties.

[33] See para 4.02 above.

[34] [1989] 1 AC 1056, 1103.

[35] [1989] 1 AC 1056, 1102.

[36] See para 4.16 above.

[37] See paras 4.21–4.28 above.

[38] *McDonnell and East Ltd v McGregor* (1936) 56 CLR 50, 60, *per* Dixon J. Thus, in *Roadshow Entertainment Pty Ltd v (ACN 053 006 269) Pty Ltd* (1997) 42 NSWLR 462, 482 the New South Wales Court of Appeal said that an assignee takes subject to cross-claims for unliquidated damages arising out of the contract which gave rise to the assigned debt, without requiring any other connection. See also *Parsons v Sovereign Bank of Canada* [1913] AC 160, 166, PC. Yet the Privy Council in the *Government of Newfoundland* case (1888) 13 App Cas 199, 212 acknowledged that, 'There is no universal rule that claims arising out of the same contract may be set against one another in all circumstances.' This accords with the generally accepted view in relation to equitable set-off. See para 4.55 above.

[39] *James v Commonwealth Bank of Australia* (1992) 37 FCR 445, 462.

[40] See now the Law of Property Act 1925, s 136(1). See para 17.04 above.

ject to all equities which would have been entitled to priority over the right of the assignee if this Act had not been passed'. It has been suggested in Australia that the equities to which the assignee took subject included not only claims which might have been set off in equity, but also cross-demands which, whilst affording no defence and giving rise only to a counterclaim, under the old system would have founded a common injunction against the enforcement of the plaintiff's claim.[41]

However, whether or not the Privy Council in the *Government of Newfoundland* **17.07** case correctly stated the relevant test for equitable set-off, it is apparent, for reasons set out in greater detail elsewhere,[42] that it proceeded on the basis that a set-off can be asserted against an assignee only because it could also be asserted against the assignor, and the case does not support a proposition that a cross-claim which is inseparable from the transaction which gave rise to the assigned debt may be asserted against the assignee in circumstances where it would not have supported a set-off as against the assignor.[43] Moreover, it is difficult to find any pre-Judicature Acts authority for the proposition that a debtor being sued by an equitable assignee of the debt, but in the name of the assignor, could obtain a common injunction to restrain the action on the basis solely of a cross-demand that would not have given rise to set-off (in its various forms) against the assignor in the absence of an assignment. In the first edition of *Kerr on Injunctions*, published in 1867 only a short time before the enactment of the Judicature Acts, there is no mention of an injunction being available in that circumstance.[44] On the contrary, the principle is stated simply in terms that: 'The assignee of a chose in action takes subject to any equitable right of set-off existing as against the assignor at the date of or before notice of the assignment . . .'[45] Further, if a common injunction would not have been available before the Judicature Acts, an argument that section 25(6) of the 1873 Act itself was the source of the debtor's right to assert the cross-demand against the assignee would run into the difficulty that the Judicature Acts were purely procedural.[46] In so far as *Young v Kitchen*[47] has been referred to as a case in which an assignee took subject to a cross-demand that might not have been available as a set-off against the assignor,[48] it is relevant to note the central point made by counsel for the defendant (Bompas QC) in his successful argument in favour of the set-

---

[41] *James v Commonwealth Bank of Australia* (1992) 37 FCR 445, 461.

[42] Derham, 'Recent Issues in Relation to Set-off' (1994) 68 Australian Law Journal 331, 334–7.

[43] See *Bank of Boston Connecticut v European Grain and Shipping Ltd* [1989] 1 AC 1056, 1110–1111, approving of Hobhouse J's first instance discussion of the *Government of Newfoundland* case in *Colonial Bank v European Grain and Shipping Ltd (The Dominique)* [1987] 1 Lloyd's Rep 239, 254–257.

[44] In Ch 4, dealing with equitable grounds for relief against proceedings at law, or in Ch 3, dealing with injunctions to restrain proceedings at law.

[45] *Kerr on Injunctions* (1st edn, 1867) 68.

[46] Meagher, Gummow and Lehane, *Equity Doctrines and Remedies* (3rd edn, 1992) 821.

[47] (1878) 3 Ex D 127.

[48] Meagher, Gummow and Lehane, *Equity Doctrines and Remedies* (3rd edn, 1992) 821–2.

off. He is reported as having argued that: 'Whatever defence might be set up against the assignor may be set up against his assignee, for the assignee cannot be in a better position than his assignor.'[49] In other words, counsel for the debtor regarded it as a case in which the assignee took subject to a defence that was available against the assignor. It was not argued in the alternative that, even if the debtor's unliquidated cross-demand could not have been set off in an action brought by the assignor in his own right, the assignee nevertheless should still take subject to the cross-demand. Nor did Baron Cleasby make any such point in his judgment.[50]

17.08 The theory proposed in Australia originated in a discussion of *Government of Newfoundland v Newfoundland Railway Co* by Dixon J in *McDonnell and East Ltd v McGregor*.[51] Dixon J suggested in the *McDonnell* case that set-off is not available against a claim for damages.[52] That proposition has now been discredited in relation to equitable set-off,[53] but it may have influenced his view that the *Government of Newfoundland* case was not a case of equitable set-off. Moreover, in so far as it has been sought to justify the decision in the *Government of Newfoundland* case by reference to a notion that an assignee of a contract cannot take the benefit of the contract without also assuming the burden,[54] that explanation would be of doubtful validity in Australia following the rejection, by the Full Court of the Victorian Supreme Court in *Government Insurance Office (NSW) v K A Reed Services Pty Ltd*,[55] of the broad benefit and burden principle advocated by

---

[49] (1878) 3 Ex D 127, 129.

[50] See Hobhouse J's discussion of *Young v Kitchen* at first instance in *Bank of Boston* (*sub nom The Dominique*) [1987] 1 Lloyd's Rep 239, 253–254. See also the explanation of *Smith v Parkes* (1852) 16 Beav 115, 51 ER 720 in Derham, 'Recent Issues in Relation to Set-off' (1994) 68 Australian Law Journal 331, 335.

[51] (1936) 56 CLR 50, 59–60.

[52] (1956) 56 CLR 50, 62.

[53] See eg *Beasley v Darcy* (1800) 2 Sch & Lef 403n; *Galambos & Son Pty Ltd v McIntyre* (1974) 5 ACTR 10 (and the cases there referred to); *Knockholt Pty Ltd v Graff* [1975] Qd R 88; *United Dominions Corp Ltd v Jaybe Homes Pty Ltd* [1978] Qd R 111; *British Anzani (Felixstowe) Ltd v International Marine Management (UK) Ltd* [1980] 1 QB 137, 145–146.

[54] *Aries Tanker Corp v Total Transport Ltd* [1977] 1 WLR 185, 193, *per* Lord Simon of Glaisdale. In *Government of Newfoundland v Newfoundland Railway Co* (1888) 13 App Cas 199, 212 Lord Hobhouse commented that: 'It would be a lamentable thing if it were found to be the law that a party to a contract may assign a portion of it, perhaps a beneficial portion, so that the assignee shall take the benefit, wholly discharged of any counter-claim by the other party in respect of the rest of the contract, which may be burdensome.' See also *Roadshow Entertainment Pty Ltd v (ACN 053 006 269) Pty Ltd* (1997) 42 NSWLR 462, 482; *Business Computers Ltd v Anglo-African Leasing Ltd* [1977] 1 WLR 578, 585 (referred to in *John Dee Group Ltd v WMH (21) Ltd* [1997] BCC 518, 530).

[55] [1988] VR 829, *per* Brooking J, with whom O'Bryan and Nicholson JJ agreed. See also *Calaby Pty Ltd v Ampol Pty Ltd* (1990) 102 FLR 186, 205; Meagher, Gummow and Lehane, *Equity Doctrines and Remedies* (3rd edn, 1992) 81, 924. In England the 'pure principle of benefit and burden' was criticized in *Rhone v Stephens* [1994] 2 AC 310, 322, which in turn was referred to in *Gallagher v Rainbow* (1994) 179 CLR 624, 648, *per* McHugh J, and see also in England *Amsprop Trading Ltd v Harris Distribution Ltd* [1997] 1 WLR 1025, 1034–1035 and *Thamesmead Town Ltd v Allotey* [1998] 3 EGLR 97. Compare Aughterson, 'In Defence of the Benefit and Burden Principle' (1991) 65 Australian Law Journal 319.

Megarry VC in *Tito v Waddell (No 2)*.[56] Indeed, the House of Lords in *Bank of Boston Connecticut v European Grain and Shipping Ltd*[57] specifically rejected the benefit and burden principle as an explanation for the *Government of Newfoundland* case.

If the claim assigned is such that as a matter of law it is not susceptible to a set-off **17.09** as between solvent parties, not because of a lack of connection between the demands but because of its nature, the assignee similarly will take free of a set-off.[58] This includes a claim for freight under a charterparty in circumstances where the charterer has a cross-claim for damages against the owner,[59] and a claim on a negotiable instrument where the issuer has an unliquidated cross-claim arising out of the transaction in respect of which the instrument was issued.[60]

(2) Statutes of Set-off

Date of notice

Mutual debts in existence between the debtor and the assignor at the date that the **17.10** debtor receives notice of the assignment may give rise to a set-off under the Statutes of Set-off enforceable against the assignee.[61] This should also apply where the cross-debt owing by the assignor to the debtor was acquired by the debtor as a result of an assignment to him before notice,[62] including where there is an effective assignment without consideration.[63] In the case of set-off under the Statutes of Set-off, the debts are not set against each other until judgment for a set-off.[64] Notice of an assignment given to the debtor itself does not effect a set-off.[65] As a

---

[56] [1977] 1 Ch 106, 289 *et seq.*

[57] [1989] 1 AC 1056, 1105–1106.

[58] *Bank of Boston Connecticut v European Grain and Shipping Ltd* [1989] 1 AC 1056.

[59] See paras 5.02–5.24 above.

[60] See paras 5.25–5.48 above.

[61] See eg *Smith v Parkes* (1852) 16 Beav 115, 51 ER 720; *Chick v Blackmore* (1854) 2 Sm & Giff 274, 65 ER 398; *Stephens v Venables (No 1)* (1862) 30 Beav 625, 54 ER 1032; *Roxburghe v Cox* (1881) 17 Ch D 520; *Lawrence v Bell* (1866) 14 WR 753; *Biggerstaff v Rowatt's Wharf Ltd* [1896] 2 Ch 93; *Re Smith & Co Ltd* [1901] 1 IR 73. See also *Peters v Soame* (1701) 2 Vern 428, 23 ER 874, which was decided before the enactment of the Statutes of Set-off. The statement in *Glencore Grain Ltd v Agros Trading Co* [1999] 2 Lloyd's Rep 410, 420, CA, that an assignment takes effect subject to any right of set-off which is available to the debtor against the assignor, should be read subject to the limitation relating to notice of the assignment. Compare para 14.63 above in relation to the situation in which a trustee obtains an order for costs against a beneficiary as a result of a failed action brought by the beneficiary against the trustee, and the beneficiary assigned his interest in the trust after commencement of the action but before judgment.

[62] See eg *Tony Lee Motors Ltd v M S MacDonald & Son (1974) Ltd* [1981] 2 NZLR 281 (company receivership). Compare *N W Robbie & Co Ltd v Witney Warehouse Co Ltd* [1963] 1 WLR 1324 (see para 17.75 below), in which the assignment occurred after notice.

[63] For a discussion of consideration in relation to assignments of choses in action, see Keeton and Sheridan, *Equity* (3rd edn, 1987) 239 *et seq.*

[64] See para 2.33 above.

[65] *Glencore Grain Ltd v Agros Trading Co* [1999] 2 Lloyd's Rep 410, 417–419.

---

corollary, there must not only be mutual debts in existence at the date of notice but the set-off must also be available when the debtor is sued by the assignee and files his defence. If therefore the cross debt is not enforceable at that time,[66] or if the court in the assignee's action would not determine the cross-debt, for example because it is subject to an arbitration clause or a foreign jurisdiction clause,[67] the assignee will not be subject to the set-off.[68]

Presently payable

17.11   It is not necessary that the pre-existing cross-debt owing by the assignor to the debtor should have been presently payable before the date of notice.[69] It should suffice if it is payable when the defence is filed.[70] It has been said however that, if the assigned debt was not presently payable at the date of notice, in order that the cross-debt may be set off it should have become payable before the assigned debt became payable.[71] The reason for the limitation is not clear. The set-off in issue is the procedural defence provided by the Statutes of Set-off. If the cross-debt owing by the assignor is in existence before notice, it should be sufficient if it is payable at the date that the defence is filed regardless of when the assigned debt became payable. Indeed, it is difficult to reconcile the suggested limitation with *Christie v Taunton, Delmard, Lane and Co.*[72] The case concerned an assignment of debentures issued by a company. Notice of the assignment was given to the company on 6 November 1890. Prior to that date, on 3 November, a call was made on shares held by the assignor, which call was payable on 20 November. The debentures on their face were not payable until 31 December, but in the event of the winding up of the company the principal moneys secured by them were to become immediately due and payable. On 19 November the company went into voluntary liquidation. Both the company's liability on the debentures and the assignor's liability for the call constituted existing debts at the date of notice, although they were not payable until after that date. Stirling J held that the company could bring them into an account, notwithstanding that, because of the occurrence of the winding

---

[66]   See para 2.49 above.

[67]   See para 2.52 above.

[68]   *Glencore Grain Ltd v Agros Trading Co* [1999] 2 Lloyd's Rep 410.

[69]   *Jeffryes v Agra and Masterman's Bank* (1866) LR 2 Eq 674; *Christie v Taunton, Delmard, Lane and Co* [1893] 2 Ch 175; *Re Pinto Leite and Nephews, ex p Visconde des Olivaes* [1929] 1 Ch 221. See also *Downes v Bank of New Zealand* (1895) 13 NZLR 723; *Business Computers Ltd v Anglo-African Leasing Ltd* [1977] 1 WLR 578, 585.

[70]   *Stein v Blake* [1996] AC 243, 251. See paras 2.08–2.12 above.

[71]   *Re Pinto Leite and Nephews* [1929] 1 Ch 221, 234–236, explaining *Jeffryes v Agra and Masterman's Bank* (1866) LR 2 Eq 674, 680. See also *Downes v Bank of New Zealand* (1895) 13 NZLR 723, 734; *Business Computers Ltd v Anglo-African Leasing Ltd* [1977] 1 WLR 578, 584.

[72]   [1893] 2 Ch 175, discussed in *Clyne v Deputy Commissioner of Taxation* (1981) 150 CLR 1, 21–22.

up, the assignor's indebtedness for the call matured after the assigned debt became due and payable.[73]

Subsequent debt arising out of a prior contract

There must be an existing debt owing by the assignor to the debtor before notice.[74] **17.12** It is not considered sufficient for a set-off that a debt accrues in favour of the debtor from the assignor after notice as a result of a contract entered into before notice.[75] Thus, where a debtor was also a lessor in respect of property leased to the creditor, and the creditor assigned the debt, it was held that the assignee was not subject to a set-off in respect of rent which accrued to the debtor/lessor after notice of the assignment, even though the lease was entered into before notice.[76] This is an undesirable result. A set-off should be allowed in circumstances where there was a possibility of a perception of a form of security in the existence of cross-demands,[77] and this should be ascertained by reference to the state of affairs existing when a binding contractual relationship was entered into, as opposed to when a debt arose as a result of the contract. It should be sufficient that there are presently payable cross-debts at the date of the action which arose out of contractual obligations incurred before notice. Consistent with that approach, an exception to the established principle may arise in circumstances where there was a temporary suspension of mutuality.[78] For example, if a debtor before notice of an assignment of the debt held a negotiable instrument upon which the creditor was liable, which the debtor indorsed to a third party before notice, and after notice

---

[73] In addition, calls were made in the winding up. See para 8.53 above.

[74] Compare para 17.19 below in relation to the debt assigned. Compare also equitable set-off. See para 17.22 below.

[75] *Stephens v Venables (No. 1)* (1862) 30 Beav 625, 54 ER 1032; *Watson v Mid Wales Railway Co* (1867) LR 2 CP 593. See also *Woodhams v Anglo-Australian and Universal Family Assurance Co* (1861) 3 Giff 238, 66 ER 397 (call on shares made after notice); *Re China Steamship Co, ex p Mackenzie* (1869) LR 7 Eq 240, 243; *Christie v Taunton, Delmard, Lane and Co* [1893] 2 Ch 175, 181; *Re Bailey Cobalt Mines Ltd* (1919) 44 OLR 1 (judgment in misfeasance action obtained after notice); *Re Pinto Leite and Nephews* [1929] 1 Ch 221, 233–234; *Business Computers Ltd v Anglo-African Leasing Ltd* [1977] 1 WLR 578 (see esp at 585). This is also consistent with *Unity Joint Stock Mutual Banking Association v King* (1858) 25 Beav 72, 79–80, 53 ER 563, 566, for which see para 3.05 above. Compare *John Dee Group Ltd v WMH (21) Ltd* [1997] BCC 518, 530 (decision affirmed [1998] BCC 972 without reference to this point) in relation to the return of the initial down payment, although Neuberger J relied on a misstatement in *Business Computers Ltd v Anglo-African Leasing Ltd* [1977] 1 WLR 578, 585 of the facts in issue in *Rother Iron Works Ltd v Canterbury Precision Engineers Ltd* [1974] 1 QB 1 (the company rather than the debtor was the seller of the goods), and in any event the question in relation to that payment concerned the quantum and the timing of the obligation, as opposed to whether there was an existing debt. Compare also the exceptional fact situation in *Ralston v South Greta Colliery Co* (1912) 13 SR (NSW) 6. See paras 4.08 and 4.09 above.

[76] *Watson v Mid Wales Railway Co* (1867) LR 2 CP 593. See also *Stephens v Venables (No 1)* (1862) 30 Beav 625, 54 ER 1032.

[77] See para 6.12 above.

[78] See paras 6.65–6.67 above in relation to company liquidation.

the debtor was obliged to take up the instrument again as a result of the creditor's default, the assignee would take subject to the debtor's right to set off his resulting claim against the creditor/assignor on the instrument. The availability of a set-off in this situation has been recognized in the context of company receivership,[79] and questions of set-off in that context are governed by the same principles which govern assignments.[80]

(3) Set-off in Australia

New South Wales and Queensland

17.13 The position may differ in some Australian states.[81] The Statutes of Set-off have been repealed in New South Wales and Queensland, which should have as a consequence that the only form of set-off to which an assignee in those jurisdictions takes subject is equitable set-off, together with analogous rights such as pursuant to the principle in *Cherry v Boultbee*[82] and combination of bank accounts.[83]

Victoria

17.14 In Victoria, on the other hand, it has been suggested that r 13.14 SCR has had the effect that any cross-claim, whether liquidated or unliquidated, may now be included in the defence and be the subject of a set-off.[84] That proposition may be debated,[85] but if the rule does operate in that manner prima facie it would have a corresponding effect on the position of an assignee. It could be said that an expanded defence under the rule would not apply to a legal assignment by a creditor which complies with section 134 of the Property Law Act 1958 (Vic).[86] The argument would be that r 13.14 is expressed to apply where 'a defendant has a claim against a plaintiff for the recovery of a debt or damages . . .', and in the case of an assignment satisfying section 134 the assignee is the plaintiff. The argument would proceed that the rule can have no application in relation to a cross-claim against the assignor, who is not the plaintiff, notwithstanding that, if the assignment had not occurred, so that the original creditor would have been the party suing, r 13.14 would have provided a defence. Therefore, in this situation the set-offs that can be asserted against the assignee are those arising under established principles, rather than pursuant to r 13.14. Section 134 nevertheless

---

[79] See *Handley Page Ltd v Commissioners of Customs and Excise and Rockwell Machine Tool Co Ltd* [1970] 2 Lloyd's Rep 459, 464–465, referred to in *Business Computers Ltd v Anglo-African Leasing Ltd* [1977] 1 WLR 578, 585–586. See also para 17.76 below.
[80] See paras 17.73–17.87 below.
[81] See paras 2.55–2.67 above.
[82] See paras 14.52–14.66 above.
[83] See para 15.113 above.
[84] See para 2.64 above.
[85] See paras 2.64–2.67 above.
[86] This is in similar terms to the Law of Property Act 1925, s 136. See para 17.04 above.

provides that the assignee takes subject to equities, and the point is that, if the assignor had sued, a defence would have been available to the debtor. The principle of taking subject to equities dictates that that defence should also be available against the assignee if it arose before notice.

But whatever the position in relation to a legal assignment, the same argument **17.15**
would not always be available in the case of an equitable assignment, because in such a case the action may be brought in the name of the assignor as plaintiff.[87] If the debtor has an unrelated damages cross-claim against the plaintiff/assignor that arose before the debtor had notice of the assignment, an expanded defence in Victoria under r 13.14 prima facie would allow the debtor to include it in its defence and set it off against the plaintiff's claim, notwithstanding the assignment, since it is not regarded as unconscionable for a debtor to rely, as against an assignee, on a defence available against the assignor that arose before notice.[88]

(4) Notice to the Debtor

It is the date of notice to the debtor,[89] as opposed to the date of the assignment, **17.16**
that determines whether an assignee takes subject to a set-off under the Statutes in relation to a cross-debt owing by the assignor to the debtor.[90] The notice need not be in any particular form.[91] It need not, for example, be in writing. Nor is it necessary that the notice should come from the assignee.[92] It would be unconscionable for the debtor to rely on a set-off otherwise available at law if the debtor knows of the assignment from whatever source. Moreover, there need only be notice of the fact that the debt has been assigned. The assignee need not be named.[93]

There is little direct authority on the question of what constitutes adequate notice **17.17**
to the debtor in order to prevent set-offs arising as between an assignor and the

---

[87] In the case of an equitable assignment of a legal chose in action it is said that the assignor should be a party to the action, either as claimant or defendant. See *McIntyre v Gye* (1994) 51 FCR 472, 480; *Three Rivers District Council v Bank of England* [1996] QB 292. See also para 17.03 above.

[88] See para 17.03 above.

[89] Notice given to an agent of the debtor may suffice. See *Moore v Jervis* (1845) 2 Coll 60, 69, 71–72, 63 ER 637, 641, 642.

[90] See eg *Moore v Jervis* (1845) 2 Coll 60, 63 ER 637; *Wilson v Gabriel* (1863) 4 B & S 243, 248, 122 ER 450, 452–453; *Watson v Mid Wales Railway Co* (1867) LR 2 CP 593, 601; *Canadian Admiral Corporation Ltd v L F Dommerich & Co Inc* (1964) 43 DLR (2d) 1; *Commercial Factors Ltd v Maxwell Printing Ltd* [1994] 1 NZLR 724, 735. See also *Brice v Bannister* (1878) 3 QBD 569, 578. The statement in *Dixon v Winch* [1900] 1 Ch 736, 742 (and see also *Turner v Smith* [1901] 1 Ch 213, 219), in so far as it appears to suggest the contrary, should be regarded as incorrect.

[91] *G & N Angelakis Shipping Co SA v Compagnie National Algerienne de Navigation (The Attika Hope)* [1988] 1 Lloyd's Rep 439, 442. For the position in relation to the notice necessary to effect a statutory assignment under the Law of Property Act 1925, s 136(1), see Oditah, *Legal Aspects of Receivables Financing* (1991) 131.

[92] See eg *Lloyd v Banks* (1868) LR 3 Ch App 488 (notice in newspaper); *Ex parte Agra Bank, re Worcester* (1868) LR 3 Ch App 555, 559; *Re Dallas* [1904] 2 Ch 385, 309; *Talcott Ltd v John Lewis & Co Ltd* [1940] 3 All ER 592.

[93] *Smith v Parkes* (1852) 16 Beav 115, 117–118, 51 ER 720, 721.

debtor, but some guidance can be obtained by reference to the approach adopted in other circumstances in relation to the adequacy of notice, for example in the case of a priorities dispute between successive assignees of a debt. The relevant principle is the rule in *Dearle v Hall*,[94] which in essence accords priority to the assignee who is the first to give notice to the debtor. In this situation the courts have emphasized that it is in the interests of an assignee to give notice so as to prevent another assignee, whether earlier or later, obtaining priority over him. If an assignee does not give notice, he acts at his peril. Accordingly, the duty is on the assignee to give notice.[95] Moreover, to be effective the assignee's notice should be clear and distinct.[96] To paraphrase Lord Cairns in *Lloyd v Banks*,[97] there must be proof that the mind of the debtor has in some way been brought to an intelligent apprehension of the assignment, so that a reasonable man, or an ordinary man of business, would act upon the information and would regulate his conduct by it. In particular, Lord Cairns indicated that proof of what would only be constructive notice would not suffice.[98] A similar approach has been adopted when the question concerns payment by the debtor. If the debtor has notice of the assignment he can only discharge his obligation by paying the assignee, unless the assignee has agreed otherwise.[99] If the debtor ignores the assignment and pays the assignor, he may be liable to pay a second time to the assignee.[100] Once again, because the debtor may obtain a good discharge by paying the assignor if he does not have notice,[101] the assignee acts at his peril if he fails to give notice, and accordingly the view is that the assignee must give clear notice in order to secure his position.[102] Thus, in *Talcott Ltd v Lewis & Co Ltd*[103] the notice sent to the debtor was ambiguous, and it was held that it was insufficient to render the debtor liable to pay the assignee after having already paid the assignor. Nor was there a duty of inquiry imposed.

17.18 Set-off is similar to payment, and the issue of notice for the purpose of whether a cross-debt owing by the assignor to the debtor can be set off against the assigned debt should be determined by like principles. In the case of an equitable assignment, where the legal title to the assigned debt remains with the assignor, the debtor prima facie has a right of set-off at law under the Statutes of Set-off in rela-

---

[94] (1828) 3 Russ 1, 38 ER 475.
[95] *Willes v Greenhill* (1861) 4 De G F & J 147, 150, 45 ER 1139, 1140; *Ward v Duncombe* [1893] AC 369, 395. See also *Mangles v Dixon* (1852) 3 HLC 702, 732–733, 10 ER 278, 291.
[96] *Bence v Shearman* [1898] 2 Ch 582, 587.
[97] (1868) LR 3 Ch App 488, 490–491.
[98] (1868) LR 3 Ch App 488, 490.
[99] See eg *First National Bank of Chicago v West of England Shipowners Mutual Protection and Indemnity Association (The Evelpidis Era)* [1981] 1 Lloyd's Rep 54, in which it was agreed that insurance payments could be made directly to the insured mortgagor until such time as the mortgagee notified the insurer of a default.
[100] See eg *Brice v Bannister* (1878) 3 QBD 569.
[101] See eg *Norrish v Marshall* (1821) 5 Madd 475, 56 ER 977.
[102] *Bence v Shearman* [1898] 2 Ch 582, 587, 591.
[103] [1940] 3 All ER 592.

tion to any cross-debt, no matter when it arises. Equity on the other hand will protect the assignee against a set-off arising after the debtor has notice of the assignment,[104] and an assignee therefore acts at his peril if he does not give notice[105] because he may not be able to take advantage of the equitable rule. The courts have emphasized that it is up to an assignee to look after his own interests and to make inquiries as to prior equities,[106] and consistent with that view, and with the attitude of the courts in relation to questions of payment and priorities, the onus should be on the assignee to give notice which is clear and unambiguous so as to prevent the debtor obtaining a subsequent right of set-off.[107] This should also be the case when the requirements for a statutory assignment set out in section 136 of the Law of Property Act 1925 are in issue,[108] particularly given the commonly expressed view that the section relates to procedure only.[109] On the other hand, if sufficient notice is given to the debtor, he cannot refuse to accept it.[110] Nor can he shut his eyes to the obvious.[111] In *Cavendish v Geaves*[112] a pass book issued by a banking firm from time to time to a customer showed changes in the firm, and principal and interest payments on some bonds given by the customer to the firm appeared as entries in the pass book. This was held to constitute notice that the bonds were assigned to the new firm whenever a change occurred.

(5) Assignment of a Future Debt

Prior contract

English law regards an unearned debt under an existing contract as an existing **17.19** debt.[113] The principle has been expressed in terms that a legal right to be paid

---

[104] See para 17.03 above.

[105] *Parker v Jackson* [1936] 2 All ER 281, 289–290.

[106] *Mangles v Dixon* (1852) 3 HLC 702, 732–733, 10 ER 278, 291; *Canadian Admiral Corporation Ltd v L F Dommerich & Co Inc* (1964) 43 DLR (2d) 1, 2, 8–9; *Helstan Securities Ltd v Hertfordshire County Council* [1978] 3 All ER 262, 266. See also *Athenaeum Life Assurance Society v Pooley* (1858) 3 De G & J 294, 299, 44 ER 1281, 1283.

[107] Thus, when the third-party interest takes the form of a charge over a debt, as opposed to an absolute assignment, the better view is that registration of the charge by itself should not suffice to constitute notice to the debtor. Unless the debtor has undertaken a search of the register or is otherwise aware of the charge, the fact of registration should simply be constructive notice. See Lightman and Moss, *The Law of Receivers and Administrators of Companies* (3rd edn, 2000) 314.

[108] See para 17.04 above.

[109] *Tolhurst v Associated Portland Cement Manufacturers (1900) Ltd* [1902] 2 KB 660, 676–677.

[110] *Higgs v The Northern Assam Tea Co Ltd* (1869) LR 4 Ex 387, 396.

[111] *Mangles v Dixon* (1852) 3 HLC 702, 732, 10 ER 278, 290.

[112] (1857) 24 Beav 163, 53 ER 319.

[113] Oditah, *Legal Aspects of Receivables Financing* (1991) 27–9, 135. See eg *Shepherd v Federal Commissioner of Taxation* (1965) 113 CLR 385 (assignment of royalties payable under a licence agreement). In *Marathon Electrical Manufacturing Corp v Mashreqbank PSC* [1997] 2 BCLC 460, 467 Mance J said that the principle embraces any contract under which payments may be received, provided at least that it is not terminable at will. Compare *Norman v Federal Commissioner of Taxation* (1963) 109 CLR 9 in relation to future interest payable on a loan which could be repaid by the borrower at any time without notice (see the explanation of the case in *Shepherd v Federal Commissioner of Taxation*).

money at a future date is a present chose in action if it depends upon an existing contract on the repudiation of which an action could be brought for anticipatory breach.[114] This broad interpretation ascribed to the concept of existing debts has not been invoked in relation to set-off when the cross-debt owing to the debtor is in issue. It is said that a debt which accrues to the debtor from the assignor after notice, albeit pursuant to a prior contract, cannot be set off against the assigned debt.[115] In New Zealand, the Court of Appeal in *Hoverd Industries Ltd v Supercool Refrigeration and Air Conditioning (1991) Ltd*[116] considered that the assigned debt is subject to a similar restriction, so that it has to be presently due when the assignment occurs[117] in order to be susceptible to a set-off.[118] However there is other authority which supports the view that the restriction applicable to the cross-debt does not apply to the assigned debt when it arises out of a prior contract. In the context of a company receivership,[119] the Court of Appeal in *Rother Iron Works Ltd v Canterbury Precision Engineers Ltd*[120] allowed a set-off in circumstances where a company entered into a contract for the sale of goods, a receiver subsequently was appointed to the company thereby crystallizing a floating charge, and after the appointment the company delivered the goods to the purchaser, whereupon the purchaser became indebted for the price. The Court of Appeal held that the secured creditor took subject to a set-off available to the purchaser in relation to a debt owing to it by the vendor before the appointment, notwithstanding that the debt for the price when it arose was embraced by a fixed charge as a result of the crystallization,[121] and notwithstanding that it arose after notice of the appointment, albeit pursuant to a prior contract.[122] The New

---

[114] Oditah, *Legal Aspects of Receivables Financing* (1991) 28–9, referring to *Norman v Federal Commissioner of Taxation* (1963) 109 CLR 9, 26, *per* Windeyer J.

[115] See para 17.12 above.

[116] [1995] 3 NZLR 577, 587–588.

[117] To be more precise, at the date of notice of the assignment. See para 17.16 above.

[118] In any event, the New Zealand Court of Appeal in the *Hoverd Industries* case concluded that a set-off would have been contrary to the intention of the parties, and therefore it was not permitted on that ground. See [1995] 3 NZLR 577, 588.

[119] See paras 17.73–17.87 below.

[120] [1974] 1 QB 1, *per* Russell, Cairns and Stamp LJJ. See para 17.78 below.

[121] It is commonly said that, when a floating charge crystallizes, any debt which is owing to the company and which comes within the ambit of the charge is assigned in equity to the chargee. See para 17.74 below.

[122] *Rother Iron Works Ltd v Canterbury Precision Engineers Ltd* has been referred to in later cases with evident approval. In addition to *Marathon Electrical Manufacturing Corp v Mashreqbank PSC* [1997] 2 BCLC 460 (see below), see *George Barker (Transport) Ltd v Eynon* [1974] 1 WLR 462, 470, 473–474, 475, CA and *Business Computers Ltd v Anglo-African Leasing Ltd* [1977] 1 WLR 578, 585 (although the facts of the *Rother Iron Works* case were there incorrectly stated, in that the goods were not delivered *to* the company but rather *by* the company). See also *Caratti v Grant* (1978) 3 ACLR 322, 331; *Roadshow Entertainment Pty Ltd v (ACN 053 006 269) Pty Ltd* (1997) 42 NSWLR 462, 483, CA; *John Dee Group Ltd v WMH (21) Ltd* [1997] BCC 518, 530 (and see also on appeal [1998] BCC 972, 976).

Zealand Court of Appeal in the *Hoverd Industries* case made the point that the *Rother Iron Works* case differed from the case before it, in that in *Rother Iron Works Ltd v Canterbury Precision Engineers Ltd* the debt which the purchaser sought to set off was already due and payable before the company entered into the contract of sale, but it nevertheless acknowledged that the judgment did not turn on that point. Russell LJ in the *Rother Iron Works* case instead emphasized that, when the debt for the price first came into existence, on delivery of the goods after crystallization, it was subject to the set-off.[123] More recently, Mance J followed the *Rother Iron Works* case in *Marathon Electrical Manufacturing Corp v Mashreqbank PSC*.[124] The case concerned a letter of credit issued in favour of a company, Munradtech, which in turn engaged Mashreqbank to collect moneys payable under the letter. Munradtech assigned the proceeds of the letter of credit to the plaintiffs, and on 2 April 1996 notice of the assignment was given to Mashreqbank. On 22 May 1996 Mashreqbank received the proceeds from the issuer of the letter of credit, whereupon it asserted that the assignees took subject to its right to set off a prior separate debt owing to it by Munradtech. Mance J accepted that the subject of the assignment was Munradtech's entitlement against Mashreqbank as collecting bank, as opposed to Munradtech's entitlement as against the issuer.[125] The date of notice was 2 April, whereas Mashreqbank did not receive the proceeds, and therefore it did not become indebted in respect of them, until later, on 22 May.[126] Nevertheless its indebtedness arose out of a prior engagement, and Mance J held that the prior debt of Munradtech could be set off against it. The approach adopted in the *Rother Iron Works* and *Marathon Electrical* cases should be followed in preference to that favoured by the New Zealand Court of Appeal in *Hoverd v Supercool*. It is difficult in any event to support the restriction in the case of the debt owing to the debtor,[127] and there is no reason for extending it also to the assigned debt.

An expectancy not derived from a present contract

Consider on the other hand that the subject of an assignment is a future debt (or an expectancy) that is not the product of an existing contract. If value has been **17.20**

---

[123] See [1974] 1 QB 1, 6.

[124] [1997] 2 BCLC 460.

[125] See [1997] 2 BCLC 460, 464–465.

[126] Mance J accepted that the notice was effective, notwithstanding that it was given before the debt accrued, since Mashreqbank had been appointed prior to the assignment to act as collecting bank. He therefore considered that there was an existing debt at the date of notice, in accordance with the principle referred to above. See [1997] 2 BCLC 460, 465–467. *Quaere* whether that was correct. It is not clear from the report why the authority to collect was not simply revocable, as opposed to constituting an existing contract on the repudiation of which an action could be brought for anticipatory breach.

[127] See para 17.12 above.

given the assignment will be effective in equity, so that the assignment attaches to the debt as soon as it is acquired.[128] The determinative date for a set-off is the date of notice of the assignment, as opposed to the date of the assignment itself, and a set-off would be denied to the debtor if the contract out of which the assigned debt arose was entered into after notice.[129] But what constitutes notice in the case of an expectancy? In the context of a priorities dispute between successive assignees under *Dearle v Hall*,[130] notice of assignment of a future debt is regarded as ineffective while the debt remains an expectancy.[131] In *Roxburghe v Cox*[132] Baggallay LJ considered that the principle applies also to set-off so that, until the assigned debt has become a present debt,[132a] the assignee could not give notice which would prevent rights of set-off accruing to the debtor in relation to cross-debts which may become owing by the assignor. Similarly its application to set-off was assumed by Mance J in *Marathon Electrical Manufacturing Corp v Mashreqbank PSC*,[133] although the debt in that case was held not to be a future debt since it arose out of a prior engagement. Those views are also consistent with descriptions of notice given before an assigned debt has become an existing debt as 'perfectly useless and idle' and 'void altogether'.[134] But notwithstanding those views, it is suggested that the principle which applies to *Dearle v Hall* should not extend to set-off. The fact that, as between successive assignees of an expectancy, notice to the debtor is ineffective while the assigned debt is still an expectancy is not to the point. As far as the debtor is concerned, his conscience should be affected as from the time that he becomes aware of the assignment.[135] There is support for that approach in Canada in the context of a debt factoring agreement. The Ontario Court of Appeal accepted that the agreement in question operated as a present assignment of future accounts receivable, and held that notice of it

---

[128] *Tailby v Official Receiver* (1888) 13 App Cas 523; *Norman v Federal Commissioner of Taxation* (1963) 109 CLR 9, 20–22. Note that, if an assignee of future debts becomes bankrupt and the trustee in bankruptcy proceeds to earn the future debts by carrying on the bankrupt assignor's business, the assignee's title to the receipts is inoperative as against the title of the trustee in bankruptcy. See eg *Wilmot v Alton* [1897] 1 QB 17 and *Re Collins* [1925] Ch 556, and paras 13.46–13.47 above.

[129] This has been established in the context of receiverships (see paras 17.73–17.87 below). See *Felt and Textiles of New Zealand Ltd v R Hubrich Ltd* [1968] NZLR 716; *Rendell v Doors and Doors Ltd* [1975] 2 NZLR 191; *Leichhardt Emporium Pty Ltd v AGC (Household Finance) Ltd* [1979] 1 NSWLR 701; *Cheviot Australia Pty Ltd v Bob Jane Corp Pty Ltd* (1988) 52 SASR 204.

[130] (1828) 3 Russ 1, 38 ER 475.

[131] *Somerset v Cox* (1865) 33 Beav 634, 55 ER 514; *Re Dallas* [1904] 2 Ch 385; Oditah, *Legal Aspects of Receivables Financing* (1991) 133–5.

[132] (1881) 17 Ch D 520, 527.

[132a] See para 17.19 above.

[133] [1997] 2 BCLC 460, 465–467.

[134] *Re Dallas* [1904] 2 Ch 385, 395, *per* Buckley J.

[135] See para 17.03 above, and Meagher, Gummow and Lehane, *Equity Doctrines and Remedies* (3rd edn, 1992) 720–1.

precluded the subsequent accrual of rights of set-off in relation to future debts.[136] In truth, notice for the purpose of establishing priorities serves a different function to notice for the purpose of set-off. In the case of priority under *Dearle v Hall,* notice is given to the debtor because it is regarded as the method by which the assignee gets in possession of the debt,[137] with the first to obtain possession in that sense having priority. But while a debt is still an expectancy, there is nothing in respect of which possession can be taken, and therefore notice at that time is ineffective.[138] In the case of set-off, on the other hand, notice defines the point beyond which the debtor's conscience is affected, which can occur whether the debt is present or future. It has nothing to do with obtaining possession of the debt.

This assumes that there is a present (although an inchoate)[139] assignment of a future debt. If on the other hand an agreement contemplates a further agreement in order to effect the assignment of a future debt, as is often the case when book debts are factored, the first agreement itself would not constitute an assignment, in which case notice of it would not be notice of a present assignment which would prevent the accrual of rights of set-off as against future debts. It would be necessary to have regard instead to each subsequent agreement which effects a present assignment of a debt, and then to determine set-off rights in relation to each such debt by reference to the position as at the date of notice of the assignment of that debt.[140] **17.21**

(6) Equitable Set-off

The preceding discussion concerned the exercise of a right of set-off against an **17.22** assignee based upon the Statutes of Set-off. For that form of set-off both demands must be liquidated. On the other hand, an unliquidated demand possessed by the debtor against the assignor[141] may be set off against the assigned debt if the case is

---

[136] *L F Dommerich & Co v Canadian Admiral Corp Ltd* (1962) 34 DLR (2d) 530 (esp at 537). The decision to refuse a set-off in the *Dommerich* case was reversed on appeal by the Supreme Court of Canada, not because of a principle that notice of an assignment of a future debt is ineffective to prevent set-offs accruing to the debtor, but rather because the agreement in question itself did not operate as a present assignment of future book debts. Rather, it contemplated a further agreement before a particular book debt was assigned, and it was by reference to notice of each such subsequent assignment of a debt that rights of set-off in relation to that debt were to be determined. See *Canadian Admiral Corp Ltd v L F Dommerich & Co Inc* (1964) 43 DLR (2d) 1.

[137] See *Dearle v Hall* (1823) 3 Russ 1, 12, 14, 22–24, 38 ER 475, 479, 480, 483–484, and on appeal (1827) 3 Russ 48, 58–59, 38 ER 492, 494–495, *per* Lord Lyndhurst.

[138] See the discussion in Oditah, *Legal Aspects of Receivables Financing* (1991) 28, 134.

[139] Goode, *Legal Problems of Credit and Security* (2nd edn, 1988) 34.

[140] *Canadian Admiral Corp Ltd v L F Dommerich & Co Inc* (1964) 43 DLR (2d) 1 (SC of Canada); *New Zealand Factors Ltd v Farmers Trading Co Ltd* [1992] 3 NZLR 703, 711. One may query Master Kennedy-Grant's view in *New Zealand Factors* (at 710–711) that the circumstances were such as to give rise to an equitable set-off.

[141] See also *Horrobin v Australia and New Zealand Banking Group Ltd* (1996) 40 NSWLR 89, 93 in relation to the situation in which the cross-demand is directly against the assignee, in that case for fraud inducing the contract subsequently assigned to the assignee.

one in which the demands are sufficiently closely connected to give rise to an equitable set-off as between the debtor and the assignor.[142] In contrast to set-off under the Statutes, it is not necessary in this situation that the cross-claim sought to be set off should have arisen before notice of the assignment. The assignee may take subject to an equitable set-off where the cross-claim arose after notice, if the claims are otherwise sufficiently closely connected.[143] Using the traditional formulation of equitable set-off, the title to sue is impeached, and in that circumstance it should not matter when the cross-claim accrued. Mutuality is not in all cases necessary for this form of equitable set-off,[144] and if the cross-demands are sufficiently closely connected to give rise to an impeachment of title, the title of an assignee to sue should be equally affected.[145]

---

[142] See ch 4 above. In addition to the cases cited below, see *Popular Homes Ltd v Circuit Developments Ltd* [1979] 2 NZLR 642. It is not sufficient in this regard that the claims arose out of the same contract. See *Government of Newfoundland v Newfoundland Railway Co* (1888) 13 App Cas 199, 212, PC; *G and T Earle, Ltd v Hemsworth RDC* (1928) 44 TLR 605, 609. Compare *Phoenix Assurance Co Ltd v Earl's Court Ltd* (1913) 30 TLR 50, 51. See also *Packer & Co Pty Ltd v Aksha Pty Ltd* (1995) 12 BCL 143 (SA) in relation to a subcontractor's lien under the Worker's Liens Act 1893 (South Australia).

[143] *Coba Industries Ltd v Millie's Holdings (Canada) Ltd* [1985] 6 WWR 14 (repudiation by assignor after notice); *Telford v Holt* (1987) 41 DLR (4th) 385; *Roadshow Entertainment Pty Ltd v (ACN 053 006 269) Pty Ltd* (1997) 42 NSWLR 462 (receivership). See also Bovill CJ in *Watson v Mid Wales Railway Co* (1867) LR 2 CP 593, 598 (referring to *Smith v Parkes* (1852) 16 Beav 115, 51 ER 720); *Business Computers Ltd v Anglo-African Leasing Ltd* [1977] 1 WLR 578, 585 (see below); *Re Wirragana Nominees Pty Ltd* (1991) 9 ACLC 1168, 1179–1180. In relation to a court-appointed receiver, see *Parsons v Sovereign Bank of Canada* [1913] AC 160, and para 17.89 below. In *Government of Newfoundland v Newfoundland Railway Co* (1888) 13 App Cas 199 (discussed below) the assignment occurred a number of years before the breach, although the report does not state when notice of the assignment was given. Given however that the assignee was a trustee for bondholders of the company, and the company was empowered to issue bonds by an Act of the Newfoundland legislature embodying the contract between the Government and the company, it may be assumed that the Government was aware of the assignment. See also the reference to *Government of Newfoundland* in *John Dee Group Ltd v WMH (21) Ltd* [1997] BCC 518, 530 in relation to set-off against charges incurred after notice of the receivership. Reference also may be made to *Bank of Boston Connecticut v European Grain and Shipping Ltd* [1989] 1 AC 1056. The bank in that case gave notice of assignment on 14 July 1982, whereas the repudiation occurred after then, on 19 July, and the Court of Appeal accepted that an equitable set-off was available against the bank. The decision was reversed by the House of Lords, but on the separate ground that an equitable set-off is not available against a claim for freight. See para 5.04 above. In New Zealand, compare *Popular Homes Ltd v Circuit Developments Ltd* [1979] 2 NZLR 642, 660 and *Hoverd Industries Ltd v Supercool Refrigeration and Air Conditioning (1991) Ltd* [1995] 3 NZLR 577, 586 (in relation to the relevance of the charge being fixed or floating), where the contrary seems to have been assumed. Compare also in Canada *Re Jason Construction Ltd* (1972) 29 DLR (3d) 623, 627–628.

[144] See paras 4.48–4.54 above.

[145] Compare the comments of Viscount Haldane in *Parsons v Sovereign Bank of Canada* [1913] AC 160, 167–168, although that was in the context of a court-appointed receiver who ordinarily contracts personally, as opposed to a receiver appointed by debenture holders who contracts as agent of the company (see para 17.89 below). The question in the *Parsons* case was whether the debt sued for was under the same contract with the company which had been repudiated, and in respect of which the cross-claim for damages arose.

It has been suggested that the transaction out of which the cross-claims arose **17.23** should have been entered into before the debtor had notice of the assignment.[146] However there should not be any such limitation. Consider for example that a receiver appointed to a company under a crystallized floating charge enters into a contract on behalf of the company, which the company proceeds to breach, and the resulting damages claim against the company is such that it would give rise to an equitable set-off against a debt due to the company under the contract. The debtor in that circumstance should not be denied a set-off on the ground that he was aware of the receivership, and of the consequent equitable assignment of the company's assets (including the debt under the contract) to the secured creditor.[147] If the claims are such that the title to sue would be impeached, it should not matter that the contract was entered into after the receivership.

In an often-quoted passage in *Business Computers Ltd v Anglo-African Leasing* **17.24** *Ltd*,[148] Templeman J summarized the position in relation to set-off in the context of assignments in the following terms:

> The result of the relevant authorities is that a debt which accrues due before notice of an assignment is received, whether or not it is payable before that date, or a debt which arises out of the same contract as that which gives rise to the assigned debt, or is closely connected with that contract, may be set off against the assignee. But a debt which is neither accrued nor connected may not be set off even though it arises from a contract made before the assignment.

The reference to 'a debt which arises out of the same contract as that which gives rise to the assigned debt, or is closely connected with that debt', contemplates equitable set-off.[149] The statement suggests, correctly, that the cross-claim need not have accrued due before notice.[150] On the other hand, it is not necessary that the cross-claim be for a debt, and indeed in the majority of cases of equitable set-off a damages claim is in issue.[151] Moreover, notwithstanding the suggestion to the

---

[146] Wood, *English and International Set-off* (1989) 768, 793, 1056. Wood uses transaction set-off as a compendious term encompassing both equitable set-off and common law abatement. See *op cit*, 9–10.

[147] It is commonly, though often inaccurately, said that crystallization of a floating charge brings about an equitable assignment of a debt owing to the company and coming within the ambit of the charge. See para 17.74 below.

[148] [1977] 1 WLR 578, 585. See also eg *Glencore Grain Ltd v Agros Trading Co* [1999] 2 Lloyd's Rep 410, 420–421.

[149] See the references in *Business Computers Ltd v Anglo-African Leasing Ltd* (at [1977] 1 WLR 578, 583–584) to *Government of Newfoundland v Newfoundland Railway Co* (1888) 13 App Cas 199 (as explained in *Bank of Boston Connecticut v European Grain and Shipping Ltd* [1989] 1 AC 1056, 1102–1103, 1110–1111) and *Hanak v Green* [1958] 2 QB 9, which concerned equitable set-off.

[150] See above.

[151] In *Business Computers v Anglo-African Leasing* itself, the debtor's cross-claim was based upon a repudiation of a contract, which sounds in damages, although in that case there was an 'agreed damages' clause.

contrary in that passage, the courts have emphasized that it is not sufficient for an equitable set-off that the demands arose out of the same contract.[152] The question is whether there is a sufficiently close connection, which is to be determined by reference to principles canvassed earlier.[153]

17.25 In *Young v Kitchin*,[154] a sufficiently close connection provided the basis for a set-off against an assignee of a sum of money owing under a building contract when the debtor had a damages claim against the assignor for failure to complete and deliver the building by the specified date. Similarly, in *Government of Newfoundland v Newfoundland Railway Co*[155] the Privy Council held that an assignee of a sum payable to a construction company under a railway construction contract took subject to a claim for damages against the company for not completing the line, while in *Lawrence v Hayes*[156] the purchaser of a business was allowed to set off against an assignee's claim for the sums due to the vendor under the contract the amount of a judgment obtained against the vendor for damages for breach of warranty. The breach arose from the fact that chattels included in the sale either were not the property of the vendor or were the subject of a charge which had not been paid off. In Canada, a damages claim available to a mortgagor against the mortgagee for breach of an obligation to renew the insurance on the mortgaged premises was set off against the mortgage debt, notwithstanding that the debt had been assigned.[157]

17.26 Those cases should be contrasted with *Stoddart v Union Trust Ltd*.[158] In the *Stoddart* case, the defendant in an action brought by an assignee for payment of a debt due under a contract was not allowed to bring into account a claim for damages against the assignor for fraud inducing the contract. The court reasoned that the damages claim was not a claim arising under the contract, or for breach of the contract,[159] but rather it was said to be a claim 'dehors' the contract.[160] That analysis is not convincing,[161] and indeed there is an apparent conflict between the

---

[152] See para 4.55 above.

[153] See ch 4 above.

[154] (1878) 3 Ex D 127. See also *Mitchell v Purnell Motors Pty Ltd* [1961] NSWR 165.

[155] (1888) 13 App Cas 199.

[156] [1927] 2 KB 111.

[157] *Campbell v Canadian Co-operative Investment Co* (1906) 16 Man LR 464.

[158] [1912] 1 KB 181. See also *Cummings v Johnson* (1913) 4 WWR 543; *Provident Finance Corp Pty Ltd v Hammond* [1978] VR 312; *Birchal v Birch, Crisp & Co* [1913] 2 Ch 375, 379.

[159] See Buckley LJ [1912] 1 KB 181, 192. On the other hand, a debtor sued by an assignee may set up the defence that the contract under which the debt arose ought to be set aside and cancelled for fraud.

[160] See Kennedy LJ at [1912] 1 KB 181, 194.

[161] In *Banco Santander SA v Bayfern Ltd* [2000] 1 All ER (Comm) 776 Waller LJ (at 780) noted that *Stoddart v Union Trust* has been the subject of criticism. In any event, the Court of Appeal in *Banco Santander* said that *Stoddart* does not apply where the fraud itself, as opposed to a cross-claim for damages for fraud inducing the contract, gives rise to a defence to an action for payment.

decision in the *Stoddart* case, on the one hand, and on the other the principle applied in the context of insolvency set-off, that a claim for damages for misrepresentation inducing a contract is not a mere personal tort, but rather it constitutes a breach of the obligation arising under the contract so that, even apart from the reform set out in the Insolvency Act 1986 by which tortious demands became provable, it could be employed in a set-off in the event of a bankruptcy.[162] Both Vaughan Williams and Buckley LJJ in the *Stoddart* case[163] emphasized that the plaintiff was an assignee for value without notice of the fraud. However that should not have affected the question whether there was an equitable set-off available as against the assignor, and if there was it should have been available against the assignee. The point was also made in the judgments that the debtor in such a case may be entitled to set aside the contract,[164] but if the contract has not been set aside the remedy of set-off should still be available.[165] *Stoddart v Union Trust Ltd* should be compared to the decision of Mann CJ in the Victorian Supreme Court in *Sun Candies Pty Ltd v Polites*.[166] The fraudulent misstatement inducing the purchaser to buy the business in that case constituted a breach of a warranty which determined the amount of the purchase price. Since the cross-claim arose out of the contract, the Chief Justice held (following *Government of Newfoundland v Newfoundland Railway Co*) that it gave rise to an equitable set-off to which the assignee from the vendor took subject.[167]

Consider that a debtor has an unliquidated cross-claim against the creditor which **17.27** is not sufficiently closely connected to give rise to an equitable set-off. If the

---

[162] See para 8.45 above. The leading authority is *Jack v Kipping* (1882) 9 QBD 113. In Australia it has been questioned whether the claim for fraudulent misrepresentation inducing the contract in *Jack v Kipping* instead should be treated as illustrating the availability of equitable set-off. See *Re NIAA Corp Ltd (in liq)* (NSW SC, McLelland CJ in Eq, 2 December 1994), referred to in *Aliferis v Kyriacou* (2000) 1 VR 447, 463 para 48, *per* Charles JA. If that view were correct, the conflict between *Jack v Kipping* and *Stoddart v Union Trust* would be heightened. In *Jack v Kipping* itself however the set-off was treated as arising under the bankruptcy section (see eg the reference to *Peat v Jones & Co* (1881) 8 QBD 147), and it has been regarded in later cases as an authority on insolvency set-off. See eg *Re Mid-Kent Fruit Factory* [1896] 1 Ch 567, 571–572; *Tilley v Bowman Ltd* [1910] 1 KB 745, 751; *Gye v McIntyre* (1991) 171 CLR 609, 630–631.

[163] [1912] 1 KB 181, 188, 192.

[164] [1912] 1 KB 181, 189, 192, 194–195. See also *Provident Finance Corp Pty Ltd v Hammond* [1978] VR 312, 318.

[165] See *Tilley v Bowman Ltd* [1910] 1 KB 745, 751 in relation to insolvency set-off.

[166] [1939] VLR 132.

[167] Compare *Provident Finance Corp v Hammond* [1978] VR 312, in which the damages claim for breach of warranty related to a different contract to that assigned. The action for the price was brought by an assignee of a bill of sale given by the purchaser of a business for the outstanding amount, rather than on the contract of sale itself. Lush J considered (at 321) that one of the objects of the contract of sale in providing for the execution of a bill of sale was to give the debt aspects of the contract a separate existence in a separate contract, and that the rights embodied in the bill of sale were not intended to be 'intertwined' with the various other rights and obligations of the contract of sale. While that may have been true in the particular circumstances of that case, it nevertheless should be borne in mind that it is not a prerequisite to an equitable set-off that the demands should have arisen under the same contract. See paras 4.55 and 4.69 above.

cross-claim has been converted into a judgment before the debtor has notice of an assignment of the debt by the creditor, the judgment would constitute a debt which should be able to be set off against the assignee under the Statutes of Set-off, since the case would then be one of mutual debts in existence before notice.[168]

(7) Insolvency

Insolvent assignor

17.28   An assignee takes subject to a right of set-off that would have been available as a defence to an action brought by the assignor against the debtor, either pursuant to the Statutes of Set-off in the case of mutual debts or because of a defence of equitable set-off when the demands are inseparably connected. If the assignor has become bankrupt the assignee does not take subject to the wider right of set-off that would otherwise have been available under the insolvency set-off section.[169] The debt, having been assigned, will not have passed to the assignor's trustee in bankruptcy as property of the bankrupt, in which case, unless the assignment is set aside as a preference or on a similar ground, it may be enforced outside of the operation of the insolvency legislation.[170]

17.29   As Wood has noted,[171] the bankruptcy of an assignor may give rise to a problem for the debtor.[172] The insolvency set-off section would not apply. Further, a set-off against the assignee, whether by way of equitable set-off or under the Statutes of Set-off, depends upon the continued existence of a claim against the assignor. But if the assignee delays in suing the debtor, so that in the interim the assignor is discharged from bankruptcy, the assignor would be released from liability.[173] The debtor would no longer have a cross-claim, and the House of Lords held in *Aries Tanker Corp v Total Transport Ltd*[174] that a claim that has ceased to exist cannot be employed in a set-off. In the case of an equitable set-off, Wood has suggested that the debtor could avoid that result by exercising a 'self-help remedy', in the sense that he could act unilaterally to bring about a set-off.[175] That view is doubtful, however. Equitable set-off admittedly is a substantive

---

[168] See para 2.72 above.
[169] *Re Asphaltic Wood Pavement Co. Lee & Chapman's Case* (1885) 30 Ch D 216, 225. See also *De Mattos v Saunders* (1872) LR 7 CP 570; *Re City Life Assurance Co Ltd, Stephenson's Case* [1926] 1 Ch 191, 214 (as explained in *Hiley v The Peoples Prudential Assurance Co, Ltd* (1938) 60 CLR 468, 501–505); *Popular Homes Ltd v Circuit Developmnents Ltd* [1979] 2 NZLR 642. See also *Boyd v Mangles* (1847) 16 M & W 337, 153 ER 1218; *Hunt v Jessel* (1854) 18 Beav 100, 52 ER 40 (assignment to a trustee under a deed of arrangement).
[170] See para 11.06 above.
[171] Wood, *English and International Set-off* (1989) 894–5.
[172] See also para 4.34 above.
[173] Insolvency Act 1986, s. 281.
[174] [1977] 1 WLR 185. See para 4.31 above.
[175] Wood, *English and International Set-off* (1989) 895.

defence,[176] but the judgment of Lord Wilberforce in the *Aries Tanker* case is authority against the view that the equitable defence enables a debtor to extinguish the debts in that manner.[177] One possibility would be to permit a debtor faced with the prospect of losing the benefit of the equitable defence to apply before the assignor's discharge for a declaration and a permanent injunction to restrain a future action by the assignee against him, although this is unsupported by authority.

Insolvent debtor

Consider that the debtor is bankrupt or is a company in liquidation.   **17.30**

A set-off would not be available in that circumstance under the insolvency set-off **17.31** section, given that the assigned debt is held by the assignee and the insolvent debtor's claim is against the assignor. There would be a lack of mutuality.[178] The only possible rights of set-off are equitable set-off and set-off pursuant to the Statutes of Set-off. If the demands are sufficiently closely connected to give rise to an equitable set-off, the better view is that the fact of the bankruptcy or the liquidation does not affect the debtor's right, although there is authority which suggests that equitable set-off is not available in bankruptcy or company liquidation in circumstances which are outside the operation of the insolvency set-off section.[179] The position is more complicated when one considers the defence of set-off conferred by the Statutes of Set-off in the case of mutual debts. The Statutes provide a procedural defence to an action at law.[180] Therefore, when it is said that an assignee takes subject to an equity constituted by this form of set-off, it is meant that the assignee, when suing the debtor, takes subject to the procedural defence that would have been available to the debtor in an action at law brought against him by the assignor. If however the debtor is bankrupt or is in liquidation, the assignee could not sue the debtor without the leave of the court,[181] and so the issue ordinarily would not arise in the context of an action against the debtor. Rather, the debtor's trustee or liquidator would assert a set-off when a proof is lodged by the assignee, so as to reduce the proof by the amount of the debt owing by the assignor to the debtor.[182] If the trustee or the liquidator rejects the proof lodged by the assignee because of the assignor's debt, the assignee could apply to the court to

---

[176] See paras 4.29–4.43 above.
[177] See para 4.32 above.
[178] See para 11.04 above.
[179] See paras 6.16–6.20 above.
[180] See para 2.33 above.
[181] See the Insolvency Act 1986, s 130(2) in relation to a court-ordered winding up, and for bankruptcy s 285(3).
[182] The trustee in bankruptcy or liquidator would only wish to assert a set-off if recovery from the assignor is unlikely, for example because of the assignor's own insolvency. Normally it would be to the advantage of the debtor's estate to pay a dividend to the assignee on the assigned debt and proceed against the assignor for payment in full of what the assignor owes. Compare *Re Parker* (1997) 80 FCR 1.

reverse the decision,[183] but the question would still not arise in the context of pleading set-off as a defence to an action. On a strict analysis, therefore, the Statutes would not justify a set-off. There is nevertheless authority to the effect that a trustee or a liquidator may reduce an assignee's claim in the debtor's bankruptcy or liquidation to the extent of a debt owing by the assignor before notice.[184] Moreover, a similar approach was adopted in another situation. Prior to the enactment of the Supreme Court of Judicature Act 1875, the insolvency set-off section in the bankruptcy legislation did not apply to company liquidation. Set-offs had been enforced in liquidations,[185] but these were founded upon the right of set-off conferred by the Statutes of Set-off in the case of mutual debts as a defence to an action at law,[186] rather than upon the bankruptcy set-off section. In that context, Lord Romilly MR in *Re South Blackpool Hotel Co, ex p James*[187] allowed a set-off against a proof lodged by a creditor, as opposed to the set-off operating as a defence to an action. He said that:[188] 'These cases are not to be decided on technicalities, but on principles of common sense.'

Insolvent assignee

17.32   The bankruptcy or liquidation of the assignee will not affect the principle that an assignee takes subject to equities. If, however, the debtor's cross-demand against the assignor is not such as to provide a set-off under the Statutes or in accordance with the principles of equitable set-off, the debtor could not rely on the insolvency set-off section in the assignee's bankruptcy or liquidation. The debtor's liability to the assignee, and the claim against the assignor, would not be mutual. But if the assignee happens to be separately liable to the debtor, the insolvency set-off section may apply in relation to that liability and the assigned debt.[189]

(8) Agreement not to Assert Set-offs

17.33   If a term in the contract between a debtor and a creditor provides for payment without set-off,[190] the term is equally applicable when payment is sought by an

---

[183] For company liquidation see the Insolvency Rules 1986, r 4.83, and for bankruptcy the Insolvency Act 1986, s 303.

[184] *Re Richard Smith & Co, Ltd* [1901] 1 IR 73; *Re China Steamship Co, ex p MacKenzie* (1869) LR 7 Eq 240; *Re Pinto Leite and Nephews* [1929] 1 Ch 221. See also *Christie v Taunton, Delmard, Lane and Co* [1893] 2 Ch 175 (members' voluntary winding up).

[185] See eg *Re Agra and Masterman's Bank, Anderson's Case* (1866) LR 3 Eq 337; *Smith, Fleming & Co's Case* (1866) LR 1 Ch App 538; *Re South Blackpool Hotel Co, ex p James* (1869) LR 8 Eq 225; *Re Progress Assurance Co; ex p Bates* (1870) 22 LT 430; *Sankey Brook Coal Co Ltd v Marsh* (1871) LR 6 Ex 185.

[186] *Brighton Arcade Co Ltd v Dowling* (1868) LR 3 CP 175, 182, 184; *Ex parte Price, re Lankester* (1875) LR 10 Ch App 648, 650.

[187] (1869) LR 8 Eq 225.

[188] (1869) LR 8 Eq 225, 226.

[189] See para 11.07 above.

[190] See paras 5.78–5.118 above.

assignee.[191] Alternatively, a debtor may have contracted with the creditor on terms that, in the event of an assignment, he will not avail himself against an assignee of any equities which he may possess against the creditor or any intermediate assignee.[192] This agreement will bind the debtor[193] as against an assignee who is a bona fide purchaser for value.[194] An agreement to that effect may also arise by implication. In one case, a company issued debentures to a person who also became a shareholder. The articles of the company provided that the company was to have a lien on the debentures held by a member who was indebted to it, and that the company could sell the debentures in order to obtain payment of the debt. The shareholder assigned the debentures, and was also liable for unpaid calls, which the company asserted as a set-of against the assignee. Since however it was contemplated by the parties that the debentures could be sold and assigned, including possibly by the company through the lien, and since it would have been difficult to sell debentures if a transferee would have had to take subject to an uncertain set-off available to the company against the member, it was held that the company and the member must have intended that a transferee of debentures should take free from set-offs available to the company against the member.[195] A similar implication has been held to arise when a company issues bearer debentures,[196] and in one case where a bank issued an open letter of credit pursuant to which the bank held out to persons negotiating bills drawn by its customer upon the bank that it would honour the bills.[197] In the latter case the bank had gone into liquidation. The liquidator argued that the letter constituted a contract with no one but the customer, and that it did not preclude the bank from setting off the customer's debt to it against the claim of

---

[191] *John Dee Group Ltd v WMH (21) Ltd* [1998] BCC 972 (receivership).

[192] See also *Society of Lloyd's v Leighs* [1997] 6 Re LR 289, in which the clause excluded set-off in respect of a cross-claim available directly against the assignee enforcing the assigned debt, although in that case the assignee itself was a party to the contract containing the exclusion.

[193] *Re Agra and Masterman's Bank, ex p Asiatic Banking Corp* (1867) LR 2 Ch App 391, 397; *Re Blakely Ordnance Co, ex p New Zealand Banking Corp* (1867) LR 3 Ch App 154, 159–160; *Phoenix Assurance Co Ltd v Earl's Court Ltd* (1913) 30 TLR 50; *Southern British National Trust Ltd v Pither* (1937) 57 CLR 89, 113; *Hilger Analytical Ltd v Rank Precision Industries Ltd* [1984] BCLC 301. See also *Re Goy & Co Ltd. Farmer v Goy & Co Ltd* [1900] 2 Ch 149 with respect to the rule in *Cherry v Boultbee* (1839) 4 My & Cr 442, 41 ER 171 (see para 14.65 above), and compare *Re Rhodesia Goldfields Ltd* [1910] 1 Ch 239 in which the debentures did not contain a stipulation to the effect that they should be paid without regard to equities.

[194] *Re Goy & Co. Ltd* [1900] 2 Ch 149, 153. See also *Re Blakely Ordnance Co* (1867) LR 3 Ch App 154, 159; *Re Brown & Gregory Ltd, Shepheard v Brown & Gregory Ltd* [1904] 1 Ch 627, affirmed [1904] 2 Ch 448.

[195] *Higgs v The Northern Assam Tea Co Ltd* (1869) LR 4 Ex 387. See also *Re Northern Assam Tea Co, ex p Universal Life Assurance Co* (1870) LR 10 Eq 458.

[196] *Re Blakely Ordnance Co* (1867) LR 3 Ch App 154.

[197] *Re Agra and Masterman's Bank, ex p Asiatic Banking Corp* (1867) LR 2 Ch App 391, explained in *Rainford v James Keith and Blackman Co Ltd* [1905] 1 Ch 296, 303. Compare *Graham v Johnson* (1869) LR 8 Eq 36.

an indorsee of the bills. The argument to that effect was rejected by the Court of Appeal, Turner LJ commenting:[198]

> The whole effect of the letter is, that the Agra Bank held out to the persons negotiating the bills a promise that it would pay the bills; and it would be impossible, according to my view of the doctrines of Courts of equity, to allow the bank, after having sent that letter into the world, addressed to the persons who were to negotiate the bills, and so held out to them that it would be answerable for their payment, to say that because there was a debt due to it from the persons to whom it had given the letter of credit, therefore it would not pay the bills.

On the other hand, a transferee who is not a bona fide purchaser for value cannot rely on the agreement. In *Re Brown and Gregory, Ltd*[199] a trustee under a creditors' deed executed by the assignor was held not to be a purchaser, so that he took subject to equities available against the assignor notwithstanding that the debentures in question contained a clause protecting transferees from equities. Similarly, neither a trustee in bankruptcy nor a judgment creditor is considered to be a purchaser.[200]

17.34 The principle is stated in the cases in terms whether the assignee or transferee is a bona fide purchaser for value. If those requirements are satisfied, notice of a prior right of set-off available to the debtor against the assignor should not affect the assignee's position.[201] The debtor has held out that it will not enforce equities against assignees, in which case notice of any such equities should not be relevant.

17.35 Debentures issued by a company may provide that, upon registration of a transfer, the transferee will take free from equities. The effect of this provision is that the company reserves the right to assert equities against a transferee prior to registration. However, the fact that the company has a right of set-off available to it against the transferor under the Statutes of Set-off should not entitle the company to refuse to register a transfer. For reasons given earlier,[202] this should be so notwithstanding the decision of Street J in New South Wales in *Stewart v Latec Investments Ltd*,[203] which stands as authority to the contrary when equity acts by analogy with the Statutes.

(9) Conduct of the Debtor

17.36 The debtor may be precluded by his conduct from setting up equities against the assignee.[204] This does not mean that the debtor is bound to volunteer information

---

[198] (1867) LR 2 Ch App 391, 395.

[199] [1904] 1 Ch 627, affirmed [1904] 2 Ch 448.

[200] *Kilworth v Mountcashell* (1864) 15 Ir Ch Rep 565, 581; *Re Marquis of Anglesey* [1903] 2 Ch 727, 732,

[201] Compare *Hilger Analytical Ltd v Rank Precision Industries Ltd* [1984] BCLC 301, 304, in which the principle was discussed in terms of notice.

[202] See para 3.07 above.

[203] [1968] 1 NSWR 432.

[204] *Athenaeum Life Assurance Society v Pooley* (1858) 3 De G & J 294, 299, 302, 44 ER 1281, 1283, 1284.

to an assignee as regards any prior equities,[205] including the existence of a set-off agreement between the debtor and the assignor.[206] An assignee is expected to look after his own interests and to make inquiries as to prior equities which may affect his position.[207] If on the other hand the notice given to the debtor indicated that the assignee may have been deceived, and that the assignee was advancing money to the assignor upon a ground which he misunderstood, or if the debtor was otherwise aware of a deception but stood by and allowed the assignment to proceed, it may be inequitable to allow him to rely on the right of set-off otherwise available at law under the Statutes if he failed to inform the assignee of the true facts.[208] It is not sufficient to render it inequitable for the debtor to rely on the set-off that the debtor knew of the assignment, if there was nothing to indicate that the assignor was deceiving the assignee.[209] If however the debtor was aware of a deception and he did not inform the assignee, it may be unconscionable for him to assert a set-off. This would also be the case if the assignee inquired of the debtor but the debtor concealed the truth.[210]

In the case of a transfer of debentures, the company may lose the right to set up **17.37** prior equities if the company registers the transferee as the holder, and subsequently treats him as such.[211]

(10) A Set-off Agreement as an Equity

There is surprisingly little authority on the effect on an assignee of a set-off agree- **17.38** ment entered into between the assignor and the debtor before the debtor had notice of the assignment.[212]

---

[205] *Canadian Admiral Corp Ltd v L F Dommerich & Co Inc* (1964) 43 DLR (2d) 1, 2, 8–9; *Higgs v The Northern Assam Tea Co Ltd* (1869) LR 4 Ex 387, 396.

[206] *Mangles v Dixon* (1852) 3 HLC 702, 732–733, 10 ER 278, 291; *Rolt v White* (1862) 3 De G J & S 360, 46 ER 674; *Toronto-Dominion Bank v Block Bros Contractors Ltd* (1980) 118 DLR (3d) 311. See paras 17.38–17.46 below in relation to set-off agreements.

[207] See para 17.18 above.

[208] *Mangles v Dixon* (1852) 3 HLC 702, 733, 10 ER 278, 291; *Canadian Admiral Corp Ltd v L F Dommerich & Co Inc* (1964) 43 DLR (2d) 1, 2–3. See also *Rolt v White* (1862) 3 De G J & S 360, 365, 46 ER 674, 676; *Wilson v Gabriel* (1863) 4 B& S 243, 247, 122 ER 450, 452; *Bank of Nova Scotia v Hellenic Mutual War Risks Association (Bermuda) Ltd (The Good Luck)* [1989] 2 Lloyd's Rep 238, 265.

[209] *Mangles v Dixon* (1852) 3 HLC 702, 734–735, 741, 10 ER 278, 291–292, 294. See also *Canadian Admiral Corp Ltd v L F Dommerich & Co Inc* (1964) 43 DLR (2d) 1, 2, 8.

[210] See *Woodhams v Anglo-Australian and Universal Family Assurance Co* (1861) 3 Giff 238, 66 ER 397; *Athenaeum Life Assurance Society v Pooley* (1858) 3 De G & J 294, 299, 44 ER 1281, 1283.

[211] *Re Northern Assam Tea Co, ex p Universal Life Assurance Co* (1870) LR 10 Eq 458, following *Higgs v The Northern Assam Tea Co Ltd* (1869) LR 4 Ex 387.

[212] For the situation in which the set-off agreement is entered into after the debtor has notice of the assignment, see para 17.46 below.

Set-off, as a matter of course

17.39 Consider first the situation in which the agreement contemplates that a set-off will occur, not at the discretion of the one of the parties, but as a matter of course so as to constitute an agreed method of payment. This should be effective as against an assignee.[213] In *Watson v Mid Wales Railway Co*[214] an assignor of a debt was also a lessee of property from the debtor. The Court of Common Pleas held that the debtor could not set off rent which accrued after the debtor received notice of the assignment, notwithstanding that it arose out of a prior contract.[215] On the other hand, the tenor of the judgments of Willes and Montague Smith JJ suggests that the result would have been different if it had been agreed that the rent was to be set off against the debt, so that only the balance was to be owing.[216] This is consistent with the earlier decision of the House of Lords in *Mangles v Dixon*.[217] The owners of a vessel chartered it to merchants for a voyage, and later assigned the freight payable. Notice of the assignment was given to the charterers before the voyage was completed. There was a second contract between the owners and the charterers, of which the assignee was not aware, the effect of which was that the profit or loss resulting from the voyage was to be shared between them. The second contract was entered into at the same time as the first contract, and before the charterer had notice of the assignment. The voyage resulted in a loss, half of which accordingly was payable by the owners. When the assignees sought payment of the freight which was due upon termination of the voyage, the charterers sought to deduct the owners' share of the loss. Lord St. Leonards held that the question was not one of set-off, strictly so called, because there were not cross-demands. Rather, he said that the effect of the agreement between the owners and the charterers was that freight never became due upon termination of the voyage to the extent that the owners were responsible for a part of the loss.[218] This was an equity to which the assignees took subject, notwithstanding that they were unaware of the second agreement. They should have inquired of the charterers before the assignment.[219]

---

[213] In addition to the cases referred to below, see *Re Moss Bay Hematite Iron and Steel Co* (1892) 8 TLR 63, 475; *Bank of Montreal v Tudhope, Anderson & Co* (1911) 2 Man R 380. See also *Lambarde v Older* (1853) 17 Beav 542, 547, 51 ER 1144, 1146 in relation to a set-off against a deceased's estate. See paras 13.121–13.127 above.

[214] (1867) LR 2 CP 593.

[215] See para 17.12 above.

[216] See (1867) LR 2 CP 593, 600, *per* Willes J, 601, *per* Montague Smith J.

[217] (1852) 3 HLC 702, 10 ER 278.

[218] (1852) 3 HLC 702, 729, 10 ER 278, 289–290.

[219] (1852) 3 HLC 702, 732–733, 10 ER 278, 291. See also *Toronto-Dominion Bank v Block Bros Contractors Ltd* (1980) 118 DLR (3d) 311.

Option to effect a set-off

A set-off agreement may take a different form, in that it gives one of the parties a **17.40** right, or an option, to set off various cross-debts. This may apply not only bilaterally, as between a debtor and creditor, but also in a multi-party situation, for example where a bank has an agreement with a group of companies entitling the bank to set off deposits of any of the companies against debts owing by that company or any other company in the group. The principle that an assignee takes subject to equities is sometimes referred to in terms suggesting that 'equities' means defences,[220] whereas in this form of set-off agreement a defence as such is not in issue. The right of a party to the agreement is positive in nature, to effect a set-off, and the question is whether an assignee of a debt who gives notice of the assignment will be bound by the debtor's positive right to effect a set-off after that date pursuant to the prior agreement. It has been said the word 'equities' should be given a wide meaning.[221] In *Mangles v Dixon*[222] Lord St Leonards equated the principle that an assignee takes subject to equities with the notion that the assignees in that case 'took precisely the same interest, and were subject to the same liabilities' as the assignor.[223] He also said that, 'if a man does take an assignment of a chose in action he must take his chance as to the exact position in which the party giving it stands'.[224] In *Cockell v Taylor*[225] Sir John Romilly MR expressed the principle in terms that, 'the purchaser of a chose in action takes the thing bought subject to all the prior claims upon it'. The principle has been expressed in similar terms on other occasions.[226] Those statements on their face would extend to a positive right to apply the assigned debt in reduction of another debt, whether owing by the assignor or another party, which is the preferred view.[227]

---

[220] For example, in *Roxburghe v Cox* (1881) 17 Ch D 520, 526 James LJ said that an assignee 'takes subject to all rights of set-off and other defences which were available against the assignor'. Joyce J in *Edward Nelson & Co Ltd v Faber & Co* [1903] 2 KB 367, 375 remarked that, 'an assignee [of a chose in action] takes it subject to all equities—in other words, whatever defence by way of set-off or otherwise the debtor would be entitled to set up against the assignor's claim . . .'. *White and Tudor's Leading Cases in Equity* (9th edn, 1928) vol 1, 136 states the principle in terms that an assignee 'takes subject to all defences existing in respect of the right assigned which would be available against the assignor seeking to enforce the right assigned.' See also *Clyne v Deputy Commissioner of Taxation* (1981) 150 CLR 1, 20–21.

[221] *Re H Simpson & Co Pty Ltd* [1964–5] NSWR 603, 605, *per* Jacobs J.

[222] (1852) 3 HLC 702, 10 ER 278.

[223] (1852) 3 HLC 702, 731, 10 ER 278, 290.

[224] (1852) 3 HLC 702, 735, 10 ER 278, 292.

[225] (1852) 15 Beav 103, 118, 51 ER 475, 481.

[226] See eg *Athenaeum Life Assurance Society v Pooley* (1858) 3 De G & J 294, 299, 44 ER 1281, 1283; *Re H Simpson & Co Pty Ltd* [1964–5] NSWR 603, 605; *Clyne v Deputy Commissioner of Taxation* (1981) 150 CLR 1, 20.

[227] See the concession by counsel in *First National Bank of Chicago v West of England Shipowners Mutual Protection and Indemnity Association (The Evelpidis Era)* [1981] 1 Lloyd's Rep 54, 57 with respect to the deduction allowed by the club rules, and also the cheque swapping arrangement in issue in *Commercial Factors Ltd v Maxwell Printing Ltd* [1994] 1 NZLR 724. In Canada, see *Toronto-Dominion Bank v Block Bros Contractors Ltd* (1980) 118 DLR (3d) 311.

Transaction entered into before notice

17.41   An assignee should take subject to a set-off agreement in so far as it applies to a debt which has accrued and is owing to the debtor as a result of a transaction entered into before notice of the assignment, whether the debt itself arose before or after notice.[228] A set-off agreement may also be expressed to extend to contingent debts. This should be effective against an assignee when the cross-debt sought to be set off by the debtor has its source in a transaction entered into before notice, but is still contingent at the date of the assignee's action.[229] Professor Goode's analysis of the operation of a set-off agreement in relation to contingent debts is instructive.[230] Depending on the circumstances, he has suggested that the agreement may be interpreted in either of two ways. The more likely construction is that the creditor is entitled to suspend payment of the debt that he owes until such time as the assignor's contingent liability may vest, followed, if it does vest, by a set-off. Alternatively, there may be cases where the effect of the agreement is that the debtor's liability is immediately cancelled to the extent of the assignor's maximum contingent liability, with an obligation to recredit the assignor if and to the extent that the contingent liability does not become an actual liability. In either case, the agreement should be binding on the assignee given his duty of inquiry.[231]

Transaction entered into after notice

17.42   The more difficult question, about which academic writers have expressed differing opinions,[232] is whether a prior set-off agreement will be effective as against an assignee where the transaction out of which the cross-debt sought to be set off arose was entered into after notice. There are two competing views on this. The first, which is consistent with the tenor of Lord St Leonards' judgment in *Mangles v Dixon*,[233] is that an assignee takes the same interest and is subject to the same liabilities as the assignor at the date of notice, and the effect of the prior agreement is that the assigned debt is liable to be used in a set-off against cross-debts both present and future, including where they arise out of new transactions. Moreover, when a chose in action is assigned the courts have emphasized that it is up to the assignee to

---

[228] This assumes that an assigned debt would come within the terms of the set-off agreement. Compare the submission in *Marathon Electrical Manufacturing Corp v Mashreqbank PSC* [1997] 2 BCLC 460, 469, 471. In *Watson v Mid Wales Railway Company* (1867) LR 2 CP 593, 601 Montague Smith J seems to have been of the opinion that a set-off against subsequently accruing rent would have been permitted if there had been an agreement for a set-off.

[229] Compare Oditah, 'Financing Trade Credit: Welsh Development Agency v Exfinco' [1992] JBL 541, 559.

[230] Goode, *Legal Problems of Credit and Security* (2nd edn, 1988) 173.

[231] See para 17.18 above.

[232] Compare Wood, *English and International Set-off* (1989) 862 para 16-36, with Oditah, (1990) 106 LQR 515, 518–19.

[233] (1852) 3 HLC 702, 731, 735, 10 ER 278, 292.

make inquiries as to prior equities so as to protect his position,[234] and the inquiry should extend to the terms of any set-off agreement in place which may affect the debt. The contrary view is that, when the debtor receives notice, he should regulate his conduct accordingly[235] and, to paraphrase the language of James LJ in *Roxburghe v Cox*,[236] he should not rely on debts arising out of new transactions to diminish the rights of the assignee as they stood at the time of notice. In the second edition of this book[237] it was suggested that the second approach was more likely to appeal to the court. After further reflection my opinion on the matter has changed, and it is suggested that the first view should be preferred.[238]

This is consistent with the approach adopted in *George Barker (Transport) Ltd v*   **17.43**
Eynon[239] in the context of a contractual lien. A carrier entered into a contract with a company to carry the company's goods, the contract being on terms that the carrier was to have a general lien on the goods for any money whatsoever due from the company to the carrier. In addition, the company had granted a floating charge over its assets to a debenture-holder. The charge crystallized as a result of the appointment of a receiver after the contract with the carrier but before the carrier obtained possession of some of the goods. Crystallization of a floating charge brings about, or at least it has an effect similar to, an equitable assignment of a debt owing to the company which comes within the ambit of the charge.[240] The Court of Appeal held that the debenture-holder's charge took subject to the carrier's general lien. The Court rejected the receiver's argument that the case involved a priorities dispute between a lien and a crystallized floating charge, and that, since the lien was a possessory lien which did not come into existence until the carrier was in possession of the goods, the lien did not arise until after the charge had crystallized, and therefore it was subject to the charge. The carrier's rights did not simply come into existence at the time it took possession of the goods. The rights were created by the contract, albeit that they were not exercisable until a future event, and it was the prior contractual rights to which the debenture-holder took subject.[241]

---

[234] See para 17.18 above.

[235] *Lloyd v Banks* (1868) LR 3 Ch App 488, 490–491.

[236] (1881) 17 Ch D 520, 526. In *Brice v Bannister* (1878) 3 QBD 569, 578 Cotton LJ expressed it in terms that, after notice of an assignment, the debtor cannot defeat or prejudice the assignee's right. See also *Long Leys Co Pty Ltd v Silkdale Pty Ltd* (1991) 5 BPR 11,512, 11,519 (NSW CA).

[237] *Set-off* (2nd edn, 1996) 588.

[238] This is subject to the assumption referred to in n 228 above. Note also *Commercial Factors Ltd v Maxwell Printing Ltd* [1994] 1 NZLR 724, in which a cheque swapping arrangement was held to be effective against an assignee of book debts. However the question whether the cross-debts the subject of the arrangement in relation to each assigned invoice arose before or after notice of the assignment of that invoice was not considered.

[239] [1974] 1 WLR 462. See also *Re Diesels and Components Pty Ltd* [1985] 2 Qd R 456; *Mercantile Credits Ltd v Jarden Morgan Australia Ltd* [1991] 1 Qd R 407.

[240] See para 17.74 below.

[241] See in particular the discussion by Stamp LJ at [1974] 1 WLR 462, 472–473, and also *Re Diesels and Components Pty Ltd* [1985] 2 Qd R 456, 461. Nor did it matter whether the carrier received notice of the appointment of the receiver before or after obtaining possession of the goods.

17.44   *George Barker (Transport) Ltd v Eynon* differed from the situation under discussion in a number of respects. In the first place, the contract was for the creation of a security interest in the form of a contractual lien. A set-off agreement on the other hand may not constitute a security interest as such,[242] although it performs a similar function. In addition, the contract which gave rise to the lien was also the contract which authorized the carriage of the goods, and therefore it could be said that the debenture-holder should not take the benefit of the contract without at the same time accepting the liabilities under it.[243] Further, the lien in the *George Barker* case arose as a matter of course from a contract of carriage entered into before crystallization, and while in the circumstances under discussion the set-off agreement is entered into before the assignment, the transaction which gives rise to the cross-debt from the assignor to the debtor is not entered into until after notice of the assignment to the debtor. Nevertheless, the approach of Edmund Davies LJ in the *George Barker* case[244] would appear to be relevant. He considered that the company could not simply shrug off the contract it had entered into for the creation of the lien, and he said that the debenture-holder could assert its position as assignee of the company's property and contractual rights only by itself recognizing and giving effect to the pre-appointment contractual rights of the carrier. Similarly, an assignee of a debt should not be able to assert its position as assignee of the assignor's contractual rights without itself recognizing and giving effect to the pre-assignment contractual right of set-off available to the debtor as against the assignor. The assignor's rights, and therefore the rights of the assignee, are circumscribed by the prior set-off agreement. If on the other hand the debtor is aware that the assignee is being deceived but fails to inform him of the true facts, the circumstances may render it inequitable to permit the debtor to assert the set-off against the assignee.[245]

Security over a debt

17.45   The notion that an assignee takes subject to a prior set-off agreement should also apply where a debt constitutes property the subject of a security.[246] The security holder takes subject to equities, which should include prior contractual rights of set-off. In Australia, an exception has been recognized in the situation in which an administrator is appointed to a company under Part 5.3A of the Corporations Act 2001 (Cth), and the administrator has a lien over property of the company,

---

See Stamp LJ at [1974] 1 WLR 462, 465. See also *Re Diesels and Components Pty Ltd* [1985] 2 Qd R 456, in which the customs agent became aware of the appointment of the receiver before it received the bill of lading relating to the goods.

[242]   See paras 16.78–16.91 above.
[243]   See [1974] 1 WLR 462, 475, *per* Sir Gordon Willmer.
[244]   [1974] 1 WLR 462, 470. See also Sir Gordon Willmer at 475.
[245]   See para 17.36 above.
[246]   See paras 17.73–17.87 below.

consisting of a debt due to the company, out of which he is entitled to be indemnified for debts incurred in the performance or exercise of the functions and powers as administrator. This follows from the decision of the New South Wales Court of Appeal in *Cinema Plus Ltd v Australia and New Zealand Banking Group Ltd*,[247] which was considered earlier.[248]

Subsequent set-off agreement

A set-off agreement entered into by a debtor and an assignor after the debtor has **17.46** notice of the assignment ordinarily would not be effective as against the assignee. On the other hand, the assignee may have agreed with the debtor that, notwithstanding the assignment, the debtor can pay the assignor until such time as the assignee notifies the debtor that payment must be made directly to the assignee. Ordinarily payment to the assignor would be construed as including payment by way of an agreement for a set-off.[249] However the set-off should have been carried into effect before the debtor receives notice from the assignee in accordance with their agreement. If the debtor and the assignor enter into an agreement for a set-off to occur in the future, and the settlement in account has not taken place when the assignee gives notice that payment is to be made directly to him, it would not be a case of a payment already having been made to the assignor, and (subject to the terms of the agreement with the assignee) the assignee therefore should be entitled to demand payment in full.[250] Further, the assignee's agreement that the debtor may pay the assignor ordinarily would not be interpreted as authorizing a set-off involving liabilities owing by parties other than the assignor to the debtor.[251]

(11) Successive Assignments

Consider the case of successive assignments. For example, A may assign a debt to **17.47** B, who in turn assigns it to C. The debtor in that circumstance should be entitled to a set-off in respect of a cross-debt owing to him by C as the ultimate assignee. However, would C take subject to a set-off in respect of a debt owing to the debtor by the intermediate assignee, B? A similar issue arose in *Re Milan Tramways Co, ex p Theys*.[252] The case concerned a number of debts for which proofs had been lodged in the liquidation of the debtor company. Subsequently the creditors assigned the debts to H, who happened to be the subject of an allegation of misfeasance in relation to the company. H then assigned the debts to T, who gave notice of the assignment to the liquidator. After this second assignment an order

---

[247] (2000) 49 NSWLR 513.
[248] See para 16.22 above.
[249] *First National Bank of Chicago v West of England Shipowners Mutual Protection and Indemnity Association (The Evelpidis Era)* [1981] 1 Lloyd's Rep 54, 63.
[250] [1981] 1 Lloyd's Rep 54, 64–65, 66 (and see also counsel's argument summarized at 62–63).
[251] [1981] 1 Lloyd's Rep 54, 65.
[252] (1884) 25 Ch D 587.

was made that H should pay £2,000 to the company on account of his misfeasance. The Court of Appeal held that the liquidator could not set off that sum against the assigned debts under the insolvency set-off section, because at the date of the liquidation the debts were held by the original creditors, and there was no right of set-off at that date available against them.[253] Alternatively, the liquidator argued that he could make a deduction from the dividend payable on the debts to the extent of H's obligation to contribute to the fund consisting of the company's assets available for distribution in the liquidation. Essentially this was based on the principle considered in *Cherry v Boultbee*,[254] although the case was not mentioned in the judgments. The argument to that effect also failed. The order against H for payment of the £2,000 was made after the assignment to the ultimate assignee, T, and before the dividend was declared. Fry LJ considered that the principle could not be invoked unless at the time the dividend was declared the entitlement to the dividend belonged to a person who was indebted to the company.[255] It was not evidently regarded as sufficient that the liability arose out of an obligation incurred by H before the debts were assigned.[256] Cotton LJ reached the same conclusion but expressed his reasoning in different terms. He said that T in seeking payment of the dividend was not enforcing the rights of H, but rather the rights of the original creditors, and there was no equity available against the original creditors to which T could be made to take subject.[257] This was in the context of the *Cherry v Boultbee* principle, but the statement was expressed generally, in terms of 'equities', and it would extend also to set-off. If in *Re Milan Tramways* H had been an equitable assignee, it would have been a powerful argument. It is consistent with the later discussion by Dixon J in the High Court of Australia in *Southern British National Trust Ltd v Pither*,[258] and it also coincides with the view

---

[253] See paras 6.46–6.48 above.

[254] (1839) 4 My & Cr 442, 41 ER 171. See ch 14 above.

[255] (1884) 25 Ch D 587, 594.

[256] Note however the criticism of *Stephens v Venables* (1862) 30 Beav 625, 54 ER 1032 in paras 14.58–14.62 above. It could not be said in *Re Milan Tramways Co, ex p Theys* that H had a monetary liability before the assignment, because the company had the right to elect to take the shares the subject of the misfeasance allegation rather than compensation. See Kay J at first instance (1882) 22 Ch D 122, 125–126. See also the similar case of *Re Bailey Cobalt Mines Ltd* (1919) 44 OLR 1.

[257] (1884) 25 Ch D 587, 593.

[258] (1937) 57 CLR 89, 108–109. Dixon J commented: 'Confusion sometimes arises between the two very different applications of the statement that the assignee of a chose in action takes subject to all equities affecting the assignor. When this statement is made in relation to the rights and liabilities of the debtor or obligor, it means that every assignee takes subject to all defences available as between the original parties to the obligation up till the completion of the first assignment by notice. The debtor's liabilities may be discharged in whole or in part by some transaction with the immediate assignee, as for instance, by payment to him. In that case an assign of an assignee would take subject to that defence also. But it is not every defence open to the debtor against such an intermediate assignee that is available against a subsequent assignee. Set-off is an instance.' See also Latham CJ at 102–103. Dixon J distinguished set-off from an equity which affects the intermediate assignee's title as against the assignor, such as a right in the assignor to set the assignment aside for fraud. A second assignee takes subject to that equity, on the basis of the principle *nemo dat quod non habet*. See also Rich J at 105.

of Parker J in *The Raven*,[259] his Lordship commenting that:[260] 'The rule that an assignee takes subject to equities means, in my judgment, equities as against the assignor and does not include claims against an intermediate assignee.'[261] It is true that in *Cavendish v Geaves*[262] Sir John Romilly said that an ultimate assignee takes subject to rights of set-off available to the debtor against an intermediate assignee, and in *Pellas v Neptune Marine Insurance Co*[263] Bramwell LJ expressed agreement with the principles laid out in *Cavendish v Geaves*. However the views of Cotton LJ, Dixon J and Parker J are to be preferred. The point is that, in the case of an equitable assignment, the assignor has the legal title to the assigned debt. The reason that an equitable assignee takes subject to a set-off available against the assignor under the Statutes of Set-off is that there is mutuality at law, and therefore there is a right of set-off at law, and if the debtor's cross-claim against the assignor arose before the debtor had notice of the assignment there is nothing unconscionable in the debtor asserting this legal right of set-off against the assignee.[264] On the other hand, when there are successive equitable assignments, and the debtor is owed a debt by the intermediate assignee, the position is different. There is no mutuality at law, given that the legal title to the debt being enforced is in the assignor whereas the debtor's claim is against the intermediate assignee, and therefore there is no right of set-off at law. Nor would an equitable set-off be available by analogy with the Statutes,[265] since the cross-demands are not equitably mutual. The beneficial title to the assigned debt is in the ultimate assignee, whereas the debtor's claim is against the intermediate assignee.

In *Re Milan Tramways*, however, it appears that H was not an equitable assignee, **17.48** but rather he had taken a statutory assignment of the debts in accordance with the Judicature Act 1873, section 25(6),[266] so that he had the legal title. In Cotton LJ's opinion this did not make any difference, because 'there is nothing to prevent the ultimate assignee from suing in the name of the original creditors, free from any equities which only attach on the intermediate assignee.'[267] Yet Lord Esher MR later commented in *Read v Brown*[268] in relation to a statutory assignment that:

---

[259] *Banco Central SA v Lingoss and Falce Ltd (The Raven)* [1980] 2 Lloyd's Rep 266.
[260] [1980] 2 Lloyd's Rep 266, 273.
[261] Compare the suggestion in Treitel, *The Law of Contract* (10th edn, 1999) 637 n 65, that this should be understood in the context of a cross-claim available to the debtor against the intermediate assignee which arose before the assignment to the intermediate assignee. Parker J's comments were not qualified in this manner, however, and indeed it is not expressly made clear in his judgment when the cross-claim in that case arose.
[262] (1857) 24 Beav 163, 53 ER 319.
[263] (1879) 5 CPD 34, 39 (*arguendo*).
[264] See para 17.03 above.
[265] See paras 3.06–3.08 above.
[266] See (1884) 25 Ch D 587, 590, 593. See now the Law of Property Act 1925, s 136(1), and para 17.04 above.
[267] (1884) 25 Ch D 587, 593. See also *Southern British National Trust Ltd v Pither* (1937) 57 CLR 89, 109, *per* Dixon J.
[268] (1888) 22 QBD 128, 132.

'The debt is transferred to the assignee and becomes as though it had been his from the beginning; it is no longer to be the debt of the assignor at all, who cannot sue for it, the right to sue being taken from him.'[269] If therefore the assignment to the intermediate assignee complies with the statute and the ultimate assignee is an equitable assignee, the ultimate assignee would sue in respect of the intermediate assignee's legal title, which should have as a consequence that the ultimate assignee takes subject to equities available against the intermediate assignee that arose before the debtor had notice of the second assignment.[270] It has been said that the statutory form of assignment only relates to procedure,[271] although it may be that it has a substantive effect upon the rights of a sub-assignee.

17.49 It may be that the intermediate assignee and the debtor entered into an agreement to set off the assigned debt against a debt owing by the intermediate assignee to the debtor. Provided that the agreement is entered into before the debtor has notice of the second assignment it should bind the ultimate assignee, whether the first assignment was equitable or statutory.[272] The agreement is equivalent to payment, and payment by the debtor to the intermediate assignee before notice of the second assignment would be effective to discharge the debtor as against the ultimate assignee.[273]

17.50 The ultimate assignee would take subject to equities available against the original assignor before notice. If the assignment to the intermediate assignee and the assignment to the ultimate assignee were both merely equitable, the ultimate assignee would be enforcing the legal rights of the original assignor, and therefore the principle of taking subject to equities should apply in relation to the original assignee.[274] If the original assignment complied with the statute, the intermediate assignee would take subject to any equity available against the original assignor,[275] which in turn should constitute an equity available against the intermediate assignee to which the ultimate assignee takes subject, whether the ultimate assignment was statutory or equitable.

---

[269] See also *Bennett v White* [1910] 2 KB 643; *Re Pain; Gustavson v Haviland* [1919] 1 Ch 38, 45.

[270] *Re Richard Smith & Co Ltd* [1901] 1 IR 73 may support this view, given that the transfer of the debentures by Murphy and Smith (the original assignors) to Fitt (the intermediate assignee) was by deed, and the conditions attached to the debentures required that the transfer in writing be delivered to the company in order to be registered. For a valid legal assignment, express notice in writing of the assignment must be given to the debtor. However, there are no formal requirements for a valid notice (see *Van Lynn Developments Ltd v Pelias Construction Co Ltd* [1969] 1 QB 607, 613), and the delivery of a transfer ordinarily should suffice. On that basis the requirements for the statutory form of assignment may have been satisfied, this having been introduced into Ireland by the Supreme Court of Judicature Act (Ireland) 1877, s 28(6).

[271] *Tolhurst v Associated Portland Cement Manufacturers (1900), Ltd* [1902] 2 KB 660, 676–677.

[272] See para 17.39 above.

[273] *Southern British National Trust Ltd v Pither* (1937) 57 CLR 89, 108–109.

[274] See above.

[275] See para 17.04 above.

(12) Marshalling

Consider that a creditor is owed two debts by the one debtor.[276] One of the debts **17.51** (debt 1) is assigned to an assignee, and the other (debt 2) is retained by the creditor/assignor. In addition, the debtor is owed a cross-debt by the assignor. The debtor would appear to have a choice. He could employ the cross-debt either as a defence under the Statutes of Set-off to an action by the assignor for payment of debt 2, or as a defence to an action by the assignee to enforce debt 1 on the basis of the principle that an assignee takes subject to equities. A similar analysis would apply if debt 2, instead of being retained by the assignor, was the subject of an assignment to a second assignee. The debtor prima facie could assert the set-off against either of the assignees. The result suggested in the cases is that, if the assignor has retained debt 2, any set-off in relation to the cross-debt should occur first as against debt 2 so as not to diminish the rights of the assignee in relation to debt 1,[277] while, if debt 2 similarly has been assigned to a second assignee, the set-off should operate rateably as against both debt 1 and debt 2.[278] This has been justified on the basis of the equitable doctrine of marshalling. It is argued elsewhere,[279] however, that marshalling is inappropriate to a situation in which a defence of set-off in relation to debts is in issue, as opposed to a positive right to have recourse to more than one fund. This is not to suggest that the assignee of debt 1 is without a remedy if the debtor asserts the cross-debt as a defence to the assignee's action. The assignee should be entitled to be indemnified by the assignor or, if debt 2 has also been assigned, he should be entitled to claim contribution from the second assignee. Alternatively, subrogation may provide relief, in the sense that the assignee may be entitled to be subrogated to the assignor's rights against the debtor on debt 2 or, if debt 2 has also been assigned, to a rateable proportion of the benefit of debt 2 as against the second assignee.

Different rights

There is in any event a limitation on the application of the doctrine of marshalling which is relevant to the question of set-off, and that is that marshalling cannot apply when different rights are in issue. In *Webb v Smith*[280] the defendants **17.52**

---

[276] For marshalling to apply there must be at least two separate debts. See *Re Bank of Credit and Commerce International SA (No 8)* [1996] Ch 245, 271–272, CA, [1998] AC 214, 230–231, HL.

[277] *Cavendish v Geaves* (1857) 24 Beav 163, 53 ER 319; *Smit Tek International Zeesleepen Berginsbedrijf BV v Selco Salvage Ltd* [1988] 2 Lloyd's Rep 398.

[278] *Cavendish v Geaves* (1857) 24 Beav 163, 53 ER 319; *Moxon v Berkeley Mutual Benefit Building Society* (1890) 62 LT 250.

[279] Derham, 'Set-off Against an Assignee: The Relevance of Marshalling, Contribution and Subrogation' (1991) 107 LQR 126.

[280] (1885) 30 Ch D 192. Compare *Moxon v Berkeley Mutual Benefit Building Society* (1890) 62 LT 250, criticized in Derham, 'Set-off Against an Assignee: The Relevance of Marshalling, Contribution and Subrogation' (1991) 107 LQR 126, 138–140.

were auctioneers who had sold a brewery for a customer. The proceeds of sale of the brewery remained in the auctioneers' hands subject to a particular lien for their charges incurred in connection with the sale. However the customer had charged the proceeds of sale in favour of the plaintiff. In addition, the auctioneers had in their hands the proceeds of sale of some furniture which they had sold for the customer. The auctioneers had two courses of action open to them. They could have deducted their charges from the brewery proceeds pursuant to their lien, and delivered the furniture proceeds to the customer and the balance of the brewery proceeds to the plaintiff in accordance with the charge. Alternatively, they could have delivered all of the brewery proceeds to the plaintiff, and asserted a right to set off the customer's indebtedness for the charges against their own indebtedness for the furniture proceeds.[281] The auctioneers adopted the first approach, to the disadvantage of the plaintiff. The plaintiff sued the auctioneers, arguing that because of the doctrine of marshalling the auctioneers should have acted in accordance with the second possible approach so as not to disappoint the plaintiff. The Court of Appeal held that marshalling was not applicable. Brett MR noted that the auctioneers had a lien upon the brewery proceeds and a right of set-off against the furniture proceeds, and said that marshalling is not applicable when different rights exist in respect of different funds. Similarly Lindley LJ said that the auctioneers had a 'superior right of lien as to the fund produced by the sale of the brewery,'[282] and they could not be deprived of this superior right.

(13) Assignment Merely of the Proceeds of a Debt

17.53 When a debt is assigned the assignee obtains an equitable interest in the debt, and once the debtor has notice of this equitable interest it is unconscionable for him to rely on subsequent events to diminish the rights of the assignee.[283] But what if the assignment is confined to the proceeds of the debt when received? It has been said that it is not possible to separate a debt from its proceeds,[284] but that was in the context of a charge on a debt. While a charge on or an assignment of a debt ordinarily would extend also to the proceeds, the converse does not apply. There may be an assignment of the proceeds of a debt when they are received, but not

---

[281] There is authority for the view that an auctioneer is entitled to a set-off against proceeds of sale in his hands, and this would seem to apply notwithstanding that the proceeds may be impressed with a trust. See *Palmer v Day & Sons* [1895] 2 QB 618, and para 10.17 above.

[282] (1885) 30 Ch D 192, 202.

[283] See para 17.03 above.

[284] *Royal Trust Bank v National Westminster Bank plc* [1996] 2 BCLC 682, 704, *per* Millett LJ.

of the debt itself.[285] Nothing would pass, even in equity, until the subject of the assignment, being the proceeds, comes into existence.[286]

Where an assignment is confined to the proceeds of a debt when received, the as- **17.54** signee does not have an interest in the debt. If the debtor has a defence to an action for payment, there would not be any proceeds received, and therefore there would not be anything to which the assignment could attach. Moreover, because the assignee's interest does not extend to the debt, the better view is that there is nothing unconscionable in the debtor relying on a set-off or other defence to an action on the debt that accrues after notice of the assignment, notwithstanding the consequential effect that this would have on the assignee's position. A person who takes an assignment merely of the proceeds of a debt, and not of the debt itself, should take subject to all defences of set-off available against the assignor whether arising before or after notice.

(14) Assignment of Part of a Debt

A part of a debt may be assigned in equity.[287] In that circumstance, if the debtor **17.55** has a cross-claim against the assignor which, apart from the assignment, is eligible for a set-off against the debt, the cross-claim should be available as a set-off against the unassigned part of the debt.[288] Furthermore, if the cross-claim is also otherwise eligible for a set-off against the assignee, the set-off should occur first against the part of the debt in which the assignor alone is beneficially interested, and after that as against the unassigned part. The assignor, as the party liable on the cross-claim, should be the first to bear the burden of a set-off which arises in relation to it.

(15) Instruments Transferable at Common Law

The principle that an assignee takes subject to equities is relevant when there is **17.56** a chose in action which, before the Judicature Acts, was assignable only in equity.[289] It does not apply when a transferee is suing upon an instrument which

---

[285] See eg *Glegg v Bromley* [1912] 3 KB 474. An assignment of proceeds may nevertheless be interpreted in a particular case as an assignment of the right to receive them. See eg *Marathon Electrical Manufacturing Corp v Mashreqbank PSC* [1997] 2 BCLC 460, 464–465 in relation to a letter of credit. Moreover, an assignor of proceeds may be under an equitable obligation to the assignee in respect of the chose in action itself, in that the assignor is bound to exercise his rights in respect of the chose in action in such a way as will not defeat or impair the assignment. See *Southern British National Trust Ltd v Pither* (1937) 57 CLR 89, 107–108.

[286] *Glegg v Bromley* [1912] 3 KB 474, 490.

[287] *Durham Brothers v Robertson* [1898] 1 QB 765, 769; *Brice v Bannister* (1878) 3 QBD 569; *Re Steel Wing Co Ltd* [1921] 1 Ch 349, 355.

[288] *Hiley v Peoples Prudential Assurance Co. Ltd* (1938) 60 CLR 468, 497–498, *per* Dixon J, referring to *Re Asphaltic Wood Pavement Co. Lee & Chapman's Case* (1885) 30 Ch D 216, 222.

[289] *Ord v White* (1840) 3 Beav 357, 365–366, 49 ER 140, 143–144; *Southern British National Trust Ltd v Pither* (1937) 57 CLR 89, 109. See also *Ashwin v Burton* (1862) 7 LT 589.

is transferable at common law in its own right.[290] While an assignee of a debt may now sue in his own name if the requirements of section 136(1) of the Law of Property Act 1925 are satisfied,[291] the section is merely procedural in its operation, in the sense that it only applies where, prior to the Judicature Acts, the assignee would have had to proceed in the name of the assignor in a common law action for payment.[292] Where however an instrument is transferable at common law in its own right, the transferee before the Judicature Acts could have sued in his own name, and in respect of his own legal title. He need not have relied on the legal title of the assignor. A mere personal equity such as a right of set-off under the Statutes of Set-off that could have been asserted against the transferor in an action brought by the transferor could not be asserted against the transferee suing in his own name, irrespective of when the transferor's indebtedness may have arisen. The reason for the distinction is plain enough. When an equitable assignee sues for payment of the debt but in respect of the assignor's legal title, there is mutuality at law in relation to that debt and a cross-debt owing by the assignor to the debtor, and the question is whether it is unconscionable for the debtor to rely on the consequent right of set-off available at law.[293] Where however the transferee of an instrument can sue at common law in his own name and in respect of his own legal title, there is not mutuality at law in relation to the transferred debt and a debt owing by the transferor, and accordingly the question does not arise as to whether it is unconscionable for the debtor to rely on a defence that would have been available if regard were had only to legal titles. Nor is there mutuality in equity to support an equitable set-off. There is no basis then for a set-off, either at common law or in equity.

Negotiable instruments

17.57   The principle is illustrated by the case of a holder in due course of a negotiable instrument, but the holder of a negotiable instrument takes free of the personal defence of set-off under the Statutes even if he is not a holder in due course. This appears from the overdue bill cases, such as *Oulds v Harrison*.[294] An indorsee of an overdue bill is not a holder in due course.[295] Nevertheless, it was confirmed in

---

[290]   *Taylor v Blakelock* (1886) 32 Ch D 560, 567. *See also Rolt v White* (1862) 31 Beav 520, 523, 54 ER 1240, 1242. Compare the discussion in *Byles on Bills of Exchange and Cheques* (27th edn, 2002) 231.

[291]   See para 17.04 above.

[292]   *Torkington v Magee* [1902] 2 KB 427, 435.

[293]   See para 17.03 above.

[294]   (1854) 10 Ex 572, 156 ER 566. See also *Burrough v Moss* (1830) 10 B & C 558, 109 ER 558; *Stein v Yglesias* (1834) 1 Cr M & R 565, 149 ER 1205; *Whitehead v Walker* (1842) 10 M & W 696, 152 ER 652; *Re Overend, Gurney & Co, ex p Swan* (1868) LR 6 Eq 344. Compare *Goodall v Ray* (1835) 4 Dowl 76, the accuracy of the report of which has been doubted. See Parke B in *Oulds v Harrison* at 576, 568.

[295]   Bills of Exchange Act 1882, s 29(1).

Oulds v Harrison that, while the indorsee of the bill takes subject to all equities that had attached to the bill[296] in the hands of the holder when it was due (this includes an agreement with the holder that the bill was to be satisfied by a set-off against a debt owing to the acceptor),[297] he does not take subject to claims arising out of collateral matters such as a right of set-off available to the acceptor against a prior holder pursuant to the Statutes.[298] Furthermore, it made no difference that the indorsee in that case was aware of the set-off available against the indorser,[299] that the indorsement was made solely in order to defeat the set-off, and that the indorsement had been made without consideration. If on the other hand an indorsee did not give value, it may be the case that he is a trustee for the indorser, and if he is simply a trustee he would take subject to any right of set-off available against the indorser.[300] The indorsee would also be subject to a set-off if he is merely an agent for collection.[301]

The view that a holder who is not a holder in due course takes free of a right of set-off available under the Statutes of Set-off as against a prior holder is not universally accepted by text-writers.[302] However it is consistent not only with a first-principles **17.58**

---

[296] This expression is synonymous with the term 'defect of title' in the Bills of Exchange Act 1882, s 36(2). See *Chalmers and Guest on Bills of Exchange, Cheques and Promissory Notes* (15th edn, 1998) 317 para 981. For a non-exhaustive list of some defects of title, see the Bills of Exchange Act 1882, s 29(2).

[297] *Oulds v Harrison* (1854) 10 Ex 572, 579, 156 ER 566, 569; *Ching v Jeffrey* (1885) 12 OAR 432 (promissory note). See also *Holmes v Kidd* (1858) 3 H & N 891, 157 ER 729, and *Merchants Bank of Canada v Thompson* (1911) 23 OLR 502, 514–515. Compare *Re Overend, Gurney & Co, ex p Swan* (1868) LR 6 Eq 344, in which the agreement was with the drawer (that the funds remitted to the acceptor were to be used to satisfy the bills), as opposed to the holders when the bills were dishonoured.

[298] While the contrary view has been expressed (see eg Wood, *English and International Set-off* (1989) 700–1), the better view is that the issuer of a negotiable instrument being sued for payment can rely on a defence of set-off under the Statutes if the person suing on the instrument is indebted to him. See paras 5.35–5.40 above.

[299] Parke B in *Oulds v Harrison*, referring (at (1854) 10 Ex 572, 579, 156 ER 566, 569) to *Whitehead v Walker* (1842) 10 M & W 696, 152 ER 652.

[300] *Agra and Masterman's Bank Ltd v Leighton* (1866) LR 2 Ex 56, 65; *Churchill and Sim v Goddard* [1937] 1 KB 92, 103–104; *Barclays Bank Ltd v Aschaffenburger Zellstoffwerke AG* [1967] 1 Lloyd's Rep 387. See also *Watkins v Bensusan* (1842) 9 M & W 422, 152 ER 179; *Mayhew v Blofield* (1847) 1 Ex 469, 154 ER 199; *Tolhurst v Notley* (1848) 11 QB 406, 116 ER 529.

[301] *Re Anglo-Greek Steam Navigation and Trading Co, Carralli & Haggard's Claim* (1869) LR 4 Ch App 174.

[302] See Wood, *English and International Set-off* (1989) 901, and also *Paget's Law of Banking* (11th edn, 1996) 414, where it is suggested that a holder for value who is not a holder in due course takes subject to personal defences available to prior parties among themselves. On the other hand, for the preferred view see Crawford and Falconbridge, *Banking and Bills of Exchange* (8th edn, 1986) vol 2, 1524 *et seq.* and *Chitty on Contracts* (28th edn, 1999) vol 2, 214 para 34-097. See also *Chalmers and Guest on Bills of Exchange, Cheques and Promissory Notes* (15th edn, 1998) 246 para 762 in relation to a holder for value. *Byles on Bills of Exchange and Cheques* (27th edn, 2002) 231 also appears to support this view in relation to set-off of unconnected cross-debts under the Statutes of Set-off.

analysis,[303] but also with the overdue bill cases. The contrary view has been said[304] to be supported by the decision in Manitoba of Major J in *Del Confectionery Ltd v Winnipeg Cabinet Factory Ltd*,[305] but the circumstances were unusual and the case is distinguishable. The plaintiff had entered into a contract with a cabinet maker to install some fixtures in his business premises by a certain date. Attached to the contract was a promissory note which was expressed to be payable at a date after the agreed completion date. The promissory note was security for payment of the unpaid balance of the price, together with interest calculated from the date of delivery. Because the date from which interest was to be calculated depended upon delivery, which was uncertain, the note was undated. After the agreed completion date but before actual completion, the cabinet maker assigned the contract to a finance company. This included the promissory note attached to the contract. Major J held that the finance company's claim on the promissory note was subject to the plaintiff's claim for damages against the cabinet maker for non-completion by the fixed date. However this does not support a general proposition that a subsequent holder of a negotiable instrument takes subject to a set-off between prior parties. In the first place, Major J postulated that the note may not have been a promissory note, given that it encompassed the payment of exchange and collection charges and accordingly it may not have provided for payment of a sum certain in money.[306] But in any event, the peculiar circumstances upon which the cross-claim was based, in particular that the note was attached to the contract, appear to have been regarded as giving rise to a defect in title to which the finance company took subject, as opposed to a mere personal equity.[307]

(16) Privity of Estate

17.59 A similar issue may arise when a purchaser of land is entitled to sue for rent in his own right as a result of privity of estate,[308] or when rent is claimed by a mortgagee in possession. In a number of cases the question has arisen whether the tenant could assert an equitable set-off that would have been available against the obligation to pay rent if the original landlord had been suing, in circumstances where a mortgagee in possession instead is claiming rent.

---

[303] See para 17.56 above.

[304] Wood, *English and International Set-off* (1989) 901.

[305] [1941] 4 DLR 795, [1941] 2 WWR 636.

[306] See the discussion at [1941] 2 WWR 636, 641.

[307] See the discussion at [1941] 2 WWR 636, 641–642. Thus, Major J relied on the earlier decision in *Edie v Turkewich* [1940] 1 WWR 554, in relation to which he said (at 642): 'Here it was held that an uncompleted contract of which certain promissory notes formed a part *affected the title of a subsequent holder*, that such holder had notice of the uncompleted conditions which put him on inquiry and he made none. Under these circumstances he was not a holder in due course.' (emphasis added).

[308] See para 17.66 below. See also para 13.58 above, and the Landlord and Tenant (Covenants) Act 1995.

Mortgage of leased premises

Contrary to views that formerly were expressed, it is now accepted that a personal **17.60** claim for damages available to a tenant against the landlord may be employed by the tenant as an equitable set-off against a liability for rent if there is a sufficiently close connection between the demands.[309] Consider, however, that the landlord has mortgaged the premises, and the mortgagee, having gone into possession of the rents and profits, is the party seeking payment of the rent. *Reeves v Pope*[310] is authority for the proposition that a personal cross-claim available to the tenant against the landlord[311] cannot be set off by the tenant when rent is being claimed by the mortgagee. The principle has since been affirmed in Victoria[312] and in South Australia,[313] but it is not universally accepted by commentators.[314] The decision in *Reeves v Pope* has been said to constitute an attempt to confer a special insulation in favour of mortgagees from the application of the principle applicable in the case of an assignment of a debt, that the assignee takes subject to an equitable set-off available to the debtor against the assignor.[315] However there is nothing special or exceptional about the mortgagee's position, and *Reeves v Pope* was correctly decided.

Reeves v Pope concerned the old form of common law mortgage that took effect as **17.61** a conveyance.[316] The land was conveyed to the mortgagee, subject to an obligation to re-convey upon satisfaction of the debt. Since the mortgagee had the legal title to the land, he had the legal entitlement to the rent. Prior to intervention by the mortgagee, the mortgagor had the 'tacit agreement' of the mortgagee to receive

---

[309] See paras 5.56–5.58 above.

[310] [1914] 2 KB 284.

[311] In *Reeves v Pope*, for breach of contract for failure to complete the construction of a hotel on the leased land by the specified date.

[312] *Citibank Pty Ltd v Simon Fredericks Pty Ltd* [1993] 2 VR 168 (cross-claim for damages for loss of profits arising from breaches of the covenant for quiet enjoyment in an earlier lease); *Piazza Grande Pty Ltd v Portis Pty Ltd* (1993) V ConvR 54-460 (breach of covenant by the lessor to provide a manager for the shopping complex of which the leased premises formed part, and breach of covenant that only one restaurant would be operated in the complex). Compare *Westend Entertainment Centre Pty Ltd v Equity Trustees Ltd* (2000) V ConvR 54–619.

[313] *Ory and Ory v Betamore Pty Ltd* (1993) 60 SASR 393 (overpayment of rent to the landlord/mortgagor not able to be set off by the tenant against rent subsequently claimed by the mortgagee).

[314] See Wood, *English and International Set-off* (1989) 886–7, and also Waite, 'Disrepair and Set-off of Damages Against Rent: The Implications of British Anzani' [1983] The Conveyancer 373, 384–386 in relation to an absolute sale of the reversion (see below). In a note in (1992) 66 Australian Law Journal 313, *Citibank Pty Ltd v Simon Fredericks Pty Ltd* [1993] 2 VR 168 was described as a good illustration of a situation whose solution is clear on the authorities but which might be reconsidered.

[315] Wood, *English and International Set-off* (1989) 886–7. See also Lightman and Moss, *The Law of Receivers and Administrators of Companies* (3rd edn, 2000) 309 para 16–020.

[316] See generally Sykes and Walker, *The Law of Securities* (5th edn, 1993) 39 *et seq.*

rent.[317] The mortgagor received the rent for his own absolute use, and not for the use of the mortgagee.[318] The mortgagee however could put an end to this tacit agreement at any time,[319] in which case, given his legal entitlement, he could sue for future rent as it accrued, and also for any rent in arrears as from the date of his legal title.[320] Indeed, prior to 1873 a mortgagor's remedies at common law to enforce payment of rent before intervention by the mortgagee were limited. A landlord who subsequently mortgaged the reversion could not sue or distrain for rent in his own name or bring proceedings for ejectment.[321] The mortgagor's position was ameliorated with the enactment of section 25(5) of the Supreme Court of Judicature Act 1873, which empowered the mortgagor to sue in his own name for unpaid rent. A similar provision is now set out in the Law of Property Act 1925, section 98, and it has also been adopted in all Australian states.[322] However, this applies only until such time as the mortgagee gives notice of intention to enter into the receipt of the rents and profits. Once the mortgagee gives notice, the mortgagor has no right to sue.

17.62   Real property mortgages in England no longer take effect by way of conveyance. As a result of reforms introduced by the Law of Property Act 1925, sections 85 and 87, a mortgage of freehold now operates either as a demise to the mortgagee for a term of years absolute, subject to a provision for cesser on redemption, or alternatively as a charge by deed expressed to be by way of legal mortgage, in which case a mortgagee of an estate in fee simple is expressed to have the same protection, powers and remedies as if a mortgage term of three thousand years had been created in his favour. Both give the mortgagee a legal estate in possession, and a

---

[317] *Moss v Gallimore* (1779) 1 Dougl 279, 283, 99 ER 182, 184.

[318] *Trent v Hunt* (1853) 9 Ex 14, 22–23, 156 ER 7, 10.

[319] *Moss v Gallimore* (1779) 1 Dougl 279, 283, 99 ER 182, 184.

[320] See eg *Burrows v Gradin* (1843) 12 LJQB 333 (referring to *Moss v Gallimore* (1779) 1 Dougl 279, 99 ER 182). The same principle applies when the lease is entered into after the mortgage. See *Re Ind, Coope & Co Ltd* [1911] 2 Ch 223, 231–232. Compare the position of an equitable mortgagee, discussed in *Finck v Tranter* [1905] 1 KB 427.

[321] *Doe d Marriott v Edwards* (1834) 5 B & Ad 1065, 110 ER 1086; *Trent v Hunt* (1853) 9 Ex 14, 156 ER 7; *Matthews v Usher* [1900] 2 QB 535, 538–539. A different principle applied if the mortgagor leased the premises *after* the mortgage. The lease was void as against the mortgagee, so that the tenant was liable to be ejected by the mortgagee, unless the mortgagee adopted or otherwise authorized the lease. If that occurred, the mortgagee upon giving notice to the tenant was entitled to all arrears of rent as well as rent which accrued due afterwards. See *Pope v Biggs* (1829) 9 B & C 245, 109 ER 91. If the lease was not adopted or authorized by the mortgagee, the tenant as against the mortgagor was estopped from disputing the validity of the lease. Accordingly, the mortgagor could enforce the covenants in the lease against the tenant, and could distrain for unpaid rent in his own name. See *Cuthbertson v Irving* (1859) 4 H & N 742, 157 ER 1034; *Trent v Hunt* at 22–23, 10. In England a mortgagor in possession now has a power to lease, pursuant to the Law of Property Act 1925, s 99. For the position in the various Australian States, see Sykes and Walker, *The Law of Securities* (5th edn, 1993) 102–4. If a lease is granted pursuant to this power, the mortgagee is entitled to the rent on the same basis as for a prior lease. See eg *Re Ind, Coope & Co Ltd* [1911] 2 Ch 223, 231–232 (power in mortgage document to create leases).

[322] See Sykes and Walker, *The Law of Securities* (5th edn, 1993) 99.

consequent legal right to go into possession by receipt of the rents and profits,[323] so that the position with respect to rent should be the same as under the old form of mortgage.[324]

The position of a mortgagee suing for rent is not the same as that of an assignee of a debt. Unless the requirements of section 136 of the Law of Property Act 1925 have been satisfied,[325] an assignment of a debt does not pass the legal title. It is only effective in equity, and therefore the assignee generally can only enforce payment of the assigned debt in an action at law if the assignor as the legal owner of the debt is joined as a party.[326] On the other hand, a mortgagee in possession can sue for rent in his own name and in respect of his own legal title.[327] He is not a mere assignee from the mortgagor of the tenant's indebtedness for rent,[328] but rather has a legal entitlement to it as a result of his legal estate in possession.[329] Therefore, for the same reason that a transferee of an instrument transferable at law does not take subject to rights of set-off that would have been available against the transferor,[330] a set-off otherwise available to a tenant against the landlord/mortgagor under the Statutes of Set-off cannot be asserted against the mortgagee. Nor would a substantive defence of equitable set-off be available in this situation independently of the principle that an assignee takes subject to equities.[331] Using Lord Cottenham's traditional formulation of the principle in *Rawson v Samuel*,[332] a claim by a mortgagee for rent is not impeached by a damages claim available to the tenant against the mortgagor. Since the mortgagee's claim is based on his own title, and not that of the mortgagor, the cross-demands could not be said to be inter-dependent.[333]

17.63

---

[323] See Megarry and Wade, *The Law of Real Property* (6th edn, 2000) 1200 para 19–067, 1223 para 19–112. If at the time of the mortgage the premises are already the subject of a lease, the demise to the mortgagee operates to vest the reversion in the mortgagee, including the right to the rents and profits. See *Harmer v Bean* (1853) 3 Car & K 307, 175 ER 566.

[324] See generally *Fisher and Lightwood's Law of Mortgage* (11th edn, 2002) 527–529 para 19.59.

[325] See para 17.04 above.

[326] See para 17.03 above.

[327] See eg *Burrows v Gradin* (1843) 12 LJQB 333 (referring to *Moss v Gallimore* (1779) 1 Dougl 279, 99 ER 182). See now the Landlord and Tenant (Covenants) Act 1995, s 15(1)(b).

[328] *Reeves v Pope* [1914] 2 KB 284, 287, 289. The point is illustrated by *Re Ind, Coope & Co Ltd* [1911] 2 Ch 223. Leasehold premises were mortgaged to debenture-holders. The mortgagor then assigned the rent to a third party, who gave notice of the assignment to the tenants before the debenture-holders went into possession of the rents and profits. The dispute as to who was entitled to the rent was not determined by reference to the rule in *Dearle v Hall* (1828) 3 Russ 1, 38 ER 475, as one would have expected if the dispute was regarded as being between two assignees of a chose in action. Rather, the case was decided on the basis that it was not within the power of the mortgagor to assign the rents in priority to the debenture-holders.

[329] See *Reeves v Pope* [1914] 2 KB 284, 289–290 in relation to a mortgage by way of conveyance.

[330] See paras 17.56–17.58 above.

[331] This involves, on the one hand, a claim by the mortgagee against the tenant, and on the other a cross-claim by the tenant against the mortgagor, but mutuality is not a strict requirement of equitable set-off. See paras 4.48–4.54 above.

[332] (1841) Cr & Ph 161, 41 ER 451. See para 4.02 above.

[333] See *Grant v NZMC Ltd* [1989] 1 NZLR 8, 13, and para 4.03 above.

Similarly, relief would not be available on the basis of the formulation endorsed by the House of Lords in *Bank of Boston Connecticut v European Grain and Shipping Ltd*,[334] that the cross-claim should flow out of and be inseparably connected with the dealings and transactions which gave rise to the claim. The mortgagee's claim is derived from his legal estate in possession consequent upon the mortgage, whereas the tenant's cross-claim does not flow out of and is not inseparably connected with the mortgage. The circumstances do not support an equitable set-off, and *Reeves v Pope* therefore was correctly decided.

Australia

17.64   A different form of mortgage also now applies in Australia in relation to Torrens title land. The legislation of all Australian states provides that a mortgage under the relevant Act does not operate as a transfer of the land, but rather it takes effect as a security, or a statutory charge,[335] with the consequence that the legal estate remains in the mortgagor.[336] While the general approach is universal, there are nevertheless differences under the Acts as regards the rights and powers of the mortgagee, and as a result *Reeves v Pope* may not be applicable in all states in so far as Torrens mortgages are concerned. Beach J in *Citibank Pty Ltd v Simon Fredericks Pty Ltd*[337] held that it applies in Victoria, and it has also been adopted in South Australia,[338] but its application to Torrens mortgages in Queensland was rejected in *Re Partnership Pacific Securities Ltd*.[339]

17.65   The facts of *Re Partnership Pacific Securities Ltd* were similar to those in *Reeves v Pope*. It concerned a leased property registered under the Queensland Torrens legislation, the legislation current at the time being the Real Property Act 1861 (Qld). That Act has since been replaced by the Land Title Act 1994 (Qld), but the relevant principles remain the same. The lessor decided to redevelop the property, and agreed with the lessee that it would cause the work to be completed in a good workmanlike manner by a particular date. The lessee alleged a breach of this agreement, and claimed damages from the lessor. The applicant had a registered mortgage over the premises and, after default by the lessor/mortgagor, went into possession by claiming all arrears of rent up to the date of possession together with all rental and other monies coming due in respect of the lease. The question was whether the lessee was entitled to set off its damages claim against the lessor. The claim for rent was the subject of two actions, the first before de Jersey J.[340] His

---

[334] [1989] 1 AC 1056. See para 4.15 above.
[335] See eg the Transfer of Land Act 1958 (Vic), s 74(2), and generally Sykes and Walker, *The Law of Securities* (5th edn, 1993) 227 *et seq.*
[336] *Figgins Holdings Pty Ltd v SEAA Enterprises Pty Ltd* (1999) 196 CLR 245, 279, *per* McHugh J.
[337] [1993] 2 VR 168.
[338] *Ory and Ory v Betamore Pty Ltd* (1993) 60 SASR 393.
[339] [1994] 1 Qd R 410.
[340] Unreported, 12 May 1992.

Honour held that, unlike the corresponding Victorian legislation considered in *Citibank v Simon Fredericks*, the Queensland Torrens legislation did not allow a mortgagee to sue for rent. In Victoria, section 81 of the Transfer of Land Act provides that a first mortgagee has the same rights and remedies at law and in equity as he would have had if the legal estate in the mortgaged land had been vested in him as mortgagee, with a right of quiet enjoyment in the mortgagor until default. This has the effect that, following default, the mortgagee has the same entitlement to sue for rent as an old title mortgagee,[341] which would justify the application of the *Reeves v Pope* principle in relation to a Torrens title mortgage in Victoria. The Victorian legislation should be compared to the Real Property Act in Queensland, which did not have an equivalent of section 81, and that remains the case under the Land Title Act 1994 (Qld). Section 60 of the Real Property Act provided that a mortgagee could enter into possession of the mortgaged land by receiving the rents and profits thereof.[342] However, de Jersey J held that this only entitled the mortgagee to receive the rents and profits as they were paid, in the sense that it was not wrongful for him to do so, but without conferring an independent right to sue for them.[343] This accords with views expressed by text-writers.[344] De Jersey J nevertheless found another source of power for a mortgagee to sue for rent, in section 117(2) of the Property Law Act 1974 (Qld), and said that this was sufficient to bring the case within *Reeves v Pope*. When it came to making his order, de Jersey J noted that the claims for declarations set out in the summons only related to the obligation to pay rent as from the date that the mortgagee went into possession. Accordingly, he declined to make declarations as to the mortgagee's entitlement to rent in arrears before that date. This was the subject of the second action, before Williams J.[345] In this action his Honour agreed with de Jersey J that the Real Property Act in Queensland did not confer upon a mortgagee an independent

---

[341] See the discussion in Sykes and Walker, *The Law of Securities* (5th edn, 1993) 260–2, and in Francis and Thomas, *Mortgages and Securities* (3rd edn, 1986) 146–7. In *Figgins Holdings Pty Ltd v SEAA Enterprises Pty Ltd* (1999) 196 CLR 245, 284 McHugh J said in relation to s 81(1) that, 'the mortgagee must . . . have the same rights against any tenant of the mortgaged property as the mortgagor would have if there were no mortgage.'

[342] See now the Land Title Act 1994 (Qld), s 78(2).

[343] In *Citibank v Simon Fredericks*, Beach J justified the decision in that case by reference to s 78 of the Transfer of Land Act, which is in similar terms to s 60 of the Queensland Act, and not s 81, as suggested by de Jersey J. Indeed, s 81 was not referred to in the Beach J's judgment. This suggests a broader operation for s 78 than de Jersey J ascribed to s 60 in Queensland. Subsequently the Full Court of the South Australian Supreme Court in *Ory and Ory v Betamore Pty Ltd* (1993) 60 SASR 393, 406 referred with approval to Beach J's reliance on s 78, although without referring to *Re Partnership Pacific Securities Ltd*. But whatever the position in relation to s 78 following *Re Partnership Pacific Securities*, the decision in *Citibank v Simon Fredericks* in any event would appear to have been justified by s 81. Compare *Westend Entertainment Centre Pty Ltd v Equity Trustees Ltd* (2000) V ConvR 54-619 at p 64,431.

[344] Sykes and Walker, *The Law of Securities* (5th edn, 1993) 258–9; Francis and Thomas, *Mortgages and Securities* (3rd edn, 1986) 147–8.

[345] [1994] 1 Qd R 410.

right to sue for rent,[346] a view with which Moynihan J also later expressed agreement.[347] Williams J disagreed however with de Jersey J's conclusion that the Property Law Act 1974 (Qld), section 117(2) conferred a power to sue. Section 117(2) provides that: 'Any such rent, covenant, obligation, or provision shall be capable of being recovered, received, enforced, and taken advantage of, by the person from time to time entitled . . .' While section 60 of the Real Property Act entitled a mortgagee to receive rents and profits, section 117(2) should be read in the light of section 117(1), which provides that: 'Rent reserved by a lease . . . shall be annexed and incident to and shall go with the reversionary estate in the land.' As Williams J noted,[348] the section is concerned primarily with defining the rights of the owner of the reversionary estate from time to time,[349] and a mortgagee of Torrens title land is not the owner of the reversionary estate in the land. Accordingly, he concluded that the section did not assist the mortgagee.[350]

Sale of leased premises

17.66 Given that the mortgage in issue in *Reeves v Pope* took effect as a conveyance, the views expressed in that case in relation to the availability of a set-off to a tenant against a mortgagee should also be relevant when there is an absolute sale of the reversion.[351] The purchaser should be able to sue for rent[352] unaffected by an equitable set-off that the tenant could have asserted against the vendor as a result of the vendor's own breach of contract. One writer has disagreed with this view.[353] The essence of his argument is that the tenant's right of set-off against the vendor/landlord is not a personal equity, but rather it has a proprietary character. The

---

[346] [1994] 1 Qd R 410, 420.

[347] *Re FAI Leasing Pty Ltd* [1994] 2 Qd R 482, 486. See also *Lensworth Properties Pty Ltd v Entera Pty Ltd* [1994] ANZ ConvR 564 [Ext].

[348] [1994] 1 Qd R 410, 421.

[349] This includes an owner in equity who is entitled to the rent to the exclusion of all others. See *Schalit v Joseph Nadler Ltd* [1933] 2 KB 79, 82–83.

[350] See also *Re FAI Leasing Pty Ltd* [1994] 2 Qd R 482, 487; *Lensworth Properties Pty Ltd v Entera Pty Ltd* [1994] ANZ ConvR 564 [Ext]. While the mortgagee in *Re Partnership Pacific Securities* was entitled pursuant to a separate agreement with the lessee to sue for rent, Williams J held that the mortgagee's right to do so was only as an assignee from the lessor, and that in suing in that capacity the mortgagee took subject to equities available to the lessee against the lessor, including an equitable set-off. See [1994] 1 Qd R 410, 421–424.

[351] See eg Buckley LJ's reported response during argument in *Reeves v Pope* [1914] 2 KB 284, 286 to counsel's statement regarding a purchase.

[352] In relation to new tenancies under the Landlord and Tenant (Covenants) Act 1995, this would not include arrears of rent accrued prior to the assignment. See s 23(1), and also s 30(4), which provides that the Law of Property Act 1925, s 141 does not apply to new tenancies. Compare *Arlesford Trading Co Ltd v Servansingh* [1971] 3 All ER 113.

[353] Waite, 'Disrepair and Set-off of Damages Against Rent: The Implications of British Anzani' [1983] The Conveyancer 373, 384–6. In addition to the argument set out below, Waite advanced an argument (at 385–6) based upon an assignment of the indebtedness for rent, although, as in the case of a mortgagee, a purchaser is not an assignee of the rent but rather has a right to sue for rent because of his own legal title.

proprietary character is said to arise because the set-off impeaches the landlord's entitlement to rent, and therefore it is incidental to the tenancy. Further, the courts have said that a purchaser of land has constructive notice of any interest that a tenant in possession has in land,[354] so that the purchaser will have constructive notice of the tenant's right of set-off. Accordingly, the argument proceeds that the purchaser is not a bona fide purchaser for value without notice. There are a number of difficulties with that analysis. In the first place, it is not clear that the equitable doctrine of constructive notice would apply in the case of a set-off operating as a mere equity.[355] More importantly, it is not easy to accept the notion that the equity in question has a proprietary character. Indeed, in *Reeves v Pope* the Court of Appeal emphasized that the tenant's damages claim in that case did not create an estate or interest in the land.[356] The suggestion that the tenant's equitable set-off has a proprietary character based, *inter alia*, on a on the proposition that the right is capable of transmission to a successor tenant by assignment.[357] The problem with this is that equitable set-off is a defence, albeit a substantive defence. It is not easy to see how a defence available to a tenant against his obligation to pay rent can be 'assigned' to a successor tenant in respect of the latter's own rental obligation. This is not to suggest that the fact that something is not capable of being assigned is a sufficient reason for saying that it is not proprietary in nature.[358] Rather, the position simply is that it is difficult to see how a defence can be regarded as anything other than a personal equity. The kind of equity to which a purchaser of land with notice will take subject is an equity which is ancillary to or dependent upon an equitable estate or interest in land,[359] in the sense that it will involve an adjustment of the rights of the person possessed of the equity to the land in question.[360] Examples include the right of a tenant to have the lease rectified,[361] and the right of a mortgagor to have a sale by the mortgagee set aside on the ground that the mortgagee's exercise of the power of sale was fraudulent.[362] At common law a purchaser of land does not take subject to a personal obligation

---

[354] See eg *Jones v Smith* (1841) 1 Hare 43, 60, 66 ER 943, 950.

[355] See *Smith v Jones* [1954] 1 WLR 1089 (equity of rectification in relation to a lease), although compare *Downie v Lockwood* [1965] VR 257.

[356] [1914] 2 KB 284, 288, 289, 290.

[357] Waite, 'Disrepair and Set-off of Damages Against Rent: The Implications of British Anzani' [1983] The Conveyancer 373, 386.

[358] *R v Toohey, ex p Meneling Station Pty Ltd* (1982) 158 CLR 327, 342–343, *per* Mason J; *Federal Commissioner of Taxation v Orica Ltd* (1998) 194 CLR 500, 537, 542–543. Compare *National Provincial Bank Ltd v Ainsworth* [1965] AC 1175, 1247–1248. See also para 16.88 above.

[359] *National Provincial Bank Ltd v Ainsworth* [1965] AC 1175, 1238, *per* Lord Upjohn.

[360] See Meagher, Gummow and Lehane, *Equity Doctrines and Remedies* (3rd edn, 1992) 121.

[361] See *National Provincial Bank Ltd v Ainsworth* [1965] AC 1175, 1238, *per* Lord Upjohn, and compare *Smith v Jones* [1954] 1 WLR 1089.

[362] Compare *Latec Investments Ltd v Hotel Terrigal Ltd* (1965) 113 CLR 265, in which the purchaser did not have notice of the equity.

of the vendor which does not run with the land, even though it may relate to the use of the land.[363] In the case of a tenant's equitable set-off, while it may be said to relate to his leasehold interest, it does not involve any adjustments to his right to the land itself, and accordingly it is not an equity to which a purchaser of the land with notice may be obliged to take subject.

Breach of covenant by the mortgagee or purchaser

17.67 The preceding discussion concerned the situation in which a tenant seeks to set off a personal liability of the original landlord to the tenant against a claim for rent by a mortgagee in possession or a purchaser of the reversion. *Reeves v Pope* established that a set-off is not available in those circumstances. The position would be different if the mortgagee or the purchaser himself breaches a covenant in the lease which is binding on him personally, and thereby becomes liable to the tenant. Pursuant to the Landlord and Tenant (Covenants) Act 1995, the burden of all 'landlord covenants' (as defined in section 28(1)) passes on an assignment of the reversion, and subject to some exceptions they bind the purchaser as from the assignment.[364] This is expressed to extend to a mortgagee in possession.[365] In an appropriate case a breach of a landlord covenant by a mortgagee or a purchaser should be able to be the subject of a set-off in a claim by the mortgagee or the purchaser for rent.[366]

Tenant's right of recoupment against a mortgagee or purchaser

17.68 If leased premises have fallen into disrepair, and responsibility for the repairs is on the landlord, the tenant may expend money in executing the repairs and recoup himself from future payments of rent.[367] This is sometimes described as a set-off,[368] but set-off is not an accurate description of the tenant's right.[369] Rather, it gives rise to a question of payment. The money spent by the tenant on repairs

---

[363] *National Provincial Bank Ltd v Ainsworth* [1965] AC 1175, 1253–1254, *per* Lord Wilberforce, referring to Buckley LJ in *London CC v Allen* [1914] 3 KB 642, 657.

[364] The Landlord and Tenant (Covenants) Act 1995, s 3. A purchaser of the reversion is not bound by a covenant which is expressed to be personal to the vendor. See s 3(6).

[365] See s 15(2).

[366] In Australia, see *Westend Entertainment Centre Pty Ltd v Equity Trustees Ltd* (2000) V ConvR 54–619. It was argued in that case that the covenant in question, relating to the refurbishment of the leased premises, was not personal to the mortgagor/landlord, but rather it ran with the land, so that the mortgagee in possession could not claim the benefit of the rent under the lease without accepting the burden of the covenant. Mandie J, while commenting that the argument faced substantial legal obstacles, nevertheless said that it raised a serious question to be tried.

[367] See paras 5.63–5.66 above.

[368] See *Waters v Weigall* (1795) 2 Anst 575, 145 ER 971; *Knockholt Pty Ltd v Graff* [1975] Qd R 88, 91, 92.

[369] *Lee-Parker v Izzet* [1971] 1 WLR 1688, 1693; *British Anzani (Felixstowe) Ltd v International Marine Management (UK) Ltd* [1980] 1 QB 137, 148.

is regarded as a payment pro tanto of future rent,[370] or of any arrears of rent.[371] The tenant's right to take this course of action is based upon a policy consideration, that 'he shall be otherwise at great mischief, for the house may fall upon his head before it be repaired; and therefore the law alloweth him to repair it, and recoupe the rent'.[372] If the tenant's expenditure constitutes payment of rent in advance, it should be binding upon a mortgagee or purchaser. This occurred in *Lee-Parker v Izzet*,[373] in which Goff J enforced as against a mortgagee a tenant's right to have expenditure on repairs regarded as a payment of future rent.

The decision in *De Nichols v Saunders*[374] is not inconsistent with this view. In that **17.69** case the Court of Common Pleas held that a payment by a tenant to the landlord, which was expressed to be and was accepted as a payment of rent in advance,[375] was not effective as against a mortgagee who had obtained the mortgage before the payment. The mortgagee on going into possession was allowed to sue for the rent that, according to the terms of the lease, accrued after the tenant had notice of the mortgage,[376] and the tenant could not rely on the advance payment to the mortgagor/landlord as a defence. In this regard, if a landlord mortgages the premises after receiving an advance payment, the payment will be binding on the mortgagee as a discharge of the rent obligation, unless he had enquired of the tenant as to the rent and the tenant answered incorrectly or failed to answer.[377] It is in the situation in which there was a prior mortgage that the principle in *De Nichols v Saunders* applies. Willes J explained the basis of the decision in the following terms:[378]

> The receipt of the rent could not be treated here as a discharge by the landlord, because by assigning the reversion before the rent was received by him he had parted with the power of giving such a discharge. The plaintiff [mortgagee] lent his money on a contract, which was under an implied condition that the landlord should continue entitled to the rent at the time it became due, and able, therefore, then to give the plaintiff a valid discharge.

---

[370] *Taylor v Beal* (1591) Cro Eliz 222, 78 ER 478, *per* Gawdy J; *Lee-Parker v Izzet* [1971] 1 WLR 1688, 1693; *British Anzani (Felixstowe) Ltd v International Marine Management (UK) Ltd* [1980] 1 QB 137, 148; *Connaught Restaurants Ltd v Indoor Leisure Ltd* [1994] 1 WLR 501, 507, 511.

[371] *Asco Developments Ltd v Gordon* (1978) 248 EG 683.

[372] *Taylor v Beal* (1591) Cro Eliz 222, 78 ER 478, *per* Gawdy J.

[373] [1971] 1 WLR 1688.

[374] (1870) LR 5 CP 589. See also *Lord Ashburton v Nocton* [1915] 1 Ch 274.

[375] An overpayment of rent is not properly described as a payment of rent. See *Ory and Ory v Betamore Pty Ltd* (1993) 60 SASR 393, 403–404.

[376] See *Cook v Guerra* (1872) LR 7 CP 132 in relation to rent accruing before notice. Prior to the statute (1705) 4 Anne, c 16, the assignee of a reversion could not recover rent until the tenant had attorned to him. Section 9 of the Act took away the necessity for attornment, although s 10 provided protection to a tenant who paid rent before he had notice that the premises had been assigned.

[377] *Green v Rheinberg* (1911) 104 LT 149. See also *Grace Rymer Investments Ltd v Waite* [1958] 1 Ch 831.

[378] (1870) LR 5 CP 589, 594.

He said that the payment was not a fulfilment of the obligation imposed by the lease to pay rent. Rather, he characterized it as an advance to the landlord, with an agreement that on the day when the rent became due the advance should be treated as a fulfilment of the rent obligation. This could not be effective as against a prior mortgagee, because the mortgagee was the party entitled to the rent as it fell due.

17.70 *De Nichols v Saunders* essentially turned upon a question of power. The landlord, having assigned the reversion by way of mortgage, did not have power to give a discharge to the tenant before the due date. However the principle, that a tenant who expends money in repairs may treat it as an advance payment of rent if the landlord is responsible for the repairs, is not based upon a question of power, or upon an agreement (express or implied) between the tenant and the landlord regarding the payment of rent. The tenant's right to treat the cost of repairs as an advance payment of rent arises as a matter of law. It is designed to encourage the tenant to effect repairs so as to protect him against the possibility that 'the house may fall upon his head.' It is effective against the landlord whoever it may be, whether it is the person whom the tenant thinks is the landlord, or whether it is a prior assignee of the reversion of whom the tenant is not aware. In *Lee-Parker v Izzet* it is unclear from the report whether the repairs were effected before or after the mortgage, but this was not important. The decision was correct, irrespective of when the mortgage was executed.

(17) Freight Payable to a Mortgagee or Purchaser of a Ship

17.71 The principle underlying *Reeves v Pope*[379] is also relevant when a mortgagee goes into possession of a ship. The mortgagee is entitled to the freight in the course of being earned, not because he is an assignee of the debt, but rather because the mortgagee is the master or owner of the ship.[380] The mortgagee's right depends on property, not on contract.[381] In the same way, when a ship is sold, the right to freight in the course of being earned passes to the purchaser.[382] Therefore, when a mortgagee in possession or a purchaser of a ship sues for payment of freight, the charterer or shipper may not set off a debt which is owing by the mortgagor or, as the case may be, by the vendor.[383] The principle of taking subject to equities does not apply.

---

[379] [1914] 2 KB 284. See paras 17.60–17.65 above.

[380] *Keith v Burrows* (1877) 2 App Cas 636, 646. See also *Kerswill v Bishop* (1832) 2 C & J 529, 149 ER 224; *Japp v Campbell* (1888) 57 LJQB 79; *Wilson v Wilson* (1872) LR 14 Eq 32 (mortgagee's right to freight has priority over an earlier assignment of freight of which the mortgagee did not have notice).

[381] *Rusden v Pope* (1868) LR 3 Ex 269, 276–277.

[382] See eg *Morrison v Parsons* (1810) 2 Taunt 407, 127 ER 1136. As Lord Ellenborough remarked in *Case v Davidson* (1816) 5 M & S 79, 82, 105 ER 980, 981, 'freight follows, as an incident, the property in the ship'.

[383] *Tanner v Phillips* (1872) 42 LJ Ch 125.

(18) Transfer of a Torrens Mortgage in Australia

In the case of a transfer of a mortgage and the mortgage debt relating to land registered under the Torrens system in Australia, the principle of indefeasibility of title is separate from and does not affect the principle that the transferee of the debt takes subject to set-offs available against the transferor.[384] Therefore, where an equitable set-off would have provided a defence to the mortgagor to an action for possession by the original mortgagee,[385] the defence should be equally available as against a transferee of the mortgage.[386]

17.72

C. Crystallized Floating Security

An intervening third party interest in a debt may arise when a floating security over a company's assets and undertaking crystallizes. If the company continues to carry on business, a person dealing with the company may be concerned to know whether debts and credits arising before and after crystallization can be set off. This includes debts and credits contracted by the company through the agency of a receiver appointed to the company by the secured creditor.[387]

17.73

(1) Statutes of Set-off

It is commonly said that, when a floating security crystallizes, any debts owing to the company and coming within the ambit of the security are assigned in equity to the secured creditor.[388] This would be the case when crystallization results in an assignment of the company's property by way of mortgage, but a floating security often is not expressed to bring about a mortgage. The terms of a floating security commonly provide for the company's property to become subject to a charge

17.74

---

[384] *Long Leys Co Pty Ltd v Silkdale Pty Ltd* (1991) 5 BPR 11,512, 11,519–11,520.

[385] See paras 4.101–4.105 above.

[386] *Long Leys Co Pty Ltd v Silkdale Pty Ltd* (1991) 5 BPR 11,512.

[387] The receiver may be an administrative receiver as defined in the Insolvency Act 1986, ss 29(2) and 251, in other words a receiver and manager of the whole (or substantially the whole) of a company's property appointed by or on behalf of the holders of debentures of the company secured by a charge which, as created, was a floating charge. Administrative receivers are subject to ss 42–49 of the Act. The scope of administrative receivership will be affected if the Enterprise Bill is enacted. The Bill was introduced into the House of Commons on 26 March 2002. Subject to some exceptions, it prohibits the holder of a floating charge from appointing an administrative receiver. On the other hand it permits the holder to appoint an administrator to the company. An administrator, like a receiver prior to liquidation, is an agent of the company, so that the following discussion would be relevant where debts are contracted by a company through the agency of an administrator following crystallization of a floating charge.

[388] See para 11.32 above. The appointment of a receiver out of court under a floating charge does not of itself determine contracts previously entered into by the company in the ordinary course of its business. See *George Barker (Transport) Ltd v Eynon* [1974] 1 WLR 462, 468, 471. This is also the case when a receiver and manager is appointed by the court. See *Parsons v Sovereign Bank of Canada* [1913] AC 160.

upon crystallization, the difference being that, unlike a mortgage, a charge does not take effect as a transfer of ownership.[389] Sometimes when a floating security is expressed to take effect by way of charge it is nevertheless interpreted as giving rise to an assignment,[390] but the distinction between a charge and a mortgage in any event should not be crucial to a set-off. A charge should have the same effect upon the availability of a set-off as a mortgage,[391] in that, after a debtor to the company has notice that a third party has a security interest in the debt, whether by way of charge or mortgage, it would be unconscionable for the debtor to rely on subsequent dealings with the chargor to diminish the rights of the third party.[392] Therefore, whether crystallization results in an assignment by way of mortgage or a charge, questions of set-off[393] should be determined by reference to the same principles that apply to assignments of choses in action, the relevant date being the date of notice of crystallization.[394] Mere notice of the existence of a floating security at a time when cross-debts are contracted, without notice of crystallization, does not preclude a set-off. In *Biggerstaff v Rowatt's Wharf Ltd*[395] both demands were liquidated and arose before crystallization. It was held, correctly, that the debenture-holders took subject to a set-off, notwithstanding that the defendant knew of the floating security.[396]

The general principle

17.75 Consistent with the principle applicable to assignments of debts, a debtor to a company ordinarily will be denied a set-off in an action brought against him by

---

[389] Goode, *Legal Problems of Credit and Security* (2nd edn, 1988) 14. The distinction between a charge and a mortgage has not always been maintained. For example, Stamp LJ in *George Barker (Transport) Ltd v Eynon* [1974] 1 WLR 462, 471 referred to 'an equitable assignment (by way of charge)', and see also *Security Trust Co v Royal Bank of Canada* [1976] AC 503, 518, PC ('assigned to the respondent by way of equitable charge').

[390] See eg *Re ELS Ltd* [1995] Ch 11, 24–25; *National Mutual Life Nominees Ltd v National Capital Development Commission* (1975) 37 FLR 404, 409–410 (criticized in Sykes and Walker, *The Law of Securities* (5th edn, 1993) 960).

[391] See para 11.34 above. Compare Goode, 'Centre Point' [1984] JBL 172.

[392] See para 17.03 above.

[393] Set-off only provides a defence to a monetary demand. It may not be invoked when the receiver is suing for the return of goods or other specific things wrongfully detained. See *Tony Lee Motors Ltd v M S MacDonald & Son (1974) Ltd* [1981] 2 NZLR 281, and ch 9 above.

[394] See *Business Computers Ltd v Anglo-African Leasing Ltd* [1977] 1 WLR 578, 582; *B Hargreaves Ltd v Action 2000 Ltd* [1993] BCLC 1111, 1115.

[395] [1896] 2 Ch 93.

[396] See also *Edward Nelson & Co Ltd v Faber* & Co [1903] 2 KB 367; *Commercial Factors Ltd v Maxwell Printing Ltd* [1994] 1 NZLR 724, 735; *Business Computers Ltd v Anglo-African Leasing Ltd* [1977] 1 WLR 578, 582 (in relation to the instalment due before notice of the appointment); *Fire Nymph Products Ltd v The Heating Centre Pty Ltd* (1992) 7 ACSR 365, 376. *A fortiori* a set-off is available against a cross-debt arising before notice of crystallization if the defendant did not know of the floating security. See *Tony Lee Motors Ltd v M S MacDonald & Son (1974) Ltd* [1981] 2 NZLR 281, in which the defendant, before crystallization, had obtained an equitable assignment of a debt owing by the company to a third party. Notice to the company was not necessary to complete the assignment.

the company for payment of the debt where the subject of the claimed set-off is a debt incurred by the company after the debtor had notice of crystallization of a floating charge over the company's assets and undertaking. The leading authority is *N W Robbie & Co Ltd v Witney Warehouse Co Ltd*.[397] The plaintiff company had issued a debenture to a bank securing, by means of a fixed and floating charge over its assets, all moneys due from it to the bank. The bank subsequently appointed a receiver and manager under the debenture, whereupon the floating charge crystallized. Before the appointment the company had sold goods on credit to the defendant. The company continued to carry on business after the appointment, during which time the defendant purchased more goods on credit. At a later date the defendant obtained an assignment from a third party of a debt owing by the company. When the company sued the defendant for the price of the goods sold, the defendant sought to set off the assigned debt. The Court of Appeal held that a set-off was not available. The decision to deny a set-off seems correct,[398] but as Meagher, Gummow and Lehane in *Australia* explained,[399] the reasoning is questionable. Russell LJ (with whom Sellers LJ agreed) said that there was no right of set-off because there was no mutuality in equity. When the floating charge crystallized, the defendant's debt for the goods purchased before crystallization was assigned in equity to the debenture-holder, while, in the case of purchases made after that date, each debt as it arose became the subject of an immediate equitable assignment in favour of the debenture-holder.[400] This meant that, at the later date when the defendant first obtained the assignment of the company's debt from the third party, there was no identity between the person beneficially interested in the claim (the debenture-holder) and the person against whom the cross-claim existed (the company). The assumption inherent in this analysis is that mutuality under the Statutes of Set-off is determined by reference to the equitable rather than the legal interests of the parties, and that, if the demands are not and never have been equitably mutual, a set-off is not available under the Statutes. However the point was made earlier that this fails to explain why a debtor on an assigned debt is permitted a set-off when the cross-debt from the assignor to the debtor arose after the assignment but before the debtor had notice of the assignment, because in that circumstance there never has been mutuality in equity.[401] The preferred analysis is that the Statutes prima facie confer a right of set-off at law

---

[397] [1963] 1 WLR 1324. See also *Lynch v Ardmore Studios (Ireland) Ltd* [1966] IR 133, which concerned a similar fact situation, and *United Steel Corp Ltd v Turnbull Elevator of Canada Ltd* [1973] 2 OR 540.

[398] Compare Barwick CJ In *Ferrier v Bottomer* (1972) 126 CLR 597, 603, who left open the question whether *Robbie v Witney* was correctly decided.

[399] Meagher, Gummow and Lehane, *Equity: Doctrines and Remedies* (3rd edn, 1992) 719–21.

[400] See also *Ferrier v Bottomer* (1972) 126 CLR 597; *Roadshow Entertainment Pty Ltd v (ACN 053 006 269) Pty Ltd* (1997) 42 NSWLR 462, 482.

[401] See para 11.09 above.

when there is mutuality at law, although a lack of mutuality in equity may render it unconscionable for a debtor to rely on the legal right.[402] *Robbie v Witney* is better explained on the ground that, since the cross-claim against the company was acquired after the defendant was aware of the crystallization of the charge, and the consequent equitable interest of the debenture-holder in the defendant's debt to the company, it was unconscionable for the defendant to rely on the right of set-off that otherwise was available at law.[403]

Cross-debt arising after notice

17.76 There is authority for the proposition that a defendant in an action brought by a company for payment of a debt which is the subject of a crystallized floating charge will be denied a set-off under the Statutes where the cross-debt owing by the company arose after the defendant had notice of crystallization, notwithstanding that the cross-debt may have had its source in a contract entered into between the defendant and the company before notice.[404] This is consistent with the principle applied in relation to assignments generally, and it was criticized earlier in that context.[405] It suffices to say that, if there was a binding contractual relationship in existence before notice, it is not clear why it should be considered unconscionable for the defendant to rely on a right of set-off otherwise available at law under the Statutes when the company's debt arose under that contract but after notice. In any event, similar to the principle that applies in bankruptcy and company liquidation,[406] there is an exception in the case of a temporary suspension of mutual credit. Thus, if a person holding a negotiable instrument upon which a company is liable indorses it to a third party before crystallization, and after crystallization the person is obliged to take up the instrument again as a result of the default of the company, the resulting claim on the instrument against the company may be the subject of a set-off.[407]

Set-off asserted by the company

17.77 The preceeding discussion concerned the situation in which the debtor to the company is the party seeking to base a set-off upon a debt owing by the company

---

[402] See paras 11.08–11.10 and 17.03 above.

[403] The report of the case does not establish when the defendant first became aware of the crystallization of the floating charge, but Russell LJ said that the defendant should be fixed with knowledge of crystallization before it acquired the cross-claim against the company. See [1963] 1 WLR 1324, 1338.

[404] *Business Computers Ltd v Anglo-African Leasing Ltd* [1977] 1 WLR 578, 585. Compare *West Street Properties Pty Ltd v Jamison* [1974] 2 NSWLR 435 (discussed below) in the situation in which the company instead is the party claiming a set-off.

[405] See para 17.12 above.

[406] See also paras 6.65–6.67 above.

[407] *Handley Page Ltd v Commissioners of Customs and Excise and Rockwell Machine Tool Company Ltd* [1970] 2 Lloyd's Rep 459, 464–465, discussed in *Business Computers Ltd v Anglo-African Leasing Ltd* [1977] 1 WLR 578, 585–586.

that arose after notice of crystallization. A set-off ordinarily is not available to the debtor. However this is not to say that a set-off similarly would be denied to the company. The issue arose in New South Wales in *West Street Properties Pty Ltd v Jamison*.[408] The plaintiff company was a lessor of premises, and was claiming payment of arrears of rent from the lessee. Pursuant to a mortgage debenture the lessee had granted a floating charge to a creditor, which crystallized when the debenture-holder appointed a receiver to the lessee. The lease was entered into before the receivership, but the subject of the proceeding was the obligation to pay rent accruing after the appointment, the receiver having determined to continue the company's business for the benefit of the debenture-holder.[409] Jeffrey J was asked to determine a question of law, whether the company could set off against its rent obligation a debt owing to it by the lessor on an advance made before the receivership. He held that the company was entitled to the set-off. He acknowledged the existence of authority for the view that the defendant in an action brought against him by a company in receivership for payment of a debt could not set off a debt owing by the company which accrued after the defendant had notice of crystallization of the charge pursuant to which the receiver was appointed. But they were cases where the defendant as an unsecured creditor was seeking to obtain payment of the debt owing to him in priority to the secured creditor, by setting it off against a debt which he owed to the company but which in equity belonged to the secured creditor.[410] The objection to a set-off in that circumstance is not relevant when the company, and inferentially the secured creditor, is the party seeking to assert a set-off. There is no countervailing equity in that case which renders it unconscionable for the company to rely on a right of set-off otherwise available at law. The cross-demands would not have been equitably mutual at any time, but lack of mutuality in equity will only deprive a defendant of a right of set-off otherwise available at law if in the circumstances it is unconscionable for the defendant to assert the legal right. As Jeffrey J remarked:[411]

> In a case where the debenture-holder elects after crystallization to cause the company to carry on its business, debts incurred to existing debtors of the company in so doing may be met by the pro tanto collection of the debts owed by them to the company by means of set-off. This is but a method of recovery alternative to the taking of proceedings at law in the name of the company, something which, as already observed, the debenture-holder has after crystallization, an undoubted right to do. For him to direct that a debt which he owns should be applied in reduction or extinction of an indebtedness which the company incurs is merely to exercise

---

[408] [1974] 2 NSWLR 435.

[409] Jeffrey J (at [1974] 2 NSWLR 435, 439) considered that, whatever personal liability for rent the receiver may have incurred by virtue of the Companies Act 1961 (NSW), s 188(1) (see now the Corporations Act 2001 (Cth), s 419A(2)), it could not have been to the exclusion of the company's liability, given that the lease was entered into before the appointment.

[410] [1974] 2 NSWLR 435, 440–441.

[411] [1974] 2 NSWLR 435, 441.

his dominion over it. It is one thing to say that a set-off at law cannot be availed of to defeat or postpone a prior equitable title to a debt, but quite another to say that it is not available to the equitable owner who wishes to employ the legal rights over which he has control in order to collect it.

In *West Street Properties Ltd v Jamison* the company's debt arose after crystallization but pursuant to a prior contract, but the reasoning would appear to be equally relevant where the company's debt has its source in a contract entered into after crystallization.[412] The *West Street Properties* case supports the view that, in the situation in which a company after crystallization of a floating charge over its assets becomes indebted to a person who in turn is indebted to the company, it is only unconscionable for the debtor to the company to assert a legal right of set-off otherwise available under the Statutes of Set-off. There is no countervailing equity which would preclude the company and the secured creditor from relying on a set-off available at law. There is merit in that view. On the other hand, a set-off should not be available where a receiver is personally liable for a debt[413] and the receiver is sued personally.[414] In that circumstance there would not be mutuality at law or in equity, so that Jeffrey J's analysis would not apply.

Debt to the company arising after notice but pursuant to a prior contract

17.78 Consider the converse situation, in which the debt owing to the company, rather than the company's debt to the debtor, arises after notice of crystallization as a result of a contract entered into before notice. It seems that a set-off may be available in that case at the instance of either party against a debt incurred by the company before crystallization.[415] In *Rother Iron Works Ltd v Canterbury Precision Engineers Ltd*[416] a floating charge in a debenture granted by a company crystallized

---

[412] See eg the discussion at [1974] 2 NSWLR 435, 439–440.

[413] As in the case of an administrative receiver in England in relation to a contract entered into by him in the carrying out of his functions, pursuant to the Insolvency Act 1986, s 44(1)(b). In Australia, see the Corporations Act 2001 (Cth), s 419.

[414] Compare *West Street Properties Ltd v Jamison* [1974] 2 NSWLR 435, 439.

[415] In New Zealand, compare *T R Hillson Ltd v Beverley Trading Co Ltd* (1987) 3 NZCLC 100,026. A company, prior to crystallization of a floating charge over its assets by the appointment of a receiver, had paid for some goods. It was therefore at the date of the appointment entitled to delivery of the goods. However the right to delivery itself could not have been the subject of a set-off. The goods were not delivered, and after the appointment the company accepted the failure to deliver as a repudiation and claimed the return of the price paid. McGechan J held that the circumstances were not such as to entitle the defendant to set off a pre-receivership cross-claim against the company.

[416] [1974] 1 QB 1. See also *State Bank of South Australia v Kralingen Pty Ltd* (1993) 172 LSJS 438, a decision of Cox J in the South Australian Supreme Court. A lease required the lessor to purchase the tenant's fixtures upon determination of the lease. The lessee granted a floating mortgage debenture over its rights under the lease to the plaintiff bank. The security crystallized and, after that, the lessor determined the lease. Cox J held that the lessor could set off the lessee's arrears of rent against its liability to pay the price of the fixtures. The *Rother Iron Works* case was not referred to, but it is consistent with that decision.

when a receiver was appointed to the company. Prior to the appointment the company was indebted to the defendant for £124. In addition, it had entered into a contract to sell goods to the defendant for £159. However, the goods were not delivered until after the receiver was appointed, and it was only upon delivery that the defendant became indebted for the price. The Court of Appeal held that the defendant need only pay £35, after the deducting the company's debt. Russell LJ in delivering the judgment of the Court[417] said that the obligation of the defendant to pay the £159 'never . . . came into existence except subject to a right to set off the £124 as, in effect, payment in advance. That which became subject to the debenture charge was not £159, but the net claim sustainable by the plaintiff for £35'.[418]

Rother Iron Works v Canterbury Precision Engineers has been referred to with evident approval in later cases,[419] and Mance J followed it in *Marathon Electrical Manufacturing Corp v Mashreqbank PSC*[420] when he allowed a set-off against an assignee of a debt where the assigned debt arose after the debtor had notice of the assignment but pursuant to a prior engagement. On the other hand, the British Columbia Court of Appeal declined to apply the *Rother Iron Works* case in *CIBC v Tuckerr Industries Inc*.[421] A debenture-holder appointed a receiver to a lessor of premises, which crystallized a floating charge under the debenture. Notice of the appointment was given immediately to the lessee. Prior to the appointment the lessor was indebted to the lessee on a transaction independent of the lease. The question was whether the lessee could set off the prior debt against rent accruing after the appointment. The Court of Appeal held that there was a lack of

17.79

---

[417] Russell, Cairns and Stamp LJJ.

[418] [1974] 1 QB 1, 6.

[419] In addition to *Marathon Electrical Manufacturing Corp v Mashreqbank PSC* [1997] 2 BCLC 460 (see below), see *George Barker (Transport) Ltd v Eynon* [1974] 1 WLR 462, 470, 473–474, 475, CA and *Business Computers Ltd v Anglo-African Leasing Ltd* [1977] 1 WLR 578, 585 (although the facts of the *Rother Iron Works* case were incorrectly stated, since the company rather than the debtor was the seller of the goods). See also *Caratti v Grant* (1978) 3 ACLR 322, 331; *Roadshow Entertainment Pty Ltd v (ACN 053 006 269) Pty Ltd* (1997) 42 NSWLR 462, 483 (CA). In *John Dee Group Ltd v WMH (21) Ltd* [1997] BCC 518, 529–531 Neuberger J accepted that, were it not for a clause in the contract in issue which required payment without set-off, a set-off would have been available in relation to transport charges payable to a company in receivership for services performed after notice of the receivership but pursuant to a prior contract, notice of the receivership also constituting notice of crystallization. However, while Neuberger J referred to the *Rother Iron Works* case, it is not clear if the availability of a set-off was thought to be on the basis of a set-off under the Statutes of Set-off or an equitable set-off, for which it is not necessary that the demands should have arisen before notice. See para 17.82 below. See Neuberger J's reference (at 530) to *Government of Newfoundland v Newfoundland Railway Co* (1888) 13 App Cas 199, and (at 531) to the extract from *Business Computers Ltd v Anglo-African Leasing Ltd* [1977] 1 WLR 578, 585 in relation to closely connected claims. Neuberger J's decision was affirmed on appeal [1998] BCC 972 but without reference to this point.

[420] [1997] 2 BCLC 460.

[421] (1983) 149 DLR (3d) 172. See also *Re Associated Investors of Canada Ltd* (1989) 62 DLR (4th) 269, but compare *Clarkson Company Ltd v The Queen* (1988) 88 *Dominion Tax Cases* 6256.

mutuality, and therefore there was no set-off, since on the one hand the lessor was indebted to the lessee, and on the other the subsequently accruing rent was owed to the debenture-holder as equitable assignee. While the *Rother Iron Works* case appears to have been a similar case, it was distinguished on the ground that it was an example of an equitable set-off,[422] the basis of which was said to be that the two companies in that case had traded with each other in such a way that every debt that arose between them in the course of their trade was subject, at the time it arose, to being set off against every subsequent cross-debt that arose within the trading relationship. That explanation is doubtful. There is nothing in Russell LJ's judgment in the *Rother Iron Works* case to suggest that there was an agreement for a set-off,[423] so as to support an equitable set-off on that ground,[424] and nor do the demands appear to have been sufficiently closely connected to give rise to a substantive equitable set-off.[425] The court in deciding against a set-off in *CIBC v Tuckerr* seems to have assumed that mutuality under the Statutes of Set-off is determined solely by reference to equitable titles, but that assumption does not accurately describe the position.[426] In the *Rother Iron Works* case there was mutuality at law, and therefore prima facie there was a right of set-off at law under the Statutes of Set-off, and the case is authority for the proposition that in the circumstances in issue there was nothing inequitable in the defendant relying on the legal right. This should be equally relevant to a case such as *CIBC v Tuckerr*.

17.80 In *Hoverd Industries Ltd v Supercool Refrigeration and Air Conditioning (1991) Ltd*[427] the New Zealand Court of Appeal noted that the debt which the defendant was permitted to set off in *Rother Iron Works Ltd v Canterbury Precision Engineers Ltd* was already due and payable before the company entered into the contract which gave rise to the receiver's later claim. However that was not the basis of the decision in the *Rother Iron Works* case. The point that Russell LJ made was that, when the debt for the price first came into existence, it was already subject to the set-off,[428] and the debt came into existence when the goods were delivered. Whether the debt which the defendant was allowed to set off arose before or after the date of the contract which gave rise to the claim for the price was not important. The New Zealand Court of Appeal was also critical of Russell LJ's comment that the set-off was 'in effect, payment in advance',[429] pointing out that set-off is a defence which can only be pleaded against a claim which is presently due.[430] That

---

[422] Mutuality is not necessary in all cases for equitable set-off. See para 4.48 above.
[423] Indeed, the contrary is inherent in Stamp LJ's comment in *George Barker (Transport) Ltd v Eynon* [1974] 1 WLR 462, 474.
[424] See para 3.03 above.
[425] See ch 4 above.
[426] See paras 11.08–11.10 and 17.03 above.
[427] [1995] 3 NZLR 577, 587–588.
[428] See [1974] 1 QB 1, 6.
[429] [1974] 1 QB 1, 6.
[430] [1995] 3 NZLR 577, 588.

observation is true enough, but Russell LJ's comment should not be taken literally. A set-off does not occur at the date of notice of an assignment,[431] and so it should not suffice to deny a set-off that the assigned debt was not in existence at that date if it arose out of a prior contract. The debt must of course be in existence and be presently payable when it is sued upon, and the question then is whether it is unconscionable for the defendant to rely on a right of set-off which is available at law given the intervening equitable interest of the secured creditor. It is in the context of the question of unconscionability that the decision in the *Rother Iron Works* case should be considered.

Contract entered into after notice

Russell LJ emphasized in the *Rother Iron Works* case that the delivery of the goods **17.81** in that case occurred pursuant to a contract made by the company before crystallization, and that the court was not concerned with a claim made by the receiver against the defendant which arose out of a contract made by the receiver subsequent to crystallization.[432] It may be thought unconscionable to allow a defendant to assert a set-off otherwise available at law when the defendant's liability to the company arose out of a dealing transacted after the defendant was already aware that the company's assets were charged to a secured creditor, and that the dealing was being conducted for the benefit of the secured creditor. Thus, there are a number of cases in which a person who purchased goods from a company known to be in receivership was not allowed to set off the debt for the price against a pre-receivership debt owing to him by the company,[433] the receivership having crystallized a floating security over the company's assets. *Robbie v Witney* is authority for the view that this also applies when the cross-claim against the company was acquired after notice through an assignment.[434] In New Zealand, Richmond J in *Felt and Textiles of New Zealand Ltd v R Hubrich Ltd*,[435] in denying the appellant a set-off against the price of goods sold to it after a floating charge over the vendor's assets crystallized upon the appointment of a receiver, emphasized that: 'the

---

[431] *Glencore Grain Ltd v Agros Trading Co* [1999] 2 Lloyd's Rep 410, 417–419.

[432] [1974] 1 QB 1, 6.

[433] In addition to the cases discussed below, see *Leichhardt Emporium Pty Ltd v AGC (Household Finance) Ltd* [1979] 1 NSWLR 701; *Cheviot Australia Pty Ltd v Bob Jane Corporation Pty Ltd* (1988) 52 SASR 204. Compare *F Suter & Co Ltd v Drake and Gorham Ltd* (1910), unreported but noted in Weaver and Craigie, *The Law Relating to Banker and Customer in Australia* (looseleaf) vol 3, para 22.590, in which, apparently, the Divisional Court (Darling and Phillimore JJ) allowed a set-off in this situation.

[434] While *Robbie v Witney* also concerned a sale of goods by a company, it is not stated in the report whether the defendant purchaser had notice of the appointment of the receiver, and therefore of crystallization, at the time of the sale of the goods. Russell LJ simply remarked ([1963] 1 WLR 1324, 1338) that the defendant should be fixed with knowledge of the assignment some time before it acquired the cross-claim against the company.

[435] [1968] NZLR 716.

appellant had notice of the fact that it was buying an asset then charged in favour of the debenture-holder from a company empowered by the debenture to sell that asset through the agency of the receiver for the purpose, primarily, of discharging the company's indebtedness to the debenture-holder'.[436] The sale in the *Felt and Textiles* case arose in the course of the realization of the company's assets by the receiver after crystallization. Richmond J tentatively suggested that there may be a distinction between that case and a case in which the receiver was carrying on the company's business. Subsequently, however, Chilwell J in the New Zealand Supreme Court in *Rendell v Doors and Doors Ltd*[437] rejected this as a ground for distinction, and held that a creditor of a company who purchased goods from a receiver known to be carrying on the company's business could not set off the price against the company's pre-receivership debt to him. There is nevertheless a suggestion in the judgment that, in some cases in which a company's business is being carried on after crystallization, an equity could possibly arise which would justify a set-off against the secured creditor.[438] The situation postulated by Chilwell J was one in which a person supplied material to a company after crystallization, which material was used in the manufacture of goods subsequently purchased by that person. The basis of any supposed equity was not explored further, but, as Jeffrey remarked in New South Wales,[439] there is something to be said for the view that a secured creditor should expect to take subject to a set-off when both demands arose out of dealings with the company while the company's business was being carried on for the benefit of the secured creditor, notwithstanding that it is contrary to the generally accepted position in relation to assignments of debts, that the line is drawn at the date of notice.

(2) Equitable Set-off

17.82 When the argument for a set-off is based upon the procedural defence provided by the Statutes of Set-off in the case of mutual debts, the company's liability to the defendant as a general rule must have come into existence before notice. However, consistent with the principle applicable in the case of an assignment of a debt,[440] this should not be necessary when an equitable set-off is in issue based upon cross-

---

[436] [1968] NZLR 716, 718.

[437] [1975] 2 NZLR 191.

[438] This would be better expressed in terms that in some cases it would not be unconscionable for the defendant to rely on a right of set-off which is available at law under the Statutes of Set-off.

[439] *West Street Properties Pty Ltd v Jamison* [1974] 2 NSWLR 435, 440. See also *Leichhardt Emporium Pty Ltd v AGC (Household Finance) Ltd* [1979] 1 NSWLR 701, 706–707, although compare *Business Computers Ltd v Anglo-African Leasing Ltd* [1977] 1 WLR 578, 585. An equitable set-off in any event should be available when both demands arose out of the same contract entered into by a receiver on behalf of the company and the demands are inseparably connected. This form of equitable set-off is considered below.

[440] See para 17.22 above.

demands which are inseparably connected.[441] The point is illustrated by *Parsons v Sovereign Bank of Canada*.[442] A company prior to the appointment of a receiver and manager at the instance of debenture-holders had entered into a number of contracts with the defendants for the supply of quantities of paper to them on a periodic basis. The receiver immediately after his appointment continued to supply paper under the contracts,[443] but subsequently repudiated the contracts. The receiver assigned the defendants' debt for the price of paper delivered after the appointment to the plaintiff, but when the plaintiff sued for payment it was held that the defendants could set off their unliquidated damages claim against the company for breach of contract.[444] The fact that the demands arose after the appointment of the receiver was not sufficient to deny a set-off as against either the debenture-holders or the assignee. The receiver in the *Parsons* case was appointed by the court rather than by the debenture-holders, but the principle should be the same for both forms of appointment.[445]

(3) Debt Owing to the Company Exceeds the Secured Debt

In the preceding discussion of the circumstances in which a set-off is denied to a **17.83** defendant in an action brought against him by a company for payment of a debt which arose after notice of crystallization of a floating charge, it was assumed that

---

[441] See ch 4 above. The judgment of Mocatta J in *Handley Page Ltd v Commissioners of Customs and Excise and Rockwell Machine Tool Co Ltd* [1970] 2 Lloyd's Rep 459 is confusing in this respect. If indeed the demands arose under the same contract and were sufficiently closely connected to give rise to an equitable set-off (see at 465, in particular the reference to *Hanak v Green* [1958] 2 QB 9), a set-off should have been available without any need to have recourse to the principle of a temporary suspension of mutual credit (see para 17.76 above) as a means of overcoming the perceived difficulty that the bills were returned to Rockwell after crystallization by the appointment of a receiver under the debenture issued by Handley-Page. In *Business Computers Ltd v Anglo-African Leasing Ltd* [1977] 1 WLR 578, 585–586 these were treated as alternative grounds for allowing a set-off in the *Handley Page* case.

[442] [1913] AC 160. See also *Forster v Nixon's Navigation Co* (1906) 23 TLR 138 (court-appointed receiver); *West Street Properties Pty Ltd v Jamison* [1974] 2 NSWLR 435, 439; *Re Wirragana Nominees Pty Ltd* (1991) 9 ACLC 1168, 1179–1180; *Roadshow Entertainment Pty Ltd v (ACN 053 006 269) Pty Ltd* (1997) 42 NSWLR 462 (see esp at 481 *et seq*). In New Zealand, compare *Popular Homes Ltd v Circuit Developments Ltd* [1979] 2 NZLR 642, 660 and *Hoverd Industries Ltd v Supercool Refrigeration and Air Conditioning (1991) Ltd* [1995] 3 NZLR 577, 586 (in relation to the relevance of the charge being fixed or floating), where the contrary seems to have been assumed.

[443] The Privy Council accepted that the paper was delivered under the old contracts with the company, and not pursuant to new contracts made with the receiver personally.

[444] When an equitable set-off is in issue based upon an inseparable connection, it is not necessary that the demands be liquidated. See eg *Sun Candies Pty Ltd v Polites* [1939] VLR 132 (receivership). Compare *W Pope & Co Pty Ltd v Edward Souery & Co Pty Ltd* [1983] WAR 117. A company in receivership was suing for the price of goods supplied to the defendant. The defendant was not permitted to set off a claim for unliquidated damages arising out of defects in an earlier consignment under a separate contract. There was not in that case a sufficiently close connection so as to give rise to an equitable set-off.

[445] See para 17.89 below.

the defendant's debt to the company is less than the debt for which the charge to the secured creditor constitutes a security. If the defendant's debt to the company exceeds the company's debt to the secured creditor, so that the company alone is interested in the excess, and the defendant is solvent,[446] the defendant may set off the excess against the company's debt to the defendant.[447]

(4) Liquidation

17.84 A company may go into liquidation after a floating charge over its assets has crystallized.[448] If at the commencement of the liquidation the secured creditor has not been paid in full, and the security operates as an equitable mortgage, any debts owing to the company and coming within the ambit of the security will be the subject of a prior equitable assignment in favour of the secured creditor. Since the secured creditor rather than the company has the beneficial title to the debts, the set-off section in the insolvency legislation would not be relevant in the liquidation,[449] and rights of set-off should continue to be determined by reference to the principles outlined above.[450] Nor should the result differ if a charge rather than a mortgage is in issue,[451] even assuming that the stipulation for a charge is not interpreted as operating by way of assignment in any event.[452] If on the other hand the security is redeemed before the commencement of the liquidation by payment to the secured creditor, the secured creditor will no longer have an interest in the debts owing to the company. The company itself would be the beneficial owner of the debts, and so the insolvency set-off section should determine the existence of any right of set-off in its liquidation.[453] Alternatively, redemption of the security may occur after the liquidation. The question of set-off in that circumstance was considered earlier.[454] Further, a set-off may occur under the insolvency set-off section as between the company and the debtor if, and to the extent that, the debt owing to the company exceeds the company's debt to the secured

---

[446] See para 11.28 above.

[447] See Dixon J in *Hiley v Peoples Prudential Assurance Co* (1938) 60 CLR 468, 497–498, referring to *Re Asphaltic Wood Pavement Co. Lee & Chapman's Case* (1885) 30 Ch D 216, 222. See also para 11.27 *ff* above.

[448] Compare *Re Parker* (1997) 80 FCR 1, in which the liquidation was deemed to have commenced prior to the appointment of the receiver, as a result of the appointment of an administrator to the company pursuant to Part 5.3A of the Corporations Law, and Mansfield J held that the question of the application of the insolvency set-off section fell to be determined as at the earlier date. See paras 6.36–6.45 above.

[449] See para 17.28 above, and also *Re Parker* (1997) 80 FCR 1, 16–18.

[450] See eg *Handley Page Ltd v Commissioners of Customs and Excise and Rockwell Machine Tool Co Ltd* [1970] 2 Lloyd's Rep 459; *Rendell v Doors and Doors Ltd* [1975] 2 NZLR 191; *Hoverd Industries Ltd v Supercool Refrigeration and Air Conditioning (1991) Ltd* [1995] 3 NZLR 577, 585 *et seq.*

[451] See para 17.74 above.

[452] See *Re ELS Ltd* [1995] Ch 11, 24–25.

[453] See *Rendell v Doors and Doors Ltd* [1975] 2 NZLR 191, 202–203.

[454] See para 11.36 above.

creditor, but a set-off should not be available in that circumstance unless the debtor is solvent.[455]

(5) Preferential Debts

When a receiver is appointed to a company on behalf of the holders of debentures secured by a charge which, as created, was a floating charge, the Insolvency Act 1986, s 40(2)[456] accords preferential status to certain debts, so that they are required to be paid out of the assets of the company coming into the hands of the receiver in priority to any claims for principal or interest payable to the debenture-holders. The concept of preferential debts also applies in company liquidation.[457] If a creditor has two debts owing to it, one preferential and the other non-preferential, and at the same time the creditor is indebted to the company, the prevailing view in company liquidation is that a set-off under the insolvency set-off section occurs rateably as between the preferential and the non-preferential debts,[458] and it has been suggested that a similar principle should apply in receivership.[459] That proposition is doubtful, however. **17.85**

The point is that different forms of set-off are in issue. In company liquidation, the courts have adopted the view that a set-off under the insolvency set-off section occurs automatically at the date of the liquidation.[460] In that situation there is no difficulty in saying that a set-off may operate rateably as between the debts. The same cannot be said, however, in the case of receivership. A set-off does not occur automatically upon the appointment of a receiver, and nor can the receiver act unilaterally to effect a set-off. The form of set-off in issue is the procedural defence provided by the Statutes of Set-off. A set-off under the Statutes is pleaded as a defence to an action, and the set-off is effected by a judgment of the court.[461] **17.86**

Consider that a receiver wishes to make a payment to the debenture-holders before suing for a debt owing to the company by a person who is a creditor in relation to two debts, one of which is preferred. In that circumstance, the receiver could only make the payment by complying with the Insolvency Act, which requires that he must pay preferential debts first. He would be required to pay the amount of the preferential debt to the creditor as it exists at the time, and the receiver could not reduce or extinguish the preferential debt by effecting a set-off himself. Alternatively, the receiver may commence an action against the creditor **17.87**

---

[455] See paras 11.27–11.29 above.

[456] In Australia, see the Corporations Act 2001 (Cth), s 433(3).

[457] Insolvency Act 1986, s 175. In Australia, see the Corporations Act 2001 (Cth), ss 555–563AAA.

[458] *Re Unit 2 Windows Ltd* [1985] 1 WLR 1383. See paras 6.114–6.119 above.

[459] Lightman and Moss, *The Law Relating to Receivers and Administrators of Companies* (3rd edn, 2000) 215 para 10–009, 406 para 21–053.

[460] See paras 6.79–6.103 above.

[461] See para 2.33 above.

for payment of the debt owing to the company before making any payment to debenture-holders. In that circumstance, it would be up to the creditor as to which debt is pleaded by way of defence. If the creditor relies only on the non-preferential debt as a set-off, it is difficult to see how a set-off could then occur rateably as against that debt and the preferential debt, when the preferential debt has not been pleaded as a defence. Indeed, it would be unsatisfactory if different results were to occur depending on whether the receiver sued before or after using the company's available cash to pay debts.

D. Court-appointed Receiver on the Application of a Secured Creditor

17.88 A receiver may be appointed by the court. One situation considered later is an appointment by way of equitable execution,[462] but the court's power is not confined to that circumstance. The court has a broad jurisdiction to appoint a receiver in all cases in which it appears to be just and convenient to do so.[463] This includes the appointment of a receiver and manager[464] of the company's business on the application of a secured creditor in order to protect the creditor's security. Court appointments in this situation are rare, given that secured creditors usually now reserve the right to appoint a receiver out of court. It may nevertheless occur if in a particular case the security document does not empower the creditor to appoint a receiver, or the validity of an appointment made by the creditor is in dispute.[465]

17.89 In *Robbie v Witney*,[466] Russell LJ said that it should not make any difference in relation to questions of set-off whether a receiver has been appointed out of court under a crystallized floating security or whether he is court-appointed. In both cases, he said, the receiver and manager is merely a piece of administrative machinery designed to enforce a security. This requires further comment. The incidents of the two forms of receivership in fact differ in a fundamental respect. A receiver appointed by a creditor pursuant to a power conferred by a security is usually expressed to be the agent of the company,[467] whereas a court-appointed receiver is the agent of neither the company nor the creditor on whose application he was appointed.[468] Any new contracts ordinarily are made by him personally, in

---

[462] See paras 17.114–17.116 below.

[463] Supreme Court Act 1981, s 37(1), and see also RSC, O 30.

[464] See *Halsbury's Laws of England* (2nd edn, 1996) vol 7(2) 1008 para 1358.

[465] See generally Lightman and Moss, *The Law of Receivers and Administrators of Companies* (3rd edn, 2000) 415–17. See also *Bank of Credit and Commerce International SA v BRS Kumar Brothers Ltd* [1994] BCLC 211.

[466] [1963] 1 WLR 1324, 1340. See also *Roadshow Entertainment Pty Ltd v (ACN 053 006 269) Pty Ltd* (1997) 42 NSWLR 462, 483–484.

[467] In relation to an administrative receiver, see the Insolvency Act 1986, s 44(1)(a).

[468] *Parsons v Sovereign Bank of Canada* [1913] AC 160, 167.

reliance on his right of indemnity from the company's assets.[469] When a receiver is appointed at the instance of a secured creditor the same result usually would follow in relation to set-off whether the receiver is appointed by the court or out of court, not because of the incidents attaching to the appointment as such, but rather because the debtor to the company will have notice of a fixed security attaching to his debts to the company, and once he has notice he cannot rely on subsequent events to diminish the rights of the creditor.[470] In any event, in the case of a court appointment a debtor to the company could not rely by way of set-off on a debt which is incurred by the receiver pursuant to a contract entered into with the receiver personally, because there would be a lack of mutuality. On the other hand, contracts entered into by the company before the court appointment remain the company's contracts, and an equitable set-off against a liability under the contract where there is a sufficiently close connection remains available to the debtor, even where the cross-claim accrued after notice of the security. This is the effect of the decision of the Privy Council in *Parsons v Sovereign Bank of Canada*,[471] and it is consistent with the principle applicable in the case of an assignment.[472]

E. Trusts[473]

(1) Set-off Between the Trustee and a Party

Equitable set-off

A trust is not a legal entity separate from the trustee.[474] When a trustee incurs a debt **17.90** in that capacity, the trustee is personally liable. The creditor does not have direct recourse either to the trust assets[475] or to the beneficiaries. Further, when the trust property includes a debt owing to the trustee, the trustee, although possessed of the legal title to the debt, is not the beneficial owner. Prima facie there would not be mutuality in equity as between, on the one hand, a debt incurred by a trustee, and on the other a cross-claim available to the trustee in his capacity as such against the

---

[469] *Parsons v Sovereign Bank of Canada* [1913] AC 160, 167. See also *Burt, Boulton and Hayward v Bull* [1895] 1 QB 276; *Moss Steamship Co Ltd v Whinney* [1912] AC 154.

[470] See para 17.03 above.

[471] [1913] AC 160. See also the similar case of *Forster v Nixon's Navigation Co* (1906) 23 TLR 138.

[472] See paras 17.22 and 17.82 above.

[473] If a trustee is liable for distinct breaches of trust, one of which has resulted in a gain to the estate and the other a loss, it is said that the trustee cannot set off the gain against the loss unless they arise in the same transaction. See *Bartlett v Barclays Bank Trust Co Ltd* [1980] 1 Ch 515, 538; Underhill and Hayton, *Law Relating to Trusts and Trustees* (15th edn, 1995) 848. This is not a case of set-off of cross-demands, however, but rather of fixing the amount of compensation payable.

[474] *Kemtron Industries Pty Ltd v Commissioner of Stamp Duties* [1984] 1 Qd R 576, 584.

[475] *Worrall v Harford* (1802) 8 Ves Jun 4, 8, 32 ER 250, 252; *Re Evans* (1887) 34 Ch D 597, 600; *Jennings v Mather* [1902] 1 KB 1, 5; *General Credits Ltd v Tawilla Pty Ltd* [1984] 1 Qd R 388.

creditor on the first-mentioned debt.[476] Consider, however, that a trustee has entered into a transaction with a third party out of which cross-demands arise which are sufficiently closely connected to give rise to an equitable set-off. In such a case, given that equity in any event has never insisted upon mutuality as a strict requirement for this form of set-off,[477] the apparent lack of mutuality should not be a sufficient ground for denying a set-off to the third party. This was the view of Giles J in the New South Wales Supreme Court in *Murphy v Zamonex Pty Ltd*,[478] and in Victoria the Appeal Division of the Supreme Court in *Doherty v Murphy*[479] accepted in a summary judgment application that a cross-claim for damages against a trustee in this situation provided an arguable defence. Nor was Giles J persuaded to adopt a different view by the argument that the trustee in that case may have lost his right to an indemnity from the trust estate in respect of the liability because it was in breach of trust.[480] The equitable set-off was justified on the ground that the beneficiaries of a trust should not have the benefit of the transaction without also bearing the burden of the trustee's conduct.[481] Moreover, while in both *Murphy v Zamonex* and *Doherty v Murphy* there had been a change in trustee, that did not affect the views expressed. The new trustee takes subject to equities, so that the defendant can assert the set-off notwithstanding that the action is brought by the new trustee.

Abatement

17.91 The fact of a trust similarly should not affect the availability of a common law defence of abatement.[482] This defence applies in an action for the agreed price of goods sold with a warranty or of work to be performed according to a contract. If the goods are delivered in a defective condition or the work is improperly performed, the purchaser on being sued for the price can defend himself by showing how much less the subject-matter of the action was worth by reason of the breach, and can obtain an abatement of the price accordingly. The rationale for the defence should not be affected by the circumstance that either the purchaser or the vendor is a trustee.

Statutes of Set-off, and insolvency set-off

17.92 What if the case is one of unrelated cross-debts, so that the question concerns the Statutes of Set-off or, in the event of a bankruptcy or liquidation, the insolvency set-off section? In the first place, if the trustee is indebted to the third party in his personal capacity as a result of a dealing unrelated to the trust, lack of mutuality

---

[476] Compare the discussion below of the effect of the trustee's right of indemnity. In *Murphy v Zamonex Pty Ltd* (1993) 31 NSWLR 439, 464 Giles J left the question open.

[477] See paras 4.48–4.54 above.

[478] (1993) 31 NSWLR 439.

[479] [1996] 2 VR 553.

[480] (1993) 31 NSWLR 439, 464.

[481] (1993) 31 NSWLR 439, 465, 468.

[482] See paras 2.87–2.97 above.

would preclude a set-off under either the insolvency set-off section[483] or the Statutes of Set-off[484] against a debt held on trust, unless in the case of the Statutes the principle of taking subject to equities applies.[485] Consider however that the trustee incurred the debt in the proper execution of the trust, so that he has a right of indemnity from the trust assets, and at the same time the trustee is a creditor of the third party in respect of a debt which is held on trust for the beneficiaries. In *Nelson v Roberts*[486] the defendant was an executor of an estate, and he had also been appointed receiver and manager. In his capacity as executor he had a claim against one Joseph Grimes. On the other hand, as receiver and manager he incurred a debt to Joseph Grimes. While different representative capacities were involved, in that the claim was held in the capacity of executor and the debt was incurred in the capacity of receiver and manager, they both related to the same estate. Nevertheless, when the defendant was sued for payment of the debt he had incurred as receiver and manager, Mathew and Wright JJ held that he was not entitled to set off the debt due to the estate under the Statutes, notwithstanding that he may have had a right of indemnity from the estate in respect of his indebtedness. It was still his personal liability. Mathew J said that the same principle applies in the case of an executor, an agent and a trustee. However the issue of an indemnity from the estate was not satisfactorily dealt with,[487] and where it is clear in a particular case that the trustee is entitled to be indemnified an argument for a set-off would have merit.

Trustee's lien

A trustee who properly incurs a liability in the execution of the trust is entitled to be indemnified from the trust assets,[488] and for the purpose of giving effect to the indemnity the trustee has an interest which has been described as a first charge or a lien over the assets.[489] This is not a mere right of retainer,[490] but rather courts in Australia have emphasized that it confers an equitable proprietary interest in those

17.93

---

[483] See para 11.04 above.

[484] See para 11.08 above.

[485] See para 17.96 below.

[486] (1893) 69 LT 352. See also *Staniar v Evans* (1886) 34 Ch D 470, 476–477; *Rex v Ray, ex p Chapman* [1936] SASR 241, 249; *Kent v Munroe* (1904) 8 OLR 723.

[487] Mathew J simply commented that: 'It is clear that the debt of the defendant was a personal debt; it may be that the Court of Chancery will say that it was rightly incurred by him as receiver and manager of the estate of John Grimes, but as between himself and Joseph Grimes it was purely personal.' (1893) 69 LT 352.

[488] See the Trustee Act 1925, s 30(2).

[489] *Re Exhall Coal Co Ltd* (1866) 35 Beav 449, 452–453, 55 ER 970, 971; *Re Pumfrey* (1882) 22 Ch D 255, 262; *Stott v Milne* (1884) 25 Ch D 710, 715; *Jennings v Mather* [1902] 1 KB 1, 6, 9; *Re Spurling's Will Trusts* [1966] 1 WLR 920, 930; *Octavo Investments Pty Ltd v Knight* (1979) 144 CLR 360, 367; *Chief Commissioner of Stamp Duties (NSW) v Buckle* (1998) 192 CLR 226, 247. In the *Buckle* case the High Court of Australia held that, while the trustee's right is referred to as a charge, it is not a security interest as such, but rather it confers a beneficial interest in the trust assets which has priority over the interests of the beneficiaries.

[490] The right nevertheless is sometimes discussed in terms of retainer. See eg *Jennings v Mather* [1901] 1 QB 108, 113–114, and on appeal [1902] 1 KB 1, 9.

assets[491] which has priority over the interests of the beneficiaries.[492] In an appropriate case[493] the court may order a sale of trust property in order to satisfy the trustee's claim.[494] The trustee's first charge should extend also to a trust asset in the form of a debt owing to the trustee in his capacity as such. Furthermore, it is not necessary that the trustee should first have paid the debt before claiming against the trust assets.[495] If the trustee has not paid the debt from his personal assets he is entitled to apply the trust property in discharging it, in other words the trustee has a right to exoneration, and he has a charge on the trust property in that circumstance as well.[496] Accordingly, when a trustee is sued by a third party for payment of a debt properly incurred in the execution of the trust, and at the same time the trustee as a result of his right of indemnity has a charge on a debt owing to the estate by the third party, there is much to be said for the view that the trustee's interest may suffice to bring about mutuality in equity[497] for the purpose of equity acting by analogy with the Statutes.[498] This should also be relevant to insolvency set-off.[499] It assumes however that the trustee has a right of indemnity. In a particular case the right may be limited by the trust instrument,[500] or it may be restricted

---

[491] *Octavo Investments Pty Ltd v Knight* (1979) 144 CLR 360, 367, 369–370; *Chief Commissioner of Stamp Duties (NSW) v Buckle* (1998) 192 CLR 226, 246–247. See also *Re Byrne Australia Pty Ltd* [1981] 1 NSWLR 394, 398; *Re Suco Gold Pty Ltd* (1983) 33 SASR 99; *Murphy v Zamonex Pty Ltd* (1993) 31 NSWLR 439, 464; *Re Matheson, ex p Worrell v Matheson* (1994) 49 FCR 454.

[492] Underhill and Hayton, *Law Relating to Trusts and Trustees* (15th edn, 1995) 796–7; *Octavo Investments Pty Ltd v Knight* (1979) 144 CLR 360, 367; *Chief Commissioner of Stamp Duties (NSW) v Buckle* (1998) 192 CLR 226, 246–247. Compare *Re Pumfrey* (1882) 22 Ch D 255, 262, which was criticized in *Re Staff Benefits Pty Ltd* [1979] 1 NSWLR 207, 213–214;

[493] Compare *Darke v Williamson* (1858) 25 Beav 622, 53 ER 774, in which a sale would have had the effect of destroying the trust.

[494] McPherson, 'The Insolvent Trading Trust' in Finn (ed), *Essays in Equity* (1985) 142, 149, referring to *Grissell v Money* (1869) 38 LJ Ch 312 and *Re Pumfrey* (1882) 22 Ch D 255, 261–262; *Chief Commissioner of Stamp Duties (NSW) v Buckle* (1998) 192 CLR 226, 247.

[495] *St Thomas's Hospital v Richardson* [1910] 1 KB 271, 276; *Re Blundell* (1889) 40 Ch D 370, 376–377; *Savage v Union Bank of Australia Ltd* (1906) 3 CLR 1170, 1197; *Re Suco Gold Pty Ltd* (1983) 33 SALR 99, 104–105.

[496] In *St Thomas's Hospital v Richardson* [1910] 1 KB 271, 276 Cozens Hardy MR said that: 'A's [the trustee's] right of indemnity exists before payment . . . In respect of this right of indemnity A has a first charge or lien upon the trust property . . .' See also *Savage v Union Bank of Australia Ltd* (1906) 3 CLR 1170, 1197; *Re Matheson, ex p Worrell v Matheson* (1994) 49 FCR 454; *Chief Commissioner of Stamp Duties (NSW) v Buckle* (1998) 192 CLR 226, 245–247.

[497] See para 11.34 above in relation to an equitable charge.

[498] See para 3.06 above.

[499] *Quaere* if this would explain the set-off in *Re Last, ex p Butterell* (1994) 124 ALR 219, given that Rawilla Pty Ltd was the trustee of a discretionary trust.

[500] See Underhill and Hayton, *Law Relating to Trusts and Trustees* (15th edn, 1995) 788–9. In Queensland it is not possible to exclude the trustee's right of indemnity conferred by the Trustee legislation. See the Trusts Act 1973 (Qld), s 65. In any event, it has been suggested that the trustee's right of indemnity is inseparable from the office of trustee and therefore is incapable of being excluded. See *Kemtron Industries Pty Ltd v Commissioner of Stamp Duties* [1984] 1 Qd R 576, 585, *per* McPherson J; *JA Pty Ltd v Jonco Holdings Pty Ltd* (2000) 33 ACSR 691, 708, 713–714; McPherson, 'The Insolvent Trading Trust' in Finn (ed), *Essays in Equity* (1985) 142, 149–150. Compare *RWG Management Ltd v Commissioner for Corporate Affairs* [1985] VR 385, 395.

to certain assets, as where a testator has authorized the executor to carry on a business but only by utilizing those assets.[501] Moreover, an executor or an administrator of a deceased person who carries on the deceased's business other than for the purpose of its realization or winding up may not be entitled to an indemnity at the expense of creditors of the deceased, unless those creditors had authorized the executor or the administrator to carry it on.[502] Authority in the testator's will is not sufficient in that regard.[503] Further, the trustee may be in default or otherwise may have an obligation to contribute to the trust fund, so that the right to an indemnity out of the trust fund is subject to the principle in *Cherry v Boultbee.*[504] It has been suggested in Australia that a breach of trust will only debar the trustee from indemnity if the breach is related to the subject matter of the indemnity.[505] However the principle underlying *Cherry v Boultbee*, that the person entitled to participate in the fund already has an asset of the fund in his hands in the form of the obligation to contribute which should be appropriated in satisfaction of the right to participate,[506] would appear to be equally relevant when the breach is unrelated to the subject matter of the indemnity.[507] Indeed, the contrary view does not sit comfortably with *Re Johnson,*[508] in so far as the right of indemnity in that case for debts incurred in running the Cambridge business was affected by the failure of the trustee to account for amounts in relation to the London business.

---

[501] *Ex parte Garland* (1803) 10 Ves Jun 110, 32 ER 786.

[502] *Dowse v Gorton* [1891] AC 190. Compare *Re Oxley* [1914] 1 Ch 604, and *Vacuum Oil Co Pty Ltd v Wiltshire* (1945) 72 CLR 319.

[503] *Vacuum Oil Co Pty Ltd v Wiltshire* (1945) 72 CLR 319, 335.

[504] (1839) 4 My & Cr 442, 41 ER 171. See ch 14 above. In particular, see *Re Johnson* (1880) 15 Ch D 548; *Re Evans* (1887) 34 Ch D 597, 601–602; *Re British Power Traction and Lighting Co Ltd* [1910] 2 Ch 470; *RWG Management Ltd v Commissioner for Corporate Affairs* [1985] VR 385, 397–399.

[505] *Re Staff Benefits Pty Ltd* [1979] 1 NSWLR 207, 214, and see also the comment by Giles J in *Murphy v Zamonex Pty Ltd* (1993) 31 NSWLR 439, 464 regarding a 'breach of trust related to the indemnity'.

[506] See para 14.03 above, and also in this context *Re British Power Traction and Lighting Co Ltd* [1910] 2 Ch 470, 475. On this formulation of the principle, it is not accurate to say that the trustee loses or is deprived of his right of indemnity. Compare *Re Staff Benefits* [1979] 1 NSWLR 207, 214, and *Jacobs' Law of Trusts in Australia* (6th edn, 1997) 631. Rather, he is required to satisfy it from a particular source. Thus, if the trustee's claim for an indemnity exceeds the amount due from the trustee by way of compensation, it has been said that the trustee may recover from the estate to the extent of the balance without first having to bring into the estate the whole of the amount for which he is liable. See *RWG Management Ltd v Commissioner for Corporate Affairs* [1985] VR 385, 397–398, criticizing statements suggesting the contrary in *Re Frith* [1902] 1 Ch 342, 346. However compare *Staniar v Evans* (1886) 34 Ch D 470. See para 14.12 above.

[507] See, for example, the formulation of the principle in *Jennings v Mather* [1902] 1 KB 1, 5 and *RWG Management Ltd v Commissioner for Corporate Affairs* [1985] VR 385, 398. See also para 14.70 above.

[508] (1880) 15 Ch D 548. See also *General Credits Ltd v Tawilla Pty Ltd* [1984] 1 Qd R 388, 389–390.

Subrogation

17.94 Where there are other trust creditors, an additional issue is whether the subrogation rights of those creditors would prevent mutuality in equity. A creditor whose debt was properly incurred in the execution of the trust is entitled to be subrogated to the trustee's right of indemnity from the trust assets, as well as to the charge consequent upon that right,[509] so as to give the creditor an indirect claim against the assets. The circumstances in which the subrogation right may be enforced remain unclear, however.[510] A creditor may enforce the right if the estate is under the administration of the court,[511] or if the trustee is bankrupt.[512] The judgment of Byrne J in *Re Raybould*[513] suggests that the court in other circumstances may order that a trust creditor can claim directly against the trust estate, but in that case the creditor seeking the order may have been the sole trust creditor,[514] and moreover the trustee supported the creditor's claim to be paid directly out of the estate. If that approach is to be adopted generally, it may be a requirement that other trust creditors are not prejudiced.[515] In Australia it has been suggested that it is no longer necessary to have a full administration suit before a creditor can be paid out of the assets of a trust, but it was also said that in such a case there should be reliable evidence establishing that the judgment debt was a liability properly incurred by the trustee, and that the trustee has an unqualified right to be indemnified out of the trust assets in priority to the claims of beneficiaries and perhaps of other trust creditors.[516] This in turn raises the issue of *Cherry v Boultbee*, which was referred to above. If however the trustee is solvent, so that judgment at law against the trustee would not be fruitless, the traditional view is that a trust creditor should proceed against the trustee personally rather than have recourse to the trust assets by means of the right of subrogation.[517] In light of these principles, how would the subrogation rights of other trust creditors affect the availability of a set-off to the third party? Trust creditors are not

---

[509] *Re Johnson* (1880) 15 Ch D 548, 552; *Re Blundell* (1890) 44 Ch D 1, 11; *Vacuum Oil Co Pty Ltd v Wiltshire* (1945) 72 CLR 319, 335–336.

[510] See generally Ford and Lee, *Principles of the Law of Trusts* (3rd edn, 1996) para 14080, and McPherson, 'The Insolvent Trading Trust' in Finn (ed), *Essays in Equity* (1985) 142, 151.

[511] See eg *Re Evans* (1887) 34 Ch D 597 and *Re Frith* [1902] 1 Ch 342.

[512] *Octavo Investments Pty Ltd v Knight* (1979) 144 CLR 360, 367.

[513] [1900] 1 Ch 199.

[514] See McPherson, 'The Insolvent Trading Trust' in Finn (ed), *Essays in Equity* (1985) 142, 151.

[515] *Jacobs' Law of Trusts in Australia* (6th edn, 1997) 639. This may require that the claims of other creditors be before the court. See Mitchell, *The Law of Subrogation* (1994) 156.

[516] *General Credits Ltd v Tawilla Pty Ltd* [1984] 1 Qd R 388, 390, and see also Ford and Lee, *Principles of the Law of Trusts* (3rd edn, 1996) para 14080.

[517] *Owen v Delamere* (1872) LR 15 Eq 134; *Re Morris* (1889) 23 LR Ir 333; Underhill and Hayton, *Law Relating to Trusts and Trustees* (15th edn, 1995) 802. See also *Murphy v Zamonex Pty Ltd* (1993) 31 NSWLR 439, 464. It is not necessary, however, that the trust creditor should pursue his common law claim against the trustee to judgment if the circumstances are such as to lead to the reasonable inference that a judgment would be fruitless. See *Re Wilson* [1942] VLR 177, 183.

equitable assignees or chargees of the assets the subject of the trustee's right of indemnity,[518] and the fact that there are other trust creditors apart from the third party prima facie should not be a sufficient reason for denying a set-off as between the trustee and the third party. On the other hand, the point has been made that the trustee's equitable charge to which a subrogation claim relates is available for the benefit of all trust creditors, and the consequence of allowing a particular trust creditor to enforce it may be to give him an advantage over other creditor.[519] If in the situation posited the third party as a trust creditor could look upon the charge that the trustee has over the particular trust asset represented by his own liability to the trustee as sufficient to bring about mutuality as between that liability and the debt in respect of which he is a trust creditor, the third party through a set-off may obtain an advantage over other trust creditors, particularly if the trustee is insolvent. If that would be the case, and if other trust creditors have an enforceable right of subrogation, the indirect interest that they have as a result of subrogation may suffice to prevent mutuality in equity arising. The approach of the courts to the issue has yet to emerge, however.

Debt owing to the trustee in his personal capacity

Given that a trustee who incurs a debt in that capacity is personally liable, there **17.95** should be mutuality as between that debt and a cross-debt owing by the creditor to the trustee in the trustee's personal capacity.[520]

(2) Taking Subject to Equities

The third party may not have been aware that he was dealing with a person who **17.96** was a trustee. Notwithstanding that the beneficiaries have the equitable title to a debt which accrues to the trustee as a result of the dealing, the beneficiaries should take subject to equities available to the third party against the trustee on the same basis described earlier in the context of assignments.[521] This should apply whether or not the cross-debt owing by the trustee was incurred in his private capacity or in his capacity as trustee. The general principle applicable to taking subject to equities is that, when there are unconnected cross-debts, the debts must have arisen before the third party had notice of the trust,[522] although there is no such requirement when a substantive defence of equitable set-off is in issue.[523]

---

[518] McPherson, 'The Insolvent Trading Trust' in Finn (ed), *Essays in Equity* (1985) 142, 156; *Staniar v Evans* (1886) 34 Ch D 470, 477. Compare *Napier v Hunter* [1993] AC 713, 736, 738 in relation to insurance subrogation.

[519] McPherson, 'The Insolvent Trading Trust' in Finn (ed), *Essays in Equity* (1985)142, 151. See also *Jacobs' Law of Trusts in Australia* (6th edn, 1997) 639.

[520] *Daniels v Imperial Bank of Canada* (1914) 19 DLR 166.

[521] See paras 17.02–17.72 above.

[522] See para 17.10 above.

[523] See para 17.22 above.

(3) Receipt of Trust Moneys in Breach of Trust

17.97 The application of the principle of taking subject to equities assumes that the beneficiary's entitlement is to a beneficial interest in a debt which at law is owing to the trustee. Alternatively, a beneficiary may claim that another has knowingly received trust moneys in circumstances where the trustee paid the moneys to the recipient in breach of trust.[524] The beneficiary in that circumstance may assert an equitable tracing claim to recover the moneys. This gives rise to a proprietary remedy to recover trust property, and it cannot be the subject of a set-off.[525] But even if the moneys are no longer traceable so as to preclude a proprietary remedy, and the beneficiary's claim instead is that the recipient has a personal liability as a constructive trustee on the basis of knowing receipt of trust property,[526] the recipient could not assert a set-off in respect of a separate debt owing to him by the trustee. The principle that a beneficiary takes subject to equities available against the trustee is based on the notion that there is mutuality at law as between the debt held on trust and the cross-debt owing by the trustee, and the question is whether it is unconscionable for the debtor to rely on this defence at law, given the trust.[527] However, when a recipient of trust money has a personal liability as a constructive trustee to the beneficiary on the basis of knowing receipt, there is not mutuality either at law or in equity in relation to that liability and a debt owing by the trustee to the recipient. This should also be the case when the basis of liability as a constructive trustee is as an accessory to a breach of trust.[528] It is only when the beneficiary's claim is based on an equitable interest in a debt owing by the third party to the trustee that the principle of taking subject to equities becomes relevant. In some cases this may be the position when a trustee pays trust money to a third party in breach of trust under circumstances where the third party as a result is indebted to the trustee. If the beneficiary acquiesced in the breach, an equitable proprietary remedy would not be available to him, and nor would the third party be personally liable to the beneficiary as a constructive trustee.[529]

---

[524] A similar question may arise in the context of combination of bank accounts, when a trustee has deposited trust moneys into an account with a bank and the bank asserts that the account may be regarded as combined with the trustee's personal overdrawn account. See paras 15.81–15.112 above.

[525] See ch 10 above.

[526] See generally *Snell's Equity* (30th edn, 2000) 223–4.

[527] See para 17.03 above in relation to assignments.

[528] See *Royal Brunei Airlines Sbd Bhd v Tan* [1995] 2 AC 378 and *Twinsectra Ltd v Yardley* [2002] 2 AC 164

[529] *Target Holdings Ltd v Redferns* [1996] AC 421, 433, and see *Snell's Equity* (30th edn, 2000) 341 (referring to *Blake v Gale* (1886) 32 Ch D 571) in relation to tracing. Acquiesence is used in the sense described by Lord Cottenham in *Duke of Leeds v Earl of Amherst* (1846) 2 Ph 117, 123, 41 ER 886, 888, that: 'If a party, having a right, stands by and sees another dealing with the property in a manner inconsistent with that right, and makes no objection while the act is in progress, he cannot afterwards complain.'

(4) Set-off Between a Beneficiary and a Third Party

Beneficiary has a personal claim against a trust creditor

When a debt accrues to a trustee in his capacity as such the debt belongs in equity **17.98** to the beneficiaries, while a debt incurred by the trustee is his own personal liability. A trustee who has incurred a debt in the proper performance of his duties as trustee is entitled to apply the trust assets in discharge of the debt, and to that end he has a first charge or lien on the trust assets which has priority over the interests of the beneficiaries.[530] It was suggested earlier that this interest may justify a set-off in relation to that debt, for which the trustee otherwise is personally liable, and a cross-claim possessed by the trustee against the creditor in the trustee's capacity as such.[531] This avenue for a set-off would not be available, however, when a beneficiary's claim against a trust creditor against which the trust creditor wishes to assert a set-off arose out of a dealing unrelated to the trust, so that it is not trust property over which the trustee has a charge. Prima facie the trustee's personal liability to the creditor and the beneficiary's separate claim against the creditor would not be mutual. It may nevertheless be possible in that circumstance to support a set-off on the basis of the trustee's right to an indemnity from the beneficiary personally.

A beneficiary who is sui juris and absolutely entitled ordinarily is personally liable **17.99** to indemnify the trustee against debts properly incurred in the execution of the trust.[532] This applies also while the debt is still outstanding, so that the trustee is entitled to be exonerated by the beneficiary. Furthermore, Underhill suggests that the right of indemnity against the beneficiaries personally should be the subject of the same right of subrogation as subsists in respect of the trustee's right of indemnity out of the trust property,[533] and indeed there is authority to that effect in Australia.[534] It is probably also subject to restrictions similar to those applicable in the case of a trustee's right of indemnity from the trust assets, for example that the trustee should be insolvent or the circumstances otherwise should be such as to

---

[530] See para 17.93 above.

[531] See para 17.93 above.

[532] Underhill and Hayton, *Law Relating to Trusts and Trustees* (15th edn, 1995) 787–8, 798–800. This applies not only in the case of a sole beneficiary (see *Hardoon v Belilios* [1901] AC 118), but also where there are a number of beneficiaries who between them are absolutely entitled and sui juris. See Underhill and Hayton, *op cit* 788, 800; *Balkin v Peck* (1998) 43 NSWLR 706; *Hurst v Bryk* [1999] Ch 1, 14–15; *Ron Kingham Real Estate Pty Ltd v Edgar* [1999] 2 Qd R 439. The indemnity obligation is in proportion to their beneficial interests. See *Matthews v Ruggles-Brise* [1911] 1 Ch 194. A trustee's right to indemnity from the beneficiaries personally can be excluded by the trust instrument. See *Hardoon v Belilios* at 127; *RWG Management Ltd v Commissioner for Corporate Affairs* [1985] VR 385, 394.

[533] Underhill and Hayton, *Law Relating to Trusts and Trustees* (15th edn, 1995) 799, and see para 17.94 above. See also *Re Richardson* [1911] 2 KB 705.

[534] *Ron Kingham Real Estate Pty Ltd v Edgar* [1999] 2 Qd R 439; *Belar Pty Ltd v Mahaffey* [2000] 1 Qd R 477, 487. See also Ford and Lee, *Principles of the Law of Trusts* (3rd edn, 1996) para 14090.

suggest that judgment against the trustee would be pointless.[535] If a trust creditor is entitled to be subrogated to the trustee's claim for an indemnity against a beneficiary, it would open the possibility of a set-off against the beneficiary's cross-claim against the trust creditor. A difficulty is that, when a third party as a trust creditor is subrogated to the trustee's claim for an indemnity from a beneficiary, the trustee does not hold the claim on trust for the third party. This is apparent when one considers the position in the event that the trustee becomes bankrupt. In that circumstance the benefit of the trustee's claim for an indemnity passes to the trustee in bankruptcy,[536] whereas if it were trust property that would not be the case. The trustee in bankruptcy admittedly would be required to apply the proceeds received from the beneficiary in reduction only of the trust debts, as opposed to all debts provable in the trustee's bankruptcy,[537] but that is because the trustee is not permitted to profit from the trust, which would occur if the proceeds of the indemnity were used to pay his personal creditors.[538] If there is more than one trust creditor, the proceeds received by the trustee in bankruptcy would be divisible amongst all trust creditors.[539] In relation to the question of set-off, because the claim for an indemnity that the trustee has against the beneficiary is not held on trust for the third party, there is not mutuality in a strict sense as between that claim and the debt owing by the third party to the beneficiary. Nevertheless, when there is an enforceable right of subrogation and there are no other trust creditors,[540] so that no one other than the third party would benefit in any event from proceeds of the indemnity received from the beneficiary, there is much to be said for the view that a set-off should be permitted in equity notwithstanding the absence of strict mutuality.[541]

Beneficiary personally liable to a trust debtor

17.100 There is also the possibility of a set-off in the converse situation, of a debt owing by a third party to the trustee in that capacity and a cross-debt owing by the bene-

---

[535] Underhill and Hayton, *Law Relating to Trusts and Trustees* (15th edn, 1995) 802, and see para 17.94 above.

[536] *Re Richardson* [1911] 2 KB 705, 715, *per* Buckley LJ.

[537] *Re Richardson* [1911] 2 KB 705.

[538] *Re Richardson* [1911] 2 KB 705, 711, *per* Cozens-Hardy MR; *Re Suco Gold Pty Ltd* (1983) 33 SASR 99 (esp at 106–107); Ford, 'Trading Trusts and Creditors' Rights' (1981) 13 Melbourne University Law Review 1, 20.

[539] Ford and Lee, *Principles of the Law of Trusts* (3rd edn, 1996) para 14090, and see also, with respect to the indemnity from the trust estate, *Re Byrne Australia Pty Ltd* [1981] 1 NSWLR 394, 399; *Re Suco Gold Pty Ltd* (1983) 33 SASR 79, 109, 111; *Re ADM Franchise Pty Ltd* (1983) 7 ACLR 987, 988–989; *Re Matheson* (1994) 49 FCR 454. In Victoria, on the other hand, the right of indemnity has been said to be an asset available for distribution amongst creditors generally, and not just trust creditors. See *Re Enhill Pty Ltd* [1983] VR 561, and also *Young v Murphy* [1996] 1 VR 279, 303.

[540] This appears to have been the case in *Re Richardson* [1911] 2 KB 705.

[541] Mutuality is not an indispensable requirement of equitable set-off. See paras 4.48–4.54 above.

ficiary to the third party on another account. The beneficiary is personally liable on his separate debt and at the same time may have a sufficient equitable interest in the debt held on trust so as to bring about mutuality in equity, and therefore to justify an equitable set-off by analogy with the Statutes.[542] For a set-off to occur, however, the beneficiary's interest in the trust should be such that he has an interest in possession in the debt as trust property, in the sense that he has a present right to claim the benefit of the debt.[543] This does not describe the entitlement of a residuary legatee under a will or a person entitled under an intestacy where the administration of the estate has not been completed.[544] Prior to completion of the administration the legatee or the person entitled does not have a beneficial interest in the assets of the trust. Rather, the legatee or the person only has an equitable chose in action to have the estate properly administered.[545] An object of a discretionary trust is in a similar position.[546] Furthermore, the beneficiary must be the sole party beneficially interested in the debt, unless, if the debt is held on trust for two or more beneficiaries, those beneficiaries are also jointly liable to the debtor. This is necessary in order to satisfy the requirement of mutuality. It has been suggested that a set-off in this circumstance will not be permitted unless the beneficiary's interest in the debt is clear and ascertained without inquiry.[547] This concept was considered earlier.[548]

A trustee who properly incurs costs and expenses in the administration of the trust **17.101** is entitled to be indemnified from the trust assets,[549] and for the purpose of enforcing the indemnity the trustee has a charge or lien over the assets.[550] The trust assets may include a debt held on trust by the trustee. While the charge may be thought to have the effect of destroying mutuality as between that debt and a cross-debt owing to the debtor by the beneficiary otherwise entitled under the trust to the benefit of the first-mentioned debt, the better view is that a set-off nevertheless may still occur as between those parties if the trustee's position, and

---

[542] *Bankes v Jarvis* [1903] 1 KB 549, 552.

[543] See *Gartside v IRC* [1968] AC 553, 607.

[544] *Bishop v Church* (1748) 3 Atk 691, 26 ER 1197; *Ex parte Morier, re Willis, Percival & Co* (1879) 12 Ch D 491; *Phillips v Howell* [1901] 2 Ch 773.

[545] *Commissioner of Stamp Duties (Queensland) v Livingston* [1965] AC 694. This applies equally in the case of a specific bequest. See *Official Receiver in Bankruptcy v Schultz* (1990) 170 CLR 306, 312.

[546] *Gartside v IRC* [1968] AC 553; *Chief Commissioner of Stamp Duties v ISPT Pty Ltd* (1998) 45 NSWLR 639, 655.

[547] Wood, *English and International Set-off* (1989) 779–80.

[548] See paras 11.11–11.23 above.

[549] The right of indemnity is restricted however when a testator has authorized the trustee to carry on a business though only by utilizing a certain part of the estate. See *Ex parte Garland* (1803) 10 Ves Jun 110, 32 ER 786.

[550] *Stott v Milne* (1884) 25 Ch D 710; *Re Spurling's Will Trusts* [1966] 1 WLR 920, 930; *Octavo Investments Pty Ltd v Knight* (1979) 144 CLR 360, 367.

that of other trust creditors who are subrogated to the trustee's right, is otherwise sufficiently secured.[551]

(5) Set-off Between Trustee and Beneficiary

17.102 There may be cross-claims between a trustee and a beneficiary, for example when the trustee is entitled to an indemnity from the beneficiary personally and at the same time is liable to the beneficiary on another account. The availability of a set-off in such a case should be determined according to normal principles. The beneficiary's claim may be for payment of the trust fund itself. Issues of set-off in that context were considered earlier.[552] Alternatively, the beneficiary's liability may not be to the trustee personally, but may take the form of an obligation to contribute to the trust fund. The question in that situation is whether the principle in *Cherry v Boultbee*[553] applies.

F. Execution of Judgments

(1) Introduction

17.103 Consider that a creditor has obtained judgment against the debtor, which the debtor has failed to satisfy, and the creditor accordingly wants to enforce the judgement against the debtor's assets. If one of the assets is a debt owing to the judgment debtor by a third party, and the judgment creditor obtains an order for the enforcement of the judgment against that asset, the question may arise whether the third party can set off a cross-claim that he has against the judgment debtor. The principal method of enforcing a judgment by attaching a debt owing to the judgment debtor is a garnishee order, although a charging order and the appointment of a receiver by way of equitable execution may also be relevant. The effect of each of these is considered below.

(2) Garnishee Orders

17.104 The procedure for obtaining a garnishee order is set out in RSC O 49. Where a judgment creditor has obtained a judgment or order for payment of a sum of money amounting in value to at least £50, and another person within the jurisdiction (the 'garnishee') is indebted to the judgment debtor, the court may order the garnishee to pay the judgment creditor the amount of the debt due or accruing due from the garnishee to the judgment debtor, or so much of it as is sufficient to satisfy the judgment. In the first instance the judgment creditor obtains an

---

[551] See paras 11.27–11.29 above. This is consistent with comments by McPherson J in *Kemtron Industries Pty Ltd v Commissioner of Stamp Duties* [1984] 1 Qd R 576, 587.
[552] See ch 10 above.
[553] (1839) 4 My & Cr 442, 41 ER 171. See ch 14 above.

order nisi, which must be served personally on the garnishee. This is an order to show cause, and it specifies the time and the place for further consideration of the matter. The debt is attached in the hands of the garnishee as from the time of service of the order.[554] When the matter comes on for further consideration the order may be made absolute.

Attachment only relates to a debt which is due or accruing due. There is a considerable body of case law as to what this encompasses, for which reference should be made to specialist texts on the subject. One thing that is clear, however, is that it is not confined to debts which are presently payable. A debt which is presently existing but not payable until a future day may be attached,[555] although the garnishee cannot be required to pay before the contract date.[556] **17.105**

While it is generally agreed that service of a garnishee order does not operate as a transfer of the property in the debt,[557] there is a solid body of judicial opinion to the effect that it gives rise to an equitable charge.[558] The notion that there is a charge is not universally accepted,[559] however, and indeed it does not sit easily with the view that the holder of a floating security granted by a judgment debtor has priority over a judgment creditor with a garnishee order where crystallization occurs after the order absolute but before payment by the garnishee.[560] If the garnishee has a substantive defence of equitable set-off available against the judgment debtor, the nature of the judgment creditor's right as a result of the garnishee order should be immaterial. The judgment debtor's title to sue the garnishee is impeached,[561] and the judgment creditor cannot obtain a better title.[562] Similarly, the precise characterization of the nature of the right should not be crucial to the **17.106**

---

[554] RSC O 49 r 3(2).

[555] *Tapp v Jones* (1875) LR 10 QB 591; *Webb v Stenton* (1883) 11 QBD 518, 522–3; *O'Driscoll v Manchester Insurance Committee* [1915] 3 KB 499, 516–7; *Joachimson v Swiss Bank Corp* [1921] 3 KB 110, 131.

[556] *Tapp v Jones* (1875) LR 10 QB 591.

[557] *Re Combined Weighing and Advertising Machine Co* (1889) 43 Ch D 99; *Norton v Yates* [1906] 1 KB 112.

[558] *Emanuel v Bridger* (1874) LR 9 QB 286, 291; *Galbraith v Grimshaw and Baxter* [1910] 1 KB 339, 343 (decision affirmed [1910] AC 508); *Joachimson v Swiss Bank Corp* [1921] 3 KB 110, 131; *Plunkett v Barclays Bank Ltd* (1936) 52 TLR 353; *Re Caribbean Products (Yam Importers) Ltd* [1966] 1 Ch 331, 343, 350, 353; *Choice Investments Ltd v Jeromninon* [1981] 1 QB 149, 155, CA; *Commissioner of Taxation v Donnelly* (1989) 25 FCR 432, 456. In *Re Combined Weighing and Advertising Machine Co* (1889) 43 Ch D 99, 104 Cotton LJ described it as a lien.

[559] See Lightman and Moss, *The Law of Receivers and Administrators of Companies* (3rd edn, 2000) 320 para 17–002, 322 para 17–006; Picarda, *The Law Relating to Receivers, Managers and Administrators* (3rd edn, 2000) 196; *Hall v Richards* (1961) 108 CLR 84, 92, *per* Kitto J; *Clyne v Deputy Commissioner of Taxation* (1981) 150 CLR 1, 27, *per* Brennan J; *Blacktown Concrete Services Pty Ltd v Ultra Refurbishing and Construction Pty Ltd* (1998) 43 NSWLR 484; *Macquarie Health Corp Ltd v Commissioner of Taxation* (1999) 96 FCR 238, 258, 267.

[560] *Cairney v Back* [1906] 2 KB 746.

[561] *Rawson v Samuel* (1841) Cr & Ph 161, 179, 41 ER 451, 458. See para 4.02 above.

[562] *Hale v Victoria Plumbing Co Ltd* [1966] 2 QB 746.

question whether a judgment creditor takes subject to a defence of set-off under the Statutes of Set-off in the case of mutual debts as between the judgment debtor and the garnishee. The relevant question is not so much what rights have priority according to the law of set-off, but rather the circumstances in which the court in its discretion will make a garnishee order absolute. The Statutes of Set-off strictly have no application in any event in garnishee proceedings. They provide a defence to an action at law for payment of a debt[563] whereas, when a garnishee order is made absolute, the judgment creditor may proceed directly to execution without the necessity of bringing a separate action on the order. If the judgment creditor brings an action when there is no necessity to do so, he runs the risk of having it stayed as an abuse of the process of the court.[564] RSC O 49 r 1 provides that the court 'may' order the garnishee to pay the judgment creditor. The making of a garnishee order is discretionary,[565] and the question is under what circumstances the court will make an order notwithstanding that the garnishee has a cross-claim against the judgment debtor. The principle which the courts have applied is analogous to that which governs assignments.[566] In other words, the judgment creditor takes subject to equities available to the garnishee against the judgment debtor before service of the order nisi,[567] equities in this sense including rights of set-off, whether equitable or contractual[568] or under the Statutes of Set-off, as discussed in the context of assignments.[569] Thus, when there is a cross-debt owing by the judgment debtor to the garnishee at the time that the order nisi is served on the garnishee, the judgment creditor takes subject to a right of set-off that the garnishee otherwise would have had in an action at law under the Statutes of Set-off,[570] even though a garnishee order generally does not result in an action. On the other hand, the garnishee does not take subject to a set-off where the cross-debt arose after service of the order nisi.[571] In the case of an assignment, the courts have denied a set-off against an assignee in relation to a cross-debt accruing after

---

[563] See paras 2.33–2.48 above.

[564] Compare *Pritchett v English and Colonial Syndicate* [1899] 2 QB 428.

[565] *Martin v Nadel* [1906] 2 KB 26.

[566] In addition to the cases referred to below, see *Wolfe v Marshall* [1997] EWCA Civ 1329 at para 8.

[567] *Norton v Yates* [1906] 1 KB 112, 121. See also *Re Stanhope Silkstone Collieries Co* (1879) 11 Ch D 160; *Blacktown Concrete Services Pty Ltd v Ultra Refurbishing and Construction Pty Ltd* (1998) 43 NSWLR 484, 495.

[568] As in *Rymill v Wandsworth District Board* (1883) Cab & El 92, and see also *Hutt v Shaw* (1887) 3 TLR 354.

[569] See paras 17.02–17.72 above.

[570] *Tapp v Jones* (1875) LR 10 QB 591, 593, 594. See also *Sampson v Seaton and Beer Railway Co* (1874) LR 10 QB 28, 30; *Bishop v Woinarski* (1875) 1 VLR (L) 31; *Rymill v The Wandsworth District Board* (1883) Cab & El 92 (set-off agreement). Compare *Fitt v Bryant* (1883) Cab & El 194, in which the debt attached, to the knowledge of the garnishee, was held by the judgment debtor on trust for the judgment creditor.

[571] *Tapp v Jones* (1875) LR 10 QB 591, 593.

notice even when the cross-debt had its source in a prior contract.[572] But notwithstanding the position adopted in relation to assignments, there is much to be said
for the view that the court in its discretion should not make a garnishee order absolute where the judgment debtor became indebted to the garnishee after service
of the order nisi but before the order absolute if the debt had its source in a prior
transaction. Nor should it be an objection to a substantive equitable set-off that
the cross-demand arose after notice.[573]

Cross-debt payable at a future date

It may be that the cross-debt is in existence at the date of service of the order nisi, **17.107**
but that it is not payable until a future date. In order to give rise to a set-off under
the Statutes of Set-off, the cross-debt must be due and payable when the defence
is filed.[574] A judgment creditor may proceed directly to execution against the garnishee without bringing an action, so that the question of filing a defence does not
arise, but an analogous principle should apply. When a garnishee asserts that there
is a set-off available to him under the Statutes of Set-off against the attached debt,
the cross-debt should not only be in existence at the date of the order nisi, but it
should also be presently payable when the order absolute is made, because at that
point payment is to be made. If the attached debt itself is not payable at that date,
it is suggested that the cross-debt should be presently payable before the attached
debt becomes payable.[575]

Trust money

In *Stumore v Campbell & Co*[576] the judgment creditor sought to attach money **17.108**
which the garnishee held on trust for the judgment debtor. A sum held on trust is
an equitable debt which may be attached,[577] but generally it cannot be the subject
of a set-off.[578] In *Stumore v Campbell* the garnishee accordingly was required to account for the trust money without deduction in respect of a debt owing to him by
the judgment debtor.

Debt owing by the judgment creditor

RSC O 49 r 5 provides a mechanism for determining a dispute by the garnishee **17.109**
as to his liability to the judgment debtor.[579] There is no machinery however for

---

[572] See para 17.12 above.
[573] See para 17.22 above.
[574] See paras 2.29–2.31 above.
[575] See also para 17.11 above in relation to assignments.
[576] [1892] 1 QB 314.
[577] *Webb v Stenton* (1883) 11 QBD 518, 526.
[578] See ch 10 above.
[579] RSC O 49, r 5.

determining the state of the account as between the garnishee and the judgment creditor, and accordingly a garnishee cannot set off a debt owing to him by the judgment creditor,[580] at least where the garnishee has not yet proceeded to judgment. The courts have power to set off judgments and orders as part of their inherent jurisdiction,[581] and if the garnishee already has a judgment or an order (for example, for costs) against the judgment creditor, it should be able to be set off against the amount payable under the garnishee order.[582]

Insolvency

17.110 If a bankruptcy petition is pending against the judgment debtor or if the debtor has been adjudged bankrupt, the court may stay execution or other legal process against the property or person of the debtor,[583] and similarly after the bankruptcy order a person who is a creditor in respect of a provable debt has no remedy against the property or person of the bankrupt.[584] Further, the Insolvency Act 1986, section 346 provides that, where a creditor of a person who is adjudged bankrupt has, before the commencement of the bankruptcy,[585] attached a debt[586] due to the person from a third party, the creditor is not entitled as against the official receiver or trustee of the bankrupt's estate to retain the benefit of the attachment[587] unless it was completed before the commencement of the bankruptcy. Similar principles apply in the case of a company liquidation.[588] The Act stipulates that an attachment is completed by receipt of the debt,[589] by which is meant receipt of the proceeds.[590]

17.111 Section 346 is not confined to attachment of debts, but extends to other forms of execution against the goods or land of the bankrupt. A creditor is not entitled to

---

[580] *Sampson v Seaton and Beer Railway Co* (1874) LR 10 QB 28.

[581] See paras 2.78–2.86 above.

[582] See *Walters v D Miles-Griffiths, Piercy & Co* (1964) 108 Sol Jo 561 in relation to the solicitors' costs of the appeal.

[583] Insolvency Act 1986, s. 285(1).

[584] Insolvency Act 1986, s 285(3). This is expressed to be subject, however, to ss 346 (enforcement procedures) and 347 (limited right to distress).

[585] A bankruptcy commences on the date on which the order is made. See the Insolvency Act 1986, s 278.

[586] Attachment is not defined in the Insolvency legislation, although it was said in relation to the equivalent provision in the Bankruptcy Act 1914 (s 40) that it is not a term of art. See *Re Lupkovics* [1954] 1 WLR 1234, 1241. In Australia the Federal Court held in *Commissioner of Taxation v Donnelly* (1989) 25 FCR 432 that attachment in the context of s 118 of the Bankruptcy Act 1966 (which in its terms is similar to s 346 of the English Insolvency Act) means attachment by curial order, and it did not include a notice under s 218 of the Income Tax Assessment Act 1936 (Cth).

[587] For a discussion of the meaning of this expression, see *Re Caribbean Products (Yam Importers) Ltd* [1966] 1 Ch 331.

[588] Insolvency Act 1986, ss 126, 130 and 183. The commencement of a winding up is defined in s 129.

[589] Insolvency Act 1986, s 346(5)(c), and, for companies, s 183(3)(b).

[590] *George v Tompson's Trustee* [1949] 1 Ch 322.

retain the benefit of the execution as against the trustee in bankruptcy unless the execution was completed before the bankruptcy. The corresponding provision in Australia differs from section 346 in that it captures executions which occurred six months before the bankruptcy. Where a creditor has issued execution against the property of a debtor within six months before the presentation of a petition against the debtor, and the debtor becomes bankrupt, the creditor must pay to the trustee an amount equal to the amount received by the creditor as a result of the execution. The creditor may then prove in the bankruptcy for his debt as an unsecured creditor as if the execution had not taken place.[591] There is a similar provision in the Corporations Act 2001 (Cth), section 569 in the context of company liquidation.[592]

The application of an earlier equivalent of section 569 in Australia produced an **17.112** unjust result in the circumstances in issue in *Findlay v Trevor*.[593] The owner of a farm, A, mortgaged it to B to secure a debt owing to B. In addition, B leased the farm from A. B breached the lease, as a result of which the lease was terminated and A sued B for damages. After A recovered judgment a writ of *fi fa* was issued against B's asset in the form of the mortgage. The mortgage was offered for sale by the sheriff at a public auction, and A was the successful bidder. It was then agreed that the purchase price payable by A to B should be set off against the amount of the judgment debt owing by B, and that only the balance should be payable to B. This was a convenient course of action to adopt, but some two months later B went into insolvent liquidation, whereupon the liquidator challenged the arrangement. The Supreme Court of Western Australia[594] held that A had received an amount as a result of an execution issued within six months of B's liquidation, the reference to 'the amount . . . received' in the section being held to include satisfaction of a debt by way of set-off. As a result, A had to pay to the liquidator the amount of B's liability received in this manner, with a resulting right of proof in the liquidation for the amount paid. This seems unjust because, if A had not issued execution, the mortgage debt and the judgment debt would have been set off in the liquidation. The problem is that the legislation does not give the judge a discretion in the matter. Indeed, if there was a second debt owing by B to A, it would appear that this debt could not have been set off against A's obligation to account to the liquidator. The demands in such a case would not have been mutual, since the amount payable to the liquidator would have been payable to him in his own right as liquidator, and not because it was payable to B before the

---

[591] Bankruptcy Act 1966 (Cth), s 118.
[592] The company liquidation and bankruptcy provisions are not identical. See *Findlay v Trevor* (1993) 11 ACLC 483, 488.
[593] (1993) 11 ACLC 483. The provision in issue was the Companies (Western Australia) Code, s 455(1), which was in the same terms as the Corporations Act 2001 (Cth), s 569(1).
[594] Malcolm CJ and Murray J, Pidgeon J dissenting on this point.

liquidation.[595] Moreover it is unlikely that the unwinding of the contractual set-off in relation to the debt for the price and the judgment debt would have resulted in a set-off as between those debts in the liquidation. When the sale occurred, A presumably would have had notice of B's insolvency, so that the qualification to the insolvency set-off section[596] would have operated to preclude a set-off. On the other hand, if A had a separate liability to B, and A paid the liquidator and therefore obtained a provable debt pursuant to section 569, a set-off may have been available in relation to A's separate liability and A's provable debt.

(3) Charging Orders

17.113 A charging order may be made in favour of a judgment creditor under the Charging Orders Act 1979. Its application to debts is limited, however. The only debts to which it extends are government debentures, or debentures issued by a body corporate that is either incorporated in England or Wales or has the register for the debentures in England or Wales.[597] When a charging order is made it operates as a charge securing payment of any money due or to become due under the judgment.[598] It has a like effect and is enforceable in the same manner as an equitable charge,[599] and it should be subject to the same principles as a garnishee order in relation to questions of set-off.

(4) Appointment of a Receiver by Way of Equitable Execution

17.114 A receiver may be appointed by way of equitable execution in circumstances where execution at common law for some reason cannot be had,[600] and included amongst the property which the receiver is authorized to receive may be a debt owing to the judgment debtor by a third party.[601] The use of the term 'execution' in this context is a misnomer. The obtaining of a receivership order in truth is not execution, but rather it constitutes equitable relief on the ground that there is no adequate remedy by execution at law.[602] The appointment by itself does not create a charge or other security interest in favour of the judgment creditor, unless in a particular case the order in its terms has specifically charged the third party not to deal with the debt except by payment to the judgment creditor.[603] Rather, it

---

[595] See, in a different context, Fletcher Moulton LJ in *Re A Debtor, ex p Peak Hill Goldfield Ltd* [1909] 1 KB 430, 437. See also paras 13.07–13.28 above.

[596] Corporations Act 2001 (Cth), s 553C(2). See para 6.49–6.64 above.

[597] Charging Orders Act 1979, s 2(2), 'stock' being defined in s 6(1) as including debentures.

[598] See s 1(1).

[599] See s 3(4).

[600] *Re Shepherd* (1889) 43 Ch D 131, 135–136, 137, 138.

[601] For an illustration of circumstances held sufficient to justify the appointment of a receiver in relation to debts owing to the judgment debtor, see *Goldschmidt v Oberrheinische Metallwerke* [1906] 1 KB 373.

[602] *Re Shepherd* (1889) 43 Ch D 131, 135, 137, 138; *Ideal Bedding Co Ltd v Holland* [1907] 2 Ch 157, 169.

[603] See *Re Pearce* [1919] 1 KB 354, 363, *per* Swinfen Eady MR, referring to *Re Potts, ex p Taylor* [1893] 1 QB 648, 659, *per* Lord Esher. See also *Re Whitehart* (1972) 116 Sol Jo 75.

operates as an injunction to restrain the judgment debtor from receiving the proceeds of the debt the subject of the order, and from dealing with the debt to the prejudice of the judgment creditor.[604] In addition, it would prevent the judgment debtor from using the debt as a set-off against a separate debt that he owes to the third party.[605]

In so far as the third party is concerned, Greer J in *Giles v Kruyer*[606] considered that, **17.115** if the third party is not a party to the order, his rights and duties are not affected and, while the order has the consequence as against the judgment debtor that the debtor cannot give a discharge, it does not prevent the third party from paying the debtor. This view has been criticized, however.[607] If the third party is aware of the order, and therefore of the injunction restraining the judgment debtor from receiving payment, he may be in contempt if he nevertheless pays the debtor, in which case he should not obtain a valid discharge.[608] On that basis, the third party similarly should not be entitled to a set-off in respect of a cross-claim that he has against the judgment debtor, unless the demands are sufficiently closely connected so as to impeach the judgment debtor's title by way of equitable set-off, or possibly, if a set-off under the Statutes of Set-off is in issue, if the cross-debt against the judgement debtor arose before the third party had notice of the order.

What if the judgment debtor becomes bankrupt after the appointment but before **17.116** payment is received from the third party? Because the appointment generally does not give rise to a charge, the judgment creditor is not a secured creditor in the insolvency. Therefore he does not have priority over other creditors, and the proceeds of the debt will form part of the estate available for distribution generally.[609] According to views expressed in the Court of Appeal in *Re A Debtor, ex p Peak Hill Goldfield Ltd*,[610] this does not have as a consequence that the third party will then be entitled to a set-off under the insolvency set-off section in respect of a cross-claim that he has against the judgment debtor.[611] While after the bankruptcy the debt is payable to the trustee in bankruptcy, the problem is that, because of the appointment, the debt immediately before the bankruptcy was not payable to the

---

[604] *Tyrrell v Painton* [1895] 1 QB 202, 206; *Re Marquis of Anglesey* [1903] 2 Ch 727, 730–731; *Ideal Bedding Co Ltd v Holland* [1907] 2 Ch 157, 169–170; *Stevens v Hutchinson* [1953] 1 Ch 299, 305. See also *Re Potts, ex p Taylor* [1893] 1 QB 648.

[605] See *Re A Debtor, ex p Peak Hill Goldfield Ltd* [1909] 1 KB 430, 437, *per* Farwell LJ.

[606] [1921] 3 KB 23, referring to *Re Potts, ex p Taylor* [1893] 1 QB 648.

[607] *Kerr on Receivers and Administrators* (17th edn, 1989) 135, and in Australia O'Donovan, *Company Receivers and Administrators* (2nd edn, looseleaf) para 22.480.

[608] *Kerr on Receivers and Administrators* (17th edn, 1989) 135, referring to *Eastern Trust Co v McKenzie, Mann & Co Ltd* [1915] AC 750. As Wood has noted (*English and International Set-off* (1989) 963), *Eckman v Midland Bank Ltd* [1973] 1 QB 519, a case on sequestration, is consistent with this view.

[609] *Re Potts, ex p Taylor* [1893] 1 QB 648; *Ideal Bedding Co Ltd v Holland* [1907] 2 Ch 157, 169.

[610] [1909] 1 KB 430, in particular Cozens-Hardy MR at 434–435 and Fletcher Moulton LJ at 436–437.

[611] *Re A Debtor, ex p Peak Hill Goldfield Ltd* [1909] 1 KB 430.

judgment debtor. In the *Peak Hill Goldfield* case[612] Fletcher Moulton LJ expressed the relevant principle in terms that: 'Moneys which under a bankruptcy became payable to the trustee . . . because they were payable to the debtor, come prima facie within the mutual credits clause, but not if they are moneys which, upon bankruptcy, become payable to the trustee in his right as trustee and not by virtue of their being payable to the debtor.' This nevertheless seems a harsh result.

G. Notice Under Section 260-5 of the Tax Administration Act in Australia

17.117   In Australia, section 260-5 in Schedule 1 of the Tax Administration Act 1953 (Cth) deals with the collection and recovery of amounts in satisfaction of a debt to the Commonwealth for a tax-related liability. It provides that, where a tax-related liability is payable to the Commonwealth by an entity ('the debtor'), the Commissioner may give a notice to a third party who owes or later may owe money to the debtor, requiring the third party to pay to the Commissioner the lesser of the tax-related liability and the amount owed by the third party to the debtor.[613] Section 260-5 was inserted in the Tax Administration Act in 1999, re-placing a similar provision in section 218 of the Income Tax Assessment Act 1936 (Cth).[614] A recipient of a notice under section 260-5 who fails to comply with it is guilty of an offence, and where a person is convicted of an offence for failing to pay an amount under the notice the court may order the person to pay to the Commissioner an amount not exceeding that amount. A question which has yet to be determined is whether the Commissioner takes subject to a right of set-off available to the third party against the debtor.

17.118   The Commissioner should take subject to a substantive defence of equitable set-off. The taxpayer's title to sue the third party would be impeached, and the Commissioner could not have a better title. The position is more complicated in relation to the procedural defence of set-off under the Statutes of Set-off, in those jurisdictions in which the defence conferred by the Statutes is relevant.[615] Section 260–5 applies where the third party owes money to the debtor. One view is that the availability of a set-off under the Statutes does not mean that there is nothing owing by the third party to the debtor to the extent of the set-off. There is money owing, but there is a procedural defence to an action at law to enforce payment.[616]

---

[612]   [1909] 1 KB 430, 437.

[613]   There are similar provisions in the Sales Tax Assessment Act (No 1) 1930 (Cth), s 38 and the Child Support (Registration and Collection) Act 1988 (Cth), s 72A.

[614]   Section 218(8) of the 1936 Act provides that the Commissioner must not issue a notice under s 218 on or after 1 July 2000.

[615]   See paras 2.55–2.67 above.

[616]   See para 2.33 above.

The section on its face therefore may be said to apply. However a notice under section 218 of the Income Tax Assessment Act was said to create a charge in favour of the Commissioner over a debt owing to the taxpayer which was the subject of the notice,[617] and it was considered as having an effect similar to a garnishee order.[618] A section 260-5 notice is likely to be regarded in the same way. The Commissioner therefore should take subject to set-offs by reference to principles analogous to those applicable to chargees[619] and judgment creditors.[620] On the other hand, unless a substantive equitable set-off is in issue,[621] the third party should not be entitled to a set-off in respect of a debt that arises after the third party receives a notice under the Act.[622] Further, if the debtor becomes bankrupt or goes into liquidation after the third party is given a notice, the third party could not rely on the wider right of set-off under the insolvency set-off section. This is because the charge that arises in favour of the Commonwealth consequent upon service of the notice would destroy mutuality for the purpose of the insolvency set-off section.[623]

H. Subrogation

Insurance subrogation

It was suggested earlier that a person who has an assignment merely of the proceeds of a debt should be in a different position to that of an assignee of the debt itself as regards set-off.[624] Unless a substantive defence of equitable set-off is in issue,[625] when a debt is assigned the assignee as a general rule only takes subject to rights of set-off available to the debtor against the assignor when those rights arose before the debtor had notice of the assignment, whereas an assignee merely of the

17.119

---

[617] *Commissioner of Taxation v Donnelly* (1989) 25 FCR 432; *Macquarie Health Corp Ltd v Commissioner of Taxation* (1999) 96 FCR 238. See also *Commissioner of Taxation v Government Insurance Office of New South Wales* (1993) 45 FCR 284, 292–294; *Deputy Commissioner of Taxation v Conley* (1998) 88 FCR 98, 99–100, 106.

[618] *Clyne v Deputy Commissioner of Taxation* (1981) 150 CLR 1, 19, *per* Mason J; *Commissioner of Taxation v Donnelly* (1989) 25 FCR 432, 442, 456; *Macquarie Health Corp Ltd v Commissioner of Taxation* (1999) 96 FCR 238, 267.

[619] See paras 17.73–17.87 above.

[620] See paras 17.103–17.116 above.

[621] See para 17.22 above.

[622] See paras 17.10 and 17.20 above.

[623] See para 11.34 above. Since a notice under s 260–5 creates an interest in the debt owing to the debtor in the form of a statutory charge, a notice served after the commencement of the debtor's liquidation would be rendered void by the Corporations Act 2001 (Cth), s 468 as a disposition of the company's property after the commencement of its winding up. See *Macquarie Health Corp Ltd v Commissioner of Taxation* (1999) 96 FCR 238. In any event, if a notice were served after the debtor's bankruptcy or liquidation, the Commissioner would take subject to a set-off as between the debtor and the third party under the insolvency set-off section, since a set-off would have occurred automatically at the date of the bankruptcy or liquidation. See paras 6.79–6.103 above.

[624] See para 17.54 above.

[625] See para 17.22 above.

proceeds should take subject to a defence whenever it arises, notwithstanding that this would have the effect that nothing would be received to the extent of the set-off to which the assignment could attach. A similar issue arises in the context of insurance subrogation. An insurer that has indemnified its insured is subrogated to any claim possessed by the insured against a third party that reduces the loss. This entitles the insurer to use the insured's name in order to sue the third party, and also to claim any moneys recovered by the insured from the third party in reduction of the loss. The insurer has an equitable proprietary interest in moneys recovered by the insured, in the form of an equitable lien or charge.[626] But what about the right of action itself? Lord Browne-Wilkinson in *Napier v Hunter*[627] declined to express a concluded view on whether subrogation gives the insurer a proprietary interest in the claim, but the tenor of his judgment suggests that he doubted that it has that effect. If a subrogated insurer is without a proprietary interest in the claim, the insurer's subrogation entitlement should not affect set-off as between the insured and the third party, notwithstanding the insurer's proprietary interest in sums that are paid directly to the insured. Lord Goff of Chieveley on the other hand, although expressing reluctance to reach a conclusion without a full examination of the authorities, said that he could see no reason in principle why an equitable proprietary interest should not be capable of attaching to the chose in action.[628] Lord Templeman adopted a similar approach. He initially suggested that the insurer does have an equitable interest in the right of action,[629] but later in his judgment he expressed himself more cautiously, commenting that, since reading in draft the speech of Lord Goff, he agreed that, if the point should become material, his initial view may require reconsideration in the light of further research.[630] Consistent with the interest that attaches to moneys recovered by the insured from the third party,[631] if the insurer has an interest in the right of action it probably would be characterized as an equitable charge or lien.[632] The

---

[626] *Napier v Hunter* [1993] AC 713, 738, 744–745, 752. On the other hand, when the insurer obtains recoveries which exceed the sum to which it is entitled in order to recoup itself, the insurer holds the surplus on trust. See *Lonrho Exports Ltd v Export Credits Guarantee Department* [1999] Ch 158, 181–182.

[627] [1993] AC 713, 752–753.

[628] [1993] AC 713, 745.

[629] [1993] AC 713, 736–738.

[630] [1993] AC 713, 740.

[631] See above.

[632] Lord Templeman and Lord Goff seem to have assumed that this would be the case. See [1993] AC 713, 740, 745. Thus, it has been said that the interest of a subrogated insurer in the insured's right of action is not that of a cestui que trust. See *Linsley v Petrie* [1998] 1 VR 427, 445. On other occasions however the epithet 'trust' has been used. See *Hartford Fire Insurance Co v Hurse* [1962] WAR 187, 191; *Levesque v Co-operative Fire & Casualty Co* (1976) 68 DLR 553, 557. It has also been said that the insurer is not an assignee of the insured's claim. See *Linsley v Petrie* at 445 and *Esso Petroleum Co Ltd v Hall Russell & Co Ltd* [1989] 1 AC 643, 663, although Morison J in *Schiffahrtsgesellschaft Detlev von Appen GmbH v Voest Alpine Intertrading GmbH* [1997] 1 Lloyds Rep 179, 186 described the effect of subrogation as a 'transfer' (on appeal [1997] 2 Lloyd's Rep 279,

determination of set-off rights in the case of a fixed equitable charge is governed by the same principles as apply in the case of an equitable assignment.[633] Therefore, if the tentative views of Lord Goff and Lord Templeman are adopted, questions of set-off in the case of insurance subrogation, to the extent of the insurer's subrogation entitlement in the insured's claim,[634] should be governed by principles similar to those outlined earlier in the context of assignments of debts.

On that basis, if a third party liable to an insured has notice that an insurer is **17.120** interested in the insured's claim through a right of subrogation,[635] the third party would not be entitled to rely on a subsequently accruing right of set-off against the insured to diminish the right of the insurer,[636] unless the demands are sufficiently closely connected to give rise to an equitable set-off.[637] Admittedly a fundamental principle underlying insurance subrogation is that a subrogated insurer can only make such claim as the insured himself could have made,[638] and consistent with that view it has been said that a subrogated insurer takes subject to all defences available to the third party against the insured.[639] The expression of the principle in those terms prima facie would extend to a cross-claim available by way of set-off against the insured which accrued after the third party was aware of the insurer's interest. But the circumstance of the third party obtaining a cross-claim against the insured after notice of the insurer's interest has yet to be addressed, and if, as tentatively suggested in *Napier v Hunter*, the insurer has a proprietary interest in the

---

286 Hobhouse LJ referred to counsel's characterization of the right in terms of a transfer without comment either way). Some of the effects of subrogation on the other hand have been said to be similar to an equitable assignment. See *Hobbs v Marlowe* [1978] AC 16, 39; *Linsley v Petrie* at 445.

[633] See para 17.74 above.

[634] In the event that the insured's claim against the third party exceeds the insurer's subrogation entitlement, so that to the extent of the excess the insured alone is beneficially interested, the third party's set-off rights as against the excess should not be affected by the insurer's interest. See para 17.55 above in relation to an assignment of part of a debt.

[635] While it is said that an insurer has a contingent right of subrogation when the policy is effected (*MacGillivray on Insurance Law* (9th edn, 1997) 542, referring to *John Edwards & Co v Motor Union Insurance Co* [1922] 2 KB 249, 254–255), the right cannot be exercised until payment under the policy. See *Page v Scottish Insurance Corp* (1929) 140 LT 571. The latter should be the relevant date for the purpose of set-off.

[636] Similarly, if the insured becomes bankrupt after the insurer has obtained a proprietary interest in the insured's claim against the third party, in the form of an equitable charge or lien on the claim, the insurer's interest should have the effect that the insolvency set-off section does not apply as between the insured and the third party. See paras 17.28 and 17.84 above.

[637] See para 17.22 above.

[638] *Simpson v Thomson* (1877) 3 App Cas 279, 286; *Lister v Romford Ice and Cold Storage Co Ltd* [1957] AC 555, 600, *per* Lord Somervell of Harrow ('The insurer, when he has paid, succeeds to such rights as the assured possesses'); *Ross Southward Tire Ltd v Pyrotech Products Ltd* (1975) 57 DLR (3d) 248, 251, *per* Laskin CJC ('The subrogated insurer's position in this litigation against the tenant is, admittedly, no better than that of the landlord itself.').

[639] *Sydney Turf Club v Crowley* [1971] 1 NSWLR 724, 734, *per* Mason JA (the action 'is brought in the name of the insured and it is subject to all the defences which would be available if the action had been brought by the insured for his own benefit.'). See also Mitchell, 'Defences to an Insurer's Subrogated Action' [1996] LMCLQ 343, 356, 360.

insured's claim against the third party, and if the demands are not sufficiently closely connected to give rise to an equitable set-off, it should be unconscionable in that circumstance for the third party to rely on the right of set-off otherwise available against the insured to diminish the rights of the insurer.[640] Having said that, this situation in all likelihood would seldom arise. The third party in a subrogation action is often a tortfeasor, with a consequent liability in damages, so that the right of set-off under the Statutes of Set-off in the case of mutual debts would not apply.

17.121   The preceding discussion concerned the case of a subrogated insurer standing behind a claimant. Alternatively, a defendant raising a cross-claim by way of defence may have been indemnified by an insurer for the loss the subject of the cross-claim. This may arise, for example, where a claimant is suing for the price of equipment delivered to the defendant, and the defendant alleges that the equipment is defective so as to give rise to a defence either on the basis of equitable set-off or the common law defence of abatement.[641] If the defendant in that circumstance has been indemnified by an insurer, the insurer is entitled to insist that the defendant raise the cross-claim by way of defence, and if the defence succeeds the defendant must account to the insurer for the benefit that the defendant has obtained through the reduction or extinction of the liability for the price.[642]

Subrogation in other circumstances

17.122   It has been said that insurance subrogation forms a category of its own,[643] but a proprietary interest may also arise in other areas of subrogation.[644] For example, *Jenner v Morris*[645] concerned a person who made loans to another's deserted wife for the purpose of purchasing necessaries. While a person who supplied necessaries to a deserted wife could sue the husband at common law for payment, the

---

[640]   See para 17.03 above. In *Lewenza v Ruszczak* (1959) 22 DLR (2d) 167, a subrogated insurer's interest in a judgment obtained by the insured against the third party was held to preclude the third party from setting off a judgment that he had obtained against the insured. The set-off in issue was a set-off of judgments, which involves a question of the court's inherent jurisdiction, as opposed to a defence of set-off under the Statutes of Set-off. See paras 2.78–2.86 above. See also *Co-operators Insurance Association v Brown* (1989) 69 OR (2d) 135 (no counterclaim against the insured in a subrogation action, although in that case the insurer was suing in its own name). Compare *Page v Scottish Insurance Corp* (1929) 140 LT 571, in which a set-off was denied for a number of reasons, including that the insurer had not indemnified the insured so that it was not entitled to be subrogated to the insured's right of action. Compare also *Re Casey; A Bankrupt* (Irish High Court, Hamilton P, 1 March 1993), noted by O'Dell [1995] RLR 193. It is not clear from the note when the rates were due, and in any event the decision appears to have turned on the statutory right of set-off in the Local Government Act 1941, s 58.

[641]   See paras 2.87–2.97 above.

[642]   *National Oilwell (UK) Ltd v Davy Offshore Ltd* [1993] 2 Lloyd's Rep 582, 624.

[643]   *Barclays Bank Ltd v TOSG Trust Fund Ltd* [1984] 1 AC 626, 639, *per* Oliver LJ.

[644]   Compare a trust creditor's right to be subrogated to the trustee's claim for an indemnity from the trust assets, for which see para 17.94 above.

[645]   (1860) 1 Dr & Sm 218, 62 ER 362, affirmed (1861) 3 De G F & J 45, 45 ER 795.

common law did not recognize a similar right in a person who merely lent money for the purpose of acquiring them. It was held in *Jenner v Morris* however that the person advancing money for this purpose was entitled to be subrogated to the claim that the supplier would have had against the husband, and further that this could be set off against a judgment debt owing by the person to the husband. The fact that a set-off was permitted suggests that the person who made the advance was regarded as having an equitable proprietary interest in the claim as a result of the right of subrogation, and indeed Lord Campbell LC suggested that the subrogation could possibly be explained as an equitable assignment of the supplier's claim against the husband.[646] A similar comment may be made in relation to the judgment of Powell J in the New South Wales Supreme Court in *A E Goodwin Ltd v A G Healing Ltd*[647] in the context of a surety's right of subrogation as against the principal debtor.[648] Powell J contemplated that the right of subrogation may bring about mutuality so as to allow a set-off in respect of the principal debtor's debt to the creditor to which the surety is subrogated and a separate debt owing by the surety to the debtor, which once again suggests that it was thought to confer an interest in the creditor's claim. On the other hand, Powell J also said that the right of subrogation is in the nature of a class right, so that if there is more than one surety subrogated to the creditor's claim there would be a lack of mutuality as between the subrogation claim and a debt owing by one of the sureties to the debtor.[649]

I. Contracts (Rights of Third Parties) Act 1999

Subject to various qualifications and exceptions, the Contracts (Rights of Third **17.123** Parties) Act 1999 permits a person who is not a party to a contract (referred to as a 'third party') to enforce a term of the contract in his own right if the contract expressly provides that he may, or if the term purports to confer a benefit on him.[650] If a third party brings proceedings pursuant to the Act to enforce a term of the contract, s 3 sets out three circumstances in which the person against whom the term is enforceable ('the promisor')[651] may avail himself of a set-off.

In the first place, the promisor has available to him by way of defence or set-off any **17.124** matter that arises from or in connection with the contract and is relevant to the

---

[646] (1861) 3 De G F & J 45, 52, 45 ER 795, 798.

[647] (1979) 7 ACLR 481, 488–489.

[648] Wood, *English and International Set-off* (1989) 943–4 also regards *Re Jeffrey's Policy* (1872) 20 WR 857 as authority for the proposition that subrogation in the context of suretyship affects mutuality, although the case may be explained on the ground that the payment of the money into court by the creditor constituted an admission that it was not entitled to retain the money but rather it was a trustee.

[649] (1979) 7 ACLR 481, 489. See also *Rowlatt on Principal and Surety* (5th edn, 1999) 157.

[650] See in particular s 1, and note the exceptions in s 6.

[651] See s 1(7).

term being enforced.[652] However this is subject to the qualification that the matter must have been available to the promisor by way of defence or set-off if the proceedings had been brought by 'the promisee', being the party to the contract by whom the term is enforceable against the promisor. [653] This has the consequence that the third party takes subject to defences of equitable set-off or common law abatement that arise out of the contract. Second, the promisor may also invoke a set-off against the third party if an express term of the contract provides for it to be available to him in proceedings brought by the third party and, in addition, if it would have been available to him by way of defence or set-off if the proceedings had been brought by the promisee. This refers to rights of set-off that would have been available to the promisor if the action had been brought against him by the promisee as the other contracting party. Third, section 3(4) provides that the promisor may rely on a defence of set-off that would have been available to him against the third party if the third party had been a party to the contract.[654] This picks up set-offs arising from the third party's own circumstances. Thus, if the third party's claim is for a debt under the contract, it would permit the promisor to set off a separate debt owing to him by the third party.

---

[652] This is subject to an express term of the contract as to matters that are not to be available to the promisor by way of set-off. See s 3(5).

[653] See s 1(7).

[654] This is subject to an express term to the contrary. See s 3(5).

18

SURETIES

This chapter is concerned with contracts of suretyship, and the availability of **18.01** rights of set-off as between a creditor, the debtor and a guarantor of the debt.

A. Principal Debtor's Right to Require a Set-off

If a principal debtor has a cross-claim against the creditor which is available as a **18.02** set-off against the guaranteed debt, equitable considerations dictate that the creditor should not be able to avoid the set-off by proceeding against the guarantor. If it were otherwise, and the creditor recovered from the guarantor, the guarantor would be entitled to be indemnified by the principal debtor. The debtor could still proceed separately against the creditor on the cross-claim, but he would have lost the benefit of the set-off. There are some early cases which support the principal debtor's right to relief in this situation.

In *Ex parte Hanson*[1] the assignees in bankruptcy of a creditor sued Hanson and **18.03** Williamson on a bond given by them jointly as security for a loan made to Hanson alone. Hanson therefore was the principal debtor, and Williamson had only joined in the bond as a surety. Hanson also had a separate claim against the creditor. Lord Eldon held, on Hanson's petition, that the assignee's action should be

---

[1] (1811) 18 Ves Jun 232, 34 ER 305, affirming (1806) 12 Ves Jun 346, 33 ER 131.

restrained, and that Hanson's separate claim should be deducted from and set off against the joint debt on the bond. The creditor in that case was bankrupt, but Lord Eldon's analysis did not turn on any peculiarity of insolvency set-off.[2] Rather, he invoked a general equitable principle that,[3] 'the joint debt was nothing more than a security for a separate debt; and upon equitable considerations a creditor, who has a joint security for a separate debt, cannot resort to that security without allowing what he has received on the separate account . . .'. The set-off in issue was based upon 'equitable considerations'. Because of the lack of mutuality[3a] it was not a set-off of mutual debts pursuant to the bankruptcy set-off section. Subsequently Lord Eldon adopted a similar approach in *Ex parte Hippins, Re Sikes*.[4] Hippins had accepted two bills of exchange for the accommodation of the drawer, one Harrison, who discounted them with a firm of bankers. The banking firm became bankrupt, at which time it was indebted to Harrison in an amount greater than the indebtedness on the bills. The firm's assignees in bankruptcy claimed to be entitled to sue Hippins as the acceptor, which would have had the consequence that Harrison would have been denied the benefit of the set-off that would have been available if he had been sued. Harrison and Hippens accordingly brought this petition to restrain the threatened proceedings. Lord Eldon affirmed an order of the Vice Chancellor, Sir John Leach, that the assignees should deliver up the bills and that all proceedings against Hippins in respect of the bills should be stayed. The important point was that the bills were accommodation bills. Therefore, as between Hippins and Harrison, equity considered that Harrison as the party accommodated was principally liable,[5] and if Hippins paid the bills he would have been entitled to be reimbursed by Harrison. If on the other hand a bill of exchange is not an accommodation bill, the acceptor rather than the drawer is principally liable, and the drawer is not entitled to restrain the holder from suing the acceptor despite a set-off that otherwise would have been available to the drawer.[6]

18.04   *Hamp v Jones*[7] evidences a similar approach. A tenant had obtained a verdict at law against the landlord and his bailiff for damages for trespass. The landlord had agreed to indemnify the bailiff, and the landlord also had a separate claim for rent against the tenant which exceeded the amount of the verdict. Sir Lancelot

---

[2] Compare Lord Erskine in earlier proceedings (1806) 12 Ves Jun 346, 348, 33 ER 131, 132.

[3] (1811) 18 Ves Jun 232, 233–234, 34 ER 305.

[3a] See paras 12.02–12.20 above.

[4] (1826) 4 LJOS Ch 195, 2 Gl & J 93.

[5] The common law on the other hand considered that the accommodation acceptor was principally liable. See *Coles Myer Finance Ltd v Commissioner of Taxation* (1993) 67 ALJR 463, 466–467, 481–484.

[6] *Ex parte Banes, re The Royal British Bank* (1857) 28 LTOS 296; *Ex parte Burton, Franco and Corea, re Kensington* (1812) 1 Rose 320. In *Ex parte Hippins* (1826) 2 Gl & J 93, 96 Lord Eldon confirmed, after an examination of the secretary's book, that *Ex parte Burton* did not involve an acceptance for accommodation.

[7] (1840) 9 LJ Ch 258.

Shadwell VC granted an injunction to restrain the tenant from issuing out execution or taking other proceedings upon the judgment. In the course of his judgement the Vice Chancellor commented that a set-off was not available at law, because there was a joint demand against the landlord and the bailiff and only a 'single' demand against the tenant. But if the landlord had agreed to indemnify the bailiff, the Vice Chancellor said that that seemed a reason for the interference of the Court of Chancery.

Lord Eldon in *Ex parte Hanson* ordered that the action against the joint debtors be **18.05** restrained and that the securities given by them be delivered up, this being the method by which equitable set-offs were enforced before the Judicature Acts.[8] Since the Judicature Acts, an equitable set-off may be pleaded directly as a defence in the claimant's action. An order setting off cross-demands may occur when the principal debtor claiming the set-off is a party to the creditor's action, as was the case in *Ex parte Hanson*. If however the principal debtor is not a party, he should still be entitled to apply to the court for a declaration as to his set-off entitlement, and for an order restraining the creditor from proceeding against the guarantor without giving credit for the set-off. If the principal's cross-claim exceeds the debt, the action against the guarantor should be stayed and there should be a consequential order for delivery up of the guarantee.[9]

B. Set-off Available to the Guarantor

A guarantor being sued by the creditor for payment under the guarantee may base **18.06** a set-off upon a cross-claim that he has against the creditor, including in circumstances where the creditor gave warranties to the guarantor in relation to the transaction the subject of the principal obligation.[10] On the other hand, while a principal debtor should be entitled on equitable grounds to insist that the creditor not avoid a set-off available to the principal by proceeding against a guarantor,[11] a similar equity does not arise in the situation in which the creditor is liable to the guarantor. The creditor is not obliged to sue the guarantor so as to give effect to a set-off, but can look instead to the principal for payment.[12] But if the guarantor contracted in terms that he was to be liable as a principal debtor, and the

---

[8] See para 3.01 above.

[9] See also *Rowlatt on Principal and Surety* (5th edn, 1999) 106.

[10] *BOC Group plc v Centeon LLC* [1999] 1 All ER (Comm) 53. Compare *Continental Illinois National Bank and Trust Co of Chicago v Papanicolaou* [1986] 2 Lloyd's Rep 441 (sale of mortgaged property at an undervalue), in which the guarantee excluded a defence of set-off. See para 18.32 below.

[11] See paras 18.02–18.05 above.

[12] *Lord v Direct Acceptance Corp Ltd* (1993) 32 NSWLR 362, 369. See also *Ex parte Burton, Franco and Corea, re Kensington* (1812) 1 Rose 320 and *Ex parte Banes, re The Royal British Bank* (1857) 28 LTOS 296, for which see para 12.22 above.

creditor has become bankrupt or is a company in liquidation, the guarantor's liability and a claim possessed by the guarantor against the creditor may be the subject of an automatic set-off under the insolvency set-off section, and the creditor's trustee in bankruptcy or liquidator could not avoid that result by commencing proceedings against the person who in substance is the principal debtor.[13]

C. Guarantor's Right to Rely on the Principal Debtor's Set-off

18.07 Consider once again the case of a creditor who is suing a guarantor, and the principal debtor, who is not being sued, has a cross-claim against the creditor which would provide a defence if the creditor sued him. The principal debtor in that circumstance should be entitled to an order restraining the creditor's action so that the debtor's defence can be given effect.[14] If however the debtor fails to take the point, the question arises whether the guarantor can defend the creditor's action on the basis of the set-off available to the debtor.[15] This differs from the assignment cases discussed in the preceding chapter. In the case of an assignment of a debt, the question is whether the debtor can assert a set-off available to him against the assignor in an action brought against him by a third party assignee. In the guarantee cases, on the other hand, it is the third party surety who is endeavouring to obtain the benefit of a set-off arising out of dealings between the principal debtor and creditor.

(1) Set-off Agreement

18.08 A surety is entitled to the benefit of an agreement between the principal debtor and the creditor that cross-demands between those parties are to be set off, since this operates as a payment.[16]

(2) Solvent Set-off—The Various Approaches

18.09 The position is more complex in relation to the availability of defences of equitable set-off, common law abatement and set-off under the Statutes of Set-off. On a general level, three distinct approaches to the question of set-off have been suggested. These should be noted before considering specifically each of the forms of set-off.

---

[13] *M S Fashions Ltd v Bank of Credit and Commerce International SA* [1993] Ch 425. See paras 12.23–12.25 above.

[14] See paras 18.02–18.05 above.

[15] Compare the exceptional fact situation in *R v Shaw* (1901) 27 VLR 70 (fidelity policy), in which the issue was not set-off as such but rather whether the guaranteed debt had been reduced by payment.

[16] See *Aurora Borealis Compania Armadora SA v Marine Midland Bank NA (The Maistros)* [1984] 1 Lloyd's Rep 646; *Cheetham v Crook* (1825) M'Cle & Yo 307; *Wreckair Pty Ltd v Emerson* [1992] 1 Qd R 700, 708. See also *Re Bank of Credit and Commerce International SA (No 8)* [1996] Ch 245, 268.

One view, which represents the preferred approach, is that the surety can defend **18.10** himself on the basis of any of these defences of set-off or abatement available to the principal debtor,[17] subject possibly to a requirement that the debtor be joined as a party to the action.[18] This view is supported by a statement in *Halsbury*, to the effect that a surety can avail himself of any right of set-off or counterclaim that the principal debtor has against the creditor,[19] which Roskill LJ quoted with evident approval in *Hyundai Shipbuilding and Heavy Industries Co Ltd v Pournaras*,[20] as did Scott LJ in *Barclays Bank plc v Gruffydd*.[21]

A second view, which is favoured by some text-writers,[22] is that a surety can invoke **18.11** an equitable set-off available to the debtor arising out of a sufficiently close connection with the guaranteed debt (once again, possibly subject to a requirement that the principal debtor be joined[23]), but not a defence of set-off under the Statutes of Set-off. This is suggested by a comment by Willes J in *Bechervaise v Lewis*,[24] that 'the plea is a special plea by a surety, of a set-off by the principal, arising out of the same transaction out of which the liability of the surety on the note arose'.

A third view, which has support in Victoria[25] and New South Wales,[26] and possi- **18.12** bly also in England in the judgment of Finlay LJ in *Wilson v Mitchell*,[27] is that a

---

[17] In addition to the authorities referred to below, see *Diebel v Stratford Improvement Co* (1917) 33 DLR 296, 301. See also *Mann v Secretary of State for Employment* [1999] UKHL 29 in relation to a set-off available to a principal debtor pursuant to statute.

[18] See below.

[19] *Halsbury's Laws of England* (4th edn, 1978) vol 20, 102 para 190 ('On being sued by the creditor for payment of the debt guaranteed, a surety may avail himself of any right to set off or counterclaim which the principal debtor possesses against the creditor . . .'). Compare the formulation in the 1993 reissue (at vol 20, 143 para 225), in terms of a set-off or counterclaim which the principal debtor could set up against the creditor in reduction of the guaranteed debt. In relation to a counterclaim which is not available as a set-off, see para 18.29 below.

[20] [1978] 2 Lloyd's Rep 502, 508. Stephenson LJ agreed with Roskill LJ's judgment.

[21] Court of Appeal, 30 October 1992. Scott LJ said that the passage in *Halsbury* is a correct statement of the law. Compare *National Westminster Bank v Skelton* [1993] 1 WLR 72, 78–79, *per* Slade LJ, with whose judgment Anthony Lincoln J agreed.

[22] Wood, *English and International Set-off* (1989) 641, 645; O'Donovan and Phillips, *The Modern Contract of Guarantee* (3rd edn, 1996) 549, 551–2.

[23] See O'Donovan and Phillips, *The Modern Contract of Guarantee* (3rd edn, 1996) 549 and *Paget's Law of Banking* (11th edn, 1996) 625.

[24] (1872) LR 7 CP 372, 377. See also *Sun Alliance Pensions Life and Investments Services Ltd v RJL* [1991] 2 Lloyd's Rep 410, 416.

[25] *Indrisie v General Credits Ltd* [1985] VR 251, although compare *Doherty v Murphy* [1996] 2 VR 553. It appears from the report of the *Indrisie* case that the High Court refused special leave to appeal from the decision, but it is not clear whether this was because of a view that a set-off available to the principal debtor can never be invoked by the surety, or whether it was because the principal debtor was not a party to the action, or whether it was simply on the ground that the demands in any event were thought to be insufficiently connected to give rise to an equitable set-off.

[26] *Cellulose Products Pty Ltd v Truda* (1970) 92 WN (NSW) 561; *Covino v Bandag Manufacturing Pty Ltd* [1983] 1 NSWLR 237, 240–241.

[27] [1939] 2 KB 869, 871. Finlay LJ commented: 'There is here a cross-claim for damages, and this cannot be prayed in aid by a surety against the claim on the guarantee. Even if my view is wrong as to this, it certainly could not be prayed in aid without bringing in the principal debtor whose claim it was.'

defence of set-off available to the principal debtor cannot be invoked by a surety. On the other hand, the rigour of this approach has been said to be ameliorated in two respects. In the first place, an exception has been recognized when the debtor is bankrupt or is a company in liquidation. This has been justified on the ground that the creditor otherwise might recover in full against the surety whereas the surety would only receive a dividend from the debtor,[28] but it could also be explained on the basis that the insolvency set-off section usually would apply in that circumstance as against the principal debt, in which case a set-off would have occurred automatically upon the occurrence of the bankruptcy or the liquidation.[29] If the principal debt has been extinguished in a set-off, so should the surety's liability under the guarantee.[30] Second, while this third approach generally would deny the surety a defence, it is said that the surety nevertheless may achieve a similar result by a procedural means. In New South Wales, Isaacs J in *Cellulose Products Pty Ltd v Truda*[31] explained this in the following terms:

> This review of the cases lends no support to the submission that a surety when sued is entitled to set up in equity or at law as an equitable plea any cross action for unliquidated damages which the debtor may have against the creditor in respect of the transaction, the performance of which the guarantor had entered upon his guarantee; that is, in the absence of the debtor being before the court in the proceeding so as to be bound by verdict and judgments. This of course does not mean that the guarantor is without remedy; when he is sued he has a right immediately to join the debtor as a third party and claim complete indemnity from him. The debtor has then a right to join the plaintiff as a fourth party, claiming damages for breach of warranty and so obtain indemnity either in whole or in part. All the actions would be heard together, the rights of all persons determined and appropriate set-off's made after verdict, and if there be any surplus of damages over and above that which is required to meet the guarantee, the debtor will have recovered that from the creditor who, in the result, will get no more than that to which he would be justly entitled.

Isaacs J referred generally to cross-actions for unliquidated damages, but the case itself was concerned with the common law defence of abatement, and it is evident that his statement was intended to encompass the availability of that defence to the debtor. Moreover, one of the proposed pleas related to equitable set-off, and it is clear that the discussion extended also to that defence.[32]

18.13 Isaacs J referred to an exception where the debtor is before the court, although by that he would appear to have had in mind the procedure he described of joining

---

[28] *Cellulose Products Pty Ltd v Truda* (1970) 92 WN (NSW) 561, 585 (referring to *Alcoy and Gandia Railway and Harbour Co Ltd v Greenhill* (1897) 76 LT 542, 553). See also *National Westminster Bank plc v Skelton* [1993] 1 WLR 72, 79.

[29] See paras 6.79–6.103 above.

[30] See para 18.30 below.

[31] (1970) 92 WN (NSW) 561, 588.

[32] See eg (1970) 92 WN (NSW) 561, 574–575, and also *Indrisie v General Credits Ltd* [1985] VR 251 and *Langford Concrete Pty Ltd v Finlay* [1978] 1 NSWLR 14, 18.

the principal as a party and setting off the judgments. That procedure however does not provide a defence, and as such it would not assist in a summary judgment application.[33] Similarly, because the guarantor does not have a defence, the procedure may have different costs consequences. It may also be the case that the debt and the guarantee have been assigned, and the assignee is suing, in which case it is difficult to see how the procedure of setting off judgments could apply. Moreover, the approach suggested by Isaacs J may not be as advantageous when the debtor has available a substantive defence of equitable set-off. For example, the debtor's cross-claim may be unenforceable as a result of the expiration of a limitation period, although this would not preclude the debtor from relying on it as a defence of equitable set-off if it is sufficiently closely connected with the debt owing to the creditor.[34] But if the creditor instead could sue a guarantor and the guarantor could not invoke the debtor's defence, it would not be a case of the guarantor joining the debtor and the debtor in turn claiming from the creditor, because the creditor could assert the expiration of the limitation period as a defence to the debtor's claim. If Isaacs J's approach were adopted, the debtor would have to take steps to protect his position in that circumstance, by applying for an order restraining the creditor's action against the surety, on the basis referred to above.[35]

18.14 In England, Slade LJ in *National Westminster Bank plc v Skelton*,[36] with whose judgment Anthony Lincoln J sitting in the Court of Appeal agreed, commented that he found the reasoning of Isaacs J impressive. Nevertheless he went on to say that he did not think it right, in a striking out application, to decide whether there is a general rule that a guarantor cannot avail himself of the remedies that otherwise may be open to the principal debtor as against the creditor. Subsequently however a differently constituted Court of Appeal in *Barclays Bank plc v Gruffydd*[37] was not as reticent. Scott LJ said that he had difficulty in accepting that the statements of principle in *Wilson v Mitchell* and *Cellulose Products v Truda* are correct statements of the law, while Purchas LJ considered that the cases were either wrongly decided or that they do not represent English law.

(3) Equitable Set-off and Common Law Abatement

18.15 Consider the case of an unliquidated damages claim available to the debtor as an equitable set-off against the creditor or, if it relates to a breach of warranty under a contract for the sale of goods or for the performance of work, as a common law defence of abatement.

---

[33] As in *Indrisie v General Credits Ltd* [1985] VR 251.
[34] See para 4.39 above.
[35] See para 18.05 above.
[36] [1993] 1 WLR 72, 79.
[37] CA, 30 October 1992 (Purchas, Nolan and Scott LJJ).

Australia

18.16   In Australia, differing views have been expressed as to whether a guarantor can invoke the debtor's defence. There is on the one hand authority for the view that a surety cannot rely on a cross-claim for damages which may be available to the principal as against the creditor.[38] This includes the judgment of the Full Court of the Victorian Supreme Court in *Indrisie v General Credits Ltd*.[39] Subsequent to the *Indrisie* case however the Appeal Division of the Victorian Supreme Court in *Doherty v Murphy*,[40] without referring to that case, allowed a guarantor leave to defend in a summary judgment application, inter alia on the basis of an arguable equitable set-off available to the principal debtor against the creditor.[41] This reflects more liberal formulations of the principle that have been expressed on other occasions in Australia, in terms suggesting that the surety can invoke the debtor's defence if the debtor has been joined as a party to the action,[42] and it represents the preferred view.

England

18.17   But whatever the position in Australia, the view in England is that a surety can rely on a defence of equitable set-off or abatement available to the debtor against the

---

[38] In addition to *Cellulose Products Pty Ltd v Truda* (1970) 92 WN (NSW) 561 (see para 18.12 above), see *Covino v Bandag Manufacturing Pty Ltd* [1983] 1 NSWLR 237; *Australia and New Zealand Banking Group Ltd v Harvey* (1994) ATPR (Digest) 46–132 at p 53,643; *Australia and New Zealand Banking Group Ltd v Ringrong Pty Ltd* (Federal Court of Australia, Ryan J, 11 September 1995, at [83]); *Citic Australia Commodity Trading Pty Ltd v Lau* (Vic SC, Byrne J, 11 November 1997); *Citic Commodity Trading Pty Ltd v JBL Enterprises (WA) Pty Ltd* (Federal Court of Australia, Heerey J, 16 March 1998); *Florgale Uniforms Pty Ltd v Orders (No 1)* [2000] VSC 427 at [26].

[39] [1985] VR 251, 253–254. The Full Court in the *Indrisie* case (at 254) noted that the principal debtor was not before the court as a party, but that was said to provide an *additional* reason for deciding against the surety. Compare however the interpretation of the *Indrisie* case in *Elkhoury v Farrow Mortgage Services Pty Ltd* (1993) 114 ALR 541, 549, *Re Kleiss* (1996) 61 FCR 436, 439–440 and *Dougan v Conias* [2000] FCA 1556 at [18].

[40] [1996] 2 VR 553.

[41] This was subject to a condition that an application be made to join the principal debtor as a defendant. See paras 18.23–18.25 below. The principal debtor was in liquidation, so that the leave of the court would have been required to join it as a party. See the Corporations Act 2001 (Cth), s 471B.

[42] *Langford Concrete Pty Ltd v Finlay* [1978] 1 NSWLR 14, 18, 19, CA; *Re Kleiss* (1996) 61 FCR 436, 439; *Elkhoury v Farrow Mortgage Services Pty Ltd* (1993) 114 ALR 541, 549, *per* Lockhart, Gummow and Lee JJ; *Dougan v Conias* [2000] FCA 1556 at [18]. See also *Commonwealth Development Bank v Windermere Pastoral Co Pty Ltd* [1999] NSWSC 518 (in which a guarantor successfully resisted a summary judgment application by the creditor on the basis of an arguable equitable set-off available to the principal debtor, without the imposition of a requirement that the debtor be joined as a party), *Electricity Meter Manufacturing Co Ltd v D'Ombrain* (1927) 44 WN (NSW) 131 (which was criticized in *Cellulose Products* (1970) 92 WN (NSW) 561, 582–583), *Tooth & Co v Rosier* (NSW SC, Wood J, 7 June 1985) (to the extent that Wood J referred to equitable set-off as well as insolvency set-off), and the submission to which Sheller JA referred without adverse comment in *Lord v Direct Acceptance Corp* (1993) 32 NSWLR 362, 368–369.

creditor.[43] On two occasions a passage in *Halsbury*[44] to that effect has been referred to with approval in the Court of Appeal.[45] In *BOC Group plc v Centeon LLC*[46] Rix J held that a guarantor could avail itself of the principal debtor's set-off, and in *Oastler v Pound*[47] Blackburn J accepted that the surety in that case could have relied on any defence of abatement that the debtor had against the creditor, although it was held that the circumstances were not such as to give rise to the defence. More recently, the House of Lords in *Trafalgar House Construction (Regions) Ltd v General Surety and Guarantee Co Ltd*[48] accepted that the characterization of a bond as a guarantee had the consequence that an equitable set-off[49] that could have been relied upon by the principal obligor by way of defence could also be relied on by the guarantor in an action by the obligee for payment under the bond. Those cases should be contrasted with *Sun Alliance Pensions Life and Investments Services Ltd v RJL*.[50] Mr Anthony Colman QC (as he then was),[51] sitting as a Deputy Judge, suggested that a set-off available to the principal debtor which arose out of the same transaction as the principal debt and which was for a 'limited amount' could be relied on by the guarantor to reduce or extinguish his personal liability on the guarantee. By 'limited amount' it appears that the Deputy Judge meant a liquidated sum, but if the circumstances are such as to give rise to an equitable set-off the nature of the debtor's cross-claim which the guarantor can invoke should not be restricted in that manner.

---

[43] See also in Canada *420093 BC Ltd v Bank of Montreal* (1995) 128 DLR (4th) 488, 500–501, Alberta CA; *Diebel v Stratford Improvement Co* (1917) 33 DLR 296, 301, Ontario SC, Appellate Division.

[44] See para 18.10 above.

[45] *Hyundai Shipbuilding and Heavy Industries Co Ltd v Pournaras* [1978] 2 Lloyd's Rep 502, 508 and *Barclays Bank plc v Gruffydd* (CA, 30 October 1992, Scott LJ). Compare *National Westminster Bank v Skelton* [1993] 1 WLR 72, 78–79, which pre-dated *Barclays Bank v Gruffydd*, and in which the Court of Appeal left the question open. In *Aliakmon Maritime Corp v Trans Ocean Continental Shipping Ltd (The Aliakmon Progress)* [1978] 2 Lloyd's Rep 499, which was decided on the same day as *Hyundai v Pournaras*, it was not disputed that if an equitable set-off had been available to the charterer it would have provided a defence to the guarantor, but Lord Denning, with whom Geoffrey Lane LJ agreed, considered that the circumstances were not such as to give rise to an equitable set-off. *Murphy v Glass* (1869) LR 2 PC 408, a case which is also often cited as support for the surety's right to have recourse to the benefit of the set-off, possibly may be explained on an alternative basis, that the debt secured by the bills of exchange was regarded as having been reduced so that a possible set-off of cross-demands was not in issue. This appears to have been the view of the Victorian Supreme Court, whose decision was affirmed on appeal by the Privy Council. See Isaacs J in *Cellulose Products Pty Ltd v Truda* (1970) 92 WN (NSW) 561, 580–582.

[46] [1999] 1 All ER (Comm) 53.

[47] (1863) 7 LT 852.

[48] [1996] 1 AC 199.

[49] While the House of Lords did not characterize the nature of the set-off in issue, since the liability of the obligor was in damages it could only have been an equitable set-off, and indeed counsel for the surety referred in his argument to equitable set-off.

[50] [1991] 2 Lloyd's Rep 410, 416.

[51] Now Colman J, a judge of the High Court of Justice.

18.18 *Bechervaise v Lewis*[52] is also sometimes referred to in this context.[53] The plaintiff
and a third party, one Rowe, were in partnership. A number of debts were due to
them as partners, and the plaintiff sold his interest in the debts to Rowe. As security for Rowe's obligation to pay the purchase price, the plaintiff was given a joint
and several promissory note made by Rowe and the defendant, the defendant
joining in only as a surety for Rowe. The plaintiff sued the defendant on the note,
whereupon the defendant pleaded a defence on equitable grounds that the plaintiff was indebted to Rowe as a result of the plaintiff having received the proceeds
of some of the assigned debts, so that the plaintiff could not have recovered from
Rowe. The judgment of the Court of Common Pleas[54] was delivered by Willes J,
who described the plea 'as a special plea by a surety, of a set-off by the principal'.[55]
He commented:[56]

> Thus we have a creditor who is equally liable to the principal as the principal to him,
> and against whom the principal has a good defence in law and equity, and a surety
> who is entitled in equity to call upon the principal to exonerate him.
>   In this state of things, we are bound to conclude that the surety has a defence in
> equity against the creditor . . .

It is not clear what form of set-off was thought to be in issue between Rowe and
the plaintiff. While the argument of counsel for the plaintiff centred on the right
of set-off available at law under the Statutes of Set-off in the case of mutual debts,
Willes J emphasized in his judgment that the set-off arose out of the same transaction out of which the liability of the surety on the note arose,[57] which suggests
that it may have been regarded as an equitable set-off arising out of a sufficiently
close connection between the demands.[58] Another interpretation of the case has
been proposed, that in truth it was not concerned with set-off at all. In *Cellulose
Products v Truda*[59] Isaacs J said that it was part of the arrangement in *Bechervaise v
Lewis* that the plaintiff was to collect the debts, and that the proceeds received by
the plaintiff had the effect of reducing the liability of Rowe which the defendant
had guaranteed. However the report does not mention that the plaintiff was
intended to collect payment, and moreover the case was argued on the basis

---

[52] (1872) LR 7 CP 372.
[53] *Rowlatt on Principal and Surety* (5th edn, 1999) 103–4 para 4–91. See also *Alcoy and Gandia
Railway and Harbour Co v Greenhill* (1897) 76 LT 542, 552–553 (Stirling J commenting that the
set-off in *Bechervaise v Lewis* arose out of the same transaction as that out of which the suretyship
arose).
[54] Willes, Keating, Montague Smith and Brett JJ.
[55] (1872) LR 7 CP 372, 377.
[56] (1872) LR 7 CP 372, 377.
[57] (1872) LR 7 CP 372, 377.
[58] Willes J referred during argument to equitable set-off, although that possibly could be explained on the ground that the principal had a set-off at law under the Statutes of Set-off as against
the creditor which could be invoked on equitable grounds by the surety.
[59] (1970) 92 WN (NSW) 561, 583–584. 586.

of set-off. Nor does the judgment suggest Isaacs J's analysis. On the contrary, Willes J commented that 'in our law set-off is not regarded as an extinction of the debt between the parties', and that 'we have a creditor who is equally liable to the principal as the principal to him'.[60] These comments indicate that subsisting cross-debts were thought to be in issue, which would not have been the case if the receipt of the proceeds by the plaintiff itself had the effect of reducing the debt.

Explanation of the set-off

However *Bechervaise v Lewis* is regarded, a surety ordinarily should be able to rely on the debtor's defence of equitable set-off or abatement.[61] The surety's right to invoke the defence may be explained on either of two grounds. **18.19**

In the first place, the guarantee as a matter of construction may require that de- **18.20** fences of set-off available to the principal be taken into account in determining the extent of the liability of the guarantor.[62] Thus, in *Langford Concrete Pty Ltd v Finlay*[63] a guarantor guaranteed 'the payment . . . of all moneys which are now payable or may in the future become payable' to the creditor by the principal.[64] The subject of the guarantee was moneys due under a contract for the performance of work, but it was alleged that the work was defective. The New South Wales Court of Appeal held that the guarantor could rely on the principal's cross-claim, commenting that:

> [T]his guarantee is so formulated that the guarantor can take advantage of the proposed cross-claim. All that the appellant undertook to pay was what was payable, that is, payable by the debtor. It was not a guarantee to pay the price, or the

---

[60] (1872) LR 7 CP 372, 377.

[61] *Williston on Contracts* (3rd edn, 1967) vol 10, 799 para 1251 sets out five objections to allowing the defence, which were reproduced in *Cellulose Products v Truda* (1970) 92 WN (NSW) 561, 575 from an earlier edition. The first and the second are considered below. In relation to the third, Isaacs J in the *Cellulose Products* case (at 573) doubted, correctly, whether the plea would succeed. The fifth is cured by requiring joinder of the debtor (see below). In so far as the fourth is concerned, regarding a number of sureties who are severally liable, this is more likely to arise when a set-off of unrelated debts under the Statutes of Set-off is in issue, and it is considered in that context below. In addition, the objection raised in Wood, *English and International Set-off* (1989) 636, 643, that the principal debtor as an alternative to equitable set-off may be entitled to rescind the guaranteed contract altogether because of the breach giving rise to the cross-claim, should not be a reason for denying a guarantor's right to invoke the defence generally. The debtor should retain the right to rescind, and if he exercises the right the guaranteed obligation in any event may fall away. Compare *Hurst v Bryk* [2002] 1 AC 185, 193, referring to *McDonald v Dennys Lascelles Ltd* (1933) 48 CLR 457, 476–477.

[62] Compare paras 18.32–18.35 below in relation to the situation in which the terms of the guarantee are such as to preclude reliance on the debtor's set-off.

[63] [1978] 1 NSWLR 14.

[64] Compare a guarantee which is expressed in terms of guaranteeing the payment of any monies advanced. See *Beri Distributors Pty Ltd v Pulitano* (1994) 10 SR (WA) 274, Western Australian District Court.

price without deduction, but to pay only what the debtor could have been compelled to pay.[65]

Similarly, if the guarantee is expressed to apply in the event of a default in payment
by the principal, and the principal has a cross-claim giving rise to an equitable set-
off for a sum which exceeds the debt, the substantive nature of the defence[66]
should have as a consequence that there has not been a default by the principal, so
that the creditor should not be entitled to proceed against the guarantor.[67] In *BOC
Group plc v Centeon LLC*[68] the guarantor guaranteed the 'prompt payment when
due of the obligations of Purchaser'. Rix J at first instance said that the guarantor
had not guaranteed more than the purchaser was obliged to pay.[69] If at the time
when the purchaser's payment obligation fell due the purchaser was entitled to a
set-off, the purchaser would not have been obliged to pay anything, and nor
should the guarantor.

18.21 But even apart from the question of construction of the guarantee,[70] the surety
should be entitled to invoke the principal debtor's defence on equitable grounds,
based upon the right that the surety has in equity to be exonerated by the debtor.[71]
The debtor, as the person principally liable to the creditor, should exonerate (or
relieve) the guarantor from liability to the creditor through the defence of set-off

---

[65] [1978] 1 NSWLR 14, 17. See also *Re Kleiss* (1996) 61 FCR 436, 440. *Langford Concrete Pty
Ltd v Finlay* should be compared to *Westco Motors (Distributors) Pty Ltd v Palmer* [1979] 2 NSWLR
93. The guarantee in that case related to amounts which were due and payable for goods supplied.
The debtor's cross-claim did not relate to the goods supplied, but rather was for damages for breach
of the Trade Practices Act (Cth) consequent upon allegations relating to restraint of trade, misuse of
market power and resale price maintenance. Sheppard J said that the cross-claim was separate and
distinct from the cause of action which the creditor had for the moneys it was owed, so that, in contrast to the *Langford Concrete* case, the cross-demand as a matter of construction did not reduce the
subject of the guarantee. Sheppard J went on to doubt whether the circumstances gave rise to an equitable set-off, but he said that that was not the real question. The real question was, what was it that
was guaranteed by the guarantor? The subject of the guarantee was the amount owing on the creditor's cause of action, which was not reduced by the cross-claim. See also the explanation of the case
in *Westpac Banking Corp v Eltran Pty Ltd* (1987) 14 FCR 541, 559. Subsequently Wood J in *Tooth
& Co Ltd v Rosier* (NSW Supreme Court, 7 June 1985, at pp 16–18) doubted the applicability of
the *Westco Motors* case when an equitable set-off is in issue.
[66] See paras 4.29–4.43 above.
[67] For a similar argument in a different context, see *Ashley Guarantee plc v Zacaria* [1993] 1 WLR
62, 67–68, 71.
[68] [1999] 1 All ER (Comm) 53, decision affirmed [1999] 1 All ER (Comm) 970, CA.
[69] [1999] 1 All ER (Comm) 53, 67. Rix J's analysis should not extend to a right of set-off under
the Statues of Set-Off which, unlike equitable set-off (see paras 4.29–4.43 above), is merely a procedural defence. See para 2.33 above.
[70] In Australia, Wood J in *Tooth & Co Ltd v Rosier* (NSW SC, 7 June 1985) commented (at 18)
that the ultimate question might not always turn on the construction of the guarantee alone.
Compare *Westco Motors (Distributors) Pty Ltd v Palmer* [1979] 2 NSWLR 93, 99.
[71] *Bechervaise v Lewis* (1872) LR 7 CP 372, 377; *Alcoy and Gandia Railway and Harbour Co Ltd
v Greenhill* (1897) 76 LT 542, 553; *Re Kleiss* (1996) 61 FCR 436, 440. This point was not considered in *Beri Distributors Pty Ltd v Pulitano* (1994) 10 SR (WA) 274, Western Australian District
Court.

that the debtor has against the creditor. The burden of the debt should be borne by the principal debtor,[72] and the surety's right to be exonerated should override the right that the debtor otherwise would have had to elect to waive the defence and to prosecute the cross-claim against the creditor in a separate action.[73] It is in a sense related to another principle considered earlier, that the creditor should not be able to avoid the set-off available to the principal by resorting to the guarantee. If the creditor sues the guarantor, the principal should be entitled to apply for orders restraining the action and for the court to give effect to the set-off.[74] The surety's right to be exonerated by the principal therefore should require the principal to relieve the surety by insisting that the set-off available to him is given effect.

Objection to the set-off

In *Indrisie v General Credits Ltd*[75] the Full Court of the Victorian Supreme Court **18.22** raised as an objection to the defence that it would involve a transference of the principal's claim in order to meet the surety's liability. This objection is without foundation, however.[76] As Willes J expressed the nature of the surety's defence in *Bechervaise v Lewis*,[77] 'the plea is a special plea by a surety, of a set-off *by the principal* . . .'. The surety is not seeking to employ the principal's claim against the creditor in a set-off against the surety's own liability on the contract of guarantee. Rather, the surety's argument is that the principal has a cross-claim against the creditor which is available to the principal as a set-off against the debt to the creditor, and because of the surety's right to be exonerated by the principal it is appropriate that the principal rather than the guarantor should bear the burden of the debt through a set-off against the principal's cross-claim.

Joinder of the principal

In *Bechervaise v Lewis*[78] the Court of Common Pleas was of the view that **18.23** the surety had a defence in equity against the creditor based upon the debtor's

---

[72] See generally *Rowlatt on Principal and Surety* (5th edn, 1999) 143 and O'Donovan and Phillips, *The Modern Contract of Guarantee* (3rd edn, 1996) 553–4.

[73] Compare the second objection in *Williston on Contracts* (3rd edn, 1967) vol 10, 799 para 1251. The equivalent passage in an earlier edition is referred to in *Cellulose Products Pty Ltd v Truda* (1970) 92 WN (NSW) 561, 575.

[74] See paras 18.02–18.05 above.

[75] [1985] VR 251, 254. See also the first objection referred to in *Cellulose Products Pty Ltd v Truda* (1970) 92 WN (NSW) 561, 572, 575.

[76] It was not apparently regarded as an objection by the Appeal Division of the Victorian Supreme Court in *Doherty v Murphy* [1996] 2 VR 553, 565.

[77] (1872) LR 7 CP 372, 377 (emphasis added). Similarly Drummond J in *Re Kleiss* (1996) 61 FCR 436, 441 referred to the situation in which 'a guarantor seeks to rely on an equitable set-off available to the principal debtor . . .'.

[78] (1872) LR 7 CP 372, 377. See para 18.18 above.

cross-claim, notwithstanding that the principal debtor was not a party to the proceedings. The question of the availability of a set-off arose upon a demurrer, but the case nevertheless is curious because the attitude of courts of equity[79] usually is that all parties materially interested in the subject of a suit should be made parties to the suit.[80] The debtor is the party who has the legal right to sue the creditor on the cross-claim, and therefore he should be present so that he may be bound by a determination as to a set-off. The creditor would then be protected against a subsequent claim by the debtor.[81] On that basis, one would have thought that the debtor should be a party in these cases. The surety should be entitled in that circumstance to have the debtor joined as a defendant, since the debtor's presence would be necessary to enable the surety to set up a defence to the creditor's action.[82] Further, when a creditor is applying for summary judgment against the surety, it would be consistent with that view to impose a condition upon the grant of leave to defend that the debtor be joined.

18.24 There is support for that approach in Australia[83] and in England,[84] but in England there is also support for the proposition that joinder is not necessary in the case of equitable set-off. Thus *Rowlatt on Principal and Surety*[85] expresses the principle in terms that: 'Where the principal is entitled to a set-off against the creditor's demand arising out of the same transaction as the debt guaranteed, and in fact reducing that debt, the surety is entitled to plead it in an action by the creditor against the surety alone.' Similar views have been expressed on other occasions.[86]

---

[79] While *Bechervaise v Lewis* was decided by a common law court (the Common Pleas), the Common Law Procedure Act 1854 (17 & 18 Vict c 125, ss 83–86) made provision for equitable defences to be pleaded at law.

[80] See *Daniell's Chancery Practice* (8th edn, 1914) vol 1, 147.

[81] See *Daniell's Chancery Practice* (8th edn, 1914) vol 1, 151.

[82] *Amon v Raphael Tuck & Sons Ltd* [1956] 1 QB 357, 386.

[83] *Cellulose Products Pty Ltd v Truda* (1970) 92 WN (NSW) 561, 588; *Indrisie v General Credits Ltd* [1985] VR 251, 254; *Doherty v Murphy* [1996] 2 VR 553 (summary judgment application); *Re Kleiss* (1996) 61 FCR 436, 441; O'Donovan and Phillips, *The Modern Contract of Guarantee* (3rd edn, 1996) 549. Compare *Commonwealth Development Bank v Windermere Pastoral Co Pty Ltd* [1999] NSWSC 518, in which a guarantor successfully resisted a summary judgment application by the creditor on the basis of an arguable equitable set-off available to the principal debtor, without any condition being imposed that the debtor be joined, and *Electricity Meter Manufacturing Co Ltd v D'Ombrain* (1927) 44 WN (NSW) 131 (which was criticized in *Cellulose Products* (1970) 92 WN (NSW) 561, 582–583) in relation to an application to strike out the guarantor's plea of set-off. When a creditor suing for a debt has joined both the principal debtor and the surety as defendants, both defendants may be granted leave to defend on the basis of a possible right of set-off available to the debtor. See *Petersville Ltd v Rosgrae Distributors Pty Ltd* (1975) 11 SASR 433.

[84] *Wilson v Mitchell* [1939] 2 KB 869, 871; *National Westminster Bank plc v Skelton* [1993] 1 WLR 72, 81 (which was argued on the basis of equitable set-off notwithstanding that the company was in liquidation); *Chitty on Contracts* (28th edn, 1999) vol 2, 1338 para 44-075.

[85] *Rowlatt on Principal and Surety* (5th edn, 1999) 103–4.

[86] In *Hyundai Shipbuilding and Heavy Industries Co Ltd v Pournaras* [1978] 2 Lloyd's Rep 502, 508 the Court of Appeal referred to the corresponding passage in an earlier edition of *Rowlatt* ((3rd edn, 1939) 137–8) without adverse comment. See also *Halsbury's Laws of England* (4th edn reissue,

The statement should be read cautiously, however. A set-off between the principal debtor and the creditor pursuant to a set-off agreement between them would operate as a payment, and therefore it would reduce the debt,[87] but the passage in *Rowlatt* does not identify expressly the forms of set-off to which it was intended to apply.[88] According to the transcript of Scott LJ's unreserved judgment in the Court of Appeal in the unreported case of *Barclays Bank plc v Gruffydd*,[89] he commented, in the context of an application by a guarantor for leave to defend on the basis of the principal debtor's set-off, that: 'A set-off, whether legal or equitable, available to the principal debtor extinguishes, or reduces pro tanto, the amount of the creditor's claim.'[90] Prior to judgment, however, neither an equitable set-off nor a defence of set-off under the Statutes of Set-off has the effect of reducing or extinguishing the debt.[91] The reference in *Rowlatt* to the 'same transaction' suggests that the passage had in contemplation equitable set-off, which admittedly is a substantive defence. But by 'substantive defence' it is meant that, where circumstances exist which give rise to the set-off, the creditor is not permitted in equity to regard the debtor as being indebted to the extent of the set-off. Because of the substantive nature of the defence its effect in equity is similar to a discharge of the debt *pro tanto*, but it does not bring about a reduction in or an extinguishment of the demands at law until judgment for a set-off.[92] Moreover, *Barclays Bank plc v Gruffydd* itself seems contrary to the view in *Rowlatt*. The principal debtor in that case was in liquidation, and Scott LJ said that the insolvency set-off section rather than equitable set-off was in issue. Unlike equitable set-off, insolvency set-off, does bring about an automatic extinguishment of the debts to the extent of the set-off, at the date of the liquidation,[93] but it was still accepted in the *Gruffydd* case that a grant of leave to defend should be subject to a condition that an application be made to join the principal debtor as a party. That view is debatable in relation to insolvency set-off,[94] but it nevertheless should apply *a fortiori* to equitable set-off which

---

1993) vol 20, 143–144 para 225. In *Barclays Bank plc v Gruffydd* (CA, 30 October 1992) Scott LJ accepted that the corresponding passage in an earlier edition of *Halsbury* correctly stated the law.

[87] See para 18.08 above.

[88] The statement in *Rowlatt* would extend however to the circumstances in issue in *Murphy v Glass* (1869) LR 2 PC 408, as explained in *Cellulose Products Pty Ltd v Truda* (1970) 92 WN (NSW) 561, 580–582. See also the explanation of *Bechervaise v Lewis* (1872) LR 7 CP 372 in *Cellulose Products v Truda* at 583–4 and 586, for which see para 18.18 above.

[89] CA 30 October 1992 (Scott, Nolan and Purchas LJJ).

[90] In referring to 'legal set-off', Scott LJ may have had in contemplation the common law defence of abatement, which in England is regarded as a substantive defence (see para 2.93 above), as opposed to set-off under the Statutes of Set-off, which is a procedural defence. See paras 2.33–2.48 above.

[91] *Langford Concrete Pty Ltd v Finlay* [1978] 1 NSWLR 14, 18. See also para 2.33 above in relation to the Statutes of Set-off.

[92] See paras 4.30 & 4.31 above. See also para 2.94 above in relation to abatement.

[93] See paras 6.79–6.103 above.

[94] See para 18.30 below.

does not operate to extinguish the debts at law until judgment. On the other hand, the decision of the House of Lords in *Trafalgar House Construction (Regions) Ltd v General Surety and Guarantee Co Ltd*[95] suggests that joinder may not be required in the case of an equitable set-off. The House of Lords accepted that a consequence of characterizing the bond in issue in that case as a guarantee was that an equitable set-off[96] that could have been relied on by the principal obligor as a defence could also be relied on by the guarantor. The case concerned an application for summary judgment by a creditor on a bond against a guarantor. Their Lordships held that the guarantor was entitled to leave to defend on the basis of the principal's set-off entitlements, without imposing a condition that the principal be joined.[97] But notwithstanding that it was not made a condition in that case, the better view is that the principal debtor should be a party when the action is tried.[98]

18.25 In Australia, where the weight of authority favours the view that joinder is necessary,[99] one situation in which it nevertheless has been recognized that joinder is not required is in an application to set aside a bankruptcy notice. In *Re Kleiss*[100] a creditor issued a bankruptcy notice against a guarantor, whereupon the guarantor applied to set it aside on the basis of an equitable set-off available to the principal debtor against the creditor. Drummond J commented that, while joinder may well be necessary in an action brought by a creditor against a guarantor, failure to comply with the procedural requirement would not prevent the Bankruptcy Court determining that, because of the debtor's entitlement to an equitable set-off, there was no debt truly owing by the guarantor.[101]

(4) Statutes of Set-off

18.26 It is sometimes said that, while a guarantor may be able to invoke the debtor's equitable set-off as a defence to an action by the creditor, a similar right is not available when the debtor's set-off arises under the Statutes of Set-off.[102] However

---

[95] [1996] 1 AC 199.

[96] Lord Jauncey of Tullichettle in delivering the judgment of the House of Lords referred simply to set-off, without commenting upon the nature of the set-off in issue. However, since the liability of the obligor was in damages, it could only have been an equitable set-off, and indeed counsel for the surety referred in his argument to equitable set-off.

[97] See also in Australia *Commonwealth Development Bank v Windermere Pastoral Co Pty Ltd* [1999] NSWSC 518 and *Electricity Meter Manufacturing Co Ltd v D'Ombrain* (1927) 44 WN (NSW) 131 (application to strike out the guarantor's plea of set-off).

[98] See also Phillips, 'When Should the Guarantor be Permitted to Rely on the Principal's Set-off?' [2001] LMCLQ 383, 387.

[99] See para 18.24 above.

[100] (1996) 61 FCR 436.

[101] (1996) 61 FCR 436, 441.

[102] Wood, *English and International Set-off* (1989) 645; O'Donovan and Phillips, *The Modern Contract of Guarantee* (3rd edn, 1996) 551–2; Andrews and Millett, *Law of Guarantees* (3rd edn, 2000) 366; *Re Kleiss* (1996) 61 FCR 436, 440–441; Phillips, 'When Should the Guarantor be Permitted to Rely on the Principal's Set-off?' [2001] LMCLQ 383.

there is no compelling reason for restricting the defences available to the guarantor in that manner.[103] Set-off under the Statutes admittedly differs from equitable set-off in that it is a procedural rather than a substantive defence.[104] But given that the right of the surety to invoke the debtor's defence of equitable set-off is not based upon the substantive nature of the defence, but rather the surety's right to be exonerated by the principal debtor,[105] the fact that set-off under the Statutes is procedural should not preclude the surety from relying on it.[106] It is not a convincing argument that the debtor may owe other debts to the creditor which he may have preferred to set off against the cross-debt owing by the creditor,[107] since the surety's right to be exonerated should override the debtor's entitlement to utilize the debt as he chooses. Nor is *Harrison v Nettleship*[108] contrary to this view.[109] In that case the surety's unsuccessful argument for a set-off was based upon cross-debts which it was said were owing by the creditor to the debtor 'at one time' during the course of their dealings, as opposed to presently existing debts. A right of set-off under the Statutes is a procedural defence which does not bring about an automatic extinction of the debts in question. A surety could only have a defence to the extent that a defence is still open to the debtor at time of the creditor's action.

The argument in favour of the surety's right to rely on the defence is consistent **18.27** with a broad statement in *Halsbury*,[110] which has been quoted with evident approval in the Court of Appeal,[111] to the effect that a surety can avail himself of any right of set-off that the principal debtor has against the creditor. The statement

---

[103] In Australia, in addition to the cases referred to below, see the submission to which Sheller JA referred without adverse comment in *Lord v Direct Acceptance Corp* (1993) 32 NSWLR 362, 368–369.

[104] See paras 2.33–2.48 above, and compare paras 4.29–4.43 above in relation to equitable set-off.

[105] See para 18.21 above.

[106] Compare *York City and County Banking Co v Bainbridge* (1880) 43 LT 732 in relation to the current account, assuming that the defendant was indeed a surety.

[107] See Steyn, 'Guarantees: The Co-extensiveness Principle' (1974) 90 LQR 246, 263.

[108] (1833) 2 My & K 423, 39 ER 1005.

[109] Compare Wood, *English and International Set-off* (1989) 645–6, and also Andrews and Millett, *Law of Guarantees* (3rd edn, 2000) 366. Andrews and Millett (*loc cit*) have also referred to *National Bank of Australasia v Swan* (1872) LR 3 VR (L) 168, but the issue in that case did not concern a set-off available to the principal debtor.

[110] *Halsbury's Laws of England* (4th edn, 1978) vol 20, 102 para 190. Compare the formulation in the 1993 reissue (at vol 20, 143 para 225).

[111] *Hyundai Shipbuilding and Heavy Industries Co Ltd v Pournaras* [1978] 2 Lloyd's Rep 502, 508, *per* Slade LJ, with whose judgment Stephenson LJ agreed. See also Scott LJ in *Barclays Bank plc v Gruffydd* (CA, 30 October 1992). Compare *National Westminster Bank v Skelton* [1993] 1 WLR 72, 78–79, *per* Slade LJ, with whom Anthony Lincoln J agreed. In Canada, see *Diebel v Stratford Improvement Co* (1917) 33 DLR 296, 301, *per* Hodgins JA ('equity would require that [the guarantor] should be allowed to set off that which the debtor himself could set off').

was not limited to any particular form of set-off.[112] Further, since the Statutes do not require any connection between the debts the subject of a proposed set-off, it should not be necessary that the debt owing to the principal should have arisen out of the same transaction as the guaranteed debt.[113] On the other hand, for the reason set out earlier in the context of equitable set-off,[114] the debtor should be made a party to the proceedings. Set-off under the Statutes is a procedural defence,[115] and it could not be said that the entitlement to the set-off itself reduces the debt.[116]

18.28 *Williston on Contracts* raises as an objection to the recognition of the defence that there may be a number of sureties severally liable.[117] This circumstance should not prevent the application of the principle, however. If the sureties are jointly and severally liable for the same debt, an order for a set-off in an action against one surety would give rise to a payment to the creditor to the extent of the set-off, which should provide a defence to other sureties as well.[118] Alternatively, a number of sureties each may be severally liable for distinct parts of the same debt, or there may be separate guarantees in place in relation to separate debts owing by the principal to the creditor. Since the right of a surety to rely on the principal's right of set-off is based on equitable grounds, the maxim that equality is equity may apply in relation to sureties who are the subject of an action at the time when the issue arises, so that each may be entitled to a defence to the extent of a proportionate part of the cross-debt owing to the debtor. But what if a particular surety is not the subject of a present action? Because the Statutes of Set-off do not result in an automatic extinction of cross-demands, the better view is that the surety not being sued should be disregarded. If the rule instead were adopted that the defence

---

[112] In Story *Commentaries on Equity Jurisprudence* (6th edn, 1853) vol 2, 931 para 1437, *Ex parte Hanson* (1811) 18 Ves Jun 232, 34 ER 305 (see para 18.03 above) is referred to as authority for the proposition that, if one of two joint debtors is only a surety for the other, he may in equity set off against the joint debt a separate debt owing to the principal by the creditor. The set-off was said to be available in equity, and was not limited to bankruptcy

[113] Compare *Sun Alliance Pensions Life and Investments Services Ltd v RJL* [1991] 2 Lloyd's Rep 410, 416–417. While in *Bechervaise v Lewis* (1872) LR 7 CP 372 the principal's cross-claim was for a liquidated sum, and Willes J noted in his judgment that it arose out of the same transaction out of which the surety's liability arose, the set-off in issue may have been regarded as an equitable set-off. See para 18.18 above. In any event, it is doubtful whether the comment regarding the same transaction was intended to lay down a rule applicable generally whenever a surety seeks to rely on the debtor's set-off.

[114] See para 18.23 above.

[115] See paras 2.33–2.48 above.

[116] Compare para 18.24 above in relation to equitable set-off. Scott LJ's comment in *Barclays Bank plc v Gruffydd* (CA, 30 October 1992), to the effect that a legal set-off available to the principal debtor reduces the amount of the creditor's claim, may have been a reference to the common law defence of abatement, which in England is regarded as substantive in its operation. See paras 2.93–2.96 above.

[117] *Williston on Contracts* (3rd edn, 1967) vol 10, 799 para 1251. See also Steyn, 'Guarantees: The Co-Extensiveness Principle' (1974) 90 LQR 246, 263.

[118] See para 12.21 above.

available to a surety the subject of an action must be reduced in order to take into account the possibility of a future action against another surety, the creditor could pay off the remainder of the cross-debt not set off in the first action before the second surety is sued, in which case the defence would be lost to the second surety in any event.

(5) Cross-action not Available as a Set-off

A statement in *Halsbury*,[119] to which the Court of Appeal has referred with evident approval,[120] suggests that a surety on being sued by the creditor can avail himself of a cross-action which the principal debtor could have asserted by way of counterclaim in an action on the guaranteed debt. This statement would appear to be expressed in unduly wide terms in so far as it may extend to a mere counterclaim not available as a set-off.[121] The surety should only be entitled to a defence to the creditor's claim if the principal's cross-action in turn would have provided a defence to the principal against a claim on the guaranteed debt.[122] Indeed, this point is made in a subsequent reissue of the relevant volume of *Halsbury*.[123] On the other hand, the procedure outlined by Isaacs J in *Cellulose Products v Truda*[124] should still be relevant in the case of a mere counterclaim, so that the surety could join the principal as a third party and claim an indemnity, and the principal in turn could join the creditor as a fourth party in relation to the cross-claim.

18.29

(6) Insolvency Set-off

If the principal debtor is bankrupt or is a company in liquidation, the surety should be entitled to assert a set-off under the set-off section in the insolvency

18.30

---

[119] *Halsbury's Laws of England* (4th edn, 1978) vol 20, 102 para 190. See para 18.10 above.

[120] *Hyundai Shipbuilding and Heavy Industries Co Ltd v Pournaras* [1978] 2 Lloyd's Rep 502, 508, and see also Scott LJ in *Barclays Bank plc v Gruffydd* (CA, 30 October 1992). Compare *National Westminster Bank v Skelton* [1993] 1 WLR 72, 78–79.

[121] While the House of Lords in *Trafalgar House Construction (Regions) Ltd v General Surety and Guarantee Co Ltd* [1996] 1 AC 199, 207 referred to the appellants (as guarantors) as having been entitled to raise 'all questions of sums due and cross-claims' which would have been available to the principal debtor, it is apparent that a defence of set-off was thought to be in issue. See in particular [1996] 1 AC 199, 206, and also the argument of counsel for the appellant at 201.

[122] *Oastler v Pound* (1863) 7 LT 852; *The Aliakmon Progress* [1978] 2 Lloyd's Rep 499. See also *Westco Motors (Distributors) Pty Ltd v Palmer* [1979] 2 NSWLR 93, and the judgment of Hutley JA in *Covino v Bandag Manufacturing Pty Ltd* [1983] 1 NSWLR 237, 238. Compare *Sun Alliance Pensions Life & Investments Services Ltd v RJL* [1991] 2 Lloyd's Rep 410, 416–417, where it is suggested that a guarantor can rely on the debtor's unliquidated cross-claim not arising out of the same transaction to extinguish or reduce the guarantor's own liability if the principal debtor is joined as a party, and also *Chitty on Contracts* (28th edn, 1999) vol 2, 1338 para 44-075, which suggests a similar proposition.

[123] *Halsbury's Laws of England* (4th edn reissue, 1993) vol 20, 144 para 225 n 2, referring to *Aliakmon Maritime Corp v Trans Ocean Continental Shipping Ltd (The Aliakmon Progress)* [1978] 2 Lloyd's Rep 499.

[124] (1970) 92 WN (NSW) 561, 588. See para 18.12 above.

legislation as between the debtor and the creditor.[125] According to the prevailing view as to the nature of insolvency set-off,[126] a set-off as between the debtor and the creditor would have occurred automatically upon the occurrence of the debtor's bankruptcy or liquidation. The debt to the extent of the set-off would have been paid, and a discharge of the principal debtor in that manner by way of a set-off should also discharge the surety.[127] If the debt to the creditor has been reduced by an automatic set-off so as to discharge to that extent the surety as well as the principal, prima facie the surety should be entitled to plead the discharge as a defence to an action by the creditor without joining the principal debtor.[128] In Australia it has been said that the debtor need not be joined if the debtor is insolvent,[129] although it has also been suggested that the creditor, if he wishes, may join the debtor so as to have the debtor bound by the court's determination.[130] In England on the other hand there are cases which suggest that joinder is

---

[125] In addition to the cases referred to below, see *Wreckair Pty Ltd v Emerson* [1992] 1 Qd R 700 (Full Court). In New South Wales, see also *Tooth & Co v Rosier* (NSW SC, Wood J, 7 June 1985). In *Westco Motors (Distributors) Pty Ltd v Palmer* [1979] 2 NSWLR 93 the principal debtor was in liquidation. In rejecting the surety's claim for a set-off, Sheppard J held that the cross-demands between the principal and the creditor were not sufficiently connected to give rise to an equitable set-off. The insolvency set-off section was not considered, however. A similar comment may be made in relation to *Re Kleiss* (1996) 61 FCR 436. *Beri Distributors Pty Ltd v Pulitano* (1994) 10 SR (WA) 274, 276–277, Western Australian District Court, should also be considered in that context. Cockburn CJ in *Rouquette v Overmann* (1875) LR 10 QB 525, 541–542, in explaining *Allen v Kemble* (1848) 6 Moore 314, 13 ER 704, seemed to doubt that English law permits a surety to invoke a set-off as between a bankrupt creditor and the principal debtor, but that was before the courts adopted the automatic theory of insolvency set-off.

[126] See paras 6.79–6.103 above.

[127] *Re Bank of Credit and Commerce International SA (No 8)* [1996] Ch 245, 268, CA, referring to *Ex parte Hanson* (1806) 12 Ves Jun 346, 33 ER 131 and see generally *McDonald v Dennys Lascelles Ltd* (1933) 48 CLR 457, 479–480. On the other hand, the Court of Appeal in *BCCI (No 8)* suggested (at 268–269) that a discharge of the surety by way of a set-off under the insolvency set-off section may not discharge the principal debtor. That proposition seems doubtful. See paras 12.26–12.36 above.

[128] A standard clause in a guarantee, to the effect that the liability of the guarantor is not to be affected by any act matter or thing which but for the clause might release the guarantor, would not assist when a set-off occurred automatically on the date of liquidation. See *National Mutual Royal Bank Ltd v Ginges* (NSW SC, Brownie J, 15 March 1991).

[129] *Langford Concrete Pty Ltd v Finlay* [1978] 1 NSWLR 14, 18–19 (referring to *Cellulose Products v Truda* (1970) 92 WN (NSW) 561, 585); *Re Kleiss* (1996) 61 FCR 436, 440. Admittedly the conclusion that the principal debtor need not be joined was not expressly justified in those cases on the basis of the automatic nature of insolvency set-off, and indeed the insolvency set-off section was not referred to. The basis of the conclusion instead was the perception that the requirement of joinder is one for the benefit of the creditor, and that joinder can be of no practical benefit to the creditor where the debtor is in liquidation or insolvent. See the *Langford Concrete* case at 19. See also *Westco Motors (Distributors) Pty Ltd v Palmer* [1979] 2 NSWLR 93, 97 and *Tooth & Co Ltd v Rosier* (NSW SC, Wood J, 7 June 1985). Compare *Elkhoury v Farrow Mortgage Services Pty Ltd* (1993) 114 ALR 541, 548–549 in which the creditor was in liquidation, but the court considered only equitable set-off and not insolvency set-off.

[130] *Langford Concrete Pty Ltd v Finlay* [1978] 1 NSWLR 14, 19.

required,[131] a conclusion that seems curious given views that have been expressed to the effect that the principal need not be joined if the set-off reduces the debt.[132] In *Sun Alliance Pensions Life and Investments Services Ltd v RJL*[133] the principal debtor was a company in liquidation. The company had a cross-claim for unliquidated damages against the creditor, and Mr Anthony Colman QC, sitting as a Deputy Judge, said that, in order for the guarantor to rely on the company's cross-claim as a defence, the guarantor would have had to join the company as a party, for which leave of the Companies Court would have been required given the liquidation.[134] However the possible effect of the insolvency set-off section was not considered. *Barclays Bank plc v Gruffydd*[135] also concerned a corporate principal debtor in liquidation. The creditor applied for summary judgment against the guarantor, who sought leave to defend on the basis of a set-off as between the creditor and the company. Scott LJ noted that set-off under rule 4.90 of the Insolvency Rules 1986 was in issue, as opposed to equitable set-off. He said that, if the company's claim could be regarded as having sufficient substance, leave to defend should be granted on terms that, unless the liquidator of the company agreed that the company would regard itself as bound by an adjudication on the claim in the company's absence, an application would have to be made for leave to join the company as a party. He went on to hold that the circumstances were not such as to justify leave to defend. Nolan and Purchas LJJ differed from Scott LJ on that issue, but Nolan LJ also said that leave to defend should be subject to the condition that an application be made to join the company.

Two debts owing to the creditor

Where the principal debtor owes two debts to the creditor, one of which is guaranteed and the other is not, and the creditor is separately liable to the debtor, a set-off under the insolvency legislation should take effect rateably as between the two debts.[136] **18.31**

---

[131] In addition to the cases referred to below, see *National Westminster Bank plc v Skelton* [1993] 1 WLR 72, 81. Compare *Alcoy and Gandia Railway and Harbour Co Ltd v Greenhill* (1897) 76 LT 542, the principal debtor being Murrietas Ltd which was not a party (although compare the discussion of the case *in Cellulose Products* (at (1970) 92 WN (NSW) 561, 585)).

[132] See para 18.24 above.

[133] [1991] 2 Lloyds Rep 410.

[134] [1991] 2 Lloyds Rep 410, 418. Leave of the court is required to commence a proceeding against a company in liquidation. See the Insolvency Act 1986, s 130(2). In the case of bankruptcy, see the Insolvency Act 1986, s 285. Since the purpose of seeking to join the bankrupt or the company in liquidation would be to assist the surety in defending the action brought against him on the basis of a prior right of exoneration, rather than to determine a point in the insolvency, it is suggested that leave ordinarily should be granted. See *Re Hutton (A Bankrupt)* [1969] 2 Ch 201 with respect to an application to stay proceedings already commenced against a bankrupt.

[135] CA 30 October 1992 (Purchas, Nolan and Scott LJJ).

[136] Consistent with *Re Unit 2 Windows Ltd* [1985] 1 WLR 1383, for which see para 6.116 above. Compare para 18.26 above in relation to the Statutes of Set-off.

(7) Contract Excluding the Defence

18.32 A guarantor's right to rely on the debtor's cross-claim as a defence may be excluded by contract. In the first place, if the contract between the debtor and the creditor is effective to exclude set-off as between those parties,[137] it should be equally effective as against the guarantor. If the debtor's cross-claim would not provide the debtor with a defence, the guarantor should not be in a better position. Alternatively, the contract of guarantee may be formulated in terms evidencing an intention that the surety is not to have the benefit of any defence of set-off that is available to the debtor.[138] This may be the case if the guarantor's liability is expressed to be primary,[139] and similarly the set-off would not apply if the instrument in question is an irrevocable letter of credit or a bank guarantee given in circumstances such that it is equivalent to an irrevocable letter of credit,[140] or if it takes the form of a bond which is not a guarantee.[141] On the other hand, a promise in a guarantee not in those forms to pay whatever is payable by the principal would not preclude reliance by the guarantor on the principal debtor's set-off. A guarantee in those terms only obliges the guarantor to pay what the principal debtor could have been compelled to pay, and if the principal could not have been compelled to pay anything because of a defence of set-off available against the creditor, the guarantor similarly should not be liable.[142]

---

[137] An agreement purporting to exclude rights of set-off will not be effective in a bankruptcy or a company liquidation. See paras 6.71–6.72 above.

[138] In addition to the cases referred to below, see *Continental Illinois National Bank and Trust Co of Chicago v Papanicolaou* [1986] 2 Lloyd's Rep 441 (although in that case the cross-claims seem to have been regarded as belonging to the guarantors); *Coca Cola Financial Corp v Finsat International Ltd* [1998] QB 43; *Try Build Ltd v Blue Star Garages Ltd* (1998) 66 Con LR 90. In Australia, see *Re Kleiss* (1996) 61 FCR 436, 439–440; *Dougan v Conias* [2000] FCA 1556. A stipulation that a debtor is to pay 'without deduction' on occasions has been said to be insufficient to preclude the debtor from relying on an equitable set-off available against the creditor (see *Connaught Restaurants Ltd v Indoor Leisure Ltd* [1994] 1 WLR 501, and paras 5.82–5.86 above), and if that is the case it similarly should not suffice to preclude reliance by a guarantor on the debtor's set-off. In Australia, compare *Langford Concrete Pty Ltd v Finlay* [1978] 1 NSWLR 14, 17 and *Australia and New Zealand Banking Group Ltd v Harvey* (1994) 16 ATPR 46–132 at p 53,643. Note also the possible application of the Unfair Contract Terms Act 1977. See paras 5.94–5.100 above, and Phillips, 'When Should the Guarantor be Permitted to Rely on the Principal's Set-off?' [2001] LMCLQ 383, 384.

[139] *National Westminster Bank plc v Skelton* [1993] 1 WLR 72, 79–80. Prima facie a 'principal debtor' clause in a guarantee should have a similar effect. See *Elkhoury v Farrow Mortgage Services Pty Ltd* (1993) 114 ALR 541, 549. Compare *Langford Concrete Pty Ltd v Finlay* [1978] 1 NSWLR 14, 19 (where the guarantor was described as a principal debtor) and *Commonwealth Development Bank v Windermere Pastoral Co Pty Ltd* [1999] NSWSC 518 (see the terms of the guarantee at [28]-[29]), in neither of which was the point considered.

[140] *Intraco Ltd v Notis Shipping Corp (The Bhoja Trader)* [1981] 2 Lloyd's Rep 256; *Power Curber International Ltd v National Bank of Kuwait SAK* [1981] 1 WLR 1233.

[141] Compare *Trafalgar House Construction (Regions) Ltd v General Surety and Guarantee Co Ltd* [1996] 1 AC 199.

[142] *Langford Concrete Pty Ltd v Finlay* [1978] 1 NSWLR 14, and compare *Westco Motors (Distributors) Pty Ltd v Palmer* [1979] 2 NSWLR 93, 98–99. See para 18.20 above.

The court may examine the factual or business background of the guarantee in **18.33**
order to ascertain the intention of the parties in relation to the availability of a set-
off.[143] In *Hyundai Shipbuilding and Heavy Industries Co Ltd v Pournaras*[144] a ship-
yard had contracted to build a number of ships for a buyer, with the defendants
guaranteeing 'the payment in accordance with the terms of the contract of all
sums due or to become due by the buyer to you under the contract, and in case the
buyer is in default of any such payment the undersigned will forthwith make the
payment in default on behalf of the buyer'. The buyer repudiated the contracts,
and the yard, having accepted the repudiation, sued the guarantors for payment
of instalments which had accrued and were unpaid. The buyer had paid an
amount on account to the yard which may have exceeded the damages payable
by the buyer consequent upon the repudiation, and the Court of Appeal[145] was
prepared to assume that the buyer could have claimed back from the yard so much
of the amount already paid as exceeded the yard's loss and damage.[146] On that
assumption, the guarantors argued that they were entitled to take advantage of the
buyer's right so as to reduce or extinguish the liability under the guarantees.[147]
Their argument to that effect failed.[148] In delivering the judgment of the Court of
Appeal, Roskill LJ commented that the guarantees could have been more clearly
drafted, but he said that, having regard to the factual and business background of
the guarantees,[149] the avowed object was to enable the yard to recover from the
guarantors the amount due, irrespective of the position between the yard and the
buyer, so that the yard could get the money from the guarantors without difficulty
if they could not get it from the buyer. If the guarantors' argument were given
effect, he said that the commercial utility of the guarantee would have been nulli-
fied.[150] In a later discussion of the *Pournaras* case,[151] Rix J emphasized that the
guarantees in that case concerned shipbuilding contracts where the guaranteed
instalments were necessary to give the shipbuilders cash flow necessary to complete the ships, that the guarantees were drafted in terms of a conditional agreement to pay forthwith (in other words, the guarantors would pay if the debtor
failed to pay) as opposed to an undertaking by the guarantors that the debtor

---

[143] In *Barclays Bank plc v Gruffydd* (CA, 30 October 1992) Scott LJ commented that the terms
of a guarantee, either express or to be implied from the commercial background to the transaction,
may disentitle the surety from reliance on a set-off defence.

[144] [1978] 2 Lloyd's Rep 502. Compare *BOC Group plc v Centeon plc* [1999] 1 All ER (Comm)
53.

[145] Stephenson and Roskill LJJ.

[146] In accordance with *Dies v British and International Mining and Finance Corp Ltd* [1939] 1 KB
724. See however Andrews and Millett, *Law of Guarantees* (3rd edn, 2000) 227–30.

[147] See the discussion at [1978] 2 Lloyd's Rep 502, 507–508.

[148] For a criticism of the decision, see Andrews and Millett, *Law of Guarantees* (3rd edn, 2000)
227–8.

[149] See the discussion of the 'factual matrix' at [1978] 2 Lloyd's Rep 502, 506.

[150] [1978] 2 Lloyd's Rep 502, 508.

[151] *BOC Group plc v Centeon LLC* [1999] 1 All ER (Comm) 53, 63–67.

would carry out its obligations,[152] and that the guarantors' obligation to pay 'forthwith' accrued at a time when the principal debtor did not have an arguable set-off, since the debtor's right to the return of the amount paid on account did not accrue until the later repudiation.

18.34 Subsequent to the *Pournaras* case the House of Lords in *Trafalgar House Construction (Regions) Ltd v General Surety and Guarantee Co Ltd*[153] said that clear and unambiguous language must be used to displace the normal consequences of a contract of suretyship, but nevertheless agreed that the language of the guarantees in the *Pournaras* case was sufficient to enable recovery from the guarantors irrespective of the position between the yard and the buyer.[154]

Insolvency set-off in the debtor's bankruptcy or liquidation

18.35 If the principal debtor has become bankrupt or has gone into liquidation, so that the insolvency set-off section applied automatically on the occurrence of the bankruptcy or the liquidation so as to extinguish the debt owing to the creditor to the extent of the debtor's cross-claim,[155] it is suggested that the clearest words would be required to preserve the guarantor's liability to the creditor.[156]

D. Mortgage Given to Secure Another Person's Debt

18.36 A contract of suretyship may take the form of a mortgage given to secure a debt owing by another person to a creditor. The question whether the creditor is entitled to possession of the mortgaged premises, or to exercise security rights which are dependent upon default, in circumstances where the principal debtor is entitled to an equitable set-off, was considered earlier.[157]

---

[152] See Lord Reid's discussion of the distinction in *Moschi v Lep Air Services Ltd* [1973] AC 331, 344–345.

[153] [1996] 1 AC 199, 208.

[154] See also *Hyundai Heavy Industries Co Ltd v Papadopoulos* [1980] 1 WLR 1129, 1137–1138, *per* Viscount Dilhorne, 1142–1143, *per* Lord Edmund Davies, 1152, *per* Lord Fraser of Tullybelton.

[155] See para 18.30 above.

[156] As a general principle, but subject to some qualifications and exceptions, discharge of the principal debtor also discharges the surety. See *McDonald v Dennys Lascelles Ltd* (1933) 48 CLR 457, 479–480. Compare *Westco Motors (Distributors) Pty Ltd v Palmer* [1979] 2 NSWLR 93, although the possible application and effect of the insolvency set-off section was not considered. A similar comment may be made in relation to *National Westminster Bank plc v Skelton* [1993] 1 WLR 72, which was concerned with a claim for possession under a mortgage given by a third party as surety, as opposed to a personal claim against the surety for payment of the debt. See paras 4.91 and 4.92 above.

[157] See paras 4.88–4.105 above.

E. Surety's Right to Rely on a Co-surety's Set-off

A right of exoneration similar to that available to a surety as against the principal **18.37**
debtor[158] does not apply as between co-sureties on a joint and several covenant. If
one of the sureties is sued by the creditor, that surety may not set off a debt owing
by the creditor to a co-surety.[159]

F. Set-off Between the Surety and the Principal Debtor

As between a surety and the principal debtor, the surety after paying the creditor **18.38**
may employ his claim for an indemnity as a set-off under the Statutes of Set-off.[160]
Since however the Statutes extended only to the case of mutual debts which were
both presently existing and payable at the date of the action,[161] a mere contingent
right to an indemnity, where the surety has not paid the creditor, will not give rise
to a defence under the Statutes.

The position with respect to insolvency set-off is more complex, and was consid- **18.39**
ered earlier.[162]

---

[158] See para 18.21 above.
[159] *Bowyear v Pawson* (1881) 6 QBD 540; *Lord v Direct Acceptance Corp Ltd* (1993) 32 NSWLR
362, 371–372.
[160] *Rodgers v Maw* (1846) 15 M & W 444, 153 ER 924.
[161] See para 2.29 above.
[162] See paras 8.07–8.26 (contingent debt owing by the insolvent) and paras 8.27–8.37 (contingent debt owing to the insolvent) above.

BIBLIOGRAPHY

1. Books

ANDREWS AND MILLETT, *Law of Guarantees* (3rd edn, 2000), London: Sweet & Maxwell

Arnould's Law of Marine Insurance and Average (16th edn, 1981), London: Stevens and Sons

Australian Law Reform Commission Report No 45, *General Insolvency Inquiry* (1988) ('the Harmer Report')

BABINGTON, *The Law of Set-off and Mutual Credit* (1827), London: Henry Butterworth

Bacon's Abridgement of the Law (7th edn, 1832), London: J and W T Clarke

BEATSON, *The Use and Abuse of Unjust Enrichment* (1991), Oxford: Clarendon Press

Benjamin's Sale of Goods (5th edn, 1997), London: Sweet & Maxwell

BIRKS, *An Introduction to the Law of Restitution* (1989), Oxford: Clarendon Press

Blackstone, *Commentaries on the Laws of England* (3rd edn, 1768), Oxford: Clarendon Press

Blagden Committee Report ('Report of the Committee on Bankruptcy Law and Deeds of Arrangement Amendment') (Cmnd 221, 1957)

Bowstead and Reynolds on Agency (17th edn, 2001), London: Sweet and Maxwell

BRANDON, *The Customary Law of Foreign Attachment* (1861), London: Butterworths

BRINDLE AND COX (ed), *Law of Bank Payments* (2nd edn, 1999), London: Sweet & Maxwell

Broom's Legal Maxims (10th edn, 1939), London; Sweet and Maxwell

Buckley on the Companies Acts (14th edn, 1981), London: Butterworths

Bullen and Leake and Jacob's Precedents of Pleadings (14th edn, 2001), London: Sweet & Maxwell

BURROWS, *The Law of Restitution* (1993), London: Butterworths

Byles on Bills of Exchange and Cheques (27th edn, 2002), London: Sweet and Maxwell

Carver's Carriage by Sea (13th edn, 1982), London: Stevens and Sons

Chalmers and Guest on Bills of Exchange, Cheques and Promissory Notes (15th edn, 1998), London: Sweet & Maxwell

Chitty's Blackstone (1826), London: William Walker

Chitty's Practice (3rd edn, 1837)

Chitty's Precedents in Pleadings (2nd edn, 1847)

Chitty on Contracts (28th edn, 1999), London: Sweet & Maxwell

CHRISTIAN, *Bankrupt Law* (2nd edn, 1818), London: W Clarke and Sons

Civil Procedure (2nd edn, 1999), London: Sweet & Maxwell

Clerk and Lindsell on Torts (18th edn, 2000), London: Sweet & Maxwell

Coke's Institutes (1648)

Comyns' Digest (5th edn, 1822), London: Butterworths

COOKE, *The Bankrupt Laws* (8th edn, 1823), London: Charles Hunter

Cooper's Parliamentary Proceedings (1828), London: John Murray

Coote on Mortgages (9th edn, 1927), London: Stevens & Sons Ltd

Cork Committee Report on Insolvency Law and Practice (Cmnd 8558, 1982)

COUSINS, *The Law of Mortgages* (1989), London: Sweet & Maxwell

CRANSTON, *Principles of Banking Law* (1997), Oxford: Clarendon Press

CRAWFORD AND FALCONBRIDGE, *Banking and Bills of Exchange* (8th edn, 1986), Toronto: Canada Law Book Inc

CRESSWELL, BLAIR, HILL, HOOLEY, PHILLIPS AND WOOD, *Encyclopedia of Banking Law* (looseleaf), London, Butterworths

DAL PONT, *Law of Agency* (2001), Australia: Butterworths

Daniell's Chancery Practice (8th edn, 1914), London: Stevens and Sons

DERHAM, *Subrogation in Insurance Law* (1985), Sydney: Law Book Company

DICEY AND MORRIS, *The Conflict of Laws* (13th edn, 2000), London: Sweet & Maxwell

DORIA, *The Law and Practice in Bankruptcy* (1874), London: Law Times Office

DORIA AND MACRAE, *The Law and Practice of Bankruptcy* (1863), London: John Crockford

ELLINGER, LOMNICKA AND HOOLEY, *Modern Banking Law* (3rd edn, 2002), Oxford: Oxford University Press

FARRANDS, *The Law of Options* (1992), Sydney: Law Book Co

FINN, *Fiduciary Obligations* (1977), Sydney: The Law Book Company

Fisher and Lightwood's Law of Mortgage (11th edn, 2002), London: Butterworths

FORD AND LEE, *Principles of the Law of Trusts* (3rd edn, looseleaf), Sydney: LBC Information Services

FRANCIS AND THOMAS, *Mortgages and Securities* (3rd edn, 1986), Sydney; Butterworths

FRIDMAN, *The Law of Agency* (7th edn, 1996), London: Butterworths

GOFF AND JONES, *The Law of Restitution* (5th edn, 1998), London: Sweet & Maxwell

GOODE, *Payment Obligations in Commercial and Financial Transactions* (1983), London: Sweet & Maxwell

GOODE, *Legal Problems of Credit and Security* (2nd edn, 1988), London: Sweet & Maxwell

GOODE, *Principles of Corporate Insolvency Law* (2nd edn, 1997), London: Sweet & Maxwell

GOODE, *Commercial Law* (2nd edn, 1995), London: Penguin Books

GOODINGE, *The Law Against Bankrupts* (2nd edn, 1701), London: John Hartley

Gore-Browne on Companies (44th edn, looseleaf), Bristol: Jordans

GOUGH, *Company Charges* (2nd edn, 1996), London: Butterworths

GRAY AND GRAY, *Elements of Land Law* (3rd edn, 2001), London: Butterworths

Halsbury's Laws of England, (4th edn), London: Butterworths

HENLEY, *A Digest of the Bankrupt Law* (3rd edn, 1832), London: Saunders and Benning

Hill and Redman's Law of Landlord and Tenant (17th edn, 1982), London: Butterworths

HOGG AND MONAHAN, *Liability of the Crown* (3rd edn, 2000), Canada: Carswell

HOLDEN, *The Law and Practice of Banking* (5th edn, 1991), London: Pitman

HOLDSWORTH, *A History of English Law,* London: Methuen

HOULDEN AND MORAWETZ, *Bankruptcy Law of Canada* (1960), Toronto: The Carswell Company

Hudson's Building and Engineering Contracts (11th edn, 1995), London: Sweet & Maxwell

JACKSON, *Principles of Property Law* (1967), Sydney: Law Book Company

Jacobs' Law of Trusts in Australia (6th edn, 1997), Sydney: Butterworths

JONES AND GOODHART, *Specific Performance* (2nd edn, 1996), London: Butterworths

Keating on Building Contracts (7th edn, 2001), London: Sweet & Maxwell

KEATING, *Law and Practice of Building Contracts* (3rd edn, 1969), London: Sweet & Maxwell

KEETON AND SHERIDAN, *Equity* (3rd edn, 1987), England: Kluwer Law Publishers

Kerr on Injunctions (1867), London: William Maxwell & Son

Kerr on Receivers and Administrators (17th edn, 1989), London: Sweet & Maxwell

Lewin on Trusts (17th edn, 2000), London: Sweet & Maxwell

LIGHTMAN AND MOSS, *The Law of Receivers and Administrators of Companies* (3rd edn, 2000), London: Sweet & Maxwell

Lindley and Banks on Partnership (18th edn, 2002), London: Sweet & Maxwell

Lindley on Companies (6th edn, 1902), London: Sweet & Maxwell

MacGillivray on Insurance Law (9th edn, 1997), London: Sweet & Maxwell

MACKEN, McCARRY AND SAPPIDEEN, *The Law of Employment* (4th edn, 1997), Sydney: LBC Information Services

MADDOCK, *Principles and Practice of the High Court of Chancery* (3rd edn, 1837), London: J & W T Clarke

MAITLAND, *Equity* (2nd edn (rev by Brunyate), 1936), Cambridge: Cambridge University Press

MANN, *The Legal Aspect of Money* (5th edn, 1992), Oxford: Clarendon Press

MARSHALL, *The Assignment of Choses in Action* (1950), London: Sir Isaac Pitman & Sons

McCRACKEN, *The Banker's Remedy of Set-off* (2nd edn, 1998), London: Butterworths

McPHERSON, *The Law of Company Liquidation* (4th edn, 1999), Sydney: LBC Information Services

MEAGHER, GUMMOW AND LEHANE, *Equity Doctrines and Remedies* (3rd edn, 1992), Sydney: Butterworths

MEGARRY, *The Rent Acts* (10th edn, 1967), London: Stevens and Sons

MEGARRY AND WADE, *The Law of Real Property* (6th edn, 2000), London: Sweet & Maxwell

MITCHELL, *The Law of Subrogation* (1994), Oxford: Clarendon Press

MONTAGUE, *Summary of the Law of Set-off* (2nd edn, 1828), London: Joseph Butterworth and Son

New South Wales Law Reform Commission Report, No 94, *Set-off,* February 2000

NUSSBAUM, *Money in the Law National and International* (1950), Brooklyn: The Foundation Press Inc

ODITAH, *Legal Aspects of Receivables Financing* (1991), London: Sweet & Maxwell

O'DONOVAN, *Company Receivers and Administrators* (2nd edn, looseleaf), Sydney: Law Book Company

O'DONOVAN AND PHILLIPS, *The Modern Contract of Guarantee* (3rd edn, 1996), Sydney: LBC Information Services

Paget's Law of Banking (11th edn, 1996), London: Butterworths

Palmer's Company Law (looseleaf), London: Stevens and Sons

Palmer's Company Precedents (16th edn, 1952), London: Stevens and Sons

PALMER, *The Law of Set-off in Canada* (1993), Ontario: Canada Law Book Co

Parry and Clark on the Law of Succession (10th edn, 1996), London: Sweet & Maxwell

PENN, SHEA AND ARORA, *The Law Relating to Domestic Banking* (1987), London: Sweet & Maxwell

PENNINGTON, *Company Law* (7th edn, 1995), London: Butterworths

PENNINGTON, HUDSON AND MANN, *Commercial Banking Law* (1978), Plymouth: MacDonald and Evans

PETTIT, *Equity and the Law of Trusts* (9th edn, 2001), London: Butterworths

PICARDA, *The Law Relating to Receivers, Managers and Administrators* (3rd edn, 2000), London: Butterworths

POWELL, *The Law of Agency* (1952), Sir Isaac Pitman & Sons

RABEL, *The Conflict of Laws* (2nd edn, 1964), Ann Arbor: Michigan Legal Publications

ROBSON, *The Law of Bankruptcy* (7th edn, 1894), London: William Clowes and Sons

Robson's Annotated Corporations Law (4th edn, 1999), Sydney: LBC Information Services

Rowlatt on Principal and Surety (5th edn, 1999), London: Sweet & Maxwell

Salmond on Jurisprudence (12th edn, 1966), London: Sweet & Maxwell

SCOTT, *The Law of Trusts* (4th edn, 1987), Boston: Little, Brown and Co

SHELFORD, *The Law of Bankruptcy and Insolvency* (3rd edn, 1862), London: Sweet & Maxwell

Smith's Leading Cases (12th edn, 1915), London: Sweet & Maxwell

Snell's Equity (30th edn, 2000), London: Sweet & Maxwell

SPENCER BOWER AND TURNER, *The Law of Actionable Misrepresentation* (3rd edn, 1974), London: Butterworths

SPENCER BOWER AND TURNER, *The Law Relating to Estoppel By Representation* (3rd edn, 1977), London: Butterworths

SPENCER BOWER, TURNER AND HANDLEY, *The Doctrine of Res Judicata* (3rd edn, 1996), London: Butterworths

SPRY, *Equitable Remedies* (6th edn, 2001), Sydney: LBC Information Services

STOLJAR, *The Law of Agency* (1961), London: Sweet & Maxwell

STORY, *Commentaries on Equity Jurisprudence* (14th edn, 1918), Boston: Little, Brown and Co

SYKES AND WALKER, *The Law of Securities* (5th edn, 1993), Sydney: The Law Book Company

The Supreme Court Practice (1999), London: Sweet & Maxwell

TIDD, *The Practice of the Courts of King's Bench and Common Pleas in Personal Actions and Ejectment* (9th edn, 1828), London: Joseph Butterworth and Son (*Tidd's Practice*)

TREITEL, *The Law of Contract* (10th edn, 1999), London: Sweet & Maxwell

TUDSBERY, *Equitable Assignments* (1912), London: Sweet & Maxwell

UNDERHILL AND HAYTON, *Law Relating to Trusts and Trustees* (15th edn, 1995), London: Butterworths

Viner's Abridgment (2nd edn, 1741), London: G Robinson

WALDOCK, *The Law of Mortgages* (2nd edn, 1950), London: Stevens and Sons

WATERS, *The Constructive Trust* (1964), London: The Athlone Press

WEAVER AND CRAIGIE, *The Law Relating to Banker and Customer in Australia* (looseleaf), Sydney: LBC Information Services

White and Tudor's Leading Cases in Equity (9th edn, 1928), London: Sweet & Maxwell

Williams on Wills (7th edn, 1995), London: Butterworths

WILLIAMS, GLANVILLE, *Joint Obligations* (1949), London: Butterworth & Co

WILLIAMS, N, *Civil Procedure Victoria* (looseleaf), Sydney: Butterworths

WILLIAMS, W, *The Law Relating to Assents* (1947), London: Butterworth & Co

WILLIAMS AND MUIR HUNTER, *The Law and Practice in Bankruptcy* (19th edn, 1979), London: Stevens & Sons

WILLIAMS AND WILLIAMS, *The New Law and Practice in Bankruptcy* (1870), London: Stevens & Sons

Williams, Mortimer and Sunnucks on Executors, Administrators and Probate (18th edn, 2000), London: Sweet & Maxwell

Williston on Contracts (3rd edn, 1967), New York: Baker, Voorhis & Co

Withers on Reversions (2nd edn, 1933), London: Butterworth & Co

WOOD, *English and International Set-off* (1989), London: Sweet & Maxwell

Woodfall's Law of Landlord and Tenant (looseleaf), London: Sweet & Maxwell

YALE, *Lord Nottingham's Chancery Cases* vol 1, 73 *Selden Society* (1957), London: Bernard Quaritch

2. Articles, Notes etc

ABRAMS, 'Talisman: A Legal Analysis' (1980) 1 The Company Lawyer 17

ADAMS, ' "No Deduction or Set-off" Clauses' (1994) 57 Modern Law Review 960

AMES, 'Undisclosed Principal—His Rights and Liabilities' (1909) 18 Yale Law Journal 443

ANDREWS, 'The Proper Limits of Set-off' [1992] Cambridge Law Journal 239

AUGHTERSON,'In Defence of the Benefit and Burden Principle' (1991) 65 Australian Law Journal 319

BAKER, 'The Future of Equity' (1977) 93 Law Quarterly Review 529

BENNETTS, 'Voidable Transactions: Consequences of Removing Avoidance Powers From the Liquidator and Vesting Them in the Court' (1994) 2 Insolvency Law Journal 136

BERG, 'Arbitration: Legal Set-off and Enforcing Admitted Claims' [2000] Lloyd's Maritime and Commercial Law Quarterly 153

BERG, 'Charges Over Book Debts: A Reply' [1995] Journal of Business Law 433

BERG, 'Contracting Out of Set-off in a Winding Up' [1996] Lloyd's Maritime and Commercial Law Quarterly 49

BERG, 'House of Lords Clarifies Liquidation Netting' International Financial Law Review, August 1995, 20

BERG, 'Liquidation Set-off: The Mutuality Principle and Security Over Bank Balances' [1996] Lloyd's Maritime and Commercial Law Quarterly 176

BIRKS, 'Equity in the Modern Law: An Exercise in Taxonomy' (1996) 26 University of Western Australia Law Review 1

BISHOP, 'Set-off in the Administration of Insolvent and Bankrupt Estates' (1901) 1 Columbia Law Review 377

BLAIR, 'Charges Over Cash Deposits' International Financial Law Review, November 1983, 14

BRESLIN, 'Set-off under Irish Law' (1997) 18 Company Lawyer 198

BRYAN, 'The Liability of Banks to Make Restitution for Wrongful Payments' (1998) 26 Australian Business Law Review 93

BRYSON, 'Restraining Sales by Mortgagees and a Curial Myth' (1993) 11 Australian Bar Review 1

BURROWS, 'We Do This at Common Law But That in Equity' (2002) 22 Oxford Journal of Legal Studies 1

BURTON, 'Negotiability: Set-offs and Counterclaims' in Burton (ed), *Directions In Finance Law* (1990), Sydney, Butterworths

CALNAN, 'The Insolvent Bank and Security Over Deposits' (1996) 11 Journal of International Banking and Financial Law 185

CALNAN, 'Security Over Deposits Again: BCCI (No 8) in the House of Lords' (1998) 13 Journal of International Banking and Financial Law 125

CALNAN, 'Fashioning the Law to Suit the Practicalities of Life' (1998) 114 Law Quarterly Review 174

CAPPER, 'Deceit, Banker's Set-off and Mareva Undertakings—The Abbey's Bad Habits' [1999] Lloyd's Maritime and Commercial Law Quarterly 21

CASTLES, 'The Reception and Status of English Law in Australia' (1963) 2 Adelaide Law Review 1

CHORLEY, 'Del Credere' (1929) 45 Law Quarterly Review 221, (1930) 46 Law Quarterly Review 11

COLEMAN, 'Netting a Red Herring' (1994) 9 Journal of International Banking and Financial Law 391

DEAN, LUCKETT AND HOUGHTON, 'Notional Calculations in Liquidations Revisited' (1993) 11 Companies and Securities Law Journal 204

DERHAM, 'Set-off and Netting of Foreign Exchange Contracts in the Liquidation of a Counterparty' [1991] Journal of Business Law 463, 536

DERHAM, 'Set-off Against an Assignee: The Relevance of Marshalling, Contribution and Subrogation' (1991) 107 Law Quarterly Review 126

DERHAM, 'Some Aspects of Mutual Credit and Mutual Dealings' (1992) 108 Law Quarterly Review 99

DERHAM, 'Recent Issues in Relation to Set-off' (1984) 68 Australian Law Journal 331

DERHAM, 'Set-off in Victoria' (1999) 73 Australian Law Journal 754

DUNS, Note (1998) 6 Insolvency Journal 4

EARLEY, 'Set-off Rights Available to Banks in Ireland' [1997] 4 Journal of International Banking Law 153

EVERETT, 'Security Over Bank Deposits' (1988) 16 Australian Business Law Review 351

EVERETT, 'Multi-Party Set-off Agreements' [1993] Journal of Banking and Finance Law and Practice 180

FARRAR, 'Contracting Out of Set-off' (1970) 120 New Law Journal 771

FORD, 'Trading Trusts and Creditors' Rights' (1981) 13 Melbourne University Law Review 1

GOODE, 'Centre Point' [1984] Journal of Business Law 172

GOODE, 'Security: A Pragmatic Conceptualist's Response' (1989) 15 Monash University Law Review 361

GOODE, 'Charges Over Book Debts: A Missed Opportunity' (1994) 110 Law Quarterly Review 592

GOODE, 'Charge-Backs and Legal Fictions' (1998) 114 Law Quarterly Review 178

GOODHART AND HAMSON, 'Undisclosed Principals in Contract' (1932) 4 Cambridge Law Journal 320

GOODHART AND JONES, 'The Infiltration of Equitable Doctrine into English Commercial Law' (1980) 43 Modern Law Review 489

GRANTHAM, 'The Impact of Security Interest on Set-off' [1989] Journal of Business Law 377

GUMMOW, 'Compensation for Breach of Fiduciary Duty', in Youdan (ed), *Equity, Fiduciaries and Trusts* (1989), Toronto: Carswell

HANDLEY, 'Anshun Today' (1997) 71 Australian Law Journal 934

HAPGOOD, 'Set-off Under the Laws of England' in Neate (ed), *Using Set-off as a Security* (1990), London: Graham & Trotman

HERZBERG, 'Bankers' Rights of Combination' (1982) 10 Australian Business Law Review 79

HIGGINS, 'The Equity of the Undisclosed Principal' (1965) 28 Modern Law Review 167

HOFFHEIMER, 'The Common Law of Edward Christian' [1994] Cambridge Law Journal 140

HOGAN, 'Set-off, Members' Rights and Winding Up' (1998) 19 Company Lawyer 16

HORACK, 'Insolvency and Specific Performance' (1918) 31 Harvard Law Review 702

HORRIGAN, 'Combining Bank Accounts in Different Currencies—A Conceptual Analysis' (1991) 65 Australian Law Journal 14

JONES, Comment [1980] Cambridge Law Journal 275

KLEINER, 'Foreign Exchange Claims Against Banks in Dispute' International Financial Law Review, May 1989, 204

LADBURY, 'Introduction to the Law of Contractual Set-off in Australia' in Neate (ed), *Using Set-off as a Security* (1990), London: Graham & Trotman

LOYD, 'The Development of Set-off' (1916) 64 University of Pennsylvania Law Review 541

LUCKETT AND DEAN, 'Cross-Debts: Notional Calculations in Liquidations' (1983) 11 Australian Business Law Review 69

McCORMACK, 'Charge Backs and Commercial Certainty in the House of Lords' [1998] Company Financial and Insolvency Law Review 111

McPHERSON, 'The Insolvent Trading Trust' in Finn (ed), *Essays in Equity* (1985), Sydney: Law Book Company

MANIRE, 'Foreign Exchange Sales and the Law of Contracts: A Case for Analogy to the Uniform Commercial Code' (1982) 35 Vanderbilt Law Review 1173

MARTIN, 'Fusion, Fallacy and Confusion: A Comparative Study' [1994] The Conveyancer 13

MATTHEWS, 'Restitution 0, Trusts 0 (After Extra Time)—A Case of Set-off' [1994] Restitution Law Review 44

MELVILLE, 'Disclaimer of Contracts in Bankruptcy' (1952) 15 Modern Law Review 28

MILLETT, 'Equity—The Road Ahead' (1995) 9 Tolley's Trust Law International 35

MILLETT, 'Equity's Place in the Law of Commerce' (1998) 114 Law Quarterly Review 214

MILLETT, 'Restitution and Constructive Trusts' (1998) 114 Law Quarterly Review 399

MILLETT, 'Tracing the Proceeds of Fraud' (1991) 107 Law Quarterly Review 71

MILLETT, (Richard) 'Pleasing Paradoxes' (1996) 112 Law Quarterly Review 524

MITCHELL, 'Defences to an Insurer's Subrogated Action' [1996] Lloyd's Maritime and Commercial Law Quarterly 343

MOKEL, 'Resolving the *M S Fashions* "Paradox"' [1999] Company Financial and Insolvency Law Review 106

MONTROSE, 'Liability of Principal for Acts Exceeding Actual and Apparent Authority' (1939) 17 Canadian Bar Review 693

NICHOLLS (Lord), 'Knowing Receipt: The Need for a New Landmark' in Cornish (ed), *Restitution Past, Present and Future* (1998), Oxford: Hart Publishing

NOTE, 'Set-off in Case of Mutual Dealings' (1882) 26 Solicitors' Journal 575

NOTE, (1992) 66 Australian Law Journal 313

ODITAH, 'Assets and Treatment of Claims in Insolvency' (1992) 108 Law Quarterly Review 459

ODITAH, 'Financing Trade Credit: Welsh Development Agency v Exfinco' [1992] Journal of Business Law 541

PHILLIPS, 'When Should the Guarantor be Permitted to Rely on the Principal's Set-off?' [2001] Lloyds Maritime and Commercial Law Quarterly 383

POLLARD, 'Credit Balances as Security—II' [1988] Journal of Business Law 219

POLLOCK, (1887) 3 Law Quarterly Review 358

POLLOCK, (1893) 9 Law Quarterly Review 111

POLLOCK, 'Re Wait' (1927) 43 Law Quarterly Review 293

RANK, 'Repairs in Lieu of Rent' (1976) 40 The Conveyancer and Property Lawyer 196

REYNOLDS, 'Practical Problems of the Undisclosed Principal Doctrine' (1983) 36 Current Legal Problems 119

ROSE, 'Deductions From Freight and Hire Under English Law' [1982] Lloyd's Maritime and Commercial Law Quarterly 33

RUSSELL, 'Defences by Way of Set-off, Counterclaim and Cross Action' (1928) 2 Australian Law Journal 80

SALTER, 'Remedies for Banks: An Outline of English Law' in Blair (ed), *Banks and Remedies* (2nd edn, 1999), London: Lloyds of London Press

SEGAL, 'Conceptual Implausibility in the Court of Appeal' [1996] 8 Journal of International Banking Law 307

SHEA, 'Further Reflections on Statutory Set-off' (1987) 3 Journal of International Banking Law 183

SHEA, 'Foreign Exchange Contracts and Netting in the UK' International Financial Law Review, January 1990, 19

SHEA, 'Statutory Set-off' (1986) 3 Journal of International Banking Law 152

SMART, 'International Insolvency: Banks and Set-off' (1999) 1 Journal of International Banking and Financial Law 10

Spry, 'Equitable Set-offs' (1969) 43 Australian Law Journal 265

STEYN, 'Guarantees: The Co-Extensiveness Principle' (1974) 90 Law Quarterly Review 246

TAYLOR, 'The Year in Review—New Zealand Insolvency Law in 1999' [1999] Insolvency Law Journal 212

TETTENBORN, Note (1997) 113 Law Quarterly Review 374

TETTENBORN, 'Remedies for the Recovery of Money Paid by Mistake' [1980] Cambridge Law Journal 272

TIGAR, 'Automatic Extinction of Cross-Demands: *Compensatio* From Rome to California' (1965) 53 California Law Review 224

TREITEL, 'Specific Performance in the Sale of Goods' [1966] Journal of Business Law 211

WAITE, 'Repairs and Deduction from Rent' [1981] The Conveyancer 199

WAITE, 'Disrepair and Set-off of Damages Against Rent: The Implications of British Anzani' [1983] The Conveyancer 373

WALLACE, 'Set Back to Set-off' (1973) 89 Law Quarterly Review 36

WALLACE, 'Set Fair for Set-off' (1974) 90 Law Quarterly Review 21

WEIR, 'A Tenant's Right of Set-off' (1994) 68 Australian Law Journal 857

WILLIAMS, GLANVILLE, 'Mistake as to Party in the Law of Contract' (1945) 23 Canadian Bar Review 380

WOOD, 'Netting Agreements in Organised and Private Markets' in Kingsford-Smith (ed), *Current Developments in Banking and Finance* (1989), London: Sweet & Maxwell

WOOD AND TERRAY, 'Foreign Exchange Netting in France and England' International Financial Law Review, October 1989, 18

YEOWART, 'House of Lords Upholds Charge-Backs over Deposits' International Financial Law Review, January 1998, 7

INDEX